Oman, UAE
& Arabian Peninsula

Jenny
Stuart Butler, Terry Carter, Lara

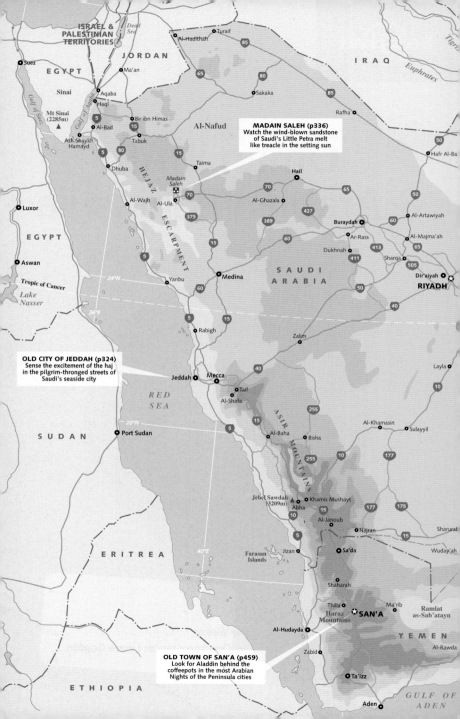

MADAIN SALEH (p336)
Watch the wind-blown sandstone of Saudi's Little Petra melt like treacle in the setting sun

OLD CITY OF JEDDAH (p324)
Sense the excitement of the haj in the pilgrim-thronged streets of Saudi's seaside city

OLD TOWN OF SAN'A (p459)
Look for Aladdin behind the coffeepots in the most Arabian Nights of the Peninsula cities

ISRAEL & PALESTINIAN TERRITORIES
JORDAN
IRAQ
EGYPT
Sinai
SAUDI ARABIA
RIYADH
RED SEA
SUDAN
ERITREA
ETHIOPIA
YEMEN
SAN'A
GULF OF ADEN

Dead Sea
Euphrates
Tigris

Suez
Ma'an
Aqaba
Haql
Mt Sinai (2285m)
Al-Bad
Bir ibn Himas
Ash Shaykh Hamayd
Tabuk
Dhuba
Al-Wajh
Al-Ula
Taima
Madain Saleh
Yanbu
Medina
Rabigh
Jeddah
Mecca
Taif
Al-Shafa
Al-Baha
Bisha
Khamis Mushayt
Abha
Al-Janoub
Najran
Jizan
Sa'da
Shaharah
Thilla
Haraz Mountains
Al-Hudayda
Zabid
Ta'izz
Aden

Al-Hadithah
Turaif
Sakaka
Rafha
Hafr Al-Ba
Al-Artawiyah
Al-Majma'ah
Sharqa
Dir'aiyah
Hail
Al-Ghazala
Buraydah
Ar-Rass
Dukhnah
Zalim
Layla
Al-Khamasin
Sulayyil
Jebel Sawdah (3209m)
Farasan Islands
Ma'rib
Ramlat as-Sab'atayn
Al-Rawda
Sharural
Wuday'ah

Luxor
Aswan
Tropic of Cancer
Lake Nasser
Port Sudan

HEJAZ ESCARPMENT
ASIR MOUNTAINS
Al-Nafud

85
65
80
85
50
15
80
15
5
5
5
15
70
65
50
375
427
70
60
389
411
413
505
50
65
60
15
60
5
40
255
255
40
10
177
15
177
175
15
10
10
10
5
5

24°N
20°N
36°E
40°E

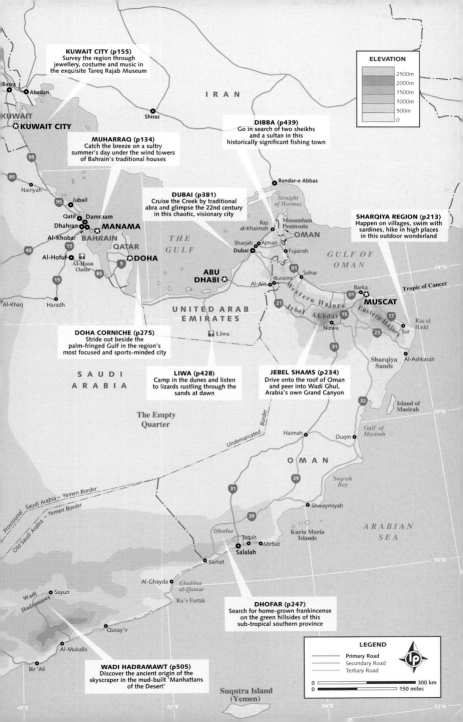

ELEVATION

2500m
2000m
1500m
1000m
500m
0

KUWAIT CITY (p155)
Survey the region through
jewellery, costume and music in
the exquisite Tareq Rajab Museum

IRAN

Basra
Abadan

KUWAIT
⊙ KUWAIT CITY

Shiraz

MUHARRAQ (p134)
Catch the breeze on a sultry
summer's day under the wind towers
of Bahrain's traditional houses

DIBBA (p439)
Go in search of two sheikhs
and a sultan in this
historically significant fishing town

Bandar-e Abbas

DUBAI (p381)
Cruise the Creek by traditional
abra and glimpse the 22nd century
in this chaotic, visionary city

*Straight
of Hormuz*

Ras
al-Khaimah

Musandam
Peninsula

SHARQIYA REGION (p213)
Happen on villages, swim with
sardines, hike in high places
in this outdoor wonderland

95

85

Nairiyah

Jubail

95

Qatif
Dhahran
Damman

Al-Khobar

Al-Hofuf

BAHRAIN
MANAMA

QATAR ⊙DOHA

*THE
GULF*

Sharjah
Ajman
Dubai

OMAN

Fujairah

*GULF OF
OMAN*

Sohar

24°N

40

15

Al-Hasa
Oasis

5

85

ABU
DHABI ⊙

Al-Ain

Buraimi

01

Barka

01 ⊙ MUSCAT

Tropic of Cancer

15

Al-Kharj

Haradh

*UNITED ARAB
EMIRATES*

21

Western Hajars

*Jebel
Akhdat*

15

Eastern Hajar

17

Ras al
Hadd

DOHA CORNICHE (p275)
Stride out beside the
palm-fringed Gulf in the region's
most focused and sports-minded city

Liwa

Nizwa

23

Sur

*SAUDI
ARABIA*

LIWA (p428)
Camp in the dunes and listen
to lizards rustling through the
sands at dawn

JEBEL SHAMS (p234)
Drive onto the roof of Oman
and peer into Wadi Ghul,
Arabia's own Grand Canyon

31

*Sharqiya
Sands*

Al-Ashkarah

32

*Island of
Masirah*

20°N

*The Empty
Quarter*

Undemarcated Border

Haimah

Duqm

*Gulf of
Masirah*

O   M   A   N

Provisional Saudi Arabia – Yemen Border

Old Saudi Arabia – Yemen Border

31

39

*Suqrah
Bay*

Shwaymiyah

39

*ARABIAN
SEA*

Dhofar

Taqah
Mirbat

Salalah

*Kuria Muria
Islands*

Sarfait

16°N

Al-Ghayda

*Ghubbat
al-Qamar*

Ra's Fartak

DHOFAR (p247)
Search for home-grown frankincense
on the green hillsides of this
sub-tropical southern province

Wadi
Hadramawt

Sayun

Qusay'ir

Al-Mukalla

Bir 'Ali

WADI HADRAMAWT (p505)
Discover the ancient origin of the
skyscraper in the mud-built 'Manhattans
of the Desert'

*Suqutra Island
(Yemen)*

LEGEND

Primary Road
Secondary Road
Tertiary Road

LP

0 ——————— 300 km
0 ——————— 150 miles

48°E   52°E   56°E   12°N

On the Road

JENNY WALKER Coordinating Author
Here in Oman, 'lovely weather' refers exclusively to rare days of rain. On such occasions, people leave work early to rejoice in the sudden appearance of water. And that's what I'm doing here – catching the precious moment of flood in gorgeous Wadi Bani Awf. I'm looking pensive because I wasn't the only one enjoying the unexpected deluge: a viper slithered out of the rocks, flicking his tongue at the end of my shadow. I was just wondering whether he could swim when my husband, Sam, took the photo. The viper swam – and so did I!

STUART BUTLER This photo was taken in Suqutra during my first surf trip to Yemen. That morning we'd been chased out of the water by an eight-foot hammerhead shark and this photo was taken in the afternoon as I tried to pluck up the courage to go back in. The kids wanted me to take fishing nets in and try and catch one of the numerous sharks. The kids in Suqutra are nuts!

TERRY CARTER Ajman is a tiny laid-back emirate with a lovely resort. We were on the white-sand beach at sunset waiting for the classic photo op of a camel framed by a brilliant sunset. A couple of hours later we were watching a Chinese waitress carve up a Peking duck at our dinner table before heading out for *sheesha* with the locals. Welcome to the UAE.

LARA DUNSTON I'd lived in the UAE for years, seeing Emirati women gracefully gliding about in their elegant *abeyyas* and *shaylahs*, but the first time I wore local dress was on this research trip to Jumeirah Mosque. Unfortunately it wasn't as flattering on me as it is on the gorgeous local girls I know, but I enjoyed wearing it. Just as my Emirati friends always told me, it's wonderfully freeing rather than inhibiting.

FRANCES LINZEE GORDON I've always been fascinated by the ancient art of falconry. Coming to Saudi Arabia was the chance I've always craved to see it practised. Since time immemorial, the Bedu have used falcons to seek out the scant resources of the desert. To my delight, an interview with a royal official resulted in an invitation to see his own birds. I shall never forget that day in the desert with them.

See full author bios page 575-6

Arabian Peninsula Highlights

The essence of Arabia resides in the tangible: in desert landscapes, in a gazelle licking dawn dew from a thorn tree, in towers ancient and modern, in a brushed carpet draped over concrete. It resides also in the intangible: in the evocation of spirit in the legends of an oral tradition, the waft of incense recalling past kingdoms, the taste of fresh fruits in summer madness. But most of all, the essence of Arabia lies in its people: good-natured haggling in souqs, cursing on long journeys, sharing of sweet tea on the edge of odd places. Unifying all, there's Islam, a way of life, the call to prayer carried on an inland breeze.

JENNY WAL

1 THE EDGE OF NOWHERE

For centuries, travellers have been attracted to the great desert wildernesses of Arabia, drawn by the limitlessness yet repelled by the void. 'This cruel land,' wrote Thesiger, after crossing the Empty Quarter on foot with the Bedu, 'can cast a spell which no temperate clime can hope to match'. Feel the magical allure of the desert but beware: the summer sands don't take prisoners, and the only stranger you're likely to meet between dunes is yourself.

The Empty Quarter, Saudi Arabia

RUINS OF EMPIRE

They rise out of the gravel plains like lost camels, or sit crumbling to dust on mountain ridges. They speak of past greatness, of prophets and kings, and forgotten dynasties. Sit among these ruins of empire – at Madain Saleh (p336) in Saudi, the Great Ma'rib Dam (p496) in Yemen, or Bat (p236) in Oman – and contemplate human frailty.

Qasr Farid, Madain Saleh, Saudi Arabia

2

ANTHONY HAM

WADI DEEP, MOUNTAIN HIGH

They can be as truculent as camels and as thirsty as donkeys, but the modern 'ships of the desert' can transport the traveller into unimagined dimensions – including stuck in sand and mired in mud. However, with some careful planning, and sticking resolutely to prior tracks, a 4WD off-road trip in Arabia is guaranteed to be an unforgettable experience. Follow the locals over the dunes, through floodwater, up mountains and over the escarpment to see the best of the Peninsula's varied landscape, and discover the myriad plants and animals that call it home.

Off-road, Oman

3

JENNY WALKER

TONY WHEELER

4

FORMIDABLE FORTS

Cresting a hill top, guarding the coastline, walling a village or securing a dried-out river bed, there is barely a town in Arabia without some kind of crumbling battlement. Learn your forts from your castles before exploring some of these mighty military edifices.

Nizwa Fort, Oman

TOPPLING OVER THE PAST

Cooling wind towers of the Gulf, watchtowers guarding the interior, enigmatic towers of mountain burial: the peoples of the Peninsula have for centuries favoured the vertical. Stroll the mud Manhattans of southern Arabia (p505), with their coloured glass, and see where the trend for high-rise living came from.

Wind tower, Dubai, UAE

PHILIP GAME

5

HOLGER L

6

TOWERING OVER THE FUTURE

Slicing through the gulf stream of the sky's superhighways, there is no more potent symbol of the Peninsula's future than the tower block. Dine on top of the modern world in one of these totems of steel-and-glass and peer down the centuries at 'business-as-usual' carrying on at ground level.

Burj al-Arab, Dubai, UAE

FRANCES LINZEE GORE

7

ARABIAN REFLECTIONS

When Jonathan Raban referred to 'Arabia Through the Looking Glass' he could have had mirror images in mind. They're everywhere – in the repeated forms of geometric design on a mosque carpet, in the arrangement of daggers at the souq. By the same token, smile at anyone on the Peninsula and you will be sure to see it reflected back.

***Jambiyas* for sale, Sa'da, Yemen**

THE PAST IS PRESENT

In Arabia the new often rises phoenix-like out of the rubble of the old, without any sense of irony. In Bahrain join in a football match between burial mounds or catch the reflection of a mosque in the windows of a neighbouring building, and you'll quickly see there's no useful distinction between then and now.

Minaret, Dubai, UAE

TONY WHEELER

PUSHING BACK THE TIDE

Visually, modernity for many Peninsula countries can be summed up in two words: reclaimed land. Take part in the promenade of nations along any of the Gulf corniches, or join the march of the malls, and chances are you'll be walking on water – or at least where water once was. But then again, you can climb any mountain in the Peninsula and claim the same: most of Arabia was once under the sea and it would appear that modern architects are keen to reverse the tide on prehistory.

Al-Corniche, Doha, Qatar

NEIL SETCHFIELD

CHRIS MELLOR

8 MONUMENTAL ICONS

Icons are not usually created but made – as illustrated by the commissioning of faintly ridiculous giant coffeepots and pearl monuments for town centres. There are exceptions, however, and the Kuwait Towers (p160) is a case in point. Visit these iconic water towers to understand the strategic significance not just of a monument, but of the country the towers have come to represent in this much-fought-over corner of the Middle East.

Kuwait Towers, Kuwait

CHRIS MII

11 RICH IN TRADITION

It's easy to spot the ostentatious wealth of the few, but Arabia's riches can be counted by more than the latest car or designer handbag. Gold twine in a dress cuff, a bead of carnelian threaded for a loved one, a basket woven with camel leather, the tinge of indigo, woollen threads on a loom, words of wisdom entwined in a silver amulet – these are the riches of heritage. Watch for the waving of a hennaed hand, the learnt flash of eyes beneath wedding gold, a rising inflection on a piece of Bedouin poetry, the practised parcelling of infant in the arms of the aged and that's where you'll find the most precious of the Peninsula's pearls.

Detail of coat of arms, Sultan's Palace, Muscat, Oman

S.M. AMIN/SAUDI ARAMCO WORLD

12 THE HAJ: THE ULTIMATE TRAVELLER'S TALE

They come from Mali and from Morocco, from the Maldives and Malaysia, pouring through the airports of Arabia, as upon the caravans of old. They come in excited anticipation or quiet reflection, in family groups or carrying the memories of those who cannot make the journey themselves. They come robed in white, anonymous and equal before Allah, to satisfy religious duty and to fulfil spiritual ambition. They come to be part of the largest annual migration of people on earth. They come to Mecca and Medina; they come to meet God. Non-Muslims cannot follow them into Islam's holiest cities, but they can watch in awe one people engaged in the pursuit of one journey spilling through all the cities of Arabia and rejoicing in horn-blowing joy on their return.

Pilgrims at Mount of Mercy, Arafat, Saudi Arabia

TRADING PLACES

They may not match the stock exchanges of New York, London or Tokyo in terms of dollars traded, but they claim a far more ancient lineage. Get lost in any of the region's labyrinthine souqs and participate in brisk trading in olives, the haggle-to-the-death technique of cloth merchants, and a collusive wink and a nod over gulled customers.

Mutrah souq, Oman

13

CHRIS MELLOR

'AHLAN WA SAHLAN' – WELCOME

There isn't a home without a set; they're often seen in giant form on roundabouts; they circulate at every meeting. They are of course coffee cups. Buy a half-dozen, together with a brass coffeepot, as a reminder of Arabia's most endearing and most enduring characteristic – the legendary habit of hospitality.

Woman serving coffee, Dubai, UAE

14

CLINT LUCAS

JENNY WALKER

15
MEETING THE LOCALS

Apparently 'mad, bad and dangerous to know', the wild men of Arab tribal lands, begirt with dagger, are disarmingly charming and educated up close. Talk about the big three (firing, siring and expiring) and you'll win friends for life. Philosophy and football are handy topics in reserve.

Local man, Oman

MANNA FROM HEAVEN

Giant copper trusses of dates hang pendulous in the palms in early summer. Learn how to crunch a half-ripe date, fresh from the tree, and the explosion of taste will register in parts of the brain you didn't know you had. You can sleep off the shock under the fronds – in company with the rest of Arabia's oases inhabitants.

**Dates ripening,
Wadi Hoqain, Oman**

JENNY WAL

17

TOR EIGELAND/SAUDI ARAMCO WORLD/PADIA

16 HEAVEN SCENTED

Gifted by wise men to babes (according to the Bible), and queens to kings (Queen Sheba to King Solomon), harvested from the barks of ugly trees in the mist-swirling magic of Oman and Yemen, frankincense is responsible for the history of Arabian empires. Catch its tantalising aroma in the house of a new-born, buy the beads of amber-coloured sap in the souq, or better still visit the trees of Dhofar.

Frankincense, Oman

CHRIS MELLOR

18 UNDER THE (RED) SEA

Who would imagine that beneath the surface of the Red Sea, whole dramas are played out by fantastical characters in costume? Wing-finned angel fish dance over death as midnight-blue stalkers and lurkers cruise the coral gardens for heroic small fry. You don't need to dive with the conga eels for a balcony view: hang from the gods with a snorkel and pluck empty handfuls of sardines as they boil by, or dangle a leg among the floating pipe fish.

Coral reef, Red Sea, Saudi Arabia

Contents

Regional Map Contents

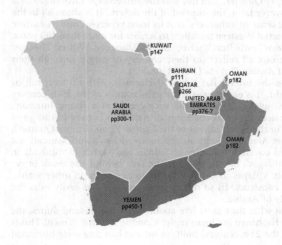

KUWAIT p147

BAHRAIN p111

QATAR p266

OMAN p182

UNITED ARAB EMIRATES pp376-7

SAUDI ARABIA pp300-1

OMAN p182

YEMEN pp450-1

Destination Oman, UAE & the Arabian Peninsula

For centuries Arabia has excited the interest and inspired the imagination of Western countries. As early as 1829, Victor Hugo, in the preface to *Les Orientales*, wrote that Europe was 'leaning towards the East'. Since that time, an astonishing 60,000 books have been written about Arabia in Britain alone.

Thanks to this literary relationship, say the word 'Arabia' (rather than 'Middle East') and a set of images is instantly conjured: Queen of Sheba holding court at Ma'rib in Yemen; camel caravans of frankincense from Dhofar in Oman; dhows laden with pearls from Dilmun; ruins of empire picked over by crows in Saudi Arabia's Madain Saleh. The caravans and the dhows may be plying different trades these days on more mechanised routes, but the colour of a modern camel market in Najran, and the click of amber prayer beads in Doha belong to the lexicon of *The Thousand and One Nights* that brought Scheherazade's exotic and vulnerable world to English-speaking countries. This text continues to inform the way we relate to the modern countries of the Arabian Peninsula today.

What binds the seven countries of Arabia into a single entity for Western on-lookers are the elements that are most 'other' (to borrow Edward Said's term) to Western concepts. There's the emphasis on race, grounded in Bedouin roots and expressed through tribal allegiance, family values and hospitality; Islam and the haunting call to prayer rising above the daily grind; a shared language – not just any language, but God's own words, spoken through the Quran. And then there's the desert, a physical and metaphorical reduction of life to essential principles.

'No man,' wrote Wilfred Thesiger of his travels with the Bedu in *Across the Empty Quarter*, 'can live this life and emerge unchanged...He will carry, however faint, the imprint of the desert.' It is above all in the desert that the sense of 'otherness' is at its most powerful, and its austere allure has attracted Western travellers to Arabia for more than 400 years. Marco Polo, Jean Lewis Burckhardt, Charles Doughty, Wilfred Thesiger and Paul Theroux all reflect on their country of origin through their experiences of *Arabia Deserta* (Desert Arabia).

Standing on the utterly flat Jiddat al-Harrasis, with no tree, hill or boulder in sight, it is easy to share the exhilaration of the 19th-century writer, AW Kinglake, at being 'the very centre of a round horizon'. This egoism raises the great challenge of Arabia: it is hard not to go in search of self in the blank canvas of the Rub al-Khali (Empty Quarter); not to look for Aladdin's lamp in the souqs of San'a and Muscat; not to peer behind covered balconies in Jeddah and search for Sinbads in Gulf fishing villages', nor to imagine the face behind the mask in remote mountain villages. It is hard not to go in search, in other words, of a Western construct. In so doing, however, one can easily miss the modern reality of Arabia.

When asked what they most like about their land of sand dunes, the Bedu near Al-Hashman in Oman reply: 'Coming to town'. Town! This is the Arabia of the 21st century, built on oil and banking – sophisticated communities looking to the future with vision and creating empires out of sand – or rather on land reclaimed from the sea.

As a traveller to Arabia, it's easy to become aware of the responsibility towards the fragile structures of the desert, but there is a greater responsibility to see a region for what it is rather than how the media, literature or tradition portrays it. The Peninsula Arabs are proud of their heritage but they are not sentimental about infant mortality rates, lack of education and the desiccating summer months without air-conditioning. If they are not sentimental about the passing of the past, then neither perhaps should we be.

Getting Started

Tell your neighbour you're off to the Arabian Peninsula for a holiday and they'll probably think you have a death wish. Many people think of the Peninsula under the generic term 'Middle East' and immediately assume that it's virtually a no-go area. For the most part, however, this is not the case. Even in countries that continue to give the visitor cause for concern and where it's imperative to check with your embassy before travelling (namely, Saudi and Yemen), there is an overwhelming determination to increase tourism. Hand in hand with that determination is a greater commitment to the visitor's safety (see p532). Even in Kuwait, on the doorstep of Iraq, you would never know that this is a country bordering a war zone.

Pockets of political troubles aside, the Arabian Peninsula is actually one of the *safest* places you're likely to visit: crime rates are low, people run after you with shopping you've left on the shop counter, unlocked cars are still there when you get back, and people mostly want to give (a greeting, coffee, some dates) rather than take.

So how easy is it to visit? Most countries in the region now offer visas on arrival. Only entering Saudi Arabia remains challenging – particularly for single women (see p366). With some planning, however, it's possible to obtain a Saudi transit visa, giving you the ability to travel overland between most Peninsula countries.

The world-class hotels and restaurants of the Gulf States are no secret, but for those who remember films such as *Lawrence of Arabia* it may come as some surprise that the Peninsula is crisscrossed with an excellent set of roads. With widespread electricity, clean water provision and access to car hire, you can penetrate mountain villages and desert wilderness with a minimal lack of creature comforts.

DON'T LEAVE HOME WITHOUT

The following items shouldn't be overlooked when packing for the Arabian Peninsula:

- **Appropriate clothing** (p51) People of the Peninsula are usually impeccably dressed and you may feel embarrassed without something smart; long sleeves, trousers (not jeans) and a head scarf (for women) are useful for visiting mosques or family homes. Pack some warm attire too: this may seem odd in a region with some of the hottest temperatures on earth but many places of interest in the region are above 2000m (including San'a, Abha and Jebel Akhdar) and at ground level the air-conditioning can be ferocious.

- **International Driving Permit** (p553) Some regional car-hire companies won't accept your home licence.

- **Mosquito net and repellent** Mosquitos are an irritating problem of low-lying areas in the region.

- **Personal items** While condoms and tampons are available in the big cities, they are hard to find elsewhere.

- **Travel insurance** (p553) With a high regional incidence of road traffic accidents, health insurance is strongly advised.

- **Vaccinations** (p560) Thankfully few are essential for the region.

- **Visas** (p541) Anyone carrying an Israeli passport or an Israeli stamp in their passport may be denied entry.

The challenge the Peninsula presents for the visitor is more in terms of cost. To make the best of the region, you ideally want to be staying in four-star hotels and hiring a 4WD. Facilities have been deliberately developed for the affluent tourist and there's almost no tradition of backpacker travel. Public transport seldom leads to sites of interest, there are no 'cheap-and-cheerful' hostelries where budget travellers can meet each other and *foul madamas* (a bean dish with olive oil) is more likely for breakfast than banana pancakes.

Yemen is something of an exception: with a much less developed infrastructure, tourism (particularly of the outdoor-adventure kind) has for decades been targeted as a useful source of income. Even here, however, most tourists rely on hiring a vehicle or taking a tour.

So, does this mean you shouldn't go if you can't afford Northern European prices? If you can muster a group of four to share the cost of car hire, pack camping equipment and eat locally (kebabs and salad), it's possible to target areas of the United Arab Emirates (UAE), Oman, and Yemen especially, for prices similar to a touring holiday in the USA. In addition, package tours from Europe are making Dubai and Salalah more affordable.

If you're aiming to work in the Peninsula, it's usually better to find a job before you arrive; bear in mind too that it's illegal to work on a 'visit visa'. If you do find casual work (in Dubai or Muscat) you will most likely be recruited on local pay rates. This usually means no air tickets home, less salary and less leave. If you arrange a job in advance, your sponsor will take care of your visa, housing arrangements and furniture, and can advise on schooling if you're bringing the family. Setting up house, opening bank accounts and buying a car are easy in any of the cities throughout the region. It's worth picking up a copy of *The Complete Residents' Guide* to your country (published by Explorer). See also the Expats chapter (p91) for more information.

WHEN TO GO

The Peninsula is ideally visited between November and March. At this time, the temperature hovers between 25°C and 35°C, occasional rains bring a blush of flowers to the desert and the interior can be explored without the worry of heat stroke.

Winter may be optimum but it's not the only time to go. If you want to know the real meaning of desert, then the summer (which regularly reaches 50°C) is certainly an experience: this is when you can spot mirages, visible heat waves and melting roads; when you appreciate the importance of the afternoon siesta, and when you finally understand why water, not oil, is the lifeblood of the region. Without water (and without a hat) heat exhaustion is an everyday hazard.

There are two other advantages to travelling in summer: firstly, this is considered off-season in most parts of the Peninsula (except for Salalah in Oman) and hotel prices are considerably lower. Secondly, in Salalah and parts of Yemen, the summer brings light drizzle, cooler temperatures than the rest of the Peninsula and a magnificent green landscape. For more information on weather, see the Climate sections in the individual country chapters.

Travelling during the region's religious festivals can be an interesting experience. During Ramadan, the Muslim month of fasting, visitors are more restricted (eating or drinking during the day must be kept hidden, and restaurants are often closed for the month). There's the chance, however, to try night-time culinary treats in the Ramadan tents

One night in the top suite at the Burj al-Arab seven-star hotel in Dubai costs US$7000.

See Climate Charts (p530) for more information.

When the temperature reaches 50°C, employers in the Peninsula are meant to send workers home. National weather centres, however, seem to be stuck on 49.9°C.

FAVOURITE FESTIVALS & EVENTS

Mention the word 'holiday' while at work in the Arabian Peninsula and your colleague will have left the building before you've got past the letter 'h'. The people of the Peninsula love their holidays and make the most of them, usually with some kind of traditional celebration such as camel racing, dancing or poetry recital. Most of these occasions are small, ad hoc affairs: a spontaneous gathering of *sheiba* (old men) in a fishing village, singing the ancestral songs of toil and harvest; or the convergence of young cousins on a mountainside to drum up good omens for a wedding. If you chance upon one of these events in your travels, it is sure to be a highlight, as no-one will let you stand on the sidelines. They provide a particularly exciting opportunity for women travellers to gain a window onto a world of henna-painted hands and feet, intimate discussions about married life and the jubilant wearing of magnificent gold.

For a more formal version of these kinds of local festivals, it's worth timing your visit around **Muscat Festival** (p204), held annually in January/February in Oman. The festival is a pageant of traditional craft making, moneymaking and merrymaking, with dancers from Sur (Oman), Egyptian caftan-sellers and clowns from Eastern Europe all sharing in a cultural exchange that has typified the region for centuries.

Then there is **Jenadriyah National Festival** (p314) outside Riyadh, Saudi Arabia, in late February and early March, where the King's Cup (an epic camel race) takes place with all the fluffing-up of plumage, and smoothing of coats that one would expect of the accompanying falconry displays and horse-racing events.

In the summer months, Emiratis, Bahrainis, Kuwaitis and Qataris migrate south to Oman's Dhofar region to chew on camel kebabs under the rain in the **Khareef Festival** (p257), held annually in August in Salalah. In December each year, the Dubai International Film Festival takes place under the auspices of Sheikh Ahmed bin Saeed al-Maktoum. Inaugurated in 2004, this not-for-profit event attracts prominent figures from the film industry from over 45 countries. Dubai is even being slated for use as a location in one or two high-flying future film projects.

And let's not forget the region's two great annual shopping festivals: the **Hala Shopping Festival** (p166) held in Kuwait City during the third week of February and the **Dubai Shopping Festival** (www.mydsf.com), usually held between December and February (see p442). While the bargains attract people from around the world, there is no greater gathering of regional people (other than during the haj, of course) on the Peninsula. Like the bazaars of ancient times, it matters little what is on sale or under what kind of roof: people come instead to ask *'Shay akhbar?'* (What's the news?), and on hearing there's no news, settle down for a week's tea and talk.

attached to hotels. Public transport can be erratic, driving habits deteriorate and business hours are reduced but, as if to compensate, the nights involve great socialising and public congregation. The two *eids* (Islamic feasts) tend to be family occasions but there's usually an opportunity to catch local dancing, singing and poetry recitals. See p534 for the dates of religious holidays, and When to Go sections in individual country chapters.

COSTS & MONEY

It's hard to generalise about costs across the entire Arabian Peninsula as different countries are good value for different things. In Saudi, for example, domestic airfares are reasonably priced; in Oman, street food and quick eats haven't increased in price for ten years; in Yemen, accommodation is cheap; in the Gulf countries, electrical goods are markedly lower than in Western countries. The table (opposite) gives an idea of some typical prices in each of the region's countries. Minimum daily expenses are based on a cheap eat, budget hotel and public transport; maximum daily expenses reflect dinner, top-end accommodation and car hire.

HOW MUCH?

Kebab snack US$0.70

Local newspaper US$0.55

Litre bottle of water US$0.40

Litre of petrol US$0.35

Packet of *khobz* (Arabic bread) US$0.25

ATMs are found in most major cities and even in many rural towns. Except in Yemen, credit cards are widely accepted. A combination of cash and credit cards is the best bet with a few travellers cheques tucked in the sock for an emergency! For more details, see p536.

TRAVEL LITERATURE

There are some wonderful publications about the Peninsula, covering every kind of subject including history, the Bedu and wildlife. Included here are some highlights. See also Books in the Directory of each country chapter.

- *The Arab World: Forty Years of Change,* by Elizabeth Fernea and Robert Warnock. A wide-ranging and readable overview of the recent history of the Middle East.
- *Arabia Through the Looking Glass,* by Jonathan Raban. One of the most readable of English travel writers, Raban's observations on expatriate life in the region are as valid today as they were when he visited the region during the oil boom of the 1970s.
- *Arabia Without Sultans,* by Fred Halliday. A detailed and incisive account of the development of the Arab Gulf countries in recent decades.
- *Arabian Sands,* by Wilfred Thesiger. One of the last great adventurers, Thesiger was as much anthropologist and ethnographer as traveller. In this classic book he records the nomadic life of the Bedu before the discovery of oil changed the region forever.
- *A History of the Arab Peoples,* by Albert Hourani. This comprehensive and insightful history, written with the author's characteristic sensitivity, is a must for anyone keen to understand the peoples of the Peninsula.
- *The Merchants,* by Michael Field. Possibly the best single overview of life, business and culture in the Gulf.
- *Orientalism,* by Edward Said. This seminal discourse on the nature of the relationship between Arab lands and the West examines the stereotypes behind the mythologised view of the region in Western literature and media.
- *The Prize,* by Daniel Yergin. Winner of the Pulitzer Prize, this book is an epic history of oil.
- *Sandstorms,* by Peter Theroux. A memoir of the author's seven years stationed as a journalist on the Peninsula (chiefly at Riyadh), it's a witty and candid portrait of culture and politics in the Middle East.
- *Seven Pillars of Wisdom,* by TE Lawrence. The account of the Arab campaign of 1915–18 is widely regarded as the most evocative description ever written about Arabia and the foundation of the modern states of the Peninsula.

DAILY EXPENSES (US DOLLARS)

Country	Cheap Eat	Dinner	Budget Hotel	Mid Hotel	Top Hotel	Car Hire	Min. Expenses	Max. Expenses
Bahrain	$4	$39	$47	$66	$184	$37	$66	$261
Kuwait	$5	$50	$83	$200	$333	$53	$100	$437
Oman	$4	$38	$64	$167	$282	$38	$77	$359
Qatar	$5	$27	$110	$192	$330	$44	$69	$401
Saudi Arabia	$5	$27	$27	$80	$133	$43	$40	$203
UAE	$5	$20	$68	$136	$218	$44	$82	$282
Yemen	$2	$5	$14	$24	$0	$60	$16	$90

- *Travels With a Tangerine,* by Tim Mackintosh-Smith. This readable set of extracts from the journals of Ibn Battuta, a 14th-century Arab Marco Polo, traces his journeys across the Arab world.

INTERNET RESOURCES

There are a wealth of good websites connected with the region. A good place to start is **Lonely Planet** (lonelyplanet.com), where succinct summaries on travelling to the Peninsula are combined with travel news and 'postcards' from other travellers. The Thorn Tree forum allows you to ask questions before you go or dispense advice when you get back.

Al-Bab (www.al-bab.com/arab/countries/egypt.htm) Meaning 'The Gate', this is indeed a gateway to the Arab world with links to dozens of news services, country profiles, travel sites and maps.

Al-Jazeera (www.al-jazeera.com) The controversial satellite service runs this very popular news-and-views-oriented website (see p294).

Arab Cafe (www.members3.boardhost.com/arabcafe/) A lively message and discussion board on Arab-world related issues (as well as adolescent Arab preoccupations).

Arabia.com (www.arabia.com) Self-styled as the 'Arab world's leading online destination', it has chat forums and covers a wide range of subjects including news, shopping, travel, women and entertainment.

Arabnet (www.arab.net) Useful Saudi-run online encyclopaedia of the Arab world. It collects news and articles, and links to further resources, organised by country.

RESPONSIBLE TRAVEL

Travelling sensitively often means following local custom (see p50), especially in choosing what to wear or how to interact socially. There are times, however, when following local custom is not such a good idea. Saving water, turning the air-conditioning off when leaving a room, avoiding buying items such as turtle shell and coral, and disposing of litter appropriately are not always a priority of locals, but they are commonsense measures that can help protect the environment.

We've all heard the saying 'take only pictures; leave only footprints', but it's not always that simple. In the Arabian Peninsula, people (women in particular) are very sensitive about being photographed and it's worth asking before clicking. Military sites are another touchy subject; quite what the visitor can reveal from a photo that Google Earth cannot is not a conversation you want to have with a policeman.

Footprints may seem harmless enough but if you can see them, chances are you've just cut a new trail across the desert – in all probability over seeds that were lying dormant, ready to germinate at the first hint of rain.

In addition to pictures and footprints, one could add 'Bag it and bin it'. But bear in mind that bagging live shells is banned across the Peninsula and avoid binning your rubbish in receptacles that are never emptied.

In summary, perhaps the best advice is 'take it or leave it as found'!

Parts of the classic film *Lawrence of Arabia,* based on the life of TE Lawrence, were filmed in the sand dunes of South Wales in the UK.

Lonely Planet, with other concerned parties in the industry, supports the carbon offset scheme run by climatecare.org. Lonely Planet offsets all of its staff and author travel.

Itineraries
BEST OF THE ARABIAN PENINSULA

OMAN   Two Weeks

Puzzle out **Old Muscat** (p197) for two days and get lost in Mutrah's gossipy, garrulous **souq** (p197). On day three, experiment with a trip on the wild side to **Al-Seifa** (p213), returning via **Wadi Mayh** (p212). If you felt at home in the wilderness, hire a 4WD and follow the gulls from **Qurayat** (p213) to **Sur** (p217) on day four, pausing to wade with the toads in **Wadi Shab** (p215). Spend day five inspecting Sur's boat-builders and potter round to **Ras al-Jinz** (p221) on day six. Rise at dawn on day seven to salute last-minute turtles. Swim with the sardines near **Al-Ashkara** (p222) and reach for the stars at a desert camp in **Sharqiya (Wahiba) Sands** (p225). Follow the resourceful Bedu into nearby **Ibra souq** (p226) on day eight and drive to **Nizwa** (p231), Oman's spiritual heartland. During days nine to 11, head for high places on **Jebel Shams** (p234), slide down under in **Al-Hoota Cave** (p233), and on day 12 go over the top on the **mountain road** (p233) to the formidable **Nakhal Fort** (p238). Celebrate the journey's end with a squid kebab in **Seeb** (p210).

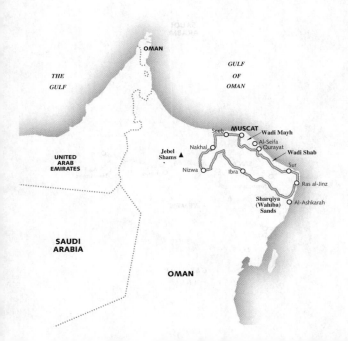

Unveil the very soul of the desert in this two-week, 1000km round trip to some of the Peninsula's loveliest sands, seas and souqs. This is the chance to see what Chelsea Tractors (4WDs) were made for.

YEMEN
Two Weeks

Spend the first couple of days savouring the sublime townscape of **San'a** (p459) before heading out on a day trip to the improbable rock palace of **Wadi Dhahr** (p467). Hike through the terraces to nearby fortified mountain villages such as **Kawkaban** (p468). The following morning leave San'a and clamber breathlessly through the Haraz Mountains for a couple of days of trekking around the cheerful town of **Manakhah** (p470). Wind down the escarpment to the hot and dusty plains of the **Tihama** (p478). Pause at the steamy port of **Al-Hudayda** (p478) and search out a fish supper. Aim to arrive here on a Thursday afternoon and let the noisy, early morning crowds at the Friday market in **Beit al-Faqih** (p480) sweep you off your feet. Spend the rest of the day searching for shade in the narrow lanes of Unesco-listed **Zabid** (p480), the hottest town in the world. Pause for a day or so in the cosmopolitan university town of **Ta'izz** (p485), which gives a radically different view of Yemen, and then head back to San'a for a night.

The following morning take your sanity and better judgement by the hair and head for wild and crazy **Ma'rib** (p494) for a date with the Queen of Sheba. From Ma'rib take a deep breath and, plunging into the Empty Quarter, let your armed Bedouin escort lead you to the ruined city of **Shabwa** (p498) and the exciting desert trail to **Wadi Hadramawt** (p505). Spend the last couple of days recuperating among the magnificent mud palaces and tower blocks of Arabia's largest wadi before flying from **Sayun** (p507) back to San'a.

Meet the Queen of Sheba in the oral legends of Arabia's hot and heady heartland. Height is what this 2000km, two-week route around Yemen is all about: high buildings of mud, high mountain terraces, high tribal tensions, and the mythical qat-chewing high.

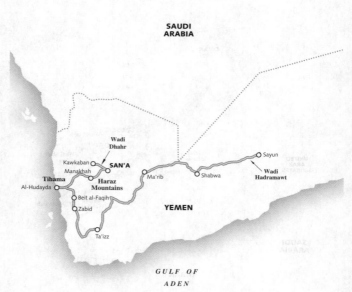

SAUDI ARABIA   Three Weeks

Challenge preconceptions of Arabia in the desert city of **Riyadh** (p311) with its 21st-century **Kingdom Tower** (p313) and dizzying **Sky Bridge** (p314). Wind the clock back a century by visiting **Masmak Fortress** (p313) and put the famous 1902 raid by Ibn Saud into a wider context at the **National Museum** (p313). After three days in Riyadh, take the long-distance bus to the **Al-Ula** (p333), with its distinctive wind blown desert formations. Save Saudi's best-kept secret for the morning: chances are you'll have the Nabataean site of **Madain Saleh** (p336) to yourself. Catch evocations of TE Lawrence along the ruins of the Hejaz railway, then fly to liberal **Jeddah** (p322) at the start of week two. Bake on the **beach** (p325), or shop in the city's **souqs** (p324). Better still, meander through **old coral houses** (p324) in Jeddah's balconied merchant quarter and learn who lurked behind the shuttered windows at the **museums** (p325). End week two by exploring the pristine underwater world of the **Red Sea** (p332). Journey south via the misty mountain tops of **Abha** (p340), and relax the eye among neat crops, impossibly green after the burnt-earth tones of the desert fastness. Begin week three in **Najran** (p344), with its cantankerous camels, part-Yemeni locals and mud-brick fortresses framed by shady palms. Travel north towards **Al-Khamasin** (p351) and step into the uniquely remote Empty Quarter, with memories of Thesiger and the Bedu pacing through the shifting dunes. Look out for other desert inhabitants, including magnificent Arabian oryx, in the shimmering sands of **Uruq Bani Ma'arid Protected Area** (p349). Return to Riyadh, stopping briefly to visit the ruins of **Dir'aiyah** (p318), a lonely remnant of Al-Saud's rapid rise to power.

Feel the allure of the desert firsthand in this three-week, 3000km epic that dances along the backbone of Arabia and unwraps the secret side of Saudi. The distances are great but so are the footsteps you'll be following.

UAE
Two Weeks

Indulge in the 21st-century experience in the happening city of **Dubai** (p381), cruise the **Dubai Creek** (p387) and admire head-in-the-clouds **Burj al-Arab** (p389) from **Jumeirah Beach** (p390) for three days. When the shopping wears thin, transfer to the more sophisticated city of **Abu Dhabi** (p417), capital of the UAE. Save enough funds for a pastry in **Emirates Palace** (p422) – the hotel where chandeliers and light bulbs outnumber people. On day five, escape on an overnight trip to enjoy lights of a different kind under the starry skies of the **Liwa Oasis** (p428), exploring the apricot-coloured dunes in the morning.

Having acquired a taste for the desert, try another overnight trip to **Al-Ain** (p429) on the Omani border, and wander through souqs of grumbling camels and date plantations for a sense of life in the slow lane. On day nine, give your desert experiences some context in the excellent **Heritage Area** (p405) and **Arts Area** (p407) in Sharjah. Move up the coast to **Ajman** (p410) on day 10 to relax at the **Ajman Kempinski Hotel & Resort** (p410). If you can tear yourself away from the *sheesha* (water pipe used to smoke tobacco) on the corniche, wander up the coast to **Umm al-Quwain** (p412) and explore the old town.

You then have the option of spending the last few days heading north to Oman's **Musandam Peninsula** (p242), pausing to visit the well-curated **National Museum of Ras al-Khaimah** (p414) or travelling across the country to the beautiful east coast. Make the bull-butting town of **Fujairah** (p433) your base and explore the fishing village of **Dibba** (p439), dive or snorkel off **Snoopy Island** (p437), or laze on the lawns of **Khor Fakkan** (p436).

Discover the Bedouin head behind the modern façade in this 1500km, two-week circuit through the Emirates. This is one country where you can enjoy the sublime to the ridiculous (top dollar chic and shared loo camp sites – or vice versa) within 24 hours.

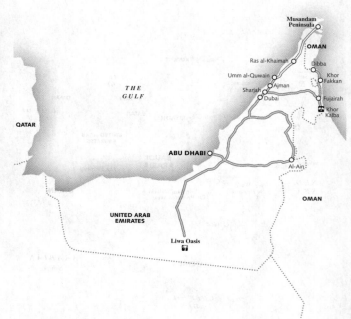

VENTURE FURTHER

THE TOWER TOUR: DUBAI TO SAN'A   Four Weeks

Start this journey in Dubai under **Burj al-Arab** (p389), symbol of the Gulf's modernity. After a couple of days exploring the city's new multi-floored architecture, go in search of its inspiration in the wind-tower constructions of Sharjah's **Heritage Area** (p405). See how the theme is redefined in the **Ajman Kempinski Hotel & Resort** (p410). Cross to the east coast and search for sand towers: ghost-crabs build these around the bays of any eastern Peninsula beach. Enter Oman via **Khatmat Malahah** (p242) and overnight in **Sohar** (p240), home to Oman's white-towered fort. Cut inland on a circuit through the Hajar Mountains via **Rustaq** (p238) and **Nakhal** (p238), two former capitals famous for their forts and watchtowers, before spending two days in **Muscat** (p192). Travel the coast road to **Sur** (p217) and see how the lighthouses of **Ayjah** (p219) guide dhows to safe haven. Complete your second week at the turtle sanctuary in **Ras al-Jinz** (p221). Head for culture-capital **Nizwa** (p231) via a stop over in **Sharqiya (Wahiba) Sands** (p225) and spend four days in the mountains of Jebel Shams. See Yemeni tower houses in the old village of **Al-Hamra** (p234). Hop on the bus to Salalah, and pass the **Sarfait border** (p254) to see more tower houses, particularly in **Wadi Hadramawt** (p505). Finish week three at **Shibam** (p505), which British explorer Freya Stark called the 'Manhattan of the Desert'. Spend four days in the skyscraper villages of mud in the **Haraz Mountains** (p467), leaving time to see the whitewashed window frames in the towers of **Old San'a** (p459).

Travel back in time on this ambitious 4000km, four-week route along the eastern rim of the Arabian Peninsula. Towers are the theme of this three-country trip: from UAE's glass-and-steel tower blocks, to Oman's crenulated watchtowers and Yemen's historical tower houses.

PAN-PENINSULA: SIX COUNTRIES IN SIX WEEKS   1½ Months

Fly into **San'a** (p456) and get acquainted with the sensory vocab of Arabia: haggling souqs, haunting call to prayer, wafts of *sheesha* and chaotic driving. Learn more about the lexicon of Arabia at Queen of Sheba's **Ma'rib** (p494) and chase other legends through **Wadi Hadramawt** (p505) along ancient frankincense routes. In week two, cross the **Sarfait border** (p254) into Oman to find your own **Boswellia sacra** (frankincense tree; p34) in the hills of **Dhofar** (p247) and visit **Khor Rouri** (p252) where the aromatic resin was exchanged for spices from India. Cross the desolate desert to **Muscat** (p192), noticing how a modern exchange between Arabia and Asia involves money and expatriate workers. In the towns of the **Al-Batinah Region** (p237), where many Omanis speak Baluchi and Farsi, see how ethnic integration is no new phenomenon. Cross into the UAE at the **Wajaja border** (p242) in week three, and discover how overseas trading powers the modern cities of the Gulf. Visit **Palm Island** (p378) and downtown **Abu Dhabi** (p417) and walk on water – or at least on reclaimed land. In week five, fly to **Doha** (p272) and see more land reclamation in the **Al-Corniche** (p275) and **Pearl Qatar** (p268). See how pearls gave the Gulf its former livelihood by flying to Bahrain in week six, visiting the **Museum of Pearl Diving** (p122) and buying loose pearls from **Gold City** (p129). Land is responsible for Arabia's modern wealth: see where it all started in **Bahrain's Oil Museum** (p134) before flying to Kuwait City and counting the cost of black gold at the **Kuwait House of National Memorial Museum** (p163). Trace similarities between the countries you've just visited in the stunning ethnographic collection of **Tareq Rajab Museum** (p163).

Trace the social history of the Peninsula from Yemen to Kuwait on an epic 5000km, six-week journey, focusing on the region's highlights. If you're lucky enough to get a Saudi visa, continue overland from Kuwait to Riyadh for a 'seven countries in seven weeks' experience.

IN THE FOOTSTEPS OF THE FAMOUS

IBN BATTUTA

Follow me – though in imagination only! I'm the legendary ghost of the Arab world's most famous traveller. I was born in Morocco in 1304 and at the age of 20, set out for Mecca. What started as a pilgrimage grew into a journey that lasted three decades and 120,000km, and took me from North Africa to China. But it was Arabia, and the land of the holy cities that drew me back. To this day, my shadow keeps crossing the flame of desert campfires and in the true oral tradition of my fellow Arabs, my travels lengthen the more each generation embellishes them for me.

I began my Arabian adventures in **Al-Ula** (p333), where Syrian Christians must end their journey and only Muslims may continue on the path of Abraham to Medina. From here I travelled on in pilgrim clothes to Mecca (p70). It was a pious journey filled with prayer in which I was conscious that the 'burdens of sin are effaced' by the merit of pilgrimage.

It was some years before I returned to Arabia – I arrived in **Jeddah** (p322) in a year of little rain. I took a *jalbah* (boat) from here. It was my first time at sea and I was fearful of the troublesome camels and of the high waves that threw us off course. We landed on the **Tihama** (p478) and drank water from ostrich shells. The merchants of Al-Yemen were open-handed and generous, and assisting of pilgrims. We rode to the great city of **Zabid** (p480) amid luxuriant gardens and where the women were of exceeding beauty. They travelled in camel litters and had an exceeding 'predilection for strangers' whom they agreed readily to marry. I left, without a wife, for **Ta'izz** (p485) and **San'a** (p456), a 'large and well-constructed city of bricks and plaster'. Then I set sail for East Africa from the port of **Aden** (p489), returning many moons later to **Al-Baleed** (p247) where people ate bananas and coconuts and fattened their livestock on plentiful sardines. In **Hasik** (p253) Arabs gathered gum from incense trees and lived in houses built with fish bones and roofed with camel hides.

From here I sailed in violent winds past **Masirah** (p228) – where people ate nothing but fish and cormorants, killed in an improper way – and landed at **Sur** (p217). I hired an Indian guide to take me to the great city of **Qalhat** (p217), which we reached in a state of great exhaustion – partly from trying to hinder the guide from making off with my garments, and partly through thirst, 'this being the season of heat'. I visited the **Tomb of Bibi Miryam** (p217) and then, after six days of traversing the desert, reached **Nizwa** (p231). At the foot of the mountain 'with fine bazaars', it had 'corrupt women' for whom the men showed no jealousy nor disapproval. I travelled next to Hormuz in Persia but stepped once again into Arabia, landing in **Bahrain** (p109) to watch **pearl divers** (p122) and shelter from the ravages of the sun in orchards of pomegranates and citrons. From Al-Bahrain I returned to Mecca and was honoured by God to perform the pilgrimage again.

WILLIAM GIFFORD PALGRAVE

I am no ghost – as an Englishman and Arabic scholar of the mid-19th century, I don't believe in them. I'm no scientist either: unlike many of my topographically minded contemporaries, I prefer to study 'the men of the land, rather than the land of the men'. I don't have the colourful genius of my compatriot, Richard Burton, under whose popular shadow my own figure has faded, but I am sincere in my desire to reveal the Arab temperament. Follow me through my *Personal Narrative of a Year's Journey through Central and Eastern Arabia,* if you care – and if you dare.

I had the courage to pass through Wahhabi territory in disguise and stay in Riyadh for six weeks where Burton eight years earlier was too scared to enter. I'm not scared of anything, not even criticism – minor exaggerations improved the story of my travels as well they might improve yours.

I trained as a Jesuit and when Napoleon III sponsored my mission to Arabia, Pope Pius IX summoned me to Rome to test my missionary zeal. Dressed as a middle-class merchant from Syria, with my assistant (a Greek I asked to be ordained for the purpose of accompanying me) and speaking Arabic passably well, I arrived in the heart of Arabia. My first great test was crossing the Nafud, 'an immense ocean of loose reddish sand'. In the midsummer heat, it was not unlike a scene from Dante's *Inferno.* We reached **Jubba** (p321) thirsty and exhausted, our leather bottles empty on the camel's flanks. In **Hail** (p320), enclosed by high mud walls, the people showed us Bedouin courtesy – and so we stayed. I ministered to the sick and watched the market erupt into life like the dawn chorus, and noted the humanity of Islamic daily life. When we came to leave, 'we carried with us the goodwill of all the court'.

It took us time to find guides willing to escort us to **Riyadh** (p311). The Najd is genuine Wahhabi country and 'to the rest of Arabia a sort of lion's den, on which few venture and fewer return'. Faisal's great city was surrounded by a sea of palm trees and echoed with the 'singing droning sound of waterwheels'. Fearful of spies and infidels, the old king fled on news of our arrival. After a month, Faisal's son Abdullah discovered we were Christian and threatened to have us killed. We negotiated a safe departure and left for the prosperous city of Hufuf, in the heart of a great oasis.

We took a ship to **Bahrain** (p109) and in January 1863, I bid farewell to my companion and sailed again for **Qatar** (p264). From here I tried several times to make the voyage to Oman and succeeded at length in reaching **Sohar** (p240). I was shipwrecked soon after and in **Muscat** (p192) suffered great weariness and depression which I blamed on my year and 10-month's journey. I was in fact suffering from typhoid. In March 1864 I returned to Europe and retreated to a monastery in Germany; a year later I renounced my Roman Catholic faith but remained an Englishman, spending my remaining days as a diplomat.

History

If there is one name in Arab history that most Western people will recognise, it's surely that of TE Lawrence, better known as Lawrence of Arabia – the same Lawrence, in fact, who wrote to his sceptical biographer that 'History isn't made up of the truth anyhow, so why worry'. This is an interesting question when it comes to the history of the Arabian Peninsula as there appears to be no definitive version of events. The story assumes a different shape – particularly since the beginning of the 20th century – according to whose account you read.

Lawrence's own account of Arabian history, so eloquently described in *The Seven Pillars of Wisdom,* is a case in point. You might imagine, from what he writes, that Lawrence and Allenby single-handedly brought the modern Arabian Peninsula into being during the Arab Revolt from 1915 to 1918: 'on my plan, by my effort', he states triumphantly on the taking of Akaba.

But where are the Arabs in Lawrence's account? What did they make of the pale-skinned, blue-eyed eccentric? The central drama of one of the most famous pieces of 'historical literature' of the 20th century imposes an essentially Western complexion upon the Arabs' greatest moment of unification. Read Suleiman Mousa's account of the same campaign in *TE Lawrence: An Arab View* and you barely recognise the same moment in history: Lawrence's advice is ignored; while he is busy taking credit for little skirmishes, larger battles led by the Arabs are only briefly mentioned; Lawrence arrives triumphant in cities where the Arab leaders, Feisal and Auda have been waiting for days. Far from the great, white hunter, he is remembered in many Arab accounts as a sickly individual with boils who, like a spoof in a Western, shot his own camel by mistake. But then such is history from an *Arab* perspective.

We'll never know whether Lawrence was hero or sideshow. What the example illustrates, however, is the caution with which you need to approach the history of the Peninsula. In the early 21st century, this must surely sound familiar to anyone following current events in the region in local as well as Western newspapers. It's tempting to agree with Lawrence that history can at times be more about fiction than fact.

Given that the Peninsula is a compact region shared by countries of small population, you'd think it would have a common history. It doesn't – or only in the most general terms. What follows is therefore only a broad summary where sometimes a passing reference is made to an important historical event. See the History section of each country for the details.

The American journalist Lydell Hart made 'El-Lawrence' into a media superhero. *Sunday Times* of June 1968 hailed Lawrence as a 'Prince of Mecca, riding across Arabia'. Hollywood did the rest with a theme tune that more people can hum than can name the capital of Saudi.

EARLY BEGINNINGS

Stand in the middle of Wadi Fanja on the outskirts of Muscat and you may just uncover more than the toads and grasshoppers of today's arid vista. This was where archaeologists discovered a herbivorous dinosaur, not unlike Zalmoxes or Rhabdodon dinosaurs from France and Romania. What is interesting about this discovery is that it shows that the climate of eastern Arabia, some 66 million years ago, was far more verdant than it is today, with savannah-like grasslands and abundant rainfall. Crocodiles also inhabited places like Wadi Fanja, suggesting that permanent rivers helped to cut the deeply incised mountain rages of today's Peninsula.

BOSWELLIA SACRA (THE FRANKINCENSE TREE) & THE INCENSE ROUTE

Drive along the road from Salalah to the Yemeni border, and you may be forgiven for missing one of the most important aspects of the Arabian Peninsula's history. Sprouting from the limestone rock as if mindless of the lack of nutrition, leafless and (for much of the year) pretty much lifeless, *Boswellia sacra* must be one of the least spectacular 'monuments' on a traveller's itinerary. With its peeling bark and stumped branches, the frankincense tree looks more like something out of *The Day of the Triffids*. Yet, hard though it is to imagine, its sacred sap sustained entire empires across the Peninsula; found its way into the inner sanctum of temples in Egypt, Jerusalem and Rome; is recorded in the Bible and the Quran and is used to this day in many of the world's most sacred ceremonies. According to Pliny, writing in the 1st century AD, it was thanks to the frankincense trade that the people of southern Arabia became the richest people on earth.

But what exactly is frankincense? It is formed from small beads of white- or amber-coloured sap that ooze from incisions made in the bark, which are then left to harden in the sun. It has a natural oil content, allowing it to burn well, and the vapour is released by dropping a bead of the sap onto hot embers. The pungent aroma is wafted at the entrance of a house to ward away evil spirits or to perfume garments. The sap has medicinal qualities and was used in just about every prescription dispensed by the Greeks and the Romans. It is still used in parts of the Peninsula to treat a wide range of illnesses, including coughs and psychotic disorders, believed to be the result of witchcraft.

Although the tree also grows in Wadi Hadramawt in neighbouring Yemen as well as in northern Somalia, the specimens of Dhofar in southern Oman have been famed since ancient times for producing the finest-quality sap. The tree favours the unique weather system of this corner of Dhofar, just beyond the moisture-laden winds of the *khareef* (summer season) but near enough to enjoy their cooling influence. As such it is notoriously difficult to root elsewhere.

Tradition dictates that the tree is a gift from Allah, and is thus not to be propagated, bought or sold, only harvested if it happens to be within your plot of land. Needless to say, that didn't stop people from trying. In an attempt to protect their precious resources, the Jibbali, descendants of the ancient people of Ad, honed the art of misinformation. Flying red serpents and toxic mists were just some of the mythical tribulations rumoured to protect groves from evil eye and thieving hand.

At the height of the trade in the 2nd century AD, no less than 3000 tonnes of frankincense were transported each year (mostly by sea) from south Arabia to Greece and Rome. The trade was centred on Sumhuram, which the Greeks called Moscha and which is now known as Khor Rouri. Today the ruins of this once great port are a short drive from Salalah, the capital of Dhofar

---

Homo erectus was attracted to the rich hunting and gathering grounds of southern Arabia more than a million years ago, though quite where they came from no-one knows for sure. *Homo sapiens* arrived on the scene 100,000 years ago and began more organised settlement. Visitors to museums across the region, particularly the National Museum in Bahrain (see p122) and the newly opened Bait al-Barandar in Muscat (see p196) will see plenty of evidence of their distant descendants, dating from 10,000 BC, including charcoal burners and spear heads. Excavations at Thumamah, in central Saudi Arabia, have uncovered similar Neolithic finds, suggesting that early human settlement wasn't confined to the seaboard rim of the Peninsula.

Arabia & the Arabs: From the Bronze Age to the Coming of Islam, by Robert G Hoyland, is one of the few histories of the Peninsula to describe the pre-Islamic period in detail.

It's hard to get too excited about any of the loose groups of stone-age or bronze-age individuals that followed, but it must have been a busy 7000 years because by 3000 BC an intricate set of trade routes had been established between Arabia and Mesopotamia (Iraq) and the Indus Valley. Copper was the main cargo, it was mined in Majan (the ancient name of Oman) and traded through the growing empire of Dilmun.

and the second-largest city in modern Oman. Looking out to sea on a wet and windy day in July, when the grazing camels and flamingos shelter in the upper reaches of the lagoon and leave the violent shore to the ghost crabs, it's little wonder that easier ports would be found for readier cargo, and Khor Rouri left to slip back to nature.

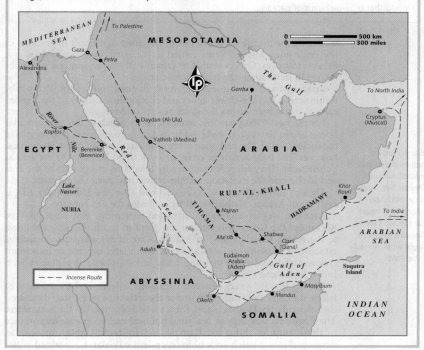

Dilmun was the first great civilisation in the Peninsula, founded on the sweet waters of ancient springs off the coast of Bahrain and extending from Failaka Island (off the coast of present-day Kuwait) towards the copper-bearing hills of Oman.

It's easy to simplify the lives of the ancients but these early seafaring traders were no barbarians: they enjoyed complex legends, ate too many dates and suffered bad teeth; took the time to thread beads of carnelian to hang round their beloveds' necks; and expressed their interest in life through their administrations of death – much like their contemporaries in Egypt.

The Dilmun people were not the only ones to be fastidious about death. During a similar period of history in Oman (3000–2000 BC), the defiant tombs at Bat and Gaylah, dramatic in the waning sun, were erected along mountain ridges by the Hafit and the Umm an Nar cultures – people who belonged to the low-lying territories of the modern UAE (United Arab Emirates).

Death was on the mind of the Sabaeans of southern Arabia too, but in a more practical sense. The mighty Ma'rib dam (Yemen; see p449), upon which the livelihoods of 50,000 people depended, burst its banks in AD 570,

Travel to the museums of Pakistan and the Mediterranean and you'll be sure to find the small round seals that were the hallmark of Dilmun traders – their personal signatures – and evidence of the extent of their trading influence.

THE HUMAN SIDE OF A HOLY MAN

Accounts describe Mohammed as enjoying good health; being fond of milk, honey, plaiting his hair in two or four braids (like some inhabitants of the Asir today) and cleaning his teeth with a stick from the toothbrush tree – such as can still be bought in bundles from souqs across the region. Touchingly, he said that dearest to him were 'prayer, perfumes, and women', all in this world that is 'reminiscent of paradise'.

---

scattering the people of Adz in one of the most significant migrations in the Peninsula's history. Some settled in the north and helped drive out Persian invaders. Others settled in Oman's Dhofar region and no doubt helped in developing the frankincense trade.

Exuding from the ugliest and most famous tree of the Peninsula, frankincense was the chief export and economic mainstay of the region, carried by caravan across the great deserts of Arabia.

For the next 5000 years this aromatic resin, which to this day pervades homes across the region, made southern Arabia one of the richest regions of the ancient world. The gathering of the aromatic gum was not so glamorous, however. The collectors were often slaves or those banished to the area as punishment. They fell sick from deadly infections indigenous to the area and life beyond the monsoon catchment was a wickedly harsh affair.

Though the frankincense trade declined after the 3rd century AD, it kept south Arabia relatively wealthy well into the 6th century.

Arabia's wealth inevitably attracted attention, not least that of Alexander the Great who was on the point of mounting an expedition to the region when he died in 323 BC. One of his admirals, Nearchus, established a colony on Failaka Island, which later became an important commeracial centre maintaining trade links for several centuries with India, Rome and Persia.

During the 950 years between Alexander's death and the coming of Islam, much of the Gulf came under the influence of Persian dynasties: the Seleucids, the Parthians and, from the 3rd century AD, the Sassanians. The Peninsula was only of marginal political and economic importance to these empires, however. Central and western Arabia, meanwhile, developed into a patchwork of independent city-states, sustained either by the frankincense trade or by farming. Around 25 BC, a Roman legion marched down the western coast of the Peninsula in an attempt to conquer the frankincense-producing regions, but it met with little success.

Between about 100 BC and AD 100 the Nabataean Empire controlled most of northwestern Arabia and grew extremely rich by taxing the caravans travelling between southern Arabia and Damascus. The remains of the Nabataean civilisation can be seen today at Madain Saleh (see p333) in Saudi Arabia, where the Nabataeans carved spectacular tombs into the desert cliffs, similar to those of their capital Petra (Jordan).

THE RISE OF ISLAM

Given that today four of every five people and three of every four countries are Muslim, there can be no greater moment of historical importance on the Arabian Peninsula than the birth of the Prophet Mohammed in the year AD 570 – the same year, incidentally, that the great dam at Ma'rib collapsed, signalling an end to the old order.

As one of the world's most influential spiritual leaders, it's easy to focus on Mohammed's teachings and forget his historical context, but in many ways the limited descriptions of his childhood give a good indication

Bahrain Island is a 'vast sea of sepulchral mounds', announced Theodore Bent, a traveller in the 19th century: 170,000 burial mounds cover 5% of the island's land mass, forming the largest ancient necropolis in the world.

Charismatic cities, such as the golden-pillared city of Ubar, were founded on the frankincense trade. Ubar (called by TE Lawrence, 'the Atlantis of the Sands') was only recently resurrected from the sands by using satellite imaging to locate it.

of life in the desert at that time. As his father died before he was born, Mohammed became the poor ward of his grandfather. Although his family were settled Arabs, he was given to a Bedouin foster mother, as was the custom at the time, to be raised in the desert. Perhaps it was this experience that gave him a sense of moderation and the preciousness of resources. In the desert, too, there were no intermediaries, no priests and no prescribed places of worship – nothing separating people from the things they believed in. Mohammed went on caravans and became a trusted trader before returning to Mecca, which at that time was a large and prosperous city that profited from being the centre of pilgrimage. It was the home of the Kaaba (see p76), a sanctuary founded by Abraham but occupied by the images and idols of many other tribes and nations.

Mohammed received his first revelation in 610 and began to lay the foundations of a new, monotheistic religion that condemned the worship of idols. As such, with an eye to the annual pilgrimage income, it is not surprising that the Meccans took fright. Mohammed and a small band of followers were forced to flee Mecca for Medina in 622, a date that marks the beginning of the first Islamic state.

From 622 to 632, the new religion spread across the Peninsula and within a century Muslim armies commanded an enormous empire that stretched from Spain to India. As the Islamic empire grew, however, Arabia became increasingly marginalised. Within 30 years of the Prophet's death (in 632) the Muslim capital was moved to Damascus. By the early 9th century, Mecca and Medina were stripped of their earlier political importance but grew in importance as spiritual centres.

As far as the rest of the world was concerned, the Peninsula was at this time something of a backwater. The European Crusades were focused more on the Levant and the Holy Land, and the old trade routes across Arabia more or less collapsed. From the 9th to the 11th centuries most of the Peninsula declined in wealth and importance. It remained an area of petty sheikhdoms bickering over limited resources, under the control of Tartar moguls, Persians and Ottoman Turks until the 14th century.

THE EUROPEANS ARRIVE

There is something satisfying about standing under the Tomb of Bibi Miriam in Qalhat (p217) in Oman and knowing that two of the world's great medieval travellers, Marco Polo and Ibn Battuta, stood there too.

Frankincense permeates the great oral histories of the region. The Queen of Sheba is fabled to have laid it at the feet of King Solomon, and then there were a certain three wise men who took some of the precious resin to Jerusalem.

Frankincense & Myrrh: A Study of the Arabian Incense Trade, by Nigel Groom, is a lively account of how these exotic fragrances made Arabia rich, examining the region's connections with other great empires of the time.

IBN BATTUTA – THE ARAB MARCO POLO

Ask anyone in the Arabian Peninsula to name a great traveller in history, and they'll be sure to mention Ibn Battuta, the 14th-century Muslim pilgrim born in 1304 in Tangier, Morocco.

Although it was the aspiration of all Muslims to attempt the pilgrimage to Mecca, most regarded it as the journey of a lifetime. Not so for Ibn Battuta: he set off on his travels at the age of 21 intending to perform the haj and study with the best scholars. But he reached Islam's holy cities having enjoyed the adventure so much that he simply went on going. He quickly discovered that with a combination of his own wit and charm (as well as a certain amount of toadying), he could win the patrimony of rich merchants along the caravan routes. This, along with an Islamic education that gained him access to lodgings at the *madrassas* (Muslim theological seminaries), allowed him to prolong his time on the road. He could be called the world's first budget traveller!

During his lifetime, his insatiable curiosity regarding the customs and manners of those from 'foreign countries' led him to spend no less than 24 years travelling across Asia, including parts of modern-day Saudi Arabia, Yemen and Oman, clocking up an impressive 120,000km. As such, he far out-travelled his contemporary, Marco Polo.

Their travels prefigured a revival in Western trading interests in Arabia and it wasn't long before the pilgrim caravans of Mecca were once again transporting spices and drugs from the Orient to Europe via the ports of Istanbul and Venice.

Meanwhile, a great Omani seafarer, Ahmed bin Majid, helped Vasco da Gama navigate the Cape of Good Hope in 1498 and, in good faith, told him of his own wondrous country on the Straits of Hormuz. The Portuguese quickly understood the strategic significance of their 'discovery' and by 1507 Portugal had annexed the Yemeni island of Suqutra, occupied Oman and colonised Bahrain. Travel along the coast of the Gulf today and Portuguese forts appear with regularity: cut inland, and there's no trace of them. The Portuguese were only interested in protecting their trade routes and made no impact on the interior of these countries at all – a suitable metaphor for the negligible cultural exchange that took place. When they were eventually ousted by the mid-17th century, they left not much more than a legacy of military architecture – and the Maria Theresa dollar.

'One great distinguishing feature of Muscat', wrote the English diplomat James Silk Buckingham in 1816, 'is the respect and civility shown by all classes of its inhabitants to Europeans.' It is an interesting comment because it appears to show that the intimate British involvement with Oman and the 'Trucial States' of the Gulf over the next two centuries was founded on mutual benefit rather than solely on colonisation and exploitation. On the one hand, the various treaties and 'exclusive agreements' that Britain signed with the sultan and emirs of the region

> According to Pliny, only 3000 families had the inherited right of harvesting frankincense and could only do so under certain conditions: those in contact with a woman, for example, or who had recently been to a funeral, were not allowed to cut the trees.

THE TRAVELLING TRIBE

And is there then no earthly place
Where we can rest in dream Elysian,
Without some cursed, round English face,
Popping up near, to break the vision?

When the English poet, Thomas Moore, wrote these words about great Middle Eastern destinations in the 18th century, he could have no idea how relevant they seem today – at the pyramids in Giza, for example, or at Petra in Jordan. Interestingly, however, the Arabian Peninsula remains one of the less visited corners of the old Orient.

While trade brought European merchant ships to the ports of the Red Sea and the Gulf, for much of the four hundred years before WWII the interior of Arabia was largely the subject of speculation only – and intense curiosity. That curiosity provoked an extended era of Western exploration by serious scholars, on the one hand, and by adventurers on the other. The first group (including Niebuhr, Burckhardt, Palgrave, Doughty and Blunt) were intent on learning about a land that gave birth to one of the most compelling creeds on earth. The latter group included a marvellously colourful collection of characters, such as Burton, better known to his contemporaries as Ruffian Dick.

Though he was obliged in his *Personal Narrative of a Pilgrimage to Al-Madinah and Meccah* to make his 'love of adventure minister to the advance of a geographical science', Burton found plenty of time to learn Arabic fluently, dress in local clothing and pass himself off as a *haja* (pilgrim) in Mecca. He also found time to write copious, salaciously detailed footnotes to *The Thousand and One Nights* tales.

Men were not the only adventurers to the region. In the 19th century, Lady Anne Blunt accompanied her husband to the Peninsula in search of Arab horses, and on leaving her womanising husband, abandoned her stud farm in England for an apricot orchard in Cairo. Today, most Arabian horses, even those in Arabia itself, can be traced back to the Crabbet stock that she helped to establish – a fitting dispersal of influence for one of the 'travelling tribe'.

THE PEARLING INDUSTRY

One of the mixed pleasures of visiting a Gulf jewellery shop is to hold a natural pearl in the palm of one's hand and see reflected in its gorgeous lustre the not so illustrious history of the region.

Although pearls have come to be associated with Bahrain, they were harvested throughout the Gulf – many cities, including Salalah, Doha and Manama, have famous modern monuments commemorating the lost industry. Each region gave rise to a specific type of pearl. Pteria shells, or winged oysters, were extensively collected for their bluish mother-of-pearl off the coast of Ras al-Khaimah. The large shells known in the trade as 'Bombay Shells' were found in Omani waters and chiefly exported to London for pearl inlay and decorative cutlery. With an annual export of 2000 tonnes, worth UK£750,000, the most common pearl oyster of the Gulf was *Pinctada radiata*, collected off the coasts of Kuwait, Bahrain and the UAE.

Given the volume of the trade, it is not surprising that it supported the local economies of much of the Gulf. Trading in pearls has existed since the 3rd millennium BC but it was only in the 19th century, with the collapse of other trade routes in the region, that pearls assumed their economic value.

The pearling season began each year in late May, when the boats would leave Bahrain and the other settlements around the Gulf for the pearl banks lying offshore. There they remained at sea, through the blistering summer, without interruption until mid-October. Supplies were ferried out by dhow.

Workers were divided into divers (who descended for the shells with a weight between their feet) and pullers (who would hoist the divers back up again by rope). Neither were paid wages. Instead, they would receive a share of the total profits for the season. A puller's share was half to two-thirds of a diver's. Boat owners would usually advance money to their workers at the beginning of the season. But the divers were often unable to pay back these loans and got further into debt with each year. As a result they were often bound to a particular boat owner for life. If a diver died, his sons were obliged to work off his debts for him. It was not unusual to see quite elderly men still working as divers.

British attempts in the '20s to regulate and improve the lot of the divers were resisted by the divers themselves. Many failed to understand the complex accounting system the British had imposed. Riots and strikes became a regular feature of the pearling seasons in the late '20s and early '30s.

Around 1930 the Japanese invented a method of culturing pearls. This, combined with the Great Depression, caused the bottom to drop out of the international pearl market. The Peninsula's great pearling industry petered out almost overnight; although the collapse brought great hardship to the Gulf in the decades before the discovery of oil, few had the heart to regret it. For more information on pearls, see p123.

kept the French at bay and thereby safeguarded British trading routes with India. On the other hand, the British navy helped maintain the claims to sovereignty of the emerging Gulf emirates against marauding Turkish and Persian interests.

The chief British officer in the region was the political resident based in Bushire, on the coast of what is now Iran. The resident supervised the political agents, usually junior officers, stationed in the various sheikhdoms of the Gulf. This system was designed to keep the British presence low-key, while permitting swift action if the need arose.

In the early years of the 20th century, two things threatened British interests in the Gulf. The first came from the north: the Ottomans (in allegiance with the Germans) were also keen to establish their presence in the region. The second threat came from within Arabia itself. In 1902 Abdul Aziz bin Abdul Rahman al-Saud, known as Ibn Saud, began a series of conquests which would eventually lead to the formation of the state of Saudi Arabia. By 1912 the Saudis posed a serious threat to the

Plants of Dhofar, by Anthony Miller and Miranda Morris, is an exquisitely illustrated scientific guide to the plants of the region. It includes a wonderfully eclectic account of the social and historical importance of the frankincense tree from a botanist's viewpoint.

Gulf sheikhdoms. Had it not been for British protection, there's little doubt that Saudi Arabia would today include most or all of Kuwait, Qatar and the UAE.

With the outbreak of WWI in 1914, the Ottoman Empire sided with Germany. Sultan Mohammed V, as leader of the empire, declared jihad, or holy war, calling on Muslims everywhere to rise up against the allied powers of Britain, France and Russia.

To counter the sultan, the British negotiated an alliance with Hussein bin Ali, the Grand Sherif of Mecca. In 1916 Sherif Hussein agreed to lead an Arab revolt against the Ottomans in exchange for a British promise to make him 'King of the Arabs' once the conflict was over. To the famous disgust of TE Lawrence, the British never had any intention of keeping this promise, preferring to negotiate with the French on the carving up of the Ottoman Empire.

Of even more significance for the future, Britain had also promised to assist the Zionist movement. Known as the Balfour Declaration (named after the British foreign secretary), Britain viewed 'with favour the establishment in Palestine of a national home for the Jewish people' after the war.

Meanwhile, Sherif Hussein was forced to confine his kingdom (and his dreams of pan-Arabism) to the Hejaz. Less than a decade later, this region was also overrun by Ibn Saud, who became 'King of the Hejaz and Sultan of Najd'. In 1932 Ibn Saud combined these two crowns and renamed his country the 'Kingdom of Saudi Arabia' (see p301).

OIL

During the first decade of the 20th century, a rare resource was discovered on the Peninsula that was to change the face of the region forever. The first commercially viable oil strike in the Gulf was made at Masjid-i-Suleiman, in Persia, in May 1908. On the Arab side of the Gulf, the search for oil began shortly after WWI.

Sidebar (left margin):

It would seem that Ibn Battuta is once again to become a household name – and not wholly in a way he might have liked. The Ibn Battuta mall has just opened in Dubai, celebrating the great traveller in various themed entertainments (see p399).

The Maria Theresa dollar was a large silver coin used in currency in the region for several centuries after the Portuguese left. As it was made of very pure silver, it became a thing of value in itself. It was often fashioned into Bedouin jewellery.

PEAK OIL – FACT OR FALLACY?

In an address to OPEC in Vienna in 2006, the President of Saudi Aramco, Abdallah Jum'ah, stated that recoverable barrels of oil would last for 140 years at current rates of consumption: in other words, the world has only consumed about 18% of reserves. 'That fact alone,' he stated, 'should discredit the argument that peak oil is imminent and put our minds at ease concerning future petrol supplies'.

Put more simply, some would argue (albeit controversially) that there's more than enough oil to meet demand, and the Middle East, while having two thirds of *proven* oil supplies, controls considerably less *potential* oil supplies. In fact there is more oil outside the region than there is within it.

Why then are so many Western governments panicking about oil? Why have the policies of US and British leaders in particular been influenced by the perceived dependency of the West on Middle Eastern resources? George W Bush stated in 2002 that the 'dependency on foreign oil is a matter of national security. To put it bluntly [no surprises there] sometimes we rely upon energy sources from countries that don't particularly like us.'

Sentiment such as this has led to the shoring up of nascent oil industries in Africa and Russia, Norway and other countries. The irony is that this is leading to a faster depletion of non-Middle Eastern reserves, due to peak by 2025, which will lead to an even greater dependency on Middle Eastern reserves thereafter. As such, it's about time the old 'us and them' dialogue was replaced with a less diametrical rhetoric. In the current political climate, however, this doesn't seem very likely.

The British and the local rulers were initially very sceptical about the prospects of finding oil in the Gulf. Their interest only picked up after oil was found in commercial quantities in Bahrain in 1932. Among the Gulf's Arab rulers, interest in oil was spurred on by the collapse, around 1930, of the pearling industry, which for centuries had been the mainstay of the Gulf's economy.

Within a few years almost every ruler in the Gulf had given out some kind of oil concession in a desperate attempt to bolster their finances. The region's nascent industry was suspended temporarily during WWII but resumed soon after, increasing output to rival that of Iran, the world's biggest producer. By 1960 the Middle East was producing 25% of the non-Communist world's oil.

The 1960s brought the winds of change and by 1961, Kuwait gained independence from the British. In late 1971 Bahrain and Qatar followed suit and a few months later the small sheikhdoms of the lower Gulf combined to form the United Arab Emirates. Hand in hand with independence came a sense of national and regional identity; making decisions about how to spend the new oil revenue helped shape each regime into a more modern and inclusive political and social entity. Generous welfare programmes that emphasised primary health care and universal education were established and women began to have a voice in national affairs.

The new wealth, and the threat of cutting off oil supplies to Europe and the US, gave Middle Eastern countries an international influence they hadn't enjoyed for centuries. After each embargo, a surge in oil prices increased both their wealth and their power, triggering an enormous building boom in the Gulf. Western expatriates took part in the Black Gold Rush, providing engineering and financial expertise while hundreds of thousands of Asian expats were brought in as manual labour, the legacy of which continues to have profound effects on the indigenous populations (see p46).

Meanwhile, events in Iran (the revolution of 1979 and the Iran–Iraq war of 1980) began to cause concern, scaring off potential foreign investors, particularly in Kuwait, which lay only a few kilometres from the front line. In May 1981 Saudi Arabia, Kuwait, Bahrain, Qatar, the UAE and Oman formed the Gulf Cooperation Council (GCC) in an effort not only to increase economic cooperation, but also in response to the perceived threat posed by Iran.

Despite regional cooperation, in 1985 the bottom fell out of the oil market and times began to change. To varying extents all of the Gulf countries had trouble keeping up their building programmes while maintaining the generous welfare states that their people had come to expect. In many senses it was a timely reminder to each of the GCC countries to consider their future. Various countries are anxious about nearing peak production and exploration of new potential oil sites, both on and off shore, has intensified over the past decade. Some countries, like Bahrain, fear that their days of oil production are numbered – giving rise to market panic in other parts of the world. The issue of peak oil, however, is very much open to debate and some would argue that the evidence isn't entirely conclusive (see boxed text, opposite).

While regionally each country is hopeful that new oil discoveries and improved methods of extraction will help provide for future security, none of the Peninsula governments can afford to be over optimistic. Hence, the buzz word of the past 10 years in particular has been 'diversification'. Diversification of regional economies has assumed various guises.

Explorers of Arabia, by Freeth and Winstone, is a readable book describing the adventures of European travellers from the Renaissance to the Victorian era who penetrated the Arabian Peninsula.

British administration in the Gulf fell under the jurisdiction of the British Raj in India and, until India became independent, the rupee was the common currency of all the Gulf States. After 1948 it was replaced by a 'Gulf rupee' – in circulation until 1971.

What came to be called the 'oil weapon' (the embargo by the Gulf States of oil supplies to the West) was first used to powerful effect during the Arab–Israeli war of 1973 to protest against the West's support for Israel.

Oman, which has limited oil supplies, has developed gas and shipping industries and is involved in major port projects. The UAE has attracted international investment through high-flying projects like the film festival inaugurated in 2004, residential developments such as Palm Island and the World, and a Disneyland is in the making. Bahrain is marketing itself as a commercial and banking hub, and is currently building its showpiece Financial Harbour in Manama. Qatar has promoted itself as the Middle East's international forum for sports, holding the Asian Games in 2006, and all countries, including the heavily oil-dependent states of Kuwait and Saudi Arabia, are looking to tourism as a major future source of income. To this end, large commercial, cultural and tourist developments are taking shape across the region, including some of the most expensive and prestigious hotel and resort complexes in the world (see the Economy sections of each country for further details of diversification).

HOSTILITIES IN THE REGION

When Iran and Iraq grudgingly agreed to a ceasefire in August 1988, the Gulf breathed a collective sigh of relief but this was merely the calm before the storm. In August 1990 Iraq invaded Kuwait and a few days later annexed the state. King Fahd of Saudi Arabia appealed to the USA for help and the US and Allied Forces launched Operation Desert Storm. After a six-week intensive bombing campaign and a four-day ground offensive, the Iraqis retreated, leaving in their wake hundreds of burning oil wells and an environmental disaster (see p154). Iraqi president Saddam Hussein, previously supported by the West in the war against Iran, suddenly became public enemy number one.

Many Western newspapers described the war as a 'clean war', a demonstration of precision bombing. This wasn't true. It was feared and fought over on the streets of Kuwait City; it rattled the walls of Indian-run corner stores; it stopped Pakistani taxi drivers flying home to their loved ones; it plucked young Arab Muslims from the streets and threw them behind the lines of brother Arab Muslims. The Kuwait House of National Memorial Museum (p163) is an interesting place to visit from this point of view because it reminds the visitor that this may have been an Allied war (and the museum is quick to give thanks where due), but it was first and foremost a humiliating, traumatic experience for the people of Kuwait and their fellow Arabs across the region. Indeed, there is a touching sequence in the animated displays of the museum: lit up against the shell-shocked night sky is a group of women, marching resolutely into gunfire. They played an important role in the resistance to the invasion and lost a generation of their sons in unaccounted-for prisoners of war.

After Desert Storm, despite the strong sense of solidarity between Peninsula countries and Western allies, there was a feeling among many in the region that they were pleased with the help but not the way it was delivered. The infamous 'turkey shoot' of trapped convoys returning to Baghdad up Mutla Ridge was an ominous case in point.

In the aftermath of the September 11 attacks on the US in 2001, people in Oman, Saudi and the Gulf countries watched with horror as the atrocity unfolded. Al-Jazeera television in Qatar showed footage of Saddam Hussein applauding the attack (just as many other Western TV channels were to do thereafter) and the broadcasters were accused – with little justification – of being apologists for terrorism (see p294).

As the US response to 9/11 over the succeeding years led first to the high-handed removal of the Taliban in Afghanistan and then the invasion

---

Seafarers of the Emirates, by Ronald Codrai, is a remarkable record re-creating the lives of pearl divers, merchants, ship builders and seafarers, with photos taken in Dubai in the middle of the 20th century.

Abu Dhabi's oil is predicted to last for 100 to 130 years. Dubai's oil, on the other hand, is rumoured to run out in 20 years. Dubai is borrowing $10 billion to improve infrastructure and for new developments in a bid to keep big multinationals on side.

War in a Time of Peace, by David Halberstam, is an engaging and easy-to-read modern history of the Middle East by a Pulitzer prize–winning journalist.

of Iraq on the flimsiest of pretexts, the trust that was won in the 1990s quickly evaporated. Interestingly, photographs played a large part in that process – of mistreated prisoners at Abu Graib, of Saddam Hussein being checked for dental problems after being pulled from hiding, and the final horror show released on video of his hanging on the first day of *eid* (Islamic feast) in 2006 – these made a huge impact on the ordinary person in the street. 'How could we celebrate *eid* with our families,' many said, 'with such indignities being heaped on that man?' Overnight, many who had no sympathy for the 'Butcher of Baghdad' declared him a martyr, a symbol of the bullying of the Arab world by Western powers. If ever there was a mismanaging of public relations in a war, it was surely evidenced during the hostilities of the past seven years – the late condemnation by Western governments of the bombing of Beirut in 2006 included.

> Yitzhak Rabin was tragically assassinated in 1995 by an Israeli extremist. Relations between Israel and Palestine descended into chaos for much of the next decade as he was replaced by hardliners like Binyamin Netanyahu and Ariel Sharon.

THE RELATIONSHIP WITH ISRAEL

The fact that most Arabs are desirous of peace with *all* their neighbours comes only as a surprise to those reading Western newspapers. Many people across the Peninsula were suspicious of Israel's role in 9/11 and conspiracy theories abounded in the coffeehouses of the regions' capitals. Students continue to write political slogans across college notice boards in support of the Palestinian people, but despite these local 'posturings', when it comes to Arab–Israeli interaction at a grass-roots level, most Peninsula Arabs express a wish to see peace and accommodation in the region for all.

Many initiatives have occurred over the past couple of decades between Peninsula countries and within the Arab–Israeli peace process. After the historic 'Oslo Accord', for example, between the PLO's Yasser Arafat and Israeli prime minister, Yitzhak Rabin, the latter was welcomed in Muscat by Sultan Qaboos. In early 2002 the Saudis put forward a radical peace plan proposing recognition of Israel in exchange for the establishment of a Palestinian state on the West Bank, Gaza and East Jerusalem (based on pre-1967 boundaries). Unfortunately, it failed to impress either side; the Saudis' recent initiative in 2007 has met with American disapproval, and so the stalemate continues.

> *A History of the Middle East*, by Peter Mansfield, is a well-regarded account that is particularly enlightening on the politics and economics of the modern Arab world.

Palestinians who work in leadership roles throughout the region express their frustration, but even they can't articulate a solution. While there is a great deal of sympathy for their predicament, the nationals of the Peninsula are not silly: they have enjoyed the benefit of several decades of education (often in the UK or the USA), good commerce, fine housing and comfortable lifestyles and that's a lot to put on the line for a neighbour, however just the cause.

BUILDING REPRESENTATIVE GOVERNMENT

Quite quietly and in the least expected corner of the Peninsula, while everyone else was busy with Iraq or Iran or both, Yemen made regional history by becoming the first multiparty democracy on the Arabian Peninsula. It may have been the first but it is certainly not the only country to espouse a more open style of government and now all countries in the region have some kind of *majlis ashura* (public representation) that advises or contributes to public policy.

> *Sheikhdoms of Eastern Arabia*, by Peter Lienhardt and Ahmed Al-Shahi, gives an insight into how oil wealth has altered Arabia's tribal structure, gender relations and the interaction between ruling sheikhs and their subjects.

The last decade has been a good time for women in this respect. Every Arab man knows, even in Saudi Arabia, that there is only one governor when it comes to the household and control of the private purse, and that's his wife. Now to the chagrin of more traditional men, women are beginning to join the ranks of government ministers, propelled ahead of their male colleagues by a greater willingness, on the whole, to work at their education and with less sense of being constrained by matters of *wusta* – the nepotistic system of (traditionally male) influence.

This doesn't mean to say that everyone thinks that democracy is a good idea. In many ways, the countries of the Peninsula, with their prosperous, well-fed, well-educated, well-housed, well-looked after and peaceful populations are reasons to be cheerful about alternative systems of governance. Ironically, the only exception is the relatively poor, relatively unstable, democratic country of Yemen.

CURRENT CHALLENGES

The Merchants: the Big Business Families of Saudi Arabia and the Gulf States, by Michael Field, is a brief sketch of the rise of Dubai as a trading centre, illustrating the role played by its powerful tribal relationships – relationships that affect the entire region.

Grandparents across the Peninsula can remember when a trip to the capital or the interior of their country meant a long journey by camel, donkey or on foot; when education was reserved only for the rich or well connected and when housing was hot, dusty and inadequate. In addition, droughts brought further hardship, and infant mortality rates were heart-breakingly high and life expectancy disappointingly low. If born into one kind of life, it was difficult to aspire to any other as families were tied to the land or dependent on the sea for their livelihoods.

Within the space of 50 years, and considerably less in Oman and Yemen, the condition of people's lives in most of the Peninsula has changed beyond all recognition. This is of course largely due to the discovery of oil but it's also due to a willingness to embrace a different way of life on behalf of the 'ordinary' person.

Of course there are problems. The process of diversification is slow; large industries draw people away from their villages; the social pattern of rural life thereby unravels; unfamiliarity with critical thinking hampers education; swapping to indigenous workforces entails hardship on immigrants and less efficiency in the short term. Frustrations with the entire process of modernisation and the perceived threat of encroaching ideologies inevitably lead to political repercussions – a situation that Al-Qaeda and other fundamentalist groups are quick to exploit.

Inside Al Qaeda: Global Network of Terror, by Rohan Gunaratna, is a comprehensive and courageous account of the inner workings of Al-Qaeda and the religious fervour and alienation which drives attacks on the West.

But read any book on management and it will be sure to highlight the challenges involved in implementing change. If it is difficult to manage change within a small business environment, how much more difficult must it be to manage change for an entire nation? The populations of all the countries in the region have encountered the shock of the new, anger at the passing of valued traditions, rejection of external pressures, but they are beginning to complete the cycle with an acceptance of their new lives. The healing process will be complete when each country finds a way in which to honour its heritage within newfound environments.

It's easy to be patronising about Arabia – thinking of it growing like a child. But how foolish is that? For centuries it has attracted Western academics, enthralled creative minds, enriched Western study of mathematics, medicine and literature. Above all, it has given birth to the world's most holistic religion. TE Lawrence summed up the spiritual core of the Peninsula: 'It is the old, old civilisation, which has refined itself clear of household gods and half the trappings which ours hastens to assume.' What a pity we're still peddling the trappings.

The Culture

'The manners of mankind,' wrote the 18th-century, British traveller Lady Wortley Montagu, 'do not differ so widely as our voyage writers would make us believe.' Lady Montagu's common sense account of the 'customs and manners' of the people she met in Arab lands in the 18th century, however, were a disappointment to many of her contemporaries who had hoped to read about the people of literary speculation: the wild men of the desert, the passionate Islamic fundamentalist, the dusky-eyed maiden. Montagu was even tempted 'to add a few surprise customs' of her own invention to placate readers. It's to her credit that she resisted.

It's easy to focus on the elements of difference between cultures, but the more one travels in Arab lands, it's the similarities that prove more persuasive.

Geographia at www.geographia.com contains interesting features on the peoples and cultures of the Arabian Peninsula.

PEOPLE

The Western stereotype of the male Peninsula inhabitant has changed over the last century. Where once he was characterised as gaunt, austere in habit and fierce of temper, he's now portrayed as rich and extravagant; invariably fat; Arab-nosed; an owner of two camels, four wives, eight children and six cars; and robed in sheet and teacloth. Male youths are wiry and neurotic, wearing Semtex vests. Women only feature in relation to the hejab (veil) debate and in cartoons they appear as indefinable black shapes.

Let's see if any of these absurd stereotypes have a grain of truth.

In The Arabs: Myth and Reality, by Gerald Butt, the ex-BBC Middle East correspondent traces the geopolitical history of the region and examines its complex relationship with the West, including the stereotypical images of the Peninsula Arab.

Lifestyle (Rich & Extravagant?)

Drive through the suburbs of Peninsula cities and you'll see domed villas with spangled concrete that glistens in the sun. Walk through the gold souqs and you'll see women with Gucci handbags, buying diamonds and pearls. Park outside the Ritz-Carlton in Manama, Burj al-Arab in Dubai and you'll be embarrassed to be driving a Toyota Echo. Undoubtedly, huge private fortunes have been made in the oil rush and building expansion.

But that isn't the whole picture. Universal education and the mass media have increased expectations, and people who were content with one floor, now want two. Cement and steel prices have doubled in a decade and the burgeoning Arab 'middle class' frets over securing loans to finish the house. If shopping before pay day is anything to go by, most families are left with little at the end of the month.

The rest of the picture is completed by stepping out of the city altogether. Lives in mountain villages, in desert oases, on the dunes or in coastal fishing villages may seem to have been little impacted by city incomes, but then you spot the satellite dish attached to the barasti (palm frond) walls; the electricity poles marching up the wadis (often-dry river beds); the communally owned truck that has allowed settlement to replace nomadic existence. Water, electricity, roads, education and health care, this is the real wealth of the region today and it is remarkably evenly spread given the challenges of geography and topography.

In a straw poll run by student nurses in Muscat, 99% listed heart disease and obesity as possible outcomes of increased fatty food and reduced exercise. However, 95% said they eat hamburger and fries at least twice a week. 'It's too good to give up,' one said.

Health & Life Expectancy (Invariably Fat?)

A more modern lifestyle, be it in the city or the interior, has brought changes to the health of many Peninsula people. Not all those changes

---

PENINSULA LIVES

Ahmed is a fisherman near Shwaymiya in Oman. He gets up before dawn, performs his ablutions and walks to the mosque for dawn prayers. By the time he returns, his sons have dragged the boat to the water's edge. His wife has prepared something light to break the night's fast and will have rice waiting on their return from sea; his daughters are out collecting firewood. A flotilla of 10 or 20 boats tears up the calm waters on the age-old hunt for tuna. Half asleep in the middle of the afternoon, the day's work accomplished, the catch drying in the sun or dispatched to town in the freezer truck, his family arranged around him in various states of slumber and repose, Ahmed asks why anybody else would want another life: 'I have my children, my wife and my fishing. What more could a man wish for?' What indeed? But they do wish for more, and that's why two of his seven sons are now enrolled in the military, and his eldest daughter is hoping to train in Salalah to become a nurse.

Fatima is married to Faisal, an administrator in the Wildlife Commission in Riyadh. Fatima remembers the days when her father took her brothers on hunting parties looking for houbara bustard (near-endangered large birds prized for their meat). She never imagined she'd marry someone involved in their protection. She's not quite sure what all the fuss is about but the steady income helps pay for the education of their two children. She was adamant about that: both daughters were to have the best. One is studying pharmacy and the other is good with figures and will make an able accountant. She could do with some help with the family accounts – especially with the investments she's made. She recently bought a part share in a truck for one of the construction companies. It's already returning a profit. She dons her *abeyya* (body-covering black robe) and sinks into the street outside, glad to be anonymous – she'll have to sort out the feud with the neighbours soon because Faisal is clearly never going to muscle up to that task!

---

are for the better. Take the statistics regarding diabetes, for example: four of the five countries with the world's highest rates of diabetes are the UAE (United Arab Emirates; 20.1%), Qatar (16%), Bahrain (14.9%) and Kuwait (12.8%).

A sweet tooth is partly to blame. Dates play an inextricable role both in the Arab diet and in matters of hospitality. No-one is eating fewer dates, but everyone now eats ice cream and burgers as well – just as unremitting TV advertisements bid them to.

But it's not all doom and gloom! Wander the terraces of southern Arabia 20 years ago, and you'd see women bent double in the fields, baked by the sun, arthritic in the mud, or weighed down with herbage, trudging back to their homes, pausing to stack stones in the crumbling terrace walls. For many of the Peninsula inhabitants, it's hard to be too nostalgic about the passing of hard manual labour, even if it comes at the price of an extra kilo or two carried around the hips.

Thanks to immunisation programmes and increasing standards of health care, the Peninsula Arab has a healthy average life expectancy of 72 years (up to 79 for Kuwaiti women) – considerably more years in which to die of a heart attack than their predecessors.

Population & Ethnic Diversity (Arab-Nosed?)

In the Gulf, people with a hooked nose are teased in a region that admires straight noses. Noses tell a lot about who is from where, and each country is acutely mindful of such distinctions: 'with a name like that, he must be a Baluchi (not real Emirati); he speaks Swahili so he must be Zanzibari (not real Omani); he's from the coast (not real Yemeni).' And so it goes on until you wonder if there's any such thing as a 'real anybody'. Such gossiping about ethnicity makes you realise that Arab allegiances are linked to tribe before nation.

There are over 50,000 Western expats in the UAE alone.

Centuries of trading and pilgrimage have resulted in an extraordinarily mixed population and only a few pockets of people, such as the Jibbalis of southern Oman – the descendents of the ancient people of Ad – or Jews in the northern parts of Yemen, can claim ethnic 'purity'.

Oddly, for the visitor, it is not always Arabs you'll notice much anyway. The indigenous population of the entire Peninsula numbers less than 20 million.

The large presence of other nationals on the Peninsula came about after the discovery of oil. Many thousands of expatriate workers were brought in to help develop the region's industries, and provide skills and knowledge in creating a modern infrastructure. Although none of these nationals were permitted citizenship, many have stayed a lifetime and set up businesses under local sponsorship, changing the demographics of the entire Peninsula.

The issue now is how to reduce the dependence on expatriate labour and train the local population to fill their place: inevitably, few expats willingly train locals to take over their jobs.

In many Gulf countries, foreigners outnumber locals: in the UAE about 80% of the population is made up of foreign residents; in Qatar, the government vowed not to allow their own nationals to be outnumbered by immigrants, but the indigenous population currently represents only 25%.

Bedouin Roots (Owners of Two Camels?)

Some Arabs still own two camels. In fact, many own considerably more. The donkey played just as important a role in transportation in the mountains of the Peninsula, but no-one is breeding those for fun. Of course, racing has something to do with it, but the camel is more deeply involved in the Arab psyche than mere racing. Camels evoke ancient nomadic lifestyles, the symbol of community through hardship and endurance – the inheritance, in short, of Bedouin roots.

The term 'Bedu' (Bedouin in singular and adjectival form) refers not so much to an ethnic group as to a lifestyle. Accounting for their appeal to Western imaginations in the 18th century, the Danish explorer Niebuhr claimed that man is 'fond even of the very shadow of that liberty, independence, and simplicity which he has lost by refinement'. City Arabs today, stressed by familiar modern anxieties regarding wealth and how to keep it, are similarly wistful of a bygone era, even if they are more likely to be descendants of townspeople and seafarers.

Bedouin: Nomads of the Desert, by Alain Keohane, is a beautiful photographic and textual testimony to the Bedu, including descriptions and images of their lifestyle, traditions, arts and customs.

Most Bedu have modernised their existence with 4WD trucks (it's not unusual to find the camel travelling by truck these days), fodder from town (limiting the need to keep moving), and purified water from bowsers.

EXPAT PECKING ORDER

Though officially treated equally, there's clearly a pecking order among the Peninsula's expats. At the top of the order are the Westerners. For the hundreds of thousands of Western expats, life is a tax-free merry-go-round, usually with rent and annual airfare home included in generous packages. The life, at least in the big Gulf cities, includes sun, sea, sand and a good social life in a lifestyle few could afford back home.

Next come the middle-income workers from other Middle Eastern countries. Their first and foremost preoccupation is to save money. Typically these expats stay just long enough to stockpile enough dollars to build a house back home and send their children to college. In some countries such as Egypt and Yemen, remittances from nationals working abroad constitute the backbone of the economy.

Languishing at the bottom are the labourers from India, Pakistan and Bangladesh. While a minority (around 5% to 10%) enjoy a standard of living similar to the Western and Peninsula communities, the majority are manual labourers. Though working conditions are tough – digging roads in 45°C heat or working on building sites that lack any safety provisions – many prefer this to poverty back home. Often a single labourer can support his entire extended family in his home country from his monthly pay packet. Some Asians remain on the Peninsula for up to 20 years, only seeing their families for two months once every two years. Wealth is highly relative it would seem.

THE BEDU – SURVIVAL OF THE MOST GENEROUS

Meaning 'nomadic', the name Bedu is today a bit of a misnomer. Though thought to number several hundred thousand, very few Bedu are still truly nomadic, though a few hang on to the old ways. After pitching their distinct black, goat-hair tents – the *beit ash-sha'ar* (literally 'house of hair') – they graze their goats, sheep or camels in an area for several months. When the sparse desert fodder runs out, it's time to move on again, allowing the land to regenerate naturally.

The tents are generally divided into a *haram* (forbidden area) for women and an area reserved for the men. The men's section also serves as the public part of the house, where guests are treated to coffee and dates, or meals. It's here that all the news and gossip – a crucial part of successful survival in a hostile environment – is passed along the grapevine.

The Bedouin family is a close-knit unit. The women do most of the domestic work, including fetching water (sometimes requiring walks of many kilometres), baking bread and weaving. The men are traditionally the providers in times of peace, and fierce warriors in times of war. Though most Bedu are more peaceful these days, warring still goes on in northern parts of Yemen.

The hospitality of the Bedu is legendary, even in a region known for its generosity. Part of the ancient and sacrosanct Bedouin creed is that no traveller in need of rest or food should be turned away. Likewise, a traveller assumes the assured protection of his hosts for a period of three days, and is guaranteed a safe passage through tribal territory. Even today the Bedu escort travellers safely across the desert in Yemen (though now you pay for the service).

The philosophy is simple: you scratch my back, I'll scratch yours – only in the desert it's a matter of survival. Such a code of conduct ensures the survival of all in a difficult environment with scant resources. It allows the maintenance of a nomadic lifestyle and the continuation of trade. It's a kind of survival, in other words, of the most generous.

Some have mobile phones and satellite television, and most listen to the radio. Many no longer move at all. Bedouin customs, dating from the earliest days of Islam, remain pretty much unchanged, however – especially their legendary hospitality towards strangers.

Camels were memorably first called 'ships of Arabia'; their seas are the deserts' by the British diplomat, George Sandy, in 1615.

Marriage & the Role of Women (Four Wives?)

Islam allows men to have four wives, but only if a man can treat each equally. In reality, there are few Peninsula Arabs who can afford the luxury of two houses, two sets of gold, two extended families of in-laws – let alone four. Nor, with the greater demands of the modern work place, can many aspire to satisfying more than one partner in equal share – though only wives will let you in on this secret.

But it's not just about expense either. While law permits a man four wives, even two centuries ago no 'man of quality' would make use of this and no 'woman of rank' would suffer it. In fact, Peninsula women are far more empowered than might be supposed, and they don't like sharing their husbands and his income any more than Western women. If the wife doesn't like something, she can and often does make the man's life a misery and, as controller of the household, often co-opts the children into her camp. Divorce is easily enacted and is becoming less of a taboo, especially in Oman and the Gulf countries, because women will put up with less these days. Modern Peninsula women are educated, usually far harder working at college than men and therefore often more successful in the workplace. They are entitled to earn and keep their own income (unlike the man who surrenders his salary to the household) and as such have an independence unthinkable by their grandmothers.

The Bedu are found across the Arabian Peninsula, mostly on the fringes of the great Rub al-Khali, in Oman's Sharqiya Sands, Khor al-Adaid in Qatar and on Kuwait's plains. Exact numbers are unknown due to the difficulty of taking a census of nomadic peoples.

Or was it ever thus? 'The Europeans are mistaken in thinking the state of marriage so different among the Mussulmans from what it is with Christian nations,' wrote Niebuhr in the 18th century. 'Arabian women enjoy a great deal of liberty, and often a great deal of power, in their families'.

It's hard to imagine women letting go of their tight-knit sisterhood, but now that they also want a slice of the man's traditional role too, something's got to give. The time-honoured, slightly mystical respect shown by men to wives and mothers, sanctified in Islam, may be one casualty of the redefining of roles that most Arab women haven't considered yet.

Family Size & Welfare (Eight Children?)

The family, guided by Muslim principles, is still at the centre of the Arab way of life. The family is an extended unit often comprising whole villages, united around a common tribal name. Avoiding actions that may bring shame to the family is of paramount importance. Saving face is therefore more than a reluctance to admit a mistake, it's an expression of unwillingness to make a family vulnerable to criticism. Equally, promotion or success is not calculated in individual terms, but in the benefits it bestows on the family. Of course, everyone knows someone who can help in the collective good, and accruing *wusta* (influence) is a Peninsula pastime.

The efforts of one generation are reflected in the provision of education and opportunity for the next. This comes at a cost and few Arabs these days can afford eight children; indeed the average is around 3.3 children.

The governments of each country have made generous provision for families across the region – in terms of free education and health care – but the resources won't last forever and the younger generation are beginning to see that they have to work hard to secure the same opportunities for their children.

Travel & Pilgrimage (Six Cars?)

When tax is minimal and petrol cheaper than bottled water, owning two cars isn't the extravagance one might imagine. The car is a status symbol but it's also a symbol of travel. The Arabs love to travel – to family members at the weekend, foreign countries for honeymoons, and of course to Mecca for haj or *umrah* (literally 'little pilgrimage'). See p70).

Dress & Fashion (Robed in Sheet & Teacloth?)

The very thought of calling the quintessentially cool and elegant dress of the Arabs 'sheet and teacloth' would appal most inhabitants of the Peninsula. Men take huge pride in their costume, which, in its simplicity and uniformity, is intended to transcend wealth and origin.

A loose headscarf, known as *gutra,* is worn by many Peninsula males: in the Gulf States it is of white cloth, while in western Kuwait and Saudi Arabia it is checked. The black head rope used to secure the *gutra* is called *agal.* It's said to originate in the rope the Bedu used to tie up their camels at night. The Omanis and Yemenis usually wear a turban, wrapped deftly about a cap. In Oman these are pastel-hued and decorated with intricate and brightly coloured embroidery.

Most Peninsula men also wear the floor-length 'shirt-dress' which in Saudi Arabia, Bahrain and Qatar is known as a *thobe,* and in Kuwait, the UAE and Oman as a *dishdasha.* Most are white, and some have collars and cuffs, while others are edged with tassels and white-thread embroidery at the neck. On ceremonial occasions, the dress is completed with a finely wrought belt and ceremonial dagger, and a silk outer garment. In Yemen and cold areas in the winter, men wear tailored jackets.

The Bedu are known for their sense of humour, which they list – alongside courage, alertness and religious faith – as one of the four secrets of life, encouraging tolerance and humility. So beware: if stuck in the sand, expect to be laughed at!

The 18th-century traveller, Lady Montagu, noted that Arab women were more at liberty to follow their own will than their European counterparts and that the *abeyya,* the 'black disguise', made it easier for women to take a lover.

Nine Parts of Desire, by Geraldine Brooks, is an objective and well-balanced investigation into the lives of women under Islam, covering various countries of the Middle East.

Women's dress is more varied. It often comprises colourful long dresses or an embroidered tunic with trousers and heavily decorated ankle cuffs. In the cities, modern dress is common. Over the top, women usually wear a black gown known as an *abeyya*. This can either be worn loose and cover the head as well (as in Saudi Arabia) or it can be worn as a fashion item, tailored to the body (as in Oman). In Yemen, the women's outer costume comprises a startling layer of coloured cotton cloth.

All Arab women cover their hair but they don't all wear the *burka* (veil) – in Oman and the UAE, they mostly do not cover the face. Veils can be of a thin gauze completely covering the face; a cloth which covers the face but not the eyes; or a mask concealing the nose, cheeks and part of the mouth – in Sana'a, women wear striking red and white tie-dye cloth to cover the face.

Many Western people assume that men force women to cover up. In fact, this is generally not the case. Women often opt for such coverings in order to pass more comfortably through male company. Nor is it a stated part of Islam. Indeed, Bedu women maintain that the custom, which protects the skin and hair from the harsh penalties of sun and sand, predates Islam.

Arabian Youth (Wiry, Neurotic Youths?)

They wear baseball caps with the peak reversed, they've got the latest iPods and Blackberries, they stay out late with friends and are rude to their elders. A few drink, fewer take drugs. They watch unsavoury things on satellite TV and they communicate 'inappropriately' via the internet. They sleep a lot and aren't interested in learning. In this regard, Arab youth are no different from any other youths. The difference in Arab countries is that really wanton behaviour is rare and the period of abandonment relatively short.

Religious Zeal (Semtex Vests?)

Only a tiny minority of people on the Peninsula are involved in religious fundamentalism, and most of those channel their zeal into peaceful attempts to reconcile the liberties of modern life with the traditional values of Islam. Those who resort to violence to accomplish largely political aims are mistrusted by their own communities and considered misguided by most religious leaders. It is unfortunate that this small minority gain maximum media coverage and are the very people upon whom the entire culture of the mostly peaceful, amiable, adaptable and tolerant Arabian Peninsula is judged.

MEETING LOCALS

Etiquette plays a very important part in Arab culture. Even though Arabs are forgiving of foreigners, they also greatly appreciate the visitor who tries to master a few civilities. It's worth remembering too that the Peninsula is still highly conservative in terms of public behaviour. This particularly applies to dress; even in more liberal cities like Dubai, the locals are easily affronted by the sight of too much flesh.

General Etiquette

When meeting either for the first time or on subsequent occasions, people usually stand up and shake hands. In some areas (Saudi being one), people may touch their heart after and in other areas they may kiss on the cheek (as in the Gulf States), or even knock noses (as in areas of

---

Sidebar notes:

Six children is about the average number of children per family in poorer and rural regions of the Peninsula, where children are seen as a resource, not an expense – another pair of hands to work the land or provide support in old age.

The Peninsula's low crime rate is partly due to sociological factors, such as wealth and low unemployment; it is mostly attributable, however, to strict codes of moral conduct expounded by Islam; a legal system sometimes rigorously enforced; traditional Arab values; and the concept of honour.

Guests are usually seen to the door, or even to the end of the corridor or garden. Traditionally this represents the secure safe passage of guests from your tribal territory to theirs. Be sure to do the same, if you have Arab visitors.

TEA & TALK

A *diwaniya* (gathering), usually conducted at someone's home – in a tent or on cushions just outside it, to be precise – is an important aspect of Gulf life, and any visitor who has the chance to partake in one will find it the best opportunity to observe Arab social life first-hand. The object of the gathering is to drink endless cups of hot, sweet tea – oh, and to chew the political cud, of course. It is usually a 'man thing'. As one Kuwaiti woman explained, the women of the house are usually too busy living life to waste time discussing it.

Oman). For the male visitor, a handshake is sufficient, but don't shake a woman's hand unless she offers hers first. Some devoutly religious men will not touch a woman's hand; the key is to take your cue from the other person.

Before any kind of transaction – at the checkout in a supermarket, if the traffic police stop you, before a meeting begins, on the telephone between strangers – people greet each other thoroughly and preferably enquire after the other person's health. As a visitor, you should never 'get down to business' without at least a few polite exchanges regarding family health. Men, however, should never enquire after another man's wife or daughters.

Shoes should be removed before entering a mosque or someone's house. The soles of feet are considered unclean and it's insulting to point them at anyone. This means taking care not to stretch your legs out. The left hand is used for ablutions, so always use the right hand when touching, or when offering things. It's impolite to beckon with a finger.

Guests are always offered coffee or tea on social or business occasions. As a guest, it's impolite to refuse at least one cup (see p84).

The Thousand and One Nights, translated by Richard Burton, is a collection of tales that originate from Arabia, India and Persia. The narrator, the beautiful Scheherazade, entertains the brutal King Shahryar with tales of genies and magical transformations, including the stories of Ali Baba and Aladdin.

What to Wear

Nothing offends Arabs quite as much as inappropriate clothing. Here are a few tips on what travellers should wear to avoid offending anybody.

MEN

Traditional dress has acquired complex nationalist connotations, visually setting apart natives of the region from the large population of foreigners. As such, Western men should avoid wearing local *thobes* or *dishdashas* – at best, Arab people think it looks ridiculous. Locals dress smartly if they can afford to and visitors are similarly judged by their dress. Some hotel bars and nightclubs have a strict dress code and on the whole it's unacceptable to be seen anywhere in public, including hotel foyers and souqs, in shorts and vests.

WOMEN

Wearing an *abeyya* and covering hair denotes that a woman is Muslim. Except in Saudi Arabia where foreign women are obliged to wear an *abeyya* (but not cover their hair), it is better for Westerners to avoid this practice, as it can lead to uncomfortable conversations about religion. There are some exceptions – for example, when visiting mosques or attending traditional weddings. Female visitors should wear loose-fitting clothing that covers their knees, shoulders and cleavage. On public beaches, women may feel more comfortable in shorts and a t-shirt than in swimming costumes. Bikinis (except in tourist resorts) cause a local sensation.

The Son of a Duck is a Floater, by Arnander and Skipworth, is a fun collection of Arab sayings with English equivalents. It's worth buying just to see how wisdom is universal – not to mention the thoroughly enjoyable illustrations.

Forms of Address

Correct address is an important part of Arab etiquette. Use Arab given names, as opposed to family names when addressing Arabs in the Peninsula. Instead of Mr Hussein, it's Mr Saddam. In the same way, a foreign visitor will become 'Mr John' as opposed to 'Mr Smith', or 'Mrs Jane' as opposed to 'Mrs Smith'. The correct formal address (or equivalent of 'Mr') is usually *'asayid'* (meaning 'Sir') or *'asayida'* for a woman.

Codes of Conduct

Arab people don't like confrontation. They prefer to smile during 'difficult' conversations and then let off steam later. Equally, the word 'sorry' is not a big part of their vocabulary. Such behaviour is part of the custom of 'saving face' and visitors are better respected if they also refrain from public outbursts of anger or from forcing an apology. Note too, that it's an offence in many Peninsula countries to gesture rudely while driving. Just smile sweetly and mutter under your breath, like they do!

ARTS

If you chose one feature that distinguishes art in the Arabian Peninsula (and in the Arab world in general) from that of Western tradition, it would have to focus on the close integration of function with form. In other words, most Arab art has evolved with a purpose. That purpose could be as practical as embellishing the prow of a boat with a cowry shell to ward off 'evil eye', or as nebulous as creating intricate and beautiful patterns to intimate the presence of God and invite spiritual contemplation. Purpose is an element that threads through all Peninsula art – craft, music, architecture and even literature.

Literature

Nothing touches the heart of a Peninsula Arab quite like poetry. Traditionally dominating Arab literature, all the best-known figures of classical Arabic and Persian literature are poets, including the famed Omar Khayyam, the 11th-century composer of *rub'ai* (quatrains), and the 8th-century Baghdadi poet, Abu Nuwas. All great Arab poets were regarded as possessing knowledge forbidden to ordinary people and, as such, they served the purpose of bridging the human and spirit worlds.

To this day, poetry recitals play an important part in all national celebrations, and even the TV-watching young are captivated by a skilfully intoned piece of verse.

Poetry is part and parcel of the great oral tradition of story telling that informs the literature of all Peninsula countries, the roots of which lie with the Bedu (see the boxed text, opposite). Stories told by nomadic elders to the wide-eyed wonder of the young serve not just as after-dinner entertainment, but as a way of binding generations together in a collective oral history. As such, story telling disseminates the principles of Islam and of tribal and national identity. It extols the virtues of allegiance, valour, endurance and hospitality – virtues that make life in a harsh environment tolerable.

Modern Arab written literature, in the form of novels and short stories, is a relatively recent addition to Peninsula arts. No-one of the calibre of the Nobel prize winning Egyptian, Naguib Mahfouz (the most important writer of Arabic fiction in the 20th century), has yet emerged from the Peninsula but the Saudi writer, Abdelrahman Munif (who wrote *Cities of Salt*) has a reputation in the West.

'Drums were beating, and the crowd swaying,' wrote Bertram Thomas in *Alarms & Excursions in Arabia*, 1931, 'quivering sword blades flashed in the sun as sword dancers leapt hither and thither.' Travel in the Peninsula today during a festival, and the scene is very similar.

In the souqs of Oman, silver jewellery is often sold according to weight measured in *tolahs* (1=11.75g). *Tolahs* are sometimes called *thallers* after the Maria Theresa dollar, an 18th-century Austrian coin used in much of Arabia's currency in the 19th and early 20th centuries.

The Craft Heritage of Oman, by Richardson and Dorr, is a comprehensive survey of all craft industries in the Sultanate. It makes valuable reading for travellers in any part of the Peninsula as many of the crafts are common to other Arabian countries.

ARABIC WHISPERS – ORAL LITERATURE ON THE PENINSULA

For the nomadic Bedu of Arabia, life is lived on the move. Permanence is virtually unknown – even the footsteps that mark their passing shift with the sands. The artistic expression of their culture has evolved to be similarly portable – weaving that can be rolled up and stowed on a camel, beadwork that can be tucked in a pocket, stories unfurled round the campfire at night.

Bedu tales, and their endless digressions, serve not just as entertainment. Allegories and parables are used to clarify a situation, to offer tactful advice to a friend, or to alert someone diplomatically to trouble or wrongdoing. More often, they lampoon corrupt leaders and offer a satirical commentary on current affairs – particularly those of the mistrusted 'townspeople'. They can be very funny, highly bawdy and verging on the libellous, depending on the persuasions of the teller.

On the Peninsula, there is said to be a tale for every situation. Travellers may be surprised how often the Bedu resort to proverbs, maxims or stories during the course of normal conversation. It is said that the first proverb of all is: 'While a man may tell fibs, he may never tell false proverbs'!

Sadly, the modern world has encroached on the oral tradition. The advent of television and other forms of entertainment has meant that the role that storytelling plays in Bedouin life has diminished. Now this valuable oral patrimony is in danger of disappearing forever.

Music

Like the oral tradition of story telling, Arabian song and dance have also evolved for a purpose. Generally, music was employed to distract from hardship – like the songs of the seafarers, marooned on stagnant Gulf waters, or the chanting of fishermen hauling in their nets. There are also harvest songs and love ballads, all of which are either sung unaccompanied or to syncopated clapping or drum beats. East African rhythms, introduced into Arab music from Arab colonies, lend much Peninsula music a highly hypnotic quality and songs can last for over an hour.

While the austere sects of Wahhabi and Ibadhism discourage singing and dancing, no wedding or national celebration in the Peninsula would be the same without them. Men dance in circles, flexing their swords or ceremonial daggers while jumping or swaying. If they get really carried away, volleys of gunfire are let off above the heads of the crowd. Women have a tradition of dancing for the bride at weddings. Unobserved by men, they wear magnificent costumes (or modern ball gowns) and gyrate suggestively as if encouraging the bride towards the marital bed.

It shouldn't be supposed that just because traditional music plays a big part in contemporary Arab life, it's the only form of music. Pop music, especially of the Amr Diab type, is ubiquitous and nightclubs are popular. There's even a classical orchestra in Oman and there are bagpipe bands.

Geoffrey Bibby's book, Looking for Dilmun, gives a very good account of barasti housing in the region.

Crafts

If there's one area in which function and form are most noticeably linked, it's in the craft traditions of the Peninsula – in the jewellery, silversmithing, weaving, embroidery and basket-making crafts that form the rich craft heritage of the Peninsula. Take jewellery, for example – the heavy silver jewellery, so distinctively worn by Bedouin women, was designed not just as a personal adornment but as a form of portable wealth. Silver amulets, containing rolled pieces of parchment or paper, bear protective inscriptions from the Quran, to guarantee the safety of the wearer. At the end of the life of a piece of jewellery, it is traditionally melted down to form new pieces as an ultimate gesture of practicality.

Contemporary Architecture in the Arab States, by Udo Kultermann, is billed as the 'first comprehensive reference on the modern architecture of the Middle East'. The book is well written and well illustrated.

GENUINE BEDOUIN – MADE IN INDIA?

One of the highlights of the Peninsula is undoubtedly a trip to the covered souqs and bazaars, some of which (especially in Jeddah, Doha, Muscat and Sana'a) have occupied the same chaotic labyrinthine quarters for hundreds of years. In these forerunners of the shopping mall, merchants sit behind piles of dates and olives, gold, frankincense and myrrh, in small shops often no bigger than a broom cupboard. Passing in between them are the water-sellers, itinerant cloth vendors, carters (complete with wheelbarrow in Kuwait) and carriers.

The scene (of haggling and gossiping, pushing and shoving, laughing and teasing) may not have changed much in centuries, but many of the goods have. Mostly practical items are on offer – aluminium pans, plastic trays, imports from China – but if you look hard, you can usually find items of traditional craft, even in the most modern of souqs.

There are *kilims* (rugs) and carpets; cotton clothing including *gutras* (white head cloth), *thobes* or *dishdashas* and embroidered dresses; Bedouin woven bags; decorative daggers and swords; copperware and brassware; olive and cedar woodcarvings; kohl (black eyeliner); old trunks and boxes; water pipes; embroidered tablecloths and cushion covers; leather and suede. But, the question is, is it real?

All tourists have seen them: the Roman coins from Syria, the Aladdin lamps from Cairo, the Bedouin jewellery torn from the brow of a virgin bride – the stories attempt to make up for the shameless lack of authentic provenance on the part of the item. While the region is home to some magnificent craft, only relatively few pieces make their way to places like Souq Waqif in Qatar, Mutrah Souq in Oman or Bab al-Bahrain in Bahrain. The vast majority of items on sale to tourists is imported from India, Pakistan and Iran and either sold as such, or more frequently passed off as 'genuine Bedouin' by less-scrupulous shopkeepers.

Recognising that this is lamentable and a wasted opportunity, one country in the region is actively doing something about it. The Omani Heritage Documentation Project was launched in 1996 to document Oman's great craft heritage and envisage ways to ensure its survival. The resulting two-volume book, *The Craft Heritage of Oman*, is the definitive guide to Oman's cottage industries and took eight years to complete. It is an inspiration to anyone with an interest in the arts and crafts of Oman and an invitation to other Peninsula countries to follow suit.

Islamic Arts, by Jonathan Bloom and Sheila Blair, is a lavishly illustrated introduction to Islamic arts from weaving and calligraphy to architecture and the decorative arts.

The sad fact of practical craft is that once the need for it has passed, there is little incentive to maintain the skills. Where's the point of potters in Al-Hufuf in Saudi Arabia and Bahla in Oman making clay ewers when everyone drinks water from Masafi branded bottles? Aware of this fact, many governments throughout the region have encouraged the setting up of local craft associations in the hope of keeping alive such an important part of their heritage. Some of the best-supported ventures in the region are the Bedouin weaving project at Sadu House (p161) in Kuwait City, the Oman Craft Heritage Documentation Project (p188) and the women's centres in Manama (p129) and Abu Dhabi (p422). Inevitably, however, when craft is hollowed of its function, when it provides a mere curiosity of the past or is redefined as souvenirs for tourists, it becomes only a shadow of itself.

Architecture

The veneration for the written word is reflected in the treatment of the calligrapher who until recent times was the most sought-after and highly paid artist in a community.

Styles across the region vary so considerably, it's hard to talk about Peninsula architecture under one umbrella – there's the multistorey mud edifices of Yemen and Southern Saudi; the round mud huts more akin to sub-Saharan architecture on the Tihama; the *barasti* dwellings of eastern Arabia; the coral buildings of Jeddah; or the gypsum decoration of Gulf design.

In common with other arts, Peninsula architecture is traditionally steered by purpose. The local climate plays an important role in this.

The wind towers of the Gulf, for example, not only look attractive, they function as channels of cooler air (see boxed text, p56); the gaily painted window frames of Yemeni and Asir dwellings in Saudi help waterproof the adobe. Security is another issue: the positioning of forts around and on top of rocky outcrops in the Hajar Mountains gives a foundation more solid than anything bricks and mortar might produce. And then there's the question of space: in the mountain areas of Saudi, Yemen and Oman, whole villages appear to be suspended in air, perched on top of inaccessible promontories, storeys piled high to save from building on precious arable land.

The one 'art form' that a visitor to the Peninsula can hardly miss is the modern tower block. In many Gulf cities, cranes almost outnumber buildings in the race to build the most extravagant confection of glass and steel. In the process, Peninsula architecture has become diverted from the traditional principle of functionality. Take the magnificent Emirates Palace hotel in Abu Dhabi, for example, where you need to pack your trainers to get from bed to breakfast.

Increasingly, architects are expected to refer, in an almost talismanical way, to the visual vocabulary of Arab art: hence the pointed windows, false balconies, wooden screens and tent motifs of modern buildings across the Peninsula. Perhaps this is because many traditional buildings, with their economy of style and design, achieve something that modern buildings often do not – they blend in harmoniously with their environment.

Islamic Architecture, by Robert Hillenbrand, looks at religious buildings across the region. Covering the period from about AD 700 to 1700, this well-illustrated volume is a definitive guide to the subject.

The Bahrain Arts Society's interesting and involving website, www.bahartsociety.org.bh, chronicles not just Bahrain's art scene but Arabic culture in general.

ARCHITECTURAL HIGHLIGHTS

The architecture of the Arabian Peninsula may not be as well known as that in neighbouring countries, but it does have some gems. The following is a highly subjective top 10 of architectural wonders, ancient and modern, that adorn the region (listed approximately by age):

- **Ma'rib Dam, Yemen** (p496) Though there's not much to see, the sense of one of the largest building projects of the ancient world lingers round the standing stones.

- **Madain Salah, Saudi Arabia** (p333) Imagine having Petra to yourself: the Nabataean monuments of this 'petit Petra' lie in a wind-sculpted desert of sandstone.

- **Nakhal Fort, Oman** (p238) It's impossible to choose just one of Oman's 1000 forts but the setting of Nakhal Fort, at the knee-bend of mountains and plains, is hard to beat.

- **Houses of Shibam, Yemen** (p505) Called 'Manhattan of the Desert' by Freya Stark, this medieval town is where the art of high-rise began.

- **Beit Sheikh Isa bin Ali, Bahrain** (p135) This house has the best example of the air-conditioning wizardry of 18th- and 19th-century wind-tower architecture, prevalent in the Gulf.

- **Arab Fund Building, Kuwait** (p162) For a demonstration of the unity of Islamic art, there's no finer modern example than the interior of this discreet 20th-century building.

- **Muscat Grand Mosque, Oman** (p201) There are many spectacular mosques across the region, but the elegant, understated masterpiece in Muscat has the largest hand-loomed carpet in the world.

- **Burj al-Arab, UAE** (p389) For the quintessential postmodern experience, a tour of this iconic tower is a must.

- **Bahrain International Circuit, Bahrain** (p133) Evocative of a Bedouin tent, this Formula One racetrack is a good illustration of the way modern building design incorporates traditional design.

- **Doha Corniche, Qatar** (p275) A monument to 21st-century modern architecture, the buildings that grace Doha's corniche set the benchmark for daring and diversity.

THE ART OF AIR CONTROL

Called *barjeel* in Arabic, wind towers are the Gulf States' own unique form of non-electrical air-conditioning. In most of the region's cities a handful still exist, sometimes attached to private homes, and sometimes carefully preserved or reconstructed at museums. In Sharjah (the UAE) a set of massive wind towers is used to cool the modern Central Market building.

Traditional wind towers rise 5m or 6m above a house. They are usually built of wood or stone but can also be made from canvas. The tower is open on all four sides and so can catch even the breathiest of breezes. These mere zephyrs are channelled down a central shaft and into the room below. In the process, the air speeds up and is cooled. The cooler air already in the tower shaft pulls in and subsequently cools the hotter air outside through a simple process of convection.

Sitting beneath a wind tower on a hot and humid day, the temperature is noticeably cooler with a consistent breeze even when the air outside feels heavy and still.

Islamic Art

There can be no greater example of function at the heart of art than Islamic art. For a Muslim, Islamic art remains first and foremost an expression of faith, and to this day people are cautious of 'art for art's sake', or art as an expression of the self without reference to community. Ask Arab students to draw a picture, and they'll often draw something with a message or a meaning, rather than just a pretty picture.

A good example of instructive or inspirational visual art is calligraphy. Arabic is not just a language for Arabs – for Muslims throughout the world it is the language of the Quran, so it's a cohesive and unifying factor, imbued with a reverence that is hard for non-Muslims to understand. Islamic calligraphy, the copying of God's own words, is seen by many as a pious act and remains to this day the highest aesthetic practised in the Arab world. All over Arabia one can see magnificent examples of this highly refined art (see especially Beit al-Quran in Bahrain; p122) with its repetition of forms and symmetry of design.

The most visible expression of Islamic art, however, is surely the mosque. It too is built on mostly functional principles. In fact, the first mosques were modelled on the Prophet Mohammed's house. To this day the basic plan in providing a safe, cool and peaceful haven for worship has changed little – there's the open *sahn* (courtyard), the arcaded *riwaq* (portico), and the covered, often domed, *haram* or prayer hall. A vaulted niche in the wall is called the mihrab; this serves to indicate the qibla, or direction of Mecca, towards which Muslims must face when they pray. The *minbar* (pulpit) is traditionally reached by three steps. The Prophet is said to have preached his sermons from the third step. Abu Bakr, his successor, chose to preach from the second step, and this is where most *imams* (prayer leaders) stand or sit today when preaching the Friday sermon.

The first minarets appeared long after Mohammed's death. Prior to that time, the muezzin (prayer caller) often stood on a rooftop or some other elevation so that he could be heard by as many townsfolk as possible.

Traditionally, mosques had an ablution fountain at the centre of the courtyard, often fashioned from marble. Today most modern mosques have a more practical row of taps and drains alongside.

The mosque serves the community in many ways. Groups of children receive Quranic lessons or run freely across the carpet; people sit in quiet contemplation of carved wood panels, tiled walls and marbled pillars; others simply enjoy a peaceful nap in the cool. As such, there is no greater expression of the way that art remains at the service of people –

The *masjid* or *jamaa* (mosque) is considered 'the embodiment' of the Islamic faith, and the Peninsula is home to Islam's holiest: the Grand Mosque in Mecca and the Prophet's Mosque in Medina. Several times larger than any football stadium, each accommodates many thousands of worshippers.

Betting is against Islamic principles, but at camel races, vast sums of money change hands in terms of prize money, sponsorship and ownership. A prize-racing camel can fetch over US$100,000.

something that surprises secular, Western onlookers. By the same token, it will be interesting to see what Muslims make of the decorative art of Europe – the Jean Nouvel–designed 'Louvre of the Desert' is about to open in Abu Dhabi (see p422), showcasing work from the Louvre in Paris. The decadence of the project, never mind the work on display, is bound to ruffle conservative feathers and challenge Peninsula people to reconsider what else could be meant by the term 'Art'.

SPORT

The people of the Arabian Peninsula love sport, and some Gulf countries, especially Qatar, are trying to promote themselves as venues for international events. This is no new phenomenon. For centuries, Arab men have been getting together in flat patches of desert to demonstrate their prowess in agility, speed and courage. Most of these traditional games, which involve bare-foot running, ball games, wrestling and even rifle throwing, are hard for a visitor to fathom, but since 2007, the GCC (Gulf Cooperation Council) countries have been trying to encourage greater participation in these kinds of sports and they may well receive more popular promotion in future.

Many traditional sports involve skill in handling animals. To this day, camel racing and horse racing are popular events, and falconry is of course the fabled sport of kings. A curiosity of the east coast of Arabia (in the UAE and Oman) is bull-butting – the kindly pitching of one Brahmin bull against another in a contest of strength, non-harmful to the animals involved. It takes place in a dusty arena where the animals are nudged into a head-down position, and push and shove from one side of the arena to the other. The bulls are precious to their owners and much beloved so the minute the going gets tough, thankfully the tough get going. As such, it isn't exactly the most spectacular sport to watch, though it always draws a huge crowd of locals. The best places to see bull-butting are near Muscat in Oman (see p237) and at Fujairah in the UAE (see p434).

Camel Racing

Camel racing is a grumbling affair of camels (who'd really rather not run) and owners (who make sure they do). The rider, traditionally, is almost immaterial. Racing usually involves a long, straight track (camels are not very good at cornering) with very wide turns. Camel fanciers race alongside in their 4WDs to give their favourite camel encouragement.

Camel racing can be seen throughout the region from October to May, although authorities are sensitive about the bad press associated

> The Dubai Cup offers prize money of US$6 million, making it the richest horse race of its kind in the world.

> It is estimated that 2000 falcons are still 'worked' across the Peninsula today. The Bedu use them for hunting.

CAMEL ON COMMAND

Traditionally, camels were raced by child jockeys, who were often 'bought' from impoverished families in Pakistan and Bangladesh, trained in miserable conditions, kept deliberately underweight and then exposed to the dangers of regular racing. The plight of these young boys has attracted international condemnation over the years. Qatar and the UAE, among other Gulf States, recently banned the use of child jockeys but were then left with the problem of finding something similarly light-weight to replace them. Their novel solution could best be described as 'robo-rider'. These robotic jockeys are remote-controlled, look vaguely humanoid and can crack an electronic whip. The camels appear to respond just as well (or just as badly) to their new mounts, and future versions of this gadget will sport bug-eyes from which the corpulent owner can pretend he's thin again as he takes virtual strides at 60km/h around the racetrack.

BENDING IT LIKE AL-BECKHAM

One sure-fire entrée into conversation across the region is to talk about Beckham – or rather Al-Beckham – and football in general back home. Peninsula men are obsessed with the game. But what distinguishes the sport in Arabia is not so much the players or the fans, but the extraordinary places where it's played.

There are pitches between fast lanes in Bahrain; motorway intersection pitches in Kuwait; shifting pitches, like the one in the UAE sand dunes, which has usually blown away before kick-off.

It's in Oman, however, that pitches are taken to new heights – like the one on the top of Jebel Shams, with goals strung out between two locally woven rugs, redefining the term 'mile-high club'. Omanis specialise in wet pitches, like the one near Bandar Khayran where the goalkeeper's job is to keep out the incoming tide or the one cradled in the mouth of Wadi Shab and cropped by donkeys. Soccer even stops traffic in Oman. Best in the road-stopping category is the pitch bisected by the road from Hat to Wadi bani Awf. When a game is on, all traffic on the only road that links both sides of the Hajar Mountains has to stop until half-time – a full 40 minutes of holding up one goat and me!

---

with the recruitment of young jockeys (see boxed text, p57) and less keen to promote races for tourism. Nonetheless, visitors can see races in Al-Shahaniya in Qatar (see p290) and Nad al-Sheba Camel Racecourse in Dubai (see p391).

Horse Racing

The breeding of horses, shipped from ports like Sur in Oman, has been a source of income in Arabia for centuries. Now, partly thanks to the efforts of Lady Anne Blunt, a 19th-century British horse-breeder, the fleet-footed, agile Arab horse is raced all over the world.

> The highlight of the year for many fanatics is the Gulf Cup, which involves all the Peninsula countries. When a national team wins a game, the capital city comes to a standstill with horn-blowing, flag-waving and even gun-firing in the interior.

Horse racing is a major spectator event for Peninsula people and the event doesn't get more glamorous than the Dubai Cup (p392). Heads of states, royalty, celebrities and top international jockeys gather for the occasion. Like Ascot in the UK it's *the* place to be seen.

Falconry

The ancient art of falconry is still practised across the Peninsula. It dates back at least to the 7th century BC when tradition has it that a Persian ruler caught a falcon to learn from its speed, tactics and focus. Modern owners continue to admire their birds and lavish love and respect upon them.

Many raptors are bred for falconry on the Asir escarpment in Saudi but the easiest place to see a peregrine up close is in the Falcon Souq in Doha (see p285). The magical spectacle of birds being flown can be seen in Dubai (see p389) and at most festivals, such as the Jenadriyah National Festival in Riyadh (see p314).

Modern Sports

A range of modern sports are popular in the region, including rally-driving, quad-biking, volleyball, cricket (especially among Asian expats), hockey and even ice-skating (see p204). In Dubai, locals have even taken to the slopes on real snow (see p391).

You can't possibly talk about sports in the area, however, and not mention football. At 4pm on a Friday, the men of just about every village in Arabia trickle onto the local waste-ground to play, all hopeful of joining international European clubs one day like some of their compatriots. Football is usually a shoeless business, on a desert pitch (see boxed text, above), played in *wizza* (cotton underskirt) and nylon strip.

Islam

You don't have to stay in the Arabian Peninsula for long to notice the presence of a 'third party' in all human interaction. Every official occasion begins with a reading from the Holy Quran. A task at work begins with an entreaty for God's help. The words *al-hamdu lillah* (thanks be to god) frequently lace sentences in which good things are related. Equally, the words *in sha' Allah* (god willing) mark all sentences that anticipate the future. These expressions are not merely linguistic decoration, they evidence a deep connection between society and faith.

For most Muslims, in other words, Islam is not just a religion, it's a way of life. It suggests what a Muslim should wear and what a Muslim should eat. It directs how income should be spent, who should inherit and by what amount. It guides behaviour and suggests punishment for transgression. Few other religions are as all-encompassing.

It is hard for most people in Western countries, where church and state are rigorously separated, to understand that for Muslims, there's little distinction between politics, culture and religion: each flows seamlessly through the other.

Understanding the religious integrity of Peninsula people makes sense of certain customs and manners. In turn, it guides the traveller in appropriate conduct and minimises the chance of giving offence.

> Turkey is the only Muslim country that has formally separated the religious sphere from the secular sphere.

> 'Travelling is a portion of punishment.' The Prophet Mohammed.

HISTORY
The Birth of Islam

Islam was founded in the early 7th century by the Prophet Mohammed. Born around AD 570 in the city of Mecca, Mohammed began receiving revelations at the age of 40 that continued for the rest of his life. Muslims believe these revelations, some received in Mecca, others in Medina, came directly from Allah through the angel Gabriel.

AND YOUR RELIGION IS...?

After exchanging pleasantries with acquaintants on the Peninsula, the conversation inevitably tends towards three subjects that most Western people shy away from: sex, politics and religion. The level of frankness involved in some of these discussions can come as a surprise. Forewarned is forearmed, however, and there's no better way of getting under the skin of a nation than talking about the things that matter most in life.

While all three subjects may seem like potential minefields (don't talk about sex with the opposite gender, especially if you're male; if you're talking politics, avoid saying 'you' when you mean 'your government'), religion is the one topic of conversation that takes a bit of practice. Christians and Jews are respected as 'People of the Book' who share the same God (see p65). Many a Bedouin encounter begins with a celebration of that fact with greetings such as 'Your God, my God same – Salam (Peace)!'

For most Muslims, however, tolerating Hindus, Christians or Jews is not the problem – knowing what to do with a heretic is the problem. Stating you don't believe in God is as good as saying you doubt the very foundation of a Muslim's life. So how do you say you're an atheist without causing offence? Try saying 'I'm not religious'. This will likely lead to understanding nods and then, on subsequent meetings, a very earnest attempt at conversion. Words like 'You'll find God soon, God-willing' should be seen as a measure of someone's like for you not as a rejection of your 'position'; as both of you have equal chances of being right, a reasonable response would be *shukran* (thank you).

WHO WAS MOHAMMED?

Very little is known about the early years of Mohammed, other than that he was born around AD 570. His biography was written a century after his death and is more adulatory than factual.

Mohammed's early life doesn't appear to have been easy. His father died before he was born, and his mother when he was six years old. Adopted by his grandfather, who shortly also died, he was eventually sent to live with his uncle. With few means, the boy was obliged to work early as a caravan trader. Mohammed's honesty, integrity and efficiency, however, didn't escape the eye of a much older, wealthy widow called Khadijah, who soon took him on as her agent. Eventually the couple married and had four daughters. After Khadijah's death, Mohammed married several other wives (polygamy was acceptable) for political and altruistic reasons. In addition he had at least two concubines.

As Mohammed came from an oral tradition, he memorised the revelations, rather than writing them down, and then repeated them to friends and family. His contemporaries recognised the revelations as divine and they formed the basis of the Quran (meaning 'recitation' in Arabic). In turn, the Quran, as well as a series of suras (verses), became the basis of the new religion of Islam.

Sunnis & Shiites

Islam split into different sects soon after its foundation, based not so much on theological interpretation but on historical event.

Al-Bab (www.al-bab .com) is a comprehensive site providing links to information on and discussions of Islam.

When the Prophet died in 632, he left no instructions as to who should be his successor, or the manner in which future Islamic leaders (known as caliphs) should be chosen. The community initially chose Abu Bakr, the Prophet's closest companion and father-in-law, as the new leader of the Muslim faith but not everyone was happy with this decision. Some supported the claim of Ali bin Abi Taleb, Mohammed's cousin and son-in-law. They became known as *shi'a* ('partisans' of Ali). Ali eventually became caliph, the fourth of Mohammed's successors, in 656. However, five years later he was assassinated by troops loyal to the Governor of Syria, Mu'awiyah bin Abu Sufyan (a distant relative of the Prophet) and Mu'awiyah became caliph.

From that point hence, the Muslim community separated into two competing factions. The Sunnis on the one hand favoured the Umayyads, the dynasty which was established by Mu'awiyah. According to Sunni doctrine, the caliph was both the spiritual leader of the Muslim community and the temporal ruler of the state. So long as a Muslim ruled with justice and according to the Sharia'a (Islamic law), he deserved the support of the Muslim community as a whole. Shiites, on the other hand, believed that only a descendant of the Prophet through Ali's line should lead the Muslims. Because Shiites have rarely held temporal power, their doctrine came to emphasise the spiritual position of their leaders, the *imams*.

Muhammed: A Biography of the Prophet, by Karen Armstrong, is a sensitive, well-researched and highly readable biography of the Prophet set against the backdrop of modern misconceptions and stereotypes about Islam.

In 680, Ali's son Hussein was murdered in brutal circumstances at Karbala (in today's southern Iraq), an event that further widened the gap between the two factions. The division and hostility between the two sects continues to this day.

As with any religion approaching one billion adherents, Islam has produced many sects, movements and offshoots within the traditional Sunni–Shiite division. The two most important Sunni sects in the Gulf States are the Wahhabis (see p307), whose austere doctrines are the official form of Islam in Saudi Arabia, and the Ibadis (see p187), who also espouse a strict interpretation of Islam and are the dominant sect in Oman.

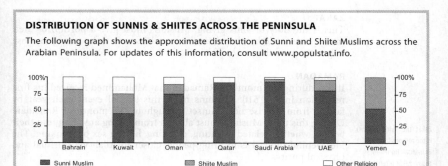

DISTRIBUTION OF SUNNIS & SHIITES ACROSS THE PENINSULA

The following graph shows the approximate distribution of Sunni and Shiite Muslims across the Arabian Peninsula. For updates of this information, consult www.populstat.info.

TEACHINGS

Despite modern connotations with fundamentalism and the violent beginnings of Islam in the Peninsula itself, Islam is an inherently peaceful creed. The word 'Islam' means 'submission', or 'self-surrender'. It also means 'peace'. Taken as a whole, Islam is the attainment of peace – with self, society and the environment – through conscious submission to the will of God. To submit to the will of God does not just entail paying lip service to God through ceremony, but through all daily thoughts and deeds.

The principal teaching of Islam is that there is only one true God, creator of the universe. Muslims believe that the God of Islam is the same god of Christians and Jews, but that he has no son or partner and he needs no intermediary (such as priests). Muslims believe that the prophets, starting with Adam, including Abraham and Jesus, and ending with Mohammed, were sent to reveal God's word but that none of them were divine.

Historically, this creed obviously had great appeal to the scattered people of the Peninsula who were given access to a rich spiritual life without having to submit to incomprehensible rituals administered by hierarchical intermediaries. Believers needed only to observe the transportable Five Pillars of Islam in order to fulfil their religious duty. This is true to this day and is perhaps one of the reasons why Islam is one of the world's fastest growing religions.

> Around 90% of all Muslims are Sunnis. In the Arabian Peninsula, however, Shiites constitute a clear majority in Bahrain (though Bahrain's ruling family are Sunnis), and there are significant Shiite minorities in Kuwait, the UAE (United Arab Emirates) and Saudi Arabia's Eastern Province.

The Five Pillars of Islam

SHAHADA

This is the profession of faith that Muslims publicly declare in every mosque, five times a day across the land: 'There is no God but Allah and Mohammed is his Prophet'. To convert to Islam, one needs only to state this with conviction three times.

SALAT

Muslims are expected to pray five times a day: at sunrise, noon, mid-afternoon, sunset and night (usually 1½ hours after sunset). It's acceptable to pray at home or at the office, except for Friday noon prayers, which are performed preferably at a mosque. Prayer involves prostration in the direction of the Kaaba in Mecca (arrows in aircraft and in hotel rooms indicate the right direction) and the ritual recital of passages of the Quran. Before praying, a Muslim must perform 'ablution' (washing arms, hands, head and feet with water or sand) to indicate a willingness to be purified in spirit.

> Over the centuries Sunnism has developed into the 'orthodox' strain of Islam and today comprises about 90% of the world's more than 1100 million Muslims. There are large Shiite minorities, however, spread across the Middle East.

ZAKAT

This is the duty of alms giving. Muslims must give a portion of their salary (one-fortieth of a believer's annual income to be exact) to those in greater need than oneself.

RAMADAN

It was during the month of Ramadan that Mohammed received his first revelation in AD 610. Muslims mark this special event each year by fasting from sunrise until sunset throughout the month of Ramadan. During this time, Muslims must abstain from taking anything into their bodies, whether related to eating, drinking, having sex or smoking. The idea behind the fast is to bring people closer to Allah via spiritual and physical purity.

> Zakat (the giving of alms) is the responsibility of the individual. Nonetheless, today, zakat often works as a kind of welfare system, collected by the state as an annual tax and redistributed through mosques or religious charities.

HAJ

Every Muslim capable of doing so (whether physically or financially) is expected to perform the haj pilgrimage to Mecca, the holiest of cities, at least once in their lifetime. For a pilgrimage to qualify as a 'true' haj, it can only be performed during a few specific days of the Muslim year. Visiting Mecca at any other time of the year is known as *umrah* (the 'lesser pilgrimage' or 'visitation'). Performing the haj is richly rewarded: all past sins are forgiven. Additionally, pilgrims are entitled to call themselves *al-haj* and doing so still evokes much respect in the community. See the Haj chapter for a fuller description of haj.

Sharia'a

As there is no distinction between life and religion in Islam, it follows that a set of principles or 'laws' based on Islamic teaching should shape the general conduct of life. The 'legal' implications of those principles is referred to as Sharia'a, although it is not 'law' in a Western sense and is widely open to differences of interpretation.

In matters of dispute, or where someone breaks the moral code of Islam, Muslim scholars turn either to the Quran or to the Sunnah, a body of works recording the sayings and doings of the Prophet (and some of his companions) for guidance. However, there are many Sunnah authorities, and their reliability is in turn determined by different schools of Islamic jurisprudence.

> Some people are excused the rigours of Ramadan, including young children and those whose health will not permit fasting. Travellers on a journey are also excused, although they are expected to fast on alternative days instead. (For more details on Ramadan, see p534.)

Sharia'a law has come to be associated with extreme forms of punishment meted out to transgressors in some Arab countries: amputation of limbs for repeat-offending thieves, flogging of those caught committing adultery, public beheading for murderers. These punishments, associated mostly with the austere Hanbali school of jurisprudence in Saudi Arabia, are intended as a deterrent first and foremost and are seldom enforced.

In some instances the Sharia'a is quite specific, such as in the areas of inheritance law and the punishments for certain offences. In many other cases it provides only guidelines. A learned scholar or judge has to determine the proper 'Islamic' position or approach to a problem using his own discretion. This partly explains the wide divergence in Muslim opinion on some issues – such as today with regard to jihad.

Jihad

If there is one term that is more misunderstood than Sharia'a by people in the West, it is the term 'jihad'. This has come to be seen as the rallying cry-to-arms of so-called Muslim fundamentalists against Western regimes and is assumed to apologise for acts of terrorism. It is true that

> **THE QURAN**
>
> Muslims believe that the Quran is the literal word of God, unlike the Bible or Torah which they
> believe were inspired by God but were recorded subject to human interpretation. For Muslims,
> the Quran is therefore not just the principal source of doctrine in Islam, but also a source of
> spiritual rapture in its own right. It is recited often with emotional elation, as a blessing to the
> reciter and the hearer. The use of the 'sacred' language of Arabic, with its unique rhythms, gives
> the recitation a sacramental quality that eludes translation, and many Muslims around the world
> still learn large portions of the Quran in its original form to feel closer to God's words.

for some fundamentalists jihad represents a violent struggle to preserve
the Islamic faith from the encroachment of a different set of moral values (or, as they would see it, a lack of moral values). For these people, it
also represents a struggle against what they consider to be the bullying
of countries whose political and economic dominance impinge upon
the rights and freedoms of Islamic peoples – in Palestine and Iraq in
particular.

The interpretation of jihad as being solely about waging war on alternative ways of governance and of living, however, is a very narrow
definition that most Islamic people wholeheartedly reject. Indeed, violent
behaviour runs counter to Islamic teaching regarding justice, tolerance
and peace. In fact, the word jihad means 'striving' or 'struggle' and has
much broader connotations than the translation usually ascribed to it by
the Western media. Far from 'holy war', it more often means 'striving
in the way of the faith' – struggling against one's own bad intentions, or
rooting out evil, 'indecency' or oppression in society. Islam dictates that
this struggle should occur through peaceful, just means and the prevailing of wisdom, not through anger and aggression.

Jihad in a political context, as the 'struggle to defend the faith', has
been the subject of intense debate among Muslim scholars for the last
1400 years. In as much as it refers to the right of a nation to defend itself
against oppression, there isn't a nation on earth that wouldn't claim
the same right. Nevertheless, for most scholars (both past and present)
jihad refers primarily to a spiritual rather than nationalistic, political or
military concept.

*Given the belief in
the Quran's physical
sacredness, Islamic law
forbids the touching
or reciting of an Arabic
Quran without special
ablution. Travellers
should be aware of this
when visiting mosques
and refrain from touching
the holy book.*

CUSTOMS & CEREMONIES

Other areas of Islamic belief and practice that attract heated Western
commentary are those concerned with daily life, and in particular, marriage, the role of women, dress and diet. When looked at from an Islamic
or even a historical perspective, however, none of them seem to deserve
the reproach they receive. For the social implications of each of these
elements of Peninsula life, see the sections on marriage and the role
of women (p48), and dress (p49) in the Culture chapter, and Habits &
Customs (p85) in the Food & Drink chapter.

Marriage

It is true that a Muslim is permitted by Islam to have up to four wives
(but a woman may have only one husband). As with many things within
Islam, however, this came about through consideration of a particular
historical context where women were left without a provider through
war, natural disasters or divorce. Uniquely, it allows a 'certain latitude
of nature' on behalf of men within the framework of the law, but holds
men responsible for their actions.

Marriage has to be entered into freely on behalf of both the man and the woman or else it is invalid.

Role of Women

Islam regards women, whether single or married, as individuals in their own right, with the right to own property and earnings without anyone dictating how they dispose of that income. A marriage dowry is given by the groom to the bride for the woman's personal use and she keeps her own name in marriage.

Although Islam permits four wives, each wife must be treated equally: 'if ye fear that ye shall not be able to deal justly, then only one.' Modern Muslim interpretation emphasises the impossibility of loving two wives equally, thereby resigning the practice to history.

Mothers are highly honoured in Islam and far from being excluded from the mosque, as is sometimes believed by non-Muslims, they are exempted the duty to make it easier to fulfil their function as carer of children. Most mosques have separate prayer halls where women can worship without feeling uncomfortable by the presence of men. Men are never permitted to enter the women's prayer hall but in some of the Grand Mosques, women are permitted, except during prayer times, to enter the men's prayer hall. In Mecca, all Muslims, male and female, stand shoulder to shoulder in the sacred places and pray together.

Dress

Islam prescribes modest dress in public places for both men and women, which involves covering the legs, arms and head for men, and the hair and neck for women. It does not, however, mention the use of a veil. It is unclear where the custom of covering the body originated from; it certainly predates Islam and to a large degree makes excellent sense in the ravaging heat of the Arabian Peninsula where exposure to the midday sun is dangerous to health.

Diet

Muslims are forbidden to eat or drink anything containing pork or alcohol. Nor are they permitted to consume the blood or the meat of any animal that has died of natural causes. These strictures made good sense in the Arabian Peninsula where tape worm was a common

A BATTLE FOR BODY & SOUL Jenny Walker

I remember travelling with my father on the Peninsula, 20 years ago, and often being the focus of a bizarre bidding war involving the price of marital upkeep weighed against a number of camels. My own father only stopped the bidding (an unavoidable topic of conversation between men over coffee in a Bedouin tent) when a shipping bill for two dromedaries arrived at our house in Surrey and there clearly wasn't going to be enough grass to graze them.

Gone are those days, thankfully, but solo women travelling in the Peninsula today may still be surprised at the number of times they receive a marriage proposal. Before assuming that this is a ruse to engage in sexual relations, you may find that your suitor is after your soul as much as your body. The sight of a single woman brings out the protective instincts of many a Peninsula male – and besides they earn more points in heaven if they extend the security of their name and home to a woman in need.

One day at work in Muscat, a young Arabic woman came looking for a job. I left her in the company of one of my team while I collected an application form. When I came back a few minutes later, he'd married her! I asked whether the speed of attachment to wife number three was anything to do with his youth, or her beauty, or her talents. My colleague was pleased his new wife could cook, he said, but his prime motivation was, with the grace of Allah, to scoop her out of harm's way. Such is the confidence of man!

problem with pork meat and where the effect of alcohol is exaggerated by the climate.

Meat must be halal (permitted) or in other words slaughtered in the prescribed manner, involving consideration of the animal and minimal cruelty.

ISLAM & THE WEST

In his Introduction to the new *Concise Encyclopaedia of Islam*, Professor Huston Smith quotes a *Newsweek* journalist commenting on the 1979 US–Iran crisis: 'We are heading into an expansion,' ran the article, 'of the American relationship with that complex of religion, culture and geography known as Islam…no part of the world is more hopelessly and systematically and stubbornly misunderstood by us.'

These are strong words and they reflect 1000 years of misinformation, mistrust and misrepresentation of the Muslim world by the West and vice versa. But to what extent can the same comment be made today when each country in the West has a sizable Muslim community, large proportions of Gulf students attend Western colleges, and expat workers from Peninsula countries return with a different story? For once in the history of East–West relations, the ordinary person in the street is better informed about alternative cultures than ever before. So why does the myth-making persist?

Historically, Muslims and Christians confronted each other during the Inquisition, the Crusades and in numerous encounters throughout history. Religious propaganda was used as a way of helping each side achieve its purpose and those prejudices persist to this day. Add to this the behaviour of a small minority who call themselves Muslim but who are not good ambassadors for the faith, and it would appear that the religion is doomed to be 'hopelessly and systematically and stubbornly misunderstood' for millennia to come.

On the other hand, if there is one positive outcome of the tensions between Islam and the West since 9/11 it is surely the high-profile dialogue between ordinary people on what constitutes Islam and how it relates to Western culture. In newspapers and TV programmes in every country of the West, the lexicon of Islam is becoming less alien and less needful of definition. Debates about the wearing of the hejab (veil) that dominated many media stories in 2006, for example, start with the premise that people are no longer ignorant of the custom.

Of course the dialogue hasn't always been a comfortable one as the publication of derogatory cartoons in Denmark showed, nor has the outcome always made good sense, as with censoring Christian expression in case it causes offence to Muslims. Nonetheless, slowly but surely, each 'side' is lurching towards a better understanding of the limits of tolerance expected by the other, and the threatening aspect of the encounter is receding in the process.

This may not be entirely welcome to the governments on either side of the equation. Surely there's an element of political convenience involved in anti-Islamic rhetoric at national levels. After all, how does a power persuade its people that it needs to invade another without drawing on old animosities? Where those old animosities came from in the first place is the subject of the following paragraphs.

Shared Foundations of Monotheism

When in 2003 US general William Boykin, referring to a Muslim soldier, said 'I knew that my God was real, and his was an idol', it offended the

The Concise Encyclopedia of Islam, by Cyril Glasse, is a definitive volume regarding the Islamic religion, detailing an A to Z of facts, concepts and premises in a factual, authoritative style. An essential point of reference for anyone wanting to become better acquainted with this world religion.

With about one billion people professing the faith, Islam is the world's second-largest religion after Christianity; around 50 countries have Muslim majorities and another 35 have significant minorities. Six million Muslims live in the USA – around 2% of the population.

Contrary to general expectation, Indonesia, not Arabia, has the largest Muslim population, followed by India.

A Middle East Mosaic,
by Bernard Lewis, is a
fascinating miscellany
compiled from many and
varied sources, a grab
bag of impressions of the
'other' by Muslim, Chris-
tian and Jewish observers
through the ages.

Muslim world not so much because of the implied hierarchy of deities but because of the heretical nature of the comment. For all Muslims there is no God but God, and this uniqueness of God is the defining principle of all three major monotheistic religions: Islam, Christianity and Judaism.

Islam, Muslims believe, is not a new religion but the refinement and ultimate manifestation of the monotheistic religions. As such, Muslims are respectful of the other two religions and their adherents (known as the 'people of the book'), and acknowledge the debt to the revelations of the Bible and Torah that came before the Quran.

The three religions have much in common as they all revere Jerusalem (the third holiest city after Mecca and Medina for Muslims) and they share the same prophets, including Abraham, Moses and Jesus. Crucially, however, Islam denies the divinity of any of these figures and teaches that Mohammed was the last prophet who will come before the Day of Judgement.

Foray into Europe

The knights of the
Spanish Reconquista
expelled the last Muslim
monarch from Spain in
1492, the very year coin-
cidentally that Columbus
reached the Americas,
signalling the waxing of
the cross and the waning
of the crescent in a new
world order.

The monotheistic faiths became powerful cultural and political entities in the world because they broke the geographic confines of their origins. Islam is no exception and it soon spread across neighbouring countries, shifting capitals from Mecca to Damascus and thence peacefully to Jerusalem. From here traders from Eastern Europe, the Mediterranean and North Africa were exposed to the new religion and recognised in it a practical, portable faith which they voluntarily took home with them.

The first major impact that Islam made on the West was through the campaigns of the Muslim armies who spread into Spain from North Africa in 711 and settled in Andalusia. During their occupation of this part of Spain, they built the great citadels and mosques of Granada and Cordoba and entered into a creative and largely peaceful dynamic with Christendom that lasted for seven centuries.

This early Islamic encounter with Europe resulted in much cultural cross-pollination. The scholars of Muslim Spain translated the classical works of medicine, astronomy, chemistry, philosophy and architecture from Greek and Roman sources, lost to the Europe of the Dark Ages, and thereby helped bring about the Renaissance, upon which modern Europe is built.

HAPPY CHRISTMAS IN THE ARABIAN PENINSULA

Living in the Arabian Peninsula and reading about the annual whipping that Western countries give themselves over Christmas, it's hard not to chuckle at the underlying misconceptions involved.

In Britain particularly, where there are laudable intentions on behalf of local councils to be equitable to Islamic immigrant families, there are thoroughly daft outcomes: three out of four small firms banned Christmas decorations in 2006; the Royal Mail scotched religious stamps; carols were called 'seasonal songs', nativity scenes banned in public places and cards sent with 'Season's Greetings'. In Birmingham they even tried to call Christmas 'Winterval'.

While Britain tiptoed round a Weary Winterval, however, the Arabian Peninsula immersed itself in a 'Merry Christmas'. In the malls and shopping centres, there were lights and carols, mangers with babies and neon cribs, cards with angels and the three wise men, and Arab Muslims queuing up to take little Ahmed to see Santa.

Even for atheists it's hard to see why, if Muslims can celebrate the birth of their prophet, Jesus, why on earth can't Christians?

MUSLIM CONTRIBUTORS

Muslims contributed widely to the world's body of knowledge at a time when Europe was lost in the Dark Ages, but few of their names are recognised by people in the West today. Here are four of the many that deserve a better billing in Western history books:

■ **Al-Khwarizmi** (AD 780–850), known as the 'Father of Algebra', combined Indian and Greek mathematical traditions and introduced Arabic numerals to Europe. He also built on Ptolemy's work to produce the first map of the world.

■ **Ibn Sina** (AD 980–1037) was a great medical scholar who wrote the *Book of Healing* and the *Canon of Medicine* – a medical encyclopaedia which was used throughout the West for over 600 years.

■ **Ibn Khaldun** (AD 1332–95), who wrote *The Book of Examples and Collections from Early and Later Information Concerning the Days of Arabs, Non-Arabs and Berbers*, was the first historian to write on the philosophy of history and civilisation.

■ **Ibn Battuta** (AD 1304–69) was a famous traveller whose pilgrimage to Mecca became a journey of 120,000km across North Africa, the Middle East and Asia (see p31).

The Crusades

Not everyone was pleased with the Muslim legacy, however, and pockets of resistance to the spread of Islam finally took a militant shape in the form of the Crusades. In the ominous name of a 'just war', Christian zealots wrested the Holy Land from the Muslims in 1099. Unfortunately, the Crusades attracted not only the pious but also every kind of adventurer and miscreant out looking for a fight, and victory was marked by wanton bloodletting.

Despite the atrocities, later travellers to the Holy Land were surprised to find Christians and Muslims settled into comfortable cohabitation, with the former imitating many of the customs and manners of the latter.

Ottoman Expansion

The second great Islamic excursion into Europe came with the Ottoman Turks. They've come to be seen as an oppressive people, but during the height of their reign – in an empire that stretched from Hungary to Libya – they treated Christians and Jews with the respect accorded to monotheistic faith by the Quran.

Meanwhile in Arabia's arid Najd region, a new spirit of 'fundamentalism', or return to pure Islamic principles, was taking shape in the form of Abd al-Wahhab. The Wahhabis' various bids for political power based on Islamic zeal prefigured movements such as the Brotherhood of Islam two centuries later.

Colonialism

When Napoleon's armies took aim at the Sphinx in the early 19th century, it marked a turning point in the relationship between the West and the Muslim world. The great powers of Europe, self-assured and wealthy, with large overseas colonies built on the industrial revolution, began to make incursions into Arab territory that were more to do with strategic influence than with faith. The Middle East became the puppet of European ambition for over a century, suffering a mortal blow in 1948 with the founding of the state of Israel (p37).

There were positive interactions during the era of colonialism, however. European explorers came to Arabia with a genuine interest in a

Muslim Arabs introduced the concept of zero into European mathematics – without which there would be no computer age – not to mention other civilising influences such as coffee, papermaking and chess.

Infidels, by Andrew Wheatcroft, is a study of Islam and Christianity's troubled relationship from the birth of Islam to the 21st century.

The Desert and the Sown, by Gertrude Bell, first published in 1907, gives an account of Arabia through the travels of this extraordinary woman at the turn of the last century that is remarkable for its common sense and objectivity.

culture that seemed less tainted by the effeteness of Western society. By the mid-20th century, the desire for learning drifted in the opposite direction, with many wealthy Muslims studying in Europe. They returned to their own countries bearing Western ideas, including democracy and individualism.

Pan-Arabism

European control of the Middle East diminished with the Suez Crisis of 1956 – the era in which Nasr became President of Egypt, bringing with him the notion of pan-Arabism. First appearing in 1915, pan-Arabism was a movement for unification among the Arab nations of the Middle East. It was a secular and mostly socialist movement with national overtones that opposed any kind of Western influence or intervention in Arab affairs. Unity based on race only fulfilled half the equation and soon unity based on Islam became a more suggestive prospect. Movements such as the Muslim Brotherhood in Egypt, led by the radical Sayyid Qutb, pursued a universal Islamic society through whatever means necessary, including violence and martyrdom. With this movement, an entirely different dynamic towards the West came into being. The revolution in Iran, in which the monarchy was replaced by Muslim clerics, was a further indicator of a new expression of the old alliance of faith and the sword.

The Crisis of Islam – Holy War and Unholy Terror, by Bernard Lewis, is a new book examining the relationship between Muslims and non-Muslims, and tracing the origin of Islamic resentment, frustration and terrorism.

'The War on Terror'

The politics of oil since the 1970s has dominated relations between the West and the world of Islam. From a Muslim perspective it was the prime motivator behind the 2003 invasion of Iraq. The wealth that has resulted from oil has been equally divisive, giving rise to fundamental Islamic elements who perceive in this relationship a threat to traditional Islamic and Arabic values.

The other major area of confrontation that continues today is resentment regarding the plight of the Palestinians, coupled with the perceived Western bias towards Israel. Until a solution to the relentless problem of cohabitation between Jews and Arabs is reached, the entire region will remain in a state of flux.

George W Bush's use of the term 'crusade' in the early days of the so-called War on Terror was a fundamental tactical error. It reopened old wounds between the West and Islam and reminded Arabs that the provocation for war in this region has generally been the bullying of the weak by the powerful.

KEEPING THE FAITH TODAY

Covering Islam – How the Media and the Experts Determine How We See the Rest of the World, by the late Edward W Said (an expert on the Middle East), examines the way in which the media portrays the Islamic world.

It's 11pm on the last Thursday night before Ramadan, and last orders were called half an hour ago. On the bar, lined up in discreet carrier bags, are the takeaway orders of the last remaining men in the bar: there are six Tigers, Pocari Sweat for the non-drinkers, a box of fried king fish and some packets of Heinz tomato ketchup. No-one is moving very far because the evening is convivial and the crack of cue on ball on the billiard table, or the thud of dart on board, is reassuringly familiar and male. The inevitable – the move downtown to a nightclub, watching skimpy-skirted women from the Philippines or from Egypt, in thick tights, gyrating mechanically on stage to Zairian music – is delayed. 'Moving on' always involves a lecture from the wife in the morning, so perhaps tonight everyone will give it a miss.

Perhaps they'll buy some kebabs with chopped cabbage and tongue-curling pickles from the coffeehouse and eat them on the waste ground

OTHER RELIGIONS ON THE PENINSULA TODAY

All the indigenous people of the Peninsula today are Muslim. One or two Muslim converts to Christianity wander in a state of miserable purgatory on the periphery of society, barred from all social interaction with family and friends by a decision that most Muslims would consider not just heretical but also a rejection of common sense, history and culture.

This is not the case with expatriate Christians whose religion is respected and provision for worship catered for in Church services across the region. In Kuwait a huge church stands in the middle of downtown. In Oman a Christian mission set up the first hospitals in Muscat and in consequence, Christian worship is respectfully tolerated with many services in English, Malayalam and languages of other local expats, conducted throughout the week. There are also Hindu and Buddhist temples tucked away in small suburbs of the region's big cities and travelling missions visit expat camps in rural areas to bring comfort to those separated from the familiar props of their home communities. Small enclaves of Jewish people who have lived on the Peninsula for centuries are given private latitude in Yemen as part of the Muslim culture of religious tolerance.

Saudi, as keeper of Islam's holiest shrines, is the exception: no religious observance is permitted other than Islam. That said, a blind eye is turned towards pockets of private worship among Christians. In fact, the key word regarding non-Islamic religious observance in the Arabian Peninsula today is discretion: whatever worship happens behind closed doors and which doesn't interfere with the beliefs of Muslims is a matter between the individual and their conscience.

and enjoy the stars, because God is good, and chat about not very much. If they time it right, by the time they get home, the maid will have put the kids to bed and perhaps it's a no headache night for the wife. Perhaps she's finished her MBA assignment and made it to her friend's wedding in the red dress – the one that hangs off the shoulders and that no other man will ever see. Then again, the football's tempting: the flat screen TV in the corner of the family room will still be on, no doubt, competing quietly with the hum of the air-con. Tonight as every night it's showing the national team being fouled by the neighbouring Gulf team. Everyone knows the referees are a biased bunch of cheating ... well it can be said tonight, but tomorrow, tomorrow is different.

Such is the scene in modern Peninsula cities throughout the Gulf, throughout most of the region in fact – maybe only minus the booze. The men in one place, the women in another, enjoying public company but coming together for family, intimacy and private time – this is the age-old pattern of Arab communities, indulging human passions but reining them in with the unconscious guidance of religion and culture and looking forward to the self-denial of Ramadan.

Modern life requires daily compromises with religion, but then it always has. As such, there's not much that separates a Peninsula life from a Western one, except perhaps in the degrees of temptation and opportunity.

The Haj: the Ultimate Traveller's Tale

The haj. Nothing quite compares. In religious as well as cultural and commercial terms, it is the single largest event in the world. Comprising one of the Five Pillars of Islam (see p61), the pilgrimage to Mecca (or haj, as it is known in Islam) is a duty every Muslim must perform at least once in their lives (so long as they are physically and financially able).

It was the prophet Ibrahim who first founded the tradition over 4000 years ago. Since then, pilgrims have been coming from all corners of the world to carry out their religious obligation.

Many Muslims save all their lives to make this journey. For most, the haj is a profoundly spiritual experience: performing the haj cleanses them of previous sins, serves to reaffirm their faith, and often brings a new meaning and direction to their lives. Additionally, pilgrims who complete the haj return to reverence and respect in their home countries. For most Muslims, the haj is the greatest achievement of their lives.

In this way, the haj has historically played a key contribution to the social cohesion of one of the world's great religions. Mecca, and nearby Medina – which many pilgrims also visit – are considered Islam's two holiest cities. Because of their status, the towns are off limits to non-Muslims, and a wall delineating the *haram* (forbidden) area surrounds the two cities.

HAJ HISTORY

Until quite recently, the haj represented a dangerous, drawn-out and difficult enterprise from which there was no guarantee of safe return. In the days before air travel and mass tourism, many pilgrims walked; for some it could take up to two years just to arrive. Still living today are pilgrims across the world – in Africa, Asia and elsewhere – who proudly retell their remarkable journeys.

Hardship was not just endured in the past, it was expected. Before setting off, pilgrims would draw up wills and appoint executors, in case they should fail to return. Many did not make it back home. Bandits, highwaymen, robbers, warring tribes, kidnappers and disease were some of the hazards pilgrims were exposed to.

The journey could also prove very costly, even for wealthier pilgrims. Some rich travellers brought with them slaves on the journey, some of whom were sold along the way, cashed like an early form of travellers cheque in order to pay for expenses.

Merchants sometimes funded their way by bringing goods to barter. This tradition continues even today. In Jeddah, Saudi Arabia's 'gateway to the holy cities', you can find pilgrims selling home-grown products straight out of their suitcases – rolls of brightly coloured cloth from West Africa, coffee from Yemen, saffron and pistachios from Iran, spices from India, kites and toys from Indonesia, juicy dates from Tunisia, and before the days of bird flu, bright-green parrots from Africa.

It was King Abdul Aziz, the founder of the modern Kingdom of Saudi Arabia, who first concerned himself with the safety, security and comfort of the pilgrims. One by one, accommodation, health care, sanitation and transportation became the focus of his attentions. It was not all

Pilgrims who successfully complete the haj are permitted to prefix their names with 'Al-Haj'. In communities around the world, this appellation still invites much respect, though Islamic teachers warn that the haj should be performed as a mark of religious commitment, not as a way of attaining a higher social status within the community.

philanthropic: no ruler could claim real control of his domain without guaranteeing the safe passage of pilgrims.

Even today, the haj is considered a massive exercise in PR terms for the Saudis as a nation and for the Al-Sauds as a family, reinforcing as it does the state's image as the self-proclaimed protector of the two holy cities (Mecca and Medina), and the head of Islamic nations.

HAJ TOURISM
Pilgrim Numbers
During 2006 (1427 Hejira), a record-breaking 2.4 million pilgrims officially performed the haj. A large proportion of these (33%) came from Saudi Arabia itself, though many were actually non-Saudi residents. Factoring in the unofficial figures as well (every year, hundreds of thousands of locals slip into Mecca without official permits), the real total probably nears the three million mark.

Just over 50 years ago, the number was not thought to exceed 10,000 pilgrims. In the last decade alone, the number is up 36%, and figures are expected to keep rising.

Millions more around the world also watch the haj live on TV and via the internet. Like the pilgrims, TV crews come from across the world, working for networks including the BBC, Fox News and CNN. Since 2004, Saudi radio has transmitted a round-the-clock coverage of the haj in eight languages, including Turkish, Farsi, Hausa, French, Indonesian and Urdu.

Pilgrim Origins
In 2006, pilgrims arrived from over 160 countries stretching from Mali to the Sudan, from Algeria to Azerbaijan, and from Russia to Bangladesh and Indonesia. An estimated 24,000 pilgrims came from the UK; 16,000 from the US.

Pilgrim Economics
Before the oil era, the haj was the economic backbone of the whole country. Nowadays, with its vast oil resources, Saudi Arabia is no longer dependent upon the event.

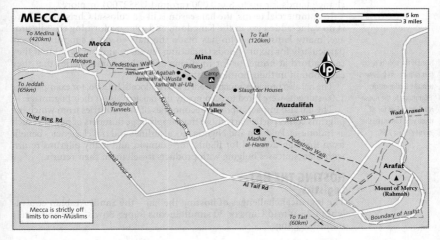

Nevertheless, the haj is still a vital source of income for the Kingdom's private sector. Millions of dollars are generated annually by the event and Saudi's service industries (including hotels, restaurants and travel agencies) benefit greatly, as does the retail industry. Across the desert in Saudi Arabia, vast camel caravans can be seen crossing the Kingdom on their way to Mecca. It's a profitable time, as prices rise dramatically: camels can change hands for up to SR10,000 (around US$2700) or more.

In commercial terms, the haj season is like a colossal Christmas. There is no value-added tax in the Kingdom, and after performing the pilgrimage, many *hajis* (one who has made the haj) go on a shopping spree, particularly for luxury goods (including jewellery and perfume) that they can't afford at home, or for medicine and other commodities that they can't obtain in their home countries.

The haj also provides much-needed jobs for locals. In 2006, for example, over 1500 students were hired to accompany the haj arrivals on their pilgrimage.

The haj also impacts upon the economies of the countries from which the pilgrims come, particularly those that supply large numbers of pilgrims such as Indonesia, Pakistan and Nigeria. Local airlines and travel agencies benefit from the high demand for flights, for example, and many pilgrims return with their suitcases bulging with products to sell upon their return.

Islam is the only religion that requires its followers to make a pilgrimage: 'Pilgrimage to the House is a duty to God for all those who can make the journey' *(sura 3:98)*.

HOSTING THE HAJ
Logistics

The logistical challenges of hosting the haj – the Saudi Arabian equivalent of 25 World Cups or 30 simultaneous Super Bowls – are absolutely mind-boggling.

'Health and Safety' for example takes on a new meaning in the Kingdom. With the coming together and close contact of so many people from so many countries (some still wracked by infectious disease), the haj is the ultimate breeding ground for infection.

If an epidemic were to occur, it could be catastrophic, not just for the pilgrims and Saudi Arabia but across the world, as infected pilgrims return to their home countries. A famous phenomenon among pilgrims is the 'haj cough', akin to the school cold picked up in the playground and passed around the whole household – but on a global scale.

One of the biggest challenges therefore is the control of this health risk. In order to qualify now for a haj visa, pilgrims are obliged to have certain vaccinations. Certificates are checked meticulously upon entry to Saudi Arabia and if pilgrims are found without them, they are administered on the spot. If pilgrims refuse, they are deported.

During the 2006 haj, no less than 9600 doctors, nurses and medical technicians assisted with this and other health-related matters. All medical treatment is administered free of charge.

As many pilgrims are elderly (some have saved all their lives to make the trip) and others are already ill (keen to make the haj while they still can), serious illness and even death are not uncommon during the pilgrimage. In Mecca and Medina alone, 21 hospitals (each with 3932 beds) remain on constant stand-by during the haj.

Other logistics include the organisation of the following:

- 50,000 armed security men who patrol the whole area using high-tech communication equipment. In the past, the haj has been targeted by terrorists (see Haj Hazards, p74).
- Over 26 fire brigades, 27 rescue units, 11 monitoring towers and 1224 fire-fighting points at the mountain of Arafat alone.
- The distribution of free food and drinks (and alms to those in need).
- The replenishing of the Zamzam well. Supplying the pilgrims' needs for centuries, today the well must be refilled before the pilgrims arrive.
- The laying on of special pilgrim flights by Saudi Arabian airlines. At the height of the haj, planes arrive at Jeddah airport every minute. Planes also fly pilgrims direct to Medina airport (which only opens during the haj). Boarding passes are issued two months in advance, and multilingual cabin crew are posted to assist pilgrims with their flights. Some pilgrims have never been in an airplane before and require help even operating the plane's toilets.
- An entire government department (the Ministry of Haj) dedicates itself solely to the annual organisation of the haj. As soon as one haj ends, preps for the next begin. The reputation of ministers and civil servants are made or mangled by the outcome of a single haj. For the accomplishment of a successful haj, the king shows his appreciation by handing out gifts, including promotions, cash bonuses and even expensive cars, to those involved.

Hajj: Reflection on Its Rituals, by Ali Shariati, is considered a masterpiece. Translated from the original Persian, the writer discusses the significance of each step of the haj.

One Thousand Roads to Mecca: Ten Centuries of Travelers Writing About the Muslim Pilgrimage, by Michael Wolfe, relates 20 accounts of the haj, spanning 10 centuries, through the eyes of people who have undertaken the journey.

STANDING ATOP THE MOUNT OF MERCY AT ARAFAT

I'm lucky. I've travelled a lot, seen a lot, done a lot. But that day that I stood on the Mount of Mercy topped everything: nothing else comes close. Stretching out beneath me were over two million people, all calling upon God to forgive their sins and bestow upon them his great blessings. The emotion I felt was overwhelming. As I came down that mountain, I realised that I was sobbing.

Haj Abdi Hussein, a British Muslim who performed his haj in 2006.

HAJ CALENDAR

The table below shows the dates of the haj. *Yawm 'Arafat* (the main haj day) is actually on the 9th of the month, but most pilgrims are already in Mecca by *yawm al-tarwiyah,* the 8th of the month.

Islamic Calendar	Estimated Equivalent in Western Calendar
8–14 Dhul Hijja 1428H	18–24 Dec 2007
8–14 Dhul Hijja 1429H	6–12 Dec 2008
8–14 Dhul Hijja 1430H	25 Nov–1 Dec 2009
8–14 Dhul Hijja 1431H	14–20 Nov 2010
8–14 Dhul Hijja 1432H	4–10 Nov 2011
8–14 Dhul Hijja 1433H	24–30 Oct 2012

Haj Hazards

With millions of people surging from one pilgrimage station to the next, many desperate to set eyes upon the holy sites they've travelled so far to see, or to perform the prescribed rites within the prescribed time, it's perhaps inevitable that accidents should happen at the haj.

One of the worst hazards in the past has been the stampedes of panicking people. The Jamarat Bridge that leads to the stone pillars in Mina Valley has seen some of the worst incidents. In July 1990, 1426 pilgrims were trampled to death in a tunnel on their way to the plains of Arafat.

The term 'mecca' has come to be used in English to mean any place that draws a large number of people. As Mecca is the holiest city of Islam, many Muslims find this use of the term offensive, and travellers should be sensitive to this.

Other hazards include fire (in July 1997, 343 pilgrims were killed and 1500 injured when a tent caught alight); road accidents (in December 2006, a coach carrying pilgrims from Medina to Mecca crashed, killing three Britons and injuring 34 others); and disease (there was an international outbreak of meningitis following the haj in 1987).

With the huge international media coverage the event attracts, the haj has also proven a tempting target for terrorists, or for political protest and activity. In July 1987, Iranian Shiite pilgrims rioted, leading to the death of over 400 people; in July 1989, two bombs attributed to Kuwaiti Shiites exploded, killing one pilgrim and wounding 16 others.

For some, the mere physical effort required in making the haj, or the stress and excitement it can generate, can be a hazard. Before the haj had even got under way in December 2006, 243 pilgrims had died (the majority elderly) as a result of heart attacks apparently brought on by heat exhaustion, fatigue or excess physical exertion. The Nigerian government reported the death of 33 of their nationals 'as a result of hypertension, diabetes, heart attack and pneumonia' (2006 was the coldest winter for 20 years).

In the 1980s, the Saudi government changed the spelling of Mecca to Makkah, or more officially, Makkah al-Mukkaramah (The Holy City of Makkah). This spelling has yet to be adopted world-wide and throughout this book we have used Mecca.

OVERSTAYERS & OFFENDERS

The biggest headache for Saudi authorities are the 'overstayers' – foreigners who enter the Kingdom on a haj visa, but who do not exit at the end.

It's now well known that many Third World citizens use the haj visa purely as a means of sneaking into the Kingdom. Recent research indicates that over 50% of haj 'pilgrims' coming from some Third World countries are actually Christian.

Of those that enter the Kingdom, an estimated 9% to 20% are believed to fail to return to their homelands annually. In real terms, this means an increase in the Saudi Arabian population of at least a quarter of a million people every four years.

Crackdowns on illegal immigrants include dawn raids on houses suspected of harbouring illegal immigrants, and tight checkpoint controls at strategic points around Mecca and Medina. In 2006, the Saudi Arabian government stopped issuing *umrah* (the 'lesser pilgrimage' or 'visitation' to Mecca outside the haj season) visas to those individuals under 40 travelling alone from any of nine South Asian and African countries (Bangladesh, Chad, Egypt, Ethiopia, India, Nigeria, Pakistan, Sudan and Yemen).

Since these overstayers cannot find legal work, some resort to illegal activities such as selling goods (especially clothes, shoes and toys) brought with them from their home countries.

A few resort to other crimes including prostitution, theft, mugging or burglary; the manufacture of illegal *raki* (firewater); or smuggling (firearms, alcohol or qat – the mildly narcotic leaf), despite the severe penalties if apprehended (the amputation of hand or feet for thieves caught three or more times, and an immediate death penalty if caught smuggling, or for armed bank robberies). Many of the public executions held in Saudi Arabia are of such unfortunates.

The holy stone, built into the Kaaba, is believed by some non-Muslims to be a meteorite (measuring around 30cm in diameter). In fact, it was long revered in pre-Islamic times by the local Bedu of the desert, who constructed a shrine around it.

PICKPOCKETS

In the pilgrim areas themselves, pickpocketing has become rampant. According to the Ministry of Justice, specialised gangs from abroad now operate, arriving especially in time for the haj. Over 100 arrests are made every year and punishments are strictly imposed.

TROUBLESOME TRAVEL AGENCIES

Unscrupulous foreign haj agencies pose another problem. Some promise guides, transport and even accommodation that never materialise. In Jeddah, disappointed pilgrims can often be seen sleeping on the streets around town.

The Ministry of Haj registers complaints, investigates them and has the power to withdraw haj operator licences, but with more than 1000 agencies worldwide, it's a tall order.

CARCASS CLEARANCE

Another problem peculiar to the haj is the disposal of the thousands of animals sacrificed annually at Mina, as part of the haj ritual.

In the past, pilgrims were permitted to keep only what they themselves could eat during the Eid al-Adha (the holiday immediately following the end of the haj). The rest of the animal was buried in huge pits.

Recently, Islamic banks have set up official abattoirs on the holy sites. On the payment of a fee, the bank will vouch to slaughter an animal on behalf of the pilgrim on the appointed day, and additionally export the meat to Third World countries around the world, so combining personal piety with international charity.

THE GREAT LEVELLER OF MEN

For many Muslims, the haj is considered the ultimate leveller of men. Pilgrims may share food, water, a corner of a prayer mat or even a bed with a king, emperor or statesman and never know it.

Dressed in the same, simple white cloth (the *ihram*), performing the same rituals and making the same sometimes challenging and exhausting journey, all people – of whatever class, colour, culture, material means or Muslim creed – are equal within the surrounds of the holy cities.

For the same reason, the haj is also said to be a kind of 'dress rehearsal' for Judgement Day when, according to the Quran, 'all people will stand equal before God'.

THE ORIGINS OF THE HAJ

The tradition of the haj extends back centuries. Ibrahim (known by Christians as Abraham) is considered the haj's founding father. The story goes like this:

During his lifetime, Ibrahim had his faith put to the test many times. One of the most testing trials was when he took his wife Hajar and infant son Ismail (Ishmael) to Arabia. Obeying Allah's command to leave them in Allah's hands, Ibrahim left Hajar and Ismail in a dry valley with little food. Soon, the supplies ran out and Hajar began to roam the valley in a frantic search for sustenance. Eventually, failing to find anything, she fell to the ground in despair.

Pilgrims today commemorate that search for water by performing the sa'ee, walking seven times between the two hills of Safa and Marwah.

Hajar's baby, Ismail, was now crying from hunger and thirst, so Hajar began to pray to Allah to help her. As Ismail wailed, he stamped his foot upon the ground, and suddenly up gushed a spring of water.

They named the spring Zamzam and in time, caravans and nomads began to stop in this valley to water their camels. A desert city began to spring up around the well of Zamzam.

That city was Mecca, and Zamzam is the only natural source of water in the city to this day.

But Ibrahim's greatest trial was still to come. Allah commanded him to take his son Ismail to the mountains and there slay him. Grief stricken, Ibrahim took his son and left Mecca. But Ibrahim's faith was stronger than his despair. On the way to the mountains, however, Shaitan (the Devil) tempted him not to kill his son. He harried Ibrahim, cajoling, taunting and mocking him. Ibrahim, finally despairing, began to throw stones at Shaitan.

This act is commemorated by the stoning of the jamrah (pillars) in Mina today.

When Ibrahim arrived at the appointed place and so passed his test of faith, Allah commanded him to allow Ismail to live, and to sacrifice a ram in his place.

Holy City Expansion

Each successive monarch since the time of King Abdul Aziz, the founder of modern-day Saudi Arabia, has sought to make his mark on the holy cities. Through the haj, the monarchs hope to secure a place not just in history, but also in heaven.

As the 'Head of Operations', the king must take personal responsibility for the pilgrimage, and every year the king, along with his entire government, uproots lock, stock and barrel from the capital in Riyadh to Jeddah, the 'gateway to the haj' on the Red Sea.

In the past, the greatest royal preoccupation has been simply how to increase the pilgrim-holding capacity of the holy cities. The evolution is startling.

Richard Burton's *Personal Narrative of a Pilgrimage to Al-Madinah and Meccah* is a classic of its genre and offers a rare (and politically incorrect) Western insight into the holy cities of Mecca and Medina.

Growing from little more than a dusty, desert shack, the Great Mosque in Mecca now boasts a total area of 356,000 sq metres, with a capacity for 773,000 people (and up to a million people during the haj season). A straight comparison with the largest stadiums or arenas in the Western world (the UK's Wembley Stadium holds 90,000 people; the Dolphin Stadium in Miami, which hosted the 2007 Super Bowl, holds 74,512 people) gives some indication of the cosmic scale and size of the holy sites.

The buildings are also designed to impress. With soaring minarets, acres of marble, and celestial proportions, many pilgrims are completely overawed by their first sight of the cities.

Some of the big plans billed for the future include the development of a state-of-the-art port in the new 'King Abdullah Economic City', planned to be constructed north of Jeddah, which will boast a dedicated haj terminal capable of receiving over half a million pilgrims every haj season.

This is remembered during the Eid al-Adha, or Festival of Sacrifice, when pilgrims of the haj and Muslims all over the world sacrifice an animal.

Ibrahim continued to visit Mecca. One day, Allah commanded him to build a house of worship and call all who believed in him to make a pilgrimage there. With Ismail's help, Ibrahim constructed the Kaaba, a cube-shaped building, for worship.

This is the building which, to this day, the pilgrims go around when performing the tawaf (circling).

After the death of his father, Ismail continued to maintain the Kaaba and kept up the pilgrimage each year. Gradually, however, as idolatry began to spread throughout Arabia, worship at the Kaaba began to descend also into paganism. Before he died, Ismail prayed: 'Our Lord! Send amongst them a messenger of their own, who shall recite unto them your *aayaat* (verses) and instruct them in the book and the Wisdom and sanctify them.' (sura Al-Baqarah 2:129)

Many prophets were sent through the ages. Then, in AD 570, a man by the name of Mohammed ibn Abdullah was born in Mecca. For 23 years, the Prophet spread a message of obedience to Allah and a law of peace and order in Arabia.

Initially, the Meccans (many of them powerful merchants) objected to the rise of Islam, as the new religion jeopardised profits and revenues collected from visiting pilgrims.

Mohammed was finally forced into exile in Medina in 622, and there he established a model Islamic community. Six years later, however, he returned to Mecca with thousands of followers. Destroying the idols, he purified the Kaaba and rededicated the House for the worship of Allah alone.

Thousands of followers gathered to hear his sermon at the haj. There he expounded the concept of a united Muslim community. The Kaaba had once again become the centre of Islam.

THE PILGRIMS
The Visa

Currently, one visa is issued per 1000 Muslim inhabitants of a country's population, with a total of 800,000 haj or *umrah* visas issued annually. Recently, restrictions on Saudi pilgrims have been introduced in order to allow more foreign Muslims to visit. Saudis can now perform the haj no more than once in every five years.

In order to obtain a haj visa, pilgrims must first have a medical check-up and obtain certain compulsory vaccinations, such as meningitis.

The wait for a haj visa varies from country to country, but some pilgrims have claimed they've waited 20 years or more. Every year, reports emerge of rampant corruption existing in some countries regarding the issuing of haj visas. Although the Saudi Arabian authorities charge nothing for them, haj visas abroad are reported to change hands for thousands of dollars, or else are used as useful political leverage by politicians.

Why Perform the Haj?

For most Muslims, the haj represents the greatest spiritual encounter of their lives. Many are profoundly affected by it both spiritually and psychologically; some claim to be changed forever by the experience.

Apart from reaffirming religious commitments, one of the major draws of haj for many Muslims is the element of redemption. After successfully performing the haj, Muslims are traditionally washed of their sins and emerge like 'newborns'. Some Muslims, who in the past led relatively secular lives, or who indulged in un-Islamic activities such as drinking, gambling or womanising, actively seek redemption and determinedly try to lead an altered life as a result of completing the haj.

The Hajj, by FE Peters, gives firsthand accounts of travellers to the haj, together with a history and detailed steps of the ritual.

Other Muslims – particularly the young – prefer to wait a few years before doing the haj until they feel fully ready and prepared to implement these changes in their lives.

If you break one of the rules of *ihram* during the haj, you must pay a *kaffarah*. Depending on which rule you've broken, there are three ways to redeem yourself: by offering a sacrifice; by feeding six impoverished people; or by fasting for three days.

Famous Faces

The haj holy cities have seen many famous faces pass through their portals. Past pilgrims include Ibn Battuta, one of history's greatest travellers, American heavyweight boxer Mohammed Ali, British pop singer Yusuf Islam (aka Cat Stevens), King Abdullah of Jordan, President Nasser and Pakistani cricketer Imran Khan.

One such personality who famously wrote about his experience was a certain 'Al-Haj Malik el-Shabazz', otherwise known as Malcolm X, the American black activist. Writing a letter to his followers back in Harlem, he declared: 'Never have I witnessed such sincere hospitality and overwhelming spirit of true brotherhood as is practiced by people of all colours and races here in this ancient Holy Land.'

Mirroring the experience of many Muslims, the haj had a profound effect on Malcolm X both personally and in his thinking and writing (see boxed text, p80).

The Cultural Exchange

With the meeting of over two million minds from all parts of the planet, the haj could be described as the most cosmic conference on earth.

Indeed, for scholars in the past the haj was as much about a voyage of learning and exchange of ideas as it was a spiritual journey. Some scholars took advantage of the opportunity to buy books, meet with colleagues and even attend courses. For a few, the haj marked a turning point in their thinking, or a new direction in their school of thought, such was the impact of the intellectual experience.

The 12th-century courtier from Arab Spain, Ibn Jubayr, performed the haj and stayed in Mecca for a period of eight months. His *Travel of Ibn Jubayr* recounts his experiences and is considered the first traveller's diary in Arabic.

Among the many momentous events attributed to the haj was the launch of the Almoravid dynasty, catalysed by a visit to Mecca by one of its leaders, Yahya ibn Ibrahim, at the beginning of the 11th century.

THE HAJ STEP BY STEP

The haj, one of the Five Pillars of Islam (see p61), consists of a series of ancient and elaborate rites that are carried out over the course of several days.

Performed at the Great Mosque of Mecca and its immediate surrounds (Mina, Muzdalifah and Arafat), the haj takes place annually at a predetermined date, which advances some 10 days annually according to the lunar calendar on which the Islamic calendar is based (see the Haj Calendar, p74).

HAJ HOPES

As we travelled, we talked and as we talked we gradually grew to know one another. One day, without any warning or explanation, Omar decided that we should get married.

'One day, when we are old, when we are bent like old donkeys, when we have legs like crooked sticks, and old shoes, we will do the haj together. Your hand in my hand, we will hold onto one another as best we can and we will be swept along with the crowd. We will be happy,' he declared turning towards me his face full of emotion.

I never did discover why Omar thought I would make him a good wife, but the beauty of that image stuck in my mind for a long time afterwards.

From the author's diary during a trip to Yemen

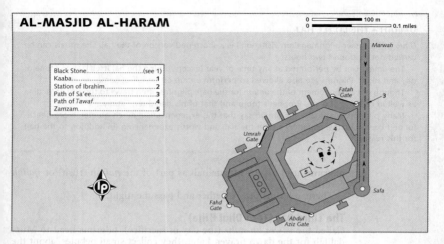

AL-MASJID AL-HARAM

Black Stone.................................(see 1)
Kaaba..1
Station of Ibrahim.............................2
Path of Sa'ee....................................3
Path of Tawaf...................................4
Zamzam...5

The haj is obligatory for those who can 'make their way' – that is, those who are of sufficient health and have the financial means to be able to do so. Following is a (greatly simplified) description of some of the most important events and ceremonies that make up the haj.

The First Day (8th Dhul Hijja)

Known as *yawm at-tarwiyah* (the day of deliberation or reflection), pilgrims must put on the *ihram* (the two seamless, unsown sheets that symbolise the state of consecration) at a place outside Mecca, and recite the *an-niyyah* (the stating of intent).

Pilgrims then perform the *tawaf al-qudum,* the circling seven times of the Kaaba. After praying between the Black Stone and the door of the Kaaba, pilgrims head to the Station of Ibrahim for more prayers.

Next, pilgrims drink some of the holy waters of Zamzam, before proceeding to the ritual *sa'ee.* This is the famous running and walking seven times back and forth between the two hills of Safa and Marwah (though this can also be performed after the second ambulation, *tawaf al-ifadah*). This ritual is the re-enactment of Hajar's frantic search for food and water, before Ismail stamped his foot and a spring gushed forth.

Later, pilgrims head to the Great Mosque for the performance of more rites, before leaving for Mina to spend the night until summoned for the dawn prayer.

The Second Day (9th Dhul Hijja)

Named the *yawm al-wuquf* (the day of standing), or *yawm 'Arafat* (the day of Arafat), pilgrims head for Arafat after the dawn prayer at Mina. Forming a key component of the haj, the *wuquf* (standing) involves pilgrims passing part of the day and night there.

Most stay from noon until after sunset, during which time pilgrims are expected to pray and recite frequently the *talbiyah* (the main, ritual, recitation of the haj, and the words attributed to Ibrahim when he first summoned mankind to Mecca). Traditionally, this day is one of solemnity, reflection and the examination of conscience for pilgrims.

Some pilgrims like to climb the Mount of Mercy (Rahmah) at Arafat (though the crowds often prevent most from doing so). Later, most

Islamic protocol dictates that 'PBUH' (Peace Be Upon Him) follow every mention of the Prophet's name. Travellers are advised to show the same sensitivity and respect when discussing the Prophet (PBUH).

UMRAH – THE LITTLE HAJ

Umrah (the 'lesser pilgrimage' or 'visitation') is a shortened version of the haj. The rituals can be carried out in around two hours.

The umrah can be performed at any time of year (except during the haj itself), at any time of day and night. Pilgrims are also allowed to perform umrah on behalf of someone else.

Though not a requirement of the umrah (or the haj), pilgrims often travel to the city of Medina as well in order to visit the Prophet's tomb and that of his daughter, Fatima.

Many pilgrims who make the umrah say that the experience is a much quieter, more peaceful and contemplative experience than the haj, and worth experiencing (in addition to the haj) for this reason.

---

pilgrims head off for Muzdalifah as part of the *nafrah* (rush) or *ifadah* (overflowing).

There, pilgrims pray together and pass the night.

The Third Day (10th Dhul Hijja)

Called the *yawm an-nahr* (the day of sacrifice), pilgrims head to Muzdalifah for the dawn prayer. Later, they collect small pebbles 'about the size of a chickpea' – 49 pebbles if they're planning to remain in Mina for two days, 70 pebbles if they're staying for three days.

At Mina, pilgrims then throw seven stones at the *jamarah* – the pillars symbolising the temptation of Ibrahim by the devil (see boxed text, p76).

Afterwards, pilgrims are free to perform the required sacrifice, which must take place any time up until the end of the 13th Djul Hijja. A camel is considered the worthiest sacrifice, but an ox or ram are also acceptable.

It is at this point that the pilgrim's hair is clipped. Though only a lock of hair is required to be cut, many men choose to have their whole heads shaved (look out for them all over the Muslim world and beyond after the end of the haj). The shaving is a symbol of rebirth – showing that the sins of the pilgrim have been cleansed through the successful completion of the haj.

Though *ihram* is now over and pilgrims can wear ordinary clothes again, they must still abstain from those things proscribed during the state of *ihram*. In greatly simplified terms, these boil down to three basic tenets: not disturbing or harming other living things; not indulging in any form of sexual behaviour; and not beautifying or adorning oneself.

Men are also not allowed to wear sewn clothes, or anything that covers the whole of the foot or the head. Women are not allowed to cover their faces with any kind of veil.

In Saudi Arabia today (particularly in Medina, Mecca and Jeddah), some citizens, and many residents, are old pilgrims (or their descendents) who have chosen to stay on after the haj and make their homes there.

THE SAME PLATE

During the past 11 days here in the Muslim world, I have eaten from the same plate, drunk from the same glass and slept on the same rug – while praying to the same God – with fellow Muslims, whose eyes were the bluest of blue, whose hair was the blondest of blond, and whose skin was the whitest of white. And in the words and in the deeds of the white Muslims, I felt the same sincerity that I felt among the black African Muslims of Nigeria, Sudan and Ghana.

We were truly all the same – because their belief in one God had removed the white from their minds, the white from their behaviour, and the white from their attitude.

From 'The Autobiography of Malcolm X' by Alex Haley

FOR GOD & COUNTRY

Home to the two holiest cities of Islam (Mecca and Medina), Saudis consider themselves supremely set apart. This blessing is also viewed as the gravest and most onerous responsibility. The opportunities offered by hosting the haj are also seen as a strong force for good. By serving its own citizens (such as by employing young people as guides), it aspires to serve the pilgrims (by providing an organised and enjoyable haj), and ultimately serve God (in facilitating his worship on earth).

On this day or the following, pilgrims head for the Masjid al-Haram in Mecca to carry out the *tawaf al-ifadah* (or *tawaf az-ziyarah;* the second circling), and the *sa'ee* (if it hasn't been carried out earlier).

The Final Days (11th, 12th & 13th Dhul Hijja)

Known as *ayyam at-tashriq* (the days of drying meat), pilgrims spend their remaining days at Mina, each day casting seven stones at the three symbolic stone pillars between sunrise and sunset.

Before leaving Mecca, pilgrims usually perform the *tawaf al-wada* (circling of farewell).

FAMOUS NON-MUSLIMS IN MECCA

For a long time, the forbidden cities of Mecca and Medina fascinated European travellers. Arousing in them an incurable curiosity, some set off to try and penetrate the cities, even on threat of death should they be discovered. Among the most famous of these was Richard Burton (1821–90), who disguised himself as a Qadiri Sufi from Afghanistan, and who, it is said, even went as far as getting himself circumcised.

Other famous 'haj explorers' included the Swiss scholar, John Lewis Burkhardt (1784–1817), and the British eccentric Harry St John Philby (1885–1960), who was a convert to Islam. His close friendship with King Abdul Aziz permitted him access to almost all areas including Mecca and Medina, which allowed him to explore, map and describe more of the Arabian Peninsula than any other traveller.

Food & Drink

Anyone who has read of the lovers' feast prepared by Keats' Porphyro in the *Eve of St Agnes* may be fairly lusting to venture into the land of 'lucent syrups, tinct with cinnamon', 'Manna and dates', not to mention 'spiced dainties' from 'silken Samarkand to cedared Lebanon'. The Arabic Orient has long been the fabled land of extravagant feasting and to this day eating is a central part of Peninsula life, love and community. The delicacies and staple dishes may not immediately appeal to a Western palette, but with a little knowledge of some of the customs that lurk behind their preparation, they can take on a whole new flavour.

STAPLES & SPECIALITIES
Arabian

For most Arab people on the Peninsula, breakfast means eggs in some shape or form and locally produced salty white cheese with a glass of buttermilk or *laban* (thin yogurt) and tahini sweetened with date syrup. It might come with *foul madamas,* a bean dish lubricated with olive oil, garnished on high days and holidays with pickles and eased along with olives. There may be lentils, heavily laced with garlic, to the chagrin of co-workers, and of course bread.

Known generically as *khobz*, bread (in up to 40 different varieties) is eaten in copious quantities with every meal. Most often it's unleavened and comes in flat disks about the size of a dinner plate (not unlike an Indian *chapati*). It's traditionally torn into pieces, in lieu of knives and forks, and used to pinch up a morsel of meat, a scoop of dip and a nip of garnish.

Lunch means one word only, and that is rice. Rice is often flavoured with a few whole cardamoms (one of which always lurks beguilingly in the last mouthful) and at feasts with saffron and sultanas. Buried in or sitting on top of the rice will be some kind of delicious spiced stew, with ladies' fingers or grilled and seasoned chicken, lamb, goat or even camel – but of course never pork, which is *haram* (forbidden) for Muslims (see p64). Popular seasoning includes some or even all of the following: cardamom, coriander, cumin, cinnamon, nutmeg, chilli, ginger, pepper and the all-important, health-giving and almost flavourless turmeric. In Yemen no-one can escape the bitter, livid green froth of fenugreek used to put a punch in a minimal broth or bean dish.

Not surprisingly for a Peninsula with such a rich coastline, fish (fresh or dried) is an equally important lunchtime staple. Hamour (a species of grouper), *beya* (mullet), king fish, Sultan Ibrahim and tuna are grilled, fried or barbecued and served with rice and chopped raw cabbage with the essential half lime or lemon. Sardines, piles of which spangle the shore in season and are raked into malodorous heaps between houses, are seldom eaten: they're usually dried for animal fodder.

Peninsula people are not big on 'puddings', preferring fruits after (or often before) the meal, and thick fruit juices, but on high days and holidays baklava (made of filo and honey) or puddings, including *mahallabiye* (milk based) and *umm ali* (bread based), might put in an after-lunch appearance.

The evening meal is a ragged affair of competing interests – children clamouring for hot dogs or burgers, maids slipping them 'keep-quiet food', mothers going for a sandwich in Starbucks and grandmothers

---

The world's oldest cultivated fruit has been the staple diet of millions of Arabs for centuries and they are grown in every country in the Peninsula. Indeed, of the 90 million date palms growing in the world, 64 million are in Arab countries.

Pork is *haram* (forbidden) to Muslims but it's sometimes available in Gulf supermarkets. Pork sections are easy to spot: customers slink out with a pork sausage wrapped in the *Gulf Times*, as if it's something naughty for the weekend. At Gulf prices for pork, high days and holidays are about the only time most people can afford to eat it.

making sweetmeats and aubergine dips, nibbling on dates and trying to persuade 'bother-it-all' fathers from going out for a kebab or a *shwarma*.

City people in the Peninsula enjoy going out and they are as likely to dine on Mongolian lamb chops, crab rangoon or spaghetti bolognaise as any other city dweller. More often than not, however, they'll opt for Lebanese food with its copious selection of hot and cold appetisers known as *mezze*. The peeled carrots, buffed radishes, whole lettuce and bunches of peppery spinach leaves, provided complimentary, are a meal in themselves.

Locals invariably entertain guests at home and go out to eat something different. For travellers to the region, it can therefore be difficult finding indigenous food. Ask locally where to sample indigenous food and you may find you're taken home for supper.

Asian

All across Arabia large populations of expatriate peoples have brought their own cuisine to the Peninsula. For many Asian expats – often men on nonfamily contracts – breakfast, lunch and dinner consists of the same thing: rice and dhal, or rice and meat or vegetable curry, separated into three round metal lunchboxes, stacked one on top of the other, and including a bag of rolled up *chapati* (Indian flat bread).

Providing a cheap and cheerful alternative to 'the lunchbox', and serving samosas, biryani or spicy mutton curry, a whole string of Indian and Pakistani restaurants have sprung up across the region, catering for hungry workers who would normally be looked after by wives and daughters. Those who do have their families with them enjoy as varied a cuisine as their nationality and local supermarket allow. British teachers eat roast beef for Friday lunch, Filipino nurses make chicken *adobo*, Sri Lankan maids try to win over their adoptive families to furious fish curries. In many of the big cities, the traveller can sample all these delights too, often in world-class restaurants.

Bedouin

When round him mid the burning sands, he saw
Fruits of the North in icy freshness thaw
And cooled his thirsty lip, beneath the glow
Of Mecca's sun, with urns of Persian snow.

Thomas Moore

Thomas Moore's 19th-century description of Bedouin delicacies, elaborated with sherbets and dainties, sounds enticing but the reality is far more prosaic. TE Lawrence memorably describes a feast with the Arab Sheikh, Nasir, in which he dips his fingers into a mess of boiling-hot lamb fat while ripping the meat from the carcass. This was probably *kebsa* – a whole lamb stuffed with rice and pine nuts. The most prized piece of this dish is the sheep's eyeballs, which irreverent hosts delight to this day in waving towards horrified Western guests.

Mostly, Bedouin food consists of whatever is available at a particular time, and hunger and thirst are far more attendant on a day's travelling in the desert than sumptuous feasting. Camel's milk and goat's cheese are staple parts of the diet as are dried dates and of course water. Water takes on a particularly precious quality when it is rationed and the Bedouin are renowned for consuming very little, particularly during the day when only small sips are taken, mostly to rinse the mouth.

Every town has a baklava or pastry shop, selling syrupy sweets made from a mixture of pastry, nuts, milk powder, honey, syrup and sometimes rosewater. Sweets are ordered by weight and 250g is generally the smallest amount sold – more than enough for one person.

In a good Lebanese restaurant the number of *mezze* (hot and cold appetisers) offered can run to 50 or more dishes and include chopped liver, devilled kidney, sheep brain and other offal. These are considered great delicacies across the region.

THE COFFEE CARRY-ON

Throughout the Peninsula there is an old and elaborate ritual surrounding the serving of coffee. In homes, offices and even at some hotels, you may well be offered a cup. To refuse is to reject an important gesture of welcome and hospitality, and you risk offending your host. 'Arabic' or 'Bedouin coffee' as it's known, is usually poured from an ornate, long-spouted pot known as a *dalla*, into tiny handleless cups. You should accept the cup with your right hand.

It's considered polite to drink at least three cups (the third is traditionally considered to bestow a blessing). More may be impolite; the best advice is to follow your host's lead. To show you've had sufficient, swivel the cup slightly between fingers and thumb.

The legendary hospitality of the Bedu will mean that travellers in the Empty Quarter (in Saudi) or the Sharqiya Sands (Oman) who bump into a Bedouin camp are bound to be invited to share 'bread and salt'. At the least this will involve Arabic coffee, camel's milk and a thatch of dried meat, usually with a host of flies dancing in the bowl. The flies don't harm the Bedu and it's unlikely they'll bother the traveller much either, but the milk can upset a sensitive stomach.

DRINKS
Nonalcoholic Drinks

If you want to try camel's milk without the stomach ache, you can often find it in supermarkets – next to the *laban*, a refreshing drink of yogurt, water, salt and sometimes crushed mint.

The best part of travelling in the region is sampling the fresh fruit juices of pomegranate, hibiscus, avocado, sugarcane, mango, melon or carrot – or a combination of all sorts – served at juice stalls known as *aseer*. Mint and lemon or fresh lime is a refreshing alternative to sodas.

Tea, known as *shai* or 'Chi-Libton', could be tea *min na'ana* (with mint, especially in Saudi and Yemen), tea with condensed milk (in the Gulf) or plain black tea (in Oman), but whatever the flavour of the day, it will definitely contain enough sugar to make the dentist's fortune. The teabag is left dangling in the cup and water is poured from maximum height to prove what an able tea-maker your host is.

Coffee, known locally as *qahwa*, is consumed in copious quantities on the Peninsula and is usually served strong. Arabia has a distinguished connection with coffee. Though no longer involved in the coffee trade today, Al-Makha in Yemen (p483) gave its name to the blend of chocolate and coffee popularly known as 'mocha'. The traditional Arabic or Bedouin coffee is heavily laced with cardamom and drunk in small cups. Turkish coffee, which floats on top of thick sediment, is popular in the Gulf region.

Nonalcoholic beer is widely available. Incidentally, travellers shouldn't think that cans of fizzy drink will suffice for hydration in the desert: they often induce more thirst than they satisfy.

Alcoholic Drinks

Despite its reputation as a 'dry' region, alcohol is available in all Peninsula countries, bar Saudi Arabia, Kuwait and some of the Emirates (where both possession and consumption for locals and foreigners is strictly forbidden).

In the more liberal countries (such as Bahrain and Qatar and some parts of the UAE), bars, cocktail bars and even pubs can be found; in others (such as Yemen and Oman) usually only certain hotels (often mid-

On highly significant Bedouin occasions, in an emir's tent in Saudi, or in an extravagant gesture in the Qatari interior, a camel is stuffed with a sheep, which is stuffed with a goat, which is in turn stuffed with a chicken.

If as a traveller you try to opt out of the fifth spoonful of sugar in your tea or coffee, you will inevitably be assumed to have diabetes. From the Arab's perspective, why else would anyone think of drinking tea without sugar?

or upper range) are permitted to serve alcohol. Wine is served in most licensed restaurants in Bahrain, Oman, Qatar and the UAE.

Officially, no Peninsula country produces its own alcoholic drinks, though rumours abound where dates ferment. Where alcohol is available it's imported from the West and the high prices are intended to keep consumption low – not very successfully. The legal age to be served alcohol is usually 18 years old. You can't buy alcohol to take off the premises unless you are a resident and are eligible for a monthly quota.

> You may prefer to taste Saudi 'champagne', which is less exciting than it sounds: it's a mixture of apple juice and Perrier water!

HABITS & CUSTOMS

The main meal for most Peninsula people is usually a home-cooked family affair involving rice. There the similarities end. Here are a few snapshots of differing eating habits across the region.

Let's start with a 'middle-class' Qatari family on a weekend. Mohammed is dispatched to the Thursday wholesale market on Salwa Rd to buy 'live chicken' and he takes his two kids to see the pink and green chicks. His wife is meeting with friends at Eli France for pastries, half to be left on the plate. The maid boils the rice, strips the vegetables and fries the spices. Dinner will be set formally on a high, polished dining table under the crystal chandelier. When the in-laws arrive, the men lounge in the tent in the garden with freshly squeezed fruit juice, while the women occupy the sofa in the family room and the kids play on the computer. There's a hand-washing alcove in the dining room with soap, which everyone uses before having lunch.

> When it comes to customs and manners, there's one thing all Peninsula families have in common: after you eat, you leave. After the main meal of the day, once the coffee has been served, all anyone wants to think about is sleeping.

In common with the Qataris, it's principally the man's role to go shopping in Oman. Moosa, whose family lives in a village on Jebel Akhdar but who works for the government in Muscat, loads the Carrefour trolley with six packs of long-life milk, industrial-sized buckets of yogurt, and sacks of tea and sugar before his weekly three-hour drive

---

EATING ETIQUETTE

Sharing a meal with a Peninsula Arab is a great way of cementing a newly formed friendship. But Arabian eating etiquette is refined and complex. Here are a few tips. Note that food is traditionally shared by all from the same plate without the use of cutlery.

Eating in Someone's House

■ Bring a small gift of flowers, chocolates or pastries, fruit or honey.

■ It's polite to be seen to wash hands before a meal.

■ Don't sit with your legs stretched out – it's considered rude during a meal.

■ Use only the right hand for eating or accepting food. The left is reserved for ablutions.

■ Don't put food back on the plate: discard in a napkin.

■ Your host will often lay the tastiest morsels in front of you; it's polite to accept them.

■ The best part – such as the meat – is usually saved until last, so don't take it until offered.

Eating in a Restaurant

■ Picking teeth after a meal is quite acceptable and toothpicks are often provided.

■ It's traditional to lavish food upon a guest; if you're full, pat your stomach contentedly.

■ Leave a little food on your plate: traditionally, a clean plate was thought to invite famine.

■ It's polite to accept a cup of coffee after a meal and impolite to leave before it's served.

SHEESHA CAFÉS

In any city across the Peninsula, two sensations mark the hot and humid air of an Arabian summer's evening: the wreaths of scented peach-flavoured smoke that spiral above the corner coffeehouse and the low gurgle of water, like a grumbling camel, in the base of the water pipe. Periodically banned by governments concerned for public morality (the pipes are not narcotic – only time-wasting), and inevitably returned to the street corners by the will of the people, *sheesha* cafés are an indispensable part of Arabian social life.

In most countries in the region, these cafés are a male affair: men perch under a tree in Yemen, or lounge on white plastic chairs in the souqs of Doha, and indolently watch the football on the café TV, occasionally breaking off from the sucking and puffing to pass a word of lazy complaint to their neighbour, snack on pieces of kebab, or hail the waiter for hot coals to awaken the drowsy embers of the *sheesha* bottle.

In Dubai, Manama and Muscat, however, the *sheesha* cafés are beginning to attract mixed company. Here, women in black *abeyyas* (full-length robe) and sparkling diamante cuffs, drag demurely on velvet-clad mouthpieces, their smoking punctuating a far more animated dialogue as they actively define the new shape of society.

home. The weekend is starting already with returned children from school, neighbours (mostly relatives) bringing the season's pomegranates, elders sitting in the corner contentedly coughing and swatting flies off the newborn. The kitchen is alive with his wife Khadija's busy preparations, tomatoes and onions dispatched deftly into a pan, while sisters-in-law moan and giggle over inconsistent husbands and grind herbal potions plucked from the hillside. There are special guests today, so incense curls around the house and eating is in batches. Ahmed, the eldest son, is deputed to spread the plastic cloth on the carpet in the *majlis* (sitting room), and pour *laban* while Moosa kneels to peel mango for the male guests, lounging against the goat-hair cushions. The guests eat first, using their right hand to dip into dishes that are carried in one by one throughout lunch. The women are already tucking in next door. Moosa and the boys will join the feasting as the guests begin to flag. A dish of rose-water, the petals harvested that spring, marks the end of the meal.

Wedged between the ruby sand dunes of Zilfi, Abdullah selects a kid from the herd and with one clean slice across the throat, lays the animal down gently to die, staying until the life is gone. He thanks Allah for the blessing and then hangs the carcass by the back leg under an acacia and begins the meticulous process of unzipping the animal from its coat. The skin is carefully set aside for washing and the organs preserved for cooking. Abdullah prides himself on a job well done; he's disdainful of town folk who can't cut cleanly and leave piles of entrails on the street corners. The women are preparing the spicy date paste that will coat the meat, while the lads poke at the underground oven. The meat will be ready '*bukara insha'allah*' (tomorrow, God-willing) and be so tender it'll fall off the bone. Everyone – the women semienclosed in their half of the tent, the men open to the gritty wind in theirs – will be so hungry by then, there won't be much decorum. The men eat first from a huge round aluminium *fadl* (dish), reserving the choicest parts for the women whose eager black-hennaed hands and licked fingers tear at the flesh with hunger, practice and gusto. In the absence of spare water, sand suffices for cleaning both hands and dishes and then there'll be the usual arguments as to who watches what on the satellite TV under the date palm.

There's much etiquette involved in date-eating. Eat them when half ripe, biting the fruit lengthwise, savouring the bitter zest with the melting, decadent ripe part. Discard the pip discreetly: Sinbad spat his out and blinded the son of a genie who then claimed mischievous revenge.

WHERE TO EAT & DRINK

One of the undoubted pleasures of the modern cities of the Peninsula is the variety and quality of the restaurants. In the Gulf in particular, there is world-class dining in magnificent surroundings. One way for a visitor to experience some of the best of these dining experiences is to skip breakfast on a Friday and visit the local five-star hotel for Friday brunch – a regional speciality much beloved by locals and expats alike. A spectacular array of local, Middle Eastern and international dishes will be on display, decorated with ice carvings and garnished extravagantly, for a relatively modest price. Similarly, many hotels arrange weekly seafood nights often with belly dancing or local entertainment. Again, this is often a more economic way of sampling the region's famous oysters, lobsters and prawns than reserving a table at an exclusive seafood restaurant.

On the whole, restaurants are open (mostly for expats) during lunch; they're closed in the afternoon and open from about 6pm to midnight to cater for the late-night eating habits of most people across the region. In Saudi Arabia restaurants must comply with certain strict regulations (regarding segregation of men and women and the observation of prayer hours for example).

In very local restaurants, seating is sometimes on the floor on mats. Shoes should be left outside the perimeters of the mats. Food is served from a communal plate placed on a tray.

One pleasant, practical advantage of travelling around the Arabian Peninsula is the easy availability of street food. Across most of the Peninsula, small eateries sell kebabs, *shwarma*, felafel and other types of sandwiches, usually served with some form of salad. These meals are quick, cheap and usually safe to eat, as the food is prepared and cooked in front of you.

There's also a good range of well-stocked supermarkets (selling many international foods) in the large cities and, increasingly, food halls are found in the malls.

> The venue of preference for 'that special meal' for many Peninsula families is a well-lit grassy verge on a highway, in the company of relatives. Picnicking takes on a whole new meaning when kebabs are brought in by the kilo (see p252).

> Visitors to *sheesha* cafés are welcome in all but the most traditional coffeehouses and even for nonsmokers there's a rich sense of union in sharing a pipe among strangers. In Yemen the pipe extends halfway across the room, so no-one needs to move to pass it on.

SEASONAL SPECIALITIES

The traveller who wants to eat truly local, seasonal food could have enormous fun on the Peninsula. With no worries about time, visas and border crossings, these could be some of the treats in store.

Start your tour at the top of the Green Mountain in Oman at the beginning of spring for citrus delights such as oranges, sweet lemons and limes. Descend to the coast near Dhofar for the sea's annual harvest of abalone and conches. Sample the delights of the Gulf coastal plains for fresh corn and irregular but delicious local tomatoes, capsicums and chillies. Cut across to Al-Hasa region in Saudi and sink your teeth into the first exquisite ripening of dates (p304).

Search the plantations for papayas and green mangos, salted and pickled, and eaten with lamb stew. Follow the Toyota trucks carrying watermelons across their asphalt caravan routes, and watch as a melon rolls off and smashes on the road like a mini firework. Ascend the Asir Mountains in time for the *mishmish* (apricot) season and then just as the hot months decline, venture into the hornbill-frequented wadis of Yemen for pomegranates, almonds and walnuts.

For Ramadan, hop on a plane to the Gulf cities and choose a different hotel each night: they will all have a Ramadan tent for Iftar supper where regional date-filled, coconut-rolled, honey-dipped and sesame-seeded sweetmeats help ease the hungry guest into an evening of seasonal dishes.

Let's hope that someone invites you home for *eid* (feast) in the desert towns of the interior where killing the fatted calf is often more than just a metaphor.

VEGETARIANS & VEGANS

While Arab people are traditionally thought of as full-blooded, red meat eaters, the reality is that meat for many of the poorer sections of the community across the region, especially in Yemen, is a treat for high days and holidays. This fact, coupled with the influence of southern Indian cuisine introduced by large expat communities of vegetarian Hindus, means that vegetable dishes appear more often than might be expected on a restaurant menu.

Vegetarian staples include many bean and pulse dishes such as soup, foul and dhal, or lentil stews. Chickpeas, either fried into felafel or ground into a paste with oil and garlic (hummus), are a ubiquitous ingredient. Aubergines and okra are used in many delicious stews, and salad vegetables are usually locally grown and organic.

EATING WITH KIDS

Eating out as a family is becoming an increasingly popular pastime in the Peninsula for Arabs and expats: whole minibuses of relatives arrive to the outdoor, seaboard city venues, particularly in the winter months when huddling round a mobile stove is part of the fun. Equally, many parents join their children for a 'MacArabia' chicken roll-up or a beef pepperoni pizza in the spreading rash of Western fast-food outlets.

Children are welcome in restaurants across the Peninsula, except in the more exclusive, chic establishments of the Gulf, and many midrange restaurants provide children's menus. High chairs are not commonly available.

Fresh milk or powdered milk is widely available except in remote areas. Ice cream and yogurt are considered safe to eat except during the summer in rural areas, where a break in the power supply often results in partial defrosting.

EAT YOUR WORDS

For country-specific food-and-drink information, see the Food & Drink entries in the individual country chapters.

Useful Phrases

Do you have...?	haal indaak...?
Arabic coffee	kawah arabeeya
with/without sugar	ma'a/bidoon sukkar
with/without milk	ma'a/bidoon haleeb
I'd like ...	ana areed...
Does anyone here speak English?	haal yoogaad ahad yatakaallam ingleezi?
Do you have a table for one/two?	haal indaak tawilah lil waahid/ithnayn
What do you recommend?	bi maza tinsahnee?
May I have the menu?	ana areed al-kaart?
Do you have vegetarian dishes?	haal indaak akl nabati laahm?
Nothing more, thanks.	kafee mashkur (UAE)/yakfee shukran (Saudi)
Water please.	maa min fadhlach
I'd like the bill please.	ana areed al-hisaab min fadhlach
That was delicious.	kan al-aakl lazeez
It's to take away.	sa 'aakhodho maa'ee

Food Glossary

Note that because of the imprecise nature of transliterating Arabic into English, spellings will vary; for example, what we give as kibbeh may appear variously as kibba, kibby or even gibeh.

In most Peninsula countries mixed dining is common in more expensive or modern city restaurants. In smaller establishments men eat on the ground floor, while women and families eat upstairs in a section reserved for them. Women travellers are advised to follow suit.

Vegetarians beware! Some Peninsula carnivores (including chefs) may regard vegetarianism either as an incomprehensible Western indulgence or even a kind of culinary apostasy. Given that soups and stews are often based on meat stock, and to avoid uncomfortable conversations about ingredients, stick to Indian restaurants.

There are over 600 species of date and each country contends it has the best variety. Most experts, however, claim the best come from Al-Hasa, near Hufhuf in Saudi Arabia, where a variety called khlas is presold to regular customers before it's even harvested.

MIDDLE EASTERN MEZZE

baba ghanooj	smoky-flavoured dip of mashed, baked aubergine, typically mixed with tomato and onion and sometimes pomegranate
batata hara	hot, diced potatoes fried with coriander, garlic and capsicum
börek	pastry pockets stuffed with salty white cheese or spicy minced meat with pine nuts; also known as *sambousek*
fatayer	small pastry triangles filled with spinach
fattoosh	a fresh salad of onions, tomatoes, cucumber, lettuce and shards of crispy, thin, deep-fried bread
fool	a kind of paste made from beans, tomatoes, onions, and chilli; also spelt *foul*
hummus	chickpeas ground into a paste and mixed with tahini, garlic and lemon
kibbeh	minced lamb, bulgur wheat and pine nuts shaped into a lemon-shaped patty and deep fried
kibbeh nayye	minced lamb and cracked wheat served raw
kibda	liver, often chicken liver (*kibda firekh* or *kibda farouj*), usually sautéed in lemon or garlic
labneh	a yogurt paste, heavily flavoured with garlic or mint
lahma bi-ajeen	small lamb pies
loubieh	French bean salad with tomatoes, onions and garlic
mashi	baked vegetables, such as courgettes, vine leaves, capsicums, or aubergines, stuffed with minced meat, rice, onions, parsley and herbs
mujadarreh	a traditional 'poor person's' dish of lentils and rice garnished with caramelised onions
muttabal	similar to *baba ghanooj,* but the blended aubergine is mixed with tahini, yogurt and olive oil to achieve a creamier consistency
shanklish	a salad of small pieces of crumbled, tangy, eye-wateringly strong cheese mixed with chopped onion and tomato
soojuk	fried, spicy lamb sausage
tabouleh	a bulgur wheat, parsley and tomato based salad, with a sprinkling of sesame seeds, lemon and garlic
tahini	a thin sesame seed paste
waraq aynab	vine leaves stuffed with rice and meat

MIDDLE EASTERN & ARABIAN MAIN COURSES

bamiya	an okra-based stew
fasoolyeh	a green-bean stew
felafel	deep-fried balls of mashed chickpeas, often rolled in Arabic bread with salad and hummus
hareis	slow-cooked wheat and lamb
kabbza	lamb or chicken cooked with onion, tomato, cucumber, grated carrot and other fruit
kebab	skewered, flame-grilled chunks of meat, usually lamb, but also chicken, goat, camel, fish or squid; also known as *sheesh* or shish kebab
kebab mashwi	meat paste moulded onto flat skewers and grilled
kebsa	whole stuffed lamb served on a bed of spiced rice and pine nuts; also known as *khuzi*
kofta	ground meat peppered with spices, shaped into small sausages, skewered and grilled
makbus	casserole of meat or fish with rice
mashboos	grilled meat (usually chicken or lamb) and spiced rice
mashkul	rice served with onions
mihammar	lamb cooked in yogurt sauce and stuffed with nuts, raisins and other dried fruit
muaddas	rice served with lentils
mushkak gamel	seasoned camel meat grilled on a skewer – usually tough as old boots!

samak mashwi	fish barbecued over hot coals after basting in a date purée
shish tawooq	kebab with pieces of marinated, spiced chicken
shuwa	lamb cooked slowly in an underground oven
shwarma	the Middle Eastern equivalent of Greek *gyros* or Turkish *döner kebap*; strips are sliced from a vertical spit of compressed lamb or chicken, sizzled on a hot plate with chopped tomatoes and garnish, and then stuffed or rolled in Arabic bread
ta'amiyya	see felafel

MIDDLE EASTERN PASTRIES & DESSERTS

asabeeh	rolled filo pastry filled with pistachio, pine and cashew nuts and honey; otherwise known as 'ladies' fingers'
baklava	a generic term for any kind of layered flaky pastry with nuts, drenched in honey
barazak	flat, circular cookies sprinkled with sesame seeds
isfinjiyya	coconut slice
kunafa	shredded wheat over a creamy, sweet cheese base baked in syrup
labneh makbus	sweet yogurt cheese balls, sometimes made into a frittatalike creation or rolled in paprika; sometimes eaten for breakfast
mahallabiye	milk-based pudding
mushabbak	lace-work shaped pastry drenched in syrup
umm ali	a bread-based pudding made with sultanas and nuts, flavoured with nutmeg
zalabiyya	pastries dipped in rosewater

Expats

FROM HARDSHIP POSTING TO DREAM JOB

Fifteen years ago, a job in the Arabian Peninsula was considered to be a 'hardship posting'. While working in the Gulf was financially lucrative, with short hours and easy work, the conditions – the unbearable heat for much of the year, the conservative environment, the personal restrictions, the lack of a social life – made life difficult. Although the Kingdom of Saudi Arabia is still a tough place to live, especially for women, life in the rest of the Gulf is relatively easy and, in places such as the United Arab Emirates (UAE), Qatar and Bahrain, it's even exciting. So much so that a position on the Peninsula is now considered a dream job.

Ironically, inflation is on the rise, rents are higher than they've ever been, and wages haven't increased in years (and are now only slightly higher than salaries in the West). For many, these conditions are offset by the fact that the salary is tax free, and that myriad perks are still considered standard in many expat packages, such as a relocation allowance, annual plane tickets home, housing, health insurance, kids' education allowance, professional development grants, long paid holidays, and generous gratuity payments for when you decide you've had enough.

'The greatest thing has been finding a whole international gang of new friends. I now have a huge network from nationalities I had never in my life encountered before.'
Rachel Ball, English, six months abroad

THE WORLD IS YOUR OYSTER

These days many people are moving to the Gulf for reasons that are less to do with financial reward, and more to do with job satisfaction and being part of the exciting developments that are taking place in the region. The opportunities are limitless. Expats don't have to be here long before they get that 'the world is my oyster' feeling. Competition exists, but it's nowhere near as tough as it is back home.

Here it's possible to create your own opportunities. If you do your research, network well, make friends in the right industry, and are flexible, prepared to start at the bottom and work hard, you'll probably land a great job, be quickly promoted and may even have a position created for you. An Australian we recently met in Dubai started out with accounting qualifications and a dull financial job before deciding to throw it all in to teach English in Japan; she then secured a position as a flight attendant with Emirates Airlines, and recently became a production manager on a morning TV breakfast show. She's started doing a masters degree in journalism by distance and is planning a career in TV.

'I've developed a stronger personality, become more mature, I'm a better decision maker, and am fully independent. I appreciate life more.'
Hoda Beckdash, Lebanese, one year abroad

THE NEW EXPAT

Whereas the expat of the oil-boom days was in his or her 40s or 50s, white, middle class, and more than likely worked in oil, gas, petroleum, construction, nursing, teaching or foreign relations, times have changed. The new expats come in all ages, races, nationalities and classes, and work in every sector of industry, including in jobs that didn't exist in the Gulf a few years ago. You're just as likely to meet a mature male Indian IT CEO or a female middle-aged Danish hotel general manager as you are a 30-plus female South African TV editor or a 20-something male Bulgarian snowboard instructor.

These days the work itself is more glamorous, with the most coveted opportunities being in tourism, hospitality, marketing, PR and advertising, real-estate development, project management, architecture, interior design, fashion and entertainment. While the work itself is

'I love meeting people from all walks of life. But I hate those "my maid/driver" conversations and people who feel they have some right to be vaguely colonial, even racist, in a way they never would back home.'
Antonia Carver, English, six years abroad

exciting, the opportunity to work on fantastic projects is even more so – some of the world's biggest and whackiest housing projects, buildings, shopping malls, cities and even islands are being developed in the UAE, Qatar, Bahrain, Oman and Saudi Arabia, ranging from floating cities in Bahrain to pearl-shaped developments in Qatar to an island development shaped like the world in Dubai.

A COSMOPOLITAN LIFE

For many expats, the multicultural environment in which they're able to work is more attractive than the job itself. Expatriate populations outnumber national populations in all Gulf States. There are over 10 million expats in the Gulf, with expats comprising 88% of the workforce in the UAE, 83% in Qatar, 81% in Kuwait, 72% in Saudi Arabia, 55% in Bahrain and 54% in Oman. The Arabian Peninsula is one of the most multicultural places on the planet.

Companies in the Gulf boast about how many nationalities they have working for them. A director of one women's university gets up at the first staff gathering of every new academic year to proudly announce where his new recruits have come from and how many countries they've travelled to – the more obscure the country they're from and the greater the number they've visited, the bigger the director's smile will be. Proudly displayed in the lobby of one city hotel are little cut-out photos of the staff, which are pinned on to their home countries on a big map of the world – most of North and East Africa, nearly all of the Middle East and Asia, and much of Europe is scattered with their smiling faces.

Another young graduate we met, fresh out of a media degree in London and working in hotel PR, had barely been six months in the Gulf when she was offered work as a radio presenter, a job she would be waiting years to get in the UK. While she admitted that she's earning less than she would be in an assistant role in the media in London, she said she's here more for the experience. She too boasts of the number of nationalities she works with and the Argentine boyfriend she's dating; he's only been speaking English since he arrived here a few months ago, and she's now learning Spanish as well as Arabic. An acquaintance who is a cocktail bar manager tells us that he loves the fact that he can have a dinner party with friends from Iraq, France, South Africa and Australia, and his girlfriend is from the Philippines – none of this would be possible in his home of Serbia.

THE OPPORTUNITY TO TRAVEL

What the 21st-century expat does have in common with the expat of the last century is their motivation to travel. A trading hub a thousand years ago, when camel caravans used to crisscross Arabia transporting frankincense, gold, spices and dates, the Gulf is now one of the world's busiest travel hubs, at the crossroads between Europe and Australasia, Africa and Asia. While Bahrain's Gulf Air leads the way in the airline stakes, and Dubai's Emirates Airlines has pioneered new air routes and markets, the UAE's Etihad Airways, Qatar Airways and Oman Air are fast catching up – as are newer lower-budget airlines such as Air Arabia and Jazeera.

Gulf Cooperation Council (GCC) tourism figures for 2006 were impressive, with the UAE having welcomed nearly 7 million visitors by January 2007, Bahrain over 800,000, Oman 750,000, Qatar 650,000 and Yemen 390,000. Even with these figures, all of the Gulf States have ambitious long-term tourism strategies in place aimed at dramatically increasing numbers of tourists.

'The best thing is the travel. We've seen more of the world in two years than most people see in a lifetime.'
Greg Unrau, Canadian, six years abroad

'Coming here was the best thing that we ever did. No matter how hard we worked there we were only moving backwards. Even though it takes a lot of effort to settle in, we're able to support our families and invest back home.'
Ann Scrilec, Filipina, two years abroad

'The best thing about living in the Gulf region is its close proximity to many exciting and exotic travel destinations.'
Mostafa Tawfik, Egyptian-American, three years abroad

The same airlines are not only bringing tens of millions of tourists to the region each year, and scores of millions to duty-free shops as they wait for connections, they're providing expats with myriad opportunities to travel. While the older expat used to focus on seeing the Middle East region if they weren't using their leave to visit family back home, the new expats are spending their five-day *eid* breaks in the Maldives or Mumbai, and their longer summer holidays (when the temperatures soar and every expat evacuates) doing Europe, Africa and Asia. These days, the older expats are taking more adventurous trips, with Ethiopia, Yemen and Iran currently topping the list.

A HOME AWAY FROM HOME

A recent change to laws in the UAE, Qatar and Bahrain to allow foreigners to own property and, in the process, get a residence visa has seen new expats buying small studios in marina-tower developments and the older expats buying villas on green golfing estates, creating a second home away from home.

Unfortunately, while everyone talks up the multicultural aspects of living in the Arabian Peninsula, when it comes to affording these properties the divide between the educated Western expat and the often equally educated Asians becomes apparent. Westerners (mostly Europeans, North Americans and Australasians) work in highly skilled jobs for which most locals are only just receiving their qualifications, while non-Western expats (primarily Pakistanis, Afghanistanis, Bangladeshis, Indians and Sri Lankans) perform much of the unskilled labour (taxi driving, construction work, domestic help). While there are exceptions to the rule (the burgeoning Indian middle class, for example), the expat divide still exists.

> 'The greatest challenge is to not be too work oriented. Many people move here and end up putting in long hours at the office. Companies then have an expectation that their staff will "live to work" – meanwhile the desert and the beach beckon.'
> *Antonia Carver, English, six years abroad*

YOU'RE MOVING WHERE? *Terry Carter*

When my wife Lara was offered an interview for a job in Abu Dhabi nearly 10 years ago, I admit that I did have to look it up in an atlas. Sure we'd travelled extensively and Lara was just back from South America, but this was potentially quite a sea change. Friends offered advice. Some of it was good ('Just do it! You can always come back if you don't like it.'), some of it misguided ('You'll be living in a compound and you'll have to smuggle in alcohol!') and some of it was negative ('You're going *where*?'). But we decided to do it anyway. We didn't want to spend our whole working lives only living in Australia, and despite having a well-paid position as a design manager in Sydney, the whole inner-city work-hard-play-hard lifestyle was not as appealing to me as it once was.

By the time Lara was offered her position, I was already packing up the apartment and just had to hit 'send' on my carefully crafted resignation letter – no bridge burning, just in case! Arriving in Abu Dhabi was surreal and life continued to be so for the first few months, with a thankfully in-tune call to prayer punctuating the air several times a day as a constant reminder that we were somewhere very different than Kings Cross, Sydney! While some things took a while to adjust to – such as dealing with bureaucracy, the fan-forced-oven summer heat, the woeful cinema offerings, our favourite magazines with the 'racy' photos ripped out of them, and hard-to-find ingredients for our favourite meals – the complete change of lifestyle was welcome. Sure there were some bigger problems: working with power-crazed expat managers (ironically, some from Australia), taking a position only to never see a contract (I walked out of that dysfunctional disaster after two weeks), and the lurking feeling that if one of us were fired we'd probably be leaving the country, perhaps hastily. But in hindsight we wouldn't change a thing – except maybe arriving in the Arabian Peninsula in one of the hottest months. That *really* makes you doubt your sanity!

LIVING IN A FOREIGN CULTURE

A major motivation for many people to move overseas is the opportunity to live within another society, and to experience the rich and fulfilling process of becoming familiar with a foreign culture. The Middle East, Islam and Arabs have all been the subjects of unprecedented and often negative Western media coverage since 9/11. Living in the Gulf allows you to make up your own mind through first-hand experience.

If you're prepared to enter the country with an open mind and learn a little about Islam, Arab culture and Bedouin society, the opportunity to enjoy the rich traditions and gracious hospitality of Arabs can be a rare privilege.

Learn as much as you can about your host nation's culture and Islam. Read (p99), do a cross-cultural course or participate in cultural activities run by local organisations such as the Sheikh Mohammed Centre for Cultural Understanding (p388), which runs visits to Jumeirah Mosque (p389), the only mosque in the UAE that non-Muslims can enter. The centre also runs cultural breakfasts and lunches, where you get to meet locals over a casual meal and ask them everything you always wanted to know about their culture and religion. Local museums and heritage villages – there's one in virtually every city in the Gulf – are a great place to learn about the history, heritage and culture of the country.

While Arabic is by no means essential to communicate in the Arabian Peninsula – and in fact, Urdu, Hindi or Tagalog would probably be more useful – you'll have a much greater chance of making friends with Gulf Arabs if you can at least learn the lengthy greetings. Few expats take up the opportunity to learn Arabic, and most end up regretting it. Don't make the same mistake.

Life on the Arabian Peninsula

Life in Oman, the UAE, Bahrain, Qatar and Kuwait isn't as 'foreign' as life in Yemen or Saudi Arabia, and new expats rarely suffer the kind of culture shock they did 10 years ago. While there are some aspects of life in the Arabian Peninsula that are distinctly Arabic (such as the language and cuisine) or very much Arabian (such as the tradition of hospitality, the architecture and the Bedouin heritage), the countries are much more multicultural than most expats would expect – much more so, in fact, than the UK, the USA or Australia.

Expats are therefore not only adjusting to the Middle East and Arab way of life, they're also adjusting to living with myriad cultures. If you live in the neighbourhood of Mankhool in Dhabi, for example, you'll probably live in a building that predominantly houses middle-class Indians; you're more likely to see the celebrations for the Diwali festival than for the Muslim festival Eid al-Adha.

Everyday life in most of the Gulf states contrasts dramatically with life in Saudi Arabia. While all are Islamic states practising Sharia'a (Islamic law), most have civil courts and penalties often aren't as harsh. Most Gulf Arabs – particularly Omanis, Emiratis, Bahrainis and Kuwaitis – are very open and tolerant. You can live wherever you want; compounds don't exist outside of Saudi Arabia. You can eat pork in most good restaurants and buy it in many supermarkets. You can get a licence to buy and drink alcohol, although you shouldn't drink and drive, and you certainly shouldn't stagger through the streets if intoxicated; to do so will most definitely land you some time in jail. Affectionate behaviour, even among married couples, is a no-no in all states and should be especially avoided during Ramadan.

'The opportunity to live and work in a place where you can contribute to its dynamic social and developmental change is very rewarding.'
Susan Brown, American, three years abroad

'We were living in Kuwait when I got a job offer in the UAE. We knew that Dubai was the best place in the Gulf to live, in terms of quality of life, so it was an easy decision.'
Steve Terney, American, 19 years abroad

'The best thing is the accessible luxury – I earn very little money, yet I'm able to treat myself to gourmet-standard food and drink for much less than it would cost me in the UK.'
Rachel Ball, English, six months abroad

Negotiating the arcane workings of the legal system and government bureaucracy across the Gulf will test the nerves of the most patient of people. Long arduous lines at government offices, and the feeling of being ushered from one place to the next are compounded by the frequent lack of courtesy shown by officials. The best advice is to be patient; losing your temper only creates a confrontation, which you cannot win and certainly will not defuse the situation, even if it does make you feel better at the time.

While historically Oman, Qatar, Bahrain and Kuwait, have not seen anywhere near the number of expats as the UAE and Saudi Arabia, they are increasingly becoming attractive to expats as the UAE becomes more expensive and crowded, and Saudi becomes less secure. Qatar is the country of the moment, having attracted the eyes of the world during Doha's extravagant Asian Games event in late 2006. Over the last few years, it has been developing an outstanding educational sector, with prestigious universities from all over the world setting up shop there. Oman is popular for its laid-back lifestyle, traditional culture and natural beauty, while Bahrain is seen as the most open and tolerant society.

> 'The most wonderful thing about living in Dubai is the opportunities that are opened to you by being part of a process of a town no-one has heard of turning into a global city that everyone has heard of.'
> *Antonia Carver, English, six years abroad*

Life in the UAE

Life in the UAE is appealing for most expats – despite the traffic problems, the soaring rents and the inflation. Dubai is an exciting city, with shops, hotels, restaurants, bars and clubs that have as much style, glamour and sophistication as any you'll find in Sydney, London or New York. And Abu Dhabi seems to be following suit with the announcement that the city will host a Formula One race, while construction of a Guggenheim Museum and a branch of the Louvre will commence soon.

The UAE's cities are also uniquely Arabian, with as much Emirati heritage and culture as any in the Gulf – it's just hard to find in Dubai.

> 'While I look forward to going home, there's this feeling when you're there, you start to miss the friends and cycle of life you've got accustomed to in Dubai. I simply enjoy my period here because when I go home for good, there'll be no coming back. There are still so many places to see.'
> *Bessie Sagario, Filipina, three years abroad*

Life in Saudi Arabia

Money has obviously been the biggest incentive for expats to move to Saudi Arabia but the trade-off has been the lack of a social life; the restrictions of living in a country that has adopted a puritanical form of Islam that segregates society by gender, outlaws alcohol, forbids women from driving, and requires all women to cover up; and in recent years, the all-important issue of security.

Entertainment is thin on the ground, and there are neither cinemas nor bars. Within the compounds (and in some workplaces), you're generally free to do as you like, but the Saudi authorities are very serious about enforcing social segregation outside the compounds, and if you're caught there's a high probability of spending time in jail. The possibility of transgressing some seemingly obscure local law is a constant worry.

On the other hand, the opportunity to experience first-hand the fascinating social and geographical landscape of Saudi Arabia is attractive to the intrepid. For many, the opportunity to live in a country which is all but closed to tourism carries personal rewards which ultimately outweigh the financial factor.

> 'The best and worst thing about being an expat is being an "outsider".'
> *Liz Maxwell, Australian, eight years abroad*

EXPAT LIFE FOR WOMEN

Expat women are generally treated with a great deal of respect in the Arabian Peninsula, outside of Saudi Arabia. You're just as likely to see a woman (local or foreign) in a management position as you are a man. Women can drive and there's no problem with women having male friends – although women shouldn't live with men they're not married to or related to.

THE ACCIDENTAL EXPAT Lisandro Palabrica,

I came to Dubai accidentally and I've been here for two-and-a-half years now. I love and hate Dubai at the same time. Actually, I hate two things and love many things about Dubai! I hate the traffic and the never-ending construction. I love the dynamic environment, the food, the sun, the sea, and the people I've met from many different cultures. People from different walks of life; some who only care how beautiful their tan looks on Jumeirah Beach, people who work hard to send money to their family back home while living in a small room in Satwa or Karama just to save rent, others with an Imeldific [named after Imelda Marcos, the shopaholic former First Lady of the Philippines, known for her colossal shoe collection] attitude who shop every week, a female CEO from an investment company who is a volunteer in a charity that takes care of African kids, or even the people I've met from the dance clubs scattered around the city, partying like there is no tomorrow! Dubai is a big oasis in the middle of the desert. A one-time chance for some to change their lives and have a better life, and a quicksand for others who are unlucky to end up in a situation where they are sinking and have no choice but to pack up and go home.

I let go of the things I have been accustomed to when I set foot in Dubai for the first time – culture, traditions, beliefs, my family, friends and environment back home. Yet there never was a moment of incongruity. Not a moment of hesitation or regret. I knew it would be a challenging journey for me, finding a home away from home, and I always believe that life is not a matter of chance, but a matter of choice. So I struggled, trying to survive the challenges and reach for my goals, though deep inside me I missed my family and friends (sometimes spending Dh300 a month on phone calls) until I started to explore and meet wonderful new friends, and became attached and breathed new air in a strange land.

Now, plans have changed. For three years I have been waiting to move to Canada, thinking that the honey tasted sweeter on the other side of the world. My wait is now over, as I've been granted an immigrant visa and might move there in April, letting go of the things I've started in Dubai. The hardest part of letting go will be not seeing the future of Dubai, the skyscrapers which I have witnessed laying their foundations and the dust from their construction that I have breathed when I've travelled around Dubai. I'll miss the weather, the sun, my dear friends who are my extended family and, importantly, the career opportunity of growing with the city.

Life must go on. Life is a choice. I'm sure I will be back here and if that happens, I will never again be an accidental expat in Dubai.

Lisandro is a Filipino marketing and public-relations executive, who spontaneously gave his CV to a recruiter and was packing his bags two weeks later.

While women are free to wear what they want, female expats should dress respectfully (p544) as, after all, you're a guest in an Islamic country. You'll also be treated with greater respect if you dress modestly.

While some women take offence to designated 'ladies queues' in banks and government departments, and to being shunted off to 'family rooms' in cheap eateries, expats who've been around for a while know to take advantage of the privilege of speedy service and the refuge from the occasional leers of guest workers who haven't seen their wives in a long time.

Saudi Arabia is a different story. Segregation between male and female is the norm, and public life is an uncompromisingly male domain that women cannot freely enter. Apart from the indignity of such treatment, this can seriously inhibit the freedom of movement for women.

MEETING PEOPLE

One of the biggest complaints of expats living in the Gulf is that they rarely befriend nationals, and in some cases never get to meet them at all. Compound life and the strictly segregated nature of Saudi society make it especially difficult in Saudi Arabia, but it's not so hard in the other Gulf countries if you make an effort.

Start by avoiding the formal expat groups. From the time you arrive you'll be inundated by invitations to attend Australia-New Zealand (insert your country here) Club get-togethers and embassy barbecues to celebrate national holidays, and to join global expat organisations such as the Hash House Harriers. Sporting clubs and charities, while worthwhile and fun, also provide few opportunities for meeting nationals, who tend to prefer to exercise privately (ladies' clubs are the exception), and to donate to their local mosque and community rather than work in a formally organised charity.

Instead, focus on meeting nationals and expats from countries other than your own. There's nothing stopping you from going to the Indian Social Club or the Iranian Club. Dance clubs also have ethnic club nights where you get to party with expats from that particular country and make friends in the process. For instance, Tuesday nights at SAX (p427) in Abu Dhabi is a great way to meet Lebanese as you dance to a live Lebanese band and Lebanese DJ. Restaurants provide the same opportunity, and there are generally a few where different nationalities congregate. If you want to meet Gulf nationals and Arab expats, head to a *sheesha* café – but go late. Local sports matches, popular activities such as barbecuing in parks (late again!), and local hobbies such as shopping (also late) all present opportunities to meet Gulf nationals. While you may have to make the effort first – and that's where those Arabic greetings come in – once you receive an invitation to coffee, accept immediately!

'I really enjoy the multicultural nature of life here and the cultural events. I've learned so much about many different cultures and made friends from all over the world.'
Monica Gallant, Canadian, 11 years abroad

CHILDREN

For anyone, an international experience is a life-changing experience for the better, but for kids this is especially the case. Many expat parents say they'd rather bring their kids up in the Gulf than in the UK/USA/Canada/ Australia, citing myriad reasons ranging from education to safety.

The standard of international schools in the Arabian Peninsula is excellent. You find schools from all countries, from America to Britain, Australia to New Zealand, and Germany to France, all offering identical or similar curriculum to that in their home countries, enabling a smooth transition into universities and colleges back home. In Saudi Arabia, large companies like Aramco and British Aerospace also operate their own schools; other expats send their children to boarding schools in their home countries. Many employers provide an allowance for education, whether it's taking place locally or abroad. Enrolling a non-Muslim, non-Arabic-speaking child in a local school is generally not an option.

BRINGING UP THE BUTLER BABIES

Leigh Butler is an expat academic who generously runs a website (http://dwc.hct.ac.ae/expatinfo /index.htm) that helps recently arrived expats settle into their new lifestyle. Having lived abroad with his wife Trish and their two daughters for 11 years, Leigh sees their family as a stronger unit for living overseas. The friendships the children form are stronger as well, although this comes at a price. 'The downside is that friends move far more often than at "home" and they have been broken hearted at times [at] losing their best friend.' The location of 'home' is itself also an issue and when travelling back to Australia their accents are often mistaken for British or American accents, leading to the problematic question of 'Where am I really from?'. While Dubai is an especially safe place to live, Leigh feels that the kids lack street smarts that similar-aged children in big-city Australia would have. 'They could catch a plane to Germany without a problem, but to catch a tram or train in Melbourne would be a major operation.'

Crime across the Arabian Peninsula is extremely low by Western standards. In small towns in Oman, the UAE, Bahrain, Qatar and Yemen, people still leave their cars unlocked when they go to the shop. (And even in Saudi Arabia, compounds have high levels of security.) Expat kids may find that they have more freedom in the Arabian Peninsula than they do back home, as parents feel safe in the knowledge that they are not going to be preyed upon in parks or offered drugs.

Children meet kids from all over the world at school and in the many sporting and extracurricular activities, including international trips. Growing up in a multinational surrounding gives them a broader view of life, creating more open-minded and tolerant young people who are accepting of other cultures.

There have been some outstanding books written specifically about the expat experience for children:

■ *Raising Global Nomads: Parenting Abroad in an On-Demand World*, by Robin Pascoe, draws on her family's personal experiences of living in a dozen countries over 25 years. Pascoe frankly shares her own family's trials and tribulations, and how they coped with the difficulties of adapting to expatriate life.

■ *When Abroad – Do as the Local Children Do: Ori's Guide for Young Expats*, by Hilly van Swol-Ulbrich and Bettina Kaltenhauser, is intended to help children of expat families overcome the challenges of living in a foreign country. This colourful kids' book contains activities to help children build the confidence to explore and embrace their new environment.

■ *Club Expat: A Teenager's Guide to Moving Overseas*, by Aniket and Akash Shah, deals with the everyday intricacies of expatriating (from what to take to what to leave at home) while looking at the bigger picture. This engaging read by two expat brothers prepares teens for the negative aspects of moving while showing them how to focus on the positive, thereby helping teens make the most of their international experience.

■ *Unrooted Childhoods: Memoirs of Growing Up Global*, edited by Faith Eidse and Nina Sichel, is an anthology of enlightening essays by writers who grew up mobile, whether as diplomats' kids or army brats – the people Pico Iyer calls the 'privileged homeless'. Writers from Isabel Allende to Ariel Dorfman write about their experience of being rootless, of the impact of their international education, and how it opened their minds to cultures around the globe.

■ *The Third Culture Kid Experience: Growing Up Among Worlds*, by David C Pollock and Ruth E Van Reken, is an enlightening read examining the 'third culture', the shared common expat lifestyle that is different to both the expats' own 'home' cultures and that of their host culture. It looks at the challenges faced by people who have spent a significant part of their development years in this 'third culture', and explains why they get bitten by the travel bug, and are drawn back to the place or the places they lived in.

DOING BUSINESS

New arrivals hoping to do business in the Gulf States should be aware of differences in outlook, particularly with regard to the favourite Western preoccupation of 'getting things done'.

Arabs are famous for their fatalism, which stems from Islam and their belief that only God can determine their fate. When you make an appointment, agree to undertake a project together, or just arrange to

'The best thing about living here is learning about different cultures and making new friends from around the world. The worst thing is feeling lonely, not alone; work takes up most of your time.'
Hoda Beckdash, Lebanese, one year abroad

'The most difficult thing is getting used to the different ways of doing things, such as telling people how to get to your place when there aren't any street addresses, but you somehow adapt.'
Helen Pearce, Canadian, four years abroad

'The worst thing is missing family, especially during a crisis back home, and the good people who come into your life, and then leave soon after…it's the expat shuffle.'
Greg Unrau, Canadian, six years abroad

have dinner, you'll more than likely hear the response *insha'allah*. Literally meaning 'if Allah wills it', it means the outcome is in God's hands. Although not necessarily 'no', it can permit both a procrastination and a polite 'no'. Unlike Westerners who often masochistically flog a problem to death, an Arab enjoys patiently pondering a situation or simply walking away.

Equally, Western business practices such as good timekeeping, decisiveness, prompt action, accepting blame and designating responsibility are all lost on Gulf Arabs. Instead, hard bargaining, the ability to find loopholes and the honouring of one's word are dearly cherished.

Another adjustment expats need to make is to the notion of time and the segmentation of the day, which is more pronounced in some countries than others. While Dubai has adjusted to Western practices, with straight work days in the private sector, businesses everywhere else in the Gulf will often close in the afternoon so people can head home for lunch and a siesta.

In Saudi Arabia, there are also breaks for prayer, with each lasting for about 25 minutes, although these don't usually affect health-care workers.

Avoid doing business in the Gulf during the month of Ramadan, when nationals work considerably reduced hours and many offices run on skeleton staff.

For practical information on doing business and working in the Arabian Peninsula, read *Living and Working in the Gulf States and Saudi Arabia* by Robert Hughes, a comprehensive, practical 'how-to' guide to everyday work and study; *Live and Work in Saudi and the Gulf* by Louise Whetter, a good general introduction to starting a business, working and buying a property in the Arabian Peninsula; and *The Arab World Handbook* by James Peters, which gives a good overview of the region, including business opportunities and available employment.

FURTHER READING

Read everything and anything you can about the country you're moving to before you leave, especially about the culture and Islam. Nothing beats talking to someone who has lived or is currently living in the Arabian Peninsula, and there are some excellent expat websites with discussion forums where you can get advice and share experiences. There are also a lot of informative books about the expat experience, both personal narratives and practical resources.

Once you've arrived, get a copy of one of the many excellent local expat guides available, such as the *Explorer* series, which cover all the practical details, from doing business, to setting up your house, and getting your kids into school.

Books

Arabia by Jonathan Raban chronicles the author's journey through the Gulf during the oil-boom years of the 1970s, introducing us to the early cities and villages, to the rich and poor, sheikhs and Bedu. It's essential to understanding how dramatic the changes have been in the region in the last few decades.

Sandstorms: Days and Nights in Arabia, by Peter Theroux, was written after the Iran–Iraq War and before the first Gulf War, and provides an excellent introduction to the complexities and contradictions of politics, religion, society and alliances in the Middle East, especially Saudi Arabia.

'The multicultural environment is what's best about life here. You hear every language spoken in the streets and see people in Western, Asian, African and Arab clothing, and it's all just so natural and normal. No-one is a foreigner.'
Steve Terney, American, 19 years abroad

'The hardest thing about coming here was leaving our family and friends. To quote my mother: "You are taking my grand-daughters *where?*" She didn't care about my wife and me.'
Leigh Butler, Australian, 11 years abroad

'Dealing with people who use their nationality as an advantage against some expatriates here can be challenging. In our first year we encountered all different people who could be brutally unethical. It's hard if you're Asian. Only whites get most of the privileges.'
Ann Scrilec, Filipina, two years abroad

SOLVING THE EXPAT SOJOURN SLUMP

When you've been living the expat lifestyle for a while, it's easy to get into a routine of visiting the same restaurants, bars, shops, neighbourhoods and friends. Here are our Top 10 tips for breaking the pattern.

■ Leave the car at home. If something is within walking distance, walk. Like the song on *Sesame Street* says, find out who the people in your neighbourhood are.

■ Take a drive to an interesting destination, such as Nizwa in Oman, or Al Ain in the United Arab Emirates (UAE), but stop at every small town on the way. Find out what the rural areas of your country of residence are really like.

■ Skip the big supermarkets. Head to the corner grocery store – chances are you'll find out far more about how other expats and locals live by not visiting the 'pork room'.

■ Eat locally. Don't understand the menu? Go right in! Find out why that local Pakistani/Indian/Sri Lankan/Iranian eatery is so popular! Do one a week, every week.

■ Be a tourist for the day. Got guests? Don't just write them a list and send them off for the day. If you haven't done all the local sights, make a point of visiting them all; you might be surprised at how much you know – or don't know – about where you live.

■ Expand your circle of friends. So, just who do you hang out with? Make a list now. Are all of your friends from the same country, or in some cases, city? Expand your horizons. Make friends with expats from other parts of the world.

■ Make local friends. While this one might appear to be the most obvious of tips, you'll be surprised how many expats leave the Arabian Gulf without one local name on speed dial. Don't let that be you, you'll regret it!

■ Have a multicultural meal. Invite these new friends to dinner at your place – mix expats from a variety of backgrounds with some locals. Make sure you cater for everyone and then let the cross-pollination of ideas, opinions and dreams begin.

■ Learn a language. Some basic Arabic is a great idea, but Tagalog, Hindi or Farsi can open doors that you might never have dreamed of.

■ Visit a local park on the weekend. Instead of having a barbecue in your backyard, why not head to the local park and mix it with other weekend chefs cooking up their local specialities. Find out why kebabs taste better when cooked with a battery-powered fan hovering over them!

Expats: Travels in Arabia, from Tripoli to Teheran by Christopher Dickey, a former *Newsweek* Middle East bureau chief, draws on interviews with compelling characters, ranging from oil-tanker captains to diplomats, to provide a fascinating insight into expat life in the Middle East in the late '80s. Read this and you might make more of an effort to chat to that craggy-faced old English bloke propping up the bar at Hemingways in Abu Dhabi, or any other expat pub in the Gulf.

A Moveable Marriage: Relocate Your Relationship Without Breaking It, by Canadian journalist Robin Pascoe, recounts the challenges to her marriage as she follows her diplomat husband to 25 countries, writing very frankly about their ups and downs, and how they kept their relationship alive.

Leaving Paradise: My Expat Adventures and Other Stories by Sonia Harford, a journalist for Australia's *Age* newspaper, recounts her years working as a foreign correspondent and what it's like to be an Australian living abroad, reflecting on everything from the glamour of expat life to the pain of nostalgia. She also investigates the boom in Australian expatriatism and examines why one million Australians now live overseas.

GenXpat: The Young Professional's Guide to Making a Successful Life Abroad by Margaret Malewski is the first book aimed at helping the new generation of culturally mobile global professionals – the kind of young creative types who work the freelance desks at Dubai Media City – succeed overseas.

Websites

There are countless websites and discussion forums managed by and aimed at expats.

Expat Exchange (www.expatexchange.net)

Expat Forum (www.expatforum.com)

Expats in Saudi Arabia (www.expatsinsaudiarabia.com)

Living Abroad (www.livingabroad.com)

Survive Abroad (www.surviveabroad.com) Has a useful 110-frequently-asked-questions section about Saudi Arabia.

Environment

The harsh lands of Arabia have for centuries attracted travellers from the Western world, curious to see 'a haggered land infested with wild beasts, and wilder men… What could be more exciting?' writes Burton, 'What more sublime?'

To this day, people come to the desert expecting 'sand, sand, sand, still sand, and only sand and sand again'. The traveller who wrote those words (Kinglake), curiously had only passed through gravel plains at that point, but so strong is the connection between the words 'desert' and 'sand', he felt obliged to comment on what he thought he should see rather than on what was there.

For anyone who has travelled extensively in Arabia, or had the privilege of being in the region after exceptional rains, it quickly becomes apparent that the lands of the Peninsula are far from a monotonous, barren wasteland of undulating sand dunes. They are richly diverse and support a remarkable range of carefully adapted plants and animals. Indeed, one of the principal joys of the region is the exceptional landscapes that form the backdrop for dramas of survival and endurance by all that makes the desert fastness home.

> The Al-Hasa Oasis, near the town of Al-Hofuf in eastern Saudi Arabia, is the largest oasis in the world. Covering 2500 sq km, it's home to over three million palm trees.

THE LAND
Geology

The Arabian Peninsula is a treasure trove for the geologist. Though not particularly rich in minerals or gems (though copper is found in northern Oman), the Peninsula is highly revealing of the earth's earliest history (see boxed text, p239), supporting theories of plate tectonics and continental shift. Indeed, geologists believe that the Peninsula originally formed part of the larger landmass of Africa. A split in this continent created both Africa's Great Rift Valley (which extends from Mozambique up through Djibouti, into western Yemen, Saudi Arabia and Jordan) and the Red Sea.

As Arabia slipped away from Africa, the Peninsula began to 'tilt', with the western side rising and the eastern edge dropping, a process that led to the formation of the Gulf.

Geologists speak of the Peninsula in terms of two distinct regions: the Arabian shield and the Arabian shelf. The shield, which consists of volcanic sedimentary, rock makes up the western third of today's Arabian Peninsula. The shelf is made up of the lower-lying areas that slope away from the shield, from central Arabia to the waters of the Gulf.

Extensive flooding millions of years ago led to the remains of marine life (both planktonic plants and micro-organisms) being deposited in layers of sediment across the tilted landmass – as the rich fossil remains found across Arabia indicate. When sufficient dead organic matter is laid down and trapped under the surface in conditions where a lack of oxygen prevents it from decaying to water and carbon dioxide, the raw material of hydrocarbons is produced – the origin, in other words, of oil and gas. The conversion from dead organic matter to a hydrocarbon, described as maturation, is subject to many other conditions such as depth and temperature. Arabia's geology is uniquely supportive of these conditions, and 'nodding donkeys' (drilling apparatus, capable of boring holes up to 5km deep) can be seen throughout the interior of the Peninsula, and offshore platforms dot the Gulf, tapping into hidden seams of 'reservoir rock', to which hydrocarbons have migrated over time.

Newspapers across the region agonise over if and when the reserves will reach their peak (see boxed text, p40). Given that the economies of all the Peninsula countries rely to a lesser or greater extent on oil and gas, this is one issue that can't be left to *insha'allah* (God's will). As such, Peninsula countries are busy diversifying their economic interests (see p40) in case their reserves run out sooner rather than later.

Geography

Stand on top of Kuwait Towers and the eye roams unhindered along flat country. The low-lying coastal plains and salt flats stretch all along the limp waters of the northern Gulf, barely managing to make a mountain out of a molehill until the Mussandam Peninsula brings the plain to an abrupt close. This is the land of mudhoppers and wading birds and long stretches of dazzling-white sands.

Much of the interior is flat too but some major mountain ranges, like the Hajar Mountains of Oman and the Haraz Mountains of Yemen, bring an entirely different climate and way of life to the high ground.

There are no permanent river systems in the Peninsula. Water-laden clouds from the sea break across the mountains, causing rainfall to slide along wadis with dramatic speed. Smaller tributaries of water collect in the wadis from natural springs and create oases in the desert. In much of the Peninsula, the water table is close enough to the surface to hand-dig a well – a fact not wasted on the Bedu who survive on a system of wells and springs discovered or made by their forefathers. Irrigation, in the form of elaborate ducts and pipes (called *falaj* in Oman – see p216), helps channel water through plantations, allowing more extensive farming in the region than might be supposed (see p87).

Gulf Landscapes, by Elizabeth Collas and Andrew Taylor, is a beautifully illustrated book that shows there's much more to the Gulf than its high-profile cities.

ECOSYSTEMS
The Desert

There's such awe in the words 'Arabian desert'. It's been described by so many famous writers and travellers, it's bound up so inseparably in Western fantasies of escape, that it's hard to begin a description of it. The

---

LANDSCAPES TO CRY FOR

The following Top 10 list of spectacular landscapes in the region are stunning enough to raise a tear or two.

- Al-Ula, Saudi Arabia (p333) – Copper-coloured wind-eroded sandstone at sunset.
- Al-Soudah, Saudi Arabia (p343) – Peregrine-eye views of the coastal plain from soaring escarpment summit.
- Uruq Bani Ma'arid, Saudi Arabia (p349) – Wind rustling sand over the dunes of the Empty Quarter.
- Wadi Dhabat, Oman (p252) – Camels and cows sharing abundant herbage in seasonal mists.
- Wadi Ghul, Oman (p234) – Vertiginous peeps into the Grand Canyon of Arabia.
- Sharfat al-Alamayn, Oman (p233) – Panoramic mountain vista of vertical cliffs and fertile wadis.
- Mughsail, Oman (p253) – Blowholes piping sardines beneath the dramatic undercliff.
- Shaharah, Yemen (p474) – Switchback glimpses of livid green, terraced fields.
- Suqutra, Yemen (p502) – Floating islands of cormorants off pristine coastline.
- Khor al-Adaid, Qatar (p287) – Sun sparking off the inland sea, netted by dunes.

Arabian Wildlife at www
.arabianwildlife.com is
the online version of the
Arabian Wildlife Magazine
and covers 'all facets of
wildlife and conservation
in Arabia'.

very words 'Empty Quarter' invite imaginative speculation, a pull towards exploration and discovery. 'Quarter' is about right: the Rub' al-Khali, as it is known locally, occupies a vast area in the heart of the Peninsula, straddling Saudi, Yemen, Oman and UAE; but 'empty' is not the case.

The sands dunes of the Empty Quarter may be the most famous geographical feature but they are not the only desert of interest. Much of the Peninsula is made up of flat, gravel plains dotted with outcrops of weather-eroded sandstone in the shape of pillars, mushrooms and ledges. Fine examples of these desert forms can be seen in Saudi Arabia, near Al-Ula (see p333), Bir Zekreet in Qatar (see p289) and Duqm and the Huqf Escarpment in Oman (see p246).

There are many other kinds of desert too, including flat coastal plains and the infamous volcanic black Harra of northern Arabia. The stoic traveller, Doughty, described the area as 'iron desolation…uncouth blackness…lifeless cumber of volcanic matter!' Even camels hate to cross it as the small rocks heat in the sun and catch in their feet.

Once upon a time, ostriches roamed the savannah-like plains of Arabia and crocodiles lurked in the rivers, but changing climate and human encroachment has resulted in a change of inhabitants.

Travels in Arabia Deserta,
by CM Doughty, was
first published in 1926.
Described by one critic
as 'Big book, big bore',
the powerful, eccentric
descriptions of the
author's laborious travels
across Arabia have a long
list of devotees, including
TE Lawrence.

Nowadays, camels (few of which are wild) and feral donkeys dominate the landscape of thorny acacia (low, funnel-shaped bush) and life-supporting *ghaf* trees. Sheltering under these trees, and licking the dew from the leaflets in the morning, are fleet-footed gazelle, protected colonies of oryx, and a host of smaller mammals – hares, foxes and hedgehogs – providing supper for the raptors that wheel overhead. Easier to spot are lizards, snakes and a network of insects that provide the building blocks of the desert ecosystem (see p225).

See the National Parks section (p107) for the location of some of these species, many of which are endangered.

Mountains

They may not be the mightiest mountains in the world but the ranges of the Peninsula are nonetheless spectacular. This is partly because they rise without preamble from flat coastal plains.

The Peninsula has two main mountain ranges. In western Arabia, the Hejaz range runs the length of Saudi Arabia's west coast, gener-

---

DESERT YES – DESERTED NO

Visiting any wilderness area is a responsibility and no more so than in a desert, where the slightest interference with the environment can wreak havoc with fragile ecosystems. The rocky plains of the interior may seem like an expanse of nothing, but that is not the case. Red markers along a road, improbable as they may seem on a cloudless summer day, indicate the height of water possible during a flash flood. A month or so later, a flush of tapering grasses marks the spot, temporary home to wasp oil beetles, elevated stalkers and myriad other life forms.

Car tracks scar a rock desert forever, crushing plants and insects not immediately apparent from the driver's seat. Rubbish doesn't biodegrade as it would in a tropical or temperate climate. The flower unwittingly picked in its moment of glory may miss its first and only opportunity for propagation in seven years of drought.

With a bit of common sense, however, and taking care to stick to existing tracks, it's possible to enjoy the desert without damaging the unseen communities it harbours. It also pays to turn off the engine and just sit. At dusk, dramas unfold: a fennec fox chases a hedgehog, a wild dog trots out of the wadi without seeing the snake slithering in the other direction, tightly closed leaves relax in the brief respite of evening and a dung beetle rolls its reward homewards.

ON THE WING IN ARABIA

The Peninsula is an ornithologist's dream, as it is positioned on migration routes between Asia, Europe and Africa. The Gulf is a particularly attractive stopover and, in Dubai alone, there are annually recorded sightings of over 400 different species. Similarly, Muscat in Oman is dubbed 'Eagle capital of the world' on account of the large numbers of raptors that can be spotted during the annual migration in November. The Hawar Islands (Bahrain) and Suqutra Island (Yemen) are important indigenous breeding grounds. The houbara bustard, a sort of desert-camouflaged crane, still roams areas of the interior despite being hunted to near extinction.

For those with a casual interest in birds, flamingos, spoonbills, kingfishers, hoopoe, cormorants, herons, green parrots and Indian rollers are some of the more colourful and characterful birds that grace the desert and towns of Arabia.

Several organisations are helpful in learning more about Peninsula birds and their haunts: **Oman Bird Records Committee** (PO Box 246, Muscat); **UAE Emirates Bird Records Committee** (☎ 9714-472 277; fax 9714-472 276; PO Box 50394, Dubai); **Yemen Ornithological Society** (☎ 01-207 059; cyos@y.net.ye; San'a).

ally increasing in height as it moves southwards. The term 'mountain' may seem a misnomer for much of the range. Saudi's landmass looks like a series of half-toppled books, with flat plains ending in dramatic escarpments that give way to the next plain. The last escarpment drops dramatically to the sea. If you follow the baboons over the escarpment rim, from the cool, misty, green reaches of Abha to Jizan on the humid, baking plains of the Tihama, the effect of this range is immediately felt. The settlers of the fertile mountains in their stone dwellings live such a different life to the goat herders in their mud houses on the plains, they may as well belong to different countries.

The Haraz Mountains of Yemen are home to Jabal an-Nabi Shu'ayb (3660m), the highest peak on the Peninsula. Forming part of the Rift Valley, the landmass of Yemen is predominantly mountainous, commonly rising 2000m or more and making farming a challenge. To compensate, Yemeni farmers cut elaborate terraces up the hillside to keep soil from washing away. These are shored up by stones and the maintenance of the terrace walls is a constant concern now that younger generations head for town for easier work than farming.

Arabia's other principal mountain range is found in the east of the Peninsula. Here, Oman's Hajar Mountains protect the communities around the Gulf of Oman from the encroachment of deserts from the interior. Terracing similar to that of Yemen can be seen on Jebel Akhdar and on pocket-handkerchief scraps of land in the Mussandam Peninsula. The southern mountains of Oman, in the hills of Dhofar, catch the edge of the monsoon from India. Light rains bring the otherwise arid hills to life during the summer when most of the rest of the Peninsula is aching under the heat.

This is where the elusive leopard, one of Arabia's most magnificent animals, stalks. It's the largest but not the only predatory mammal of the Peninsula: caracal, striped hyena and sand cat are all resident (though in small and diminishing numbers) in the mountains and wadis, preying on rodents. In Oman, the many wolf-traps dotting the Hajar Mountains (see p233) are still sometimes used if a wolf harasses herds.

The mountains are the best (though far from the only) place to see wild flowers. After rains they bloom in abundance. In the wadis there are delights like pink-flowering oleander and tall stands of Sodom's apples; on the mountainsides there's juniper, wild olive, lavenders and many plants with medicinal properties.

Peninsula species have adapted to the demands of desert life. The sand cat, sand fox and desert hare have large ears, giving a large surface area from which to release heat, and tufts of hair on their paws that enable them to walk on blistering desert floors.

Handbook of Arabian Medicinal Plants and *Vegetation of the Arabian Peninsula*, both by SA Ghazanfar, are good, illustrated guides to their subjects.

Seas

Remote and isolated Suqutra Island (p502) in Yemen, is particularly interesting botanically with 300 endemic species.

The Peninsula is bordered by three distinct seas, each of which has its own character.

The Red Sea, with its magnificent underwater wonderland, is mostly calm, and its shores flat and sandy. It teems with a thousand species of fish. Grouper and wrasse, parrotfish and snapper nose round the colourful gardens of coral, sea cucumbers and sponge, while shark and barracuda swim beyond the shallows, only venturing into the reefs to feed or breed.

The Arabian Sea, home to dolphins and whales and five species of turtle, many of which nest along the eastern Arabian shore, has a split personality. Calm like a pussy cat for much of the year, it rages like a tiger in the *khareef* (summer monsoon), casting up the weird and wonderful on some of the most magnificent, pristine, uninterrupted beaches in the world. Rimmed by cliffs for much of its length, this sea is punctuated with fishing villages that continue a way of life little changed in centuries, supported by boiling seas of sardine and tuna.

Atlas of the Breeding Birds of Arabia, by Michael C Jennings, gives comprehensive details on each of the 268 breeding species, plus general ornithological and conservation information.

The Gulf is a different kettle of fish. Flat, calm, so smooth at times it looks solid like a piece of shiny coal, it gives onto the shore so gently that fishermen can be seen standing only waist-deep, a kilometre from the shore. With lagoons decorated with mangroves this is a heron's delight. It's also a developer's delight: much of the rim of the Gulf has been paved over or 'reclaimed' for the improbable new cities at its edge.

TELLING YOUR CONES FROM YOUR COWRIES

Walk on any beach in the Peninsula and it doesn't take long before you start noticing that it is strewn with a remarkably wide variety of shells. Over a thousand species of mollusc occur off the east coast alone, several hundred of which are virtually microscopic. Learning how to identify them may seem a bewildering task and tackling a shell guide disappointingly complex, but even a rudimentary knowledge of a few major families helps to enhance the enjoyment of beachcombing.

The first feature to look out for is the 'segmentation' – does the shell consist of one part (like a snail) or does it have two parts hinged in the middle? The former is known as a 'gastropod' and the latter is known, predictably, as a 'bivalve'.

Some major families within the gastropods include murex, which have an assortment of spines and protrusions; cones, which are conical in shape and gorgeous in colour and pattern; cowries, which are hump-backed, glossy-coated beauties, and top shells which have a variety of flattened or elongated whirls on a flat base. It's hard to generalise but gastropods are often found on rocky shores, thrown up onto the dry tide-line.

Some major families within the bivalves include ark shells with their long straight hinges; outrageously colourful oysters with unequal halves pinched together or fused onto a neighbouring shell; fan shells like those used to edge a cottage garden, and heart shells that, in profile, live up to their name. Many bivalves live in sand where you'll find them burrowing as you walk on the low tide-line, or else opened up and winkled out by gulls.

Shells are localised and seasonal so there are no guarantees. The following, however, are fairly easy to see: look for the architectonic whorls of wentletraps in the muddy banks of the western Gulf; the fragile, crumbly shells of oysters, upon whose nacreous mother-of-pearl interiors whole nations relied, off the coast of Bahrain; sun-bleached ark shells on the sandy coasts of eastern UAE; Venus clams popping seductively out of the sand at dusk in northern Oman; and drifts of tiny pink top shells, tinging the beaches of southern Oman.

It's very tempting to form a collection but remember that collecting live molluscs is illegal and some shells are toxic and dangerous to handle (especially some of the cones). In addition, you may assemble your collection around the tent at night only to find they've walked off by the morning: hermit crabs are very quick to make a home of a stray gastropod.

No-one has told that yet to the molluscs, whose gorgeous shells keep rolling up the tide-line.

NATIONAL PARKS & OTHER PROTECTED AREAS

The idea of setting aside areas for wildlife runs contrary to the nature of traditional life on the Peninsula which was, and to some extent still is, all about maintaining a balance with nature, rather than walling it off. The Bedu flew their hunting falcons only between certain times of the year and moved their camels on to allow pasture to regrow. Fishermen selected only what they wanted from a seasonal catch, and threw the rest back. Goat and sheep herders of the mountains moved up and down the hillside at certain times of the year to allow for regrowth. Farmers let lands lie fallow so as not to exhaust the soil.

Modern practices, including settlement (of nomadic tribes), sport hunting, trawler fishing and the use of pesticides in modern farming, have had such an impact on the natural environment over the past 50 years, however, that all governments in the region have recognised the need to actively protect the fragile ecosystems of their countries. This has resulted in a rather spasmodic setting up of protected areas (less than 10% of regional landmass) but, with tourism on the increase, there is a strong incentive now to do more and many fine initiatives are in place.

Most countries have established conservation schemes. Five per cent of the Emirate of Dubai is a protected area, thanks to the example set by the late Sheikh Zayed, posthumously named 'Champion of the Earth' by the UN Environment Programme (UNEP) in 2005 (see p381). Saudi Arabia's Asir National Park (p343) is the largest on the Peninsula, comprising 450,000 hectares of Red Sea coast, escarpment and desert. In addition, Saudi authorities have designated 13 wildlife reserves (which amount to over 500,000 hectares) as part of a plan for more than 100 protected areas. Suqutra in Yemen has recently become a Unesco biosphere reserve and there are plans to designate the forests around Hawf (p511) and the Bura'a Forest in the Tihama into national parks. The Hawar Islands, home to epic colonies of cormorants and other migrant birds, are protected by the Bahrain government (see p136).

Although it has no national parks as such, Oman has an enviable record with regard to protection of the environment – a subject in which the sultan has a passionate interest. His efforts have repeatedly been acknowledged by the International Union for the Conservation of Nature (see p191). Sanctuaries for oryx (see p246), the internationally important turtle nesting grounds of Ras al-Jinz (see p221) and the leopard sanctuary (see p253) provide protection for these endangered species.

ENVIRONMENTAL ISSUES

The major concern for all Peninsula countries, particularly those of the Gulf, is water – or rather the lack of it. Good rains in 2007 brought relief to an area that has suffered drought for five years, but not enough fell to make much difference to the depleted water table. Saudi Arabia will run out of ground water long before it runs out of oil. Bahrain's freshwater underground springs have already dried up, leaving the country relying on expensive desalinated water. Yemen's ground-water levels have in recent years dropped dramatically, due to use of pumps for irrigation. Higher demand for residential use is another factor forcing countries to rethink ways of managing water. Modernisation of irrigation systems appears to be the way forward although public awareness has a role to play too. At present, it would be unthinkable to impose a hose-pipe ban

Breeding Centre for Endangered Arabian Wildlife at www .breedingcentresharjah .com is a site dedicated to programmes preserving the endangered species of the Peninsula.

A multinational initiative to tag tuna in the Arabian Sea was launched in 2007 in response to concerns about over fishing. So far 120,000 tuna have been tagged in a project that hopes to assess the stocks.

To make the most of the Arabian Peninsula's extensive coastlines, pick up the handy *Collectable Eastern Arabian Seashells* by Donald Bosch, or the magnificent definitive guide *Seashells of Eastern Arabia,* which he co-authored.

GO LIGHT ON THE LITTER

There's a wonderful tale in *The Thousand and One Nights* that describes the inadvertent chain of devastation caused by a merchant spitting out his date pip and unknowingly blinding the son of a genie. It may not be immediately apparent to a visitor watching pink and blue plastic bags sailing in the breeze that Peninsula authorities are making concerted efforts to clean up the countryside. It's immensely difficult not to add to the rubbish, especially when local attitude still maintains that every soft-drink can thrown on the ground represents one more job for the needy. Attitudes are beginning to change, however, thanks in part to educational schemes that target children and the adoption of Environment Days in Oman, UAE and Bahrain. 'Bag it' and 'out it' is a pretty good maxim as, hardy as it seems, the desert has a surprisingly fragile ecosystem that once damaged is as difficult as a genie's son's eye to mend.

(such as marks most summers in rainy Britain) on municipal and private gardens as flowering borders are considered the ultimate symbol of a modern, civilised lifestyle.

That said, mostly gone are the days when you could cross parts of Saudi and see great green wealds dotted across the desert. There was much to regret in the attempt to make the desert bloom: while Saudi became an exporter of grain, it used up precious mineral deposits and lowered the water table, and to no great useful purpose – the country can easily afford to import grain at the moment; there may be times to come when it cannot, and many experts are of the opinion it's better to retain precious resources for an emergency.

In a region where oil is the major industry, there is always a concern about spillage and leakage, and the illegal dumping of oil from offshore tankers is a constant irritation to the countries of the Gulf. The oil spillage following the Gulf War (see p154), however, mercifully did not result in the environmental catastrophe predicted and is now, thanks to international rescue efforts, completely cleaned up.

Two other issues pose an environmental threat. As one of the Peninsula's fastest-growing industries, tourism is becoming a major environmental issue – as seen at the turtle beaches of Ras al-Jinz (see p191), where many tourists show a dismal lack of respect for both the turtles and their environment. The other issue is rubbish: indeed, for several decades the Arabian Peninsula has been affected by the scourge of the plastic bag. Bags are unceremoniously dumped out of car windows or discarded at picnic sites and can be seen drifting across the desert, tangled in trees or floating in the sea. Many Peninsula Arabs don't feel it is their responsibility to 'bag it and bin it' – that would be stealing the job, so the argument goes, of the road cleaner. You can see these individuals on a scooter or even walking in the middle of summer with a dust pan and brush and a black bin liner, 100km from the nearest village. The idea that Arabs have inherited the throw-away culture from the Bedu and can't distinguish between organic and non-biodegradable is often cited but lacks credibility. As the aged and illiterate will delight in telling you, an orange peel, let alone a coke can, does not decompose in a hurry in the dry heat of the Peninsula.

The Arab response to litter, like the Arab response to conservation in general, probably has more to do with a lack of interest in the great outdoors for its own sake. But times are changing, and school trips to wild places may just be the answer.

See Responsible Travel (p24) for advice on how travellers can minimise their effect on the environment.

The Gulf War and the Environment, edited by Farouk El-Baz and RM Makharita, is a provoking analysis of the long-term environmental consequences of the Gulf War: thankfully, the recuperative powers of nature have exceeded expectation.

According to an article in a British newspaper in 2007, the average person uses 167 plastic bags a year. Plastic bag usage in the Arabian Peninsula cannot be far behind, a fact that has prompted Friends of the Earth Middle East to run a 'Say No to Plastic Bags' campaign. For more information, see www.foeme.org/projects.

Bahrain بحرين

Bahrain is defined by its relationship with water. Take the country's name: 'Two Seas' in Arabic, the focus is not the island's minimal landmass, but the water that laps its shores. So shallow is the water lapping Bahrain's coastline that the inhabitants regularly 'reclaim' pieces of land, filling in the gaps between sand bars, as if winning back lost territory. The new Bahrain Financial Harbour of Manama is currently rising like Neptune from such reclaimed land, and its proud buildings, such as the Dual Towers, appear to be holding back the sea.

Of course land reclamation in the Gulf has become the fashion. Dubai and Abu Dhabi, Doha and Muscat all have ambitious projects involving a tamed sea in a human landscape. Only Bahrain, however, can claim a truly integral connection between the two: the sweet-water springs that bubble off-shore helped bring about 4000 years of settlement, the layers of which are exposed in rich archaeological sites around the island. The springs also encouraged the most lustrous of pearls – the trade in which helped build the island's early fortunes.

Like an oyster, Bahrain's rough exterior takes some prising open, but it is worth the effort. From the excellent National Museum in Manama and the traditional houses of Muharraq to the extraordinary burial mounds at Sar, there are many fine sites to visit. For more modern pearls, there's the spectacular Bahrain World Trade Centre, King Fahd Causeway and the new islands project at the southern tip. Presumably the engineers have factored in the projected effects of global warming or the sea may yet have the last laugh.

FAST FACTS

- **Official name** Kingdom of Bahrain
- **Capital** Manama
- **Area** 706 sq km
- **Population** 723,000
- **Country code** ☎ 973
- **Head of State** King Hamad bin Isa al-Khalifa
- **Annual number of tourists** 3.5 million
- **Stereotypes** The 'pleasure dome' of the Gulf for regional visitors
- **Surprises** Five percent of Bahrain's land-mass is occupied by burial tombs

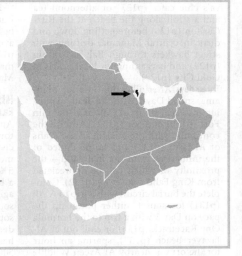

HIGHLIGHTS

- **Bahrain National Museum** (p122) Open the door on ancient Dilmun, with its legacy of burial chambers honeycombing the island.
- **Qala'at al-Bahrain** (p130) Take an interesting 16th-century view of the sea from the battlements of Bahrain Fort, bequeathed by the Portuguese.
- **Beit Sheikh Isa bin Ali** (p135) Catch the whisper of a breeze under the wind towers of Muharraq's 19th-century residences.
- **Formula One Racetrack** (p133) Sample life in the fast lane in a behind-the-scenes tour at Bahrain's 21st-century racetrack.
- **Al-Areen Wildlife Park & Reserve** (p133) Experience the timelessness of Bahrain's desert landscape and some of its beautiful inhabitants.

ITINERARIES

- **Bahrain stopover** Examine snapshots of the ancient and modern in Bahrain National Museum (p122) before wandering around the real thing in the wind-tower residences and post-modern alleyways of neighbouring Muharraq (p134). Share communal space with Islam at the giant Al-Fatih Mosque (p123) and complement the visit with manuscript-viewing at Beit al-Quran (p122). Pause for matters more corporal at one of Adliya's chic cafés (p127) or afternoon tea and a stroll along the beach at the Ritz-Carlton (p126) before getting down and dirty in central Manama, drifting with street hawkers through Bab al-Bahrain (p122) and bargaining for local pearls in Gold City (p129).
- **Three days** After allowing time for Manama, spend Day 2 with the dead, exploring the excavations at Qala'at al-Bahrain Fort (p130) and Sar (p132). Admire the continuity with the ancient in the crafts of Al-Jasra (p132) and be reminded of the influences from the mainland – the proximity of which can be appreciated from King Fahd Causeway (p132). Complete the burial circuit with a trip to A'Ali (p131) for sunset. Either pump up the pace on Day 3 with a trip to the Formula One Racetrack (p133) or chill out at Al-Jazayer beach (p133), sparing an hour for the oryx at nearby Al-Areen Wildlife Park & Reserve (p133).

- **For expats** For those wanting to escape the high life of Manama, cut across the desert to the Oil Museum (p134) to see what the city's wealth is founded upon and visit the nearby Tree of Life (p133) that rests on even sparser foundations. If island fever sets in, dive off the edge with a nose-peg and knife, and collect pearls with one of the city's diving operations (p124). For something altogether less painful, take a weekend package to the Hawar Islands (p136) for a spot of bird-watching and ponder what a tidal rise of two inches might do to the islands' waistlines.

CLIMATE & WHEN TO GO

Naturally enough, tourist brochures warn visitors away from the intensely hot summer months (early June to mid-September), when the sea is flat and vaporous, the cold tap runs hot and even the grass is too peppery to walk on. Yet, in many ways, this is the most character-full time of the year – when you realise the importance of a wind tower or a well in the desert, shade from the Tree of Life or a headscarf to keep out the hot, dry winds of a dust storm. Even the humble cardigan in the over-air-conditioned malls takes on a new meaning when it is heading up to 50°C in the car park outside.

If braving the most extreme that heat and humidity can muster doesn't appeal, the best time to visit is November to March, avoiding Ramadan and Eid holidays (see p139), when an influx of Saudi tourists can make it hard to find a room. See p530 for a Manama climate chart.

HISTORY
Early Civilisation

Anyone with the mildest interest in history cannot help but be curious about the civilisation that left behind 85,000 burial mounds that lump, curdle and honeycomb 5% of the island's landmass. Standing atop a burial mound at A'Ali, it is easy to imagine that the people responsible for such sophisticated care of their dead were equally sophisticated in matters of life. And, indeed, such was the case. Although Bahrain has a Stone-Age history that dates back to 5000 BC, and evidence of settlement from 10,000 BC, it has recently been confirmed

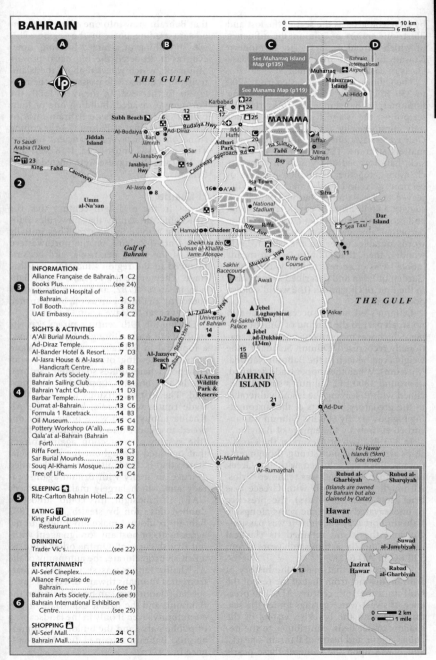

BAHRAIN

0 — 10 km
0 — 6 miles

THE GULF

See Muharraq Island Map (p135)

Bahrain International Airport

See Manama Map (p119)

Muharraq
Muharraq Island
Al-Hidd

MANAMA

Karbabad
22
17
24
25

Subh Beach
6
12

Al-Budaiya
Bani Jamrah
Ad-Diraz
9
Budaiya Hwy
Jidd Haffs
20

Adhari Park

Isa Sulman Hwy
4
Juffair
Mina Sulman
Tubli Bay

Jiddah Island

To Saudi Arabia (12km)
23

King Fahd Causeway

Al-Janabiya
Janabiya Hwy
3
Sar
19
Al-Jasra
8

Umm al-Na'san

A'Ali
16
Isa Town
1
National Stadium
Sitra

Dar Island

Gulf of Bahrain

5
Hamad
Ghadeer Tours
Riffa Ave
Riffa
18
Riffa Golf Course
Sea Taxi

Sheikh Isa bin Sulman al-Khalifa Jame Mosque
Sakhir Racecourse
Muaskar Hwy

7
11

Awali

THE GULF

Al-Zallaq
Al-Zallaq
University of Bahrain
14
As-Sakhir Palace
Jebel Lughaybirat (83m)
Askar

Jebel ad-Dukhan (134m)

Al-Jazayer Beach
15

Al-Areen Wildlife Park & Reserve
BAHRAIN ISLAND

10

21
Ad-Dur

To Hawar Islands (5km) (see inset)

Al-Mamtalah

Ar-Rumaythah

Rubud al-Gharbiyah
(Islands are owned by Bahrain but also claimed by Qatar)
Rubud al-Sharqiyah

Hawar Islands

Suwad al-Janubiyah

Jazirat Hawar
Rabad al-Gharbiyah

0 — 2 km
0 — 1 mile

by archaeologists as the seat of the lost and illustrious empire of Dilmun, the influence of which spread as far north as modern Kuwait and as far inland as the Al-Hasa Oasis in eastern Saudi Arabia.

The Dilmun civilisation lasted from 3200 to 330 BC, during which time, according to Sumerian, Babylonian and Assyrian inscriptions, the island's residents were not only commercially active, plying the busy Gulf waterways, but were also attentive to matters at home. The proper burial of the sick, handicapped and young in elaborate chambers, together with their chattels of ceramic, glass and beads (meticulously displayed at the Bahrain National Museum), suggest a civilisation of considerable social and economic development, assisted by the perpetual abundance of 'sweet', in other words potable, then, water on the island. Little wonder, then, that Dilmun (which means 'noble') was often referred to as the fabled Garden of Eden and described as 'paradise' in the Epic of Gilgamesh (the world's oldest poetic saga).

Dilmun's economic success was due in no small part to the trading of Omani copper, which was measured using the internationally recognised 'Dilmun Standard' (the weights can be seen in the Bahrain National Museum). When the copper trade declined, in around 1800 BC, Dilmun's strength declined with it, leaving the island vulnerable to the predatory interests of the surrounding big powers. By 600 BC Dilmun was absorbed entirely by the empire of Babylon.

In 323 BC, two of Alexander the Great's ships arrived, and such strong, though temporary, links were forged with the Greek empire that the island was renamed Tylos. Although the flirtation with Greece was brief (less than 100 years), the presence of unexcavated Hellenistic ruins alongside Bahrain Fort may yet show it was passionate, and the island retained its classical name for nearly a thousand years (from 330 BC to AD 622).

There is little that makes the history of Bahrain distinct from that of the rest of the Gulf until the 16th century AD. The presence of sweet-water springs under the sea, mingling with the brackish waters of the shallow oyster beds, contributes to the peculiar colour and lustre of Bahrain's pearls, and it was upon the value of these pearls that Bahrain grew into one of the most important trading posts in the region. This was something of a mixed blessing, however, as it attracted the big naval powers of Europe, which wheeled about the island trying to establish safe passage for their interests further east. In the early 1500s the Portuguese invaded, building one of their typical sea-facing forts on Bahrain's northern shore (Qala'at al-Bahrain) – the coping stone on seven layers of ancient history. Their rule was short-lived, however, and by 1602 the Portuguese were ousted by the Persians.

Al-Khalifa

It was in the mid-18th century that the Al-Khalifa, the family that now rules Bahrain, first arrived in the area. They initially settled at Al-Zubara, on the northwestern edge of the Qatar peninsula, and became involved in the region's lucrative pearling trade. They drove the Persians out of Bahrain in about 1782, and were themselves routed by an Omani invasion, but returned in 1820 never to leave again.

During the 19th century, piracy was rife in the Gulf and, although it never gained a foothold in Bahrain as such, the island gained something of a reputation as an entrepôt, where pirates sold their captured goods and bought supplies for the next raid. The British, anxious to secure their trade routes with India, brought the Al-Khalifa family, who were professedly opposed to piracy, into the 'Trucial system' (the system of protection against piracy that operated throughout the old Trucial States; that is, the Gulf states which signed a 'truce' or treaty with Britain against piracy and which largely make up today's UAE). In hindsight, this could almost be dubbed 'invasion by stealth', as by 1882 Bahrain could not make any international agreements or host any foreign agent without British consent. On the other hand, as a British protectorate, the autonomy of the Al-Khalifa family was secure and threats from the Ottomans thwarted. To this day, a special relationship can be felt between the Bahrainis and the sizable expatriate British community, even if only in the landscaping of public parks and the building of roundabouts. Bahrain regained full independence in 1971.

Black Gold

In the middle of the desert, roughly in the middle of the island, stands a small museum sporting marble pillars and a classical architrave, wholly unbefitting of the landscape of nodding donkeys in the vicinity. But the museum has a right to certain pretensions of grandeur; it marks the spot where, in 1932, the Arab world struck gold – black gold, that is – and with it, the entire balance of power in the world was transformed forever. The first well is in the museum grounds, perhaps no longer pumping oil, but with polished pipes and cocks, worthy of the momentousness of its role in modern history. The discovery of oil could not have come at a better time for Bahrain as it roughly coincided with the collapse of the world pearl market, upon which the island's economy had traditionally been based. Skyrocketing oil revenues allowed the country, under the stewardship of the Al-Khalifa family, to steer a course of rapid modernisation that was a beacon for other countries in the region to follow well into the 1970s and '80s.

When the oil began to run out, so did the fortunes of the government, and in the last decade of the 20th century the country was shocked by sporadic waves of unrest. The troubles began in 1994 when riots erupted after the emir refused to accept a large petition calling for greater democracy. There was more unrest in April 1995, and again in the spring of 1996, when bombs exploded at both the Diplomat and Meridien (now the Ritz-Carlton Bahrain) hotels.

Recent History

On 6 March 1999 Sheikh Isa bin Sulman al-Khalifa died and was replaced by his son, Sheikh Hamad bin Isa al-Khalifa. Upon his accession, Sheikh Hamad pledged to introduce a fully elected parliament, hold municipal elections and set up a constitutional monarchy. He also released political prisoners, allowed exiles to return and declared all nationals equal. As a result, the violence of the previous years came to a timely halt. In 2001 a national charter for constitutional reforms was endorsed by the country's first ever national referendum and a year later, on 14 February, Bahrain was declared a constitutional monarchy and Sheikh Hamad its king. Under this new charter, both men and women are eligible to vote and stand for office, and a system of financial controls and administration has been created to ensure transparency in the government's finances. Despite rumours of a new design, the familiar red-and-white flag of Bahrain still flutters unmolested along the main thoroughfares of the country's tree-lined highways – a symbol of a nation contentedly taking its place as an offshore banking centre and commercial hub in the international environment of the 21st century.

GOVERNMENT & POLITICS

Bahrain is a constitutional monarchy with an independent legal and judiciary system and a strong framework of commercial laws. The country is ruled by His Majesty, the popular King Sheikh Hamad bin Isa al-Khalifa, and assisted by Prime Minister Sheikh Khalifa bin Sulman al-Khalifa, together with the Shura Council, a 30-member consultative body active since 1993. Sheikh Sulman bin Hamad al-Khalifa is the crown prince and Commander-in-Chief of the Bahrain Defence Force. Bahrain observes a strict rule of primogeniture within the royal family, whereby the eldest son is the sole heir. Bahrain is a member of the United Nations, the Arab League and the Gulf Co-operation Council (GCC).

ECONOMY

Recognising the pitfalls of relying on income from oil revenues alone, the government took early steps to diversify the economy and Bahrain is now an important offshore banking centre, a growing industrial and commercial hub, and a major destination for international investment. Heavy industry is evident along the eastern seaboard of the island, and the interior is crisscrossed by gas and oil pipelines. International tourism was adversely affected by the onset of hostilities in Iraq although regional tourism, from Saudi Arabia in particular, continued unabated. The inauguration of the Grand Prix in April 2004 has helped to win back international visitors and has attracted considerable overseas investment to the island. Large-scale projects, like the new Bahrain Financial Harbour in Manama and the resort complex on the southern tip of the island, are visible expressions of the island's continuing prosperity.

BAHRAIN'S MEGA PROJECTS

Visitors to Bahrain can't help but notice that the island is in the grip of a building frenzy. Multi-billion dollar projects are sparking a new gold rush that is attracting investors in epic proportions. Unlike previous economic miracles (focused previously on pearls and recently on oil), however, the current boom is based on a wing and a prayer – how else to describe no less than 20 mega projects of 'sky-kissing towers, luxurious resorts, green golf clubs and massive man-made island developments' all proceeding at the same time in an island the size of postage stamp? Still, Bahrain successfully pulled off the first Formula One circuit in the region, so it doesn't pay to be too cynical. High-profile developments to watch are the Al-Areen complex (p309); Health Island with specialist hospitals and hotels; Durrat al-Bahrain, a city to be built on a 30 million sq foot horseshoe of man-made islands at the southern tip of the country, complete with more canals than Glasgow and Michael Jackson in residence; and Bahrain World Trade Centre with twin 50-storey towers, partially sustained by wind turbines.

PEOPLE
The National Psyche
Bahrain is so close to the mainland it is joined by a causeway to Saudi Arabia, and preparations are continuing for a second causeway to link the island to Qatar as well (see boxed text, p297). Bahrain is nonetheless an island, and there is something of an island mentality to be felt in Manama and microcosmically in Muharraq, too. It is difficult to pinpoint the differences between Bahrainis and other *jizari* (people of the Gulf) inhabitants, but perhaps it lies somewhere in the Bahraini identification with the wider world, a feeling engendered by the centuries of international trade and, in more recent times, by the earliest discovery of oil in the region. This latter fact enabled Bahrain to engage in an international dialogue well before its neighbours, and as such helped in developing a sense of greater affinity with Western nations, as well as a tolerance and even acceptance of many (and some would argue not altogether the best) Western practices. Even a one-time visitor cannot fail to notice the many bars serving alcohol, the largely unchecked social freedoms and the general party atmosphere that engages the streets of Manama.

Naturally enough, a greater degree of conservatism prevails outside the capital area, but this is still not the land of the censorious: on the far-flung Al-Jazayer Beach, there is a notice that asks the beachgoer to be quiet out of respect for visitors wishing to escape the noise of the city. In a beach hut, not 5 metres away and with the door shut against the wind, the fully amplified, Afro-Arabic beat of an ad-hoc jam session

bulges against the surrounding austerity of the desert. It speaks volumes.

Lifestyle
It's the prerogative of the inhabitants of busy seaports to select from the 'customs and manners' that wash up on the shore. Watching young Bahraini men on the nightclub floor in one of Manama's central hotels, for example, sporting a crisp white *thobe* (floor-length shirt-dress) or the international uniform of jeans and leather jacket, a visitor could be forgiven for thinking that the young have sold out to the West. These same young men, however, would probably have been to the barber, aged three to six years old, one auspicious Monday, Thursday or Friday in spring, and come out clutching their coins – and loins. These same young men will no doubt send their sons on similar rituals of circumcision and maturation, because beneath the urbane exterior, the sweet waters of the island run deep.

As for Bahraini women, while Islam requires surrender to the will of God, it does not imply surrender to the will of man. Bahraini women take their place in many walks of public life, and, as such, 'surrender' is the last word that comes to mind. Only an outsider considers it contradictory that women who choose to cover their hair in the presence of men should at the same time give them instructions on all matters of life, cardinal and profane.

Bahraini people have enjoyed the spoils of oil for over half a century and it's tempting to think that wealth has created a nation of idlers – you won't see many Bahrainis engaged in manual labour, for example, nor waiting on tables. A modern, enterprising, wealthy nation isn't built on money alone, however, and the burgeoning financial sector is proof that the locals have chosen to invest their energies and creativity in their traditional trading strengths while importing labour for the jobs they no longer need to do themselves.

As for most Arab nationals, 'home is where the heart is' for Bahrainis. Despite the imperatives of international business, time with the family is cherished, and the sense of home is extended to the Bahraini community at large through many public-funded amenities and educational opportunities.

Population

About 720,000 people live in Bahrain; half of these are under 25 years old, a factor that will continue to fuel the urbanisation of the island in years to come. Despite the urban sprawl, the population is still mostly concentrated in the northern third of Bahrain Island and in the southern edge of Muharraq Island, although this may well change as more and more ambitious developments reach into open country. The indigenous Bahrainis are Arabs, though many are at least partially of Persian ancestry.

Multiculturalism

Behind Bab al-Bahrain, at the heart of Manama, there is little besides shop signs in Arabic to indicate that this is indeed part of Arabia. There are Indian and Pakistani shop owners, Filipino hotel workers and occasional groups of US servicemen. The same could be said of Al-Seef, where the manicured gardens and bars of the Ritz-Carlton Bahrain Hotel or the international chain stores of Al-Seef Mall, are peopled largely by Western expatriates.

Indeed, in a country where nearly 40% of residents (and 60% of the workforce) are non-Bahrainis or expatriates (Western expats comprise about 15% of the resident population), it is surprising to find that such a strong sense of local identity has survived the influx of migrant workers. This imbalance, however, while harmonious for the most part, has been a source of political agitation too. In 1997, for example, a series of arson attacks were carried out by unemployed local Bahrainis, angry that jobs were being taken by workers from Asia. While the government is now actively pursuing a policy favouring the indigenous workforce, tensions will continue to prevail as educated Bahrainis find it difficult to compete in sectors with entrenched (and often experienced and skilled) expatriate workforces.

In common with other Gulf nationals, and despite a free and excellent education system, many Bahrainis choose to study abroad, particularly in the USA and UK. They generally come back, however!

SPORT

Soccer (football) is the major sport played in Bahrain. Games are held at the immense National Stadium and at smaller grounds in the residential areas of Muharraq, Riffa and Isa Town – and on just about any vacant patch of level ground, including the interchanges along the highway to the Saudi Arabian causeway. Also popular among locals are volleyball, badminton, basketball, cricket and handball.

The horse is very close to the Bahraini heart, and the Equestrian & Horse Racing Club holds races every Friday between October and March at the **Sakhir Racecourse** (☎ 17 440 330) near Awali.

RELIGION

Most Bahrainis are Shiite Muslim, although a sizable minority, including the royal family, are Sunni. A good introduction to the often misunderstood tenets of Islam is provided through the *Discover Islam* series. These pamphlets, written in clear and concise English, are published in Bahrain and available free of charge from the visitors desk inside the Al-Fatih Mosque (p123).

ARTS
Traditional Arts & Crafts

There is something of a revival of interest in the artistic heritage of the country, and several cultural centres, such as the Craft Centre (p129) in central Manama, and workshops, such as Al-Jasra Handicraft Centre (p132), have been set up to encourage the continuation of skills such as weaving and pottery.

Pottery and ceramics are made in the village of A'Ali, while traditional weaving of brightly coloured, woollen carpets, wall hangings and cushions is carried out in the villages of Ad-Diraz and Bani Jamrah. In Karbabad, basket weaving with palm leaves is an old village speciality.

Exquisite gold and silver jewellery featuring tiny natural pearls (p129) is made in the workshops of Manama and sold in the gold souqs of the city.

The art of *tatrees* (traditional Bahraini embroidery) has been passed from one generation of Bahraini women to another. Particularly popular are *al-nagde* (intricately embroidered ceremonial gowns decorated with gold and silver threads, worn by women). Some areas of Muharraq Island are renowned for *tatrees*, and the industry is enjoying a revival.

All of these crafts can be seen in action at the craft centres mentioned above. If you go out to the villages, A'Ali in particular, you may get a glimpse of work in progress there too, though these crafts are generally carried out in cottage industries or cooperatives with people working from the privacy of their own inner courtyards.

Contemporary Arts

In addition to traditional activities, there's a vibrant contemporary arts scene in Bahrain. Exhibitions of local paintings regularly take place at the Bahrain National Museum, while small ad hoc displays in temporary spaces, such as in the foyers of large hotels, draw large local audiences. There are a few private galleries in the country, often showcasing the work of the owner. These include the Rashid al-Oraifi Museum (p136) in Muharraq and the Muharraqi Gallery in A'Ali, which features the surreal works of Abdullah al-Muharraqi.

The best way to find out what's going on where is to consult the listings in the English-language newspapers.

ENVIRONMENT
The Land

Most people think of Bahrain (706 sq km) as a single flat island with a couple of low escarpments in the middle of a stony desert and surrounded by a very shallow, calm sea. In fact, such is the description of Bahrain Island only, which, at 586 sq km, is the largest in an archipelago of about 33 islands, including the Hawar Islands, and a few specks of sand that disappear at high tide. The visitor may or may not have the

chance to visit the bird havens of Hawar, nor the little resort island of Dar, but the airport is situated on Muharraq Island and has many interesting sites. Both Muharraq and some other small islands are joined to Bahrain Island by causeways that are in themselves worth a look. When crossing any of the causeways, including the King Fahd Causeway which links Bahrain with the Saudi mainland, it is easy to see how the whole archipelago was once attached to the rest of the continent.

Wildlife

A plaque in the Bahrain National Museum, introducing a delightful diorama of Bahrain's wildlife, states that for one of the smallest countries in the world, Bahrain has a surprisingly diverse range of habitats; it then lists sea lavender and saltwort as occurring in three out of the five zones! Bahrain does have some noteworthy wildlife, however, including the Ethiopian hedgehog, Cape hare, various geckos and the endangered Rheem gazelle, which inhabits the dry and hot central depression.

ANIMALS

There's not much in the way of visible animals in Bahrain, except the odd appearance of the usual desert companions – foxes, hares and hedgehogs. A naturalist will have better luck with birds, particularly on the Hawar Islands, with their resident cormorant and flamingo populations, and plenty of winter migrants.

The casual visitor to Bahrain is most unlikely to see, at least in the wild, the Rheem gazelle, terrapin, sooty falcon, and the seafaring dugong, all of which appear on the endangered species list. Some of them can be seen, however, along with a beautiful herd of oryx, at Al-Areen Wildlife Park & Reserve (p133).

PLANTS

The deserts of Bahrain may look sparse, but they're a surprising source of healing. Various cardboard boxfuls of twigs turn up in the souq to be applied in poultices or pastes in a rich tradition of herbal medicine. Applying the sap of the al-Liban tree or inhaling incense is an apparent cure for measles; for a skin infection, there's rock salt or the bark of the *dawram* tree; or for jaundice there's *agool* soup made of boiled wild thorns. Herbal medicine is still widely practised and locals swear it is more effective than expensive 'modern' medicines.

Another useful plant is the endangered mangrove, which provides a rich habitat for a variety of birds and molluscs. In fact, mangrove is not so much the name of a plant as the name of a genus, the members of which share the characteristic of being anchored to the muddy, brackish waters of tropical coastlines by a scaffolding of aerial roots. The black mangrove, *Avicennia marina*, is the only species existing in Bahrain; it has suffered 40 years of habitat erosion and landfill in the Tubli Bay area near Manama.

The bay supports another unique ecosystem, that of the seagrass *Halodule uninervis*. Important for the dugong and a large number of migrating birds, this tough plant is remarkably resilient against extreme temperatures and high salinity.

National Parks

Located in the middle of Bahrain Island, Al-Areen Wildlife Park & Reserve (see p133) was set up to conserve natural habitats in order to support research projects in the field of wildlife protection and development. In common with most Gulf States, the 20th-century passion for hunting left the island virtually bereft of natural inheritance. At least at Al-Areen, visitors can see well-looked-after specimens of indigenous fauna, such as gazelles and bustards (large ground-living birds). The park also provides a free-roaming natural habitat for certain native Arabian species, including the endangered oryx. Al-Areen is usually a peaceful spot, despite the decision to build the Formula 1 Racetrack virtually next door. This will probably change, however, with the enormous new Al-Areen development that promises a 'desert spa' themed water park, luxury resort, and residential and retail complexes all overlooking the park. Billed as enhancing Bahrain's reputation as a 'friendly destination for family and health-oriented tourists', it seems a bizarre way to celebrate the island's last vestige of wilderness.

In addition to Al-Areen, there are two other protected areas in Bahrain: the mangroves at Ras Sanad (Tubli Bay) and the Hawar Islands. With a huge residential development project underway in one and oil exploration around the other, it's hard to see what is meant by 'protection'.

Environmental Issues

Bahrain has made a big effort in recent years to clean up its act environmentally, and the visitor will certainly appreciate the landscaping of roads with avenues of palms, beds of annuals for a splash of seasonal colour and the topiary of citrus hedges in Manama and along all major thoroughfares throughout the island. Nonetheless, the perennial Middle Eastern curse of the plastic bag is still prevalent beyond the city limits.

The main threats to the Bahraini environment take the form of unrestrained development; perpetual land reclamation; rampant industrialisation; an inordinate number of cars (about 200 per sq km); and pollution of the Gulf from oil leakages. In addition, little appears to have been done to curb emissions from heavy industry (such as the aluminium smelting plant) to the east of Bahrain Island.

During the standoff between Bahrain and Qatar over ownership of the Hawar Islands, the wildlife, which includes dugongs and turtles and many species of migratory bird, was left in peace. Immediately after the territorial dispute was resolved, however, Bahrain invited international oil companies to drill for oil. The impact of this is a source of great topical debate.

Despite the poor record of wildlife protection in the past, the government has taken a number of initiatives in the last decade to raise awareness of environmental issues.

FOOD & DRINK

Bahraini cuisine is pretty much the same as that of the other Gulf States (see p82). *Makbus* (rice and spices) with chicken, lamb or fish can usually be found on the menus at Arabic-style restaurants around town. Other local dishes, such as spicy bean soups, *nekheh, bajelah* and *loobah*, as well as very sweet desserts, like *akil* (cardamom cake), *rangena* (coconut cake), *khabees* (dates, dates and more dates) and *balaleet* (sweet vermicelli with cardamom), can all be sampled at various tented buffets organised by hotels during Ramadan.

BAHRAIN

> **WATER: TOO MUCH OF A GOOD THING**
>
> Since the installation of modern water-treatment techniques, the presence of doubled-over elderly people in the villages of Bahrain may have come to an end. The condition is associated with a fusion of bones, particularly of the spine, through a disease called 'fluorosis'. Fluorosis, which is also typified by a staining of the teeth, was common in Bahrain on account of there being double the normal levels of fluoride in the abundant natural spring water. Studies have revealed that many of the inhabitants of Bahrain's many burial chambers suffered from the same disease.

Beyond local fare, Bahrain has a huge variety of restaurants serving international cuisines. There are also plenty of fast-food outlets in shopping centres and along the main streets of Manama.

Anyone staying for a while may like to pick up the *Bahrain Hotel & Restaurant Guide* by Redhouse Publishing (BD1). This excellent booklet highlights the best of the 2000 or so restaurants throughout the country and is updated every year.

Nonalcoholic drinks include soft drinks, fruit juice and milk shakes. Tap water is now safe to drink though most people prefer to stick to bottled water (see box p82). Alcohol is widely available, but high tariffs help discourage a growing problem with alcoholism: a pint of beer costs upwards of BD1.600 and spirits start at BD1.500 a shot.

Modern cafés can be found throughout Manama, especially in the district of Adliya where some very chic venues offer excellent coffee, light bites and pastries. Any place called a 'coffeehouse' in all but the top-end hotels is usually a bar and intended for men only.

MANAMA منامة

pop 147,894

Manama means 'Sleeping Place', but with its central atmosphere, its late-night shopping, and its lively bars and nightclubs, it's hard to see when the city gets a chance to sleep. Manama is a night bird and people flock in on weekends for fine dining and an off-duty drink. For those who prefer an early start to a late night, however, the city is sleepy enough by day, and it's unlikely there'll be much of a queue for the excellent Bahrain National Museum.

HISTORY

Manama appears in Islamic chronicles as far back as 1345 AD but, in all probability, there were settlements on and around the best springs on the island for centuries.

Invaded by the Portuguese in 1521 and then by the Persians in 1602, Manama then passed into the hands of the Al-Khalifa, the current ruling family, in 1783. It became a free port in 1958 and the capital of independent Bahrain in 1971. With a third of Bahrain's population living in the city, modern Manama continues to grow at a cracking pace, thanks to oil revenues and a vibrant banking sector. Some new buildings, like the Bahrain World Trade Centre and the developments in the Bahrain Financial Harbour, all built on reclaimed land, are helping to bring the city into line with its more modern regional counterparts.

ORIENTATION

Visitors arriving by air touch down at the airport on Muharraq, a small island connected by two causeways to Bahrain Island. Manama occupies the top northeastern corner of Bahrain Island, bounded on two sides by corniches. The northeastern corniche is built on reclaimed land and is in danger of retreating inland as land is evermore tacked onto the city rim. Most of the tourist activity is sandwiched between Bahrain's famous Pearl Monument (nicknamed rather unkindly by expatriates as 'Ball's Up Corner') and the Sail Monument, close to the causeways. The main thoroughfare is Government Ave, punctuated by Bab al-Bahrain, a veritable hub of activity day and night, and the gateway to the streets and alleys that make up the souq. Most of the city's budget and midrange hotels are near this gateway, while top-end accommodation centres on the Diplomatic Area near the two causeways to Muharraq Island, extending into the suburbs. The new malls are also largely outside the city centre, especially around Al-Seef.

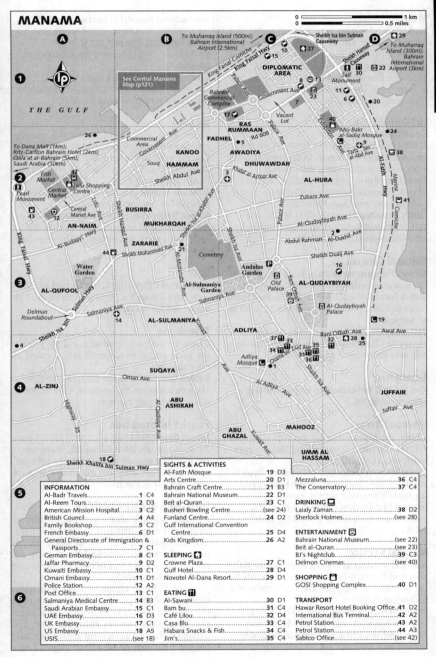

MANAMA

0 ————— 1 km
0 ————— 0.5 miles

Maps

For an informative city map, the *Bahrain Map & Pocket Guide* (BD1), published in cooperation with Tourism Affairs, Ministry of Information, is regularly updated. It is available free at the airport, or you can buy a copy from the tourist office and Bahrain National Museum.

INFORMATION
Bookshops

Al-Hilal Bookshops (Map p121; ☎ 17 224 860; Shera-ton Bahrain, Palace Ave) Branches located in many top-end hotels, modern shopping centres and in the souq.

Books Plus (Map p111; ☎ 17 582 263; Al-Seef Mall, off Sheikh Khalifa bin Sulman Hwy) Offers a wide range of books, including some Lonely Planet titles.

Family Bookshop (Map p119; ☎ 17 211 288; Bldg 1874, Sheikh Isa al-Khebir Ave) Stocks some attractive coffee-table books on the region.

Cultural Centres

Alliance Française de Bahrain (Map p111; ☎ 17 683 295; www.afbahrain.com; off 16th December Hwy, Isa)

British Council (Map p119; ☎ 17 261 555; www.british council.org/bahrain; Ahmed Mansour al-Ali Bldg, Sheikh Isa bin Sulman Hwy)

USIS (Map p119; ☎ 17 273 300; www.bahrain.us embassy.gov; US embassy, off Sheikh Khalifa bin Sulman Hwy) Has a library open to the public.

Emergency

Fire, Police & Ambulance The number to call in an emergency is ☎ 999.

Internet Access

There are many internet centres scattered around Manama including the conveniently situated two here:

Hawar Internet Centre (Map p121; Manama St; per hr 500 fils; ☼ 9am-1am) Centrally located alongside Gold City, this facility has voice chat with webcam.

Internet Plus Services Centre (Map p121; 1st fl, Batelco Commercial Centre, Government Ave; per hr 500 fils).

Medical Services

Medical treatment is easy to obtain in Bahrain and the standard of care is high. Medical services or supplies are available at the following facilities:

American Mission Hospital (Map p119; ☎ 17 253 447; www.amh.org.bh; Sheikh Isa al-Khebir Ave) Over 100 years old, this is the oldest and smallest hospital in Manama, but it is well equipped.

International Hospital of Bahrain (Map p111; ☎ 17 591 666; www.ihb.net; just off Budaiya Hwy)

Jaffar Pharmacy (Map p119; ☎ 17 291 039; Tarfa bin al-Abd Ave; ☼ 24 hr) Located near McDonald's, off Exhibition Rd.

Salmaniya Medical Centre (Map p119; ☎ 17 255 555; Salmaniya Ave) Emergency treatment is available for residents and expats at a nominal fee of BD3.

Money

There are a number of banks and money-changers on Government Ave between the central post office and the Delmon International Hotel. There are ATMs at most banks including HSBC.

American Express (Map p121; ABN-Amro Bank Bldg, Al-Furdah Ave) Exchanges currency.

No Noo Money Changer (Map p121; behind Bab al-Bahrain Ave) Don't be put off by the name; this hole-in-the-wall in central Manama keeps late but unspecified hours.

Post

Central Post Office (Map p121; Government Ave, op-posite Bab al-Bahrain Ave; ☼ 7am-7.30pm Sat-Thu) Poste restante facilities are available.

Telephone

There are telephone booths and payphones for local and international calls located all over the city.

Batelco Commercial Centre (Map p121; ☎ 17 881 111; www.batelco.com.bh; Government Ave) International calls can also be made from here.

Tourist Information

Tourist Department (Map p121; ☎ 17 231 375; www .bahraintourism.com; Bab al-Bahrain Bldg, Government Ave) A variety of brochures on Bahrain's tourist sights are available here. The souvenir shop sells a dusty collection of cards, books and wooden dhows.

DANGERS & ANNOYANCES

Bahrain is a safe and agreeable country to visit, with very little in the way of dangers and annoyances, with the possible exception of the taxi drivers and the slightly nefarious nature of some of the city hotels (see the boxed text, p125).

Sadly, Bahrain seems to deserve its reputation for sharp practice when it comes to the city taxi service in Manama and Muharraq. Countless visitors complain that taxi drivers refuse to switch on the meter, and heaven help anyone who hasn't agreed on a

CENTRAL MANAMA

0 — 200 m
0 — 0.1 miles

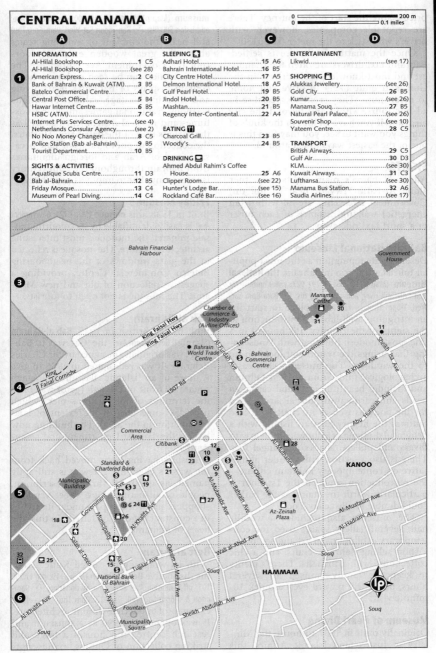

INFORMATION		
Al-Hilal Bookshop	**1**	C5
Al-Hilal Bookshop	(see 28)	
American Express	**2**	C4
Bank of Bahrain & Kuwait (ATM)	**3**	B5
Batelco Commercial Centre	**4**	C4
Central Post Office	**5**	B4
Hawar Internet Centre	**6**	B5
HSBC (ATM)	**7**	C4
Internet Plus Services Centre	(see 4)	
Netherlands Consular Agency	(see 2)	
No Noo Money Changer	**8**	C5
Police Station (Bab al-Bahrain)	**9**	B5
Tourist Department	**10**	B5

SIGHTS & ACTIVITIES		
Aquatique Scuba Centre	**11**	D3
Bab al-Bahrain	**12**	B5
Friday Mosque	**13**	C4
Museum of Pearl Diving	**14**	C4

SLEEPING		
Adhari Hotel	**15**	A6
Bahrain International Hotel	**16**	B5
City Centre Hotel	**17**	A5
Delmon International Hotel	**18**	A5
Gulf Pearl Hotel	**19**	B5
Jindol Hotel	**20**	B5
Mashtan	**21**	B5
Regency Inter-Continental	**22**	A4

EATING		
Charcoal Grill	**23**	B5
Woody's	**24**	B5

DRINKING		
Ahmed Abdul Rahim's Coffee		
House	**25**	A6
Clipper Room	(see 22)	
Hunter's Lodge Bar	(see 15)	
Rockland Café Bar	(see 16)	

ENTERTAINMENT		
Likwid	(see 17)	

SHOPPING		
Alukkas Jewellery	(see 26)	
Gold City	**26**	B5
Kumar	(see 26)	
Manama Souq	**27**	B5
Natural Pearl Palace	(see 26)	
Souvenir Shop	(see 10)	
Yateem Centre	**28**	C5

TRANSPORT		
British Airways	**29**	C5
Gulf Air	**30**	D3
KLM	(see 30)	
Kuwait Airways	**31**	C3
Lufthansa	(see 30)	
Manama Bus Station	**32**	A6
Saudia Airlines	(see 17)	

price before the start of the journey. There are reputable companies, however, with drivers who stick to the meter (see p130).

Once the matter of the fee is settled, Bahraini taxi drivers are often the friendliest and most knowledgeable drivers in the Gulf, and quite likely to drive you home to meet mum. They seem to specialise in ad hoc tours, within and beyond the city area, and if you have an idea of the kinds of things you want to see, you may find this is one of the easiest ways to get around.

SIGHTS

All of Manama's main sights are either along Al-Fatih Hwy or near (if not on) Government Ave. They are all within (an energetic) walking distance of each other or a short taxi ride away.

Bahrain National Museum

Deserving its reputation as the most popular tourist attraction in Bahrain, the **National Museum** (Map p119; ☎ 17 292 977; www.bnmuseum .com; Al-Fatih Hwy; admission 500 fils; ⏰ 8am-8pm Sat-Wed, 1-5pm Thu) is the best place to start for an intriguing, well-labelled introduction to the sights of the country. It's housed in a fine, post-modern building with landscaping that brings the waterfront location up to the windows. The museum showcases archaeological finds from ancient Dilmun and includes beautiful agate and carnelian beads and earthenware burial jars – used for the body as well as its chattels. It also outlines the history of pearl fishing with a delightful diorama of a dhow, complete with divers and pullers, sharks and angel fish. There is also a section with wonderful narrative on contemporary Bahraini culture – the reproduction souq on the 1st floor is particularly worth the stairs, as the barber could double for Sweeney Todd.

The museum also includes a wildlife hall, several gallery spaces used for contemporary exhibitions of art and sculpture, a shop selling Bahraini crafts, and a chic coffeehouse with armchairs. There's plenty to keep the family amused for several hours, but it will reward even a quick 10-minute visit.

Museum of Pearl Diving

Originally built in 1937 to house the Ministry of Justice and Islamic Affairs, this **museum** (Map p121; ☎ 17 210 600; Government Ave; admission 500 fils; ⏰ 8am-noon Sat-Wed, 9am-6pm Thu) still bears the emblem of weighing scales above the great wooden entrance doors (not the Government Ave entrance). The rooms, which can be seen within an hour, contain displays of Bahrain's pearl-diving and seafaring heritage, exhibits of antique weapons, traditional games, medicine, costumes and musical instruments, as well as the various uses of the date palm. Upstairs, the collection of photographs of state occasions and of Arab and foreign dignitaries from Bahrain throughout the 20th century is interesting. Photography is prohibited.

Friday Mosque

Built in 1938, this **mosque** (Map p121; Government Ave) is easily identifiable by its colourful mosaic minaret, the mosque's most interesting architectural feature. The mosque is reflected in the glass windows of the neighbouring Batelco Commercial Centre, providing a suggestive reflection of old and new Manama. The mosque is not open to tourists.

Bab al-Bahrain

Built by the British in 1945, **Bab al-Bahrain** (Map p121; Government Ave), the 'Gateway to Bahrain', was originally designed by Sir Charles Belgrave. It was redesigned in 1986 to give it more of an 'Islamic' flavour. The small square in front of the *bab* (gate) was once the terminus of the customs pier (which provides some idea of the extent of land reclamation in the area). The building now houses the Tourist Department and a souvenir shop.

Despite having been moved back from the water's edge, the gateway is still aptly named, as goods of various description, people of all nationalities, street vendors, shoppers and workers pass under its arches in a constant pageant of activity in this, the heart of Manama.

Beit al-Quran

With its wrapping of carved Kufic script, the distinctive **Beit al-Quran** (Map p119; ☎ 17 290 101; off Exhibition Ave; admission by donation; ⏰ 9am-noon & 4-6pm Sat-Wed, 9am-12.30pm Thu) is a fine example of modern Bahraini architecture. It was opened in 1990 as a museum and research centre, and houses a large and striking collection of Qurans, manuscripts

PAIN & PEARL

It seems rather ironic that something as lovely as a pearl can be born of an out-and-out pain in the neck. Pearls are potentially created when a grain of sand or grit enters the shell of any nacreous mollusc, most especially an oyster or a clam; the animal coats the intrusive irritant with a layer of nacre (mother-of-pearl) to make it smooth and less irksome. The longer the problem is nursed, the bigger it gets. One man's grit is another man's grain, however, and large pearls have attracted large sums of money throughout history. Size counts, but it's not everything. Other factors that gem specialists take into consideration are the depth and quality of the lustre, the perfection of the shape and of course the colour, which can range quite naturally from peach to iron.

In Bahrain, it is thought that the fabled sweet water from under the sea tempers the salt water to produce a pearl of a distinctive hue. So valuable were the pearls from the island's shallow waters that the country's entire prosperity was built on the collection and trading of the pearl for over four centuries. A 'fish eye' (the ancient name for pearl) dating back to 2300 BC has even been found in the excavations at Sar, suggesting that pearling was an activity of the Dilmun period, too. Despite the beauty of the catch, pearling was an unglamorous industry that entailed local 'divers' working with little more than a nose peg and a knife in shark-infested waters, and being hauled up with their bounty by 'pullers' working long and sun-baked shifts from June to October. At the height of the pearling industry, some 2500 dhows were involved in the industry and loss of life was common.

Commercial pearling on this scale has long since vanished from Bahrain's waters, thanks primarily to a slump in the international pearl market in the 1930s and subsequently on account of the cultured pearl industry, pioneered in Japan. A cultured pearl is usually created through the artificial injection of grit, or more often a bead, into the shell of an oyster. The uniformity of the bead generally guarantees a more uniform pearl and is created in a much shorter space of time. Nonetheless, at the heart of the gem is a piece of plastic.

In Bahrain, on the other hand, natural pearls are still garnered from the island's healthy oyster beds in something of a revival of this cottage industry, and are crafted locally into astonishingly lovely pieces of jewellery. Occasionally, the sea bed renders up the larger, uniquely coloured pearls that once made the area so famous, but more usually Bahraini pearl jewellery features clusters of tiny, individually threaded, ivory-coloured pearls, which are then set in 21 carat gold.

Naturally enough, there are many places to visit in Bahrain to learn more about the pearl, including the Bahrain National Museum (p122) and the Museum of Pearl Diving (p122) – the more adventurous of bounty hunters can even dive for their own (see p124). For those not too keen on modelling the nose peg, however, the pearls don't come much closer than in the gorgeous gold shops (p129) of central Manama.

and woodcarvings. It functions as a good introduction to Islam in general, and Islamic calligraphy in particular. Look out for the miniature Qurans, the smallest of which (from 18th-century Persia) measures only 4.7cm by 3.2cm. The exhibits are well labelled in English and can be superficially perused within an hour. The bookshop in the foyer sells crafts. Visitors should dress conservatively. The building is next to the Bahrain Red Crescent Society, off Exhibition Ave, but the main entrance and car park are at the back.

Al-Fatih Mosque

A visitor wanting to learn more about Islam could not do better than to visit this grand

mosque (Map p119; Al-Fatih Hwy; ☉ non-Muslims 8am-2pm Sat-Wed), with its unpatronising, informative guides. Built on reclaimed land in 1984, Al-Fatih Mosque is the largest building in the country and is capable of holding up to 7000 worshippers. The mosque was built with marble from Italy, glass from Austria and teak wood from India, carved by local Bahraini craftspeople, and has some fine examples of interior design. The dedicated guides lead visitors through the mosque, explaining aspects of religious etiquette while pointing out special features of mosque architecture.

Visitors begin their guided tour at the small library immediately to the right inside the main entrance, where women will be given a black cloak and headscarf to wear while visiting the prayer hall. Wearing shorts is prohibited. After the tour, visitors are welcome to free booklets in the *Discover Islam* series (published by the Muslim Educational Society of Bahrain) which help to dispel some of the commonly held misconceptions about Islam.

ACTIVITIES
Bowling
A good venue for bowling is **Busheri Bowling Centre** (Map p119; ☎ 17 292 313; Funland Centre, Marina Corniche; from 800 fils; ◷ 9am-midnight). Also recommended is the bowling alley at **Al-Bander Hotel & Resort** (Map p111; ☎ 17 701 201).

Ice-Skating
Ice-skating clearly carries some kind of magical enchantment for people in the Gulf and no capital is worth its salt, it seems, if it can't generate a piece of ice in the 50°C heat that is good enough for a Muscovite ice-skating team. Manama is no exception and it has a fine rink at **Funland Centre** (Map p119; ☎ 17 292 313; Marina Corniche; incl shoe hire BD3; ◷ 9am-midnight). There's even ice disco for travelling Travoltas – don't forget your white T-shirt for the ultraviolet lighting.

Look out for a new development called Iceberg Tower. When built, it will apparently have a ski-run that will compete in piste and permafrost with the one in Dubai.

Pearl Diving
Pearl diving in Bahrain has been a tradition (and was the backbone of the economy) for centuries. While the industry has come to an end, the oysters have continued to grow, uncollected, on the shallow sea beds. If you're interested in learning about pearls, and even diving for them, **Aquatique Scuba Centre** (Map p121; ☎ 17 271 780; Sheikh Isa Ave; ◷ 8am-12.30pm & 4-7.30pm Sat-Thu) runs a very informative pearl-diving course. It covers everything from the history of the pearl industry to what sort of oysters are likely to contain pearls; the grand finale is a dive trip to one of Bahrain's abandoned pearl beds.

COURSES
Courses in traditional Bahraini and Arabic art and music are sometimes offered for a nominal fee by **Bahrain Arts Society** (Map p111; ☎ 17 590 551; www.bhartsociety.org.bh; Budaiya Hwy).

Occasional Arabic language courses are run by the **Ministry of Education** (☎ 17 714 795; www.education.gov.bh) as and when there is sufficient demand.

MANAMA FOR CHILDREN
Bahrainis welcome visiting children to their amenities. You'll find plenty of information about what's on for children in the media; in particular, the 'Teens & Kids' section in *Bahrain this Month* has heaps of information on fun activities, including lessons in hip hop and salsa.

The principal amusement area is **Funland Centre** (Map p119; ☎ 17 292 313; www.funlandcentre.com; Marina Corniche). An amusement park called **Kids Kingdom** (Map p119; King Faisal Corniche) has a few rides if the nearby construction work isn't off-putting.

TOURS
One of the best tour agencies is the friendly **Al-Badr Travels** (Map p119; ☎ 17 710 077; www.albader.com). In addition to sightseeing trips around Manama and Bahrain Island, dhow and fishing trips can also be arranged.

If you're interested in ecotourism, it's well worth contacting **Al-Reem Tours** (Map p119; ☎ 17 710 868; www.alreem.com) before your visit. This unique company specialises in environmental tours. It runs daily birdwatching and wildlife trips to remoter parts of the Hawar Islands and to the mainland desert. It also has a special six-day birdwatching package. Check the excellent website for more details.

SLEEPING
There is a wide range of city accommodation on offer, particularly on or around Government Ave, in the heart of central Manama. Many of the budget and midrange hotels in this area entertain weekend visitors from Saudi Arabia – in more ways than one (see boxed text, opposite) – so it may pay to spend a little more to enjoy one of the good-value, top-end hotels. Beautiful resort accommodation is available at the edges of the city, particularly on the causeway towards Muharraq Island and at Al-Seef, close to the shopping centre.

Budget
All of the following hotels have air-con, TV (but not satellite) and an attached bath-

room with hot water, but if you can stretch your budget to midrange, it's worth it.

Jindol Hotel (Map p121; ☎ 17 227 227; www.jindol hotel.com; Municipality Ave; s/d BD12/18) Step up to the desk of the tiny reception in this newly renovated hotel in the heart of downtown, and you may wonder what you are signing up for as the receptionist covertly telephones the madam of the upper floors. If you manage to get beyond the desk, however, the rooms and attached showers are clean and given an Arabic flourish. Note that breakfast is not included in the price. An added attraction is the attached coffeehouse: with its sedans, *sheesha* and roasted coffee, it caters to a heady mix of regional nationalities whose jobs don't cover the price of a pricier hotel, however women may feel conspicuous here.

Adhari Hotel (Map p121; ☎ 17 224 343; adhari@ batelco.com.bh; Municipality Ave; s/d BD20/25) What often makes a hotel is not the fancy plumbing and designer decoration but a friendly reception and a bit of character. You can forgive the Adhari the noisy, no-frills rooms and the smell of stale smoke in the corridors, because of the unfailingly helpful manager – and character-full Hunter's Bar. The latter is a trophy bar full of military paraphernalia that dishes up sizzling steaks to home-sick US soldiers. If you want a lively alternative perspective on the Middle East, this is one place to find it.

City Centre Hotel (Map p121; ☎ 17 229 979; www .city-centre-hotel.com; Government Ave; s/d BD20/25) This hotel has had its finger on the nighttime pulse of Manama for years but it has retained its suitable-for-the-family atmosphere. The foyer doubles as a popular Lebanese restaurant that's always humming with locals, and the upper floors offer renowned entertainment venues including Likwid (a hot-spot disco), an Italian restaurant and an ambient Moroccan-style café. The rooms with wine-red carpets and dingy corridors are basic, but with so much else going on in the hotel, you may be enticed to spend more time outside the room than in. Breakfast is not included.

Midrange

Most of the hotels listed have excellent-value rooms, but others offer carpetless broom cupboards, without windows, or rooms overlooking stairwells. It pays, therefore, to ask to see the room first, and to stipulate a room with a view.

Bahrain International Hotel (Map p121; ☎ 17 211 313; byhot@batelco.com.bh; Government Ave; s/d BD23/28) The curious mix of Parisian Art Deco (in the Al Banco Café) and the Seoul Subway kiosk on the ground floor gives a certain character to the hotel but rooms vary widely from unacceptable with paper-thin walls, to comfortable and almost elegant with full-length drapes. The Filipino entertainment in the Rockland Café Bar keeps merchant traders, who most commonly use this hotel, amused.

Gulf Pearl Hotel (Map p121; ☎ 17 317 333; gphbah@ batelco; Government Ave; s/d BD25/30) Clean and well furnished, with commodious bathrooms, this is a good bachelor's choice. The 5th floor is supposedly reserved for women and families, but with its 1st-floor disco and 24-hour Intensity Bar, it has dubious family

---

HOTEL NO-SLEEP

You don't have to be Richard Gere to know that pretty women hanging around a hotel foyer does not bode altogether well for a quiet night's sleep. Indeed, many male visitors have reported being harassed with phone calls in the middle of the night, and the paper-thin walls of some of the more budget accommodation leave little to the imagination. Ask the price of a night's sleep in the infamous Hotel Bahrain, for example, and you may well receive the same reply given to us: 'this hotel no-sleep – sleep cost more'.

Ironically, the Muslim holidays – when a wave of Saudi tourists floods over the causeway – seem to turn even the midrange hotels into a rendezvous for mostly discreet and unobtrusive liaisons. One word of warning: when a hotel says it has a floor especially for women, it often means just that, with a variety of women of the night plying their trade. As such, women travelling on their own are better off avoiding it. Despite Manama's alter ego, however, solo women are unlikely to feel threatened on the capital's streets, which are so a-throng with people engaged in 'no-sleep' they seem disinclined to mess with yours.

appeal. Breakfast is not included but the set lunch is good value at BD3.

Delmon International Hotel (Map p121; ☎ 17 224 000; delmonbn@batelco.com.bh; Government Ave; s/d BD30/35; ☒) In a central location, with a distinctly Arabic character, the once family-friendly Delmon has reinvented itself as a hot night spot with a range of bars and clubs to suit 'all tastes' (that is, there are bands from Russia, the Philippines and India). The new Yemeni-style foyer with Artex plaster and stained glass is homely, however, and the well-furnished rooms with giant mahogany beds belong to the days when the Delmon had chandeliers and marble in the foyer. The excellent Marrakesh Restaurant on the premises offers a tasty family Friday lunch (*tangeen pilpil* and saturated shrimp) from noon to 4pm for BD5.

Mashtan (Map p121; ☎ 17 224 466; mashtanb@ batelco.com.bh; off Government Ave; s/d BD30/40) In a cavernous building, with wild-wood chairs in the foyer and fake fires blazing on each floor, the accommodation in this brand new hotel boasts, for some reason, the most enormous bathrooms. The rooms are small enough but comfortable and no doubt the atmosphere will liven up once it attracts more clientele.

Top End

The Crowne Plaza, Regency InterContinental and Gulf Hotel all operate under a pricing cartel and hence charge the same rates, including tax but without breakfast.

HOTELS

Crowne Plaza (Map p119; ☎ 17 531 122; www.crowneplaza.com; King Faisal Hwy; s/d BD70/80; ☒) Situated across from the Bahrain National Museum, this low-rise hotel has a relaxed and pleasant atmosphere, with a large pool area surrounded by cerise-coloured bougainvillea. The rooms, which are arranged almost motel-style around a central hub, are bright and attractive and the Tracks Sports Pub is a local favourite. The hotel offers a complimentary bus service to Bab al-Bahrain twice a day.

Regency InterContinental (Map p121; ☎ 17 227 777; www.ichotelsgroup.com; King Faisal Hwy; s/d BD70/80; ☐ ☒) In the middle of downtown but offering uptown accommodation, this luxurious, glamorous hotel is an excellent

choice for visitors who want to step off a marble foyer into the bustling hubbub of Bab al-Bahrain. The grand entrance, decorated with giant floral displays and bronze statues is matched in elegance by its famous French restaurant, Le Versailles.

Gulf Hotel (Map p119; ☎ 17 713 000; www.gulfhotelbahrain.com; Bani Otbah Ave; s/d BD70/80; ☐ ☒) Despite being 4km from the city centre, this old favourite is the most convenient location for the Gulf International Convention Centre. With an extravagant foyer at the top of a huge flight of stairs, velvet lounges and marble halls, the interior appears to belong to an Italian palazzo rather more than a concrete skyscraper. The excellent Japanese restaurant, one of six restaurants in the hotel, is an additional drawcard, as is the hotel's proximity to the most popular Western expat eating haunts in Adliya.

Movenpick Hotel Bahrain (Map p135; ☎ 17 263 300; Muharraq Town; s/d BD80/90; ☐ ☒) It's usually hard to recommend a hotel near to the airport but with the Movenpick chain's usual inimitable feel for a landscape, this is one airport hotel that comes highly recommended. Built around an infinity pool that is contiguous with the flat-calm waters of the Gulf, the hotel whispers 'holiday' from the orchid-strewn foyer to the gorgeous gardens of hibiscus. For ardent soakers, the pool compensates for the lack of bathtubs in the rooms. Although the hotel is on Muharraq Island, it is only a five minute taxi ride over the causeway to Manama. Breakfast is not included.

RESORTS

ourpick Novotel Al-Dana Resort (Map p119; ☎ 17 298 008; aldana@novotel-bahrain.com; Sheikh Hamad Causeway; s/d from BD60/65; ☐ ☒) This Novotel resort has the kind of distinctive style and character that is all too scant in many international hotels. Built like a *qasr* (castle or palace) around elegant central courtyards, and punctuated at the edges by whimsical adaptations of the Bahraini wind tower, this luxurious resort commands wonderful views of the bay from its vantage point on Sheikh Hamad Causeway. The fact that the neighbour has just built the mother-of-all-tower-blocks next door hasn't spoilt this hotel's charm.

Ritz-Carlton Bahrain Hotel (Map p111; ☎ 17 588 000; Al-Seef; s/d from BD105/120; ☐ ☒) While this is undoubtedly Bahrain's most luxurious and opulent hotel, boasting its own private beach and secluded island, some may find the dark, polished interior of black marble and gilt-edged furniture rather oppressive and pretentious. The service is faultless, but it would be hard to describe the staff as friendly. Nonetheless, if yours is a Bentley, you'll be in good company and the Friday brunch (from BD15) is worth saving your appetite for.

EATING
There is a wide selection of restaurants in Manama to satisfy every palette, from a Full Monty of an English breakfast to a plate of French oysters overlooking the bay. For a full listing of what's on offer, it's worth buying the informative *Bahrain Hotel & Restaurant Guide* (BD1).

Restaurants
Manama has restaurants to suit all palettes and pockets, from cheap and cheerful grills and curries to the finest *haute cuisine*. While all the top-end hotels naturally offer excellent options for international-style dining, the selection here represents a small sample of independent restaurants chosen for their distinctive character.

Charcoal Grill (Map p121; Bab al-Bahrain; mains BD1.200-1.600) Plain, simple and clean, the meals in this no-frills grill are nonetheless spiced up by the panorama of life in the heart of the city. Tuck into a kebab and salad (BD1.500) while watching a procession of hawkers, street-walkers, lurkers, shirkers and tourists as they cruise by the city's famous gate.

Habara Snacks & Fish (Map p119; ☎ 17 715 461; Osama bin Zaid Ave, Adliya; mains BD1.200-1.600) No-one could fail to enjoy the name of the best diner in Adliya with its cheery streamers of plastic flowers. And there's more than just the name to enjoy: try the fish and chips (BD2) or pluck up courage for the liver with cheese sandwich (450 fils). If you're looking for pudding and don't fancy the carrot with ice-cream juice (600 fils), pop into Al-Jazeera supermarket next door.

Jim's (Map p119; ☎ 17 710 654; Adliya; mains from BD6; ☽ 11am-2.30pm & 6-11pm) If you're feeling homesick this is one venue that might cheer you up with regular roasts (BD6.500) and a cosy cottage interior. It also serves

a 'Full Monty' breakfast (BD4.900) on a Friday with home-cooked eggs, bacon and black pudding. With a convivial atmosphere and legendary homemade chocolate vodkas (BD1 for a double), Jim's is highly popular with Western expats, so it's worth booking.

Bam Bu (Map p119; ☎ 17 714 424; Adliya; set lunch BD3, with desert BD5) Practical, filling, tasty, fresh-to-the-table home-cooking is what makes this Shanghai establishment worth a visit. The cooking may be traditional but the venue certainly isn't: the open-kitchen restaurant is painted lime-green, has electronic sliding doors and is wi-fi enabled. The set-price dinner option (BD11.800), which includes unlimited beverages, is excellent value.

Al-Sawani (Map p119; ☎ 17 290 797; Al-Fatih Hwy; set dinner BD13; ☽ noon-3.30pm & 5-11pm) If you're curious to know where Bahraini families go to celebrate that special occasion, join a buffet lunch at this plush Arabic restaurant, next to the Bahrain National Museum. Housed in a traditional wind-towered building overlooking the sea, the brightly-lit, cavernous restaurant is best visited with a group of friends or you may feel rather conspicuous.

ourpick **Mezzaluna** (Map p119; ☎ 17 742 999; Adliya; mains BD15; ☽ 6-11pm Sat-Tue, 6-11.30pm Wed-Fri) If you're looking for that 'somewhere special' but don't want to lose sight of the country you are in, then you can't do better than the atmospheric and sophisticated Mezzaluna. Occupying a stylish Bahraini courtyard house, the high-ceilinged restaurant has a live Latin band on Fridays and jazz music at other times. It offers a Mediterranean menu with imported cheeses from France and an excellent wine list. The Algerian fillet mignon (BD9.800) is a melt-in-the-mouth classic. Book to avoid disappointment.

Cafés
There's a vibrant café culture in Manama, centred particularly on the Adliya district in the southeastern part of the city near the Convention Centre. They all serve good coffee, a range of teas, and an assortment of snacks or light dishes – and not forgetting some divine pastries. The following venues in Adliya are also popular meeting places.

BAHRAIN

Café Lilou (Map p119; ☎ 17 714 440; ⏱ 8am-10.30pm Sat-Tue, 8am-11pm Wed-Fri) This elegant balconied venue, with its velvet upholstery, wrought-iron banisters and polished wood floors, is reminiscent of a 19th-century Parisian brasserie. The Trio du Chef (BD1.800) of pannacotta, chocolate brownie and peanut ice cream is worth missing lunch for.

Casa Blu (Map p119; ☎ 17 710 424; snacks BD2.500; ⏱ 10am-2am) This fashionable Arabic-style café has a personality as large as the giant TV screens suspended from the ceilings. Antique typewriters, tills, cameras and gadgetry strewn around the walls will keep you occupied if your companion's conversation doesn't. The plush divans, kofta kebabs (BD2.500), *sheeshas* (BD2.300) and live hip hop music add to the mixed messages of this quirky venue. Dress code stipulates 'no *thawb* without *gutra*' – in other words, don't wear shorts. Bare legs are not the only things stopped at the door: the 'blue' in the title discourages 'evil eye' from entering too.

The Conservatory (Map p119; ☎ 17 712 917; ⏱ 8.30am-7pm Sat-Thu) One of the oldest cafés in Manama, this has earned a fine reputation for its excellent teas and homely atmosphere. Step through the door of the town house and it feels like stepping into a secret garden.

Quick Eats

There are plenty of *shwarma* stands in the centre of Manama, around the back of Bab al-Bahrain and in the souq, where the large turnover of customers ensures the freshness of the snack. Woody's (Map p121), near the rear of Bahrain International Hotel, is one such establishment, where roll-up sandwiches cost 250 fils and a mixed-fruit juice 500 fils – there's no charge for the ringside view of life behind Government Ave.

Self-Catering

Dozens of grocery stores (cold stores) are dotted around the residential areas, and are usually open from about 7am to 10pm. The French franchise Geant has a giant store in Bahrain Mall. Al-Jazeera Supermarket, on Osama bin Zaid Ave in Adliya, is open from 8am to 1am. For fruit, spices, vegetables and meat, try the Central Market; for fish there's the Fish Market (no surprises here) – or a hook over the side, anywhere along the corniche, should do it.

DRINKING

One of the surprisingly few decent traditional coffeehouses in Bahrain is **Ahmed Abdul Rahim's Coffee House** (Map p121; Government Ave). The sign is in Arabic, but you'll find it hard to miss: just look for a line of old *sheyba* (venerable men) sitting on benches and puffing away on apricot *sheesha*. **Laialy Zaman** (Map p119; ☎ 17 293 097; Marina Corniche) is also an excellent place for views, the breeze, teas and a *sheesha*.

All top-end hotels have sophisticated bar areas, often with jazz or other live music, and usually featuring a 'happy hour' or cut-price cocktails. These include the generic **Clipper Room** (Map p121; Regency InterContinental), the bizarrely thematic **Sherlock Holmes** (Map p119; Gulf Hotel) and the Polynesian-themed **Trader Vic's** (Map p111; Ritz-Carlton Bahrain Hotel). There are bars in most of the midrange hotels too, but these can range from cosy to positively dire. The **Rockland Café Bar** (Map p121; Bahrain International Hotel) is one of the better ones.

Stepping into **Hunter's Lodge Bar** (Map p121; ☎ 17 224 242; Adhari Hotel) is like walking back into '70s 'Nam: you expect the DJ to bellow above the rock music 'Good Morning, Bah-ha-rayn.' The bar is periodically packed with US military on R&R in the Gulf, so there's something rather poignant about the sober gloom when it's empty.

ENTERTAINMENT

To find out what's going on around Bahrain, see the What's On listings of the *Gulf Daily News*, the *Bahrain this Month* magazine or the *What's On in Bahrain* booklet, all of which are available in good bookshops.

Cinemas

Delmon Cinemas (Map p119; GOSI Shopping Complex) and **Al-Seef Cineplex** (Map p111; ☎ 17 864 666; Al-Seef Mall) regularly screen recent Western films, and tickets cost BD2. Programmes are advertised in the English-language newspapers. Special films are also shown at the **Bahrain National Museum** (Map p119; ⏱ evening Sun) and the **Alliance Française de Bahrain** (Map p111; ⏱ evening Wed).

The Bahrain **Cinema Club** (☎ 17 725 959; www.bahraincinemaclub.tv; Juffair, southern Manama) features Arabic and foreign films. All films are subtitled in English. For film lists and screening times, check the English-language newspapers or call the club for information about these popular events.

Nightclubs

The coolest nightspots include **Likwid** (Map p121; City Centre Hotel) and **BJ's Nightclub** (Map p119; ☎ 17 742 323; Al-Bustan Hotel, off Bani Otbah Ave, Adliya), which plays a mix of world music, house, R&B, hip hop and Latin grooves.

Serious night clubbers should pick up the *Bahrain Hotel & Restaurant Guide*, which lists recommended bars and nightclubs. Live shows are listed in the 'Nitelife' section of *Bahrain This Month*, and in the English-language newspapers.

Live Music

The **Bahrain International Exhibition Centre** (Map p111; ☎ 17 558 800; www.bahrainexhibitions.com; Sheikh Khalifa bin Sulman Hwy) often has recitals of Bahraini music. Beit al-Quran (Map p119) also features occasional Quran recitals and Qala'at Arad (Map p135) on Muharraq Island often features traditional music on Thursday and Friday afternoons.

SHOPPING

From markets to malls, central Manama has heaps of shopping opportunities. Manama Souq (Map p121), in the warren of streets behind Bab al-Bahrain, is the place to go for electronic goods, bargain T-shirts, nuts, spices, *sheesha* bottles and a plethora of other Bahraini essentials. Most shops in the souq are open from about 9am to 1pm and 4pm to 9pm Saturday to Thursday, and open in the evening on Friday.

Many Bahrainis, however, prefer the more sophisticated shopping experiences of modern complexes, such as the **Yateem Centre** (Map p121; Al-Muthanna Ave) and **GOSI Shopping Complex** (Map p119; Exhibition Ave). Dana Mall (Map p119) and Al-Seef Mall (Map p111), on opposite sides of Sheikh Khalifa bin Sulman Hwy and a short taxi ride into the suburbs, are the biggest and best of the malls.

For regional souvenirs (most of which are imported from Yemen, India, Pakistan and Iran), there are many shops selling silver jewellery, brass coffeepots, lapis lazuli and coral beads, carpets and *kilims* in the streets of Adliya district (near the Gulf

Hotel and Convention Centre), especially along Osama bin Zaid Ave.

Traditional Crafts

Bahrain has a diverse and thriving arts community. The **Bahrain Arts Society** (Map p111; ☎ 17 590 551; www.bahartsociety.org.bh; Budaiya Hwy) is just one of the many centres promoting local art and artists. The relaxed and friendly **Bahrain Craft Centre** (Map p119; ☎ 17 254 688; Sheikh Isa al-Khebir Ave; ☼ 8am-2pm Sun-Thu), managed entirely by Bahraini women, is home to a variety of studios and workshops, and promotes the contemporary revival of traditional crafts, such as weaving, palm-leaf papermaking, pottery and ironwork. All the work is for sale.

Pearls

Bahrain is the only country in the world to sell almost exclusively natural pearls. While the odd imported, artificial pearl creeps in, shop owners are very quick to tell you which ones are and which ones are not genuine, natural Bahraini pearls; when it comes to Bahrain's most famous heritage item, it is more than their license is worth to mislead the customer.

A good place to start for pearls is **Gold City** (Map p121; Government Ave), an arcade of jewellery shops in Central Manama. The owner of **Kumar** (Map p121; ☎ 17 214 248; Shop 49, Centre Point) and **Natural Pearl Palace** (Map p121; ☎ 17 213 248; Shop 21, Centre Point) is particularly knowledgeable and has some priceless pearls in the shop's collection. **Alukkas Jewellery** (Map p121; ☎ 17 229 914; main entrance to Gold City) is also well respected in the Gulf.

While the sky is the limit with regard to the price of a pearl, a pair of cluster earrings starts at US$100, a gold-and-pearl bangle from US$200 and a set (necklace plus earrings) costs around US$400 to US$800. A discount of 15% may be negotiable, but prices for pearl jewellery are more or less fixed. An oyster shell with a growing pearl (US$50) makes a fine souvenir.

GETTING THERE & AWAY

Air

Bahrain International Airport (Map p135; ☎ 17 321 013, flight information 17 339 339; www.bahrainairport .com; Muharraq Island) is one of the busiest airports in the Gulf.

BAHRAIN

Most airline offices are situated around Bab al-Bahrain, in the Chamber of Commerce & Industry building, or inside the Manama Centre, which is where you'll find **Gulf Air** (Map p121; ☎ airport 17 338 844, Manama 17 335 777; www.gulfairco.com), the main national carrier.

Since there is only one airport in Bahrain, domestic flights aren't available to other locations in the country.

GETTING AROUND
To/From the Airport

The airport is on Muharraq Island, approximately 6km from central Manama. Bus 1 runs from outside the airport (ask for directions as the bus stop is a five-minute walk, off the nearest roundabout, and not part of the airport complex) to the Manama bus station on Government Ave. It leaves about every 40 minutes between 6am and 8.45pm.

A metered taxi from central Manama to the airport should cost about BD2. For trips from the airport there is a BD1 surcharge, and drivers are very reluctant to use their meters.

There are ATMs for a range of bank cards, including American Express (Amex), in the transit lounge of the airport, and plenty of car-hire outlets in the arrivals hall.

Bus

Bahrain has a reasonable public bus system that links most of its major towns to the bus terminals in Manama and Muharraq. Buses run every 40 minutes to one hour from approximately 6am to 8pm, depending on the route. The fares range between 150 to 200 fils per trip. A few private buses ply the same routes for 100 fils per trip. Very few people use the bus system, preferring to travel in and around Manama by car or taxi.

Taxi

Taxis are easy to find, and there are taxi stands outside Bab al-Bahrain and many hotels. Taxis in Bahrain have meters, but foreigners have to be very persistent before drivers will use them (see p120). The flag fall is 800 fils for the first 2km. Thereafter the meter ticks over in increments of 150 fils for every subsequent kilometre. Fares officially increase by 50% between 10pm

and about 6am. For a better guarantee of meter use, try **Radio Meter Taxis** (☎ 17 682 999) or Speedy Motors, which both share the same telephone number. Alternatively, for a far more comfortable experience, try **Bahrain Limo** (☎ toll free 801 999) which charges 900 fils for 2km and 200 fils per each half kilometre thereafter.

AROUND BAHRAIN ISLAND

Although dominated by its capital city, there's more to Bahrain Island than Manama, as those coming for the Grand Prix are sure to discover. The island is particularly rich in archaeological sites. Bahrain is small and the southern end is presently occupied by the military, so all of the sights covered in this section make easily accessible day trips from the capital by car, and some can even be visited by bus. It's hard to get lost, because all road signs point to Saudi!

QALA'AT AL-BAHRAIN (BAHRAIN FORT)   قلعة البحرين

A 10-minute drive from central Manama, and standing guard on an ancient tell (mound created by centuries of urban rebuilding) overlooking the northern coast, restoration on the impressive **Bahrain Fort** (Qala'at al-Bahrain; admission free; ☼ daylight hrs) is at last complete. Built by the Portuguese in the 16th century as part of a string of defences along the Gulf, the moated fort is particularly attractive at sunrise, when the surrounding history of the site seems to rise out of the excavations.

And what a remarkable set of excavations they are. The site appears to have been occupied from about 2800 BC and there are seven layers of history represented in the various digs surrounding the fort, including the remnants of two earlier forts. You would need to be an expert – and have rather more knowledge than proffered by the heritage sign boards – to work out the significance of each site. A glimpse, however, of an Assyrian doorway, 3m high, a carefully fitted set of stone slabs and the sea lapping up to a fragment of defensive wall (all without a piece of barbed wire to keep the visitor from wandering into history) are good provocation to find out more about the excavations. One good way of doing that is to read Geoffrey Bibby's celebrated book on the subject, *Looking for Dilmun*.

The site is well signposted about 5km west of Manama near the village of Karbabad and easy to reach by car. Drive along King Faisal Hwy and its extension, Sheikh Khalifa bin Sulman Hwy, and follow the signs. The houses of the surrounding village are newly covered in colourful murals of palm trees, animals and geometric patterns.

BARBAR TEMPLE   معبد بربر

A complex of 2nd- and 3rd-millennium BC temples, **Barbar** (suggested donation BD1; ☼ daylight hrs) was probably dedicated to Enki, the God of Wisdom and the Sweet Water From Under the Sea. It is some 15 minutes' drive (10km) from central Manama.

The excavated complex can be seen from a series of walkways, which provide a great overview, but it's hard to understand without a detailed map (such as *In Bahrain: A Heritage Explored* by Angela Clark) or a knowledgeable tour guide. There is officially no admission fee, but a guard is on hand to suggest visitors sign a guestbook and make a donation.

Take the Budaiya Hwy west from Manama and turn right at the sign for Barbar. The temple is on the right. The closest bus stop is near Ad-Diraz Temple, about 30 minutes' (2km) walk away and, unless you have specialist knowledge, you may feel the site is not altogether worth the walk.

AD-DIRAZ TEMPLE   معبد الديراز

Near the Barbar Temple complex, to which it is related, this **temple** (admission free; ☼ daylight hrs) dates from the 2nd millennium BC. The site is small and possibly only worth visiting for the archaeologically inclined. The turn-off for the temple is clearly signposted along Budaiya Hwy from Manama (but not if you're driving in the other direction). Bus 5 from Manama stops near the temple.

BANI JAMRAH   بني جمرة

It is still possible to see work in progress at huts on the edge of this village, famous as a centre for traditional textile weaving. Visitors are discouraged from walking around

the village itself, but in the hut across the road from the cemetery, demonstrations are given and there is plenty of highly patterned cloth available for purchase.

To reach the village, located about 10km west of Manama, take a bus to Ad-Diraz Temple and walk the remaining few hundred metres.

AL-BUDAIYA   البديع
pop 34,451
This small village marks the western edge of Bahrain Island. At sunset, the beach affords a fine view of King Fahd Causeway, as it snakes and humps across the interminable flats and shallows of the Gulf. The Windsor Castle of a building overlooking the sea is Sheikh Hamad's Fort House, a private residence not open to the public. Al-Budaiya is at the end of Budaiya Hwy and is accessible by bus 5, a 30-minute ride from Manama.

SOUQ AL-KHAMIS MOSQUE
مسجد سوق الخميس
The original mosque is believed to have been built in the early 8th century, but an inscription dates the construction of most of the remains as the second half of the 11th century. Nevertheless, it was the first mosque to be built in Bahrain and one of the oldest in the region.

The **complex** (admission free; ☼ 7am-2pm Sat-Wed, 8am-noon Thu & Fri) is about 2.5km southwest of Manama. Buses 2 and 7 from Manama run to the complex (50 fils, 10 minutes, about every 40 minutes to one hour). To get here, take the Sheikh Sulman Hwy to Al-Khamis village; the mosque is on the right-hand side of the road.

A'ALI   عالي
pop 57,024
To gain an idea of the significance of the **burial mounds** that dominate the approach to A'Ali, it's worth spending time at the Bahrain National Museum (p122) in Manama beforehand. The mounds, which date from the Dilmun period, encase burial chambers used for all members of society, young and old. At 15m in height and 45m in diameter, the tallest of the mounds are referred to as the 'Royal Tombs'; it's easy to see why they deserve the name, as they give this scruffy town of potters and bakers a regal presence.

A'Ali is the site of Bahrain's best-known **pottery workshop** and ceramics are on sale at several stalls nearby (as well as in the souvenir shop at Bab al-Bahrain in Manama). Look out for the votive display of curiosities in the workshop and the traditional mud-bricked kilns. A'Ali also boasts a 'traditional' **Arabic bakery** (the flat bread is delicious when newly flipped from the oven). The townsfolk seem to be fond of their pigeons – there are some elaborate dovecotes around town, particularly near the pottery.

From Manama, take the Sheikh Sulman Hwy south past Isa Town, then turn west along A'Ali Hwy and follow the signs to the pottery workshop or mounds. Buses are problematic: take bus 2 or 7 from Manama to Isa Town, and then bus 9 or 15 to A'Ali (150 fils), which leave approximately every 40 minutes to one hour for each leg of the journey.

Travelling by car takes just 20 minutes, while bus travel takes over an hour. Keep your eyes open either side of the highway for the burial mounds: there are more than 100,000 of them in Bahrain.

SAR   سار

The excavations at Sar have revealed a honeycomb of **burial chambers** dating from the Dilmun period. They have all long since been plundered, but the systematic removal of the coping stones has at least revealed the inner sanctum of the site and there is still a feeling that this is 'hallowed ground'. When excavations are finished, there are plans to turn the site into a major tourist attraction, including a museum. For now, while the explanatory heritage board is not very illuminating (in fact, the English version seems to have been appended to the wrong site), there is a special privilege in being able to wander unchecked among the cradles of the dead.

Although the site is visible from the main road, there is no access from the Causeway Approach Rd. Instead, follow signs for the village of Sar, heading south from Budaiya Hwy, or from Janabiya Hwy, and then heritage signs lead to the site. Bus 12 goes to Sar village (80 fils, 25 minutes, every 40 minutes to one hour), from where it's about a 1.5km walk. Sar is 10km from Manama and takes 25 minutes to travel there by bus or car.

KING FAHD CAUSEWAY   معبر الملك فهد

There is something immensely evocative about a border and there could be few more impressive heralds of a border than the 26km causeway that links Saudi Arabia with Bahrain. Built in a series of humpbacked rises and long flat stretches across the shallows of the Gulf, this remarkable piece of engineering, completed in 1986 at a cost of US$1.2 billion, is worth a visit just to marvel at the construction. On either side of an island, roughly in the middle of the causeway, are two observation towers that invite the visitor as close to the border as visas allow. For an egg rollup and chips while watching the sun dip behind the Saudi mainland at sunset, try the **King Fahd Causeway Restaurant** (admission 500 fils; ☻ 9am-11pm), halfway up the tower on the Bahraini side. Leave enough time to queue for the tiny lift that services the viewing platform near the top of the tower. From there it's possible to see the 26km, four-lane causeway in full, with its 12,430m of viaducts and its five separate bridges, all made from 350,000 sq metres of concrete and reinforced by 147,000 tonnes of steel.

All drivers (and passengers in taxis) must pay a toll at a toll booth (per vehicle BD2) along the Causeway Approach Rd, whether going to Saudi or not. No local public bus travels along the causeway. The island in the middle of the causeway is 25km from Manama and it takes 30 minutes to drive there.

AL-JASRA   الجسرة

One of several historic homes around Bahrain that have been restored to their original condition, **Al-Jasra House** (☎ 17 611 454; admission 200 fils; ☻ 8am-2pm Sat-Wed, 8am-5pm Thu) was built in 1907 and is famous as the birthplace in 1933 of the former emir, Sheikh Isa bin Sulman al-Khalifa. It is constructed in the traditional way from coral stone, supported by palm-tree trunks. The gravel in the courtyard is made up of a 'hundreds and thousands' mixture of tiny mitre and auger shells.

In the residential area, a few hundred metres from Al-Jasra House, is the government-run **Al-Jasra Handicraft Centre** (☎ 17 611 900; ☻ 8am-2pm). This modern, well-laid-out collection of workshops specialises in textiles, basket weaving and mirrors. It's adjacent to a stop for Bus 12 from Manama.

From the Causeway Approach Rd, look for the exit to Al-Jasra (before the toll booth); both the house and the handicraft centre are well signposted. The town is 15km from Manama and takes 20 minutes to travel by bus or car.

RIFFA FORT   قلعة ريفا

Commanding the only piece of high ground overlooking the Hunanaiya Valley, this **fort** (☎ 17 779 394; admission 500 fils; ☽ 7.30am-2pm Sat-Wed, 10am-3pm Thu) was originally built in the 19th century. It was completely restored in 1983. The limited captions and explanations are in Arabic, and the rooms are mostly empty, but it's interesting enough and the views over a valley of a golf course, nodding donkeys and tree-lined highways is appealing.

The fort is easy to spot from several main roads near the town of Riffa and is well signposted. Access to the fort is only possible along Sheikh Hamood bin Sebah Ave, which is off Riffa Ave. Buses 7 and 11 (80 fils) pass the turn-off along Riffa Ave, from where it's a 20-minute walk. Riffa is 25km from Manama and a 30-minute ride by car or bus. Along the journey, note all the magnificent avenues of palms, orange-flowering cordias and topiaried citrus trees that line the suburban part of the highways.

BAHRAIN INTERNATIONAL CIRCUIT

The distinctive Al-Sakhir Tower of the **Formula One Racetrack** (☎ 17 450 000; www.bahraingp .com; admission BD5) rises above the surrounding desert like a beacon. If you are visiting Bahrain out of season and are curious to see what a state-of-the-art race track looks like, then you can join a 90-minute tour of the grounds, including the media centre and race control room, and even take a lap around the circuit. Tours are offered every Sunday, Tuesday and Thursday and begin at 10am and 2pm. See p138 for more details about the circuit.

In October each year, there is an opportunity to see drag racing at the circuit.

From Manama, just about all roads point to the circuit. The circuit is about 30km from Manama and takes about 35 minutes to get there by car. There is no public transport.

AL-AREEN WILDLIFE PARK & RESERVE   حديقة حيوانات العرين

This interesting little (10 sq km) **reserve** (☎ 17 836 116; bncftpw@batelco.com.bh; admission BD1; ☽ 9am-5pm Sun-Thu, 2-5pm Fri) in the southwest of the island is a conservation area for species indigenous to the Middle East and North Africa. After a short introductory film (in Arabic only), a small bus leaves roughly every hour for a tour (with commentary in Arabic and English) past some of the 240 species of birds and mammals housed in the park. There are several herds of mature oryx with fabulous horns that make it easy to appreciate, firstly, how this gracious animal could be mistaken for a unicorn and, secondly, what an enviable choice of national animal it makes.

As the park is given to changing its opening times at regular intervals, it's best to call or check the 'What's On' listings in the *Gulf Daily News* before heading out.

About a five to 10 minute drive west from the park is **Al-Jazayer beach**, which has some scanty shade and reasonable swimming, though the beach can get very noisy at weekends.

From Manama, follow the signs to Riffa and then Awali along Sheikh Sulman Hwy, and then continue towards Al-Zallaq. The turn-off to the park is along the Zallaq Beach Hwy. The park is 35km from Manama and it takes about 40 minutes to get there by car, travelling past the Bahrain International Circuit. Al-Jazayer Beach is signposted from the park. There is no public transport to either destination.

TREE OF LIFE   شجرة الحياة

The Tree of Life is a lone and spreading mesquite tree, famous not because it somehow survives in the barren desert (plenty of trees and thorn bushes do that) but because it has survived so long. No one is sure what sustains this remarkable old knot of thorny branches, but it has presumably tapped into an underground spring. It won't be a change in the climate, however, that will signal its downfall, but the all-too-visible change in the kind of visitor it attracts, as daubs of spray paint all over the venerable old bark forewarn.

Follow signs to the tree along the Muaskar Hwy. It is just off the sealed road (take a right turn by Khuff Gas Well 371 and turn right

---

GARDEN OF EDEN

And the Lord God planted a garden eastward in Eden; and there He put the man whom He had formed. And out of the ground made the Lord God to grow every tree that is pleasant to the sight, and good for food; the tree of life also in the midst of the garden, and the tree of knowledge of good and evil.

Genesis 2:8-9

When standing under the spreading limbs of the lone mesquite tree that graces a patch of Bahrain's southern desert, with earth movers scraping the escarpment for cement, and oil and gas pipelines running the length and breadth of the wadi (often-dry valley or river bed), it's hard to imagine anywhere less deserving of the name 'Garden of Eden'. And yet, that is precisely what some tourist promoters would have us believe. Their claims are not entirely without foundation, however. Modern scholars point to several ancient sources that suggest that Bahrain may indeed have been the locus of paradise. In the Babylonian creation myth, the Epic of Gilgamesh (the world's oldest poetic saga), for example, Dilmun (Bahrain's ancient incarnation) is described as the home of Enki (the god of wisdom), the Sweet Water From Under the Sea, and Ninhursag (goddess of the Earth). Likewise, in the Old Testament, which combines two separate creation stories, it is possible that Hebrew and Sumerian traditions of paradise are similarly conflated. Certainly, the lush oases in parts of Bahrain testify to perpetual springs of sweet water if nothing more.

On encountering the Tree of Life (p133) in southern Bahrain, however, you may well urge archaeologists searching for Eden to keep looking!

---

again along the power lines). There's no need for a 4WD, but take care not to drive into soft sand. Delightfully, there is a signboard at the site telling the visitor how to get there. Just before leaving the tarmac road, look out for a low escarpment: for those interested in desert erosion, there's a fine example of what is known as a 'desert mushroom'. Chiselled out of the limestone by the wind, this rounded lump of rock, about 2m wide, sitting proud on the cliff face, looks very much like a giant white toadstool. Don't be tempted to drive over: there are deep pockets of sand that even a 4WD couldn't negotiate easily. The Tree of Life is 40km from Manama and a 45-minute drive away.

OIL MUSEUM

Built in 1992, to mark the 60th anniversary of the discovery of oil, this **museum** (☎ 17 753 475; admission free; ⏰ 9am-6pm Thu & Fri) is housed in a grand, white-stone building quite out of keeping with the surrounding nodding donkeys and sprawling pipelines. In the shadow of Jebel ad-Dukhan (Mountain of Smoke) – Bahrain's highest point at a very modest 134m – the building is befitting as a landmark of the country's wealth, for it marks the point at which 'Black Gold' was struck for the first time on the Arabic side of the Gulf. The museum has exhibits,

photographs and explanations about the oil industry in Bahrain. A few metres away, you can see the country's first oil well, which was constructed in 1932.

Ring ahead to check opening times, as the museum is seldom visited despite being clearly signposted along an unmarked road south of Awali. There is no bus service to this region. By car, it takes about 40 minutes to reach the museum, which is 35km south of Manama.

MUHARRAQ ISLAND محرق

pop 98,967

Just over the causeways from Bahrain Island, Muharraq Island could in many respects belong to a different country. With some interesting old houses, a fort and a shore full of moored dhows and lobster pots, there's enough to keep a visitor occupied in the atmospheric back streets for at least half a day.

The attractions on the island are easy to reach on foot from Muharraq bus station – buses 2 and 7 travel between the bus stations in Muharraq and Manama (80 fils, 10 minutes, at least every hour). Alternatively, hop in a taxi (around BD1.200 from central Manama) to one place, and walk to one or more of the other attractions.

BEIT SHEIKH ISA BIN ALI
بيت الشيخ عيسى بن علي

Offering a fascinating look at pre-oil life in Bahrain, **Beit Sheikh Isa bin Ali** (☎ 17 293 820; admission 200 fils; ☒ 8am-2pm Sat-Tue, 9am-6pm Wed & Thu, 3-6pm Fri) was built around 1800. The upper quarters with the shuttered, colourful windows were used in summer, while winter accommodation was provided for in some of the windowless downstairs rooms. The chief sitting room downstairs was kept cool in summer by the down draft from the wind tower, the shutters on which could be closed in the

chilly months. There is some very fine gypsum and woodcarving throughout the house, and it's worth spending some time looking at the collection of old black-and-white photographs. Spare a glance, too, for next door's fine dovecote: keeping doves seems to be something of a national pastime.

While the rooms are bare, the different sections of the house are well captioned in English and a good half-hour could be spent rambling up and down the different staircases.

From Manama take the Sheikh Hamad Causeway and turn right at the roundabout (with cropped lemon trees in the middle) on Sheikh Abdullah bin Isa Ave. Brown signs indicate the way.

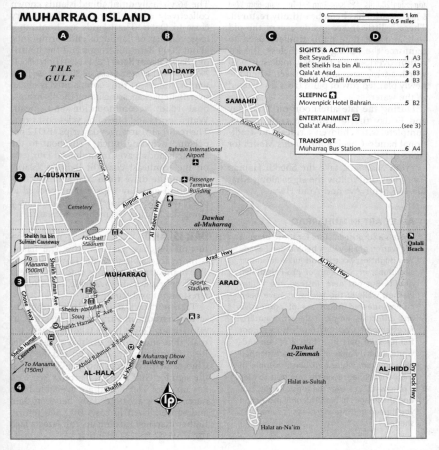

MUHARRAQ ISLAND

0 ——— 1 km
0 ——— 0.5 miles

SIGHTS & ACTIVITIES
Beit Seyadi.....................................1 A3
Beit Sheikh Isa bin Ali..................2 A3
Qala'at Arad.................................3 B3
Rashid Al-Oraifi Museum..............4 B3

SLEEPING
Movenpick Hotel Bahrain.............5 B2

ENTERTAINMENT
Qala'at Arad...............................(see 3)

TRANSPORT
Muharraq Bus Station....................6 A4

THE GULF

AD-DAYR   RAYYA

SAMAHIJ

Aradous Hwy

AL-BUSAYTIN

Bahrain International Airport

Passenger Terminal Building

Cemetery

Avenue 20

Airport Ave

Al Kabeer Hwy

Dawhat al-Muharraq

Qalali Beach

Sheikh Isa bin Sulman Causeway

Football Stadium

Arad. Hwy

Al-Hidd Hwy

To Manama (500m)

Sheikh Sulman Ave

Chose Hwy

MUHARRAQ

Sports Stadium

ARAD

Sheikh Abdullah Ave

Souq

Sheikh Hamad Ave

Abdul Rahman al-Fadel Ave

Dawhat az-Zimmah

AL-HIDD

Dry Dock Hwy

Sheikh Hamad Causeway

To Manama (150m)

AL-HALA

Khalifa al-Khebir Ave

Muharraq Dhow Building Yard

Halat as-Sultah

Halat an-Na'im

BAHRAIN

BEIT SEYADI بيت سيادي

Another traditional house from the pre-oil period, **Beit Seyadi** (admission free; 4-6pm Thu) is a smaller house of similar age that once belonged to a pearl merchant. Quite the best part of the house is the fine exterior, with its peculiar rounded corners decorated with emblems of stars and crescent moon. An old mosque is attached to the house, so take care to find the correct entrance.

The route to this house is clearly signposted from Beit Sheikh Isa bin Ali.

QALA'AT ARAD قلعة عراد

Built in the early 15th century by the Portuguese, **Qala'at Arad** (Arad Fort; ☎ 17 672 278; admission 200 fils; 8am-2pm Sat-Tue, 9am-6pm Wed & Thu, 3-6pm Fri) has been beautifully restored. There is little to see inside except the old well and the date-palm timbers used to reinforce the ceiling. Nonetheless, the location overlooking the bay makes it well worth a trip, especially at sunset, when the newly planted row of palm trees is reflected in the water.

During the late afternoon on Thursday and Friday the fort hosts a craft market, complete with children's rides and traditional bands. Check *Bahrain this Month* for more details.

From Manama, take the Sheikh Hamad Causeway and follow the signs along Khalifa al-Khebir Ave and Arad Hwy.

ALLEY ART IN MUHARRAQ

There's a surprise in store for those braving the warren of alleyways behind Beit Seyadi. You might expect the odd lurker in similar situations, or a stream of pro-Palestinian graffiti. But not here: instead, the white-washed walls of the alleyways have been commandeered in an act of aggressive and effective en-plein-air art. Painterly faces emerge from DIY brushstrokes, door frames take part in a frenzy of red-and-white daubs, flanks of houses are slapped with the red, white and black insignia of the Bahraini flag. Even the sun gets to play a role as it slices over the tops of walls, cutting the images in half. The only protection you'll need in these alleyways is some dark shades.

RASHID AL-ORAIFI MUSEUM متحف راشد العريفي

Dedicated to the art and artefacts of the Dilmun era, this private **collection of art and sculpture** (☎ 17 535 112; admission BD1; 8am-noon & 4-8pm Sat-Thu, 8am-noon Fri) has over 100 works of art from this era. Inspired by these artefacts, the artist owner paints Dilmun-related canvases which he displays in the museum's gallery. From Manama, take the Sheikh Isa bin Sulman Causeway and follow the signs along Airport Ave.

OTHER ISLANDS

HAWAR ISLANDS جزيرة حوار

The 16 virtually uninhabited islands known collectively as the Hawar Islands are very close to Qatar. The islands are home to a large number of flamingos and cormorants, about 2000 Bahraini troops and the luxurious **Hawar Resort Hotel** (☎ 17 849 111, city office 17 290 377; www.hawarresort.com; s/d BD30/48;). In winter, the resort runs comparatively cheap overnight packages, including the 45-minute boat road, accommodation and meals. Water sports and hire of bicycles cost extra. The resort also arranges day trips (BD12 per person, including lunch). The boat to the Hawar Islands leaves from the Ad Dur jetty on the southeast coast of Bahrain Island, a 40-minute drive from Manama. Accommodation and day trips can be booked at the Hawar Resort Hotel's city office located along the Marina Corniche in Manama.

DAR ISLAND جزيرة الدار

Just off the coast south of Sitra, Dar Island is more accessible than the Hawar Islands. The main attraction is the sandy beach, but water sports are also available, and there is a restaurant and bar.

Transport to Dar Island leaves from the scruffy harbour in Sitra, on the east of Bahrain Island. To get there, take Avenue 1, the road that ends in the exclusive Al-Bander Resort (private members only) and the Yacht Club, which welcomes tourists. Turn left at the sign for Gulf Ports & Harbour Services. Sea taxis for Dar Island are available from here, leaving anytime daily between 9am and sunset. The trip costs BD2.500 return. Rather than just turning up, call **Jazeera Taxis** (☎ 17 535 557; fax 17 527 853) first.

BAHRAIN DIRECTORY

ACCOMMODATION

Bahrain's main sights are all within day-trip distance of the capital. As a result, most visitors stay in the large selection of hotels available in Manama and its suburbs. Bahrain has accommodation to fit most pockets, although travellers will find it difficult to find single/double rooms for less than BD12/18 per night.

The suitability of budget accommodation for many travellers, especially women and children, is another matter, as many of the cheaper hotels (and some midrange hotels) double as brothels for visiting Saudi patrons. It seems to be that the cheaper the room, the more overt the night-time activity.

Midrange accommodation usually implies a carpet, minibar and view of something other than an internal stairwell.

Bahrain has some excellent top-end accommodation, including resorts. These often offer substantial discounts to the published rack rate.

Camping is not a recommended option.

In this chapter, we've defined budget hotels as those that charge no more than BD25 for a double room, midrange hotels as those that charge no more than BD50 for a double room and top-end hotels as those that charge more than BD50 for a double room. All prices are based on high-season rates (from November to March). In the low season (April to October), prices can drop by at least 10% in some hotels. During *eid* holidays (see p534), prices rise by 20%.

ACTIVITIES

Dolphin Watching

Dolphin watching is a popular pastime in the still Gulf waters around Bahrain. The friendly and efficient **Bahrain Yacht Club** (Map p111; ☎ 17 700 677; www.bahrainyachtclub.com.bh) organises trips and a range of activities for families.

Golf

No-one is surprised that you can play golf in the desert these days, but coming upon bright green lozenges of grass in the sand-blasted interior is still a startling – if not exactly environmentally sound – sight. The following clubs are open to visitors:

Awali Golf Club (☎ 17 756 770; www.awaligolf club.com)

Riffa Golf Club (☎ 17 750 777; www.riffagolf club.com)

Horse Riding

Horse riding is possible at the **Awali Riding Club** (☎ 17 756 525) or at **Bahrain Riding School** (☎ 17 593 267).

Running

Long-established running clubs for those who prefer to share their pain are the **Bahrain Hash House Harriers** (☎ 17 862 620; www .bahrainhash.com) and the **Bahrain Road Runners** (☎ 3 9685 547; www.bahrainroadrunners.com).

Water Sports

Bahrain is a good place to enjoy the sea, but not necessarily from the beach. Low tides and large expanses of shallow water make it difficult to swim close to the shore. That said, there are plenty of options for getting into deeper water, and snorkelling is a popular activity.

Other water sports on offer include swimming, diving, sailing, water-skiing and game fishing. A number of clubs and resorts can arrange these activities, particularly the friendly **Bahrain Yacht Club** (☎ 17 700 677; www.bahrainyachtclub.com.bh). With a private beach, swimming pool, fully-equipped diving school and sailing school, it has all the expected amenities of a professional yacht club, including bars and restaurants.

Alternatively, try the following, who welcome nonmembers on a day-fee basis:

Al-Bander Hotel & Resort (☎ 17 701 201)

Bahrain Sailing Club (☎ 17 836 361)

BOOKS

Bahrain Island Heritage by Shirley Kay is a useful and informative book on Bahrain. *Resident in Bahrain* by Parween Abdul Rahman and Charles Walsham is particularly helpful for businesspeople.

A celebrated book on Bahrain is Geoffrey Bibby's *Looking for Dilmun*, which provides a fascinating picture of life in Bahrain in the 1950s and '60s.

For those interested in archaeology and history, *Bahrain Through the Ages: The Archaeology* and *Bahrain Through the Ages:*

The History by Sheikh Haya Ali al-Khalifa and Michael Rice offer in-depth coverage at a justifiable BD22 each.

See p20 in the Getting Started chapter for more general Middle East titles, some of which contain coverage of Bahrain.

BUSINESS HOURS

The weekend in Bahrain has recently changed from Thursday and Friday to Friday and Saturday for most commercial and government organisations (see p529 for further details). Business hours are as follows:

Banks 7.30am to 3pm Sunday to Thursday

Government offices 7am to 2pm Sunday to Thursday

Internet cafés 8am to 1pm and 4pm to 10pm

Post offices 7am to 2pm (and 4pm to 6pm at alternating offices)

Restaurants 11am to 3pm and 6pm to 1am

Shopping centres 9am to 10pm Saturday to Thursday, 10am to 10pm Friday

Shops 8am to noon and 3.30 to 7.30pm Saturday to Thursday

CHILDREN

Bahrain is a family-friendly country and there are many attractions to keep children amused in the capital (see p124), though, disappointingly, the coast is not the paddling paradise that one would expect of a desert island. See also p133 for information on the Al-Areen Wildlife Park & Reserve.

CUSTOMS

Bahrain, unlike some of the other countries in the region, is not a dry state, so the importation, purchase and consumption of alcohol is permissible. Visitors (but only non-Muslims) can import 1L of wine or spirits, or six cans of beer duty-free. If you're returning to Saudi via the causeway, don't forget to empty the coolbox! Take care not to drink alcohol (or any beverage) in public during the holy month of Ramadan. See also Customs p532 for other import restrictions.

DANGERS & ANNOYANCES

Bahrain is an extremely safe place to visit. Travellers should note, however, that the country has one of the highest pedestrian fatality rates in the region, so take care when you're crossing any of Manama's busy streets.

EMBASSIES & CONSULATES
Bahraini Embassies & Consulates

Bahraini embassies in major cities around the world are as follows. For Bahraini embassies in neighbouring Arabian Peninsula countries, see the relevant chapters.

Canada (☎ 450-931 7444; fax 931 5988; Rene, Levesque West Montreal, Quebec H3H IR4)

France (☎ 01 45 53 01 19; fax 01 47 20 55 75; 15 Ave Raymond Poincar, 75116 Paris)

Germany (☎ 228-957 6100; fax 957 6190; Plittersdorfet Str 91, 53173 Bonn)

UK (☎ 020-7370 5132; fax 7370 7773; 98 Gloucester Rd, London SW74 AU)

USA (☎ 202-342 0741; fax 362 2192; 3502 International Dr, NW Washington DC 20008)

Embassies & Consulates in Bahrain

The nearest embassies representing Australia, Canada and Ireland are in Riyadh, Saudi Arabia, which is not much use to anyone other than those resident in Saudi Arabia. Most of the embassies in Bahrain are located in the Diplomatic Area in Manama, between King Faisal Hwy and Sheikh Hamad Causeway.

Opening hours are generally from around 8am or 8.30am to somewhere between noon and 2pm. The Saudi embassy is only open from 9am to 11am. All embassies and consulates are closed on Thursday and Friday.

France (Map p119; ☎ 17 298 660; fax 298 637; Al-Fatih Hwy)

Germany (Map p119; ☎ 17 530 210; fax 536 282; Al-Hassaa Bldg, Sheikh Hamad Causeway)

Kuwait (Map p119; ☎ 17 534 040; fax 536 475; King Faisal Hwy)

Netherlands (Map p119; ☎ 17 713 162; fax 212 295; ABN Bldg, Al-Furdah Ave) Handles Benelux countries.

Oman (Map p119; ☎ 17 293 663; fax 293 540; Al-Fatih Hwy)

Saudi Arabia (Map p119; ☎ 17 537 722; fax 533 261; King Faisal Hwy)

UAE (Map p119; ☎ 17 723 739; fax 727 343; off Sheikh Daij Ave, Juffair)

UK (Map p119; ☎ 17 534 404; fax 536 109; Government Ave)

USA (Map p119; ☎ 17 273 300; fax 272 594; just off Sheikh Isa bin Sulman Hwy, Al-Zinj)

FESTIVALS & EVENTS
Formula One Grand Prix

This is the biggest international event of the year and is held at **Bahrain International Circuit** (☎ 17 450 000; www.bahraingp.com), a 25-minute drive south of Manama. The event opens with great fanfare and entertainment, both at the race track venue and around Manama. See p133 for information on visiting the venue out of Grand Prix season.

Annual All-Fleets Open Regatta

This regatta, inaugurated 20 years ago by **Bahrain Yacht Club** (☎ 17 700 667), now attracts over 60 participants from all over the Middle East. It's organised over a weekend each November. Admission for spectators is free.

HOLIDAYS

In addition to the main Islamic holidays described in the Arabian Peninsula Directory (p534), Bahrain celebrates the following public holidays:

New Year's Day 1 January

Ashura 10th day of Muharram (month in the Hejira calendar; date changeable) – Ashura marks the death of Hussein, grandson of the Prophet. Processions led by men flagellating themselves take place in many of the country's predominantly Shiite areas.

National Day 16 December

INTERNET ACCESS

The only internet service provider (ISP) is Batelco and it's called **Inet** (www.inet.com.bh). With a modem and access to a phone line, it's easy to buy prepaid dial-up cards (Inet Pre-paid) from the Batelco Commercial Centre on Government Ave. They come in denominations of BD3 (215 minutes), BD5 (415 minutes) and BD8 (800 minutes).

There are many wi-fi hotspots around town, especially in Starbucks and McDonald's and in most major hotels. Prepaid wi-fi cards cost BD1 (60 minutes), BD3 (200 minutes) and BD5 (one day).

There are also many internet centres in Manama (see p120).

INTERNET RESOURCES

Some useful Bahrain-specific websites include the following:

Al-Reem Tours (www.alreem.com) A 'green' site that promotes Bahrain's wildlife, as well as highlighting some of the environmental problems the island is facing and how these are being addressed.

FAST FACTS AT BAHRAIN INTERNATIONAL CIRCUIT

With more than a billion people in worldwide audiences, the highlight of Bahrain's sporting calendar is undoubtedly the Grand Prix. No-one was sure whether it would be a success, especially when the authorities insisted on a respect for local sensibilities that seemed to run counter to the event's high-glamour profile. Race organisers quickly found an alternative to champagne for the podium celebrations, however, and winners are now sprayed with *wardt*, made from locally-grown pomegranate and rosewater. Instead of scantily-clad pit girls, women working in the reception area sport Gulf costumes with golden hair braids. With the magnificent Arabian-style stadium, 'tented' grandstands and allusions to the country's wind towers, this is one circuit that truly matches its context and as such is a befitting showcase for this modern, sophisticated and self-confident country. Below are the 'fast facts' to date:

- **Where** A 30-minute drive south of Manama
- **When** Completed in 2004
- **How much** US$150 million
- **How many workers** Over 1000 people were employed to build the venue
- **How many hours** An estimated 3.5 million hours of work were clocked up on the project
- **Capacity of stadium** 70,000 people
- **Number of tracks** The circuit contains six individual tracks, including a 1.2km drag strip and a 2km test oval
- **Barriers** 4100m of tyre barriers using 82,000 tyres are erected around the circuit
- **Winners** Michael Schumacher for Ferrari (2004) and Fernando Alonso for Renault (2005 and 2006)
- **Fastest lap** One minute and 31 seconds
- **Other non-alcoholic drinks used in celebrations** The Williams team, sponsored by Saudia Airlines in the late 1970s, were asked to shake orange juice.

Bahrain Tourism (www.bahraintourism.com) Official government site with information on hotels and tourism.

Clickbahrain (www.clickbahrain.com) Complete island guide for restaurants, hotels and tourist information.

Gulf Daily News (www.gulf-daily-news.com) One of Bahrain's English-language newspapers.

MAPS

The *Bahrain Map & Pocket Guide* (BD1), published in cooperation with Tourism Affairs, Ministry of Information is available from the airport, Tourist Department and Bahrain National Museum. It has useful up-to-date information on the reverse, together with a good map of Manama.

MEDIA
Magazines

The monthly *Bahrain This Month* magazine (BD1.500) is an excellent information source for entertainment, sports and local events. *Woman This Month* (BD1.500) is another popular publication. International magazines are available in all major hotels and bookshops the day after publication.

Newspapers

The *Gulf Daily News* and the less-interesting broadsheet, *Bahrain Tribune*, are both English-language dailies with good international news and sports coverage. They each cost 200 fils. The former contains a good classifieds section and a useful What's On listing. International newspapers are available in all major hotels and bookshops the day after publication.

Radio

Radio Bahrain broadcasts in English 24 hours a day on several FM and MW frequencies, the main ones being 96.5FM and 101FM. FM and MW radio stations established for US forces based in the Gulf are also easy to pick up, as are Voice of America, the BBC World Service and other European services on short wave.

TV

Bahrain Television broadcasts Channel 55 in English (from late afternoon), and the BBC World Service is shown in English on Channel 57. Most satellite programmes, such as CNN and MTV, are available at most top-end hotels. All radio and TV programmes are listed in the two English-language newspapers, and in *Bahrain This Month* magazine.

MONEY
ATMs & Credit Cards

Major credit cards are widely accepted throughout Bahrain. With a PIN number it's also very easy to obtain money from ATMs. Most banks have ATMs that accept Visa, Cirrus and MasterCard cards, while the Bank of Bahrain & Kuwait (BBK) has ATMs that take Visa, MasterCard, Cirrus, Maestro and Amex cards.

Currency

Bahrain's currency is the Bahraini dinar (BD). One dinar is divided into 1000 fils. There are 500 fil and 1, 5, 10 and 20 dinar notes. Coins come in denominations of 5, 10, 25, 50, 100 and 500 fils. The Bahraini dinar is a convertible currency and there are no restrictions on its import or export.

Exchange Rates

The dinar is pegged to the US dollar and rarely fluctuates. The rates below were current when this book went to print.

Country	Unit		Bahraini dinar
Australia	A$1	=	BD0.31
Canada	C$1	=	BD0.33
Euro	€1	=	BD0.51
Japan	¥100	=	BD0.32
Kuwait	KD1	=	BD1.30
New Zealand	NZ$1	=	BD0.28
Oman	OR1	=	BD0.98
Qatar	QR1	=	BD0.10
Saudi Arabia	SR1	=	BD0.10
UAE	Dh1	=	BD0.10
UK	UK£1	=	BD0.75
USA	US$1	=	BD0.38
Yemen	YR1	=	BD0.002

Exchanging Money

Money (both cash and travellers cheques) can be changed at any bank or money-changing office. There's little to choose between banks and moneychangers in terms of exchange rates (as little as BD0.010 per US dollar usually), and it's rare for either to charge a commission – although it's always wise to check first.

Currencies for other Gulf States are easy to buy and sell.

Tipping & Bargaining

A service charge is added to most bills in restaurants and hotels in Bahrain, so tipping is at your discretion. An appropriate tip for good service would be around 10%. Airport porters expect 200 fils per bag despite their services being covered by the airport tax. Taxi drivers do not expect a tip for short journeys. For longer journeys (over 5km), 10% would be appropriate.

Bargaining in the souqs and in most shops, together with asking for a discount, is expected.

PHOTOGRAPHY & VIDEO

Plenty of shops in Manama, and elsewhere around Bahrain, sell batteries and memory cards for digital cameras as well as popular brands of print film and video cassettes. Prints from digital images cost 500 fils. A roll of 36-exposure colour print film costs about BD2. Colour print film can be developed in many places, often in less than 30 minutes, for 600 fils, plus 100 fils per print. Many photo shops around central Manama can also take passport photos for about BD2 (for four copies).

POST

Sending postcards to Europe/North America and Australasia costs 150/200 fils. Letters cost 200/250 fils per 10g. Parcels cost a standard minimum of BD3 for the first 500g to all Western countries, and BD1/1.500 for every extra 500g.

Mail to/from Europe and North America takes about one week; allow 10 days to/from Australia. The central post office is in Manama, and there are smaller post offices in major residential areas around the country and at the airport.

Most major international express mail and package companies have offices in Manama.

SHOPPING

Bahrain's specialities – pearls and gold – are good value and fun to purchase from the knowledgeable shopkeepers. Locally produced items include pottery from A'Ali, hand-woven cloth from Bani Jamrah and textiles from Al-Jasra. Bahrain also has art galleries and craft centres selling quality, locally produced contemporary arts and crafts.

TELEPHONE & FAX

Bahrain's telephone country code is ☎ 973 and there are no area or city codes. The international access code (to call abroad from Bahrain) is ☎ 00.

Bahrain's excellent telecommunications system is run by the government monopoly, Bahrain Telecommunications Company (Batelco). Virtually every country can be dialled direct from most payphones, and some specially marked booths also accept Visa and MasterCard. International calls from Bahrain cost BD0.180 per minute to Europe, Australia and North America. Rates are reduced to BD0.160 between 7pm and 7am every day, as well as all day Friday and on public holidays. There are several help lines including local directory assistance (☎ 100) and international directory assistance (☎ 191). Local calls anywhere within Bahrain cost 21 fils for three minutes. Blue payphones take coins. Red payphones take phonecards, widely available in denominations of BD1, BD2, BD3.500, BD6.500 and BD15. Phonecards are available from most grocery stores.

Fax

Fax services are available at most midrange and top-end hotels, and at the Batelco Commercial Centre in Manama.

Mobile Phones

Bahrain's mobile phone network runs on the GSM system through Batelco and Vodafone. Visitors can also purchase SIM cards for BD8 at all Batelco and Vodafone outlets. Recharge cards come in denominations of BD3, BD5 and BD10.

VISAS

People of most nationalities need a visa, which can be conveniently obtained at Bahrain International Airport or at the border with Saudi Arabia. A two-week visa on arrival costs BD5 for citizens of Australia, Canada, the EU, New Zealand, USA and 29 other nations. There is a foreign-exchange office next to the immigration counter at the airport and at the border with Saudi Arabia.

Multiple-entry business visas are available for citizens of the above nationalities and are valid for 6 months. They cost BD42. This visa does not entitle you to work. For addresses of Bahraini embassies in the Middle East, see the relevant country chapters.

If you're transiting through Bahrain and travelling on to Saudi Arabia by land (and can prove it), the visa fee on arrival for all nationalities is BD2.

For details of visas for other Middle Eastern countries, see the Visa section in the Arabian Peninsula Directory (p541).

Visa Extensions

Visa extensions of up to a month are available in Manama from the **General Directorate of Immigration & Passports** (☎ 17 535 111; Sheikh Hamad Causeway). You must first find a sponsor (a Bahraini friend or your hotel may oblige for a small fee). Extensions cost BD15 for one week and BD25 for more than one week up to one month; they will take up to a week to process. Foreigners overstaying their visas are rigorously fined.

WOMEN TRAVELLERS

Bahrain is fairly liberal compared to some of the other Gulf countries, which can be both a blessing (less of the staring) and a nuisance (more of the hassle). See also the advice offered in the same section in the Arabian Peninsula Directory (p542).

TRANSPORT IN BAHRAIN

GETTING THERE & AWAY

See also the Arabian Peninsula Transport chapter (p545) for more information on the following.

Air

Bahrain International Airport (☎ 17 325 555; flight information ☎ 17 339 339) is on Muharraq Island, 12km from the centre of Manama, and handles frequent services to many intercontinental destinations as well as other countries in the region. It is modern and efficient and has one of the largest duty-free shopping areas in the region. Check-in time is officially two hours before flight departure.

The national carrier is **Gulf Air** (☎ 17 222 800; www.gulfairco.com; Manama Centre, Government Rd, Manama), which flies to destinations worldwide. It is a highly regarded airline with a

good safety record and reliable departure times. Reconfirmation of tickets 48 hours ahead of departure is necessary on many Gulf Air flights.

OTHER AIRLINES FLYING TO/FROM BAHRAIN

Air Arabia (G9; ☎ 17 505 1111; www.airarabia.com; hub Sharjah)

British Airways (BA; ☎ 17 214 584; www.ba.com; hub Heathrow Airport, London)

EgyptAir (MS; ☎ 17 209 264; www.egyptair.com.eg; hub: Cairo)

Emirates (EK; ☎ 17 588 700; www.emirates.com; hub Dubai)

Etihad Airways (EY; ☎ 17 519 999; www.etihad airways.com; hub Abu Dhabi)

Kuwait Air (KT; ☎ 17 223 332; www.kuwait-airways .com; hub Kuwait City)

Lufthansa (LH; ☎ 17 828 762; www.lufthansa.com; hub Frankfurt)

Oman Air (WY; ☎ 17 225 650; www.omanair.com; hub Muscat)

Qatar Airways (QR; ☎ 17 216 181; www.qatarairways .com; hub Doha)

Saudi Arabian Airlines (SV; ☎ 17 211 550; www .saudiairlines.com; hub Jeddah)

Flight	Price	Frequency
Manama to Doha (Qatar)	BD32	daily
Manama to Muscat (Oman)	BD109	daily
Manama to Kuwait City (Kuwait)	BD71	daily
Manama to Abu Dhabi (UAE)	BD61	daily
Manama to Riyadh (Saudi Arabia)	BD52	6 per week
Manama to San'a (Yemen)	BD232	2 per week

Land
BORDER CROSSINGS

The only 'land' border is with Saudi Arabia, across the King Fahd Causeway (p132).

Tourists are not permitted to drive between Saudi and Bahrain in a hired car. Residents of Saudi who have their own cars may use this crossing providing they have car insurance for both countries. For those coming from Saudi this can be purchased at the border. A transit visa must be obtained from the Saudi authorities for those driving by car between UAE and Bahrain.

BUS

The **Saudi Bahraini Transport Co** (Sabtco; ☎ 17 266 999; www.sabtco.biz) runs a bus service between

Manama and Dammam in Saudi Arabia. Buses leave six times a day between 8am and 8.30pm, and cost BD5 one way. From Dammam there are regular connections on to Riyadh (Saudi Arabia) and Doha (Qatar).

From Manama, **Saudi Arabian Public Transport Co** (Saptco; ☎ 17 266 999; www.saptco.com) also has daily buses as far as Amman (Jordan) and Damascus (Syria) for BD17.500; Abu Dhabi, Dubai and Sharjah (UAE), all for around BD11; and Kuwait BD10. All departures are from the international bus terminal in Manama, where the Sabtco office is located. It acts as the agent for Saptco. You must have a valid transit visa for Saudi Arabia in advance and an onward ticket and visa for your next destination beyond Saudi's borders.

CAR & MOTORCYCLE

To get on the causeway to Saudi Arabia, all drivers (and passengers in taxis) must pay a toll of BD2, regardless of whether they're travelling to Saudi or just as far as the border. The toll booth is on the western side of the intersection between the appropriately named Causeway Approach Rd and Janabiya Hwy.

Anyone crossing the border from Bahrain to Saudi will be given a customs form to complete, and drivers entering Bahrain from Saudi must purchase temporary Bahraini insurance and also sign a personal guarantee.

Sea

The Valfajr 8 Shipping Company operates a fortnightly ferry service between Manama and the Iranian port of Bushehr. A one-way fare, including two meals, costs BD35. The ship departs from the Mina Sulman port in Manama and the agent in Bahrain is **International Agencies Company** (☎ 17 727 114; www .intercol.com); for helpful additional information on this service, call the **shipping agent** (☎ 39 450 911).

GETTING AROUND
Bus

Bahrain has a public bus system linking most of the major towns and residential areas. The fare is a minimum of 150 fils per trip. Buses run about every 40 minutes between 6am and 9pm from the **Manama bus station** (Government Ave), and there are user-friendly bus terminals in Isa Town, Muharraq and Riffa. A few private buses and minibuses ply the main routes and cost about 100 fils per trip. The only difficulty with the bus system is working out the routes.

Car & Motorcycle

Driving around Bahrain is straight forward and roads are well signposted to the main sites of tourist interest. Some roads south of the Tree of Life are currently off limits to the public though this will change with the new developments.

Speed limits, the wearing of seat belts and drink-driving laws are rigorously enforced. Speed limits are 60km/h in towns, 80km/h in the outer limits of suburbs and 100km/h on highways. Petrol stations are well signposted, especially along highways.

HIRE

Although there is a bus service to various points around Bahrain Island, it is much more convenient to rent a car, as the buses are not wholly reliable and don't go directly to the points of interest for a visitor.

Car-hire companies have offices in Manama and at the airport, charging from BD15/72 for one day/week for the smallest four-door sedan.

Rates exclude petrol, but include unlimited mileage and insurance. To avoid the excess of BD200 to BD300 in case of an accident, it's wise to pay the extra BD2 Collision Damage Waiver (CDW) per day. Rates are for a minimum of 24 hours. Companies normally only accept drivers over 21 years old (over 25 for more expensive models), and foreigners must (theoretically at least) have an International Driving Permit, although a driving licence is often sufficient. There is nowhere to rent a motorcycle.

Local Transport
TAXI

Taxis in Bahrain have meters, but foreigners need to be very persistent before drivers will use them. The flag fall is 800 fils, which will take you 2km. Thereafter the meter ticks over in increments of 150 fils every subsequent kilometre. Fares officially increase by 50% between 10pm and about 6am. It's rare that taxis will even consider using the meter for longer trips, so expect to negotiate an hourly rate (a charge of BD7 to BD8 per hour is reasonable). However, if you're visiting more than one tourist attraction a fair distance from town, it's probably cheaper to hire a car than charter a taxi.

Kuwait

الكويت

Kuwait, in the cradle of one of the most ancient and most-contested corners of the world, is best described as a city state. The burgeoning capital, Kuwait City, is like a magnet: indeed it has been attracting Bedouin people from the Arabian interior, in search of a sea breeze and an escape from recurring drought, for centuries. Today the metropolis is still an oasis in a land of desert plains, but rather more of the cultural and epicurean kind. Excellent museums; a corniche ornamented with combed beaches and extravagant restaurants; modern shopping complexes and marinas, and long and lazy retreats at new beach resorts mark the Kuwait City experience.

Between one ostentatious building project and another, it's almost possible to overlook the Iraqi invasion – almost, but not quite. A decade has passed, but Kuwaitis are still smarting from the devastating experience and there are many visible reminders of the war (high security around hotels, and museums dedicated to the invasion). As such, it's surprising to find there is little ostensible animosity between Kuwaitis and their northern neighbours.

Outside Kuwait City there are few attractions, except at resorts dotted along the coast. Tourist development of the historical island of Failaka is still in the planning stage, flat desert plains are given over to oil excavation and, with the exception of Mutla Ridge, there are few distinctive geographical features. That said, there is always something to see in a desert, with a bit of patience and an eye for detail; when it comes to the ritual camping expedition, Kuwaiti people seem to have plenty of both.

FAST FACTS

- **Official name** Kuwait
- **Capital** Kuwait City
- **Area** 17,818 sq km
- **Population** 2.8 million
- **Country Code** ☎ 965
- **Head of State** Emir Shaikh Sabah al-Ahmad al-Sabah
- **Annual number of tourists** 91,000
- **Stereotypes** 'Filthy rich' with 10% of the world's oil reserves
- **Surprises** Wealth not as conspicuously evident as may be expected

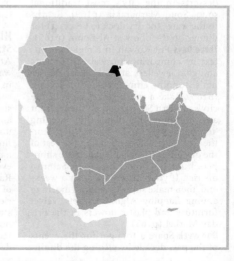

KUWAIT

HIGHLIGHTS

- **Scientific Center Aquarium** (p158) Appreciate the life of a mudhopper in the magnificent display of marine life at the Scientific Center.
- **Tareq Rajab Museum** (p163) Compare regional headdresses in this gem of an ethnographic collection that escaped the Iraqi invasion.
- **Kuwait Towers** (p160) Take an eagle's eye view of the city and the Gulf from Kuwait's famous triple towers.
- **Al-Boom restaurant** (p169) Dine in a dhow in the shadow of the largest wooden boat on earth, Al-Hashemi II.
- **Kuwait House of National Memorial Museum** (p163) Be reminded of war and its heroes in a country that has put its tribulations to rest.

ITINERARIES

- **Kuwait Stopover** Spend the morning learning about Kuwait's marine inheritance at the Al-Hashemi Marine Museum (p164), then come eye to eye with the incoming tide at the Scientific Center's aquarium (p158). Potter the length of the Corniche (Arabian Gulf St), pausing at Kuwait Towers (p160) for an aerial view of the city. Get a feel for the country's Bedouin history at Sadu House (p161), take lunch around the courtyard in a typical Kuwaiti house at Beit 7 (p168), and sample local desserts in the city's most traditional souq, Souq Marbarakia (p169). Return to the water (or dry dock to be exact) for dinner on the dhow at Al-Boom (p169).
- **Three Days** Put Kuwait in a regional context by comparing musical instruments and gold jewellery at Tareq Rajab Museum's stunning ethnographical collection (p163). Take a more global view in the city's modern Sharq souq on the seafront and continue the theme by lunching 'internationally' at Le Notre (p169) on the Corniche before spending the rest of the day joining local and expatriate shoppers hunt for brand names in Salmiya district. If your three days span a weekend, then make sure you enjoy a morning among flapping Afghan carpets, velvet furniture and plastic flowers in the Friday Market (p163).
- **One week** Spare a thought for the events of the past decade by visiting the dimin-ished National Museum (p161), sense the still-smarting scars of war in the Kuwait House of National Memorial Museum (p163) or Al-Qurain Martyrs' Museum (p165), and drive out to Al-Jahra's Mutla Ridge (p172). Brighten up a sobering day with picnicking Kuwaiti families on the road to Sabiyah or gauge the city's remarkable reconstruction with a tour of modern architecture, including the Arab Fund Building (p162). For an altogether more tranquil experience, book in for a day of R&R at the Hilton Kuwait Resort (p168), on a silky stretch of coastline with sequined waters, or explore Wafra Farms (p172) to enjoy some greenery in the unremitting desert.

CLIMATE & WHEN TO GO

In summer (April to September) Kuwait is intensely hot. The fact that it is not quite as humid as neighbouring Gulf States is not much consolation. There are plenty of air-conditioned amenities, however, to make a summer visit tolerable.

The winter months are positively chilly in the evenings, but with pleasant daytime temperatures hovering around 18°C. Sand-storms occur throughout the year, and are particularly common in spring (February to April). During spring, the desert is laced in a gossamer of lime green and the city is decorated with petunias, making it the most pleasant time to visit. See p530 for a Kuwait City climate chart.

HISTORY
Strategic Importance

At the time of the Iraqi invasion of Kuwait in 1990, there was some speculation, in Western countries at least, as to why such an unprepossessing splinter of desert should be worth the trouble. Of course, anyone watching the retreating Iraqi army, under skies black from burning wells, could find an easy answer: oil. But oil was only half of the story. Kuwait is not, nor has it ever been, simply a piece of oil-rich desert. Rather, it represents a vital (in all senses of the word) piece of coast that for centuries has provided settlement, trade and a strategic staging post. The latter is a point not lost on US military forces, who until recently camped out on Failaka Island. A decade ago, the same island, at the mouth

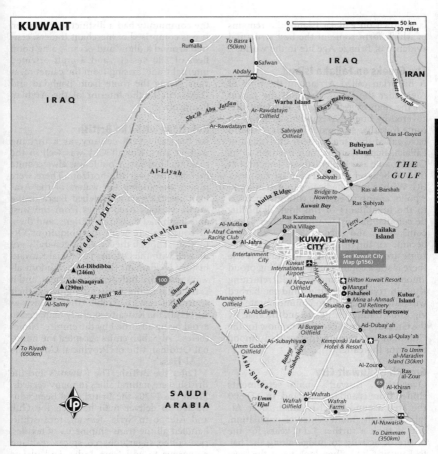

KUWAIT

To Basra
(50km)
Rumalla
Safwan
Abdaly
IRAQ
IRAN
IRAQ
She'ib Abu Jatfan
Warba Island
Ar-Rawdatayn
Oilfield
Khawr Bubiyan
Ar-Rawdatayn
Sabriyah
Oilfield
Ras al-Gayed
Al-Liyah
Subiyah
Bubiyan
Island
THE
GULF
Ras al-Barshah
Mutla Ridge
Bridge to
Nowhere
Ras Subiyah
Kuwait Bay
Ras Kazimah
Ras al-Quly'ah
Failaka
Island
Al-Mutla
Doha Village
Al-Atraf Camel
Racing Club
Al-Jahra
Salmiya
KUWAIT CITY
See Kuwait City
Map (p156)
Ad-Dibdibba
(246m)
Ash-Shaqayah
(290m)
Entertainment
City
Al-Salmy
Kora al-Maru
Kuwait
International
Airport
Al-Maqwa'
Oilfield
Al-Atraf Rd
Shuaib
al-Humaiyyat
100
Manageesh
Oilfield
Al-Abdaliyah
Fahaheel
Mangaf
Mina al-Ahmadi
Oil Refinery
Al-Ahmadi
Shuaiba
Hilton Kuwait Resort
Kubar
Island
Fahaheel Expressway
To Riyadh
(650km)
Al Burgan
Oilfield
Ad-Dubay'ah
Umm Gudair
Oilfield
As-Subayhiya
Kempinski Jalal'a
Hotel & Resort
Ras al-Qulay'ah
To Umm
al-Maradim
Island (30km)
Bahrat
ar-Subayhiya
Ash-Shaqeeq
Al-Zour
Ras
al-Zour
69
Al-Khiran
SAUDI
ARABIA
Umm
Hjul
Wafrah
Oilfield
Al-Wafrah
Wafrah
Farms
Al-Nuwaisib
To Dammam
(350km)

KUWAIT

of Kuwait Bay, was occupied by the Iraqis. Roughly 2300 years before that, it was the turn of the ancient Greeks, attracted to one of only two natural harbours in the Gulf; and 2000 years earlier still, it belonged to the great Dilmun empire, based in Bahrain. The country has a curious way of cleaning up history once the protagonists have departed, and just as there's very little evidence of recent events without some determined (and ill-advised) unearthing, the same could be said of the rest of Kuwait's 10,000 years of history.

Early History

Standing at the bottom of Mutla Ridge on the road to Bubiyan Island, and star-ing across the springtime grasslands at the estuary waters beyond, it's easy enough to imagine why Stone Age man chose to inhabit the area around Ras Subiyah, on the northern shores of Kuwait Bay. Here the waters are rich in silt from the mighty river systems of southern Iraq, making for abundant marine life. Evidence of the first proper settlement in the region dates from 4500 BC, and shards of pottery, stone walls, tools, a small drilled pearl and remains of what is perhaps the world's earliest sea-faring boat indicate links with the Ubaid people who populated ancient Mesopotamia. The people of Dilmun also saw the potential of living in the mouth of two of the world's great river systems and built a large town on Failaka Island, the remains of which form some of the best structural evidence of Bronze Age life in the world.

The Greeks on Failaka Island

A historian called Arrian, in the time of Alexander the Great, first put the region on the map by referring to an island discovered by one of Alexander's generals en route to India. Alexander himself is said to have called this, the modern-day island of Failaka, Ikaros, and it soon lived up to its Greek name as a Hellenistic settlement that thrived between the 3rd and 1st centuries BC. With temples dedicated to Artemis and Apollo, an inscribed stele with instructions to the inhabitants of this high-flying little colonial outpost, stashes of silver Greek coins, busts and decorative friezes, Ikaros became an important trading post on the route from Mesopotamia to India. While there is still a column or two standing proud among the weeds, and the odd returning Kuwaiti trying to resettle amid the barbed wire, there's little left to commemorate the vigorous trading in pearls and incense by the Greeks. There's even less to show for the Christian community that settled among the ruins thereafter.

Growth of Kuwait City

Over time, Kuwait's main settlements shifted from island to mainland. In AD 500 the area around Ras Khazimah, near Al-Jahra, was the main centre of population, and it took a further 1200 years for the centre of activity to nudge along the bay to Kuwait City. When looking at the view from the top of the Kuwait Towers, it's hard to imagine that 350 years ago this enormous city was comprised of nothing more illustrious than a few Bedouin tents clustered around a storehouse-cum-fort. Like a tide, its population swelled in the intense summer heat as nomadic families drifted in from the bone-dry desert and then receded as the winter months stretched good grazing across the interior.

Permanent families living around the fort became able and prosperous traders. One such family, Al-Sabah, whose descendants now rule Kuwait, assumed responsibility for local law and order, and under their governance, the settlement grew quickly. By 1760, when the town's first wall was built,

the community had a distinctive character. It was comprised of merchant traders, centred around a dhow and ocean-going boom fleet of 800 vessels, and a craft-oriented internal trade, arising from the camel caravans plying the route from Baghdad and Damascus to the interior of the Arabian Peninsula.

Relations with the British

By the early 19th century, as a thriving trading port, Kuwait City was well in the making. However, trouble was always quite literally just over the horizon. There were pirates marauding the waters of the Arabian coast; Persians snatched Basra in the north; various Arab tribes from the west and south had their own designs; and then, of course, there were the ubiquitous Ottomans. Though the Kuwaitis generally got on well with the Ottomans, official Kuwaiti history is adamant that the sheikhdom always remained independent of them, and it is true that as the Turks strengthened their control of eastern Arabia (then known as Al-Hasa), the Kuwaitis skilfully managed to avoid being absorbed by the empire. Nonetheless, Al-Sabah emirs accepted the nominal Ottoman title of 'Provincial Governors of Al-Hasa'.

Enter the British. The Kuwaitis and the British were natural allies in many regards. From the 1770s the British had been contracted to deliver mail between the Gulf and Aleppo in Syria. Kuwait, meanwhile, handled all the trans-shipments of textiles, rice, coffee, sugar, tobacco, spices, teak and mangrove to and from India, and played a pivotal role in the overland trade to the Mediterranean. The British helped to stop the piracy that threatened the seafaring trade, but were not in a position to repel the Ottoman incursions – that is until the most important figure in Kuwait's modern history stepped onto the stage. Sheikh Mubarak al-Sabah al-Sabah, commonly known as Mubarak the Great (r 1896–1915), was deeply suspicious that Constantinople planned to annex Kuwait. Concerned that the emir was sympathetic towards the Ottomans, he killed him, not minding he was committing fratricide as well as regicide, and installed himself as ruler. Crucially, in 1899, he signed an agreement with Britain: in exchange for the British navy's protection, he promised not to give territory to, take support from or negotiate with any other foreign power without British consent. The Ottomans continued to claim sovereignty over Kuwait, but they were now in no position to enforce it. For Britain's part, Prussia, the main ally and financial backer of Turkey, was kept out of the warm waters of the Gulf and trade continued as normal.

Rags to Riches in the 20th Century

Mubarak the Great laid down the foundations of a modern state. Under his reign, government welfare programmes provided for public schools and medical services. In 1912, postal and telegraphic services were established, and water-purification equipment was imported for the American Mission Hospital. According to British surveys from this era, Kuwait City numbered 35,000 people, with 3000 permanent residents, 500 shops and three schools, and nearly 700 pearling boats employing 10,000 men.

In the 1920s a new threat in the guise of the terrifying *ikhwan* (brotherhood) came from the Najd, the interior of Arabia. This army of Bedouin warriors was commanded by Abdul Aziz bin Abdul Rahman al-Saud (Ibn Saud), the founder of modern Saudi Arabia. Despite having received hospitality from the Kuwaitis during his own years in the wilderness, so to speak, he made no secret of his belief that Kuwait belonged to the new kingdom of Saudi Arabia. The Red Fort, currently being restored at Al-Jahra, was the site of a famous battle in which the Kuwaitis put up a spirited defence. They also hurriedly constructed a new city wall, the gates of which can be seen today along Al-Soor St in Kuwait City. In 1923 the fighting ended with a British-brokered treaty under which Abdul Aziz recognised Kuwait's independence, but at the price of two-thirds of the emirate's territory.

The Great Depression that sunk the world into poverty coincided with the demise of Kuwait's pearling industry as the market became flooded with Japanese cultured pearls. At the point when the future looked most dire for Kuwait, however, an oil concession was granted in 1934 to a US-British joint venture known as the Kuwait Oil Company (KOC). The first wells were sunk in 1936 and by 1938 it was obvious that Kuwait was virtually floating on oil. WWII forced KOC to suspend its operations, but when oil exports took off after the war, Kuwait's economy was launched on an unimaginable trajectory of wealth.

In 1950, Sheikh Abdullah al-Salem al-Sabah (r 1950–65) became the first 'oil sheikh'. His reign was not, however, marked by the kind of profligacy with which that term later came to be associated. As the country became wealthy, health care, education and the general standard of living improved dramatically. In 1949 Kuwait had only four doctors; by 1967 it had 400.

Independence

On 19 June 1961, Kuwait became an independent state and the obsolete agreement with Britain was dissolved by mutual consent. In an act of foreboding, the President of Iraq, Abdulkarim Qasim, immediately claimed Kuwait as Iraqi territory. British forces, later replaced by those of the Arab League (which Kuwait joined in 1963), faced down the challenge, but the precedent was not so easily overcome.

Elections for Kuwait's first National Assembly were held in 1962. Although representatives of the country's leading merchant families won the bulk of the seats, radicals had a toehold in the parliament from its inception. Despite the democratic nature of the constitution and the broad guarantees of freedoms and rights – including freedom of conscience, religion and press, and equality before the law – the radicals immediately began pressing for faster social change, and the country changed cabinets three times between 1963 and 1965. In August 1976 the cabinet resigned, claiming that the assembly had made day-to-day governance impossible, and the emir suspended the constitution and dissolved the assembly. It wasn't until 1981 that the next elections were held, but then parliament was dissolved again in 1986. In December 1989 and January 1990 an extraordinary series of demonstrations took place calling for the restoration of the 1962 constitution and the reconvening of parliament.

The Invasion of Iraq

Despite these political and economic tensions, by early 1990 the country's economic prospects looked bright, particularly with an end to the eight-year Iran–Iraq War, during which time Kuwait had extended considerable support to Iraq. In light of this, the events that followed were all the more shocking to most people in the region. On 16 July 1990, Iraq sent a letter to the Arab League accusing Kuwait of exceeding its Organization of Petroleum Exporting Countries (OPEC) quota and of stealing oil from the Iraqi portion of an oilfield straddling the border. The following day Iraqi president Saddam Hussein hinted at military action. The tanks came crashing over the border at 2am on 2 August and the Iraqi military was in Kuwait City before dawn. By noon they had reached the Saudi frontier. The Kuwaiti emir and his cabinet fled to Saudi Arabia.

On 8 August, Iraq annexed the emirate. Western countries, led by the USA, began to enforce a UN embargo on trade with Iraq, and in the months that followed more than half a million foreign troops amassed in Saudi Arabia. On 15 January, after a deadline given to Iraq to leave Kuwait had lapsed, Allied aircraft began a five-week bombing campaign nicknamed 'Desert Storm'. The Iraqi army quickly crumbled and on 26 February 1991, Allied forces arrived in Kuwait City to be greeted by jubilant crowds – and by clouds of acrid black smoke from oil wells torched by the retreating Iraqi army. Ignoring demands to retreat unarmed and on foot, a stalled convoy of Iraqi armoured tanks, cars and trucks trying to ascend Mutla Ridge became the target of a ferocious Allied attack, nicknamed 'the turkey shoot'.

Physical signs of the Iraqi invasion are hard to find in today's Kuwait. Gleaming shopping malls, new hotels and four-lane highways are all evidence of Kuwait's efforts to put the destruction behind it. However, the emotional scars have yet to be healed, particularly as hundreds of missing prisoners of war are yet to be accounted for, despite the fall of Saddam Hussein.

Kuwait After the Demise of Saddam Hussein

In March 2003 the Allied invasion of Iraq threw the country into paralysing fear of a return to the bad old days of 1990, and it was only with the death of Saddam Hussein (he was hanged on 30 December 2006)

that Kuwaitis have finally been able to sigh with relief. Without having to look over its shoulder constantly, Kuwait has lost no time in forging ahead with its ambitious plans, including that of attracting a greater number of regional tourists. The annual Hala Shopping Festival in February is proving a successful commercial venture, attracting visitors from across the region, and resorts offer R&R mostly to the international business community. More significantly, cross-border trade with Iraq (particularly of a military kind) has helped fuel the economic boom of the past five years.

GOVERNMENT & POLITICS

On 15 January 2006, the much beloved Emir of Kuwait, Sheikh Jaber al-Sabah, died, leaving Crown Prince Sheikh Sa'ad al-Sabah at the helm. Poor health, however, led to Sa'ad's abdication and the prime minister, Sheikh Sabah al-Ahmad al-Sabah, took over.

Under Kuwait's 1962 constitution, the emir is the head of state. By tradition the crown prince serves as prime minister. The prime minister appoints the cabinet, usually reserving key portfolios (such as the interior, and foreign affairs and defence) for other members of the ruling family.

The powers of the emir, crown prince and cabinet are tempered somewhat by the 50-member National Assembly, which must approve the national budget and also has the power to question cabinet members. The emir has the power to dissolve the assembly whenever he pleases, but is required by the constitution to hold new elections within 90 days of any such dissolution (a requirement that, historically, has not always been honoured).

Kuwait boasts an elected National Assembly, the role of which is beginning to live up to the hopes of those who support a more Western-style democracy. In May 2005, after years of campaigning, women were at last enfranchised and permitted to run for parliament. A few months later, Aasuma al-Mubarak, an academic by training, was named as the Minister of Planning and Administration. Despite the reticence of hard-line clerics and traditional tribal leaders, women now hold positions of importance in both private and public sectors

Despite greater equality between the genders, only 'original' Kuwaiti nationals over the age of 30 are eligible to contest parliamentary seats. Only indigenous Kuwaitis are eligible to vote, although members of the police and armed forces are not eligible. Elections are held every four years, with the next scheduled for 2007.

The country's parliament is still viewed with some scepticism, as it is considered to stall rather than achieve reforms, but slowly and surely democracy is developing.

ECONOMY

During the late 1970s Kuwait's stock exchange (the first in the Gulf) was among the top 10 in the world, but a decade later the price of oil collapsed together with a not-entirely-legal parallel financial market, leaving hundreds of people bankrupt. The scandal left behind US$90 billion in worthless post-dated cheques and a mess that the Kuwaiti government is still trying to sort out. The mid-1980s brought further trouble to the economy as tensions with Iran (including the highly publicised bombings of the US and French embassies) scared away foreign investors. The invasion of the 1990s was an unmitigated financial disaster and the country is still paying back its military debts, while trying not to count the cost of rebuilding the country. As such, it is remarkable to see how spectacularly the economy has bounced back since the turn of the 21st century.

With the country home to 10% of the world's oil reserves, oil and oil-related products naturally dominate the economy

---

FAREWELL TO THE 14TH EMIR OF KUWAIT

Several days of public mourning were declared in January 2006, not just in Kuwait but across the region, to mark the death of Kuwait's popular 14th emir, Sheikh Jabir al-Ahmad al-Sabah. On the throne since 1977, he survived an assassination attempt in 1985 and was forced into exile in Saudi Arabia during the Iraqi invasion. Subsequently, he helped instigate economic and political reforms that helped bring about the modernisation of Kuwait and for this he won plaudits both at home and abroad.

---

and, with more than 100 years' worth of remaining oil, the need to diversify has not been as urgent as it has been in neighbouring countries. Nonetheless, the economy is also buoyed by vibrant banking and commercial sectors, and the encouragement of overseas investment. In addition, Shuwaikh Port still boasts the largest cargo fleet in the Arab world. Tourism is a negligible part of the economy.

The government established a free trade zone in 1998 to offer a combination of incentives to investors, including tax-free personal or corporate income, monetary restrictions and, joy oh joy, minimal bureaucracy.

PEOPLE
The National Psyche

It's easy to imagine that recent events have fashioned a suspicious and bitter mindset among Kuwaitis: young Kuwaiti men (together with family heirlooms) snatched from homes; national treasures ripped from the nation's museum; the Kuwait Towers used for target practice – these and countless other horrors marked the Iraqi invasion. And then there was the almost as agonising threat of the same occurring only a decade later.

Despite the trauma, however, it is a credit to the national temperament that life in Kuwait is characterised not by suspicion and bitterness but by affable handshakes, courteous business meetings and spending sprees in the capital.

Of course, Kuwaitis haven't forgotten the invasion; indeed, in the past few years, there has been an increase in the number of memorials and plaques appearing around the city as if, since the demise of Saddam, people are daring to look back and place the event in a historical context at last, rather than trying to forget about the possibility of a repeat occurrence. Groups of school children can be seen shepherded through the Kuwait House of National Memorial Museum knowing this was their parents' war and not a threat they need to feel defensive about for their own sake.

Kuwaitis are an ambitious and sophisticated people, determined to grasp the commercial opportunities that the 21st century has laid at the doorstep of their continuing wealth but mindful, as Muslims, that what

KUWAIT

is written will be. As such, there's not much point in fretting about the future.

Lifestyle

In common with the rest of the Gulf, Kuwaiti people value privacy and family intimacy at home, while enjoying the company of guests outside. In many instances, 'outside' is the best description of traditional hospitality: while female guests are invited into the house, men are often entertained in tents on the doorstep. These are no scout camp canvases, however, but lavish striped canopies made luxurious with cushions and carpets.

Any visitor lucky enough to partake in tea and homemade delicacies in these 'majlis al fresco' may be inclined to think that life in Kuwait has retained all the charm and simplicity of its Bedouin roots.

Kuwaitis take a different view, however. Some blame the war for a weakening of traditional values: theft, fraudulent practice, a growing drug problem, higher rates of divorce and incidents of suicidal driving have all increased. Others recognise that the same symptoms are prevalent in any modern society. With a cradle-to-grave welfare system, where 94% of Kuwaiti nationals are 'employed' in government positions, and an economy that has run ahead faster than the culture has been able to accommodate, many Kuwaitis feel their society has become cosseted and indulgent, leaving the younger generation with too much time on their hands to wander off course.

Whatever the reasons, life in Kuwait has clearly changed out of all recognition in the past decade: women work, couples hold hands in public, taboo subjects find expression, and people spend money and raise debts. Indeed, the galloping pace of change is proving a divisive factor in a country of traditionally conservative people. It would be ironic if a society that had survived some of the most sophisticated arsenal of the 20th century fell under the weight of its own shopping malls.

Population

The last census, at the end of 2004, put Kuwait's population at 2.8 million. Of these, about 35% are Kuwaitis, many of Bedouin ancestry, and the remaining 65% are expats. After liberation, the government announced that it would never again allow Kuwaitis to become a minority in their own country, implying a target population of about 1.2 million. With an unquenchable desire for servants and drivers, and an equal antipathy for manual labour, it is unlikely the Kuwaitis will ever achieve this target.

There are small inland communities but, to all intents and purposes, Kuwait is a coastal city-state.

A generation of young men are missing after the Iraqi invasion.

Multiculturalism

The origin of the non-Kuwaiti population has changed considerably in the last decade. Before the Iraqi invasion, 90% of the expat population was from Arab countries, with large volumes of Egyptian labourers, Iranian professionals and over a million Palestinian refugees who arrived after the creation of the Republic of Israel in 1948. Since the invasion, Arab nationalities make up less than 15% of the expat population, with large numbers of Palestinians, in particular, being forced to return to their country of origin – a bitter phrase in the circumstances. As Yasser Arafat was widely regarded as a supporter of the invasion, all Palestinians were tarred with the same brush; some were even court martialled on charges of collaboration.

Today Kuwait resembles other parts of the Gulf in its mix of mainly Indian and Filipino immigrants. Alas, a two-tier society appears to have developed wherein some immigrant workers (Filipino maids, in particular) are subject to virtual slave labour. Talk to many Pakistani or Indian traders, taxi drivers, pump attendants or restaurant workers, however, and they evince a warmth towards the country that is somewhat surprising to the Western bystander: just as the friendly reflections regarding the Iraqi man in the street comes as a surprise when speaking to elder Kuwaitis. In comparison with other countries in the region, Kuwait has a relatively small Western expat population, working almost exclusively in higher-paid professions.

RELIGION

Most Kuwaitis are Sunni Muslims, though there is a substantial Shiite minority. During the 1980s there was considerable tension, mostly inspired by Iran, between the two communities, a worry that has returned with sectarian violence over the border in Iraq.

Before the Iraqi invasion, Kuwait was still governed by a strict code of conduct, steered by a devout following of Islam. The invasion shook belief in all kinds of areas, including religious observance. Materialism is beginning to exert as strong an influence on the young as religion used to affect the customs and manners of their Bedouin or seafaring ancestors. Kuwaiti society certainly can't be described as permissive, but the veil in many areas of social exchange is discernibly slipping.

A tolerance towards other religions is evinced through the provision of services at Coptic, Anglican, Evangelical and Orthodox churches in Kuwait City. Kuwait is the only Gulf country to have a strong relationship with the Roman Catholic Church.

ARTS

Kuwait's artistic endeavours are influenced by the country's Bedouin roots and its seafaring tradition.

The Bedouin arts of weaving, folk tales, songs and dancing are to less and less an extent passed on in the daily lives of modern Kuwaitis, but attempts to preserve them by the activities of cultural centres such as Sadu House (p161) are reassuring.

The seafaring tradition of Kuwait has manifested artistically in the form of sea shanties and seafaring folklore. Shipbuilding developed into an art form, too, in its 18th-century heyday, as can be seen at the Al-Hashemi Marine Museum (p164). Two modern wooden sailing boats, *Mohammedi II* and *Al-Hashemi II*, on the same site as the museum, showcase the aesthetic side of shipbuilding. A tradition of lavish feasting upon the return of ships, which were often out pearling for months at a time, is also heartily alive.

Kuwait City has also developed a lively contemporary art scene with a growing regional reputation for the quality of exhibitions shown at venues such as Boushahri Art Gallery (p170) and Dar Al-Funoon (p170).

ENVIRONMENT
The Land

It has to be said that Kuwait is not the most well-endowed patch of earth, either in terms of the sublime or the picturesque. The interior consists of a mostly flat, gravelly plain with little or no ground water. Its saving grace is the grassy fringe that greens up prettily across much of the plain late in the spring, providing rich grazing for the few remaining Bedu who keep livestock. The only other geographic feature of any note in a country that measures 185km from north to south and 208km from east to west is Mutla Ridge, just north of Kuwait City. The coast is a little more characterful, with dunes, marshes, salt depressions around Kuwait Bay and an oasis in Al-Jahra.

Of the nine offshore islands, the largest is Bubiyan Island, while Failaka Island is the most historic: there are plans afoot to develop a container port on the former and a vast tourist complex on the latter, but at present there is nothing much to see on either island.

Wildlife

The anticlockwise flow of Gulf currents favours Kuwait's shoreline by carrying nutrients from the freshwater marshes of Shatt al-Arab and the delta of the Tigris and Euphrates in southern Iraq. The result is a rich and diverse coastline, with an abundance of marine life that even the poisoning of spilt oil has failed to destroy.

ANIMALS

Pearly goatfish, the oddly spiked tripod fish and the popular dinner fish of silver *pomphrey* are just some of the myriad species of fish that frequent the fishermen's nets along Kuwait Bay. Crabs tunnel in the mud flats near Doha Village, surviving in extreme temperatures and aerating the mud for other less durable bedfellows – such as the tiny mudskipper that sorties out for a mouthful of mud and water with which to build the walls of its castles in the sand. Propped up on their fins for a gulp of oxygen, they provide a tasty titbit for black-winged stilts, teals, lesser-crested terns and huge nesting colonies of soccotra cormorants, which share the coastline, and they trap algae in their geometric homes that feed the flamingos.

Inland, birds of prey, including the resident kestrel and the short-toed eagle, roam the escarpments. The desert comes alive at night with rare sightings of caracal, and hedgehog, big-eared fennecs – the smallest canines in the world – and jerboas, which gain all the liquid they need from the plants and insects they eat. It is easier to spot the dhoubs, a monitor lizard with a spiny tail, popular as a barbecue snack. And, of course, no Arab desert is the same without the diligent dung beetle or the scorpion.

In terms of endangered species, given the events of the past few years, it's remarkable that a few more species have not been added to the familiar list of desert mammals, like oryx and gazelle, made regionally extinct through hunting. The desert wolf has apparently made something of a comeback in recent years and has been spotted near residential areas.

PLANTS

After the winter rains, corridors of purple-flowered heliotrope bloom everywhere, and the highways are decorated with borders of assorted wild flowers. There are about 400 plant species in Kuwait. One of the most common is the bright-green *rimth*, which, along with red-flowered *al-awsaj*, is a favourite of grazing camels. The Bedu still use herb poultices for snake bites. In spring, truffles sprout through the cracked ground in desert wadis, as if remembering that Kuwait was once a delta land of the long-extinct Arabian River.

A particular blow to the country's ecology was the loss of many kilometres of

BLOOMS OF HOPE IN THE DESERT

A coalition of 28 nations fought to drive Iraq's military out of Kuwait in January and February 1991. In the months that followed, an equally impressive international effort helped clean up the ensuing mess.

The environmental damage caused by the Iraqis occurred on an unprecedented scale. On 20 January 1991, the third day of the war, Iraqi forces opened the valves at Kuwait's Mina al-Ahmadi Sea Island Terminal, intentionally releasing millions of litres of oil into the Gulf. The resulting oil slick was 64km wide and 160km long. Between six and eight million barrels of oil are thought to have been released, at least twice as much as in any previous oil spill. At least 460km of coastline, most of it in Saudi Arabia and Bahrain, was affected, with devastating consequences for the region's cormorants, migratory birds, dolphins, fish, turtles and large areas of mangrove.

The slick was fought by experts from nine nations and oil companies eventually managed to recover, and reuse, around a million barrels of crude oil from the slick.

The Iraqis were also to blame for the systematic torching of 699 of the emirate's oil wells. By the time the war ended, nearly every well was burning. At a conservative estimate, at least two million barrels of oil per day were lost – equivalent to about 5% of the total daily world consumption. One to two million tonnes of carbon dioxide streamed into the air daily, resulting in a cloud that literally turned day into night across the country.

Like the slick, the fires devastated wildlife throughout the region, but they also had a direct impact on public health. Black, greasy rain caused by the fires was reported as far away as India, and the incidence of asthma increased in the Gulf region.

Initial reports that it would take five years to put all the fires out proved pessimistic. A determined international effort, combined with considerable innovation on the part of the firefighters, extinguished the fires in only eight months. The crews did the job so quickly that one well had to be reignited so that the emir of Kuwait could 'put out the final fire' for reporters in November 1991.

Cleaning up the 65 million barrels of oil, spilt in 300 oil lakes covering around 50 sq km of desert, was not so speedily effected. In a joint project between the Kuwait Institute of Scientific Research (KISR) and the Japanese Petroleum Energy Center (PEC), a bioremediation project was launched to rehabilitate the oil-polluted soil. Through a variety of biological processes, which included composting and bioventing, more than 4000 cubic metres of contaminated soil were treated, resulting in soil of such high quality that it was good enough for landscaping and could be used as topsoil. The Japanese Garden in Al-Ahmadi is a showcase for the miracle 'oil soil'. The garden's 'blooms of hope' are a testimony to international cooperation and the ability of man and nature to outwit the worst that disaster can throw at them. The gardens are currently closed to the public.

black mangrove roots and beds of seagrass to oil spillage. These precious and endangered species help to stabilise and extend the country's shoreline, and their damage has been devastating.

National Parks

Larger than the state of Bahrain, the 863 sq km nature reserve on the northern end of Bubiyan Island is home to many species of birds and animals. Comprised of marshland and creeks, it is a haven for waders. It was heavily mined during the Gulf War and the causeway destroyed. The future could be just as alarming with a port and residential complex planned for the southern part of the island.

Environmental Issues

While Kuwait shares many of the same environmental concerns as its Gulf neighbours, it has also had to contend with the extraordinary circumstances inflicted by war (see boxed text, opposite). Over a decade later, the casual visitor is unlikely to detect any signs of war either in the desert or along the coast. A thorough cleanup by Pakistani and Bangladeshi troops, and subsequent diligence with regard to the removal of unexploded ordnance, means that Kuwaitis can once again enjoy the ritual camping expedition without fear of danger. Perversely, however, it is now the campers who are threatening the environment with discarded rubbish and heavy use of delicate grazing lands. In addition, relaxed standards with regard to waste and oil dumping have led to concerns about polluted seas along Kuwait's shoreline.

Every year on 24 April, the country observes Regional Environment Day, with school competitions and raised public awareness regarding marine and land resources.

FOOD & DRINK

Not surprisingly, a particular emphasis on fish occurs in Kuwaiti cuisine. It is often baked or stewed with a particularly Kuwaiti blend of Indian spices, such as coriander, turmeric, red pepper and cardamom, but without the chilli hit. Parsley, onions and dill are used to stuff *hammour* or *pomphrey*, two white-fleshed fish, similar to cod, while pine nuts, cashews and almonds are added to the stuffing on special occasions. Late

autumn and early winter are the best times for sampling Gulf prawns.

Kuwait's seafaring past has brought to this patch of desert an eclectic taste for international cuisine, and visitors can choose from a large selection of restaurants specialising in anything from Iranian stews to a burger and fries.

All drinks are nonalcoholic, but the elaborate mixed fruit cocktails are just as engaging.

Note that in addition to the usual prohibition on eating and drinking, it is illegal to chew gum in public during Ramadan.

KUWAIT CITY

مدينة الكويت

With its landmark triple towers looming over a clean and accessible corniche; a first-class aquarium and some excellent museums; stunning pieces of marine and land architecture; malls and souqs to please the most discerning or eclectic of shoppers; and a selection of restaurants to whet the appetite of the fussiest gourmands, Kuwait City is a sophisticated and interesting destination in its own right. Add to its sights and attractions a harrowing layer of modern history, the effects of which rumble invisibly below the surface, and there is enough to keep all but the dedicated nightclubber intrigued for days.

HISTORY

Kuwait City evolved from a collection of Bedouin tents around a well into a small military outpost with a *kout* (small fort adjacent to water), built in 1672 by the Bani Khalid tribe who came from the Arabian interior to escape drought. The word '*kout*' evolved to give the city (and indeed the country) its name. The outpost continued to attract Arab nomads who migrated east in the hot weather, but its natural harbour also made it an ideal location for a port. Indeed, it proved such an excellent port that it soon came to handle a lucrative trade in frankincense from Oman, pearls from Bahrain, spices from India, textiles from China and dates from just about everywhere. The port also facilitated the transshipment of goods across the desert to the Syrian port of Aleppo, a journey of two to three weeks. Pilgrims returned in the other direction, great caravans taking sustenance for the onward journey to Mecca.

Walls were built around the city in 1760, 1814 and 1920 in an attempt to define as well as confine the city, and five of the original districts – Qibla, Murgab, Sharq, Dasman

and Salhiya – remain. But no number of walls could restrain the oil boom. Within the memory of the older generation, Kuwait City was a nomadic port town and Salmiya consisted of a few mud huts around a tree. Suddenly, within the last two decades, a booming Middle Eastern metropolis has burst from its skin and the city gates are all

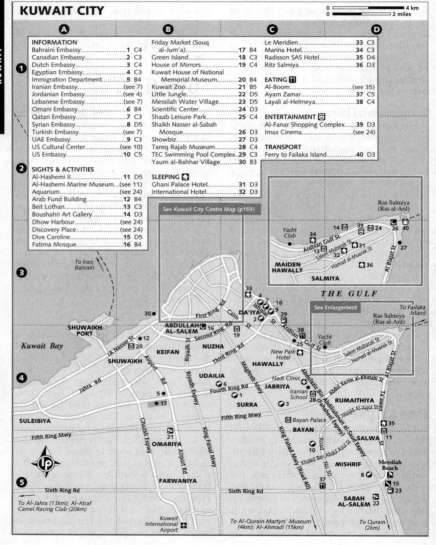

KUWAIT CITY

0 — 4 km
0 — 2 miles

INFORMATION
Bahraini Embassy.....................**1** C4	
Canadian Embassy....................**2** C3	
Dutch Embassy.........................**3** C4	
Egyptian Embassy.....................**4** C3	
Immigration Department..........**5** B4	
Iranian Embassy..................(see 7)	
Jordanian Embassy..............(see 4)	
Lebanese Embassy.................(see 7)	
Omani Embassy........................**6** B4	
Qatari Embassy........................**7** C3	
Syrian Embassy........................**8** D5	
Turkish Embassy...................(see 7)	
UAE Embassy............................**9** C3	
US Cultural Center..............(see 10)	
US Embassy.............................**10** C5	

SIGHTS & ACTIVITIES
Al-Hashemi II...........................**11** D5	
Al-Hashemi Marine Museum...(see 11)	
Aquarium.............................(see 24)	
Arab Fund Building.................**12** B4	
Beit Lothan.............................**13** C3	
Boushahri Art Gallery.............**14** D3	
Dhow Harbour.....................(see 24)	
Discovery Place....................(see 24)	
Dive Caroline..........................**15** D5	
Fatima Mosque......................**16** B4	

Friday Market (Souq	
al-Jum'a)...........................**17** B4	
Green Island...........................**18** C3	
House of Mirrors....................**19** C4	
Kuwait House of National	
Memorial Museum............**20** B4	
Kuwait Zoo.............................**21** B5	
Little Jungle...........................**22** D5	
Messilah Water Village...........**23** D5	
Scientific Center....................**24** D3	
Shaab Leisure Park................**25** C4	
Shaikh Nasser al-Sabah	
Mosque...........................**26** D3	
Showbiz.................................**27** D3	
Tareq Rajab Museum.............**28** C4	
TEC Swimming Pool Complex.**29** C3	
Yaum al-Bahhar Village.........**30** B3	

SLEEPING
Ghani Palace Hotel.................**31** D3	
International Hotel..................**32** D3	

Le Meridien...........................**33** C3	
Marina Hotel..........................**34** C3	
Radisson SAS Hotel................**35** D4	
Ritz Salmiya...........................**36** D3	

EATING
Al-Boom..............................(see 35)	
Ayam Zamar..........................**37** C5	
Layali al-Helmeya..................**38** C4	

ENTERTAINMENT
Al-Fanar Shopping Complex...**39** D3	
Imax Cinema........................(see 24)	

TRANSPORT
Ferry to Failaka Island............**40** D3	

See Kuwait City Centre Map (p159)

Ras Salmiya (Ras al-Ard)

Yacht Club

MAIDEN HAWALLY

SALMIYA

THE GULF

See Enlargement

Ras Salmiya (Ras al-Ard)

To Failaka Island

SHUWAIKH PORT

Kuwait Bay

SHUWAIKH

DA'IYA

ABDULLAH AL-SALEM

KEIFAN

NUZHA

New Park Hotel

Yacht Club

HAWALLY

UDAILIA

SURRA

JABRIYA

Hadi Clinic

Iranian School

RUMAITHIYA

SULEIBIYA

Fifth Ring Mwy

BAYAN

Bayan Palace

SALWA

OMARIYA

Messilah Beach

MISHRIF

FARWANIYA

Sixth Ring Rd

Sixth Ring Rd

SABAH AL-SALEM

To Al-Jahra (13km); Al-Atraf Camel Racing Club (20km)

Kuwait International Airport

To Al-Qurain Martyrs' Museum (4km); Al-Ahmadi (15km)

To Qurain (2km)

To Iran; Bahrain

that remain of the redundant walls. Three successive master plans have tried to give direction to city growth, allowing for generous mortgages and free housing for the needy, but the growth is organic and unstoppable.

The Iraqi invasion in 1990 tore a piece of the heart out of the city, but remarkably most of the landmark buildings remained standing. Barring the fortifications around hotels and embassies, and the mirror searches under cars, a visitor today is never likely to know how much the city suffered.

ORIENTATION

Kuwait City is vast. Extending 25km or more from east to west and 12km from north to south, one district runs seamlessly into the next. For the visitor, there are several key landmarks. Most of the city centre, sites of interest and souqs are encased by the First Ring Rd and by Arabian Gulf St, which forms the corniche. Near the northernmost point of the corniche are the distinctive triple Kuwait Towers and in the middle of central Kuwait City is the unmistakable Liberation Tower, used for telecommunications.

The main shopping and commercial street is Fahad al-Salem St in the city centre, which becomes Ahmed al-Jaber St north of Safat Sq. The souq is buried in the area between the municipal park and Mubarak al-Kabir St. More international shopping areas are clustered along the lower end of Fahad al-Salem St (near the Kuwait Sheraton hotel), behind the JW Marriott Hotel, along Arabian Gulf St and, for designer labels, further southeast in the shopping district of Salmiya.

The city spreads inland gradually, ringed and bisected by major highways.

Maps

GEO Projects publishes two maps of Kuwait City found on the back of the country map in its Arab World Map Library. These are available from hotels and bookshops for KD5.

INFORMATION
Bookshops
Kuwait Bookshop (Map p159; ☎ 242 4289; kbs1935b@qaulitynet.net; Basement, Al-Muthanna Centre, Fahad al-Salem St, Safat; ⊙ 9am-12.30pm & 5-9.30pm

Sat-Thu, 9am-noon & 5-9pm Fri) With a wide selection of bestsellers, books on current affairs and local-interest, this is the best place to look for English-language books.

Cultural Centres
Beit Lothan (Map p156; ☎ 575 5866; baytlothan@hotmail.com; Arabian Gulf St, Salmiya) Located in a traditional Kuwaiti house and dedicated to the promotion of arts and crafts; offers courses on crafts, poetry, drawing and painting.
British Council (Map p159; ☎ 251 5512; www.british council.org/kuwait; Al-Arabi St, Mansouria; ⊙ 8am-3pm Sat-Wed) Located next to Nadi al-Arabi stadium. The British Council runs a library, with a comprehensive video section, and gives guidance regarding studying in the UK as well as information on local and regional arts events. It also runs a number of English-language courses and testing services such as IELTS.
Centre Culturel Francais de Koweit (Map p159; ☎ 257 1061; Villa 24, Block 1, Street 13, Mansouria) Located at the French embassy, there is a library and video cinema; concerts, plays and exhibitions are sometimes organised.
US Cultural Center (Map p156; ☎ 539 5307; Plot 14, Block 14, Al-Masjid al-Aqsa St, Bayan) Located at the US embassy, about 17km south of the city centre, the Cultural Center provides information on studying in the US and runs a library.

Emergency
Fire, Police & Ambulance (☎ 777)

Internet Access
Many of the top-end hotels offer free internet access to guests. There is a growing number of internet cafés in the city centre and in Salmiya.
Kuwait Internet Café (Map p159; 2nd fl, Al-Dawliah Centre, Fahad al-Salem St; per hr 250 fils) Located behind the Kuwait Airways building, it offers reasonably fast connections.

Medical Services
Services in an emergency are provided free or at a minimal charge on a walk-in basis in most city hospitals. The biggest hospital is **Al-Amiri Hospital & Casualty** (Map p159; ☎ 245 0080; Arabian Gulf St).

Money
Banks are evenly distributed throughout the city. Moneychangers can offer slightly better rates than banks (and usually charge lower commissions); try some of the side streets that run from Safat Sq. Travellers

cheques can be changed at the following places:

Al-Ghanim Travel (Map p159; 2nd fl, Salhiya Commercial Centre; ⊗ 8am-1pm & 4-7pm Sat-Thu) American Express (Amex) is found here and card holders can cash personal cheques, but the office will not hold mail for Amex clients.

Al-Muzaini Exchange (Map p159; Fahad al-Salem St)

UAE Exchange (Map p159; Basement, Burgan Bank Bldg, Fahad al-Salem St)

Post

Kuwait City Post Office (Map p159; Fahad al-Salem St; ⊗ 7am-2pm Sat-Wed, 7am-noon Thu) Located by the intersection with Al-Wattiya St.

Telephone & Fax

Main Telephone Office (Map p159; cnr Abdullah al-Salem & Al-Hilali Sts; ⊗ 24hr) Located at the base of the telecommunications tower. Prepaid international calls can be booked, but international cardphones are cheaper. Fax services are also available.

Tourist Information

There is still no official tourist information office in Kuwait despite rumours to the contrary. However, there is a useful website (www.kuwaittourism.com). The Kuwait Tourism Services Company (p166) is a private company with many years of experience in supplying tourist information.

Travel Agencies

Lots of small travel agencies are to be found on Fahad al-Salem and Al-Soor Sts, between Al-Jahra Gate and the Radio and TV building. For helpful service, try the following:

Al-Ghanim Travel (Map p159; ☎ 802 112; travel@alghanim.com; 2nd fl, Salhiya Commercial Centre, Fahad Al-Salem St)

Al-Hogal Travels (Map p159; ☎ 243 8741; Al-Dawliah Centre)

Sanbouk Travels and Tours (Map p159; ☎ 245 7267; Arabian Gulf St) Located opposite Sharq Souq.

SIGHTS

Many of Kuwait's sights are concentrated along the corniche and around the National Museum area. While some of the downtown sights are within walking distance of each other, the most convenient way of visiting outlying attractions, or of covering longer stretches of the corniche (Arabian Gulf St), is by taxi.

Scientific Center

With time to do nothing else, it would be hard to beat a trip to the excellent **Scientific Center** (Map p156; ☎ 848 888; www.tsck.org.kw; Arabian Gulf St, Salmiya; ⊗ 9am-9.30pm Sun-Thu, 2-9.30pm Fri). Housed in a fine, sail-shaped building on the corniche, the centre's mesmerising **aquarium** is the largest in the Middle East. A sign of contentment, perhaps, turtles perch on the back of lazy crocodiles, hedgehogs mate, prickles notwithstanding, in the adjacent eco-display, and even the aquarium's guards have taken to humming Arabic love songs. The unique intertidal display, with waves washing in at eye level, is home to shoals of black-spotted sweetlips and the ingenious mudskipper. But the most spectacular part of the display (with giant spider crabs at 3.8m leg to leg, a living reef and fluorescent jellyfish coming in at a close second) is undoubtedly the wraparound, floor-to-ceiling shark and ray tanks. Ring to inquire about current feeding times.

The **IMAX cinema** includes a sensitive feature entitled *Fires of Kuwait*, charting the post-invasion cleanup. **Discovery Place** is an interactive learning centre for children, who can make their own sand dunes or roll a piece of road. There is a pleasant **dhow harbour**, where the *Fateh al-Khair*, the last surviving dhow of the pre-oil era, is moored.

Admission prices vary, depending on which parts of the centre are visited. A ticket to the aquarium or IMAX, for example, costs KD3/2 per adult/child while entrance to Discovery Place is KD2/1.500 per adult/child. A family could easily spend a day here and not get bored.

Salmiya bus stop, for buses 15, 17, 24, 34 and 200, is a short 10-minute (shaded) walk away.

Corniche

Comprising over 10km of winding paths, parks and beaches on Arabian Gulf St (sometimes referred to locally as Gulf Rd), the corniche is marked at its southern end by the Scientific Center and at its northernmost point by the Kuwait Towers. Stop off at any one of these beaches, restaurants or coffeehouses to watch a desert sunset, or, on hot summer evenings, enjoy being part of the throng of people flocking to the sea to catch the breeze.

KUWAIT CITY CENTRE

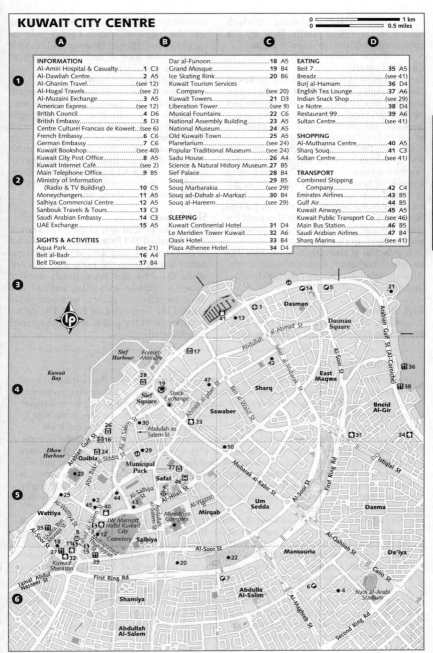

The private residences, some of which belong to the ruling family, light up the opposite side of the corniche at night.

Kuwait Towers

Kuwait's most famous landmark, the **Kuwait Towers** (Map p159; ☎ 244 4021; Arabian Gulf St, Dasman; observation deck admission KD1; ☯ observation deck 9am–midnight), with their distinctive green 'sequins', are worth a visit for the prospect of sea and city that they afford.

Designed by a Swedish architectural firm and opened in 1979, the largest of the three towers rises to a height of 187m, and houses a two-level revolving observation deck, gift shop and café. The lower globe on the largest tower stores around one million gallons of water. The middle tower is also used for water storage, while the smallest tower is used to light up the other two.

A **collection of photographs** show how the so-called 'barbarian invaders' tried to destroy the symbol of Kuwait during the Iraqi invasion.

Beit Dickson

A modest, white building with blue trim, **Beit Dickson** (Map p159; ☎ 243 7450; Arabian Gulf St; admission free; ☯ 8am–12.30pm & 4–7.30pm Sat–Wed) was the home of former British political agent Colonel Harold Dickson and his wife Violet whose love of and contribution to Kuwait is well documented.

Freya Stark spent most of March 1937 in the house and, while she adored Kuwait, she described the house as a 'big ugly box'. Nonetheless, a collection of photographs taken during Kuwait's British protectorate era; a replica museum of the Dixons' living quarters; and an archive of Kuwaiti-British relations that dates from the 19th century to the 1960s, when Kuwait was granted independence, make the museum an interesting place in which to spend an hour.

Sief Palace

This is the official seat of the emir's court. The L-shaped **Sief Palace** (Map p159; Arabian Gulf St) that faces the roundabout is the original palace dating from the early 20th century, while the new and ponderously opulent palace, complete with lake, helipad and dock for visitors' yachts, was completed around the beginning of 2000. The palace is not open to the public and photography is prohibited.

BUILDING WEALTH

There are few buildings in the region as iconic as the Kuwait Towers (above). Their slender columns and plump water reservoirs are symbolic of the way in which a city has blossomed from humble beginnings. Nor are they Kuwait's only bid for the skies: Liberation Tower (p162), the fifth-largest communication tower in the world, illustrates how the city, despite the troubles of the past 20 years, is keen to win international status as concrete as the oil reserves upon which it sits.

Kuwait's extraordinary modern wealth has been expressed in many other pieces of civic pride. The flamboyant National Assembly Building (opposite), designed by Jørn Utzon of Sydney Opera House fame, resembles a piece of unfurled silk, evoking both the canopy of a Bedouin tent and a sail-furled dhow, while expressing modernist concepts of negative space and the sculpture of light and shade. Then there's the Arab Fund Building (p162), with its expression of the integrity of space and function, light and communication, and combining modern interior design with a traditional Islamic aesthetic.

Considerable wealth has also been channelled into religious architecture, with some 60% of Kuwait's mosques financed and built by individuals. The Grand Mosque (opposite), across from Sief Palace on Arabian Gulf St, with the tallest minaret in the country; the green-and-white pudding bowl of Fatima Mosque (Map p156) in Abdullah al-Salem; and the pyramid-shaped Shaikh Nasser al-Sabah Mosque in Ras Salmiya (also known as Ras al-Ard) all contend as exceptional pieces of modern mosque design.

But, descending from god to mammon, it is the shopping malls that have been constructed during the last few years that have provided the modern architect with the greatest scope. Sharq Souq (p170) on Arabian Gulf St is a case in point; with its wind-tower design and adjoining marina, architects are clearly free to build on the city's humble Bedouin and seafaring beginnings both metaphorically and literally.

Grand Mosque

Also known as Masjed Al-Kabir, and located opposite Sief Palace, the **Grand Mosque** (Map p159; ☎ 246 7058, 241 8447; www.freekuwait .com/mosque; Mubarak al-Kabir St) was opened in 1986 and cost KD14 million to construct. The largest of the city's 800 mosques, it boasts Kuwait's highest minaret (74m) and can accommodate up to 5000 worshippers in the main hall, with room for another 7000 in the courtyard. Prebooked tours are possible between 9am and 4pm Saturday to Wednesday and it is respectful to dress modestly, covering arms and legs.

National Museum Complex

Once the pride of Kuwait, the **National Museum** (Map p159; ☎ 245 1195; Arabian Gulf St, Qibla; admission 250 fils; ⏰ 8.30am-noon & 4-7pm Sun-Fri, 4-7pm Sat) is still under restoration. The centrepiece of the museum, the **Al-Sabah collection**, was one of the most important collections of Islamic art in the world. During the Iraqi occupation, however, the exhibition halls were systematically looted, damaged or set fire to.

Following intense pressure from the UN, the majority of the museum's collection was eventually returned, but many pieces had been broken in transit, poorly stored and, some suggest, deliberately spoiled. Nonetheless, this beleaguered collection has since been displayed in London's British Museum and the Metropolitan Museum of Art in New York while waiting to be restored in its entirety to Kuwait's National Museum.

Over 2000 items are now on display, covering various aspects of Kuwait's national heritage, and a newly opened hall displays ancient treasures from Failaka Island, including stamps and seals from the Bronze Age, axe heads and a wonderful Hellenistic limestone dolphin. The dhow in the courtyard (a replica of *Muhallab II* that was destroyed by the Iraqis) makes a good photo opportunity at sunset.

The quaint **Popular Traditional Museum** (☎ 272 9158) – variously described as the Heritage Museum and Culture Museum – is in Building 2, in the rear of the museum complex. It illustrates daily life in pre-oil Kuwait through a diorama of full-sized figures going about their various businesses – be sure to see the bead maker and what the museum booklet describes as the 'men's over-robe tailor'.

The wonderful, modern **Planetarium** (☎ 245 6534) in the museum complex has shows at around 6pm daily: local children, convinced the room is spinning, clap in syncopated beats every time the accompanying music begins.

Buses 12 and 16 (departing from the main bus station) stop a couple of blocks from the museum complex.

Sadu House

Forming part of the National Museum complex, **Sadu House** (Map p159; ☎ 243 2395; www.sadu-house.com; Arabian Gulf St, Qibla; admission free; ⏰ 8am-1pm & 4-7.30pm Sat-Thu) is a cultural foundation dedicated to preserving Bedouin arts and crafts. It is also the best place in Kuwait to buy Bedouin goods, such as pillows (KD5) and small bags (KD7 to KD15). The house is built of gypsum and coral, with fine decorations in the courtyard and an elegant use of light and space.

The **Kuwait Textile Arts Association** (☎ 390 3462; ktaaworkshop@yahoo.com) holds a variety of *sadu* (Bedouin-style) and other weaving courses, taught by Bedouin women, at Sadu House.

Beit al-Badr

A traditional mud-built house, with heavy carved doors, **Beit al-Badr** (Map p159; ☎ 242 9158; Arabian Gulf St, Qibla; admission free; ⏰ 8am-1pm & 4-7pm Sat-Wed) was built between 1838 and 1848 and is one of the last examples of pre-oil residential architecture in the city. It is located alongside Sadu House.

National Assembly Building

Close to the National Museum, the interesting white building with its distinctive canopy, the **National Assembly Building** (Map p159; ☎ 241 8949, 243 6381; Arabian Gulf St, Qibla), was designed by Jørn Utzon, the Danish architect who also designed the Sydney Opera House, and was completed in 1985. The two sweeping roofs were designed to evoke Bedouin tents and the building is befitting of the first parliament of the region.

Old Kuwaiti Town

Situated just west of the dhow harbour, near the National Assembly Building, the houses in this complex of **replica 19th-century** dwellings (Map p159; Arabian Gulf St, Qibla; admission free) gives a good idea of what Kuwait City would have looked like before the discovery of oil. Part of the complex is lived in, while the other part is given over to some of the city's best restaurants.

Souq

True to its origins, Kuwait City has retained the **old souq** (Map p159; btwn Mubarak al-Kabir, Ahmad al-Jaber & Ali al-Salem Sts; ☀ 9am-1pm & 4-9pm Sat-Thu, 4-9pm Fri) in all of its complex, bustling and convoluted glory in the city centre. Albeit partly housed now in a smart, modern building, complete with cubby-holes of lockable wooden shutters, it nonetheless exudes antique practices, from the sharp haggling over ribands of offal and tails of ox, to the quick-witted trading of olives and dates in the extensive food halls of **Souq Marbarakia**. It's a wonderful place to idle a few hours, and indeed an entire lunch time could be spent sampling delicacies without ever setting foot in one of the numerous snack shops that line the outer rim of the souq.

The souq also comprises the small, covered **Souq al-Hareem**, where Bedouin women sit cross-legged on cushions of velvet selling *kohl* (black eyeliner), pumice stones,

---

SNACKING WITH HISTORY

If you can find it, try a dozen mixed samosas (250 fils) from the Indian snack shop (p169) at the edge of Souq Marbarakia. Approaching from the heritage section of the souq (for incense and perfumes), the shop is in the corner of a small outdoor seating area. Next to a clothing shop and around the corner from the date souq, the shop is identified by the small window in a wall of sheet metal.

This isn't just any old hole-in-the-wall. It hasn't been included in the surrounding modernisations because this ramshackle wooden building is one of the least known and most important of Kuwait's historic buildings. In the early 20th century it was here that Mubarak the Great held his daily *diwaniya* (gathering), walking each day from Sief Palace through the old souq to this building where he would sit, talk to the people and feel the pulse of the street.

---

and gold-spangled dresses (KD1) in the red, white and green livery of the Kuwaiti flag. Beyond the covered alleyway, the souq opens out into alleyways stocked with woollen vests and Korean blankets.

The close-by **Souq ad-Dahab al-Markazi** is the city's central gold market.

Liberation Tower

Not to be confused with the distinctive Kuwait Towers, **Liberation Tower** (Map p159; ☎ 242 9166; cnr Al-Hilali & Abdullah al-Salem Sts, Safat) in the city centre is the tallest building in the city, and at a height of 372m claims to be the fifth-tallest communications tower in the world. Started before the invasion, the tower took its new name when it was completed in 1993.

Science & Natural History Museum

For an eclectic range of exhibits from electronics and space paraphernalia to fossils, stuffed animals and an 18m whale skeleton, this **museum** (Map p159; ☎ 242 1268; Abdullah al-Mubarak St, Safat; adult/child 150/100 fils; ☀ 9am-noon & 4.30-7.30pm Sat-Wed), near Liberation Tower, also has a **planetarium** with a Galaxy Sky-show at 6pm.

Old City Gates

Al-Shaab, **Al-Shamiya**, **Al-Jahra** and **Al-Maqsab** are the names of Kuwait City's gates in Safat on Al-Soor St, the street that follows the line of the old city wall ('*soor*' is the Arabic word for 'wall'). Despite their ancient appearance, the wall and gates were only constructed around 1920. The wall was demolished in 1957.

Yaum Al-Bahhar Village

With traditional wind-tower architecture, this small area of **craft workshops** (Map p156; Arabian Gulf St, Shuwaikh; admission free) is part of a development along the coast that includes walking paths and fountains. The workshops are open at variable times and some of the items are for sale. Not-for-the-faint-hearted crafts include stuffed bustard, an endangered bird, and shell decorations that you wouldn't wish on your enemy.

Arab Fund Building

Although not strictly open to the casual caller, the impressive **Arab Fund Building** (Map p156; ☎ 484 4500; www.arabfund.org/aohq;

Airport Rd, Shuwaikh; admission free), with a host of exceptionally beautiful rooms, is worth the trouble of gaining access. Call first to request an appointment and explain that you wish to see the building's interior and you'll be given a guided tour by one of the employees.

The gravity of the exterior belies the light and airy interior, designed upon Arabic architectural principles of integrity of space, decoration and function. The magnificent eight-storey atrium with wooden lattices, opening onto a transparent corridor or an exquisite hidden *majlis* (meeting room), is an exciting reinterpretation of a familiar theme. Traditional craftsmanship from around the Arab world is represented in lavish concoctions of ceramic, carpet and woodwork in one of the most extraordinary expressions of postmodern eclecticism in the Gulf.

Beit Lothan

The cultural centre, **Beit Lothan** (Map p156; ☎ 575 5866; lothan@hotmail.com; Arabian Gulf St, Salmiya; ☻ 9am-1pm & 4.30-9pm Sat-Wed), promotes the work of Kuwaiti and Gulf artists and craftspeople through regular exhibitions in a 1930s house that was originally the home of the country's late emir, Sheikh Sabah al-Salem al-Sabah.

Kuwait House of National Memorial Museum

This innovative **museum** (Map p156; ☎ 484 5335; opposite prime minister's residence, Shuwaikh; admission KD1; ☻ 8.30am-1pm & 4.30-8.30pm) encapsulates the horror of the Iraqi invasion and honours the sacrifices that ordinary Kuwaiti citizens, the Kuwaiti military and the allies made in order to beat back Saddam's forces. The exhibits comprise a set of well-crafted models of the city that are illuminated in time with an audio recording in English. Despite the nationalist propaganda, the experience of walking through the darkened corridors, lit only by simulated gun blasts and mortar attacks, and focusing on the heroism of the few for the safety of the many, has a contemporary resonance that transcends the exhibit's narrow remit. The museum is best reached by taxi and can be combined with a visit to the nearby Arab Fund Building. In case you are wondering, the state-of-the-art steel and concrete building nearby is the brand new headquarters of Kuwait Petroleum Corporation.

Friday Market (Souq al-Jum'a)

For a plastic pot plant, a second-hand dress, an Afghan coat or a smuggled antique from Iran, this enormous open-air, weekly **market** (Map p156; south of 4th Ring Rd & west of Airport Rd, Shuwaikh; ☻ 8am-4pm Fri) is more than a shopping extravaganza – it offers an insight into contemporary Kuwaiti culture and cross-border relations. Five minutes sitting in the shade of sun-fading textiles and sipping on the good-natured coffee of a friendly vendor delivers more in the way of insight into the complex web of Kuwaiti affairs, domestic and international, than one could absorb in a month of lectures on Arabic culture. Bring a hat and water in summer.

House of Mirrors

For a quirky art-in-action experience, visit this small **museum** (Map p156; ☎ 251 8522; House 17, Street 94, Block 9, Qadisiya; admission free) in a residential house in the suburbs of Qadisiya. Reputedly, 77 tons of mirror and 102 tons of white cement have been used in the creation of the mirror mosaics that spangle the entire house – both inside and out. The creation of Lidia al-Qattan, the widow of Khalifa al-Qattan, a renowned Kuwaiti artist, the project was inspired by the decorating of an old piece of dining-room furniture and grew to incorporate epic scenes, as in the Room of the Universe (bedroom) and the Basin of the Sharks (hallway). Ring ahead to request a tour; you should bring a small gift in exchange for the hospitality you will no doubt receive.

Tareq Rajab Museum

Housed in the basement of a large villa, this exquisite ethnographic **museum** (Map p156; ☎ 531 7358; www.trmkt.com; House 16, Block 12, Street 5, Jabriya; admission free; ☻ 9am-noon & 4-7pm Sat-Thu, 9am-noon Fri) should not be missed. It was assembled as a private collection of Islamic art by Kuwait's first minister of antiquities and his British wife. A pair of ornate doors from Cairo and Carl Haag's 19th-century painting of Lady Jane Digby el-Mesreb of Palmyra, who lived in tents in the winter and a Damascus villa in the summer, mark the entrance to an Aladdin's cave of beautiful items. There are inlaid musical

---

WEARING A THREE-PIECE

When visiting the Friday Market (p163), spare a thought for the ubiquitous men in yellow who scout the aisles of the market looking for customers. They are more than just carters and humpers, they are the backbone of the market.

The lucky ones get to wheel a green three-wheeled barrow of chirping plastic birds or second-hand light bulbs; they load the barrows high with repaired microwaves or used bicycle bells; or they wait patiently for Kuwaiti women to haggle in the open corridors of curtains and wall-to-wall sticky-backed carpeting. On rare occasions, they might win a commission from a Western tourist, wherein they have to fade into the fluffy-sleeved Afghan jackets while the customer tries on badly cut leather jackets from Pakistan or barters old lamps for new in the artisan corner of the market.

But it's the unlucky ones that are the heroes of the souq. They are the men that have to heave second-hand fridges that didn't work the first time, or lever Hoover pipes and old armchairs over the cogs and wheels of discarded machinery. In particular, watch out for the 'three-piecers' – three-piece sofas, that is, carried aloft on the head of a single, extraordinary strong, and conspicuously small, person from Bangladesh. With their king-sized upholsteries perfectly balanced, these mini-Goliaths of the souq trot through the aisles of fluttering caftans to the tune of Tagalog, Erdu, Hindi, Arabic and Malayalam as unphased by their impossible loads as a sherpa on Everest, and generous enough to spare a smile for a passing stranger.

---

instruments suspended in glass cabinets; Omani silver and Saudi gold jewellery; head dresses, from the humble prayer cap to the Mongol helmet; costumes worn by princesses and by goatherds; necklaces for living goddesses in Nepal; Jaipur enamel; and Bahraini pearl. Despite all these superbly presented pieces from around the Muslim world, it is the Arabic manuscripts that give the collection its international importance.

The museum is all the more prized given the fate that befell the treasures in the National Museum during the Iraqi invasion. When news of the invasion spread, the owners bricked up the doorway at the bottom of the entry steps and strewed the way with rubbish. The Iraqis questioned why the stairs led to nowhere, but mercifully didn't pursue the issue and the collection survived intact.

The museum is in Jabriya, near the intersection of the Fifth Ring Motorway and the Abdulaziz Bin Abdilrahman al-Saud Expressway (also known as the Fahaheel Expressway). There is no sign on the building, but it is easily identified by its entrance – a carved wooden doorway flanked by two smaller doors on each side. All four of the door panels are worked in gilt metal.

Allow an hour to visit, although anyone with a passion for textiles will inevitably want to stay longer. Buses 102 and 502

stop at Hadi Clinic. Walk south along the Fahaheel Expressway for five minutes and turn right just before the Iranian School. Walk for a further 50m and the museum is on the left.

Al-Hashemi Marine Museum

For proof that the Vikings made it to the Middle East, albeit only model ones, it's worth visiting this **museum** (Map p156; ☎ 565 7000; behind Radisson SAS Hotel, Ta'awen St, Salwa; admission free) with its impressive collection of large, scaled-model dhows. A novel shop sells 21-piece knot boards (KD25) and Gipsy Moth lanterns (KD16.500) among other nautical souvenirs, such as barometers and sextants. You can even buy your own Nelson figurine, incomplete with one arm, at the bargain price of KD12.

On the wall of the museum is a certificate, dated 2002, from the Guinness World Records announcing that **Al-Hashemi II**, the huge and unmissable wooden dhow adjacent to the museum, is the largest wooden boat on earth, measuring a world record–breaking 80.4m long, 18.7m wide and weighing an estimated 2500 tonnes. The vision of Husain Marafie, owner of the Radisson SAS Hotel, the dhow was completed in 1998 from mahogany and ekki logs from Cameroon, planks from the Ivory Coast and pine logs from Oregon. It's worth taking a five-minute walk inside the lavish, parquet-floored interior, used for conferences and banqueting.

A smaller dhow in the complex, called Al-Boom (p169), is a restaurant; it's a great place for dinner.

Al-Qurain Martyrs' Museum

Located in the residential suburb of Qurain, a 20-minute taxi ride southeast of the city centre, this small **museum** (Rd 208, Qurain; admission free; ⊙ 8am-2pm Sat-Thu) is a memorial to a cell of young Kuwaiti patriots who tried to resist arrest in February 1991. Early in the morning, a minibus (the one that is still parked outside) drew up outside the house. When no-one answered the door, the Iraqis bombarded the house for hours with machine guns, bombs and eventually a tank. Nine of those under siege were captured and tortured to death, while four hid in a roof space.

General Schwarzkopf, who visited the house on 14 April 1994, commented that 'when I am in this house it makes me wish that we had come four days earlier then perhaps this tragedy would not have happened'. The Iraqi occupation lasted for seven long months, during which time many similar raids on the homes of Kuwaiti families were made: or, as the editor of a local publication put it, the Iraqi army 'was like a locust that ate both the green and the dry'.

To understand what invasion meant to the ordinary Kuwaiti family, allow half an hour to visit this sobering museum, if only to see copies of documents issuing instructions to 'burn and destroy' homes and 'fire on demonstrations'. Bus 101 stops within a 10-minute walk of the museum, but it is difficult to find the precise location without assistance. Go by taxi.

ACTIVITIES

Kuwait City's location on the seafront provides many opportunities for fun with water – in it (swimming), on it (water sports, and ice skating), alongside it (jogging along the corniche) and through it (ferry rides). One tour operator that can help you with a wide range of activities is **Nuzha Tourist Enterprises** (☎ 575 5825; www.nuzha.com.kw).

Green Island

For activities ranging from strolling in the gardens, swimming in a lagoon, cycling or listening to an impromptu concert, this artificial **island** (Map p156; ☎ 252 6153; Arabian Gulf St, Dasman; admission adult/child 500/250 fils; ⊙ 8am-11pm), joined to the mainland by a pedestrian causeway, houses a 700-seat amphitheatre, restaurants, and a game park for children. On 25 February (National Day) and 26 February (Liberation Day), Green Island becomes the launching pad for firework displays.

Swimming

All the way along Arabian Gulf St there are splendid beaches and there is nothing to stop a committed paddler from taking a dip in any of them, though the water tends to be on the shallow side for serious swimming and worries prevail as to the state of pollution in the water.

For those who prefer facilities, **Messilah Water Village** (Map p156; ☎ 565 0505; Arabian Gulf St, Messilah; admission KD3; ⊙ 8am-11pm), some 20km south of the city centre, has a good range of pools, floats and slides. The water is chilled in summer and heated in winter. Between April and August the beach is reserved for women only on three days of the week. The same company manages the centrally located **Aqua Park** (Map p159; ☎ 243 1960). Call first, as it is not always open.

If the turquoise sea doesn't tempt, there's always Touristic Enterprises Company. Affectionately known as the **TEC Swimming Pool Complex** (Map p156; Arabian Gulf St, Dasman), there are three large pools available, one for women and families, one for men only and a shallow one for children.

Diving

Diving in Kuwait's warm, shallow waters is a pleasant way to spend time. There are several dive outfits, but the best-established is **Dive Caroline** (Map p156; ☎ 371 9289; divecaroline .com) at the Messilah Water Village. It offers day trips for KD15 to KD20 or half-day trips to Donkey Reef leaving at 8am and 2pm daily. You can also try the five-star PADI dive establishment at the **KIM Center** (Map p156; ☎ 371 6002; www.kimcenter.com; Hilton Kuwait Resort, Fahaheel) for diving and snorkelling trips to the outer islands of Kubar and Umm al-Maradim (from around KD20).

Other Water Activities

Water taxis run regularly from the tourist enterprise office in Shaab to Kuwait

Towers for 500 fils per person. **Nuzha Touristic Enterprises** (☎ 575 5825; www.nuzhatours.com) can organise half- and whole-day boat trips to Failaka Island and other locations.

Both diving companies organise a range of other water sports including kayaking (KD7.500 for four hours).

Ice Skating

One of the best in the region, Kuwait City's **ice-skating rink** (Map p159; ☎ 241 1151; Al-Soor St & First Ring Rd, Shamiya; admission KD1.500; ⏰ 8.30am-10pm) gives the public a chance to sample an Olympic-sized rink. With a spectator capacity of 1600, it's home to the Kuwaiti Falcons, the country's official ice-hockey team, and the only Arab team to win membership of the International Ice Hockey Federation.

COURSES

Beit Lothan (p157) offers a range of courses, including crafts, poetry, drawing and painting. Weaving is taught by Bedouin women at Sadu House (p161).

KUWAIT CITY FOR CHILDREN
Fun Parks

Occupying a large, open area, **Shaab Leisure Park** (Map p156; ☎ 561 3777; www.shaabpark .com; Arabian Gulf St, Salmiya; admission 500 fils; ⏰ 4pm-midnight Sat-Wed, 10am-midnight Thu & Fri) offers rides, bungee jumping and pony riding. For a unique souvenir, try the video cinema, where visitors can make their own music video.

For a less-crowded experience, try **Showbiz** (Map p156; ☎ 571 4094; Al Blajat St, Salmiya; admission free; ⏰ 4-11pm), which offers the same kind of activities but on a smaller scale. Attractions inside the funfair cost between 500 fils and KD1.

Zoos

The **Kuwait zoo** (Map p156; ☎ 473 3389; cnr Airport Rd & 5th Ring Rd, Omariya; admission 500 fils; ⏰ 8am-10pm winter, 8am-noon & 4pm-midnight Sun-Fri summer) has 65 species with an emphasis on desert dwellers.

Another, smaller zoo, called **Little Jungle** (Map p156; ☎ 390 2635; www.littlejungle.net; off Fahaheel Expressway, Funaitees; admission 250 fils; ⏰ 4-11pm), is designed for smaller children, who can pat a pony, grab a goat or kiss a camel while parents puff on a *sheesha* (water pipe

used to smoke tobacco) and think of caterpillars instead.

Musical Fountains

Located next to the ice-skating rink, this outdoor **music and water display** (Map p156; ☎ 242 8394; Al-Soor St & First Ring Rd; admission 250 fils; ⏰ 4-11pm) is said to have the 4th-largest set of fountains in the world.

TOURS

The **Kuwait Tourism Services Company** (Map p159; ☎ 245 1734; www.ktsc-q8.com; Ice-skating Rink, Al-Soor St & First Ring Rd, Shamiya) runs tours around the various city sights and out to the oilfields. It mainly caters for large tour groups, but can also arrange similar tours for individuals. Half- and full-day city tours (depending on the choice of activities) cost around KD15/25 per person for a minimum of two people.

Nuzha Tourist Enterprises (☎ 575 5825; www .nuzha.com.kw) can organise a wide range of tours and offers camel and horse rides, desert safaris, climbing tours and many other activities.

FESTIVALS & EVENTS

During the month of February, the city goes crazy with the **Hala Shopping Festival**. There are lots of draws giving away valuable prizes in the shopping centres, and special promotions lure customers in. Many shops offer discounts of up to 70%. Ask your hotel reception where to go for the best bargains.

The festival coincides with National Day on 25 February and Liberation Day on 26 February. During this time, there are fireworks displays on Green Island and the city is draped in lights. Check the *What's On* listings in the English-language dailies to check the cultural programmes on offer.

SLEEPING

All of the hotels mentioned here have aircon, private bathrooms, satellite TVs and minifridges. Prices quoted are inclusive of the 15% service charge that most hotels add to their tariff, though it's always worth asking for a discount.

Budget

The following are about as budget as hotels get in Kuwait.

International Hotel (Map p156; ☎ 574 1788; www.internationalhotel-kw.com; Dumna St, behind Al-Fannar Complex, Salmiya; s/d KD20/25) This 1970s hotel, in its distinctive round building and period-piece lobby of varnished wood and mirror, is something of a Kuwaiti institution. The oddly shaped rooms with their curved balconies, chocolate brown carpets and grilled radiators, are dated but spacious. There is 24-hour room service but no restaurant.

Kuwait Continental Hotel (Map p159; ☎ 252 7300; www.kcontl.net; Road 30, opposite Dasma Roundabout, Bneid Al-Qar; s/d KD30/35; ✉) Popular with regional sporting personalities, as the trophies behind reception testify, this no-nonsense hotel on a busy intersection is not the friendliest place in town. If you can see past the tired and hideous blue corridors, the rooms and bathrooms are recently refurbished with quality, Arabian-style décor and furnishings and as such represent good value. There is a Budget car-hire desk in the foyer.

Oasis Hotel (Map p159; ☎ 246 5489; www.oasis.com.kw; cnr Ahmad al-Jaber & Mubarak al-Kabir Sts, Sharq; s/d KD30/35) One can only sympathise with this friendly hotel with its tolerant staff: the adjacent buildings either side of the hotel were being demolished at the time of research. If you're not troubled by the noise of rebuilding and can overlook the dingy corridors and stained carpets, then this lime-green hotel, with its sea-green reception area, has simple, clean rooms and is in a prime downtown location.

Midrange

All the following midrange hotels offer good value.

Plaza Athenee Hotel (Map p159; ☎ 846 666; www.plazaatheneekuwait.com; Port Said St, Block 18, behind Al-Manar Complex, Bneid Al-Qar; s/d KD34/65) If you're wondering at the discrepancy in price between single and double in this brand new boutique hotel, it is not a printing error! The singles are pigeon-sized, with tiny, angular shower rooms and linoleum floors. In contrast, the doubles, with heavy Arabian-style furniture and thick wooden doors all have marble-topped kitchenettes, balconies and separate sitting areas.

Ghani Palace Hotel (Map p156; ☎ 571 0301; www.ghanipalace.com; Salem Mubarak St, Salmiya; s/d KD35/45; ✉ ✉) Located in an extraordinary Yemeni–style building next to the Central Plaza shopping mall, this hotel is a flight of Arabian fancy with furniture from Syria, lanterns from Morocco and local plaster work. Each wood-panelled room is split level with kitchenette and balcony and gives in character what it lacks in finish. There is a billiard room and internet café downstairs, and a rather lovely swimming pool on the rooftop. This is one of the few hotels where you don't have to check the address to remember you're in the Middle East.

Ritz Salmiya (Map p156; ☎ 571 1001; www.ritzkuwait.com; Qatar St, Salmiya; r KD40-57) With the opportunity of using the facilities (including swimming pool and sauna) of the sister Ritz hotel on the corniche, this good value, bright and friendly hotel, opposite the City Center shopping mall, has an appealingly busy atmosphere. Rooms are modern and bright.

Le Meridien (Map p156; ☎ 251 0999; www.lemeridien-kuwait.com; Arabian Gulf St, Bneid al-Qar; r KD59.500; ✉) This small and tasteful boutique–style hotel with wonderful views of Kuwait Towers has a French Rococo foyer and a bright and intimate atmosphere. The floors and ceilings need a bit of TLC but the rooms, with their CD players, polished floors, floral-design bedsteads, huge bolster pillows and enormous luxury bathrooms are state-of-the-art.

Top End

The prices quoted here are rack rates: with a bit of persuasion, you can usually negotiate some sort of 'corporate' rate.

HOTELS

There are plenty of five-star hotels to choose from. The following are well-located options that have something different to offer.

Le Meridien Tower Kuwait (Map p159; ☎ 247 9000; www.lemeridienkuwait.com; Fahad al-Salem St, Wattiyah; s/d KD57/69; ✉ ✉) Located in the heart of downtown Kuwait, this stylish hotel prides itself as being the first 'art and tech' hotel in the Gulf with designer features such as LCD TV screens, powered showers, DVD, VCD, CD and interactive TV in each room. The illuminated glass panels behind the bedstead and the glass washbasin in the bathrooms help complete the impression of 22nd-century living. Live cooking shows in the chrome and wood Cascade Restaurant cater for individual guests.

Radisson SAS Hotel (Map p156; ☎ 575 6000; www .radissonsas.com; Ta'awen St, Rumaithiya; s/d KD 96/110; ▣ ▣) If it wasn't for the armed guard on the gate, it would be hard to imagine that a decade ago there wasn't a window remaining in this quiet hotel. While the hotel is ordinary enough, the presence of Al-Hashemi Marine Museum (p164) and the intimate Al-Boom restaurant (opposite) in the back garden give this old warhorse of a hotel a welcome added dimension, together with the excellent staff, small but cosy rooms and beach access.

ourpick Marina Hotel (Map p156; ☎ 224 4970; www.marinhotel.com; Arabian Gulf St, Salmiya; s/d KD110/ 122; ▣ ▣) Situated within walking distance from the shopping district of Salmiya, this beautiful circular, low-rise hotel floats like a lily on the water's edge and is a welcome addition to the corniche. Many of the stunning rooms have direct access onto the beach. Sophisticated, elegant and modern, this is one boutique hotel that succeeds in being practical as well as aesthetically pleasing. If you get bored of gazing at the sea outside your bedroom window, you could always sit in the lobby and enjoy the aquarium behind reception instead. The hotel's Atlantis restaurant, in the shape of a ship's prow, is an excellent place to sample the catch of the day (KD12.500), together with six oysters (KD6).

RESORTS

There are many resorts along Kuwait's sandy seashores, but they mostly cater for private membership. The following, which are well out of town, welcome tourists.

Hilton Kuwait Resort (Map p147; ☎ 372 5500; www.hilton.com; Coast Rd, Mangaf; s/d KD75/88; ▣ ▣) Situated on 1.8km of white-sand beach with spotless water, this resort provides the perfect antidote to the proverbial 'hard day in the office', whether 'office' equates with a business meeting, a day of committed shopping or sightseeing, or even a day of peacekeeping over the border. While the hotel is still popular with allied officers on R&R, it is equally attractive as a family holiday destination, with plenty of activities for children, and an excellent spa, restaurants and exercise opportunities for mum and

dad. Lessons in Thai cuisine at the Blue Elephant Royal Thai Restaurant may occupy those who can't sit still and there is a dive centre here. An apartment or chalet offers good value, but if the cost is still prohibitive, check the current rate for use of the resort's facilities for the day. At 35km and a 20-minute drive south of the city centre, it's pushing it to call it a city resort, but it still makes an easily accomplished afternoon's outing.

Kempinski Jalai'a Hotel & Resort (Map p147; ☎ 844 444; www.kempinski-kuwait.com; Rd 245, Fahad Motorway, Jalai'a; s/d KD94/106; ▣ ▣) Located about 70km south of Kuwait City, this is definitely not what one could call 'conveniently located'. If you are looking to get away from the city for a weekend, however, this palm tree, pool and beach complex, with its desert-castle architecture, Ayurvedic Centre and health club could be just the thing. With a spa, water-sports facilities, cinema, entertainment centre and bicycle hire, it's unlikely you'll notice that's there's precious little surrounding the resort.

EATING

Perhaps the city's best-loved activity, dining out is something of an institution, and there are literally hundreds of restaurants to suit all wallets and palates. The following represent an eclectic hotchpotch of choices that have a flavour of the region either in the cuisine or in the ambience.

Restaurants

Burj Al-Hamam (Map p159; ☎ 252 9095; fax 254 1308; Arabian Gulf St, Dasman; meals KD2-5; ☽ 9am-midnight) This circular restaurant at the end of a pier is like a piece of punctuation along the corniche – but don't let the rather unattractive steel exterior put you off. This is a great place to sample Middle Eastern fare in a thoroughly convivial atmosphere among loudly chatting local families. There is an inner and outer core to the restaurant with 280 degrees open to the sea – that's if you can glimpse it above the heaps of primarycoloured cushions and through the haze of peach-flavoured *sheesha* (KD2.500). Try the *kheshkhash* (spiced mince meat with onions and parsley) priced at a very reasonable KD2.250.

Beit 7 (Map p159; ☎ 245 0871; www.beit7.com; Behbehani Houses No 7, Usama Ben Monqiz St, off Al-Soor St,

Wattiya; meals KD5-8) With tables tucked around the interior courtyard of this old coral-and-gypsum house, dating from 1949 and included on the government's list of heritage sites, this restaurant, with its beaded lanterns, palm fans and wicker chairs, has retained the feeling of house and home. It serves international fare and is a firm favourite with the expat community. Try the herb-crusted lamb chops (KD6.500) and the naughty date pudding (KD2.500).

Ayam Zamar (Map p156; ☎ 474 2000; Crowne Plaza Hotel, Farwaniya; meals KD6-9) Perched in an eyrie high in the atrium of the lively and 'happening' Crowne Plaza Hotel, this whimsical Lebanese restaurant is spread over a number of split levels, taxing the dexterity of the waiters who have to climb dozens of steps per serving. Somehow they still manage to bring the mezze steaming hot and crispy from the kitchens, and deliver the devilled chicken livers with truly Arabian grace and hospitality. It's not surprising that it's a favourite with Gulf nationals and is packed on Fridays when a comprehensive Arabian brunch is on offer.

our pick **Al-Boom** (Map p156; ☎ 575 6000; Radisson SAS Hotel, Ta'awen St, Rumaithiya; set 3-course meal KD12) Located in the hull of a boat, this inventive restaurant takes some beating, particularly as this isn't just any old boat: this is *Mohammedi II*, built in Culicut, India in 1979. A replica of the largest dhow ever built (*Mohammedi I*, 1915), it took three years to construct from teak wood and 2.5 tonnes of copper, and was completed with 8.8 tonnes of handmade iron nails. Not that one spares much thought for the 35,000 days of labour that was invested in one of the most characterful cargo holds in the history of boat building: when ensconced in the curving hull, under a ship's lantern hung from the beams, the attention is much more carefully focused on the set-piece of grilled grouper or sirloin, delivered sizzling to a personalised brass dinner setting. As the ship is dry, in all senses of the word, seasickness is not a prime concern.

Cafés

Restaurant 99 (Map p159; Al-Soor St; sandwiches from 300 fils) Near Al-Jahra Gate, this is one of the city's best bets for a quick bite. Hummus, *shwarma* (meat sliced off a spit and stuffed in a pocket of pita-type bread with chopped tomatoes and garnish) and a wide variety of Arabic-bread fillings are on offer for a few hundred fils.

Layali al-Helmeya (Map p156; ☎ 263 8710; Arabian Gulf St, Salmiya; snacks 300 fils-KD1) A block north of the New Park Hotel, this is a lovely place to sit and enjoy the view overlooking Kuwait Bay. A modern version of a traditional Egyptian coffeehouse, it offers kebabs and *ta'amiyya* (deep-fried bean-paste ball) sandwiches for 250 fils to 500 fils, *shish tawouk* (chicken kebab) for KD1 and *sheesha* for 500 fils.

Le Notre (Map p159; ☎ 805 050; Arabian Gulf St; lunch buffet KD3, meals KD5-9) Fantastic views of the Kuwait Towers, a discerning buffet lunch, an exclusive *chocolatier*, and a landmark building of steel and glass, make this French café one of the chicest in town.

English Tea Lounge (Map p159; ☎ 242 2055; Sheraton Kuwait Hotel, Wattiya; high tea KD6-10; ☼ 10am-1pm & 4pm-midnight) The newly renovated Sheraton, with its multiple marble pillars and extravagant Persian carpets, looks like the last place to find a Welsh tea with rarebit (KD6.500). But if scones and cucumber sandwiches beckon, choose from a Yorkshire tea with fruit cake (KD7), or a Royal Windsor tea with smoked salmon (KD7).

Quick Eats

Souq Marbarakia (Map p159; btwn Mubarak al-Kabir, Ahmad al-Jaber & Ali al-Salem Sts; kebabs KD1.500) One of the best ways to get a feel for the heart of the city is to pull up a chair at one of the casual tables strewn around the western edge of the old souq on the semi-pedestrianised Abdullah as Salem St. If you order kebabs at lunchtime, a generous helping of green leaves, pickles, hummus and Arabic bread arrives to garnish the meat.

Breadz (Map p159; ☎ 240 7707; Ground fl, Sharq Souq, Arabian Gulf St, Sharq; sandwiches & salads from KD1.500) Serving a deliciously fresh selection of pastries, sandwiches and salads, as well as fresh fruit juices, tea and coffee, the outdoor terrace overlooking the Sharq marina makes this a pleasant spot for a snack. The decadent dessert bar is worth a look.

Self-Catering

Indian snack shop (Map p159; Shop 8/9, off Money Exchange Sq, Souq Marbarakia; 12 samosas 250 fils) This hole-in-the-wall shop on the edge of the souq is famed for its fresh samosas. Ask for a mixed bag and then finish off lunch around the corner at the date souq.

Sultan Centre (Map p159; Sharq Souq, Arabian Gulf St, Sharq) This modern chain of supermarkets has all the wherewithal for a budget picnic. The closest store to the city centre is in Sharq Souq, which has lots of opportunities for a portable pudding that'll blow the budget.

DRINKING
Coffeehouses & Teahouses
There are a number of Arabic cafés around town where mostly men go to chat over a *sheesha* and numerous small cups of sweet, black coffee. The following coffeehouses are the equivalent of a commercial *diwaniya* (gathering) and business preliminaries are often conducted informally on the premises.

Souq Marbarakia (Map p159; btwn Mubarak al-Kabir, Ahmad al-Jaber & Ali al-Salem Sts) Women may feel rather uncomfortable in the covered inner courtyard of the old souq, near the cafés on the western edge of the souq, but men will love the convivial atmosphere.

Beit Lothan (Map p156; ☎ 575 5866; Arabian Gulf St, Salmiya) Coffee, tea and a *sheesha* are available in a quiet garden, adjacent to the Beit Lothan cultural centre (see p157).

The best high tea in town is served at the English Tea Lounge (p169).

ENTERTAINMENT
In the absence of bars, entertainment in the city is pretty much confined to shopping and dining, although film and theatre are popular with locals.

Cinemas
Considering its size, Kuwait has an overwhelming number of cinemas, which unfortunately show the same films (usually heavily edited to exclude kissing, nudity and sex – violence, however, is left uncensored). The more popular and modern of the cinemas are at **Sharq Souq** (Map p159; Arabian Gulf St, Sharq) and in the **Al-Fanar Shopping Complex** (Map p156; ☎ 575 9306; Salem Mubarak St, Salmiya). Admission to all films costs KD2.500. Call ☎ 80 3456 for What's On and Where.

There is also an Imax cinema in the Scientific Center (p158).

Theatre
Arabic theatre has enjoyed a long history in Kuwait, dating back to 1922 when the first amateur plays were performed, and are highly popular with Arab audiences.

Two groups perform in English. The Kuwait Players began in 1952 and stage about 10 productions per year, from pantomime to Shakespeare. The other company is **Kuwait Little Theatre** (☎ 398 2680; www.theklt.com; Main St, Al-Ahmadi), which has been performing comedies and dramas in its own venue in Al-Ahmadi (see opposite) since 1948.

For performance times and venues, check What's On listings in the local papers.

SHOPPING
Salmiya is undoubtedly *the* shopping district of Kuwait. The main street, Hamad al-Mubarak St, is known as the 'Champs Elysée' of the Middle East and is filled with dazzling shopping malls. **Sharq Souq** (Map p159; Arabian Gulf St, Sharq) is another modern complex, and boasts its own marina.

For something more traditional and locally produced, the Kuwaiti Bedouin weavings at Sadu House (p161), a cultural foundation dedicated to preserving Bedouin art, are recommended. Alternatively, some attractive Iranian and Pakistani antiques often turn up at the Friday Market (p163). The old souq (p162) in the heart of Kuwait City is a great place to shop for anything from olives to blankets – or just to snack and watch the world go by.

Contemporary Arts
Galleries showcasing contemporary regional work include the long established **Boushahri Art Gallery** (Map p156; ☎ 571 4883; off Arabian Gulf St, Salmiya; ⏰ 9am-1pm & 4-7pm) and **Dar Al-Funoon** (Map p159; ☎ 243 3138; www.daralfunoon .com; Salhiya; ⏰ 10am-1pm & 4-8pm Sat-Wed, 10am-1pm Thu). Situated behind the churches near the Sheraton Hotel and housed in an old Kuwaiti-style house with a courtyard, the popular Dar Al-Funoon gallery and restaurant complex is the best place to buy a piece of contemporary local art.

GETTING THERE & AWAY
Kuwait being more or less a city-state, the information for getting to Kuwait City are the same as for those to Kuwait in general, so please see p178 for details.

GETTING AROUND
To/From the Airport

Taxis charge a flat KD5 between the airport (16km south of the city), and the city centre. It's 20- to 45-minute journey. Bus 501 runs between the main bus station and the airport every half-hour from 5.30am to 9pm daily (250 fils). Car-rental agencies have booths on the ground floor of the airport.

Bus

The main bus station (Map p159) is near the intersection of Al-Hilali and Abdullah al-Mubarak Sts in the Safat district. On printed timetables the station is referred to as 'Mirqab bus station'.

Buses run from approximately 5am to 10pm. Fares are 100, 150 or 200 fils, depending on the distance travelled. An office on the ground floor of the Kuwait Public Transport Company (KPTC) building at the main bus station sells a route map for 150 fils.

Taxi

Any trip within the city centre costs 250 fils plus 100 fils per kilometre. Longer trips outside the city centre (eg to Salmiya) cost about KD3. Some reliable taxi companies are **Al-Salmiyah Taxi** (☎ 572 2931) and **Al-Ghanim Taxi** (☎ 481 1824).

Call taxis often offer tours of the city for a flat rate of KD5 per hour, but finding a driver that doesn't have a death wish is not always easy. One highly recommended driver for safe and knowledgeable service is **Mohammed Hanif** (☎ 962 5140). Another is Mr Ramsi of **Taxi Al-Amana** (☎ 656 8270). Both are available 24 hours a day and have many years of experience driving in and around the city.

AROUND KUWAIT

Kuwait, to all intents and purposes, is a city-state wherein most of the attractions and activities are centred in the capital. There are few towns outside Kuwait City and even less in the way of physical attractions in the oil-producing interior.

Despite these drawbacks, however, Kuwait is comprised of a long and beautiful stretch of coast, and future tourist developments include the multi-billion-dollar holiday resort and entertainment complex on Failaka Island, expected to take 10 years or so to complete.

FAILAKA ISLAND   جزيرة فيلكا

Failaka Island has some of the most significant archaeological sites in the Gulf. With a history dating from the Bronze Age, evidence of Dilmun and Greek settlements, a Classical name to die for (the Greeks called it 'Ikaros') and a strategic location at the mouth of one of the Gulf's best natural harbours, this island could and should be considered one of Kuwait's top tourist attractions.

Alas, recent history has deemed otherwise. First, the Iraqis established a heavily fortified base on Failaka, paying scant regard to the relics over which they strewed their hardware, and then the island was billeted by Allied forces with equally pitiful regard for antiquities.

The island is once again open to visitors but there is not much to see at present, although it does make a pleasant place for a picnic. If you like it enough to stay, the **Safir Hotel** (☎ 252 0600; www.safirpalace.com; Failaka Heritage Village; s/d KD30/35; 🏊) has a range of facilities including a children's zoo, lake, horse-riding and *shwarma* outlets, all of which cater mainly for the local community. There are also some homemade crafts available for sale.

Kuwait Public Transport Company Ferries (☎ 571 3544; www.q8boatc.com) to Failaka Island depart from Ras Salmiya (also known as Ras al-Ard) on Arabian Gulf St in Salmiya. The trip takes 1½ hours, costs KD2.500 and leaves daily except Saturday and Monday at 8.15am, returning at 12.30pm. A guide would be handy for interpreting the various ruins. If you take your own vehicle it costs KD20 for the return fare. The ferry terminal in Kuwait City can be reached via buses 15, 24, 34 and 200.

AL-AHMADI   الأحمدى
pop 41,556

Built to house the workers of Kuwait's oil industry in the 1940s and '50s, the town of Al-Ahmadi was named after the emir of the day, Sheikh Ahmed. It remains, to some extent, the private preserve of KOC.

The **Oil Display Centre** (☎ 398 9111; www.kpc .com.kw; Mid 5th St; admission free; ⏱ 7am-3pm Sat-Wed) is a well-organised introduction to KOC and the business of oil production. The Kuwait Little Theatre (p170) has performances in the town.

Bus 101 runs from the main bus station in Kuwait City to Al-Ahmadi (passing by the oil display centre as it enters town). To get here by car from Kuwait City, take the King Fahad Motorway south until the Al-Ahmadi exit. First follow the blue signs for North Al-Ahmadi and then the smaller white signs for the display centre.

FAHAHEEL   فحاحيل
pop 74,175

The traditional town of Fahaheel was, until quite recently, a distinct village in its own right. It now merges into the city suburbs but retains a distinctive atmosphere, reminiscent of its Bedouin roots. The fish souq and dhow harbour are more characterful, in many ways, than their modern counterparts in the city centre. The oil refinery at neighbouring Mina al-Ahmadi is one of the largest in the world.

The Hilton Kuwait Resort (p168) is just north of here.

RAS AL-ZOUR   رأس الزور
One-hundred kilometres and about an hour's drive of the capital, Ras al-Zour (also spelt Ras Azzor) is one of the most pleasant beach areas in Kuwait. The Saudi Texaco compound is only open to guests of members, but the public beach alongside is clean and attractive too.

WAFRAH FARMS
While not the most obvious of tourist destinations, Wafrah Farms, about 1½ hours drive south of the capital, on the Saudi Arabian border, is a soothingly green oasis of vegetable gardens and papaya trees. It makes a pleasant excursion from Ras al-Zour.

ENTERTAINMENT CITY
Located in Doha Village, this huge **park** (☎ 487 9545; admission KD3.500; ☼ 3.30-10pm Sun-Thu, 10am-10pm Fri) is located 20km west of Kuwait City. It comprises three theme parks (Arab World, International World and Future World), a miniature golf course, a small lake with landscaped parkland and railway, a small zoo, and a variety of restaurants. The entrance fee covers most of the rides

but there is an additional charge for some of the more elaborate rides. Admission times vary slightly from season to season, so call ahead. There is no public transport to the park and a taxi (KD4 from the city centre) is not easy to hail for the return journey.

AL-JAHRA   الجهراء
pop 28,387

Al-Jahra, 32km west of Kuwait City, is the site where invading troops from Saudi Arabia were defeated (with British help) in 1920. It was also the site of the Gulf War's infamous 'turkey shoot' – the Allied destruction of a stalled Iraqi convoy as it lumbered up Mutla Ridge in an effort to retreat from Kuwait. The highway and surrounding desert are now completely clear of evidence, picked over by scrap-metal dealers and dubious souvenir hunters.

Sights & Activities
The town's only sight is the **Red Fort** (☎ 477 2559; admission free; ☼ 8am-1pm & 4-6pm), which played a key role in the 1920 battle. Also known as the Red Palace, this low, rectangular, mud structure near the highway has recently been restored. Coming from Kuwait City, take the second of the three Al-Jahra exits from Jahra Rd. The Red Fort is on the right, about 200m south of Jahra Rd.

Between November and April camel racing can be seen early in the morning (races start around 7am or 8am) at **Al-Atraf Camel Racing Club** (☎ 539 4014; Salmi Rd; admission free). Phone ahead for details of races, which are held most Thursdays and Fridays, or check the What's On listings in the English-language dailies. The track is located 7km west of Al-Jahra.

Getting There & Away
Al-Jahra can be reached conveniently by bus 103 from Kuwait City, which passes directly in front of the Red Fort. By car, take the Sixth Ring Rd west out of Kuwait City. For the racing club take the turn-off where there is a faded sign of a camel, after skirting Al-Jahra.

MUTLA RIDGE   مطلا
While not a particularly spectacular line of hills, Mutla Ridge is about as good as it gets in Kuwait. The ridge at least offers a wonderful view of the full expanse of Kuwait

---

WATER, WATER EVERYWHERE BUT NOT A DROP TO DRINK

Kuwait has long been known for its fine natural harbour but, like so many places in the Middle East, it is chronically short of water. Indeed, from 1907 until 1950, traders had to buy fresh water from the Shatt al-Arab waterway near Bubiyan Island, at the head of the Gulf, and ship it by dhow to Kuwait. The trade peaked in 1947 when it was estimated that 303,200L of water per day was arriving in Kuwait by boat – thankfully the country didn't have a golf course.

Early investment of oil revenues into the search for ground water was unsuccessful, but the country's first desalination plant in 1950 signalled the end of the sea trade in water. An exorbitant way to acquire fresh water, desalination nonetheless satisfies the country's huge thirst for water, which jumped from 6822L per capita in the 1950s to 83,380L per capita in the mid-1980s.

Natural resources are precious and, as every Bedouin knows (and any mid-summer visitor can guess at), water in the desert is far more valuable than oil. In Kuwait, it's also more expensive.

KUWAIT

Bay. Although the land mines have been cleared, you should stick to the paths in case of explosive remnants.

For a taste of the desert, take the road to **Bubiyan Island** that runs along the southeastern flank of the ridge. Either side of the road, large numbers of camels roam along its edge, grazing on the coarse grass that is common to the area. In spring, the slope down to the coastal marshes is pale green with new shoots and full of wild flowers. It is also a popular area for camping, both for Bedu (black tents and goats) and city dwellers (white tents and aerials) keen to touch base for a while.

By following signs to Subiyah, you'll eventually reach the **Bridge to Nowhere**, some 50km northeast of Al-Jahra. There's a checkpoint in front of it, preventing further excursion, but the bridge spans more than just the narrow passage to Bubiyan Island: it also reinforces Kuwait's claim to the island in the face of erstwhile claims by both Iraq and Iran. So keen was Kuwait to maintain its claim to the uninhabited, flat and barren island and its neighbouring water supply (see the boxed text, above), when the Iraqis blew up the middle section of the bridge, the Kuwaitis quickly rebuilt it even though it goes to nowhere.

KUWAIT DIRECTORY

ACCOMMODATION
There are few options for budget travellers in Kuwait but some excellent value choices in the midrange category. In this chapter, we have defined budget hotels as being those that charge no more than KD35 for a double room, midrange hotels as those that charge between KD36 and KD65 for a double room, and top-end hotels as those that charge over KD65 for a double room. All prices are inclusive of the 15% service charge and unlike other countries of the peninsula, there are no particularly high or low seasons. Prices do not include breakfast unless otherwise stated.

The northern shore of Kuwait Bay is a popular camping spot with locals: just look for the tents from October to April. Alternatively, there are some good places to camp on the coast near the Saudi Arabian border. Camping equipment is available in the many sporting goods shops in the city malls and a 4WD is necessary to find a suitable spot.

ACTIVITIES
Most activities are either organised, or take place, in Kuwait City (see p165).

For swimming outside of Kuwait City, there are many public beaches along the coast, particularly to the south. One-piece swimsuits for women are encouraged.

Fishing and boating are offered to visitors by **Kuwait Offshore Sailing Association** (☎ 973 1859; www.kosaq8.com). Camel racing takes place just outside Al-Jahra (opposite).

BOOKS
There are several excellent, recently published books on Kuwait available. *Pearling in the Arabian Gulf,* by Saif Marzooq al-Shamlan, offers an interesting collection of memoirs and interviews on Kuwait's pearling industry. *Women in Kuwait,* by Haya al-Mughni, paints a clear and illuminating picture of the lives and roles of Kuwaiti

women, as well as society's attitudes towards them. Sheikha Altaf al-Sabah's *Traditions & Culture* is a beautifully produced coffee-table book, with excellent photographs depicting old Kuwait, its people and traditional culture.

The Ministry of Information publishes the *Welcome Visitors' Guide to Kuwait*, updated regularly. It is pricey at KD12 but has some lovely photographs.

The definitive work in English on the Iraqi invasion is John Levin's *Days of Fear* (1997). Levin, an Australian long-term resident of Kuwait, lived through the Iraqi occupation.

For more general Middle Eastern titles, some of which contain coverage of Kuwait, see p23.

BUSINESS HOURS

The following opening hours prevail throughout Kuwait (see p529 for general details for the entire region):

Banks 8am to 1pm Sunday to Thursday
Government offices 7am to 2pm Saturday to Wednesday
Internet cafés 8am to 10pm
Post offices 7am to 2pm Saturday to Wednesday, 7am to noon Thursday
Restaurants 11am to 3pm and 7pm to 11pm
Shopping centres 10am to 10pm
Shops 8am to 1pm and 4pm to 7pm or 8pm Saturday to Thursday.

CHILDREN

Kuwait is a safe, easygoing, family-oriented country, and children are welcome and catered for everywhere. See p166 for ideas of what to do while you're here.

CUSTOMS

No alcohol or pork-related products are permitted in the country. Up to 500 cigarettes and 500g of tobacco are acceptable. Duty-free items are on sale at the duty-free shop in the arrivals and departures section of the airport. See also p532 for general information.

DANGERS & ANNOYANCES

The many spectacularly twisted bits of metal left by the roadside are testament to the fact that Kuwait has one of the highest road accident rates in the world. Indeed, one third of all deaths in Kuwait are driving-

related. The horrifying scenes on TV have not deterred Kuwait's drivers, despite government efforts to slow the pace down with radar surveillance. As such, it's hard to recommend driving in Kuwait unless you're confident of holding your own in the face of sheer lunacy. A police sign at traffic lights speaks volumes: 'Crossing the red signal leads to death or prison.'

Although the country has now been cleared of mines after the Gulf War, you should still remember *not to pick up any unfamiliar object* in the desert and to stick to established tracks.

For some reason, smoking appears to be much more prevalent in Kuwait than in neighbouring Gulf countries. While smokers may be glad to enjoy a smoke on buses, in taxis, at the airport, and in restaurants and hotel rooms without fear of vilification, nonsmokers are sure to find the dense atmosphere in public places quite irritating.

EMBASSIES & CONSULATES
Kuwait Embassies & Consulates

Kuwaiti embassies in major cities around the world are as follows. For Kuwaiti embassies in neighbouring Arabian Peninsula countries, see the relevant chapters.

Canada (☎ 613-780 9999; www.embassyofkuwait.ca; 80 Elgin St, Ottawa, ON, K1N 1J9)
France (☎ 01 47 23 54 25; 2 Rue Lubeck, Paris 75116)
Germany (☎ 228-378 081; Griegstrasse 5-7 D, Berlin 14193)
Netherlands (☎ 070-3603 813/6; Carnegielaan 9, KH den Haag)
UK (☎ 020-7590 3400; 2 Albert Gate, Knightsbridge, London SW1X 7JU)
USA (☎ 202-966 0702; 2940 Tilden St NW, Washington DC 20008)

Embassies & Consulates in Kuwait

Many embassies are located in the Diplomatic Area. Embassies are usually open from about 8am to 1pm Saturday to Thursday. A more complete list appears on www.kuwaitiah.net/embassy.html.

Bahrain (Map p156; ☎ 531 8530; fax 533 0882; Villa 35, Block 6, Surra St, Surra)
Canada (Map p156; ☎ 256 3025; www.dfaitmaeci.gc.ca /kuwait; House 24, Block 4, Al-Mutawakil St, Diplomatic Area, Da'iya) Located adjacent to the Third Ring Rd.
Egypt (Map p156; ☎ 251 9956; fax 256 3877; Villa 1, Block 5, Street 58, Diplomatic Area, Da'iya)

France (Map p159; ☎ 257 1061; www.ambafrance.kwt
.org; Villa 24, Block 1, Street 13, Mansouria)
Germany (Map p159; ☎ 252 0857; fax 252 0763; Villa
13, Block 1, Street 14, Abdulla al-Salim)
Iran (Map p156; ☎ 256 0694; iranembassy@hotmail.com;
Block 5, Diplomatic Area, Dai'ya)
Jordan (Map p156; ☎ 253 3261; joremb@qualitynet.net;
Villa 20, Block 3, Akkah St, Nuzha)
Lebanon (Map p156; ☎ 256 2103; fax 257 1628; Block 6,
Diplomatic Area, Dai'ya)
Netherlands (Map p156; ☎ 531 2650; kwe@minbuza
.nl; House 76, Block 9, Street 1, Jabriya)
Oman (Map p156; ☎ 256 1956; fax 256 1963; Villa 25
Block 3, Street 3, Udailia) Located by the Fourth Ring Rd.
Qatar (Map p156; ☎ 251 3606; fax 251 3604; Istiqlal St,
Diplomatic Area, Dai'ya) Located off Arabian Gulf St.
Saudi Arabia (Map p159; ☎ 240 0250; fax 242 0654;
Arabian Gulf St, Sharq)
Syria (Map p156; ☎ 539 6560; fax 539 6509; Villa 1,
Block 6, Al-Khos St, Mishref)
Turkey (Map p156; ☎ 253 1785; fax 256 0653; Block 5,
Istiqlal St, Diplomatic Area, Dai'ya) Opposite Green Island.
UAE (Map p156; ☎ 252 8544; fax 252 6382; Plot 70,
Istiqlal St, Diplomatic Area, Dai'ya) Located off Arabian
Gulf St.
UK (Map p156; ☎ 240 3336; visa@britishembassy-kuwait
.org; Arabian Gulf St, Dasman) Located west of Kuwait
Towers.
USA (Map p156; ☎ 539 5307; www.kuwait.usembassy
.gov; Plot 14, Block 14, Al-Masjid al-Aqsa St, Bayan) About
17km south of the city centre.

FESTIVALS & EVENTS
See p166 for information on festivals and
events in Kuwait.

HOLIDAYS
In addition to the main Islamic holidays
described on p535, Kuwait celebrates the
following public holidays:
New Year's Day 1 January
National Day 25 February
Liberation Day 26 February

INTERNET ACCESS
Internet access is easy for those travelling
with a laptop as many hotels and cafés are
now wi-fi enabled. Prepaid dial-up internet cards are available in denominations
of KD1, KD5 and KD10, and can be purchased at *bakalas* (corner shops) and supermarkets. A KD10 card gives around 150
hours of internet access.

There are also many internet centres in
Kuwait City (see p157).

INTERNET RESOURCES
Some useful Kuwait-specific websites in-
clude the following:
Arab Times (www.arabtimesonline.com) An on-line
version of the local newspaper.
Complete Guide to Kuwait (www.kuwaitiah.net) An
excellent guide to Kuwait.
Kuwait Information Office (www.kuwait-info.org)
Contains lots of information and links on Kuwaiti history,
culture and lifestyle.
Kuwait Petroleum Corporation (www.kpc.com.kw)
Gives a rundown on the nation's number-one resource and
industry.
Kuwait Pocket Guide (www.kuwaitpocketguide.com)
Comprehensive expat site giving information on all aspects
of living and working in Kuwait.
Kuwait Tourism Services Company (www.ktsc-q8
.com) Provides information on accommodation, sights and
specific tours, as well as the Kuwaiti lifestyle.

MAPS
GEO Projects publishes a good country
map on the reverse of two useful maps of
Kuwait City in its Arab World Map Library,
available from car-rental offices, hotels and
bookshops for KD5.

MEDIA
Newspapers & Magazines
The *Arab Times* and *Kuwait Times* are Kuwait's two English-language newspapers
(150 fils each). Both provide adequate foreign coverage, largely reprinted from British newspapers and the international wire
services. They include useful What's On
listings. International newspapers are available (usually a day or two late) at major
hotels.

The *Kuwait Pocket Guide* (KD5) covers
everything from doing business in the country to where to find horse-riding lessons,
and is essential for anyone intending to
spend any length of time in the country.

International glossy magazines, complete
with large tracts of blackened text courtesy of
the government censor, or even with pages
torn out, are also available from hotels.

Radio & TV
Radio Kuwait – also known locally as the
Superstation – broadcasts on 99.7 FM; it
plays mostly rock and roll, with some local
news and features thrown in for good measure. The US military's Armed Forces Radio
& TV Service (AFRTS) can be heard on

107.9 FM; it broadcasts a mixture of music, news and chat shows. On 92.5 FM there is a nonstop music station that broadcasts '60s to '90s hits, with the occasional piece of classical music.

Kuwait TV's Channel 2 broadcasts programmes in English each evening from around 2pm to midnight. Many hotels, even the smaller ones, have satellite TV.

MONEY
ATMs & Credit Cards
Visa and Amex are widely accepted in Kuwait, and all major banks accept most credit cards and are linked to the major networks. Most banks accept Visa (Electron and Plus), MasterCard and Cirrus.

Costs
Kuwait is an expensive country to visit. While it's easy to eat for KD3 (about US$9) or less per day, sleeping cheap is another matter. Visitors are hard pressed to get away with spending less than KD25 per night on accommodation. Add to this other costs, such as transport, dining out, and admission prices to museums and other attractions, and an average daily budget of at least KD40 needs to planned for.

Currency
The currency used in Kuwait is the Kuwaiti dinar (KD). The dinar is divided into 1000 fils. Coins are worth five, 10, 20, 50 or 100 fils. Notes come in denominations of 250 fils, 500 fils, KD1, KD5, KD10 and KD20. The Kuwaiti dinar is a hard currency and there are no restrictions on taking it into or out of the country.

Exchanging Money
Moneychangers are dotted around the city centre and main souqs, and change all major and regional currencies. Only banks and the larger money-exchange facilities will change travellers cheques. Since the dinar has been pegged to the dollar, there's little difference between exchange rates from place to place.

Exchange Rates
Since 2003, the Kuwaiti dinar has been pegged to the US dollar. The following exchange rates were correct at the time of printing.

Country	Unit		Kuwaiti dinar
Australia	A$10	=	KD2.31
Bahrain	BD10	=	KD7.71
Canada	C$10	=	KD2.47
Euro zone	€10	=	KD3.86
Japan	¥1000	=	KD2.47
New Zealand	NZ$10	=	KD2.04
Oman	QR10	=	KD7.56
Qatar	QR100	=	KD7.98
Saudi Arabia	SR100	=	KD7.74
UAE	Dh100	=	KD7.91
UK	UK£10	=	KD5.66
USA	US$10	=	KD2.90
Yemen	YR1000	=	KD1.65

Tipping & Bargaining
A tip is only expected in the upmarket restaurants where 10% for service is often already added to the bill. For longer journeys, 10% is a suitable tip for a taxi driver.

Bargaining is *de rigueur* in Kuwait's souqs but also in many Western-style shops and some hotels. It is always acceptable to ask for a discount on the original price offered, particularly as discounts have generally already been factored into the quoted price.

PHOTOGRAPHY & VIDEO
Photographing obvious 'tourist' sites, such as the Kuwait Towers or the Red Fort in Al-Jahra, is no problem, but aiming a camera at military installations, embassies or palaces is not advisable. Remember to ask before taking pictures of people and bear in mind that photographing local women is considered *haram* (forbidden).

Any photo lab can print digital images, and memory cards and an assortment of batteries is obtainable throughout the city. Colour print film is quick and cheap to develop. Slide and B&W film is much more expensive and is very hard to find. Small photo studios throughout the city centre process passport photos for about KD4.

POST
Post boxes are a rare sight around Kuwait City, so there's little alternative to braving the lines at post offices. The postal rate for aerograms and for letters or postcards weighing up to 20g is 150 fils to any destination outside the Arab world. Postage for cards or letters weighing 20g to 50g is 280 fils. Ask at the post office for parcel rates

as these vary significantly from country to country.

There is no poste-restante service in Kuwait. Large hotels will usually hold mail, but only for their guests.

TELEPHONE & FAX

The country code for Kuwait is ☎ 965, and is followed by the local seven-digit number. There are no area codes. The international access code (to call abroad from Kuwait) is ☎ 00.

Kuwait's telephone system is very good, though getting an overseas connection on weekends and public holidays can take time. Local calls are free, but international calls are expensive: per minute to Australia, Canada and the UK costs around 300 fils; New Zealand, the Netherlands and Japan 400 fils; and the USA 150 fils. Payphones take 50 fils and 100 fils coins, though they are increasingly giving way to cardphones. Phonecards are available in units of KD3, KD5 and KD10.

Fax

Fax services are available from government communications centres, though there are usually long queues. The best bet is the business centres in the larger hotels, which charge according to their IDD rates.

Mobile Phones

Users of mobile phones can link into the GSM services of Mobile Telecommunications Company (MTC) or Wataniya. Prepaid SIM-cards are widely available in malls and from Wataniya (there's a booth at the airport).

VISAS

Visa requirements for Kuwait have relaxed considerably in an effort to encourage more people to visit the country. It is now possible – indeed easy – to obtain a visitor visa at Kuwait International Airport on arrival for nationals of 34 countries including Australia, Canada, the EEC, New Zealand and the USA. A visa costs KD3, except for the citizens of the UK, USA, Italy, Norway and Sweden for whom entry is free. The five-star hotels listed in the sleeping section of this chapter are usually able to sponsor guests not eligible for a visa at the airport, if they intend to stay at the hotel.

Visitor visas are valid for 90 days from the date of issue and allow a maximum stay of 30 days from the date of entry.

Anyone holding a passport containing an Israeli or Iraqi stamp will be refused entry to Kuwait.

Multiple-entry visas are only valid for business requirements. They are valid for 12 months but need to be applied for in advance. For general details on visas for other Middle Eastern countries, see p541.

Transit Visas

A transit visa can be obtained from any Kuwaiti consulate or from the Kuwait Port Authority if you arrive by sea; it is valid for a maximum of seven days and costs KD2. To be eligible, applicants must have a valid visa for their next destination and a confirmed onward ticket.

Visa Extensions

Up to two one-month visa extensions are possible. To do this, an application needs to be made to the **Immigration Department** (Map p156; 28 Street, off Airport Rd) in Shuwaikh before the existing visa expires. There is a hefty fine (KD10 per day) for overstaying once the visa has expired.

WOMEN TRAVELLERS

Women travellers may find the increased attention from men in Kuwait a nuisance. From being tailgated while driving to being followed around shopping centres, expat women are frequently the targets of young men's harmless (read mindless) fun. Despite dressing conservatively, refusing to respond to approaches and avoiding eye contact with men, it's still hard to avoid attracting unwanted attention. Generally, if the situation becomes uncomfortable, the best way to defuse it is to stop being an object and become a foreign person: this can be accomplished by turning towards the men in question, giving them a firm but frosty greeting (all the better in Arabic) and offering the right hand for shaking. Ask the offending parties where they come from and to which family they belong. This is usually so unexpected and traumatising for these men that the threat disappears.

For tips on avoiding or dealing with harassment from males, see Women Travellers (p542) in the Arabian Peninsula Directory.

TRANSPORT IN KUWAIT

See also the Arabian Peninsula Transport chapter (p545).

GETTING THERE & AWAY
Air
AIRPORTS & AIRLINES

Kuwait International Airport (☎ 433 5599, flight information 181) is a reasonably modern enterprise and plans are afoot to upgrade it with the building of a second terminal. Visas are obtained from a counter on the upper storey of the airport, before descending to passport control and baggage claim. Check-in time is two hours before flights are due to depart. Given the limited attractions of the airport and the heavy smoking of regional users, this can seem like a long time. Note that Gulf Air still insists on reconfirmation of tickets 48 hours ahead of departure.

Kuwait's national carrier is **Kuwait Airways** (☎ 434 5555; www.kuwait-airways.com; cnr Abu Bakr al-Siddiq St & Al-Hilalli St, Safat), which flies to many destinations in the Middle East, Europe (including London, Paris and Frankfurt), Asia and the USA. It has an excellent safety record and is reliable and punctual.

Kuwait also has a no-frills, private carrier called **Jazeera Airways** (☎ 177; www.jazeeraairways .com; Kuwait International Airport) with flights to 30 destinations within the Middle East and the Indian subcontinent.

OTHER AIRLINES FLYING TO/FROM KUWAIT

British Airways (BA; ☎ 242 5635; www.ba.com; hub Heathrow Airport, London)
EgyptAir (MS; ☎ 243 9576; www.egyptair.com; hub Cairo)
Emirates Airlines (EK; ☎ 242 5566; www.emirates .com; hub Dubai)
Gulf Air (GF; ☎ 245 0180; www.gulfairco.com; hub Bahrain)
Lufthansa (LH; ☎ 242 2493; www.lufthansa.com; hub Frankfurt)
Oman Air (WY; ☎ 241 2284; www.oman-air.com; hub Muscat)
Qatar Airways (QR; ☎ 242 3888; www.qatarairways .com; hub Doha)
Saudi Arabian Airlines (SV; ☎ 242 6310; www.saudi airlines.com; hub Jeddah)
Yemen Airways (IY; ☎ 240 8933; www.yemenia.com; hub San'a)

DEPARTURE TAX

There is an airport departure tax of KD2, payable in cash at the airport. Some tickets sold outside Kuwait already include this charge. To check, look for 'KD2' or something similar in the 'tax' box just below the part of the ticket that indicates the destination.

FARES

Kuwait is not a particularly cheap place to fly into or out of. The airlines and travel agents control prices tightly, and few discount fares are available. The following fares represent walk-in prices from Kuwait City with Gulf Air, one of the most flexible and comprehensive airlines in the region.

Flight destination	Price	Frequency
Doha (Qatar)	US$207	daily
Manama (Bahrain)	US$175	daily
Muscat (Oman)	US$360	daily
Abu Dhabi (UAE)	US$280	daily
Riyadh (Saudi Arabia)	US$411	daily
San'a (Yemen)	US$245	2 per week via Manama

Land
BORDER CROSSINGS

Kuwait has borders with Iraq (currently closed to visitors) and Saudi Arabia. The border-crossing situation with Iraq changes frequently and it's best to check with embassy officials before contemplating this option. It is certainly not currently open to the curious tourist; in fact, it's not possible, at present, to get beyond the checkpoints on Mutla Ridge without a good reason and paperwork to back it up.

The crossings with Saudi Arabia are at Al-Nuwaisib (for Dammam) and Al-Salmy (for Riyadh). You must have a valid visa for Saudi Arabia or a transit visa, an onward ticket and a visa for your next destination beyond Saudi's borders before you can cross the border. You cannot obtain these at the border. See p547 for further details.

Bus

Kuwait Public Transport Company (☎ 246 9420; www.kptc.com.kw) operates comfy, modern buses to a number of different destinations beyond Kuwait's borders. Buses also operate between Kuwait and Cairo, via Aqaba in Jordan and Nuweiba in Egypt. Agents specialising in these tickets (the trip takes about two days) are in the area around the main bus station.

Modern, air-con buses, operated by the Saudi bus company **Saptco** (www.saptco.com .sa) and handled in Kuwait by **Kuwait & Gulf Transport Company** (☎ 484 9355), travel between Kuwait and Dammam (Saudi Arabia) and cost KD6.500. The trip takes six hours.

Car & Motorcycle

For those planning on driving through Saudi Arabia, a three-day transit visa is required. Inquire at the **Saudi Embassy** (☎ 240 0250; Arabian Gulf St, Sharq) for more details.

Sea

The **Combined Shipping Company** (Map p159; ☎ 483 0889; www.csc-kw.com; Ahmed al-Jaber St, Sharq) operates a return service twice a week from Kuwait's Shuwaikh Port (Map p159) to the Iranian port of Bushehr. A one-way/return economy passage costs US$70/140; an extra US$250 is required to take a car. You can book online (www.irantraveling center.com).

Speedboat services leave from Shuwaikh Port for Manama (KD45, five hours) in Bahrain. The easiest way to book tickets for these services is through one of the city travel agents (p158).

Nuzha Touristic Enterprises (☎ 575 5825; www .nuzhatours.com) run charter trips to Manama and Doha but this is not likely to be a cheap way of getting to those countries.

GETTING AROUND

Boat

Kuwait Public Transport Company Ferries (KPTC; ☎ 571 3544; www.q8boatc.com) goes to Failaka Island from Kuwait City (see p171 for more details). **Nuzha Touristic Enterprises** (☎ 575 5825; www.nuzhatours.com) run half- and whole-day boat trips.

Bus

Kuwait has a cheap and extensive local bus system but it's designed for the convenience of local residents rather than for visiting tourists. The routes therefore don't often coincide with the places of tourist interest. Nonetheless, if a 10-minute walk either side of the bus stop isn't a problem, pick up a bus timetable from the main bus station in the city centre.

Most bus routes are operated by **Kuwait Public Transport Company** (KPTC; ☎ 880 001; www .kptc.com.kw), which has air-conditioned and comfortable vehicles. Intercity trips cost between 150 fils and 250 fils. Route 101 runs from the main bus station in the city centre to Al-Ahmadi and Fahaheel. Route 103 goes to Al-Jahra. The **Citibus** (☎ 882 211) alternative follows KPTC routes but doesn't always go the full nine yards; a route map can be obtained from the bus – by which time it may be too late! Both services are used primarily by lower-income workers travelling to their place of work.

Car & Motorcycle

If you have an International Driving Permit (IDP), or a license and residence permit from another Gulf country, driving in Kuwait is possible, without any further paperwork, for the duration of your visa.

Fair warning is given of the dangers of driving on Kuwait's roads. See Dangers & Annoyances (p174), as well as Road Hazards (p556) for information.

HIRE

Expect costs of between KD10 (for a Toyota Corolla) to KD30 (for a Toyota Prado) per day for car hire. This rate usually includes unlimited kilometres and full insurance. Those driving on an IDP are required to pay an additional KD10.500 for a one-month period to cover insurance. **Al-Mulla** (☎ 243 7333; travel@almulla.com.kw) is one of the better local agencies, with desks at the airport and in many of the city hotels.

Local Transport

TAXI

Taxis are a useful and popular way of getting around, though they are comparatively expensive when travelling outside the city area, when costs can increase to KD9 per hour. If you want to do some exploring around Kuwait by taxi, it's better to agree on a half- or full-day rate in advance. See p171 for more details.

Oman عمان

It's a curious observation about travelling in Oman that the moment you tuck behind a sand dune and begin erecting your tent, however discreetly, someone will park alongside and start camping too. Never mind that it is the only car you've seen all day; never mind that there are 2700km of beautiful, empty sandy beaches; never mind that the mountains are so lonesome in parts that only wolves and hedgehogs meander into the night; and never mind that memories of Thesiger are the only evocations of the living to issue from the dunes of the Empty Quarter – the one-car-per-day will find yours and camp alongside.

What makes this observation a particularly topical one is that it's only relatively recently that a network of roads and graded tracks, such as the coast road from Filim to Shwaymiyah, or the adventurous mountain track to the ancient tombs at Gaylah, has made it possible to penetrate Oman's pristine landscapes. Those who are sufficiently intrepid to get off the beaten track will find that they can have the desert to themselves quite easily without mounting a major expedition. Now that the secret of Oman's great untouched beauty is out, however, it surely can't be long before groups of visitors are a common sight and it will no longer be necessary to seek the company of strangers at the end of a day's exploration.

In the meantime, what should you say to the happy camper who parks in 'your space'? As every hospitable Omani you'll meet on your travels will tell you, there's only one answer: *'Ahlan wa salan!* Welcome!'

FAST FACTS

- **Official name** Sultanate of Oman
- **Capital** Muscat
- **Area** 309,500 sq km
- **Population** 3.1 million
- **Country code** ☎ 968
- **Head of State** Sultan Qaboos bin Said
- **Annual number of tourists** 1.2 million
- **Stereotype** A country that has only relatively recently emerged from isolation
- **Surprise** An infrastructure that any country would be proud of

HIGHLIGHTS

- **Jebel Shams** (p234) Haggle with insouciant local carpet sellers for vertiginous rugs on a precipice above Wadi Ghul.
- **Nakhal Fort** (p238) Survey the flat panorama of the Al-Batinah Region from the battlements of Oman's most spectacular castle.
- **Sharqiya Sands** (p225) Put your driving and navigational skills to the test in an auburn sea of sand.
- **Ras al-Jinz** (p221) Attend the night-time drama of labour and delivery at the green turtle's favourite nesting site.
- **Dhofar Region** (p247) Explore the subtropical terrain of a region famed for gold, frankincense and myrrh.

ITINERARIES

Itineraries covering Oman and other parts of the Arabian Peninsula can be found starting on p25.

- **Muscat Stopover** Rise with the dawn to see fishermen bring in the weird and wonderful at Mutrah's fish market (p196). Join the ebb and flow of the city's residents by strolling along the corniche (p196), under the overhanging balconies of the harbour residences. Duck into Mutrah Souq (p197) to learn the art of good-natured argument and lose your way among the pink, plastic and implausible. Spare an hour for the sights of Muscat proper (p197), the walled heart of the capital, before a spot of R&R and an extravagant dinner at one of the city's whimsical hotels (p204).
- **Two weeks** Make the most of the mountains by circling the Western Hajar range and making your base the lively town of Nizwa (p231). Climb the beanstalk to Jebel Akhdar (p230), famed for giant pomegranates and hailstones. Hike the rim of Oman's Grand Canyon for a spot of carpet-buying on Jebel Shams (p234). Engage with *jinn* (spirits created by Allah) at the remarkable tombs and forts of Bat (p236), Bahla (p235) and Jabrin (p236). Finally, take the long way home to Muscat, via a dizzying mountain drive (p233) to Rustaq (p238), and wash the dust off in a sparkling sea at Sawadi (p240).
- **Three weeks** Go in search of wild places on an adventurous route from Muscat to Oman's second city, Salalah (p247), 1000km to the south. Follow the Qurayat–

Sur coast road to Sur (p214), home of the dhow, pausing to explore the celebrated wadis of Shab (p215) and Tiwi (p216). Learn about turtles at Ras al-Jinz before cutting inland to the sea of sand near Mintirib (p225). Acclimatise to nights under the stars before the camping journey to Salalah via Duqm, Ras Madrakah and Shwaymiyah (p250). Leave time to explore Salalah's beautiful beaches and go in search of frankincense.

CLIMATE & WHEN TO GO

The best time to visit Oman is between November and mid-March, when the cooler air brings the mountain scenery sharply into focus and daytime temperatures average 25°C. For the rest of the year, much of Oman is oppressively hot and hazy, particularly between May and August.

The redeeming summertime feature is the *khareef*, the mid-June to late-August rainy season in southern Oman. Many Gulf visitors flock to this area to picnic under the drizzle on Dhofar's grassy hills. The rain (and the green) vanishes by mid-September.

The peak tourist season in the north is from November to mid-March. See also p530 for a climate chart for Muscat.

HISTORY

'Renaissance' is a term any visitor to Oman will hear, as it refers to the current period under Sultan Qaboos, a leader held responsible by most of the population for easing the country into modernity. Before he came to the throne after a bloodless coup in 1970, Oman had no secondary and only two primary schools, two hospitals run by the American mission and a meagre 10km of sealed roads. In addition, the country was in a state of civil war. Oman has since caught up with its more affluent neighbours, and it boasts efficient, locally run hospitals, universities, electricity to remote villages and an ever-improving infrastructure of roads. Furthermore, Oman is peaceful and stable, with an enviably low crime rate and a well-trained local workforce.

Early Oman: Gold, Frankincense & Copper

The term 'renaissance' is an appropriate one, as it suggests equally rich periods through Oman's long history.

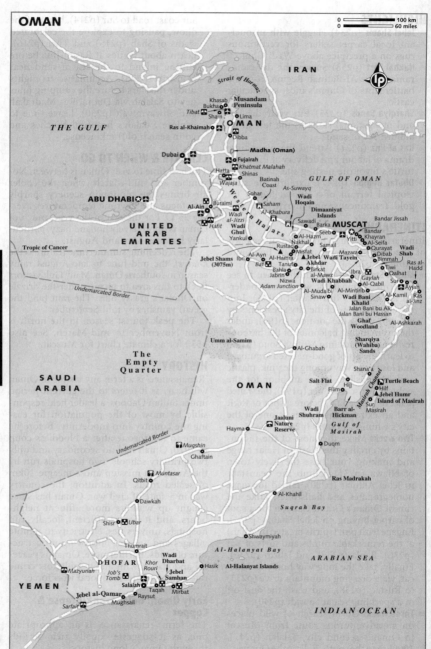

OMAN

0 — 100 km
0 — 60 miles

IRAN

Strait of Hormuz

THE GULF

Khasab
Bukha
Sham
Tibat
Lima
Musandam Peninsula
OMAN

Ras al-Khaimah
Dibba

Dubai
Fujairah
Madha (Oman)
Khatmat Malahah
Hatta
Shinas
Wajaja
Batinah Coast
As-Suwayq
GULF OF OMAN

ABU DHABI
Buraimi
Sohar
Wadi Hoqain
Saham
Dimaaniyat Islands
Bandar Jissah

Al-Ain
Wadi al-Jizzi
Al-Khabura
Sawadi
MUSCAT

UNITED ARAB EMIRATES
Hafit
Wadi Ghul
Yankul
Rustaq
Al-Hazm
Nakhal
Samail
Seeb
Barka
Bandar
Khayran
Al-Seifa
Qurayat
Wadi Shab

Tropic of Cancer
Ibri
Al-Ayn
Al-Hamra
Misfat
Jebel Akhdar
Wadi Tayein
Mazara
Dibab
Bimmah
Ras al-Hadd

Jebel Shams (3075m)
Bat
Bahla
Birkat al-Mawz
Tanuf
Jabrin
Ibra
Wadi Khabbah
Tiwi
Qalhat
Sur
Ayijah

Undemarcated Border
Nizwa
Adam Junction
Al-Mudaibi
Sinaw
Al-Mintirib
Gaylah
Al-Qabil
Wadi Bani Khalid
Al-Kamil
Ras al-Jinz

Umm al-Samim
Jalan Bani bu Ali;
Jalan Bani bu Hassan
Ghaf Woodland
Al-Ashkharah

The Empty Quarter

Al-Ghabah
Sharqiya (Wahiba) Sands

SAUDI ARABIA
OMAN
Shana'a
Salt Flat
Filim
Hijj
Turtle Beach
Hilf
Jebel Humr
Island of Masirah
Barr al-Hickman
Sur Masirah

Undemarcated Border
Hayma
Jaaluni Nature Reserve
Wadi Shuhram
Gulf of Masirah
Duqm

Muqshin
Ghaftain
Ras Madrakah

Muntasar
Qitbit
Dawkah
Suqrah Bay

Shisr
Ubar
Al-Khahil

Thumrait
Shwaymiyah

DHOFAR
Wadi Dharbat
Al-Halanyat Bay
ARABIAN SEA

Mazyunah
Job's Tomb
Khor Rouri
Jebel Samhan
Hasik
Al-Halanyat Islands

YEMEN
Salalah
Taqah
Mirbat
Jebel al-Qamar
Raysut
Sarfait
Mughsail

INDIAN OCEAN

Western Hajars

Masirah Channel

As far back as 5000 BC, southern Oman (now called Dhofar) was the centre of the lucrative frankincense trade. This highly prized commodity, produced from the aromatic sap of the frankincense tree, was traded for spices with India and carried by caravans across all of Arabia. While the trees grew in Yemen and one or other two locations, they grew best in the monsoon-swept hills of Dhofar, where they continue to be harvested to this day. So precious was the sap of these trees, that even the part-mythical Queen of Sheba hand-delivered Dhofari frankincense to King Solomon. Equally legendary, of course, are the gifts borne by the three wise men of biblical report.

The Bible also mentions the golden-pillared city of Ubar, built by the people of Ad. This fabled city, which has excited the curiosity of explorers for hundreds of years, grew out of the frankincense trade to become one of the most powerful cities in the region. The remains of the city were reputedly rediscovered in the 1990s by English explorer Ranulph Fiennes. Nonetheless, it is hard to believe this claim, looking at the virtually barren plot near Thumrait – much more persuasive is the fact that the presumed descendents of the remarkable civilisation of Ad still occupy the surrounding desert, speaking the distinct and ancient language of Jibbali, whimsically known as the 'language of the birds'.

Oman enjoyed further prosperity in pre-Islamic times through the trading of copper. Indeed, Oman is referred to in some sources as 'the Mountain of Copper', and the Bahrain National Museum provides evidence of vigorous trading in copper between Oman and its Gulf neighbours. The country then slipped into a long period of isolation that prevailed until the 7th century AD when Islam was introduced by Amr ibn al-As, a disciple of the Prophet Mohammed. Oman was quick to embrace the new faith – it even gained a reputation for its proselytising zeal.

For about the next 500 years Oman came under the leadership of the Bani Nabhan dynasty (1154–1624).

Hostilities: the Portuguese

Frequent civil wars during the Bani Nabhan dynasty, between the sultan's forces and tribal factions, left the country vulnerable to outside hostilities that eventually came in the form of the Portuguese.

Alarmed by Oman's naval strength and anxious to secure Indian Ocean trade routes, the Portuguese launched a succession of attacks against Omani ports; by 1507 they managed to occupy the major coastal cities of Qalhat (near Sur, and mentioned in the journals of Ibn Battuta and Marco Polo), Muscat and Sohar. Ironically, it was a talented sailor from Sohar, Ahmed bin Majid, who unwittingly helped Vasco da Gama navigate the Cape of Good Hope in 1498, leading to the Portuguese invasion a few years later.

Over the next 150 years Oman struggled to oust the occupying forces. Eventually, under the guidance of the enlightened Ya'aruba dynasty (1624–1743), Oman was able to build up a big enough fleet to succeed. The Portuguese were interested in Oman only as a sentry post for their maritime adventures and had barely ventured into the country's interior. They were therefore easy to rout, given Oman's newly established naval might. Other than Al-Jalali Fort, Al-Mirani Fort and Mutrah Fort, all of which dominate the centre of Muscat, the Portuguese left little behind, although their legacy of military architecture shaped fort construction in Oman.

Unified & Wealthy

By 1650 Oman became a settled, unified state of considerable wealth and cultural accomplishment, with influence extending as far as Asia and Africa. Many of Oman's other great forts were built during this period, including the impressive, round-towered Nizwa Fort.

By the 19th century, under Sultan Said bin Sultan (r 1804–56), Oman had built up a sizable empire controlling strategic parts of the African coast, including Mombasa and Zanzibar, and parts of what are now India and Pakistan. Today it is easy to see the influence that Oman had on the coastal areas of those countries, and even more tangibly the extent to which its own culture and population was enriched by the contact. The Batinah coast, for example, is home to the Baluchi people originally from Pakistan; as a result, mosque design along the highway between Barka and Sohar bears more resemblance to the florid architecture across the neck of the Gulf than it does to the more austere Ibadi tradition of Oman's interior.

When Sultan Said died, the empire was divided between two of his sons. One became the Sultan of Zanzibar and ruled the African colonies, while the other became the Sultan of Muscat and ruled Oman. The division of the empire cut Muscat off from its most lucrative domains, and by the end of the century, the country had stagnated economically, not helped by British pressure to end its slave and arms trading.

Coastal vs Interior: Isolation

The new century was marked by a rift between the coastal areas, ruled by the sultan, and the interior, which came to be controlled by a separate line of *imams* (religious teachers). In 1938 a new sultan, Said bin Taimur, tried to regain control of the interior, sparking off the Jebel Wars of the 1950s. Backed by the British, who had their own agenda, Said successfully reunited the country by 1959.

In all other respects, however, Said reversed Oman's fortunes with policies that opposed change and isolated Oman from the modern world. Under his rule, a country that a century earlier had rivalled the empire builders of Europe became a political and economic backwater. While neighbours such as Bahrain, Qatar and Kuwait were establishing enviable welfare states and sophisticated modern patterns of international trade, Oman slumped into poverty, with high rates of infant mortality and illiteracy. Even the communist insurgency in Dhofar during the 1960s failed to rouse Said from his reclusive palace existence in Salalah, and by the end of the decade his subjects, the most powerful of which had been either imprisoned or exiled, lost patience and rebellion broke out across the country.

The unrest led to a palace coup in July 1970 when Said's only son, Qaboos, covertly assisted by the British, seized the throne. With a face-saving shot in the foot, Said was spirited off to the Grosvenor Hotel in London, where he spent the remainder of his days. Some suggest that Said was not a greedy or malicious leader, just fiercely protective of his country's conservative traditions, which he feared would be eroded by the rapid modernisation experienced in neighbouring countries. Perhaps the country's contemporary balance between old and new, so skilfully maintained by his son, owes something to Said's cautious approach to Western influence.

Present-Day Renaissance

As soon as Qaboos bin Said was enthroned, the young sultan began to modernise Oman's economy, and set in motion the social, educational and cultural renaissance that prevails to this day. With the help of British forces, he also resolved the Dhofari skirmishes, though they simmered on until 1982 when the Yemeni government in Aden cut off its assistance to the communist insurgents.

Each year, the anniversary of Sultan Qaboos' reign is celebrated with due pomp and ceremony, including the Sultan's 'meet the people' tour where he and his ministers camp in different regions of the country to listen to local requests. Any visiting dignitaries are obliged to go camping too. A royal camp can be a spectacular affair of pennant-carrying camel riders bringing their petitions across the desert with gifts of goats for His Majesty. Requesting lighting in their village on day two of the sultan's visit, petitioners may well expect to see the pylons delivered by day four of the same trip. It is this accessibility on the part of the Sultan, together with his reputation for delivering promises, that makes him such an effective and beloved leader. Anyone from a Western country who has waited a year to get a street light mended, may well wonder exactly what democracy means.

GOVERNMENT & POLITICS

The sultan is the ultimate authority, with jurisdiction over even minor policy decisions. In January 1992 an elected Majlis ash-Shura (Consultative Council) was convened as a first step towards broader participation in government. Female representation on the council is growing and there are currently three women holding high office in government, including the ministers of higher education, tourism and social development.

Sultan Qaboos is not married and has no children. The constitution stipulates that an heir to the throne must be chosen by the royal family within three days of the throne falling vacant, an event that most people in Oman hope will be delayed for many a year yet.

In foreign affairs, Sultan Qaboos has shown himself to be a distinguished peacemaker. In 1998 he was awarded the International Peace Award from the National Council on US-Arab Relations in recognition of his role in maintaining stability in the region. During the invasion of Kuwait, his government was unequivocally behind the Allies. After 11 September 2001, it skilfully navigated the path between Allied support against terrorism (expressed with practical assistance) and a strong identity with pan-Arab issues, particularly with regard to Palestine. Oman opposed the Allied invasion of Iraq in 2003, however, and many Omanis share the regional suspicion that the Allies have a hidden agenda for remaining in Iraq. For decades, Oman received help from Iraq's professional bodies in building a modern infrastructure. Now the tables are turned and Oman is stretching out a helping hand in rebuilding Iraq's broken institutions.

ECONOMY

In building a modern state, Sultan Qaboos' chief strategy has been to create a highly trained local workforce through intensive investment in education. Schooling is free, even at tertiary level, and provision is made (until recently by helicopter) for children of even the remotest villages.

With limited oil revenues, Oman cannot sustain costly expatriate labour, so a policy of 'Omanisation' in every aspect of the workforce is rigorously pursued. In contrast to the rest of the region, it is refreshing to find locals – often of both sexes – working in all sections of society, from petrol pump attendants to senior consultants.

Two central planks of the economy are self-sufficiency in food production, realised through intensive agriculture along the Batinah coast, and diversification of the economy. These schemes include the export of natural gas from a successful plant near Sur; an enormous port project in Salalah, the first phase of which is now complete; and the Sohar port project. The latter has already helped turn Sohar into a city reminiscent of its illustrious past with a university

and large hospital complex. The decision to disperse new economic initiatives across the regions has helped keep local communities buoyant and helped slow the exodus of villagers migrating to the capital.

A third central plank of the economy is tourism, which is growing rapidly. A large resort complex, Bandar Jissah, opened in the capital area in 2005, and in 2006 the Wave, a seafront residential and tourism development, started offering expats the opportunity to own property in Oman for the first time. In addition, one of the largest development projects on the Arabian Peninsula, called Blue City, is underway, with plans for an entire new town, canals and marinas, luxury hotels and recreational facilities, carved out of the desert around Sawadi.

Much investment continues to be made in Oman's infrastructure – no mean feat given the challenges presented by the country's size, remoteness and terrain. It is now possible to drive on sealed roads to most towns and villages across the country.

PEOPLE
The National Psyche

Since the sultan came to power in 1970, Oman has trodden a careful path, limiting outside influence while enjoying some of the benefits that it brings. The result has been a successful adoption of the best parts of the Gulf philosophy, marked by a tolerance of outside 'customs and manners', without the sacrifice of national identity that often characterises rapid modernisation. Oman takes pride in its long history, consciously maintaining tribal customs, dress, architecture and rules of hospitality, as well as meticulously restoring historical monuments.

Omani people have had to work hard to make their country what it is today, and perhaps that is why the arrogance that may be seen in neighbouring countries is conspicuously absent here – indeed, Omanis are some of the most gracious, friendly and hospitable people in the region.

Lifestyle

It would be hard to imagine any country that has changed so dramatically in such a short space of time. Within the living memory of most middle-aged people outside

OMAN

Muscat, travelling to the next village used to mean hopping on a donkey or bicycle, education meant reciting the Quran under a tree and medication comprised of a few herbs (very effective ones) from the mountainsides. Modern farmers contemplate GMC crop rotations, yet also look at the cloudless sky and realise that their grandmothers and children haven't been praying loud enough. Little wonder that some families have buckled under the pressure of such an extraordinary pace of change; divorce, alcoholism, drug abuse and manic driving are all social ills that have increased proportionately.

On the whole, however, Oman is a success story; it has embraced the new world with just enough scepticism to allow people to return to their villages on the weekend, park their Toyotas at the end of the tarmac and walk the rest of the way to see grandfather.

It's possible to recognise people's ethnic origins, even the regions from which they hail, by observing women's clothing. Heads, arms and legs are always covered, but costumes range from a patterned cotton cloth to a transparent *abeyya* (woman's full-length black robe), worn with a peaked face mask. In the capital, the silk *abeyya*, often worn over Western clothing, has become a fashion item. During festivals, sisters and even friends often wear clothes cut from the same cloth with elaborately embroidered trouser cuffs. Men wear a *dishdasha* (shirt-dress, usually white) and a white hat, traditionally embroidered by a loved one. On official occasions, they wear a turban (made of pashmina and usually imported from Kashmir) and tuck a silver *khanjar* (ceremonial dagger) into their belt. For an especially formal occasion, they may wear a silk outer garment with gold trim and carry a short, simple camel stick.

A BETTER PILL TO SWALLOW

Omanis have had to work especially hard to achieve a modern economy. Unlike in wealthy neighbouring countries with enormous oil revenues, the government of Oman was not in a position to lavish money on extravagant public welfare provision, or spend unlimited resources on higher education. The population of Oman has had to share in the burden of paying towards their health and education.

The result has had an effect on the size of the population. Encouraged by active community health campaigns, many modern parents realise that small is beautiful when it comes to the number of children they choose to nurture and educate, especially when the younger generation, benefactors of a universal secondary schooling, now aspire to costly tertiary education.

In turn, smaller families are beginning to reshape the socioeconomic profile of the country. There are the obvious improvements to the general health of women who are spared the dangers and inconveniences of multiple pregnancies, but there are also subtle knock-on effects on the extended family too. With a good education behind them, higher combined incomes, and less mouths to feed, parents of the new generation are able to invest in the wider community. Large modern villas are springing up not just in the suburbs of Muscat but also in the heart of regional towns. Even small villages are given a make-over as prosperous city-earners return to their roots at weekends to spend their disposable income to the common good. While many have migrated to the capital never to return, an equal number are planning for the day they will retire to the homes they have invested in.

If the days of producing seven sons and seven daughters are now numbered, the method by which the size of a family is controlled has not been quite so uniformly embraced. While contraception is catching on in the towns – 'something for the weekend' can now be bought even at Al-Maha petrol stations – not everyone is so quick to adopt modern methods in the *willayats* (villages). On a helicopter visit with a paramedical team to a remote mountain village, I saw local ladies gather up precious medicine – talismans from His Majesty – and stock them in their cave dwellings, together with the unopened medicine boxes from last month. The population of this village had not grown in a decade. Asked how they achieved this, the women replied with collusive grins: 'It's easy, see that *jebel* (mountain) over there? See this *jebel* over here? When I don't want another baby, I sleep behind that one and my husband sleeps behind this one.' If only all of life's solutions were that simple!

Population

Attracted by work and modern amenities, many people are moving to the capital, with the result that Muscat is spreading along the coast towards Seeb. In an effort to stem this flow, graded roads and water have been supplied to even the smallest *willayat* (village), and electricity cables can be seen travelling as resolutely as a camel caravan hundreds of kilometres across the desert.

Other centres of population at Sohar, Nizwa, Sur and Oman's second city of Salalah rank more as large towns than cities, although this is beginning to change with the expansion of various industrial projects in or near each of these regional centres.

Omani people have a strong sense of tribe and their tribal names (for example, al-Nabhani, al-Wahaybi, al-Balushi) indicate very clearly to which area they belong. Some families, such as the Al-Abris from Wadi Sahten, can be pinpointed to specific wadis in the Hajar Mountains.

Multiculturalism

Oman's population is predominantly Arab, although the country's imperial history has resulted in intermarriage with other groups, particularly from East Africa. As such, some Omanis speak Swahili better than Arabic. An Indian merchant community has existed in Muscat for at least 200 years, and people of Persian or Baluchi ancestry inhabit the Batinah coast. The Jibbali people form a separate group in Dhofar. Many of them live a mostly nomadic life with their own distinct customs; their language, completely distinct from any other, is dubbed 'the Language of the Birds'. Kumzari, the compound language spoken in parts of the Musandam Peninsula, is a mixture of Portuguese, Arabic and Farsi.

SPORT

Omani people are, on the whole, athletic. Campaigns by the Ministry of Health even send text messages to encourage people to walk more and avoid fast food. Obesity, however, is beginning to affect the new generation in the Muscat area. Traditionally energy was channelled into working the land or walking from village to village. Today it often takes the form of organised sport, particularly basketball, table tennis and rally driving. And, of course, football (soccer).

Ever since an Omani footballer Hani Adhabet was named top goal scorer in the world in 2001, football has become a national obsession – as anyone can see at 5pm on a Friday when the beaches of Oman are turned into ad hoc pitches (see the boxed text, p58). The **Bawshar Stadium** (☎ 24 592197) in Muscat hosts regular games.

A variety of traditional Omani sports are being actively encouraged by the Sultan, consisting of long jumps, strength and endurance activities. Two more comprehensible traditional sports are camel racing and bull-butting. Camel races are held on Friday mornings at tracks around the country from mid-October until mid-April, but particularly around National Day in November. The very young age of the camel jockeys has for some time been a source of consternation and plans are afoot to replace the child riders with light-weight adults. Until this is accomplished, there is a strong sense that judgmental foreigners are not welcome at these events. If you are determined to watch a race, however, contact one of the tour companies – or check with the **Directorate-General of Camel Affairs** (☎ 26 893804; fax 26 893802).

Perhaps surprisingly, bull-butting is altogether a less controversial affair. These unscheduled events involve pitting Brahmin bulls in a push-and-shove around a dirt arena. It doesn't involve blood or injury and the bulls are much beloved by their owners. The best place to see bull-butting is between November and March at Barka (p237), 45km west of Muscat, on a Friday from 4pm to 6pm (but timings are erratic).

RELIGION

About 75% of Omanis follow the Ibadi sect of Islam, an austere form of Islam that eschews decadence of any kind, even in mosque architecture. That said, modern Omanis tend to be pragmatic in their interpretation of religion, are tolerant of other forms of Islamic worship, and allow expats to express their own religions in and around Muscat.

Magic plays a tangible role in the spiritual life of many Omanis. The 'evil eye' is not mere superstition; it is regarded as a hazard of everyday life. Amulets containing verses from the Quran, or hung around the necks of infants, are considered an effective way of warding off such problems. An expat member of the Magic Circle (an exclusive and international society of professional magicians who vow never to reveal to the public the tricks of their trade) was invited to do a magic show in a nearby village: when he conjured a white rabbit from his hat, his entire audience ran away.

ARTS

In a village between Dibab and Tiwi on the Qurayat–Sur coast road, the porches of several houses sport splendid pink or lime-green bathroom tiles, complete with fern motif. Next door to one of these houses, the remains of an intricately, hand-carved door lay disintegrating for years until weather, or an entrepreneur from Muscat, or both, put paid to it. It's not a case of out with the old and in with the new, but a demonstration of Oman's commercial relationship with art: a job lot of Indian tiles for a camel-bag of incense (or the modern-day equivalent) is the kind of international exchange that has characterised the pragmatic nature of Omani arts and crafts for centuries. It's not unusual, for example, to find the family silver (particularly grandmother's jewellery) making the journey to Muscat, because wife No 2 prefers gold. Before they became items of tourist value, exquisite pieces of silver were readily melted down and returned in kind from the gold souq. In fact, for centuries most silver jewellery was fashioned from Oman's old currency (smelted Maria Theresa dollars, or *thalla*), prized for its 80%-plus silver content.

Oman's arts and crafts are all the more wonderful for being about the living rather than the dead, the practical rather than the purely decorative. Whether this heritage can withstand rapid modernisation is another matter.

Traditional Crafts

There are many wonderful crafts in Oman, all of which have been meticulously documented through the Omani Craft Heritage Documentation Project, under the auspices of His Highness Seyyid Shibab bin Tariq al-Said and endorsed by Unesco.

Each region of Oman is associated with a different craft – Bahla is famous for pottery, Nizwa for silver jewellery, Jebel Shams for rug-weaving, Sur for boat-building, Shwaymiyah for basket-making. For a definitive survey of Omani crafts, the twin-volume *The Craft Heritage of Oman,* by Neil Richardson and Marcia Dorr (OR49), makes a superb souvenir. Avelyn Forster's book, *Disappearing Treasures of Oman* (OR14.300), focuses on the silver Bedouin jewellery of Oman.

Music & Dance

There are dozens of traditional song and dance forms in Oman, over 130 of which have been documented by the **Oman Centre for Traditional Music** (☎ 24 601317; www.octm-folk .gov.om), which was set up in 1984 to preserve the country's musical heritage. Oman was the first Arab country to become part of the International Council for Traditional Music, under Unesco.

Oman's music is diverse, due to the country's seafaring and imperial heritage. The *naham* is a particularly famous call to crewmembers to pull together during a long sea voyage.

Sultan Qaboos is a Western classical-music lover. The Royal Oman Symphony Orchestra set up in his honour has been a surprising success, given the difficulties involved in learning a completely different musical idiom. Concerts are regularly given at the Al-Bustan Palace Hotel (see p199) and are listed in the What's On columns of the English-language newspapers.

Each branch of the armed forces has a band of international calibre, including the highly popular bagpipe contingent – no official ceremony in Oman would be the same without the pipes and drums. The massed bands perform annual tattoos, giving lavish horse- and camel-back displays. Some of the military bands have regularly participated in the Edinburgh Tattoo.

Architecture

Oman may no longer boast pillars of gold like the fabled city of Ubar, but it does have another architectural trump card: its forts – there is barely a village without one (see boxed text, opposite).

Oman has mercifully largely escaped the skyscraping obsession of its neighbours, settling for more restrained public buildings in keeping with a more modest budget. However, what the buildings lack in multiple floors, they make up for in imaginative design. Muscat, in particular, abounds with serene and elegant examples, such as the ministry buildings and embassy buildings in Al-Khuwair. The Grand Mosque (p201) in Al-Ghubrah, completed in 2001, is the ultimate expression of restraint, with the simplicity of its exterior masking an exuberantly rich interior.

Not all of Muscat's buildings are grave, however; take the whimsical Grand Hyatt Muscat (p206), with its confection of arabesques and crenulations, or the venerable but distinctly quirky Al-Bustan Palace Hotel (p199). Whatever individual flights of fancy are indulged in by the architect, the result is a remarkably harmonious affair of whitewashed or sand-coloured buildings that illustrate a respect for traditional architectural values.

Outside the towns are a variety of homesteads, including marbled villas with pillars and domes, and more modest houses made from local materials. *Barasti* (palm-leaf) and other palm-constructed housing is still common along the coast from Duqm to Shwaymiyah. In Masirah, 'tin-can housing' is made out of flattened oil drums. In the Sharqiya Sands, Bedu use goat-hair tents, and many people on the mountains live in caves with an improvised front door. Most interesting of all are the round houses made from constructed, interlocking sticks that cling to the hills of Dhofar. They were once thatched but these days are more likely to be covered in bright plastic.

Painting & Sculpture

Set up to provide a forum for contemporary arts, the **Oman Fine Arts Society** (Map pp194-5;

FORTS OF OMAN

You don't have to be terribly observant while travelling around Oman to notice the number of forts and castles that dot the countryside; once you start to look, you realise that there is barely a hilltop without some kind of stronghold or watchtower.

It is telling that at a time when you'd imagine there were higher priorities to worry about than the replastering of a pile of crumbling mud and splintering wood, the Ministry of National Culture & Heritage invested in an extensive fort restoration project. This act of historical preservation, begun in the 1970s when there were only a handful of schools and hospitals, was more than just a whim and it certainly had nothing to do with the embryonic tourist industry; rather it was a central plank of the renaissance – a shoring up of the country's identity, the securing of a foundation upon which to build the new image of Oman.

Fortifications, be it a simple walled enclosure, or a grand edifice such as the fort at Nakhal (p238), have a longer lineage than the country itself. Some, such as Rustaq Fort (p238), partly predate Islam. Erected by local tribes to protect trade routes or, like the fort at Barka (p237), built to withstand marauding forces from the sea, they have been part and parcel of the birth of a nation. Fort-building may be a dying skill in Oman (most of the specialists involved in the restoration projects are from overseas), but the need to save these landmarks for posterity is very much alive. Take the on-going Bahla project, a Unesco world heritage site: this is the fort's fourth makeover, following restoration in the 9th, 17th and 19th centuries.

So what is a fort? A fort is a military structure designed, such as the imposing Al-Hazm Fort (p239), to protect a community. A castle, on the other hand, such as Bait Na'aman in Barka (p237), is primarily a large fortified private residence. As such, the fort is a piece of civic pride. It is a symbol of a community's independence and interdependence – something the Portuguese failed to appreciate when they conquered Muscat with Forts Mirani, Jalali (p198) and Mutrah (p197) but failed to conquer the people within.

It would be easy to conclude by looking at the splendidly spruced up little fort in Ayjah (p219), a village that has yet to be touched by much of the modern world, that Oman is retrospective in its outlook. But then you notice that the bus stop, the payphone, the brand new ministry buildings in Muscat all echo some feature of fort architecture; the fort has been reinvented for a new age. When you consider how completely other countries in the region have eschewed their past, this expression of, and respect for the continuity between history and heritage, is part of what makes Oman unique.

☎ 24 694969; Shatti al-Qurm, Muscat) has a regular programme of exhibitions that showcase local painters and sculptors. Omani artists are engaged in international debate and some established artists show their work across the region.

Another venue for contemporary painting, much of which is inspired by the landscape, is the **Bait Muzna Gallery** (Map p199; ☎ 24 739204; www.omanart.com; Old Muscat), which also stocks some fine pieces of Omani craft.

ENVIRONMENT

Oman is blessed with a remarkable environment of spectacular landscapes and a wealth of flora and fauna. However, it doesn't render up its treasures easily and a 4WD is required to visit many of the places of natural beauty and interest. Accommodation near these places is often restricted to ad hoc camping, but many regard this as a joy in its own right. Indeed, waking up to the sound of a turtle retreating down the beach, or falling asleep to the croak of toads, is an unforgettable experience. To help explore these places, *Off Road in the Sultanate of Oman*, by Lonely Planet author Jenny Walker, and Sam Owen, describes how to reach just about every corner of the country.

If hiring a vehicle is not an appealing option, there are plenty of tours available from Muscat and Salalah that will reveal the country to the visitor (see p260).

The Land

Geographically, Oman is large and diverse, with an untrammelled coastline, rugged mountains, a share of the Empty Quarter and a unique monsoon catchment. It extends from the fjords of the Musandam Peninsula to the intermittently green Dhofar Region of southern Oman. Most of the country's population is concentrated on the Batinah coast, a semifertile plain that runs from the border with the United Arab Emirates (UAE) to Muscat, and is separated from the rest of Arabia by the Hajar Mountains. These mountains are internationally famed for their geological heritage (see the boxed text, p239) and even the layperson will enjoy the candy-striped rocks. The highest peak is Jebel Shams (Mountain of the Sun) at 3075m, alongside which runs Wadi Ghul, dubbed the Grand Canyon of

Arabia. On the slopes of nearby Jebel Akhdar (Green Mountain), temperate fruits are grown.

Much of the country between the Hajar Mountains and Dhofar is flat and rocky desert, but there are also areas of sand dunes. Most notable are the Sharqiya (Eastern) Sands, formerly known as Wahiba Sands, and the less-accessible sands of the Rub al-Khali (Empty Quarter). Oman is not as rich in oil as its neighbours, but it does have some extensive fields in the gravel plains around Mumul in Al-Wusta Region and Fahood in Al-Dakhiliyah Region.

Thriving and diverse marine life exists off Oman's long coastline and there are many islands, the chief of which is the desert island of Masirah.

Wildlife
ANIMALS

Oman's isolated mountains and wadis provide a haven for a variety of animals. These include over 50 types of mammals, such as wolves, foxes, hedgehogs, jerboas and hares. The largest land mammal that a visitor is likely to see is the gazelle, a herd of which lives in a protected area along the Qurayat–Sur coast road (see p216).

There are 13 different species of whale and dolphin in Omani waters, and Oman has an important biodiversity of molluscs (see p106). Indeed, the rich variety of shells adds to the pleasure of visiting the coast.

The *Oman Bird List* is updated regularly and published by the Oman Bird Records Committee (OR1, available in Muscat bookshops); there are over 400 recorded species. Spoonbills and flamingos frequent salt lagoons, even in Muscat, but the country is internationally renowned for its migrating raptors. For more information, it's worth buying *Birdlife in Oman* (OR12), by Hanne and Jens Eriksen. Keen ornithologists should contact the **Oman Bird Group** (☎ 24 695498; www.birdsoman.com).

There is a thrilling diversity of insects in Oman – from the mighty minotaur beetle to the fig tree blue, orange pansy and other butterflies – attracted to Oman's fertile wadis or desert acacias.

Endangered Species

Oman is of global importance to the survival of the endangered green turtle and has one of the largest nesting sites in the world at Ras al Jinz (p221). There are five endangered species of turtle supported by the coasts of Oman, all protected by royal decree.

Oman's varied terrain is home to a large number of endangered species, including houbara bustard, ibex, *tahr* (an Omani species of the goat-like animal) and Arabian leopard. The latter frequents Jebel Samhan in Dhofar and has even been known to stroll onto the runway at Salalah. There are also declining numbers of sand cat, caracal, honey badger and mongoose.

The Arabian Oryx Sanctuary (p246), a Unesco World Heritage Site in Jiddat al-Harasis, continues to protect a herd of wild oryx.

PLANTS

Oman built an empire on the frankincense trees that grow in Dhofar. The trees are still bled for the aromatic sap, but dates, covering 49% of cultivated land, have overtaken them in economic importance. Oman has a very rich plant life thanks to its fertile wadis, many irrigated year-round by spring water. It is common to see tall stands of pink oleander flowering in the wadis throughout the year.

A government-sponsored herbal clinic in Muscat uses many locally occurring plants and shrubs to treat a wide range of illnesses, most commonly diabetes and hypertension. Sultan Qaboos University has a small botanical garden of local plants and is building a new, extensive collection.

National Parks

While there are several reserves, such as the Qurm Nature Reserve in Muscat, set up to protect the endangered mangrove, and the Arabian Oryx Sanctuary, a Unesco World Heritage Site, there are no formal national parks as such.

Environmental Issues

Oman has an enviable record with regard to its protection of the environment – a subject in which the sultan has a passionate interest. His efforts have been acknowledged by the International Union for the Conservation of Nature (IUCN), which awarded him the John C Philips Prize in 1996, and cited Oman as a country with

one of the best records in environmental conservation and pollution control. Oman is still the only Arab country with membership of IUCN. The sultanate's first environmental legislation was enacted in 1974, and in 1984 Oman was the first Arab country to set up a ministry exclusively concerned with the environment. The prestigious Sultan Qaboos Prize for Environmental Conservation, first awarded in 1991, is awarded every two years to a conservation body or individual chosen by Unesco for environmental performance.

On 8 January each year the sultanate celebrates Environment Day, during which children learn about habitat erosion, rubbish dumping and depletion of freshwater reserves. One of the environmental problems that visitors will most readily notice is the amount of oil washed up on Oman's beaches, dumped illegally from container ships. Despite heavy penalties if caught, offenders often get away with it, as it's almost impossible for Oman's military services to police such a long and exposed coastline.

Until recently, Oman's shores were otherwise pristine. Unfortunately, the sudden influx of tourists has led to previously unknown problems including dirty beaches where people insist on leaving their litter behind. Plastic bags are fast becoming a serious environmental hazard, mistaken by land and marine animals for food.

By far the most upsetting issue, however, has been the insensitivity of tourists towards the turtle population at Ras al-Jinz (see p221). The government is clearly going to have to employ more staff in the area to minimise the disruption of the celebrated nesting sites.

FOOD & DRINK

While local cuisine outside the Omani home tends to be of Lebanese origin, home cooking is nutritious and varied, reflecting Oman's ethnic diversity. Cardamom, saffron and turmeric are essential ingredients, but Omani cooking is not exceptionally spicy.

With access to a long coastline, Omanis are particularly fond of fish – sardines can be seen drying in noisome piles from Sohar to Salalah. Until recently, however, shellfish, including the local lobster (actually a large, clawless crayfish), were not considered fit for eating.

OMAN

OMAN

A SWEET TOOTH

Omanis have a decidedly sweet tooth which they indulge during every important social occasion. At official ceremonies, such as graduations and National Day celebrations, halwa is offered to guests. Lumps of the sticky, glutinous confection are pinched out of a communal dish between right finger and thumb, much to the chagrin of those who forgot to bring a hanky. This sweetmeat is made of sugar or dates, saffron, cardamom, almonds, nutmeg and rosewater in huge copper vats heated over the fire and stirred for many hours by men wielding long, wooden pestles; it's hard and hot work and is displayed as an entertainment during eids and festivals. Every region thinks it produces the best halwa but Barka is generally understood to have the edge and many outlets around the town sell it piled up in colourful plastic dishes.

If no-one quite got round to making the halwa for a party, then dates will suffice. Dates are not only an indispensable part of a meal, but also of Omani hospitality. Dates are always served with one or two cups of strong qahwa (Arabic coffee laced with cardamom) and it is impolite to refuse to share at least two cups with a host (but not too many more).

The other sop to a sweet tooth is honey, dubbed by some as the 'liquid gold' of the region. At OR10 to OR70 a kilo, it's easy to see why apiculture is on the increase. It's not a new trend, however: boiling honey was used in Oman as a weapon against enemies – just look for the holes above fort doors. The most expensive honey is still collected in the traditional way from wild beehives in the upper reaches of the Hajar Mountains. Pale, golden honey indicates the bees were raised on date-palm pollen; deep amber suggests sumar-tree blossom; while sidr, a mountain shrub, produces a molasses-coloured honey.

With so many sugar-laden temptations in the Omani heritage, it's little surprise that Oman has a particularly high incidence of diabetes. What is more surprising is that most Omanis have a fine set of teeth.

Perhaps the most typical Omani dish is harees, made of steamed wheat and boiled meat to form a glutinous concoction. It is often garnished ma owaal (with dried shark) and laced with lime, chilli and onions, and is a popular dish used to break the fast in Ramadan.

Visitors should try shuwa (marinated meat cooked in an earth oven) if given the chance. It is the dish of parties and festivals, and comprises goat, mutton, calf or camel meat, prepared with a potpourri of date juice and spices, and wrapped in banana leaves. The result, at least 12 hours later, is a mouth-wateringly tenderised piece of meat, aromatically flavoured with wood smoke and spices. It is served with rukhal (wafer-thin Omani bread) and rice on a fadhl (giant, communal eating tray), and eaten, of course, with the right hand only. Guests traditionally eat first, followed by men, who are expected to reserve the best pieces for women.

A surprisingly delicious traditional dish from southern Oman is rabees. It is made from boiled baby shark, stripped and washed of the gritty skin, and then fried with the liver.

Fruit is a very important part of an Omani meal, usually served before the meat course. Oman grows its own prize pomegranates, bananas, apricots and citrus fruit on the terraced gardens of Jebel Akhdar.

Camels' milk is available fresh and warm from the udder in Bedouin encampments. Like mares' milk, it's an experience many prefer to miss! Alcohol cannot be purchased 'over the counter' in Oman without a residents permit. It is available, however, in most of the more expensive hotels and restaurants.

MUSCAT مسقط

☎ 24 / pop 1 million

'Muscat is a port the like of which cannot be found in the whole world where there is business and good things that cannot be found elsewhere.'

As the great Arab navigator Ahmed bin Majid al-Najdi recognised in AD 1490 Muscat, even to this day, has a character quite different from neighbouring capitals.

There are few high-rise blocks, and even the most functional building is required to reflect tradition with a dome or an arabesque window. The result of these strict building policies is an attractive, spotlessly clean and whimsically uniform city – not much different in essence from the 'very elegant town with very fine houses' that the Portuguese admiral Alfonso de Alburqueque observed as he sailed towards Muscat in the 16th century.

Muscat means 'anchorage', and the sea continues to constitute a major part of the city: it brings people on cruise ships and goods in containers to the historic ports of Old Muscat and Mutrah. It contributes to the city's economy through the onshore refinery near Qurm, and provides a livelihood for fishermen along the beaches of Shatti al-Qurm and Athaiba. More recently, it has also become a source of recreation at Al-Bustan and Bandar Jissah, and along the sandy beach that stretches almost without interruption from Muscat to the border with UAE, over 200km to the northwest.

Muscat is a forward-thinking, progressive city much loved by its citizens, and a beacon for those who live in the interior. In 2006 a new museum, Bait al-Baranda (see p196), was opened in the city's honour. Its inauguration coincided with the choice of Muscat as Arab Cultural Capital – a fitting celebration of Muscat's renaissance.

HISTORY

The 2nd-century geographer Ptolemy mentioned a 'concealed harbour', perhaps the first documented reference to Muscat, but the settlement's location, surrounded on three sides by mountains, made it all but inaccessible from the land. Indeed, the supposed original settlers, Arab tribes from Yemen, almost certainly approached from the sea.

Little is known about the early days of Muscat, except that it grew into a small port in the 14th and 15th centuries. Although it gained importance as a freshwater staging post, it was eclipsed by the busier port of Sohar. By the beginning of the 16th century, however, Muscat gathered momentum as a trading port in its own right, used by merchant ships bound for India. Inevitably it attracted the attention of the Portuguese who conquered the town in 1507. The city walls were constructed at this time (a refurbished set remains in the same positions), but neither they nor the two Portuguese forts of Mirani and Jalali could prevent the Omani reconquest of the town in 1650 – an event that effectively ended the Portuguese era in the Gulf.

Muscat became the capital of Oman in 1793, and the focus of the country's great seafaring empire of the 18th and 19th centuries. Having been party to the control of much of the coast of East Africa, Muscat's 20th-century descent into international oblivion, under Sultan Said bin Taimur, was all the more poignant.

The city gates remained resolutely locked and bolted against the inevitable encroachments of the outside world until 1970. Under the auspices of a progressive leader, Sultan Qaboos, the city reawakened. To facilitate the growing number of cars needing access to the city, a hole was driven through the city walls. Goods and services flooded in and Muscat flooded out to occupy the surrounding coastline. Touchingly, the city gates continued to be locked at a specific time every evening, despite the adjacent hole in the wall, until the gates were replaced with an archway. In many respects, that little act of remembrance is a fitting metaphor for a city that has given access to modern conveniences while it continues to keep the integrity of its character.

ORIENTATION

Wedged into a relatively narrow strip of land between mountains and sea, Muscat comprises a long string of suburbs. The city spans a distance of 50km or so by road from the airport to Al-Bustan, serviced by plenty of public transport.

Muscat is sometimes referred to as the 'three cities': Muscat, Mutrah and Ruwi. Muscat proper, a small area with few shops and no hotels, comprises the *diwan* (palace administration and reception). The neighbouring port of Mutrah has most budget accommodation, while shopping centres and transport terminals are located in the commercial district of Ruwi.

It's best to navigate by reference to landmarks (eg the HSBC in Qurm, the Clock Tower roundabout in Rusayl) rather than street addresses, especially when asking for directions or speaking with taxi drivers.

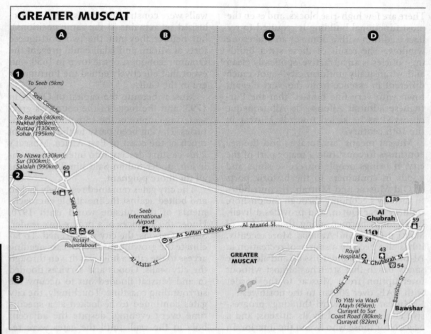

GREATER MUSCAT

Maps

The *Apex Map of Oman* (OR3; Apex Publishing, 1998) has some excellent city maps, as well as a large road map of Oman and is available from good bookshops and hotel foyers.

INFORMATION
Bookshops

Most large hotels stock a wide range of coffee-table books, specialist guides and a selection of Lonely Planet guides. Try the following:

Family Bookshop (Map pp194-5; ☎ 24 604245; Qurm commercial district) Stocks a good selection of English-language titles on Oman and a few bestsellers.

House of Prose (Map pp194-5; ☎ 24 564356; Al-Wadi Centre, Qurm) Stocks second-hand paperbacks with a great buy-back scheme.

Turtles (Map pp194–5; ☎ 24 793590; www.turtles oman.com; Terminal Bldg, Seeb International Airport; ⏲ 24hr) Includes a wide range of topical publications.

Cultural Centres

British Council (Map pp194-5; ☎ 24 681000; www .britishcouncil.org; Al-Inshirah St) Runs English-language

courses and offers advice on studying in the UK. It has a small library and stocks a selection of English newspapers and magazines.

USA Information Service (Map pp194-5; ☎ 24 698989 ext 201; www.muscat.usembassy.gov; US embassy, Jameat ad Duwal al-Arabiyah St; ⏲ 10am-noon & 1-3pm Sat-Wed) Maintains a comprehensive resource centre for studying, working and travelling in the USA.

Emergency

Ambulance, Fire & Police (☎ 9999)

Royal Oman Police (☎ 24 560021) Organises emergency care at the scene of an accident.

Internet Access

Internet cafés can be found all over Muscat. The standard rate is 500 baisa per hour.

Fastline Internet (Map p200; ONTC bus station, Al-Jaame St, Ruwi; per hr 500 baisa; ⏲ 10am-midnight Sat-Thu, 2pm-midnight Fri)

First Internet Café (Map pp194-5; CCC Shopping Centre, Qurm; per hr 800 baisa; ⏲ 9.30am-1.30pm & 5-10pm Sat-Thu, 5-10pm Fri)

Internet Café (Map p197; Corniche, Mutrah; per hr 400 baisa; ⏲ 9.30am-noon & 4.30-midnight Sat-Thu, 4.30-10pm Fri)

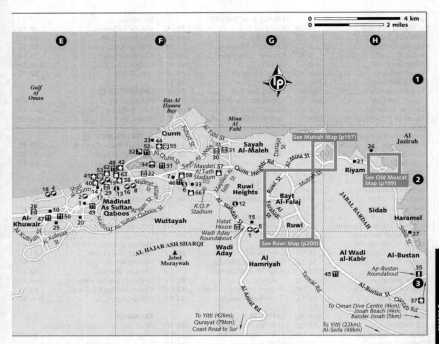

Left Luggage

Seeb International Airport (Map pp194-5; ☎ 24
510385; per piece per day OR1; ☉ 24hr) Located in the
departures side of the building.

Medical Services

International-standard health care is available at the main city hospitals. An ambulance service, under the auspices of the police, was introduced in April 2004. Initial emergency treatment may be free, but all other health care is charged. English is spoken in all hospitals and clinics in Muscat.

Pharmacies rotate to provide 24-hour coverage in all regions; check *Oman Observer* to learn which ones are on duty on a given day. Pharmacies can advise which local doctors or dentists are on duty.

Al-Nahdha Hospital (Map pp194-5; ☎ 24 831255;
Al-Nahdha St, Wattiyah) Emergency cases are generally
brought here.

Money

The big banks are centred in Ruwi's Central Business District (CBD), but there are numerous branches with ATM facilities throughout Muscat. Most are able to give cash advances on international credit cards and will exchange travellers cheques (though they charge a large commission).

The most convenient moneychangers are in Qurm, along Souq Ruwi St in Ruwi and on the Mutrah Corniche at the entrance to the Mutrah Souq. Most are open 8am to 1pm, and some from 5pm to 7pm; all are open Saturday to Thursday.

Amex (Map pp194-5; Dawhat al-Adab St, Madinat as-
Sultan Qaboos; ☉ 8am-1pm & 4-6.30pm Sat-Thu) Inside
Zahara Tours, behind the large City Plaza department store.
HSBC (Map p197; Markaz Mutrah al-Tijari St; ☉ 8am-
1pm Sat-Wed, 8am-1pm Thu)

Post

Branch Post Office (Map p200; Markaz Mutrah al-Tijari
St, CBD Ruwi; ☉ 8am-2pm & 4-6pm)
Main Post Office (Map pp194-5; Al-Matar St; ☉ 8am-
2pm & 4-6pm) Located off the airport roundabout. There
are also branches in Old Muscat and Mutrah.

Telephone

There are numerous cardphones around the city for making local and international

OMAN

OMAN

calls. Hayyak cards, for making international and local calls from a mobile phone, can be bought at the airport and most corner shops and supermarkets.

Telephone Office (Map p200; Al-Burj St, CBD Ruwi; ☷ 8am-2pm & 4-6pm) Faxes can be sent from here.

Tourist Information

Brochures and maps are available from foyers in larger hotels.

Ministry of Tourism (Map pp194-5; ☎ 24 588831; www.omantourism.gov.om) Staff can answer limited telephone inquiries.

National Travel & Tourism (Map pp194-5; ☎ 24 566046; nttoman@omantel.net.om; Ar-Rumaylah St, Wattayah; ☷ 8am-1pm & 4-7pm Sat-Thu) Next to the Kia showroom in Wattayah, this is one of the best places to ask for information. Staff are experienced and helpful.

SIGHTS

Many of Muscat's sights are in and around Mutrah and the neighbouring Old Muscat. There are a number of things to see in the suburbs, including some lovely beaches.

Mutrah   مطراح
CORNICHE

Mutrah stretches along an attractive corniche of latticed buildings and mosques; it looks spectacular at sunset when the light casts shadows across a serrated crescent of mountains, while new pavements, lights and fountains invite an evening stroll. Despite being the capital's main port area, Mutrah feels like a fishing village. The daily catch is delivered to the **fish market** (Map p197; ☷ 6-10am), by the Marina Hotel, from sunrise everday.

BAIT AL-BARANDA

This new **museum** (Map p197; ☎ 24714262; Al-Mina St, Mutrah; adult/child OR1/500 baisa; ☷ 9am-1pm & 4-6pm Sat-Wed, 9am-1pm Thu) in a renovated 1930s house, traces the history – and prehistory – of Muscat through imaginative, interactive displays and exhibits. A 'cut-and-paste' dinosaur, using bones found in the Al-Khoud area of Muscat and topped up with borrowed bones from international collections, is one of many striking exhibits in this excellent museum. The ethnographical displays help set not just Muscat but the whole of Oman in a regional, commercial and cultural context.

MUTRAH SOUQ

Many people come to Mutrah Corniche just to visit the **souq** (Map p197; ⊙ 8am-1pm & around 5-9pm Sat-Thu; 5-9pm Fri), which retains the chaotic interest of a traditional Arab market albeit housed under modern timber roofing. There are some good antique shops selling a mixture of Indian and Omani artefacts among the usual textile, hardware and gold shops. Bargaining is expected but the rewards are not great, any discount will be small. Entrance to the souq is via the corniche, opposite the pedestrian traffic lights. Take care not to wander into the historic, Shiite district of Al-Lawataya by mistake, as the settlement is walled for a good purpose. A sign under the archway politely requests visitors to keep out. Turn right immediately inside the entrance and follow your nose along to the **gold souq**; or walk straight ahead, fork right at the first junction and left at Muscat Pharmacy for Al-Ahli Coffeeshop (see p208).

MUTRAH FORT

Built by the Portuguese in the 1580s, this **fort** (Map p197) dominates the eastern end of the harbour. Used for military purposes, it is generally closed to visitors although you can scale the flank of the fort for a good view of the ocean.

AL-RIYAM & KALBUH BAY PARKS

Beyond the fort, the corniche leads to the leafy **Al-Riyam Park** (Map pp194-5; ⊙ 4-11pm Sat-Wed, 9am-midnight Thu & Fri), with fine views of the harbour from the giant, ornamental incense burner and small fun fair. Further along the corniche, **Kalbuh Bay Park** (Map pp194–5), juts into a sea that's boiling with sardines – a good place for an evening stroll from Mutrah.

WATCHTOWER

The restored Portuguese **watchtower** (Map p203) on a promontory out to sea, half way along the corniche, affords a lovely view of the water. Access to the staircase is from

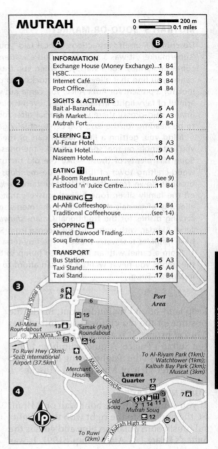

behind the Al-Inshirah Restaurant. The area is a popular place to catch the evening breeze and is decorated with colourful fountains at night.

Old Muscat

The main road leads via the corniche to the tiny, open-gated city of Muscat, home now to the palace and *diwan*. It sits cradled in a natural harbour surrounded by a jagged spine of hills.

MUSCAT GATE MUSEUM

Straddling the road between the corniche and the old walled city, this **museum** (Map p199; ⊙ 9.30am-12.30pm & 4.30-7pm Sat-Thu), with the original gates used until the 1970s to

OMAN

MUTRAH'S 'SOUQ-OR-MARKET'

Describing Mutrah's attractions, a local said 'you must visit the souq-or-market'. Thinking he said 'supermarket', it was a surprise to find a warren of alleyways with no checkouts – but there are some similarities. For a start, just when you thought you'd fathomed where to find the frankincense, you find that alleyway now stocks Thai clothing. Secondly, though you fully intended to look for a present for Aunt Alice, you came out with a toy helicopter, two melamine trays and an armful of fairy lights instead. Thirdly, even though you definitely didn't want to buy a *dishdasha* (man's shirt-dress), there was a special offer for three. And finally, although all alleyways seem to be heading for the exit, you can't actually get out.

Mind you, getting a little lost is part of the fun of the souq, as that is the most likely time you'll stumble on the 'special offers' – the ones unique to 'that place' at 'this time'. And Mutrah Souq has plenty of those – like the old picture frames, complete with woodworm, from the wood-crafting town of Ibra; antique *mandoos* (wedding chests) with brand-new thumbtacks brought down from the Hajar Mountains; a *khanjar* (traditional curved dagger) shop selling off the family silver; rope-twined muskets that saw action in the Dhofar wars of the 1970s; an alleyway of sandals that complete the men's smart Omani costume; and another of aluminium serving dishes for the traditional Omani *shuwa*; a fruit-juice shop serving pomegranates from Jebel Akhdar, with wafts of frankincense from Salalah outside the door; and a tea palace whose host sprinkles rosewater made in the tiny terraced village of Al-Ayn.

From a camel with an illuminated hump to that favourite, the kitsch mosque alarm clock, all the things you never wanted but can afford to buy (plus a few you did and can't) are available in Mutrah Souq.

---

keep land-bound marauders out, marks the position of the old city wall and introduces Muscat proper. It is also a vantage point for the Sultan's Palace. A quick climb up to the aerial mast on the neighbouring hill gives an even better view of Mutrah and Muscat.

SULTAN'S PALACE

If you stand by the harbour wall on Mirani St, the building to the right with the delightful mushroom pillars in blue and gold is the **Sultan's Palace** (Al-Alam; Map p199). It was recently extended over the site of the former British embassy. In the grounds, there used to be the stump of a flagpole: the story goes that any slave (Oman was infamous for its slave trade from East Africa) who touched the flagpole was granted freedom. There's a fine view of the palace from the roundabout on the inland side; some streets of houses have recently been cleared (to the chagrin of some) to make a new colonnade befitting of a royal residence and more appropriate to officially 'meet and greet' – particularly spectacular when the mounted guard is in attendance.

AL-JALALI FORT

Guarding the entrance to the harbour to the east, **Al-Jalali Fort** (Map p199) was built

during the Portuguese occupation in the 1580s on Arab foundations.

The fort is accessible only via a steep flight of steps. As such, it made the perfect prison for a number of years, but now it is a museum of Omani heritage, open only to visiting dignitaries and heads of state.

Neither this fort nor Al-Mirani (below) is open to the public, but photographs are permitted. During palace military occasions, bands of bagpipers perform from the fort battlements, and the royal dhow and yacht are sailed in full regalia into the harbour. With fireworks reflected in the water, it makes a spectacular sight.

AL-MIRANI FORT

To the west, **Al-Mirani Fort** (Map p199) was built at the same time as Al-Jalali Fort. It contributed to the fall of the Portuguese through a curious affair of the heart: legend has it that the Portuguese commander fell for the daughter of a Hindu supplier, who refused the match on religious grounds. On being threatened with ruin, he spent a year apparently preparing for the wedding, but in fact convincing the commander that the fort's supplies needed a complete overhaul. Instead of replacing the removed gunpowder and grain, he gave the nod to

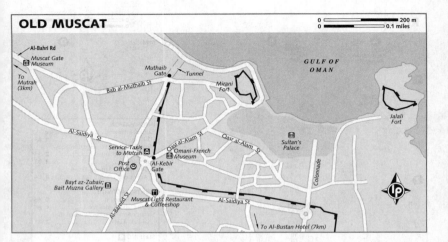

OLD MUSCAT

Imam Sultan bin Saif, who succeeded in retaking the defenceless fort in 1649. The Portuguese were ousted from Muscat soon after.

BAYT AZ-ZUBAIR
In a beautifully restored house, this **museum** (Map p199; ☎ 24 736688; Al-Saidiya St; admission OR1; ⏰ 9.30am-1pm & 4-7pm Sat-Thu) exhibits Omani heritage in photographs and displays of traditional handicrafts and furniture.

OMANI-FRENCH MUSEUM
With galleries detailing relations between the two countries, this **museum** (Map p199; ☎ 24 736613; Qasr al-Alam St; admission 500 baisa; ⏰ 9am-1pm Sat-Thu) provides an interesting snapshot of mostly 19th-century colonial life in Muscat. From October until March, the museum is also open from 4pm to 7pm Saturday to Thursday.

Al-Bustan البستان
AL-BUSTAN PALACE HOTEL
Set in lush gardens, this sumptuous **hotel** (Map pp194-5; ☎ 24 799666; ⏰ closed until January 2008) was built as a venue for the Gulf Cooperation Council (GCC) summit in 1985. Remarkable for its enormous domed atrium, the hotel has won numerous awards as the best hotel in the Middle East. It's worth coming just to look at the building's interior and the location. It was being refurbished at the time of research and is scheduled to re-open in 2008.

AL-BUSTAN ROUNDABOUT
Just outside the Al-Bustan Palace Hotel, a small roundabout is home to the *Sohar* (Map pp194–5), a boat named after the hometown of the famous Omani seafarer, Ahmed bin Majid. The boat is a replica of one sailed by Abdullah bin Gasm in the mid-8th century to Guangzhou in China. It was built in the dhow yards of Sur from the bark of over 75,000 palm trees and four tonnes of rope. Not a single nail was used in the construction. Tim Severin and a crew of Omani sailors undertook a famous voyage to Guangzhou in this boat in 1980 – a journey of 6000 nautical miles that took eight months to complete.

Ruwi روي
Oman's 'Little India' is the commercial and transport hub of the capital, with plenty of budget-priced places to eat, shop (especially along Souq Ruwi St) and socialise.

NATIONAL MUSEUM
With displays of jewellery, costumes and dowry chests, this **museum** (Map p200; ☎ 24 701289; An-Noor St; admission 500 baisa; ⏰ 9am-1pm & 4-6pm Oct-Mar) has its moments. A mural and collection of boats celebrating Oman's seafaring heritage are probably the best part of a tired collection.

SULTAN'S ARMED FORCES MUSEUM
Despite the less than appealing name, this excellent **museum** (Map p200; ☎ 24 312642;

OMAN

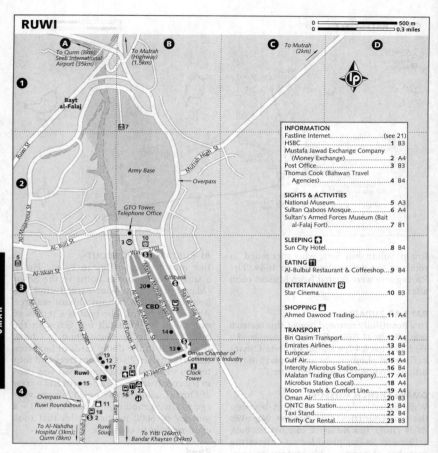

RUWI

admission OR1; ☾ 8am-1pm) is far more than just a display of military hardware. The museum is housed in Bayt al-Falaj, built in 1845 as a royal summer home but used mostly as the headquarters of the sultan's armed forces. The lower rooms give a comprehensive outline of Oman's history, and the upper rooms explore Oman's international relations and military prowess. The museum is on the itinerary of visiting dignitaries and you'll be given a mandatory military escort. There's a *falaj* (irrigation channel) in the grounds outside.

Qurm   القرم

Most of this area comprises modern shopping centres and residences, but there are several places to visit. Surprisingly, one of the best places to buy Omani silver and handicrafts is inside a modern mall called the **Sabco Centre** (see p209).

In addition to the small displays of artefacts and interesting rooms on Omani architecture, the **Oman Museum** (Map pp194-5; ☎ 24 600946; admission 500 baisa; ☾ 8.30am-1.30pm Sat-Wed, 9.30am-12.30pm Thu) is worth trying to find for its view over dazzlingly white suburbs and sea, though it's not always open as stated. A taxi from Qurm up the steep 1.3km climb costs OR1. From October to March, the museum is also open from 4pm to 6pm, Saturday to Wednesday.

Petroleum Development Oman (PDO) is responsible for much of the rapid growth of infrastructure throughout the country, as outlined in the **PDO Oil & Gas Exhibition** (Map pp194–5; ☎ 24 677834; Sayh al-Malih St; admission free; ☺8am–noon & 1–4pm Sat-Wed, 8am–noon Thu). The neighbouring **Planetarium** (☎ 24 675542) is open for two shows per week in English (at 7pm Wednesday and 10am Thursday) but book one day ahead.

To reach both from Qurm, follow the signs for the Crowne Plaza Hotel and turn at the first right along Sayh al-Malih St.

A popular venue during the annual Muscat Festival in January, **Qurm Park** makes a good place for a picnic even in the hot summer months; the adjacent **Qurm Nature Reserve** (closed to visitors) protects a rare stretch of mangrove. A road runs along the edge of the reserve towards the Crowne Plaza Hotel, giving access to a long, sandy **beach**. Women bathing on their own have been accosted here, so avoid skimpy swimwear.

There are two pleasant cafés along the beachfront with a view out to sea above the palm trees.

Shatti al-Qurm & Al-Khuwair
شاطي القرم و الخوير

Near the Hotel InterContinental Muscat, along Way 2817, there is a small shopping complex where you will find the **Omani Heritage Gallery** (Map pp194–5; ☎ 24 696974; www.omanheritage.com), which sells local handicrafts (see p209).

The Ministry of National Heritage houses the small but lovely **Natural History Museum** (Map pp194–5; ☎ 24 641510; Way 3413; admission 500 baisa; ☺9am–1pm Sat-Thu). The museum is a must for anyone interested in the local flora and fauna, and there are also some excellent displays on Oman's geography and geology.

It's worth driving around the elaborate **ministry and embassy buildings** bunched in this area. Make time to stop at the beachside **Grand Hyatt Muscat** to enjoy a Yemeni prince's flight of fancy; love it or hate it, tea in the foyer is a delight.

Ghala & Al-Ghubrah
الغبرة و غلا

Also known as the **Grand Mosque** (Map pp194–5; Sultan Qaboos St; ☺8–11am Sat-Wed for non-Muslims), this glorious piece of modern Islamic architecture was a gift to the nation from Sultan Qaboos to mark the 30th year of his reign. Quietly imposing from the outside, the main prayer hall is breathtakingly rich. The Persian carpet alone measures 70m by 60m wide, making it the largest carpet in the world; it took 600 women four years to weave.

When visiting the mosque, long sleeves and trousers (not jeans) or long skirts should be worn, and women should cover their hair. As when entering all mosques, you should remove your shoes and take care not to touch the Quran. If you sit on the carpet, make sure your feet are tucked behind you – it is offensive to Muslims if you point the soles of your feet at them.

Al-Ghubrah and Ghala lie some 8km west of Al-Khuwair. If you are visiting the mosque from Muscat in the summer, it's easier to take a taxi (OR5) rather than catch the bus: it is a hot walk crossing the highway via the overpass. Plenty of buses bound for Ruwi stop outside the mosque.

ACTIVITIES
The sea and the mountains dominate Muscat, giving plenty of amenities for water-related sports and some independent hiking. **Muscat Diving & Adventure Centre** (☎ 24 485663; www.holiday-in-oman.com) can help with activity-based trips in the capital area and beyond.

For other companies offering much the same, see p260.

4WD Trips
Muscat's rocky mountains and soft-sand dunes offer some exciting and challenging 4WD driving. Close to the city there are plenty of places to explore, especially near Yitti and en route to Al-Seifa (see p213). Many routes further afield are covered in this book (such as the mountain road from Al-Hamra to Wadi Bani Awf, p233. For more adventurous routes, pick up a copy of *Off-Road in the Sultanate of Oman*, by Lonely Planet author Jenny Walker, and Sam Owen; see p255.

Many people refer to this activity as 'wadi-bashing' – taking a 4WD into remote terrain can lead, through careless or insensitive driving, to irreparable degradation of the environment. For information on limiting the negative effects of this activity, see p554.

OMAN

It's also possible to take 4WD tours to many off-road destinations (see p260).

Beaches

Many of the big hotels have attractive beach-side facilities open to nonguests for a fee. Women may feel more comfortable here than on public beaches. The Crowne Plaza Hotel is at the head of a beautiful, sandy bay and has its own private scrap of beach. Admission costs OR6 per day. A taxi from Mutrah should cost OR3. At present, all beaches in Muscat are 'public', so there's nothing to stop a keen walker starting at Qurm Nature Reserve and walking all the way to Seeb, a distance of some 20km or so.

Bird-Watching

With your own transport, it's easy to access a number of places in Muscat for bird-watching opportunities, including the reed beds and mangroves at Qurm Nature Reserve, where a number of waders can be seen year-round. Contact the Oman Bird Group (☎ 24 695498) for specialist information.

Hiking

There are some rewarding mountain walks in the Muscat area. Several two- to three-hour walks in and around Mutrah and Old Muscat afford excellent views of the two port areas and take the rambler up past ruined villages. These walks are covered in Anne Dale and Jerry Hadwin's *Adventure Trekking in Oman*, with good maps, directions and safety precautions. Their Muscat–Sidab route is a one-hour walk that could be added, for energetic walkers, onto our walking tour (see right).

The Ministry of Tourism (☎ 24 588831; www .omantourism.gov.om) has developed a set of walking tours and a booklet describing these routes. Brown information signs mark the trailheads of some routes. One, the C38 from Al-Riyam Park to Mutrah (a walk of 2km taking about 1½ hours), is an option on our walking tour. Be prepared for rough conditions in remote territory on all trails: stout walking shoes, water and a hat are essential at any time of year, even on the shortest route.

Horse-Riding

There are two horse-riding schools in Muscat that are open to the public:

Al-Sawahil Horse Riding (☎ 24 590061)
Qurm Equestrian School (☎ 99832199)

Water Sports

Water sports in Muscat include diving and snorkelling. There are also boat trips around scenic Bandar Khayran (and nearby rock arch), and dolphin and whale watching. The following centres offer a full range of water sports and activities, and run diving courses.

DiveEco (Map pp194–5; ☎ 24 602101; diveco@omantel .net.om; beachside, Grand Hyatt Muscat, Shatti al-Qurm), a well-established centre, is situated on a long, sandy beach.

The Marina Bander al-Rowdha (Map pp194–5; ☎ 24 737288; www.marinaoman.com; Sidab St) offers a full range of boating amenities. (Also see p211 for the Oman Dive Centre.)

Bait Al-Bahar (☎ 24 693223; Hotel InterContinental Muscat; Shatti al-Qurm) is one of the newest additions to the water-sports scene.

MUSCAT WALKING TOUR: A DAY IN THE LIFE OF THE ARABIAN SEA

> **Start** Fish Market, Muscat
> **Finish** Al-Bahri Rd, Old Muscat
> **Distance** 8km
> **Duration** 4 to 5 hours

This walking tour follows the sea through the ancient ports of Mutrah and Muscat. Pack a snack and take water. The walk can be segmented if time, energy or summer heat forbids the whole circuit.

Begin where the morning tide beaches fishermen and their catch at the Fish Market (1; p196). Stop for breakfast at nearby Al-Boom Restaurant (p207).

Turning right at fishy Al-Samak roundabout (2), visit nearby Bait al-Baranda (3; p196) and learn about the history of Muscat's relationship with the sea. Return to the corniche (p196) and head towards 16th-century Mutrah Fort (p197). Look left at dhows and right at the merchants' houses of the Lawataya people, who built their fortunes on the sea-faring trade.

Just before the fort, turn into Mutrah Souq (4; p197) where items such as handmade silver dhows and ship chandlery are on sale; this souq grew from seaborne cargo. Ward

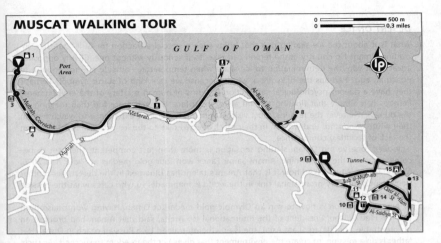

MUSCAT WALKING TOUR

GULF OF OMAN

off the scurvy with a mixed fruit juice at **Al-Ahli Coffeeshop** (p208) in the heart of the souq. Return to the corniche and turn right.

At the **goldfish monument and fountains (5)**, a heron often snacks in view of the royal dhow and the visiting navy. Continue towards the giant incense burner; Oman's former prosperity was built on Dhofar frankincense.

On reaching **Al-Riyam Park (6**; p197), you could, with stout shoes, head back to Mutrah on the Ministry of Tourism's walking route C38, past panoramic views. Alternatively, continue along the corniche to the **watchtower (7**; p197) and scan for dolphins: some real and some carved from marble.

After **Kalbuh Bay Park (8**; p197) cut inland via Al-Bahri Rd and enter the 'city proper' via **Muscat Gate Museum (9**; p197).

Turn right towards Sidab on Al-Saidiya St and visit **Bayt az-Zubair (10**; p199) for photographs showing the sea's influence on Muscat and buy a souvenir of your tour in **Bait Muzna Gallery (11**; p209) opposite.

Continue along Al-Saidiya St, still heading for Sidab. Pause for fried fish at **Muscat Light Restaurant & Coffeeshop (12**: p208) on the corner before turning right along an elegant avenue of date palms.

At the roundabout, march left through the colonnade towards the grand front entrance of the **Sultan's Palace (13**; p198). Follow the palace walls left, past beautiful gardens and mature trees (favourite roost of minar birds) on Qasr al-Alam St.

At the junction, turn left for the **Omani-French Museum (14**; p199) and a display on shipbuilding, or right for **Muscat Harbour**. The Portuguese built forts, such as **Al-Mirani (15**; p198), towering to the left, and **Al-Jalali** (across the bay), to protect their maritime interests. Look across the harbour for a graffiti log book left by maritime visitors.

Turn left at the harbour wall, and duck under the tunnel before the naval base. Turn right under the **old city gate** onto Bab Muthaib St. This soon runs into Al-Bahri Rd – and from here, it's an easy taxi ride back to Mutrah.

COURSES
Language
Muscat isn't a great place to learn Arabic, as many people speak English proficiently and relish the chance to practise.

For the determined, however, **Polyglot** (Map pp194-5; ☎ 24 835777; www.polyglot.org; off Wadi Aday roundabout, Ruwi; per course OR105) runs 10-week courses in six different levels of Arabic proficiency, from beginners to advanced. The teachers are usually from Sudan and the courses concentrate on classical Arabic rather than the Omani dialect.

MUSCAT FOR CHILDREN
Muscat is a safe and friendly city with a few attractions for children, including the following:
Children's Museum (Map pp194-5; ☎ 24 605368; off Sultan Qaboos St, Qurm; admission 500 baisa;

OMAN

DESERT ON ICE

What is it about the ice-skating rink that holds such a special attraction for Gulf countries, including Oman? No country in the region can take itself seriously without one. Clearly opposites attract, but why the determination to ice-skate when temperatures outside are hot enough to poach an egg? Perhaps the rinks are a 'we do because we can' kind of status symbol? Perhaps they have a deeper psychological satisfaction in terms of human mastery of the environment? Perhaps it is simply that floating around a frozen surface is much more fun than roasting on the dunes? Whatever the reasons, most visitors will find it a unique experience to watch men in their white *dishdashas* and women in their black *abeyyas* take to the ice with a surprising (given the lack of facilities) competence.

Indeed, one young Omani skating sensation is more than just competent, she's set to become a star. At the age of nine, Amani Samir Fancy won four gold medals at Skate Asia 2006, held in China. When asked how it is that Amani's talent has bloomed in the desert, her mother points out that every professional rink in the world is manmade, so who cares what the outside temperature is.

Amani's ambition is now to win an Olympic gold medal for Oman. Having won praise from the top (Ted Wilson, President of the international Ice Arena, said that Amani had brought an unforgettable 'sparkle' to Skate Asia), she is now being trained by a Russian coach in Dubai. Her father is on a mission 'to create the environment that gives her the freedom to succeed'. As such, Muscat could be looking forward to a bigger, better rink in the near future.

(Ⓨ) 9am-1pm Sat-Thu) Well-signposted, domed building with lots of hands-on science displays.

Ice skating (Map pp194-5; ☎ 24 489492; Al-Khuwair St, Al-Khuwair; admission OR2.500 incl skate hire; Ⓨ 9am-10pm) A good way to beat the summer heat (see above).

Markaz al-Bahja (Map pp194-5; ☎ 24 540200; Mawaila) A fair way out of town, this covered play area with themed rides is in the new shopping mall, 5km northwest of Seeb Airport on the highway towards Seeb.

Qurm Park (Map pp194-5; admission free; Ⓨ 4-11pm Sat-Wed, 9am-midnight Thu & Fri) Attractively landscaped park, with ponds, shade for picnics, a model village (active during Muscat Festival) and a funfair with Ferris wheel.

TOURS

As Muscat's attractions are so spread out, a tour is recommended. Generally, tours can be organised on a bespoke basis from any of the main tour operators (see p260).

National Travel & Tourism (Map pp194-5; ☎ 24 660376; www.nttoman.com; Ar-Rumaylah St, Wattayah; Ⓨ 8am-1pm & 4-7pm Sat-Thu) can arrange half-day city tours for OR40 for a car of up to four people with an English-speaking driver.

FESTIVALS & EVENTS
Muscat Festival

Lasting for a month from around the beginning of January, Muscat Festival has become a highlight of the capital's year. The event is organised around two main venues; one in Qurm Park and the other at a semi-permanent site along the seafront between Athaiba and Seeb.

In Qurm Park, there are nightly fireworks at about 8pm, a 'living' replica of an Omani village with *halwa*-making and craft displays, exhibitions from regional countries and events such as laser shows and traditional dancing. At the beachside venue, there is a funfair, international pavilions selling crafts, bargain clothing and bedding and a range of items from cheap imports to inlaid furniture from Pakistan. International dance troupes perform on the open-air stage and fashion shows take place nightly; other acts, such as highwire acrobatics, occupy the periphery. In addition, many shops offer grand draws and discounts. Check the English-language newspapers and FM radio for the festival programme.

National Day

On 18 November, National Day is marked with fireworks, city buildings are draped with strings of colourful lights, and Sultan Qaboos St is spectacularly lit and adorned with flags and framed images of the Sultan.

SLEEPING

Muscat is not a cheap city to sleep in, but it does have some splendid hotels. Some of these are almost holidays in their own right. The hotels of Qurm, Shatti al-Qurm and Al-Khuwair are all located on or near the same stretch of sandy beach. For a location within walking distance of the capital's main attractions, however, the less expensive hotels in Mutrah are the best bet.

Budget

Al-Fanar Hotel (Map p197; ☎ 24 712385; fax 24 714994; Mutrah Corniche, Mutrah; s/d OR8/15) Near the fish market and neighbouring the Marina Hotel, this is a familiar travellers' haunt, but is in dire need of a face-lift. If you can ignore the down-at-heel interior, the basic rooms are clean and the cheapest in town. Breakfast is not included.

Naseem Hotel (Map p197; ☎ 24 712418; fax 24 711728; Mutrah Corniche, Mutrah; s/d OR12/16.500) In need of a make-over, this tired old Mutrah favourite has large, clean, comfortable rooms, some with stunning views of the harbour. Given its location, plum in the middle of the city's finest row of merchant houses, it's remarkable that this hotel has survived in the budget category – or survived at all for that matter. What it lacks in décor and sophistication, however, it makes up for in friendly, helpful service and of course, its prime location.

Sun City Hotel (Map p200; ☎ 24 789801; fax 24 789804; Al-Jaame St; s/d OR15/20) Beside Ruwi bus station, this new hotel, with its bright and cheerful lobby, large rooms with shiny floor tiles and big windows, is recommended if you have an early bus to catch. Friendly staff can help you navigate the vagaries of the bus station.

Qurm Beach House (Map pp194–5; ☎ 24 564070; qbhotel@omantel.net.om; Way 1622, Qurm; s/d OR14/32) In a quiet location and within walking distance of the beach, this hotel is on the approach to the Crowne Plaza Hotel. Don't be put off by the appearance of the lobby; the rooms are clean and appealingly quirky with an ill assortment of furniture. Right next door is Rocklands, one of the hottest nightclubs in town.

Midrange

Marina Hotel (Map p197; ☎ 24 713100; irfansyed1@ yahoo.com; Mutrah Corniche, Mutrah; s/d OR15/35) For those who have come to Muscat to discover its soul, then the Marina Hotel, overlooking the fish market and participating in the character of the corniche, offers a

very good vantage point. In fact, you can see what the city is all about over breakfast: the comings and goings of the ancient port of Mutrah can all be enjoyed from the restaurant window. The rooms are on the cramped side but the staff are interested and the clientele interesting, making for an enjoyable rag-bag atmosphere in the foyer.

Majan Continental Hotel (Map pp194–5; ☎ 24 592900; www.majanhotel.com; s/d OR40/46; ☒) Perched on top of a hill overlooking the pearly white suburbs of Muscat, this comfortable, Arabic-style hotel is hugely popular with Omani and regional visitors. If you think of Muscat as a prudish city, then think again: quiet and decorous by day, with a dome fit for an Italian palazzo, the hotel reinvents itself at night into the city's liveliest nightspot. With a pleasant pool area, coffee shop and large, chintzy rooms, this hotel best suits male travellers wanting to feel the pulse of local life.

Beach Hotel (Map pp194–5; ☎ 24 696601; beachhtl@omantel.net.om; Way 2818, Shatti al-Qurm; s/d OR48/52; ☒) In a pristine white building with tiled blue trim, big rooms with armchairs, balconies with sun shades and a lobby with sky blue domes, this is a rare residential-style hotel. There's no alcohol on the premises and the breakfast menu includes *fuul medamas* (beans) and *khoubs* (Arabic flat bread). With hospitable, helpful staff, an Arabic restaurant with live music on Monday, Wednesday and Thursday, an easy walk to the beach, and plenty of options for local exploration, this hotel offers a genuine Omani experience.

Coral Hotel (Map pp194–5; ☎ 24 692121; www.coral international.com; Shatti al-Qurm; s/d OR65/76) Fun and quirky, and with a nautical theme, this ship's bow-shaped hotel is only a seagull's glide from the sea. With sailor-suited staff and compass carpets, ships' wheel banisters and a dhow-shaped reception, guests will be glad to learn that rooms bear little resemblance to cabins. The bathrooms are particularly attractive with swan-shaped fixtures and fittings. All in all, this fun, well-priced option is a sail short of a fleet but a boom more than a tanker.

Top End

Prices quoted here are rack rates and you can almost certainly arrange a discount of

OMAN

some sort. Disconcertingly, rates literally change by 20% or more from one day to the next. Nonsmoking rooms are available.

Hotel InterContinental Muscat (Map pp194-5; ☎ 24 680000; muscat@interconti.com; Shatti al-Qurm; s/d from OR110/120; 🖳 ☎) If anything is 'happening' in Muscat, chances are it is doing so at the 'InterCon'. From Scottish balls and bagpipes to the latest cover show, regular entertainment is featured under the swaying coconut palms or in the hotel's English-style pub. While not the prettiest building in town, this hotel has a fine interior, quality rooms, shady gardens and access to the beach, making it a popular resort-style hotel. A handy shopping complex, including coffee shops and restaurants, is within walking distance.

Grand Hyatt Muscat (Map pp194-5; ☎ 24 641234; www.muscat.grand.hyatt.com; Shatti al-Qurm; s/d OR155/165; 🖳 ☎) This hotel is pure kitsch! The exterior owes much to Disney, while its stained-glassed and marbled interior is a cross between Art Deco and a royal Bedouin tent. Apparently a Yemeni prince designed the hotel and, like it or loathe it, it has an interior to be experienced. While traditionally more focused on the well-heeled business community, there is much in this majestic, marble-clad hotel to appeal to the sophisticated holiday-maker too, including luxurious, balconied rooms and Muscat's best Italian restaurant, Tuscany. With watersports offered on the beach and limitless walks along the sand, this is a hotel with more than one angle.

ourpick Chedi (Map pp194-5; ☎ 24 505035; www.ghmhotels.com; Al-Ghubrah North; s/d OR165/205; 🖳 ☎) With a hint of the *kasbah* (desert castle) combined with Oriental minimalism, the Chedi has been designed to make the best of its mini sand-dune location. Don't let the occasional groan of aircraft lowering into Seeb airport put you off: for most of the day, the only audible sound from the poolside of one of Muscat's most stylish hotels, is the whisper of crickets and the odd chink of wine glasses. The gardens, rhythmically punctuated by Zen ponds, raked pebbles and an infinity pool virtually contiguous with the sea, are satisfying to the soul. Satisfying to the palette, the Restaurant (p207) for once lives up to a rather presumptuous name. Chocolates, or should we say, 'Les Chocolates', are handmade on site by a French chef. Hanging suits and accommodating the etceteras of working life may be difficult in the minimally furnished rooms, but if all you brought is a swimsuit and a good book, then very little will intrude on your sense of getting away from it all.

Al-Bustan Palace Hotel (Map pp194-5; ☎ 24 799666; albustan@interconti.com; Al-Bustan; 🖳 ☎) In a secluded bay ringed by spectacular mountains, the Al-Bustan is more palace than hotel. It has an atmosphere and class of its own, partly engendered through the impeccable service, exceptional Arabian-style interior and some top-quality restaurants. It's closed for refurbishment until 2008.

EATING

There are plenty of opportunities for fine dining in Muscat, particularly at the top-end hotels. Equally, it's hard to go 10 paces without tripping over a *shwarma* (meat sliced off the spit and stuffed in pita-type bread with chopped tomatoes and garnish) stand.

Dozens of cafés around Muscat sell a variety of largely Indian snacks, such as samosas and curried potatoes. It is more difficult to eat typical Omani food – the best option is Bin Atique. For a comprehensive roundup of Muscat's restaurants and cafés, it's worth buying a copy of *Oman Today* (OR1). Below is a selection of restaurants that give a flavour of the region, either in menu or venue.

Restaurants

Automatic Restaurant (Map pp194-5; ☎ 24 487200; behind the Sabco Centre, Qurm; mains OR2) There is nothing automatic about the Lebanese fare from this chain of Lebanese restaurants: they serve uniformly good-quality food with friendly service in cheap and cheerful surroundings. Whatever you order, a dish of leaves (lettuce, radish and mint) is provided free and makes a good garnish for the kebabs, felafel and hummus staples.

Al-Daleh Restaurant (Map pp194-5; ☎ 24 813141; National Hospitality Institute, An-Nuzha St, Al-Wadi al-Kabir; 3-course lunch OR2; ☉ 1-2.30pm Sat-Wed, 7-8.30pm Tue) Nervous Omani hospitality students practise their culinary and waiting skills at this exceptionally good-value restaurant. Menus comprise mostly top-notch international dishes. Ring to book a table as it gets busy.

Al-Boom (Map p197; ☎ 24 713100; Marina Hotel, Mutrah Corniche, Mutrah; dishes OR5, breakfast OR1.800) This small restaurant, with large windows overlooking the harbour, is a good place to get a feel of Muscat's age-old relationship with the sea. It is in an ideal location for breakfast (from 7.30am to 10.30am) after visiting the Fish Market opposite.

Bin Atique (Map pp194-5; ☎ 24 478225; Al-Khuwair; meals OR4) One of the few places in town to serve a variety of local Omani dishes. As the restaurant caters mainly for homesick Omani traders, you'll be seated on an old carpet in a private room. If you can put up with the unglamorous surroundings, however, the food is generally good quality and authentic. Try *harees*, a glutenous, Omani dish often mixed with chicken (OR2).

Meknes Restaurant (Map pp194-5; ☎ 24 475497; Al-Khuwair Slip Rd, Al-Kuwair; meals OR5) If Bin Atique didn't appeal, try nearby and newly opened Meknes for a more comfortable Arabian ambience. Serving excellent Moroccan dishes in a tiled interior with brocade armchairs, this is a good place to sample *tajine* (lamb stew) with potatoes and green olives (OR2.950) and mint tea poured with relish from silver kettles.

our pick Mumtaz Mahal (Map pp194-5; ☎ 24 605907; Way 2601, Qurm; meals from OR8) The Mumtaz Mahal is more than just the best Indian restaurant in town, it is part of the landscape of Muscat. Perched on a hill overlooking Qurm Nature Reserve, and with an intimate atmosphere created by live sitar performances, traditional seating at low tables, and lantern-light, it is little surprise that this restaurant, specialising in Northern Indian Mughlai cuisine, is a local legend. Try the snake coffee, which the head waiter prepares by setting fire to an orange peel.

Al-Kiran Terrace (Map pp194-5; ☎ 24 799666; Al-Bustan Palace Hotel, Al-Bustan; brunch buffet OR11) For Muscat's best Friday brunch, in gorgeous surroundings and with a bar licence after 2pm, this is more of a day out than just an excellent dining experience. Walk off that extra slither of smoked salmon under the coconut palms, or snooze away the rest of the afternoon on the beach lounge chairs – if the management sees sense and allows its customers out after lunch! The restaurant is closed until early 2008 due to hotel renovation.

Restaurant (Map pp194-5; ☎ 24 524400; Chedi Hotel, Al-Ghubrah North; meals from OR15) Repeated winner of awards for the best ambient dining in Muscat, this restaurant, with Arabian chandeliers and modern open kitchens, serves delicate international fare but includes melt-in-the-mouth *hamour* (a succulent local white fish), and some truly wonderful regional dishes such as *harira* (a thick soup with beef, lentils and chickpeas spiked with coriander). The French pastry chef makes wicked confections, including handmade chocolates. A walk under the stars in the hotel's gorgeous grounds is a good way to conclude an evening.

Cafés

A new café culture is blossoming in Muscat. These are a few of the city's favourite venues.

D'Arcy's Kitchen (Map pp194-5; ☎ 24 600234; Way 2817, Shatti al-Qurm; dishes from OR2) Next to the Omani Heritage Gallery, this friendly and award-winning establishment serves Western favourites at reasonable prices and is open when most other cafés are taking a siesta. An English breakfast for OR3.500 will set you up well for a 'constitutional' along the nearby beach.

Tche Café (Map pp194-5; ☎ 24 602757; Shatti Beach, Shatti al-Qurm; dishes from OR3) This modern venue, near to Starbucks, has one of the few seafront views in Muscat. It is on the pricy side but the locally caught fish on the menu will probably tempt you to savour the ocean for longer than the intended iced latte.

Khargeen Café (Map pp194-5; ☎ 24 692269; Medinat Qaboos complex; mains from OR4) With a choice of open-air, *majlis*-style dining or a cosy, indoor coffee-and-a-chat, this café-cum-coffeehouse has spilt into a courtyard of lighted trees to make a wonderfully relaxed, atmospheric and Arabian experience. With hubbly-bubblies croaking, fountains splashing, kebabs sizzling and people propped on a variety of cushions and throws, this could almost be part of a Bedouin caravan. Try the hibiscus or cacao drinks or the avocado milkshake.

Quick Eats

Fastfood 'n' Juice Centre (Map p197; Mutrah Corniche, Mutrah; sandwiches 200 baisa) Left of the entrance to the Mutrah Souq, with tables on the pavement, this thoroughly typical, local-style

OMAN

restaurant is an ideal place to people-watch over a *shwarma* and a 'chi lipton' (tea-bag tea with sweet condensed milk).

Muscat Light Restaurant & Coffeeshop (Map p199; Al-Saidiya St, Old Muscat; shwarma 250 baisa) Have an egg roll up in view of Fort Al-Mirani in this corner-street café, ideal as a rest-stop on a walking tour of Muscat (p202).

Al-Bulbul Restaurant & Coffeeshop (Map p200; Al-Jaame St, Ruwi; snacks 200 baisa) Just across the road from Ruwi bus station, this 'Arab and Turkish' street-side café is a good place for a quick *shwarma* before catching the bus.

Self-Catering

The ubiquitous Al-Fair supermarket chain is the perfect shop for picnic ingredients with good fruit and vegetable counters and items to suit Western palettes; the one in Medinat Qaboos makes excellent bread. Another good place to buy bread and savoury pastries is the Al-Bustan Bakery in the Qurm Commercial District.

Lulu's is the region's favourite supermarket chain and its food halls include many Middle Eastern favourites such as *hummus* (ground chickpea dip) and *muttabel* (smoked aubergine dip). There is a convenient branch off Sultan Qaboos St in Al-Khuwair. You can pick up a coolbox and freezer packs while you're at it to keep the picnic edible in the searing summer temperatures.

DRINKING

Arabic coffee is surprisingly hard to find in Muscat outside an Omani home or a hotel lobby. The coffeehouses all over town are oriented more to snacking than sipping coffee.

The best place for delicious, layered fruit juices of pomegranate, custard apple and mango is **Al-Ahli Coffeeshop** (Map p197; ☎ 24 713469; Mutrah Souq; large mixed juice 800 baisa) in the middle of Mutrah Souq. There is a traditional coffeehouse, on the left, just inside the souq, where Omani elders (men) trade news.

Each of the top hotels has an elegant café and a bar where alcohol is expensive but unrestricted.

Grand Hyatt Muscat (Map pp194–5; ☎ 24 641234; Shatti al-Qurm; afternoon tea OR8) If you sit sipping tea long enough in the extravagant foyer of this sumptuous hotel, chances are you'll

worry that the tea was laced: the statue of the Arab on Horseback that graces the central podium moves just slowly enough to make you suspect you've joined the flight of fancy that inspired the architects.

John Barry Bar (Map pp194–5; ☎ 24 641234; Grand Hyatt Muscat, Shatti al-Qurm) Named after the raised ship and its booty of silver treasure that made the fortunes of the Hyatt's owner, this bar is a sophisticated setting for some live piano music and a cocktail.

Trader Vic's (Map pp194–5; ☎ 24 680880; Hotel Inter-Continental Muscat, Shatti al-Qurm) When it comes to cocktails (try the Samoan fogcutter), nowhere competes with this fun and lively Polynesian-style venue. With live Latin music and wafts of Mongolian barbequed lamb chops, you'll probably be seduced into staying for dinner.

Al-Ghazal Bar (Map pp194–5; ☎ 24 680000; Hotel Inter-Continental Muscat, Shatti al-Qurm) More of a pub than a bar, this is a popular expat meeting place, with live music, a quiz night, televised sport and excellent Western-style bar food.

ENTERTAINMENT

Muscat is rather thin on entertainment options, although the five-star hotels and some of the smaller ones have bars and nightclubs, usually with live acts. *Oman Today* is the best source for information. For Muscat's latest hotspot, try **Rocklands** (Map pp194–5; ☎ 24 564443; Ramee Guestline Hotel, Way 1622, Qurm), which stays open until 3am.

The **Star Cinema** (Map p200; ☎ 24 792360; Way 2703; tickets OR2.500) screens both Western and Indian films. It occupies the unmistakable round building with flashing lights near the telephone office in Ruwi.

There is a newer cinema, **Al-Shatti Plaza** (Map pp194–5; ☎ 24 692656; tickets OR2.500), in Shatti al-Qurm and another one at Markaz al-Bahja mall.

You can take in a football (soccer) game at Bawshar Stadium.

SHOPPING

Muscat doesn't have the exhaustive range of shopping options on offer in other parts of the region, nor is it particularly cheap. However, with one of the most characterful old souqs in the region and a few new malls in the suburbs (Muscat City Centre near Rusayl roundabout and nearby Markaz al-

Bahja), there's enough to keep a dedicated shopper happy.

Souq Ruwi St is worth highlighting for all manner of cheap and cheerfuls from souvenir T-shirts to don't-ask DVDs and gold from India.

Crafts, Souvenirs & Gifts

Some popular Omani-produced items include highly worked, silver *khanjars* (curved daggers) that start at OR30 for a tourist replica to OR500 for an exquisite genuine item; baskets worked with pieces of camel or goat hide (from OR5); *kuma* (Omani hats), which start at OR2 for a machine-made one to OR50 for a highly crafted handmade piece; hand-loomed, goat-hair rugs (from OR15); frankincense (from 500 baisa) and a range of local and imitation perfumes; and dates (from 600 baisa per 500g).

Mutrah Souq (Map p197; Mutrah Corniche, Mutrah; ⏲ 9am-10pm & 5-10pm Sat-Wed, 5-10pm Fri) From *khanjars* to framed silverwork, gold and spices, this labyrinth of alleyways under a *barasti* (palm leaf) roof is the top spot in town for crafts and souvenirs.

Sabco Centre (Map pp194-5; Qurm shopping complex) A surprisingly comprehensive little souq inside the Sabco Centre sells crafts (mostly from India and Iran), *pashmina* shawls and Omani headdresses. Bargaining is recommended, although prices are reasonable. The souq's excellent cobbler can repair any leather item.

Bateel (Map pp194-5; ☎ 24 601572; www.bateel.com .sa; Oasis by the Sea complex, Shatti al-Qurm) For a regional gift-with-a-difference, the chocolate dates from Bateel are utterly world class.

Amouage (Map pp194-5; Sabco Centre; Qurm shopping complex) It sells the most expensive (and exquisite) perfume in the world, produced from frankincense, musk and other exotic ingredients in premises near Rusayl. You'll find the ultimate Arabian gift here.

Bait Muzna Gallery (Map p199; ☎ 24 739204; www .omanart.com; Al-Saidiya St; Old Muscat) Beautiful collectors' pieces, such as *mandoos* (wooden, brass-fitted dowry chests), Omani doors, Bedouin jewellery and contemporary paintings are sold in this gallery opposite Bayt Az-Zubair. Prices are high, but the quality is assured.

For guaranteed 'Made in Oman' crafts, try the **Omani Heritage Gallery** (Map pp194-5; ☎ 24 696974; www.omanheritage.com; Way 2817, Shatti

al-Qurm), a nonprofit organisation set up to encourage cottage industries through the sale of handicrafts. Prices are high, but so is the quality. See also **Omani Craftsman's House** (Map pp194-5; ☎ 24 568553; Qurm shopping complex) opposite the Sabco Centre in Qurm.

Camping Equipment

Most of what you will need for a night under the stars is sold at Al-Fair supermarkets. For more specialised equipment, try **Ahmed Dawood Trading** (Map p197; ☎ 24 703295; Al-Mina St, Mutrah) or Muscat Sports in Markaz al-Bahja.

GETTING THERE & AWAY
Air

Situated 37km west of Mutrah is **Seeb International Airport** (☎ 24 519223, 24 519456). See p261 for details of international flights. The only domestic flights currently available are with **Oman Air** (☎ 24 707222) between Muscat and Salalah (one way/return OR36/72, 1½ hours, twice daily at variable times), and Muscat and Khasab (one way/return OR24/48, one hour, variable times on Monday, Wednesday, Friday and Saturday).

Bus

The national bus company **ONTC** (☎ 24 490046; www.ontcoman.com) provides comfortable intercity services throughout Oman. Its main depot is the **ONTC bus station** (Map p200; ☎ 24 701294) in Ruwi. Timetables in English are available on the website (with fares); a summary is printed in the *Oman Observer*.

ONTC buses run to Salalah (one way/return OR6/11, 12 hours, twice daily at 6am and 7pm). However, there is some competition on this route from **Malatan Trading** (Map p200; ☎ 24 702091; Way 2985), which has a daily bus at 4.30pm (one way/return OR6/11), and **Bin Qasim Transport** (Map p200; ☎ 24 785059; Way 2985), which has a daily bus at 3.30pm (one way/return OR6/11), but note that arrival in Salalah is before dawn. Both companies are located around the corner from the bus station, near Moon Travels.

For buses to the UAE, see p262.

Car

Car hire can be arranged with several agencies in the area around the Ruwi roundabout, as well as at the usual desks in hotels and at the airport. See p262 for details.

OMAN

Taxi & Microbus

Taxis and microbuses leave for all destinations from Al-Jaame St, opposite the main (ONTC) bus station in Ruwi. There is an additional departure point at Rusayl roundabout (also known as Burj al-Sahwa – the Clock Tower), the next roundabout west of the airport roundabout.

Some sample taxi/microbus fares are:

To	Contract (OR)	Shared (OR)	Microbus (OR)
Barka	5	1	0.300
Buraimi	30	n/a	n/a
Nakhal	10	2	1
Nizwa	15	1.500	1
Rustaq	15	2	2
Samail	10	1	0.500
Sohar	15	2.500	1.700
Sur	16	4	3

GETTING AROUND
To/From the Airport

Taxis running between the airport and Qurm, Al-Khuwair and Ruwi cost OR5, and OR6 for Mutrah and Muscat. Alternatively, you can walk 300m to the roundabout outside the airport and wait for a microbus. Microbuses pass the airport fairly frequently between 7am and 10pm, and cost 500 baisa to Ruwi, Mutrah or Muscat. There is no regular direct bus service to/from the airport, despite the bus stop located there.

Microbus & Taxi

In Mutrah, local microbuses cruise the corniche and congregate around the Mutrah bus station. In Ruwi they park en masse along Al-Jaame St, opposite the main bus station. Trips from one suburb to the next cost 200 baisa to 300 baisa. No microbus journey within greater Muscat should cost more than 500 baisa.

Muscat's taxis, like all others in Oman, are orange and white and do not have meters. Even if you bargain you will inevitably pay two or three times the going rate for locals – fix the rate before you get in. A taxi between suburbs in Muscat should cost no more than OR5 engaged or OR1 shared (getting to/from the airport excepted). Expect to be charged double the going rate to/from hotels.

A shared taxi from Ruwi to Rusayl roundabout costs 500 baisa. Microbuses charge 300 baisa for the same trip. From Mutrah Corniche to Rusayl roundabout, the taxi/microbus fare should be 700/400 baisa.

AROUND MUSCAT

For an easy and rewarding day-trip from Muscat, a trip to the *khors* (rocky inlets) is recommended. The area, southeast of the city, is a popular snorkelling spot for weekend boat trips but it's also possible to reach many of the *khors* by car.

If you are looking for peaceful alternatives to staying in Muscat, the traditional town of Seeb, located to the west of Muscat, and the spectacular resort of Bandar Jissah, to the east of Muscat, are well worth considering.

SEEB السيب
☎ 24 / pop 252,864

If you are looking to experience a typical Omani town close to Muscat that barely sees a tourist, you can't do better than a trip to Seeb. A 20-minute drive northwest of the airport, this thriving coastal town has much to offer: there's a watchtower, a lively souq with a colourful textiles market, a gold souq with competitive prices, a magnificent stretch of sandy beach and some of the best squid kebabs in Oman.

Orientation

It's easy to find your way around Seeb. The high street (it's a one-way road) runs in a circle through the heart of the town, with banks, the gold souq, supermarkets and tailors either side of the road. The main souq is on the right in a purpose-built sandy-coloured complex of buildings before you reach the main mosque; it includes a fruit and vegetable area and a fish market. The road loops back to the entrance of the town. Lying to the other side of the fish market is the corniche.

Sights & Activities

There are no 'tourist' sights as such but Seeb is a great place to experience everyday Omani life. The wonderful 8km corniche has a landscaped area for walking, enjoying sea views, sniffing drying sardines and watching the fishermen net-mending.

One place to get a feel for the culture is on the main loop road as it returns to the entrance to the town. Along this section of the high street, there are many **shops** selling Omani-style **traditional ladies' clothing** with colourful anklets and embroidered smocking. Interspersed with the tailors are 'Wedding Services' shops selling strings of lights and outrageous bridal thrones. Towards the end of the street, there are many **carpentry workshops** selling *mandoos* (bridal chests). Usually black or terracotta-red and decorated with brass-tacks, these make a fun souvenir. A small box costs OR5 or a larger trunk OR16.

Seeb is an excellent place to find a tailor. Bring a favourite shirt or skirt, buy some material in neighbouring textile shops and take both into **MAS Tailoring** (☎ 95037004; cnr High St & Street 3850). For between OR3 to OR10, the Bangladeshi tailors will make you a replica in half a day. If you've been invited to a special 'do' in Muscat and forgot to pack the dinner jacket, this is the place to get one made for a bargain OR50, including material.

The other drawcard in Seeb is the beach. For shell-collectors, the long flat sands at low-tide make a great place to see horn, turret and auger shells.

Sleeping & Eating

There are a couple of pleasant places to stay in Seeb.

Al-Bahjah Hotel (☎ 24 424400; www.ramee -group.com; Seeb High St; s/d OR20/25) It's right in the heart of town (turn towards the sea by Oman International Bank). With a dhow and a giant coffee pot in the foyer, this is a traditional Omani hotel. It has a good Indian restaurant with a license. Try *palak paneer* (spinach and cottage cheese), which comes with rice, roti and pickles for a give-away OR1.800.

Dream Resort (☎ 24 453399; drmuscat@omantel .cnet.om; Dama St; s/d OR40/50; 🏊) This place is as close to a beach holiday that a bargain tariff can buy around Muscat. Though not literally on the sands, the beach is a five-minute walk along the hotel's own private *khor* (inlet) and guests can watch great grey herons parachute in to the hotel's tidal pools. The rooms, all with sea views, are comfortable and spacious, with split-level 'duplex' options for families. There is also an atmospheric nightclub, featuring live music from Africa. The resort is located 1km west along the corniche from Seeb fish market.

There are several other places to eat in town such as the beachside **Seeb Waves Restaurant** (☎ 24 425556; Corniche; mains OR2) with tasty chilli chicken (OR1), but the best option is to buy squid kebabs (500 baisa for three sticks) from the vendors on the corniche (opposite the souq) and eat them sitting on the sea wall.

A taxi from the highway near Seeb International Airport takes 20 minutes along Sultan Qaboos Hwy (OR5). Frequent minibuses connect Muscat with Seeb; to reach Muscat from Seeb it's easy to take one that plies the streets of Seeb (300 baisa).

BANDAR JISSAH   بندر الجصة
☎ 24

Until recently, Bandar Jissah was no more than a rocky promontory with a small, inaccessible beach. It now offers activities to suit most budgets and is home to Muscat's most prestigious resort development.

Picturesque **Jissah beach** (sometimes referred to as Qantab Beach) offers perfect bathing on weekdays (it gets too crowded on Thursday and Friday). For OR5 per boat (five people), entrepreneurial fishermen will take visitors on a 10-minute tour to see the famous **sea arch** that is now almost incorporated into the resort.

Lying just over the next headland to the resort, is the friendly **Oman Dive Center** (Map pp194-5; ☎ 24 824240; www.omandivecenter.com; Bandar Jissah; cabin s/d OR46/57). It makes a good place for lunch (try the carpaccio) and there are even a few (expensive) *barasti* huts on the beach if you fancy a dawn view of the bay. Camping is possible at the discretion of the management for a small charge. Perhaps one of the most easy-going places to enjoy some water sports, the centre offers half-day snorkelling trips (OR9, including equipment hire), and dolphin and whale-watching trips (OR15). You can enjoy its peaceful, secluded beach (and club facilities) for the day for a nominal OR1.300 (OR3 on Thursday and Friday). You'll need your own transport or a taxi to get here (about OR5 from Mutrah).

OMAN

The **Shangri-La's Barr Al-Jissah Resort & Spa** (☎ 24 776666; www.shangri-la.com; Barr Al-Jissah; 🔳 🔝), comprised of three kasbah-style hotels around a shared beach and garden, has brought modern tourism and a first-class holiday experience to Muscat – even for those staying at **Al-Bandar** (s/d OR170/180), the more business-oriented of the three hotels. The sophisticated six-star **Al-Husn Hotel** (s/d OR260/270) was toned down on instructions of the Sultan and is now less pink, but it's still majestic on its perch above the hightide. **Al-Waha** (s/d OR130/140), the easy-going, family hotel, accessed via a tunnel through the cliff, has luxurious rooms overlooking the pool.

Meandering between hotels, a lazy river offers a fun way of getting from one watering hole to another. The richly carpeted foyers, marble corridors and designer bedrooms and bathrooms in all three hotels make choosing one over the other a matter of whim. There is a complimentary bus service from Seeb airport, or it is a 15-minute drive by car from Mutrah. The resort includes some of the country's top restaurants: the Bait al-Bahr (nouvelle cuisine), Samba (international buffet) and Al-Tanoor (Middle Eastern fare).

If you have your own transport, pause at the spectacular **viewing point** between Bandar Jissah and the long descent into Al-Bustan. On the opposite side of the road, those after serious exercise can ascend to Muscat's hidden **40km cycle and walking track** that snakes above Bandar Jissah. A new road is being cut spectacularly through the mountains to link Bandar Jissah with Yitti, due to open in 2008.

YITTI
يتي

☎ 24

About 25km from Muscat, Yitti boasts a beautiful, sandy **beach** surrounded by craggy, mountain scenery. The beach is at the end of a large, muddy inlet that is regularly picked over by wading waterbirds.

If the tide is low, walk past a clump of serrated rocks at the end of the inlet. It was believed these rocks were inhabited by *jinn* and offerings used to be left at their base. Alas, the spirits have gone somewhere more private, according to the local fishermen, due to the scandalous behaviour of visitors from Muscat. Wade to a sandbar and

look left for a great view of Bandar Jissah's famous **sea arch**.

It is possible to stay on Yitti beach at **Al-Moosa Beach Resthouse** (☎ 24 886119; anosh@omantel.net.om; apt OR25). It has eight furnished apartments that each sleeps five people, with satellite TV, kitchen, dining room and the most glorious views out to sea. A small shop has minimal provisions, but it's better to bring a few kebabs from Al-Fair supermarket and cook them on the barbeque in the courtyard.

A resort is planned for Yitti, and development is expected to start in 2008. For now, however, it's a peaceful backwater.

There is no public transport here. There are currently two routes to Yitti (a third is being built from Al-Jissah). The shortest way (26km, about 30 minutes) is to take the winding sealed road from Souq Ruwi St in Muscat. Follow signs for Yitti (a right turn at 700m from Hamriya roundabout) through a maze of houses to a steep hill. Yitti is signposted again after 15.7km, soon after the road runs out of the hills. The route is easier to find going from Yitti to Muscat. The longer way (about 45km), via Wadi Mayh, is easier to find and takes about an hour.

WADI MAYH
وادي مياح

For a taste of a typical Omani wadi within an afternoon's drive of Muscat, look no further than Wadi Mayh. With towering limestone cliffs, sand-coloured villages, back-garden date plantations, straying goats and feral donkeys – not to mention a compulsory watchtower or two – Wadi Mayh has it all. Look out for a pair of stout *falaj* that have been shored into either side of the wadi, and which carry water from one village plantation to the next (see the boxed text, p216).

The wadi has areas where multi-coloured layers of rock have been forced into a vertical wall. The rocks of the wadi are smooth, round and strikingly colourful, making them a valuable building commodity, hence the piles ready for collection near the villages.

The entrance to the wadi is about 24km from Wadi Aday roundabout in Muscat. To reach the wadi, follow the Quryat road from the roundabout. After 16km, turn left at the roundabout with the gold eagle. Turn left at the sign for Yitti (at 24km) and the road leads directly into the wadi. The wadi can be negotiated by car although the last section of road (about 10km) is not sealed. There is no public transport.

BANDAR KHAYRAN & AL-SEIFA

بندر خيران و السيفا

Even if you don't manage to reach Al-Seifa, with its wonderful camping beaches, it's worth driving for 30 minutes in that direction from Yitti to get a flavour of the *khors*.

The first *khor* is popular with fishermen, but the second *khor* (at 4.8km) is one of those rare entities – a tidal football pitch, giving a new meaning to the term Mexican wave, perhaps, especially as the spectators of this busy pitch include crabs and mud creepers.

Thereafter (at 6km), the road hugs the side of **Bandar Khayran**, a large, mangrove-fringed lagoon, more usually visited by boat from Muscat. It is a beautiful spectacle late in the afternoon when the sandstone, and its reflection in the water, seem to vibrate with colour. Be sure to turn right at the mosque in the middle of the village, taking care to dodge the goats and the small boys selling seashells. Turn left at the junction for Al-Shaikh (at 12.5km) and some excellent **snorkelling** (watch out for seahorses), or continue to Al-Seifa.

There's not much to the scenically appointed village of Al-Seifa, resting in the shadow of the Hajar Mountains. Nearby beaches to the east, however, offer protected camping for those who bring equipment and provisions. The beaches are worth a closer look as they are a lapidary's dream: in between the sandy bays, pebbles of yellow ochre, burnt sienna and olive green beg to be picked up. For those interested in bugs, the giant-skipper butterfly frequents the surrounding wadis in spring.

To reach Al-Seifa by car, head to the power sub-station near Yitti and follow the sign. The latter is touchingly precise about it being '25.5km': it's not, but near enough. Although the road to Al-Siefa is now sealed, allow 40 minutes to reach Al-Seifa village beach and beware some steep descents. You will need 10 minutes more and preferably a 4WD to find your own beach beyond Al-Seifa along unpaved tracks.

QURAYAT

قريات

☎ 24 / pop 43,356

There are a number of features to enjoy in this attractive fishing village an hour's drive east of Muscat. It includes the 19th-century **fort** (admission 500 baisa; ⏲ 8.30am-2.30pm Sun-Thu) and a unique triangular **watchtower** overlooking the corniche. The sandy **beach** to the east of the tower extends for many kilometres with only the occasional football team to interrupt it.

The town was once an important port, famous for exporting horses that were reared on the surrounding plains. Sacked by the Portuguese in the 16th century, the town never regained its importance, although it retains a lively fishing industry and is celebrated for its basket makers. The large, porous baskets are made from local mangrove, and are used for keeping bait fresh aboard the small boats that pack the harbour.

Qurayat is well signposted from the Wadi Aday roundabout in Muscat, a pretty and at times spectacular 82km drive through the Eastern Hajar foothills. Look out for Indian rollers (blue-winged birds) in the palm trees lining the avenue into town. Shared taxis cost OR2 and microbuses OR1 from the Wadi Aday roundabout. A taxi costs OR8.

There are no places to stay in Qurayat, but it makes a pleasant day trip from Muscat or a good stop off before heading along the Qurayat–Sur coast road.

SHARQIYA REGION

المنطقة الشرقيه

This eastern-most corner of the Arabian Peninsula holds some of Oman's main attractions, including beautiful beaches, spectacular wadis, turtle-nesting sites and the strawberry-blond Sharqiya sand dunes. As many of the sites of interest lie en route rather than in the towns, it's worth having your own vehicle, although tours cover the whole area (see p260).

A great introduction to this region is to follow the Qurayat–Sur coast road. This route ideally forms the first day of a two- or three-day circular tour, returning to Muscat via the sealed road through Al-Mintirib. When the new motorway linking Quarayat with Sur is complete (2008) it will be possible to use a saloon car. For now, a 4WD is needed to complete the circuit.

A trip to Sharqiya can easily be combined with a visit to the Dakhliyah Region without having to return to Muscat. It's not possible, however, to get along the coast from Sur to Hijj (also known as Hay) in Al-Wusta Region without expert knowledge of sand-driving and navigation. Even tour company drivers regularly get stuck in the soft sand and unexpected high tides south of Al-Ashkara.

QURAYAT–SUR COAST ROAD

The four- to five-hour drive from Muscat to Sur, running along the northern base of the Eastern Hajar Mountains, is rugged and scenic. The new dual carriageway that will eventually link Muscat with Sur via Qurayat is still under construction so the following section describes the graded, off-road route. Don't be fooled by the odd saloon car you may pass on this route: 4WD is necessary to negotiate rough wadi bottoms and several sharp descents, especially after rain. There are no hotels between Muscat and Sur, but plenty of beaches for camping for those with equipment and supplies.

To reach the graded Qurayat–Sur coast road, follow the sealed road from Muscat to Qurayat, but turn right onto Daghmar Street by the Toyota showroom at the roundabout before you reach the town centre. After 6km, turn right for Fans, Tiwi and Sur (113km to the southeast). (Note that there's no public transport east from Qurayat.)

The tarmac soon runs out and the route continues along the bottom of Wadi Dayqah (one of the longest wadis in the Sharqiya Region) before meandering across a dusty and desolate moonscape for 30km. A small watchtower signals a sharp descent into **Dibab** and arrival at the Qurayat–Sur coast road. Some sections of the old coast road are now sealed, but there are no petrol stations between Qurayat and Sur.

Mazara   مزارع

A longer but rewarding way of reaching the Qurayat–Sur coast road is to take a more inland route via the small village of Mazara. Positioned half way along Wadi Dayqah, protected by a fort perched on a rocky outcrop, surrounded by copper-toned mountains and half-buried in thick plantations, the village is one of the most attractive in the region.

There is a picnic site by the side of the wadi, on the outskirts of the village. Popular with Omani day-trippers from Muscat at weekends, it's left to a loose assemblage of toads, kingfishers and goats at most other times. The picnic site marks the beginning of the Wadi Dayqah Walk, an impressive six-hour hike through the chiselled heart of the Eastern Hajar Mountains (see the boxed text, opposite).

The *barasti* hut accommodation near the picnic site is not recommended; camping is a better bet although it's hard to find a discreet spot.

To reach Mazara, turn off the Muscat to Qurayat road at the Omanoil petrol station (1km before you reach Qurayat roundabout) onto Hail al-Ghaf St and follow the signs for 21km through the foothills. The picnic site is signposted as a 'Rest Site', 500m off the sealed road, just before reaching the centre of the village. There is no public transport, but it is possible to engage a return taxi from Wadi Aday roundabout in Muscat (OR15, 1½ hours). The fare includes a 90-minute wait while you explore the pools at the neck of the wadi.

You can reach Mazara from Muscat in a saloon car but a 4WD is necessary if you want to continue on from Mazara to Dibab and the old Qurayat–Sur coast road.

Desert Mushrooms

Near to Mazara, on the graded track that leads to the Qurayat–Sur coast road, are two wonderful examples of a sandstone formation known as 'desert mushrooms'. These form when the wind sculpts away the softer sedimentary rock, leaving a cap of harder rock on top of the eroded column.

To reach the mushrooms from Mazara, follow the road through the village, over the wadi and past the fort. The road climbs steeply through the plantation towards a school. Turn left before the school, veer left over two *falaj* bridges and join the main graded road. From here it is about 8km to the mushrooms.

Turn left at the following junction and next right to join the graded Qurayat–Sur coast road 12km before the watchtower that marks the descent into Dibab.

A WALK ON THE WILD SIDE

Described by a 19th-century explorer as the 'most singular piece of earth sculpture in Arabia', the upper reaches of Wadi Dayqah are spectacularly chipped out of the Eastern Hajar Mountains to create a steep-sided, narrow gorge. For many centuries this gorge, otherwise known as the 'Devil's Gap', was an important thoroughfare from the interior to the coast, and an ancient pathway still picks a cautious route past obstructive boulders and irritable streams.

Tracing this route through the wadi bottom into neighbouring Wadi Tayein, on the other side of the Eastern Hajar Mountains, makes an exciting if strenuous six- to seven-hour hike, past polished wadi walls, and aquamarine pools fringed with bright-green algae and maiden hair fern. To avoid having to make the return journey, you can arrange for friends to tackle the walk in the opposite direction – a particularly large boulder in the middle of the main bend in the wadi marks the midway point and a good place to exchange car keys.

As the way follows the wadi bottom for much of the route, be prepared to wade or even swim through large pools of water. You may have to scramble over large boulders at the Wadi Tayein end of the route; if these are not passable because of recent rains, then follow a donkey track higher up the sides of the wadi for the last part of the walk.

Strong walking boots, a set of dry clothes and a bag for your camera are helpful. In addition, bring plenty of water and a hat as the route is unremittingly hot for most of the year. The hike is not suitable for young children and should not be attempted after heavy rains or on a cloudy day: occasional flash floods rip through the narrow channel with great ferocity, and near the Mazara end of the walk, the vertical wadi walls make escape to higher ground impossible.

To reach the beginning of the walk, park at the picnic site in Mazara and walk upstream, past the reservoir, and aim for the gap in the mountains. For directions on how to reach the other end of the walk, see Wadi Tayein (p224).

Bimmah Sinkhole   بمّا سنخول

The blue-green, brackish water at the bottom of this peculiar 40m by 20m limestone hole invites a swim and a snorkel. Known locally as Bayt al-Afreet (House of the Demon), you could come face to face with more than you bargain for in the water, the depth of which is still unknown. If the demon eludes you, look out for the equally elusive, blind cavefish instead.

The sinkhole is 1km inland, 6km east of Dibab, right by the new dual carriageway. It's not signposted, but look for a ring of *barasti* shelters on your right that is currently being developed into a picnic site.

Mountain Road to Gaylah

Making your way southeast along the Qurayat–Sur coast road, you'll notice several roads zigzagging up the mountainside into the clouds that often top the Eastern Hajar range. They mostly connect with small villages, such as Umq, in the heart of the mountains from where there is no onward route except on foot.

One exception, however, is the new graded track that has just been carved out of the rock face that leads to the cliff-hugging village of **Qaran**. The route is strictly 4WD and is not for the faint-hearted as the last part of the ascent is a near-vertical climb with sharp hairpin bends. The road is not on official maps yet but it is worth making the ascent for a panoramic view of the coast and an idea of the arid plateau that characterises the top of the Eastern Hajar range. If you're feeling brave, have a good sense of direction and spare petrol, you can follow the road across the plateau to the tombs at Gaylah (see p224).

The mountain road begins 35km southeast of Dibab (5km northwest of Wadi Shab) and is signposted 'Qaran'. Beware, there are no facilities whatsoever on top of this desolate plateau and the nearest petrol station is in Sur (or Hwy 23 on the Ibra side of the mountains).

Wadi Shab   وادي شعب

Aptly named in Arabic the 'Gorge Between Cliffs', Wadi Shab is still one of the most lovely destinations in Oman – despite the new dual carriageway being slung across the entrance. The wadi rewards even the most reluctant walker, with turquoise pools, waterfalls, and terraced plantations;

kingfishers add glorious splashes of colour and all year-round trusses of pink oleander bloom by the water's edge. There is an opportunity for (discreet) swimming during a visit to a partially submerged cave in the upper reaches of the wadi.

To begin the walk, cross the footbridge at the entrance of the wadi and follow the path through plantations, crossing and recrossing the wadi several times before reaching a small pumping station. Be prepared to wade up to your knees in places and beware of slipping on algae-covered rocks. After heavy rains, it may even be necessary to swim across some of the pools, so bring a bag for your camera and some dry clothes just in case. The path has been concreted (not very sympathetically) for part of the way and passes close to several villages, hidden in the plantations. At times the path follows an impressive *falaj* (see the boxed text, right) complete with underground sections and laced with ferns. The wadi eventually broadens into an area of large boulders and wild fig trees with many pools of deep water. Look for a ladder descending into one of these pools as Wadi Shab bends to the left. If you duck through a short underwater channel in this pool, you will find the partially submerged cavern. Allow up to two hours of walking to reach this pool.

Unfortunately, some visitors have caused offence to the local residents of the wadi by swimming and behaving inappropriately. It may look as though you are on your own but shepherds roam the cliffs and farmers tend their crops invariably unseen by the passer-by. As such it's better for both men and women to wear shorts and a T-shirt over swimwear and to confine swimming and sunbathing to the upper reaches of the wadi, beyond the plantation areas.

It's possible to walk beyond the pools to other small villages clustered along the wadi floor but the paths are not so well-trodden and they follow, sometimes steeply, goat tracks over the wadi cliffs. Walking shoes are necessary and plenty of drinking water. The wadi becomes drier the higher you climb into the mountains.

From Dibab, Wadi Shab is 40km southeast along the Qurayat–Sur coast road. Watch for grazing **gazelle** along the route. You can't miss Wadi Shab: the vista of mountains opening into a pea-green lake

---

WATER ON TAP

It may not have pipes and U-bends, but Oman's ancient *falaj* system is as sophisticated as any Western water mains. The channels, cut into mountainsides, running across miniature aqueducts and double-deckering through tunnels, are responsible for most of the oases in Oman. The precious water is diverted firstly into drinking wells, then into mosque washing areas and at length to the plantations, where it is siphoned proportionately among the village farms. Traditionally, a *falaj* clock like a sun dial was used to meter the time given to each farm; nowadays, some *falaj* are controlled by automatic pumps. There are over 4000 of these channels in Oman, some of which were built more that 1500 years ago. The longest channel is said to run for 120km under Sharqiya Sands. Although they can be seen throughout the mountains, the best, most easily accessible examples are in Wadi Dayqah, Wadi Shab and Wadi Bani Awf.

---

is sublime after the barren plain. Vehicles, thankfully, cannot navigate the wadi beyond a small parking area – even if they are shortly to cruise high over the wadi entrance on the new road.

Tiwi طيوي

There's not much to the little fishing village of Tiwi, but being flanked by two of Oman's beauty spots, Wadi Shab and Wadi Tiwi, it has found itself very much on the tourist map. Not that it has made many concessions to tourism – there's no hotel and no public transport, either to Muscat or to Sur. The locals are nonetheless forbearing of the convoys of passing 4WDs and are delighted when a driver bothers to stop for a chat. If you do stop, ask about Ibn Mukarab. The story goes that this Saudi fugitive paved the steps from his house (the ruins are still visible on the hill) to his tomb in gold. As anticipated, the locals dug the steps up for the booty, making the tomb inaccessible. Ibn Mukarab has since been able to enjoy the peace in death that he couldn't find in life.

The new dual carriageway is due to pass the very doorstep of the town, no doubt bringing with it considerable change. For now, the only access to Tiwi is via the old Qurayat–Sur coast road, 42km southeast of Dibab and 2km up a very sharp incline from Wadi Shab.

Tiwi also makes an easy day trip from Sur, 48km southeast. You might be able to persuade a taxi driver from Sur to take you to Tiwi (OR8) and wait for an hour or so while you explore either Wadi Shab or Wadi Tiwi. Occasional private microbuses ply the Qurayat–Sur coast road, but there is no regular service and this option shouldn't be relied upon.

There is plenty of ad hoc camping along nearby beaches. The most popular is Tiwi Beach (White Beach), a large sandy bay 9km northwest of Tiwi towards Dibab.

Wadi Tiwi   وادي طيوي

With its string of emerald pools and thick plantations, Wadi Tiwi almost rivals Wadi Shab in beauty, especially in the spring when the meadows turn a vivid green. Known as the 'Wadi of Nine Villages', there are excellent walking opportunities through the small villages that line the road. For the more ambitious hiker, there is a strenuous but rewarding two-day hike that begins at Sooee, the last of the nine settlements. Indeed, the route over the mountain to Wadi Bani Khalid (p223) has become a popular camping excursion with walking groups.

Wadi Tiwi can be accessed by 4WD but villagers prefer visitors to approach on foot. The road is narrow and steep in parts towards the upper reaches and it is easy to get a large vehicle stuck between the plantation walls.

Tours to the area, including Wadi Tiwi and Wadi Shab, can be arranged through all the hotels in Sur. To reach the wadi by car, drive through the village of Tiwi. Turn right at a small roundabout by the block factory at the Sur end of the village. If coming from Sur, you'll spot the donkeys and herons knee-deep in the grass at the mouth of the wadi before you reach Tiwi. Unfortunately, you will also now spot the giant pylons that are striding across the once picturesque entrance of the wadi, in preparation for the new dual carriageway. There is no reason why, however, the new road should disturb the peace of the wadi beyond the first couple of bends.

Qalhat   قلهات

The 2nd-century AD settlement of Qalhat is one of the most ancient sites in Oman. Although there's not much left to see, it's worth pausing to have a photo taken under the picturesque **Tomb of Bibi Miriam**. You'll be in excellent company: both Marco Polo in the 13th century and Ibn Battuta in the 14th century stopped here on their travels. You'll also have the satisfaction of knowing that your journey to Qalhat was a lot more adventurous than theirs. In their day, Qalhat was a 'very good port, much frequented by merchant ships from India' and a hub for the trade in horses from the interior. Today only the tomb and water cistern (both of which were being renovated at the time of writing), and the remnants of city walls, are visible, and in place of barques and dhows, all that the sea brings to the shore are sharks, sardines and rays. If you camp nearby, the water is often spangled at night with green phosphorous.

Qalhat is 22km southeast along the Qurayat-Sur coast road from Tiwi and 26km from Sur. The unsealed part of Qurayat-Sur coast road runs out near the gas works and a sealed road leads to the centre of Sur. A return taxi from Sur, if you can find a driver willing to take you, should cost around OR5.

SUR   سور

☎ 25 / pop 73,423

With an attractive corniche, two forts, excellent beaches nearby and a long history of dhow-building, there is much to commend Sur to the visitor. In addition to its attractions, Sur is a convenient base for day trips to Wadi Tiwi and Wadi Shab, the turtle reserve at Ras al-Jinz and the desert camps of the Sharqiya Sands.

History

Watching the boat-builders at work in the dhow yards in Sur, hand-planing a plank of wood, it is easy to recognise a skill inherited from master craftsmen. Sur has long been famed for its boat-building industry and even in the 19th century – when the Portuguese invasion and the division of Oman into two separate sultanates had delivered a heavy blow to the port town's trading capability – Sur still boasted an ocean-going fleet of 100 or more vessels. Demand for ocean-going boats declined once the British India

Steamer Navigation Company became preeminent in the Gulf and the town's fortunes declined correspondingly. Sur is currently enjoying a resurgence, however, thanks to the state-of-the-art liquid gas plant, which has generated lots of new jobs locally, and the newly opened fertiliser factory.

Orientation

The sealed road from Muscat (via Ibra) lies a few kilometres inland and ends at a clock tower roundabout with a marine mural. The Qurayat-Sur coast road also ends at this roundabout. Main St, running parallel with the coast and punctuated by five roundabouts, begins at this clock tower (Roundabout 1) and ends at the souqs and

Sur Hotel. Sur Plaza Hotel, the forts, banks, museum and restaurants lie on or just off this road.

Information

There are numerous banks, most with ATMs, along Main St and Souq St.

The **Internet Café** (Souq St; per hr 400 baisa; ☾ 8am-1pm & 4-10pm Sat-Thu; 4-10pm Fri) occupies the upper floor of the Digital Photo Express shop.

Sights

BILAD SUR CASTLE

Built to defend the town against marauding tribes from the interior, 200-year-old **Bilad Sur Castle** (admission 500 baisa; ☾ 8.30am-2.30pm Sun-

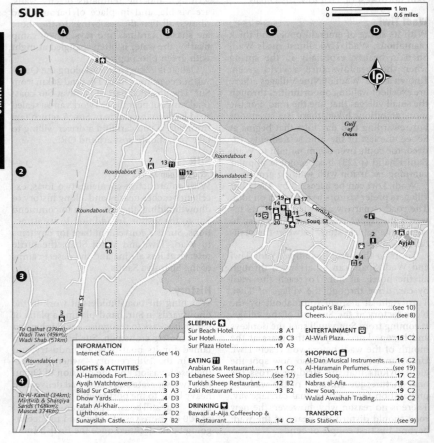

SUR

0 — 1 km
0 — 0.6 miles

INFORMATION	
Internet Café	(see 14)

SIGHTS & ACTIVITIES	
Al-Hamooda Fort	1 D3
Ayajh Watchtowers	2 D3
Bilad Sur Castle	3 A3
Dhow Yards	4 D3
Fatah Al-Khair	5 D3
Lighthouse	6 D2
Sunaysilah Castle	7 B2

SLEEPING	
Sur Beach Hotel	8 A1
Sur Hotel	9 C3
Sur Plaza Hotel	10 A3

EATING	
Arabian Sea Restaurant	11 C2
Lebanese Sweet Shop	(see 12)
Turkish Sheep Restaurant	12 B2
Zaki Restaurant	13 B2

DRINKING	
Bawadi al-Aija Coffeeshop & Restaurant	14 C2
Captain's Bar	(see 10)
Cheers	(see 8)

ENTERTAINMENT	
Al-Wafi Plaza	15 C2

SHOPPING	
Al-Dan Musical Instruments	16 C2
Al-Haramain Perfumes	(see 19)
Ladies Souq	17 C2
Nabras al-Afia	18 C2
New Souq	19 C2
Walad Awashah Trading	20 C2

TRANSPORT	
Bus Station	(see 9)

To Qalhat (27km); Wadi Tiwi (49km); Wadi Shab (51km)

To Al-Kamil (34km); Mintirib & Sharqiya Sands (168km); Muscat 374km)

Gulf of Oman

Ayjah

Thu) is the more interesting of the town's two fortresses. Look out for the unusually shaped towers. To reach the castle, turn left off Main St, 1.3km from Roundabout 1, at an elaborately kitsch residence.

SUNAYSILAH CASTLE

Perched on a rocky eminence, this 300-year-old **castle** (Main St; admission 500 baisa; ⏰ 8.30am-2.30pm Sun-Thu) is built on a classic square plan with four round watchtowers. It was the most important part of the defensive system of Sur, a town that was greatly fortified to protect its illustrious overseas trade. The entrance is a few metres off Roundabout 3, but access is via Roundabout 4.

CORNICHE & DHOW YARDS

The corniche affords a wonderful view across to the picturesque village of **Ayjah**. Dhows used to be led to safe haven by Ayajh's three **watchtowers**, which mark the passage into the lagoon. It is still possible to see the boats being made by hand alongside this passage.

To reach the dhow yards, turn left at the T-intersection at the end of the main road and follow the road in a semicircle past the corniche to the great lagoon. The road circles back eventually to the new souq, passing by **Fatah al-Khair**, a beautifully restored dhow built in Sur 70 years ago and brought back from retirement in Yemen. A new maritime museum is being constructed in the grounds. Look out for a small workshop opposite the dhow: Sur is famous for carpentry and some finely crafted model dhows are on sale here (opening hours at the whim of the owner).

AYJAH العيجة

Now that renovations to **Al-Hamooda Fort** (admission 500 baisa; ⏰ 8.30am-2.30pm Sun-Thu) are complete it is worth hopping on the ferry to the pretty, white-washed village of Ayjah, where the fort seems to have been built as part and parcel of the surrounding merchant houses with their elaborately carved doors and lotus-pillared porches. If you wander over to the old **lighthouse**, there is a fine view of Sur.

To reach Ayjah, you can either drive around the lagoon or, for a much quicker option, take the small ferry that leaves intermittently from a jetty on the corniche, next to the dhow yards. It costs only a few baisa and takes about five minutes.

Sleeping

There are only three places to stay in Sur. The two more comfortable options publish a 'rack rate' at greatly inflated prices; the following prices should be available if you ask, however, with some seasonal variation.

Sur Hotel (☎ 25 540090; fax 25 543798; off Souq St; s/d OR13/16 excl breakfast) In the middle of the new souq area, the location of the Sur Hotel is both a bother and a boon. On the downside, the rooms are noisy and the views from the window distinctly 'urban'. On the upside, this is a very convenient hotel within walking distance of the bus stop, cinema and corniche. Rooms are clean and adequate and meals are catered for in the good-value Arabian Sea Restaurant (p220) next door. Turtle-watching trips to Ras al-Jinz can be arranged through the hotel (OR25 for up to four persons) as well as trips further afield to Wadi Tiwi, or Wadi Bani Khalid and even Sharqiya Sands (OR30 per person for transport and one night's full-board accommodation).

Sur Beach Hotel (☎ 25 542031; surbhtl@omantel .net.om; s/d OR30/35; 🏊) This three-star, beachside hotel benefits from its location at the start of a 2km path along the shore. It receives a large number of visitors at weekends during the winter season and is beginning to look weary under the strain. It's probably going to take more than a lick of paint to bring this hotel back to its former high standard but it's still good value. The rooms have balconies overlooking the sea from which you can watch for phosphorescent waves at night. Try the excellent Indian chicken dishes and fresh *japathi* in the restaurant. The hotel offers free transport to a sister hotel at Ras al-Hadd (p222), near the turtle reserve.

Sur Plaza Hotel (☎ 25 543777; resvnsur@omantel .net.om; s/d OR30/35; 🏊) With the Captain's Bar open from 6pm to 3am offering live entertainment (usually a Filipino band), this hotel is popular with tour groups despite being several kilometres inland. Rooms are grand and bathrooms have magnificent marble basins – ideal for arranging the ill-gotten-gains of a day's beachcombing. Some rooms have fine views across the

OMAN

OMAN

mountains. Oyster's Restaurant has a good choice of international dishes but the king-fish (OR2.500) steals the show.

Eating

For international-style food, the restaurants inside the Sur Beach Hotel and Sur Plaza Hotel offer the best choices, and there is a Pizza Hut. For something more local, the following are recommended:

Zaki Restaurant (Main St; mains OR1) Located between Roundabouts 3 and 4, next to the BP petrol station, this place serves the best rotisserie chickens in town, complete with Arabic bread, chopped salad and tasty dhal. If the road-side location doesn't appeal, then ask for a 'take-away' and park at one of the picnic shelters near the Sur Beach Hotel.

Arabian Sea Restaurant (☎ 99746423; off Souq St; mains OR1-1.500; ❂ 11.30am-1.30pm & 5pm-midnight Sat-Thu, 5pm-midnight Fri) On the ground floor of the Sur Hotel (the entrance faces the other side of the block), this is a popular and lively local restaurant. It serves tasty bean dishes and kebabs.

Turkish Sheep Restaurant (Main St; mains OR2) Between Roundabouts 3 and 4, this popular venue offers sizzling kebabs, marinated in the chef's best spices, reputedly from Ottoman origin, and naughty triple-decker fruit juices. If these aren't hitting the spot, then the fresh-baked baklavas right next door from the Lebanese sweet shop surely will.

There are many small grocery shops in the New Souq area of town. Nabras al-Afia shopping centre, opposite Sur Hotel, sells everything needed for a picnic.

Drinking

From the outdoor seating area of **Bawadi al-Aija Coffeeshop and Restaurant** (☎ 25 360 1030; Souq St; ❂ 1pm-3am), it is fun to watch the residents of Sur amble along the brightly lit shops of Sur's liveliest street over a cup of mint tea or a mixed fruit juice.

The best place to meet other tourists or Western expats is the cosy **Captain's Bar** (☎ 25 543777; Main St; ❂ 6pm-3am) in the Sur Plaza Hotel, which has live entertainment, usually in the form of a Filipino band. The East African entertainment in **Cheers** (☎ 25 542031; ❂ 6pm-3am) in the Sur Beach Hotel features an odd 'on all-fours' dance routine

performed by heavily clad women. It raises polite applause from bemused Omani men but is definitely not the place to take your granny. Indian expats prefer the bingo on the beach next door: a cast of thousands regularly assemble on a Thursday evening hoping to strike the jackpot.

Entertainment

You can't miss the **Al-Wafi Plaza** (☎ 25 540666; www.filmcityoman.com; English/Hindi film OR2/1.500) cinema complex, next to the Friday market, as it is a tall, new building decorated with lights. It screens some films in English (though most are in Hindi) and is a non-smoking establishment.

Shopping

Sur has grown considerably in the last few years, largely as a result of the nearby gas and fertiliser plants. The souqs of Sur reflect the town's greater prosperity and there are some interesting shops to explore. In the **Ladies' Souq** (Main St) there are many textile shops, some selling braided ankle parts for women's trousers.

In the adjacent **New Souq** (Souq St) look out for Al-Haramain Perfumes. The elaborate bottles alone are temptation enough to enter the shop, and being daubed in exotic musk and ambergris is one of Arabia's great experiences.

Near to the livestock, fruit and vegetable souqs, **Al-Dan Musical Instruments** (☎ 99475588) has some beautifully crafted wooden ouds on sale.

For camping equipment, try **Walad Awashah Trading** (☎ 92262265), next to the musical instrument shop. It has tents for rent and for purchase and an assortment of camping gear.

Getting There & Around

Public transport leaves from or near the Sur Hotel. Buses to Muscat (OR3.400, 4¼ hours, twice daily) depart at 6am and 2.30pm. Shared taxis to the Rusayl roundabout in Muscat cost OR5 (engaged cost OR25). Microbuses make the same trip for OR3 and leave early in the morning. All public transport takes the inland route via Ibra. There is no public transport along the graded Qurayat–Sur coast road.

Taxis cost 150 baisa per ride anywhere in Sur.

RAS AL-JINZ   رأس الجِنز

Ras al-Jinz (Ras al-Junayz), the easternmost point of the Arabian Peninsula, is an important **turtle-nesting site** for the endangered green turtle. Over 20,000 females return annually to the beach where they hatched in order to lay eggs.

Oman has an important role to play in the conservation of these endangered species and takes the responsibility seriously, with strict penalties for harming turtles or their eggs. The area is under government protection and the only way to visit the site is by booking through the **Directorate General of Nature Reserves** (☎ 24 602285; fax 24 602283) and joining an escorted tour at around 9.30pm every evening.

While the tour is intended for the well-being of the turtle, the sudden influx of tourists has overwhelmed resources and the wardens at Ras al-Jinz simply aren't able to cope at peak holiday times with the number of people flocking to the reserve. There is something immensely intrusive about large, noisy groups gawping at such an intimate act, especially when flippers are lifted out of the way for better viewing and the frightened turtles are chased down the beach by mobile-phone wielding individuals.

A new museum and scientific centre is being built on the approach to the site (due

for completion by the end of 2007) and tourist numbers are being restricted. Perhaps this will help ease the pressure on the beach itself; if not, you may wish to avoid the area. For further information about the conservation measures in place to protect Oman's turtles, contact the **Ministry of Regional Municipalities, Environment & Water Resources** (☎ 24 692550 ext351; aid@mrmewr.gov.om).

For a more rewarding experience, you could get up at dawn in the hope of seeing the last of the late-comers. At this time of day, you are permitted to go to the beaches alone and can set your own limits of discretion around the few remaining laying turtles. If the turtles have already departed, then don't be too disappointed: at dawn the sandstone cliffs are burnished rose-red by the rising sun, and the turtle tracks of last night's heavy traffic inscribe the sand like ancient calligraphy. At this time, you'll most likely, except at weekends and during holidays, have the magical bay to yourself.

July is the peak laying season for the greens when over 100 turtles come ashore each night. September to November, however, is the best time to witness both laying and hatching at Ras al-Jinz. At least one turtle arrives on the beach every night of the year. Full-moon nights make it easier to walk and to witness the spectacle but

---

TURTLE-WATCHING ETIQUETTE

Watching labour and delivery on Oman's sandy beaches can be an awe-inspiring sight. Serene and patient, the female turtles that quietly lumber up the beach are sure to win the hearts of anyone lucky enough to see the spectacle of egg-laying on one of Oman's sandy beaches. Witnessing these gentle giants slip back into the darkness of the returning tide is one those unforgettable wildlife experiences – at least, that is, if the turtle is permitted to make her exit *after* rather than *before* the job is done and without the disheartening spectacle of bullish tourists trying to take a photograph at any cost.

Turtles are no land-lovers, and they are very easily dissuaded from making the journey up the beach. In fact, any disturbance during the turtle's approach to the shore will most probably result in a U-turn and it may be days before the turtle plucks up courage to try again. Once the digging of pits is over and the laying begun, however, the process cannot be interrupted. Nonetheless the following points should be avoided:

■ touching or approaching a moving turtle

■ standing in front of a nesting turtle

■ riding or sitting on a turtle (it happens!)

■ lighting a fire or using a torch near a turtle beach

■ taking a photograph with a flash or a mobile phone

■ leaving litter – turtles often mistake plastic bags for jellyfish

turtles prefer dark nights so as not to attract the unwanted attentions of predators which often dig up the eggs as soon as they are laid. The beach is about a 10-minute walk from the car park across soft sand.

A permit (per person OR1) is purchased at the park entrance and includes the guided tour to the beach.

Sleeping & Eating

There is a small, noisy and not very attractive camp site of basic wooden huts and shared washrooms that can be reserved through the **Directorate General of Nature Reserves** (☎ 24 602285; fax 24 602283; huts OR4). Food is not available so you need to bring all your own supplies. Apart from the price, the only advantage of the camp site is the instant access to the beach.

Offering more comfortable accommodation, **Desert Discovery Tours** (☎ 24 493232; www .desert.discovery.com; per person OR16) has a number of *barasti* huts with beds and reasonable shared bathrooms at A'Naseem Tourism Camp. The communal meals are healthy and sociable and the location, 4km outside the reserve on the approach road to Ras al-Jinz, is handy for a dawn visit to the beach.

Getting There & Around

Ras al-Jinz can be visited as an evening trip from Sur (organised through Sur Hotel, and with a one-hour journey time each way, costing OR25 for a car and driver with up to four passengers). There is no public transport.

If you have your own vehicle (4WD is no longer necessary), at Sur follow the signs to Ayjah. From Ayjah, follow the coast road. You'll eventually reach a T-junction where you can turn left for Ras al-Hadd or right for Ras al-Jinz. Ras al-Jinz can also be reached in a saloon car via a new sealed road from Al-Kamil on the Muscat–Sur Hwy (about an hour's drive) via Al-Ashkarah.

RAS AL-HADD راس الحد
☎ 25

A **castle** (admission 500 baisa; ☼ 8.30am-2.30pm Sun-Thu), some shops and attractive lagoon scenery nearby make this fishing village a useful supply point or alternative stopover to camping at Ras al-Jinz.

For a comfortable night's sleep in a room with sea views, **Ra's al-Hadd Beach Hotel**

(☎ 99376989; fax 25 542228; s/d OR25/30; 🖳) offers good-value accommodation on the edge of a flat-calm lagoon. In the early morning and late afternoon you can spot a variety of wading birds on the lagoon, dodging the outgoing or incoming dhows. If you walk along the beach at dusk, the water bobs with the backs and heads of turtles, queuing up to come ashore in the dark. For their protection, it's not permitted to camp or picnic at night on this beach. The hotel restaurant offers simple Indian fare or a buffet of international-style dishes. To reach the hotel, turn off the main road, by the castle in Ras al-Hadd, and follow the signs.

Offering *barasti* huts with reasonable shared bathroom and meals included, **Turtle Beach Resort** (☎ 25 543400; fax 25 543900; per person OR18) offers alternative accommodation in a camp situated on another glorious lagoon. The location is picture perfect and the sea gentle enough for the whole family to enjoy. The only drawback is that the huts are so close together you are at the mercy of noisy neighbours. The open-air dining area, in the shape of a wooden dhow, is a sociable spot, particularly with families of Indian expats from Muscat. Turn left immediately after entering Ras al-Hadd; the resort is 7km along a bumpy road.

To reach Ras al-Hadd, follow the signs for Ras al-Jinz but veer left after Khor Garami. It is clearly signposted. There is no public transport to this area.

AL-ASHKARAH الأشخرة

Wedged between two glorious sandy beaches, Al-Ashkarah is a lively fishing village and important supply point for the Bedouin communities of the Sharqiya Sands. It looks particularly attractive at sunset when it could well be called the 'pink city of the east coast' as the local cement has a pinkish hue. There is nothing to see or do, and nowhere to stay in Al-Ashkarah, but it does have a few picnic umbrellas on the beaches on the southern side of the town, and some camping opportunities. The sea here is much rougher and more characterful than on the beaches north of town and if you choose to break your journey here from Ras al-Jinz to Al-Kamil, you can look forward to large waves and flocks of gulls itching to join your picnic.

A major road is under construction between Al-Ashkarah and Shana'a, the ferry terminal for Masirah, but as it has to cross some of the most inhospitable terrain in the country, it's likely to be several years in the making. For now, the only way to reach points south of Khuwaymah (a supply town with hand-pumped petrol, about 70km south of Al-Ashkarah), is by 4WD and expert knowledge of sand-driving.

JALAN BANI BU HASSAN & JALAN BANI BU ALI جعلان بني بو حسن جعلان بني بو علي

☎ 25 / pop 82,383

These towns comprise a conglomeration of watchtowers, old fortified houses, forts and ancient plantation walls, all of which lie crumbling in various states of beloved dereliction. There's been little attempt to court the modern world and none at all to woo the visitor, making a visit all the more rewarding. It's worth trying to stumble on **Jami al-Hamoda Mosque** in the middle of Jalan Bani Bu Ali, with its unique structure of 52 domes and a *falaj* used for ablutions running through the courtyard. To get to the mosque, turn off the Al-Kamil to Al-Ashkarah road at the sign for Jalan Bani Bu Ali and drive towards the fort (closed to the public but obvious above the palm trees). Take the small road behind the fort and look around for the mosque, 300m away. To get a good view of the multidomed roof, climb the ramparts of a derelict house nearby. Tracks lead from here into the Sharqiya Sands but should not be attempted without a 4WD, and preferably a guide (or off-road guidebook) as these routes are seldom explored by visitors.

If the quiet authenticity of the two towns attract, or their gateway location on the fringe of the Sharqiya Sands invites further exploration, then consider staying at **Al-Dabi Jalan Bani Bu Ali Tourist Motel** (☎ 25 553307; s/d OR12). If you can ignore the sleeping bodies in the foyer (guests are not very common and staff may well be surprised to see you), you'll find the rooms are simple, a bit dusty, but perfectly serviceable. There's a small restaurant next door for rice and dhal.

The towns are signposted 17km from Al-Kamil on the Al-Ashkarah road. They make a good diversion en route to/from Ras al-Jinz.

AL-KAMIL الكامل

☎ 25 / pop 21,160

Despite some interesting old architecture, including a **fort** and **watchtowers**, this small town is more commonly known as an important junction with Al-Ashkarah road and the Muscat-Sur Hwy, punctuated by local-style cafés. It is something of a rarity in Oman, however, for being one of the few towns in the country surrounded by trees. The low-lying **acacia and ghaf woodland** is a special feature of the area, much prized by the Bedouin who use the wood for shade, shelter (as props for their tents) and firewood. Their camels nibble the nutritious new shoots and livestock lick the moisture from the small leaves in the early morning.

Al-Kamil, as an importance staging post between Muscat, Ibra and the Sharqiya Sands, and Wadi Bani Khalid, Sur, Al-Ashkarah and Ras al-Jinz, is a good place to break a long journey. There are no hotels in the town of Al-Kamil but the **Oriental Nights Rest House** (☎ 99354816; www.onrh.net; s/d OR14/16), on the Muscat–Sur Hwy near the Al-Ashkarah junction, offers very friendly, simple accommodation in clean but basic rooms. The hotel has a dining room that offers a familiar choice of home-cooked Indian curries, dhal and spicy soups in large portions. The hot bird satellite channel is a surprising addition to in-room entertainment.

There is public transport to Al-Kamil from Sur (OR1, 45 minutes) and Muscat (OR3.500), but note that there is no public transport to Ras al-Jinz from Al-Kamil.

WADI BANI KHALID وادي بني خالد

Justly famed for its natural beauty, this wadi just north of the town of Al-Kamil, makes a rewarding diversion off the Muscat–Sur Hwy. The approach road, which climbs high into the Eastern Hajar Mountains, zigzags through some spectacularly colourful rock formations, green with copper oxide and rust-red with iron ore, and passes by a natural spring or *'ayn'*, which is signposted by the side of the road.

Wadi Bani Khalid comprises a long series of plantations and villages that lie in or close to the wadi floor. All year-round, water flows from a natural spring in the upper reaches of the wadi, supporting the abundant vegetation that makes it such a beautiful spot. Most people visiting Wadi Bani Khalid head for the source of this water, which collects in a series of deep **pools** in the narrow end of the wadi, and **Moqal Cave**. Both are well signposted from the Muscat–Sur Hwy.

The pools have been developed into a tourist destination with a small (too small) car park, a concrete pathway and a series of picnic huts. Swimming is possible here but only if clothed in shorts and T-shirt over the top of a swimming costume. The site is rather unattractive or crude but at least efforts have at last been made to enhance access to this beauty spot. It is heavily crowded at weekends and during public holidays but it is possible to escape the visitors relatively easily by going in search of the cave or by climbing above the wadi on the marked path. The path eventually leads to Tiwi by the coast. It takes three days to walk (with donkeys carrying camping equipment) and is a popular hike organised by tour agents in Muscat (p260).

To reach the cave, look for a lower path above the picnic area and walk along the bottom of the wadi. You will have to scramble over and squeeze under boulders and ford the water several times. For precise directions, ask the goatherds. If they don't tell you the right place, it's because they don't like tourists swimming deeper into the wadi. Then again, they may just be worried you'll be lured into the land of gardens and cool streams revealed to all who strike the rocks of Moqal Cave and utter the magic words 'Salim bin Saliym Salam'. The cave, however, is more likely to reveal evidence of bats and previous visitors. The narrow entrance is finally accessed by a concrete stairway. A torch is needed to see anything and to find the underground pools, you will need to be prepared to scramble and slither through the mud.

GAYLAH الجيلة

This exciting destination on top of the Eastern Hajar Mountains is worth the effort as much for the journey through crumbling cliffs and past remote, mountain villages as for the reward of ancient tombs on the summit.

The route, which can only be negotiated in 4WD, begins at a right turn for Souqah,

just before the town of Ash-Shariq (also known as Simayiah – located at the entrance of Wadi Khabbah). Make sure you have water, map, compass and a full tank of petrol. At 3.1km after you leave the sealed road, take the right fork for Gaylah (often pronounced 'Jaylah' and sometimes spelt Al-Gailah). The track traces a precarious route through walls of unhinged black shale, waiting for a good storm to collapse. The last 6km of the ascent to the plateau, past shepherd enclosures, is currently poorly graded and progress is slow. At 21.4km, turn steep left by the water filling 'station' and follow the road to the top of the plateau.

A myriad of car tracks thread from village to village on the top of the plateau and numerous little communities survive on very little on the more or less barren plain. Until recently, the only access to many of these villages was by foot with an occasional helicopter visit landing supplies and/or health officials.

The numerous tombs (there are 90 or so) scattered across the hilltops date back to the Umm an Nar culture of 2000 to 2700 BC and, if you've been to Bat (see p236) you'll recognise the meticulous stone towers, carefully tracing the ridges of the high ground. Local belief has it that they were built by the spirit Kebir Keb, which is as good a way as any of describing the collective consciousness of the ancients.

If you are feeling adventurous, you can continue over the unmapped plateau to the village of Qaran and drop down to the Qurayat–Sur coast road, 5km northwest of Wadi Shab (see p215).

WADI KHABBAH وادي كبة
& WADI TAYEIN وادي الطائين

These two wide and luscious wadis meander along the western base of the Eastern Hajar Mountains and provide a fascinating alternative route between Muscat and Sur. A 4WD is needed to navigate the off-road sections, which invariably involve fording water. The picture of rural wadi life that unfolds as you meander through the spectacular mountain scenery is a highlight. There are numerous plantations and small villages in these wadis and it's much appreciated if you travel through the wadis with sensitivity.

To find the start of the western end of the Wadi Dayqah Walk (see p215), head for the village of Tool, some 10km east of the town of Mehlah. Mehlah is at the end of the sealed road through Wadi Tayein. You can park outside Tool and wade across the wadi entrance. Deep pools invite a swim but don't for a minute think you're alone: the steep ravine is a favourite with silent-walking shepherds.

AL-MINTIRIB   المنترب

This small village on the edge of the dunes is an important navigational landmark for visits to the Sharqiya Sands. Camp representatives often meet their guests here and help them navigate (in 4WD only) the route to their site – usually impossible to find independently unless you've been before. Al-Mintirib has a small **fort** and a picturesque **old quarter** of passing interest for those breaking the drive from Muscat, 220km to the northeast. The village is 10km southeast of Al-Qabil Rest House (p226) on the Muscat–Sur Hwy.

SHARQIYA (WAHIBA) SANDS
رمال وهيبه (الشرقية)

A destination in their own right, or a diversion between Muscat and Sur, these beautiful dunes, formerly known as Wahiba Sands, could keep the visitor occupied for days. Home to the Bedu (Bedouin), the sands offer the visitor a glimpse of a traditional way of life that is fast disappearing as modern conveniences limit the need for a nomadic existence. The Bedu specialise in

raising camels for racing and regular **camel races** take place throughout the region from mid-October to mid-April. Contact the **Ministry for Camel Affairs** (☎ 26 893804) for details.

The sands are a good place to interact with Omani women whose Bedouin lifestyle affords them a more visible social role. They wear distinctive, brightly coloured costume with peaked masks and an *abeyya* (outer garment) of gauze and are accomplished drivers, often coming to the rescue of tourists stuck in the sand. They are also skilful craft-makers and may well approach you with colourful woollen key rings and camel bags for sale.

It is possible, but highly challenging, to drive right through the sands from north to south, camping under the seams of native *ghaf* trees or tucking behind a sand dune. There are, however, no provisions available, petrol stations or any other help at hand in the sands, beyond the desert camps at the northern periphery. As such, it is imperative that you go with a guide, or at least with another vehicle, driven by someone who knows the route. Off-road guidebooks describe this route but all will advise you not to venture through the sands alone. In the summer the sands don't take prisoners so avoid exploring too far off-the beaten track between April and October.

For the casual visitor, the best way to explore the sands is by staying at one of the desert camps (p226). The owners of the camp will meet you at the Muscat–Sur Hwy, and guide you, usually in convoy across the sands. Needless to say, it is essential to have

---

SAND OF THE LIVING

If you drive through the sands in the spring, when a green tinge settles over the dunes, you'll notice that they are not the static and lifeless heap of gold-coloured dust that they might at first appear. Not only do they move at quite a pace (up to 10m a year) but they are also home to a surprising number of mobile inhabitants.

The Royal Geographical Society of London, in cooperation with the Omani government, conducted a survey in 1986 and concluded that among the 180 species of plants, there were 200 mammals, birds, reptiles and amphibians in the sands. The best way to spot these inhabitants is to look for the prints that slither, wriggle and otherwise punctuate the sand early in the evening and then lie in wait above the point where the tracks end. Sooner or later, the animal will burrow to the surface and scuttle off for twilight foraging.

While each animal has its place in the delicate ecosystem of the sands, the health of the environment as a whole is largely due to one six-legged, black-boxed insect called a dung beetle. Rolling its prize up and down the dunes, it can cover many acres of land and in so doing helps fertilise the fragile plants in its path.

4WD and prior knowledge of off-road driving is very helpful!

If you don't fancy the prospect of getting your vehicle stuck in the sand, there are plenty of tours available (see below) and some camps will come and collect their nondriving guests for an extra fee.

Sleeping

DESERT CAMPS

Accommodation in the sands takes the form of tented or *barasti* camps that offer the full desert experience, including camel rides (from OR5 per hour), camel-racing, dune-driving, sand-skiing and trips to Bedouin settlements. Don't confuse camping here with budget. The camps are often quite expensive for what they offer. The best value camps are as follows:

Al-Raha Tourism Camp (☎ 99343851; per person OR15) Located deep in the dunes, this friendly and efficient camp offers *barasti*-style huts at the end of a long corridor of orange sand. It can be rather noisy during holidays but at other times is a magical retreat and one that makes exploration deeper into the sands feasible.

Desert Discovery Tours (☎ 99317874; www.desert .discovery.com; r incl meals OR20) This company runs a spectacular camp, called Al-Areesh, on the edge of a silver sand dune with local Bedouin villages nearby. Staff can organise transport (OR20 per person) from Al-Qabil Rest House to the camp. Accommodation is in tents with shared bathroom.

Nomadic Desert Camp (☎ 99336273; www.nomadic desertcamp.com; r incl meals OR28) This experienced, intimate camp, run by a Bedouin family, offers a personal service in the heart of the dunes. Accommodation is in *barasti*-style huts with clean, shared bathrooms. Included in the price is transport to and from Al-Wasil on the Muscat-Sur Hwy, a camel ride and a visit to a Bedouin village.

HOTEL

For those wanting to experience the dunes as a day trip rather than an overnight experience, the following hotel offers easy, escorted access to the dunes.

Al-Qabil Rest House (☎ 25 581243; fax 25 581119; s/d OR13.100/17.500) On the Muscat–Sur Hwy 10km northwest of Al-Mintirib, this small and friendly guesthouse offers comfortable rooms around a courtyard and a range of sand dune explorations.

Getting There & Around

To get to the edge of the Sharqiya Sands by public transport, take a Muscat–Sur bus (from Muscat/Sur OR2/1.400) and ask to be dropped off at the Al-Qabil Rest House. It takes three hours from Muscat and 1½ hours from Sur. There are two buses per day in either direction.

The sands run parallel to the Muscat–Sur Hwy and the easiest access into the sands (with your own vehicle) is at Al-Mintirib.

IBRA إبرا

☎ 25 / pop 26,072

Ibra, the gateway to the Sharqiya Region, enjoyed great prosperity during Oman's colonial period as the aristocratic locals set sail for Zanzibar and sent money home for plantations and luxury residences, still in evidence in the old quarter of town. The tradition of farming is continued today, with rich plots producing vegetables, bananas, mangos, and, of course, dates. It makes a pleasant stop off for those heading to Sharqiya Sands.

Sights & Activities

Ibra has a lively **souq** that is at its most active early on a Thursday morning. Arranged around a double courtyard, the greengrocery takes pride of place in the centre, with local melons and aubergines making colourful seasonal displays. A working silver souq, where *khanjars* and veil pins are crafted, occupies several of the shops around the outer courtyard, muscling in between carpentry shops where elaborately carved doors are still made. Look out for a shop called 'Sale and Maintenance of Traditional Firearms & Rifle Making': there's always an energetic huddle of old men engaged in comparing ancient weaponry around the tables outside. You will probably notice piles of flattened and dried fish – a local delicacy, still prized despite the modern road system that has brought fresh fish to Ibra via the neighbouring wet fish market.

To reach the souq by car, turn right off the Muscat–Sur Hwy (if coming from Muscat) at the Omanoil station and turn immediately left, parallel to the main road. A watchtower punctuates the top of each surrounding hill, indicating the prior importance of the town. Pass the office of the local *wali* (governor) and the souq is on the right about 3.5km from the main road. Alternatively, take the first right off the Muscat–Sur Hwy, after Sultan Qaboos Mosque at the signpost for Al-Yamadi. If coming by bus, say you're heading for the souq and ask to be set down near the Al-Yamadi turning.

Women may be tempted to make a special visit on a Wednesday morning when the nearby **women's souq** attracts women-only buyers and sellers from all over the region, selling a variety of handicrafts (such as baskets, woven cushions and camel bags). Men, however, are not welcome.

If you continue past the souq area and turn right at the T-junction toward Al-Yamadi, you'll come to one of the old parts of Ibra with plenty of crumbling **mud-built houses** of two or three storeys. One or two houses across the wadi have been restored by local residents and it makes an intriguing place to take a discreet stroll.

Sleeping & Eating

There is adequate accommodation in Ibra to suit all pockets.

Ibra Motel (☎ 25 571777; ibramtl@omantel.net.om; Naseeb Rd; s/d OR9/10.500) It's cheap and it's central and for the price, not much more can be expected of it. Nonetheless, this modest hotel has clean rooms with wildly painted wardrobes and a job lot of 1970s-style patterned carpets. The tiny bathtubs have built-in seats for some reason. Breakfast is provided (OR2) in the adjoining restaurant, **Fahad bin Saleh Al-Hooti Restaurant** (☎ 92 416105; Naseeb Rd; mains 300 baisa), which cooks fresh food on the premises; the prawns in ginger sauce are a tasty option. The hotel is just off the Muscat–Sur Hwy, behind the Omanoil station.

Nahar Tourism Camp Oasis (☎ 99387654; www.emptyquartertours.com; s/d OR20/26, ste incl dinner & breakfast OR28/32) A very pleasant place to get a feel of the surrounding rock desert, this camp has a rural and remote atmosphere despite being only 3km from Ibra. With a pretty garden of vincas, a *barasti*-roofed dining area and its own camel race track, the camp is popular with European tour groups. Accommodation is in traditional mud-built rooms with decorative wind-towers, although a generator supplies air-con during the sweltering summer months. It's worth paying the extra for a suite: traditionally decorated, with painted ceilings and mosquito-netted beds, they are charm-

ing enough to persuade you to stay an extra night. For the rare visitor who enters Ibra by bus, the owners of this camp will pick you up from the town centre. Ask to be set down at the Omanoil station so at least you have shade while you wait or you can pop into the neighbouring cafes for a bit of air conditioning.

The owners have another camp deep in the Sharqiya Sands called the **1000 Nites** (s/d incl dinner and breakfast OR25/50) and can arrange 4WD transport at extra cost.

Al-Sharqiya Sands Hotel (☎ 99205112; fax 99207012; s/d OR22/28; 🏊) On the Muscat–Sur Hwy just south of Ibra, this attractive hotel is arranged around a central courtyard with a swimming pool and heaps of colourful lantana. The rooms are spacious, comfortable and have polished floors and large bathrooms. There is a rather loud 'local' bar and a more family-oriented restaurant with a very large international menu.

Eating in Ibra outside the hotels and camp is confined to small coffee shops. Opposite the souq is a large supermarket called Al-Najah shopping centre and there are lots of small groceries, *shwarma* stands and rotisseries dotted along the high street.

Getting There & Around

The Muscat–Sur Hwy passes through the modern town centre. The Muscat to Sur bus stops in Ibra (from Muscat OR2, about 2¼ hours, three times daily both ways).

SINAW   سناو

The reason most people pay a visit to Sinaw is to see its rather wonderful **souq**, which, like most other souqs in the country, is at its most active early on a Thursday morning. What makes this particular souq such fun to visit is that it attracts large numbers of Bedouin from nearby Sharqiya Sands who throng to the town to trade livestock for modern commodities. Local ladies wearing bronze peaked masks and transparent gauzy *abeyyas* add to the exoticism of the spectacle. Just before Eid the centre of town comes to a virtual standstill as camels are loaded (with inordinate difficulty) onto pick-up trucks and goats are bartered across the street. Spirals of smoke emanating from almost every house in the vicinity over the holiday period indicate that the livestock are not traded in vain.

The souq is on the edge of the town, on the Sinaw to Hijj (also known as Hay) road. It is arranged around a central courtyard and the souq gates are decorated with a green car for some reason. If you pass this gate on your left and veer around to the right, a left turn after about 500m takes you up the hill towards a **cemetery**. After a couple of kilometres more, you'll come to the old town of Sinaw. Well-preserved multistorey **mud houses** make this a fascinating place to wander around and give an idea of how this town has always been an important trading post.

Sinaw is 65km west of Ibra. Although you can catch a bus from Muscat (OR2, three hours), it's not very useful as it leaves late in the afternoon and there's nowhere to stay.

MASIRAH   مصيرة
☎ 25

With its rocky interior of palm oases and gorgeous rim of sandy beaches, Masirah is the typical desert island. Flamingos, herons and oyster-catchers patrol the coast by day, and armies of ghost crabs march ashore at night. Home to a rare shell, the Eloise, and large turtle-nesting sites, the island is justly fabled as a naturalist's paradise. Expats stationed here affectionately termed Masirah 'Fantasy Island' – not because of wildlife, but because anything they wanted during the long months of internment was the subject of fantasy only.

Masirah is still remote, with minimal facilities, but the island's splendid isolation is under threat with hotel chains negotiating for a portion of the eastern shore. For now, though, Masirah continues to offer a rare chance to see nature in the raw: if you can get there it promises a rare trip on the wild side.

History
Little is known about the island, except through hearsay. At one point it was inhabited by Bahriya tribes people, shipwrecked from Salalah. Wiped out by an epidemic 300 years ago, their unusual tombstones can still be seen at Safa'iq. The island has been used variously as a staging post for trade in the Indian Ocean, and as home to a floating population of fishermen attracted by the rich catch of kingfish, lobster and prawn.

> **FANCY A SNACK?**
>
> Masirah must be the only place in Oman without a fort – unless the air base counts. The local population tolerates the overseas militia with good grace, but outsiders have not always been welcome. In 1904 a British ship called the *Baron Inverdale* was wrecked off the rugged eastern coast. Her crew struggled ashore expecting Arab hospitality, but found a very different reception. A monument to their massacre in the shape of a concessionary Christian cross is all that remains of the luckless crew.
>
> There were rumours of cannibalism and as a result the Sultan decreed the destruction of all local houses – there are surprisingly few permanent settlements, even for the tiny population of 6000. You'll be glad to know that nowadays the only meat on the kebabs is likely to be camel or goat.

Orientation
Masirah is 63km long, 18km wide and lies 15km off the Barr al-Hickman coast near the southern end of the Sharqiya Sands. The rough Indian Ocean contrasts with the calm and shallow Masirah Channel. Jebel Humr (274m) is the highest point of Masirah's hilly backbone. Hilf, a 3km string of shops and fish factories in the northwest, is home to most of the native population. There are no shops or petrol stations beyond the town, but Hilf caters for most basic needs from food stuff to simple camping gear.

Sights
There are few attractions to draw the visitor away from the beach, but it is worth visiting the 300-year-old **grave sites** at Safa'iq, just inland from the island road (look for a red flag 6km north of Sur Masirah). Two rocks are usually the only indication of a grave for men, three rocks for women, but some of the Safa'iq graves have surprisingly elaborate headstones.

The **Baron Inverdale Monument** (see the boxed text, above) is next to the old BERS camp at the far northwest of the island. A climb up **Jebel Humr**, the flat-topped mountain, is recommended, but wear good shoes as the scree can be quite dangerous towards the top. The effort is rewarded by a wonderful view of the island, especially at sunset, and the plateau is strewn with fossils. To get there, head out of Hilf in the direction of Sur Masirah, turn left at the sign for A'Samar and scout around the wadi until the mountain comes into view. It takes about 30 minutes to hike up the left rump of the mountain and scramble over the rim.

Masirah is internationally renowned for its turtles: four species frequent the island, including the hawksbill, olive ridley and green, but the most numerous are the loggerheads. Thirty thousand come ashore each year, making Masirah the largest **loggerhead turtle-nesting site** in the world – the favourite nesting beach is by the old BERS camp. To reach 'Turtle Beach', drive towards the northwestern tip of the island.

For their sheer diversity, the shells of the island are hard to beat. Spiny whelks (murex) used to be harvested here for their purple dye, and ancient shell middens near Sur Masirah indicate that clams were an important food source for early settlers. Latterly, the island has become famous for the Eloise', a beautiful, rare shell unique to Masirah. Needless to say, the collection of live specimens of molluscs and corals is strictly prohibited.

Activities
Nightlife on Masirah is limited to 'labour and delivery' among the turtle population – all other entertainment is left to the imagination. High tide on the southwestern shore offers idyllic swimming, but the other coast should be treated with caution due to strong currents.

Bait is available from the fish factories – during winter you can expect to catch something using the simplest hand line.

Sleeping
With a 4WD, camping in any of the deserted bays on the west coast or at the southern tip is recommended. If you choose the east coast, don't forget you cannot light fires on a turtle beach. Without a car, hitch to Sur Masirah and walk 10 minutes southwest to secluded beaches.

Currently the only hotel on the island, **Masirah Hotel** (☎ 25 504401; fax 25 504035; r OR15) is in Hilf, to the immediate left of the main jetty on the main street. It has six rooms with multiple beds, commodious bath-

rooms and a lot of Arabic chintz, but no other facilities. It receives so few visitors there is no resident staff – if you fax them your dates, someone will switch the aircon on before your arrival. A Golden Tulip hotel is under construction on the north eastern side of the island. It should be completed by 2008.

If you get stuck at the ferry in Shana'a on the mainland, the grubby **Shanah Hotel** (☎ 99034216; s/d OR8/10) will do if you're desperate and haven't got camping gear.

Eating & Drinking
Dining options used to be limited to kebabs along the main road. Now, under the guise of the ubiquitous coffeehouse, you can find Indian (Timah Trading Restaurant), Chinese (Suhol Adam) and seafood (Ibn Al-Quramshi Restaurant), in addition to the usual Arabic fare.

Basic provisions can be found in the souq in Hilf. The bakery on the main road sells good samosas from 9.30am to 10.30am daily. Abu Sanidah is the most comprehensive supermarket in town but if you require any 'must-haves', bring them with you.

Getting There & Away
Getting to the ferry terminal at Shana'a is theoretically feasible by public transport but not very practical as there is no direct service from Muscat. If you are determined to try, however, take the Route 52 bus from Muscat to Sinaw, leaving at 5.30pm (3½ hours, OR2.800). The bus stops in Sinaw and there is no place to stay. You will then have to try to find a shared taxi to Shana'a (2½ hours, OR5) – not that easy late at night. You will arrive around midnight at the earliest. If you're lucky you can catch a ferry before morning but then the hotel in Hilf will not be open (it's not manned 24 hours – in fact, it's barely manned at all!). You may have better luck in reverse (from Shana'a to Muscat) as taxis often wait at the jetty for passengers to disembark. It's better to drive.

A left turn off the Sinaw–Duqm road leads, after 18km, to Hijj (also known as Hay). Shana'a is a further 45km away along a sealed road. Turn right across the salt flats (which turn a stunning red when the algae is in bloom) at the bus stop. Muscat to Shana'a takes about five or six hours by car.

OMAN

The trip by **ferry** (☎ 25 5040134) from Shana'a, near the desolate salt flats of Barr al-Hickman, is certainly characterful. The journey to Hilf, the main town on Masirah, usually takes 1½ hours – a lot longer when the boat gets beached on a sand bar, and the cost is OR15 each way per car; foot passengers travel free. Ferries run from morning until evening, but only during high tide.

Getting Around

There is a limited bus service in Hilf, but the only way to explore the island is to hike or rely on the few cars per day using the road.

There is no car-hire service on Masirah so the most feasible option for getting around is to bring your own 4WD. A sealed road circumnavigates the island but if you want to camp you'll need 4WD to get close to the water.

AL-DAKHILIYAH REGION منطقة الداخلية

This dramatic, mountainous region is one of the biggest tourist destinations in Oman, and for good reason. The area has spectacular scenery, including Jebel Shams (Oman's highest mountain), Wadi Ghul (the Grand Canyon of Arabia) and Jebel Akhdar (the fruit bowl of Oman). In addition, some of the country's best forts can be seen in Nizwa, Bahla and Jabrin.

Many of the sights from Nizwa to Jabrin can be managed on a long day trip from Muscat, and all tour companies in the capital (p260) organise such trips. The region deserves more than just a fleeting visit, however, especially if adding 4WD trips into the *jebel*.

With a 4WD, an exciting three-day round trip from Muscat can be made via Nizwa, taking in the sights of Al-Dakhiliyah Region, before crossing over the mountains from nearby Al-Hamra and descending to the Al-Batinah Region near Rustaq.

BIRKAT AL-MAWZ بركة الموز
☎ 25

The name of this pretty village roughly translates as 'Banana Pool' – a suitable name, as a quick drive through the village

plantation will reveal. Although there is a restored fort, **Bait-al-Radidah** (admission 500 baisa; ☽ 8.30am-2.30pm Sun-Thu), on the edge of the village, most people only venture into Birkat al-Mawz to begin the drive (or strenuous day hike) up Wadi Muaydin to the Saiq Plateau on Jebel Akhdar.

Birkat al-Mawz lies on the Muscat–Nizwa Hwy, 111km from the Rusayl roundabout in Muscat and 24km from the *khanjar* roundabout in Nizwa.

JEBEL AKHDAR الجبل الأخضر
☎ 25

Without a guide or some inside information Jebel Akhdar (Green Mountain) may seem something of a misnomer to the first-time visitor. Firstly, Jebel Akhdar refers not to a mountain as such, but to an area that encompasses the great **Saiq Plateau**, at 2000m above sea level. Secondly, the *jebel* keeps its fecundity well hidden in a labyrinth of wadis and terraces where the cooler mountain air (temperatures during December to March can drop to -5°C) and greater rainfall (hailstones even) encourage prize pomegranates, apricots and other fruit.

With a day or two to explore this 'top of the beanstalk', the determined visitor will soon stumble across the gardens and **orchards** that make this region so justly prized. If you stay at the hotel in Saiq, collect a hand-drawn map picking out some of the highlights of the area. It helps to think of Jebel Akhdar as two separate areas – an upper plateau, and a lower plateau on which the main town of **Saiq** is located. On the edge of the lower plateau, in a south-facing crescent, high above Wadi al-Muaydin, are spectacularly arranged terraced villages, where most of the market-gardening takes place.

In a weekend, you could spend one day exploring the upper plateau by car (turn first right after the hotel), picnic among magnificent mature juniper trees (in a perfect camp site about 2km after the Sultan's experimental farm) and hike through wild olive and fig trees to sunset point (a right turn before the school). The following day, explore the lower plateau by dangling over Diana's Viewpoint – named after the late Lady Diana of Britain who visited this vertiginous vista, with its natural pavement of fossils and dizzying view of the terraces

IN THE PINK

If you are lucky enough to find yourself in the small village of Al-Ayn on Jebel Akhdar in April, then you will be sure to have your nose assailed by the redolent Jebel Akhdar rose. Each rose has a maximum of 35 petals, but if you spend time counting them, you may well be missing the point. The point in cultivating these beautiful briars is not for the flower but for the aroma. For hundreds of years, the rose petals have been harvested here to produce rosewater (*attar* in Arabic) – that all-important post-dinner courtesy, sprinkled on the hands of guests from slender, silver vessels.

The yellowing bottles lined up in the sticky shed of a rosewater workshop suggest the petals have been boiled and discarded. This in fact is not the case. While the exact production of the precious perfume is kept a family secret, anyone on Jebel Akhdar will tell you the petals are not boiled but steamed over a fire with an arrangement of apparatus that brings to mind home chemistry sets. But the alchemy, according to Nasser 'bin Jebel' whose father's hands are ironically blackened each spring with rosewater production, is not so much in the process of evaporation but in the process of picking. If you see people dancing through the roses before dawn, chances are they are not calling on the genies of the *jebel* to assist the blooms, but plucking petals when the dew still lies on the bushes and the oil is at its most intense.

---

below. Then, allowing extra time to adjust to the thin, high-altitude air, hike from Al-Aqor to Seeq around the edge of the crescent. This is particularly rewarding during spring when the fragrant, pink roses from which rosewater is made are in bloom.

Jebel Akhdar was the centre of fierce fighting during the Jebel Wars (see p184), and until recently access was restricted to residents and the military. Although a permit is no longer necessary to make the ascent, you are only permitted to approach the area in 4WD. There have been many accidents caused by people trying to make the long descent in a saloon car, using their brakes with disastrous consequences rather than changing gears.

The only alternative to 4WD is a walking trail through the terraced villages of Wadi al-Muaydin to the Saiq Plateau. You'll need a guide and you should allow six hours from Birkat al-Mawz at the bottom of the wadi to reach the plateau (12 hours return). Beware: it's an unrelenting uphill slog!

Sleeping

Perched like an eyrie on the edge of Saiq Plateau, for most of the year **Jebel al-Akhdar Hotel** (☎ 25 429009; jakhotel@omantel.net.om; s/d OR26.200/36) is as empty as the land it sits upon. Even the open fire in the lobby in winter doesn't manage to make it cosy. But with a wind howling around the wacky stained-glass domes, and chilling the corridor, the hotel has at least character. There's

no bar but you can bring a bottle to drink with dinner.

Getting There & Around

Access to Jebel Akhdar is via the town of Birkat al-Mawz. Following the signs for Wadi al-Muaydin, off the Muscat–Nizwa Hwy, turn left in Birkat al-Mawz and pass the fort on your right. After 6km you will reach the second of two checkpoints, where you will have to satisfy the police that your car has 4WD. The hotel is 28km beyond the checkpoint – keep to the main road and you shouldn't have difficulty finding it.

As yet there is no public transport to the area, but several tour companies, including **National Travel & Tourism** (☎ 24 660376), offer day trips for OR110 per person. It may be cheaper (and possibly more rewarding) to hire a 4WD and stay at the hotel.

NIZWA نزوى

☎ 25 / pop 75,459

Nizwa lies on a plain surrounded by a thick palm oasis and some of Oman's highest mountains. About two hours from Muscat along a new highway, the town is a gateway to the historic sites of Bahla and Jabrin, and for excursions up Jebel Akhdar and Jebel Shams.

Only half a century ago, the British explorer Wilfred Thesiger was forced to steer clear of Nizwa: his Bedouin companions were convinced that he wouldn't survive the ferocious conservatism of the town and

OMAN

refused to let him enter. He'd have been amazed to find that Nizwa is now the second-biggest tourist destination in Oman. The seat of factional imams until the 1950s, Nizwa, or the 'Pearl of Islam' as it's sometimes called, is still a conservative town, however, and appreciates a bit of decorum from its visitors.

Orientation

Nizwa's fort dominates the town centre and all of Nizwa's sights are either inside or within walking distance of the fort. The hotels, however, lie along the Muscat-Nizwa Hwy, a few kilometres (100 baisa by microbus) from the town centre.

Coming from Muscat, the bus stop and taxi stand are situated in the middle of the wadi in front of the fort complex, 800m past the *khanjar* roundabout. When the wadi is flowing, the road is impassable at this point, hence the bridge further upstream that leads to the book roundabout. Buses for Ibri leave from the book roundabout.

Information

Banks and moneychangers are along the main street that runs from the fort complex to the book roundabout. The post office is inside the souq.

For those with a special interest in Nizwa, a website (www.nizwa.net) offers interesting insider information.

Sights

NIZWA FORT

Built in the 17th century by Sultan bin Saif al-Yaruba, the first imam of the Ya'aruba dynasty, the **fort** (admission 500 baisa; ⏰ 9am-4pm Sat-Thu, 8-11am Fri), which took 12 years to build, is famed for its 40m-tall, round tower. It's worth climbing to the top of the tower to see the date plantations encircling the town and the view of the Hajar Mountains.

NIZWA SOUQ

The fruit and vegetable, meat and fish markets are housed in new buildings, behind the great, crenulated piece of city wall that overlooks the wadi. If you're not put off by the smell of heaving bulls and irritable goats, the **livestock souq** (in full swing between 7am and 9am on Thursday) is worth a look. It occupies a small plot of land beyond the souq walls, left of the entrance.

You will have to try hard to find a bargain for antiques and silver at the other end of the souq (nearest the fort), but local craftsmanship is good. Nizwa is particularly famous for crafting silver *khanjars*. Today Indian or Pakistani silversmiths often work under an Omani master craftsman, especially for pieces designed for tourists, but the workmanship is exquisite. Prices range from OR30 for a tourist piece to well over OR100 for an authentic piece.

Sleeping

All the following hotels are on the road between Birkat al-Mawz and Nizwa.

Tanuf Residency (☎ 25 411601; fax 25 411059; s/d OR10/12) With huge rooms and even bigger beds, scenic views across the foothills and a competent restaurant, this is a good-value hotel that welcomes individual travellers – although English is limited. It is next door to the Arab World restaurant, 4.5km from the *khanjar* roundabout.

Majan Hotel (☎ 25 431910; fax 25 431911; s/d OR14/18) There is nothing memorable or charming about this hotel but if all you are looking for is a bed for the night, this hotel, which caters mostly for local business clientele, is clean and serviceable. Single women may feel uncomfortable in the all-male environment. It is 5km from the *khanjar* roundabout.

Falaj Daris Hotel (☎ 25 410500; fdhnizwa@omantel .net.om; s/d OR29.500/37.500; 🏊) This delightful hotel, wrapped around two swimming pools and a bar and with a vista of toothy mountains beyond, is the most characterful hotel in Nizwa. The low-ceilinged, marble foyer is a good place to sit on divans and discuss route plans over Omani coffee and dates. The rooms are more pleasant in the new block, but the older courtyard and pool have some welcome shade under which is arrayed the evening buffet – a friendly, tasty affair with long tables for tour groups. The hotel is 4km from the *khanjar* roundabout.

Golden Tulip Nizwa Hotel (☎ 25 431616; www .goldentulip.com; s/d OR59/64; 🏊) This rather pretentious, marble-clad hotel has a vast foyer and large pool but somehow misses the feeling of hospitality that is so prevalent elsewhere in Oman. It has plush rooms, however, with an arena of mountains visible in the garden, a bar and a good restaurant. It is situated some way out of town, near the turning for Jebel Akhdar, 18km from the *khanjar* roundabout.

Eating

Al-Zuhul Restaurant (meals OR2) This is a simple venue with outdoor seating on the pavement but it has one of the best night-time views in Oman. Situated opposite the souq, the café overlooks the fort and mosque, both of which are lit up spectacularly at night. It sells *shwarma* and kebabs, and is always busy with locals who generally pull up in the car and toot for a take-away.

Arab World Restaurant (meals OR2.500) Located on the Muscat–Nizwa Hwy, next to Tanuf Residency, this Lebanese-style restaurant has indoor seating, welcome in the summer after a dusty day's drive in the *jebel*. Kebabs and mezze are the most popular fare.

Bin Atique Restaurant (☎ 25 410466; meals OR3) Part of a small chain of Omani-style restaurants, this is one of the few places where you have the opportunity to sample local dishes. It is just a pity that the restaurant hasn't risen to the challenge of increased tourists looking for an authentic experience because the rather grubby private rooms are not the best ambience for dinner on the ground. Still it's worth a try – especially the cuttlefish with tomato.

Getting There & Away

ONTC buses run from Muscat to Nizwa (OR1.800, two hours 20 minutes, 8am and 2.30pm daily). Buses for Muscat from Nizwa (OR1.800) leave at 8.30am and 5.30pm.

You can catch the southbound bus from Muscat to Salalah at the roundabout at the end of the Muscat–Nizwa road (or 5km from the *khanjar* roundabout if coming from Nizwa). The fare from Nizwa to Salalah is OR5, and the journey takes 10 hours. Telephone the **Ruwi bus station** (☎ 24 701294) in Muscat to reserve a seat and check times.

Shared-taxi/microbus fares from Nizwa to Rusayl roundabout in Muscat are OR2/1 (to Ruwi add 500 baisa). Nizwa to Ibri costs OR2.500/1.500 by taxi/microbus.

AL-HOOTA CAVE   كهف الهوتة

Having announced the opening of this **cave** (☎ 24 490060; www.alhottacave.com; admission OR5; ⏱ 9am-2pm & 3-6pm Tue-Thu & Sun, 9am-noon & 2-6pm Fri Sep-Jun) in December 2006, the Ministry of Tourism was surprised to find half the population of Muscat queuing up outside. Such is the newly awakened spirit of tourism here that everyone is hungry for something to do at the weekend. Unfortunately, this cave, which is richly embellished with stalactites and stalagmites only has room for 750 visitors per day. As such, you should ring first to make a reservation. If you do manage to gain access, a train takes you into the cave and a 40-minute walking tour passes by an underground lake with blind cave-fish.

MOUNTAIN ROAD VIA HATT & WADI BANI AWF   الحمراء الروادي بني عوف

This truly spectacular road over the Western Hajar Mountains affords some of the best views in Oman. It can be accomplished as a long round-trip from Muscat or as a more leisurely outing from Nizwa to Rustaq. Although the mountain part of the route is only 70km long, it takes about four hours to drive and a 4WD is essential to negotiate the sustained, off-road descent into Wadi Bani Awf. This route passes through remote, rugged country and you should take the necessary precautions (spare tyre, jack, water, warm clothing, walking shoes and basic provisions).

From the book roundabout in Nizwa, take the road towards Bahla and turn right to Al-Hamra after 30.6km. After 3.5km turn right again for Al-Hoota Cave (Hoti Cave) and head for Bilad Sayt (Balad Seet).

The mountain road, zigzagging up the mountain in front of you, is well-signposted and sealed for much of the ascent. Look out for wild palms and clumps of aloe. At 23.9km you will come to the Sharfat Al-Alamayn viewpoint, on the saddle of the ridge: this is the highest point in the road. It's worth spending time here to enjoy the scenery and to look for wolf traps (piles of stone with a slate trap door) before the long descent into the village of **Hatt**.

After Hatt, the road continues for another 6km, skirting past **Bilad Sayt**, which is off the road to the left. The village is well-worth a detour. With its picture-postcard perfection of terraced fields and sun-baked houses, it's one of the prettiest villages in the area. The villagers prefer visitors to park outside and walk in or simply view the village from a distance.

At 43.8km, the road passes the entrance to aptly named **Snake Gorge**, a popular destination for adventure hikers and climbers (see the boxed text, opposite), and through the middle of a football pitch. From here the main track meanders around the mountain to the exit of Snake Gorge at 49.6km, signalled by a neat row of trees. If you're here in the spring, look out for a beautiful yellow-flowering tree (*Tecomella Al-Zamah*) that some say is indigenous to the area. Continue along the main track into **Wadi Bani Awf** (see p238) ignoring the left fork at 57.2km. At 59.4km you will pass through the small wadi village of Al-Teekah and eventually arrive at Hwy 13 at 69.7km. Turn left for Rustaq, or right for Nakhal and Muscat.

AL-HAMRA الحمراء
☎ 25

This venerable village at the foot of the Hajar Mountains is one of the oldest in Oman, and is interesting for a wonderfully well preserved row of two- and three-storey **mud-brick houses** built in the Yemeni style. It's best to park in the new part of Al-Hamra and walk through the old city gates to explore. There are many abandoned houses in the upper parts of the village and it's easy to gain an idea of a life that has only changed in the past three decades.

Al-Hamra can be reached by turning right off the Nizwa–Bahla road, 30.6km from Nizwa, past the junction for Jebel Shams. At the second roundabout in Al-Hamra, turn left to reach the old part of the village.

MISFAT مسفاه

There is a sealed road from Al-Hamra up to this mountain-hugging village, making it one of the few mountain villages that is easily accessible by saloon car. The mountain flank draped in date plantations and a terraced sequence of stone houses in the foreground make a picturesque landscape. For the best view of the village, turn right just before reaching the houses. The road ends after some modern villas, a viewpoint ideal for a photograph.

JEBEL SHAMS جبل شمس

Oman's highest mountain, Jebel Shams (Mountain of the Sun; 3075m), is best known not for its peak but for the view into the spectacularly deep **Wadi Ghul** lying alongside it. The straight-sided Wadi Ghul is known locally as the Grand Canyon of Arabia as it fissures abruptly between the flat canyon rims, exposing vertical cliffs of 1000m and more. Until recently, there was nothing between the nervous driver and a plunge into the abyss but now an iron railing at least indicates the most precipitous points along the track and a couple of rough car parks along the rim pick out some of the best viewpoints into the canyon.

While there is nothing 'to do' exactly at the top, the area makes a wonderful place to take photographs, have a picnic (there are no shops or facilities so bring your own), enjoy a hike (see the boxed text, opposite)… or buy a carpet.

You need only step from your vehicle and you'll find **carpet sellers** appear from nowhere across the barren landscape clutching piles of striped, red-and-black goat-hair rugs. Weaving is a profitable local industry, but don't expect a bargain. A large, striped rug can cost anything from OR30 to OR50, depending on the colours used and the complexity of the pattern. Weaving is men's work on Jebel Shams: spinning the wool is women's work. If you can't find room for a carpet, a spindle made from juniper wood makes a more portable souvenir.

Jebel Shams is a feasible day trip from Nizwa (or a long day-trip from Muscat), but to savour its eerie beauty, consider camping at the plateau near the canyon rim (no facilities or supplies nearby). Alternatively, **Jebel Shams Hotel** (☎ 99382639; s/d OR12/24; breakfast OR2) has attractive and cosy stone cabins with bathroom, veranda and heater. The hotel is situated close to the canyon rim, 39km from the start of the road. Another hotel is sprouting up nearby. Be warned, it is freezing in winter.

The junction for Jebel Shams is clearly signposted off the Nizwa–Bahla road, 30.6km from the book roundabout in Nizwa. Turn right at the BP petrol station then left after 11.8km at a Shell petrol station and follow the sealed road along the bottom of the wadi. At 9.1km after the Shell petrol station, the road passes the vacant village of Ghul at the entrance of the Wadi Ghul canyon (you can access the canyon for a short distance only), providing a wonderful photo opportunity.

ON EDGE IN THE HAJAR MOUNTAINS

Most people would be content with peering gingerly over the rim of Wadi Ghul (Oman's Grand Canyon) but there are those for whom this isn't close enough. If you are the kind who likes to edge to the ledge, then try the hike from the rim village of Al-Khateem to the well-named hanging village of Sap Bani Khamis. Abandoned over 30 years ago, it is reached along the popular but vertiginous **Balcony Walk**: one false step in this five-hour 'moderate hike' will send you sailing (without the 'ab') 500m into the void.

If you're comfortable with this angle of dangle, then you might like **Snake Gorge** – the upper reaches, that is, where expat enthusiasts have thrown up 'via ferrata' lines allowing those with a head for heights to pirouette on a tightrope 60m above certain death.

Mind you, this experience palls in comparison with the descent into Hades: the 158m drop into the **Majlis al-Jinn**, is the stuff of legend. Fabled as the second-largest cavern in the world – bigger than St Peter's Cathedral in Rome, bigger than Cheop's pyramid in Giza – this is one mighty hole. Don't count on *jinn* for company; the only spirit you're likely to feel is your own – petering out with the rope as you reach for rock bottom. Named after the first person to descend into the shaft of sunlight at the bottom of the cavern, Cheryl's Drop is the deepest free-fall rappel in Oman.

With dozens of challenging hikes, 200 bolted climbing routes, and an almost uncharted cave system, Oman is one adrenalin rush still pretty much waiting to happen. If you want to be in with the pioneers, contact **Muscat Diving and Adventure Center** (☎ 24 485663; www.holiday-in-oman .com), which can tailor-make trips for the extremely edgy.

The road continues past a recharge dam and climbs through a series of sharp hairpin bends to the top of Jebel Shams. The road then gives way to a well-graded track that climbs eventually to the military radar site on the summit (closed to visitors). There's a right turn just before the summit that leads, after 10 minutes' drive or so, to the canyon rim, 28km from the Shell station.

It is possible but foolhardy to attempt the drive without a 4WD and car-hire agencies won't thank you for the uninsurable abuse of their car. There is no public transport here.

BAHLA
بهلا

☎ 25/pop 57,539

Ask anyone in Oman what Bahla means to them and historians will single it out for its fort, expats for its potteries; but any Omani not resident in the town will be sure to respond with 'jinn'. These devilishly difficult spirits are blamed for all manner of evil-eye activities, but you're unlikely to encounter them unless you understand Arabic, as they are considered a living legend in the folklore of the country.

A remarkable set of **battlements** are noticeable at every turn in the road, running impressively along the wadi and making

Bahla one of the finest walled cities in the world. These walls extend for 7km and are said to have been designed 600 years ago by a woman. Part and parcel of the battlements is the 12th-century fort, built by the Bani Nebhan tribe. It has been under restoration as a Unesco World Heritage site since 1987 and is still closed to the public.

Bahla has a traditional **souq** (☉ 6-10am), with homemade ropes and *fadl* (large metal platters used for feeding the whole family) for sale, and a beautiful tree shading the tiny, central courtyard. To find the souq, turn off Hwy 21, the main Nizwa-Ibri road, opposite the fort; the souq entrance is 100m on the right.

To find Bahla's famous **potteries**, follow the main road through town towards the plantations. After 500m you will come to a number of potteries; the traditional unglazed water pots cost a couple of rials.

Microbuses to/from Nizwa cost 300 baisa and shared taxis 500 baisa. A taxi should be OR2.500 – *if* you can haggle like a local! The trip takes about 45 minutes. There is an excellent branch of the Nizwa-based **Al-Huzaily Travel** (☎ 25 419313; fax 25 419009) opposite the bus stop on the corner of the road that leads to the souq. It acts as an ad hoc information centre.

OMAN

JABRIN جبرين

Rising without competition from the surrounding plain, **Jabrin Castle** (admission 500 baisa; 9am-4pm Sat-Thu, 8-11am Fri) is an impressive sight. Even if you have seen a surfeit of forts at Nizwa and Bahla, Jabrin is one of the best preserved and most whimsical of them all.

Built in 1675 by Imam Bil-arab bin Sultan, it was an important centre of learning for astrology, medicine and Islamic Law. Look out for the **date store**, to the right of the main entrance on the left-hand side. The juice of the fruit would have run along the channels into storage vats, ready for cooking or to assist women in labour. Note the elaborately painted ceilings with original floral motifs in many of the rooms.

Head for the flagpole for a bird's-eye view of the latticed-window courtyard at the heart of the keep. Finding these hidden rooms is part of the fun, and the defensive mechanism, of Jabrin. Try to locate the **burial chambers**, remarkable for the carved vaults. The **falaj** was not used for water but as an early air-con system. There is even a room earmarked for the Sultan's favourite horse.

From Bahla, turn left off the Bahla–Ibri road after 7km and Jabrin is clearly signposted from there. Beware of hitching from the junction, as it is an exposed 4km walk if you're out of luck. It may be better to engage a return taxi (OR2) from Bahla.

AL-DHAHIRAH REGION منطقة الظاهرة

A region of flat plains, copper-bearing hills and edged by the orange sands of the UAE, it's fair to say that this region has the least attractions for the visitor. That said, there is one big drawcard: the Unesco-protected tombs of Bat. If you have plenty of time to explore Oman, a loop can be made from Muscat via Nizwa, Bat and Ibri, through the mountains along the newly sealed Hwy 8 to Sohar and back along the coast to Muscat – a trip of at least three days.

IBRI ابرى

☎ 25 / pop 105,926

Ibri, the capital of Al-Dhahirah Region is a modern town with a major highway, Hwy 21, linking it to the border town of Buraimi in the north. There are not too many sights to keep a visitor busy, though there is a well-preserved **fort** (admission 500 baisa; 8.30-2.30 Sun-Thu) and a lively shopping area.

The only place to stay in town is the delightful and elegant **Ibri Oasis Hotel** (☎ 25 689955; fax 25 492442; Hwy 21; s/d OR21.800/29.500) on the Buraimi side of town. It has a glorious polished marble staircase and stained-glass windows, the rooms are large and well-furnished and the restaurant makes a fine chicken curry. You will be sure of a hearty welcome as it sees so few tourists.

There are plenty of *shwarma* and rotisserie-chicken restaurants in town if you want to get a feel for local life.

To reach Ibri by public transport, microbuses cost OR1.500 from Nizwa and take two hours. Buses from Muscat cost OR3.200 and take five hours. It has to be said, however, that without your own transport, it would be hard to make much of the trip.

BAT & AL-AYN بات والعين

Unlike the discreet modern cemeteries of Oman, where a simple, unmarked stone indicates the head and feet of the buried corpse, the ancient tombs of Bat rise defiantly from the tops of the surrounding hills, as in a bid for immortality. Not much is known about the tombs except that they were constructed between 2000 BC to 3000 BC, during the Hafit and the Umm an Nar cultures.

Known as 'beehive tombs' (on account of their shape) these free-standing structures of piled stones were designed to protect the remains of up to 200 people. There is barely a hilltop without one, and because of the extent of the site, which lies on an ancient caravan route, the whole area has been declared a Unesco World Heritage Site.

While Bat has the largest concentration of tombs, the best preserved tombs are another 30km away, near Al-Ayn. If you time your visit for an hour or so before sunset, **Jebel Misht** (Comb Mountain) makes the most stunning backdrop for the highly charged site.

To reach Bat, take the road signposted for Ad Dariz off Hwy 21 in Ibri. After 16km or so, turn right for Bat. The sealed road soon runs out but there's a good graded road that tends southeast through russet-coloured foothills. It takes a while to rec-ognise the tombs, but once you've spotted one, you will see them on almost every hill-top either side of the track.

To reach Al-Ayn from Bat, you need to skirt around to the west of Jebel Misht (one of the Oman 'Exotics' – a limestone mass that is out of sequence with the surround-ing geology), following signs for Sint (Sant on some maps). The *jebel* forms a sharp spine but if you want to be sure of the roads, take an off-road guidebook with you or ask the helpful staff in the Ibri Hotel if they can find you a guide. A 4WD is preferable but you can get by without. There is no public transport.

BURAIMI البريمي
☎ 25 / pop 79,917

For many years the inseparable twin of Al-Ain, in the UAE, Buraimi has just been divided from its alter-ego by a large barbed wire fence. This shouldn't be interpreted as a cooling of relations between Oman and its neighbour, just an attempt to sort out a border that leaked in both directions.

Although Buraimi has an interesting ren-ovated fort, noisy camel market and places to stay, there's not much reason to make a special visit other than if you're using the UAE border for Al-Ain and Abu Dhabi. At the time of writing, the border post (which is in Wadi Jizzi – uniquely 50km *before* the border) was closed to non-GCC (Gulf Cooperation Council) citizens.

If you are determined to go, however, **Al-Buraimi Hotel** (☎ 25 642010; fax 25 642011; s/d OR25/27; 🖳) offers comfortable rooms near the camel market. Two daily buses run a service between Buraimi and Muscat (OR3.600, 4½ hours) and an engaged taxi makes the trip for OR30.

AL-BATINAH REGION
منطقة الباطنة

This flat and fertile strip of land between the Hajar Mountains and the Gulf of Oman is the country's breadbasket and most pop-ulous area. Interesting sites include the old castle towns of Nakhal and Rustaq, exhila-rating off-road destinations such as Wadi Bani Awf and Wadi Hoqain, the fishing towns of Barka and Sohar, and an attractive resort at Sawadi.

Many of the sights can be managed on day trips from Muscat, with a tour com-pany or even by public transport. A more enjoyable way of visiting, however, is to hire a saloon car and visit Nakhal and Rus-taq en route to Sohar, returning via Sawadi and Barka on a three-day trip. This is diffi-cult to accomplish if relying only on public transport, particularly as there is limited accommodation. With a 4WD (even better with camping equipment), side trips into Wadi Bani Awf or Wadi Hoqain open the door to some of the most dramatic land-scapes in the country.

It's also possible to combine the above route with a visit to (or preferably *from*) the Western Hajar Mountain region by using the 4WD mountain road via Hatt and Wadi Bani Awf (see p233).

On the Muscat-Sohar Hwy, elaborately decorated mosques reflect the Persian influ-ence of the Farsi people who have settled in the region. Also look out for forts guarding the coastal strip at As-Suwayq, Al-Khabura and Saham. None particularly warrant get-ting off a bus for, but they may be worth a leg stretch from your own vehicle.

BARKA برقح
☎ 26 / pop 88,274

The main reason for visiting Barka, 80km west of Muscat, is to see **bull-butting**. This is where great Brahmin bulls, specially raised by local farmers, are set nose-to-nose in a push-and-shove that supposedly hurts nei-ther party. To get to the bullring by car take the turning for Barka off the Muscat–Sohar Hwy and turn left at the T-intersection in the centre of town. After 3.4km you will see the shallow, concrete ring on your right. Bull-butting rotates from village to village along the Batinah coast on selected weekends. Ask locally to find out when and where, or chance your luck on a Friday be-tween November and March from 4pm to 6pm. There's no admission charge.

Barka's **fort** (admission 500 baisa; ☺ 8.30am-2.30pm Sun-Thu) has an unusual octagonal tower. To get there, turn right at the T-in-tersection and it's 300m on the left.

Barka's other point of interest is the 18th-century **Bayt Nua'man** (admission 500 baisa; ☺ 8.30am-2.30pm Sun-Thu), a restored merchant house. The turn-off for the house is sign-posted off the Muscat–Sohar Hwy, 7km west of Barka roundabout. There's no pub-lic transport to the house.

Barka is famous for its **halwa**, a unique, laboriously made Omani confection (see the boxed text, p192), as distinct from the sesame confection known as *halvah*, found across the rest of the region. A pot from dedicated *halwa* shops in town costs from OR3.

There's nowhere to stay in Barka, but the town makes an easy diversion en route for Sawadi or Sohar.

Getting There & Away

ONTC buses run between the Barka roundabout and Muscat's Ruwi bus sta-tion (OR1.300, four times daily). Taxis and microbuses can be found both around the T-intersection in town and at the Barka roundabout. A shared taxi from Rusayl roundabout to Barka costs OR1 per per-son and around OR5 engaged. Microbuses charge 300 baisa.

NAKHAL   نخل
☎ 26

Nakhal is a picturesque town dominated both by the Hajar Mountains and one of Oman's most dramatic forts. Built on the foundations of a pre-Islamic structure, the towers and entrance way of this **fort** (ad-mission 500 baisa; ◷ 9am-4pm Sat-Thu, 8am-11pm Fri) were constructed during the reign of Imam Said bin Sultan in 1834. There are excellent views of the Batinah plain from the ram-parts and the *majlis* (seating area) on the top 'storey' of the fort makes a cool place to enjoy the tranquillity. The windows are perfectly aligned to catch the breeze, even in summer.

There are many features to look for: gaps where boiling cauldrons of honey would have been hinged over doorways; spiked doors to repel battering; round towers to deflect cannon balls; *falaj* in case of a siege. The entire structure is built around a rock – a common feature of Omani forts, which saves the problem of having to construct sound foundations.

Continue past Nakhal Fort through date plantations for a couple of kilometres to find the hot spring of **Ath-Thowra**. The spring emerges from the wadi walls and is chan-nelled into a *falaj* for the irrigation of the surrounding plantations. There are usually children and goats splashing in the over-spill. Look out for the flash of turquoise-winged Indian rollers, among other birds, attracted to the oasis. Picnic tables with shelters make it a popular place on Thurs-day and Friday.

Microbuses and taxis are the only vi-able transport to Nakhal and leave from the junction with the main road and in the area below the fort. Microbuses charge OR1 for the trip to Rusayl roundabout (a jour-ney of about an hour), and 300 baisa to/ from the Barka roundabout (30 minutes). A taxi charges about OR3 for the same trip if you can find one that doesn't only travel locally.

WADI BANI AWF   وادي بني عوف

This spectacular wadi often flows year-round and looks particularly gorgeous when mountain rain causes the *falaj* to cas-cade over its walls. That said, the trip (4WD only) should be avoided if there is any hint of stormy weather. It is possible to reach the **rock arch** (a fissure in the cliff, through which the graded road passes en route to neigh-bouring Wadi Sahten, about 17km into the wadi) as a day trip from Muscat or Sawadi. If treating the wadi as a side trip en route from Muscat to Sohar, you probably won't have time to penetrate the wadi for more than 5km or 6km.

To reach Wadi Bani Awf, turn left 43km from Nakhal, off the Nakhal–Rustaq road. There is no access by public transport. Dis-creet wild camping is possible in the upper reaches of the wadi.

Wadi Bani Awf can also be reached via the mountain pass from Al-Hamra on the other side of the Western Hajar Moun-tains. For details of this spectacular route, see p233.

RUSTAQ   الرستاق
☎ 26 / pop 84,870

Some 175km southwest of Muscat, Rustaq is best known today for its imposing **fort**, though it enjoyed a spell as Oman's capital in the 17th century. The small **souq** near the entrance to the fort has a few antiques and souvenirs, but the smart **new souq** on the main street, about 1.5km from the high-way, has left the old one for dead. If you've time to spare, you could visit the **hot springs**,

ROCK & ORE IN BATINAH'S WADIS

If geology seems like a frankly 'anorak' pursuit, then a trip through the wadis of the Western Hajar Mountains might change your mind. Seams of iridescent copper minerals; perfect quartz crystals glinting in the sun; stone pencils and writing slates loose in the tumbling cliff; walls of fetid limestone that smell outrageously flatulent when struck; pavements of marine fossils, beautiful for their abstract design and the pattern of history they reveal – these are just a few of the many stone treasures of Batinah's wild wadis.

Although many of these features can be spotted in Wadi Bani Awf, it is neighbouring Wadi Bani Kharus that excites geologists. They go in search of the **classic unconformity** that is revealed half way up the canyon walls a few kilometres into the wadi. At this point, the upper half of the cliff is a mere 250 million years old while the lower half is over 600 million years old. What created this hiatus, and what it reveals about tectonic forces, is the subject of speculation in numerous international papers. For the layperson, what makes Wadi Bani Kharus remarkable is that it appears to have been opened up as if for scientific study: the opening of the wadi is comprised of the youngest rocks, but as you progress deeper into the 'dissection', some of the oldest rocks in Oman are revealed, naked and without the obscuring skin of topsoil and shrubs. While you're inspecting the rocks, look out for **petroglyphs** – the ancient images of men on horseback is a common feature of all the local wadis.

All the main wadis in the area – Mistal, Bani Kharus, Bani Awf and Sahten – have their share of geological masterpieces and can be easily accessed with 4WD, a map and an off-road guide-book. Take along Samir Hanna's *Field Guide to the Geology of Oman* too, to help identify some key features.

signposted through the plantation off the high street.

The only place to stay in the area is the simple but friendly **Shimook Guesthouse** (☎ 26 877071; r OR15), at the start of the road from Rustaq to Ibri. The rooms are basic to say the least and the taps drip irrepressibly in the bathrooms, but the waft of extravagant incense makes up for these shortcomings. You can ask for dinner (freshly cooked and tasty) in the front yard or go for kebabs at one of the small restaurants on the corner (a two-minute walk towards the great mosque).

Microbuses can be found a few hundred metres from the fort on the main road to Nakhal (500 baisa), the Barka roundabout (400 baisa) and Muscat (OR1). A taxi to Muscat costs OR2. Alternatively, you can head for Sohar by taxi for OR3.

WADI HOQAIN   وادي الحوقين

This fertile wadi, accessible only by 4WD, offers one of the easiest and most reward-ing off-road experiences of the region. A reasonable graded road meanders through wadi-side **plantations** and **villages**, bustling with activity in the late afternoon. Add cop-per-coloured cliffs and a stunning **castle** to the rural mix, and it's a wonder that this wadi has remained a secret for so long.

To reach the wadi from the Rustaq roundabout at the entrance of town, turn left after 3.4km at the big mosque round-about, on the road towards Al-Hazm, and turn right after 9km for Wadi Bani Ghafir and Ibri. Despite being a rough, graded road at this point, this is the major thor-oughfare from Rustaq to Ibri and is there-fore busy and dangerous: use headlights in the fog of dust thrown up by speeding vehicles. At 15.5km, turn right into Wadi Hoqain. It is not signposted, but the track follows the wadi bottom. After 17km, you reach the fortified 'castle' in the middle of the wadi. On closer inspection, you'll find the castle is better described as a walled set-tlement. The best view of the fortification is the approach, with watchtowers and date plantations in the foreground and the wadi escarpment behind.

The track continues past an abandoned settlement for 24.5km, and eventually comes out in a plantation and block-mak-ing village at 35km. If you get lost in the village, locals will steer you to the other side of town, which eventually meets up with a sealed road at about 60km. Turn right for **Al-Hazm** (where there is yet an-other magnificent fort), 20km from Rustaq and left to reach the Muscat-Sohar Hwy.

OMAN

The whole route from Rustaq to Al-Hazm takes about three hours.

SAWADI السوادي

☎ 26

A sandy spit of land and some **islands** scattered off the shore make Sawadi a popular day trip, an hour or so drive west of Muscat. At low tide, you can walk to one **watchtower** on one of the islands, but beware: the tide returns very quickly. There's good **snorkelling** off the islands and local fishermen will take you around for OR5.

There is an abundance of **shells** at Sawadi. The resort shop sells a handy volume called *Collectable Eastern Arabian Seashells,* by Donald Bosch, if you want help identifying the booty on the beach.

Al-Sawadi Beach Resort (☎ 26 795545; www .alsawadibeach.com; s/d OR90) Forty minutes west of Seeb International Airport, Sawadi Resort makes a pleasant alternative to city accommodation. This may soon change once The Blue City development, one of the largest in the Middle East, starts transforming the surrounding desert into a visionary housing and tourist complex. In the meantime, with a limitless beach peppered with pink top-shells, and bungalow-style rooms set in landscaped gardens of jasmine and Rangoon creeper, the hotel is almost worth the high tariff. A variety of water sports, snorkelling and diving is on offer, including boat trips to the nearby Damanayat Islands and 4WD excursions into the nearby wadis. Beware, it gets noisy at weekends with holidaymakers from Muscat.

From the turn-off to Sawadi off the Sohar-Muscat Hwy, it's a further 12km to the coast. The resort is for most of the year 1km before the end of the headland. A microbus from Muscat or Rustaq to the junction costs 700 baisa or 500 baisa respectively, but hitching is the only option to reach the coast – unless you can hail a passing taxi (OR2).

DAMANAYAT ISLANDS

جزيرة الدمنيات

These government-protected, rocky islands about an hour's boat ride off the coast of Sawadi are rich in marine life and make an exciting destination for snorkelling and diving. Turtles feed off the coral gardens

here and at certain times of the year can be seen congregating in large numbers. Angel and parrot fish are commonly seen and colourful sea snakes are another feature of the area, though be warned, the latter are highly dangerous if disturbed. Day trips (OR26 for two dives) can either be arranged through Al-Sawadi Beach Resort (see left) or through one of the dive centres in Muscat (see p202).

SOHAR صحار

☎ 26 / pop 112,286

Rumoured home of two famous sailors, the historical Ahmed bin Majid (see p183) and the semifictional Sinbad, Sohar is one of those places where history casts a shadow over modern reality. A thousand years ago it was the largest town in the country: it was even referred to as Omana, though its ancient name was Majan (seafaring). As early as the 3rd century BC, the town's prosperity was built on copper that was mined locally and then shipped to Mesopotamia and Dilmun (modern-day Bahrain).

Now it is one of the prettiest and best-kept towns in the country, but with little more than legend – and a triumphal arch over the Muscat–Sohar Hwy – marking its place in history. A new port-side industrial area is helping to change that.

Orientation

Most of Sohar's sites of interest lie along or near the corniche. To get there, take the town centre exit off the highway, turn right at the An-Nahdah roundabout and head for the fort. A brand-new road linking Sohar to Ibri via Yankul was completed in December 2006 and makes a pleasant and easy drive across the mountains.

Sights

Sohar's glorious **beach** runs for kilometres, with glossy-smooth strands of sand. Access to the beach is easiest from a car park next to Sohar's **municipal park** (admission free; ☒ sunrise-sunset). Look under the hedges for the mighty minotaur, the largest beetle in Arabia. The park is next to Sohar Beach Hotel, west along the sea front.

The **fish market** next to the corniche is fun early in the morning. Also worth a visit is the **traditional handicraft souq** (☒ 8am-noon & 4-9pm Sat-Thu). Only half the workshops

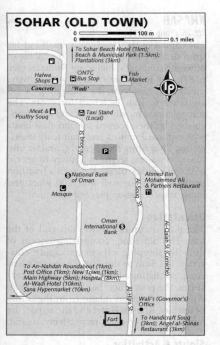

SOHAR (OLD TOWN)

0 ——— 100 m
0 ——— 0.1 miles

To Sohar Beach Hotel (1km);
Beach & Municipal Park (1.5km);
Plantations (3km)

Halwa Shops
ONTC Bus Stop
Fish Market

Concrete
'Wadi'

Meat & Poultry Souq

Taxi Stand (Local)

Al-Souq St

National Bank of Oman

Mosque

Ahmed Bin Mohammed Ali & Partners Restaurant

Al-Souq St

Oman International Bank

Al-Qalah St (Corniche)

To An-Nahdah Roundabout (1km);
Post Office (1km); New Town (1km);
Main Highway (5km); Hospital (8km);
Al-Wadi Hotel (10km);
Sana Hypermarket (10km)

Al-Hijra St

Wali's (Governor's) Office

Fort

To Handicraft Souq (3km); Angel al-Shinas Restaurant (3km)

in this modern arcade are open but there's a few mat-weaving establishments and an apothecary, where you can pick up some *bukhorr hassad*, a mixture of natural ingredients to ward off the evil eye. Try sage for sore throats, frankincense for constipation and myrrh for joint pains. The souq is signposted after the An-Nahdah roundabout.

Built in the 13th century, Sohar's distinctive white **fort** (admission 500 baisa; ☺ 8.30am-2.30pm Sun-Thu) apparently boasts a 10km tunnel intended as an escape route during a siege. Easier to find is the small **museum** in the fort's tower, which outlines local history, and the **tomb** of one of Oman's 19th-century rulers, namely, Sayyid Thuwaini bin Sultan al-Busaid, the ruler of Oman from 1856 to 1866.

Sohar is in the heart of a fertile **oasis**, and a pleasant hour can be spent wandering through the local plantations and farms. To reach the plantations, drive beyond Sohar Beach Hotel on Al-Nuz'ha St and turn right for fishing settlements or left for the Muscat-Sohar Hwy.

Sleeping & Eating

If you're looking for somewhere plain and simple just to have a night's rest, then look no further than **Al-Wadi Hotel** (☎ 26 840058; fax 26 841997; s/d OR41/52; ᗰ). With a distinctly local atmosphere (due partly to the enormously popular taxi bar – decidedly men-only in character), it caters mostly for travelling businessmen. Its ground-floor rooms are nothing special but they are clean and quiet and the small restaurant serves excellent Indian dishes. It is on a service road off the main Muscat-Sohar Hwy, 10km from the town centre.

If, on the other hand, you're looking for a holiday experience in Sohar, then the more-luxurious, fort-shaped **Sohar Beach Hotel** (☎ 26 841111; www.soharbeach.com; s/d OR45/50; ᗰ) is a far better bet. Situated northwest of the corniche, on a long sandy beach, the good restaurant, coffee shop, pretty gardens and pools make this a peaceful retreat. The rooms are palatial with big balconies.

There are a number of good biryani restaurants within easy walking distance of the fort and along the corniche, including Ahmed Bin Mohammed Ali's, a sea-fronting café popular with locals. For an evening of *sheesha* (water pipe used to smoke tobacco) and Hindi pop videos try **Angel Al-Shinas** (mixed fruit juice OR1.500) inside the handicraft souq. The huge Sana hypermarket is virtually next door to Al-Wadi Hotel, selling everything you might need for tomorrow's journey and a Lulu's Hypermarket is planned.

Getting There & Away

ONTC buses from Muscat (OR2.500, three hours, four times daily) drop passengers off at the small hospital near the centre of town and then continue to Buraimi or Dubai. Check with **Ruwi bus station** (☎ 24 701294) for accurate times.

Microbuses and taxis come and go from a car park across the street from the hospital. Microbuses charge OR1.700 for the trip to Rusayl roundabout in Muscat and OR2 to Ruwi. Shared taxis charge OR2.500 to Rusayl roundabout and OR3 to Ruwi. You can expect to pay around OR15 for an engaged taxi to Rusayl roundabout. An engaged taxi from Sohar to Rustaq or Nakhal costs OR15.

OMAN

WAJAJA & KHATMAT MILAHAH الوجاجة و خطمة الملاحة

These two border crossings are the most common entry and exit points for the UAE. Wajaja is the post that buses use (it takes about an hour for a full bus to clear customs) while Khatmat Milahah is more useful for those with their own transport wanting to explore the eastern coast of the UAE. See p261 for more on border crossings.

MUSANDAM المسندم

Separated from the rest of Oman by the east coast of the UAE, and guarding the southern side of the strategically important Strait of Hormuz, the Musandam Peninsula is a land of beautiful *khors,* small villages and dramatic, mountain-hugging roads. No longer difficult to reach, this beautiful peninsula with its cultural eccentricities is well worth a visit if you're on an extended tour of Oman, or if you're after a taste of the wilderness from Dubai. A boat trip is a must, as this is the only way to see the best of the area.

KHASAB خصب

☎ 26 / pop 38,370

The capital of the province is small but far from sleepy. Its souq resounds to a babble of different languages, including Kumzari (see p187), and its harbour bursts with activity, much of it involving the smuggling of US cigarettes to Iran in return for goats. The smugglers are mostly Iranian and are distinguished by their souped-up fibreglass boats with outboard motors and their lusty moustaches. They bring money and character into town, so no-one seems in a hurry to get rid of them; besides, piracy has been a tradition in these parts for well over 200 years and locals respect a good piece of tradition.

Orientation

The port occupies the western end of the bay. The old souq, comprising dozens of dubious shipping offices packaging cigarettes, is 1.5km to the east. The town's new souq, consisting of restaurants and grocery stores, the post office, banks and the Oman Air office, is 1.5km inland from the centre of the bay. Khasab Hotel and the airport are a further 3km to 6km, respectively, inland.

Sights & Activities

With a command of the mud flats on the edge of the bay, **Khasab Fort** (admission free; ⏲ 8.30am-2.30pm Sun-Thu) cuts quite a dash from a distance. A new levee in front of the fort means the sea no longer washes up to the walls – a good thing from a preservation point of view, a disappointment aesthetically. If you continue past the fort and turn right at the T-junction, you'll circuit some fine modern villas with nautical themes: one house has a scaled model of a dhow over the entrance while another sports fine Iranian tiles with a sea-faring theme.

There is a small **beach** with palm umbrellas just outside Khasab. Follow the road from the port towards Bukha for 2km or so. Don't be alarmed by the 1.8m sharks that often circle in the shallow bays near Khasab – apparently they're not interested in human flesh.

The Musandam Peninsula offers fine coral-reef diving at over 20 dive sites within an hour's boat ride of the harbour. The conditions are suitable only for experienced divers with a minimum of a PADI Open Water Certificate and 50 logged dives. Located at the Golden Tulip Khasab Hotel Resort, **Extra Divers** (☎ 99877957) organises full-day dive trips for OR55, including permits and hire of all equipment.

Tours

For friendly and personal service, **Musandam Sea Adventure Tourism** (☎ 26 730069; www.msaoman .com) comes highly recommended. The owner is proud of being local and employs knowledgeable Omani guides who speak a variety of languages. The company offers a range of services, including full-day dhow trips around the *khors* for OR40, or OR60 to Kumzar. If you share the boat, the price is OR20 per person. If you have a specific interest (such as bird-watching) the guides will be happy to tailor a trip for you.

Situated in the old souq, **Khasab Travel & Tours** (☎ 26 730464; www.khasabtours.com) have a somewhat variable reputation for being curt and inefficient, but can offer a two-night B&B package at any of the Khasab hotels, with a full-day dhow trip, a half-day 4WD visit to the mountains and a city tour for OR180 per person, or OR140 per person for two or more people.

Sleeping & Eating

Camping is not officially permitted in Musandam (there are security issues) but authorities usually turn a blind eye if you're discreet. Khor an-Najd is the best place to head for but as there are no facilities, you'll need to bring all your own equipment.

The hotels listed here organise half-/full-day dhow trips (OR15/20).

Al-Kaddar Hotel (☎ 26 731664; fax 26 731676; r OR20) Within walking distance of the fort and the old souq, this friendly, Omani-run hotel offers comfortable rooms with views over the town. At sunset the cliffs on the opposite side of the bay dissolve like liquid gold.

Khasab Hotel (☎ 26 730267; fax 26 730989; s/d OR23/35; ⊠) A kilometre south of the new souq roundabout, this long-established hotel recently expanded to include a rather stark new block. Nonetheless, the new rooms are bright and fresh and some have excellent views of the mountains.

Golden Tulip Khasab Hotel Resort (☎ 26 730777; www.goldentulip.com; s/d OR75/88; 🖳 🕾) Perched on a headland, just outside Khasab, this modish resort has transformed tourism in the Musandam Peninsula. Surrounded on three sides by water and with a terrace overlooking the sea, you can enjoy the crystal clear water and mountain scenery over a glass of wine. There are a variety of stylish rooms, some with split level, windows for walls and balconies aligned to the sunset. The terraced restaurant offers a comprehensive buffet with a Lebanese twist for OR13.500. As this hotel is highly popular as a weekend getaway from the UAE, it's worth booking ahead.

Bukha Restaurant (old souq; meals 600 baisa) Biryanis are available at lunchtime, and roast chicken and kebabs are added to the menu in the evening. Expect to keep company with a smuggler or two.

Shopping

Walking sticks (OR3) make an unusual buy from the old souq. With their axe-tops, used traditionally for cutting wood, killing snakes and keeping children in order (at least according to one local), these sticks are the emblem of the Shihuh tribespeople – the main ethnic group in the Musandam Peninsula. They carry them in place of the camel stick on formal occasions.

Getting There & Away

Despite the fact that the Musandam Peninsula belongs to Oman, it's easier to visit the area from the UAE, not least because the flights from Muscat preclude a weekend excursion. With a car, driving to and from Muscat (eight hours in either direction) involves getting a road permit (for residents), insurance for two countries, and passing through checkpoints no less than eight times. On an Omani visit visa, this makes a trip to the area something of a challenge.

AIR

Oman Air (☎ in Muscat 24 707222, Khasab 26 730543) has flights between Khasab and Muscat (one way/return OR24/48, 1¼ hours) every Thursday (10.30am) and Friday (4.05pm). The office in Khasab is on the new souq roundabout, and flights depart and arrive from the military air base.

CAR

The only border post currently allowing access to the Musandam Peninsula is at Al-Darah/Tibat, on the western coast of the

OMAN

UAE. There is a Dh20 road tax to leave the UAE and Dh60 visa charge to enter Musandam Peninsula. A 4WD is only necessary to explore the mountainous area around Jebel Harim.

Residents driving from Muscat must have a road permit and insurance for UAE. Currently the best border crossing to use is Wajaja (see p261 for more border crossing information).

LONG-DISTANCE TAXI

Public transport is erratic at best, if not nonexistent. You can try to engage a taxi in Khasab's old souq to Bukha (OR5), Tibat or Khor an-Najd (OR10) and Muscat (OR75).

Although it's only about 70km from Ras al-Khaimah in the UAE to Khasab, there are no shared taxis making the run on a regular basis. Khasab drivers in pick-ups charge OR15 for the trip to Ras al-Khaimah, but you may get marooned at the border in the opposite direction.

Getting Around
TO/FROM THE AIRPORT

It's best to arrange transfers with your hotel in advance as there are no taxis near the airport.

TAXI

The orange-and-white taxis in town are almost permanently booked by locals. If they stop for you, shared trips around town cost 200 baisa to 300 baisa.

CAR

Car hire (2WD/4WD OR12/40) is available from **Khasab Rent-a-Car** (☎ 99447400). A 4WD with a driver costs OR80 per day from **Khasab Travel & Tours** (☎ 26 730464; khastour@omantel.net.om).

KHASAB–TIBAT ROAD
طريق خصب – طيبات

The cliff-hugging 90-minute drive from Khasab to Tibat is a highlight of a trip to Musandam. The sealed road is a feat of engineering and affords spectacular views across the Strait of Hormuz. There are a few sites of interest along the way and you could spend a day pottering along the road, enjoying a swim – and watching very large sharks basking in the shallows.

About 8km from Khasab harbour lies the village of Tawi, site of a few **prehistoric rock carvings** of boats, houses and warriors on horseback. To reach the carvings, follow a track up Wadi Quida, just before Quida village, for 2.3km. The carvings are etched into two rocks on the left, just before a large white house.

Scenically positioned **Bukha Fort** commands a good view of the bay. Prisoners used to be pegged to the lower courtyard and drowned by the incoming tide.

The road ends in Tibat at the Al-Darah border with UAE; the post is open 24 hours and passing through customs on either side is quick and efficient.

THE MUSANDAM KHORS
أخوار المسندم

A dhow trip around the *khors* of Musandam, flanked by dolphins, is a must and well worth the expense. Trail a fishing line from the back of the boat, and your skipper will cook your catch for lunch. So remote are some of these *khors* that people still have their water delivered by boat and speak a dialect almost unrecognisable to Arabic speakers from Muscat.

Khor Ash-sham
خور الشم

This beautiful inlet is interesting for its stone **fishing villages**, accessible only by boat, and for **Telegraph Island**, which you can cruise past but not land upon as it used for military exercises. You are free, however, to snorkel and swim in the pristine surrounding waters.

It makes a good day tour from Khasab or you can try your luck renting a fishing boat for OR20.

Khor An-najd
خور رنجد

At 24.5km southeast of Khasab, this is the only *khor* accessible by car, but beware the steep approach. You can camp on the rim of this wild bay although it's often too shallow and muddy for a good swim. The view from the top of the road is stunning.

From Khasab head towards the mountains for 15km and follow the sign for 'Khor an-Najd 10km'. After 5.6km turn left and head for the road that winds up the mountain. After 2.3km there's a great outlook, from where a steep 2.8km descent brings you to the water's edge.

GOING ROUND THE BEND

Ever wondered where the term 'Going round the bend' comes from? If you take a trip to Khor ash-Sham, you'll learn first-hand what the saying means. In the middle of the *khor*, a tiny island, not much bigger than a postcard and considerably less attractive, was home to a British telegraphic relay station in the 19th century. The utter isolation of the island, tucked around the bend of this remote inlet, with no diversions other than sleeping and swimming, drove many of the workers stationed there to madness. The saying 'going round the bend' persists to this day… and so perhaps does the associated implication of being 'driven round the bend'. From time to time, the military set up camp on the rocks and see how long it takes to run out of things to do. Personnel stationed there run straw polls estimating the number of days endurable at a stretch. 'We get very good at counting cormorants', said Captain Ahmed Saif. Another volunteered the improvement of their fishing skills. They could tell us what they were really doing being driven round the bend, but then of course they'd have to shoot us.

Kumzar   كمذار

☎ 26

Set on an isolated *khor* at the northern edge of the peninsula, the surprisingly modern town of Kumzar is accessible only by boat. The villagers speak their own language, known as Kumzari – a combination of Farsi, Hindi, English, Portuguese and Arabic. There is nowhere to stay in Kumzar, and there are no sights of special interest in the town. It is nonetheless fascinating to wander around the **old stone houses** and the **souq** area to see how this outpost has developed its own unique character.

Water taxis travel between Khasab and Kumzar most days, charging OR5 per person. This can be a pretty harrowing trip, however. Most of the speedboats used as water taxis have no seats and boast maximum clearance between deck and gunwale of 15cm. Consider hiring your own boat and skipper through **Musandam Sea Adventure Tourism** (☎ 26 730069; www.msaoman.com) in Khasab.

JEBEL HARIM   جبل حارم

If you have a 4WD, the mountain scenery around **Jebel Harim** (Mountain of Women) makes a rewarding day-trip, especially in spring when the mountains are full of delicate blooms such as wild geraniums and miniature iris.

The graded road switchbacks through limestone formations until it reaches the **Sayh plateau**, a startling patchwork of fields and grazing donkeys, surrounded by stone settlements. The road climbs a further 8km to a pass below the telecommunica-

tions tower (off-limits to the public) that marks the top of the mountain. Even if you don't intend to make the descent to Rawdah Bowl, it's well worth unravelling the helter-skelter of road for a few kilometres beyond the pass: the views of improbable homesteads, clinging to the crescent-shaped canyons, with terraces in various states of livid green or grey abandonment are spectacular.

RAWDAH BOWL   مدرّج الروضة

From Jebel Harim, the descent towards the Omani checkpoint (currently only open to Omani nationals) is via a narrow ridge with remarkable views of striated sedimentary rock.

At the bottom of the descent, a right turn leads to the checkpoint while a left turn crosses the wadi bottom and meanders into the Rawdah Bowl – a beautiful depression of mature acacia and *ghaf* trees. The bowl has several interesting features including the local stone-built houses known as the **'house of locks'**. So called on account of the elaborate locking mechanism, the homes (which are left empty during the summer months) are built low to the ground and the floor is excavated to about 1m below the door with beds and eating area raised on platforms.

The area has a long history of settlement, as can be seen from the **pre-Islamic tombstones** (lying close to the road), made either from luminous yellow sandstone, or from grey limestone and etched with script or pictographs. The entire area, with its diagonal slants of sandstone takes on a surreal quality at sunset.

OMAN

AL-WUSTA REGION
منطقة الوسطى

Stretched between a wild and empty coast and the unchartered sands of the Empty Quarter, the flat, desolate oil-bearing plains of Al-Wusta comprise the remotest and least-populated part of the country. Too far to explore thoroughly on a visit visa and not the first choice for expats on leave, the region sees few visitors and tends to be written off as a joyless transit between the mountains of the north and the subtropical south. For those with a 4WD, camping equipment and time on their hands, however, the region has some surprising wonders – not least the oryx reserve near Hayma and a superb coastline of traditional fishing villages, stunning rock formations and gulls in their thousands. There is only space here to highlight a few of these attractions.

HAYMA
هيما

☎ 23

This is the chief town of the region and an important transit point between the interior and the coast. Although there is little to commend the town itself, it does have basic accommodation and makes a good base for visiting the oryx reserve in Jaaluni.

The **Hayma Motel** (☎ 92189784; fax 23 436061; Hwy 31; r OR15), on the highway opposite the main turning into town, primarily caters for Asian businessmen and has the worst beds in the country with springs that sprung years ago. You're better off sleeping on the floor. The hotel does have air-con, though, and this makes it a useful stopping-off point after the five-hour drive from Muscat.

There are a number of unremarkable chicken-and-rice restaurants dotted around the petrol station opposite the motel.

JAALUNI
جالوني

The return of the oryx is one of the great wildlife success stories of the region and watching these magnificent animals paw the dust in the summer heat, or slip gracefully through the dawn mists in winter, makes the long journey to the desolate Jiddat al-Harasis plain worthwhile.

> ### A WILDLIFE SUCCESS STORY
>
> In 1962 the Fauna Preservation Society captured the last remaining oryx close to the border with Yemen and sent them to a zoo in the USA. By 1982, protected by new laws banning the hunting of wild animals, a herd of 40 Arabian oryx was returned to Jiddat al-Harasis. Despite intermittent bouts of poaching the programme has met with success, in part due to the commitment of the Harasis tribe designated to look after them.
>
> The return of the oryx to Oman was the occasion of great rejoicing, which prompts the question: what it is about this antelope that provokes such emotion? Perhaps it's the uncanny resemblance of a mature bull, with rapier-like antlers, to the mythical unicorn. This is not as far-fetched as it seems. The ancient Egyptians used to bind the antlers of young oryx so they would fuse into one. Seeing a white, summer-coated herd-bull level up to a rival in profile, it's easy to confuse fact with fiction.

A permit is needed to visit the reserve, easily organised through the **Office of the Advisor for Conservation of the Environment** (☎ 24 693536, 24 593537; acedrc@omantel.net.om; OR20 per party) in Muscat. The permit covers the cost of a mandatory guide, usually a member of the Harsusi tribe, who will show you the excellent on-site portacabin **museum**, show you the resident, captive breeding herd and help you spot a wild oryx. You will also more than likely see gazelle. If you ask, the guide will also show you the remarkable, windblown formations of the Huqf Escarpment, an hour deeper into the reserve. Unfortunately most guides don't speak English. Most tour operators can arrange trips for you.

You can camp in the reserve at a designated site but you will have to bring your own food. Keep your clothes under canvas as there is always a heavy dew by the morning – indeed this is how the animals survive in the absence of surface water.

Additional information on the reserve can be found through the website of the **Arabian Oryx Project** (www.oryxoman.com). The reserve is 50km off the Hayma-Duqm road (Hwy 37) on a well-graded track, marked by a brown nature reserve sign. It takes about an hour to drive from Hayma to the reserve.

DHOFAR   ظفار

The southernmost province of Oman is a world away from the industrious north and separated geographically by an interminable gravel desert. With its historic frankincense trade, great beaches, a laid-back atmosphere and an interesting ethnic mix, it's a fascinating place to visit, particularly during or just after the *khareef*.

There are many intriguing sites to visit as day trips from Salalah, including Job's Tomb; the heroic town of Mirbat with its beautiful beaches; and Mughsail, famed for the violent blowholes in the undercliff and for nearby groves of wild frankincense.

If you are travelling during the *khareef* and can put up with the unremittingly tedious journey from Muscat or Nizwa, it is worth going overland to Salalah across the largely featureless Al-Wusta Region (see the boxed text, p250) and returning by plane. This is the best way to sense the full spectacle of the *khareef* across the top of the *jebel*; after eight hours of gravel plains, Dhofar seems like a little miracle.

SALALAH   صلاله
☎ 23/pop 169,881
Salalah, the capital of Dhofar, is a colourful, subtropical city that owes much of its character to Oman's former territories in East Africa. Flying into Salalah from Muscat, especially during the *khareef*, it is hard to imagine that Oman's first and second cities share the same continent. From mid-June to mid-September, monsoon clouds from India bring a constant drizzle to the area and, as a result, the stubble of Salalah's surrounding *jebel* is transformed into an oasis of misty pastures. Year-round, Salalah's coconut-fringed beaches and plantations of bananas and papayas offer a flavour of Zanzibar in the heart of the Arabian desert.

Orientation
The intersection of An-Nahdah and As-Salam Sts forms the commercial hub of Salalah. The ONTC bus station is a 15-minute walk northeast of this intersection.

Information
INTERNET ACCESS
There are numerous internet cafés, particularly along 23 July St, charging between 500 baisa and 800 baisa per hour.

MONEY
There are several banks and a few exchange houses around the intersection of An-Nahdah and As-Salam Sts.
Amex (lobby, Crowne Plaza Resort Salalah) Zubair Travel represents Amex in Salalah. It cannot cash cheques for clients, but it will hold mail, which should be addressed to: American Express (Clients' Mail), c/o Zubair Travel & Services Bureau, Salalah Branch Office, PO Box 809, Postal Code 211, Oman.
HSBC (As-Salam St) Cash advances are available from the ATM.

POST & TELEPHONE
Main Post Office (An-Nahdah St; ☽ 8am-2pm Sat-Wed, 9-11am Thu) The entrance is at the rear of the building.
Telephone Office (cnr An-Nahdah & Al-Montazah Sts; ☽ 8am-2.30pm & 4-10pm) Offers fax and telex facilities.

Sights & Activities
Part of the Cultural Centre, Salalah's **museum** (Ar-Robat St; admission free; ☽ 8am-2pm Sat-Wed) is housed in the large white building (access is from the back, via Markaz al-Muhafdhah St). Although there's not much to see, the exhibit on Khor Rouri (see p252) is interesting, and don't miss Wilfred Thesiger's 1940s and '50s photographs of Arabia in the lobby.

For the best place to buy genuine Dhofari frankincense and be daubed with locally made perfumes, head for **Al-Husn Souq** (Sultan Qaboos St). Quality silver *khanjars*, swords and jewellery are also on sale here. *Halwa* shops selling Oman's traditional confection monopolise the corner of Al-Hafah and Sultan Qaboos Sts. For a distinctive local souvenir, look out for the intricately beaded perfume bottles (OR2 for a small one) in African bands of colour.

The main sight of interest in Salalah is the ancient site of **Al-Baleed** (admission free; ☽ variable). The comprehensive set of ruins, which are open on an ad hoc basis, and are atmospherically lit at night, belong to the 12th-century trading port of Zafar. From here, frankincense was shipped across the sea to India in exchange for spices. The surrounding plantations of coconut, papaya,

SALALAH

INFORMATION
HSBC...1 C2
Internet Cafés..................................2 C2
Main Post Office..............................3 B1
Telephone Office.............................4 C2

SIGHTS & ACTIVITIES
Al-Fawaz Travel & Tourism.............5 B2
Cultural Centre...........................(see 6)
Museum..6 B1
Zahara Tours....................................7 C2

SLEEPING
Al-Haffa House Coffeeshop.........(see 9)
Al-Hanaa Hotel................................8 D2
Haffa House......................................9 D1
Salalah Tourist Hotel......................10 C1

EATING
Al-Fareed Tourist Restaurant.........11 C2
Omar al-Khayyam...........................12 C2

ENTERTAINMENT
Al-Ahkhaf Cinema..........................13 C3

SHOPPING
Lulu Shopping Centre....................14 D1

TRANSPORT
Avis...(see 7)
Bin Qasim Transport.......................15 C2
Malatan Trading.............................16 C2
Oman Air.....................................(see 9)
ONTC Bus Station..........................17 C2
Sixt Rent-a-car...............................18 C2
Taxi & Microbus Stands.................19 C2

---

sugar cane and banana illustrate the fecundity of the region and it is little wonder that the port was a prosperous one. Little is known, however, about the port's demise. You can buy fruit from the many colourful stands by the roadside nearby.

For diving and snorkelling opportunities in the region, contact **Samharam Dive Centre & Partners** (Crowne Plaza Resort Salalah; ☎ 99099002; www .divesalalah.com). A day trip (two dives) including transport and equipment costs OR45.

It's great to visit Salalah during the Khareef Festival (p250).

Tours

Local agents **Zahara Tours** (☎ 23 235581; www .zaharatours.com; An-Nahdah St, Salalah; ☻ 8am-1pm & 4-6pm Sat-Thu) offer city tours for OR36 for one to four people.

Also available is a half-day tour to Job's Tomb and Mughsail blowholes, or to Taqa and Mirbat, for OR36. For the romantic, there is a backbreaking day trip in a 4WD to the lost city of Ubar, 175km from Salalah (OR105), but be warned, you'll need a lively imagination or Ranulph Fiennes' book *Atlantis of the Sands* (see p255) to make any sort of sense of the site. All prices quoted are for a vehicle with an English-speaking driver and a maximum of four people.

Similar tours for similar prices are offered by **Al-Fawaz Travel & Tourism** (☎ 23 294324; alfawaz_tours@yahoo.com; An-Nahdah St).

Sleeping

During the *khareef,* all accommodation in Salalah is heavily booked, so you will need to organise your stay in advance to be sure of a room. Prices during the *khareef* may be significantly greater than those quoted here. Camping is possible around Mirbat, but you'll need to bring your own equipment. Alternatively, you can buy supplies in any of the major shopping centres in Salalah.

BUDGET

Al-Hanaa Hotel (☎ 23 298305; 23 July St; s/d incl breakfast OR10/13) This characterful, Arabic-style hotel with tiled foyer is recommended for its bright, clean rooms. It is conveniently situated in the middle of town, in walking distance of the main shopping areas.

Salalah Tourist Hotel (☎ 23 295332; fax 23 292145; off 23 July St; s/d incl breakfast OR10/12) Opposite the ONTC bus station, this good-value hotel has large, comfortable rooms and friendly staff. It is close to the new souq area and attracts an interesting mixture of Omani salesmen and regional travellers. It's often full in the summer.

MIDRANGE & TOP END

Haffa House (☎ 23 295444; haffa@omantel.net.om; cnr Al-Matar & Ar-Robat Sts; s/d OR25/28; ☑) Located within a small commercial complex near the clocktower roundabout, the hotel is one of the city's main landmarks. Don't be put off by the rather cavernous, gloomy foyer: the rooms are old-fashioned but comfortable, the staff helpful and there is a pool. The restaurant, with city views, serves tasty Asian-style fare among less appealing international dishes.

Salalah Beach Villas (☎ 23 235999; www.geocities .com/sllbeachspa; s/d OR20/28) On the beach one block east of the Crowne Plaza Resort Salalah, this family-style and welcoming hotel has lovely views: the sea is so close you can taste it through the window. Walk off breakfast (included in the room rate) along the magnificent white sand beach and hazard a splash in the surf on calmer days. Car hire (2WD/4WD OR14/35, including 200km free mileage) is available.

Hilton Salalah Hotel (☎ 23 211234; www.salalah .hilton.com; s/d OR60/66; ☑ ☒) It was a surprise when the Hilton skipped Muscat and plummed for Salalah instead. It was an even greater surprise they located the hotel, 12km from the city centre along the highway to Mughsail, within view of the enormous Raysut Port. Despite the cargo boats queuing up on the horizon, the hotel still has a fine situation on a smooth sand beach of scurrying ghost crabs, touched by angel-wings (delicate bivalve shell). The hotel, with its chic interior, designer bar, marbled foyer and beautiful gardens, provides a welcome piece of glamour in this otherwise casual city. The excellent, beachside Palm Grove Restaurant (try the lobster for OR11.500) is an added attraction.

Crowne Plaza Resort Salalah (☎ 23 235333; www.cpsalalah.com; s/d OR70/80; ☑ ☒) The main rendezvous for expats, the Crowne Plaza, with its marble foyer and terraced restaurants, has pleasantly landscaped gardens and a good water-sports facility. A fine sandy beach, stretching for kilometres in either direction, is an additional bonus of this sociable hotel.

Eating

Al-Haffa House Coffee Shop (☎ 23 295444; snacks from 500 baisa; ☷ 7–11am & 4–8pm) Located on the ground floor of Haffa House, this a central place to enjoy a coffee and a bun.

Omar al-Khayyam (☎ 23 293004; 23 July St; mains OR1.500–2; ☷ 6pm–midnight) This no-frills restaurant serves a wide range of Chinese and Indian food. It is a popular place in the evening when it attracts a lively local crowd.

Al-Fareed Tourist Restaurant (☎ 23 292382; 23 July St; mains OR1.200–2; ☷ 6pm–12.30am) Across the road from Omar al-Khayyam, this atmospheric venue serves excellent Indian meals and an Arabic-Indian buffet dinner on Thursday. It also has private dining areas for Omani-style food. Needless to say it is always abuzz with locals and is a great place to gain a flavour of cultural exchange – such as has been occurring in Dhofar for centuries.

There are plenty of small Indian restaurants along As-Salam St. Both the top-end hotels have good restaurants and cafés, with Western menus and prices to match.

Entertainment

Check *Oman Today* to see what bands or dancers are performing at the Crowne Plaza Resort Salalah or at the Hilton Salalah Hotel.

ROADS ACROSS NOWHERE

It comes as some surprise to see a sign off the Rusayl roundabout in Muscat that says 'Salalah 998km'. There are other such signs in Ibri, Sohar and Nizwa. Salalah may be Oman's second city, but it would be inconceivable to see a sign pointing to Edinburgh from the outskirts of London, or Washington from New York. The signs are partly to help Emirati visitors in their annual migration during the *khareef* (rainy season in Oman's southern-most province of Dhofar). More tellingly, however, there's the implication that there is precious little in between – that once on the lonely Hwy 31 from Nizwa, there is nothing between you and Salalah.

And that's pretty much the case! The eight-hour journey between Nizwa and Thumrait across Al-Wusta Region is punctuated by one lone limestone hump near Adam, the excitement of a small town at Hayma and precious little else. One Thorn Tree correspondent called it 'the least memorable journey in the world' and as you gaze across the big sky, midpoint along Hwy 31, without a rock, without a bush, without any kind of interruption of the level plain, it's hard not to agree.

With your own 4WD, however, there are a few points of interest en route: excellent bird-watching spots at the oases of **Muqshin** and **Muntasar** (near Qitbit), famous for the daily fly-by of thousands of sandgrouse; relatively easy access to the magnificent ghaf woodlands and seams of soddom's apple that decorate the edge of the **Empty Quarter**; the chance to exercise the imagination at Shisr, the supposed site of the fabled gold-pillared **Ubar** (p254), a relatively short detour along Hwy 43. If the prospect of exploring this 'Road Across Nowhere' appeals, you can make this 10-hour, 1047km journey more bearable by stopping off at the friendly, simple, courtyard guesthouses of **Al-Ghabah Hotel**, **Al-Ghaftain Hotel** and **Qitbit Resthouse** – all run by the same management, and all of which provide simple Asian-style meals. There's no need to book ahead!

During the *khareef*, the Ittin road comes alive with the **Khareef Festival**. There is usually a fun fair, clothes stalls and lots of small stands selling kebabs and *shwarma*. Check *Oman Today* for a programme of traditional dancing and music, among other activities.

The **Al-Ahkhaf Cinema** (☎ 23 291318; Sultan Qaboos St; 1st-class/balcony seats 700/900 baisa) adjoining the Al-Husn Souq screens films in English (unlike the two modern cinemas in town).

Shopping

Among Dhofar's most distinctive souvenirs are small, bead-covered *kohl* (black eyeliner) bottles (OR3 to OR5 from the new souq). Baskets made of rush and camel's leather from the fishing village of Shwaymiyah make another good souvenir (OR5 to OR30 at the new souq).

Don't visit Dhofar without treading in the paths of ancient traders! A small bag of locally harvested frankincense from Al-Husn Souq costs 500 baisa, and a decorative pottery incense burner costs OR1.500 to OR10.

Salalah has some master silversmiths. Ash-Sharooq St, behind Al-Husn Souq, is one of the best places in Oman to buy a new silver *khanjar*. They are beautifully crafted and cost OR100 to OR250. Visit the gold souq for Salalah's distinctive silver necklaces and bracelets, which cost OR4 to OR20.

For camping equipment and supplies, try Lulu Shopping Centre, south of Haffa House.

Getting There & Away

AIR

National carrier **Oman Air** (☎ 23 295747; Haffa House) flies to Muscat (one way/return OR36/72, 1½ hours, twice daily) at variable times.

BUS

To Muscat, **ONTC** (☎ 23 292773) buses (one way/return OR6/11, 12 hours, four daily) leave from the bus station in the new souq. You can store luggage in the adjoining ticket office free of charge. There are also services to Nizwa and Buraimi.

Also try **Malatan Trading** (☎ 23 211299; As-Salam St), which has a 4.30pm service (OR6/11, 12 hours, daily) that leaves from near the cemetery, or **Bin Qasim Transport** (☎ 23 291786), which has a 4pm service (one

There is an altogether more scenic way of getting to Dhofar along the shores of the beautiful Arabian Sea but it is not for those in a hurry. The coastal trip from Muscat to Salalah takes at least three days and the beauty of the coast will make you wish you'd allowed more time. There are no hotels along this route and, despite the new sealed road that at last extends from Hijj to Thumrait, if you want to explore the best of the route, you'll need a 4WD. There are also precious few amenities so you need to take all your provisions with you. Stop each time you see a garage – they frequently run out of petrol.

Some of the highlights of this route include the traditional **barasti fishing villages** at Filim; **ancient rock formations** such as blue-green algae (the Earth's original animate form) in the laminations of Wadi Shuhram (near Shital); wind-eroded sandstone in the **rock garden** at Duqm; superb shells and cosy camping in the coves of Ras Madrakah; **pink lagoons** and **flamingos** near Al-Kahil, and **basket-weaving** in Shwaymiyah. Shwaymiyah's long bay, under the looming presence of Jebel Samhan, lair of the leopard, is one of the most beautiful sights in Oman. For full descriptions of how to make the best of this area, refer to an off-road guide.

So is it worth the effort – the heat, the flies, the prospect of getting stuck, dust-storms and mirages, lonesomeness, and a constant battle to stay awake on unremitting roads? Perhaps it's better to fly or take the magic carpet (nickname for the overnight-bus)? If you choose to drive, either inland or along the coast, you will most likely enter Salalah on Hwy 31. If you attempt the journey in summer (between July and mid-September), there is a point along that road, just after Thumrait, where you will notice something quite remarkable: the *jebel*, suddenly, unexpectedly and with ruler-like precision, turns green. After 10 hours or three days of hard desert driving, it is an unforgettable, almost Zen-like experience that can only be fully experienced through the force of contrast. Worth it? In the words of the Bedu, 'There's nothing sweeter than water after drought.'

way/return OR6/11, 12 hours, daily) that leaves from near the new souq.

For buses to Yemen, see p262.

TAXI & MICROBUS

Salalah's taxis and microbuses hang out in front of HSBC on As-Salam St. Microbus fares from Salalah include Mirbat (500 baisa) and Mughsail (OR1). Taxis will generally only make intercity trips on an engaged basis, which is invariably expensive (OR10 to Taqa, for example).

Getting Around

There is no public transport from the airport. Taxis charge a fixed price of OR3 from the airport to anywhere in Salalah. A microbus ride within the city costs around 300 baisa and a taxi about 800 baisa. Expect to pay OR3 to the Crowne Plaza Resort Salalah and OR3.500 to Hilton Salalah Hotel from the city centre.

Hiring a car in Salalah is recommended for exploring, especially during the *khareef*. You don't strictly need a 4WD unless you want to enjoy some of the country's best camping, or explore the more rugged roads, but beware of the soft sand on the beaches.

Sixt Rent-a-Car (☎ 23 297125; An-Nahdah St) has 2WD cars for OR12, including insurance and 200km free, per day. **Salalah Beach Villas** (☎ 23 235999) hires 2WD/4WD for OR14/35, with 200km free. **Budget** (☎ 23 235581) has a desk at the airport and **Avis** (☎ 23 202582) is on An-Nahdah St.

During the *khareef* the roads into the *jebel* are notoriously dangerous. They are slippery and local drivers fail to make allowances for the fog. Camels often cause accidents by wandering onto the road – if you hit one, you can be sure it will be an extremely expensive female, prize-winning, racing camel.

AROUND SALALAH

Salalah is sandwiched on the plain beneath the mountains. As such, it makes a good base for a day trip or overnight camping trip east towards Mirbat, with side trips to Khor Rouri and Wadi Dhabat en route, followed by a trip out west exploring Mughsail and the Sarfait road.

Beaches

There are very good beaches along the entire coastal plain of Salalah. For the most beautiful, head beyond Mirbat (4WD advisable) and follow any graded road going east. After 5km to 10km there is a string of glorious bays of striking red rock and white sand suitable for protected camping. Beware of strong currents anywhere along the coast during the *khareef,* which makes swimming ill-advised.

Khor Rouri خور روري

Looking across the estuary at grazing camels and flocks of flamingos, it's hard to imagine that 2000 years ago Khor Rouri was the trading post of the frankincense route and one of the most important ports on earth. Today little remains of the city except some nondescript ruins, currently closed to visitors. It is worth making the trip to Khor Rouri, however, to enjoy the bird-watching and to take a cautious swim (beware strong currents) in one of the coast's prettiest bays.

Khor Rouri is about 35km east of Salalah. Take the Mirbat road and turn right 5km beyond the Taqa roundabout at the signpost. The site is 2.5km along a graded road and the beach is a further 3km to 4km. A microbus to the junction on the highway is 400 baisa.

Wadi Dharbat وادي دربات

A popular picnic site during the *khareef* and a great place to enjoy the *jebel* in any season, Wadi Dharbat is the source of the estuary that flows into Khor Rouri. During a good *khareef,* an impressive waterfall spills over the cliff face, 300m to the plain below. Above the falls, water collects in limestone pools ideal for a swim. In the dry months, October to May, the Jibbali tribespeople set up their camps in this area. The caves in this area were used by the Sultan's forces, together with the British SAS, to infiltrate areas of communist insurgency in the mid 1970s. Now the most surreptitious activity you are likely to see is the scuttling away of a small, fur-clad rock hyrax (an unlikely relative of the elephant) that lives among the rocks. Chameleons share the same territory and are equally clandestine, changing colour when abashed.

To get to Wadi Dharbat, take the turn-off for Tawi Attair 4km after the Taqa roundabout and climb 3km to the Wadi Dhabat junction (a small coffeeshop marks the entrance). A sealed road leads to the top of the waterfall and a semipermanent lake. Don't be tempted to swim in this lake as Bilharzia is present here.

PICNICKING IN PARADISE

It came as some surprise recently when a group of Omani military officers, all trained at Sandhurst in England and perfectly at ease with the regimental silver, opted to enjoy their annual dinner, not in the HQ mess, but in a makeshift car park on the edge of the desert. Such is the desire to eat 'en plein air' in Oman that considerable logistic manoeuvres are undertaken to make it happen.

While Western expats sidle off to remote corners of the country for an apologetic lunch of wilted sandwiches from a Tupperware box, Omanis prefer to wait for night and for company and to dine on a picnic fit for kings. Under the stars, in caravans of up to a dozen cars, they bring chairs and divans, coolboxes and barbeques. Most surprising to Western onlookers, they often choose not the glorious coast, but the brightest spot on a well-lit motorway, unfurling their rice mats in family groups of loosely assorted siblings and cousins.

The most bizarre and most celebrated picnic spot in the country is at Wadi Dhabat in Dhofar. During summer, on a humid, damp and drizzling day in conditions that all Omanis would describe as 'beautiful weather', the luminous green pastureland is turned into a sticky mud slide of buzzing flies and blood-suckers. Omanis, Emiratis, Kuwaitis and just about anyone else with a week off in the region come here to spread their carpets in the rain, seemingly oblivious to the welter of insect-life around them.

Asked why they put up with such inconveniences, Omar bin Alawi, looks surprised: 'Need you ask?' he replied, 'For eight weeks of the year a piece of the *jebel* turns green and we get to live the life of our fathers. Who of us doesn't want that...?' He trailed off mid-sentence to answer his mobile. As he did, a clutch of expats huddled under the plastic awning of the candy floss vendor: this may not be the tale of Arabian nights they were looking for, but for the locals, this is picnicking in paradise.

OMAN

MIRBAT
مرباط

☎ 23

The town of Mirbat, just over 70km east of Salalah, has seen better days, but it has considerable historical significance. The town's main **fort** (admission 500 baisa; ⏰ 8.30am-2.30pm Sun-Thu) was the site of the well-documented Battle of Mirbat during the Dhofari insurrection of the 1970s.

Notice the old **merchant houses** with their wooden, latticed windows. The onion-domed **Bin Ali Tomb**, 1km off the main road, marks the entrance to the town. Glorious beaches stretch east and west of Mirbat, though 4WD is necessary if you want to get close enough to the sea for wild camping (there are no facilities). Snorkelling and diving is possible around this coast and equipment can be hired from the Samharam Dive Centre & Partners in the Crowne Plaza in Salalah for OR4 per day.

A new resort (not yet open) in Mirbat will make a good base for further exploration along the coast towards Hasik.

Microbuses charge 500 baisa for the trip from Salalah.

JEBEL SAMHAN
جبل سمحان

Although you need a permit and a good reason to visit the leopard sanctuary at Jebel Samhan, the sealed road up to the reserve entrance makes a rewarding day trip from Salalah. The road passes the entrance to Tawi Attair, a deep sink hole known as the 'Well of Birds' (accessible only with a guide), and climbs up through a variety of different flora, including rocky fields of desert roses. Sometimes known as elephant plants, they have huge bulbous trunks and beautiful pink flowers in the spring. As you near the summit, you can drive towards the cliff edge for a panoramic view of the coast. There are many exceptional vistas in Oman and this is one of them. If you're wondering about the odd spiky tree on the plateau, it's called a dragon tree and is confined to high, semi-arid elevations.

To reach Jebel Samhan, take the Tawi Attair road after the fishing town of Taqah, and follow the signs.

HASIK
حاسك

Positioned at the most eastern end of the Dhofar coast before the cliffs of Jebel Samhan interrupt, Hasik is worth the two-hour drive from Salalah for the journey more than the destination. The road is sealed and not particularly exceptional in winter, but in summer, luminous clouds billow down from the *jebel* and high winds whip across the water, sending the surf backwards as the waves roll inexorably forwards. Glossy cormorants cluster like oil slicks in the coves and waders shelter from the seasonal fury amid the drifts of pink top shells.

There is not much to see in Hasik itself, but if you continue along the road towards Hadraban, look out for a spectacular limestone waterfall overhanging the sandstone cliffs. A small car park marks the spot.

Hasik is clearly signposted from Hwy 47, just before the town of Mirbat.

JOB'S TOMB
قبر النبي أيوب

In religious terms, Job's Tomb is probably the most important site in Dhofar. Regardless of your religious convictions, the tomb, situated on an isolated hilltop overlooking Salalah, is a must-see for the beautiful drive, especially during the *khareef* and for the excellent view over the Salalah plain on a clear day.

The tomb is just over 30km northwest of Salalah. Take the main westbound road towards Mughsail and turn right along the Ittin road, after passing the Hamilton Plaza Hotel. Turn left at the signpost for An-Nabi Ayyub after 22km. A small restaurant below the tomb has wonderful views. There is no public transport.

If you are visiting Job's Tomb during the *khareef,* return to the main road and turn left for another 10km or so to reach the end of the monsoon catchment. The contrast between the green slopes and the desert floor beyond is remarkable. Continue along this road until you meet the Thumrait road and turn right for Salalah.

MUGHSAIL
مغسيل

Mughsail is 48km west of Salalah on a spectacular bay, ending in a set of sheer cliffs that reach towards the Yemeni border. Immediately below the start of the cliffs the rock pavement is potholed with **blowholes** that are active year-round, but particularly volatile during the high seas of the *khareef*.

Camping on the beach here is not permitted, but **Al-Mughsail Beach Tourist Resthouse**

(☎ 99584039; fax 23 290643; chalets OR16.300) has a few simple chalets on the beach, with bathroom, TV and sitting room, and a small restaurant from which to enjoy the superb views.

Microbuses charge OR1 for the trip between Salalah and Mughsail.

SARFAIT ROAD   طريق صرفيت

If you have your own transport, it's worth continuing from Mughsail towards the Yemeni border. The road is an impressive feat of engineering, zigzagging 1000m to the top of the cliff. Look out for a wadi full of **frankincense trees**, 8km from Mughsail (see p34). Three or four kilometres after the top of the road, there are stunning views back towards Mughsail and inland across some of the wildest wadis in Arabia. The vegetation in this area is entirely different from that on the Salalah plain, with yuccas and succulents clinging to the limestone ledges.

The Sarfait road continues to the Yemeni border, a two-hour drive from Salalah along a sealed road. There is no accommodation between Salalah and the border crossing and no facilities at the border itself. If entering Oman this way you won't find much if any onward transport to Salalah. As such, it is better, unless you have your own vehicle, to travel on a through-bus. See p262 for details and p521 for onward travel in Yemen.

UBAR   اوبار

Ubar, near the town of Shisr, is an archaeological site of potentially great importance. Lost to history for over a thousand years, the rediscovery of the remains of this once mighty city caused great archaeological excitement in the 1990s. It may be hard for the ordinary mortal to appreciate what all the fuss is about: there is almost nothing to see at present, except a small, dusty museum, and the fabled golden pillars of antiquity are still only the stuff of dreams.

If legend gets the better of you, however, then take the main Salalah-Thumrait Hwy. At just over 10km north of Thumrait, turn left to Shisr (72km) on a graded road (4WD necessary). On entering Shisr, the site is on the right.

OMAN DIRECTORY

ACCOMMODATION

Accommodation in Oman is limited and expensive though discounts can often be negotiated out of season (May to September, except in Salalah where peak season is June to August). In many places, there's no alternative to the single mid- to top-end hotel, and smaller towns often have no hotels at all. Room rates quoted in this chapter include the mandatory 17% tax and include breakfast unless otherwise stated. In this chapter, we have defined budget hotels as being those that charge less than OR35 for a double room, midrange hotels as those that charge less than OR80 for a double room and top-end hotels as those that charge OR80 and above for a double room.

The only official camp sites in Oman are at Ras al-Jinz, and some expensive 'camping experience' resorts in Ras al-Hadd and Sharqiya Sands. That said, wild camping is one of the highlights of this country, and

---

LOST CITY OF UBAR

In early 1992 the British explorer Ranulph Fiennes, together with a group of US researchers, announced that they had found (with the use of satellite imagery) the remains of Ubar, one of the great lost cities of Arabia. According to legend, Ubar, otherwise known as the Atlantis of the Sands, was the crossroads of the ancient frankincense trail. Scholars are fairly certain that the place existed, that it controlled the frankincense trade and was highly prosperous as a result, but therein lies the end of the certainties. The Quran states that God destroyed Ubar because the people were decadent and had turned away from religion, but archaeologists are more inclined to believe that it fell into a collapsed limestone cavern. Ongoing studies are hopeful of a more definitive reason for the city's demise.

Predictably, there are many who dispute the rediscovery of Ubar. At the time of writing, excavations at the site were proceeding slowly and nothing of sufficient age had surfaced to verify the claims.

providing you are discreet, outside urban areas and don't require creature comforts, a beach of your own, a dune or wadi cave is yours for the taking. Finding somewhere suitable to camp, however, can be difficult without a 4WD vehicle.

ACTIVITIES

Oman is a large country with a sparse population. There are still vast tracts of land without a road that are virtually unmapped. This is excellent news for anyone interested in the outdoors, as you have the chance of coming across an unmapped wadi or hidden cave system; finding a bed of undisturbed fossils; or discovering a species unnamed by science – the possibilities are endless.

However, there is a responsibility, firstly, to avoid getting into a dangerous situation (rescue services are either not available or stretched to the maximum in taking care of road traffic accidents) and, secondly, to limit the negative impact of each activity on the environment. To see what this entails in practical terms, see p554).

Off-Road Exploration

One of the highlights of visiting Oman is off-road exploration of its mountains, wadis, sand dunes and coastline, particularly in a 4WD with some camping equipment. An essential guide for this activity is *Off-Road in the Sultanate of Oman* (see p256). Hiring a 4WD can be expensive, but tour companies (see p260) offer all the destinations mentioned in this chapter as day trips or on overnight tours. For details regarding vehicle hire, see p262.

Hiking, Rock Climbing & Caving

With a pair of stout boots, a map, water and *Adventure Trekking in Oman*, by Anne Dale and Jerry Hadwin, you can access superb walking territory all over the country. Unless you are an accustomed outbacker, however, it is advisable to take a tour (see p260 for details of companies) that can help tailor a trip to suit your interests.

Hiking, rock climbing and caving (see the boxed texts, p235 and p215) are increasingly popular activities, but they tend to be conducted on a 'go-it-alone' basis. *Rock Climbing in Oman*, by RA McDonald, lists some exciting routes, but you need a climbing partner and equipment.

Oman has some rich cave systems, of which many have never been explored. *Caves of Oman*, by Samir Hanna and Mohamed al-Belushi, gives an excellent account of speleology in Oman and points out some local safety advice.

Fishing

A line cast from the shore (try the jetty on Athaiba beach in Muscat) almost invariably lands a fish of some description but for a big catch (marlin, swordfish and barracuda), call **Muscat Game Fishing Club** (☎ 99322779; www.mfga-oman.com), which organises deep-sea outings. Game fish is tag and release but tuna you can bring home for supper! The competitive angler might like to try a line in the three-day Sinbad Classic in Muscat each winter.

Snorkelling & Diving

There are some excellent snorkelling and diving opportunities in Oman, and the vast coastline is virtually unexplored in many places. Diving courses are available in Muscat (see p202) and Al-Sawadi Beach Resort (see p240).

Wildlife Watching

Oman is a great country for naturalists, with dolphins and whales found in large numbers off the coast; important turtle-nesting sites (see p221); a great diversity of sea shells (p106); migration routes ferrying unusual birds across the territory (see p190) and relatively easy sightings of gazelle (see p190). A pair of binoculars and a set of wheels is all that's necessary, although tour companies can arrange specialist tours (p260).

BOOKS

Oman – a Comprehensive Guide (OR12), published under the auspices of the Directorate General of Tourism, includes interesting anecdotal information. Other specialist guides and coffee-table books are available from hotel or city bookshops and cover diverse subjects from caving to camels.

An interesting account of life before the 'renaissance' is included in *The Doctor and the Teacher: Oman 1955-1970*, by Donald Bosch. Philip Ward combines modern travel narrative with the accounts of earlier travellers in *On the Track of the Early Explorers*.

The final part of Wilfred Thesiger's 1959 classic, *Arabian Sands*, describes Oman's interior. *Atlantis of the Sands*, by Ranulph Fiennes, gives an account of the Dhofar insurgency in the 1960s, while describing the search for the lost city of Ubar. On the same subject, *The Road to Ubar*, by Nicholas Clapp, is worth a read.

More practically, *Off-Road in the Sultanate of Oman*, by Lonely Planet author Jenny Walker and Sam Owen, is a must for 4WD exploration in Oman. It covers the entire country, highlights special interests and provides a useful set of maps. *Adventure Trekking in Oman*, by Anne Dale and Jerry Hadwin, lists some great hikes.

Books on specialist subjects (such as crafts, jewellery, shells, caving etc) in Oman are mentioned in the relevant sections of this chapter.

More general Middle Eastern titles, some of which contain coverage of Oman, are listed p23.

BUSINESS HOURS

Oman is rumoured to change its weekend to Friday and Saturday (see p529 for further details). For now, the following hours apply:

Banks 8am to noon Saturday to Wednesday and 8am to 11am Thursday.

Government departments & ministries 7.30am to 2.30pm Saturday to Wednesday, closing 1.30pm during Ramadan.

Post offices 8am to 1.30pm Saturday to Wednesday and 8am to 11am Thursday.

Restaurants 11.30am to 2pm and 5pm to midnight Saturday to Thursday, and 5pm to midnight Friday.

Shops 8am to 1pm and 4pm to 7pm Saturday to Wednesday, and 8am to 1pm Thursday (Mutrah Souq and upmarket Muscat shopping centres to 9pm or 9.30pm).

CHILDREN

Oman is a friendly and welcoming place for children. For younger children, beachcombing, sandcastle building and paddling make Oman a dream destination. That said, there are few specifically designed amenities for children, except for a park with swings in most town centres. See also p203.

CUSTOMS

Non-Muslims travelling by air can bring in one bottle of alcohol, but beware that it is illegal to cross by land from Oman into the UAE and vice versa carrying alcohol. A 'reasonable quantity' of cigars, cigarettes and tobacco can be imported.

DANGERS & ANNOYANCES

Oman is a very safe country and even the driving isn't that bad. Two dangers that may escape the attention of visitors, however, are flash floods and the isolation of many off-road destinations. See Road Hazards (p556) for more information.

DISABLED TRAVELLERS

Other than a few disabled car-parking spots, few other facilities exist in Oman. The **Oman Association for the Disabled** (☎ 24 605566; www.oadisabled.org.om) is set up primarily to assist nationals, but you can email with inquiries.

ELECTRICITY

The mains electricity in Oman is 220V to 240V. Adaptors are widely available at hotel shops and from supermarkets such as Al-Fair.

EMBASSIES & CONSULATES
Omani Embassies & Consulates

Canadian travellers should contact the Omani embassy in the USA. Australian or New Zealand travellers should contact the Omani embassy in Japan. For Omani embassies in neighbouring Middle Eastern countries, see the relevant country chapter. Other Omani embassies:

France (☎ 01 47 23 01 63; fax 01 47 23 77 10; 50 ave de Lena, 75116 Paris)

Germany (☎ 228-35 70 31; fax 35 70 40; Lindenallee 11, D-53173 Bonn)

Japan (☎ 3340-20877; fax 3340-41334; 2-28-11 Sendagaya, Shibuya-Ku, Tokyo, 151-0051)

Netherlands (☎ 070-361 5800; fax 360 7277; Koninginnegracht 27, 2514 AB The Hague)

UK (☎ 020-7225 0001; fax 7589 2505; 167 Queen's Gate, London SW7 5HE)

USA (☎ 202-387 1980; www.omani.info; 2535 Belmont Rd NW, Washington DC 20008)

Embassies & Consulates in Oman

Unless indicated otherwise, all the embassies listed are on Jameat ad Duwal al- Arabiyah St in the district of Shatti al-Qurm, Muscat. The British embassy looks after Irish nationals, processes visas and handles emergencies for Canadian citizens. Australians should contact the Australian embassy in Riyadh, Saudi Arabia (see p363).

Consular sections of the embassy often close an hour or two earlier than the rest of the embassy, so try to go as early in the day as possible or ring first to check. Embassies include the following:

Bahrain (Map pp194–5; ☎ 24 605133; bahrain@omantel.net.om; Way No 3017, Shatti al-Qurm; ⏱ 8am-2.30pm Sat-Wed)

Egypt (Map pp194–5; ☎ 24 600411; fax 24 603626; ⏱ 9am-12.30pm Sat-Wed)

France (Map pp194–5; ☎ 24 681800; www.amba france-om.org; ⏱ 9am-2.30pm Sat-Wed)

Germany (Map pp194–5; ☎ 24 7732482; diplofug@omantel.net.om; An-Nahdah St, Ruwi; ⏱ 9am-noon Sat-Wed)

Iran (Map pp194–5; ☎ 24 696944; fax 24 696888; ⏱ 7.30am-4pm Sat-Wed)

Iraq (Map pp194–5; ☎ 24 604178; fax 24 605112; near Al-Fair supermarket, Madinat as-Sultan Qaboos; ⏱ 8am-2pm Sat-Wed)

Jordan (Map pp194–5; ☎ 24 692760; fax 24 692762; ⏱ 8am-noon Sat-Wed)

Kuwait (Map pp194–5; ☎ 24 699626/7; fax 24 699628; ⏱ 8am-12.30pm Sat-Wed)

Lebanon (Map pp194–5; ☎ 24 695844; fax 24 695633; Way No 3019, Shatti al-Qurm; ⏱ 8am-2.30pm Sat-Wed)

Netherlands (Map pp194–5; ☎ 24 603719; nethmnus@omantel.net.om; Villa 1366, Way 3017, Shatti al-Qurm; ⏱ 9am-noon Sat-Wed)

Qatar (Map pp194–5; ☎ 24 691152; fax 24 691156; ⏱ 8am-2.30pm Sat-Wed)

Saudi Arabia (Map pp194–5; ☎ 24 601744; fax 24 603540; ⏱ 8.30am-2pm Sat-Wed)

Syria (Map pp194–5; ☎ 24 697904; fax 24 603895; Al-In-shirah St, Madinat as-Sultan Qaboos; ⏱ 9am-2pm Sat-Wed)

Turkey (Map pp194–5; ☎ 24 697050; www.turkish embassymuscat.org; Way No 3047, Shatti al-Qurm; ⏱ 8am-noon Sat-Wed)

UAE (Map pp194–5; ☎ 24 600988; uaeoman@omantel .net.om; ⏱ 8am-1.30pm Sat-Wed)

UK (Map pp194–5; ☎ 24 609000; www.britishembassy .gov.uk; ⏱ 7.30am-2.30pm Sat-Wed)

USA (Map pp194–5; ☎ 24 698989; www.muscat .usembassy.gov; ⏱ 8am-4pm Sat & Mon-Wed)

Yemen (Map pp194–5; ☎ 24 600815; fax 24 609172; Bldg No 2981, Way No 2840, Shatti al-Qurm; ⏱ 9am-1.30pm Sat-Wed)

FESTIVALS & EVENTS

When the Sultan is on his Meet the People Tour (no fixed time of year), his ministers camp with him in a spectacular pageant of camel-giving, pennant-waving and sup-

plication from his subjects – combined with state-of-the-art military protection of course.

JANUARY & FEBRUARY
Muscat Festival Around mid-January to mid-February each year, this festival has developed into a fun occasion, with fireworks displays, funfairs, concerts, dance perform-ances, sports events and shopping opportunities.

JUNE-AUGUST
Khareef Festival Check a June, July or August edition of *Oman Today* for a programme of this Salalah festival's cultural activities, which include craft sales, traditional singing and dancing, and an FM radio roadshow.

NOVEMBER
National Day Celebrated on 18 November all over Oman, with feasting, camel-racing, a spectacular military tattoo, shopping bargains, fireworks, gun-toting in the villages, and the draping of lights over buildings.

HOLIDAYS

In addition to the main Islamic holidays described, p535, Oman observes the follow-ing public holidays:
Lailat al-Mi'raj (Ascension of the Prophet) The exact date is dependent on the sighting of the moon – the date is never given until the last minute.
Renaissance Day (23 July) A day's holiday is given to mark the beginning of the reign of Sultan Qaboos, gener-ally credited for the modern rebirth of the country.
National Day (18 November) Marked by at least two days of holiday and flags decorating the highway (see also above).

INTERNET ACCESS

Internet access is now available throughout Oman and many of the larger towns have at least one internet café. If you have an ac-count with Omantel, the countrywide ac-cess number is ☎ 1311. For dialling without an account, the number is ☎ 1312 and the service is paid for through the cost of the call. The homepage of **Omantel** (www.omantel.net.om) provides up-to-date details and instructions for using the service. A prepaid Al-Ufuq card (OR6) gives 20 hours of access.

INTERNET RESOURCES

Some Oman-specific websites include the following:
Destination Oman (www.destinationoman.com) This thorough resource gives practical information about hotels, restaurants and car hire.

Ministry of Information (www.omanet.om/english
/home.asp) This official website provides a useful handbook of facts and figures about the Sultanate. It covers
politics, economics, foreign affairs and media, and provides
links to other websites on Oman.

Oman Tourism (www.omantourism.gov.om) The official
website of the Ministry of Tourism gives useful information
about sites and forthcoming events.

MAPS

The *Apex Map of Oman* (OR3; Apex Publishing), available from bookshops and hotel
foyers, has city maps, as well as a large road
map of Oman. Hildebrand's *Oman* road
map has been recommended by travellers,
but is not available in Oman.

MEDIA
Magazines

Oman Today is a monthly pocket-sized
handbook, with listings and interesting features of interest to the tourist. It is
widely available throughout the Sultanate
for OR1.

Newspapers

The *Times of Oman* and *Oman Daily Observer* are the local English-language newspapers. Foreign newspapers and magazines,
available only in top-end hotels in Muscat
and Salalah and in Muscat's shopping centres, are usually three days old.

Radio

The local English-language radio station
broadcasts on 90.4FM (94.3FM from Salalah) from 6.30am to midnight daily, and
you can hear news bulletins at 7am, 2.30pm
and 6.30pm.

TV

Oman TV broadcasts the news in English
nightly at 8pm and shows English-language
films two or three nights a week (usually
around 11pm). Satellite TV is also widely
available.

MONEY
ATMs & Credit Cards

ATMs are widespread in Oman and many
of them, particularly those belonging to
HSBC, are tied into international systems.
The most popular credit card in Oman is
Visa, but MasterCard is also widely ac-
cepted. Amex is not accepted in many

shops, and you may incur a fee of 5% for
using it in some restaurants and hotels.

Costs

The cost of living is high in the capital and
a budget of OR20 (about US$52) per day is
the minimum required, staying in a small
hotel in Mutrah, eating from local cafés
and using public transport. While general
living expenses are lower outside Muscat,
high accommodation costs and getting to
off-road destinations limit the ability to see
much of Oman for less than OR35 (US$90)
per day.

Currency

The official currency is the Omani rial (OR
but widely spelt RO). One rial is divided
into 1000 baisa (also spelt baiza and shortened to bz). There are coins of five, 10, 25,
50 and 100 baisa, and notes of 100 and 200
baisa. There are notes of a half, one, five, 10,
20 and 50 rials.

UAE dirhams can be used in some
towns at an exchange rate of about Dh10
to OR1.100.

Exchanging Money

Most banks will change US-dollar travellers
cheques for a commission. Moneychangers
keep similar hours to banks, but are often
open from around 4pm to 7pm as well.
They usually offer a slightly more competitive rate than the banks, and most charge
only a nominal commission of 500 baisa per
cash transaction.

Exchange Rates

The following exchange rates were correct
at the time of printing:

Country	Unit		Omani rial
Australia	A$10	=	OR3.14
Canada	C$10	=	OR3.34
euro zone	€10	=	OR5.16
Japan	¥1000	=	OR3.26
Kuwait	KD1	=	OR1.34
New Zealand	NZ$10	=	OR2.78
Qatar	QR10	=	OR1.06
Saudi Arabia	SR10	=	OR1.03
UAE	Dh10	=	OR1.05
UK	UK£10	=	OR7.63
USA	US$10	=	OR3.86
Yemen	YR1000	=	OR2.16

Tipping & Bargaining

A tip of 10% is customary only in large hotels and restaurants if a service fee hasn't been included in the bill. It is not the custom to tip taxi drivers or smaller establishments.

Discounts are available for most items in all shops other than supermarkets and Western-style chain stores. Haggle hard for taxi fares and souvenirs but don't expect too much of a bargain!

PHOTOGRAPHY

Shops selling memory cards and batteries, as well as print film are plentiful in Muscat. Most studios can print digital photos from a memory card. They can also transfer photos to a CD from a memory card or film. Slide film is hard to find so bring your own.

POST

Sending a postcard to any destination outside the GCC costs 150 baisa. Postage for letters is 200 baisa for the first 10g and 350 baisa for 11g to 20g. Mailing small packets to countries outside the GCC costs OR2 to OR4. For parcels of 1kg it costs OR4 to OR6.

Poste restante service is available at the post office in Ruwi. Mail should be addressed to: (Your Name), Poste Restante, Ruwi Central Post Office, Ruwi, Sultanate of Oman. Parcels received in Oman incur a 250 baisa customs charge.

RESPONSIBLE TRAVEL

Westerners are often seen wandering around supermarkets or hotel foyers in shorts, dressed in bikinis on public beaches and skinny-dipping in wadis. These practices are highly resented, though Omanis are too polite to say as much. In order to respect local customs, knees, cleavage and shoulders should be covered in public.

It's tempting when exploring off-road destinations to drive straight through the middle of villages. This is about as sensitive as taking a lorry through a neighbour's garden back home. If you want to see the village, it's better to park outside and walk in, preferably with permission from a village elder.

In addition, Oman's wild environment requires special consideration. Tyre tracks leave marks on the desert floor, often forever, and litter does not biodegrade in the hot, dry climate (see p104). See also Responsible Travel, p24.

SHOPPING

Oman is a great centre for handicrafts with expertise in silversmithing. Exquisitely crafted *khanjars* can cost up to OR500 but tourist versions are available from OR30. Genuine Bedouin silver is becoming scarce (read *Disappearing Treasures of Oman,* by Avelyn Foster). Silver Maria Theresa dollars, used as Oman's unit of currency for many years, make a good buy from OR2. Wooden *mandoos* studded with brass tacks cost OR15 for a new one and start at OR70 for an antique.

Other items commonly for sale include coffeepots (not always made in Oman), baskets woven with leather, camel bags, rice mats and cushion covers. Many items are imported, as per centuries of tradition, from India and Iran.

Frankincense is a 'must buy' from Salalah, together with a pottery incense burner (both available in Muscat). Amouage (OR50), currently the most valuable perfume in the world, is made in Muscat partially from frankincense. Omani dates make another excellent gift.

SOLO TRAVELLERS

Travelling beyond Muscat and the main towns of Nizwa, Sohar, Sur and Salalah can be a lonely experience. The interior is sparsely populated, and with no established circuit of travellers' meeting places, bumping into other foreigners is rare outside the holiday period. While Omani people are very friendly and hospitable, they are also private and you are unlikely to be invited to stay for longer than the customary bread and salt. If you hitchhike to somewhere remote, you may have a very long wait before you find a ride out again. On the whole, as with any country with large expanses of remote territory, it's better to have backup in the form of a vehicle, a companion, or at least water, map and compass.

TELEPHONE & FAX

There are central public telephone offices, also offering fax services, in both Muscat and Salalah, though the latter only has cardphones. Phonecards are available from

OMAN

grocery stores and petrol stations. International phone calls can be made with a phonecard by dialling direct from most public phone booths throughout Oman. The cost of a two-minute call to Europe and the USA is approximately OR1.

Each area of Oman has its own code (for example, 24 is the prefix for Muscat). Note that you need to use this code even if calling from within the same area.

Mobile Phones

Temporary local GSM connections can be made through the purchase of an **Omantel** (www.omantel.net.om) Hayyak SIM card (OR10), which includes OR5 worth of call time. Alternatively, **Nawras** (www.nawras.com .om) offer a similar service for OR9, including OR2.500 worth of call time. These cards can be purchased on arrival at the airport and from shopping centres in Muscat.

TOURS

Tours in Oman are generally tailor-made for the customer in private vehicles with an English-speaking driver-guide. This is great for your itinerary, but painful on the pocket unless you can muster a group of four to share.

The following are average all-inclusive prices for a full-day tour from Muscat:

Tour	Cost
Nizwa, Bahla & Jabrin	OR70
Nakhal & Rustaq	OR70
Jebel Shams	OR110
Wadi Shab & Wadi Tiwi	OR110
Sharqiya Sands	OR120
Dolphin & other	with local fisherman OR5;
boat trips	all-day dhow cruise OR90

Tour companies abound in Muscat and Salalah; they offer camel safaris, 4WD touring, camping, city tours, caving, rock climbing and combinations thereof. *Oman Today* has a complete listing of tour operators. Some recommended agencies are as follows:

Arabian Sea Safaris (☎ 24 693223; www.arabian seasafaris.com) Specialises in boat trips.

Desert Discovery Tours (☎ 24 493232; www.desert discovery.com) For trips to the Sharqiya Sands.

Explore Oman (www.exploreoman.com) An experienced UK-based company.

Mark Tours (☎ 24 565869; www.marktours.com) A popular and experienced company that can tailor-make study tours and adventure trips.

Muscat Diving and Adventure Center (☎ 24 485663; www.holiday-in-oman.com) The best company through which to organise activities such as caving, hiking and other outward-bound activities.

National Travel & Tourism (☎ 24 660376; www .nttoman.com) Offers an excellent, friendly and comprehensive tour service, including trips to the Oryx Sanctuary at Jaaluni National Reserve.

VISAS

A one-month visit visa, required by all nationalities except for citizens of Gulf countries, can be obtained by many foreign nationals (including those from the EEC, the Americas, Australia and New Zealand) at Seeb International Airport in Muscat for OR6. You may be refused admission if you have an Israeli stamp in your passport.

It is also possible to obtain a visa at those border crossings that are open to foreigners. If you have a UAE visa, it is possible to cross into Oman by land without paying a further fee.

Multiple-entry visas cost OR10. They are valid for one year with maximum stays of three weeks.

Visa Extensions

One-month extensions (OR6) are available for visit visas from the Immigration & Passports Directorate in Qurm, Muscat. Overstaying a visa will incur charges on departure (OR10 per day).

WOMEN TRAVELLERS

Women travelling alone are a novelty in Oman and you may feel uncomfortable, particularly on public transport, eating in restaurants, and when visiting public beaches. Omani men mostly ignore women (out of respect) and it's hard to meet Omani women. Many of the country's attractions lie off-road where travelling solo (for either sex) is inadvisable unless you are highly resourceful and, if driving, strong enough to change a tyre.

Harassment is not a big problem, except near hotels where attitudes are, rightly or wrongly, influenced by the sight of women in bikinis. Outside hotels, it helps (in addition to being more culturally sensitive) to be discreetly dressed in loose-fitting clothing, and to wear shorts and a T-shirt for swimming. See also p542.

WORK

To work in Oman you have to be sponsored by an Omani company before you enter the country (ie you have to have a job). Although it is illegal to work on a tourist visa, some expats take a short-term contract and hope their employer will arrange a labour card for them. The reality is a fretful experience best avoided.

TRANSPORT IN OMAN

GETTING THERE & AWAY

See also the Arabian Peninsula Transport chapter (p545) for more information on the following.

Entering Oman

Entering Oman at **Seeb International Airport** (☎ 24 519223) is straight-forward. The small airport is surprisingly efficient, queues are kept to a minimum (outside holiday periods), staff are friendly and your luggage is often waiting on the carousel before immigration is complete. Most visitors require a visa upon arrival. This is easily expedited by filling in a form (in the immigration hall) and taking it to the clearly marked visa-collection counter before queuing up to have your passport stamped.

Air

AIRPORTS & AIRLINES

There is only one truly international airport in Oman, and that is **Seeb International Airport** (☎ 24 519223) in Muscat. That said, Oman Air sometimes runs direct flights between Dubai and Salalah Airport, but you need to have a visa for Oman *before* arrival. At the time of writing, these flights were suspended due to lack of demand. Preparations for a second runway and a new terminal building are currently in progress.

DEPARTURE TAX

The departure tax is OR5 (US$13). This is invariably included in the cost of your ticket.

OTHER AIRLINES FLYING TO/FROM OMAN

British Airways (BA; ☎ 24 568777; www.ba.com; hub: Heathrow Airport, London)

Emirates (EK; ☎ 24 792222; www.emirates.com; hub: Dubai) Has an office in Ruwi (Map p200).

Gulf Air (GF; ☎ 800 72424; www.gulfairco.com; hub: Bahrain) Office in Ruwi (Map p200).

Oman Air (WY; ☎ 24 707222; www.omanair.com; hub: Muscat) Office in Ruwi (Map p200).

Qatar Airways (QR; ☎ 24 787070; www.qatarairways .com; hub: Doha)

Saudi Arabian Airlines (SV; ☎ 24 789485; www .saudiairlines.com; hub: Jeddah)

Sri Lankan Airlines (UL; ☎ 24 784545; www .srilankan.lk; hub: Colombo, Sri Lanka)

Flight Destination	Price	Frequency
Abu Dhabi (UAE)	OR98	3 per day
Doha (Qatar)	OR129	3 per day
Kuwait City (Kuwait)	OR190	2 per day
Manama (Bahrain)	OR145	3 per day
Riyadh (Saudi Arabia)	OR218	1 per day
San'a (Yemen)	OR265	2 per week

Land

Oman borders the UAE, Saudi Arabia and Yemen. Current practicalities mean, however, that you can only enter UAE and Yemen, and only through certain borderposts (see below). The situation changes frequently, however, and it's worth checking with the **Royal Oman Police** (☎ 24 4569603) before planning your trip to see which crossings are open to non-GCC visitors. Visas are obtainable at all Oman border posts.

BORDER CROSSINGS

UAE

Currently there are three border posts open 24 hours to foreigners; these are at Wajaja (for Dubai), Khatmat Milahah (for Dibba) – see p242 for details on both, and Al-Darah–Tibat (for Musandam Peninsula – see p244). It is likely that the Buraimi border (for Abu Dhabi – see p237) will open again shortly.

Yemen

There are two border posts with Yemen at Sarfait (see p254) and Mazyunah. Both are open 24 hours. Sarfait is by far the best option as new roads lead to the post on either side. Mazyunah leads into unsafe territory on the Yemeni side.

OMAN

Note that you cannot re-enter Oman on a tourist visa and, as a tourist in Oman, you cannot obtain a visa for Yemen from the embassy in Muscat. Most nationalities, however, can obtain one at the border (see p517 in the Yemen chapter).

BUS
UAE
The **Oman National Transport Company** (ONTC; ☎ 24 708522; www.ontcoman.com) has buses to Dubai (OR5, six hours, daily) departing from **Ruwi bus station** (☎ 24 701294) in Muscat at 6am, 7am and 4.30pm.

Comfort Line (☎ 24 702191), has a similarly comfortable service to Dubai at 6.30am and 4.30pm (OR5, five hours, daily). The bus leaves from a parking lot outside Moon Travels, two blocks behind the bus station on Way 2985 in Muscat.

The ONTC service from Muscat to Abu Dhabi (OR5, six hours, daily) leaves at 6.30am but check the status of the border in Buraimi first.

Yemen
The **Gulf Transport Company** (☎ 23 293303) has three buses daily per week to Mukhalla in Yemen (OR12, six hours) departing from Salalah bus station at 9.30am Monday, Wednesday and Friday.

CAR
It's possible to drive through any of the borders in your own vehicle if you obtain insurance to cover both countries.

You need extra insurance if you wish to take a hired car over the border to/from UAE and you must return the car to the country in which you hired it (unless you're willing to pay a huge premium).

Sea
There are currently no passenger services to/from Oman, although Muscat is a port of call for cruise liners.

GETTING AROUND
Air
Besides Seeb International Airport in Muscat, the only functioning airports are at opposite ends of the country in Salalah and Khasab; both these handle domestic flights only. Four new airports have been approved, however, at Sur, Sohar, Adam and Duqm, which will help open up the country for visitors.

The national carrier is **Oman Air** (☎ 24 707222). It services the domestic airports, as well as a selection of Middle Eastern and subcontinental destinations. Oman has a 50% share in Gulf Air, which services all Middle Eastern cities and many long-haul destinations.

The only domestic flights currently available in the country are on Oman Air between Muscat and Salalah (one way/return OR36/72, 1½ hours, twice daily at variable times), and between Muscat and Khasab (one way/return, OR24/48, 1¼ hours, on Thursday at 8.55am and Friday at 2.30pm). Tickets can be booked through any travel agent.

Bus
The intercity buses are operated by **ONTC** (☎ 24 490046; www.ontcoman.com), which has daily services to/from most of the main provincial towns for OR5 or less, with the exception of Salalah, which costs one way/return OR6/11 from Muscat. Buses are usually on time, comfortable and safe. It is worth making reservations for longer journeys. Tickets are available from the bus driver.

Car
Road signs are written in English (albeit with inconsistent spelling), as well as in Arabic, throughout Oman. Helpful brown tourist signs signal many sites of interest. Petrol, all of which is now unleaded, is widely available. Al-Maha petrol stations usually have modern, well-stocked shops and clean toilets.

DRIVING LICENCE
Most foreign driving licences are accepted in Oman but an International Driving Permit is preferable. Foreign residents of Oman need a road permit to leave or re-enter the country by land. This regulation does not apply to tourists.

HIRE
International car-hire chains in Oman include Avis, Budget, Europcar and Thrifty, but dozens of local agencies offer a slightly reduced rate. Rates for 2WD cars start at about OR14 and 4WD vehicles at OR35.

Always carry water with you (a box of a dozen 1.5L bottles costs OR1.500 from petrol stations) and a towrope (OR4 from any large supermarket). If you buy three 'freezer packs' at the same time (600 baisa each), they will keep your cool box cold for a day, even in summer, and you can ask hotels to refreeze the packs at night.

INSURANCE
Check the small print on all car-hire documents to see if you are covered for taking the vehicle off-road.

ROAD CONDITIONS
Travellers comment that some roads indicated in this book as '4WD only' are passable in a 2WD. Often they are right, until something goes wrong – 2WDs are not built to withstand potholes, washboard surfaces and steep, loose-gravel inclines, let alone long distances to the next petrol station.

If travellers' letters are anything to go by, who knows over what terrain the previous driver dragged your hire car! Bear in mind, you'll get no sympathy from hire companies if your 2WD breaks down off-road (and don't forget you're not insured to be off-road in a 2WD). With virtually zero traffic on some routes you are very vulnerable, especially in extreme summer temperatures.

In short, saving on the expense of a 4WD might cost more than you bargained for.

ROAD HAZARDS
Aggressive tailgating and fast, inappropriate driving is a hazard of the capital area in particular. Camels and goats often wander onto the road – with disastrous consequences in Dhofar during the *khareef,* when locals continue to drive at the same speed regardless of the fog. After rain, the roads are exceptionally slippery.

Failing brakes on mountain roads, beguiling soft sand and a salty crust called *sabkha* (that looks and feels hard until you drive on it) are further common hazards. As a rule, always stick to the tracks: if they suddenly stop, it's time to reverse! See also p556 for further information (particularly on the danger of flash flooding in wadis).

ROAD RULES
Traffic laws are strictly enforced, especially in Muscat. Seatbelt use is mandatory for passengers and there is a fine of OR10 for not wearing one. Drink-driving is completely forbidden and so is the use of mobile phones while driving. Most vehicles are fitted with a beeping device for Oman's maximum speed limit of 120km per hour.

Note that it's illegal to drive a dirty car – the fine is OR5!

RESPONSIBLE DRIVING
Before heading off over uncharted territory, it's worth asking if you really need to scar this piece of desert. It's better, generally, for your safety and for the environment if you stick to previous tracks (see the boxed text, p554).

Hitching
Hitching is possible but inadvisable as most roads outside the capital area have low volumes of traffic. Bear in mind that you may often get left between towns while the driver turns off piste to his or her village. You therefore need to be self-sufficient enough to survive the hottest part of a day – even a night or more in some parts of the interior – without any prospect of an onward or return ride.

Always carry water and avoiding hitching off-road. It is the custom to offer the driver some remuneration. If you're driving, you will often be asked to give a ride to locals but see p557 for some words of caution!

Local Transport
TAXI & MICROBUSES
Oman has a comprehensive system of cheap but slow long-distance shared taxis (painted orange and white) and microbuses. Oman's shared taxis and microbuses do not wait until they are full to leave. Instead, drivers pick up and drop off extra passengers along the way.

To visit certain places of interest, you'll often have to take an 'engaged' taxi (ie private, not shared) – generally four times the price of a shared taxi as you have to pay for all the seats. Bargain hard before you get in and try to avoid hailing a taxi from a hotel. Fares quoted in this chapter are for shared taxis unless otherwise stated.

OMAN

Qatar قطر

When looking at modern Qatar, it's easy to imagine the great Oriental scholar, Edward Said, turning in his grave.

Nineteenth-century Western travellers to the Middle East went in search of an imagined Arabia. When they couldn't find it, they described an Orient they thought their readers would prefer to the reality. Even today, it's tempting to go searching for such stereotypes and Qatar has its share: there are rock carvings to testify human endurance pitched against adversities of nature; forts to hint at the ruins of empire; and occasional goat-hair Bedouin tents to suggest the 'noble savage' nature of life in the desert.

Qatar has spent its energies (and considerable fortunes) in eschewing this stereotype, however, and showing that these 'Orientalist' flights of fancy are more a product of feverish Western imaginations than anything related to the Middle East. To this end, vast vertical 'pleasure domes' of the postmodern variety have been erected in Doha as if to demonstrate that the country is as international as any other. At least, that was until recently. Suddenly, wind-towered developments like Al-Sharq Village Resort & Spa proclaim to be 'genuinely Arabic'; Al-Waqif souq sports 'antique' passageways; tented accommodation in Khor al-Adaid comes with air-conditioning. Qatar, in other words, appears to be reinventing itself in the image of Western 'otherness' fantasies. For the visitor, it's wonderful: everything one imagined of Arabia is there in all its sanitised glory. For those who knew the Qatar of hawk souqs and dust storms, however, there's the suspicion that this country is turning Disney.

FAST FACTS

- **Official name** Qatar
- **Capital** Doha
- **Area** 11,437 sq km
- **Population** 885,000
- **Country code** ☎ 974
- **Head of State** Sheikh Hamad bin Khalifa al-Thani
- **Annual number of tourists** 732,000
- **Stereotypes** An oil rich state with more money than sense
- **Surprises** An oil rich state with more sense than money

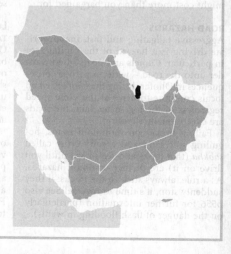

HIGHLIGHTS

- **Al-Corniche** (p275) Step into the future by walking along Doha's sparkling seafront, decorated with the region's finest modern buildings.
- **Souq Waqif** (p277) Step into the past in the city's most labyrinthine souq, with its spices and shimmering textiles.
- **Al-Khor** (p288) Discover there is more to Qatar than Doha in this former pearl-fishing village on the northeastern coast.
- **Bir Zekreet** (p289) Set up camp under a desert mushroom or watch the waders in nearby shallows.
- **Khor al-Adaid** (p287) Take a dune for a pillow and the stars for a blanket, at this beautiful 'inland sea'.

ITINERARIES

- **Qatar Stopover** Absorb the best of Doha by promenading the corniche (p275), pausing for banana-wrapped hamour and pomegranate juice in Arabian-style Al-Bandar (p282) restaurant complex. Spend the afternoon pampering to weary limbs by the beach at InterContinental Doha (p282) followed by standing-room-only at the convivial hotspot, Paloma (p284). Go cultural at one of Qatar's big four: the National Museum (p277), the Museum of Islamic Arts (p277), the Photography Museum (p279) or the National Library (p279). If they're not open, opt for retail therapy among the pots and pans, *oud* (incense made from agar wood) and odd bits at Souq Waqif (p277), followed by a hunt among the brand names for prayer beads at City Center-Doha (p286).
- **Three Days** After a day exploring modern central Doha, go in search of the city's origins by bartering for bangles in the Gold Souq (p285). Spend the discount on something you didn't really want at the Second-hand Market (p285); spare a few dirhams for a pink chick in the Animal & Bird Market (p285); and then shop for falcons at the Thursday/Friday market (p284). Hire a car and imagine the falcons flying in the shrubby interior near Al-Khor (p288), or watch them as they circle over the camel races at Al-Shahaniya (p290).
- **For Expats** Take a trip around the entire peninsula, calling in on the fishing communities of Al-Ruweis (p289) and Al-Zubara (p289). Camp out under the escarpment at Bir Zekreet and search for a pearl on a shore full of washed-up oysters. Cast an eye over the historic interior at Umm Salal Mohammed (p288) and neighbouring Umm Salal Ali (p288), or enjoy some R&R and water sports at Sealine Beach Resort (p287). For something more adventurous, stay overnight at the enchanting inland sea of Khor al-Adaid (p287), picnic in the gossiping dunes and sleep on a magic carpet of sand.

CLIMATE & WHEN TO GO

For half the year, the climate across the plains of Qatar is unforgiving. During summer (May to September), temperatures generally average 35°C, but it's not uncommon for the mercury to rise to 50°C. The 90% humidity that comes with this time of year sags over the Peninsula like a bad hangover, and frequent sandstorms are an added irritation. The winter months are much milder, with pleasant, even chilly evenings and the odd rainy day, especially in December and January.

As for when to go, that's a different matter. For the sports-minded, key international fixtures will make a trip to Qatar worth the effort whatever the season, and, in Doha at least, there are plenty of air-conditioned facilities to make even the worst summer tolerable. Summer brings to the desert its own consolations, like mirages and halos of heat above the sand. See p530 for a Doha climate chart.

HISTORY
Early Inhabitants

The written history of Qatar begins in grand fashion with a mention by the 5th-century Greek historian Herodotus, who identifies the seafaring Canaanites as the original inhabitants of Qatar. Thereafter, however, Qatar appears to be the subject more of conjecture than history. Although there is evidence, in the form of flint spearheads, pottery shards (in the National Museum), burial mounds near Umm Salal Mohammed and the rock carvings of Jebel Jassassiyeh to support the early inhabitation of Qatar (from 4000 BC), the peninsula has surprisingly little to show for its ancient lineage. Take Al-Zubara, for example: the

QATAR

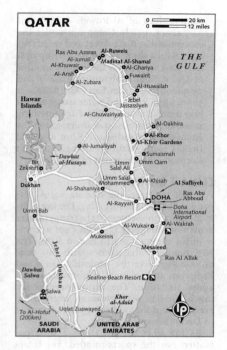

famous ancient Greek geographer Ptolemy tantalisingly includes 'Qatara' in his map of the Arab world. This is thought to be a reference to Al-Zubara, Qatar's main trading port right up until the 19th century. A visitor to the small modern town, however, would have difficulty imagining a dhow (traditional wooden boat) dodging the sandbanks at low tide, let alone a fleet of cargo ships moored in the harbour. Even Al-Zubara Fort, one of only a few in Qatar, was built as recently as 1938 and, although some 9th-century excavations further down the coast have revealed remnants of a sizable city with two mosques and a fort, as well as hints of life in other centuries, the surrounding desert is marked by absence rather than by strong historical presence.

Indeed, what is remarkable about the history of Qatar is not what has been left behind but the almost magical erasure of any visible sign of six thousand years of its human evolution. The history of Qatar, in many respects, is the history of the Bedouin, who traverse a land 'taking only memories, and leaving only footprints', footprints that

are dusted away by frequent sandstorms. As such, history in Qatar is easier to spot in the living rather than the dead, for example, by the avid racing of camels at Al-Shahaniya, the trading of falcons in the Doha souqs, the hospitality towards guests in the coffeehouses of the city, and the building of camps (albeit with TV aerials and 4WDs) in the sand dunes of Khor al-Adaid.

Documents indicate that Qatar played an important role in the early spread of Islam through the assembling of a naval fleet used to transport the warriors of the Holy Jihad. Again, however, Islam is carried rather more stoutly in the conservatism of the modern people than in any monuments to that era. Even the Portuguese, who left forts in every country in the Gulf like modern businessmen leave calling cards, bequeathed only hearsay to Qatar's coast line. The Turks helped drive out the Portuguese in the 16th century and Qatar remained under the nominal rule of the Ottoman Empire (and the practical governance of local sheikhs) for more than four centuries. Yet the comings and goings of even that great empire have made little impression on Qatar's sands of time, metaphorically or physically.

Al-Thani Family Dynasty

Enter the Al-Thani family. Al-Khalifa (the current ruling family of Bahrain) controlled much of the peninsula until the arrival, in the mid-18th century, of the charismatic Al-Thani family, which remains in power to this day. Al-Thani is a branch of the ancient Tamim tribe of central Arabia, thought to have arrived in Qatar from the Gibrin oasis in southern Najd. Originally they were nomadic Bedouins, but the region's sparse vegetation led them to settle in the peninsula's coastal areas around Zubara, where they fished and dived for pearls. The first Al-Thani emir, Sheikh Mohammed bin Thani, established his capital at Al-Bida in the mid-19th century, thereby laying the foundations of modern Doha. He strengthened his position against other local tribes by signing a treaty with the British in 1867. In 1872 the second Al-Thani emir, Jasim, signed a treaty with the Turks allowing them to build a garrison in Doha (Doha Fort). The Turks were expelled under the third Al-Thani emir, Sheikh Abdullah (the emir who lived in the palace that now houses the National Museum), after Turkey entered WWI on the opposite side to Britain. Thereafter, the British guaranteed Qatar's protection in exchange for a promise that the ruler would not deal with other foreign powers without British permission – an agreement that endured until independence was proclaimed on 1 September 1971.

Rags to Oil Riches

Qatar's history from WWI to the end of the 20th century reads rather like a fairy tale. Life in Qatar, even before the collapse of the pearl market in the 1930s, was marked by widespread poverty, malnutrition and disease. The arrival of oil prospectors and the establishment in 1935 of Petroleum Development Qatar, a forerunner of today's state-run Qatar General Petroleum Corporation (QGPC), signalled the beginning of a brave new world, even though WWII delayed production of oil for another 10 years. Although not huge in comparative terms, the oil revenue instantly turned the tiny, impoverished population into one of the richest per capita countries in the world. Qatar's first school opened in 1952 and a full-scale hospital followed in 1959, marking the beginning of long-term investment in the country's modernisation. Most of these improvements occurred under the leadership not of Sheikh Abdullah's son Ali, nor his grandson Ahmed, but under that of his nephew Khalifa bin Hamad al-Thani, who, over a period of 15 years, ran many of the country's ministries, including foreign affairs, oil and the police. On 22 February 1972 Khalifa ousted his politically apathetic kinsmen in a palace coup. Astutely, one of his first gestures was to crack down on the extravagance of the royal household. Celebrating the stability that his reign and increasing oil prices brought to Qatar, Sheikh Khalifa invested in one of the world's great, all-encompassing welfare states.

Qatar Today

In June 1995, while holidaying in Switzerland, Sheikh Khalifa was unexpectedly replaced as emir by his son Hamad. Since assuming power, the popular new emir has accelerated the modernisation of the country through political and institutional reforms. These have included allowing women to drive and vote, encouraging education and training, and opening the country to tourism.

In 2001 Qatar hosted the World Trade Organization Conference and major development in the form of hotels and infrastructure was undertaken for the 15th Asian Games in 2006. Qatar is a member of the UN, the Organisation of Petroleum Exporting Countries (OPEC), the Arab League, the International Monetary Fund (IMF) and the World Bank, and the Gulf Cooperation Council (GCC). As such, within the space of 70 years, Qatar has emerged from the virtual anonymity of its past to become a regional force to be reckoned with. Monuments to that achievement are found symbolically in the country's modern infrastructure and its social welfare programmes. But also, perhaps for the first time in its history, they're also found in a tangible, physical sense, by the growing ring of magnificent buildings that grace Doha's corniche, and in the high-profile events that the country hosts, such as the Asian Games of 2006.

GOVERNMENT & POLITICS

Qatar is ruled by the popular emir, Sheikh Hamad bin Khalifa al-Thani, who doubles as minister of defence and commander-in-chief of the armed forces. His third son, Sheikh Tamim bin Hamad al-Thani, is the official heir apparent. The prime minister and minister of the interior is Sheikh Abdullah bin Khalifa al-Thani, the emir's brother. A Council of Ministers (cabinet) assists in the implementation of the general policies of the state, advised by a 35-member Advisory Council.

In April 2003, 96.6% of Qataris voted in favour of a draft permanent constitution that became effective on 8 June 2005, transforming Qatar into a democracy. On National Day, 3 September, the country flutters with the maroon and white national flag, symbolising the bloodshed of past conflicts (particularly those of the latter half of the 19th century) and subsequent peace, a peace that has made Qatar one of the most politically stable countries in the region.

Not that there haven't been moments of trouble: in March 2005 a suicide bomber targeted the small but popular English-language theatre in Doha. One person was killed and several were wounded. This was an isolated incident, however, precipitated it would seem by widely shared anger at the Western fiasco in Iraq. Most Qataris, whatever their private opinions, try to stay out of the fray, recognising that their own country's prosperity relies to a great extent on good relations with the West.

ECONOMY

All that is left of the once major pearling industry is the oyster monument on the corniche, but with huge quantities of natural gas, estimated at 5.8% of the world's reserves, no-one is paying too much attention to the forgotten oyster beds. Qatar is one of the fastest-growing economies in the world, with a very high per capita income. Already a major global supplier of energy, it is due to become the largest exporter of liquefied natural gas in the world. Diversification of the economy includes investment in agriculture, medium-scale industry, mining, tourism and leisure.

PEOPLE
The National Psyche

Watching 4WDs racing over the sand dunes, attached to trailers holding sand buggies and skis, it's clear that this is a very rich country. Back in the 1970s it wasn't uncommon to see a brand-new Mercedes-Benz, with 21-carat gold badge and no number plate, squealing through the streets, having just been handed over to a potential customer on approval. Such enormous wealth delivered to the young, who had little or no recollection of the hardships of life before the riches of oil, came at a price calculable in terms of the arrogance of the nouveau riche; their unwillingness to work; a military staffed by officers but no privates; and jobs half started but lacking the patience to see them through.

Times have changed, however. The evident wealth of modern Doha is built not on money alone but on local vision and the growing confidence of Qatari professionals. Not all of Doha is as glittering as the new

---

A BOOM DECADE

An article in the *Gulf Times* of 1 March 2006 boasts the headline 'Qatar Set for Boom Decade'. The *New York Times* picked up on the same headline and pitched a whole piece about Qatar that makes it sound like the next Manhattan. Qatar's Ministry of Tourism must be rubbing its hands gleefully as fried eggs, white pillows and sparkling wine are given a five-star make-over by the clever marketing campaign of Qatar Airways. All in all, Qatar is being hyped to the hilt – and not without justification.

From the surrounding barren plain, Doha has risen like a magic mushroom over the past 10 years in a proliferation of elegant buildings and carefully planned developments, wrapped around the corniche. In fact, forget the mushroom – think mountain peaks. Poised to overtake Switzerland as the richest nation on earth, Qatar is building its own Alps, a set of building developments worth hundreds of millions of dollars, including such lofty projects as the 80-storey Dubai Towers. Closer to earth, but no less prestigious, are key tourist complexes such as Pearl Qatar, built on islands of reclaimed land off West Bay Lagoon, with four marinas, tourist facilities and the first development to offer freehold property to nonlocals. In addition to the refurbishment of the National Museum, there are no less than three other high-quality museums being built, including a photography museum, national library and the prestigious Museum of Islamic Art. With 37 new hotels mid-construction, a new airport and a causeway to Bahrain, Qatar is in a prime position to offer cheese for the MICE market (meetings, incentives, conferences and exhibitions) while learning to purr for the CATS (CEOs, arbitrators, tycoons and sports stars).

But does the country live up to the hype? Standing on Ring Rd B, three years ago, very much behind the corniche developments, you'd have noticed that the new projects represented a relatively thin veneer on an otherwise tired-looking 1970s wasteland. What is remarkable today is that Ring Rd B is now running through prime property. It may take a while for the reinvention of Qatar to reach the hinterland (though tourist and residential beach projects like Lusail are already addressing this issue) but there's little doubting that the country's vision and drive have now penetrated the heart of downtown Doha. I for one can't wait to return next year to see what exciting changes are in store for Ring Rd C.

BONDING BEADS

Sit in a coffeehouse in Qatar, be present at a business meeting or watch a party of *sheesha* (water pipe used to smoke tobacco) smokers and you will notice that they are bonded by a common activity: they are twirling a set of beads between thumb and forefinger, or flicking the entire set of 33, 66 or 99 beads around the wrist. At a party or wedding, they may even be whirling them overhead like a rattle.

These are not any old beads: they could be pearl or jade, coral or bone, turquoise or gold nugget; they could be spiritually precious clay from Mecca; bought in the local souq, or collected bead by bead and at great cost from around the world. Qataris favour amber beads, however, and a trip to a specialist *misbah* (prayer bead) shop in Souq Waqif, or even to a stall on the 1st floor of City Center-Doha, will gladden the eye with strands of yellow, gold and treacle-coloured amber.

Men have carried *misbah*, traditionally threaded by women, for thousands of years. It is thought they have their origins in the Hindu meditative tradition; traders brought the practice to the Middle East and strings of beads have been used for prayer since the early days of Islam to help in the contemplation of God. A user usually rolls each bead while reciting the names or attributes of Allah.

While many continue to use the beads for religious purposes, prayer beads in Qatar have become a social item, too: they are a necessary accessory to the *thobe* (floor-length shirt-dress), sitting in the pocket ready to be whipped out when the haggling gets tough or a pause threatens conversation – like the 'How are you?' that can be repeated 10 times or more in the course of an evening's engagement. They function like a piece of intuited discourse, as well as talisman and storyteller, comforter and companion: the ultimate symbol, perhaps, of male bonding.

West Bay developments, though there is a determination to maintain the quality of life that oil and gas revenues made possible. Perhaps it's this that has encouraged a commitment to work in the new industries, shopping malls, resorts and sports facilities, of which a new generation of Qataris is justly proud.

Lifestyle

Despite its significant neighbour, Saudi Arabia, with which it shares a religion (the Wahhabi sect of Islam) as well as a border, Qatar has managed to steer a remarkably independent course, seeking ties with Iran, for example, and even more contentiously with Israel in the 1990s.

Qataris aim to be equally as independent in society: while observant of a conservative form of Islam, Qataris are not afraid of extending hospitality to those of a different mind; while it is still unusual to see Qataris drinking alcohol, there is a tolerance of visitors who do; and while men and women are discreetly dressed, there's no harassment of the disrespectful tourist. Most significant is Qatar's press, which has enjoyed complete freedom of expression since 1995, resulting in one of the most exceptional media phenomena of modern times – Al-Jazeera Independent Satellite TV Channel (see p294).

Family life, at the heart of most Arab societies and equally so in Qatar, manages to reflect the espousal of Western materialism while paradoxically retaining something of the Bedouin simplicity of life: the day can stop for tea with a stranger; the emergency exit on a plane is spread with prayer carpet; and a business dinner may be rejected in favour of kebabs with friends.

Population

After witnessing Qatar's interior it's easy to appreciate that with about 885,000 people, this is one of the most sparsely populated countries in the Arab world. Almost 50% of the population lives in the capital, Doha; the remaining 50% is scattered mainly in small coastal settlements or industrial areas, like Al-Ruweis and Al-Khor in the north and Dukhan, Mesaieed and Al-Wakrah in the south. Most nationals are of Najdi (central Arabian) ancestry, though there are also people of Persian descent.

Multiculturalism

An arriving visitor will be stamped into the country by a Qatari, but thereafter they could be forgiven for thinking they had stepped into another country – or at least pockets of many. There are car-hire attendants from Pakistan, shopkeepers from India, nightclub entertainers from the Philippines, and Brits turning pink in the afternoon sun during a day off from the oil and gas industries. Forming only a quarter of the population of their own country, Qatari men are recognisable in the multiethnic crowd by their impeccable white *thobe* (floor-length shirt-dress), *gutra* (white headdress) and long, black-tasselled *agal* (head rope); women by their narrow-eyed *yashmak* (veil).

The broadmindedness of an otherwise conservative nation stems not only from interaction with the thousands of immigrant workers who have helped build the country, but also from the fact that so many Qataris have travelled or studied abroad. Alas, that broadmindedness doesn't always translate into fair treatment of the immigrant population, many of whom continue to be treated as second-class citizens.

SPORT

Qatar is proving to be a capable and popular venue for a host of international sporting events, including top-level tennis and golf, and regionally important camel and horse races (p292).

In 2006 Qatar successfully staged the 15th Asian Games, with 45 nations participating in 423 events, a new marina, hotels and beaches, together with new infrastructure to support this enormous international event.

Like everyone else in the region, Qataris are football crazy and participate in many Asian tournaments.

RELIGION

Most Qataris, like the Saudi Arabians, adhere to the austere Wahhabi sect of Islam, which enjoins strict codes of conduct. As such, many outsiders are surprised to see women driving and working outside the home. Wahhabism does not preclude either activity. However, it does forbid any activity that may incite illicit relationships between men and women. In Qatar driving and working are not considered areas of likely temptation.

ARTS

Although the rapid modernisation of Qatar has encouraged a certain Westernisation of culture, some distinctive elements of traditional cultural expression remain, particularly in terms of music and dance, as evident during Eid al-Adha or Eid al-Fitr (p292) or social occasions, such as weddings. With its Bedouin inheritance, only a specialist is likely to pick up the nuances that distinguish Qatar's music or dance from that of other Gulf States, but numerous events throughout the country make Qatar one of the easier places to encounter these art forms. For example, from 5pm on Friday during summer (May to September), you can see dance troupes performing in Montazah Park (Map pp276–7), just south of central Doha, or in Al-Khor. Contact **Qatar Tourism Authority** (☎ 441 1555; www.qatar tourism.gov.qa, www.experienceqatar.com) or check local 'What's On' listings in the *Gulf Times* and the *Peninsula* for details.

Poetry & Dance

On National Day, 3 September, you may be lucky to see a troupe of male dancers performing Al-Ardha in a display of patriotic affection for the emir and the country at large. It's hard to know whether to call the performance a dance with words or a poem in motion, as during Al-Ardha, a poet chants celebrations of horsemanship and valour while threading a path between two opposing lines of dancers, each of whom echoes a verse of the poem while fluttering his sword in the air.

Another fascinating spectacle sometimes seen on National Day is Al-Qulta. Witnessing this kind of spontaneous poetry making is remarkable for those who understand Arabic, as two facing poets extemporise with great skill on a given topic. Even without knowing what is being said, the occasion is exciting as the poets are accompanied not by instruments but by syncopated *tasfiq* (the slapping of palm to palm), while the audience gets carried away with the rhythm of the poetry.

There is a long association between the Gulf countries and those of the east coast of Africa, and an interchange of culture is an inevitable bonus of trade. One dance that reflects East Africa's more relaxed integration of the sexes is Al-Lewa, performed by a mixture of men and women for pleasure.

At weddings it is a traditional mark of respect for young women, who are often daringly dressed in the absence of men in low-fronted, backless ball gowns, to dance for the bride. Today, the music is often imported from Egypt and is a sort of pan-Arabic pop, performed by men hidden behind a screen. If lucky enough to be invited to a wedding, the visitor (strictly women only) may be treated to Al-Khammary, performed by a group of masked women, or to Al-Sameri, a thrilling spectacle in which the dancers gyrate their loosened hair in time with the accelerating beat.

For more information, contact the **National Council for Culture, Arts & Heritage** (www .nccah.com).

Theatre

Traditional Qatari drama, sometimes performed at the Qatar National Theatre (p284) in Doha, centres on stories of love, betrayal and loyalty, in performances that generally include singing, dancing and colourful costumes. Even without knowledge of Arabic, these performances can be entertaining.

Crafts

The traditional Bedouin skill of weaving for carpets, tents, rugs and curtains was practised by modern Qataris until only about two decades ago, when machinery and cheap imports shut down the industry. Carpet wool, however, is still often prepared in the traditional way. The wool is washed and soaked in lemon juice and a crystalline mixture to remove impurities and oil, boiled for about 10 hours, dried in the sun and then dyed (often with imported dyes from India and other Gulf States). Goat hair is still used to make tents (particularly the black tents with white stripes, which are now seen more readily in the garden of a wealthy villa than in the interior). Camel hair, plaited using two hands, one foot and a strangely shaped piece of wood, is used for ropes and bags. A form of basket weaving, called *al-safaf*, using palm leaves and cane, is still practised in the villages.

Jewellery making is a craft that continues to thrive: while the traditional Bedouin pieces of silver and stone are now difficult to find, expert local goldsmiths and jewellers engage in centuries-old practices of sword decoration and bridal ornamentation. The *burda* (traditional Qatari cloak) is still worn in Qatar and the cuffs and sleeves are decorated by hand, using thin gold and silver threads.

ENVIRONMENT
The Land

One would expect the area of a country to be finite. Not so in Qatar, where extensive reclamation programmes keep adding a square kilometre or two to the total. The Qatar peninsula is generally given as 11,437 sq km, about 160km long and 55km to 80km wide, and includes 700km of shallow coastline. It includes one or two islands, but not the neighbouring Hawar Islands, which were a bone of contention until a recent settlement awarded the oil-rich islands to Bahrain. While Qatar is mostly flat, the oil-drilling area of Jebel Dukhan reaches a height of 75m.

The sand dunes to the south of the country, especially around the inland sea at Khor al-Adaid, are particularly appealing. Much of the interior, however, is marked by gravel-covered plains. This kind of desert may look completely featureless but it's worth a closer look: rain water collects in *duhlans* (crevices), giving rise intermittently to exquisite little flowering plants. Roses even bloom in the desert, though not of the floral kind: below the *sabkha* (salt flats that lie below sea level), gypsum forms into rosettes, some measuring eight to 10 inches across. Stone mushrooms and yardangs, weathered out of the limestone escarpment near Bir Zekreet, offer a geography lesson in desert landscape. Anyone with an interest in sharks' teeth, shale or any other aspect of Qatari wildlife, can contact **Qatar's Natural History Group** (☎ 493 1278; gillespi@qatar.net.qa), which usually runs a slide show on the first Wednesday, and a field trip on the last Friday, of every month.

Animals

The desert wolf, sand fox, hedgehog and sand hare are features, if rarely spotted ones, of the terrain. The hare, together with the three-toed jerboa and sand rat, all have hairy feet – on the underside – to enable them to move more easily in the soft sand. Altogether easier to spot, a rich and diverse number of birds (waders, ospreys, cormorants, curlews, flamingos, larks and hawks) frequent the coastal marshes and the offshore islands. Numerous winter visitors make bird-watching a treat, and local ornithologists have identified over 200 species. A golf course may seem an unlikely birding venue, but the lush oasis of Doha Golf Club occasionally attracts the glorious golden oriole and crested crane. The mangrove plantations north of Al-Khor are another good place to get the binoculars out.

ENDANGERED SPECIES

A passion for hunting, traditionally with falcon or *sluqi* (a Bedouin hunting dog), has marked Qatar's relationship with birds (particularly the tasty bustard) and mammals, with the double consequence that there is little wildlife left. The Qataris are the first to admit this and most eager to remedy the situation. Gazelle, oryx (Qatar's national animal) and Arabian ibex are all locally extinct, but ambitious breeding programmes aim to reintroduce the animals into the wild. A herd of oryx can be seen, by permit only or while on a tour, near Al-Shahaniya (p290). There are also protected areas, north of Al-Khor, for the endangered green turtle, which nests on the shore.

Plants

Other than dates, coconuts and the ubiquitous acacia (desert thorn tree), few trees grow in the wilds of Qatar. Despite this, there are quite a few species of plant on the gravel plains. A dusting of rain or dew in the colder months and a dried-up wadi (river bed) can be transformed into a hub of activity: the trumpets of *Lycium sharwii* and the orchidlike *Indigofera intricata* are two recently classified species that have surprised botanists.

ENDANGERED SPECIES

Qatar's mangrove wetlands, which provide a breeding ground for waders and crustaceans such as shrimps, are threatened by the multiple hazards of grazing camels, oil seepages and land reclamation. Various projects are afoot to protect this important coastal habitat, including the replanting of mangroves north of Al-Khor, but there are no official nature reserves as yet.

A SOBER DECISION

In a country that adheres to the rigorous Wahhabi sect of Islam, it may come as some surprise to discover that alcohol is now available in many top-end hotel bars. One may wonder what prompted the government, once so determined on the point, to relax the laws concerning alcohol.

A cynic might point to the increasing number of international sporting and commercial events being held in the country, for which the availability of a bar is a major consideration. But whether for pragmatic reasons or through tolerance, it is no longer unusual to see Qatari men in a bar, albeit refraining from drinking alcohol.

Environmental Issues

Qatar is now 2m higher than it was 400 years ago thanks to 'geological uplift', a phenomenon where movements in the earth's crust push the bedrock up. As a result, the underground water table sinks, or at least becomes more difficult to access. In Qatar, uplift has resulted over time in increasing aridity and sparseness of vegetation. This, combined with encroaching areas of sand and *sabkha*, has given environmentalists much to be concerned about.

FOOD & DRINK

Qatar's indigenous cuisine is very similar to that of other Gulf States (p82). From a felafel sandwich to a lobster thermidor, the visitor will be able to find a taste of whatever they fancy in one of Qatar's (or should we say, Doha's) cafeterias or restaurants.

Alcohol is now widely available in all top-end hotel restaurants and bars. Officially, alcohol is only available to hotel guests or 'members', but there seems to be some flexibility to this rule. Drinking alcohol in any place other than a bar is not permitted.

DOHA الدوحه

pop 370,700

It's rare to see a great city in the making these days. It would be misleading to represent Doha as a latter-day New York: much of the new development has been given a heart but hasn't yet acquired a soul. But that will come as more people flock to Doha, fascinated by the coverage it received during the Asian Games of 2006 and bringing with them the atmosphere that puts the 'city' into the buildings. Or should that be Buildings, with a capital 'B', for these new goliaths capture the intangible sense of growth and prosperity, optimism and vision you feel when walking around old souqs and new malls alike, or while watching Doha families strolling the grounds of the city's opulent resorts. 'Watch this space' might have been a good motto for Doha a few years ago; 'enjoy this space' is probably a better motto for today as the city begins to fill its own shoes, leaving plenty of gorgeous green spots to kick off your own.

HISTORY

With more than half of the population of Qatar residing in the capital, one would expect Doha to have an ancient and powerful history. On the contrary, the city was a small and inconsequential fishing and pearling village up until the mid-19th century, when the first Al-Thani emir, Sheikh Mohammed bin Thani, established his capital at Al-Bida, now the port area of town. From a notorious safe haven for Gulf pirates, it became the British administrative centre in 1916.

After the discovery of oil, and the export of related products from Umm Sa'id (modern-day Mesaieed) in 1949, the city grew rapidly but haphazardly. New administrative centres sprang up to manage the vast revenues, and an artificial, deepwater port was excavated in 1969 to handle transhipments of cargo from other Gulf States. Shrimp processing became one of the city's major industries, remaining so to this day.

In 1971 Doha became the capital of the independent state of Qatar and, thereafter, literally thousands of foreign nationals, employed in the construction and engineering industries, poured into the city. Cheap blocks of flats and Indian-managed shops spread into the surrounding shrub desert. The University of Qatar (1973) and Qatar National Museum (1975) brought education and culture to the city, and the shape of Doha changed, not just on account of its spread westwards, but also through the ambitious relandscaping of Doha Bay, carved from reclaimed land. Since then, Doha has seen the most extraordinary expansion in international banking, sporting and tourism activities, as evidenced by the many modern towers, malls, hotels and seats of power scattered throughout the city, and through huge developments like Pearl Qatar, a whole commercial, residential, tourist and leisure complex beyond the West Bay area.

One way to chart Doha's remarkable recent growth, physically, economically and internationally, is through its airport. Built to receive small commercial Twin Otter flights at the end of the 1950s, Doha's aerodrome was a secondary affair compared with the landing strips at the oilfields of Dukhan and Mesaieed. Today, with 65 aircraft landing daily, serving 25 major airlines (including the country's high-profile flagship, Qatar Airways) and able to cope with 7.5 million passengers a year, recently modernised Doha International Airport reflects the vibrant commercial and tourist activity that the city now attracts. Furthermore, a brand-new airport is in the pipeline for 2008. At an estimated cost of QR5 billion, Doha clearly has ambitions that extend well beyond the corniche.

ORIENTATION

From the visitor's point of view, the city centre is not in the centre of Doha at all – nor is it really a centre for that matter. The 8km corniche that marks the northern parameter of the city, ending at the Sheraton Doha Hotel & Resort, the prestigious Four Seasons Hotel and the diplomatic district, is undoubtedly the main focus of interest for the visitor. Most of the other sights, such as the National Museum, Museum of Islamic Art, Souq Waqif, Doha Fort and budget hotel district (near the Clock Tower and Grand Mosque), are close at hand (but not entirely within walking distance) between the coast and Ring Rd A. Roads are haphazardly signposted at best but the concentric ring roads (A to E) serve as useful landmarks. The West Bay area, which is still continually under construction, lies at the end of the corniche, to the northwest of the Sheraton Doha Hotel & Resort – with the InterContinental Doha and the Ritz-Carlton Doha and the forthcoming Pearl Qatar complex, it's a 10-minute drive outside town.

QATAR

GREATER DOHA

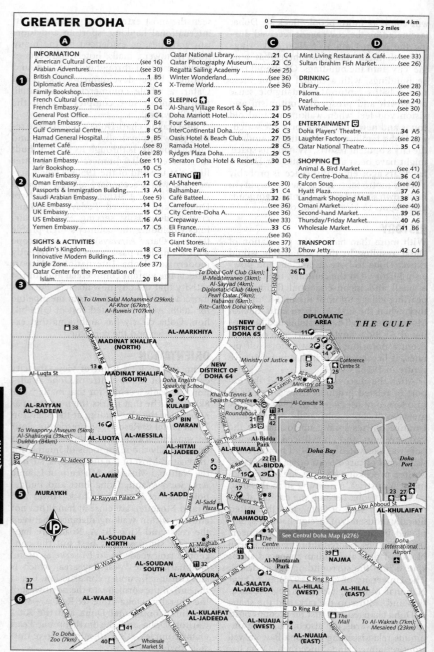

INFORMATION

American Cultural Center..................(see 16)
Arabian Adventures.........................(see 30)
British Council...**1** B5
Diplomatic Area (Embassies)...............**2** C4
Family Bookshop.................................**3** B5
French Cultural Centre........................**4** C6
French Embassy......................................**5** D4
General Post Office..............................**6** C4
German Embassy.....................................**7** B4
Gulf Commercial Centre.......................**8** C5
Hamad General Hospital.......................**9** B5
Internet Café...................................(see 8)
Internet Café.................................(see 28)
Iranian Embassy...............................(see 11)
Jarir Bookshop......................................**10** C5
Kuwaiti Embassy.................................**11** C3
Oman Embassy..**12** C6
Passports & Immigration Building..........**13** A4
Saudi Arabian Embassy.......................(see 5)
UAE Embassy..**14** D4
UK Embassy...**15** C5
US Embassy..**16** A4
Yemen Embassy.....................................**17** C5

SIGHTS & ACTIVITIES

Aladdin's Kingdom...............................**18** C3
Innovative Modern Buildings................**19** C4
Jungle Zone......................................(see 37)
Qatar Center for the Presentation of
  Islam...**20** B4

Qatar National Library.........................**21** C4
Qatar Photography Museum.................**22** C5
Regatta Sailing Academy.....................(see 25)
Winter Wonderland..............................(see 36)
X-Treme World......................................(see 36)

SLEEPING

Al-Sharq Village Resort & Spa............**23** D5
Doha Marriott Hotel.............................**24** D5
Four Seasons..**25** D4
InterContinental Doha..........................**26** C3
Oasis Hotel & Beach Club....................**27** D5
Ramada Hotel..**28** C5
Rydges Plaza Doha...............................**29** C5
Sheraton Doha Hotel & Resort............**30** D4

EATING

Al-Shaheen..(see 30)
Balhambar...**31** C4
Café Batteel...**32** B6
Carrefour...(see 36)
City Centre-Doha A............................(see 36)
Crepaway...(see 33)
Eli France..**33** C6
Eli France...(see 36)
Giant Stores...(see 37)
LeNôtre Paris......................................(see 33)

Mint Living Restaurant & Café.............(see 33)
Sultan Ibrahim Fish Market.................(see 26)

DRINKING

Library..(see 28)
Paloma...(see 26)
Pearl..(see 24)
Waterhole..(see 30)

ENTERTAINMENT

Doha Players' Theatre.........................**34** A5
Laughter Factory................................(see 28)
Qatar National Theatre.......................**35** C4

SHOPPING

Animal & Bird Market..........................(see 41)
City Centre-Doha..................................**36** C4
Falcon Souq...(see 40)
Hyatt Plaza..**37** A6
Landmark Shopping Mall......................**38** A3
Omani Market......................................(see 40)
Second-hand Market............................**39** D6
Thursday/Friday Market........................**40** A6
Wholesale Market.................................**41** B6

TRANSPORT

Dhow Jetty..**42** C4

QATAR

Maps

GEO Projects publishes two useful maps of Doha on the reverse of the *Qatar* map in its Arab World Map Library, available from car-rental offices, hotels and bookshops for QR30 to QR50.

INFORMATION
Bookshops

Family Bookshop (Map p274; ☎ 442 4148; fax 432 0828; Al-Mirghab St) A helpful store stocking a variety of books in English, including travel guides and a range of English literature. Other branches are inside the Sheraton Doha Hotel & Resort and at City Center (p286).

Jarir Bookshop (Map p274; ☎ 444 0212; Salwa Rd) A large selection of English-language books, including coffee-table books pertaining to the region, and a limited selection of best sellers.

Cultural Centres

The following represent some of the cultural centres in Doha:

American Cultural Center (Map p274; ☎ 488 4101, ext 4241; usisdoha@qatar.net.qa; 22nd February St, Al-Luqta) Located inside the US Embassy, the Cultural Center provides information on studying in the US and runs a library.

British Council (Map p274; ☎ 442 6193; www.british council.org; Al-Mirqab Al-Jadeed; ☒ 8am-8pm Sun-Fri, 8am-4pm Sat) The British Council runs a library, with a comprehensive video section, and gives guidance regarding studying in the UK. It also runs a number of English-language courses and testing services such as IELTS.

French Cultural Centre (Map p274; ☎ 493 0862; www .ccfdoha.com; Al-Muntazah St, Al-Nuaija East) This centre offers Arabic as well as French lessons.

Emergency

Fire, police & ambulance The number to call in an emergency is ☎ 999.

Internet Access

Internet access costs about QR20 per hour at the business centres of all the top-end hotels. There are also easy-to-use internet cafés in the City Center.

Internet Café (per hr QR7) Al-Bidda (Map p274; Abu Firas St); Gulf Commercial Centre (Map p274; Al-Khaleej St); Ramada Hotel (Map p274; Salwa Rd)

Medical Services

Hamad General Hospital (Map p274; ☎ 439 4444; www.hmc.org.qa; Al-Rumaila West) Subsidised medical and dental treatment is available for tourists on a walk-in basis.

Money

There are plenty of moneychangers just south of Doha Fort. ATMs are available throughout Doha.

Darwish Travel & Tourism (Map pp276-7; Al-Rayyan Rd) American Express (Amex) is available here.

Post

General Post Office (Map p274) Located in a large building off Al-Corniche near the Oryx roundabout.

Post Office (Map pp276-7; Abdullah bin Jasim St)

Telephone & Fax

Main Telecommunications Centre (Map pp276-7; Wadi Musheireb St; ☒ 24hr) Fax, telex and telegram services are available.

Tourist Information

There are no tourist information centres as such, but the **Qatar Tourism Authority** (☎ 441 1555/462 8555; www.experienceqatar.com, www.qatar tourism.gov.qa) provides good general information on its websites.

Local travel agencies are the best in-situ source of information regarding Doha (see p280 for a listing).

DANGERS & ANNOYANCES

Doha is one of the safest cities in the Middle East. Even women travelling on their own late in the evening are unlikely to feel threatened, providing they are dressed appropriately. The only danger worth commenting on is the speed and volume of traffic, which doesn't always obey the rules.

SIGHTS

Doha has an increasing number of sights to entertain and interest the visitor. Not all of the ones listed below are open yet to the public (see the boxed text, p279).

Al-Corniche

The highlight of Doha is unquestionably the corniche. Doha Bay was carefully constructed with landfill to make an attractive crescent, along which runs shaded footpaths and cycling tracks. One great way to gain an introduction to the city is to begin at the Ras Abu Abboud St Flyover at the southeastern end of the corniche and either walk or drive around to the Sheraton Doha hotel, looking out for the prominent landmarks. See the boxed text, p278 for details.

QATAR

CENTRAL DOHA

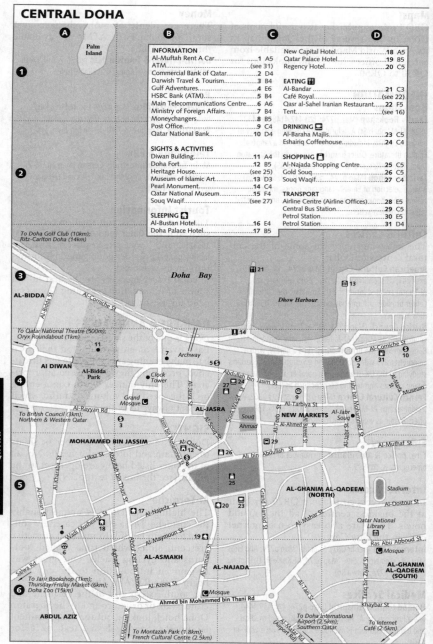

INFORMATION
Al-Muftah Rent A Car................................1 A5
ATM..(see 31)
Commercial Bank of Qatar.......................2 D4
Darwish Travel & Tourism.........................3 B4
Gulf Adventures...4 E6
HSBC Bank (ATM).......................................5 B4
Main Telecommunications Centre............6 A6
Ministry of Foreign Affairs.........................7 B4
Moneychangers..8 B5
Post Office..9 C4
Qatar National Bank................................10 D4

SIGHTS & ACTIVITIES
Diwan Building...11 A4
Doha Fort..12 B5
Heritage House...(see 25)
Museum of Islamic Art............................13 D3
Pearl Monument.......................................14 C4
Qatar National Museum...........................15 F4
Souq Waqif..(see 27)

SLEEPING
Al-Bustan Hotel..16 E4
Doha Palace Hotel....................................17 B5

New Capital Hotel....................................18 A5
Qatar Palace Hotel....................................19 B5
Regency Hotel...20 C5

EATING
Al-Bandar..21 C3
Café Royal...(see 22)
Qasr al-Sahel Iranian Restaurant.............22 F5
Tent...(see 16)

DRINKING
Al-Baraha Majlis..23 C5
Eshairiq Coffeehouse...............................24 C4

SHOPPING
Al-Najada Shopping Centre......................25 C5
Gold Souq...26 C5
Souq Waqif...27 C4

TRANSPORT
Airline Centre (Airline Offices).................28 E5
Central Bus Station...................................29 C5
Petrol Station..30 E5
Petrol Station..31 D4

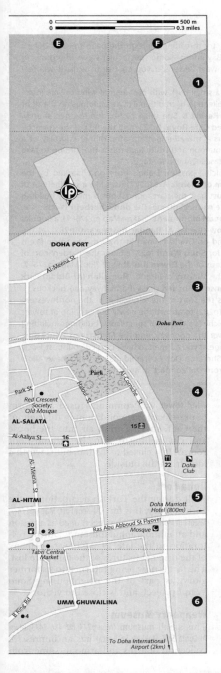

Qatar National Museum

In the last throes of a major overhaul by a top designer, it is anticipated that the **Qatar National Museum** (Map pp276-7; ☎ 444 2191; admission free; ☉ 8am-1pm & 4-7pm Sat-Thu), just off Al-Corniche, will open early in 2007. In the meantime it's possible to wander around the outer courtyard of the museum complex. Much of the museum is housed in the **Fariq Al-Salata Palace**, built in 1901 and used by Sheikh Abdullah bin Mohammed, Qatar's ruler from 1913 to 1949. The central building in the courtyard is particularly elegant. Rooms currently open to the public include exhibits of costumes, maps of Doha, antiques and jewellery, folk medicine and a traditional wedding room.

For information about the reopening of the museum, call the **National Council for Culture, Heritage & Arts** (☎ 466 8777).

Museum of Islamic Art

Rising from its own purpose-built island, this monumental **museum** (Map pp276-7; ☎ 444 2191; just off Al-Corniche), just off Al-Corniche, and designed by the renowned architect IM Pei, is shaped like a postmodern fortress, with minimal windows and a 'virtual' moat. With an avenue of palm trees extending along the approach road from the corniche, it makes a bold statement about a capital that has matured into one of the most culturally engaged cities in the region. Due to open with appropriate fanfare sometime in 2007, the museum will house the largest collection of Islamic art in the world. It will also include exhibition halls, a gallery, library and restaurant.

Souq Waqif

Currently enjoying the last phase of a major make-over, **Souq Waqif** (Map pp276-7), bounded by Al-Souq St and Grand Hamad St, is a wonderful place to explore. There has been a souq on this site for centuries, as this was the spot where the Bedouin would bring their sheep, goats and wool to trade for essentials. It grew into a scruffy warren of concrete alleyways in recent years but now its tourist potential has been recognised and it's been cleverly redeveloped to look like a 19th-century souq, with mud-rendered shops and exposed timber beams.

Despite the slight 'Disneyfication' of the area, the chief business of the souq continues

QATAR

A PROMENADE UNDER THE PALMS

If you want an encapsulation of Doha in a day, try threading through the palm trees of Doha's beautiful corniche. The 8km trip around Doha Bay affords some spectacular views of a growing city and invites plenty of rest-stops along the way. Beware, if you choose to walk, it will feel more like a hike across the Sahara in summer.

Begin at Ras Abu Abboud St Flyover, where a small park with ornamental wind towers introduces the 'heritage' zone of the corniche. The collection of traditional-style buildings on the right belongs to the new five-star **Al-Sharq Village Resort & Spa** (Map p274), due to open shortly. Breakfast is possible in the similarly wind-towered **Café Royal** (p283) and the first of the corniche roundabouts is denoted by rosewater sprinklers – the all-important after-dinner courtesy of a traditional Qatari feast. Marked by the national maroon and white flag, this is the turning to take for the **National Museum** (p277), which showcases Qatar's heritage.

Continue into the 'sea' section of the corniche, passing Doha's busy port marked by the monumental anchors on the shore. The **Museum of Islamic Art** (p277) rises like a sentinel out of the sea on the right (1.3km) while on the left, just past the port roundabout, a ministry building shaped like a ship's bridge (1.8km) continues the nautical theme. The **dhow harbour** is opposite, the entrance of which is marked by the famous **pearl monument** (2.3km; Map pp276–7), a popular spot for photos. Enjoy the sea view at the dhow-shaped **Al-Bandar Restaurant** (p282), at the end of a jetty full of lobster pots, or turn inland on Grand Hamad St towards the magnificent spiral-tapered building (Islamic Studies Centre) for **Souq Waqif** (p277). Enter the 'garden' part of the corniche, where water cascades down the steps of the **Diwan Building** (2.7km; Map pp276–7) and winter petunias decorate the approach to the Ministry of Interior. **Rumeilah (Al-Bidda) Park** (p280) is next on the left, offering a large expanse of shaded grass if a halfway nap beckons.

The honeycombed post office (5.1km) marks the start of the 'cityscape' at the northwestern end of the corniche. Have lunch at **Balhambar** (p282) to absorb the newly built skyline of towers across the bay. From here to the end of the corniche is a cluster of spectacular buildings including the **Ministry of Justice**, with a pair of scales over the doorway, and the **Ministry of Education**, featuring a mosque dome set in the glass frontage. If you happen to have packed your best frock, then dine at **Al-Shaheen** (p283) on top of the Sheraton Doha pyramid. Its stunning views allow you to retrace the route you've just travelled from the comfort of an armchair.

unabated and it remains one of the most traditional market places in Doha. This is the place to look for the national Qatari dress, including beautifully embroidered *bukhnoq* (girl's head covering), spices, perfumes and *oud*, an exotic incense made from agar wood. For a fun souvenir, take an empty glass jar and ask the spice traders to fill it with layers of colourful cumin, fenugreek, turmeric and ginger. If you get tired wandering round the antique shops or wondering what the newly built caravansary will be used for, then rest up at **Eshairiq Coffeehouse** (p284) with a mint tea and watch the world go by.

Heritage House

Formerly an ethnographic museum, this restored **Heritage Museum** (Map pp276-7; Al-Najada Shopping Centre courtyard), just off Grand Hamad St, was built in 1935 and offers the best view of the *badghir* (wind tower). The square

wind tower was commonly used as a form of pre-electric air-conditioning throughout the Gulf, sucking fresh air into the house and channelling it into the ground-floor rooms. It is closed to visitors but is worth a look from the outside.

Doha Fort

Built during the Turkish occupation in the 19th century, this **fort** (Al-Koot Fort; Map pp276-7; Jasim bin Mohammed St) has been used as a prison and an ethnographic museum. During restoration in the late 1970s, however, many of the original features of the fort were lost. The fort is now being returned to its former glory, as part of the neighbouring Souq Waqif project, and is closed to visitors.

Weaponry Museum

This small **museum** (Map p274; ☎ 486 7473; btwn Al-Luqta St & Makkah St, Luqta) has an impressive collection of arms and armour, some from the 16th century. However, what makes this museum worth a visit is the dazzling array of gold and silver swords and daggers, including a *khanjar* that belonged to Lawrence of Arabia. The museum is not generally open to the public, except by prior appointment or with a tour guide.

Doha Zoo

With more than 1500 animals from all over the world in a pleasant garden setting, this **zoo** (☎ 468 2610; Al-Furousiya St, Al-Rayyan; ☼ 8am-noon & 2.30-7.30pm Sat-Thu, 2.30-7.30pm Fri), opposite the Racing and Equestrian club, is one of the better zoos in the region. It also has a good display of local desert animals and birds, making it a worthwhile 'first stop' for those going on desert safari. It's best to ring first as opening times are erratic.

ACTIVITIES

For a chance to see the corniche from the sea, consider taking a **dhow ride** around Doha Bay. These local fishing boats leave from the jetty near Balhambar restaurant on the corniche between 8am and 4pm. A ride costs QR10/5 per adult/child. The dhows used to cruise over to Palm Tree Island, but this is currently under redevelopment. All the tour companies (p280) offer three- to four-hour evening dhow cruises with dinner, traditional music and entertainment for around QR275/200 per adult/child.

A popular pastime in Doha is **fishing**, either off the corniche or from the Dhow Jetty. Local fishermen use hand lines baited with cuttlefish or *khobz* (Arabic bread) made into a paste with water. More sophisticated fishing tackle can be bought from several outlets, including Carrefour in City Center-Doha (p286). All the big hotels or local tour companies (p280) can arrange fishing trips in the Gulf.

A sight to behold amid the surrounding barren desert, the gloriously green **Doha Golf Club** (☎ 483 2338; salespr@dohagolfclub.com; West Bay Lagoon) has an internationally recognised 18-hole course, which hosts the annual Qatar Masters in March. Open to nonmembers, it also has a flood-lit, nine-hole academy course for those in a hurry. The opulent, marble-rich clubhouse sports an excellent restaurant called Il Mediterraneo (reservations should be made through the golf club).

For those interested in stamps, the active **Qatar Philatelic and Numismatic Club** (☎ 432 3292; www.qatarstamps.com; Al-Sadd St) offers a café-style venue for enthusiasts, where the national stamp collection can be viewed and philatelic websites accessed.

COURSES

Thanks to the vibrant expatriate community in Doha, there are many courses available, from line dancing to karate, ice-skating and scuba diving. Anyone in town for a while and interested in any of these activities is advised to pick up a copy of *Marhaba, Qatar's Premier Information Guide* and consult its 'What to Do' section.

Language & Culture

Close to the Doha English Speaking School, **Qatar Centre for the Presentation of Islam** (Map p274; ☎ 441 1122; Medinat Khalifa South) runs free courses in Arabic language and culture. Classical Arabic classes are held in the mornings (two classes per week) and evenings (one class per week).

QATAR

WATCH THIS SPACE

In fact, you'll be doing more than watching the space at the **Qatar Photography Museum** (Map p274), when it puts in an appearance towards the end of 2007 – you'll be watching the walls as well. The design of this remarkable building is inspired by the camera lens, and the walls will be able to open and close to control the infiltration of light. This futuristic museum, with its flying stingray design, will be more than just a home to the government's impressive collection of photographs and photographic equipment – it will be a prominent landmark along the corniche.

Another bold new landmark to look out for along the corniche is the proposed **Qatar National Library** (Map p274). Designed by Arata Isozaki, the famous Japanese architect, it will include a natural history and science museum as well as providing shelf space for two million books. The library is due for completion in 2007, completing Doha's ambitious cultural expansion programme.

Arabic courses lasting three months are also offered by **Qatar Guest Centre** (☎ 486 1274; www.qatarguestcenter.com) and are of particular interest for those involved in Islam. The **University of Qatar** (☎ 485 2594; arabicprogram@qu.edu .qa) also runs a year-long course in Arabic.

Sailing

The **Regatta Sailing Academy** (Map p274; ☎ 550 7846; regatta@qatar.net.qa; Four Seasons Hotel Doha, Marina) offers a variety of sailing courses from beginner to advanced levels, including family weekend courses.

DOHA FOR CHILDREN

If you're travelling with children, there are several fun things to do around town.

Aladdin's Kingdom (Map p274; ☎ 483 1001; West Bay; ⏰ 4-10pm Mon-Sat), an outdoor entertainment park, has a roller coaster, dodgem cars and go-karts (for which you need a driving licence!). Some days are allocated for women or families only, so ring first – or do as the locals do, and listen for the screams. Admission is free but you pay a small fee for each ride.

Midway along the corniche, the unfenced **Rumeilah (Al-Bidda) Park** (Map p274) has some fun attractions for children, including a Ferris wheel, boats and the only train in Arabia since Lawrence (albeit a miniature one).

Winter Wonderland (Map p274; ☎ 483 1047; ⏰ 1-10pm Sat-Thu, 1-11pm Fri), located at City Center-Doha (p286), features an ice-skating rink, a 10-pin bowling alley and a water park. Also at City Center-Doha, on the top level, is **X-Treme World** (Map p274; ☎ 483 9501) – a whizz-bang collection of virtual rides, go-karts, merry-go-rounds and an indoor ski slope (with snow).

Housed in a shopping complex near Khalifa Stadium, **Jungle Zone** (Map p274; ☎ 469 4848; hyattplaza@qatar.net.qa; Hyatt Plaza; admission Thu-Sat QR45, Sun-Wed QR30; ⏰ 1-10pm Sun-Fri, 10am-10pm Sat) offers 3500 sq metres of animal-themed children's attractions.

TOURS

There are several excellent companies that organise tours around Doha, to the desert, camel farms and Khor al-Adaid. They are often able to arrange access to private museums, private zoos and other interesting sights that are not open to the independent traveller. They all offer similar sorts of packages, but some of the better ones include: **Alpha Tours** (☎ 434 4499; excursions@alphatoursqatar .com) Experienced in off-road excursions to the desert.

Arabian Adventures (Map p274; ☎ 436 1461; www .qatarvisits.com) Also has a desk at the Sheraton Doha Hotel & Resort. Tours cost from QR150/250 for half/full-day trips to QR375 for overnight desert safaris.

Gulf Adventures (Map pp276-7; ☎ 431 5555; www .gulf-adventures.com) Offers friendly and knowledgeable advice.

FESTIVALS & EVENTS

Doha has lost its reputation as one of the 'most boring places on the planet', with a huge variety of events and entertainment, largely held at the big hotels, and a lively expatriate scene. Check 'What's On' listings in the newspapers, and especially in *Marhaba, Qatar's Premier Information Guide* (published quarterly) for other events. For more information, see p292.

Without a doubt, the sports event of the decade for Qatar was the Asian Games held in December 2006. These games helped Qatar's already growing reputation as a venue for high-level international sporting events. Almost every month, you'll find some large sporting event on the city's calendar.

For a chance to meet the locals, consider attending one of the weekly horse races that occur throughout the season (October to May). Horses are in the hearts of most Qataris, and every Thursday races of purebred Arabian horses take place at the **Racing & Equestrian Club** (☎ 480 5901; www.qrec.net.qa; Al-Furousiya St, Al-Rayyan; admission free) between 4pm and 7.30pm.

SLEEPING

There is some excellent accommodation in Doha, particularly at top-end resorts, which offer wonderful views and beach locations, especially in the West Bay area. Cheaper accommodation is conveniently located near Souq Waqif, although none of the options are very cheap. In fact, prices for all hotel rooms have doubled or even tripled over the past three years, stripping Doha of its reputation for five-star accommodation at four-star prices.

All rooms at the hotels listed below have air-conditioning, a TV (normally satellite), fridge and bathroom (with hot water) but do not include breakfast unless stated.

QATAR

Budget

As in other parts of the Gulf, most budget hotels are not suitable for, nor will they accept, solo women travellers. The hotels listed below are the exceptions to this rule.

New Capital Hotel (Map pp276–7; ☎ 444 5445; capitalhotel@gmail.com; Wadi Musheireb St; s/d QR350/400; 🏊) Despite boasting a swimming pool, free breakfast and a central location, this dated hotel has been left behind by its neighbours – but fortunately the same can be said of the room rates. The 1970s rooms are basic but clean, just don't look too carefully at the balconies where the pigeons have taken up permanent residence – this place isn't too hot on housekeeping.

Regency Hotel (Map pp276–7; ☎ 436 3363; www .hotel-regency.com; 101 Al-Asmakh St; s/d QR430/520) Within walking distance of Souq Waqif, this smart, central hotel, with its Arabic-style foyer and restaurant, represents excellent value for money. The rooms are small but plush and the staff unfailingly courteous and helpful, arranging tours and transport on request. All in all, the hotel helps businesspeople on small expense accounts feel they are as valued as the big spenders.

Qatar Palace Hotel (Map pp276–7; ☎ 442 1515; www.qatarpal.com.qa; 44 Al-Asmakh St; s/d QR433/527) If you are looking for a cheerful, bright and comfortable hotel in a central position, the new Qatar Palace Hotel is a good option. The commodious rooms in pastel shades with large sofas are homely and comfortable, and the marble bathrooms are spotless. With an efficient front desk, this no-nonsense hotel is particularly suited to businesspeople or those coming to attend a sporting meet.

Midrange

Doha Palace Hotel (Map pp276–7; ☎ 436 0101; dpalace@qatar.net.qa; Wadi Musheireb St; s/d QR500/600) Positioned on one of the busiest roads in the centre of Doha, this hotel, with its pink plaster and marble foyer, has recently undergone a thorough refurbishment that makes it worth donning earplugs for. Each room has a balcony with frilly net curtains and small but adequate bathrooms. Despite the chintz, the hotel caters mainly for Indian businessmen and offers efficient service, including free breakfast and airport transfers.

Oasis Hotel & Beach Club (Map p274; ☎ 442 4424; oasis@oasishotel-doha.com; Ras Abu Abboud St; s/d QR600/900; 🏊) If it wasn't so perversely loved, it would be hard to recommend this expensive, thoroughly dated battle horse of a hotel. But the fact remains, it's a travel favourite. Perhaps it's the leatherette reception desk, or the gold lamé lift doors, the Soviet-style concrete cladding or the chintz sofas. It can't be the rooms, which smell of garlic and smoke. The hotel does have a good bay-side position, however, and a convivial atmosphere and, if it delays renovation for much longer, will be listed as a period piece.

Al-Bustan Hotel (Map pp276–7; ☎ 432 8888; albustanhotel@qatar.net.qa; Al-Muthaf St; s/d QR702/819) Only a short walk from the National Museum, this small and very popular boutique-style hotel, with its potted bonsai, primary-coloured seating and Islamic-patterned flooring in the foyer, is often fully booked. The rooms, which open onto smart, black-marble corridors with red-framed pictures, are huge and the bathrooms have the dubious distinction of frilly shower curtains.

Rydges Plaza Doha (Map p274; ☎ 438 5444; reservations_doha@rydges.com; Abu Firas St, Al-Bidda; r QR936; 🏊) This is a competent and luxurious business-oriented hotel in central Doha, a 10-minute walk from the corniche. The narrow, central atrium extending the full height of the tower block is rather oppressive and the service geared exclusively towards business clientele. Nonetheless, cresting the only 'hill' in Doha, the rooms command fine city and sea views, and the Aussie Legends Bar attracts a lively expat clientele.

Top End

Prices quoted here are rack rates. Discounts and special deals can often be negotiated, especially during summer. Many new hotels are in the pipeline, so check the media for special 'soft opening' packages, offering half-price tariffs while the staff learn the ropes.

HOTELS

Doha Marriott Hotel (Map p274; ☎ 429 8888; marriott@qatar.net.qa; Ras Abu Abboud St; r QR1135; 🏊) Situated near Doha Bay and the southeastern end of the corniche, this hotel is ideal

QATAR

for the airport. Don't let the ugly concrete exterior put you off: the interior has been royally redeveloped with a large central rotunda and conservatory. Some rooms have balconies overlooking the sea and there is a large selection of restaurants and amenities, although the pool is overshadowed by the blue-glass windows of the hotel's new tower block.

ourpick **Sheraton Doha Hotel & Resort** (Map p274; ☎ 485 4444; www.sheraton.com/doha; Al-Corniche; s/d QR1350/1460; ☒) The Sheraton Doha is more than a place to stay: it's an institution. The oldest of Doha's five-star hotels, it still boasts one of the best locations and wonderful views from attractive, split-level rooms with balconies. Rates include breakfast delivered to the room in silver salvers. With the excellent top-floor restaurant Al-Shaheen (opposite), belly dancing and a lively bar, a fascinating turnover of international sports and business personalities, and a friendly staff, this resort is near the city and its souqs, and the new lagoon area.

Four Seasons (Map p274; ☎ 294 8888; www .fourseasons.com; Diplomatic District; r QR1640; ☒) This world-class hotel occupies one of a set of matching new tower blocks, just beyond the corniche in the Diplomatic District. With its 'happening' location, its own small patch of beach with traditional watchtower, and a marina, it's giving the Ritz-Carlton a run for its money as the city's most exclusive hotel. It has a magnificent interior design and a less intimidating atmosphere than other prestigious venues. The service is friendly but, as with all new hotels, taking time to live up to the room rates.

RESORTS

Ritz-Carlton Doha (Map p274; ☎ 484 8000; www .ritzcarlton.com; West Bay Lagoon; r QR1290; ☒) No expense has been spared to ensure that this is Doha's most opulent and exclusive hotel. This is no place to come in jeans and a t-shirt: the black and white marble in the foyer, the silver service high tea with piano concert, the towels folded into a swan in the topiaried garden, are details that require a similar commitment to style and expense on the part of the guest. The resort is a fair way out of town with a splendid spa, but sadly, with the neighbouring development of the Pearl Qatar complex, the private beach and marina is not quite the haven it once was.

InterContinental Doha (Map p274; ☎ 484 444; www.intercontinental.com; West Bay Lagoon; r QR1500; ☒) Benefiting from the slightly compromised position of the Ritz-Carlton, this genteel and luxury hotel is thriving. InterCon hotels have an excellent reputation for the 'common touch' – making its establishments popular with a wide range of people (through high-quality facilities and best-in-town entertainment) without being snooty. This resort, with its attractive beach area and lively bars, is no exception and is a great choice for a family getaway.

EATING

If you're a serious foodie, make sure you pick up a copy of *Posh Nosh, Cheap Eats and Star Bars*, by Explorer Publishing, before selecting where to eat. There are literally dozens of excellent choices. The selection below offers Middle Eastern cuisine to fit a range of budgets.

Restaurants

Tent (Map pp276-7; Al-Bustan Hotel, Al-Muthaf St; mains QR60; ☒ 6pm-1am) Located under a Bedouin–style tent, this highly popular restaurant is a relaxed place to try delicious Arabic fare or a puff of *sheesha* (water pipe used to smoke tobacco; QR25) in a traditional, carpet and sedan-style setting. The waiters are accustomed to helping nonArabic people find their way around a Middle Eastern menu of *mezze* (small preparatory dishes).

ourpick **Al-Bandar** (Map pp276-7; ☎ 431 1818; www.albandarrestaurant.com; Al-Corniche; mains QR70; ☒ 1-11.45pm) On a balmy evening in the cooler months, there can't be anywhere much more pleasant than to enjoy the breeze than in the collection of restaurants at the end of the dhow jetty. Eccentrically shaped like dhows, with split-level wooden flooring and a garden of potted trees around the terrace, it's always brimful with local families. Try the whole hamour wrapped in banana leaf (QR65) or the barracuda and chef's spices (QR55) for a taste of deeper waters.

Balhambar (Map p274; ☎ 483 7807; Al-Corniche; meals QR90; ☒ 8am-11.30pm) For an authentic taste of Qatar, this elegant, gypsum-walled seafront restaurant serving traditional Qatari food is highly recommended. The turtle shell and swordfish hanging in the porch give an idea of the bygone cuisine, but there's nothing to lament in the *ghuzi* – a whole roasted lamb with rice, pine nuts and *harees*.

Al-Shaheen (Map p274; ☎ 485 4444; Sheraton Doha Hotel & Resort, Al-Corniche; mains QR130; ☼ 7pm-midnight) Boasting great views of the city and the sea, this rather chaotic restaurant with its bedevilling Arabic music is nevertheless a local favourite. Apart from its nightly à la carte menu, it also offers Friday brunch (from 8am to 3pm) for QR85.

Housed in the Ras Al-Nasaa, an extraordinary red-and-white brick complex on the southern end of Al-Corniche, **Qasr Al-Sahel Iranian Restaurant** (Map pp276-7; ☎ 441 1177; Ras Al-Nasaa, Al-Corniche; mains QR60; ☼ noon-late) serves tasty and reasonably priced kebabs and hotpots. With a pontoon on the bay, this is a pleasant place to enjoy supper with views of the harbour and occasionally live Arabic music. The adjoining **Café Royal** (Map pp276-7; ☎ 436 7036; ☼ 6pm-late) is a comfortable resting point for unaccompanied women.

A short way out of town are two places to enjoy excellent seafood. **Al-Sayyad** (Map p274; ☎ 484 7444; www.thediplomaticclub.com; Diplomatic Club, West Bay; mains QR50; ☼ 12.30-3pm & 7.30pm-midnight) is worth visiting just for a walk through the jewel-like Diplomatic Club, with its inlaid strawberry-coloured carpets. Decorated with nets and baskets, the restaurant catches the best of the sea breeze. Try the Sultan Ibrahim (QR45) for local flavour. Alternatively, visit the **Sultan Ibrahim Fish Market** (Map p274; ☎ 484 4444; www.ichotelsgroup.com; InterContinental Hotel; mains QR90; ☼ 7pm-midnight Sun-Fri) and pick the fish you fancy from the display. With a resident belly dancer and skipping lanterns, count on an evening of entertainment as well as an excellent supper.

Cafés

Café Batteel (Map p274; ☎ 444 1414; Salwa Rd, Al-Maamoura; snacks QR20; ☼ 8am-11.30pm) With a range of delicious freshly baked pastries, home-made ice creams and sorbets, and some innovative sandwiches, this café, set in a traditional Qatari house with Arabic cushions and *barasti* (palm leaf) ceilings, is a firm favourite with residents.

Mint Living Restaurant & Café (Map p274; ☎ 467 5577; Salwa Rd, Al-Muthana; mains QR20; ☼ 8am-midnight) If you've reached the limit of your fascination for Middle Eastern food, one

international-style venue that is worth singling out for a mention is the Mint. With Ron Arad furniture and other top artists featured in the interior design, this is an ultrahip location for a coffee and exotic sandwich, or for the full fusion experience.

LeNôtre Paris (Map p274; ☎ 455 2111; Al-Emadi Centre, Ramada Junction; desserts QR50; ☼ 8am-1am) Think chrome and blue-glass in this hip coffee shop that attracts busy professionals and be-seen sushi-eaters alike. If chocolate is your thing, there's plenty of wickedness in the designer desserts.

Quick Eats

Crepaway (Map p274; ☎ 465 5830; www.crepaway.com; Al-Mouthanna Complex, Salwa Rd; crepes from QR40) This hip diner, with its scarlet walls and strips of Lichtenstein pop art, is a fun place for a snack. With a live DJ, jukebox and occasional karaoke, it's little wonder it attracts such a crowd.

City Center-Doha (Map p274; ☎ 483 0582; Diplomatic District; ☼ 10am-10pm Sat-Thu, 1-10pm Fri) The food halls in this shopping complex include all the usual Western fast-food outlets in opulent surroundings.

Alternatively, try the string of restaurants at the intersection of C Ring and Salwa Rds, opposite the Ramada Hotel.

Self-Catering

One of the best bakeries in town, **Eli France** (Map p274; ☎ 435 7222; Salwa Rd; ☼ 8am-11.30pm) is next to the Ramada Junction on Salwa Rd; it also has a branch in the City Center-Doha.

There are dozens of grocery stores and supermarkets dotted around town. **Carrefour** (Map p274; ☎ 484 6265) in City Center-Doha has a very good fresh fish and vegetable counter. For a cheaper variety of edible goods, try **Giant Stores** (Map p274; ☎ 469 2991) in the Hyatt Plaza.

DRINKING
Bars

Hotel bars are generally only open to guests and 'members' (who pay a 'membership' of about QR100 per year). These rules, however, are continually relaxing and even Qataris can now be seen in some of these establishments (once strictly forbidden).

Some of the more popular bars include: the **Library** (Map p274; ☎ 441 7417; Ramada Hotel;

QATAR

⏱ 6pm-1am); the cigar and fine wine lounge, **Habanos** (Map p274; Ritz-Carlton Doha; ⏱ 6pm-late); the cocktail bar, **Pearl** (Map p274; Doha Marriott Hotel; ⏱ 4.30pm-late, happy hour until 8.30pm); and the bar and disco, **Waterhole** (Map p274; Sheraton Doha Hotel & Resort; ⏱ 6pm-1am). One of the most lively bars in town is the **Paloma** (Map p274; InterContinental Doha; ⏱ 6pm-late), which often has live music and doubles as a Tex-Mex restaurant.

Coffeehouses

The private *majlis* (meeting room) is popular around town, where men congregate over tea or coffee for a chat, or to share news or watch TV together. Try the following:

Al-Baraha Majlis (Map pp276-7; Al-Najada St) Opposite Al-Najada Shopping Centre, there is nothing to stop a male visitor sitting on a divan on the pavement or pulling up a chair in front of the TV inside this simple coffeehouse and smoking a *sheesha* with the locals. Women may not receive quite the same reception.

Eshairiq Coffeehouse (Map pp276-7; ☎ 537 9997; Souq Waqif) On the eastern (sea-facing) edge of the souq, this traditional rooftop coffeehouse is welcoming of all-comers. Stretched on a divan under the stars, sipping mint tea and listening to the muezzin call prayers at dusk while the city lights sparkle into life, is the quintessential Arabic experience.

ENTERTAINMENT

With the burgeoning number of luxury hotels in Qatar, there is plenty of entertainment on offer. Jazz evenings, live entertainment and international food promotions are on frequently. Check the 'What's On' listings in *Marhaba, Qatar's Premier Information Guide* and the English-language newspapers for anything from line dancing at the rugby club to cookery classes at the Ritz-Carlton Doha.

Cinemas & Theatre

The best cinemas are in **City Center-Doha** (Map p274; ☎ 483 0582; Diplomatic District), the **Mall** (Map p274; ☎ 467 8666; cnr D Ring Rd & Najma St) and the **Landmark Shopping Mall** (Map p274; ☎ 488 1674; cnr Al-Shamal N Rd & Al-Markhiya St) shopping complexes. They show the latest Hollywood blockbusters and the occasional film from Iran or Europe. Tickets cost about QR15. For current information on cinemas in Qatar, visit http://movies.theemiratesnetwork.com.

Qatar National Theatre (Map p274; ☎ 483 1250; Al-Corniche) Housed in an impressive building, it infrequently features Arabic plays.

Doha Players (Map p274; ☎ 487 1196; www.dohaplayers.com) In existence for 50 years, Doha Players continues to stage productions, undeterred by the suicide attack of 2005 (p267). It is trying to raise funds to rebuild its own theatre.

The Laughter Factory (Map p274; ☎ 441 7417; www.thelaughterfactory.com; Ramada Hotel, Salwa Rd; tickets QR75) Organises monthly tours of professional comics in conjunction with the Comedy Store from London. Tickets sell like hot cakes.

SHOPPING

Doha is full of wonderful shopping opportunities, and you can buy anything from a camel to a racing car, an Armani suit to a sequined *abeyya* (woman's full-length black robe), and a fishing rod to a peregrine falcon. While there aren't many locally produced crafts, half the fun of shopping in Doha is ambling through the souqs or brand-new shopping malls, stumbling over things you couldn't imagine people would want to buy and then buying one anyway, like a house for the garden birds (complete with letter box), or a dyed-pink hair extension made of ostrich feathers – the possibilities are endless.

Souqs

One of the joys of shopping in Doha's traditional souqs is that the shopkeepers take the time to chat with their customers, whether buying or not, making shopping one of the best ways to engage with the locals. Despite a bit of push and shove when it's crowded, all the souqs are safe places to visit and bargaining is expected. The souqs are open from around 9am to 1pm and 4pm to 8pm Saturday to Thursday, and 4pm to 8pm on Friday.

Falcon Souq (Map p274; B31/32, Thursday/Friday Market) This souq (next to Al-Wadi Gents Saloon) has recently dwindled to a single shop in a corner of the larger Thursday/Friday Market, just off the Salwa Rd roundabout at the junction of Wholesale Market St. It is, nonetheless, worth a visit just to see the kind of paraphernalia involved in falconry.

FLYING THE FALCON

There is something deeply unsettling about entering the falcon shop in a corner of the Thursday/Friday Market: 20 birds, some hooded in black leather, others watching intelligently with wary eyes, perch on the open railing at a hand's distance, waiting like Rottweilers to be taken home, fed less than a square meal and put straight to work. They may sit immovable and unimpressed as the shopkeeper tosses a slab of meat into the sawdust, but there is nothing placid about the 'don't-diss-me-man' raptor: these are mean machines, bred and trained for the kill.

Falconry is an ancient art that dates at least from the 7th century BC. The first falconer, according to Arabic tradition, was a violent king of Persia who was so entranced by the grace and beauty of a falcon taking a bird on the wing, that he had it captured so he could learn from it. What he learnt, according to legend, changed him into a calm and wise ruler.

It is no easy task to train birds of prey. Bedouins, the falconers par excellence, traditionally net their falcons (usually saker or peregrine) during their migration, using pigeons as bait. They train the birds through complex schedules of sleep deprivation and sparse feeding, retain them for as long as it takes to harvest fresh meat, and then set them free again at the onset of summer.

It is estimated that 2000 falcons are still employed on the Arabian Peninsula each year. Today, birds are more usually bred and 'imprinted' from hatchlings to create a bond that lasts a lifetime. Sporting achievement is measured not through the number of quarry caught but in the skill of the catch – and in the wisdom of leaving enough prey for tomorrow.

Equipment, such as *burkha* (hoods) and *hubara* (feathers), is on sale. During falcon season (October to March), you might also see a dozen or more peregrines and other assorted falcons. A truculent falcon costs about QR2000, but a well-mannered bird can be many times that figure and usually changes hands privately. The shop owner is quite happy to show off the birds to anyone who shows some interest. See also the boxed text, above.

Omani market (Map p274; Wholesale Market St) This small market, near the Thursday/Friday Market, offers a curious mishmash of items, such as Saudi dates and hand-woven baskets, Omani dried fish, tobacco and lemons, Iranian honey and pots, camel sticks and incense, and fronds of pollen-baring date flowers (to fertilise the female date palms). Buying anything here renders the satisfaction of taking part in a trade that has existed between Oman and the Gulf for centuries.

Animal & Bird Market (Map p274; Salwa Rd) Located behind the colourful Wholesale Market (selling wholesale fruit, vegetables, meat and fish), this market may be of interest to anyone who hasn't seen pink, yellow and lime green chicks before. Why the birds are dyed is a mystery of the region. Fortunately, they leave the spotted guinea fowl, ring-necked parakeets, African greys and cut-throat zebra finches untinged – possibly because the plumage of the rows and rows of domestic birds is outrageous enough already. The day before an *eid* (Islamic feast; see p292), the market is heaving with goat-buyers, camel-traders and sheep-shoppers, all looking for a suitable *eid* supper, but the animals are well shaded and watered, and respect for the livestock is shown by much inspection of teeth and smoothing of coats. It's worth visiting the market just for the sideshows: cockerels unbagged in a flourish, children tugging at rabbit ears, hooded peregrines balancing on a white-*thobed* arm and women in black picking their way through the mayhem of one of the great bazaars of modern times – repeated in similar scenes from Yemen to Kuwait.

Gold Souq (Map pp276-7; off Ali bin Abdullah St) This pageant of glorious design and spectacular craftsmanship is fun to see even without the intention to buy. The souq comes alive later in the evening, especially before a holiday, when men traditionally express the value of their relationships through buying 22kt gold bangles, or a 'set' comprised of earrings, necklace and bracelet for the women in their family. Qatari bridal jewellery can cost thousands, but sometimes pieces can be traded back after the wedding for something more readily usable, or even just for cash.

Second-hand Market (Souq al Haraj; Map p274; off Al-Mansoura St) If you're looking for something

QATAR

quirky, the best place to visit is this market in Doha's Najma area. It's a great place to find that teapot from the British administration, minus the spout no doubt, or the date palm saw that you always wanted. The souq comes alive on Friday, when sales are conducted briskly from the back of trucks.

Malls

There is a kind of subversion of expectation inside the great shopping malls of the Gulf. They appear to be even more opulent versions of American malls, complete with themed entertainment and Starbucks, but then you'll find an *abeyya* shop selling women's cloaks or a prayer bead counter next to a waffle stand that confirms that you are, indeed, shopping in the Middle East.

City Center-Doha (Map p274; ☎ 483 0582; info@citycenterdoha.com; Diplomatic District; ⏰ 10am-10pm Sat-Thu, 2-10pm Fri) The largest of the Middle East's shopping palaces is a veritable pantheon of the shopping world. With its 350 shops, from Debenhams to the Family Development Centre (top floor, selling local crafts); tented architecture, marble flooring and glass-fronted lifts; its ice-skating rink, bowling alleys and climbing walls; its congregations of juice-sipping Qataris and huddles of homesick expatriates; and trolleys laden with eggs, packets of *khobz* and Egyptian olives, it's more an event than an errand.

Landmark Shopping Mall (Map p274; ☎ 487 5222; cnr Al-Shamal N Rd & Al-Markhiya St; ⏰ 9am-10pm Sat-Thu, 3-10pm Fri) If you can't find what you're looking for in City Center-Doha, try this enormous shopping centre, with a multiplex cinema, Marks & Spencer's department store and Virgin Megastore, as well as dozens of other international chain stores.

Hyatt Plaza (Map p274; ☎ 469 4848; Al-Waab St; ⏰ 10am-10pm Sat-Thu, 2-10pm Fri) Located alongside the Khalifa Sports Stadium, this is yet another recent addition to the mall phenomenon.

GETTING THERE & AWAY

Qatar's only public airport is **Doha International Airport** (☎ 465 6666; fax 462 2044). It has offices for **Qatar Airways** (☎ 449 6666), the country's main airline, and **Gulf Air** (☎ 445 5444). Many airlines have offices in the **Airline Centre** (Map pp276-7; Ras Abu Abboud St) and

Al-Saad Plaza (Map p274; C Ring Rd), south of the city centre.

GETTING AROUND
To/From the Airport

Most top-end hotels and resorts provide free transport to/from the airport. An orange and white taxi between the airport and central Doha costs about QR25. The blue taxis use a meter but charge a surcharge from the airport.

Car

A public transport system is being developed, but in the meantime hiring a car (p297) is the best option for getting around. There are a string of car-rental companies in the arrivals area of the airport.

Driving in Doha is easy enough if you watch out for impatient drivers overtaking on both the left and right, and honking the horn at roundabouts. Parking, except in the souq areas, is not a problem: all hotels and large malls have car parks or parking services, and there is plenty of waste ground in the centre of Doha where you can park your car. A lack of street signs can make navigation difficult.

Taxi

Most people get around Doha by taxi, but these are insufficient to meet growing demand. This means that you may have to wait over half an hour to find an empty one. There are two types of taxi: the newer sea-blue cars run by **Mowasalat Karwa** (☎ 458 8888) costing QR3 plus QR1 per kilometre, and the older orange taxis. The latter seldom bother with air-con and you'll have to persuade the driver to use the meter.

AROUND QATAR

While Qatar isn't exactly blessed with sights and activities outside the capital of Doha, it does have several attractions that justify the cost of hiring a vehicle for a day or two, including a few coastal villages where life still revolves around fishing and the local mosque.

The land is arid in the extreme but that is not to say it is featureless: there are some beautiful beaches, interesting wind-eroded escarpments and large areas of sand dune.

The country's biggest natural attraction is undoubtedly Khor al-Adaid, a salt-water inlet in the south surrounded by a magical landscape of sand and salt. Camping here or at Bir Zekreet is a reminder of the achievement of the Qataris (which they have in common with their Gulf neighbours) in fashioning a complex modern state out of very limited assets.

AL-WAKRAH & AL-WUKAIR
الوكرة و الوكير

pop 34,700

The old pearling villages of Al-Wakrah and Al-Wukair are rapidly stringing out to meet the Doha suburbs. They make a pleasant afternoon outing from the capital, however, and there are several interesting old **mosques** and **traditional houses** in and around the gracious modern villas. Al-Wakrah also has a small **museum** (9am-1pm & 4-7pm) next to the buoy roundabout by the dhow harbour, featuring natural and nautical history.

The **beaches** south of Al-Wakrah offer glorious stretches of sand, interspersed with the odd *khor* (creek). The shallow water makes paddling a better option than swimming. At least the determined wader is in good company: flocks of **flamingos** roost along the coast between Al-Wakrah and Mesaieed during winter, and groups of six or seven flamingos are a familiar sight, sieving the water with their beaks, or with neck and one leg tucked up, taking a nap. **Fishing** is a popular pastime in the area, as the limestone shallows act as fish traps when the tide goes out.

Both Al-Wakrah and Al-Wukair are an easy 15-minute drive by car from Doha, following Al-Matar Rd past the airport and heading south.

MESAIEED
أم سعيد

pop 14,800

Mesaieed (formerly known as Umm Said) is an industrialised town about 45km south of Doha, but although it's not particularly attractive in itself, the nearby **beaches** with deep water make for some of the best swimming in Qatar.

Sealine Beach Resort (☎ 476 5299; sbr@qatar.net .qa; s/d with breakfast QR800/880; 🏊) is a lovely, understated, low-rise resort built on a beach just south of Mesaieed. It's far enough away from the industrial area to be unaffected by

the heavy industry, and the ring of glorious amber sand dunes doubles the resort's entertainment opportunities. The beach shelves quite steeply, allowing for good swimming, and desert quad bikes can be hired from the resort to explore the local dunes, known as the 'singing sands'. The latter are particularly beautiful at sunset, although purists may be disappointed by the myriad of bike tracks that spoil the dunes' pristine curves. Day visitors are welcome to use the hotel facilities, including pools and the beach; camel and horse rides are available (QR100 per hour); and there is a clown to entertain the children, as well as activities, like face painting. Admission costs QR50 from Thursday to Saturday and QR30 from Sunday to Wednesday.

To reach Mesaieed from Doha, follow the road past the airport and through Al-Wakrah. A shuttle bus service operates to/from Doha, which is free to hotel guests.

KHOR AL-ADAID
خور العديد

Without a doubt, the major natural attraction in Qatar is the beautiful 'inland sea' of Khor al-Adaid, near the border with Saudi Arabia. Often described as a sea or a lake, the *khor* is in fact neither: rather it is a creek surrounded by silvery crescents of sand (known as *barchan*). All sand dunes look wonderful in the late afternoon sun, but those of Khor al-Adaid take on an almost mystical quality under a full moon when the *sabkha* sparkle in the gaps between the sand.

While a night under the stars on a camping expedition is a special experience in the right company, not everyone goes to the area to enjoy the tranquillity. Sand skiing, quad-bike and 4WD racing compete with the time-honoured picnic and a song, much to the consternation of some and the pleasure of others. The area is big enough, thankfully, to satisfy both, although environmental concerns are being expressed as more and more travel agencies make the area the central attraction of their tours.

This region is *only* accessible by 4WD, and independent travellers should accompany someone who knows the area and really can drive a 4WD. Being stuck in the sand is no fun after the first hour and in summer is very dangerous. If determined to do it yourself, make sure you have at least a box of water on board for each passenger, a map and compass,

QATAR

very clear directions of the best route currently navigable, a tow rope and a shovel. If you get stuck don't dig: let out the air in the tyres and return to the nearest petrol station immediately to reinflate.

Going on an organised tour (p280) is probably the safest way to see Khor al-Adaid; overnight tours often include folkloric entertainment and a barbecue, as well as camping equipment. Rates vary but a six- to seven-hour day excursion usually costs around QR350/250 per adult/child or QR425/300 for an overnight trip.

UMM SALAL MOHAMMED   ام صلال محمد
pop 37,300

There are several old buildings dating from the 19th and early 20th century dotted around this small, modern residential district. The ruined **Umm Salal Mohammed Fort** (admission free; ☼ 8am-1pm & 4-7pm) was built for military and civil use. Neighbouring **Barzan Tower** is possibly more interesting as the triple-decker, T-shaped construction is unique in the Gulf; however, this white-washed building was closed to the public at the time of research and is unlikely to reopen any time soon.

Umm Salal Mohammed is about 22km north of Doha, just west of the main highway to Al-Ruweis. It's impossible to give directions to the fort or tower as there are no street signs, but it's easy enough to stumble across both as they are visible above the surrounding houses.

UMM SALAL ALI   أم صلال علي
A small field of **grave mounds**, probably dating from the 3rd millennium BC, is worth a visit in Umm Salal Ali if you're visiting nearby Umm Salal Mohammed, especially if you have a guide. If not, look for rounded bumps in otherwise flat land just north of the town; more mounds are scattered among the buildings in the town centre. Umm Salal Ali is clearly signposted off the main highway north to Al-Ruweis, about 27km from Doha.

AL-KHOR   الخور
pop 37,600

Al-Khor, once famous as a centre for the pearling industry, is a pleasant town with an attractive corniche, off which most of

---

FLOTSAM & GYPSUM

Look up at the door lintels or window frames of any old house or mosque in Qatar and chances are it will be decorated with a filigree of white plaster – only it isn't plaster, it's gypsum, otherwise known as calcium sulphate. Found in abundance locally, and sometimes combined with chippings of driftwood washed up on the beach, it was used to clad the exterior of houses, forts, mosques and wind towers, as an improvement on mud. Able to withstand extreme changes in temperature and humidity, this durable material lent itself to moulding and carving. Some of the abstract plant designs and geometric patterns that can be seen on important buildings across the Gulf illustrate how working with gypsum has evolved into a complex craft.

---

the sights are situated. The small **museum** (☎ 472 1866; ☼ 9am-1pm & 4-7pm Sat-Thu), on the corniche, displays archaeological and cultural artefacts from the region including traditional clothing. Exhibits showcase local craft industries like gypsum moulding (see boxed text, above) and the making of incense burners. Several old **watchtowers** are scattered around the town; many have been restored to their original form. From the old mosque, there's a fine view of the ocean.

The nearby **mangroves** are a good place for bird-watching, as are the large public **Al-Khor Gardens** (☼ sunrise-sunset), hedged with tamarisk trees. The gardens are signposted 2km north of the turn-off for Al-Khor on the main highway from Doha to Al-Ruweis.

The felafel sandwiches at **Ain Hailitan Restaurant** (☎ 472 0123) have a delicious local twist, while the **Beirut Pearl Restaurant** (☎ 472 2003) commands a good view of the sea. Both restaurants are along the corniche.

Al-Khor is a drive of around 45 minutes, or 40km from Doha.

JEBEL JASSASSIYEH   جبل الجساسية
On the road to Al-Huwailah, about 60km north of Doha, lies the rocky ridge known as Jebel Jassassiyeh; this is where you can see over 900 ancient **rock carvings** in 580 sites. Some are said to depict aerial views

of boats, which is interesting given that in an utterly flat country, on a usually utterly flat sea, there would be no opportunity for people to have an aerial view of anything. Access is by 4WD only and as it is very hard to find the ridge in a landscape of limited features, it's better to go with an organised tour.

AL-GHARIYA الغورية

Since Qatar has such a picturesque coastline, it's surprising there are not more resorts like **Al-Ghariya Resort** (☎ 472 8811; www .alghariyaresorts.com; r from QR1000; 🛌). With apartment-style accommodation and kitchen area for self-catering, it is popular with Doha families – be warned, the noise of children on sand buggies can be deafening. There's a pool; sea-swimming is only possible at the neighbouring beach.

All round Al-Ghariya there are excellent **bird-watching** possibilities, 4WD or a strong pair of boots permitting.

Al-Ghariya is signposted off the northern highway from Doha, some 85km from the capital.

AL-RUWEIS الرويس
pop 3406

Situated at the northern tip of the peninsula, at the end of the northern highway about 90km from Doha, lies Al-Ruweis, a typical fishing village where the age-old industry of net-mending or fish-pot cleaning takes place on board the stranded dhows, while waiting for the tide to return.

Several **abandoned villages**, like Al-Khuwair and Al-Arish, mark the potholed road between Al-Ruweis and Al-Zubara. They were vacated in the 1970s as the inhabitants were drawn to new areas of industry.

The lovely, **unspoilt beaches** around the northern coast are a joy, but access is only possible in a 4WD; extreme care should be taken to follow previous tracks, both for environmental and safety reasons.

AL-ZUBARA الزبارة
pop 862

Al-Zubara occupies an important place in Qatari history, as it was a large commercial and pearling port in the 18th and 19th centuries when the area was under the governance of Al-Khalifa (now the ruling family in Bahrain). At the time of research, there was not much to see, other than the tiny bustling fishing village.

Al-Zubara Fort was built in 1938 and used by the military until the 1980s. It was then converted into **Al-Zubara Regional Museum** (admission by donation QR1-2; 🕐 8am-1pm & 4-7pm Sun-Thu, 4-7pm Fri). The archaeology and pottery exhibits have sadly been neglected, but the fort is still worth visiting for the bleak views from the battlements. The fort is at the intersection of a road from Doha and Al-Ruweis, 2km from Al-Zubara.

Al-Zubara is 105km northwest of Doha along a good dual carriageway.

BIR ZEKREET بئر زكريت

There is not much in the way of altitude in Qatar, which only serves to exaggerate the little escarpment on the northwest coast of the peninsula, near Dukhan. The limestone escarpment of Bir Zekreet is like a geography lesson in desert formations, as the wind has whittled away softer sedimentary rock, exposing pillars and a large mushroom of limestone. The surrounding beaches are full of empty oyster shells with rich mother-of-pearl interiors and other assorted bivalves. The shallow waters are quiet and peaceful and see relatively few visitors, making the area a pleasant destination for a day trip. Camping is possible either along the beach or less conspicuously under the stand of acacia trees near the escarpment. There are no facilities or shops nearby, so campers should come prepared, bringing water especially in the summer months.

To reach Bir Zekreet from Doha, head west past Al-Shahaniya and take the signposted turn-off on the right about 10km before Dukhan. An ordinary car could manage the off-road portion from the Dukhan highway, but a 4WD would be advisable for exploring the escarpment area. To reach the desert mushroom, turn right 1.5km past the school at a gap in the gas pipes and bear left before the trees.

The remains of the 9th-century **Murwab Fort**, about 15km further up the northwest coast from Dukhan, may be worth a visit with a guide. Five groups of buildings, including two mosques and an earlier fort, have been partially excavated but a lack of information makes the sight of limited interest.

QATAR

AL-SHAHANIYA   الشحانية

Al-Shahaniya, 60km west of Doha along the Dukhan Rd, is a good place to see camels roaming around the desert or being exercised before the famous local **camel races**.

The races, or the 'sport of sheikhs', can be seen from a purpose-built stadium. If you have a car – a 4WD is not necessary – it's fun to drive along the 8km racetrack during the race. It can be quite an event, as female camels can maintain a speed of 40km an hour for an entire hour, and are often better at keeping in lane than the motorists. Check the English-language daily newspapers for race times or call the **racing committee** (☎ 487 2028); better still, contact one of the local tour companies, which often organise trips to the races during the season (October to May). It's easy to spot the stadium, as long before it comes into view the approach is marked by 5km of stables, exercise areas, lodgings for the trainers and breeders, and all the other facilities required of a multimillion dollar sport, not to mention a national passion befitting Qatar's Bedouin origins.

Nearby, a protected herd of oryx can be seen with prior permission from the **Ministry of Municipal Affairs & Agriculture** (☎ 443 5777), though it is usually easier to go with a tour guide who will arrange the formalities for you.

QATAR DIRECTORY

ACCOMMODATION

In this chapter we have defined budget hotels as those charging less than QR600 for a double room, midrange hotels as charging less than QR1000 for a double room, and top-end hotels as charging more than QR1000 for a double room. All prices quoted are inclusive of the mandatory 17% tax and service charge, and are based on realistic high-season rates.

There are some truly splendid resort-style hotels in Qatar, with glorious, seafront locations and carefully landscaped gardens suitable for a relaxed family holiday. Most offer weekend (Friday/Saturday) specials and other deals in association with selected airlines.

At the other end of the market, the solo traveller looking for a cheapish stopover will find plenty of clean, modern and centrally located options for about QR400.

There are no hostels in Qatar. Camping in the desert or along the gentle coastline is possible with a 4WD and knowledge of driving on soft sand and *sabkha*, but there are no specific facilities. Basic camping equipment is available from Carrefour in City Centre-Doha (p286).

ACTIVITIES

Beaches

The coast of Qatar is almost a continuous line of sandy beaches with pockets of limestone pavement. As pretty as it looks, the sea is very shallow, making it almost impossible to swim. There are some good beaches, however, at the top resorts in Doha, the Sealine Beach Resort (p287), near Mesaieed, and Al-Ghariya Resort (p289). The nearest public-access beaches close to Doha are at or near Al-Wakrah (p287). None of the beaches outside the resort areas have facilities, and shade is a problem in the summer.

Sand Sports

The sand is beginning to attract people to Qatar in the same way that the snow draws the crowds elsewhere, with sand skiing, quad-bike racing and sand-dune driving all becoming popular sports, though largely for those with their own equipment. The Sealine Beach Resort (p287), south of Mesaieed, is the best place for these activities, offering quad bikes for QR150 per hour for a 160cc model and helpful assistance if you get stuck in the dunes.

Golf, sailing and fishing are other popular activities. See p279 for information or check with any of the big hotels.

BOOKS

The definitive illustrated reference to Qatar is David Chadock's *Qatar*, revised in March 2006. If you can find a copy, Helga Graham's *Arabian Time Machine: Self-Portrait of an Oil State* is an interesting collection of interviews with Qataris about their lives and traditions, before and after the oil boom. *Qatari Women Past and Present* by Abeer Abu Said explains the changing and traditional roles of women in Qatar. More recent is Byron Augustin's *Qatar – Enchantment of the World*, which gives an overall view of life in Qatar.

For more general Middle East titles, some of which contain coverage of Qatar, see Books (p23).

BUSINESS HOURS

Qataris love their 'siesta', and Doha resembles a ghost town in the early afternoon. See Arabian Peninsula Directory chapter (p529) for details about the weekend. The following opening hours prevail throughout Qatar:

Banks 7.30am to 1pm Sunday to Thursday.

Government offices 6am to 2pm Sunday to Thursday.

Internet cafés 7am to midnight.

Post offices 7am to 8pm Sunday to Thursday, and 8am to 11am and 5pm to 7pm Saturday.

Restaurants 11.30am to 1.30pm and 5.30pm to midnight Saturday to Thursday, 5pm to midnight Friday.

Shopping centres 10am to midnight Saturday to Thursday, 2pm to midnight Friday.

Shops 8.30am to 12.30pm and 4pm to 9pm Saturday to Thursday, 4.30pm to 9pm Friday.

CHILDREN

Qatar is a wonderfully safe, easy-going, family-oriented country, and children are welcome and catered for everywhere. Even the Gulf, with its gently sloping shores and flat, waveless seas is more conducive to paddling about and building sand castles than it is to extreme sports. The large resorts all have plenty of activities for young children and Doha has a heap of attractions to keep even the most overactive kids amused. See also p280.

CUSTOMS

Doha's recently modernised airport now has a large **duty-free shop** (www.qatardutyfree.net). No alcohol, narcotics or pork-related products may be brought in through customs – and no magazines from the 'top shelf' back home. Goods originating from Israel may also pose problems if you are stopped by customs. See also Customs, p532.

DANGERS & ANNOYANCES

Many Western visitors have been deterred from coming to the Gulf on account of the hostilities in Iraq and Afghanistan. Qatar, however, is one of the safest and most politically stable countries to visit, and experiences minimal crime.

The poor quality of driving is the only danger worth pointing out, especially as intolerant local drivers are not very cautious about pedestrians.

For those hiring a 4WD, beware the pockets of soft sand and *sabkha* around the coast and in the interior that are not always apparent until it's too late. Drivers should always stick to tracks when going off the road and make sure they have all the necessary equipment (water, tow rope, jack, spare tyre etc) for an emergency, as passing cars are sometimes few and far between, especially in the interior.

DISABLED TRAVELLERS

Little provision has been made in Qatar for disabled travellers, although the new resorts have tried to make accommodation wheelchair accessible. The corniche area of Doha and the new malls are easily accessed, but many of the other sights and souqs are not. No provision is made for the visually or hearing impaired.

EMBASSIES & CONSULATES
Qatar Embassies & Consulates

The following is a list of Qatari embassies and consulates in major cities around the world. For addresses of Qatari embassies in neighbouring Arabian Peninsula countries, see the relevant chapters or visit the government's website (www.mofa.gov.qa) for more information.

France (☎ 01 45 51 90 71; paris@mofa.gov.qa; 57 Quai D'Orsay, 75007 Paris)

Germany (☎ 228-957 520; bonn@mofa.gov.qa; Brunnen alle 6, 53177 Bonn)

UK (☎ 020-7493 2200; london@mofa.gov.qa; 1 South Audley St, London W1Y 5DQ)

USA Washington (☎ 02-274 1600; washington@mofa.gov.qa; Ste 200, 4200 Wisconsin Ave, NW, Washington DC 20016); New York (☎ 212-486 9335; 4th fl, 809 UN Plaza, New York, NY 10017)

Embassies & Consulates in Qatar

Most embassies are in the 'Diplomatic Area', north of the Sheraton Doha Hotel & Resort, and few have specific road addresses. All are open from 8am to 2pm Sunday to Thursday, but telephone first.

Bahrain (Map p274; ☎ 483 9360; alkaabi50@hotmail.com; Diplomatic Area)

France (Map p274; ☎ 483 2283; www.ambafrance qa.org.qa; Diplomatic Area)

Germany (Map p274; ☎ 487 6949; germany@qatar.net.qa; Al-Jezira al-Arabiyya St, Kulaib)

QATAR

Iran (Map p274; ☎ 483 5300; fax 467 1665; Diplomatic Area)

Kuwait (Map p274; ☎ 483 2111; faisal1234@qatar.net .qa; Diplomatic Area)

Oman (Map p274; ☎ 493 1910; fax 493 2278; C Ring Rd, Al-Salata Al-Jadeeda)

Saudi Arabia (Map p274; ☎ 483 2030; fax 483 2720; Diplomatic Area)

UAE (Map p274; ☎ 483 8880; emarat@qatar.net.qa; Diplomatic Area) Off Al-Khor St,

UK (Map p274; ☎ 442 1991; www.british-in-qatar.com; Al-Istiqlal St, Al-Rumaila Rumailiah)

USA (Map p274; ☎ 488 4101; www.qatar .usembassyqatar@qatar.net.qa; 22 February St, Al-Luqta)

Yemen (Map p274; ☎ 443 2555; yemenembqa22@qatar .net.qa; Al-Jazeera St, Ibn Mahmoud) Located near Al-Sadd Plaza.

FESTIVALS & EVENTS
Eid al-Adha/Eid al-Fitr

Qatar's own brand of *eid* festivities (Islamic feasts; dates changeable) includes 'traditional-style' markets and entertainment for both adults and children, from falconry to sand skiing, shopping festivals, fireworks and laser shows, and displays of pearl-fishing. For dates, see the boxed text (p535).

National Day

Dancing, camel racing, fireworks and other cultural activities take place on and around 3 September, Qatar's National Day.

Sports

Following are some of the fixtures that have helped to make Qatar the sporting capital of the region. Most events take place in the first half of the year. For details on any of the fixtures listed below, visit **Experience Qatar** (www.experienceqatar.com) and search for 'Future Events'.

January

ExxonMobil Qatar Open Men's Tennis (www .qatartennis.org) The sporting year begins with this event, which has included top players like Federer.

February

International Sailing Regatta (☎ /fax 487 0486) The International Sailing Regatta is a firm favourite in the year's sporting calendar, with three events: international, GCC and Arab championships.

Tour of Qatar Cycling Race (☎ /fax 447 4019) Cycling as an event is gaining in popularity since the first Tour of Qatar Cycling Race in 2002.

March

Qatar Masters Golf Tournament (www.qatarmasters .com) International golf tournaments, such as this PGA European Tour event, have been a surprise success across the region. As such, many of the so-called 'browns' of local desert courses have been turned into more traditional 'greens' with a hefty investment in irrigation.

April

Class 1 World Power Boat Championship Grand Prix (www.qmsf.org) Wave on your favourite team from Doha's corniche, during this fast and furious spectacle.

May

Emir's Cup Camel racing at its very best.

HOLIDAYS

In addition to the main Islamic holidays described in the Arabian Peninsula Directory (p534), Qatar observes the following public holidays:

Accession Day 27 June
National Day 3 September

INTERNET ACCESS

Internet facilities are available at all top-end hotels, and there are an increasing number of internet cafés around the capital (p275). The only local ISP is **Internet Qatar** (☎ 125; www.qatar.net.qa), part of Qtel. It's possible to use this service on your own computer, as long as you have a modem and telephone line with either GSM or international access. Prepaid dial-up cards can be purchased from supermarkets for QR30 and QR50 and are valid for six months. A QR30 card will give you seven hours of internet access.

INTERNET RESOURCES

Some useful Qatar-specific websites include:

Experience Qatar (www.experienceqatar.com) The official website of Qatar, with comprehensive information for visitors.

Ministry of Foreign Affairs (www.mofa.gov.qa) A detailed site covering everything from getting a visa to what to see in Qatar.

Qatar Info (www.qatar-info.com) Contains useful information and links to other Qatar websites.

Qatar National Hotels Company (www.qnhc.com) Detailed information on some of the country's hotels and tour companies.

The Peninsula (www.thepeninsulaqatar.com) Qatar's leading English-language daily newspaper with news and views specific to Qatar.

MAPS

GEO Projects publishes a useful *Qatar* map in its Arab World Map Library, available from car-rental offices, hotels and bookshops for QR30 to QR50. Hildebrand's road map of Qatar has also been recommended, but it's not easily available in Qatar.

MEDIA
Newspapers & Magazines

Both of Qatar's English-language newspapers, the **Gulf Times** (www.gulf-times.com) and **The Peninsula** (www.thepeninsulaqatar.com), are published daily, except Friday and cost QR2. **Marhaba, Qatar's Premier Information Guide** (marhaba@qatar.net.qa), published quarterly, is an excellent source of information regarding events in Qatar, and includes some interesting feature articles on Qatari life and culture. It costs QR20. International newspapers and magazines are available one or two days after publication at major bookshops in Doha.

Two other magazines, *Qatar Today* and *Woman Today,* focus on business issues and women in work respectively.

A listing of monthly events is available in the free booklet called *Qatar Happening*, distributed in malls and hotels.

Radio & TV

Qatar Radio offers radio programmes in English on 97.5FM and 102.6FM, and a French service on the same frequencies each afternoon from 1.15pm until 4pm. The BBC is available on 107.4FM and Armed Forces Radio is on 104FM.

Channel 2 on Qatar TV (QTV) broadcasts programmes in English, while most international satellite channels are available at the majority of hotels. The renowned Al-Jazeera Satellite Channel is broadcast from Doha: it has become one of the most watched and most respected Arabic news channels in the Arab world.

MONEY
ATMs & Credit Cards

All major credit and debit cards are accepted in large shops. Visa (Plus & Electron), MasterCard and Cirrus are accepted at ATMs at HSBC, the Qatar National Bank and the Commercial Bank of Qatar, which also accepts American Express (Amex) and Diners Club cards.

Currency

The currency of Qatar is the Qatari riyal (QR). One riyal is divided into 100 dirhams. Coins are worth 25 or 50 dirhams, and notes come in one, five, 10, 50, 100 and 500 denominations. The Qatari riyal is fully convertible.

Exchange Rates

The Qatari riyal is fixed against the US dollar. The following exchange rates were correct at the time of printing:

Country	Unit		Qatar riyal
Australia	A$1	=	QR2.90
Bahrain	BD1	=	QR9.68
Canada	C$1	=	QR3.10
Euro zone	€1	=	QR4.85
Japan	¥100	=	QR3.11
Kuwait	KD1	=	QR12.67
New Zealand	NZ$1	=	QR2.55
Oman	OR1	=	QR9.49
Saudi Arabia	SR1	=	QR0.97
UAE	Dh1	=	QR0.99
UK	UK£1	=	QR7.08
US	US$1	=	QR3.64
Yemen	YR1	=	QR0.02

Exchanging Money

Currencies from Bahrain, Saudi Arabia and the UAE are easy to buy and sell at banks and moneychangers. Travellers cheques can be changed at all major banks and the larger moneychangers. Moneychangers can be found around the Gold Souq area of central Doha. There is little difference in exchange rates between banks and moneychangers.

Tipping & Bargaining

A service charge is usually added to restaurant (and top-end hotel) bills. Local custom does not require that you leave a tip and, although it is certainly appreciated, there is a danger of escalating the habit to the detriment of the workers involved (some establishments reduce wages in anticipation of tips that may or may not be forthcoming). It is therefore recommended that local custom is followed, unless exceptional service or assistance warrants an exceptional gesture.

Bargaining is expected in the souqs and, although Western-style shopping centres have fixed prices, it's still worth asking for a discount in boutiques and smaller shops.

AL-JAZEERA: THE BLOOM OF A THORN TREE

One of the 'blossoms' produced by the freedom of the press in Qatar since 1995 has been the establishment of Al-Jazeera Independent Satellite TV Channel in November 1996. Free from censorship or government control, it offers regional audiences a rare opportunity for debate and independent opinion, and opens up an alternative perspective on regional issues for the world at large. Its call-in shows have been particularly revolutionary, airing controversies not usually open for discussion in the autocratic Gulf countries.

The station, which means 'The Island' in English, was originally launched as an Arabic news and current affairs satellite TV channel, funded with a generous grant from the Emir of Qatar. It has been subsidised by the emir on a year-by-year basis, despite the airing of criticism towards his own government. The station was originally staffed by many former members of the BBC World service, whose Saudi-based Arabic language TV station collapsed under Saudi censorship; a close relationship with the BBC continues to this day.

Before the launch of Al-Jazeera, most citizens in the Peninsula were only able to access state-censored TV stations. Al-Jazeera brought to the public hot topics such as Syria's relationship with Lebanon and the thawing of relations between the Gulf States and Israel – hitherto unheard of. Inevitably, the station is viewed with suspicion by ruling parties across the Arab world. The station's website notes one occasion on 27 January 1999, when the Algerian government pulled the plug on the capital's electricity supply to prevent the population from hearing a live debate that alleged Algerian military collusion in a series of massacres. In response to such coverage, the station has attracted critics of its own, along with accusations of boosting audience ratings through sensational coverage.

Al-Jazeera only became internationally significant after the 9/11 attacks. The station broadcast video statements by Osama bin Laden (incidentally earning the station $20,000 per minute in resale fees) and other al-Qaeda leaders who defended the attacks. The US government accused the station of a propaganda campaign on behalf of the terrorists; however, the footage was

---

PHOTOGRAPHY

Shops selling memory cards and batteries, as well as print film and video cassettes, are plentiful in Doha. Most studios can print digital photos from a memory card. They can also transfer photos to a CD from a memory card or film. Slide film is hard to find and very difficult to get developed, so bring your own. Many photographic shops also arrange passport photos.

POST

There is a general post office in northern Doha and another in central Doha (p275). Postal rates start at 50 dirhams for an inland postcard, to QR3 for letters to Europe, and QR3.5 to the US and Australia. For a full list of postal rates, check the following website: www.qpost.com.qa.

SHOPPING

Providing you go shopping with an open mind, rather than having the usual Arabic crafts (of which there are few) on your shopping list, there is a wonderful world of curiosities to buy in Qatar. Shopping in Doha isn't just about buying, it's about a cultural and social exchange. For information about souqs and malls, see p284.

TELEPHONE & FAX

The country code for Qatar is ☎ 974. There are no specific area or city codes. The international access code (to call abroad from Qatar) is ☎ 0.

All communications services are provided by **Qtel** (www.qtel.com.qa), and the telephone system is excellent. Local calls are free, except from the blue and white Qtel phone booths, which cost QR1 per minute. To make a local or international call from a phone booth, you must buy a phonecard (which comes in denominations of QR30, QR50 and QR100), available in bookshops and supermarkets around Doha.

The cost of an International Direct Dial call to the USA, Canada, the UK or Europe is about QR4.6 per minute, while it's about QR4 to Australia or New Zealand. Rates are cheaper between 7pm and 7am, all day Friday and on holidays. An additional QR4 is charged for operator-assisted calls.

broadcast by the station without comment and later parts of the same tapes were shown by Western media channels without attracting condemnation.

Al-Jazeera continued to air challenging debate during the Afghanistan conflict, bringing into sharp focus the devastating impact of war on the lives of ordinary people. In 2003 it hired its first English-language journalist, Afshin Rattansi, from the BBC's *Today Programme* and covered Tony Blair's decision to join the USA in the invasion of Iraq. It has since been accused by American sources of sustaining an anti-American campaign, something the channel stoutly denies. It did not, for example, show the beheading of Western terrorists by masked gunmen as many Western sources claim. Nonetheless, the station has been continually undermined since 9/11, including attacks on its office in Baghdad in April 2003 by US forces and more subtly through the launch of a US-funded Arabic-language TV station called Al-Hurra in 2004.

Despite these difficulties, Al-Jazeera has earned its spurs on the frontline of journalism and is today the most widely watched news channel in the Middle East; indeed, its ratings as of 2007 number 40 to 50 million viewers, equal to that of the BBC. It has won several international awards for risk-taking journalism both on TV and through its **website** (www.aljazeera.net in Arabic & aljazeera .net/english), launched in January 2001. One year after the launch, it had received 811 million emails and 161 million visits to its website, making it one of the 50 most visited websites worldwide.

In November 2006 a 24-hour, seven-day-a-week news channel called Al-Jazeera English was launched, with broadcasting centres in London, Kuala Lumpur and Washington DC, and media observers will be watching carefully to see what impact the channel will make.

Unafraid of controversy, the stated aim of Al-Jazeera is to seek the truth through contextual objectivity (in as much, of course, as that is ever possible): 'Truth will be the force that will drive us to raise thorny issues, to seize every opportunity for exclusive reporting'. For many Western governments at least, that's proving to be an unexpected thorn among the first blossoms of democracy.

Directory inquiries can be contacted on ☎ 180. Call ☎ 190 for international inquiries.

Mobile Phones

Qtel operates a prepaid GSM mobile phone service called Hala Plus, which requires no guarantor. Cards in a variety of denominations are widely available in shops.

VISAS

All nationalities other than citizens of Gulf Cooperation Council (GCC) countries need a visa to enter into Qatar. Since Qatar opened its doors to tourism, however, 31 different nationalities can now obtain a visa at Qatar's airport, even though the regulations change in minor ways fairly frequently.

At the time of writing, citizens of the European Union, USA, Australia, New Zealand, Canada, Singapore, South Korea, Japan, Brunei and Hong Kong were eligible for a two-week, single-entry tourist visa, which is issued on arrival at the airport and costs QR55. Some visitors have reported having a three-week visa stamped in their passport upon requesting a two-week visa: there's no harm in asking! To avoid being turned back from a lengthy queue, fill out the application card (in piles on top of the visa counter) before you reach the visa counter and have your credit card ready. Note that at the time of writing, only *payment by credit card* is acceptable.

Apparently, an agreement recently made between Oman and Qatar means that anyone with a visa for Oman can now enter Qatar (and vice versa) free of charge; however, this arrangement was not being implemented at the airport at the time of writing.

You must apply for a multi-entry tourist and business visa through a Qatari embassy or consulate. Three passport-sized photos are required and an application form filled out in triplicate. Anyone requesting a business visa needs to supply a letter from their host company. These visas are issued within 24 hours.

For details of visas for other Peninsula countries, see p541.

QATAR

Visa Extensions

Tourist visas can be extended for an additional seven days. The charges for overstaying are very high – between QR200 and QR500 *per day*, according to some sources. If you obtained your visa at the airport on arrival or through an embassy/consulate, you can organise an extension at the **Passports & Immigration Building** (Map p274; ☎ 488 2882; cnr Khalifa & 22 February Sts) in Doha.

WOMEN TRAVELLERS

On the whole, Qatar is a safe place for women to travel. While it's still a largely conservative society, women can move about freely, without any of the harassment or restrictions that are often experienced in other parts of the region. Harassment of women is not looked upon kindly by officials. Despite being a safe country, women on their own will still encounter stares and unwanted curiosity. For more information on women travelling in this region, see p542.

TRANSPORT IN QATAR

See also the Arabian Peninsula Transport chapter (p545) for general information on all the following.

GETTING THERE & AWAY
Air

Doha International Airport (☎ 465 6666; fax 462 2044) is only 2.5km from the city centre. There is a departure tax of QR20.

The national carrier **Qatar Airways** (☎ 449 6666; www.qatarairways.com; Al-Matar St), near the airport, has daily direct services from London to Doha, and several direct flights a week from Paris, Munich, Jakarta, Kuala LumpUr and from most cities in the Middle East. Qatar is also serviced by several major airlines: British Airways flies direct from London to Doha daily, KLM flies direct from Amsterdam, while Emirates flies to Doha from most major hubs via Dubai. There is no airport departure tax.

OTHER AIRLINES FLYING TO/FROM QATAR

British Airways (BA; ☎ 432 1434; www.ba.com; Heathrow Airport, London)
EgyptAir (MS; ☎ 445 8401; www.egyptair.com.eg; Cairo)
Emirates (EK; ☎ 438 4477; www.emirates.com; Dubai)
Gulf Air (GF; ☎ 445 5444; www.gulfairco.com; Bahrain)
Kuwait Air (KT; ☎ 442 23920; www.kuwait-airways.com; Kuwait City)
Oman Air (WY; ☎ 432 0509; www.omanair.aero; Muscat)
Saudi Arabian Airlines (SV; ☎ 432 2991; www.saudiairlines.com; Jeddah)

Flight	Price	Frequency
Doha to Muscat (Oman)	QR1400	daily
Doha to Manama (Bahrain)	QR500	daily
Doha to Kuwait City (Kuwait)	QR1500	daily
Doha to Abu Dhabi (UAE)	QR1650	daily
Doha to Riyadh (Saudi Arabia)	QR1200	daily
Doha to San'a (Yemen)	QR2000	3 per week

Land
BORDER CROSSINGS

Residents of Qatar, Saudi Arabia and the UAE can drive across the Qatar–Saudi border, providing they have insurance for both countries. Bear in mind that if others want to travel *from* Qatar, they must have a Saudi visa (or transit visa) in advance. An exciting new project is under way to link Qatar and Bahrain via a causeway (see opposite).

BUS

From Doha, **Saudi Arabian Public Transport Co** (Saptco; www.saptco.com) has daily buses to Dammam (QR100), with onward connections to Amman (Jordan) and Damascus (Syria), both SR150; Manama (QR25, approximately five hours); Abu Dhabi (QR21, six hours) and Dubai (QR21, seven hours); and Kuwait (QR26, approximately 10 hours). All routes can be booked online. Departures are from the central bus station in Doha. You must have a valid transit visa for Saudi Arabia in advance, and an onward ticket and visa for your next destination beyond Saudi's borders.

GETTING AROUND
Bus

A new public bus system is currently being developed in Qatar. From the **Central Bus Station** (Map pp276-7; ☎ 458 8888; www.mowasalat.com; Grand Hamad St), air-conditioned buses should soon start servicing Al-Khor, Al-Wakara and Masaieed among other destinations. Prices will cost QR2 for inner-city rides and up to QR7 outside Doha. The new taxi system is designed to bridge the gap in Doha until the new bus system is fully implemented.

Car & Motorcycle

If you're driving around Doha, you'll discover that roundabouts are very common, treated like camel-race tracks and often redundant in practice. Finding the right way out of Doha can also be difficult: if you're heading south towards Al-Wakrah or Mesaieed, take the airport road (Al-Matar St); the main road to all points north is 22 February St (north from Al-Rayyan Rd); and to the west, continue along Al-Rayyan Rd.

Driving in Qatar is on the right-hand side. Numerous petrol stations are located around Doha and along the highways.

Authorities are strict with anyone caught speeding, not wearing a seat belt or not carrying a driving licence: heavy on-the-spot fines are handed out freely. Don't even think about drink driving. For more information on driving in the region, see the Arabian Peninsula Transport chapter (p552).

HIRE

A foreigner can rent a car (there's nowhere to rent motorcycles) with a driving licence from home – but *only* within seven days of arriving in Qatar (although expats resident in other GCC countries can drive for up to three months). After that, a temporary driving licence must be obtained, issued by the Traffic Licence Office. It costs QR150 and lasts three months – rental agencies can arrange this for you. The minimum rental period for all car-hire agencies is 24 hours and drivers must be at least 21 years old.

Car hire costs (which include unlimited kilometres, but not petrol) vary, so it's worth shopping around. Major agencies charge about QR120/700 per day/week for the smallest sedan, though cheaper rates can be found at some local agencies. Most agencies have a compulsory Collision Damage Waiver (CDW) of around QR10 per day, which is a good idea to avoid an excess of QR1500 to QR2500 in case of an accident. A few companies also add a compulsory Personal Accident Insurance Fee.

The cost of a 4WD can be very high (around QR300/1800 per day/week); an ordinary sedan is perfectly suitable for reaching all the places mentioned in this chapter, with the exception of Khor al-Adaid. A

> **FRIENDSHIP CAUSEWAY**
>
> Relations between Qatar and its neighbour, Bahrain, have not always been the best. Shared royal family has been a bone of contention for one thing and it was only relatively recently the two countries stopped haggling over ownership of the Hawar Islands. Driven by a growing sense of community within the Gulf region, however, and with a shared mission to attract higher volumes of tourists, the two countries have at last put their differences aside. As if consolidating the friendlier relations, a proposed 40km road link has been approved between Qatar and Bahrain. It will take over four years to complete and will involve multiple bridges supported on reclaimed land, similar to King Fahd Causeway (see p132) that links Bahrain to Saudi Arabia. When complete, it will form the longest fixed link across water in the world.

4WD is essential, however, for those wanting to explore the interior in greater depth or wishing to camp on a remote beach.

Al-Muftah Rent a Car (Map pp276-7; ☎ 432 8100; rntcar@qatar.net.qa; Wadi Musheireb St) is a reliable and cheaper alternative to the major agencies, which include **Avis** (☎ 466 7744; avis@qatar.net.qa); **Budget** (☎ 468 5515; budget@qatar.net.qa), **Europcar** (☎ 443 8404) and **Hertz** (☎ 462 2891; hertz@qatar.net.qa).

Local Transport

TAXI

The orange and white cars are a battered, scraped and barely functioning bunch, entirely out of character with the modern face of Qatar. While they probably don't have or won't use air-conditioning, Qatar's taxi drivers at least seem to possess a sense of humour and a gift of the gab. The newer sea-blue taxis belonging to Mowasalat-Karwa offer a much better service for slightly more money. They charge QR3 and QR1 for each subsequent kilometre. For travel outside the capital, it's best to negotiate a fixed fare.

The easiest way to catch a taxi is to ask your hotel to arrange one, although technically you can wave one down from the side of the road. To visit most sights outside Doha, it's better to hire a car (p179).

QATAR

Saudi Arabia
المملكة العربية السعودية

Saudi Arabia. The world's last great forbidden kingdom, and an emblem of everything most inexplicable to the West: the Middle East, Islam, oil and terrorism. For centuries the country was considered closed to outsiders, penetrable only to the bravest and the boldest, such as Richard Burton, TE Lawrence and Wilfred Thesiger, who risked life and limb to get there. Today it continues to exist only in the realms of the imagination for most people, who still relish the sensational stories surrounding it.

And yet, ever so tentatively, the country is beginning to permit travellers past its portals. For those willing to 'risk' the realm, there may well be a surprise or two. Madain Saleh, called Saudi Arabia's Petra, numbers among the most magical and monumental sites of the Middle East. Or it would if more people knew about it.

The Empty Quarter, the largest sea of sand on the planet, is home to dunes the size of ships. The Arabian oryx, one of the most beautiful animals on earth, also lives there. In the far south lies Najran, an ancient caravan stop, where mud-brick forts rise out of the palm plantations and oases. On the coast, liberal, libertine Jeddah – or so it's seen by the Kingdom's more conservative kinsmen – is home to sensation-full souqs and lovely coral houses, once the abode of its moneyed merchants. Off its shores lie Saudi's Red Sea riches – reefs that rank among the least spoilt and most spectacular in the world.

Most memorable for many, however, is the traditional Bedouin hospitality that, like the sand of the Empty Quarter, seems to go on and on forever.

FAST FACTS

- **Official name** Kingdom of Saudi Arabia
- **Capital** Riyadh
- **Area** 2,149,690 sq km
- **Population** 26.6 million
- **Country code** ☎ 966
- **Head of State** King Abdullah bin Abdul Aziz Al-Saud
- **Annual number of Western tourists** (including haj pilgrims) 95,000
- **Stereotypes** Wells spurting oil, kings as rich as Croesus, hijackers, desert
- **Surprises** Mist-covered mountains, fragrant juniper forests, freezing desert temperatures (in winter), rich coral reefs

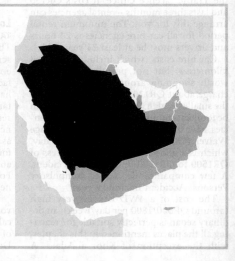

HIGHLIGHTS

- **Madain Saleh** (p336) Marvel at Madain Saleh, called 'Saudi Arabia's Petra' for its tremendous tombs set in a stunning desert setting.
- **Old City of Jeddah** (p322) Meander among the old merchants' houses, ancient markets packed with pilgrims and the myriad museums of Old Jeddah.
- **Empty Quarter** (p351) Drive the dramatic dunes of the Empty Quarter or camp out with camels under star-lit desert skies.
- **Najran** (p344) Feast your eyes on fantastic mud-brick fortresses set amid palm plantations in this lovely oasis town.
- **Red Sea Diving** (p332) Dive the dazzling depths of Saudi's Red Sea and spot sharks, sea turtles and stunning coral reefs at Yanbu or Al-Lith.

ITINERARIES

See also the Saudi itineraries on p27.

- **Riyadh and around** Take a tour of Masmak Fortress (p313) and see where the city began. Next sip coffee whilst standing on Sky Bridge (p313) with its stunning aerial summary of the town's old and new. After a whirlwind whiz through the Kingdom's culture at the National Museum (p313), lay off for lunch at Najd Village (p316). Later, fine-dine at the Globe (p316) then relax with a fruit cocktail and Cuban at the Cigar Lounge (p316) in the Al-Faisaliah Tower. At the weekend, head out to visit the colourful camel market (p318), camp in the Red Sands (p319) or wander the ghostly ruins of Dir'aiyah (p318).
- **Jeddah and around** Attend the early auction at Jeddah's frenetic fish market (p325) before taking a traditional breakfast of bread and *fool* at Restaurant Ful & Hummus (p327). Next amble the alleyways of the Souq al-Alawi (p324) and crane your neck counting the coral houses (p324) of Jeddah's maritime merchants. After a light lunch at one of the city's many Asian eateries (p327), take a stroll sizing up the famous sculptures (p325) along Jeddah's corniche. At night, taste the town's cooking and its culture at the laid-back, Al-Nakheel Restaurant (p328). At the weekend, unwind and relax at the Red Sea resort of Al-Nakheel (p329).
- **City Escapes** Head off to hike in the great Al-Nafud desert (p321) and recce the

---

VISA VICISSITUDES

Note that it is still currently impossible to visit the Kingdom as an independent traveller (though expats already in Saudi Arabia are free to travel around the Kingdom). Tourist visas are, however, granted to groups (minimum four people; women under 30 must be accompanied by their husband or brother) if booked through a recognised agency (see p366 for more details).

---

rocks for ancient art and stupendous scribblings. Take the plunge and go diving off Saudi's spectacular Red Sea shores and search the reefs (p332) for sensational riches in Jeddah, Yanbu and Al-Lith. Migrate to Madain Saleh (p336) and spend a week exploring the wonderful Nabataean necropolis, the haunting remains of the Hejaz railway and the stupendous desert scenery. Fill up the 4WD and head out to explore the great Empty Quarter (p348), driving across the dunes, setting off Thesiger-style on a spectacular camel safari, or star-gazing at night from traditional Bedouin tents.

CLIMATE & WHEN TO GO

The best time to visit Saudi Arabia is between November and February. From mid-April until October, average daily temperatures regularly top 40°C, with high humidity in the coastal regions to boot.

It's appreciably cooler in the Asir Mountains and around Taif all year. In the dead of winter (December to January), temperatures in the main cities (except Jeddah) will drop into the teens during the day and even hit zero in some places overnight. For climate chart information, see p530.

The Kingdom's Islamic holidays (p364) are another important factor in deciding when to go. Unless you've no choice, Ramadan is best avoided as getting a daytime meal can be difficult and opening hours are kept to a minimum.

HISTORY
Early Arabia

Of all the empires that profited from the lucrative trade in frankincense, few have captured the imagination like the

SAUDI ARABIA

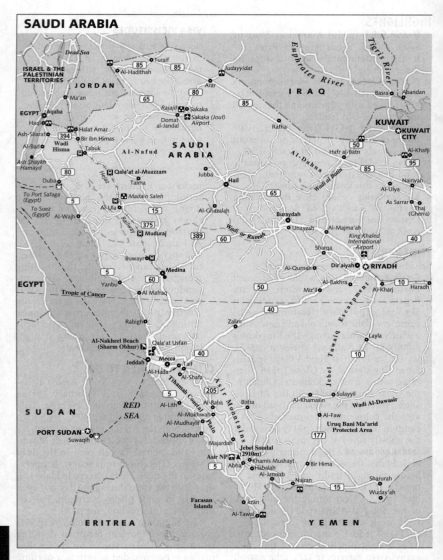

Nabataeans (see the boxed text, p336), a people of Bedouin origin who developed a specialised knowledge of the trade caravan routes.

From their extraordinary rock-hewn cities of Madain Saleh and Petra (in Jordan), the Nabataeans grew wealthy from around 200 BC by exacting tolls and protection money

from the caravans. The Nabataeans never really possessed an 'empire' in the common military and administrative sense of the word, but instead established a zone of influence that stretched as far north as Syria and south into the Hadramawt (Yemen).

In the years following the Prophet Mohammed's death in AD 632, the territory

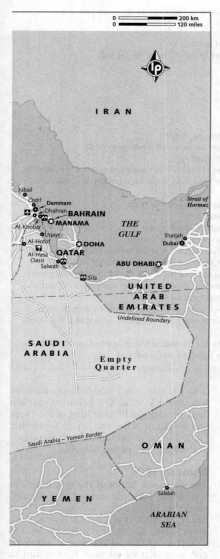

of what is now Saudi Arabia was nominally ruled from afar by the Umayyad and Abbasid caliphates, and was saved from obscurity only by the spiritual significance of the holy cities of Mecca and Medina.

By 1517 the Ottomans, under Salim I, had established their authority over Hejaz, a deeply unpopular move in Arabia.

Birth of Saudi Arabia

In 1703 Mohammed ibn Abd al-Wahhab was born in the oasis of Al-Uyaynah in the Najd. After a period of itinerant religious scholarship, Al-Wahhab returned to Al-Uyaynah to preach a zealous message calling for the purification of Islam (see 'Wahhabi Islam' p307).

Al-Wahhab's reformist zeal was initially tolerated by the local authorities, but he was expelled from the town after he meted out severe punishments to those who didn't engage in communal prayer, and led the stoning of a woman accused of adultery. He sought refuge in Dir'aiyah, 65km from Al-Uyaynah, where he was granted protection by Mohammed ibn al-Saud, the local emir.

In the meantime, there was considerable anger throughout Arabia that the holy cities of Mecca and Medina were under foreign (Ottoman) tutelage and the Saudi-Wahhabi emirate expanded rapidly.

Upon his death, Al-Saud was succeeded by his son Abdul Aziz, who captured Riyadh in 1765. In 1792 Al-Wahhab died but the inexorable expansion of the Saudi-Wahhabi emirate continued.

In 1803 the Saudi army marched on the Hejaz and defeated Sherif Hussain of Mecca. The same year, Abdul Aziz was assassinated by a Shiite fanatic in the mosque of Dir'aiyah in revenge for the Saudi-Wahhabi sacking of the Shiite cities of Iraq. Despite losing their leader, the Saudi-Wahhabi emirate was recognised by the Mecca authorities. The first Saudi empire stretched from Al-Hasa in the east to Hejaz in the west and to Najran in the south.

Second Saudi Empire

It didn't last long. The Ottoman Sultan Mahmoud II ordered his viceroy in Egypt, Mohammed Ali, to retake Hejaz in the Ottoman sultan's name. With the support of many Arabian tribes who resented the strictures of Saudi-Wahhabi rule, the Ottoman armies took Mecca and Medina in 1814, conquered the Saudi-Wahhabi stronghold of Dir'aiyah on 11 September 1818 and executed Abdullah ibn al-Saud (Abdul Aziz's successor).

In 1824 Turki ibn Abdullah, the son of the executed Abdullah, retook Riyadh. A series of assassinations and family squabbles over succession attracted the attention of the Ottomans, who captured Faisal, the emir

THE FERASA PHENOMENON

'Have you seen my camel?' A man once asked another.

'Right eye missing? Loaded all on the left side? No tail?' The other replied.

'Yes, that's exactly my camel!'

'I've no idea.'

'But you just described her perfectly!'

'I don't have her.'

'You're a liar, I tell you! A Liar!'

'I'm telling you, I don't have her.'

Eventually the first man took the second before the judge.

'This man has described my camel perfectly yet he says he's never seen her!'

The judge asked the second man to explain himself.

'It's simple,' the man replied. 'Only the left side of the bushes have been eaten, the footprints of the left feet are more heavily pressed into the sand than those on the right, and the camel's stool is clumped together and not dispersed'.

'Alright, but can you help the man find his camel?' asked the judge.

'Certainly,' replied the man. 'She went that way.'

Ferasa, as it's known in Arabic, is a gift uniquely credited to the Bedu. Translated roughly by 'perspicacity' in English, it's a kind of swift summing-up of the situation.

The talent probably evolved as a kind of survival technique in the hostile environment of the desert. Though desert days have long since past for most Saudis, don't think it doesn't have its uses: *ferasa* continues to play a vital role in many areas of Saudi life. Professional desert trackers regularly assist the police with their hunt for criminals, for example, and more recently, with the 'war on terror'. As you travel, listen out for famous local tales.

Policemen are also said to put *ferasa* to good use at checkpoints; park wardens use it in the fight against poachers; and customs officials in the combat against smuggling and illegal immigrants.

Even the present ruler, King Abdullah, is said to put his Bedouin bent to good use in his ability to quickly get the measure of his foreign guests trying to pull a fast one.

of Riyadh, and sent him into exile in Cairo. Six years later, Faisal escaped, marched on Riyadh and regained the throne, a position he would hold for another 22 years. After Faisal died, Riyadh fell to the Al-Rashids, an increasingly powerful tribe based around Hail, in the early 1890s.

The decisive battle for the future of Arabia came in 1902 when the 21-year-old Abdul Aziz ibn Abdul Rahman ibn al-Saud (Ibn Saud) and a small band of followers stormed Riyadh at night. The religious authorities in Riyadh then swore allegiance to the Al-Sauds through a series of religious edicts.

With deft diplomacy skills and the momentum of successful military campaigns, Ibn Saud orchestrated a conference at which Arabia's Islamic clergy condemned Sherif Hussain (ruler of Mecca) as a foreign puppet. Although Sherif Hussain responded by proclaiming himself the King of the Arabs, the tide of history was with Ibn Saud.

In 1925 the Saudi-Wahhabi alliance took Mecca and Medina. The following year Ibn Saud proclaimed himself King of the Hejaz and Sultan of Najd, and on 22 September 1932, Ibn Saud announced the formation of the Kingdom of Saudi Arabia.

Discovery of Oil

The economic future of the new kingdom was almost instantly secured with the discovery of oil and the signing in 1933 of Saudi Arabia's first oil concession. Four years later, the Arabian American Oil Company (Aramco) discovered commercial quantities of oil near Riyadh and in the area around Dammam in the east. In 1943 President Roosevelt established the Kingdom's political importance by stating grandly that the Kingdom was 'vital for the defence of the USA'.

Upon Ibn Saud's death on 9 November 1953, his profligate son Saud became king. Saud endeared himself to the Arab in the street by supporting Egypt in the Suez Crisis of 1956, but, with the Kingdom's finances in deep trouble, Saud abdicated in 1964.

His brother Faisal proved more willing to provide his citizens with a stake in the economic benefits of oil. He introduced, among other things, a free health service for all Saudis, and began the building boom that has transformed Saudi Arabia from an impoverished desert kingdom into a nation of modern infrastructure.

In response to the USA's unconditional support for Israel, Saudi Arabia imposed an oil embargo on the USA in 1974, a move that quadrupled world oil prices, drew support from across the region and reminded the world of Saudi Arabia's importance in a world economy dependent upon oil.

Growing Pains

On 25 March 1975 King Faisal was assassinated by a nephew. Although the throne passed to Faisal's brother Khaled, a man who was known for his piety, frugal lifestyle and closeness to his subjects, the real power behind the throne was another of Faisal's brothers, Fahd.

In November 1979 the Great Mosque of Mecca was overrun by 250 fanatical followers of Juhaiman ibn Saif al-Otai, a militant Wahhabi leader, who claimed that the Mahdi (Messiah) would appear in the mosque on that very day. During two bloody weeks of fighting, 129 people were killed. The conflict was a devastating blow to the credibility of a regime that had prided itself on being the inheritors of the Wahhabi legacy and the rulers best able to safeguard the holy places.

During the following year, riots also broke out in the towns of the Qatif Oasis, the heartland of the Kingdom's 300,000 Shiites, many of whom were inspired by the revolutionary fervour of their co-religionists in Iran and the exhortations of the Ayatollah Khomeini to export the Shiite revolution. The riots were brutally put down.

On 14 June 1982 the figurehead King Khaled died aged 69. Fahd became king and set about reinforcing the twin pillars (and contradictions) of modern Al-Saud rule. He made a priority of proving himself a moderate and reliable friend of the West, while in 1986 he proclaimed himself the 'Custodian of the Two Holy Mosques'.

Saudi Arabia Today

When Iraq invaded Kuwait in August 1990, Saudi Arabia's subsequent decision to allow foreign military forces to operate from Saudi soil would later prove one of the catalysts for propelling Osama bin Laden, a Saudi, and his Al-Qaeda movement onto the world stage.

In 1991 a petition calling for reforms and greater openness was sent to King Fahd by liberal intellectuals. It was quickly followed by a contrary petition by conservative Islamic scholars – a struggle symbolic of the two opposing sides of Saudi politics that continues to this day.

After a great deal of fanfare, the much-vaunted Consultative Council (Majlis ash-Shoura) was opened on 20 August 1993. For more on politics, see p305.

When Fahd died from a stroke in August 2005, his half-brother Abdullah ascended to the throne. Prince Sultan bin Abdulaziz al-Saud became crown prince.

An Uncertain Future

After the terrorist attacks on New York and Washington on 11 September 2001, and the discovery that 15 of the accused 19 hijackers were Saudi citizens, the world's attention focussed on Saudi Arabia. Western governments questioned both the alleged financing of terrorists in the Kingdom and the measures taken by the authorities to combat Al-Qaeda cells operating there.

In 2003 and 2004, a series of widely reported Al-Qaeda terrorist attacks targeted Westerners in Riyadh, Al-Khobar and Yanbu. It led to the subsequent departure of an estimated 50% of expat Americans and 30% of Europeans (on whom the government is so dependent for technical expertise). As a result, the Saudi authorities have been very keen to be seen to combat terrorism, including the hunting down of its main operatives. See also p363.

However, for as long as security (in the shape of international terrorism) and economic issues (in the shape of oil) remain a key concern for Washington, Saudi Arabia will remain a vital strategic partner to the USA and the West.

For the Kingdom's part, it has to play a difficult double-game. On the one hand, it's keen to show itself as a staunch supporter

SAUDI DATES

'We love dates – the dates we eat, and the dates we do!' goes the popular Saudi saying. Of the edible variety (as opposed to dating) you'll find these pressed upon you in every home you enter – and some hotels too.

Traditionally much beloved by the Bedouin, the Saudi desert-dwellers could survive for days in the dunes on just a diet of dates and camel milk.

The Kingdom's travellers also traditionally treasure them, particularly those performing the haj (annual Muslim pilgrimage to Mecca). No self-respecting pilgrim would leave home without at least a kilo. Replete with vitamins and minerals, they are the perfect source of sustenance during the still quite arduous journey. Returning *hajis* also buy dates as presents for their families.

Saudis also give dates as presents, particularly during Ramadan, and love to boast that 'These came from my own farm'. They also bring dates as gifts when visiting friends in hospital (but for the patients' visitors rather than for the patients themselves!). During Ramadan, dates (eaten in even numbers only) are famously used to break the fast. The easily-digested sugar soon satisfies the stomach. Saudi mothers traditionally eat dates mixed with herbs after child birth in order to recuperate their strength.

Because of the range of both soil type and climate, as well as the centuries of selective breeding, Saudi Arabia's dates are considered among the best in the world.

Many Saudis also like to keep date palms much as they like to keep camels – for the sake of it and for the social kudos it brings.

Nearly all the parts of a palm are traditionally used in Saudi Arabia – the fruit to eat and for cooking, the trunks for ceiling beams, and the leaves for making basket ware, straw hats and prayer mats.

Generally considered the choicest Saudi dates are the type known as *Ajua* (SR90 to SR120 per kg) from Medina, *Sukariya* (SR20 to SR50) from Qasim, and *Rotana* (SR15 to SR35) from Al-Kharj. When in Rome…a little bag of dried dates (from SR7 for 250g) goes a long way on one of those legendary long Saudi bus journeys.

of the West and its 'War on Terror' (and in doing so, continue to benefit from the trade it depends upon). On the other, it has to try and allay the growing resentment and hostility of its own people and religious establishment (who see the war in Iraq as unjustified and disastrous), and the insidious, corrupting influence of the West in general.

Saudi Arabia also fears a power imbalance in the region, so is strongly opposed to the withdrawal of US troops from Iraq. Nervous about Shiite Iran increasing its influence in the area (with neither Iraq nor America to counter it), it also fears the stirring up of sectarian tension within its own boundaries (Shiites dominate some areas, including the eastern provinces).

In the meantime, regional, tribal and sectarian discontent continues to simmer (albeit on a low flame and generally unfelt and unheard by the traveller – it's almost never reported by the country's press), as does the jockeying for power among the royal family, and an increasingly restless youth.

In response, the government continues its tried-and-tested policy of dampening the flames of any political discontent by chucking lots of money at it; a criticism long levied at the Al-Sauds by their opponents – in effect buying rather than earning the loyalty of its regions and tribes.

Another persistent threat to Saudi's future is terrorist attacks on both Western expats and the government, with the aim of destabilising what is viewed by Islamists as a corrupt and overtly pro-Western state. The security services have claimed both diligence and success in tracking down operatives. As you travel around the Kingdom, look out for the billboards proclaiming 'Together Against Terrorism' and 'Help police route out these people'.

It's worth remembering that tribal warfare and anarchy existed within the lifetime of some of the Kingdom's inhabitants. In many respects, Saudi Arabia has achieved an enormous amount (stability, peace and modernisation) in the space of about 50 years, when it took the West centuries.

GOVERNMENT & POLITICS

On paper (and many would say in practice too), Saudi Arabia is one of the least democratic countries in the world. There is no written constitution, no elected parliament and no political parties.

The Council of Ministers holds all executive and legislative power. It is headed by the king (who is also the country's prime minister), who also appoints all council ministers. The legal system is based upon Sharia'a (Islamic law).

In addition to the Supreme Economic Council (which advises ministers on economic policy), there is also the Consultative Council, though it only has a very limited influence and is made up entirely of men.

Wahhabism, the ultra-conservative interpretation of Sunni Islam, remains the cornerstone of the Al-Saud legitimacy (along with the political and moral support of its clerics). And though oil has transformed the country economically, politically it remains a deeply conservative society.

In 2005, the first and much-hailed Saudi municipal elections took place. Some commentators saw this as the first tentative – if limited – step towards the introduction of a democratic process in the Kingdom.

King Abdullah, despite initial concerns about his perceived conservatism and caution (particularly in balancing the demands of leading members of the royal family with the appeasement of the powerful clerical establishment), has won considerable credit among critics and commentators alike for his recent spate of reforms. These include even the curbing of royal family spending. He has also expressed his support for reforms for women.

Known locally as 'rolling thunder' for his decisive and widespread initiatives, he is genuinely popular among his people too.

Unless commitment to reform is genuine and far-reaching, however, and the pace of implementation quickened, Saudi's future path is still far from smooth and assured.

ECONOMY

Saudi Arabia's enormous oil wealth is the single most important factor that has shaped its economy. It is still the world's largest oil exporter with the largest proven oil reserves – estimated at over 250 billion barrels.

Since oil accounts for some 90% of exports and government revenue, the economy is highly dependent on the commodity, and very vulnerable to fluctuations in the world's oil prices. Projections based on known reserves suggest that oil will only continue to flow for the next 90 years or so.

Problems facing Saudi's economy include this high dependence on oil, the rapidly-growing population (which is expected to double by 2030), the high unemployment rate (which hovers at around 26%), and a relatively undereducated and underskilled Saudi workforce.

The education system in particular is in desperate need of reform to improve the skills and education of those entering the job markets. Currently, it is overly oriented towards religious studies and learning by rote, and fails to prepare its youth for the modern-day labour market.

Saudi's foreign workforce is also considered top-heavy (more than 50% of the total). The government is currently pursuing a 'Saudisation' programme in order both to increase the number of Saudis in the labour force, as well as to level out the balance of payments (most expat workers send a large portion of their salary to their home countries – look out for them queuing outside Western Union offices around the country). The government recently declared that it is going to limit the number of foreign workers and their dependants to 20% of the Saudi population by 2013.

Other future measures include diversification of the economy into non-oil sectors, including manufacturing and services, as well as encouraging the private sector. Saudi's accession to the WTO in 2005 should slowly lead to the liberalisation of the economy to comply with WTO rules including openness to foreign investment.

Saudi's economic forecast is fairly rosy (with a predicted annual growth of a healthy 5.2% to 2010), helped by foreign investment, increased oil production, and above all, high oil prices.

PEOPLE
The National Psyche

Residing as they do in the home of Islam, the Saudis are fiercely proud of their Islamic heritage. Religion plays a more active

VEILED FREEDOM?

'A woman's beauty is her hair,' goes one Arab saying. Walking around without a headscarf certainly seems to attract attention. Though you don't have to wear one, doing so does seem to earn you extra respect.

In the more conservative regions (the centre, far north, northwest and far south), many would prefer more. 'May God lead him to a straight path,' were the mutters my driver and I heard as we walked down a street in Najran. They assumed we were married; it was my 'husband's' shame to show me. Time to adopt the full attire.

From within the veil I could see without being seen, understand without being understood, and ogle the magnificent tribesmen without suffering inspection myself. It shielded from the sun and deterred the dust; it hid blemishes and bags brought on by a late-night's writing or a 15-hour drive. It concealed uncombed hair, a crumpled shirt or clumsy cosmetics. When I returned to London, the pressure to appear fashionable, feminine and *au fait* again seemed overwhelming. To my surprise, I secretly coveted those days in my coverings.

Don't think the Saudis themselves miss out too much either. Underneath the austere attire, many Saudi women don the finest fabrics or Milan's most fashionable fittings. Saudi men manage too:

'From the fold in a woman's ankle, you know her age; from the size of her wrist, her build; from the *abeyya* in motion, her figure; and from her hands, her complexion. From the eyes, you have everything else.'

Frances Linzee Gordon

part in the daily life of its inhabitants than perhaps anywhere else on Earth.

At the same time, many Saudis are drawn irresistibly to their satellite TV (the going rate is just SR200 for a satellite dish or cable) and their computers for the window it offers on the 'forbidden fruit' of the West (including European pornography channels), inciting in them both an envy and an utter contempt for all that the West offers.

In the same way, Saudis are both deeply suspicious of Western encroachment onto Islamic values and lands (including their own), but also can't get enough of American consumerism and popular culture including fast-food, and fast, gas-guzzling cars. A down side of all this is that a once very active people now lead a very inactive life; one of the consequences is one of the highest incidents of diabetes in the world.

Many Saudis also speak proudly of their Bedouin heritage, although few would forsake the comforts of city life for it now. One of the more positive results is a dramatic increase in life expectancy, which stands now at 75 years of age (77 for women). There has been a dramatic decrease in the fertility rate, which has fallen from a whopping 7.3 (number of live births per woman) in 1970–75, to 4.1 in 2007, though compared to the world average of 2.7, it's still high.

Lifestyle

Saudi society is strictly segregated between the public (male) and private (female) domain. Apart from Islam, family is the bedrock of Saudi society and family members only leave the family home once married.

Traditional Arabian society was formerly divided into nomadic desert dwellers, traders and sedentary town dwellers. In this pre-oil world, tribes were the main source of cultural identification and loyalty.

Since the discovery of oil, most former nomads have been encouraged to settle, and the importance of tribal loyalties has diminished a little. Nevertheless, such familial ties and bonds remain and are much stronger than the authorities and even some citizens care to admit to – even within the royal family.

Education (primary and secondary) is free (though strictly segregated) in Saudi Arabia; male professors sometimes lecture their female students via video link. The Saudi curriculum has been widely criticised for its overwhelming focus on Islam (one third of all subjects relate to the Quran).

For many women, life in Saudi Arabia is more controlled than anywhere else in the world (bar perhaps Taliban Afghanistan), particularly with regard to freedom of movement. Women are forbidden to drive and may not travel abroad without the permission of their husband or brother. Many Saudis (both men and women and including King Abdullah) are in fact strongly in favour of reform. Reforms are expected in the near future. Saudi Arabia has also signed the UN Convention to Eliminate Discrimination Against Women.

Girls also enjoy the same rights to attend (segregated) schools and universities as boys, and later work as teachers, doctors, nurses, social workers, business managers and journalists in the print media, although their numbers are proportionally small and most may deal only with women as part of their work. Many Saudis (including women) also claim that women in Saudi Arabia live free from the fear of public sexual violence.

For a look at modern-day life inside the Kingdom see the boxed text, p327.

Population

More than 80% of Saudi Arabia's population is concentrated in urban areas, with one-third of the population living in the urban agglomerations centred on Riyadh, Jeddah and Mecca.

Overall population density is low: 12 people per square kilometre, although desert regions have less than one person per square kilometre. Despite the urbanising impact of oil wealth and modernisation, around 1.8 million Bedu still claim to live a semi-nomadic lifestyle, though numbers are decreasing all the time.

Saudi's population is very young (over 40% of the population are under 15 years old), with an annual population growth rate of 2.8% (which means that the population doubles every 20 years). Saudi authorities are increasingly confronted with the dilemma of providing for a disaffected, young, undereducated population with not enough jobs (or money) to go around (see also p305).

Multiculturalism

Modern Saudi Arabia is a paradox. One of the most insular societies on earth, yet less than two-thirds (some say only half) of the population is Saudi. Official figures place the number of foreign expatriates living and working in the Kingdom on temporary visas at nine million or more.

Westerners (mainly from Europe, North America and Australasia) work in high-skilled jobs for which most Saudis do not have the qualifications. Non-Western expats (primarily Pakistanis, Bangladeshis, Indians and Filipinos) perform mostly unskilled labour (such as taxi driving, construction work and domestic help), which many Saudis consider beneath them.

A process of 'Saudisation' is underway (see p305), but foreigners still form the backbone of the Saudi economy. Many of the lower-paid immigrants complain of ill-treatment, exploitation or even abuse, although Saudi law does in theory protect its legal immigrants.

RELIGION

Islam is not just the religion of Saudi citizens, it's the religion of Saudi society and the Saudi state, and is all-encompassing.

Officially, all Saudis are Muslim, 15% of whom are Shiites who are found in different parts of the country but particularly in the Eastern Provinces. The practice of other religions is strictly forbidden in Saudi Arabia. Non-Muslims cannot even be buried there.

Wahhabi Islam

The prevailing Islamic orthodoxy in Saudi Arabia is Wahhabi Islam (also known as the Hanbali or literalist school of Islamic interpretation). It is named after Mohammed ibn Abd al-Wahhab, who preached a 'new' message in the 18th century – essentially a call to return to the roots and purity of Islam.

At the heart of the Wahhabi doctrine lies the denunciation of all forms of mediation between Allah and believers, and a puritanical reassertion of *tawhid* (the oneness of God). Under the Wahhabis, only the Quran, the Sunnah (the words and deeds of Mohammed) and the Hadith (Mohammed's sayings) are acceptable sources of Islamic orthodoxy. The worship of saints and the reverence towards tombs belonging to holy men (especially by the Sufis) are seen as acts of egregious heresy.

Obligations espoused by Al-Wahhab included the requirement to pay *zakat*, a tax (in 2007, 2.5% of net worth) payable to the leader of a Muslim community and calculated according to a person's wealth.

Communal prayers are also considered a religious duty, and rulings on personal matters are interpreted according to Sharia'a (Islamic law), which has changed little in the 14 centuries since it was revealed by the Prophet Mohammed.

One of the central questions in modern Saudi Arabia today is the battle over who can be considered the true inheritors of the Wahhabi legacy. Famously, Al-Qaeda believes that it is they, not the Saudi royal family, who are the modern guardians of the austere and fundamentalist Wahhabi vision.

Although Muslims traditionally attribute a place of great respect to Christians and Jews as Ahl al-Kitab (People of the Book), Wahhabi orthodoxy is unusually hostile to any deviations (whether they be Shiite or Christian) from Sunni Islam.

ARTS
Literature

Novelists to chronicle the impact of oil money and modernisation on a traditional desert kingdom include Hamza Bogary, Ahmed Abodehman and Abdelrahman Munif (works are available in English).

Recent translations of Saudi women writers offer an interesting perspective into the otherwise closed world of Saudi women. Among them are Saddeka Arebi, Raja Alim, Fowziyha Abu Khalid, Ruqayya ash-Shabib, Sharifa as-Shamlan, Khayriyya as-Saggaf and Najwa Hashim.

Music

Since the early 1980s the Saudi government has made recordings of folk-music traditions from almost every village of the Kingdom, and some of these are screened on Saudi TV. In the Hejaz, the Al-Sihba form of folk music interestingly blends Bedouin poetry with the songs of Arab Andalusia in mediaeval Spain.

Of the musicians whose music has found an audience in the wider Arab world, among the most important are Tariq Abdul Hakim, Mohammed Abdou, Abadi al-Johar, Mohammed Aman and Abdou Majeed Abdullah.

Architecture

Saudi Arabia boasts a good range of architecture, though sadly much built in the traditional style has either disappeared or is deteriorating fast. Recently launched restoration projects should start preserving some for posterity.

Among the finest examples of traditional architecture (high-walled homes built from mud, straw, stone and palm products) can be found at Al-Ula (p333) and Dir'aiyah (p318). Mud fortress-style architecture can find its most enchanting expression in Najran in southwestern Arabia.

Further north, the merchants of Jeddah built stunning homes from Red Sea coral with lattice-work wooden balconies.

The most startling expressions of modern Saudi architecture are found in Riyadh, such as at the Kingdom and Al-Faisaliah Towers.

Dance

The mesmerising Bedouin *ardha*, with its roots in the Najd, is the national dance of Saudi Arabia, and involves a pastiche of singers, dancers and a poet-narrator. Sword-bearing men, shoulder to shoulder, are set off by a singing poet while the men sway in unison to rhythmic drum beats.

Your best chance of seeing one of the more than 50 folkloric dance and music groups in Saudi Arabia is at the annual Jenadriyah Festival (p314).

ENVIRONMENT
The Land

Saudi Arabia takes up 80% of the Arabian Peninsula. Over 95% of Saudi Arabia is desert or semidesert, and the country is home to some of the largest desert areas in the world, including Al-Nafud (Nafud Desert) in the north and the Empty Quarter in the south.

Just 0.5% of Saudi territory is considered to be suitable for agriculture and less than 2% of the land is covered by forest.

Saudi Arabia's most elevated regions run like a spine down the west coast – from 1500m in the north, up to Jebel Soudah (2910m) lcoated in the southwestern Asir Mountains.

Wildlife

Illegal hunting is still a major problem in Saudi Arabia, and during your travels, the animal you're most likely to come across is the Arabian *hamadrya* (baboon), which is proliferating along the mountain roads of southwestern Saudi Arabia.

The waters of Saudi's Red Sea are rife with wildlife (see Diving, p359), including five species of marine turtle; the green and hawksbill sometimes breed on Saudi Arabia's Red Sea beaches. Whales and dolphins are also present in both the Red Sea and the Gulf.

For more information on the Kingdom's wildlife, contact the **National Commission for Wildlife Conservation & Development** (NCWCD; Map p312; ☎ 01-441 4333; www.ncwcd.gov.sa; ☯ 7.30am-

2.30pm Sat-Wed). The commission's small museum can be visited in Riyadh.

ENDANGERED SPECIES

At least seven mammal species are considered endangered in Saudi Arabia, including the Syrian wild ass, Arabian gazelle, Saudi gazelle, Arabian jird, Arabian oryx, Arabian leopard and Nubian ibex.

Efforts such as captive breeding and re-introduction programs are at the forefront of the government's work to arrest the slide. Also vulnerable are Geoffroy's bat, the lesser horseshoe bat and Sind bat. The Kingdom's waters are among the last remaining habitats for the dugong.

Endangered bird species include the Arabian bustard (found on the Tihamah coastal plain). The ostrich and Houbara bustard are currently being bred in captivity and the latter has been successfully reintroduced into the wild.

National Parks

At the time of writing, Saudi authorities have designated 13 wildlife reserves (which amount to over 500,000 hectares) as part of a plan for more than 100 protected areas.

Travellers wishing to visit any of the reserves must apply for permission from the **NCWCD** (☎ 01-441 4333; www.ncwcd.gov.sa;

CAMEL CULTURE

Though the traditional, Bedouin way of life has long since passed for most Saudis, a few habits die hard. The camel, traditionally much treasured and revered by the Bedu, remains an important status symbol in the Kingdom (with the obvious exception of the city of Jeddah, where it's your 'wheels' which really count).

The Saudis simper over their camels as Westerners worry over their dogs and cats. Some owners visit their cherished charges daily; others take off at weekends with coffee and dates, and friends or families in tow to admire their animals.

Unlike the keeping of sheep or goats, the keeping of camels serves no commercial purpose; in fact many owners expend vast sums on medicine and veterinary fees. A herd of 50 camels is not an unusual number to own; several hundred is not uncommon. Today, it's the Sudanese Bedu who usually care for the camels, especially those from the Al-Rashid tribe who are famous for their facility with camels.

During the school holidays, Saudi families love to go to the races. At other times of the year, camel beauty contests occur, in which several thousand camels of all shapes, sizes and colours converge from all across the Kingdom. The author visited one; first prize was no less than 100 cars. At Saudi weddings, camels given as gifts are appreciated above all. In Riyadh, the people are still partial to baby camel served on a plate – count the traditional restaurants that still serve *hashi*.

It all goes to show, you can take the Saudi out of the Bedu, but you can't take the Bedu out of the Saudi.

SAUDI ARABIA

OLD HABITS DIE HARD

Many visitors to the Kingdom are shocked by the state of Saudi's scenery. Though some cities such as Riyadh may be kept sparkling by the legions of immigrant workers, not so the countryside. Indeed, discarded tyres are so ubiquitous along the sides of the roads that they're known as 'desert dolphins'; they may be the only Saudi wildlife you see.

Until quite recently, most Saudi waste was biodegradable, consisting of natural materials such as pottery, cotton and paper. With the introduction of plastics, along with a consumer society, and a burgeoning population with the oil, bygone Bedouin habits are coming back to haunt them.

Nevertheless, environmental campaigns are slowly gathering pace. Look out for the US-inspired 'Leave No Trace' adverts, as well as the sporadic land, coastal and even coral reef clean-ups across the country.

In September 2006, stiff fines (between SR200 and SR5000) for dropping litter were introduced, though they're yet to be forcefully implemented. Wildlife awareness programmes are also underway to combat hunting and to teach locals how to care for their environment.

⏰ 7.30am-2.30pm Sat-Wed). Some of the best places to see wildlife are at the 'Uruq Bani Ma'arid Protected Area (p349) in the Empty Quarter and the Farasan Islands (p348).

Environmental Issues

Saudi Arabia's environmental problems are legion, and include desertification, pollution, deforestation, lack of local education and awareness, and the critical depletion of underground water.

Illegal hunting (even of endangered species) is a particular problem. Once part of Bedouin survival, many Saudis are struggling to cease the sport.

Expansion of human settlements to accommodate Saudi Arabia's rapid population growth, as well as overgrazing by local herds have both led to the decline in numbers of ungulate species and also ensured that a number of wildlife species are highly endangered.

On the plus side, captive breeding programmes and the subsequent reintroduction of species formerly extinct in the wild (particularly the Arabian oryx) are considered to be among the most successful in the world.

The Kingdom's water shortages are being partially addressed through the development of costly seawater desalination facilities.

FOOD & DRINK

Traditional Saudi food shares many characteristics with the cuisines of other Gulf States (see p82). But it also benefits greatly from the enormous influence of its immigrant population (particularly Asian), which spices up (literally) the traditional standard Bedouin diet of meat and rice.

Great feasts mark the momentous events of Saudi society and some dishes have been designed especially for such occasions. One of the most famous ceremonial dishes is *khouzi*. It consists of a whole lamb potroasted with almonds, sultanas, spices and hard-boiled eggs. It's served with rice, and in some areas, the eyes are a delicacy and reserved for honoured guests.

As a traveller, you will be offered food and refreshments every step of your way, often in stomach-groaning excess. It is considered mean and remiss to serve a meal that isn't far in excess of your guest's needs, even when ordering in restaurants.

Some of the Saudi fast-food chains are also well worth tasting. The most famous is the newish and wildly successful Jeddah (and Mecca) chain Al-Baik, a kind of Saudi equivalent of KFC.

Starters

Many restaurants serve mezze, truly one of the joys of Arab cooking. Similar in conception to Italian antipasti or Spanish tapas (for which it was the inspiration), mezze can include dips such as hummus (chickpea dip), a variety of nuts, *lahma bi-ajeen* (small lamb pies), *kofta* (meat balls), *wara ainab* (stuffed vine leaves) and other savoury pastries.

Main Dishes

Grilled chicken, *shwarma* (meat sliced off a spit and stuffed in a pocket of pita-type bread with chopped tomatoes and garnish) and *fool* (fava bean paste) are the ubiquitous cheap – but often delicious – dishes. You'll find restaurants specialising in them in almost every town in the Kingdom.

For a few riyals more, meat dishes are served with rice and salad. In some, the rice (hard-grain basmati) will itself be a highlight – aromatic and enlivened by a spice mix known as *baharat*, which can include cardamom, coriander, cumin, cinnamon, nutmeg, chilli, ginger and pepper, with (occasionally) turmeric and saffron added for colour.

Rosewater (or orange-blossom water), pine nuts, tomato and ghee (*samneh*; clarified butter) are sometimes used in Saudi cooking. The *baharat* spice concoction is also sometimes used in preparing soups, fish and other meat dishes.

Another enduring favourite of Gulf palates is *kebab meshwi* (shish kebab).

Seafood is another widely available highlight. Fish in Saudi Arabia is at its best when slow-cooked over coals or baked in the oven, but it's usually fried in cheaper places. Other seafood on offer includes prawns, crabs and lobster.

RIYADH الرياض

☎ 01 / pop 3.7 million

Once little more than a dusty, desert outpost, Riyadh today is one of the fastest growing cities in the world. Since the 1970s (and the influx of ample oil revenue), the population has tripled. Today, Riyadh is the country's capital as well as its financial and administrative centre, eclipsing at last Jeddah's power and influence on the coast.

Nowhere are the contradictions of modern Saudi Arabia more evident than in Riyadh. Seen from afar, soaring, sparkling, stunning modern towers rise above the desert and camels. Amid the split-new Chevrolets and luxury Lotuses, slip the *mutawwa* (religious police) hurrying and harrying the citizens to prayer.

Its considered conservative, cautious and sober, yet the Kingdom's capital boasts handsome hotels, fabulous fine-dining and cosy cafés. It's also got considerable culture, including a National Museum that numbers among the best in the region.

HISTORY

Riyadh became the Al-Saud capital in 1818 when the Al-Sauds were driven from Dir'aiyah by soldiers loyal to the Ottoman sultan. Riyadh fell to the Al-Rashids in the 1890s, and it was not until the dramatic recapture of the city in 1902 that Riyadh became the Al-Sauds' undisputed and permanent capital.

ORIENTATION

Riyadh reels and sprawls over 960 sq kms. Unfortunately, most of its street signs are in Arabic only. Al-Bathaa is the central, older portion of town. Most of what you'll require in Riyadh lies north of here, especially in Olaya and Sulaimania, the main business and shopping areas.

The main north–south thoroughfares are Olaya St and King Fahd Rd, while Makkah Rd is the main east–west artery.

Maps

The Farsi *Map & Guide of Riyadh* (SR20) is essential for navigating your way around Riyadh. It's very detailed, and contains an extensive index of street names and points of interest.

INFORMATION
Bookshops

Jarir Bookstore (Map p312; ☎ 462 6000; Olaya St; www.jarirbookstore.com; ☒ 9am-2pm & 4-11pm Sat-Thu, 4-11pm Fri) The excellent Jarir Bookstore has extensive selections in Arabic and English. The Olaya St branch is the most accessible.

Emergency

Ambulance ☎ 997
Fire ☎ 998
Police ☎ 999
Traffic accidents ☎ 993

Internet Access

There are loads of internet cafés across Riyadh, though you'll be very hard pushed to find any that admit women (even foreign women).

Manila Internet (Map p314; ☎ 403 4345; Manila Plaza, Al-Bathaa; per hr SR5; ☒ 8.30am-10pm Sat-Thu, 8.30am-10.30am & 12.30pm-10pm Fri)

Medical Services

24-Hour Pharmacy (Map p312; Mosa ibn Nosayr St) Located in Al-Akariya Centre.

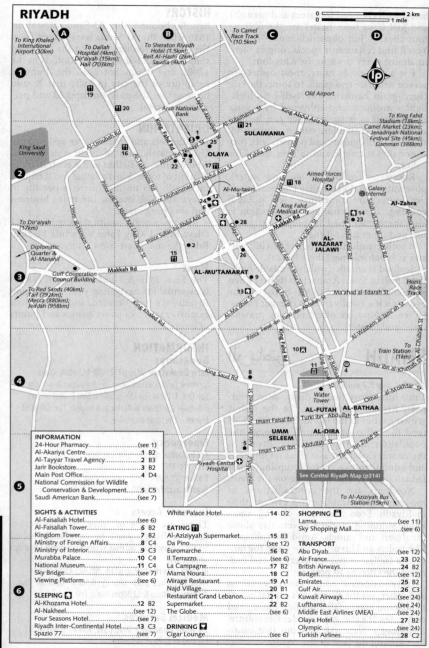

RIYADH

0 —— 2 km
0 —— 1 mile

To King Khaled International Airport (30km)

To Dallah Hospital (4km); Dir'aiyah (15km); Hail (703km)

To Sheraton Riyadh Hotel (1.5km); Beit Al-Hashi (2km); Saudia (4km)

To Camel Race Track (10.5km)

Arab National Bank

Old Airport

King Saud University

SULAIMANIA

OLAYA

To King Fahd Stadium (18km); Camel Market (23km); Jenadriyah National Festival Site (45km); Damman (388km)

Al-Mu'tasim St

Armed Forces Hospital

Galaxy @Internet

AL-ZAHRA

To Dir'aiyah (17km)

Diplomatic Quarter & Al-Manahil

Gulf Cooperation Council Building

King Fahd Medical City

Makkah Rd

AL-WAZARAT JALAWI

To Red Sands (40km); Taif (792km); Mecca (880km); Jeddah (958km)

Makkah Rd

AL-MU'TAMARAT

Horse Race Track

Ma'ahad al-Edarah St

To Train Station (1km)

King Saud Rd

Omar ibn al-Khattab St

Water Tower

AL-FUTAH   AL-BATHAA

Omar

al-Mokhtar St

AL-DIRA

UMM SELEEM

Riyadh Central Hospital

See Central Riyadh Map (p314)

To Al-Aziziyah Bus Station (15km)

INFORMATION
24-Hour Pharmacy..........................(see 1)
Al-Akariya Centre............................**1** B2
Al-Tayyar Travel Agency....................**2** B3
Jarir Bookstore................................**3** B2
Main Post Office.............................**4** D4
National Commission for Wildlife
  Conservation & Development...........**5** C5
Saudi American Bank.......................(see 7)

SIGHTS & ACTIVITIES
Al-Faisaliah Hotel...........................(see 6)
Al-Faisaliah Tower...........................**6** B2
Kingdom Tower..............................**7** B2
Ministry of Foreign Affairs................**8** C4
Ministry of Interior.........................**9** C3
Murabba Palace.............................**10** C4
National Museum............................**11** C4
Sky Bridge...................................(see 7)
Viewing Platform...........................(see 7)

SLEEPING
Al-Khozama Hotel..........................**12** B2
Al-Nakheel...................................(see 12)
Four Seasons Hotel.........................(see 7)
Riyadh Inter-Continental Hotel.........**13** C3
Spazio 77...................................(see 7)

White Palace Hotel.........................**14** D2

EATING
Al-Aziziyyah Supermarket................**15** B3
Da Pino......................................(see 12)
Euromarche..................................**16** B2
Il Terrazzo...................................(see 6)
La Campagne................................**17** B2
Mama Noura.................................**18** C2
Mirage Restaurant.........................**19** A1
Najd Village.................................**20** B1
Restaurant Grand Lebanon...............**21** C2
Supermarket.................................**22** B2
The Globe...................................(see 6)

DRINKING
Cigar Lounge................................(see 6)

SHOPPING
Lamsa..(see 11)
Sky Shopping Mall.........................(see 6)

TRANSPORT
Abu Diyab...................................(see 12)
Air France...................................**23** D2
British Airways..............................**24** B2
Budget.......................................(see 12)
Emirates.....................................**25** B2
Gulf Air.......................................**26** C3
Kuwait Airways.............................(see 24)
Lufthansa....................................(see 24)
Middle East Airlines (MEA)...............(see 24)
Olaya Hotel..................................**27** B2
Olympic......................................(see 24)
Turkish Airlines.............................**28** C2

SAUDI ARABIA

Dallah Hospital (☎ 454 5277; cnr King Fahd & Al-Imam Saud ibn Abdul Aziz ibn Mohammad Rds) This hospital northeast of Riyadh accepts emergency cases on a walk-in basis.

Money

Banks and moneychangers can be found throughout Riyadh, including on Olaya St and Al-Bathaa St.

Post

Main Post Office (Map p312; King Abdul Aziz Rd; ⊙ 7.30am-2.30pm & 4-10pm Sat-Wed, express mail window 7.30am-1pm Thu) Located north of the intersection with Al-Bathaa St.

Travel Agencies

Al-Tayyar (Map p312; ☎ 463 3667; www.altayyargroup .com; Al-Takhassasi Rd; ⊙ 9am-1.30pm & 4.30-8pm Sat-Thu) The largest travel company in the Kingdom and one of the most reputable, Al-Tayyar can organise car hire, air tickets, tourist visas, accommodation and tours.

SIGHTS
National Museum

This state-of-the-art **museum** (King Abdul Aziz Museum; Map p312; ☎ 402 9500 ext 1290; www.arriyadh .com; King Saud Rd; adult/child/student SR15/10/free; ⊙ men & schools 9am-noon Sun, Mon, Wed, Thu & 4.30-9pm Tue; women & schools 9am-noon Tue; families 4.30-9pm Sun, Mon & Wed-Fri) is without question one of the best museums in the Middle East. Its eight floors contain well-designed, engaging and informative displays on Arabia's history, culture and art, including beautiful, original rock carvings, models and even a full-scale reconstruction of a Nabataean tomb.

Films (in English via headphones) shown on 180° screens complement the exhibits, as do virtual visits to sites and other excellent interactive displays.

It's great for a sneak preview of the Kingdom's attractions, a sum-up, or a virtual visit if you don't have time to get to places. Don't miss it.

Murabba Palace

Built by King Abdul Aziz in 1946, this **fortress-palace** (Qasr al-Murabba; Map p312; ☎ 401 1999; King Saud Rd; ⊙ 8am-3pm & 6-9pm Sun-Fri) is most impressive for its formidable white-washed walls than for anything much within. Largely empty (albeit labelled) rooms surround a central courtyard.

Masmak Fortress

This **fortress** (Qasr al-Masmak; Map p314; ☎ 411 0091; Imam Turki ibn Abdullah St; admission free; ⊙ men 8am-noon & 4-9pm Sat, Mon & Wed, women & families 8am-noon & 4-9pm Sun & Tue, 9am-noon Thu) is Riyadh's most significant historical monument. It was built around 1865 on the site of an earlier fortification and has been extensively restored to its pre-Saud days.

Masmak was the scene of Ibn Saud's daring 1902 raid, during which a spear was hurled at the main entrance door with such force that the head is still lodged in the doorway. The information panels and short (but action-packed and well-produced) films on the storming and the 'reunification' afterwards are rather reverential towards the Al-Sauds, but are worth watching nonetheless.

Inside, look out for the mosque, *diwan* (meeting room), and well (in the rear courtyard). There are also displays of weapons and costumes, maps and evocative photographs dating from 1912 to 1937.

Outside, the four watchtowers stand around 18m high and the walls are 1.25m thick.

Al-Faisaliah Tower

Designed by British architect Norman Foster and built in 2000 by the Bin Laden construction company, **Al-Faisaliah Tower** (Map p312; ☎ 273 3000; www.rosewoodhotels.com; off Olaya St; admission SR35; ⊙ 10am-midnight) was the first of the startling new structures to rise above Riyadh's skyline. It's most famous for its enormous glass globe (24m in diameter and made of 655 glass panels) near the summit.

On its 34 floors can be found a five-star deluxe hotel and four exclusive restaurants (see p314), offices, apartments, the **Sky shopping mall** (☎ 273 0000; ⊙ 10am-11.30pm Sat-Thu, noon-11.30pm Fri) and a fabulous **viewing platform** (Globe Experience; per adult/family SR25/35; ⊙ 10am-11.30pm Sat-Thu, noon-11.30pm Fri). The tower's needlepoint pinnacle (with a crescent on the tip) sits 267m above the ground.

Kingdom Tower

Riyadh's newest landmark **tower** (Map p312; King Fahd Rd) is another stunning piece of modern architecture. Known as the 'necklace' for its unusual apex, it's particularly

SAUDI ARABIA

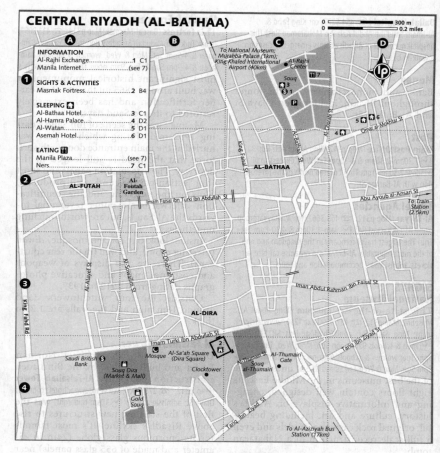

CENTRAL RIYADH (AL-BATHAA)

INFORMATION
Al-Rajhi Exchange.....................1 C1
Manila Internet.......................(see 7)

SIGHTS & ACTIVITIES
Masmak Fortress......................2 B4

SLEEPING 🏨
Al-Bathaa Hotel......................3 C1
Al-Hamra Palace......................4 D2
Al-Watan.............................5 D1
Asemah Hotel.........................6 D1

EATING 🍽
Manila Plaza.........................(see 7)
Ners.................................7 C1

conspicuous at night when the upper sweep is lit with constantly-changing coloured lights.

Rising 302m above the ground, its most distinctive feature is the steel-and-glass, 300-tonne bridge connecting the two towers. High-speed elevators fly you (at 180km/h) to the 99th floor **Sky Bridge** (☎ 201 1888; admission per child/adult SR12.50/25; ⏰ 10am-midnight) from where the views are breathtaking (you're allowed to take photos from up here). Avoid weekends and evenings after 6pm when it can get very crowded.

If you're feeling peckish, the tower is also home to some reputable restaurants, including Spazio 77 (p316).

COURSES

The **Al-Manahil** (☎ 488 1069; www.almanahil.com .sa; Ibn Zaher St, Diplomatic Quarter) offers Arabic courses to non-Arabic speakers (men and women) at 10 levels (consisting of 24 hours spread over two weeks). Lying just west of the French and Italian embassies, it specialises in tuition to women (but can also accommodate men).

FESTIVALS & EVENTS

The annual two-week **Jenadriyah National Festival** takes place in late February or early March at a special site about 45km northeast of central Riyadh.

Commencing with the King's Cup (an epic camel race with up to 2000 participants racing across a 19km track), the festival programme includes traditional songs, dances, and poetry competitions, as well as demonstrations of falconry, and exhibitions of traditional crafts from around the Kingdom. It's a colourful event; don't miss it if you're in town.

SLEEPING

Note that contrary to the rest of the country, Riyadh's hotels fill up during the week (with people on business) and are quieter at weekends. To be sure of a room, reserve three to four days in advance; several weeks in advance in the high season.

Budget

Al-Watan (Map p312; ☎ 404 3489; fax 403 1644; Rail St, Al-Bathaa; s/d SR70/100) Don't be put off by the lurid green paint; the rooms are a decent-size, fresh-smelling and sparkling. There's even a plastic potplant for company.

Al-Hamra Palace (Map p312; ☎ 403 1071; fax 409 4077; Asad Bin Al-Farat St, Al-Bathaa; s/d SR80/100) Well-hidden behind the Riyadh Hotel and with a sign in Arabic only, this is nonetheless worth finding; it's the best budget bet in town. Its 30 rooms are clean, fairly well-furnished and are quieter than most. It's next door to the Smari Pharmacy.

Midrange

Asemah Hotel (Map p312; ☎ 402 4121; fax 402 4120; www.asemah.com; Ibn Faris St, Al-Bathaa; s/d SR150/180) New and nicely decorated, the 68 rooms are arranged around a quiet central courtyard and are terrific value for money. There's also a coffee shop and a restaurant.

Al-Bathaa Hotel (Map p314; ☎ 405 2000; www.albatha-hotel.com; Al-Bathaa St; s SR180-220 d 260-300; 🖳) With large (40 sq metre) rooms designed like mini suites, professional management, a central location and breakfast included to boot, this is a great choice. There's also a good coffee shop, a paper shop and a health club.

White Palace Hotel (Map p312; ☎ 478 7800; www.hotelwhitepalace.com; King Abdul Aziz Rd; s/d 170/260; 🖳) Though it may look a bit like a polystyrene box with bubbles for balconies, it's well-maintained, well-managed and unbeatable value for money. Rooms have good views (ask for the Kingdom Tower side) and facilities include free access to the business centre, airport pick up (SR60), and

a restaurant. In the future there will be a pool which *may* open to women also.

Al-Khozama Hotel (Map p312; ☎ 465 4650; www.rosewoodhotels.com; Al-Faisaliah Tower, Olaya St; s/d 500/600, ste SR2000; 🖳 🍴) Though rooms aren't the largest, they're cosy, comfortable and well-furnished. With a lively lobby, a good patisserie (cakes SR15), a coffee shop, and three reputable restaurants offering a good variety and quality of cuisine including Al-Nakheel (Arabic) and Da Pino (Italian), it's a popular choice for those on business.

Top End

ourpick Al-Faisaliah Hotel (Map p312; ☎ 273 2000; www.rosewoodhotels.com; Al-Faisaliah Tower, Olaya St; s SR800-1000, d SR800-1250, royal ste SR10,000; 🖳 🍴) Beyond adorably decorated rooms, it's the attention to detail (including fresh orchids and chocolates) that make Al-Faisaliah stand out. It's also known for excellent service (including 24-hour butlers in tailcoats) and good facilities (such as DVD players in all rooms). Its Il Terrazzo restaurant has a good reputation too.

Riyadh InterContinental Hotel (Map p312; ☎ 465 5000; www.intercontinental.com; Al-Ma'dhar St; s/d from SR900/1100; 🖳 🍴) A great choice for those on business, each room has a little office, the hotel provides first-class service, and facilities include a nine-hole golf course, health club, squash and tennis courts, as well as laptop rental (per day SR150). Excursions can be organised.

RIYADH'S REMARKABLE ARCHITECTURE

Being less than 100 years old, Saudi Arabia is unimprisoned by its past; there's sackfuls of space and prosperous patrons falling over one another to build the biggest and the best.

Scan the Saudi skyline: there's the King Fahd football stadium with its dramatic white 'sails' that resemble a Bedouin's tent; the Ministry of Foreign Affairs that copies a *qasr* (traditional castle); and the Ministry of Interior that resembles a space ship. Look for Riyadh's most recognisable icon of all: the Kingdom Tower, known as the 'necklace', or 'bottle-opener' by the less charitable.

Love it or loathe it, Saudi's architecture is statement-making.

Four Seasons Hotel (Map p312; ☎ 211 5000; www .fourseasons.com; 15-24th fl, Kingdom Tower, King Fahd Rd; s/d SR1200/1600, ste SR11,000; ☑ ☎) Located in the Kingdom Tower, the hotel's biggest boon is its show-stopping views (ask for rooms on the upper levels) through wide-paned windows. All in grey, granite and glass, it's a slick, sleek and modern choice.

EATING

All of the following have family sections unless indicated.

Budget

There are a mass of cheap eats and *shwarma* stands along Talya St. Choose the busiest.

Mama Noura (Map p312; ☎ 470 8881; Prince Abdul Aziz ibn Mosa'ad Jalawi St; kebabs SR5-13; ☑ 6am-3am) Large, bright and clean, this Turkish place remains perennially popular among Riyadhis, who come for the succulent *shwarma* (sandwich/plate SR3/10) or famous felafel (deep-fried balls of chickpea paste with spices; SR3 to SR10). There's no family section, but takeaway is possible.

Ners (Map p314; ☎ 50-078 9927; mains SR6-15; ☑ 11am-10pm Sat-Thu & 7am-10am Fri) Located on the 2nd floor of the Manila Plaza, Ners is an old fave among Riyadh's Asian community for its freshly prepared Filipino and Thai food at fabulous prices. It's clean, waiter-served and very friendly. Dishes such as tom yum soup (SR15) or chicken chilli with coconut milk (SR12) are delicious.

Restaurant Grand Lebanon (Map p312; ☎ 463 1888; Al-Sulaimania St; mezze SR6, mains SR12-20; ☑ 6.30am-2am Sat-Thu, 1pm-2am Fri) Spotless, salubrious and serving delicious Lebanese and Syrian dishes that change daily, this is much loved locally. The mixed grill (SR20) is something of a speciality.

There are supermarkets around Olaya including Euromarche and Al-Azizyyah.

Midrange

our pick **Najd Village** (Map p312; ☎ 464 6530; Al-Ta-khassosi Rd; mains SR15-25; ☑ men only noon-midnight Sat-Thu, families only noon-midnight Fri) Serving Saudi food in a Saudi setting (designed like a central-region village), this place is almost unique in the Kingdom. It's the perfect place to sample *kasba* (meat with rice; SR25), or the Najd region speciality, *hashi* (baby camel). The set menu (SR85;

minimum five people) includes 14 different mains, coffee, dates and even *bachoor* (incense). Prices are reasonable and it's much loved by locals.

Beit al-Hashi (Map p312; ☎ 240 0000; Prince Abdul-lah bin Abdul Aziz Rd; men only; ☑ 10.30am-12.30am) Though located just over 10km north of the centre, this restaurant's worth the trek for its famous speciality, baby camel (SR35). The sign's in Arabic only (look for the appropriately camel-coloured sign). It's next to Mama Noura Juice Centre, just west of the Sheraton.

Spazio 77 (Map p312; ☎ 211 1888; open buffet per child/adult SR60/140; ☑ 10am-1am Sat-Thu, 1pm-1am Fri) Located in the nook of the 'necklace' of the Kingdom Tower, Spazio 77 consists of a coffee shop, brasserie and sushi bar – all with gorgeous views thrown in for free.

Top End

La Campagne (Rif Al-Lubnani; Map p312; ☎ 416 2006; Tahlia St; mezze SR8-25, mains SR30-85; ☑ 12.30pm-1am) Though roomy and rambling, the place gets packed – it's rated by some as Riyadh's best Lebanese. The mezze are freshly made and the grills are something of a speciality. In warm weather, head for the lovely covered terrace at the back. Reserve 24 hours in advance; 48 hours at weekends.

Mirage Restaurant (Map p312; ☎ 483 4127; Al-Takhassosi Rd; starters SR10-66, mains SR35-166; ☑ 1pm-11.30pm) Boasting 'the best Chinese chef in the Peninsula', the Mirage certainly attracts a loyal, and royal, following (the king's grandchildren were there when we visited). The décor (illuminated fish tanks and water channels running down the centre), is like the food – full of fun and panache. Reservations are essential at the weekend.

The Globe (Map p312; ☎ 273 3000; Al-Faisaliah Tower; set menus SR350-750; ☑ noon-3pm, 7.30pm-1am) Considered one of Riyadh's top-ranking restaurants, it's also one of the most romantic. Cosy, dimly-lit and with spectacular views of town, it's the place to go to gaze over candlelight. The *haute cuisine* cooking of the Austrian chef includes dishes such as pan-roasted foie gras, and butter-roasted wagu beef.

DRINKING

There's a good number and selection of cafés in the shadow of the Al-Faisaliah Tower, as well as along Tahliya St.

CREATIVE CRUISING

If you think it might be difficult to survive in a city with perhaps the most restricted entertainment scene in the world, spare a thought for young Saudis. In a country where cinema is banned, singles are kept strictly separated from members of the opposite sex and nightclubs are nonexistent, young Saudis have resorted to novel means of making contact.

The least subtle of these are the *shebab* (teenage boys) with little else to do but 'impress' other drivers with their speed. Cars also cruise up and down outside girls schools and the *shebab* sometimes throw their phone numbers from the window in the hope of receiving a call on their mobile phones.

A similar charade takes place in the shopping malls (particularly the Al-Faisaliah and Kingdom Towers). Called 'numbering', it's the Saudi version of a casual encounter. The latest Blue Tooth technology has facilitated things still further by allowing total strangers to text each other without even knowing each other's numbers.

Cigar Lounge (Map p312; ☎ 273 3000; Al-Faisaliah Tower; minimum cover charge per person SR150, cigars SR74-450; ☾ noon-2.30am) A badly kept secret among well-heeled 20- to 30-something Saudis as *the* place to take a date, it's all low-light...and discretion here. Set in the highest point of the Al-Faisaliah Tower, the views by day and night are spectacular. Snacks range from Beluga caviar (SR795) to hot mezze (SR50). Drinks include coffee (SR21 to SR30) and non-alcoholic cocktails (SR37 to SR40).

ENTERTAINMENT

Foreign embassies (see p363) frequently organise cultural and social evenings, as well as musical or theatrical performances, so it's not a bad idea to get plugged into the expat scene.

SHOPPING

In a country where there are scarce public diversions, shopping has become almost a national sport. A new shopping mall seems to mushroom up every three months, crammed with all the latest international designer outfits a woman (or man) could want. Even if you're not buyin', the malls are well worth a mosey.

Among the most famous malls are **Kingdom Tower** (Map p312; ☎ 211 2222; Al-Mamlaka Mall; ☾ 9am-noon & 4-11pm Sat-Thu, 4-11pm Fri), which even has a floor for women only ('Ladies Kingdom') and the mall in **Al-Faisaliah Tower** (Map p312; ☾ 9.30am-noon & 4-10.30pm Sat-Tue, families only 10am-11.30pm Wed-Thu & 4-10.30pm Fri) is also well known and popular.

For (mostly) Arabic handicrafts, **Lamsa** (Map p312; ☎ 401 4731; lobby, National Museum;

☾ 9.30am-noon & 4.30-10pm Sun-Thu, 4.30-10pm Fri) has a good though not inexpensive selection. Most handicrafts and 'antiques' are in fact manufactured by the Lamsa company.

For the real McCoy, head to **Souq al-Thumairi** (Map p314; Al-Thumairi St; ☾ 9am-noon & 4-9pm Sat-Thu, 4-9pm Fri) immediately south of the Masmak Fortress in the Al-Dira area. The shops in the small lanes offer everything from carpets to coffee pots and silver daggers to silver jewellery.

GETTING THERE & AWAY
Air

Riyadh's **King Khaled International Airport** (Map p312; ☎ 222 1700) lies nearly 40km north of Al-Bathaa. All domestic air services are operated by the main carrier, **Saudi Arabian Airlines** (Saudia; ☎ 450 0000; www.saudiairlines.com; Olaya St; ☾ 8am-10pm Sat-Wed), which has an office 14km north of Al-Bathaa. A number of airlines have offices around Olaya.

There are daily flights to Abha, Jeddah, Najran, Sakaka (Jouf) and Shararah for SR280 each, Medina and Taif for SR250, as well as Jizan (SR320), Dammam (SR150) and Hail (SR200).

Bus

Al-Aziziyah Bus Station (☎ 213 2318) lies around 17km south of the city centre. From Al-Aziziyah station to Al-Bathaa stop (under the bridge, around 200m from Al-Bathaa Hotel) buses (SR2, 10 to 15 minutes) run every 15 to 30 minutes. Taxis cost SR10 to SR15.

There are daily departures heading to Dammam (SR60, five to six hours, every hour); Hail (SR100, eight hours, seven daily); Al-Hofuf (SR45, three hours, three daily); Jeddah (SR135, 12 hours, every two hours); Taif (SR110, 10 hours, Jeddah bus); Najran (SR135, 13 hours, three daily); Sakaka (SR190, 15 hours, two daily); Abha (SR135, 12 hours, every two hours); Jizan (SR170, 13 hours, three daily); and Al-Ula (SR150, 12 hours, one daily).

There's also a VIP service to Al-Khobar (SR90, five hours, four daily) departing from the Olaya Hotel.

Car

Car-hire agencies in Riyadh can be found along Olaya St, near the Al-Khozama Hotel, where choices include **Budget** (Map p312; ☎ 463 3546) and **Abu Diyab** (Map p312; ☎ 464 7657); as well as at the airport domestic arrivals hall.

Train

From the **train station** (☎ 473 4444; www.saudi railways.org; off Omar ibn al-Khattab St; ⏱ 7am-2am), 2.5km east of Al-Bathaa, direct trains run to Dammam (2nd/1st/VIP class SR60/75/130, 3¾ hours, two daily) via Al-Hofuf (SR45/55/100, 2½ hours, four daily).

GETTING AROUND
To/From the Airport

Buses (SR10, every two hours) run from 8am to 10pm daily between Al-Aziziyah **Saptco Bus Station** (☎ 213 3219) and the airport, via the main bus stop in Al-Bathaa.

A taxi from the airport to the city centre costs SR70, from the city centre to the airport SR50, but negotiate first.

Taxi

Riyadh's white taxis charge SR5 for a journey of 1km to 2km, but always negotiate the price first.

AROUND RIYADH

CAMEL MARKET & RACES

Riyadh's **camel market** (Souq al-Jamal; free admission; ⏱ sunrise-sunset) is one of the largest in the Arabian Peninsula. Spread out north of the Dammam road 30km from the city centre (take the Thumamah exit), this is a fascinating place to wander. Late afternoon is when the traders really find their voices. If you want to put in a bid, you'll need a good SR5000 to SR10,000.

At 4pm on some Thursdays during season, camel races take place at the camel race track along the extension of Al-Uroubah St in the Thumamah district, 10.5km from Riyadh.

DIR'AIYAH   الدرعية

The ancestral home of the Al-Saud family and the birthplace of the Saudi-Wahhabi union, **Old Dir'aiyah** (☎ 486 0274; admission free; ⏱ 8am-4.30pm Sat-Thu, 4pm-5.30pm Fri winter, 8am-5.30pm Sat-Thu, 4pm-5.30pm Fri summer), makes a welcome escape from the frenzy of Riyadh.

Built of mud, this old, walled oasis town boasts a few restored buildings, but most lie in ruins, lending it an evocative, abandoned, even ghostly air. The ruins are among the most extensive old cities in the Kingdom.

Ask for the free colour pamphlet at the Visitor's Centre; inside there's just the odd panel with site labels.

History

The site was settled in 1446 by an ancestor of the Al-Sauds. Dir'aiyah reached its peak in the late 18th and early 19th centuries, during the first Saudi empire. The city fell to the Ottomans after a six-month siege in 1818. After Dir'aiyah was razed, the Al-Sauds moved to Riyadh.

Walking Tour

As you climb up from the car park, the **Palace of Salwa (1)** – once a four-storey complex of palaces, residential and administrative buildings and the home of Mohammed ibn Abd al-Wahhab – towers above the **visitors' centre (2)** on your left. Directly opposite, the **Al-Saud Mosque (3)** was once connected to the palace by a bridge.

The main path continues south, then east, then south again to the **Palace of Fahd (4)** and **Palace of Abdullah bin Saud (5)**. Further south are the somewhat nondescript ruins of the **Palace of Thunayyan Bin Saud (6)**, behind which are good views out over the palm groves.

Returning to the main path, walk west for around 250m, passing the ruined **Palace of Mishaari (7)** on the right and the newly restored **Al-Turaif Bath (8)**, with its decoratively painted doors. After a further 100m to the west and northwest respectively, you'll find the restored **Palace of Nasser (9)** and the **Palace of Saad bin Saud (10)**, which has turrets, wall

DIR'AIYAH

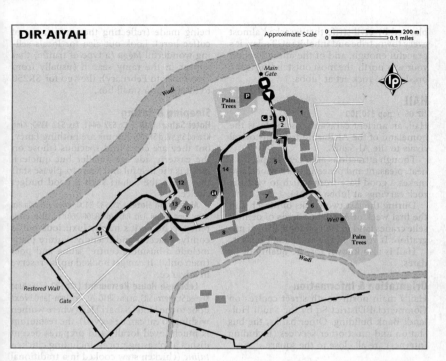

Approximate Scale

Main Gate

Palm Trees

Restored Wall

Gate

Wadi

Well

Palm Trees

Wadi

and door decorations. This is how much of Dir'aiyah must have once looked.

The main lane continues west before entering an open area where few houses remain. You can continue on to the restored sections of the wall (which once ran for 15km around the perimeter of Dir'aiyah) or branch off to the north to the **Tower of Faisal (11)**, the only restored tower in Dir'aiyah. A different path twists back to the Palace of Saad bin Saud, passing en route the ruined **Palace of Fahran bin Saud (12)** and the **Saad bin Saad Mosque (13)**.

Circle the Palace of Saad bin Saud from where a path heads north and then east back to the entry gate, passing some of the best-preserved **houses (14)** along the way; watch for decoratively painted doors hanging forlornly from their hinges.

Getting There & Away

There's no public transport to Dir'aiyah, which lies 25km northwest of Al-Bathaa. A one-way taxi costs SR30; if you want it to wait for you, you'll need to negotiate the fare back.

If you're driving, take King Fahd Rd north and follow the signs off to the west after passing the Dallah Hospital. The road then turns north again – follow the brown signs marked 'Old Dir'aiyah'.

SAND DUNES

There are numerous stretches of sand dunes just off the Riyadh–Mecca Hwy.

The **Red Sands**, just west of the turn-off to Duruma around 40km west of Riyadh, are probably the best because they boast a backdrop of the cliffs of the Jebel Tuwaiq Escarpment – a great sight at sunset. To see them properly, you'll need a 4WD.

THE NAJD نجد

Meaning 'highland', the Najd is hemmed in by the Hejaz Mountains to the west and vast stretches of sand surrounding its other three sides. Its people are known for their strict and staunch adherence to Islam, and the local women all don the traditional burka (face veil). For centuries the region was

SAUDI ARABIA

plagued by civil strife that wracked almost every town, tribe and inhabitant. Today, it's peaceful enough, and of the attractions on your way north, the most outstanding is the pre-Islamic rock art at Jubba.

HAIL   حايل
☎ 06 / pop 310,100

Hail, an ancient caravan crossroads, is the homeland of the Al-Rashid tribe, historical rivals to the Al-Sauds.

Though attractions aren't epidemic, it's a neat, pleasant and peaceful town which also makes a good base from which to visit the rock carvings at Jubba (p321).

During the last two weeks of March and the first week of April, hundreds of demoiselle cranes land in Hail on their annual migration. If you're in the area, don't miss it.

Hail is also known for the quality of its dates.

Orientation & Information

Hail's main north–south street centres on Commercial District Sq by the Saudi Hollandi Bank building. Other banks, the bus station and most other services (including internet) are all close to the square.

Sights

The mud-brick **Al-Qashalah Fortress** (☎ 533 1684; admission free; 9am-noon) in the centre of town was built in the 1930s and was used mostly as a barracks for King Abdul Aziz's troops in Hail. Recently restored, it may soon open afternoons also. The tent inside should eventually house a small museum.

Near the post office is the **Hail Museum** (☎ 533 1684; admission free; 9am-noon) which contains archaeological finds from the surrounding area.

On a hill just outside the centre of town, the impressive-looking **'Airif Fort** (admission free; 9am-noon & 4-6pm Sat-Thu, 4-6pm Fri), also mudbrick, was built around 200 years ago as a combined observation post and stronghold. Inside you can wander the (now empty) residential quarters, mosque, baths and storerooms. It makes a pleasant climb up the hill, and there are lovely views from 'Airif's main watchtower.

Hail's **souq** (7am-sunset Sat-Thu, to 10.30am Fri), found behind the elementary school, is well worth a wander, and you can watch traditional coffee pots (SR60 to SR2000)

being made (reflecting the importance of coffee here). Look out also for locals selling wonderful *fagga* (a type of truffle) that appear in the rainy season (usually from December to February); they go for SR250 to SR300 for a small box.

Sleeping & Eating

Hotel Sahari Hail (☎ 532 6441; fax 532 4390; King Khaled St; s & d SR100) Rooms are nothing fancy, but they are clean and spacious (those on the eastern side are smaller but quieter), but it is the helpful and keen-to-please staff that make the Sahari such a good budget choice.

Al-Jabalain Hotel (☎ 532 3100; www.jabalain.8m .com; King Abdul Aziz Rd; s/d SR200/260) Hail's current top hotel, it's hardly luxurious but is comfy, peaceful and friendly. Future plans include a business centre, sauna and pool (men only). It can get booked up, so reserve in advance.

Lebanese House Restaurant (☎ 532 6736; King Khaled St; mezze SR3, mains SR10-20; 1pm-1am) Next door to the Hotel Sahari Hail (where women wishing to eat can be served), the restaurant is much loved locally and prepares decent dishes at pleasing prices, including chicken *tajine* (chicken stew cooked in a traditional clay pot; SR10), *shwarma* (SR5 to SR10) and pizza (SR5 to SR15). It also sells fruit juices (small/large SR3/5).

ourpick At-Thurathy (☎ 532 9636; King Faisal St; 6am-midnight Sat-Thu, 11.30am-midnight Fri) Halfrestaurant, half-museum, you can admire the artefacts over your baby camel (SR25) or roasted, quarter kid (SR150). Seating is on the floor around a courtyard. Sadly, construction of a new road is threatening to close this all-too-rare example of Saudi tradition, but it will hopefully relocate elsewhere.

Getting There & Away

There are daily **Saudia** (☎ 532 2222; Main Rd) flights to and from Riyadh (SR200, three daily) and Jeddah (SR250, one daily), and less frequent departures to Dammam (SR360), Medina (SR160) and Sakaka (Jouf; SR110).

Saptco (☎ 531 0101) has buses to Riyadh (SR100, eight hours, three daily), Al-Ula (SR65, five hours, one daily), Jubba (SR20, one hour, two daily), Tabuk (SR100, eight hours, five daily), Sakaka (SR185, 20 hours,

---

THE ROCK ART OF ARABIA

With almost 2000 rock art sites, Saudi Arabia is one of the richest open-air museums in the world. Every year, locals discover more. Though some are in a very sad state of decay as a result of natural erosion as well as local vandalism (look out for the bullet holes riddling some!), they are well worth seeking out. All are astonishing for their extraordinary age; some give great insights into the ancient culture they represent, and a few are very beautiful.

The general rule is that the earlier carvings display a higher degree of sophistication, while later carvings are simpler, even child-like.

The most impressive examples you'll come across in Saudi Arabia date from around 5500 BC and mark the transition from hunter-gatherer communities to sedentary agricultural ones, as reflected in the images of domesticated cattle.

The most impressive and accessible sites are at Jubba (below), Al-Ula (p333) and Sakaka (p338).

---

twice daily) and Jeddah (SR110, 12 hours, one daily non-stop).

Getting Around

Hail's taxis can take you around town (around SR10 but be sure to negotiate first).

JUBBA جبة

Jubba, lying 100km northwest of Hail, is famous above all for its impressive **rock carvings** (www.jubbahil.com). Revealing a level of sophistication remarkable for their era, they include ibexes with long curved horns, and several sets of elegant and elongated human figures, and are believed to date from 5500 BC when much of the area was covered with water. There are also cruder carvings of camels and other domesticated animals dating from around AD 300. The closest carvings to Jubba are 3kms away.

A permit is necessary to visit the site. You can either obtain it from Riyadh (see p367), the Hail Museum (p320), or from the custodian of the keys himself and local guide, the energetic and entrepreneurial **Ateeq Naif al-Shamari** (☎ 057 494 877).

To find him, follow the signs to Naif's Palace of Heritage, which is just off the main street. Whilst there, cast a glance at the lovely 800-year-old well, the valuable collection of arms, and the rooms where Lady Blunt apparently rested. The **museum** (☎ 541 2103; admission SR20; ⏰ 7am-7pm) – along with the Palace – is a family heirloom, and the result of a life time's collection of antiques and artefacts. It's also well worth a wander.

Apart from guiding you to the rock carvings (all-day hikes are possible to some),

Mr Ateeq (☎ mobile 05 0749 4877) can also organise camel excursions lasting from one hour to five days or more, ranging from visits to rock carvings and local Bedu camps, to full-on traverses of the GreatNafud desert.

As Mr Ateeq doesn't speak English, you'll need to enlist the help of an Arabic speaker or go through a tour agency (see p323).

Prices range from SR300 per person for one day's sightseeing by camel, to SR1500 per person (minimum two) for a three-day trip into the Great Nafud desert. Excursions by 4WD are also possible, as are trips to see traditional falconry. All camping equipment can be supplied and a pick up from both Hail and Hail airport can be arranged.

You'll need your own transport to get to Jubba, or call Mr Ateeq.

HEJAZ الحجاز

Meaning 'barrier', the region derives its name from the great escarpment that runs along the Hejaz, separating it from the great plateaux of the interior. It also seems separate in its distinct character, culture and history. The Hejazi are fiercely proud of their heritage; a few even mutter about independence.

The Hejaz has seen a multitude of merchants and traders pass through its portals as well as pilgrims on their way to perform the haj. For this reason, it's the most multicultural and mixed of all Saudi's regions.

With its Red Sea coastline, its mountainous hinterland and the fascinating old town of Jeddah, it is a great place to pass some days.

SAUDI ARABIA

JEDDAH   جدة

☎ 02 / pop 3.2 million

A converging point for pilgrims and traders for centuries, Jeddah is probably the largest cultural melting pot in the world. The tremendous foreign influence is reflected not just in the faces of its multicultural inhabitants, or in its range of restaurants, souqs and shops, but even in the peculiar, hotpotch accent of the liberal, laidback Hejazis.

Considered the most cosmopolitan town in the Kingdom – and somewhat wild, degenerate and dangerous by some Saudis! – it has a palpably relaxed, seen-it-all feel. Don't be surprised if you see bikini-clad girls on jet skis at the beaches here.

Jeddah is also the undisputed commercial capital of Saudi Arabia. If you fancy a spot of shopping, this is the town to trawl (see p328).

The Al-Balad district, the heart of Old Jeddah, is a nostalgic testament to the bygone days of old Jeddah, with beautiful coral architecture casting some welcome shade over the bustling souqs beneath. Occupied largely by the poorest of the poor – mainly over-staying Haj pilgrims – they crumble visibly before your eyes. There's now a local race to save the old town before it too disappears under the concrete.

History

A local legend asserts that Eve died and was buried here: the name 'Jeddah' means 'grandmother'. The graveyard (Hawa Cemetery, northeast of Al-Balad) still exists, but is out of bounds to non-Muslims (who are not permitted to enter Islamic cemeteries).

Since AD 646, when Caliph Uthman officially established Jeddah as the gateway to Mecca, Jeddah's fortunes have been dominated by Islam's holiest city, which lies to Jeddah's east. The entire Hejaz came under nominal Turkish control in the 16th century, though the local rulers retained a great deal of autonomy. The Wahhabis, under Abdul Aziz, took control of the city in 1925.

Orientation

Al-Balad, the historic district, loosely represents the centre of Jeddah; King Abdul Aziz St is its main north–south thoroughfare, and has a host of restaurants, banks and

shops. Medina Rd is the principal street running north from the centre, flanked to the west by Al-Andalus St.

The corniche (Al-Kournaish Rd) runs the length of Jeddah's coastline from Jeddah Port in the south to the city's northern outskirts.

MAPS

The best map is the Farsi *Map & Guide of Jeddah* (SR20), which is available from any Jarir Bookstore.

Information

BOOKSHOPS

Jarir Bookstore (www.jarirbookstore.com; ⊙ 9am-2pm & 4.30-11pm Sat-Thu, 4.30-11pm Fri) Falasteen St (Map p323; ☎ 673 2727); Sary St (Map p323; ☎ 682 7666)

EMERGENCY

Ambulance ☎ 997
Fire ☎ 998
Police ☎ 999
Traffic accidents ☎ 993

INTERNET ACCESS

Jeddah has numerous internet cafés (open to men only), which include the following two places:

Asia Internet Café (Map p324; ☎ 668 9834; King Abdul Aziz St; per hr SR3; ⊙ 7.30am-midnight Sat-Thu, 10am-noon & 1.30pm-midnight Fri)
Hala Internet Café (Map p323; ☎ 653 0884; At-Tawbah St; per 30 mins/hr SR3/5; ⊙ 7am-2am Sat-Thu, 7am-9am & 3pm-3am Fri)

MEDICAL SERVICES

Dr Sulayman Fakeeh Hospital (Map p323; ☎ 665 5000, 660 3000; Falasteen St) A good accident and emergency department.

MONEY

Head for the row of **moneychangers** (Map p324; Al-Qabel St, Al-Balad; ⊙ 9am-1.30pm & 4.30pm-10pm), which offer good rates, and don't charge commission.

POST

Main Post Office (Map p324; Al-Bareed St; ⊙ 7.30am-9.30pm Sat-Wed)
Post Office (Map p323; off Medina Rd, Al-Hamra'a)

TELEPHONE

There are international call cabins all over the city.

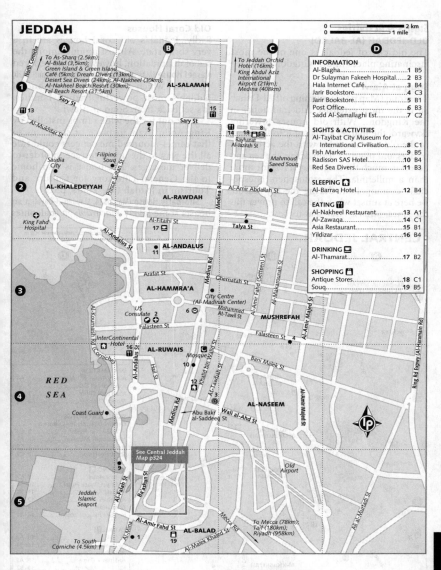

JEDDAH

INFORMATION
Al-Blagha.....................................**1**	B5
Dr Sulayman Fakeeh Hospital.....**2**	B3
Hala Internet Café......................**3**	B4
Jarir Bookstore...........................**4**	C3
Jarir Bookstore...........................**5**	B1
Post Office.................................**6**	B3
Sadd Al-Samallaghi Est...............**7**	C2

SIGHTS & ACTIVITIES
Al-Tayibat City Museum for	
International Civilisation.........**8**	C1
Fish Market................................**9**	B5
Radisson SAS Hotel...................**10**	B4
Red Sea Divers..........................**11**	B3

SLEEPING
Al-Barraq Hotel.........................**12**	B4

EATING
Al-Nakheel Restaurant...............**13**	A1
Al-Zawaqa.................................**14**	C1
Asia Restaurant.........................**15**	B1
Yildizar.....................................**16**	B4

DRINKING
Al-Thamarat..............................**17**	B2

SHOPPING
Antique Stores...........................**18**	C1
Souq..**19**	B5

TOURS

Sadd Al-Samallaghi Est (Map p323; Talya St; ☎ 668 5054; www.samallaghi.com) With a solid reputation locally, this tour company can organise Saudi visas, tours, car rental , scuba diving, desert excursions (including falconry) and boat trips. Ahmed Mostafa, the Saudi owner (who lived formerly in Germany) runs the company with a killer combination of local know-how and Teutonic efficiency.

TRAVEL AGENCIES

Alireza Travel & Tours (Map p324; ☎ 648 1380; www.alirezatravel; King Abdul Aziz St; ⏰ 9am-8.30pm Sat-Thu) The long-established Alireza Travel & Tours agency is a good place to visit to if you're after airline tickets. It issues tickets for all major airlines both inside and outside the Kingdom (as well as for airlines servicing the Peninsula).

SAUDI ARABIA

Sights & Activities

OLD JEDDAH (AL-BALAD)

The old city of Jeddah is one of the most fascinating places in the Kingdom.

Souq al-Alawi

This souq (Map p324), running off Al-Dahab St, is the most extensive and traditional in the Kingdom. With old houses towering skyward, the market stalls cut into the heart of the old city and buzz with the activity of traders and pilgrims from across the sea and desert in much the same way it has for more than a millennia. The atmosphere is especially cosmopolitan during the haj season. Be here at sunset when the call to prayer fills the lanes – this is Arabia at its best.

Old Coral Houses

Sadly, Jeddah's old coral houses are in a very sorry state. Almost unique among the sea of dilapidation, however, is the restored **Naseef House** (Map p324; ☎ 647 2280; admission SR20; ⏱ 5-9pm), which once belonged to one of Jeddah's most powerful trading families. It's set back from Souq al-Alawi.

Look out for the wide ramps installed by King Abdul Aziz in place of staircases so that camel-mounted messengers could ride all the way to the upper terrace in order to deliver messages. The house is also home to the General Directory for Culture and Tourism in Jeddah (see Tours, p326).

Shorbatly House (Map p324; Maydan al-Bayal) also boasts some lovely *mashrabiyya* (balconies

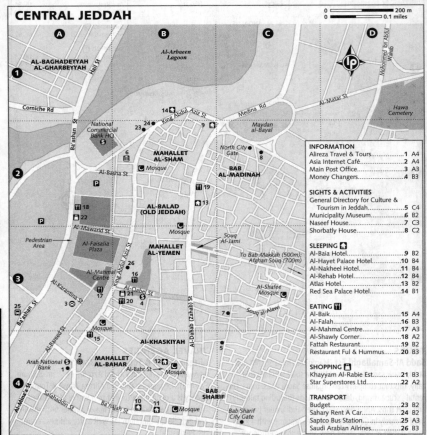

CENTRAL JEDDAH

0 .... 200 m
0 .... 0.1 miles

INFORMATION	
Alireza Travel & Tours	1 A4
Asia Internet Café	2 A4
Main Post Office	3 A3
Money Changers	4 B3

SIGHTS & ACTIVITIES	
General Directory for Culture & Tourism in Jeddah	5 C4
Municipality Museum	6 B2
Naseef House	7 C3
Shorbatly House	8 C2

SLEEPING	
Al-Baia Hotel	9 B2
Al-Hayet Palace Hotel	10 B4
Al-Nakheel Hotel	11 B4
Al-Rehab Hotel	12 B4
Atlas Hotel	13 B2
Red Sea Palace Hotel	14 B1

EATING	
Al-Baik	15 A4
Al-Falah	16 B3
Al-Mahmal Centre	17 A3
Al-Shawly Corner	18 A2
Fattah Restaurant	19 B2
Restaurant Ful & Hummus	20 B3

SHOPPING	
Khayyam Al-Rabie Est	21 B3
Star Superstores Ltd	22 A2

TRANSPORT	
Budget	23 B2
Sahary Rent A Car	24 B2
Saptco Bus Station	25 A3
Saudi Arabian Airlines	26 B3

SAUDI ARABIA

with perforated screens to allow the air to circulate). Though much restored to something approaching its original state in the 1980s, it has since been allowed to deteriorate once again. It is closed to visitors.

MUSEUMS

Jeddah now boasts no less than 13 museums. Some of them are private collections belonging to the heritage-proud and ever-entrepreneurial Hejazi, and are open by appointment only. The General Directory for Culture & Tourism in Jeddah (see Tours, p326) can arrange access if you're interested.

Don't be put off by the grandiose name: **Al-Tayibat City Museum for International Civilisation** (☎ 693 0049; www.altaybatcity.com; Rayhanat al-Jazirah St; students/adults SR20/30; ☖ 8am-noon & 5-9pm Sat-Thu) definitely merits a visit. The vast palace contains over 300 rooms crammed with a collection built over a local merchant's lifetime.

The four-floor collection ranges from exquisite Islamic manuscripts and old coins, to stunning furniture and pottery (some of it bought from international art houses). Exhibits are accompanied by good captions and information panels, as well as a few dioramas.

Note that, unfortunately, it can't open for less than 10 people; try and form a group or telephone to join one.

For those who have neither the time nor the energy to face Jeddah's 'Louvre', try the **Shallaby Museum of Traditional Handicrafts & Hejazi Heritage** (☎ 697 7442; Al-Balad; admission free; ☖ 10am-1pm & 6-11pm Sat-Thu) with a good collection of coins, silver antiques (look out for the silver-plated wedding slippers) and traditional Bedouin clothes.

FISH MARKET

The colourful and frenetic **fish market** (Map p324; west of Al-Kournaish Rd; admission free; ☖ 5am-9pm) is located in Al-Balad, just over 1km south of the Red Sea Palace Hotel. It's well worth a wander if only to admire Saudi's Red Sea riches – there's at least 50 species of fish on display ranging from hammerhead sharks to grouper, parrot fish and squid.

Don't miss, if you can, the daily auction of the morning's catch (from 5am to 9am), when the place really lights up. Note that

---

JEDDAH'S OPEN-AIR ART

Ever mindful of the serious spiritual responsibility that comes with the hosting of the haj, Jeddah's mayor had an idea: to use some of the vast oil revenue of the 1960s to beautify his city, the official portal to the pilgrims. For the next 20 or so years, Mohammed Said Farsi collected sculptures from all around the world and placed them at strategic points along the seafront.

Jeddah's corniche now comprises one of the most impressive outdoor sculpture collections in the world, and counts among it no less than four bronzes by the British sculptor Henry Moore, as well as work by, among others, the Spaniard Joan Miró, the Finnish artist Eila Hiltunen and the French César Baldaccini.

One artist, the Spaniard Julio La Fuente, contributed in particular, as a landscape architect as well as a sculptor. Hired to help beautify the city, he demonstrated how scrap metal could be recycled into art – see if you can spot his pieces.

---

as the market's situated close to the Coast Guard and Port, photos are not permitted.

CORNICHE

Do as the Saudis long have and take a walk along the 35km-long corniche (Al-Kournaish Rd; Map p323), particularly on a warm, summer's night. You'll get a real sense of what Jeddah is all about, as well as life in the Kingdom today. Students sit cross-legged and stooped over books, families share picnics spread on rugs, men gather to gossip and cut commercial deals, and young men meet to play cards and show off their latest car.

Look out for the famous corniche sculptures (see boxed text, above) that line the wide pedestrian areas for 30km north from the port. Subjects range from the mundane to the miraculous; from anchors and boats to giant sunflowers squirting water; elongated and fragmented camels to a boat made entirely out of Arabic calligraphy.

BEACHES & DIVING

Sadly, some of Jeddah's best stretches of sand are now covered in concrete. What's left often disappoints. Many beaches are swamped by beachgoers at weekends, along with their sand buggies and jet skis.

Some five-star hotels have their own private beach. The **Radisson SAS Hotel** (Map p323; ☎ 652 1234; www.radissonsas.com; Medina Rd) allows nonguests to use their beach and facilities for SR50 per person per day, or you can head for Al-Nakheel (see p329).

See p360 for information on diving around Jeddah.

Tours

The **General Directory for Culture & Tourism in Jeddah** (Map p324; Naseef House; ☎ 647 2280; www .jeddah.org.gov) organises an excellent 'lecture and walking tour' of Jeddah's history and architecture at 9am every Thursday, meeting at Naseef House (p324). To book a place, email jedsam@yahoo.com, or call the charming director, Sami Nowar. It's located south of Souq al-Alawi.

Sadd Al-Samallaghi Est (p323) is also a good option for tours.

Sleeping

Most of Jeddah's budget and midrange hotels are in Al-Balad.

BUDGET

Al-Nakheel Hotel (Map p324; ☎ 647 5127; alnakhil@icc .net.sa; Ba'najah St; s/d from SR80/130) Very much the best of the budget bunch, Al-Nakheel's rooms are reasonably sanitary, quite well-furnished (including fridge and TV) and well-maintained. Ask to see several rooms, as they vary in size.

Atlas Hotel (Map p324; ☎ 643 8520; fax 644 8454; Al-Dahab St; s/d from SR80/120) Though some of the furniture's seen happier days, and the hotel's within easy earshot of a mosque, the rooms are clean, quite spacious and well cared for.

Al-Rehab Hotel (Map p324; ☎ 647 9636; fax 647 2246; s/d from SR90/140) Similar to the Al-Nakheel above and belonging to the same owners, the Al-Rehab also offers good value for money. Clean and quite attractively decorated, all rooms also have fridges and TVs. It's just off Al-Bahr St, west of the mosque.

MIDRANGE

Al-Barraq Hotel (Map p323; ☎ 650 3366; htl_barraq@ hotmail.com; Khalid bin Walid St; s/d SR125/150) Smaller and with more character than most, the

Barraq's a little gem: rooms are all well-furnished, decent-sized and great value.

Al-Hayet Palace Hotel (Map p324; ☎ 647 7111; www.alhayethotel.com; Ba'najah St; s/d SR160/180; ☐) This new, four-star hotel, lying 50m west of Bab Sharif, is centrally-located, well-managed and unbeatable value for money; rooms are a reasonable size and the décor's very decent. There's also a choice of two restaurants. It's next door to the Tysir Hotel.

Al-Baia Hotel (Map p324; ☎ 644 4446; Maydan al-Baya; s/d SR180/250) Though the rooms aren't the largest, the lovely views from 24 of them overlooking the Al-Arbaeen Lagoon and city, plus the rational prices and well-furnished rooms (some also with balcony) more than compensate. The restaurant on the 9th floor brings you the additional boon of breakfast-with-a-view.

Jeddah Orchid Hotel (Map p323; ☎ 607 0777; jeddahorchidhotel@hotmail.com; Medina Rd; s/d from SR270/360; ☐) If you're catching an early flight, or are in town for business, this new and accommodating four-star hotel is located opposite the Jeddah Exhibition Center, just 5km from the southern terminal of the airport.

TOP END

Red Sea Palace Hotel (Map p324; ☎ 642 8555; www .redseapalace.com; King Abdul Aziz St; s/d from SR350/425; ☒) This newly renovated, five-star hotel's biggest boon is its location in the thick of things downtown, as well as its impressive views over the Al-Arbaeen Lagoon offered by 135 of its rooms. The downside is sometimes stinky seaward smells, and a booking service that could be more reliable.

Al-Bilad Hotel (☎ 694 4777; www.albiladhotel.net; North Corniche; s/d SR420/550, bungalow SR850; ☐ ☒) Situated 35km from downtown, the Bilad is much beloved for its 'escape-the-crowds' feel and cosy, homey atmosphere. Facilities include a bakery, a lovely, covered veranda (complete with air con in summer) and large, landscaped gardens with sea glimpses and birdsong.

Mövenpick Hotel Jeddah (☎ 667 6655; www .moevenpick-hotels.com; s/d from SR450/500; ☐ ☒) Lying on Medina Rd, 10km from the town centre, the recently opened Mövenpick combines Rococo razzle with its usual reputation for excellent food and hospitality. Facilities include a terrific Indo-Chinese restaurant (three-course business lunch SR49 per person), and ice-cream parlour.

InterContinental Hotel (☎ 661 1800; www.intercontinental.com; Al-Kournaish; s SR650-725, d SR800-875; 🖳 🛋) The chic InterContinental boasts three main drawcard: the waterside location, good facilities (including decent restaurants), and the attention to detail (right down to complementary underwater cameras and playing cards for the kids).

Qasr As-Sharq (☎ 659 9999; www.hilton.com; North Corniche; ste US$1500-15,000; 🖳 🛋) Decorated by the same designer that worked on Dubai's famous Burj al-Arab, the newly opened seven-star As-Sharq prides itself on 'Luxury' (with a capital L) and 'discretion'. The dazzling décor includes no less than 60kg of gold leaf, silk curtains and a 12m chandelier; rooms all have a 42-inch plasma TV (complete with gold-panelling) and 24-hour butler service. In low-season, rates are US$700 to US$15,000.

Eating
BUDGET

Restaurant Ful & Hummus (Map p324; ☎ 647 6468; off Al-Qabel St; 🕑 7am-11.30am & 5pm-10.30pm Sat-Thu, 8.30am-10.30am & 5.30pm-10.30pm Fri) For a filling breakfast of bread and *fool* (SR4), do as the locals do and head here. It lies a couple of doors down from Khayyam Al-Rabie date shop. The sign's in Arabic only – look for the Coca Cola sign.

Al-Shawly Corner (Map p324; ☎ 644 7867; Ba'ashan St; 🕑 9am-11pm) This Filipino-run restaurant remains wildly popular with Jeddah's Asian community. Though simple and unpretentious, it's clean, the food is fresh, and the service is fast and efficient. There's also a family section and a few outdoor 'cubicles'. Ask for the 'budget meal' (soup, choice of two mains, rice and Coke, SR12), which is terrific value.

Al-Baik (☎ 647 7827; meal SR10; 🕑 11am-midnight) A kind of Saudi equivalent of KFC (but considered far superior by its fans) that comes complete with its own secret recipe. Well-heeled young Saudis are said to fly in from Riyadh and back, especially for a chicken fillet fix for them and their friends.

Al-Falah (Map p324; ☎ 647 4974; entrées from SR5, mains SR10-15; 🕑 7.30am-11.30pm Sat-Thu, 4pm-11.30pm Fri) Sparkling and central, and with a large seating area, the Al-Falah serves up Arabic, Filipino and Chinese dishes ranging from *shwarma* (SR4) to fried shrimp (SR15) and sweet-corn soup (SR4). The restaurant lies down a side street east of King Abdul Aziz St – take the first left after McDonald's.

Al-Zawaqa (Map p323; ☎ 691 6004; Sary St; mains SR15-35; 🕑 7am-2am) Much loved locally, this Lebanese restaurant serves everything from great grilled chicken and succulent *shwarma* to chocolate baklava and fresh fruit juices. For something different, try the fried lamb's testicles (SR15).

For a table-with-a-view, the 7th floor of the **Al-Mahmal Centre** (Map p324; King Abdul Aziz St) has several small restaurants serving Turkish, Lebanese and Filipino fast food.

MIDRANGE

Fattah Restaurant (Map p324; ☎ 604 0620; Al-Dahab St; ✹ 6am-midnight) Don't be put off by the façade (rustic log cabin meets Santa's grotto), this Yemeni restaurant is a firm local fave; sample the food and you'll soon see why. Try the delicious shish kebabs (SR10) served with tahini and chilli sauce and freshly-baked flatbread

Asia Restaurant (Map p323; ☎ 682 8525; Sary St; mains SR20-40; ✹ 1pm-12.30am) A longstanding favourite locally (particularly among Jeddah's expats), the Asia's Thai food is much sought after, particularly the tom yum kum soup (SR15) and its fish seafood, such as deep-fried grouper with tasty chilli sauce (SR40). Reserve at weekends – it gets packed.

ourpick **Al-Nakheel Restaurant** (Map p323; ☎ 606 6644; Al-Mukhtar St; starters SR12-15, mains SR25-50; ✹ 9am-3am) Styled like a traditional tent (with open sides to let in the sea breezes), this is the place, to come for a taste of Jeddah – in the culinary and cultural sense. It's wildly popular locally; even the Jeddah women let their hair down here (literally). The food is great; the fish and seafood is a speciality.

TOP END

Yildizar (Map p323; ☎ 653 1150; off Al-Andalus St; entrées from SR15, mains SR40-60; ✹ 1pm-1am) Lavish in both décor and its dining, the Yildizar (and its Lebanese chefs) are renowned. Dishes range from boneless pigeon with truffles (SR55) to caviar (SR100), fabulous fish dishes (SR65 to SR180) and gorgeous grills (SR30 to SR60).

Green Island (Map p323; ☎ 694 0999; North Corniche; starters SR45-65, mains SR65-130; ✹ 1pm-1am) Spread across the water in the form of little chalets-on-stilts (complete with glass floor panels that reveal the fish and the water beneath), this is the place to come if you're after a final splurge or a romantic revival. The menu is a fusion of Arab, Asian and Continental cuisines. Try the locally loved rock lobster bisque (SR25), or go for the all-out 'seafood platter Green Island' (SR130).

CAFES

The perfect place for a drink at sunset or for a morning coffee-and-cake (coffee SR5 to SR6, desserts SR12 to SR15) is the **Green Island Café** (Map p324; ☎ 694 0999; North Corniche;

sandwiches SR7-25, mains SR18-48; ✹ 8am-2am Sat-Thu, 1pm-2am Fri), open to men and women, and one of Jeddah's best kept secrets. The outdoor tables have great sea views and the food is good albeit a little pricey (note the minimum charge of SR25 per person).

A popular place for breakfast among well-heeled Saudi families is **Al-Thamarat** (☎ 660 0514; breakfast dishes SR10, mains SR18-35, juices SR7; ✹ 6am-midnight), which is designed like an old-style Jeddah coffeehouse. The traditional Saudi dishes are good, but not the cheapest. It's on Al-Fitaihi St, off Talya St

Shopping

Jeddah claims to offer the best prices, latest products and greatest variety of shopping of any town in Saudi.

Popular things to purchase include photographic equipment, computers, mobile phones, electronic equipment and gold.

More 'local' souvenirs include Saudi dates (SR15 to SR120 per kg) and coffee pots (SR200 to SR4000), Yemeni coffee (from SR25 per kg), and even *Zamzam* (holy water) from Mecca (SR4 for 250ml). If you're after a souvenir, or fancy 'going local', the *thobes* (traditional shirt-dresses) are, according to one Saudi, 'great value in Jeddah!'.

For antiques, head for the string of stores on Rayhanat al-Jazirah St, right next to the Al-Tayibat City Museum for International Civilisation (Map p323) where you can find *jambiyas* (tribesmen's ceremonial daggers), old coffee pots, good-quality Bedouin jewellery and incense burners.

For dates, nuts and nibbles, head straight for the famous **Khayyam Al-Rabie Est** (Map p323; ☎ 647 6596; off Al-Qabel St), which, with its fairy lights and floor-to-ceiling rows of goodies (including over 50 varieties of dates in all shapes, shades, colours and textures), is like an Aladdin's cave for the sweet-toothed.

Jeddah's **souq** (Map p323; ✹ 10am-11pm) immediately south of Al-Amir Fahd St and Al-Balad, is well worth seeking out. It's subdivided into different sections, some populated by different immigrant groups, such as Yemenis selling Yemeni coffee and *jambiyas*. If you're immediately before, during or after the haj, don't miss it (see the Haj chapter, p71).

The largest supermarket downtown, with a reputation for reasonable prices, is the **Star Superstores** (Map p324; ☎ 643 7291; Ba'ashan St;

8am-midnight) found inside the Corniche Commercial Centre. With its selection of fresh fruit, cheeses, freshly baked breads and olives, it's a good place for preparing a picnic. It also sells baby food.

Getting There & Away
AIR
Jeddah's **King Abdul Aziz International Airport** (☎ 684 1707, 688 5526; Medina Rd) is north of the city centre. **Saudi Arabian Airlines** (Saudia; Map p324; ☎ 632 3333; King Abdul Aziz St), departs from the south terminal (25km from the city centre). Foreign airlines use the north terminal (35km from the centre). There is also a separate Haj terminal, as well as a Royal Terminal (exclusively for the use of Saudi's royals and VIPs).

Daily domestic departures include Abha (SR190), Dammam (SR390), Hail (SR250), Jizan (SR200), Medina (SR140), Najran (SR250), Riyadh (SR280), Sakaka (Jouf; SR300), Taif (SR110) and Yanbu (SR110). There are less regular departures for Sharurah (SR330).

BUS
The **Saptco Bus Station** (Map p324; ☎ 647 8500; Ba'ashan St) has daily departures to Abha (SR100, nine hours, every two hours), Dammam (SR200, 14 to 15 hours, three daily), Jizan (SR100, nine hours, every two hours), Najran (SR130, 14 hours, four daily), Riyadh (SR135, 12 hours, every two hours), Taif (SR30, three hours, every hour) and Yanbu (SR60, five hours, every two to three hours).

Buses also go to Medina (SR50, five hours, every two hours) and Mecca (SR10, one hour, every hour), though you must be Muslim to travel here.

For Al-Ula, passengers travel to Medina, then change to Al-Ula (SR55, five hours). If you're a non-Muslim, you'll need to inform the ticket vendor when you buy your ticket. The driver of your bus will be asked to drop you at a partner bus station outside the *haram* (forbidden) boundaries and another bus should come and pick you up from there. As it's all a bit of an unknown quantity, you should check details first.

CAR
Rental agencies can be found in the arrivals hall of the airport and in Jeddah's centre.

Budget (Map p324; ☎ 642 0737; www.budget.com; King Abdul Aziz St) charges the usual rates (see p371), and the local company, **Sahary Rent A Car** (Map p324; ☎ 645 0770; King Abdul Aziz St), offers a cheaper alternative (from SR70 per day for a 2WD, including full insurance with 150km daily included (SR0.30 per extra km thereafter).

Getting Around
A taxi from the town centre to the south/north terminals costs SR30/40 (add SR10 to SR20 in high season). A short hop in town costs SR10 to SR15. Hiring a taxi for a half-/full-day tours should cost no more than around SR100/150. Decide on a price with the driver beforehand.

AL-NAKHEEL النخيل
Lying 40km northwest of Jeddah's city centre in the North Obhur area, the small but pleasant **Al-Nakheel Beach Resort** (☎ 656 1177; www.saudidiving.com/al-nakheel-beach.htm; adult/child SR50/25; 🏊) is a good place to come if you fancy a day at the beach (but avoid the weekends). Claiming to be 'one of the best family resorts', it welcomes women, who are permitted to swim in both the sea and swimming pools. Well-designed and well-managed, it's also clean and very relaxed. Diving (per dive per person including equipment SR120) is also possible.

If you live in Saudi Arabia and truly want to 'get away from it all', the new, Greek-designed and luxurious **Fal Beach Resort** (☎ 656 0033; www.falbeachresort.com; North Obhur; studio SR500, ste SR1000; 🖥 🏊) styles itself on being a 'little piece of Europe'. The wearing of either *thobes* or *abeyyas* (woman's full-length black robe) is even banned within its grounds. It's beautifully designed and contains everything you could want for the weekend, including a gorgeous 70m pool complete with its own little island.

TAIF الطائف
☎ 02 / pop 760,000
After the cauldron-like coastal plain, Taif in summer can seem like a breath of fresh air. It is. Located 1700m above sea level, its gentle, temperate climate is its biggest attraction, and in summer, Taif becomes the Kingdom's capital. With its wide, tree-lined streets, remnants of old Taif, a large and lively souq and beautiful surrounding

CAMEL CHAOS

Each weekend (Wednesday to Friday), every two weeks during July and August, the town of Taif departs for the races. Open to all, the camels come from far and wide including from other Peninsula countries. It's a spectacular sight. Located on a site 10km outside Taif, the four races run from 3pm to 5.30pm and attract from between 25 to 100 participants in a single race! No wonder: first prize is SR150,000 in cash, 10 cars and 100 bags of wheat.

scenery, it's not hard to see why the King and his cronies relocate here.

Taif is also known for the cultivation of roses and fruit (particularly honey-sweet figs, grapes, prickly pear and pomegranates). Over 3000 gardens are said to grace Taif and its surrounds.

The Taif to Mecca road was one of many roads built by the Bin Laden construction company (the largest construction company of its kind in Saudi, and specialising in mountain road construction).

Orientation

The town centre stretches out from the southern end of Shubra St to south of As-Salamah St.

Information

Main Post Office (Souq area) Just south of King Faisal St.
Saudia (☎ 733 3333; Shubra St)

Sights

SHUBRA PALACE

The city's **museum** (☎ 732 1033; Shubra St; admission free; ☒ 8am-2pm Sat-Wed Sep-May, 8am-noon & 5-7pm Jun-Aug) is housed in a beautiful early 20th-century house that is the most stunning vestige of old Taif.

The exterior is lovely, with latticework windows and balconies made from imported Turkish timber, offset against pristine white walls. The interior marble was imported from Carrara in Italy. King Abdul Aziz used to stay here when he visited Taif and it was later the residence of King Faisal.

AL-KADY ROSE FACTORY

The largest rose factory in Taif and belonging to one of Taif's oldest families, the 120-year-old **Al-Kady Rose Factory** (☎ 733 4133; off As-Salamah St; admission free; ☒ 9.30am-2.30pm Sat-Thu) is well worth a visit, particularly at harvest time (May to July, when it's open 24 hours). The old distillers date to Ottoman times. The precious rose essence (SR1200 for 10g!) is apparently much in demand among the rich-and-the-royal in Gulf Cooperation Council (GCC) countries. Rose water (SR10 per bottle), used in Arabia to scent clothes, baths, cooking and drinks, is also sold and is a bargain by comparison.

SOUQ

Taif's **souq** (☒ 9am-2pm & 4.30-11pm Sat-Thu) is one of the largest in the Kingdom and is well worth a wander, particularly on a summer's evening when all of Taif is out and about. Look out for the little boxes of honeycomb (SR350 per kg), touted by Taif's citizens as 'the best in the world'.

Famous also are the local white cheeses (*jubal balidy*), *bachoor* (incense) and the gold souq area. Look out also for the dried Taif rose petals used locally to brew a fantastically fragrant tea.

The souq is southeast of the Great Mosque.

BEIT KAKI

Built in 1943 as a summer residence for one of Mecca's most important merchant families, **Beit Kaki** (As-Salamah St; currently closed) is one of Taif's oldest surviving buildings.

With its intricately carved balconies and carved window and door frames, it's a typical Hejaz building. In the future, the building should be restored and turned into a museum on the history and culture of the area.

Tours

A local guide who can give great, custom-made tours in his car of both the town and perimeters of Taif is **Mahmoud Maqsoud Alim** (☎ 050-571 0197; mmalim2004@yahoo.com; 1-day tour 1-4 people SR300 per tour). The country around Taif is very attractive and contains a range of intriguing sights.

Sites Mahmoud suggests include the ancient Al-Qu'a mosque (4km from Taif), the oldest tree in Taif – known locally as 'Al-Khafoura' (22km), the 1400-year-old Samallaghi dam (30km), the Turkish fort (32km) and the crater (250km).

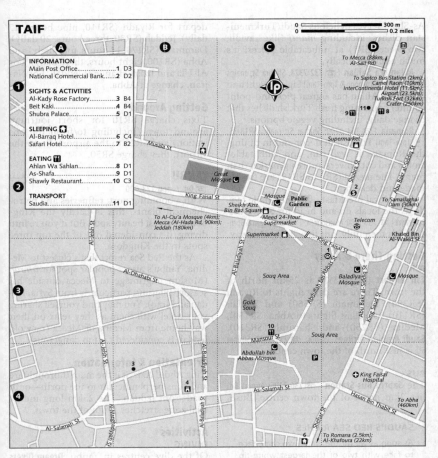

TAIF

0 — 300 m
0 — 0.2 miles

INFORMATION
Main Post Office.....................1 D3
National Commercial Bank......2 D2

SIGHTS & ACTIVITIES
Al-Kady Rose Factory.............3 B4
Beit Kaki................................4 B4
Shubra Palace.......................5 D1

SLEEPING
Al-Barraq Hotel.....................6 C4
Safari Hotel...........................7 B2

EATING
Ahlan Wa Sahlan...................8 D1
As-Shafa...............................9 D1
Shawly Restaurant...............10 C3

TRANSPORT
Saudia.................................11 D1

To Mecca (88km;
Al-Sail Rd)

To Saptco Bus Station (2km);
Camel Races (10km);
InterContinental Hotel (11.5km);
Airport (23.5km);
Turkish Fort (32km);
Crater (250km)

Musala St

Great Mosque

King Faisal St

Mosque Public Garden

Sheikh Aziz Bin Baz Square

Meed 24-Hour Supermarket

To Al-Qu'a Mosque (4km);
Mecca (Al-Hada Rd, 90km);
Jeddah (180km)

Supermarket

King Faisal St

Telecom

Khaled Bin Al-Waled St

Al-Dhahabi St

Souq Area

Al-Baladiyah St

Baladiya Mosque

Abu Bakr al-Siddiq St

Mosque

Al-Jeish St

Gold Souq

Abdullah bin Abbas St

King Saud St

Mansour St

Souq Area

Abdullah bin Abbas Mosque

As-Salamah St

King Faisal Hospital

Al-Jeish St

Al-Salamah St

Shehar St

Hasan Bin Thabit St

To Abha
(460km)

To Romana (2.5km);
Al-Khafoura (22km)

To Samallaghai Dam (30km)

Shubra

Abu Bakr al-Siddiq St

Sleeping

Taif is a still a popular summer retreat during the summer (May to September) for Saudis as well as for Kuwaitis, Emiratis and Omanis. Reservations (at least 10 days in advance) are advised.

Safari Hotel (☎ 734 6660; Musala St; low/high season s SR60/100, d SR90/150) The best budget choice (and value) is the Safari with newly renovated, pleasantly furnished rooms, all with balcony (ask for a 'mosque-side' view).

Al-Barraq Hotel (☎ 650 3366; fax 651 1322; Shehar St; low/high season s SR165/210, d SR250/270) Popular among the diplomatic expat community, it's easy to see why: rooms are spacious, comfy and recently refurbished, and the luxurious lobby, laden with marble and

chandeliers defies the prices. There are also two restaurants, a health club and Jacuzzi.

InterContinental Hotel (☎ 750 5050; www.ich hotelsgroups.com; Al-Matar Rd; s/d from SR450/585, villas SR4000-4500; 🖵 🏊) Lying 11.5km north of Taif's centre, the InterContinental looks a bit 1970s-Arabia, but the refurbished rooms are extremely comfortable and the hotel offers good facilities and services. Non-guests (men only) can use the outdoor pool and health club for SR75 per day.

Eating

The following all have family sections (unless otherwise indicated).

As-Shafa (☎ 733 0332; just off Shubra St; ⏱ noon-1am) Located behind the Saudia office,

SAUDI ARABIA

As-Shafa serves delicious Saudi/Turkmenistan dishes, including *manti* (like ravioli; two pieces SR1) at unbeatable prices; it's much admired locally.

Ahlan Wa Sahlan (☎ 732 7324; Shubra St; mains SR13-25; ☒ 7am-noon & 1pm-1am) Light, bright and clean, the Ahlan has a great pick-and-point counter containing fresh Turkish dishes that change daily, including veggie options.

Romana (☎ 743 3700; Shahar St; mains SR18-35; ☒ 1pm-1am) Turkish in décor and in dining, the Romana is well-run, and with tablecloths and cut flowers, more upmarket than many. The mezze (SR3 to SR12) are freshly made and delicious.

For a local breakfast of freshly made *fool*, do as the locals do and head for **Shawly Restaurant** (☎ 736 1180; Mansour St; ☒ 5am-11am & 5pm-1am). It's men only, but they'll do takeaway.

Getting There & Away
AIR
Taif airport (☎ 685 5527) is 25km north of the town. There are daily flights to Riyadh (SR250), Dammam (SR360) and Jeddah (SR110), as well as flights to Abha (SR150), Medina (SR250) and Sharurah (SR310). **Saudi Arabian Airlines** (Saudi; ☎ 733 3333; Shubra St) is just north of the town centre.

BUS
The **Saptco Bus Station** (☎ 736 3195; Airport Rd) lies 2km north of the town centre. Buses

---

SAUDI'S RED SEA RICHES

As soon as we hit the water, we came face to face with two of the largest white-tip sharks I have ever seen; they appeared quite unruffled by our presence. Above our heads, just below the surface, was a shimmering shoal of some of the most curious creatures I have ever seen: large, bumphead parrot fish, turquoise-green and with a large protrusion issuing from their heads. The corals – hard and soft – were magnificent, though I brushed my elbow accidentally against some fire coral and still have the scar a month later; I've never seen so much. Towards the end of the dive, a huge leatherback turtle, startled by our presence, dived deeply below us.

From the author's dive log book. Maluthu South Island, off Al-Lith

---

depart for Riyadh (SR110, nine hours, 17 daily), Jeddah (SR30, three hours, 20 daily), Dammam (SR170, 14 hours, four daily) and Abha (SR100, eight hours, three daily). For Al-Ula and Jizan, change at Jeddah. For Najran, change at Abha.

Getting Around
Taxis charge SR10 for short journeys around town (including to/from the bus station) and SR25 to the airport. From the airport, they charge SR50.

YANBU
ينبع
☎ 04 / pop 173,000
With a booming port, refineries and petrochemical plants, this is hardly the Kingdom's biggest beauty spot. But if you're into diving, it's considered one of the top three spots in the Kingdom.

As the Red Sea resort that's closest to Medina, Yanbu's also a popular spot for *umrah* (Muslim pilgrimage to Mecca outside haj season) pilgrims, particularly from Syria, Jordan and Iraq. You may find yourself sharing your hotel with them as they relax on their way home from Medina or Mecca (racy old Jeddah is considered far too dangerous).

Orientation & Information
King Abdul Aziz St is the main thoroughfare and runs perpendicular to the north–south road from Jeddah. The 25km-long industrial zone stretches south of the town.

Activities
DIVING
Of the dive centres in Yanbu, **Dream Divers** (☎ 322 0330; www.alahlam-marina.com; King Abdul Aziz St; per person per day for 2 dives incl tanks, weight belt, lunchbox SR250; ☒ 9am-noon & 2-10pm) has the best reputation. If you're without equipment, BCDs and regulators can be hired for US$25 each, a mask and snorkel for US$20. PADI scuba diving courses are also offered, including a seven-day Open Water course (per person all inclusive SR1400). Bring your own boots, fins and wetsuit.

For more details about diving in Saudi's Red Sea, see p360.

Sleeping & Eating
Middle East Hotel (☎ 322 1281; fax 322 8571; King Abdul Aziz St; s/d SR80/120) Though the rooms aren't the largest and those nearest the road

can be a bit noisy, they're sanitary, have firm mattresses and are good value.

Banat Hotel (☎ 391 2222; danat_hotel@yahoo .com; King Abdul Aziz St; s/d SR150/160) Decorated in browns and creams like a giant crème caramel, the rooms are nevertheless comfortable, clean, and conveniently situated two doors down from Dream Divers.

Arac Yanbu Resort (☎ 328 0000; www.arac.com .sa; chalets for 1/2/3 people including service charge weekdays SR590/890/1190, weekends SR890/1190/1590) The new Arac, lying 17km from town and 10km from the airport, boasts good facilities in a good location. This includes a private beach where women can swim (albeit in trousers and T-shirt), Marine Club (offering diving, and in summer waterskiing, as well as jet ski, pedalo and bike hire), a tennis court, a café and a restaurant. The comfortable two-storey chalets are built on the waterfront and the management is friendly and accommodating.

Iskenderun Restaurant (☎ 322 8465; King Abdul Aziz St; ☼ 1pm-2am) Canary-coloured, cheap and cheerful, this is Yanbu's favourite eating establishment. Buzzing with locals, the place is kept spotless and the food's fresh and finger-lickin'. Try the speciality, the *shwarma iskender* served with a special, secret sauce. Mezze (SR5 to SR6), pide (Turkish pizza SR7 to SR12), fish fillets (SR20) and fresh fruit juices (SR3 to SR5) are also served here.

Getting There & Away
The airport lies 10km northeast of the town centre. **Saudia** (☎ 322 6666; King Abdul Aziz St) has flights to Jeddah (SR110, twice daily). Coming by car, Yanbu lies 230km (around 2½ hours) from Jeddah.

MADAIN SALEH & THE NORTH

مدائن صالح و الشمال

The astonishing Madain Saleh is the single most impressive site in Saudi Arabia and should be on every visitor's itinerary.

Saudi Arabia's northern provinces are the Kingdom's richest source of pre-Islamic sites, including those at Al-Ula and the rarely visited Rajajil (Standing Stones) near Sakaka.

The substations of the Hejaz Railway and forts stand as lonely sentinels to the days of trade and pilgrim caravans that once passed through here thick and fast.

AL-ULA   العلا
☎ 04
Al-Ula, the gateway to Madain Saleh, is a small town lying in the heart of some exceptionally beautiful country, with palm groves running down the centre of the wadi (valley or river bed) and forbidding red sandstone cliffs rising up on two sides.

As well as the extraordinary nearby tombs of the Nabataeans, are the delightful if sadly decrepit mud-brick ruins of Old Al-Ula, one of the last remnants of old towns in Saudi Arabia.

The surrounding area also bears ample evidence (in the form of tombs and rock inscriptions) to habitation dating back more than two millennia.

Orientation & Information
Al-Ula lies along the western side of the wadi. The southern section of town is home to the museum, some banks with ATMs (one opposite the museum), and an internet café, **Ala-Albal** (☎ 884 3621; Khaled Bin Waled St; per hr SR10), 300m southwest of the Riyad Bank.

A terrific little book on the area is *Al-'Ula and Mada'in Salih* by AR Al-Ansary and Hussein Abu Al Hassan (SR40). It's available in Al-Ula's hotels, as well as in Al-Jarir bookshops (where's it's also cheaper).

Sights
AL-ULA MUSEUM OF ARCHAEOLOGY & ETHNOGRAPHY
Well-worth a visit, this **museum** (☎ 884 1536; Main St; admission free; ☼ 8am-2.30pm Sat-Wed) is attractively designed with some intriguing and informative displays on the history, culture, flora and fauna of the area, as well as on Madain Saleh and the Nabataeans.

OLD AL-ULA
Although crumbling as you look at it, and each year after the rains, less and less remains, Old Al-Ula is one of the most fascinating old towns in Arabia. Locals are petitioning for its preservation.

The mud-brick town stands on the site of the biblical city of Dedan, which is mentioned in Isaiah (21:13) as the home base of

SAUDI ARABIA

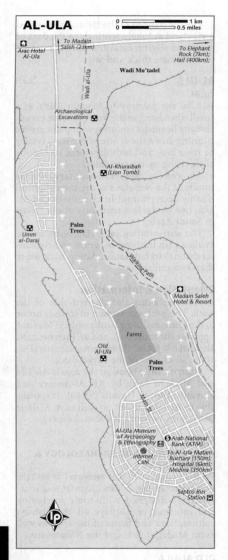

AL-ULA

0 ———————— 1 km
0 ———————— 0.5 miles

To Madain
Saleh (23km)

Arac Hotel
Al-Ula

To Elephant
Rock (7km);
Hail (400km);

Wadi Mu'tadel

Wadi al-Ula

Archaeological
Excavations

Al-Khuraibah
(Lion Tomb)

Umm
al-Daraj

Palm
Trees

Walking Path

Madain Saleh
Hotel & Resort

Farms

Old
Al-Ula

Palm
Trees

Main St

Al-Ula Museum
of Archaeology
& Ethnography

Arab National
Bank (ATM)

Internet
Café

To Al-Ula Matam
Buchary (150m);
Hospital (6km);
Medina (350km)

Saptco Bus
Station

Arab caravans, and in Ezekiel (27:20-21) as a trading partner of the Phoenician city of Tyre. The buildings that you'll see mostly date back a few hundred years, although bricks from much earlier settlements have been reused.

Originally, the old quarter was walled with just two gates and consisted of around 500 houses; it was occupied until the late 1970s. Throughout the town, there are some superb doors made from palm trunks. Rising up from the centre of the old town are the remnants of Qala'at Musa Abdul Nasser. The palm trees and maze of low mud-brick walls directly across the road from the old town were once farms whose owners lived in the old town.

AL-KHURAIBAH

Situated in the northeast of town is the impressive site of Al-Khuraibah, believed to have formed part of the ancient capital of the Kingdom of Lihyan.

Several important tombs have been found here along with inscriptions in the Lihyanite, Dadanite and Minaean scripts.

Sadly, the site is closed while it undergoes excavation, but you can get a view of it from outside the fence across from the tombs. Ask your guide to show you. Look out for the 'Lion Tomb', so-called for the two lions carved on either side of it.

UMM AL-DARAJ

At the northwestern end of town, some kilometres north of Old Al-Ula, Umm al-Daraj (Mother of Steps) is worth a brief detour. It contains a former Lihyanite sacrificial altar, weathered steps climbing up the hill, some beautiful, albeit rather weather-beaten, Lihyanite inscriptions and a few rock carvings of people and camels.

From the top of the steps there are fine views out over the wadi. You'll need a guide to find Umm al-Daraj, but it's included on most tour itineraries.

Tours

Madain Saleh Hotel & Resort (☎ 884 2888; www .mshotel.com.sa) offers a good-value weekend package of three days and two nights half-board including sightseeing of all the main attractions in both Al-Ula and Madain Saleh, and airport pick-up for SR895 to SR980 per person (depending on which airport) in a double room (single supplement SR180). With your own vehicle (a guide is provided by the hotel), it costs SR660 per person half-board.

The **Arac Hotel Al-Ula** (☎ 884 4444; hotelalula@arac .com.sa) charges SR300 per group per day for a guide. With a guide, vehicle (for up to 25 people) and driver, it charges SR650 per

SAUDI ARABIA

day. Guided excursions by 4WD into the desert (half/full day SR350/600) can also be arranged. Lunch boxes (SR40) can be prepared on request.

A local tour guide – and the author of a soon-to-be published coffee-table book (that will sell for around SR60) on Madain Saleh – is **Hamid M Al-Sulaiman** (☎ 055-435 3684; hamed699@yahoo.com). With intimate knowledge of the area, he offers tours in his 4WD of all the local sites, including up Al-Harra (a mountain from which there are good views), as well as a few not offered by the hotels (but which are very well worthwhile if you have the time). Though his English is limited, he is reliable, very keen to please and good company. Trips include: Al-Mejez (SR350, half day, one to four people) known as Al-Ula's 'Grand Canyon' for its impressive rock formations; Hejaz Railway (SR1200, full day including BBQ lunch, one to four people); camel excursions (SR350 per person); Bedu visits (SR350 per person); and even star-gazing trips in the desert.

Sleeping & Eating

Madain Saleh has just two hotels.

Medain Saleh Hotel & Resort (☎ 884 2888; www .mshotel.com.sa; r SR220, ste SR390-495, tent s/d SR145/ 165; 🏊) Located 3km east from the town centre, the hotel's big boons are its location on the eastern cliff face overlooking the wadi, and its pool set in gardens (open to men and women). The rooms are decent-sized and comfy and all have a small balcony (ask for 'garden view'). The tents, furnished attractively in a traditional style (complete with camel stool) are great value, atmospheric

and comfortable (with ensuite bathroom, TV, minibar and air con).

Arac Hotel Al-Ula (☎ 884 4444; www.arac.com .sa; s/d/ste SR390/315/1035 Dec-May, s/d SR190/220 Jun-Nov) Situated 7km from the town centre on the main road to Madain Saleh, the Arac restaurant (SR65 for three-course lunch or dinner) is also known for its great Asian and Italian-inspired food – the beef stroganoff is famous. There are plans to build a large, open-air pool that will be open to both men and women (at different times). It's located 15km from the entrance gates to Madain Saleh. Note that discounts are usually available, and reservations advised.

Of Al-Ula's small selection of restaurants, **Al-Ula Matam Buchary** (☎ 884 1124; Khaled Bin Walid St; mains SR9-16; ⏰ 1pm-1.30am Sat-Thu), which lies 100m south of Saptco, has the best reputation. It's signposted in Arabic only and there's no family section (but it does takeaway). Try the flavoursome barbecue half chicken (SR9).

Getting Around

There are no taxis or car hire companies in Al-Ula, though cars with drivers can be organised through the hotels (from SR300 per day).

Getting There & Away

A new airport located 60km from Al-Ula is planned for the future. In theory, it should be completed by 2009, but check for progress.

In the meantime, daily flights leave from Riyadh to Hail, daily from Jeddah to Medina (399km from Al-Ula), or twice weekly from Jeddah to Al-Wedjh airport (240km

---

WHO WERE THE NABATAEANS?

Little is known about the earliest origin of the Nabataeans, though it's believed they were a nomadic people. It was their tight control of the vital, overland trade routes (stretching from modern-day Jordan all the way down to modern-day Yemen) however, that brought them their greatest power and prosperity. Before long, they had transformed themselves from a simple, nomadic people into a sedentary, sophisticated and wealthy state with a king.

Establishing their capital at Petra in Jordan from the 3rd century BC, they began to expand, taking control of all of northwestern Arabia from the 2nd century BC onwards. A second great centre was then founded at Madain Saleh, and at one point they even occupied Domat al-Jandal.

Known to be great engineers and skilled masons, they were also masters in techniques of irrigation. Many Saudi Arabian sites testify to the sophistication of their agriculture.

In 106AD, the Nabataean power finally began to wane as their kingdom was annexed by Rome.

from Al-Ula). Hotels charge SR1500 for an airport pick-up from Al-Wedjh.

Saptco (☎ 884 1344) runs buses to Al-Ula from Jeddah (SR110) and Riyadh (SR170).

AROUND AL-ULA

A wonderful natural rock formation, **Elephant Rock** (Sakharat al-Fil) towers above the sands in a landscape of red rocky monoliths. Also known as Mammoth Rock, it lies 11km northeast of Al-Ula, just off the road to Hail, some 7km from the Arac Hotel Al-Ula.

MADAIN SALEH مدائن صالح

If you can only visit one place in Saudi Arabia, make it Madain Saleh. This crossroads of ancient civilisations, pilgrims, explorers, trade caravans and armies finds its most remarkable expression in the elaborate stone-carved temples of the Nabataeans.

The Nabataeans, who carved the astonishing city of Petra (Jordan), chose Madain Saleh as their second city. Although the tombs are less spectacular here than those in Petra, their setting in large landscapes of sweeping sand and remarkable rock formations, is unique and unsurpassed.

History

Madain Saleh (Mada'in Salih) was the Nabataeans' second city and stood at the midpoint of the caravan route between Mecca and Petra. When Petra was, after a period of Nabataean autonomy, finally taken by the Romans in AD 106, Madain Saleh fell into a decline from which it never recovered.

The Romans later reoriented trade away from the Arabian interior, instead preferring the ports of the Red Sea. In later centuries the pilgrim road from Damascus to Mecca passed through Madain Saleh.

Information

You need a permit (p367) to visit Madain Saleh. Both of Madain Saleh's hotels, as well as the tour operators (see p326), can arrange permits on your behalf if you fax them your details a week in advance.

Video cameras are not allowed inside the site; be aware that surveillance is carried out. Bring your passport – you will need to present it at the gate along with the permit.

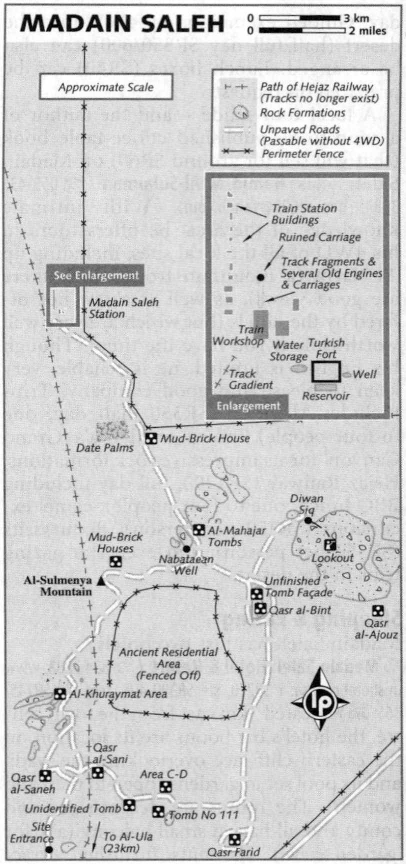
MADAIN SALEH
0 3 km
0 2 miles
Approximate Scale
Path of Hejaz Railway (Tracks no longer exist)
Rock Formations
Unpaved Roads (Passable without 4WD)
Perimeter Fence
Train Station Buildings
Ruined Carriage
Track Fragments & Several Old Engines & Carriages
Train Workshop
Water Storage
Turkish Fort
Track Gradient
Well
Reservoir
Enlargement
See Enlargement
Madain Saleh Station
Date Palms
Mud-Brick House
Diwan Siq
Al-Mahajar Tombs
Mud-Brick Houses
Lookout
Nabataean Well
Al-Sulmenya Mountain
Unfinished Tomb Façade
Qasr al-Bint
Qasr al-Ajouz
Ancient Residential Area (Fenced Off)
Al-Khuraymat Area
Qasr al-Sani
Qasr al-Saneh
Area C-D
Unidentified Tomb
Tomb No 111
Site Entrance
To Al-Ula (23km)
Qasr Farid

Sights

The extraordinary **Madain Saleh** (admission free; 8am-5pm) is home to 131 tombs, 45 of which carry inscriptions in late Aramaic script above the doors. These inscriptions detail the period of the tomb's construction; translations appear on signs in front of most tombs. The tombs were the only permanent structures built by the Nabataeans; they lived in relatively flimsy adobe houses, the remains of which are yet to be excavated, and lie in the fenced-off area in the centre of the site.

QASR AL-SANEH

Qasr al-Saneh is an appropriate place to start a tour of Madain Saleh, as it reveals many of the essential elements of Nabataean funerary architecture: a relatively unadorned façade; the two five-step motifs at the top; a simple interior burial chamber with shelves for corpses; and inscriptions above the doorway.

Built around AD 50, Qasr al-Saneh was in use for just 50 years before the Nabataean kings were overwhelmed by Rome.

AL-KHURAYMAT
This area of **tombs**, about 750m north of Qasr al-Saneh, has some of the best preserved tombs in Madain Saleh. With around 20 tombs carved into the rock face, you'll see some impressive griffin-like figures with human heads, lions' bodies and wings that adorn the corners of the pediment. Look out also for rose-like designs above some doors; these symbolise plates on which blood fell during animal sacrifice.

NABATAEAN WELL & AL-MAHAJAR
The Nabataean Well was one of around 60 wells in the area. The wall supports – added in the 20th century – were built from railway sleepers pilfered from the Hejaz Railway.

Across the track from the entrance to the well, the Al-Mahajar tombs are especially photogenic because they're all lined up in a row.

HEJAZ RAILWAY STATION
At the northern edge of the site, is the **Madain Saleh Station** of the Hejaz Railway. Though the site has been comprehensively restored, it lacks the lonely and decrepit charm of the substations elsewhere.

The complex, built in 1907, consists of 16 buildings, which include a large workshop (with a restored WWI-era engine), shells of train carriages and a rebuilt Turkish fort that served as a resting place for pilgrims travelling to Mecca.

DIWAN
The diwan, carved into a hillside to shield it from the wind, is one of the few examples of non-funerary architecture in Madain Saleh. The name owes more to modern Arab culture than to the Nabataeans, who probably used the area as a cult site. Opposite the hollowed-out room are niches cut into the rock where Nabataean deities were carved (some deeply weathered examples remain).

Running south from the diwan is the **Siq**, a narrow passageway between two rock faces lined with more small altars. At the far end is a striking natural **amphitheatre** with weird and wonderful rock formations. Carved into the eastern wall you can see *qanats* (water channels), while at the southern end there are some well-preserved sacrificial altars.

High above the canyon to the west is a lookout with breathtaking views over the site.

QASR AL-BINT
Qasr al-Bint (Girl's Palace) consists of a wonderful row of façades that make for dramatic viewing from across Madain Saleh.

The east face has two particularly well-preserved tombs. If you step back and look up near the northern end of the west face, you'll distinguish a tomb that was abandoned in the early stages of construction and would, if completed, have been the largest in Madain Saleh; only the step façade was cut.

QASR FARID
Qasr Farid in the south is the largest tomb of Madain Saleh and certainly the most stunning. Its stand-alone location makes it a spot of rare beauty, especially just before sunset. Carved from a single free-standing monolith of rock, it's visible from miles away, and the craggy mountains to the east are spectacular.

Getting There & Away
The road from Al-Ula (23km) is easy to find. The site entrance is marked off the road with a blue 'Antiquities' sign.

TAIMA   تيماء
☎ 04 / pop 65,000
Taima is famous above all for its extraordinary **well** (Bi'r Al-Haddaj; ☉ 9am-5pm Sat-Wed). Not merely the oldest well in the Kingdom, it's also the largest, measuring over 18m across and 12m in depth. It is believed to date back to Babylonians time (the early 1st millennium BC), though it may even be older.

Originally, 60 draw-wheels positioned around the rim of the well brought water up from the well bottom to the surface with the aid of camels and ropes. Stone-hewn channels then conducted the water to the labyrinth of gardens that made up the verdant oases, for which Taima was famous. The well is still in use today (except that diesel pumps have replaced the camels!).

The nearby **Taima Museum** (☎ 622 1398; admission free; ☻ 9am-5.30pm Sat-Wed) has excellent and informative displays (including photographs, maps and diagrams) on the well and the history and culture of the area, as well as archaeological finds from the region. Look out in particular for the 'silent visages' – the mysterious faces carved on Taima's unique tombstones thought to date to the 5th or 4th century BC.

With time to spare, Taima merits further exploration. One of the largest archaeological sites in the Kingdom, there are a mass of interesting sites, remains and buildings in the area.

In the 1st millennium AD, it was an important caravan stop for the holy cities to and from Damascus. German archaeologists are currently excavating the site.

An agricultural town since ancient times, Taima is known even today for the high quality of its fruit, including pomegranates, figs, peaches, melons and plums.

Sleeping & Eating
Sahari Hotel (☎ 463 5103; Prince Khaled St; s SR80-100, d SR100-150, 2-bed apt from SR200) The best bet in town at the time of writing, it's hardly the Hilton (and the carpet can tell a tale or two), but the rooms are clean, quite well-furnished and quiet. The Yemeni management is also friendly and keen to please.

Hadramawt Restaurant (☎ 463 5103; Prince Khaled St; mains SR10-15; ☻ 8am-1am) Located next door to the Sahari Hotel, the Hadramawt is loved locally for its wholesome dishes served in simple but clean surrounds. Dining is on cushions on the floor and there's family eating inside the little cubicles.

Getting There & Away
Saptco (☎ 463 2942) runs buses to Jeddah (SR110, 10 hours, 10 daily), Al-Ula (SR30, 2½ hours, one daily), Tabuk (SR45, three hours, 10 daily), Domat al-Jandal (SR75, five hours, one daily), Hail (SR65, five hours, five daily), Riyadh (SR165, 13 hours, five daily) and Sakaka (SR80, five hours, one daily).

The nearest airports to Taima are the ones at Tabuk (220km northwest of Taima) and Al-Jouf (300km northeast of Taima). Saudia flies from Riyadh to Tabuk daily (SR280) and from Riyadh to Al-Jouf (SR200).

SAKAKA   ساكاكا
☎ 04 / pop 55,000
Remote and rural Sakaka has a host of little-visited archaeological sights, particularly Rajajil (Standing Stones; opposite) 25km from town.

Lady Anne Blunt and her husband Wilfred visited Sakaka (which they called Meskakeh) in 1879; Lady Blunt's book, *A Pilgrimage to Najd*, provides a rare portrait of Arabian society in that era.

Orientation & Information
Sakaka's main street runs north from a single, large intersection for approximately 4.5km. The intersection is dominated by Sakaka's main mosque and its biggest hotel, Al-Nusl. Along or near this street you'll find most of Sakaka's restaurants and services.

Sights
At the northern end of town, **Qasr Za'abel** (admission free; ☻ 8.30am-noon & 4pm-sunset) dates from the early 19th century. Restored in 1994, the fort has lost something of its antique charm, although the hilltop perch, irregular shape and four towers make it worth a look. Inside, you'll find the usual diwan and the commander's house.

The rocky outcrop 150m north (as the crow flies) of Qasr Za'abel, Jabal Burnus, has rock carvings of dancing stick figures with their hand raised level to their face, as well as inscriptions. The carvings date from the 6th century BC.

Sleeping & Eating
Al-Nusl Hotel (☎ 625 0353; fax 625 0408; s/d incl service charge SR345/448; 🖳) Designed by a Canadian architect, the Al-Nusl is modern-meets-Moorish. The rooms, which lie around three central courtyards covered by glass domes, appear a little anodyne after the grand entry but are quiet, peaceful and comfortable. Guides, car hire and tours can be organised – though they're not the cheapest – and there's a free airport pickup.

Al-Andalus Hotel (☎ 633 1212; fax 633 1331; Main St; s SR90-120, d SR150-180) Lying on the highway 37km beyond Domat al-Jandal and 13km from Sakaka, the Al-Andalus offers good value and convenience, with a restaurant, laundry, supermarket, parking space and car rental (SR80 per day including insurance) all next door. Rooms are clean and spacious.

Sofrajy (☎ 626 111; Main St; mains SR9-12; ☀ 1pm-1am) Long the local choice, the Sofrajy has menus in both Arabic and English and a family section. Dishes such as chicken cooked in a clay pot (SR11) are fresh, filling and very reasonably priced. With its wide choice of breakfast foods (including set breakfast menus – SR10 to SR12 for two people) and fourteen fruit juices (from SR3), it's also a great place to start the day. It lies 400m north of the Al-Nusl Hotel.

Also much loved locally is **As-Safir** (☎ 635 7414; Main St; ☀ 3pm-2am), lying 800m north of Al-Nusl, which does succulent *shwarma* (sandwich/plate SR3/7).

Getting There & Away

The airport (listed as Jouf in Saudia flight timetables) lies 28km southwest of town on the road to Domat al-Jandal. There are two daily **Saudia** (☎ 624 4444; King Abdul Aziz St) flights to Riyadh (SR290), and less-frequent services to Jeddah (SR300) and Hail (SR120).

Buses go from the **Saptco Bus Station** (☎ 624 9844) to Riyadh (SR185, 12 hours, two daily) and Dammam (SR185, 12 hours, two daily), Domat al-Jandal (SR10, one hour, six daily), Tabuk (SR85, six hours, four daily), Taima (SR80, five hours, one daily). For Al-Ula and Jeddah, go to Tabuk first.

Getting Around

A taxi to/from the airport to/from Al-Andalus/Al-Nusl costs SR50/70. Car-hire agencies can be found at the airport, the Al-Nusl Hotel and the Al-Andalus Hotel.

AROUND SAKAKA

Perched on a windswept plateau and surrounded by some of the loneliest country in Arabia, approximately 25km west of Sakaka, stand the mysterious clusters of 2m-high stone pillars of **Rajajil** (Standing Stones; admission free; ☀ 8am-1pm Sat-Wed).

Little is known of their history, but they're thought to date from around 2000 BC and are covered in ancient Thamudic graffiti. Archaeologists surmise that the stones once belonged to a Bronze Age cult centre and served an astrological purpose.

According to a local legend, they are *rijal al-hajar* (men of stone) who were punished by God for their unfaithfulness.

Keep your eyes peeled for arrowheads which litter the area; but don't remove any (you may be checked for them at Hail airport).

To visit the site, you need a permit (p367); at the time of writing, a large hole in the fence allowed access, though don't count on this! The Al-Nusl Hotel can arrange access if you're staying there.

To get here, take the first right off the highway after the Saudi Aramco Bulk Plant building (65km from Domat al-Jandal), follow the road for 5.7km and the dirt track for 350m to the site. The way in is indicated by a brown sign, but it's in Arabic only.

A taxi should cost SR50 to Al-Andalus Hotel and SR70 to Al-Nusl.

DOMAT AL-JANDAL　　دومت الجندل

Domat al-Jandal is a modest town that boasts a ruined fortress, an interesting fort and a good museum. There are still no hotels in the town.

Information

The museum and Qasr Marid are 1.2km east of town, south off the main Tabuk–Sakaka road. Domat al-Jandal has few services and the only hotels are at Sakaka, 50km away.

Sights

AL-JOUF MUSEUM OF ARCHAEOLOGY & ETHNOGRAPHY

This **museum** (☎ 622 2151; admission free; ☀ 7.30am-2.30pm Sat-Wed), contains some excellent and informative displays (including old photographs, drawings, maps and diagrams) on the local history, flora, fauna and culture, ranging from 'the Arabian One-Humped Camel' to 'Desert Life' and the Nabataeans.

A new museum is scheduled to open in the building across the car park. Enquire.

QASR MARID

The foundations of **Qasr Marid** (☀ sunrise-sunset) date to at least Nabataean times, and Roman-era records of Queen Zenobia's expedition to the area in the 3rd century AD mention Marid by name.

The fortress was repaired in the 19th century and became the local seat of government until the new fort, built by the Al-Rashids, supplanted it.

The main mud structure has towers at its four corners, and beautifully hewn, squared pre-Islamic brickwork is visible around the building's lower levels. The ramparts provide great views over the town and oasis.

MOSQUE OF OMAR
One of the earliest surviving mosques in Saudi Arabia, the Mosque of Omar is believed to have been founded by the second caliph, Omar bin al-Khattab (who ruled until AD 644), when he stopped here en route to Jerusalem.

Still in use, the mosque's famous lone minaret is one of the few surviving sections of the original building and may even predate its use as a mosque. Though the exact date of its construction is unknown, the exquisite, dry-stone construction and corbelling point possibly to pre-Islamic times (notice the similarities between it and the older parts of Qasr Marid). And fascinatingly, this is confirmed by the local tradition – that the 'tower' was indeed converted into a mosque by Caliph Omar.

OLD DOMAT AL-JANDAL
The old mud quarter adjacent to the Mosque of Omar has been settled for almost 1000 years. Although the buildings standing there today are not that old, earlier building materials have been used (Nabataean inscriptions are visible on some stones).

A clear path runs through the houses, and wandering through the ruins is a pleasant way to pass an afternoon.

Getting There & Away
Taxis cost SR70/SR100 to Al-Andalus/Al Nusl hotels for the 50km trip from Sakaka, but you're better off arranging transport through your hotel in Sakaka. The same applies in the opposite direction.

ASIR   عسير

'Asir' means 'difficult' in Arabic, after the legendary difficulties involved in crossing the Asir Mountains by camel. It is perhaps this above all that has preserved the distinctive cultural heritage of the Asir region.

With much closer historical ties in fact to Yemen than the rest of Arabia, the Asir is home to beautiful (albeit fast-disappearing) stone, slate and mud-brick architecture nestled among towering mountains of rare beauty, forests barely a hundred kilometres from the Empty Quarter and valleys that drop steeply down to the Red Sea coastal plain.

In the coastal region, look out for the traditional, conical huts showing the African influence from across the water, and around Abha, keep your eyes peeled for the famous 'Flower Men', locals who traditionally wear garlands of flowers on their head (apparently to attract women and detract the flies!).

In the mountains, and easier to spot, are the ubiquitous Arabian baboons now living the easy life from the picnic leftovers thrown to them by passing Saudi tourists. Don't let children get too close; they've been attacked or bitten in the past.

Merhaban alf – 'a thousand welcomes' is the traditional greeting of the Asir people; it sums up their supreme hospitality and you'll soon find yourself pressed to accept an invitation to eat or stay overnight everywhere. If you're invited to a wedding, don't be alarmed if the whole village starts shooting off guns – it's a traditional form of celebration (as in Yemen)!

ABHA   أبها
☎ 07 / pop 163,000
Arriving in Abha, perched 2200m above sea level, is a shock to the senses. Not only is it palpably cooler – or colder (hail and ice are not unheard of in winter), but it's the neat green lawns, marigolds, mountains and mist that make the greatest impression.

Attempting to explain the stark contrast to the torrid, torpid lowlands below, the locals talk rather unkindly of the giant, invisible air-conditioner that points to Abha, with its back to Jizan.

Some tourists (particularly the Japanese) are disappointed by Abha; for some it's too much like their home country. For the Saudis, however, the cold, mist and rain is all a bit of a novelty and they flock here (along with other GCC citizens, particularly Kuwaitis) to escape the relentless heat and humidity of the lowlands during summer.

Unfortunately, this has seen the rise of un-checked and uncontrolled building, which has resulted in a rash of carbuncle-like concrete apartments on Abha's gentle hills.

Orientation

The town centre is roughly demarcated by four streets: King Saud, King Faisal, King Khaled and Prince Abdullah. Nearly everything you'll need in the town itself is found within or just outside these boundaries.

Information

There are various banks with ATMs in the centre. To change money, head for **Enjaz** (☎ 229 0271; King Saud St; ⏰ 9am-noon & 5-8pm Sat-Wed, 5-8pm Fri), which offers the best rates and

is found diagonally opposite the Mawasam Agadeer Hotel.

The proactive **Asir Tourism Board** (☎ 231 1506; off King Khaled St) can organise English-speaking guides, as well as trips to the brightly painted, traditional houses of the area; or to traditional mud-brick villages such as Alianfa or Rejal Al-Maa; or alternatively, to bird watching trips in pursuit of the 170 species which make their home in the region.

In summer, French-monitored paragliding from Al-Soudah (SR200) and rock climbing (grades from 3a to 7b) at Habalah (including all equipment SR150) are also possible. Mountain bikes can also be hired (call for prices).

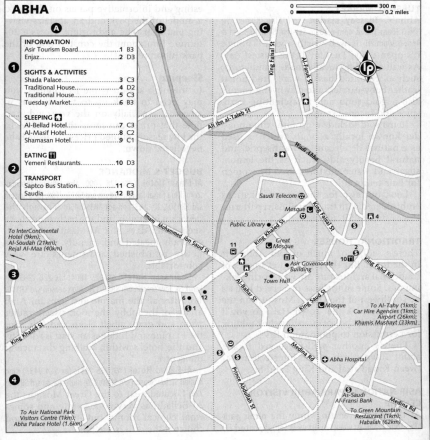

ABHA

INFORMATION
Asir Tourism Board....................1 B3
Enjaz....................................2 D3

SIGHTS & ACTIVITIES
Shada Palace............................3 C3
Traditional House.......................4 D2
Traditional House.......................5 C3
Tuesday Market.........................6 B3

SLEEPING
Al-Bellad Hotel.........................7 C3
Al-Masif Hotel..........................8 C2
Shamasan Hotel........................9 C1

EATING
Yemeni Restaurants...................10 D3

TRANSPORT
Saptco Bus Station....................11 C3
Saudia..................................12 B3

To InterContinental Hotel (9km); Al-Soudah (21km); Rejal Al-Maa (40km)

To Asir National Park Visitors Centre (1km); Abha Palace Hotel (1.6km)

King Faisal St
Al-Farit St
Ali ibn al-Taleb St
Wadi Abha
Saudi Telecom
Mosque
Public Library
King Khaled St
Great Mosque
Imam Mohammed ibn Saud St
Asir Governorate Building
Town Hall
Al-Bahar St
King Saud St
Mosque
King Fahd Rd
To Al-Tahy (1km); Car Hire Agencies (1km); Airport (26km); Khamis Mushayt (33km)
Medina Rd
Abha Hospital
Prince Abdullah St
As-Saudi Al-Fransi Bank
Medina Rd
To Green Mountain Restaurant (1km); Habalah (62km)
King Khaled St

SAUDI ARABIA

Sights

SHADA PALACE

Built in 1927 as an office-residence for a local Saudi governor, this **palace** (off King Khaled St; admission free; ☼ 9am-2pm Sat-Thu winter, 9am-6pm Sat-Thu summer) is one of the few traditional buildings left in Abha. Its squat, mud-walled tower provides an interesting counterpoint to the modern buildings that surround it.

The building itself is arguably more interesting than the exhibits (local handicrafts and household items). The whitewashed walls are adorned with brightly painted geometric patterns, particularly the staircase, which leads to the sitting rooms and the palace's former residential quarters on the upper two floors.

TUESDAY MARKET

Abha's **Tuesday market** (off King Khaled St; ☼ 6.30am-1pm & 4pm-6.30pm Sat-Thu, 8am-10.30am & 4pm-6.30pm Fri) is well worth a visit. Though it's open daily, Tuesday is the busiest day. As well as selling locally made handicrafts, such as coloured basket ware, traditional leather baby-carriers and clay ovens, there's also a gold souq and a fascinating herb, spice and incense souq.

Items sold include a ground white powder known locally as *shab*, which is used as a natural deodorant and antiseptic, and natural beauty aids (such as the lemon, sugar and water mixtures used by women for hair removal).

Look out also for the women's kaftans embroidered with traditional Asiri patterns. Prices start at SR165.

TRADITIONAL HOUSES

There's sadly not much of Old Abha left in the town. But the few good examples of traditional architecture are well worth seeking out. Some of the best-preserved houses lie southwest of the Grand Mosque, on the same square as the Town Hall, so you'll need to ask the police guarding the building for permission to photograph first.

There's another well-preserved façade about 100m north of the intersection between King Faisal and King Fahd Sts.

ASIR NATIONAL PARK ABHA VISITORS CENTRE

At the time of writing, only the **picnic park** (☼ 4pm-11pm last week Jun-1st week Sep), located in the southwest of Abha under the southern edge of the Ring Rd, was open to the public. Around five hectares in size, it contains some trails and paths, a climbing area for children, and a French-designed, artificial climbing wall (with climbs ranging from Grade 3 to Grade 7, including a 14m stretch that carries a prize of SR100,000 if you can do it in less than two minutes!). Sadly, an old Ottoman *hammam* was flattened in the construction of the cable car.

For access to the **visitors centre** (☎ 225 0920; admission free; ☼ 9am-2pm), you must first contact the **Asir National Park Office** (☎ 224 9812 ext 221222; fax 225 0920) located 4km from the centre for permission (or ask your hotel to do so).

The visitors centre contains some interesting and informative panels on the park, a model of the park and an upstairs viewing platform. The auditorium shows a 20-minute film about the construction of the park (upon request).

Sleeping

In the high season (June to August), you may need to book up to two months in advance, especially on the weekend; and note that prices can more than double. In the low season, quoted prices can usually be negotiated down.

BUDGET & MIDRANGE

Al-Masif Hotel (☎ 228 7000; almasifhotel@hotmail .com; King Faisal St; low season s/d SR125/188, high season s/d SR150/220, 2-/3-bed apt SR350/450) Though the décor's a bit lugub, and the bathrooms have seen better days, the Al-Masif is peaceful, centrally-located and friendly. The hotel's newly refurbished apartments are very comfortable.

Shamasan Hotel (☎ 225 1804; fax 228 2293; Al-Faruk St; low season s/d SR80/120, high season s/d SR110/ 165) After all the marble and gypsum Arab arches of the lobby, the rooms seem rather plain and drab, albeit clean and tidy. But the Filipino and Indonesian staff is friendly, and the hotel's within walking distance of the centre.

Al-Bellad Hotel (☎ 226 1451; fax 224 7433; King Khaled St; low season s/d SR80/120, high season s/d SR150/ 220) Located next to the Great Mosque, the Al-Bellad has very large, white and somewhat clinical rooms, but it makes a good choice if the others are full.

TOP END

Abha Palace (☎ 229 4444; www.abhapalace.com
.sa; Nahran Rd; low season s/d SR350/425, high season
s/d SR450/525, 4-bed apt from SR350, 3-bed villas from
SR750; ▢ ▣) Lying 1.5km southwest of the
town centre, the five-star Abha Palace certainly makes an impression: outside for its
bold, glass-paned architecture, and inside
for its combination of great facilities, excellent service and picturesque location overlooking Lake Saad and its dam. Facilities
include a ladies health club (and pool).

InterContinental Hotel (☎ 224 7777; www
.intercontinental.com; high season s/d SR495/675, villas
from SR1500; ▢ ▣) Perched atop the escarpment in Al-Soudah to the west of Abha
and originally designed as a palace for a
Saudi prince, the InterContinental is suit-
ably large, lavish and lush. The hotel is only
open June to September. It's about 10km
west of town.

Eating

Green Mountain Restaurant (☎ 229 1519; Green
Mountain; starters SR10-12, mains SR30-55; ◷ 8am-
midnight) Lit up at night with green lights,
this large restaurant (situated at the top of
the hill known as Green Mountain in the
southeast of Abha), is hard to miss. It's the
views overlooking Abha that you come for.
Take them in over a coffee (SR4 to SR7) and
a cake (SR8) at a table outside, or as the
locals do over a suck on a *sheesha* (water
pipe). Meals and snacks are also available,
though neither the food (nor prices) are
anything too special. It lies around 2km
south of the town centre.

Al-Tahy (☎ 228 331; Prince Sultan St; ◷ 1pm-
1am) One of the very few restaurants in
Abha with a family section (found around
the back), the Al-Tahy is also known for
its excellent Syrian chef (after whom it's
named). Large, bright and sparkling clean
it's much-beloved by the locals for its fresh
and excellent mezze (small/medium/large
SR5/10/15) and mains such as stuffed aubergine (SR10) and chicken *tajine* (SR15).
It's 1.25km from the town centre

Along King Saud St, there is a string
of small Yemeni restaurants which serve
delicious and filling *fool* (SR4) or ome-
lettes (SR4) for breakfast, as well as succulent *shwarma* sandwiches (SR4) and half
roasted chickens (SR10). Choose the most
popular.

Getting There & Away

AIR

Saudia (☎ 223 7777; King Khaled St; ◷ 9am-6pm Sat-
Thu) has several daily departures to Jeddah
(SR190), Riyadh (SR280) and Dammam
(SR390), with less frequent departures for
Medina (SR310) and Taif (SR140).

BUS

Abha's main **Saptco Bus Station** (☎ 226 3929;
King Khaled St) lies diagonally opposite the
Great Mosque. There are departures to
Jeddah (SR100, nine hours, every 90 min-
utes), Taif (SR100, eight hours, three daily)
and Jizan (SR35, four hours, three daily).
For Riyadh, take the free bus to Khamis
Mushayt (45 minutes, every 10 minutes)
and change. From Khamis Mushayt, it costs
SR135 to Riyadh and takes 12 hours. For
Najran (SR45, 3½ to four hours, four daily),
you'll also need to go to Khamis Mushayt.

Getting Around

The airport lies just over 26km from
town, signposted from the Abha–Khamis
Mushayt road.

There are no taxis in Abha, so you'll have
to make arrangements with your hotel –
most will collect you or drop you at the bus
station or airport. Car-hire agencies can be
found at the airport and in town.

During the summer months, a cable car
links the top of Green Mountain with the
Asir National Park Abha Visitor Center
and the Abha Palace hotel (one-way/return
SR30/60).

AROUND ABHA

Asir National Park

This **National Park** (◷ summer; free admission) in
the southwest of Abha was Saudi Arabia's
first and contains some of the Kingdom's
most spectacular scenery, with mountains
reaching nearly 3000m before plunging
down onto the coastal plain. The park encompasses some 450,000 hectares stretching
from the Red Sea coast, across the mountains and east into the desert. The park's
territory is not contiguous, with a number of
pockets of land – separated by towns, villages
and farmlands – fenced off for protection.

Al-Soudah

Al-Soudah, or 'the black one', so named for
the black clouds that so often surround it, is

jaw-droppingly beautiful. Located close to
the summit of the Kingdom's highest peak,
Jebel Soudah (2910m), about 22km west of
town, this is the place to come for precipitous cliffs, deep valleys and mountain-tops
disappearing behind the clouds.

There's no better way to enjoy the views
than taking the **As-Sawdah Cable Car** (☎ 229
1111; return ticket SR50; 9am-9pm Apr-Sep, winter by
special request). It's well signposted on the approaches from Abha.

It drops down off the escarpment to the
traditional mud-brick village of **Rejal Al-Maa**,
with wonderful views to accompany you all
the way, including stone villages, terraced
fields, juniper forests off in the distance and
even the occasional defensive watchtower.

Habalah

Believed to have been established by frightened villagers fleeing the invasion of the
Ottomans, the old village of Habalah is
uniquely situated halfway down a cliff face.
It lies around 63km southeast from Abha.

To reach the village, you no longer have
to climb by rope down the cliff face as the
villagers once had to do, but can take the
cable car (☎ 253 1919; adult/child return ticket SR40/30;
 9am-9pm Jun-Aug, public holidays & weekends Sep-
May) instead. Though it's only a short ride
(600m; 3½ minutes), the views en route are
impressive.

Unfortunately, the site itself is not. Almost nothing remains of the old village,
and some of the last villagers were forcibly
removed with the completion of the cable
car. And in its place is a pretty hideous,
concrete tourist complex – in parts very
litter-strewn, whose only aim appears to be
to make as much money as possible during
the high season. Nevertheless, the complex
contains several restaurants as well as activities for kids and remains a popular local
tourism attraction among Saudi families

Unfortunately Habalah symbolises the
more destructive face of privately-owned
Saudi tourism ventures. It costs SR6/3 per
adult/child to enter the tourist complex, a
fee that's waived if you take the cable car.

A via ferrata (climbing route with the
aid of fixed cables) has been established up
the rock face from Habalah. It costs SR20
including all equipment, a free cable car
ride back down to Habalah, and on-hand
assistance from Saudi guides.

NAJRAN   نجران

☎ 07 / pop 123,000
The oasis at Najran, surrounded by mountains and close to the Yemeni border, is one
of Saudi Arabia's hidden gems. With towering mud-brick, fortress-like homes known
as *qasr* strung out along the wadi and an
exceptional mud-brick fort, Najran is like
nowhere else in the Kingdom.

Throughout its long and sometimes turbulent history, Najran has been a key link
between the north and west of Arabia and
Yemen. Today, these connections can still
be seen and felt in Najran's people and its
culture.

Orientation & Information

Najran is strung out over nearly 30km. Just
about everything you'll need (hotels, restaurants, transport and banks) is located on
or just off King Abdul Aziz Rd.

Don't be alarmed about the unusually
high number of checkpoints around the
town – it's to combat the smuggling of
arms, qat (the mildly narcotic leaf), and
hashish from Yemen.

Sights
NAJRAN FORT (QASR AL-IMARA)

The town's most conspicuous monument,
the **Najran Fort** (☎ 542 1060; western end of King
Abdul Aziz Rd; admission free; 7.30am-sunset) displays all the architectural features of Najran's traditional architecture (see boxed
text, opposite). Construction began in 1942,
and the fort's 60 rooms were designed to
form a self-sustaining complex.

The main entrance is through a beautifully carved door. The highlights of the
interior at ground level include the fort's
mosque, a restored well that dates to pre-
Islamic times and the two-storey prince's
palace in the centre.

From the latter, a bridge leads to the
rooms above the fort's entrance, which
include the prince's office and the *majlis*
(meeting place) where the king held audiences. There are good views from the
ramparts.

AL-UKHDUD ARCHAEOLOGICAL SITE & MUSEUM

One of the most important archaeological
sites in Saudi Arabia and even on the southern Arabian Peninsula, is **Al-Ukhdud archaeo-**

ARCHITECTURAL DÈJÁ VU?

Rising regally out of the fertile fields, gardens and palm plantations, Najran's traditional tower houses are a stunning sight. Built with bricks made from a mixture of mud and straw, the houses usually stand three or four storeys high.

Unlike mud-brick architecture in other parts of the Kingdom however, Najran's houses are sometimes whitewashed or daubed with bright colours around the window and door frames.

The windows of the houses are usually large, and on the *majlis* (top floor) the windows are semi-circular in shape and often contain coloured glass. At night, and lit up, they look like giant lanterns lighting up the landscape. *Dèjá Vu?* Mirroring uncannily Yemen's houses across the mountains, they are yet another reminder of the close cultural ties between the two regions.

logical site (☎ 542 5292; fax 542 5120; Prince Sultan ibn Abdul Aziz St; admission free but permit required).

For 1000 years before the dawn of Islam, Al-Ukhdud was a major centre for the overland caravan trade in frankincense and myrrh which stretched from Yemen in the south all the way to Egypt and Syria in the north, and to the Gulf and Iraq in the east.

Measuring just over 5 sq km, a walk around the site will take you past the ruins of an ancient city (some buildings date back to 600 BC), which may be that of Al-Ukhdud (or, it is now thought by Saudi scholars, ancient Najran), including the remains of fortifications (in the unmistakable 'South Arabian style' found fascinatingly also in Yemen and across the water at Ethiopia's Yeha) and the remains of a moat or trench.

Look out also for the beautiful rock drawings and some stunning ancient inscriptions. You currently need permission to visit the site (see boxed text, p367), but this may change in the future.

The well-designed **museum** (☎ 542 5292; fax 542 5120; Prince Sultan ibn Abdul Aziz St; admission free; ☽ 8am-2pm Sat-Wed, 3-7pm Fri) next door contains some interesting information panels and displays on the history of the site as well as the culture of the area.

Exhibits include items excavated at Al-Ukhdud such as some very beautiful pre-Islamic, South Arabian scripts (dating to the early 2nd millennium BC), pottery, small artefacts and glass.

There are plans to open a new museum that will house items excavated at Al-Ukhdud. In the future, admission may be charged to both museums (probably SR10), but the ticket should include a guided tour around the archaeological site.

AL-AAN PALACE

This **palace** (Prince Nayef ibn Abdul Aziz Rd) is one of the best-preserved pieces of traditional architecture remaining in Wadi Najran. Set on a hill overlooking the wadi, it rises impressively to five storeys high. Many of the original windows and doors are still evident.

The palace is closed to visitors, but the views over the wadi from the car park make a visit here worthwhile, albeit if only to witness the ever-increasing encroachment of concrete on the traditional architecture.

TRADITIONAL MARKETS

Don't miss Najran's **traditional markets** (Ash Sha'abi (Public Souq); western end of King Abdul Aziz Rd; ☽ 8am-noon & 2-6pm) which are spread in different sections over a large area south of Najran Fort. The souqs sell everything from spectacularly sequined burka (headscarf covering a woman's face) and DIY *bachoor* (incense) sets complete with little spoon (SR15), to tooled, leather pistol holders, antique *jambiyas* (SR500 to SR30,000) and delightful baskets with pointed conical covers for holding dates (SR5 to SR100).

For the ultimate souvenir-hunter, what about a gold-plated Saudi ceremonial sword (SR1000)? Also worth seeking out are the gold and silver souqs; at the latter, women sell antique Bedouin jewellery, though you'll need to bring your best bartering skills.

Tours

Both the Holiday Inn Najran and Najran Hotel offer tours of Najran and the surrounds. The Najran Holiday Inn offers half-day tours (per person SR50) and full-day tours (SR100). The Najran Hotel offers full-day tours of Najran for SR150 per person.

SAUDI ARABIA

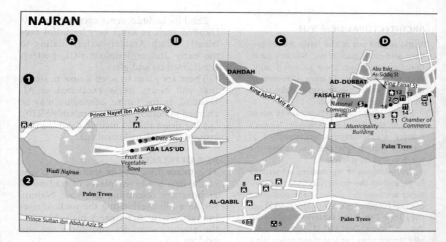

Both hotels can organise a permit to visit Al-Ukhdud Archaeological Site if given a few days' notice (you should fax the hotels your dates and a copy of your passport and visa).

Sleeping

Najran Hotel (☎ 522 1949; fax 522 1418; just off King Abdul Aziz Rd; s/d 80/150) Though the lobby's a bit lugub, the Najran is friendly, well-run and welcoming. Rooms are generously sized, clean and comfy and are great value (but be sure to ask for one of the 'tourist rooms'). Breakfast is included.

Hyatt Najran Hotel (☎ 523 3344; www.najranh .com; King Abdul Aziz Rd; s/d SR300/400; 🖳) The newly opened Hyatt wouldn't win a style contest, but it's the best midrange choice with rooms boasting good views over the town and some of its traditional houses. There's also a restaurant.

ourpick Holiday Inn Najran (☎ 522 5222; www .holiday-inn.com/najran; King Abdul Aziz Rd; s/d SR440/570; 🖳 🖭) The most comfortable place to stay in Najran, the Holiday Inn is also well-managed, friendly and accommodating.

Eating

Lahore Pakistani Restaurant (☎ 523 6777; King Abdul Aziz Rd; mains SR4-10 🕙 7.30am-2am) Simple but spotless and serving fresh, delicious food at extremely pleasing prices, it's easy to see why this is a firm local favourite. Dining is at tables or on the floor inside little cubicles, and there's a family section. Try the nicely spiced chicken tikka and fragrant biryani rice.

Hori Restaurant (☎ 523 4335; King Abdul Aziz Rd; 🕙 11am-2am Sat-Thu) For a quick bite or takeaway, head for the Hori. Its chicken with garlic sauce (SR12) is famous, but it also does excellent *shwarma* sandwiches (SR5), roast fish fillet (with chips, salad and bread; SR15) and lamb kebabs with salad (SR15). It's also got a family section.

Getting There & Away

The **Saudia** (☎ 522 3333; King Abdul Aziz Rd) booking office is 3km west of the Abha–Riyadh roads intersection. There are daily flights to Riyadh (SR280) and Jeddah (SR250), and less frequent flights to Dammam (SR390), Jizan (SR150) and Sharurah (SR120).

Saptco Bus Station (☎ 522 0005; King Abdul Aziz Rd) lies 1.7km west of the Abha–Riyadh roads intersection. Buses leave for Jizan (SR80, eight hours, three daily), Riyadh (SR135, 12 hours, three daily), Jeddah (SR130, 14 hours, four daily), Abha (SR45, 3½ hours, six daily), and Sharurah (SR50, 3½ hours, one daily).

Getting Around

The airport lies 19km northeast of Najran; there are no buses there, only taxis (SR30).

Najran's taxis operate as shared shuttles, mostly between Faisaliyeh and Najran Fort and cost SR1 to SR2 per person (though you should negotiate the fare before getting in). If you want one to yourself, expect to pay between SR5 to SR10.

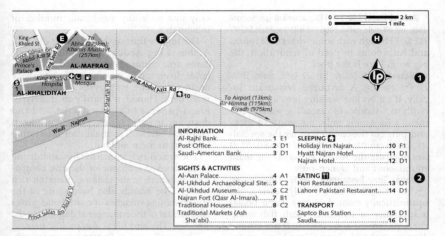

INFORMATION	
Al-Rajhi Bank	1 E1
Post Office	2 D1
Saudi-American Bank	3 D1

SIGHTS & ACTIVITIES	
Al-Aan Palace	4 A1
Al-Ukhdud Archaeological Site	5 C2
Al-Ukhdud Museum	6 C2
Najran Fort (Qasr Al-Imara)	7 B1
Traditional Houses	8 C2
Traditional Markets (Ash Sha'abi)	9 B2

SLEEPING	
Holiday Inn Najran	10 F1
Hyatt Najran Hotel	11 D1
Najran Hotel	12 D1

EATING	
Hori Restaurant	13 D1
Lahore Pakistani Restaurant	14 D1

TRANSPORT	
Saptco Bus Station	15 D1
Saudia	16 D1

AROUND NAJRAN

Lying 116km north of Najran, off the road leading north to Al-Khamasin, is **Bir Himma** (admission free; 24hr), the site of a famous and beautiful well said to be over 4500 years old but still used by the locals. It's well worth a stop if you have your own transport.

Close by are some impressive **rock carvings** (admission free with permission; 8am-sunset), albeit much damaged by vandalism, which has led to the construction of a perimeter fence. You can fetch the key from the mayor's office (though it's perfectly possible to clamber over the rocks around the fence).

Look out for the carvings showing how dates were traditionally harvested. To visit the site, you need a permit which your hotel can arrange for you in Najran.

JIZAN جازان

07 / pop 78,000

Jizan is known as the 'fruit basket' of Saudi Arabia for the variety and abundance of its agricultural produce.

The fair ladies of Jizan are considered to be great cooks, tidy housekeepers and skilful in the use of perfumes and fragrances – so are much admired by Saudi men! If you're invited to an inhabitant's house, expect a fabulous feast. The whole region of Jazan is known for its famous hospitality, in which guests are fed to the gunnels.

For the traveller, Jizan can seem muddy, grubby and drab – and in summer unbearably humid. Fruity fish market smells don't help either. Most use it merely as a jumping-off point for Farasan Island. But if you're here in the autumn (usually around September), be sure to enquire about the famous Parrot Fish Festival, which is a riotous and very colourful event.

Orientation & Information

The heart of the town is between Al-Tawhid Sq and the corniche. The bus station is just off the corniche.

Sights

If you're filling time, the **souq** is worth a wander, if only to admire the gold shops or the abundant produce for which Jizan is famous: everything from cucumbers and cabbages to tomatoes, watermelons and mandarins.

Look out also for the exquisite local honey, coffee husks from Yemen (made into a type of coffee), and the endless types of *bachoor* (incense) much loved by the Jizani women to scent their houses, clothes and hair.

Sleeping & Eating

Al-Hayat Gizan Hotel (322 1055; fax 317 1774; Corniche; s/d SR230/300;) Conveniently located 200m from the sea port south of the town centre, the hotel is also friendly and well-run. Despite the somewhat dank smell and cavernous corridors, rooms are spacious and well-furnished. Rooms on the third floor are best.

Atheel Hotel (☎ 317 1101; atheelhot-jaz@hotmail
.com; just off main roundabout; s/d with breakfast SR240/
330; ⚐) Though with somewhat small rooms
and bathrooms in need of renovation, the
big boon here is the pool.

Waterfall (As-Shalal; ☎ 322 3998; mains SR10-
25; ☽ 1pm-1am) A favourite restaurant locally, it's a bit like walking into a car wash
(with its windows of cascading water). The
menu's in Arabic only, but you can pick-
and-point at the counter, or try the speciality, *kasba* (mutton on a bed of rice; SR15). It
lies opposite the Atheel Hotel off the main
roundabout and is men-only

Happy Time Restaurant (☎ 321 7162; Corniche;
☽ 5pm-midnight) With a family section, the
optimistically named Happy Time boasts
a speciality of delicious, fresh fish oven-
roasted, Yemeni-style (SR30). It lies around
1km from the Al-Hayat Gizan Hotel on the
same road.

Getting There & Away

The airport is about 5km northeast of the
town centre; a taxi should cost SR10. There
are several daily **Saudi Arabian Airlines** (☎ 323
3333) flights to Jeddah (SR200) and Riyadh
(SR320), with less frequent departures to
Najran (SR150) and Sharurah (SR190).

Saptco Bus Station (☎ 317 1267; King Abdul Aziz
St) is just off the corniche between the junction with the main road and the entrance
to the port. Buses run to Jeddah (SR100, 9
to10 hours, every two hours), Abha (SR35,
four hours, four daily) and Najran (SR80,
eight hours, three daily).

To get to Farasan Island, the **Seaport Authority** (☎ 317 2864 for ferries from Jizan, 316 3446 for
ferries from Farasan; Jizan Port; ☽ 6am-6pm) issues
tickets (free) for the two ferries (a recent
gift to the people from King Abdullah) that
depart daily at 7am and 3pm in both directions. The journey takes one hour 20
minutes.

If you're coming with a car, it's best to
reserve two days in advance. The Seaport
Authority (and entry to the ferry departure
point) lies around 1.5km from the centre
of town.

FARASAN ISLANDS   جزر فرسان
☎ 07

The Farasan Islands form part of an archipelago which lies about 40km off the coast
of Jizan. Farasan, the main island, is the

only one with any significant number of
inhabitants.

During the time of the first ruler of Saudi
Arabia, King Abdul Aziz, political dissi-
dents and criminals were exiled to the islands. Even today, employers threaten lazy
or incompetent employees with banish-
ment here. Though it's hardly an archetypal
island-paradise (it's generally flat, arid and
dusty and in parts, is rather poor, run-down
and litter-strewn), it makes an interesting
break from the mainland.

The area *is* rich in marine life, and diving
(if pre-booked with one of the dive companies) is superb in the shallow, plankton-rich
waters. The islands also have some of the
few remaining stretches of coastal mangroves
(the habitat of the endangered dugong) in the
Red Sea. The bird life is also prolific here.

The small town of **Farasan** has several surviving traditional houses built from coral
with intricately decorated and carved doorways. These were the homes of former merchants and pearl dealers. There's also a small
Turkish Fort on the edge of the main town.

The newly opened **Coral Farasan Resort**
(☎ 316 0000; www.coralhotels.com.sa; s/d low season
SR350/460, s/d high season SR400/550; ⚐), lying
11km east of the port, offers comfortable
rooms, a private beach (where women can
swim), a restaurant, car rental (SR75/125
per day in low/high season), a ferry booking
service and boat trips (SR250 per hour per
boat for up to six people). In the future, a
dive centre should open.

If the Coral Farasan is full, the **Farasan
Hotel** (☎ 316 0876; mohdbinali@yahoo.com; s/d SR250/
375) right next to the hospital in the town
centre offers similar services and accommodation as well as fishing trips, snorkelling and reef diving if pre-booked (from
SR250 per person inclusive; minimum six
passengers). In winter, both places get busy,
so reserve one week in advance.

THE EMPTY QUARTER
الربع الخالي

The Empty Quarter (Rub al-Khali; 'the
Abode of Silence'), conjures up all that
was romantic and forbidden about Arabia. European adventurers all dreamt of
conquering it, while the Bedu, who called

AMID THE DESERT DUNES

We stopped to examine a small clump of sage grass. In the stems was a little water, and I chewed on them as I supposed the animals chewed on them as they eked out an existence in this merciless but mesmerising environment.

'I love to sleep in the desert,' Abu Ali declared. 'The sand is so smooth and restful. There is no dirt and dust – you get up and you feel refreshed.' He stood up and the sand on his *thobe* poured softly to the ground. Looking towards the horizon he said, 'I shall die here. And when I do, I want that they bury me here.'

Later we came across what he called *zaher*, a tiny *tribulus* flower with bright yellow petals, endemic to the Empty Quarter.

Turning towards me with the flower outstretched he proclaimed, 'Just as this flower is the light of the desert, so you are the light of all womanhood.' I smiled embarrassed. Even in the presence of a stranger, even in front of a foreigner, the Bedu can't resist the spontaneous poetry that still sometimes seizes them.

'Are you sad that you're no longer living the life of a Bedouin, Abu Ali?' I asked later.

'Yes,' he said. 'I long for that way of life.' After a pause he went on, 'But I don't long for those days…those terrible, difficult, desert days.'

As we slipped and struggled up another dune, a pair of Arabian oryx, the colour of the sands, spun, startled to face us. In a minute they were gone again, leaping lithely through the dunes in the fast-descending dusk. At sunset, the dunes now a deep mauve, Abu Ali fell to his knees and prayed.

From the author's diary. With thanks to Sheikh Abu Ali, Head Park Ranger, 'Uruq Bani Ma'arid Protected Area & Mr Othman A Llewellyn, Environmental Planner, NCWCD.

---

it simply the 'Sands', looked upon it as a formidable world of necessity, less enamoured with the beauty of a sand dune than concerned about the number of days' travel to the next well.

The largest area covered by sand on the planet, the Empty Quarter encompasses 655,000 sq km, an area larger than France or Texas. The breathtakingly sculpted sand dunes, for which the Empty Quarter is famous, can rise over 250m and form vast chains of longitudinal dune ridges, stretching over hundreds of kilometres, as well as individual barchan dunes. Shifted by the wind, sand dunes can move at a rate of up to 30m per year.

INFORMATION

Unfortunately, after September 11, access to the Empty Quarter was suddenly restricted and all off-road driving was banned without special permission. As a result, local hotels no longer offer day excursions and overnight trips here.

If you want to get permission, you'll need to apply to the Ministry of Interior and also justify the trip. Currently, the Ministry is also asking all embassies in the Kingdom to advise their nationals against going

there. Tour agencies in Jeddah (see p323) can obtain permission if you give them enough advance notice, but trips there are not cheap.

If you want to get an idea of the dunes without subjecting yourself to the rigmarole of obtaining the permits, one option is to take the road running from Najran to Sulayyil. You'll pass through the dunes on the way (though it's difficult to get much idea of them without going off-road). Don't try and sneak in; the area is patrolled.

A better option (though you'll need your own 4WD) is to visit the 'Uruq Bani Ma'arid Protected Area.

'URUQ BANI MA'ARID PROTECTED AREA

Lying 222km north of Najran (6km east off the main road) and about the same distance from Wadi Sulayyil, is the 'Uruq Bani Ma'arid Protected Area. Though as yet it doesn't register on tourists' or expat itineraries, it's a fantastic way of both sneaking (legally!) into the Empty Quarter, as well as seeing some of Saudi's all-too-rare but beautiful wildlife.

The dunes are as spectacular here as anywhere (up to 250m high and several

EXPLORING THESIGER

As any visitor to the great desert interior of the Empty Quarter will tell you, there is an intangible magic about sitting astride the ridge of one of its sand dunes. It is here that you come closest to the work of the wind as it catches up a few grains of sand and sneezes them over the crest in a shiver of heat and redundancy – an act performed on numberless ridges as the dunes progress to nowhere, and eventually, as the wind turns, come back again. A geode, like a hard, unripe cauliflower, and a golden dancing ant are often the only distractions in this immutable pattern of topographical inanity.

Not surprisingly, then, this celebrated sea of sand has been a holy grail of explorers for well over 200 years. In the empirically-minded 19th century, it represented one of the last frontiers of Western exploration: a place to be overcome, penetrated, civilised, acquisitioned, labelled, explained. In the more egoistical 20th century, it became a blank canvas for self-exploration through physical endurance: man (especially man) pitted against nature.

It is tempting, as such, to map the Empty Quarter in terms of the remarkable lives of the eccentric few who endeavoured to penetrate its uncharted interior. Many made or harboured dreams of the attempt but it wasn't until 1930 that the first crossing of the Empty Quarter was made by one Bertram Thomas, a softly-spoken British civil servant. His travels from Salalah in Oman to Doha in Qatar resulted in a fine book, *Arabia Felix*, that is a classic of the personal endurance genre. St John Philby travelled from Riyadh to Sulayyil, tortured by the knowledge that he'd missed the plaudit of being the first across the wilderness by only a matter of months. His accounts of the experience are poignant for the disappointment they describe.

What is easy to forget in the reading of these endurance classics is that the Empty Quarter has in fact been peopled for centuries. The Bedu know what it is to cross this desert; they know what it means to feel the menacing, maniacal must for water; they live with the grit under their eyelids,

hundred kilometres long) and so also is the wildlife. You should see at least three types of gazelle and the very beautiful Arabian oryx, but don't expect to see large numbers of any species. The best time to see animals is from dawn to 10am and from 4pm to sunset.

Information

You will still need to apply for permission to visit (from the National Commission for Wildlife Conservation & Development – see p309), but permits are usually readily and quite quickly granted, and are free. A ranger will be provided to guide you at the protected area.

To get the permit, send an email to the Commission outlining who you are, when you want to travel, how many people and vehicles will make up your party, and include a copy of your passport or *iqama* (residence permit).

AL-FAW الفاو

Nestled under the limestone cliffs of the Jebel Tuwaiq Escarpment on the western fringe of the Empty Quarter, Al-Faw was once a great trading centre, as well as a staging post for camel caravans crossing the desert between Yemen and the Gulf.

Al-Faw was at the height of its prosperity from late in the 2nd century BC until early in the 1st century AD. It was evidently a large city (1.5km by 1.7km) surrounded by 20m-high walls, beyond which lay fields of irrigated wheat. The city appears to have had a fortified two-storey souq, a palace, temple, domestic houses and a number of tombs.

The outlines (in the form of beautifully hewn stones) of many of these buildings are still evident in the remarkably atmospheric and extensive ruins. Within some of the tombs are some startlingly beautiful and well-preserved inscriptions, though you'll need a guide to find them.

A permit (p367) is required to visit the site. There are no official opening hours, but a guardian and his family live there. Photography is not allowed.

Though the site has been closed for the time being, Professor Ansary, the distinguished Saudi archaeologist who spent 25 seasons at the site, is currently finishing four volumes about it, which should be published in the near future.

wedged in the ear cavities and ground into the cracks of sunburnt heels. What they don't understand, rather like the Sherpas on Everest, is why anyone else wants to know what they know.

There was one traveller, however, who not only wanted to know what the Bedu know but who also wanted the rest of us to understand that it is wrong to assume that Western exploration conquered the Empty Quarter. That man was Wilfred Thesiger – an Eton and Oxford man who found his soul in the heart of Arabia. 'I was exhilarated by the sense of space, the silence,' he wrote of the desert in *The Life of My Choice*. But it is not just the emptiness and his own remarkable resistance to fatigue, thirst and hunger that he describes. Crucially, he describes being 'in harmony with the past, travelling as men had travelled for untold generations across the desert'. Thesiger's Empty Quarter, compellingly described in *Arabian Sands*, isn't empty at all: it's filled with the history of the people of that region and of their extraordinary patience and humour; of the comradeship of the Bait Kathir tribe (among others) and their aptitude to withstand hardship. His sensitivity to their character, his empathy with and profound respect for the Bedu (which was returned in kind), is one of the most significant aspects of his 1000km crossing of the Empty Quarter.

By the time of Thesiger's death in 2003, aged 93, his journey had become a legend. After leaving Arabia, he railed against the dubious advances of modern technology and their impact upon his Bedu friends. Even into his 80s, Thesiger lived in Kenya in a tin-roofed house with neither electricity nor running water.

It wasn't until early 1999 that three Canadian explorers and their camels successfully retraced Thesiger's footsteps, crossing from Salalah in southern Oman to Abu Dhabi in the UAE. They, too, were accompanied by the legendary Bait Kathir, immortalised in Thesiger's black-and-white photographs of the days before the pickup changed the desert forever.

Getting There & Away

Al-Faw can only be reached by private vehicles.

From Sulayyil, take the main highway west for 40km and then the turnoff south to Najran. The turnoff to Al-Faw is a further 76km south, near a petrol station and a large radio tower. The site is 700m east of the road – look for the guardian's Bedouin tent (and the fence enclosing the ruins 200m beyond). Al-Faw lies 340km from Najran.

AL-KHAMASIN (WADI AL-DAWASIR)

الخماسين

☎ 01 / pop 85,500

Lying at an important junction 475km from Najran, 445km from Abha and around 600km from Riyadh, Al-Khamasin (known locally also as Wadi al-Dawasir after the wadi it's found in) lies on an ancient caravan route and today still makes a useful place to overnight on your way to or from the South, or from where to explore the Empty Quarter.

The town is particularly famous for its *bachoor* (incense) and for the quality of its camels. It's also one of the most impor-

tant areas for the rearing of camels, and in spring, with the rains, the whole place bursts into a verdant green, attracting caravans of camels from all around.

Sleeping & Eating

Al-Rokan Hotel (☎ 784 2492; fax 784 0311; Main St; r SR100) Though considered the best bet in town, rooms can only be described as adequate. Rather small and with somewhat grubby walls, it's nevertheless welcoming and good value.

Sarawat Hotel (☎ 786 1243; fax 786 2111; Main St; s SR75-125, d SR100-150) A better bet but lying 8km from Saptco, the Sarawat is well-run by the friendly Egyptian manager and offers small-but-quiet rooms located at the back, or larger-but-roadside ones at the front.

Al-Rokan Restaurant (☎ 784 6861; Main St; ⊗ 1pm-midnight) Part of Al-Rokan Hotel, the restaurant is considered one of the best places for a bite to eat. Try the flavoursome oven-roasted quail (SR12) or juicy chicken kebab (SR10).

Getting There & Away

Saptco (☎ 784 1433) runs buses from Al-Khamasin to Riyadh (SR80, eight hours, nine daily), Al-Hofuf (SR125, 10 hours, two daily), Dammam (SR140, 12 hours, two daily), Khamis Mushayt (SR55, four hours, four daily) and Jeddah (SR160, 14 hours, two daily). For Abha, go to Khamis Mushayt and change. For Najran, go to Sulayyil (80km south of Al-Khamasin, SR10, one hour, six buses) and from there take a bus to Najran (SR65, five hours, two daily).

Saudia flies to the airport known as Wadi al-Dawasir daily from Riyadh (SR190) and from Jeddah (SR250).

EASTERN PROVINCE
المنطقة الشرقية

The Eastern Province is the centre of Saudi Arabia's colossal oil industry and, as such, you're more likely to live and work here than to visit. The province boasts the longest history of Westerners living and working in Saudi Arabia, and the sprawling satellite towns of Dammam, Al-Khobar and Dhahran are prosperous and relatively liberal.

Despite the modernity, the desert is never far away and rarely more enchanting than the Bedouin market of Nairiyah and the oasis town of Al-Hofuf.

DAMMAM
الدمام
☎ 03 / pop 836,000

The run-down provincial capital, Dammam, is the longest settled and largest town of the Dhahran–Dammam–Khobar group, but it nonetheless has the feeling of a town whose time has passed. The town is home to enormous populations of immigrant Asians – in the centre it can be hard to imagine that you're in Saudi Arabia at all.

Central Dammam spreads south of the intersection between King Abdul Aziz and 11th Sts.

There are plenty of banks and reasonably priced internet cafés. **Sharkiya Internet Café** (off King Saud St; per hr SR4; ☯ 6am-1am) is for men only; it's behind Safari Al-Danah Hotel. The main post office is on 9th St.

Sights

The **Dammam Museum of Archaeology & Ethnography** (☎ 826 6056; 4th fl, Prince Mohammed bin Fahd St; admission free; ☯ 7.30am-2.30pm Sat-Wed), at the

railroad crossing and opposite the Al-Waha Mall, contains Stone Age tools, Hellenistic pottery, Bedouin crafts, silver jewellery and information on the archaeological sites of the Eastern Province. Frustratingly, the exhibits aren't all labelled in English.

Sleeping

Gulf Flower Hotel (☎ 826 2170; fax 827 0709; 9th St; s SR99-110, d SR132) The best budget bet by a mile, and a good midrange option too, the Gulf Flower has sparkling-clean, spacious and quite well-furnished rooms. It's great value. Ask for one of the 15 rooms with a decent-sized balcony.

Golden Tulip Al-Hamra Hotel Dammam (☎ 833 3444; www.goldentulipalhamra.com; King Khaled St; s/d SR450/550; 🖳) The big boon of the four-star Tulip is its central location. There are also four restaurants and a health club (men only) offering massages, Jacuzzi etc.

Eating

As in Al-Khobar (see p352), you're spoilt for choice in Dammam. Streets such as those around Prince Mansour St and Prince Nasser St host everything from Syrian and Sudanese to Afghani and Filipino cuisine. The following all have family sections.

Al-Bahar Oriental Restaurant (☎ 833 4579; King Saud St, diagonally opp Al-Dahah Shopping Centre; ☯ 9am-11pm) Though the outside looks unpromising, this bright, clean Filipino restaurant does delicious dishes at unbeatable prices. Ask for the excellent-value set menu (SR10).

Shahnaz (☎ 833 2243; King Khaled St; starters SR8-18, mains SR25-38; ☯ noon-4pm & 7pm-12.30am) The Shahnaz is known for its pizzazz: first-class food served in a magnificent Moorish setting. The cuisine is Italian (pasta/pizza SR18 to SR24) and Iranian; the seafood cooked è l'Iranien is famous (SR42 to SR52).

Ghazi Restaurant (☎ 828 0887; Prince Nasser St; mains SR12-18; ☯ noon-3pm & 7pm-midnight) Perennially popular locally, the spotless and well-managed Ghazi serves fresh and flavoursome Pakistani food at decent prices. Specials change daily.

Getting There & Away
AIR

King Fahd International Airport, lies about 42km west of the city centre. **Saudia** (☎ 894 3333; Gulf Centre, Prince Turki St, Khobar) has flights

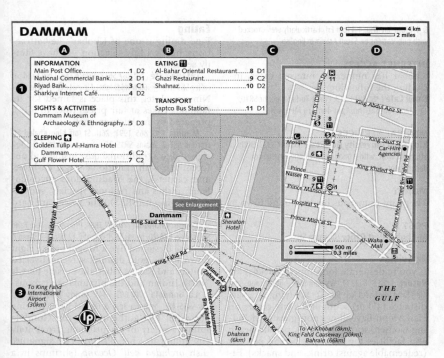

DAMMAM

0 — 4 km
0 — 2 miles

INFORMATION
Main Post Office..........................1 D2
National Commercial Bank..........2 D1
Riyad Bank.................................3 C1
Sharkiya Internet Café................4 D2

SIGHTS & ACTIVITIES
Dammam Museum of
Archaeology & Ethnography...5 D3

SLEEPING
Golden Tulip Al-Hamra Hotel
Dammam..................................6 C2
Gulf Flower Hotel........................7 C2

EATING
Al-Bahar Oriental Restaurant......8 D1
Ghazi Restaurant.........................9 C2
Shahnaz....................................10 D2

TRANSPORT
Saptco Bus Station...................11 D1

See Enlargement

Dammam
King Saud St

Sheraton
Hotel

To King Fahd
International
Airport
(30km)

Train Station

THE
GULF

To
Dhahran
(6km)

To Al-Khobar (8km);
King Fahd Causeway (20km);
Bahrain (66km)

---

leaving once daily to Abha (SR390), Hail (SR320), Najran (SR390) and Taif (SR360), three times daily to Jeddah (SR390) and eight times daily to Riyadh (SR150).

BUS
The **Saptco Bus Station** (☎ 834 2545; 11th St) is approximately 700m north of the city centre. Intercity services include Al-Hofuf (SR20, two hours, nine daily), Riyadh (SR60, 4½ to 5¼ hours, 14 daily), and Jeddah (SR200, 16 hours, three daily) via Taif (SR170, 12 hours) and Sakaka (SR185, 13 hours, four daily).

TRAIN
The **train station** (☎ 871 5071; end of Fatima Az-Zahra St; 24hr) to the southeast of the city centre has trains to Riyadh (VIP/1st/2nd class SR130/75/60, four to 4½ hours, four daily), and Al-Hofuf (VIP/1st/2nd SR40/25/20, 1½ hours, daily).

Getting Around
Buses (SR15, 50 minutes, hourly) run from the bus station to the airport. A taxi between

the airport and Dammam costs about SR50; from the bus station to the town SR10, and to Al-Khobar SR25 to SR30.

AL-KHOBAR الخبر
☎ 03 / pop 205,000
Al-Khobar (Khobar) is both the newest and the most attractive of the three cities that make up Greater Dhahran.

With its long corniche along the waterfront, it is the most pedestrian-friendly, relaxed and liberal city in the Eastern Province. It also boasts some of the finest restaurants in Saudi Arabia.

Orientation
Khobar follows a compact grid design, with the central business area bounded by Prince Faisal bin Fahd St to the north, Dhahran St to the south, the Gulf to the east and Prince Hamud St to the west.

Information
BOOKSHOPS
Jarir Bookstore(☎ 894 3311; www.jarirbookstore .com; Prince Turki St, btwn 11th & 12th Sts; 9am-2pm

SAUDI ARABIA

& 4-11pm Sat-Thu, 4-11pm Fri) Particularly well-stocked with publications on Saudi Arabia in English.

INTERNET ACCESS

Khobar has numerous internet cafés, including the following:

Email Café (☎ 893 8579; Prince Turki St; per hr SR10; ☼ 8am-4am Sat-Thu, 1pm-4am Fri) Men only.

MEDICAL SERVICES

King Fahd University Hospital (☎ 887 3333; 30th St) In the west, with a good accident and emergency department.

MONEY

There are numerous banks around town.

POST

Al-Khobar Post Office (Dhahran St)

Activities

If you're desperate for a dip, the **Holiday Inn Resort** (☎ 896 3333; www.hmb@ichotelsgroup.com; King Fahd bin Abdul Aziz Rd; ☐ ☑ ☒) lying at a safe distance (45km) south of the city centre on Half Moon Bay, allows non-guests (including women) to use its clean, private beach and facilities for SR60 per person per day (redeemable against drinks and snacks). Facilities include jet ski, buggy and boat hire, and waterskiing. By 2008, it should also have a second pool and gym (for women only). A taxi will take you here for SR50.

Sleeping

ourpick **Al-Nimran Hotel** (☎ 867 5618; www.alnimran hotel.com; Prince Faisal bin Fahd St; s/d SR288/400; ☐ ☒) Though the rooms and bathrooms could be bigger, the big boon here is the lively lobby which also doubles as the very popular Latasia Café. There's also a pool on the 9th floor, which is open to both men and women. Note that 'older rooms' are available (singles/doubles from SR100/150) if you're on a tight budget. Ask for the very accommodating English manager, Mr Neil Maitland Walker.

Gulf Meridien (☎ 896 9000; www.lemeridien-alkho bar.com; Prince Turki St; s/d SR650/700, villas SR3500, royal ste SR12,000; ☐ ☒ ☒) Though the décor's a bit anodyne, the comfort is not. Khobar's finest boasts lovely views (all rooms have sea views and balconies), a pool that's open to both men and women, and restaurants with an excellent reputation (buffets SR135).

Eating

Fine dining is one of Khobar's key attractions; here's a tiny selection. All have family sections.

Latasia Café (☎ 867 5618; Prince Faisal bin Fahd St; coffee SR5-10; ☼ 6am-midnight) Located in the Al-Nimran Hotel, this place is famed for its fabulous cakes at fair prices (SR7 to SR9), prepared by an Austrian chef.

Madina (☎ 865 1991; 26th St, off King Khaled St; starters SR6-7, mains SR15-25; ☼ 1pm-midnight) Designed like a traditional *qasr* inside and out (complete with traditional rugs, cushions and carpets), the Madina does succulent Saudi dishes and regional specials, such as grilled pigeon (SR15). The prices are hard to beat too.

Copper Chandni (☎ 887 7868; Prince Faisal bin Fahd St; starters SR8-20, mains SR20-55; ☼ 12.30pm-4.30pm & 7pm-1am) Designed like a Mogul palace right down to the gold damask screens, liveried waiters and Karma vibes, the cuisine here is North Indian and the biryanis are famous.

La Gondola (☎ 893 7345; mains SR48-128, pizzas SR35-48; ☼ noon-3pm & 6pm-11.30pm) Aiming above all for 'authenticity', the Gondola imports many of its products from Italy (including its chef, Paolo). The signature dish *orchidea dell' Oceano* (shrimps in a mascarpone cheese and mustard sauce) and tiramisu are famous in the Eastern Province, and the restaurant's the choice of princes and the press alike. It lies just east of Prince Msa'id St.

ourpick **Al-Sanbok** (☎ 865 3867; just off Dhahran St; starters SR22-28, mains from SR65, 3-course average SR150; ☼ noon-3pm & 6pm-11.30pm) Claiming the 'Kingdom's finest' crown, Al-Sanbok is particularly famous for its fish and seafood, supplied by its own fishing boats. The cuisine, 'international' in style (with Thai and Tandoori influences), is superb; the tom yum kung soup (SR22) is legendary. Much patronised locally as well as by Saudi celebs and international news crews, it's not uncommon to queue for one to 1½ hours in the high season.

If you've blown your budget on fine-dining, or fancy something fast, head for the terrific **Al-Shallal Pastry** (☎ 899 0088; 10th St; sandwiches SR1-2, pizzas SR5-6, ☼ 5.30am-2pm & 3.30pm-12.30am Sat-Thu, 6am-11am & 3.30pm-1am Fri). Its combination of fresh food, freshly baked in spotless premises at rock-bottom prices sees this place buzzing with locals and delivery vans heading off to local schools.

SAUDI ARABIA

Getting There & Away

AIR

For details of flights from King Fahd International Airport, see p352.

BUS

All intercity buses leave from Dammam (p353), with the single exception of a non-stop Saptco VIP service between Al-Khobar and Riyadh (SR90, five hours). It leaves from the **Algosaibi Hotel** (☎ 882 2882; Prince Talal St) from where you can also buy tickets.

CAR

Considered reputable among the many car rental companies are **Avis** (☎ 895 5053; www

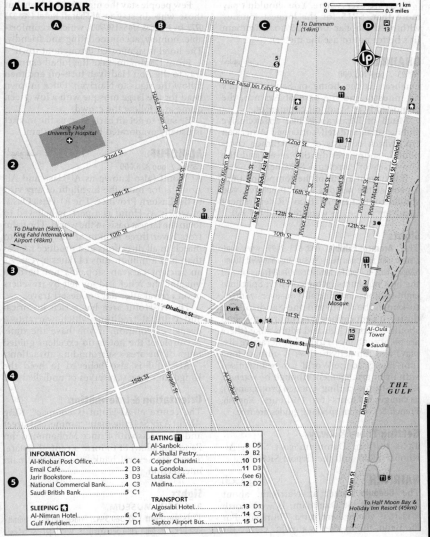

AL-KHOBAR

0 ——————— 1 km
0 ——————— 0.5 miles

To Dammam (14km)

Prince Faisal bin Fahd St

King Fahd University Hospital

22nd St

Hafid Ibrahim St

22nd St

16th St

Prince Hamud St

Prince Maiin St

Prince Mitib St

King Fahd bin Abdul Aziz Rd

Prince Naif St

16th St

12th St

Prince Bandar St

King Fahd St

King Khalid St

Prince Talal St

Prince Musaid St

Prince Turki St (Corniche)

To Dhahran (5km);
King Fahd International
Airport (48km)

10th St

10th St

12th St

4th St

1st St

Dhahran St

Park

Dhahran St

Mosque

Al-Oula Tower

Saudia

15th St

Riyadh St

Al-Khobar St

Dhahran St

THE GULF

To Half Moon Bay &
Holiday Inn Resort (45km)

INFORMATION
Al-Khobar Post Office.................1 C4
Email Café.................................2 D3
Jarir Bookstore..........................3 D3
National Commercial Bank.........4 C3
Saudi British Bank.....................5 C1

SLEEPING
Al-Nimran Hotel.......................6 C1
Gulf Meridien...........................7 D1

EATING
Al-Sanbok................................8 D5
Al-Shallal Pastry.......................9 B2
Copper Chandni......................10 D1
La Gondola.............................11 D3
Latasia Café.......................(see 6)
Madina..................................12 D2

TRANSPORT
Algosaibi Hotel.......................13 D1
Avis.......................................14 C3
Saptco Airport Bus..................15 D4

.avis.com.sa; 8am-10pm Sat-Thu, 2pm-10.30pm Fri).
Hire per day, including insurance plus 150km free, starts at
SR80, then SR0.23 per extra kilometre.

Getting Around
The easiest way to get to/from the airport is
with the Saptco airport bus (SR15, 45 minutes, hourly from 6am to 11pm). The bus stop
is on Prince Majed bin Abdul Aziz St.

Taxis are everywhere. You shouldn't pay
more than SR15 for the longest journey
within Al-Khobar or SR25 to Dammam
(it's better not to use the meter).

DHAHRAN
لظهران

☎ 03 / pop 105,000

Dhahran is the home of Saudi Arabia's
oil industry and the base of Aramco, the
granddaddy of Saudi oil companies.

Much of Dhahran is like an exclusive
club: a small and self-contained American
city, which consists of the Aramco compound, shops, residential areas and the
University of Petroleum & Minerals.

If you want a tour of the compound (and
a peek at the famous No 7 pipeline), you
should contact the Aramco PR department
in advance (see the website listed below).

Sights
The **Aramco Exhibit** (☎ 877 2499; www.saudi
aramco.com; admission free; 8am-4pm Sat-Wed, 10am-
6.30pm Thu, 3-6.30pm Fri, families only Thu & Fri) is one of
the best museums in the country. Split into
eight sections covering all-you-ever-wanted-
to-know-about-oil-and-the-Saudi-oil-in-
dustry, it's educational and informative, and
should entertain kids and adults alike (there
are plenty of buttons to push, interactive displays and fun activities). A 17-minute long
film 'Energy to the World' can be organised
with prior arrangement (though be warned,
it's mostly toe-curling Aramco propaganda),
as can guided tours (1 to 1½ hours). English,
French & German speaking guides are free.

Getting There & Away
Taxis to/from Dammam cost SR40, Al-
Khobar SR30, and the airport SR80.

NAIRIYAH
النعيرية

The **Bedouin market** at Nairiyah, about
250km north of Dammam, is well worth
a visit if you're here on a Thursday. For
the Bedu, the market is a major centre for
buying and selling sheep, goats, housewares
and the occasional camel.

For foreigners the attraction has long
been the Bedouin weavings (mostly rugs)
sold by women tending stalls off to one
side of the main market; be wary of hard-
nosed negotiating techniques, and don't
even think of getting a good price if you
point your camera at any of them.

Few people stay the night in Nairiyah, but
those who do stay at **Al-Sharafi Hotel** (☎ 373
0772; fax 373 1688; s/d SR150/200), which is comfortable, homely, accommodating and friendly.
The hotel is signposted throughout town.

From Dammam, take the Jubail expressway to the Abu Hadriyah turn-off and then
follow the signs to Nairiyah. Once in town
head for the large mosque with a low green
dome and follow the crowd.

Be sure to get an early start as the market
is usually evaporated by around 10am.

AL-HOFUF
الهفوف

☎ 03 / pop 326,000

Al-Hofuf (also known as Al-Hasa and Al-
Ahsa) is for most the highlight of any visit
to the Eastern Province. The Al-Hasa Oasis,
of which Al-Hofuf is a part, is believed to
form the largest oasis in the world. The palm
trees (over three million of them) seem to
march in all directions and produce no less
than half a million tons of dates a year. As
an ancient caravan stop, it's not hard to
imagine the relief and joy felt by travellers
upon arrival after days of desert travel.

The Al-Hofuf area has a rich historical
and cultural tradition which warrants a
deeper exploration, if you have the time.
A couple of the hotels do excellent guided
tours of the area's surrounding attractions.

Al-Hofuf is also believed to hold the
Kingdom's largest reserves of undrilled oil.

Orientation & Information
The centre of Al-Hofuf is compact. King
Abdul Aziz St is the main commercial street
and intersects with Prince Mohammed ibn
Fahd ibn Jalawi St to form a central square.
There are several banks around the main
intersection.

Sights
AL-HOFUF MUSEUM
This **museum** (☎ 580 3942; Prince Sultan St; admission free; 8am-2pm Sat-Wed) is well-presented,

with maps, photos and good information panels. There's a large map of the oasis at the entrance to the exhibit hall. Sections include those on Eastern Province archaeology, as well as displays showing the Arabian Peninsula disappearing and reappearing from under the oceans up until well after the Ice Age.

QASR IBRAHIM

With its solidity and austerity, this heavily restored **palace** (☎ 585 0852; Prince Mohammed ibn Fahd ibn Jalawi St; admission free; 7am-1pm & 4-8pm Sat-Wed, on request Thu) dominates the centre of town metaphorically and literally. Inside, the atmosphere is a bit abated by the rather insensitive permanent light fixtures – a common affliction in Saudi Arabia.

The Qasr Ibrahim fort's earliest structure is the restored, white **Al-Quba Mosque** (1571), although most of what you see dates from the beginning of the 19th century. Other structures include the **soldiers' barracks**, the **well**, the **stables** (note the high doors to allow horse and rider to enter) and the **Guard's dormitory**. King Abdul Aziz

apparently used the *hammam* (bathhouse) to store his dates. Check out the views from the ramparts.

SOUQS & MARKETS

One of the last-remaining souqs in Saudi Arabia, and one of the most extensive, the **Qaisariya souq** (8am-11.30am & 4pm-10pm) was tragically devastated by a fire in 2001. Following a patch-up job by the local authorities, King Abdullah has recently pledged his help to rebuild the famous souq in its original style.

Until then, it's still well worth a visit as it contains an excellent selection of local handicrafts including basketware, pottery and locally made coffee pots.

Look out in particular for the *besht* (the lovely, thick cloaks worn by Saudis in winter) as well as *mashlah* (the fine, lightweight cloaks sometimes bordered with gold and worn at ceremonial occasions), Bedouin silver jewellery and antiques. A little jar of Iranian saffron (SR10) would make a great pressie to take to loved ones back home.

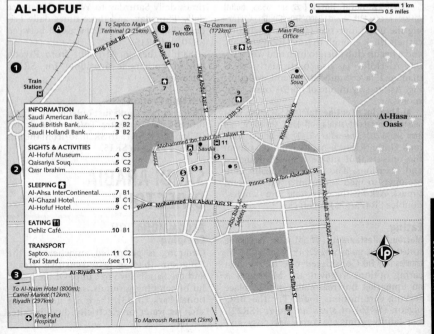

AL-HOFUF

0 ——————— 1 km
0 ——————— 0.5 miles

To Saptco Main Terminal (2.25km)
Telecom
To Dammam (172km)
Main Post Office
King Fahd Rd
King Khaled St
Imam Ali Rd
Train Station
King Abdul Aziz St
13th St
Date Souq
Al-Hasa Oasis
Mohammed ibn Fahd ibn Jalawi St
Saudia
Prince Sultan St
Prince Fahd Ibn Abdullah St
Prince Mohammed ibn Abdul Aziz St
Abu Bakr St
Sadeeq St
Prince Abdullah ibn Abdul Aziz St
Prince Sultan St
Ar-Riyadh St

To Al-Naim Hotel (800m);
Camel Market (12km);
Riyadh (297km)

King Fahd Hospital

To Marroush Restaurant (2km)

INFORMATION
Saudi American Bank...............1 C2
Saudi British Bank.................2 B2
Saudi Hollandi Bank...............3 B2

SIGHTS & ACTIVITIES
Al-Hofuf Museum..................4 C3
Qaisariya Souq.....................5 C2
Qasr Ibrahim........................6 B2

SLEEPING
Al-Ahsa InterContinental.........7 B1
Al-Ghazal Hotel....................8 C1
Al-Hofuf Hotel......................9 C1

EATING
Dehliz Café..........................10 B1

TRANSPORT
Saptco................................11 C2
Taxi Stand........................(see 11)

SAUDI ARABIA

Also well worth a visit if you're in town on a Thursday is the **camel market** (☼ 7am-noon) which takes place on the outskirts of town (around 15km west from the centre) on the Riyadh road.

Tours

The Al-Ahsa InterContinental offers 'City Tours' for SR50 per person per hour; the Al-Hofuf Hotel provides comprehensive two-day tours of the town and surrounding area (SR500 per person). Prices are cheaper if you can muster a group.

Sleeping

Al-Naim Hotel (☎ 575 5511; fax 575 8211; Riyadh St; s/d SR120/180) The best budget bet in town, rooms are simply furnished but sanitary. The hotel is also an agent for Saptco (and can issue tickets for its buses), and lies southwest of the town centre.

Al-Ghazal Hotel (☎ 582 6555; fax 586 9966; 16th St; s/d SR230/300) Set on a quieter road, the hotel is more peaceful than many. Its decoration is a bit Orientalist-glitz, but the rooms are well-furnished and comfortable. It's excellent value.

our pick **Al-Hofuf Hotel** (☎ 585 5555; hofhtl @nesma.net.sa; 13th St; s/d SR400/570; 🖵 🌊) Offering the usual four-star facilities (including carpets thick enough to leave footprints in, and a health club open to men and women), the Al-Hofuf is also particularly well-managed, accommodating and welcoming. Ask to stay in one of the 20 'oasis-side' rooms.

Al-Ahsa InterContinental (☎ 584 0000; www .intercontinental.com/alahsa; off King Khaled St; s/d from SR650/800; 3-bed villas SR2400; 🖵 🌊) It may look Gothic-church-meets-Arab-*qasr* from the outside, but inside it's well-designed and luxurious. The pool and health club are open to men and women (at different times). Ask for the corporate rate (singles/doubles SR475/575) if you can.

Eating

Marroush Restaurant (☎ 581 0000; Stadium St; starters SR6-10, mains SR12-22; ☼ noon-2am Sat-Fri, families only Fri) Considered one of the best eating options in town, the Marroush is an upmarket but reasonably priced place serving scrumptious food. Try the BBQ pigeon (SR16) or *steak au poivre* (SR22). The family rooms are comfy and cosy, and

the restaurant is 2km south of the town centre.

our pick **Dehliz Café** (☎ 587 5533; off King Khaled St; iced latte SR12, cakes SR12; ☼ 9am-12.30pm & 4pm-2.30am) Close to the Al-Ahsa InterContinental, the Dehliz is a fabulous new café decorated like a traditional *qasr*, complete with part-beamed roof and traditional Quranic chant-music. It's a great place for breakfast or a coffee-and-a-cake curled up on the comfy sofas. Look out for the old photos of Al-Hofuf hung on the walls.

Getting There & Away

There are bus services with **Saptco** (☎ 587 3688; cnr King Abdul Aziz & Prince Mohammed ibn Fahd ibn Jalawi St) including Dammam (SR20, two hours, nine daily), Riyadh (SR45, 4½ hours, five daily), Nairiyah (SR5, three hours, one daily) and Jeddah (SR190, 16 hours, one daily).

The **train station** (☎ 582 9999; King Fahd Rd; ☼ 5am-12.30am) lies 2.5km northwest of the town centre. Trains run to Riyadh (VIP/1st/2nd class SR100/55/45, 2½ hours, four daily) and to Dammam (VIP/1st/2nd class SR40/25/20, one hour 20 minutes, four times daily Saturday to Wednesday, twice daily Thursday, and three times daily Friday). Taxis to/from the town cost between SR10 and SR15.

Saudia flies to Al-Hofuf from Riyadh (among other destinations) for SR190 one-way.

Getting Around

There's a taxi stand just outside the Saptco office in the city centre. To/from the airport (25km) costs SR15 to SR20, to/from the bus stations SR10 to SR15.

SAUDI ARABIA DIRECTORY

ACCOMMODATION
Camping

Camping is permitted anywhere in the Kingdom (bar security-sensitive areas), and the Saudis love to camp. Of the handful of camping grounds, such as Asir National Park (p343), there are no facilities such as water or electricity, but the sites are free.

Hostels

These days very few Westerners stay at Saudi Arabia's men-only youth hostels *(buyut ash-shabab)*. Most are located near the stadium (they're run by the Youth Association) some distance from the centre, though they're usually clean and well maintained. Most offer rooms with a private bath (SR10 per person, maximum three nights).

Hotels

Throughout this chapter, quoted room rates include private bathroom, unless stated otherwise, and exclude the 15% service charge that is added to your bill by all five- and some four-star hotels (and restaurants).

During the haj season (particularly in Jeddah), at the end of Ramadan, during school holidays, and in summer (June to August) in Abha, Taif and other mountain regions (periods all known as the Saudi 'high season') prices can increase from between 50% to 150%, .

The cheapest budget hotels are basic and bleak, but for a few riyals more you can usually find something simple and clean, some with private bathrooms and almost all with air-conditioning. Expect to pay from around SR60 to SR80 for a single to SR100 for a double.

Midrange hotels (singles SR150 to SR200, doubles SR250 to SR400), offer good value for money, with comfortable and often spacious rooms, satellite TV (usually with English-language channels) and private bathrooms.

Saudi Arabia also has a generous selection of top-range hotels. Most offer the usual five-star facilities including business centres, internet access, swimming pools, fitness centres etc. Most hotels quote rack rates (around SR500 to SR1000 for singles, and SR700 to SR1500 for doubles), but offer decent 'corporate discounts' to tour operators, embassies and companies with whom they have prior agreements. If you're travelling independently, try to book your hotels through a local tour operator (see p366) who can get discounts of between 15% to 50%, or ask your company (if you work for one) to fax the hotel with your dates.

Note that many hotels offer 'weekend packages', which offer special rates; if you're planning a whole weekend somewhere, enquire.

During the haj season, the end of Ramadan and during school holidays, be sure to reserve well in advance. During the haj in Jeddah, two months is not too soon.

ACTIVITIES

Beaches

Saudi's beaches can disappoint. Many have been built on or over, are litter-strewn and very crowded and noisy at weekends. They're almost all men-only. The best bet is to head for the five-star coastal hotels, which often have their own private beach, where women also can swim (albeit usually covered up in a t-shirt and trousers).

Diving

With the longest coastline of any country on the eastern seaboard of the Red Sea, Saudi Arabia has huge diving potential. Those who do know it, rank it among the

---

BED BUREAUCRACY

To check in at any hotel, Saudi law requires the presentation of a passport (for those travelling on visitors' visas) or an *iqama* (for expats).

In order to share a room, you must be married – and able to prove it: either a marriage certificate, or your passports *and* visas clearly showing your marital status.

Unaccompanied women (one or in a group) have the biggest bureaucracy to battle with. You will need to present one of three documents: a letter of introduction (claiming full responsibility for you) from either your company (if you are working in Saudi Arabia), or your sponsor (and ideally stamped by the Chamber of Commerce in Jeddah or Riyadh); a confirmed hotel booking from a local tour agent if you're a tourist; or, as a last resort, a letter from the local police. Even then, lodging may be refused you, except by the five-star establishments (though not all) and some four-star hotels. Travelling in a group (minimum of four women) does simplify things, as this is considered more acceptable. Note also that with very few exceptions, hotel pools and health clubs are for men only.

best sites in the world. It is also this relative obscurity outside the Kingdom that is its greatest advantage: its reefs remain almost empty of divers and boats.

Note that women (local and foreign) are permitted to dive, though conservative behaviour is still sometimes expected (such as wearing loose clothing over your wetsuit until just before you get into the water).

Currently, just one dive operator regularly operates live-aboard diving, though a number of dive outfits operating in Jeddah cater to growing local demand.

Saudi Arabia's diving is considered forgiving. Even in winter, the water temperatures rarely drop too low (at the southern sites from 24°C to 26°C), though wetsuits of between 5mm to 6mm are advised in winter; 3mm to 4mm in summer. Saudi's greatest advantage is its visibility, which ranges from the good to the astonishing (up to 35m to 40m is not uncommon). In general, there are also few currents to contend with.

More experienced divers prefer to boat-dive off Jeddah, and particularly around Al-Lith, Yanbu and the Farasan Islands, where the diving can be spectacular. See the quick guide (right).

A local dive operator frequently recommended and with a good safety record, which also operates live-aboard boats on a regular basis (and which can arrange tourist visas) is **Dream Divers** (☎ 02-234 0473; www .dreamdiver.net; Dream Marina, Corniche Rd, South Obhur, Jeddah), the largest, privately owned diving operation in the Middle East. It has offices in Jeddah, Yanbu and Al-Lith.

Two other outfits are **Red Sea Divers** (☎ 660 6368; fax 660 2064; Al-Kournaish St, Jeddah) and **Desert Sea Divers** (☎ 02-656 1807; www .desertseadivers.ws; Al-Kournaish St, 4km north of Radisson SAS Hotel, Jeddah).

Equipment can be hired (regulators and BCDs per day SR20 to SR25), though boots, fins and wetsuits can be difficult to find; bring your own. Jeddah has a decompression chamber.

For more information on diving in Saudi, visit www.saudidiving.com, a comprehensive website that includes descriptions and maps of individual dive sites, a list of tour operators and general information about the region.

JEDDAH

- Boasts over 50 dive sites and a number of wrecks (accessible even to inexperienced divers), reached by day boats operated by dive clubs in and around town.
- A colourful selection of hard and soft corals.
- Good variety of smaller reef fishes, including Anthea, sergeant major, large-sized trevally jack, king fish, Spanish mackerel, tuna dog tooth, big eye, bump tail, skip jack.
- During the season there are yellow fin, rays, moray eels and turtles.

YANBU

- Lies 230km north of Jeddah.
- Boasts outstanding visibility (34m to 40m average).
- Hammerheads found at deeper depths (from around 40m).
- Wide variety of fish including good numbers of Napoleon wrasse, blue-spotted rays, moray eels and turtles.

AL-LITH

- Lies 180km south of Jeddah.
- Giant bumphead parrot fish (often in quite big groups) are major draw.
- Sharks (grey, white-tip and black-tip mainly) seen all year, others (hammerhead chiefly) during winter.
- Large variety of hard and soft corals as well as coloured sponges and sea whips.
- The only accommodation is currently at **Ahlam Marina & Resort** (☎ 07-733 4112; cabins per night SR300) with restaurant, and fishing and dive shop.
- Other attractions include caverns, caves and islands used as nesting site by leatherback and green turtles, and excellent birdlife (including sooty gulls, blue legged boobys, white-eyed gulls, little bitterns, crab plovers, goliath herons, night herons, pelicans, flamingos, ospreys and sooty falcon).

FARASAN ISLANDS

- Lies off coast, 40km from Jizan, 722km from Jeddah.
- Though visibility is not always so good, waters around Farasan Islands can offer the most spectacular diving of all – the nutrients and plankton attracting large pelagic species including whales, whale

sharks and mantas, and on the drop offs, many hammerheads.

- Currently, only one dive operator branch (at the Farasan Hotel p348); another operator to open soon.

4WD

There are ample opportunities to leave tarmac roads behind and explore Arabia's desert interior. Among the most rewarding are the sand seas of the Empty Quarter (p348), following the Hejaz Railway, and excursions into the Al-Nafud desert (p321).

BOOKS

If you're in Saudi for a while, there's a good variety of locally written and produced books such as *Desert Treks from Riyadh* by Ionis Thompson. *An A-Z of Places and Things Saudi*, by Kathy Cuddihy, contains everything about the *abeyya* and Islamic banking to an overview of key places around the kingdom.

Both Sandra Mackey's *The Saudis: Inside the Desert Kingdom* and the more recent *Saudi Arabia Exposed* by John R Bradley are expats' insider (and banned) accounts of life in Saudi Arabia. Though they pander slightly to the West's love of salacious Saudi stories of violence, intrigue and drama, they nevertheless offer interesting insights.

The world of Saudi women is illuminated by Saddeka Arebi's *Women and Words in Saudi Arabia*, a fascinating look through the eyes of nine female Saudi writers.

The impact of rapid modernisation upon Bedouin society is beautifully portrayed in Abdelrahman Munif's novel, *Cities of Salt*.

Of the good selection of coffee-table books, the *Kingdom of Saudi Arabia*, published by the Supreme Commission of Tourism, makes a great pictorial souvenir. Other glossy tomes include *The Traditional Architecture of Saudi Arabia* by Geoffrey King, and the beautifully produced *Travellers in Arabia – British Explorers in Saudi Arabia*, edited by Eid al Yahya, which includes maps and evocative photographs.

For more book listings, see p23.

BUSINESS HOURS

Opening hours vary according to the season and province. In general:

Banks 8.30am to noon and 4.30pm to 8pm Saturday to Wednesday. At airports, banks are open 24 hours.

Offices 7.30am to 2.30pm or 3.30pm Saturday to Wednesday

Post offices 7.30am to 10pm Saturday to Wednesday, 4.30pm to 10pm Friday

Restaurants 7am to 10.30am, noon to 3pm and 6pm or 7pm to midnight (to 1am or 2am at weekends)

Shopping centres 9am or 10am to midnight Saturday to Thursday

Shops & souqs 8am or 9am to 1pm or 2pm and 4.30pm or 5pm to 9pm to midnight, Saturday to Wednesday

Note that during prayer times (five times a day), everything shuts.

CHILDREN

For general information on travelling with children in the Peninsula, see p529. Saudi Arabia has numerous amusement parks for children. They're usually family-only affairs, cost SR10/5 per adult/child and just about any medium-sized town has one. For a small listing of some amusement parks in the Kingdom, visit www.funguide.com/parks/park.pl?saudiara.

CUSTOMS

Despite all the warnings, some travellers continue to try and enter the Kingdom with alcohol. Note that if you are caught with any amount, you will be returned home on the next flight. If you're deemed to be in possession of a quantity that exceeds 'personal consumption', punishments are severe (the death penalty if convicted of smuggling).

DVDs, videos or suspect-looking books are passed to the Ministry of Information officials for inspection. Unfamiliar or suspect-looking items may be confiscated for further inspection for up to 48 hours. Receipts are issued for later collection once inspected and passed. Laptop harddisks and computer media are not checked unless officials are suspicious. See also boxed text, p362.

DANGERS & ANNOYANCES
Dos & Don'ts

Conservative dress is the rule of thumb in Saudi Arabia. Shorts in public are a big no-no (bar the private beaches operated by some top-end hotels and expat compounds). See also Women Travellers, p367.

Unmarried couples shouldn't travel together; if they do, they may be stopped and investigated. Alcohol is strictly illegal in Saudi Arabia.

SAUDI ARABIA

PLEASE (DON'T) BRING A BOTTLE

The following items are banned in Saudi Arabia. Don't be tempted to try and sneak them in; the bags of all passengers are X-rayed upon arrival (with high-tech equipment that can detect liquids as well as metals):

- Alcohol
- Art work or any other item bearing religious symbols or motifs, such as Stars of David
- Banned books, DVDs and videos
- Firearms and explosives
- Illegal drugs and medication without a doctor's prescription
- Politically sensitive material, and material overly critical of the government or royal family
- Pork products
- Pornography or any publications containing pictorial representations of people (particularly women) in a less than conservative state of dress
- Symbols of other religions, such as Christian crosses

You should carry your passport with you at all time. If travelling independently, carry a letter of introduction (and many copies) with you from your company.

See also p50 for general information on social etiquette in the Peninsula.

Mutawwa

Formally known as the Committee for the Propagation of Virtue and the Prevention of Vice, the *mutawwa* (religious police) have an infamous reputation as a kind of squad of moral vigilantes out to enforce strict Islamic orthodoxy.

Operating independently of other branches of the security services, the *mutawwa* are at their most authoritative (and hence not to be argued with) when accompanied by uniformed police.

They have become less visible – and less welcome – in places like Jeddah and Al-Khobar in recent years, but they remain active elsewhere.

Ramadan

For Muslims, public observance of the fast is mandatory. For non-Muslims, smoking, eating or drinking anywhere in public could result in an arrest.

Road Safety

Saudi Arabia has one of the highest incidents of road fatalities in the world. If you're driving, here are the main hazards to heed:

- Be particularly careful on the coastal road that links Jeddah to Jizan (known as Road No 55), which has the highest fatality rate in the Kingdom (though a new dual-carriageway is planned for the future).
- Camels wandering onto unfenced roads, particularly at night.
- In towns, local buses and taxis suddenly veering across the road to pick up or drop off passengers.
- Pick-up trucks suddenly pulling out in front of you at junctions or after petrol stations.
- Vehicles driving with one or no lights at night on roads outside the towns.
- Vehicles trying to overtake, particularly on corners. Saudi drivers expect you – and sometimes oncoming traffic too! – to pull over onto the hard shoulder so that they can pass.

See also the boxed texts, p371 and p555.

Sexual Harassment

As elsewhere, Hollywood movies and hard-core porn channels (now all too easily available in the Kingdom) have greatly coloured the Saudi perception of Western women. As a result, stares, leers and obscene comments are sometimes reported by Western women travellers.

It's very rarely more than this, however, and the social disgrace that comes from having touched a woman in public is one of your most effective weapons. If your harasser persists, report him to the police or security men that can be found on most streets and malls.

Remember also the rule of thumb: the more conservatively you dress, the more conservatively you will be treated, particularly with regards to wearing a headscarf.

See p51 for more information.

Terrorism

Since the widely reported series of attacks on Western targets in 2003 and 2004 (see p303), security has been dramatically tightened around residential compounds and embassies.

Nevertheless, incidents are still sporadically occurring (most notably in the shooting of four French tourists near Medina in February 2006), though these are not always reported by the largely government-controlled press.

Some security analysts both in and outside the country fear that this new form of unplanned, low-tech, low-cost and spontaneous attack against Westerners may even form the future face of Al-Qaeda attacks against Westerners in Saudi Arabia. While there may be little cause for undue alarm, it pays to remain vigilant at all times, especially around Western compounds and other places frequented primarily by Westerners.

Travellers visiting with group tourist visas are currently accompanied (incognito) by a Ministry of Interior vehicle for added safety. You should also register your arrival in the Kingdom with your embassy, and keep a close eye on warnings issued by them (in the form of emails or text messages).

EMBASSIES & CONSULATES
Saudi Embassies & Consulates

Following are the Saudi embassies and consulates in major cities around the world.

Australia (☎ 612-6282 6999; 38 Guilfoyle St, Yarralumla, 2600 ACT)

Canada (☎ 613-237 4100; Ste 901, 99 Bank St, Ottawa, Ontario K1P 6B9)

France (☎ 01 47 66 02 06; 5 Ave Hoche, 75008 Paris)

Germany (☎ 030-889 250; Kurfürstendamm 63, 10707 Berlin)

Ireland Apply through Saudi embassy in UK.

Netherlands (☎ 070-361 4391; Alexanderstraat 19, 2514 JM, The Hague)

New Zealand Apply through Saudi embassy in Australia.

UK (☎ 020-7917 3000; 30 Charles St, London W1X 7PM)

USA (☎ 202-342 3800; 601 New Hampshire Ave NW, Washington DC 20037)

Embassies & Consulates in Saudi Arabia

All of the following are in Riyadh's Diplomatic Quarter in the west of Riyadh. They generally open from 9am to 4pm Saturday to Wednesday.

Australia (☎ 01-488 7788 or 01-488 7812 after hrs)

Bahrain (☎ 01-488 0044)

Canada (☎ 01-488 2288)

France (☎ 01-488 1255)

Germany (☎ 01-488 0700)

Iran (☎ 01-488 1916)

Ireland (☎ 01-488 2300)

Jordan (☎ 01-488 0039)

Kuwait (☎ 01-488 3500)

New Zealand (☎ 01-488 7988)

Oman (☎ 01-482 3120)

MINDING THE MUTAWWA

The *mutawwa* are a source of both fear and fascination for many travellers. But so long as you dress and behave appropriately, you should have little to fear. Indeed, some *mutawwa* are known to give *hawajas* (Westerners) a wide berth.

Not so for Saudi's immigrant population, however, who sometimes complain of harassment. One Filipino that the author met in Abha claimed to have been severely chided for allowing her pigtail to peep out the back of her headscarf, and on another occasion for having plucked her eyebrows, which 'Allah had given her'.

The *mutawwa* are conspicuous for their *thobes* which are worn above their ankles (according to instructions in the Quran) and for wearing *gutras* (white head cloths) without *agals* (head ropes), since God alone is entitled to wear 'crowns'.

The places where you're most likely to encounter *mutawwa* in Saudi Arabia (since they are more conservative) are in descending order: Al-Ula, Qasim, Jizan, Abha, Hail, Al-Jouf, Sakaka, Al-Hofuf, Riyadh, Taif, and Najran.

Qatar (☎ 01-482 5685)
UAE (☎ 01-482 6803)
UK (☎ 01-488 0077)
USA (☎ 01-488 3800)

FESTIVALS & EVENTS

Saudi Arabia's major festival is the **Jenadriyah National Festival**; see p314 for details. Other smaller, local festivals include Abha's summer festivals of poetry and folklore, and National Day (23 September) is usually also celebrated in some form or another across the Kingdom.

HOLIDAYS

No holidays other than **Eid al-Fitr**, **Eid al-Adha** and **National Day** are observed in the Kingdom. See the boxed text, p535, for information on Islamic holidays.

INTERNET ACCESS

Internet cafés are present in the larger Saudi towns, but are not as ubiquitous as you might imagine and are men-only domains. Connections are generally adequate and costs SR3 to SR10 per hour. It's far easier to bring a laptop or Blackberry, however, particularly for women (who should otherwise head for the business centre of a five-star hotel). Most four- and all five-star hotels and many coffeeshops now have wireless facilities.

Most three-star hotels will let you use a dialup connection.

Connecting your computer to a local internet server is relatively easy. Internet cards from Saudi Internet companies start from SR10 for 10 hours; the best companies are Awal Net, Nesma and Saudi Net. Cards are available from computer shops, Jarir Bookstores (Riyadh, Jeddah, Dammam, Al-Khobar and Al-Hofuf) and some stationery stores.

INTERNET RESOURCES

The internet is strictly policed, with more than 3000 sites blocked at the last count. Most of these are pornographic, but they also include sites discussing politics, health, women's rights and education. For a full list of internet topics prohibited by the Saudi authorities, visit www.al-bab.com/media/docs/saudi.htm.

Some useful websites on Saudi Arabia include the following:

Arabian Wildlife (www.arabianwildlife.com/archive /vol2.2/sauwhe.htm) A good listing for most of Saudi Arabia's protected areas.
Saudi-American Forum (www.saudi-american-forum .org/index.html) An informative cross-cultural dialogue with articles discussing the Saudi-American relationship and changes taking place within Saudi society.
Saudi Arabian Information Resource (www.saudinf .com) Run by the Ministry of Culture & Information, it contains nearly 2000 pages of history, culture, economics and helpful addresses.
Wahhabi Theology (http://reference.allrefer.com /country-guide-study/saudi-arabia/saudi-arabia40.html) Fairly balanced and detailed coverage of the history and central tenets of Wahhabi Islam.
Who Were the Nabataeans? (http://nabataea .net/who.html) Everything you needed to know about the builders of Madain Saleh.

LEGAL MATTERS

Saudi Arabia imposes strict Sharia'a (Islamic law), under which extremely harsh punishments are imposed.

If you're involved in a traffic accident, call ☎ 999 (it doesn't have to be an emergency), don't move your car (even by 1m) and don't leave the scene until the police arrive.

Try and get the name of the other driver, and the registration and insurance number of the vehicle. To claim insurance, a police report is obligatory. Sometimes Saudis in a hurry offer to pay for minor damages on the spot, but you should insist on a police report, as garages are not allowed to carry out repairs without one.

MAPS

The best maps of Saudi Arabia are Farsi Maps. They're available at branches of the Jarir Bookstore throughout the Kingdom (SR20 each). The series includes many general maps for most regions, and excellent city maps for Riyadh, Jeddah, Al-Ahsa (Al-Hofuf), Hail, Abha, Taif, Mecca and Medina, among other places.

MEDIA

All forms of media (other than satellite TV) are controlled by the government, though the grip has definitely loosened in recent years.

Newspapers & Magazines

The English-language dailies *Arab News* and the *Saudi Gazette* (SR2 each) are surprisingly frank, although they steer clear of any criticism of the royal family or Islam.

International newspapers (the *Guardian*, the *Times, International Herald Tribune* and *Le Monde*) and magazines (*Time* and *Newsweek*) are available from any branch of Jarir Bookstore, usually three days after publication.

Don't expect your foreign newspaper to include all of its pages; censors routinely extract articles about Saudi Arabia and any photographs considered vaguely risqué or controversial.

Radio

Jeddah Radio (96.2FM) broadcasts in English and French, while the **BBC World Service** (www.bbc.co.uk/worldservice/programmes/index.shtml) is available on short-wave frequency (11.760khz or 15.575khz).

TV

Satellite TV (CNN, BBC and RFI) is widely available in private hotels and homes. NBC2 broadcasts films in English 24 hours, and Saudi Arabia TV Channel 2 broadcasts in English (everything from Australian soap operas to *Islam Q&A*).

There's also Al-Jazeera, see p294.

MONEY
Credit Cards

More and more establishments are accepting credit cards including most medium to large-sized hotels, restaurants, airline offices and shops. Surprisingly, some tour operators do not – check first.

Currency

The unit of currency is the Saudi riyal (SR) and one riyal (SR1) is divided into 100 halalas. Coins come in 25 and 50 halala denominations. Notes come in SR1, SR5, SR10, SR20, SR50, SR100, SR200 and SR500 denominations. The Saudi riyal is a hard currency and there are no restrictions on its import or export.

Exchanging Money

Banks (with ATMs that accept international cards) are ubiquitous throughout the country. For exchanging cash, you'll get a much better rate at one of the many money changers, whose bureaus are found in most town centres. All major hard currencies are

exchanged and commission is not usually charged, but check this (and rates) first.

As everywhere, avoid the exchange desks at top-end hotels, which offer poor rates.

Exchange Rates

The riyal is pegged to the US dollar. The following exchange rates were correct at the time of printing:

Country	Unit	Saudi riyal
Australia	A$1	SR3.05
Bahrain	BD1	SR2.00
Canada	C$1	SR3.24
Euro zone	€1	SR5.01
Japan	¥100	SR3.16
Kuwait	KD1	SR13.02
New Zealand	NZ$1	SR2.70
Oman	OR1	SR9.77
UAE	Dh1	SR1.02
UK	£1	SR7.41
US	US$1	SR3.75
Yemen	YR100	SR2.08

PHOTOGRAPHY

Though the ban on photography in public places has recently been lifted, there are still areas that are off-limits (mainly because of security concerns): designated government buildings, embassies, airports, seaports, desalination or electricity plants, oil rigs, royal palaces and police stations or anything vaguely connected with the military or security services. Don't photograph people without their permission, and never photograph women (even in a general street scene).

Camcorders are prohibited at some archaeological sites; if you get caught, your camcorder may be confiscated. If you're coming to Saudi with a tour operator, ask them if they can organise a video permit for you, as well as a letter to Customs (stating that you will arrive with a camcorder).

Memory cards and batteries can be found in both Riyadh and Jeddah, as can places that burn CDs.

POST

The queues at Saudi post offices can be long, especially in the main city branches in the evenings and at weekends.

Any parcel you want to post to an address outside the Kingdom must first be taken to the post office unwrapped so that

---

UPWARDLY MOBILE

Mobiles make the world go round in Saudi Arabia. Owning one – even temporarily – can also greatly ease your path. Call:

■ Direct Enquiries (☎ 905) if you're having trouble tracing someone or something (it lists almost every hotel, restaurant and government office in the Kingdom, the service operates 24 hours, is English-speaking and is well-known for its efficiency and helpfulness)

■ Home (it's astonishingly cheap calling via the Saudi networks)

■ Hotels if you're running late (reservations are automatically cancelled by hotels' computer systems after a certain time)

■ Museums, shops or restaurants to check opening hours (which are notoriously erratic)

■ Police or emergency services in the (sadly, not too unlikely) event of a road accident or for help

■ To stay in touch with new Saudi friends or contacts (the author was handed mobile numbers belonging even to Saudi ministers and princes).

Saudi customs can inspect it. If the parcel includes video tapes, they may be viewed by customs before you can mail them.

The attempt to introduce private post boxes recently failed inexplicably. Most Saudis continue to use their company mailboxes instead. If you're living in Saudi, you should follow suit or get a post box at your local post office.

TELEPHONE

Healthy competition between the mobile companies keeps costs down. There's little difference in price between calling from a home number and a mobile number.

At the time of writing, you could buy a mobile SIM card from SR75 (from Mobily) which included 120 minutes' free credit (with a one to three month expiry date), as well as second handsets from SR100.

The mobile phone network run by STC operates on the GSM system. For directory assistance, call ☎ 905 (domestic) or ☎ 900 (international).

VISAS

Saudi Arabia is one of the most difficult places in the world to visit. Note that Jews are not granted visas to the Kingdom.

Haj & Umrah

For haj (pilgrimage to Mecca) visas there's a quota system of one visa for every 1000 Muslims in a country's population. Exactly how this system is administered varies from country to country.

Umrah (any pilgrimage to Mecca that is not haj) visas are issued to any Muslim requesting one, although if you're not from a Muslim country or don't have an obviously Muslim name, you'll be asked to provide an official document that lists Islam as your religion. Converts to Islam must provide a certificate from the mosque where they went through their conversion ceremony.

Umrah and haj visas are free and are valid only for travel to Jeddah, Mecca and Medina, and on the roads connecting them to one another.

Residence (Work) Visas

The visas required to live and work in the Kingdom are organised by your employer.

Tourist Visas

During the last six years the Saudi authorities have started tentatively to issue tourist visas, but *only* for those willing to travel as part of a group (minimum four people) organised by a recognised tour company (including dive companies).

Issued under the sponsorship of Saudia (under its 'Discover Saudi Arabia' program), you can find the list of approved international and local Saudi tour companies who can arrange the visas at: www.saudiairlines.com/tours/discoversaudiarabia.jsp. It takes 14 days from the date of request to issue a tourist visa.

Note also that passports must be valid for a minimum of six months, and women under 30 years old must be accompanied by their husband or brother (who must also arrive and leave Saudi Arabia at the same time).

Note that men and women are only allowed to travel together (and granted a visa to do so) if they are (a) married (with an official marriage licence) or (b) form part of a group.

It is not permitted for an unmarried couple to travel alone together in Saudi Arabia (and doing so runs the risk of apprehension). Regarding the tourist visa, two couples could in effect travel together, but only if they came as 'individuals in a group'.

One local tour company that can offer advice and has an excellent reputation locally is Sadd Al-Samallaghi Est based in Jeddah (see p323).

Transit Visas

Three-day transit visas are available for people driving between Jordan and either Kuwait or Yemen. Those driving between Jordan and Bahrain or the United Arab Emirates (UAE) are usually granted seven-day visas. They're only issued if you can prove that there was no other way to get to your destination.

To obtain a transit visa you must visit the embassy with your vehicle's carnet de passage and proof that you have a visa for the country you're planning to visit.

Visitor (Business) Visas

Rule number one is that you must have a Saudi sponsor (a company or an individual). The sponsor applies to the Saudi Chamber of Commerce & Industry for approval and, if granted, an invitation letter will be sent to you (or direct to the embassy).

Rule number two is that you must then make your application in your country of nationality or permanent residence.

Depending upon the Saudi embassy to whom you are making your application (always phone the embassy to check), most commonly you will require a letter from your company outlining the nature of your business in Saudi Arabia and a letter of support from your local chamber of commerce.

Armed with this paperwork, the visa is usually granted without difficulty by the embassy, sometimes even on the same day (if you visit in person), but more often within a week to 10 days if applying by post.

WOMEN TRAVELLERS

Saudi Arabia is considered the most difficult country in the world for Western

---

SITE PERMITS

Though access to Saudi's sites is gradually opening up (with plans to further facilitate access in the near future), some forts, ruins or archaeological sites still require permits in order to visit them. You can obtain these (free) from the Director General of the **Department of Antiquities** (☎ 01-404 0617; fax 01-404 1391; PO Box 3734, Riyadh 11418; 7.30am-2.30pm Sat-Wed). The office lies right in front of the water tower besides Riyadh's National Museum.

File the permit application in the morning and return a day later to collect it. If you're not in Riyadh, fax your details (passport number, a list of which sites you want to visit and when) 14 days in advance, including a fax number to which the permit can be faxed back. Email facilities aren't available yet.

Resident foreigners must present their *iqama* (residence permit); travellers their passport and visa. Local tour operators (see p323) and some local hotels (such as at Madain Saleh, p334) can usually arrange the permits if you give them enough notice.

The major sites that require permits:

- Al-Faw (p350)
- Rock art at Jubba (p321)
- Madain Saleh (p336)
- Standing Stones of Rajajil (p339)
- Al-Ukhdud archaeological site, Najran (p344)

SAUDI ARABIA

women to travel. Though the strict segregation of the sexes and the prohibition on female drivers leads to obvious limitations on movement, most women travellers (including the author) are surprised by the privilege they are accorded, and the respect and deference they are shown, and end up having a very positive experience.

Women everywhere are urged to the front of queues, for example, and are served first at banks, restaurants, check-in desks and ticket offices. It is also said that Saudi decorum dictates that no man can ever turn down the appeal for help from a woman – so take full advantage (as the author did)!

Restrictions

Access to almost all internet cafés, and most mid- and budget-range hotels is impossible, as is access to many restaurants. Most towns and villages have at least one restaurant with a 'family section' where women, whether accompanied or not, must sit; those that do not, are provided with takeaways. Museums and some sights have special family-only hours, and banks have 'Ladies' branches'.

For information on women and diving, see p359. For information on women and access to hotel facilities, see p359.

See also Internet Access information on p364.

What to Wear

Women must by law wear an *abeyya*. Though a headscarf is not compulsory, you should always have one at hand as the *mutawwa* (religious police – see p362) may insist that you wear it.

See also p543.

TRANSPORT IN SAUDI ARABIA

GETTING THERE & AWAY
Entering Saudi Arabia

Immigration is much quicker than it used to be (except during the haj and Ramadan when you can expect long queues). All bags (including hand luggage) are now X-rayed and only opened when warranting further investigation (see Customs p361. Don't forget to fill in immigration cards.

Note that upon departure, security is vigorous and is time-consuming; you're advised to arrive early, 1½ hours before departures for domestic flights, three hours before international flights. If you're travelling with Saudia, a tip to save time is to obtain your boarding pass up to 24 hours in advance.

If you're arriving by land, procedures are similar, although expect long delays if you're bringing your own car into the Kingdom.

Note that Jews are not permitted entry to the Kingdom (nor anyone showing evidence of having visited Israel).

Air

There are four airports handling international traffic in Saudi Arabia.

King Abdul Aziz International Airport (JED; ☎ 02-684 2227) Located in Jeddah.

King Fahd International Airport (DMM; ☎ 03-883 5151) In Dammam.

King Khaled International Airport (RUH; ☎ 01-221 1000) In Riyadh.

Medina International Airport (MED; ☎ 04-842 0052) Opens only during the haj and occasionally during the *umrah* season to assist haj traffic in and out of Jeddah.

The national carrier is **Saudi Arabian Airlines** (Saudia; ☎ 01-488 4444; www.saudiairlines.com), which flies to dozens of destinations across the Middle East, Europe, Asia and the USA. It has a respectable safety record (see www .airsafe.com for details) and is usually on time. In the future, it will be privatised.

Saudia also offers special fares for groups, as well as offering special advantages when travelling on its domestic network.

AIRLINES FLYING TO/FROM SAUDI ARABIA

Al-Arabiya (G9; ☎ 01-465 9826; www.airarabia.com; hub Sharjah)

Air France (AF; ☎ 01-476 9666; www.airfrance.com; hub Paris)

British Airways (BA; ☎ 01-465 0216; www.british -airways.com; hub London)

EgyptAir (MS; ☎ 02-644 1515; www.egyptair.com.eg; hub Cairo)

Emirates (EK; ☎ 01-465 5485; www.emirates.com; hub Dubai)

Etihad Airways (EY; ☎ 01-644 2871; www.etihad airways.com; hub Abu Dhabi)

Gulf Air (GF; ☎ 01-462 6666; www.gulfairco.com; hub Bahrain)

Iran Air (IR; ☎ 02-664 6449; www.iranair.com; hub Tehran)

Kuwait Air (KT; ☎ 01-463 1218; www.kuwait-airways .com; hub Kuwait)

Lufthansa (LH; ☎ 01-463 2004; www.lufthansa.com; hub Frankfurt)

Middle East Airlines (ME; ☎ 01-465 6600; www.mea .com.lb; hub Beirut)

Oman Air (WY; ☎ 02-664 8666; www.oman-air.com; hub Muscat)

Qatar Airways (QR; ☎ 02-667 5182; www.qatar airways.com; hub Doha)

Royal Jordanian Airlines (J; ☎ 01-218 0850; www .rja.com.jo; hub Amman)

Yemenia (☎ 02-644 7042; www.yemenia.com.ye; hub Sana'a)

Sample fares for flights include:

Flight	Price	Frequency
Riyadh to Doha (Qatar)	US$185	3 per week
Riyadh to Manama (Bahrain)	US$140	3 per day
Riyadh to Kuwait City (Kuwait)	US$255	1 per day
Riyadh to Abu Dhabi (UAE)	US$265	3 per day
Riyadh to Muscat (Oman)	US$420	2 per week
Riyadh to San'a (Yemen)	US$415	2 per week

Land

BORDER CROSSINGS

At the time of research, all of Saudi's land crossings were trouble free and relatively efficient (except during the haj and Ramadan when you can queue up to 12 hours at some crossings, such as Halat Ammar).

Make sure you have visas for the countries you wish to enter (see p366). And never agree to carry either passengers or baggage through borders.

See the table on p547 for information on Saudi Arabia's land crossings.

BUS

Saptco (☎ 800 124 9999; www.saptco.com.sa) offers the best international bus services, although other companies from surrounding countries also cover the same routes for similar prices. Departures are primarily from Riyadh, Jeddah and Dammam.

From Riyadh's Al-Aziziyah bus station (p317), departures include: Amman (SR175, 22 hours, one daily), Kuwait (SR180, eight hours, three weekly), Aden (SR200, 42 hours, one daily), Sana'a (SR200, 36 hours, daily), Bahrain (SR100, six hours, three

daily), Qatar (SR125, eight hours via Al-Hofuf, one daily), Dubai (SR125, 12 hours via Abu Dhabi, one daily), Cairo (SR335, 32 hours, one daily), Khartoum (SR593, 36 hours, three weekly) and Damascus (SR175, 24 hours, three weekly). There are currently no buses to Oman, Turkey, Iran or Iraq.

From Jeddah's bus station (p329), buses depart to Amman (SR175, 18 hours, daily), Cairo (SR348, duration varies according to route taken, daily), Beirut (SR180, 26 hours, daily), Damascus (SR175, about 23 hours, daily), Dubai (SR210, 30 hours, daily), Abu Dhabi (SR210, 30 hours, daily), Khartoum (SR425, 31 hours, daily), Sana'a (SR150, 24 hours, daily) among other destinations in Yemen. For Bahrain and Qatar, change at Dammam.

From the Dammam bus station (p353), there are regular daily departures to Bahrain (SR50, about two hours, six daily), and to Doha (SR190, five hours, one daily), Kuwait (SR100, five hours, one daily), Abu Dhabi (SR110, 8 hours, one daily), Dubai (SR110, 10 hours, one daily), and Sharjah (SR110, 11 hours, one daily) and to Yemen. The same bus travels to Al-Hudayda (SR250, 24 hours), Sana'a (SR300, 30 hours) and Aden (SR300, 36 hours). There are no buses for Oman. Take the Dubai bus and take a shared taxi (SR50) from there.

There are also buses from Dammam to Damascus (SR175, 24 hours, one daily); Amman (SR175, 24 hours, one daily); Aqaba (SR235, 24 hours, two to three weekly); Cairo (1st/2nd/3rd class SR378/408/458, at least two daily). There are no buses currently running to Turkey, Iran or Iraq.

CAR & MOTORCYCLE

For general information, see p547.

To avoid queues at busy times (such as during holidays), go early or late (all borders are open 24 hours). If you're driving someone else's car, make sure you carry a letter granting permission from the owner.

Sea

Car and passenger ferries operate between Saudi Arabia and Egypt: **Al-Blagha** (☎ 02-648 0334 ext 253; www.alblagha.com) is the largest shipping company in the Red Sea and operates boats from Jeddah to Suez (1st/2nd/3rd class SR845/695/395, car from SR850; 42 hours, once weekly both ways), and from

Duba to Port Safaga (1st/2nd/3rd class SR300/265/225, car from SR469, eight hours, daily both ways).

Boats also travel from Jeddah to Suwaqih, Sudan (1st/2nd/3rd SR470/370/300, cars from SR460, 10 hours, three weekly both ways). In the future, boats should also sail sporadically from Jeddah to Al-Hudayda (Yemen); check the website. Boats do not go to Massawa (Eritrea).

Ferries are modern, well-kept and professionally run. Cabins (either two- or four-bed) are simple, clean and comfortable and all have air-conditioning. First-class cabins have private bathrooms; 2nd class common bathrooms; and 3rd (also known as 'Pullman' are just seats). Bookings can be made by email or telephone and you can travel on the same day. In the high season (summer, haj and Ramadan), book one week in advance for Duba to Port Safaga and one month in advance Jeddah to Suez, and vice versa. All ferries have restaurants. Check in three hours before departure.

GETTING AROUND
Air
Domestic air services in Saudi Arabia are operated by **Saudi Arabian Airlines** (Saudia; www.saudiairlines.com). Once Saudia has been privatised, the monopoly on providing domestic passenger services will be lifted, and it's likely that new domestic air companies will spring up.

Saudia flies frequently to major towns, generally runs on time and is very reasonably priced. Unlike international tickets (which travel agents can sell at discounted prices), domestic Saudia tickets cost the same price whether bought from an agency or direct from Saudia.

Domestic tickets can also be bought from abroad. Tickets can be changed as often as you like (though SR20 is sometimes charged). You can get refunds (minus an administration charge of SR20), even on missed flights. Putting yourself on the waiting list is well worthwhile therefore as there are so many no-shows.

Check in 1½ hours prior to departure is advised for domestic flights. Note that Medina airport lies outside the *haram* (forbidden) area so can be used by tourists.

Prices are very reasonable and haven't changed in six years. Schedules also don't alter much either. Bookings by telephone can also be made if you're flying within 24 hours (you can pick the ticket up at the airport). For information on flight schedules and information, call ☎ 920-022 222.

Bus
All domestic bus services are operated by the **Saudi Arabian Public Transport Company** (Saptco; ☎ 800-124 9999; www.saptco.com.sa). The company is professionally run and has a good safety record with well-maintained buses (usually replaced every two to three years).

The buses are comfortable, air-conditioned and clean. Standing passengers are not allowed, talking to the driver is prohibited and smoking is strictly prohibited. Saptco also guarantees that if a bus breaks down, a repair vehicle is sent within two hours, a replacement within four.

All buses have on-board toilets, and make rest stops every few hours. For general information, fare prices and timetables, dial ☎ 800 124 9999, toll-free (with recorded messages in both Arabic and English).

Unaccompanied foreign women can travel on domestic and international buses with their *iqama* (residence permit) if an expat, or passport and visa if a tourist. The front seats are generally unofficially reserved for 'families' including sole women, and the back half for men.

Check in half an hour before domestic departures, one hour before international departures (though passengers with hand luggage can arrive 10 minutes before). If the bus is full, you can join the waiting list and board the bus five minutes before departure if there are no-shows.

Note that during the haj, services are reduced across the country as buses are seconded for the pilgrims.

CLASSES
There are no classes, except on one service: the Saptco VIP Express service that runs between Riyadh (see p318) and Al-Khobar (p355; SR90, five hours).

COSTS
Bus fares cost approximately half of the equivalent airfare. Return tickets are 25% cheaper than two one-way fares. Note that at the time of writing, only cash was accepted for payment.

RESERVATIONS

When purchasing your ticket, you'll need to show your passport (visitors) or *iqama* (expats). During the haj season, during Ramadan or in summer, booking at least a week in advance is advisable.

Tickets can be bought up to three months in advance for domestic journeys, six months for international. If tickets are cancelled or unused, you can get a refund (less 10%) for a one-way ticket (or unused return) or 30% for a return ticket if it hasn't expired (within three/six months for domestic/international destinations).

Note that you can only buy tickets from the point of relevant departure, and that you can't make a reservation unless you've bought a ticket (so you can only make a telephone reservation for the return portion of the ticket).

Tickets are best bought from Saptco itself (as opposed to its agents which are less reliable vis-a-vis reservations).

Car & Motorcycle

Despite its impressive public-transport system, Saudi Arabia remains a country that glorifies the private car (the large private car above all), rivalled in this regard only by the US. Roads are generally sealed and well-maintained.

Motorcycles are an extremely rare sight on Saudi roads (they're rather unfamily friendly because of the heat, dust and their price relative to cars), though in recent years Harley Davidson clubs have opened in Jeddah and Riyadh.

DRIVING LICENCE

If you have a visitors' visa and want to rent a car, you should always have your International Driving Licence (IDL) available to show.

If you're going to be in the Kingdom for more than three months, you'll need to get a local driving licence, which is arranged by your employer. You'll also have to do a driving test and purchase insurance.

FUEL

It currently costs just 47 halalas per litre for unleaded petrol (introduced in January 2007) and 60 halalas for leaded fuel. All stations charge the same (by law). Petrol stations are ubiquitous throughout the country on sealed roads.

HIRE

International and local car-hire agencies can be found in the larger towns in the Kingdom, as well as at international airports. Local companies tend to be significantly cheaper, but always check that *full* insurance is included. Prices usually stay the same throughout the year.

Rates for the smallest cars at international agencies generally start at SR75 per day (including full insurance) and can start from SR450 for 4WDs. For rental of a month or more, prices drop by around 30% or more. Be sure to negotiate.

There's usually an additional charge of around SR0.75 to SR1.5 per kilometre, although most agencies offer the first 150km free. Women travellers (who are not permitted by law to drive) will need a driver – around SR105 per eight-hour day (SR20 per extra hour).

INSURANCE

If you are travelling with a car from another GCC country, insurance and the Collision-Damage Waiver (CDW) are mandatory. With car hire, it is usually included in the price, but it pays to check very carefully that it is.

ROAD RISKS

Over the last five years, a concerted government campaign has tried hard to reduce Saudi's shocking rate of road fatalities. On the roads, look out for the billboards proclaiming 'Enough!' On TV, you may well come across the graphic interviews with real-life road-accident victims, or doctors.

Speed cameras and radars now riddle the roads – for many Saudis, a worse hazard than before! Steep speeding fines of between SR150 and SR800 are regularly demanded on the motorways, from SR300 in the towns. For jumping traffic lights, you can be arrested on the spot, fined and your car impounded. Note that the fine for failing to wear a seatbelt is a stiff SR100.

ROAD RULES

The main rules include:

- Driving on the right side of the road.
- Leaving the scene of an accident is a serious offence and can result in fines of over SR1000, imprisonment and deportation.
- Not carrying a valid driving licence can result in a night in jail and a hefty fine.
- Right turns are allowed at red lights unless specifically forbidden.
- Speed limit in towns is 60km/h, 70km/h or 80km/h.
- Speed limit on open highways is 120km/h (but can drop to 90km/h or 100km/h).

See also the boxed text, p371.

Local Transport

TAXI

Taxis are found in most of the larger towns and are known as 'limousines' locally; they can be hailed anywhere. Note that it's much better to negotiate the fare first (as the locals do) rather than using the meter.

Train

Saudi Arabia has the only stretch of train track in the entire Arabian Peninsula. Trains travel between Riyadh (p318) and Dammam (p353) via Al-Hofuf.

Future rail plans include a line from Jeddah to Hail, and a train linking Riyadh's Al-Bathaa with King Khaled international airport (scheduled for 2013) and a Tabuk to Dammam line (for 2017).

Note that schedules change often; check the website for the latest information (www .saudirailways.org). Maximum luggage allowance is 50kg (per excess kilo SR0.50); luggage is loaded onto a separate carriage.

The gate closes five minutes before departure, but you should get there one hour before departure for the sometimes time-consuming police checks and luggage x-rays.

CLASSES

There are three classes: 2nd, 1st and the new VIP class. The main difference between them is a bit of space (and TV screens and a meal in VIP class). All classes have access to the train restaurant.

Women can travel unaccompanied (with ID) and sit in any class (in 2nd – there's a separate carriage; in VIP and 1st, designated areas).

COSTS

You'll need either your passport or *iqama* to buy a ticket. Travelling by train in 2nd class is slightly cheaper than the equivalent bus fare, but note that the company will be privatised by the end of 2007/2008, so prices may change. There are discounts for Saudi students only.

RESERVATIONS

Reservations (☎ 92 000 8886) can be made a minimum of 24 hours before departure and a maximum of 90 days in advance, and from any station to any station.

Tickets can be changed up to three hours before departure though you'll forfeit 10% of the total ticket cost. Check all tickets are correct after purchase, and note that there is no refund if you miss your train.

During school holidays, Ramadan and the Haj Eid, book well in advance. At the weekend, book three to four days in advance.

United Arab Emirates
إتحاد الإمارات العربية

While the United Arab Emirates (UAE) these days appears to be little more than a stage for Dubai to strut its increasingly crazy stuff, there's far more to this fabulous little federation than Disneyesque dioramas. The UAE is a contradictory destination, an Islamic state where the DJs' turntables stop spinning just before the muezzins' morning call to prayer can be heard, and where a traditional Bedouin lifestyle and customs continue alongside a very Western version of rampant consumerism. While many visitors marvel at the fantastic (in the true sense of the word) hotel and real estate projects, the real wonder is how the savvy sheikhs manage to harmonise such disparate and seemingly opposing forces.

For Western visitors, the UAE is a very safe Middle East destination, with the comforts of home and a taste of the exotic. Here you can max out those credit cards at designer clothes shops, laze in front of a gorgeous beach and azure seas, and sip a cocktail as you plan which fine dining restaurant to book and which international DJ to dance to until the early morning. On a less hedonistic stay, you can soak up the atmosphere of the heritage areas, haggle over a Persian carpet, head out to the desert sands for a camel ride under a star-filled sky, or dive the coral-filled waters of the Gulf. Or simply mix up a blend of everything; after all, that's what makes the UAE unique.

FAST FACTS

- **Official name** United Arab Emirates
- **Capital** Abu Dhabi
- **Area** 83,600 sq km
- **Population** 4.32 million
- **Country code** ☎ 971
- **Head of State** (President) Sheikh Khalifa bid Zayed al-Nahayan
- **Annual number of Western tourists** Six million
- **Stereotypes** Local sheikhs giving a royal wave from their limo
- **Surprises** Local sheikhs fanging in a Ferrari down Sheikh Zayed Rd

HIGHLIGHTS

- **Dubai** (p387) Cruise across Dubai's chaotic creek in an *abra* (water taxi) – no matter the time of day, it never looks the same.
- **Abu Dhabi** (p417) Join the locals for an often steamy stroll along the city's stunning Corniche.
- **Sharjah** (p405) Admire the historic windtower architecture in the atmospheric heritage area.
- **Al-Ain** (p431) Lose yourself in the labyrinthine lanes of Al-Ain's shady date-palm oases.
- **Liwa** (p428) Wonder at the spectacle of the shifting sands that drift across the roads in the desert of Liwa.
- **Dibba** (p439) Count the coloured doors as you kick back in the low-key fishing town of Dibba.

ITINERARIES

Also see the Itineraries chapter (p28) for further UAE itineraries.

- **Three days or less** With only three days, your time is best spent in Dubai. Follow our Dubai itinerary (p383) and check out Lonely Planet's *Best of Dubai* and *Dubai* city guides. Keen to see more of the country? Restrict your Dubai explorations to one day ambling around the bustling creek, surrounding souqs, and historic Shindagha and Bastakia areas. On day two, hire a car and drive to Al-Ain for some sublime desert scenery, date-palm oases, and a beautifully restored fort at Al-Ain Palace Museum. On day three, wander the narrow lanes of Sharjah's heritage and arts precinct, taking in its tiny museums, then shop the souqs.
- **One week** After a few days in flashy Dubai, focusing your time on both old and 'New Dubai', hire a car to explore more of this compact country. Drive to Abu Dhabi (p417) to experience an attractive Arabian city that operates at a much more leisurely pace than fast Dubai (see the itinerary, p421). Get an early start for the drive to the Liwa (p428) and some camel-spotting, spectacular desert landscapes, and date farms. The next day take the back road to verdant Al-Ain (p429) and return to Dubai the next day via Hatta (p402) and Sharjah (p404).

- **Two weeks** With two weeks, you can also explore the stunning east coast of the country. Follow the one-week itinerary above, but from Sharjah, drive along the coast via the interesting little towns of Ajman (p410), Umm al-Quwain (p412) and Ras al-Khaimah (p413) to Oman's Musandam Peninsula (p242), where you should spend a few days. From the Musandam, head south to Dibba (p439), which you could make your base for some east coast exploration, spending time at Khor Kalba (p433), Khor Fakkan (p436) and Fujairah (p433). If you're in the area on a Friday, don't miss the bull-butting event in Fujairah.
- **One month** Extend your stay in each town by a day or two. In Dubai, spend a day on the slopes at Ski Dubai (p391) and another recovering at the Oriental Hammam (p391). Sleep under the stars on an overnight desert safari from Abu Dhabi (p424) and do a diving course on the east coast at Sandy Beach Motel (p438). Laze on the beach for a couple of days at Fujairah's Al Aqah Beach Resort (p439) or Dibba's dramatically located Golden Tulip Resort (p439) then complete your trip with a stay at one of Dubai emirate's dreamy desert resorts, such as Al Maha (p402) or Bab Al Shams (p402).

CLIMATE & WHEN TO GO

The best time to visit the UAE is between October and November and then February and March, when temperatures hang around the mid-20s and the humidity is under control. While December and January are generally considered the best months to go, the weather over the last couple of 'winters' has been unpredictable with conditions often cloudy, rainy and bleak. See p530 for climate charts.

This is also high season when most of the country's festivals, sporting events, and conferences are held, so you'll be paying rack rates for accommodation in Dubai and Abu Dhabi and will need to book well in advance. The Christmas and New Year period also gets busy, particularly on the east coast when European expat families want to get away.

Avoid the month of Ramadan if you possibly can: *iftar* (breaking the fast after sundown) is fun and it's a great way to meet locals, and hotel rates are heavily discounted, but erratic business hours, dangerous driving and not being able to eat or drink in public during the day can make it hard going. A trip to the UAE in high summer (July and August) is simply a bad idea – the only advantage being heavy discounted hotels.

HISTORY
Early History
While the country doesn't appear rich in physical history, the earliest significant settlements in the UAE date back to the Bronze Age. In the 3rd millennium BC, a culture known as Umm al-Nar arose near modern Abu Dhabi. Umm al-Nar's influence extended well into the interior and down the coast to today's Oman. There were also settlements at Badiyah (near Fujairah) and at Rams (near Ras al-Khaimah) during the 3rd millennium BC.

The Persians and, to a lesser extent, the Greeks, were the next major cultural influences in the area. The Persian Sassanid Empire held sway until the arrival of Islam in AD 636 and another religion, Christianity, made a brief appearance in the form of the Nestorian Church, which had a monastery on Sir Baniyas Island, west of Abu Dhabi, in the 5th century.

European Arrivals
During the Middle Ages, the Kingdom of Hormuz controlled much of the area, including the entrance to the Gulf, as well as most of the Gulf's trade. The Portuguese arrived in 1498 and by 1515 they had occupied Julfar (near Ras al-Khaimah) and built a customs house, where they taxed the Gulf's flourishing trade with India and the Far East. However, the Portuguese stayed on in the town only until 1633.

The rise of British naval power in the Gulf in the mid-18th century coincided with the rise of two important tribal confederations along the coast of the lower Gulf. These were the Qawassim and the Bani Yas, the ancestors of the rulers of four of the seven emirates that today make up the UAE.

The Qawassim, whose descendants now rule Sharjah and Ras al-Khaimah, were a seafaring clan based in Ras al-Khaimah. Their influence extended at times to the Persian side of the Gulf. This brought them into conflict with the British, who had forged an alliance with the Al-Busaid tribe, the ancestors of today's rulers of Oman, to guarantee that the French could not take over their all-important sea routes to India. The Qawassim felt that the Al-Busaid had betrayed the region, and launched attacks on British ships to show that they weren't going to be as compliant. As a result, the British dubbed the area 'the Pirate Coast' and launched raids against the Qawassim in 1805, 1809 and 1811. In 1820 a British fleet destroyed or captured every Qawassim ship it could find, imposed a General Treaty of Peace on nine Arab sheikhdoms in the area and installed a garrison. This was the forerunner of a later treaty, the Maritime Truce, which was imposed by the British in 1835 and increased their power in the region. In 1853 the treaty was modified yet again, when it was named the Treaty of Peace in Perpetuity. It was at this time that the region became known as the Trucial Coast. In subsequent decades, the sheikhs of each tribal confederation signed agreements with the British under which they accepted formal British protection.

Throughout this period the main power among the Bedouin tribes of the interior was the Bani Yas tribal confederation, made up of the ancestors of the ruling families of modern Abu Dhabi and Dubai. The Bani Yas were originally based in Liwa, an oasis deep in the desert, but moved their base to Abu Dhabi in 1793. The Bani Yas divided into two main branches in the early 19th century when Dubai split from Abu Dhabi.

From 1853 until the discovery of oil, the region was a backwater, with the sheikhdoms nothing more than tiny enclaves of fishers, pearl divers and Bedu. Rivalries between the various rulers occasionally erupted into conflict, which the British tried to subdue. During this time the British also protected the federation from Saudi Arabia, which had ambitions to add the territory to its own.

Black Gold
After the collapse of the world pearl market in the early 20th century, the coast had sunk into poverty. However, the sheikhs of Abu Dhabi, Dubai and Sharjah had already

THE UNITED ARAB EMIRATES

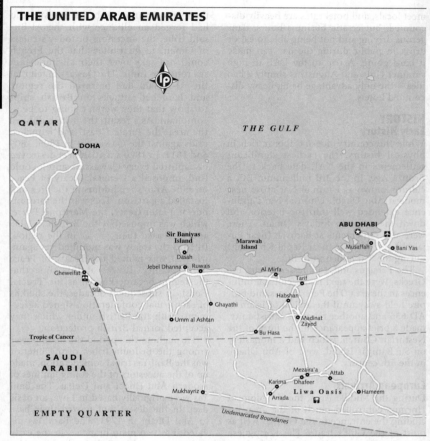

discussed oil exploration in the area, with Abu Dhabi's Sheikh Shakhbut granting the first of several oil concessions in 1939. The first cargo of crude left Abu Dhabi in 1962 and Dubai, which had been busy cementing its reputation as the region's busiest trading centre, exported its first oil in 1969. With the British hinting at an oddly timed exit from the Arabian Gulf in 1971, Abu Dhabi's ruler, Sheikh Zayed, set about negotiating with other sheikhdoms in the Trucial States to create one nation.

Independence

The British had set up the Trucial States Council (the forerunner to today's ruling council) in 1951, and with the announce-

ment of their imminent departure, the original plan (announced in February 1968) was to form a federation including Bahrain, Qatar and the Trucial Coast. With some tough negotiating by Sheik Zayed and some odd boundaries formed (such as the Omani enclaves, and Fujairah split between Fujairah, Sharjah and Oman), as well as Bahrain and Qatar deciding to drop out, the new country came into existence when six of the emirates united on 2 December 1971; Ras al-Khaimah joined the following year. While critics said the UAE wouldn't last, and with doubts about its future after the death of Sheikh Zayed in 2004, the UAE remains the only united Arab states in the region.

GOVERNMENT & POLITICS

'Emirate' comes from the word 'emir' (ruler). In practice, the seven hereditary emirs of the UAE are called sheikhs. Though there is a federal government over which one of the sheikhs presides (the president), each ruler is completely sovereign within his emirate.

Sheikh Zayed bin Sultan al-Nahyan of Abu Dhabi was the president since the country was formed in 1971, a position he held until his death in 2004. Revered by his people, and often called 'father' by Emiratis, he commanded huge respect across the Middle East. Visitors to the UAE will no doubt see enormous posters of Sheikh Zayed in a pair of Ray Ban-style sunglasses, alongside a smiling Sheikh Maktoum bin

Rashid al-Maktoum, who was the ruler of Dubai and the country's vice-president and prime minister up until his death in January 2006. He was the eldest and most introspective of Sheikh Rashid ('the Father of Dubai') al-Maktoum's sons, and was appointed heir to the throne in 1958. Upon his death, the next in line, his younger brother Sheikh Mohammed, took over, and in his year or so in office has had an extraordinary impact.

The degree of power that the sheikhs should cede to the federal government has been a hot topic of debate ever since independence. The forum where these and other issues are discussed is the Supreme Council of Rulers, the highest body in the land, which comprises the ruler of each emirate. There is also a cabinet in which the posts are distributed among the emirates. Most of the Emirates population live in Abu Dhabi and Dubai, so their representatives hold most of these posts. In reality, most of the power in the country is concentrated in these two emirates – particularly Abu Dhabi – as they are the wealthiest in the federation.

The cabinet and Supreme Council are advised, but can't be overruled, by the Federation National Council (FNC). This is a consultative body whose members are now elected. At the last election eight women were elected to the FNC.

ECONOMY

The UAE has the world's third-largest reserves of oil (with Abu Dhabi alone having 9%); unsurprisingly, this underpins the national economy, contributing approximately 28% of GDP. It is thought that at current levels of production, oil reserves will last for only another century, and, sensibly, the country is looking at other industry to take over from oil in the future. Dubai has handled this with particular foresight and its oil exports now only account for around 6%, with this reducing to a miniscule 1% by 2010. Through its development of healthy tourism, trade, manufacturing and construction industries, Dubai has become the most modern Middle East metropolis.

PEOPLE
The National Psyche

Yes, they wear different clothing and some of them are wealthy beyond our wildest dreams, but that's about as far as the

BIGGER THAN BEN HUR

Following Dubai's lead, property and tourism developments are popping up all over the country. While the trend is still to go big (as in tall like the Burj al-Arab) others are going big (as in square kilometres like the Palm Island development off the coast). While we're not going to report on some of the sillier ideas that may never see the light of day, here are some that have more concrete (so to speak) foundations.

Palm Island

Built on reclaimed land, this enormous development has added 120km of beach to the Dubai coastline. In the form of two palm-shaped islands, so far only some residents have been handed the keys to their condos. Looks good from an aircraft, the Sheik's helicopter, or Google Earth.

Burj Dubai

Currently going up at a rate of a new floor every four days, Burj Dubai (Dubai Tower) is fast headed towards being the tallest building on the planet. Just how tall? No-one's saying, just in case someone else decides to usurp the Burj before it's had its moment close to the sun. Looks good from above where it resembles a *Hymenocallis* flower. From the ground it's just damn tall at the moment.

Saadiyat Island

Abu Dhabi is turning one of its natural islands into the 'Island of Happiness'. What will make you happy? Perhaps a 'seven-star' hotel, golf courses and a 'Cultural City' (see boxed text, p422, featuring a space by Zaha Hadid and a Guggenheim designed by Frank Gehry. Given the architects, it should look good from any angle.

stereotype of Emiratis (known as 'nationals' or 'locals') stretches. Women, for instance, emerged from beneath their *shayla* (headscarf) long ago to take up educational opportunities and now hold mid- and high-level management positions in government and industry around the country. They wear the *abeyya* (a black cloak that covers the body) and *shayla* out of choice: this 'national dress', as they proudly call it, distinguishes them as Emiratis. And while there's some truth to the stereotype of shopping-obsessed 'Gulf Princesses', young Emirati women continually prove that they can be academic achievers and successful in the workplace. Part of the drive to succeed for the girls is that the vast majority of Emirati marriages are still arranged – there are very few exceptions. However, the young people see each other's photos, talk on the phone and increasingly 'meet' before the wedding night (even if it's via internet chat lines). Both can refuse to marry if they feel the person is not right for them, and women are increasingly doing this, working on their career and putting off marriage until they're in their late 20s,

when many in society consider them to be 'spinsters'.

The men often aren't the autocratic despotic rulers (of household or country) that many expect, either – it's the women who often rule the house in this manner! Emirati men have a strong sense of self-worth, which at times may appear as arrogance, but their business dealings with the outside world dictate that they be shrewd, urbane and open to different influences, while continuing to hold their proud Bedouin and Emirati heritage dear. They may not take these influences into their households wholesale, but the role of the patriarch is certainly changing because of it, and the next generation is going to be different again.

One thing that hasn't changed over decades or centuries is the notion of *wusta* (power and influence) in society. Basically, if you have the right networks (which generally means being born into one of the major tribes) you can get things done – whether it be clinching a massive business deal with the government or getting the best parking place at work. Flaunting *wusta* isn't really done though: those who have *wusta* don't need to talk about it, while those who do claim to have it, generally don't.

Lifestyle

The national household is generally the result of an arranged marriage, in most instances to a cousin or blood relative. The vast majority of national families have some type of home help – usually a Filipino, Malaysian or Indonesian housemaid, nanny and/or cook. Emirati households are generally segregated by gender, with separate women's and men's quarters. And while women can divorce their husbands, this is relatively rare. Families are usually large, with up to a dozen family members sharing the same house.

Non-*wusta* types – and that includes the 80% of the population that is not Emirati – have a very different lifestyle to nationals. The contentious 'guest workers' from the Indian subcontinent, Southeast Asia, Africa and more recently China, work for low wages and live in simple conditions, but earn far more than they could at home. They take most of the menial jobs in the country, largely in construction, but also functioning as cleaners, housemaids, taxi drivers and shop assistants, with the goal of saving enough money to buy a house or start a business back home. Conditions for these workers, especially those in the construction sector, has been much written about in the local and international press, and the government's reaction to complaints about conditions and safety have been swift, but generally seen as having mainly been prompted by the bad press.

The skills and training of Indians, and Arabs from elsewhere in the Middle East, have secured them better paid jobs in IT, the media, hospitality, government and the service sector, albeit at lower salaries than nationals. A booming economy in recent years has seen a surge of young people from all over the world, especially from Europe (the UK, Norway, Germany, the Baltic countries and Eastern Europe), South Africa and Australia, coming to Dubai to work in the media, tourism and hospitality industries, simply because the opportunities to gain experience and get ahead and live a multicultural life far outweigh any other disadvantages, such as long hours and few holidays.

Middle managers in the private sector are largely from the West, other Arab nations and India. They are paid well and treated better than the 'guest workers' and compensation comes in terms of income and 'the good life'.

Population

There are an estimated 4.3 million people living in the UAE; about 20% are nationals. The population has been growing at an average of 5% per year over the past decade, bolstered by a high birth rate and ever-growing numbers of expatriate workers.

RELIGION

Most Emiratis are Sunni Muslims subscribing to the Maliki or Hanbali schools of Islamic law. Many of the latter are Wahhabis, though UAE Wahhabis are not nearly as strict and puritanical as the Saudi Wahhabis. There are also smaller communities of Ibadi and Shiite Muslims. Other religions are tolerated, and there are a number of Christian churches throughout the country, as well as Hindu and Sikh temples in Dubai.

ARTS

The revered Bedouin heritage of the UAE dictates that the most popular art forms in the country today are the same as those that have been practised for centuries, namely traditional dance, music and poetry. The only other distinctive and significant art form is architecture (see p54). Though Sheikh Sultan bin Mohammad al-Qassimi of Sharjah has made an enormous effort to raise the profile of theatre, the visual arts and literature (other than poetry) in his emirate, these art forms are still nascent there and in the rest of the country. The announcement of a Cultural City in Abu Dhabi (p422) sees a significant raising of the arts profile in the UAE.

The UAE's most popular television show at the time of writing was *Millionaire Poet*, the local equivalent of *American Idol*.

Poetry

In Bedouin culture in the UAE, a facility with poetry and language is greatly prized. Traditionally, a poet who could eloquently praise his own people while pointing out the failures of other tribes was considered

THE UNBELIEVABLE UAE TRUTH...

You can't buy alcohol?

Partially true. You can, as a visitor, purchase alcohol in bars and clubs that are generally attached to four- and five-star hotels for consumption on the premises. Expat residents need an alcohol licence, which entitles them to a fixed monthly limit of alcohol available from alcohol stores. Except in Sharjah, of course, where even *sheesha* (water pipe used for smoking tobacco) is banned.

There's no pork?

Pork is available for non-Muslims in some supermarkets (such as Spinneys) in a specially labelled area of the shop. In many hotel restaurants, pork is a menu item and is usually clearly labelled as such. However the 'beef bacon' and 'turkey ham' that are commonly available are nothing more than a reminder of how tasty the real thing is...unless you're a vegetarian, of course.

Women don't really need to cover up anymore.

Absolutely not true. However, all that locals ask is that people dress respectfully, with clothes that are not too revealing – especially true outside of Dubai. Emiratis *will* judge you on how you dress; boys in shorts at shopping malls will be assumed to have forgotten their pants and girls who dress like Paris Hilton will be assumed to have the same morals as the heiress. It's your call.

Homosexuals are banned?

Simply being homosexual is not illegal as such, but homosexual acts are – as are any sex acts outside marriage.

What about those guys holding hands?

Simply a sign of friendship. It's OK for married couples to hold hands as well, but serious public displays of affection by couples (married or not) are frowned upon and fines and jail terms can result. Really.

If you're HIV positive you'll be kicked out?

Yes. As a worker coming to live in Dubai you will be tested for HIV as well as other things such as diabetes. If you are proven to be HIV positive, you'll be deported.

Dubai is the capital.

No! Abu Dhabi is. Both are emirates (like states) and both are the capitals of their respective state, but Abu Dhabi is the seat of UAE power. It just looks like Dubai is the capital, and Dubai acts like it's the capital, but Abu Dhabi's too busy counting the oil revenue to care...much.

---

a great asset. Modern poets of note from the UAE include Sultan al-Owais and Dr Ahmed al-Madani.

Nabati (vernacular poetry) is especially popular and has traditionally been in spoken form. These days, sheikhs such as Sheikh Mohammed bin Rashid al-Maktoum, Dubai's ruler, are respected poets in this tradition.

There are scores of well-known male poets in the UAE who still use the forms of classical Arab poetry, though they often experiment with combining it with other styles. There are also some well-known female poets, most of whom write in the *tafila* (prose) style.

Music & Dance

Emiratis have always acknowledged the importance of music to daily life. Songs have been traditionally composed to accompany different tasks, from hauling water to diving for pearls.

These days, popular local musicians include Mohammed al-Mazem, Mohammed al-Beloushy, Rashed al-Majed, Mihad Hamad and Eda bin Tanaf al-Manhaly. The most popular of all is the female singer Ahlam: nationals pay up to US$50,000 to have her sing at their weddings.

At celebrations such as weddings or *eid*, traditional dance comes into its own. Clapping and the rhythmic beating of traditional drums accompanies the dance, which is performed by groups of men with sticks, swords or rifles, or by young girls who swing their hair and sway their bodies in time to the music.

The Dubai Museum (p388) has an interesting audiovisual presentation on traditional dance.

ENVIRONMENT

Environmental awareness is increasing at the macro level in the UAE, due in no small part to the efforts of the late Sheikh Zayed, who was posthumously named a 'Champion of the Earth' by the UN Environment Programme (UNEP) in 2005. With his efforts in wildlife preservation, such as Sir Baniyas Island, where several nearly extinct Arabian wildlife species are being nurtured, as well as the ban on hunting with guns over a quarter of a century ago, Sheikh Zayed foresaw the acute threats to the endangered native species of the region.

In Dubai, the Dubai Desert Conservation Reserve (DDCR) comprises 225 sq km, or 5%, of the area of the Dubai emirate and operates as a national park as well as a luxury resort (see p402). The success story of this project is the successful breeding of the endangered scimitar-horned oryx, which is bred successfully as part of the DDCR's programme. Also in the Dubai emirate, the Ras al-Khor Wildlife Sanctuary (p390) is a haven for bird-watchers (the pink flamingos are extraordinary) and has been a reserve since 1985. A breeding centre at the Sharjah Desert Park (p408) is open to travellers, and a wetland reserve, Al Wasit lagoons, is currently being prepared.

Unlike Australia and the USA, the UAE ratified the Kyoto Protocol in January 2005 and has set targets for the reduction of domestic carbon emissions as well as greenhouse gases. In terms of the Emirates' going green at a micro level, much work needs to be done. Water wastage (all water comes from desalination plants) and littering are major issues and while more public transport systems are on the way, getting residents and visitors out of cars and taxis and onto metros and monorails will be a challenge for Dubai's government.

FOOD & DRINK

The UAE's cuisine is extraordinarily multicultural due to the presence of so many foreign workers in the country. Lebanese, Indian and Iranian (also called Persian) cuisines are the most common, and these are eaten both at home and in restaurants. The most popular streetside snack is *shwarma* – meat sliced off a spit and rolled in a pocket of pita-type bread; lamb *shwarma* generally comes with chopped tomatoes, onion and rocket leaves or parsley, while chicken *shwarma* comes with potatoes and hummus. Whether eating at a souq stall or sampling an exquisite degustation menu at a top Dubai restaurant, you'll find something suited to your budget and your tastebuds. There are few opportunities to sample 'authentic' Emirati cuisine but there *are* dishes that are worth sampling if you get the chance. Try *khuzi*, a stuffed whole roast lamb on a bed of spiced rice; *makbus,* a casserole of meat or fish with rice; *hareis,* slow-cooked wheat and lamb; and *umm ali,* a pudding with raisins and nuts. You really must sample some of the delicious local dates too.

Alcohol can only be sold in restaurants and bars in hotels or in members-only clubs, such as golf clubs, which often admit paying guests. Because of the 30% tax on alcohol in the country, prices are expensive but on par with Europe. Expect to pay around Dh22 for a pint of beer. Alcohol is not available in Sharjah or Khor Fakkan.

See Food & Drink (above) for a general discussion of typical Gulf Arab fare.

DUBAI   دبي

☎ 04 / pop 1.3 million

Glitzy, glam, over-the-top and a little overexposed, Dubai lives for attention. On the surface it's materialistic beyond anyone's wildest dreams and by treating every visitor like a VIP, visitors respond by spending like VIPs, only to need resuscitating when the next month's credit-card bill arrives. But this is the whole idea. We're talking about a city that virtually invented the 'shopping festival' (Dubai Shopping Festival, or DSF), the simple premise of which was to get people to travel to Dubai and spend money. With myriad shopping malls, flamboyant

THE DUBAI DREAM

While Dubai continues to sell itself as a dream destination, both for visitors and potential expats – particularly those looking at salaries above Dh15,000 a month plus a nice housing and travel package – many long-term expats are starting to find the dream a little disturbing. A city that was once considered a hardship posting, by the mid-1990s Dubai had become a very liveable metropolis, well, apart from during summer.

As Dubai's growth quickened, prices went up, salaries stayed the same, and many long-timers (the ones who live overseas for the experience, not just the money), were left feeling a little sidelined. Dubai had become what many expats were trying to escape – a big city with big city problems. For some, the traffic problems – both the amount of accidents and the congestion – have made the city almost unliveable. While many contemplate moving house to lessen the daily commute, finding affordable accommodation is almost impossible despite the new annual rent-cap of 7%, not to mention the constant complaints about the building quality of Dubai's new housing projects. While many see public transport projects as the saviour, even a 500m walk to your business can leave you drenched in sweat for much of the year.

A great number of expats who have lived here for more than 10 years pine for the good old days; other newer, younger expats embrace the constantly morphing city proclaiming, 'Where else can you live where things grow and change so fast!'

hotels, a dizzying array of dining options and hip clubs and bars, it's all just too easy. Driven by Sheikh Mohammed, a leader who doesn't understand the word 'no', visitors and potential residents are flocking to this Middle East metropolis in increasing numbers with the promise that Dubai is like no other city on earth. And Sheikh Mohammed is delivering. However, whether you end up loving or loathing its ostentatious nature, under the surface another Dubai exists. Head to the Heritage Village (p389) during Ramadan or the DSF (p442) and you'll witness a different Dubai, where local Emiratis take joy in their songs, dance and traditions. Spend a few fascinating hours by the creek, watching the dhow (traditional wooden boat) traffic and the *abras* weave along the waterway while smoking some *sheesha*. Walk the streets of the tranquil, re-stored Bastakia area or take a stroll through multicultural Karama or Satwa. You'll find this Dubai a million miles removed from the credit-card frenzy of the five-star hotels. Whatever you end up preferring, Dubai is a fascinating experiment and a city-state that's like no other.

HISTORY

Archaeological remains found at Al-Qusais, on the northeastern edge of Dubai, prove that there was some form of human settlement here as long ago as 8000 BC, though little is known about the development of the city until the 17th century, when the Portuguese occupied the area, followed by the French, Dutch and, finally, British. During these occupations, the people of Dubai made their living by pearling, and through a trickle of trade with India and the rest of the Gulf; the rest of the UAE was where the power and prosperity of the region was centred. This changed after 1833, when 800 members of the Bani Yas tribe under Maktoum bin Butti settled in Dubai, turning it overnight into a small town rather than a village.

In 1894 Sheikh Maktoum bin Hasher al-Maktoum (r 1894–1906) declared Dubai a tax-free port, giving birth to what would become the modern-day economic phenomenon of Dubai. By this stage the population had grown to 10,000. Though the pearling trade collapsed around 1930, Dubai's status as the region's major port continued to grow, supported by major works such as the dredging of Dubai Creek in the 1950s so as to allow large trading vessels to use the port. Under Sheikh Saeed (r 1912–58) and Sheikh Rashid (r 1958–90), the city cemented its reputation as the main trading hub in the lower Gulf.

In 1971, Dubai became one of the seven emirates of the UAE and for the next 19 years Sheikh Rashid acted as vice-president and prime minister of the federation as well as being the leader of Dubai itself. The city continued to grow and prosper during these years. Sheikh Rashid died in 1990, and was succeeded by his son Sheikh Maktoum who steered a steady course for Dubai until his death in January 2006. Now under the leadership of Sheikh Mohammed bin Rashid al-Maktoum (commonly and affectionately know as 'Sheikh Mo' by expats), the plans for Dubai Inc are as ambitious as they are audacious.

ORIENTATION

Dubai is growing at an astounding rate, and its city suburbs now extend to the border with its northern neighbour, Sharjah. In fact, the lower housing prices in Sharjah mean that many people are now basing themselves there and commuting into Dubai each day for work, making the northern roads into the city nightmarishly busy during peak hours. To the south, skyscrapers, shopping malls and construction sites line Sheikh Zayed Rd as far as Jebel Ali, where the city's major port is located, whereas just a few years ago there was nothing but desert between Jebel Ali and the Hard Rock café with its giant guitar was considered to be in the middle of nowhere. The fashionable and affluent suburb of Jumeirah is found along this stretch of coast and is accessed via Jumeirah Rd (also known as Jumeirah Beach Rd and Beach Rd). Sheikh Zayed Rd, with its signature Emirates Towers buildings, is the backbone of the city and the major artery to the national capital, Abu Dhabi. After it leaves Dubai it is called Abu Dhabi Rd.

The city was originally built around Dubai Creek, also known as Khor (creek) Dubai, an inlet of the Arabian Gulf. Today, most tourist attractions are found around here. The city is split in two, divided by the creek: Deira is to the northeast, and Bur Dubai to the southwest. The major landmark on the Deira side is the National Bank of Dubai, an impressive modern skyscraper with a golden-brown reflective surface facing the creek. The main square in Deira, Baniyas Sq, is also known as Al-Nasr Sq. Bur Dubai's major landmark is the Diwan (Ruler's Office) on the edge of the creek. There are five ways of crossing the creek: via the Al-Maktoum and Al-Garhoud bridges, the Al-Shindagha car and pedestrian tunnels or on the traditional *abras* that cross the river at all hours of the day and night. A new bridge across Dubai Creek is currently under construction and a monorail will also take people across the creek in a few years.

The airport occupies a central position in Al-Garhoud, on the Deira side of the creek. It is a short bus or taxi ride to central Deira or Bur Dubai. There are two major bus and taxi stations: one in Deira and one in Bur Dubai. See p401 for more details.

DUBAI IN...

Two Days

Start with a **Cultural Breakfast** (p388) at the Sheikh Mohammed Centre for Cultural Understanding, for a rare chance to meet locals, eat home-cooked Emirati food and learn about the local society. Next hit the **Dubai Museum** (p388) for an introduction to the history and culture of the Emirates. Wander around the historic **Bastakia quarter** (p389) before having lunch in the courtyard of the **Basta Art Café** (p396). Check out the **Bur Dubai textile souq** (p399) then in the late afternoon catch an *abra* across the creek to explore the **Dubai Souqs** (p399), particularly the glittering Gold Souq. Walk along the bustling **dhow wharves** (p387) on the creek and after another *abra* crossing, wander along the **Shindagha waterfront** (p389) for a quick look at the **Heritage and Diving Villages** (p389), and dinner, *sheesha* and spectacular views at **Kanzaman** (p397).

Day one focused on the old centre, so devote day two to new Dubai, beginning at Jumeirah, with a guided visit to **Jumeirah Mosque** (p389). Grab a bite to eat nearby at **Fudo** (p396) before heading up to Jumeirah Beach to admire the architecture of the **Burj al-Arab** (p389). If it's summer, head for **Wild Wadi Waterpark** (p391). If it's winter, hit the snow, naturally, at **Ski Dubai** (p391), where you can also check out Dubai's largest shopping centre, **Mall of the Emirates** (p399). Start your evening with a sunset drink on the veranda at **Bahri Bar** (p398), followed by a Moroccan meal at **Tagine** (p396), a *sheesha* at the **Sheesha Courtyard** (p397), followed by a nightcap at the **Rooftop Bar** (p398). Magic.

UNITED ARAB EMIRATES

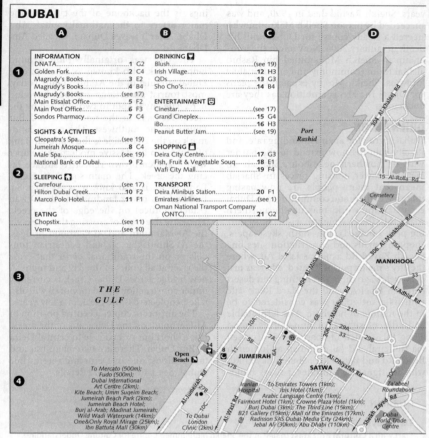

DUBAI

INFORMATION
DNATA..................................1 G2
Golden Fork..........................2 C4
Magrudy's Books....................3 E2
Magrudy's Books....................4 B4
Magrudy's Books................(see 17)
Main Etisalat Office.................5 F2
Main Post Office.....................6 F3
Sondos Pharmacy...................7 C4

SIGHTS & ACTIVITIES
Cleopatra's Spa..................(see 19)
Jumeirah Mosque...................8 C4
Male Spa...........................(see 19)
National Bank of Dubai............9 F2

SLEEPING
Carrefour.........................(see 17)
Hilton Dubai Creek................10 F2
Marco Polo Hotel..................11 F1

EATING
Chopstix..........................(see 11)
Verre.............................(see 10)

DRINKING
Blush............................(see 19)
Irish Village......................12 H3
QDs...............................13 G3
Sho Cho's.........................14 B4

ENTERTAINMENT
Cinestar..........................(see 17)
Grand Cineplex....................15 G4
iBo...............................16 H3
Peanut Butter Jam.............(see 19)

SHOPPING
Deira City Centre.................17 G3
Fish, Fruit & Vegetable Souq......18 E1
Wafi City Mall....................19 F4

TRANSPORT
Deira Minibus Station.............20 F1
Emirates Airlines.................(see 1)
Oman National Transport Company
  (ONTC)..........................21 G2

Port Rashid
15 Al-Rolla Rd
Cemetery
Kuwait St
MANKHOOL
304 Al-Mina Rd
306 Al-Mankhool Rd
Al-Adhid Rd
THE GULF
Open Beach
JUMEIRAH
SATWA
Al-Dhiyafah Rd
Za'abeel Roundabout
Sheikh Zayed Rd
Dubai World Trade Centre
Iranian Hospital
Al-Jumeirah Rd
Al-Wasl Rd
To Mercato (500m); Fudo (500m); Dubai International Art Centre (2km); Kite Beach; Umm Suqeim Beach; Jumeirah Beach Park (2km); Jumeirah Beach Hotel; Burj al-Arab; Madinat Jumeirah; Wild Wadi Waterpark (14km); One&Only Royal Mirage (25km); Ibn Battuta Mall (30km)
To Dubai London Clinic (2km)
To Emirates Towers (1km); Ibis Hotel (1km); Arabic Language Centre (1km); Fairmont Hotel (1km); Crowne Plaza Hotel (1km); Burj Dubai (3km); The Third Line (15km); B21 Gallery (15km); Mall of the Emirates (17km); Radisson SAS Dubai Media City (24km); Jebel Ali (30km); Abu Dhabi (110km)

Maps

The free *Dubai at a Glance* map is available from the Department of Tourism & Commerce Marketing welcome bureaus and hotel concierge desks. Explorer Publishing sells an *Explorer Mini Map* (Dh15), available at bookshops and supermarkets.

INFORMATION
Bookshops

Magrudy's Books Deira City Centre (Map pp384–5; ☎ 295 7744; Baniyas Rd, Al-Garhoud; ☼ 10am–10pm); Jumeirah (Map pp384–5; ☎ 344 4192; Beach Rd; ☼ 9am–9pm Sat–Thu, 4.30–8.30pm Fri); BurJuman Mall (☎ 359 3332; Trade Centre Rd, Bur Dubai; ☼ 10am–10pm Sat–Thu, 4–10pm Fri); Ibn Battuta Mall (☎ 366 9770; Sheikh Zayed Rd, Jebel Ali; ☼ 10am–10pm Sat–Thu, 4–10pm Fri)

Dubai's most comprehensive bookshop, with an excellent travel section, good books on Middle East history and politics, and gorgeous coffee-table books on the UAE.

Emergency

24-Hour Pharmacies (☎ 223 2323)
Ambulance (☎ 998)
Police (☎ 999, 800 4888, SMS 4444)
Tourist Police (☎ 800 4438)

Internet Access

Al Jalssa Internet Café (Map pp386–7; ☎ 351 4617; Al Ain Shopping Centre, Al-Mankhool Rd, Bur Dubai; per hr Dh10; ☼ 8.30am–1am) Thirty work stations with high-speed ADSL connection, web cams and head sets; you can also plug in your laptops, and get good sandwiches, juices and coffee.

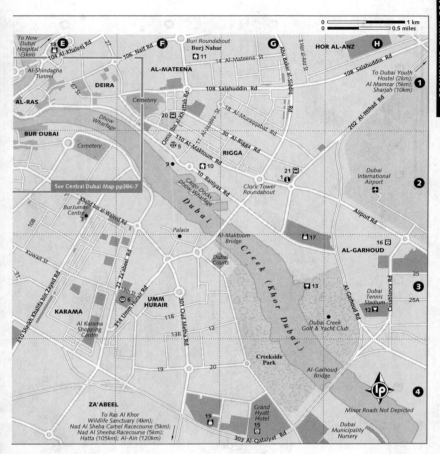

Golden Fork (Map pp386–7; ☎ 228 2662; Al-Maktoum Rd, Deira; per hr Dh5; ⏰ 1pm-3am) This fast-food restaurant offers good connections and comfortable work stations, at a bargain price.

Medical Services
American Hospital (☎ 336 7777; Oud Metha, Bur Dubai) This private hospital has an excellent 24-hour emergency department and clinic.

Dubai London Clinic (☎ 344 6663; Al-Wasl Rd, Jumeirah) A private medical centre that also has an emergency department.

New Dubai Hospital (☎ 222 9171; Abu Baker al-Siddiq Rd & Al-Khaleej Rd, Hor al-Anz) A government hospital with a decent 24-hour emergency department.

Sondos Pharmacy (Map pp384-5; ☎ 346 0660; Al-Dhiyafah Rd, Satwa) A 24-hour pharmacy that will deliver.

Money
In central Deira, especially along Baniyas Rd and on Baniyas Sq, every other building seems to contain a bank or a moneychanger. In Bur Dubai there are moneychangers around the *abra* docks. There are ATMs throughout the city, in all shopping malls and in most five-star hotel lobbies.

Post
Deira Post Office (Map pp386–7; Al-Sabkha Rd; ⏰ 8am-midnight Sat-Wed, 8am-1pm & 4-8pm Thu) Near the intersection with Baniyas Rd.

Main Post Office (Map pp384-5; ☎ 337 1500; Za'abeel Rd, Karama; ⏰ 8am-11.30pm Sat-Wed, 8am-10pm Thu, 8am-noon Fri) On the Bur Dubai side of the creek in Karama. Entrance is at the rear of the building.

CENTRAL DUBAI

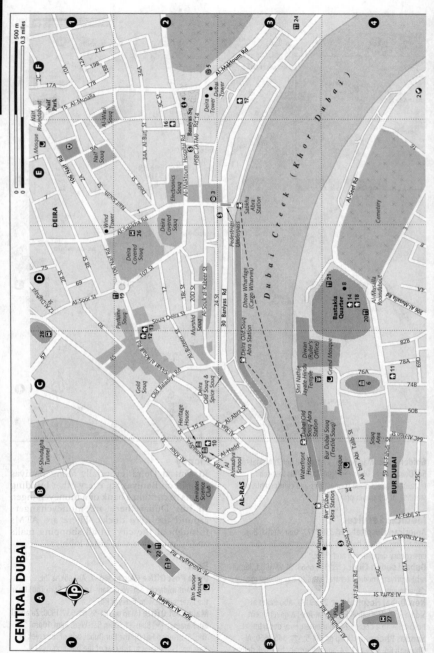

Telephone
Main Etisalat Office (Map pp384–5; cnr Baniyas & Omar ibn al-Khattab Rds, Deira; ⏰ 24hr) Wasl mobile recharge through automatic machines.

Tourist Information
The **Department of Tourism & Commerce Marketing** (DTCM; www.dubaitourism.ae; ☎ 223 0000) operates two main **branches** (airport arrivals area ☎ 224 5252, 224 4098; ⏰ 24hr; Deira Map pp386–7; ☎ 228 5000; Baniyas Sq; ⏰ 9am-11pm) and a number of information desks throughout the city at most of the major shopping malls. They usually stock a free 'Dubai at a Glance' map of the city and a range of free brochures on major attractions. The Deira branch also stocks local bus timetables.

   Dubai National Travel & Tourist Authority (DNATA; Map pp384–5; ☎ 295 1111; Head Office, Al-Maktoum Rd, Deira; ⏰ 9am-6pm Sat-Thu) is the quasi-official government-run travel agency in the UAE. It books accommodation and travel throughout the UAE and abroad.

SIGHTS
Dubai Creek
Dubai Creek is the colourful and chaotic heart of the city, bustling day and night with working dhows sailing in and out of the inlet (on their way to or from Iran); dhow tour boats taking tourists on buffet and belly-dancing cruises; and bizarre amphibious buses (yep, that's right).

   Taking an *abra* across the creek among all the craziness is one of the highlights of a trip to Dubai. Crowded *abras* make the crossing all day, to and from Bur Dubai and Deira, costing Dh1 per person per trip. You can also charter an *abra* for Dh50 per hour from any *abra* station, or an old rowing *abra* for Dh30 per hour from the Creek Park Station or Public Library Station. Most wait at the docks near the Heritage and Diving Village, Al Diwan and Al Seef Rd Park. Depending on where you get on, get the captain to do a length of the creek, taking you to Al-Maktoum bridge and back to Shindagha. Sunset is a sublime time to do the trip.

   On the Deira side, take time to explore the dhow wharves, where boats bound for Iran and other ports around the Gulf dock here to load and unload all sorts of intriguing cargo. You'll get to see the colourful wooden vessels up close and may even get invited aboard by the captain (although women shouldn't accept if alone). Early evening is a great time to do this walk and is also the best time to wander the aromatic **Spice Souq** nearby, and, not too far from there, Dubai's bustling **Covered Souq**, famous glittering **Gold Souq** and heady **Perfume Souq**. On the Bur Dubai side of the creek, take some time to shop for textiles and sequinned slippers in **Bur Dubai Souq** before exploring the labyrinthine streets of the historic **Bastakia Quarter**, home to traditional wind-tower houses, built from 1900 to 1930, that were once the residences of wealthy Persian merchants. Restored in recent years, the neighbourhood is one of Dubai's most atmospheric.

Dubai Museum

The outstanding **Dubai Museum** (Map pp386-7; ☎ 353 1862; Al-Fahidi St, Bastakia; adult/child Dh3/1; ⏲ 8.30am-8.30pm Sat-Thu, 2.30-8.30pm Fri), located in the Al-Fahidi Fort, is without doubt the most impressive in the country and is Dubai's most popular attraction. Dating from 1778, it's the oldest building in Dubai, and was once the ruler's office (now next door in the white Diwan) and residence (now at Za'abeel Palace). Built from sea rocks and gypsum, the fort has three towers (one square and two round), a big breezy courtyard, and an imposing teak door studded with enormous iron nails.

In the courtyard, there are traditional boats, cannons and buildings, including *al kaimah* (a primitive one room *barasti,* or palm-frond hut) and *al areesh* (a summer house made from palm-leaf), with a wind tower (the traditional form of air-conditioning) and *al manama* (an alfresco summer bed). Off the courtyard, within the fort walls, are fascinating displays of musical instruments and weapons, including intricately detailed old silver *khanjars* (swords inscribed with Arabic calligraphy), and wooden bows and arrows decorated with cowrie shells.

Inside the museum, a multimedia presentation charts the extraordinarily rapid development of Dubai, from a small fishing village with a bustling port, to the sprawling postmodern city it is today. The highlight, however, are the life-size dioramas with mannequins that make up most of the museum's exhibits and provide a fascinating glimpse into the social and cultural history

of Dubai. They're wonderfully kitsch and make fantastic use of video and sound to re-create Old Dubai, complete with a dhow dock and old souq from the 1950s, a traditional coffeehouse, blacksmith, carpentry, pottery and jewellery workshops, textile and spice shops, an Islamic school and a traditional home. There are also splendid displays on the desert and oasis, its flora and fauna, survival in the desert, the desert at night, the Bedu, traditional costumes and jewellery, and the excellent 'under water' sea exhibit on pearling, fishing and dhow boat building.

Any would-be Indiana Jones will also be thrilled with the small but excellent archaeology exhibition featuring many artefacts excavated at Jumeirah and Al Qusais. Look out for the wonderful grey chlorite pots decorated with geometrical designs (they say the straight lines represent the sea and the zigzag lines the sand dunes), dating from the 2nd millennium BC, the exquisite alabaster vessels from the 1st millennium BC, and the stucco decorations dating to the 9th and 12th centuries.

Sheikh Mohammed Centre for Cultural Understanding

Make the wonderful **Sheikh Mohammed Centre for Cultural Understanding** (Map pp386-7; ☎ 353 6666; www.cultures.ae; admission free; ⏲ 9am-3pm Sun-Thu) your first stop in the Bastakia area. Not only will you get the chance to check out one of the most beautifully restored courtyard houses in the neighbourhood (the staff will even let you go up to the terrace roof for fantastic views over the Bastakia) but you can also sign up for a range of interesting activities and tours as part of its 'Open Doors, Open Minds' programme, aimed at fostering greater understanding between Islam and other religions, or for those who just want to learn more about the UAE.

There are enjoyable **Cultural Breakfasts** (Dh50; ⏲ 10am Mon) and **Cultural Lunches** (Dh50; ⏲ 1pm Sun) where visitors get to meet some locals and learn about local traditions, Emirati customs and social rituals over a traditional home-cooked breakfast or lunch. Not only does the experience provide a rare opportunity to try Emirati food, not available elsewhere in eateries in the UAE, but you also get to meet Muslims (both local Emirati and foreign women married to Emiratis) and ask those questions you'd always wanted to ask, like why men wear white and women wear black.

Bastakia Walking Tours (Dh50; ☺ 10am Sun & Thu), Ramadan *iftar* dinners, and the popular **Jumeirah Mosque Guided Visits** (registration fee Dh10; ☺ 10am Sat, Sun, Tue & Thu) also operate from the centre. The mosque tour is the only means by which you can enter the mosque as a non-Muslim, but it also gives you the chance to learn about Islam, see a prayer demonstration, and dispel some myths.

Shindagha Waterfront

The historic Shindagha waterfront area is a wonderful place to wander. The creek is lined with a number of restored coral, gypsum and limestone buildings that were once the former fort-residences of Dubai's rulers and are now fascinating museums. The highlight is the **Sheikh Saeed al-Maktoum House** (Map pp386-7; ☎ 393 7139; off Al-Khaleej Rd; adult/child Dh3/1; ☺ 8.30am-10.30pm Sun-Thu, 4.30-10.30pm Fri & Sat), which was once home to the grandfather of Dubai's present ruler, Sheikh Mohammed, and is now a museum of pre-oil times. Built in 1896, the elegant 30-room house is a prototype of the traditional courtyard villa, and has two storeys and four wind towers. Occupied by the ruling family until 1958, it was extensively restored and opened as a museum in 1986. It's now home to a compelling exhibition of photographs from the 1940s, '50s and '60s documenting life on the creek and the development of Dubai, and it's extraordinary to see how very different the place was just a few decades ago.

Another highlight here are the splendid **Heritage and Diving Villages** (Map pp386-7; ☎ 393 7151; off Al-Khaleej Rd; admission free; ☺ 8.30am-10.30pm Sun-Thu, 4.30-10.30pm Fri & Sat), re-creations of traditional villages with *barasti* houses, a camel yard, dhow, a pearling display, a souvenir souq and temporary exhibitions. Quiet during the day, they come alive in the evenings during the cooler months, especially during Ramadan and the Dubai Shopping Festival (see p442). At this time, you'll barely see a tourist or expat in sight. Every night, the villages are crowded with Emiratis who bring their children to see performances of traditional Bedouin dancing and singing, and re-enactments of traditional weddings from around the Gulf

region, along with displays on falconry and Arab horses, and – our favourite – rifle-throwing competitions!

Jumeirah Mosque

Dubai's beautiful **Jumeirah Mosque** (Map pp384-5; ☎ 353 6666; www.cultures.ae; Jumeirah Rd, Jumeirah; registration fee Dh10; ☺ 10am Sat, Sun, Tue & Thu), with its rose-coloured sandstone and intricately detailed architecture (stunningly lit at night), is the only mosque in the UAE open to non-Muslims. To appreciate its austere interior, however, you have to do one of the fascinating guided visits offered by the Sheikh Mohammed Centre for Cultural Understanding (see opposite). The tour introduces visitors to Islam, the mosque, the Five Pillars of Islam (see p61), and the ritual of prayer, starting outside with ablutions (washing before prayer) through to a demonstration of the prayer inside. A large part of the tour is taken up with an often fascinating Q&A session, where you can ask questions and have those myths dispelled. Prebook as the tour is becoming increasingly popular, and make sure to dress modestly: no shorts, sleeveless tops or tight clothes, and women should cover their back and arms and wear a long skirt and headscarf. There are *abeyyas* and *shaylas* available for loan at the mosque. You will also need to remove your shoes before entering.

Burj al-Arab

A visit to the **Burj al-Arab** (☎ 301 7777; Al-Jumeirah Rd, Umm Suqeim), Dubai's iconic 'seven-star' hotel, has become almost obligatory. While the ostentatious interior of the world's tallest dedicated hotel is nowhere near as impressive as the striking exterior (inspired by the sails of the traditional dhow boat), visitors to Dubai can't seem to resist taking a peak inside. You can't just wander around – it's necessary to book two to three days in advance for lunch, afternoon tea, cocktails or dinner, and you'll be given a confirmation number to present at the security gate.

Although you won't get to see a suite (for which prices range from Dh3500 to Dh25,000 per night), you will get to watch a 'water ballet' performed by the dancing fountains; be dazzled by a use of gold leaf worthy of Versailles; catch a magnificent

UNITED ARAB EMIRATES

TOP FIVE CONTEMPORARY BUILDINGS

- **Burj al-Arab** (p389) Dubai's landmark building was inspired by the sails of the dhow and Sheikh Mohammed's desire to create an iconic symbol for the city. Mission accomplished.

- **National Bank of Dubai** (Map pp384-5) Dominates the creek with its shield-like curve, and charms with its golden-hued reflections of creek traffic.

- **Emirates Towers** These two bottle openers on Sheikh Zayed Rd scream 'look at us' and we're always happy to oblige.

- **Dubai Creek Golf & Yacht Club** Refreshingly low-rise, its sculptural form is reminiscent of Sydney's Opera House.

- **Burj Dubai** It wasn't quite finished at the time of writing, however its elegant profile will make the Burj al-Arab a little jealous. Let's hope it gets a better interior design than Dubai's 'old' icon.

---

view of the Palm Island development and the rest of Dubai from the Al-Muntaha restaurant; whiz up and down the hotel's 27 floors in a panoramic lift travelling at six metres per second; and sip a cocktail in the gaudy Skyview bar. You'll need to dress for the occasion.

Ras Al Khor Wildlife Sanctuary

Despite the construction of Dubai Festival City close by, Dubai's beautiful pink flamingo population flocks to mangroves at **Ras Al Khor Wildlife Sanctuary** (☎ 338 2324; off Oud Metha Rd; admission free; ❨ 9am-4pm Sat-Thu), at the inland end of Dubai Creek. In fact, bird numbers are on the increase, with some 3000 flamingos dwelling there at the time of research. Wooden hides (viewing platforms) allow visitors to get a close-up view of the birds without disturbing them, and there are excellent, powerful binoculars available if you want to get even closer. The juxtaposition of these elegant birds framed against the Dubai metropolis is dramatic. The best time to visit is between November and April.

The sanctuary is on the way to Nad Al Sheba Horse Racing Club.

ACTIVITIES
Beaches

Sunbathing on Dubai's white-sand beaches with their crystal-clear turquoise waters is brilliant, however most tourists can't drag themselves away from the resort swimming pool, or more precisely, the wet bar. If you want to see how the local expat community plays, it's worth checking out the city's many free, clean public beaches. Wherever

you go take care swimming: the strong currents can be dangerous, not all of the public beaches are patrolled, and there have been a number of fatalities in the past.

The ever-popular **Open Beach** (Map pp384–5) is located next to Dubai Marine Beach Resort and Spa. It's also known as Russian Beach because it gets crowded with Russian package-tourists. On Fridays a large number of male guest workers hang out here on their day off. While it's safe, women won't always feel comfortable in their bikini, but there is a kiosk, showers and toilets.

Kite Beach at Umm Suqeim 4 is popular with Dubai's board-loving expats who enjoy kite surfing (hence the name). There are no facilities but women will be relaxed sunbathing here.

Umm Suqeim, between Kite Beach and Jumeirah Beach Hotel, has fabulous views of the Burj al-Arab and is popular with Jumeirah's expat families.

On the other side of town, there's a lovely long stretch of narrow white-sand beach at calm **Khor Al-Mamzar**, just before Al-Mamzar Park. While there are no waves, this is one of the prettiest spots to swim, with the Sharjah skyline in the distance. There are also showers and picnicking facilities.

For those who are prepared to pay an entrance fee, the private **Jumeirah Beach Park** (☎ 349 2555; adult Dh5, plus car Dh20; ❨ 8am-11pm), next to Jumeirah Beach Club, is a verdant beach park that gets busy on the weekends, when local families arrive en masse. There are lifeguards on duty, grassed picnic areas, barbecues, change rooms and playgrounds.

Spas

Dubai's splendid spas are renowned and a day of pampering is a wonderful way to end a trip, especially if you've been sweating it out on the back of a camel on a desert safari.

Get the 'Royal Treatment' (Dh380) at the **Oriental Hammam** (☎ 04 315 2140; www.oneandonlyroyalmirage.com; One&Only Royal Mirage Hotel, Al Sufouh Rd, Jumeirah; 9.30am-8pm), a traditional Moroccan-style ritual that includes a deep black-soap scrub, or head to **Cleopatra's Spa** (Map pp384-5; ☎ 324 7700; www.waficity.com; Wafi City Mall, Oud Metha, Bur Dubai; 8.30am-8pm) for a frangipani body wrap (Dh380). Guys can head next door to **Male Spa** (Map pp384-5; ☎ 324 0000; 9.30am-10pm) for a signature deep-tissue massage.

Wild Wadi Waterpark

The extraordinarily popular 4.8-hectare **Wild Wadi Waterpark** (☎ 348 4444; www.wildwadi.com; Jumeirah Rd, Umm Suqeim; adult/child day pass Dh165/135; 11am-6pm Nov-Feb, 11am-7pm Mar-May & Sep-Oct, 11am-9pm Jun-Aug), next to the Jumeirah Beach Hotel, features dozens of water rides and activities, some of which reach speeds of 80km/h. The rides are ingeniously interconnected, based on the legend of Arabic adventurer Juha and his friend, Sinbad the sailor, who are shipwrecked on a lush lagoon, beyond which lies a magical oasis.

There are height restrictions on some rides (children must be 1.1m tall to be allowed on the terrifying Jumeirah Sceirah and Tunnel of Doom), but the little ones love playing with the water cannons and slides at Juha's Dhow and Lagoon, and surfers will enjoy the two Flowriders (artificial waves). The water in the rides is cooled during the warmer months and there are fast-food eateries, making it a good day out. Food and beverages are bought via clever debit card attached to your wrist, and towels and lockers can be rented (Dh10).

During summer, the park is open one night a week (9pm to midnight) to women only.

Ski Dubai

Who doesn't want to say they skied at a resort in a shopping mall in the desert? Much to the surprise of many sceptics, since its opening in late 2005, **Ski Dubai** (☎ 409 4000; www.skidxb.com; Mall of the Emirates, Sheikh Zayed Rd, Interchange 4; ski slope day pass adult/child Dh230/180, 2hr Dh140/120, 1hr extension Dh30/20; Snowpark adult/child Dh60/50, private 'discovery' lesson 1hr Dh120, group lessons adult/child Dh165/145; 10am-11pm Sat-Tue, 10am-midnight Wed-Fri), one of the world's largest indoor snow parks, has been enormously successful. While it's a hot tourist attraction, local Emiratis are heading here in droves to take their kids tobogganing (many seeing snow for the first time) and to learn to ski and snowboard, while expats use the slopes as a warm-up for ski holidays. Ski Dubai has all the bases covered: a snowpark where the kids can build snowmen; a gentle beginners area; a couple of jumps to get airborne; a quarterpipe for snowboarders (Monday freestyle nights are popular with boarders); and a couple of good runs, including the world's first indoor 'black' run for those who like it steep.

There's a quad lift taking skiers and boarders up to two stations, and a magic carpet for beginners, so apart from the shopping mall outside the windows, it is just like a mini ski-resort. There are no chemicals in the snow – it's 'real' snow that falls overnight at around -10°C and is then groomed, with the temperature rising to a comfortable -1°C to -2°C for the day. The best bit about it, though, is that you only need to bring a hat and gloves – everything else is included in the price.

Camel Racing

Racing of the much beloved camel is a popular sport in the UAE. While it's not your traditional spectator sport – don't expect to seat yourself in a grandstand – a visit to the camel racetrack is worth the early wake-up call just to take in the atmosphere. Races start at around 7am on Friday and Saturday between October and April at the **Nad Al Sheba Camel Racecourse** (☎ 338 2324; off Oud Metha Rd; admission free). Watching these ships of the desert racing at speeds of up to 60km/h is quite a sight and really only matched by the rather erratic driving of the owners who race around the inside of the track in their 4WDs urging on their pride and joy.

While the use of child jockeys was a contentious issue in the past, the practice does not exist anymore in Dubai as robot jockeys are now used (see p57). If you're not in Dubai during racing season, head here around 5pm any day to watch the training.

The camel racecourse is near Nad Al Sheba Racing Club.

Horse Racing

Dubai's well-patronised **Nad Al Sheba Racing Club** (☎ 336 3666; wwwdubairacingclub.com; Nad Al Sheba, off Sheikh Zayed Rd; general admission Dh85), 5km southeast of Deira centre, is home to the world's richest horse race, the Dubai Cup, with its dizzying prize money of US$6 million. The culmination of the winter racing carnival held from February through to March, it's a very glam event with high-profile jockeys from all over the world competing, fabulously frocked and suited expats, and members of the ruling family resplendent in their crisp white *dishdashas* (men's shirt dress). Gambling is, of course, prohibited, but the members' stand is licensed, and there are different food and beverage packages available.

Other races are held from November to April; the racing schedule varies, so check racing dates and times with **Emirates Racing Association** (www.emiratesracing.com). Book ahead for dinner with spectacular views of the track at the Dubai Restaurant or **Millennium**

Granstand Views Restaurant (☎ 332 2277, 336 1410; range of packages available).

Keen racing enthusiasts should not miss the chance to do the **Godolphin Stable Tour** (☎ 336 3666; www.godolphin.com; adult Dh170; ⏰ 7am Sat, Mon & Wed Sep-Jun) to check out these world-class stables. Visitors get to watch the morning training, tour the thoroughbred training facilities, have a delicious breakfast in the clubhouse, visit the Millennium Grandstand, then tour the Godolphin Gallery, which has various displays documenting the development of Godolphin stables, and shelves full of trophies.

Desert Safaris

If you want to get out of the city, **Desert Safari** (Arabian Adventures; ☎ 971 4 303 8888; www .arabian-adventures.com; Emirates Holidays Building, Sheikh Zayed Rd) gives you the opportunity to experience some edge-of-your-seat off-road driving, sandboarding and camel riding in Dubai's gorgeous desert. You can also get some henna done, feast on an Arabic buffet, and join the belly dancer for a bit of a shimmy.

DUBAI'S ART SCENE

Dubai has a small but vibrant art scene with exhibitions of Middle Eastern art regularly changing. Unlike some big cities where the art scenes can be clicky, in Dubai the galleries are inclusive and their buzzy champagne openings are a great way to meet locals. Email the galleries for more details.

■ **Third Line** (☎ 394 3194; www.thethirdline.com; Al-Quoz; ⏰ 11am-8pm Sat-Thu, 4-8pm Fri) Dubai's most interesting gallery, run by young curators Sunny Rahbar and Claudia Cellini, opens its adventurous contemporary art exhibitions with splashy champagne launches. Expect everything from digital media by young Emiratis to photography by Iranian female artists. It's off Sheikh Zayed Rd, between Interchange 3 and 4.

■ **B21 Gallery** (☎ 340 3965; info@B21gallery.com; Al-Quoz; ⏰ 10am-2pm Sat-Thu, 5-8pm Fri) Palestinian artist Jeffar Khaldi shows his own work, as well as wonderful exhibitions of local and regional work, such as Egyptian Youssef Nabil's retro-looking portraits. The gallery is diagonally opposite the Third Line, off Sheikh Zayed Rd between Interchange 3 and 4.

■ **Art Space** (☎ 332 5523; info@artspace-dubai.com; 9th floor, Fairmont Hotel, Sheikh Zayed Rd; ⏰ 10am-8.30pm Sat-Thu) This refreshing commercial gallery has monthly exhibitions featuring contemporary Middle Eastern art, including Emirati art, such as Mohamed Kanoo's fun pop art.

■ **XVA** (Map pp386-7; ☎ 353 5383; xva@xvagallery.com; Al Musallah Roundabout; ⏰ 10am-8.30pm Sat-Thu) This peaceful gallery, café and boutique hotel in a restored courtyard house in the Bastakia holds regular exhibitions of art, sculpture and design, with buzzy openings. The gallery is behind Basta Art Café.

Also check the Dubai Cultural Council's website (www.dubaiculturalcouncil.ae) and *Time Out* for details on the latest exhibitions.

THE DESERT IN DUBAI

If you don't have time to get out of the city to explore the desert but want to experience a bit of the desert in Dubai, head to:

■ **Dubai Museum** (p388) Sit down on the sand with the Bedouin (mannequins) around the campfire under the starry sky in the 'Desert at Night' museum display.

■ **Heritage and Diving Villages** (p389) Do a couple of circuits on camel-back in the sandy yards at the back of the Heritage Village, then sit down on the ground in a Bedouin goat-hair tent for a cardamom coffee and chat with one of the local guys.

■ **Dubai Camel Racetrack** (p391) Admire the Afghani camel trainers – their heads wrapped in their *gutras* Lawrence of Arabia–style – perched atop their beasts as they lead a long train of camels across to the race track for practice. You'll have to turn away from the city skyline to get the sense you're out in the desert, but when you do, you'll find it hard to believe Sheikh Zayed Rd is just five minutes away.

COURSES

While Arabic is by no means essential to communicate in the UAE – and in fact, Urdu or Hindi would probably be more useful – you'll have a much greater chance of making friends with Emiratis and other Arabs if you can at least learn the lengthy greetings. Many people visit with the intention of learning Arabic but unfortunately many expats leave the country years later with one of their biggest regrets being not having learnt it. If you're keen to say more than *shukran*, enrol in private lessons or courses at one of the following:

Arabic Language Centre (☎ 308 6036; World Trade Centre, Sheikh Zayed Rd; one lesson Dh30; ☟ 8.30am-5pm)

Dubai International Art Centre (☎ 344 4398; 75b St; one lesson Dh30, course Dh270; ☟ 8.30am-7pm Sat-Wed, 8.30am-4pm Thu) The centre is located near Jumeirah Town Centre.

Sheikh Mohammed Centre for Cultural Understanding (Map pp386-7; ☎ 353 6666; www.cultures.ae; Bastakia) Gulf dialect only.

If you've been to see a belly dancer at one of Dubai's Arabic restaurants, and want to learn to shimmy like a pro, sign up for some belly-dancing lessons at the **JW Marriott Hotel's Griffins Health Club** (☎ 348 0000; one lesson Dh30, 10 lessons Dh270; ☟ 8-9pm Mon).

DUBAI FOR CHILDREN

Toddlers and teenagers alike love Dubai, and who's to blame them? There truly are few cities in the world so child friendly. Little kids love Juha's Dhow and Lagoon at **Wild Wadi Waterpark** (p391), the Storytelling

Tour at **Ibn Battuta Mall** (p399), the snow park at **Ski Dubai** (p391), the life-size dioramas at **Dubai Museum** (p388), Encounter Zone at **Wafi City Mall** (p399) and the playground at **Jumeirah Beach Park** (p390).

An **abra ride** (p387) down the creek will go down well, especially with an ice-cream stop at the end. All top-end and some midrange hotels have pools, and the beach resorts have kids clubs with organised activities. Teens will be just as happy snowboarding at **Ski Dubai** (p391), hanging out at the **beaches** (p390), or escaping from their folks in the **malls** (p399). With its myriad shops, fast-food eateries, cinemas and Ski Dubai, **Mall of the Emirates** (p399) is best for keeping kids busy, while **Deira City Centre** (p399), with the added bonus of a tenpin bowling alley and Magic Planet, comes a close second, followed by **Wafi City Mall** (p399).

SLEEPING

If you want to centre your energies on Dubai Creek, the souqs and heritage areas, stay in Deira or Bur Dubai. If you're looking for a restful stopover with sun and sand at the beginning or end of your trip, then head to Jumeirah Beach. Keep in mind that you'll only pay rack rates for midrange and top-end hotels in Dubai during the December/January high season; the rest of the time you'll get up to 50% off these rates, especially if you book online.

Budget

Dubai Youth Hostel (☎ 298 8151/61; uaeyha@emirates.net.ae; 39 Al-Nahda Rd, 2 Area; House A YHA members/nonmembers s Dh150/175, d Dh170/200, House B members/nonmembers dm Dh60/75, s Dh130/150, d Dh150/170; 🖳) While it's a fair way from the centre (catch bus 3, 13, 17 or 31), this is Dubai's only hostel and the great-value rooms and good facilities – pool, gym, sauna, spa, Jacuzzi, tennis court and billiards room – make it worth the trek. The spacious spotless en suites in the newer wing (Hostel A) beat Dubai's zero star hotels hands down, although the dorms in the older block (House B) are a bit like boarding school. Breakfast is included but keep snacks handy as there's little close by in the way of decent eating.

Gold Plaza Hotel (Map pp386–7; ☎ 225 0240; fax 225 0259; Souq Deira St, Deira; s/d Dh175/225) In an excellent location at the entrance to the always-tempting Gold Souq, guests are mainly East Africans here for a spot of trading. The small, simply furnished rooms haven't had a sniff of renovation in years, but they are clean. And while the staff amusingly proclaimed that they had 'no facilities' when we visited, at least there's air-conditioning.

Deira Palace Hotel (Map pp386–7; ☎ 229 0120; marwan32@emirates.net.ae; 67 St, Gold Souq area, Deira; s/d Dh200/250) This budget hotel, a block from the Gold Souq, has been surviving for years on business from African commercial travellers (coming to do business in the souqs) and the occasional backpacker looking for Deira action. While it's certainly no palace, the location is central and it has big clean rooms with views of the vibrant streets below.

Residence Baniyas Square by Le Meridien (Map pp386–7; ☎ 224 3888; Baniyas Sq, Deira; d Dh360) These strategically located studio apartments on Baniyas Sq are a bargain. While it feels like you're staying in a private apartment block (with no public spaces or facilities to speak of), who needs a coffee shop or room service when you have a 24-hour supermarket and a string of *shwarma* stands on your doorstep? The staff make up for the lack of facilities with friendly service, and the rooms are clean and have kitchenettes.

Ibis Hotel (☎ 318 7000; www.accor.com; Sheikh Zayed Rd; d Dh380; 🖳) While the groovy egg chairs in the lobby would win this Ibis awards for being the coolest chain hotel in the world, the rooms can be a tad tight if you've been doing some serious shopping. While there is no service to speak of, it's impossible to find a hotel that's cleaner or more comfortable for this price. A last-minute godsend, the Ibis is located behind the World Trade Centre.

Midrange

Al-Hijaz Motel (Map pp386–7; ☎ 225 0085; alhijaz motel.com; Deira; d incl breakfast Dh400; 🖳) Smack bang in the middle of Deira's heritage area next to Al-Ahmadiya School, this low-key hotel offers up the rare opportunity to stay in a heritage house, with clean, huge rooms. Book well ahead.

Ramee Hotel Apartments (Map pp386–7; ☎ 352 2277; rameeapt@eim.ae; Rolla Rd, Bur Dubai; d studio Dh400) Well situated in Bur Dubai – just a 10-minute stroll to the creek and souqs – these clean, spacious self-contained studios are excellent for short stays, with a fridge, microwave, washing machine/dryer and stove-top. While the official rack rate would (amusingly) put this place in the top-end category, you'll only pay these for a few weeks in December/January – you'll generally get a room online for around Dh300.

Orient Guest House (Map pp386–7; ☎ 351 9111; info@arabiancourtyard.com; off Al-Fahidi St; d Dh550) This new boutique hotel is one of only two hotels in restored old buildings in the Bastakia area (the other being XVA). Each room is individually decorated in a traditional Arabian or Indian style (with big, spotless bathrooms), but guests prefer chilling out in the charming courtyards. Service is personable and the atmosphere intimate, but the highlight is hearing the call-to-prayer echoing through the labyrinthine streets.

Arabian Courtyard Hotel (Map pp386–7; ☎ 351 9111; www.arabiancourtyard.com; Al-Fahidi St, Bur Dubai; d Dh600; 🖳) Situated in an excellent location in the heart of Bur Dubai, overlooking Dubai Museum (and with interesting Dubai Creek views from the top floors), this comfortable hotel has spacious rooms with polished wooden floors, heavy teak furniture, and leather window seats. While there are myriad cheap eats in the surrounding streets (everything from Russian fare to *shwarma*), the hotel has a couple of terrific restaurants, including Mumtaz Mahal (p396), Silk Route (serving tasty Chinese–Thai), and Tex-Mex eatery Barry's Bench.

Riviera Hotel (Map pp386–7; ☎ 222 2131; riviera@ emirates.net.ae; Baniyas Rd, Deira; d incl breakfast Dh600; 🖳) This creek stalwart has one of the best addresses in Deira, in the heart of the action. After a sweaty stroll through the souqs you will probably be wishing you were staying next door at the Carlton Tower with its big swimming pool, but this is still a good choice if you are after creek views.

Top End
CITY HOTELS

XVA (Map pp386-7; ☎ 353 5383; www.xvagallery.com; Al-Fahidi St, Bastakia; d incl breakfast Dh750) This stylish boutique hotel in a restored wind-tower building in the historic Bastakia is a triple treat with its contemporary gallery and courtyard café. Rooms are decorated in a minimalist style with traditional Emirati touches, like the sheer curtain over the four-poster bed, made from the elegant black cloak sheikhs wear over their *dishdashas* to social functions. An added bonus is that there are no noisy distractions like TV.

Marco Polo Hotel (Map pp384-5; ☎ 272 0000; www.marcopolohotel.net; Al-Mateena St, Deira; d with breakfast Dh800; 🖳 🕿) Comfortable rooms at this four-star hotel can be had for half this price outside of high season. While the location is out of the way for those interested in Jumeirah action, it's ideal if you want to focus on the Deira souqs and heritage areas, and beautiful Al Mamzar Beach is five minutes away. While Al-Mateena (one of Dubai's hidden gems) is lined with Iraqi and Persian kebab restaurants, the hotel has several super restaurants, the excellent Chopstix (p396) and Indian eatery Bombay, offering a similar experience to Mumtaz Mahal.

Radisson SAS Dubai Media City (☎ 366 9111; www.mediacity.dubai.radissonsas.com; Dubai Media City; d Dh950; 🖳 🕿) This chic new four-star in the heart of Dubai Media City has luxe rooms with all mod cons, including complimentary wi-fi. Attracting young creative types here to do business, it's ideal for travellers who aren't fans of the beach but want to experience 'new Dubai'. There's a fabulous rooftop bar, Tamanya Terrace (p398) and an outstanding Italian restaurant, Certo.

Hilton Dubai Creek (Map pp384-5; ☎ 227 1111; www.hilton.com; Baniyas Rd, Deira; d Dh1100; 🖳 🕿) Still one of the coolest creekside addresses, this stylish hotel by Carlos Ott (architect of the Opera la Bastille in Paris) offers its guests relief from the over-the-top opulence everywhere else. The rooms are spacious and beds divine – wonderful to crawl into

after a dégustation menu at the hotel's splendid Verre (see p396). Ask for a room with views of the creek.

BEACH HOTELS

Dubai's five-star beach resorts on Jumeirah Beach between Umm Suqeim and Jebel Ali are 25 minutes from the Deira Centre in good traffic and up to 45 minutes during peak hour. Taxis cost Dh40 to Dh50, although most hotels provide complimentary shuttle buses from the airport and into Deira.

our pick One&Only Royal Mirage (☎ 399 9999; www.oneandonlyresorts.com; Al-Sufouh Rd, Jumeirah; d Dh1740; 🖳 🕿) This Moroccan-style resort is Dubai's most romantic with plush rooms and enormous marble bathrooms. Splendidly set in verdant gardens with trickling fountains, still ponds and gorgeous peacocks wandering about, it's like something out of *The Thousand and One Nights*. There are sprawling palm-shaded swimming pools, a pristine white-sand beach overlooking Palm Island, and an opulent Givenchy spa with *hammam* (bathhouse). Add to that several exceptional restaurants: Tagine (p396), Eauzone and Nina; Dubai's atmospheric Rooftop Bar (p398); and the palm-filled Sheesha Courtyard (p397). You won't want to leave.

Mina A'Salam (☎ 366 8888; www.jumeirah.com; Jumeirah Rd, Umm Suqeim; d Dh1800; 🖳 🕿) This magnificent Arabian-inspired resort is situated within the sprawling Madinat Jumeirah complex that also houses myriad restaurants, bars, clubs, a souq, theatre and the opulent Al Qasr hotel. The elegant rooms incorporate traditional touches, such as Bedouin textiles and Arabian antiques, and have balconies with wonderful views of the Burj al-Arab and the sea.

EATING
Restaurants

Bastakiah Nights (Map pp386-7; ☎ 353 7772; Bastakia, Bur Dubai; mains Dh26; 🕙 10am-11pm Sat-Thu, 3-10pm Fri) While this traditionally decorated restaurant in a restored Bastakia courtyard house serves up tasty Arabic food, the atmosphere is the highlight, especially at night when you can climb to the rooftop for fine views over the old quarter to the creek. The restaurant is unlicensed, and is located near Al-Fahadi roundabout.

Noodle House (☎ 319 8757; Emirates Towers Hotel, Sheikh Zayed Rd; mains Dh35; ☯ noon-midnight) Dubai's diners don't mind putting their names down on the door (no bookings) and heading across to the Agency for a drink while they wait for a table. The tasty appetisers, delicious pan-Asian dishes, and generous bowls of noodles are great value by any standards and definitely worth the wait. The Asian beers and New World wines by the glass are also reasonably priced.

Chopstix (Map pp384-5; ☎ 272 0000; Marco Polo Hotel, Al-Mateena St, Deira; mains Dh35; ☯ lunch & dinner) Chef Richard's Indian–Chinese heritage is evident in the fusion menu that features both classic Hong Kong–Chinese dishes and some creative variations influenced by his upbringing, and time spent training at the Taj Bengal. The crackling spinach (thin strips of deep-fried spinach sprinkled with sesame seeds and salt; Dh28) is a flavour sensation; the melt-in-your-mouth salt-and-pepper squid the best we'd ever had; dry beef with chilli garlic is truly delicious; and the crispy chilli potatoes heavenly.

YUM! (Map pp386-7; ☎ 222 7171; Radisson Deira Creek, Baniyas St; mains Dh36; ☯ noon-1am) Deira's version of Noodle House is popular with local workers and souq shoppers who pack the place out at lunch. The gorgeous displays of fresh vegetables and colourful spices are a good indicator of what to expect: fresh, fast, tasty dishes. The authentic *char kway teow* is our favourite.

Mumtaz Mahal (Map pp386-7; ☎ 351 9111; Arabian Courtyard Hotel, Bur Dubai; mains Dh45; ☯ 12.30-3pm & 7.30pm-2am) This atmospheric North Indian restaurant, decorated like a fort palace with heavy, carved teak furniture, serves excellent spicy Mughlai cuisine (we love the smoky tandoor specialities), but diners come as much for the entertainment as the food. The five-piece Indian *ghazal* band with their magical yet melancholy dancers can distract from the food. Settle in for the night; song requests from the Indian expat diners come streaming in around midnight and that's when things really start to heat up. The restaurant is opposite Dubai Museum.

Tagine (☎ 399 9999; the Palace at One&Only Royal Mirage; mains Dh70; ☯ dinner Tue-Sun) For those who've visited Marrakesh, this atmospheric restaurant will bring back memories. For those who haven't we've just saved you an airfare. From the authentic pigeon *pastilla* (sweet pastry stuffed with pigeon and aromatic spices and dusted with icing sugar) to tasty 'Couscous Royal' and melt-in-your-mouth lamb tagine with prunes, the flavours are straight from Morocco. As an added bonus, there are excellent Moroccan musicians, so book a table near them if you're fond of Maghrebi music. Don't leave without tasting the fragrant, fresh-mint tea flamboyantly poured in the traditional style, and checking out the bathroom. Book ahead.

our pick **Verre** (Map pp384-5; ☎ 212 7551; Hilton Dubai Creek, Baniyas Rd, Rigga; mains Dh90; ☯ dinner Sun-Fri) While there have been plenty of over-hyped pretenders to the throne, Gordon Ramsey's Verre (the chef's first overseas venture, which opened in 2001) remains peerless for its outstanding quality of cuisine, its attentive and efficient service, and Dubai's only true sommelier, Luca Gagliardi. While some are disappointed by the apparent simplicity of the food, it's exactly that – the purity, and delicate and clever combination of flavours – that is so impressive. Book well ahead.

Cafés

Basta Art Café (Map pp386-7; ☎ 353 5071; Al-Fahidi St, Bastakia; meals Dh28; ☯ 8am-8pm Sat-Thu) This leafy courtyard café, located in a restored wind-tower house, is one of Dubai's most characterful and makes an ideal spot for refuelling after a Bastakia walk. The fresh juices are renowned and there's none more refreshing than the 'Basta Special' (Dh16) made from fresh lime and mint. The big salads bring the regulars back, with the grilled haloumi, asparagus and mixed lettuce salad (which also includes avocado, green beans and mustard dressing) being a favourite (Dh28). The café is unlicensed.

Fudo (☎ 344 8896; 73a St, off Jumeirah Beach; mains Dh35; ☯ 8am-2am) The idea behind this stylish living room-style café actually works – it's the kind of place where you can sink into a comfy sofa and linger a while, grab a quick bite to eat if you're in a hurry, sit down at a long table with a bunch of friends, or settle in for a long night of *sheesha*-smoking. The global menu, spanning Thai, Japanese, Italian and Lebanese, is great, with a wide selection to suit all tastes. Try the crispy barbecue duck spring rolls (Dh22) and refreshing *som tam* (papaya, shrimp and roast peanut salad; Dh25) if you just want a light snack. The café is adjacent to Mercato Mall, and is unlicensed.

Almaz by Momo (☎ 409 8877; Mall of the Emirates; mains Dh40; ☼ 10am-midnight) This atmospheric Moroccan salon is a wonderful place to linger. Drop by at any time of day – there's a breakfast menu from 10am to noon, and delicious *kemia* (Moroccan mezze) all day (try the tangy red capsicum and tomato *mechouia* dip). The afternoon tea from 3pm to 5.30pm includes a selection of fresh Marrakesh Berber pancakes and Maghrebine pastries with Moroccan mint tea (Dh70). Don't leave without sticking your head into the *sheesha* café, and the fine-dining restaurant. The salon adjoins Harvey Nichols, and is unlicensed.

Quick Eats

These might take the form of a worker's cafeteria where a cook slops curries on a hot plate from a big pot, to an Arabic eatery serving *shwarma* and felafel at a stand out front. While they're cheap, they're not always cheerful, and they don't serve alcohol.

Ashwaq Cafeteria (Map pp386-7; cnr Al-Soor St & Sikkat al-Khail Rd, Deira; ☼ noon-2am) If you've been shopping the Deira souqs for hours, Ashwaq, on the corner of the Perfume Souq, is the ideal place to refuel. Pull up a white plastic chair, sip on a fresh mango juice (Dh7), try a scrumptious chicken *shwarma* (Dh3.50) and take in the Deira scene.

Nefertiti Restaurant (Map pp386-7; ☎ 355 8855; Khalid Bin Al-Waleed St, Bur Dubai; ☼ 24hr) Serving an odd combination of home-cooked Russian food and Arabic cuisine, this busy cafeteria is also a drop-in centre for Dubai's Russian community, who come to borrow the magazines, books and DVDs stacked up against the wall. Try a hearty portion of meat pelmeni (Dh14) or *pirojki kartoshkoi* (potato dumplings; Dh7) or go for an Arabic mixed grill (Dh30). Nefertiti is opposite Four Points Sheraton.

Al Mallah (☎ 398 4723; Al Dhiyafah St, Satwa; ☼ 6am-4am) Serving some of the most delicious *shwarmas* (Dh3.50) around, along with excellent Lebanese food, this busy eatery with shady outdoor seating is a great choice for a quick snack.

Self-Catering

There are supermarkets, big and small, on every street corner in Dubai. The supermarket with the largest variety and the best prices is the colossal **Carrefour** (Map pp384-5; ☎ 295 1010; Garhoud, Deira; ☼ 10am-10pm Sat-Thu, 2-10pm Fri), which has the best bakery and deli counter in town, with barrels of delicious olives and Arabic cheeses, and the best-quality fruit and vegetables. Note, there are many cheaper supermarkets, such as Choitrams, but when it comes to fresh fruit and veg you could feel like you're digging around in a backstreet garbage bin because the quality is so awful. Carrefour also has a huge range of products from Europe, Australia and North America, if you're missing some of your favourites from home.

Sheesha Cafés

Smoking fragrant *sheesha* (flavoured tobacco, also known as nargileh, hookah and hubbly bubbly) with friends is an integral part of social life in the Emirates, whether it's at a grungy neighbourhood coffeehouse or an atmospheric courtyard café in a luxury hotel.

Kanzaman (Map pp386-7; ☎ 393 9913; Al-Shindagha; ☼ 4.30pm-2.30am) There are some experiences that are quintessentially Dubai and this is one of them: joining local Emiratis and Arab expats smoking fragrant *sheesha* under the starry sky, while you watch the dhow cruise boats drift by. Aaahh. If you're peckish try a tangy lamb *shwarma* (Dh5). Kanzaman in unlicensed, and is adjacent to the Heritage and Diving Villages.

Sheesha Courtyard (☎ 399 9999; the Palace at One&Only Royal Mirage; ☼ 6pm-2am) Smoke some *sheesha* as you recline on cushions strewn about on Persian carpets in an enchanting palm-filled courtyard, the date palms twinkling above you, and you could be forgiven for thinking you're in paradise.

Tché Tché (Map pp386-7; ☎ 355 7575; Bank St, Bur Dubai; ☼ 10am-2am Sat-Thu, 3pm-2am Fri) If the exotic Oriental atmosphere isn't your glass of tea, head here for a *sheesha* with the Arab expats who are keeping it real at this street corner café with Lebanese music videos blaring. It's near BurJuman Mall.

QDs (Map pp384-5; ☎ 295 6000; Dubai Creek Golf & Yacht Club; ☼ 6pm-2am) Overlooking Dubai Creek, QDs is a sprawling one-of-a-kind *sheesha* spot that somehow manages to feel like your regular neighbourhood pub and an exotic *sheesha* café at the same time.

DRINKING

Irish Village (Map pp384–5; ☎ 282 4750; Dubai Tennis Stadium, Al-Garhoud Rd; ☉ 11am-1.30am) While the kitsch Irish-pub façade still has us shaking our heads after all these years, the Irish Village nevertheless attracts a regular Anglo expat crowd, from airline crew to teachers, who come to down beers in the big beer garden by the duck pond.

Tamanya Terrace (☎ 366 9111; Radisson SAS Hotel, Dubai Media City, Jumeirah; ☉ 5pm-2am) The spectacular views at sunset as the lights from the skyscrapers of 'New Dubai' go on are sufficient reason to settle in here for a drink, but locals love Friday's 'Favela Chic' night when Dubai's Latino community turn this rooftop lounge bar into a salsa club.

Bahri Bar (☎ 366 8888; Mina A'Salam Hotel, Jumeirah; ☉ 6pm-2am) While most come for the stunning views of the Burj al-Arab, we just love the wonderful veranda covered in Oriental carpets and comfy cane sofas, perfect for sinking into with a chilled glass of white as you watch the sunset. If it's too hot outside, the Arabian-inspired interior is attractive, but we prefer to sweat it out.

Rooftop Bar (☎ 399 9999; Arabian Court, One&Only Royal Mirage, Al-Sufouh Rd, Jumeirah; ☉ 6pm-2am) Call ahead and book the corner cushion-covered banquette seat for sunset and settle in for the night. This candle-lit rooftop bar, with its Moroccan lanterns, Persian carpets, and DJ Stickyfinger's Oriental chill-out music, is one of Dubai's most atmospheric.

our pick **Sho Cho's** (Map pp384–5; ☎ 346 1111; Dubai Marine Beach Resort & Spa, Jumeirah Rd, Jumeirah; ☉ 7pm-3am) Long the city's coolest bar for its laid-back vibe, it's during Dubai's winter months when it's really special, when the cool ocean breezes blow and the DJ spins on the wooden deck outside to a background soundtrack of waves crashing on the beach. Simply sublime.

ENTERTAINMENT
Nightclubs

With high-profile international DJs hitting town on a regular basis, Dubai's nightlife has become as much of a magnet as its shopping. **iBO** (Map pp384–5; ☎ 398 2206; www.9714.com; Airport Millennium Hotel, Al-Garhoud, Deira; ☉ 10pm-3am)

attracts a casual crowd to its retro interior for the laid-back vibe and interesting music. Super-club **Trilogy** (☎ 366 6917; www.trilogy.ae; Madinat Jumeirah, Jumeirah; ☉ 10pm-3am), Dubai's hottest dance club, attracts top DJs such as Mylo and Armand Van Helden and a mixed crowd of multicultural clubbers to its Deep nights (www.deepnights.net). Buy tickets in advance to avoid long queues.

The clubs of the moment are den-like **Apartment** (☎ 406 8000; Jumeirah Beach Hotel, Sheikh Zayed Rd; ☉ 8pm-3am) and summery rooftop bar-club **360 degrees** (☎ 352 3500; Jumeirah Beach Hotel, Sheikh Zayed Rd; ☉ 5pm-2am), popular for Friday sundowners, but ironically only doable in the cooler months when the temperatures aren't rising about 40 degrees. The seriously glam hit Friday night's **Peppermint Club** (☎ 332 0037; www.peppermint-club .com; Fairmont Dubai Hotel, Sheikh Zayed Rd; ☉ 10pm-3am Fri) while **Blush** (Map pp384–5; ☎ 324 8200; Wafi City Mall, enter through Ginseng bar; ☉ 10pm-3am Thu) is attracting a more down-to-earth crowd for its funky house. The airline crew and hospitality industry staff like to party at **Zinc** (☎ 331 1111; Crowne Plaza Hotel, Sheikh Zayed Rd; ☉ 10pm-3am). Worth a look for something different if you're at the Sheesha Courtyard is adjoining **Kasbar** (☎ 399 9999; One&Only Royal Mirage, Al-Sufouh Rd, Jumeirah), an Arabian Nights–style club attracting a sophisticated Arab expat set.

Entry fees to clubs vary – even in the one night; you can get in for free before 10pm, pay a ticket price after 10pm, then a higher one after midnight. Some clubs are free on certain nights, but when they do charge prices can range from Dh50 to Dh150 for top DJs, but may include a drink. 'Ladies' often get in free. Sign up for guest lists at www.platinumlistdubai.com. Check the listings in *Time Out* for what's on, and buy tickets online (at www.timeouttickets.com, www.boxofficeme.com or www.itptickets .com) so you don't miss out.

Live Music

If you're after live music, sink into a bean bag, get stuck into the barbecue, and enjoy the jam sessions at **Peanut Butter Jam** (Map pp384–5; ☎ 324 4100; www.waficityrestaurants.com; Wafi City Rooftop Gardens; admission free; ☉ 8pm-late Fri).

The stylish **Jambase** (☎ 366 6550; Souq Madinat Jumeirah, Al-Sufouh Rd, Jumeirah; ☉ 7pm-2am) is the place to head for live jazz, R&B and soul, and the bands know how to work a crowd.

Cinemas

You can catch English-language flicks, Bollywood movies or subtitled films from the Middle East at the multiplexes at most malls. Ticket prices are Dh35, with some cinemas offering Dh20 tickets before 6pm.

Cinestar (Map pp384-5; ☎ 294 9000; Deira City Centre)

Cinestar at Mall of the Emirates (Map pp384-5; ☎ 341 4222; Mall of the Emirates, Sheikh Zayed Rd)

Grand Cineplex (☎ 324 2000; Garhoud) Located next to Wafi City Mall.

Theatre

Dubai's performing arts scene has taken off in the last couple of years with the opening of **Madinat Theatre** (☎ 366 6546; Souq Madinat Jumeirah, Al-Sufouh Rd, Jumeirah) and **Dubai Community Theatre & Arts Centre** (☎ 341 4777; www .ductac.org; Mall of the Emirates, Sheikh Zayed Rd), both of which offer a full programme of theatre, classical music, opera, ballet, musicals and comedy.

SHOPPING
Shopping Malls

In today's UAE, the mall is the modern-day equivalent of the traditional souq, a place where Emiratis socialise, relax, do business and, of course, shop. While nationals still shop in the traditional souqs in Deira and Bur Dubai (nobody drives a bargain as hard as an Emirati woman!) they've taken malls to their hearts, revelling in the abundance

of multibrand stores, boutiques and cafés on offer. It helps, of course, that Dubai's malls are air-conditioned and offer ample parking and myriad eateries.

The most popular are sights in themselves: Wafi City is housed within kitsch Egyptian pyramids; Ibn Battuta Mall has domes and arches to rival Isfahan's, a life-size Chinese junk, and starry skies; while Mercato is an ersatz Italian city with piazza and arcades.

Deira City Centre (Map pp384-5; ☎ 295 1010; Garhoud, Deira; ✆ 10am-10pm Sat-Thu, 2-10pm Fri) Has a Carrefour supermarket, electronics stores, global fashion franchises, an amusement centre and cinema complex.

Ibn Battuta Mall (☎ 362 1900; Sheikh Zayed Rd, Jebel Ali; ✆ 10am-10pm Sat-Tue, 10am-10pm Wed-Fri) Houses many of the same shops as the other malls, but is distinguished by its extravagantly themed malls-within-a-mall representing the countries that 14th-century Arab traveller Ibn Battuta visited.

Mall of the Emirates (☎ 295 1010; Sheikh Zayed Rd, Interchange 4; ✆ 10am-10pm Sat-Thu, 2-10pm Fri) Dubai's biggest, with every kind of store imaginable, cinemas and Ski Dubai (see p391).

Mercato (☎ 344 4161; ✆ 10am-10pm Sat-Thu, 2-10pm Fri) With a Spinneys supermarket, fashion boutiques and a plethora of coffee shops.

Wafi City Mall (Map pp384-5; ☎ 324 4555; Garhoud, Oud Metha; ✆ 10am-10pm Sat-Thu, 4.30-10pm Fri) Specialising in exclusive boutiques, with several of Dubai's best bars and restaurants.

Souqs

For a contrast to the exuberance of the malls, visit the city's many traditional

---

THE REAL DUBAI

Forget gold souqs, oil wells and cargo-laden wooden dhows: nothing symbolises modern-day Dubai quite like the shopping mall. It's easy to snigger at these exercises in commercial kitsch, but they say a lot about the city and its residents. The mall coffee shops are a great example. You'll see glamorous Emirati women clad in designer clothes and filmy *abeyya* enjoying animated conversation with girlfriends over cappuccinos – hardly the cliché of the silent, sequestered woman many travellers expect. At the next table Emirati businessmen in spotless white *dishdashas* might hold a power meeting over espresso.

This modern-day version of the age-old Gulf custom of doing business over coffee is a potent symbol of how the traditional and modern seamlessly merge in Dubai. Then there are the gaggles of giggling teenage girls sipping soft drinks, chaperoned by brothers who are trying to assert their authority while at the same time being teased by their little sisters' flirtatious friends. Despite their responsibilities, these adolescent boys are as embarrassed by this as older brothers the world over.

These malls are where the true lifeblood of the city flows – be sure to visit at least one during your stay.

atmospheric souqs, located on either side
of the creek. Over the last couple of centuries, wares from the Far East, India and
the rest of the Arabian Peninsula have been
making their way to Dubai by dhow, and
into the souqs. Fragrant spices and gold
from India, richly textured carpets from
Iran, and shimmering silks from China are
still traded today, along with electronics,
kitchenware and clothes. As elsewhere in
the Middle East, everyone bargains: the key
is to keep your transaction good-natured
and be certain that you're haggling over
something you really want.

In Deira, the glittering Gold Souq (p388)
is a must-see, along with the tiny Perfume
Souq (p388), the aromatic Spice Souq
(p388) and the Deira Covered Souq (p388;
mainly selling homeware but vibrant all the
same). In the same area, the Fish, Fruit &
Vegetable Souq is worth a look to see what
the locals are eating, while in Bur Dubai, the
attractive wooden covered alleys of the Bur
Dubai Textile Souq (p388) are a wonderful
place to while away an hour. If you want to
have some clothes tailor-made, this is where
to do it.

Other Shopping Spots
For cheap electronics and digital products
try Al-Fahidi St in Dur Dubai and Al-Sabkha Rd near Baniyas Sq, although the best
prices can often be found at Carrefour Supermarket at Deira City Centre. For fake
designer goods (usually kept under the
counter) and cheap souvenirs, Al Karama
is the place to head. Other spots worth trying for souvenirs, carpets and handicrafts,
including Bedouin silver jewellery and
khanjars, are the Arabian Treasures arcade
section in Deira City Centre; Baniyas Rd
near the *abra* station; the Dubai Museum
gift shop; and the shops in the Heritage
Village at Shindagha. For carpets, try Deira
Tower and Dubai Tower on Baniyas Sq.

GETTING THERE & AWAY
Air
Dubai international airport (☎ 224 5252, flight
inquiries 216 6666; www.dubaiairport.com) The busiest air
hub in the Middle East, with a famed duty-free selection.
Emirates Airlines (Map pp384-5; ☎ 214 4444; www
.emirates.com; DNATA Airline Centre, Al-Maktoum Rd,
Deira; ☺ 9am-6pm Sat-Thu) There's another office on
Sheikh Zayed Rd, Bur Dubai.

Bus
Dubai's Roads and Transport Authority (RTA; ☎ 800
9090; www.rta.ae) operates all buses within
Dubai emirate and runs an hourly bus
service to Hatta (Dh7, 90 minutes). Bus 16
leaves for Hatta every hour from Al-Sabkha
bus station from 6am to 9.35pm.

Dubai Transport (☎ Bur Dubai 393 7014, Deira
227 0718; www.dubaitransport.com) runs regular
minibus services to other destinations in
the UAE. The buses are clean but cramped.
Only the Sharjah service returns passengers to Dubai. From other destinations,
you have to take a local taxi or bus for the
return trip.

The following services operate from
6.30am to 10pm and leave from the Deira
minibus station near the intersection of Omar
ibn al-Khattab and Al-Rigga Rds, Rigga.

Destination	Frequency	Cost	Duration
Ajman	every 20min	Dh7	1½-2hr
Sharjah	every 20min	Dh5	1-1½hr
Fujairah	every 60min	Dh25	2½hr
Ras al-Khaimah	every 60min	Dh20	2hr
Umm al-Quwain	every 60min	Dh10	1½hr

Dubai Transport (along with Al Ghazal
Transport) runs minibuses to Abu Dhabi and
Al-Ain from 7am to 10pm, departing from
the Bur Dubai bus station on Al-Ghubaiba
Rd. It's also possible to catch a bus to Shar-
jah from this station.

Destination	Frequency	Cost	Duration
Abu Dhabi	every 30min	Dh15	2hr
Al-Ain	every 60min	Dh20	1½hr
Sharjah	every 15min	Dh5	1-1½hr

By far, the most popular service between
Dubai and Abu Dhabi is the **Emirates Express**
(☎ 800 4848) jointly operated by Dubai Public
Transport and Abu Dhabi Public Transport.
There are 24 services daily, from 6.20am
until 11.40pm, seven days a week (Dh15 one
way). Buses depart every 20 to 40 minutes,
from the Bur Dubai bus station, taking two
hours. You can pick up a comprehensive
bus timetable from the bus stations.

Car
Dubai has scores of car-rental agencies,
from major global companies to no-name

local businesses. The former may charge slightly more but you get peace of mind knowing that you can get full insurance and that they'll get you out of a fix if you need assistance. In our experience, Europcar offers the best combination of low prices and efficient service – it will even drop the car at your hotel or home, which other companies don't do.

Avis www.avis.com; airport ☎ 224 5219; head office ☎ 295 7121

Budget www.budget.com; airport ☎ 224 5192; head office ☎ 282 3030)

Europcar www.europcar-dubai.com; airport ☎ 224 5240; head office ☎ 339 4433)

Hertz www.hertz-uae.com; airport ☎ 224 5222; head office ☎ 282 4422

Long-Distance Taxi

From the Bur Dubai bus station, you can catch a shared taxi to Sharjah for Dh20. To Abu Dhabi, a seat in a shared taxi will cost Dh25. If you decide to engage a cab for yourself, you'll pay around Dh150 in a regular long-distance taxi, which may not have air-conditioning. The plush **Al Ghazal Transport** (☎ Abu Dhabi 02-444 7787) taxis provide a more efficient and comfortable service from Dubai to Abu Dhabi (Dh180), Abu Dhabi to Dubai (Dh275), Dubai to Al-Ain (Dh275), and Al-Ain to Dubai (Dh175). **National Taxis** (☎ 02-622 3300) also travels from Abu Dhabi to Dubai (Dh 225), and Dubai to Abu Dhabi (Dh150).

GETTING AROUND
To/From the Airport

Only the sand-coloured Dubai Transport taxis are allowed to pick up passengers at the airport, and they impose a Dh20 surcharge on top of the metered fare. In total, it will cost about Dh30 to Dh35 to Deira Souq area (from 10 to 20 minutes depending on traffic) and Dh40 to Dh45 to Bur Dubai (around 15 to 30 minutes, again depending on the time of day). Fares to Sheikh Zayed Rd will start at around Dh40 (15 to 25 minutes), and to Jumeirah, Umm Suqeim and the beachside suburbs from Dh50 to Dh60, and take from 20 to 40 minutes depending on traffic. Fares to the airport from these destinations will be Dh20 cheaper, as they don't include the surcharge.

There are two 24-hour municipal **airport bus services** (☎ 800 9090) running every 30

minutes to Deira (route 401) and Bur Dubai (route 402). The fare on both is Dh3 and the round trip takes one hour. These buses stop at centrally located bus and taxi stands at Al-Khor St and Al-Sabkha Rd in Deira, and in Al-Ghubaiba Rd in Bur Dubai.

Abra

Dubai's Roads and Transport Authority runs the city's *abra* service, operating from early morning until midnight. To cross the creek by *abra* costs Dh1 (pay onboard) and there are three set routes, all ideally positioned for creek walks.

- **Route one** Leaves Deira from the Deira Old Souq Abra Station and goes to the Bur Dubai Abra Station, near the Bank of Baroda.
- **Route two** Leaves Deira from Al-Sabkha Abra Station and goes to the Bur Dubai Old Souq Abra Station in Bur Dubai.
- **Route three** Leaves the brand spanking-new Baniyas Abra Station near Arbift Tower and Dubai Municipality and goes to the new Al-Seef Abra Station.

Bus

The Roads and Transport Authority also runs an efficient city bus network, although unfortunately Western expat residents don't use it much and it's predominantly used by low-income guest workers. As a result, women travelling solo may feel uncomfortable. It's best to sit in the women's section at the front of the bus to avoid harassment. From the main bus stations on Al-Ghubaiba Rd in Bur Dubai or Al-Khor St in Deira you'll be able to catch a bus to most destinations in the city. Fares range from Dh1 to Dh3.50 and services are frequent. Numbers and routes are posted on the buses in English as well as in Arabic.

Taxi

Taxis around town are metered and are thick on the ground. Fares start at Dh3. If you come across a non-metered taxi, it's most likely from Sharjah or a northern Emirate, and it's illegal for the driver to collect a fare from Dubai; if you choose to take one of these, you'll have to negotiate a fare but if the driver tries to rip you off you don't stand a chance with the authorities. Women travelling unaccompanied after dark shouldn't use these taxis.

You can also phone **Dubai Transport** (☎ 208 0808) to book a taxi. If you ask for a taxi at a five-star hotel, you may be shown to an unmarked limo; ask the fare before getting in, as these are often double the price of a standard taxi, or ask for a Dubai Transport taxi.

AROUND DUBAI

Dubai has two heavenly desert retreats less than an hour from the city that are highly recommended if you want to experience the desert in luxury.

Al-Maha Desert Resort & Spa

Situated just 65km southeast of Dubai, **Al-Maha Desert Resort & Spa** (☎ 303 4224; www.al-maha.com) is a wonderful eco-tourism resort that is part of the Dubai Desert Conservation Reserve (DDCR). Al-Maha is named after the Arabic word for the endangered scimitar-horned oryx, which is bred successfully as part of the DDCR's programme.

The resort offers 40 suites and two royal suites, all luxurious, stand-alone, tent-roofed structures that come with their own large, chilled private plunge pool. Each suite has a patio with stunning vistas of the beautiful desert landscape and peach-coloured dunes, dotted by the shapes of the beautiful white oryx happily grazing on small tufts of desert grass.

There are myriad activities included in the price, from desert wildlife drives to see the oryx up close, to sunset camel rides where you're rewarded with champagne and strawberries as you watch the sun go down over the dunes. However, the resort really excels at the romantic rather than the social. Private vehicles, visitors and children under 12 are not allowed at the resort, and taking meals at your suite – or at a dining table in the desert – rather than in the dining room is a popular choice. If you can't rekindle a romance here, then sorry guys, but it's probably over.

Transfers can be arranged, or if you're driving, directions can be given upon booking.

Bab Al Shams Desert Resort & Spa

The Arabian-style **Bab Al Shams Desert Resort & Spa** (☎ 832 6699; www.babalshams.com), just 40 minutes from Dubai, may be less exclusive compared to Al-Maha (kids are welcome

for a start), but it offers a desert experience that's dream-like.

The labyrinthine medina-like layout, with hidden stairways, secluded terraces and lovely courtyards, is simply magical, especially when the candles and lanterns are lit at night. The rustic rooms with traditional Arabian décor are spacious, and the Blooms 'Dead Sea' toiletries are certainly worth finding some space for in your bag.

While the range of activities is limited by comparison to Al-Maha (there's horse riding, camel rides and desert safaris, but they cost extra), the resort makes an excellent retreat for some serious relaxing. The enormous swimming pools (recently expanded) are the main focus of daytime activity, with the attention turning to Al-Sarab bar at sunset for *sheesha*, oud (lute) music, and a view of the falconry exhibition and prettily decorated camels. The traditional Al-Hadheerah Desert restaurant offers the full Arabic experience complete with belly dancer, while Masala restaurant serves up refined Indian cuisine, and Le Dune does excellent casual Italian.

If you do plan on staying a while, there are complimentary daily shuttle buses to Jumeirah Beach Hotel in Dubai (where guests have use of the facilities), and Madinat Jumeirah Souq for some shopping. If you're driving, directions can be given upon booking.

HATTA   حتا
☎ 04

Stunningly situated over several small hills with the spectacular Hajar Mountains surrounding it, Hatta, an enclave of Dubai emirate, is a popular UAE weekend getaway. The drive from Dubai is pleasant in parts, featuring picture-postcard vistas of camels, peach-coloured sand dunes and the occasional lush oasis, all set against a backdrop of rugged mountains. Tiny Hatta was once an important source of tobacco, as well as a vital staging post on the trade route between Dubai and Oman. Nowadays, a 20km stretch of the 105km drive from Dubai takes you through Oman, and while there are no immigration or customs formalities as you cross the borders before Hatta, keep in mind that if you're driving a rental car your insurance won't cover accidents in Oman.

Hatta's main attraction is its cool, humidity-free climate (compared to Dubai and Abu Dhabi's steamy weather, that is!) and its magnificent mountain scenery. While it makes a good base for off-road trips through the mountains, Hatta itself is a wonderful place to relax.

There is little to do in the town itself. In fact there is little *in* town. Don't expect any shops. If you're after souvenirs, stop at the **Mezereh roadside market**, just over the Omani border on your way to Hatta, for cheap carpets, terracotta pots, candle holders and incense burners. The quality isn't great, but a wander around is enjoyable. If you're after cash, there's an ATM in the National Bank of Dubai on the main Hatta roundabout.

Sights & Activities

Hatta has some great **bird-watching**, ample **trekking** and **desert safari** opportunities. Ask at the Hatta Fort Hotel (p404) for information about organised tours, but be warned: they're pricey.

Don't miss the functioning *falaj* (irrigation channel) that waters small but lush agricultural plots below the Heritage Village.

HERITAGE VILLAGE

Hatta's main attraction is the **Heritage Village** (admission free; ⏰ 8am-8.30pm Sat-Thu, 2.30-8.30pm Fri), a re-creation of a traditional mountain village with a restored fort with *majlis*, a traditional courtyard house, and various *barasti* buildings dedicated to weaponry, local music, palm-tree products, handicrafts, weaving, traditional dress, social life, and old village society. It's worth an hour of your time, especially on a weekend evening during winter when there are often live performances of Bedouin song and dance.

Hatta was once known as 'The Two Rocks' because of its stone and mud-brick **watchtowers**, built in the 1880s to protect the village from external attack. These have been restored and you can climb one at the Heritage Village for awesome views over the valley. The other is on the road opposite. The turn-off for the Heritage Village is signposted on the main street, about 3km from the fort roundabout.

HATTA ROCK POOLS

Unfortunately the area's other main attraction, the once-lovely **Hatta rock pools**, a series of pools and waterfalls that nature has carved out of the rocky bed of a wadi valley, are now in a sad state. Littered with rubbish, often dry, and covered in graffiti, they're rather disappointing, though most travellers still like to see the pools for themselves. The miniature canyon has cold, clear water for much of the year, and if you're lucky to find the pools full, you can leap off the rocks into the icy water – wonderfully invigorating when it's hot. After heavy rain, the waterfalls are quite dramatic. Be warned though, the area is a popular picnic place and can get crowded at weekends. While some would argue that you don't *need* a 4WD to get to the rock pools from Hatta, it's strongly advised that you shouldn't attempt the trip without one, as the drive is very steep in parts and goes through a number of dry wadi beds. The drive should definitely not be attempted in unstable weather due to the possibility of flash flooding.

Although about 20km south of Hatta town, across the border in Oman, access is from Hatta. To get to the pools, from the main roundabout outside the Hatta Fort Hotel, turn right and drive through town, past the shops. Continue straight up the road (passing the Heritage Village turn-off) for 2.6km, then turn south past the new village at the next roundabout, and follow the main road towards the mountains. After 500m, the road forks at a mosque; stay to the right and continue to a second fork at the school, where you turn left. You'll see one of the historic towers on your left. Drive 700m and then take the right turn towards the villages of Jeema and Fay. After 2.7km the road crosses a bridge over Wadi Jeema. Continue for 3km until you come to a sign welcoming you to Oman. Don't worry about a visa as there are no border formalities. Go straight through Fay. After Fay, before the tarmac finishes, take a dirt-road turn-off to the right, continuing south for 5.9km along a particularly steep descent into the wadi after the sign to Al Bon. The track to the pools is on your left. Almost immediately, do a dogleg turn left, continuing downhill for 600m. There are a few spots to park here; the remaining distance (much of it steep) must be covered on foot. When you get to the wadi bed, walk along the stream to reach the pools and, further on, the waterfalls.

SUBLIME SAND DUNES

Avoid dull drives on drab roads by taking the following routes through stunning desert scenery:

- **Liwa: Abu Dhabi to Hameem** Take pleasure in the peach-shaded dunes dotted with date palm oases. Take the road to Hameem instead of the main route via Madinat Zayed; the turn-off is about 20km out of Abu Dhabi on the Musaffah to Tarif road.

- **Liwa: Liwa Resthouse to Moreeb Dune (Tal Mireb)** Marvel at these enormous apricot-coloured dunes on the edge of the Empty Quarter – the largest you'll see in the UAE. From Liwa Resthouse head to Moreeb Dune; at 287m it's the highest dune in the country.

- **Mahafiz: Sharjah to Kalba Rd** Count the camels, if you can! See how they blend into the camel-coloured sands on this brand-new road that wends its way through camel farms set among the sand dunes; look for road no 149.

- **Al-Ain: Dubai to Al-Ain Rd** Be amazed by the big tangerine dunes on the approach to Al-Ain around Shabat. To truly appreciate them you'll have to pull over to get a look through the roadside greenery.

- **Shwaib: Al-Ain to Hatta Rd** Gorgeous white gazelles graze on desert shrubs on the big red dunes in the grounds of a sheikh's palace at Shwaib. From Al-Ain, take the back road to Hatta via Shwaib, but instead of bypassing the village, drive down into town; you'll see rugged mountains on your right and gazelles on the dunes to your left.

If you don't have your own transport, the Hatta Fort Hotel offers a 4WD safari to the rock pools. A three-hour trip costs Dh675, including soft drinks.

Sleeping & Eating

Hatta Fort Hotel (☎ 852 3211; www.jebelali-international.com; d Dh780; 🖳 🛒) is the only place to stay and expats love it, packing the place on weekends. Families are everywhere, with kids enjoying the swimming pools and minigolf while parents tee off at the nine-hole golf course, play a few rounds of tennis or have a go at archery. While the hotel exterior and public spaces have a 1960s country-club feel about them (modernist lines, sweeping lawns), the enormous rooms would be more at home in a winter chalet with their bare stone walls and high wood-beamed ceilings. The rooms are wonderfully comfortable, with heavy Indian teak furniture and Arabian touches such as red striped bed throws, all feature private patios with fantastic views of the mountains (perfect for a sunset drink) and we love the attention to detail: flat screen TVs, tea and coffee making facilities with proper china, good hairdryers, and an El-emis 'bath menu'.

Unfortunately, the eateries are disappointing – and we can't suggest you bring your own food to the resort as an alternative as it's not allowed! Café Gazebo (mains

Dh40), overlooking the pool, may be popular with visiting day-trippers, but when we visited the food was awful. Jeema Restaurant (mains Dh30 to Dh80) boasts a 1970s a la carte menu to match the décor (tinted mirror walls and cheap chandeliers), or a dreadful buffet of bad Indian and over-cooked seafood.

The only other options for food are a couple of grungy cafeterias on the main street serving *shwarma*, kebabs and juices.

Getting There & Away

Daily minibuses leave Hatta for Dubai from near the roundabout outside the Hatta Fort Hotel every hour from 6am to 9.35pm (Dh7, 90 minutes).

THE NORTHERN EMIRATES

SHARJAH   الشارقة
☎ 06 / pop 679,000

The anti-Dubai. The only thing conservative Sharjah has in common with its glitzy neighbour is that they both have charming waterways. With no alcohol, no *shee-sha* cafés, no revealing clothing and most definitely no cohabitation by non-married couples, thankfully the third-largest emirate has plenty of other activities to keep your mind off the forbidden fruits offered elsewhere in the UAE.

Sharjah promotes itself as the cultural capital of the UAE, and its proliferation of excellent museums, galleries and theatres makes this tag well deserved. Architecturally, the restored central arts and heritage precincts are two of the most interesting neighbourhoods in the UAE, and the city's souqs give it the cachet of being the best place for souvenir shopping in the country, and well worth a couple of days' exploration – perhaps to detox from Dubai's decadent delights?

History

Like most of the emirates, Sharjah historically relied on trade, fishing and pearling for its livelihood until the discovery of oil. The ruling family, the Qawassims, once ruled both Sharjah and Ras al-Khaimah and, until the British took power in 1809, were the major power in the region. Over the period of British reign, Sharjah was probably the most important of the emirates. The establishment of the first airport in the UAE was a reflection of this, with Imperial Airways flights arriving from Britain from 1932. The present ruler, Sheikh Sultan bin Mohammad al-Qassimi, took over from his father in 1972, the same year that oil was discovered in the emirate.

Orientation

Central Sharjah surrounds Khalid Lagoon, the city's attractive heart. A leisurely stroll around the lovely lake is mandatory for all visitors. To the northwest of the lagoon are the Al-Khalidia and Al-Majaz areas, home to top-end hotels and restaurants. Across the Sharjah Bridge to the east is the city's old town, home to the heritage and arts precincts, the souqs, and most of the city's cheap hotels. Outside the centre are the anonymous and very ugly industrial areas to the southwest, and the artificially greened suburbs around University City and the airport to the southeast. Central Sharjah is not a huge area, and it's quite possible to walk around the lagoon and through the various tourist precincts; in fact, it's a good idea to do this, because the manic traffic, innumerable roundabouts and hard-to-read street signs make driving a nightmare. The main road to Dubai, Al-Wahda Rd, suffers peak-hour gridlock from around 7am to 11am, and from 4pm to 7pm every weekday.

Information

BOOKSHOP & INTERNET ACCESS
Book Mall (☎ 556 2111; www.thebookmall.ae; Al- Khan Rd, Al-Majaz; ☼ 9am-11pm Sat-Thu, 4-11pm Fri) Enormous bookshop with a small café and reasonable English-language fiction and travel books. Internet access costs Dh5 per hour. It's near Al-Qasba Canal.

EMERGENCY
Sharjah Police (☎ 563 1111)

MEDICAL SERVICES
Al Zahra Private Hospital (☎ 561 9999, 561 3311; Al-Zahra Sq, Al-Ghuair) A centrally located private medical centre with an emergency department.

MONEY
On Burj Ave (also called Bank St), nearly every building contains a bank with an ATM. Moneychangers can be found on the small streets immediately to its east and west, as well as on Rolla Sq. There are also ATMs in the Central Souq.

POST
Sharjah Post Office (☎ 572 2219; Government House Sq, Al Soor; ☼ 8am-8pm Sat-Wed, 8am-6pm Thu)

TELEPHONE
Main Etisalat Office (☎ 561 1111; Ibrahim bin Mohammed Al-Medfa'a Rd; ☼ 7am-3pm Sat-Wed) It's off Kuwait Sq.

TOURIST INFORMATION
Sharjah Commerce & Tourism Development Authority (☎ 556 6777; www.sharjahtourism.ae; 9th fl, Crescent Tower, Buheirah Corniche, Al Majaz; ☼ 7.30am-3pm Sat-Thu) Stocks a free map of the city (also available at most hotels). It doesn't offer any other services.
Sharjah National Tourist & Transport Authority (SNTTA; ☎ 351 411; Al-Arouba St; ☼ 8am-1pm & 4-7pm Sat-Thu) This huge government-run tourism agency can book transport and accommodation throughout the UAE.

Sights

HERITAGE AREA
The beautiful historic buildings in the Heritage Area, just inland from the Corniche between Burj Ave and Al-Maraija Rd, have been carefully restored and faithfully reconstructed using traditional materials

UNITED ARAB EMIRATES

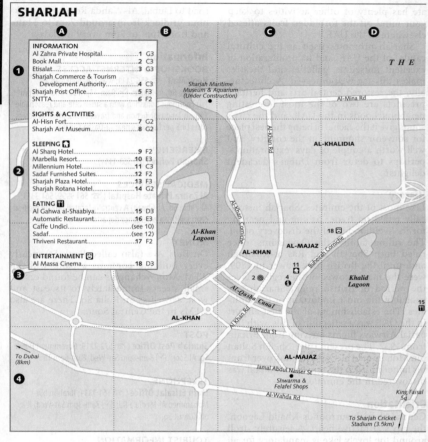

SHARJAH

INFORMATION
Al Zahra Private Hospital.................1 G3
Book Mall...2 C3
Etisalat..3 G3
Sharjah Commerce & Tourism
　Development Authority..................4 C3
Sharjah Post Office..........................5 F3
SNTTA...6 F2

SIGHTS & ACTIVITIES
Al-Hisn Fort....................................7 G2
Sharjah Art Museum........................8 G2

SLEEPING
Al Sharq Hotel.................................9 F2
Marbella Resort.............................10 E3
Millennium Hotel...........................11 C3
Sadaf Furnished Suites...................12 F2
Sharjah Plaza Hotel........................13 F3
Sharjah Rotana Hotel.....................14 G2

EATING
Al Gahwa al-Shaabiya....................15 D3
Automatic Restaurant....................16 E3
Caffe Undici..............................(see 10)
Sadaf..(see 12)
Thriveni Restaurant.......................17 F2

ENTERTAINMENT
Al Massa Cinema...........................18 D3

such as sea rock, coral and gypsum. First visit the imposing **Al-Hisn Fort**, with its fascinating historical exhibits inside, before making your way to the atmospheric **Literature Square** and the **House of Poetry**. Across from here is the splendid **Bait Sheikh Sultan Bin Saquer al-Qassimi** (☎ 569 3999; admission free; ⏰ 9am-1pm & 5-8pm Tue-Sun, 5-8pm Fri), a traditional house with wind towers set around a courtyard. Inside are wonderful displays of traditional costumes, jewellery, ceramics and furniture.

Walking past the Sharjah National Theatre, you'll come to the **Islamic Museum** (☎ 568 3334; www.sdci.gov.ae; admission free; ⏰ 9am-1pm & 5-8pm Tue-Sun, 5-8pm Fri), with interesting exhibits including a large collection of coins from

around the Islamic world and a number of beautiful handwritten Qurans. Next door, the **Sharjah Heritage Museum** (Bait al-Naboodah; ☎ 568 5500; admission free; ⏰ 9am-1pm & 5-8pm Tue-Sun, 4.30-8pm Fri) has similar traditional exhibits to Bait Sheikh Sultan Bin Saquer al-Qassimi though without the wind towers, but it is still worth a look.

At the Islamic Museum, Friday evening is women only: at the other museums, Wednesday admission is for women only, all day.

The atmospheric **Souq al-Arsa** (⏰ 9am-1pm & 4-9pm Sat-Thu, 4-9pm Fri), with its gorgeously restored *areesh* (palm leaf) roof and wooden pillars, is not far from the waterfront. The oldest souq in the UAE, it has

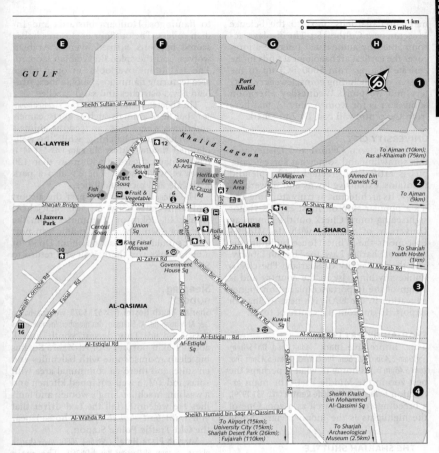

a wonderful traditional **coffeehouse**, where you can stop for a reviving mint tea and plate of dates.

ARTS AREA

Tucked behind the textile shops and souqs on the opposite side of Burj Ave is the Arts Area, home to the country's most impressive art gallery, the **Sharjah Art Museum** (☎ 568 8222; admission free; ☯ 9am-1pm & 5-8pm Sat-Thu, 5-8pm Fri). Showing contemporary art by local and foreign artists, it has a small but interesting permanent collection, a stylish café and helpful staff. It is also home to the world-class Sharjah International Art Biennale (www.sharjahbienniale.com) – widely recognised as an outstanding event

with provocative arts; check it out if you're around when it's on.

The **Bait Obeid al-Shamsi** (☎ 568 8811), opposite the art museum, is a restored house used as an international artists' studio; don't miss the intricate pillars on the upper level. Nearby are the **Very Special Arts Centre** (☎ 568 7812), a workshop and gallery for disabled artists, and the **Emirates Fine Arts Society** (☎ 568 4488), which also displays the works of local artists.

SHARJAH ARCHAEOLOGICAL MUSEUM

This fascinating **museum** (☎ 566 5466; www .archeology.gov.ae; Sheikh Rashid bin Saqr al-Qassimi Rd; admission free; ☯ 9am-1pm & 5-8pm Sat-Thu, 5-8pm Fri) is housed in an elegant building set in manicured gardens, next to the Science Museum near Cultural Sq. The displays, accompanied by audiovisual interpretations, cover the earliest archaeological finds in the emirate (dating from 5000 BC) up to the present day, including coins, jewellery, pottery and weapons. Wednesday afternoon admission is for women only. A taxi here from the centre will cost Dh7 to Dh10.

UNIVERSITY CITY

A cross between Oxford and Disneyland, this sprawling and somewhat surreal campus is artificially greened, with splendid fountains, expansive lawns and flowerbeds galore. Its architecture is truly stunning and it's a popular stop on most expat's visitor sightseeing tours. Check out the American University of Sharjah, with its Middle-East-meets-the-White-House building, the School of Sharia'a Law, the Sharjah Library, and the University of Sharjah. The city is unlike anything else in the country and is a sign of the importance placed on higher education in the UAE. It's next to Sharjah airport, 15km from the centre of town.

SHARJAH DESERT PARK

This impressive **park** (adult/child Dh15/free; 9am-5.45pm Sat, Sun, Tue & Wed, 11am-5.45pm Thu, 2pm-5.45pm Fri) is home to what is perhaps the best zoo in the Middle East. The main attraction is **Arabia's Wildlife Centre** (☎ 531 1999), a breeding centre as well as a zoo. One of the highlights is the indoor aviary, home

---

THE SHARJAH SHUTTLE

With Dubai's crazy rental market price increases over the past couple of years, many workers on lower and middle incomes in Dubai have moved to neighbouring Sharjah to be able to afford to stay in the UAE. This trend has spawned unofficial taxis that ferry workers daily to Dubai as well as some well-organised car pooling for the daily drive. With transport times of up to two hours to get to Sheikh Zayed Rd and up to 90 minutes to get back to Sharjah, what does everyone do in a car with the same people every day? 'Sleep', everyone told us. 'Conversation wears pretty thin after the first month of spending over 20 hours a week with the same people!'

---

to flamingos, Houbara bustards and Indian rollers. The outdoor enclosures house sacred baboons, striped hyenas, Arabian wolves, and the splendid Arabian leopard. The restaurant overlooks an open range area featuring flamingos, Nubian ibex, Arabian oryx, ostriches and sand gazelles.

The **Children's Farm** (☎ 531 1127; closed noon-4pm) has farm animals such as goats, camels and ducks where kids can feed the animals and watch quails hatching, while the well-planned **Natural History Museum** (☎ 531 1411) has a botanical garden with more than 120 types of wildflowers. There's also a park with café and picnic facilities.

The Desert Park is just past the airport and University City on the Sharjah/Al Dhaid Rd, 26km or 20 minutes from the centre of town. There is no public transport but it should only cost you about Dh50 for a taxi to take you there, wait and return to Sharjah.

Sleeping

BUDGET

Sharjah Youth Hostel (☎ 522 5070; www.uaeha.org .ae; Al-Mirgab Rd, Al-Shargan; dm members/nonmembers Dh35/50, s/d 105) This decent youth hostel, about 1.5km northeast of Al-Zahra Sq, has big clean rooms, some with balconies and en suite, and there's a communal area with sofas and TV, a well-equipped kitchen and a washing machine. Single women and families are welcome. Tell the taxi driver that you want *bait shabab* (youth house) near the Old Traffic Police Station.

Sharjah Plaza Hotel (☎ 561 7000; www.sharjah plazahotel.com; Al-Qassimi Rd; d Dh250) The main thing this hotel has going for it is that its modest rooms are clean and cheap. Otherwise, the beds are uncomfortable, the bathrooms need renovating, and it's on busy Government House Sq, so street noise is a problem.

MIDRANGE

Sadaf Furnished Suites (☎ 568 6111; www.sadaff .com; Al-Mina Rd; d Dh300) These clean, spacious apartments are decorated like a suburban home from the '80s with lots of mismatched florals and geometric machine-made rugs. They're fully equipped with kitchen (fridge, washing machine, stove and utensils), bathroom and sitting area, and cheaper rates can be negotiated for longer stays.

Al Sharq Hotel (☎ 562 0000; www.sharqhotel .com; Rolla Sq; s/d incl breakfast Dh400/500) This small hotel is in the centre of town, close to the arts and heritage precincts, but while it's clean, comfortable and the management are friendly, it's overpriced for what's on offer. It should be a last resort option.

Sharjah Rotana Hotel (☎ 563 7777; sharjah.hotel@ rotana.com; Al-Arouba St; d Dh450; 🖳 🗟) The excellent Rotana is Sharjah's best-value hotel with enormous, comfortable, well-equipped rooms; spotless spacious bathrooms; an expansive buffet breakfast; and interesting views over the city. The location is central, but a cheap taxi is just a hand signal away if you don't have your own wheels.

TOP END

Marbella Resort (☎ 574 1111; www.marbellaresort .net; Buheirah Corniche; junior/2-bed ste Dh690; 🖳 🗟) An old-timer on the Sharjah hotel scene, this 25-year-old Spanish-style resort is looking a little worn around the edges but Gulf Cooperative Council (GCC) and Arab expat families love the private villa accommodation, set in lush tropical gardens, with a pleasant swimming pool.

Millennium Hotel (☎ 555 6666; www.millennium hotels.com; Buheirah Corniche; d Dh850; 🖳 🗟) The hotel's unrivalled location overlooking the gorgeous lagoon, its plush amenities, and the splendid swimming pool make this an excellent choice if you're planning to spend a lot of time at the hotel. If you're not, then the Rotana represents better value.

Eating

Caffe Undici (☎ 574 1111; Marbella Resort, Buheirah Corniche; ⏲ 7am-1am) Sharjah's most sophisticated café has indoor and outdoor seating, continental breakfasts (Dh22), generous-sized sandwiches (Dh12 to Dh18) and real espresso coffee (Dh12).

Al Gahwa al-Shaabiya (☎ 572 3788; Buheirah Corniche; ⏲ 8am-2am) This traditional *barasti* coffeehouse, overlooking the lagoon, serves mint tea, local coffee, ginger milk and Arabic snacks. Extremely popular with Emiratis, it's a wonderful place to sit in the evenings, play backgammon and watch the city lights reflected in the water of the lagoon.

Thriveni Restaurant (☎ 562 6901; Rolla Sq; ⏲ 10am-midnight) This dirt-cheap Indian eatery is usually packed with guest workers from the subcontinent eating thalis (Dh6),

biryanis (Dh7) and curries (Dh7 to Dh11). As is usually the case in workers' cafeterias, women are required to sit in the family area, which in this case is rather shabby but is worth tolerating unless you enjoy being ogled.

Automatic Restaurant (☎ 572 7335, 574 1147; Buheirah Corniche; mezze Dh11, shwarma Dh3.50; ⏲ 11am-1am) A branch of the famed Lebanese chain, Automatic serves up fresh, reliable Lebanese staples in a bright, clean, cafeteria. The place gets packed with Arab expats late at night.

Sadaf (☎ 569 3344; Al-Mina Rd; mains Dh35; ⏲ lunch & dinner) Popular with local Emirati families who dine in private booths, this excellent Iranian restaurant chain serves up authentic Persian cuisine – the spicy moist kebabs are particularly good and the 'Zereshk Polo Meat: Iranian rice with Iranian red barberries and meat' (Dh25) is scrumptious.

Entertainment

Al Massa Cinema (☎ 556 3300, 562 4400; Buheirah Corniche) Shows the latest Hollywood blockbusters and odd Bollywood flick.

Shopping

Souq al-Arsa (⏲ 10am-1.30pm & 4-10.30pm) Located in the Heritage Area, this is the most atmospheric souq in the UAE and one of the few selling authentic antiques and collectables from pre-oil times, and the early development days. You'll also find good-quality handicrafts, carpets and souvenirs that you'll pay a fraction of the price for than you would in Dubai.

Central Souq (⏲ 9am-1.30pm & 4-10.30pm) Also called the Blue Souq or New Souq, this is one of the best souqs in the country. The bargains are to be found in the little shops on the upstairs balconies, specialising in carpets from Iran, Afghanistan and Turkey, Kashmiri pashminas, and silver Bedouin jewellery from Oman, Yemen, Afghanistan and India. Shop around and compare prices before purchasing, and remember to bargain; start at 50% off the price offered and you'll end up getting something for a quarter of the original price. Head here in the evenings with the locals if you can: only tourists shop here during the day.

Also worth a wander is the glittering Gold Centre, on the corner of Sheikh Humaid bin Saqr al-Qassimi and Al-Wahda Rds, which has scores of stores selling gold jewellery.

Getting There & Away

Sharjah International Airport (☎ 558 1111) is 15km from the centre. A taxi to the centre of town costs Dh40.

Dubai Transport minibuses leave every 30 minutes from Rolla Sq and cost Dh5. A taxi to Dubai can be picked up anywhere in town and will cost Dh4/20 shared/contracted. Shared taxis to Ras al-Khaimah and Umm al-Quwain leave from a sandy parking lot opposite a park on Al-Sharq Rd. They cost Dh15 shared to Ras al-Khaimah and Dh10 to Umm al-Quwain. Comfortable minibus taxis to Abu Dhabi (Dh30) and Al-Ain (Dh30) leave from the taxi rank at the southwest side of the Fruit and Vegetable Souq. A negotiated trip to Ajman should cost Dh15 to Dh20.

Getting Around

Sharjah has no local bus system, so getting around without your own car means taking taxis or walking. The taxis have no meters, so you need to negotiate the fare before you get in: trips around the centre should cost Dh5 to Dh15 depending on where you're going.

AJMAN   عجمان

☎ 06 / pop 251,000

Laid-back and unassuming, Ajman, only 10km from Sharjah, is one of the poorest and smallest of the seven emirates. While many people just pass through out of curiosity, the pretty, palm-lined, white-sand beach alone is worthy of some time. During the cooler weather locals barbecue and picnic on the sand under the palm trees, or at the picturesque white picnic tables with blue umbrellas. There's also the excellent Kempinski Hotel & Resort (with its own lovely, private beach), the *sheesha* cafés opposite the waterfront, the museum and renowned dhow building yards.

It's easy to walk around town. The Corniche (also known as Arabian Gulf St or Al Khaleej Rd) is where locals promenade in the evening; shops and the museum are found around the central square.

There are ATMs on Sheikh Humaid bin Rashed Al Nuaimi St and an internet café

in **Sanad Winner Cafeteria** (☎ 744 7538; Corniche; per hr Dh5; ⏰ 24hr).

Sights

Undergoing renovation at the time of research, the splendid **Ajman Museum** (adult/child/ student Dh4/2/1; ⏰ 9am-1pm & 5-8pm Sun-Thu, 5-8pm Fri) occupies an imposing old police fort. Built in the late 18th century, the attractive fort served as the ruler's palace and office until 1970. From 1970 to 1978 it was Ajman's main police station; hence the bizarre exhibit featuring handcuffs and police uniforms. In the fort yard is a charming reconstruction of a traditional souq.

At the sleepy harbour (next to the fishing boat wharf) there's a souq selling fresh produce and household items. It's a reasonably interesting area to explore in the morning when the souq is busiest.

Sleeping

Coral Suites (☎ 742 9999; www.coral-suitesajman .com; Corniche; d Dh375, with sea view Dh 450; 🖭) If you can't get a room at the Kempinski (see below), then Coral Suites is your only other option. Oddly, the rooms are outfitted with what looks like garden furniture, but they're nevertheless comfortable, and come with all mod cons. If you must stay here, it's worth paying extra for the sea views. There's an indoor swimming pool and a gaudy restaurant, but no alcohol is served.

Ajman Kempinski Hotel & Resort (☎ 745 1555; www.kempinski-ajman.com; Sheikh Humaid bin Rashid Al Nuaimi St; Arabian Gulf St; d Dh650; 🖳🖭) This fine hotel, with an opulent Arabian-style lobby with palm trees and *mashrabiyya*, has spacious rooms with supremely comfortable beds – the kind you never want to leave – balconies with stunning sea views, and Bulgari products. Situated on a pretty stretch of beach with soft, white sand, sea shells and palm trees, this is the perfect place to kick back for a couple of days. There are several outstanding restaurants, a pleasant swimming pool, PADI diving centre, loads of water sports, an indoor bowling alley and a good playground. There's also the highly regarded **Kempinski Softouch Spa** (☎ 745 8806; www .softouchayurveda.com; massages Dh155-465, head & face treatments Dh50-300; ⏰ 7am-9pm) specialising in Ayurvedic massages. Indulge in a massage, a head and face treatment, or try its signature 'anti-voyage fatigue' massage (Dh550).

Eating

La Croisette Café (☎ 744 4171; Corniche; coffee & croissants Dh16; ☯ 8am-2am) This is a popular breakfast spot for coffee and croissants. And it has a real espresso machine – a rarity in these parts!

India House (☎ 744 2497; Sheikh Humaid bin Abdul al-Aziz St; meals Dh3-14; ☯ 7.30am-3.30pm & 5.30pm-midnight Sat-Thu, 7.30am-noon, 1-3pm & 5pm-midnight Fri) Specialising in vegetarian dishes, this spotlessly clean cafeteria is popular with the Indian expat community for its extensive menu, featuring cheap thalis (Dh6 to Dh10), decent biryanis (Dh8 to Dh12), tandoor kebabs (Dh11 to Dh14) and curries.

Sanad Winner Cafeteria (☎ 744 7538; Corniche; meals Dh8-15; ☯ 24hr) Local guys keep coming back to this popular fast-food place (especially late at night, when the pavement is packed) for its inventive pizzas (Dh15 to Dh30) – try the 'mango craze' with beef strips, green pepper and slices of mango. There's also tangy *shwarma* (Dh4), generous club sandwiches (Dh8) and big burgers (Dh7).

Hai Tao (☎ 745 1555; Ajman Kempinski Hotel & Resort, Sheikh Humaid bin Rashid Al Nuaimi St; mains Dh50) This atmospheric restaurant is Ajman's best, by a long way. Decorated in a traditional Chinese style (complete with rickshaw), Hai Tao serves up superb Szechwan and Cantonese dishes. If you enjoy duck, try the tasty fried duck rolls (Dh32) and authentic roasted Peking duck with pancakes (Dh85), expertly prepared at your table.

Al Masa Cafeteria & Coffee Shop (☎ 747 4163; Corniche; sheesha Dh8-10; ☯ 7am-2am) The local guys love the 'Cocktail *sheeshas*' (*sheesha* made with real fruit) at Al Masa on the Corniche, just opposite the mosque. It's hard to find a spare plastic seat after midnight.

Getting There & Away

Ajman has no bus service. There's a taxi stand on Sheikh Humaid bin Abdul al-Aziz St just past the intersection with Al-Karama and Al-Ithad Sts, where you can catch shared taxis to Deira in Dubai (Dh15) and Sharjah (Dh10). Taxis to Ras al-Khaimah (Dh25) and Umm al-Quwain (Dh10) leave from the taxi stand near Ajman City Centre mall. You'll need to agree on the fare before getting into the taxi.

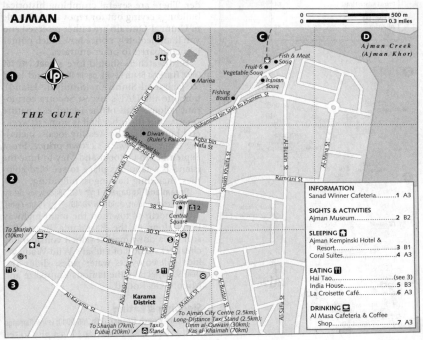

AJMAN

0 — 500 m
0 — 0.3 miles

INFORMATION
Sanad Winner Cafeteria..........**1** A3

SIGHTS & ACTIVITIES
Ajman Museum....................**2** B2

SLEEPING
Ajman Kempinski Hotel &
  Resort..............................**3** B1
Coral Suites.........................**4** A3

EATING
Hai Tao..............................(see 3)
India House.........................**5** B3
La Croisette Café..................**6** A3

DRINKING
Al Masa Cafeteria & Coffee
  Shop.................................**7** A3

UMM AL-QUWAIN أم القيوين

☎ 06 / pop 66,000

The sleepy fishing port of Umm al-Quwain offers little in the way of attractions for the visitor compared to other emirates, apart from the chance to experience the closest thing to a pre-oil town that you'll find in the UAE. Its name, 'Mother of Two Powers', refers to the emirate's power over both land and sea, and the town itself lies on a narrow peninsula of sand jutting north from the main road linking Sharjah with Ras al-Khaimah.

The old town and the emirate's tiny business district are at the northern tip of the peninsula, along King Faisal Rd (aka Muroor Rd). Banks are found in King Faisal Rd and internet access is available at the Palma Beach Hotel for Dh10 per hour.

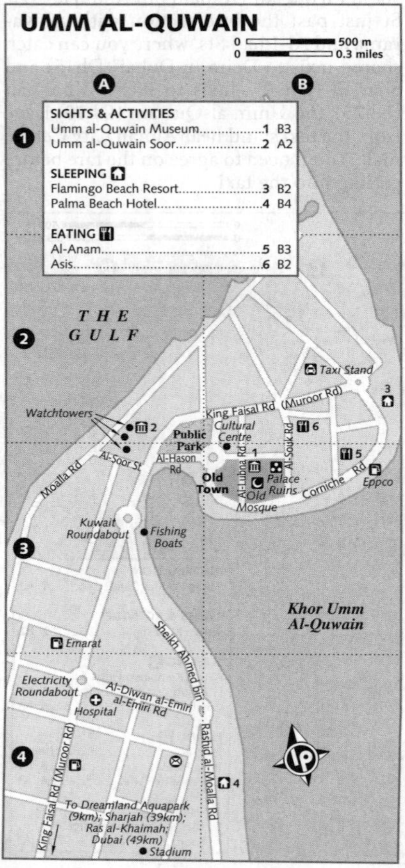
UMM AL-QUWAIN
0 500 m
0 0.3 miles
A
B
1
2
3
4
SIGHTS & ACTIVITIES
Umm al-Quwain Museum 1 B3
Umm al-Quwain Soor 2 A2
SLEEPING
Flamingo Beach Resort 3 B2
Palma Beach Hotel 4 B4
EATING
Al-Anam 5 B3
Asis 6 B2
THE GULF
Taxi Stand
King Faisal Rd (Muroor Rd)
Watchtowers
Public Park
Cultural Centre
Al-Soor St
Al-Hason Rd
Moalla Rd
Al-Lubna Rd
Al-Souk Rd
Old Town
Palace Ruins
Old Mosque
Corniche Rd
Eppco
Kuwait Roundabout
Fishing Boats
Khor Umm Al-Quwain
Emarat
Sheikh Ahmed bin Rashid al-Moalla Rd
Electricity Roundabout
Al-Diwan al-Emiri Rd
Hospital
King Faisal Rd (Muroor Rd)
To Dreamland Aquapark (9km); Sharjah (39km); Ras al-Khaimah; Dubai (49km)
Stadium

Sights

The beautifully restored **Umm al-Quwain Museum** (☎ 765 0888; www.uqmuseum; adult/child Dh4/free; 🕒 8am-1pm & 5-8pm Sat-Thu, 5-8pm Fri), on the edge of the old town, was once the town's fort. The oldest building in Umm al-Quwain, it was built in 1768 for the ruler of the time, Sheikh Rashid Bin Majid Al Mualla, and served as the residence and seat of government for the emirate's rulers until 1969. Highlights include the ruler's fine *majlis* (meeting room), an archaeological collection and displays of old Bedouin jewellery and weapons, including intricately decorated swords.

Also worth a quick look is the nearby **Umm al-Quwain Soor (Old Wall)** (☎ 765 0888; www.uqmuseum; admission free; 🕒 9am-1pm & 4-10pm). Built in 1820 from sea stones and plaster, it has an impressive wooden gate and several towers.

The sandy lanes of the old town in the area around the museum are worth a wander. There are several crumbling historical buildings crying out for renovation. People in Umm al-Quwain are rather reserved and you'll immediately notice how much poorer it is compared to other emirates.

Bird-watchers should hire a **boat** (☎ 765 0000; Flamingo Beach Resort; per hr Dh180) and head to Jazirat al-Sinniyah (Sinniyah Island), home to the UAE's largest Socotra cormorant colony. Half of the island is a nature reserve, but the other half is home to weekend houses used by wealthy locals, including Umm al-Quwain's crown prince. From September to October and May to June the island is a fabulous place to see bird colonies, including flamingos, migrating.

Dreamland Aquapark (☎ 768 1888; www.dreamlanduae.com; adult/child Dh70/40; 🕒 10am-6pm), 10km north of town on the main highway (next door to the Barracuda Beach Resort), is a downmarket (albeit considerably cheaper) version of Dubai's Wild Wadi, yet kids still enjoy its water rides, slides and pools, especially the famous Kamikaze and Mighty-Go-Round.

Sleeping & Eating

Flamingo Beach Resort (☎ 765 0000; www.flamingoresort.ae; Corniche Rd; d Dh400; 🏊) It's a pity to see

---

AN UMM AL-QUWAIN XMAS STORY

Twas the afternoon before Christmas and we were in Umm al-Quwain searching for decent places to eat – no mean feat in this tiny emirate – when we came across a small new 'restaurant' that looked inviting. We went inside and were given the usual cheery greeting by a pretty young Filipino woman. We chatted about the menu and she said that the restaurant had only opened a few weeks ago and that she hadn't had a day off since she arrived from the Philippines. She asked if we were Christians. 'Merry Christmas!' she exclaimed. 'You're the first people I've been able to say that to, everyone else here is a Muslim!'

The Filipino girl asked whether the rest of the country looked like this (err, no…) and how far away Dubai was (a two-hour drive). The poor woman admitted that she'd been told she was going to be working in Dubai and couldn't believe that she was stuck in a place that bore no relation to the city she'd heard so much about back home. We left the restaurant feeling sad so we rummaged around the car to find something to give her as a present. We found a boxed Panatone cake given to us by the hotel we just checked out of and Lara ran back inside to give it to her: 'Merry Christmas!' The poor girl shed a tear. And so did we when Lara returned to the car.

We're always hearing about construction workers getting a raw deal in the UAE, but this in many ways was just as heartbreaking.

Terry Carter & Lara Dunston

---

the glum faces of package tourists downing beers in the characterless bar who probably thought they were heading for Dubai. While it's pleasant enough to sit by the water under the palm trees, there's no reason to actually stay here. If you must, the motel-style rooms are comfortable enough with views of the big swimming pool and lagoon, and there is an Ayurveda spa (treatments from Dh125 to Dh325) and plenty of water sports, including water-skiing (per 30 minutes Dh120), speedboat rides (per 30 minutes Dh120), glass-bottom boat trips (one hour, per person Dh180) and evening crab-hunting trips (per person including dinner Dh160). The facilities are available to nonguests.

Palma Beach Hotel (☎ 766 7090; fax 766 7388; Sheikh Ahmad bin Rashid Rd; d Dh550-3650, houseboats Dh1650; 🖥 🕭) Taking its inspiration from an Egyptian theme park, with obelisks, mummies, statues of tigers, and faux Roman columns, this bizarre hotel is popular with Emirati and Gulf Arab families, who like to barbecue on the palm-lined beach. There's also a bowling alley and amusement centre, along with a restaurant, *sheesha* café and bar overlooking the water.

Barracuda Beach Resort (☎ 768 1555; www.barra cuda.ae; Dubai-Ras Al-Khaimah Rd; Spanish haciendas Dh350, cabanas Dh700; 🕭) Renowned across the country for its liquor store (the only one in the country where a liquor licence isn't required, although we understand this won't

be for long), this pleasant, whitewashed Mediterranean-style 'leisure' resort has simple yet spacious, tiled-floor apartments and cabins, a popular 'nightclub' and 24-hour check-in.

Asis (☎ 765 1751; Al Hason Rd, old town; dishes Dh5-30), a new cafeteria in the old town, serves up everything from pizzas (Dh15 to Dh30) and burgers (Dh6) to mutton masalas (Dh12) and biryanis (Dh6 to Dh10). Shabby **Al-Anam** (☎ 765 6729; King Faisal Rd; meals Dh5-15; ⏰ irregular hr), opposite Eppco and KFC, does spicy curries and biryanis.

Getting There & Away

Umm al-Quwain has no bus service. Minibuses from Dubai drop passengers off on the highway opposite the Emarat station. You'll have little luck catching a shared taxi to leave; engaged taxis can be flagged anywhere in town for travel to Sharjah (Dh40), Deira (in Dubai; Dh60), Ajman (Dh30) and Ras al-Khaimah (Dh50).

RAS AL-KHAIMAH   رأس الخيمة
☎ 07 / pop 208,000

Often overlooked in the tourist brochures, Ras al-Khaimah (usually known as simply 'RAK') is somewhat of an undervalued destination for visitors to the UAE. With its proximity to the hazy Hajar Mountains, the UAE's northernmost and most fertile emirate is often just seen as the gateway to Oman's spectacularly beautiful Musandam

Peninsula (p242), however it has a few surprises of its own. Firstly, while the town itself is a dusty ramshackle affair, the views of the mountains are spectacular and come as quite a surprise after the endless sands and dreary drive to get here. The nearby beaches are as pristine and development-free as you'll find in the UAE, and the Al Hamra Fort Hotel & Beach Resort (p416), 25km south of RAK, makes an excellent base to sample some water sports.

History

Inhabited since the 3rd millennium BC, Ras al-Khaimah's main city was for many centuries Julfar, a few kilometres to the north of the present-day city. By the 7th century Julfar was an important port of the Sassanian Empire, which was based in Iran and acted as the major power in the region. After occupation by the Portuguese in the early 16th century, Julfar was abandoned and the foundations of the modern city were laid. Ruled by the Al-Qassimi family, which also ruled Sharjah, the emirate was the major power in the Gulf from this time until the British swaggered into the region. It was because of the scars left behind from this earlier British occupation that RAK initially chose to stay out of the federation brokered by the British in 1971. Wisely, its ruler soon decided that the emirate couldn't survive as an independent state and joined shortly afterwards. Today, the emirate's economy is based on agriculture, the pharmaceutical industry and petrochemical industries, and its small reserves of oil.

Orientation & Information

Ras al-Khaimah has two parts: Ras al-Khaimah proper, the old town on a sandy peninsula along the Gulf coast; and Al-Nakheel, the newer business district on the other side of the creek and harbour. A bridge links the two. The two major roads are Sheikh Mohammad bin Salem St, which leads to Dubai, Sharjah, Umm al-Quwain and Ajman; and Oman St (aka Al-Yayiz Rd), which leads to Oman to the north and the airport to the south (this stretch is called Airport Rd).

You can change money or access ATMs at the banks along Sheikh Mohammad bin Salem St in Ras al-Khaimah or Oman St in Al-Nakheel. The main post office is a red-brick building on Sheikh Mohammad Bin Salem St. The Etisalat office is on bin Dahir St in Al-Nakheel.

Sights & Activities

The **National Museum of Ras al-Khaimah** (☎ 233 3411; www.rakmuseum.gov.ae; Al-Hisn Rd; adult/child Dh2/1; ⏰ 9am-5pm Wed-Mon Sep-May, 8am-noon & 4-7pm Wed-Mon Jun-Aug), set in an imposing 18th-century fort built of stone and gypsum, and with a wonderful wind tower, was the residence of the Qawassim rulers until the 1970s. The thoughtfully curated collection includes exhibits on the area's natural history, archaeology, ethnography and the Qawassim tribe. Highlights include intricately patterned Iron-Age softstone vessels, 18th-century terracotta urns and other splendid artefacts from Julfar, the biggest port in the UAE from the 13th until the 18th century, and Shamal (see p416).

Ras al-Khaimah's ramshackle **old town** is also worth a wander. The small but fascinating textile souq, with colourful traditional dresses on display in the doorways, is especially vibrant at night, when the local Emirati ladies come out to shop.

RAK Equestrian Club (☎ 487 6549), 5.5km from the centre of town at the foot of the mountains, offers horse riding in a spectacular setting. There are lessons, treks and pony rides.

Rock climbing is a popular activity in this part of the UAE, with the best climbs in the country being near Wadi Bih, starting from the Ras al-Khaimah side.

Tours

Most visitors to RAK are stopping off in town on their way to the magnificent Musandam Peninsula (see p242) in Oman. If you are one of them, call ahead to book some tours with **Musandam Sea Adventure Tourism** (☎ in UAE 050-750 3001, in Oman 00968 9934 6321; www.msaoman.com), an excellent Khasab-based tour company that runs fabulous half- and full-day dhow trips through the spectacular fjords for snorkelling, dolphin-spotting and traditional fishing villages. It also does fantastic half-day 4WD tours up to the Sayh Plateau and the 2000m Jebel Harim, where you'll see ancient marine fossils and jaw-dropping views over Khor Al Najd. If you are from one of the 34 countries eligible to get an on-the-spot

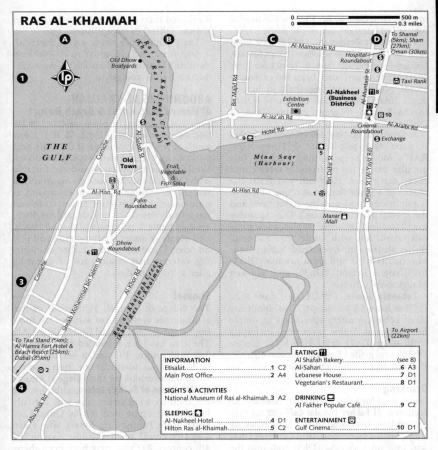

RAS AL-KHAIMAH

INFORMATION		EATING 🍴	
Etisalat..	1 C2	Al Shafah Bakery.................................	(see 8)
Main Post Office..............................	2 A4	Al-Sahari...	6 A3
		Lebanese House..................................	7 D1
SIGHTS & ACTIVITIES		Vegetarian's Restaurant......................	8 D1
National Museum of Ras al-Khaimah..	3 A2		
		DRINKING 🍷	
SLEEPING 🛏		Al Fakher Popular Café.......................	9 C2
Al-Nakheel Hotel...............................	4 D1		
Hilton Ras al-Khaimah.......................	5 C2	ENTERTAINMENT 🎭	
		Gulf Cinema...	10 D1

visa at Dubai airport, then you can also get an Omani visa at the Al Darah passport control (see p445). Everyone else has to apply in advance at the Oman embassy in Dubai.

Sleeping

Al-Nakheel Hotel (☎ 228 2822; hotelnakheel@hotmail .com; Oman St; d Dh170) Shabby, sleazy and noisy, this hotel should only be seen as a last resort. Single women staying here alone (not recommended) should expect that they might probably be mistaken for prostitutes. The dodgy Churchill Pub (open noon to 2am) on the first floor should be avoided unless you're desperate for a drink and dreadful karaoke.

Hilton Ras al-Khaimah (☎ 228 8888; rkhilton@ emirates.net.ae; Al-Jaz'ah Rd; Dh700; 🖥 🐕) It may be the only decent hotel in town, but this Hilton doesn't meet the chain's usually high standards. The low-ceilinged rooms are claustrophobic, service is slow, the lobby café is terribly smoky, and phone calls appeared on our bill that we never made. The German package tourists that fill the place don't seem to mind though.

Eating

Al Shafah Bakery (☎ 227 1855; pizzas Dh2.50-6; ☽ 8am-midnight) This hole-in-the-wall Afghani bakery, a few doors down from the Vegetarian's Restaurant, does delicious 'pizzas'. Try the cheese and *zaatar* (thyme), or mutton with cheese. Eat them while they're piping hot, straight out of the stone oven.

Vegetarian's Restaurant (☎ 228 8809; mains Dh10; ⊙ 7.30am-2.30pm & 6.30pm-11.30pm Sat-Wed, 7am-3pm & 5pm-midnight Thu & Fri) They take their vegetarianism seriously here; the extensive menu offers everything from delicious dosas (from Dh3.50) to tandooris (Dh10 to Dh15) and fragrant curries (Dh8 to Dh10).

Al-Sahari (☎ 233 3966; Sheikh Mohammad bin Salem St; mezze Dh2-15, grills Dh13-17; ⊙ 11am-midnight) RAK's locals keep coming back to this popular eatery for its friendly service and cheap tasty food. How can you resist the charm of a place that boasts 'our objective is salubrious food and the sweet taste and the special arabic kindness'? The expansive menu features Lebanese staples, a few Emirati favourites, with some 'international' dishes thrown in, from fried Sultan Ibrahim fish (Dh15) and *shish tawooq* (Dh13) to 'Chateau Briand' (Dh30) and 'chicken Maggi soup' (Dh3).

Lebanese House (☎ 228 2181; mains Dh20; ⊙ 11am-3pm & 6.30pm-midnight) This spotlessly clean Lebanese eatery specialises in simple home-cooked Arabic favourites, including lentil soup (Dh2), fried *kibbeh* (12 pieces; Dh20), and grilled Egyptian pigeon (Dh25). It's next to Al-Nakheel Hotel.

Drinking

Local guys love the traditional *barasti* coffeehouse **Al Fakher Popular Café** (☎ 228 8334; ⊙ 4pm-1am), overlooking the lagoon where they play backgammon, drink coffee (Dh4) and puff on a *sheesha* (Dh5) well into the night. It's near Mina Saqr.

Entertainment

The **Gulf Cinema** (☎ 222 3313; tickets Dh20; ⊙ 1.30pm-10.45pm) shows English-language films.

Getting There & Around

Tiny **Ras al-Khaimah airport** (☎ 228 8809) is 22.5km south of Al-Nakheel.

There are no bus services within the emirate or to other emirates. The taxi station is on Sheikh Mohammad bin Salem St just south of the Bin Majid Beach Hotel on the other side of the street. A shared taxi to Dubai will cost Dh25, and to Sharjah, Ajman or Umm al-Quwain Dh20. There are

no shared taxis to Fujairah; it will cost you around Dh160 to engage one.

Taxis within the town aren't metered. A trip from the old town to Al-Nakheel shouldn't cost more than Dh10. Agree on the fare before you get in.

AROUND RAS AL-KHAIMAH
Al Hamra Fort Hotel & Beach Resort

This old Arabian-inspired **resort** (☎ 244 6666; www.alhamrafort.com; d Dh750; 🖳 🞬), 25km south of RAK, on the edge of the Gulf, gets packed with European package tourists. While rooms are spacious and comfortable with Oriental touches such as *mashrabiyya* screens, unfortunately the interior isn't as impressive as the exterior architecture and has already dated. Set in lush gardens, there are two pools, a pristine white-sand beach, and plenty of water sports, diving and golf on offer. There are several rather uninspiring eateries that could prove frustrating after a couple of days.

Shamal سمال

The village of Shamal, 5km north of Ras al-Khaimah, is the site of some of the most important archaeological finds in the UAE. The area has been inhabited since the late 3rd millennium BC and a set of ruined buildings and fortifications spread on a small hill overlooking the village is known as the **Queen of Sheba's Palace**, although it's disputed as to whether she was actually here. Some argue that it was Queen Zenobia from Palmyra (in Syria), who ruled a sizable chunk of the Middle East in the 4th century AD who may have been there. The fortifications were used as recently as the 16th century but unfortunately there's little of the structure left today and to the untrained eye it probably looks like a pile of rubble and small stone wall. The views of the mountains are super though and the village is fascinating.

To reach the site, travel north along Oman St for 4.3km from the hospital roundabout in Al-Nakheel and turn right onto a paved road, where there is a brown sign pointing to the Shamal Folk Arts and Theatre Society (Saqr Heritage Village). Follow this road for 1.5km past the Heritage Village until you reach an oval roundabout. Turn right and follow the road for another 2.3km through a village until you come to the People Heritage Revival Association, a new building made to look like a fort. Turn left. Pass through the village, passing a small brown and orange mosque on the left. Immediately after the mosque you'll come to a fork in the road; turn left and continue until you come to a small mountain on your right. You'll see a knocked-down fence and some grey stone steps leading up to the ruins, and a UAE flag at the top.

A taxi from Al-Nakheel should charge around Dh50 to take you there, wait 30 minutes and return. Agree on the fare before you leave.

ABU DHABI أبو ظبي

☎ 02 / pop 1.7 million

With the oil predicted to run out sometime after 2100 AD, you'd forgive Abu Dhabi for wanting to just sit pretty and count the money. But this attractive, green and distinctly Arab city just appears to be hitting its stride. While not as cosmopolitan or as sophisticated as Dubai, Abu Dhabi also lacks traffic jams and the poseurs that plague its neighbour, making it a much more liveable city if you don't crave clubbing. After closely watching Dubai's phe-

nomenal growth, Abu Dhabi has chosen its development projects wisely, and while the laid-back feel might eventually change, the local Emirati flavour of the capital appears certain to remain.

The emirate of Abu Dhabi is huge by comparison to the other emirates, comprising almost 87% of the country's total area. Just as 50 years ago Abu Dhabi was little more than a fishing village comprising a fort, a few coral buildings and a smattering of *barasti* huts, the rest of the emirate is very 'Arabian Sands' with its enigmatic empty desert, dotted with oases such as Al-Ain and Liwa. While the ruling Al-Nahyan family may have become rich from what lies beneath, you get the sense that their connection to the desert and the sea is something that remains more important than petrodollars.

HISTORY

The Bedouin of the Bani Yas tribe settled on the island of Abu Dhabi in 1761. Early on, the centre of power for the tribe remained at Liwa Oasis, where the ruling Al-Nahyan family was based, but in 1793 the family moved to Abu Dhabi. At this time a haven for wildlife (Abu Dhabi literally means 'Father of the Gazelle'), the

---

GULF CUP GONE WILD

'You don't know just how important this is to us!' said my local Emirati friend in between tokes on his little tobacco pipe. 'We need to win this.' With *this* being the soccer (football) semi-final against highly fancied Saudi Arabia in the 18th edition of the Gulf Cup being held in Abu Dhabi, I wished him luck. Playing at a packed 20,000-seat stadium that night, the UAE did the impossible, scoring in extra time to defeat the strong Saudi team. Soon, across the nation, painted faces and unfurling flags hit the streets. Abu Dhabi's Corniche turned into a slow-motion drag race, with souped-up 4WDs and low-slung sports cars taking turns in burning rubber to the delight of onlookers that lined the waterfront.

These scenes were repeated in the capital a few nights later when the UAE defeated Oman in front of 60,000 wild fans to win the cup for the first time in its history. Instead of celebrating the win in *sheesha* cafés, with their wall-sized TV screens projecting the game, locals downed *sheesha* pipes and ran to their cars at the final whistle, performing a Middle Eastern version of the classic 'Le Mans' start to the celebrations. From the beginning of the Corniche to the Emirates Palace hotel, locals danced on top of, inside, and in front of, their wildly painted vehicles. For hours they burnt rubber up and down the usually tranquil waterfront, while plain-clothed police kept the crowd in relative check.

Along Sheikh Zayed Rd in Dubai a couple of days later, similar victory celebrations drew complaints of how the parade held up traffic. Stern 'letters to the editor' were printed about how laws were being broken and law enforcement officials vowed to bring the law-breakers to justice. And Abu Dhabi is the reserved city?

Terry Carter

UNITED ARAB EMIRATES

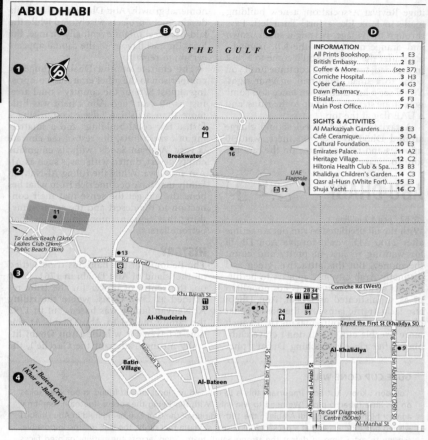

ABU DHABI

INFORMATION
All Prints Bookshop	**1** E3
British Embassy	**2** E3
Coffee & More	(see 37)
Corniche Hospital	**3** H3
Cyber Café	**4** G3
Dawn Pharmacy	**5** F3
Etisalat	**6** F3
Main Post Office	**7** F4

SIGHTS & ACTIVITIES
Al Markaziyah Gardens	**8** E3
Café Ceramique	**9** D4
Cultural Foundation	**10** E3
Emirates Palace	**11** A2
Heritage Village	**12** C2
Hiltonia Health Club & Spa	**13** B3
Khalidiya Children's Garden	**14** C3
Qasr al-Husn (White Fort)	**15** E3
Shuja Yacht	**16** C2

town expanded rapidly during the heyday of the pearl trade in the late 19th century. In 1892 its ruler, Sheikh Zayed bin Mohammed al-Nahyan (known as Zayed the Great), agreed that the emirate would become a protectorate of Britain and it joined the Trucial States. Zayed the Great died in 1909, and under five subsequent rulers the emirate's power and prosperity declined, largely due to the collapse of the pearling industry.

Everything changed in 1958 when oil was discovered, and it is from this date that the development of modern Abu Dhabi can be said to have commenced. The current ruler, Sheikh Zayed bin Sultan al-Nahyan, staged a coup against his brother, then the ineffectual ruler, in 1966. Sheikh Zayed subsequently used his vast diplomatic skills to be the main player in creating the UAE and became its first president, a role he held up until his death in November 2004. Sheikh Khalifa bin Zayed al-Nahyan, Zayed's oldest son, became ruler of Abu Dhabi and was elected President of the UAE soon after.

ORIENTATION

The city of Abu Dhabi sits at the head of a T-shaped island. The airport is about 30km from the centre, across the Al-Maqta Bridge, one of two major bridges that link the island with the mainland. Near the bridge is the colossal Sheikh Zayed bin

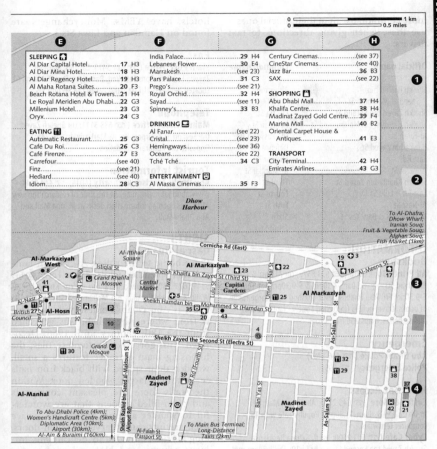

Sultan al-Nahyan Grand Mosque, nearing completion at the time of writing. Airport Rd leads into the centre of the city to Hamdan St, the city's main street. You know you've arrived when you see a number of enormous white, iconic UAE monuments in front of you, including a giant coffeepot, incense burner and a perfume sprinkler. On the other side of these is the wide Corniche road, which runs the length of the city. Its waterfront promenade is a favourite jogging/powerwalking route and its many parks are filled with families picnicking and playing with their kids, often late into the night during the cooler winter months. At the eastern end of the Corniche are the *mina* (port), the

Tourist Club area, some five-star hotels and Abu Dhabi Mall. At the western end is Emirates Palace, the public beach and Ladies Beach, the Breakwater, Marina Mall and the Heritage Village.

The main business district of Abu Dhabi is the area bounded by Sheikh Khalifa bin Zayed and Istiqlal Sts to the north, Zayed the Second St to the south, Khalid bin al-Walid St to the west, and As-Salam St to the east. Planned along a New York–style grid system, the city is easy to navigate. The main bus terminal and taxi stand is on the corner of Defence St and East Rd, slightly south of the centre. It's a Dh5 taxi ride to the centre of town from here. Some of the city's main streets have names that are in more common use than their official ones – use these when giving directions to taxi drivers:

Official name	Common name
Sheikh Rashid bin Saeed al-Maktoum St	Airport Rd
Sheikh Zayed the Second St	Electra St
Sheikh Hamdan bin Mohammed St	Hamdan St
Al-Falah St	Old Passport Rd
Haza'a bin Zayed St	Defence Rd
East Rd	Muroor Rd
Juwazat St	Al-Manhal St
Sheikh Khalifa bin Zayed St	Third St
East Rd & Lulu St	Fourth St
Al-Nasr St	Fifth St
Umm al-Nar & Bani Yas St	Sixth St
Liwa St	Tenth St

INFORMATION
Bookshop
All Prints Bookshop (☎ 633 8572; cnr Al Nasr & Tariq ibn Ziyad Sts; ☷ 8.30am-1.30pm & 5-9.30pm Sat-Thu, 5-9.30pm Fri) Abu Dhabi's best bookshop has a large range of books, travel guides (including Lonely Planet guides), phrase books, maps and magazines.

Emergency
Abu Dhabi Police (☎ 446 1461)
Police Emergency (☎ 999)

Internet Access
Coffee & More (☎ 645 2020; Abu Dhabi Mall; per hr Dh15; ☷ 8.30am-11.30pm) Popular café with 15 computer terminals.
Cyber Café (☎ 631 2600; 1st fl, Sahara Residence, Sheikh Zayed the Second St; per hr Dh10; ☷ 8.30am-midnight) Above Sea Star garments; enter through the foyer of Sahara Residence.

Medical Services
Corniche Hospital (☎ 672 4900; Al-Meena St, Al-Meena) 24-hour emergency.
Dawn Pharmacy (☎ 626 9545; cnr Hamdan & Liwa Sts; ☷ 24hr)
Gulf Diagnostic Centre (☎ 665 8090; Al-Khaleej al-Arabi St; ☷ 8am-8.30pm Sat-Wed, 8am-1pm Thu) Highly regarded private medical centre.

Money
There are myriad banks across the city with ATMs, especially in the centre of town along Hamdan and Sheikh Khalifa bin Zayed Sts. All the malls, and many of the five-star hotels, have ATMs. Moneychangers are found on Hamdan and Liwa Sts.

Post
Main Post Office (☎ 621 5415; East Rd, Madinat Zayed; ☷ 8am-8pm Sat-Wed, 8am-6pm Thu, 8-11am Fri) Located between Al-Falah and Zayed the Second Sts.

Telephone
Main Etisalat Office (☎ 633 3111; cnr Sheikh Zayed the Second St & Airport Rd, Al-Markaziyah; ☷ 24hr) Opposite the Cultural Foundation.

Tourist Information
Abu Dhabi Tourism Authority (ADTA; ☎ 444 0444; www.abudhabitourism.ae) At the time of research the new ADTA was opening information desks at Marina Mall and Abu Dhabi Mall.

SIGHTS
Qasr al-Husn
Once home to the ruling Al-Nahyan family, this splendid, white **Palace Fort** (☎ 619 5349, 621 5300; www.cultural.org.ae; cnr Khalid bin al-Walid & Sheikh Hamdan bin Mohammed Sts), built in 1761, is Abu Dhabi's oldest building. This is from where Abu Dhabi was governed from the 18th century until 1966. Decorated with gorgeous Portuguese tiles, the imposing main entrance features a small, wooden door spiked with black iron nails set within a larger wooden door. Within the walls there are pleasant courtyards and palm-filled gardens that are wonderful to wander around. Inside the palace itself are intricately carved wooden doors, long corridors divided by delicate *mashrabiyya* screens, and high-ceilinged rooms decorated with painted friezes of birds, peacocks, flowers and calligraphy. Not officially open to the public, the palace will soon be undergoing restoration to return it to its original state – until work begins you can call the Cultural Foundation to arrange an informal tour.

Cultural Foundation
Abu Dhabi's vibrant **Cultural Foundation** (☎ 621 5300, 621 1958; www.cultural.org.ae; cnr Sheikh Zayed the Second St & Airport Rd; exhibitions & lectures free, films & workshops various prices; ☷ 8am-3pm & 5-9.30pm Sun-Thu, 5-8pm Fri, 9am-noon & 5-8pm Sat) is the city's artistic and cultural centre with a regular programme of live theatre, classical music, ballet, local poetry, music and dance, art

ABU DHABI IN...

Two Days

Wander around the palm-filled gardens of **Qasr al-Husn** (White Palace Fort; opposite) first thing in the morning while the air is fresh and the light is clear, then drop into the vibrant **Cultural Foundation** (opposite) to see what's going on. Make sure you check out the local ladies practising their traditional handicrafts at **Heritage Corner** (below) and buy an authentic souvenir from them. Head to **Prego's** (p425) or **Finz** (p425) at the Beach Rotana Hotel for a lovely alfresco lunch in the sun, then laze away the afternoon (when everything is closed) by the pool. In the early evening participate in the carpet-buying ritual, an expat obsession, at the **Khalifa Centre** (p427) and **Oriental Carpet House & Antiques** (p427) then try to convince yourself that you got a good deal while you down some bubbly at the happy hour at **Cristal** (p426). Enjoy dinner and live jazz at the **Jazz Bar** (p427) then walk off the calories with a moonlit stroll along the Corniche with the rest of Abu Dhabi's population. Finish the night at one of the special coffeehouses for *sheesha* with some local Emirati lads.

Spend your second morning at the fascinating **Abu Dhabi Heritage Village** (below) on the Breakwater, taking in the displays of traditional Bedouin jewellery, costumes, weapons and old photographs in the Fort Museum. Have a bite to eat at **Al Dhafra** (p422) on the white-sand beach while you enjoy spectacular vistas of the city skyline. Do some people-watching and shopping at **Marina Mall** (p427) before heading to **Emirates Palace** (p422) to marvel at the mind-boggling amount of gold over afternoon tea. Get a bird's-eye view of the city over sunset cocktails at the revolving restaurant **Al Fanar** (p426) before heading to **Marrakesh** (p425) for a Moroccan feast, Maghrebi music and some belly dancing. If that gets you in the mood for dancing, head to **SAX** (p426); otherwise have a nightcap as you enjoy a balmy breeze at **Oceans** (p426).

and photography exhibitions, and screenings of world cinema. It's also home to the excellent Emirates Film Competition, which provides a rare insight into local culture through short films, and the Abu Dhabi International Pearl Festival (www.ad-pearl.com). Situated in the centre of the city in a modern Islamic-inspired building, with elegant arches and intricately decorated tiled passageways, it's also home to the Abu Dhabi Authority for Culture and Heritage, National Archives, the National Library, an Arts Workshop and Children's Centre. Throughout the building there are small displays of musical instruments, Islamic art, old black-and-white photographs, and a fascinating model of old Abu Dhabi.

A highlight however is the wonderful Heritage Corner upstairs, with a traditionally decorated Bedouin tent with local crafts, textiles and antiques on display. Covered, local ladies sit here and demonstrate their traditional crafts, such as *saddu* (the technique of weaving textiles for carpets and camel bags), *talli* (the embroidering of silver and gold ribbons used to decorate clothes, and other household linen and textiles), and basketweaving with palm fronds to create various baskets, such as al *goffa*

(for carrying women's belongings), *al jefeer* (for dates), and *al makabba* (a pyramid-shaped cover to protect food, ideal for picnics). All crafts are for sale.

Adjacent is Delma Corner, a pleasant café that does delicious sandwiches and juices.

Souqs

Abu Dhabi's atmospheric old souq on Hamdan St was levelled after a fire a few years ago. Construction is under way to build a fabulous new building complex that will incorporate a re-creation of an old Arabian-style central market. If you're after souq action in the meantime, you'll have to settle for a visit to the fruit and vegetable souq or fish market near the dhow wharf at the *mina*; the Iranian souq selling household goods, and Iranian carpets and crafts; and the Afghan souq for cheap machine-made carpets and red-striped *majlis* cushion sets for the floor.

Abu Dhabi Heritage Village

On the Breakwater, beside the big flagpole, is the charming **Abu Dhabi Heritage Village** (☎ 681 4455; admission free; ☽ 8am-1pm & 5-9pm Sat-Thu, 5-9pm Fri). After renovations, it's now one

---

THE CULTURAL CAPITAL

While Sharjah has its Biennale and Dubai gets Cirque de Soleil, Abu Dhabi's been quietly working behind the scenes to position itself as the cultural capital of the region. While 'Cultural City' sounds like yet another Dubai real-estate venture, it's actually a savvy move by Abu Dhabi to position itself to attract more wealthy tourists rather than the package tours that plague Dubai. With name architects such as Frank Gehry designing a new Guggenheim Museum, Jean Nouvel a classical museum (that may be a satellite of Paris' Louvre), Tadao Ando a maritime museum, and Zaha Hadid a performing arts centre, the nation's capital appears to be spending its wealth wisely.

Of course there will be hotels, housing and golf courses, but it's the sheer scale of the project, based on Saadiyat Island, that has the art world reeling, and Dubai perhaps sneaking a glance over its shoulder...

---

of the most interesting in the UAE. Set in lush gardens with trickling fountains, it's a lovely place to spend a morning, before it gets too steamy. It offers a glimpse of Abu Dhabi life in the pre-oil days, with a re-creation of a souq, a traditional old mosque, a Bedouin encampment with a goat-hair tent and camels, and a *barasti* house. Workshops are held where you can watch craftsmen making pots, blowing glass, beating brass and weaving on traditional looms.

The highlight, however, is a fascinating fort museum with wonderful displays of Bedouin jewellery, traditional costumes, cooking utensils, bronze coffeepots, and old baskets. Don't miss the goat-skin containers used for holding oil and yogurt, and the old brown-and-white porcelain dishes decorated with tiny palm trees and lions. There are some beautiful black-and-white photos of the late Sheikh Zayed, and of Abu Dhabi when it was a fishing village of *barasti* huts, and Qasr al-Husn was the only solid building in the city.

There are also interesting exhibits on pearling tools and pearl-trading implements, well-aged camel harnesses and pulleys used for drawing water from wells, and intricately detailed *khanjars*, swords and powder containers. The large and impres-

sive Heritage Village Theatre is next to the village.

If you're peckish, try some traditional Emirati dishes or Arabic mezze at **Al Dhafra** (☎ 681 8955; ⌚ noon-midnight), on the white-sand beach where you can enjoy the splendid city skyline while you eat.

Women's Handicraft Centre

If you have an interest in traditional crafts, the government-run **Women's Handicraft Centre** (☎ 447 6645; fax 447 6890; Al-Karamah St, Al Mushrif; admission free; ⌚ 8.30am-1pm Sat-Wed), in the Women's Union building, is definitely worth an hour of your time. Start with the displays of traditional weaving, costumes, textiles, camel bags and crafts in the Exhibition Hall; there are some products for sale in a small shop here. Then head to the eight workshops out the back where covered old local ladies sit on the floor, gossiping and laughing (and totally oblivious to the German and French tour groups), as they demonstrate their crafts of *saddu, talli*, textile weaving, embroidering, tailoring, basket-weaving, palm-tree frond weaving and henna. Take off your shoes before entering the rooms and leave them outside. Male travellers should keep in mind that while you're welcome, in the local culture only male relatives would get this close to women; you should keep some distance out of respect, don't take photos without asking first, and then focus on photographing the crafts rather than the women.

Ask taxi drivers to take you to the Women's Association or the Women's Union; the Exhibition Hall and workshops are at the rear of this compound. A taxi from the centre will cost around Dh7. To reach the centre by car, simply take Airport Rd south from the centre and exit at the small black-and-white sign pointing right to the 'General Women's Union' (it's easy to overshoot the turn-off, so watch the road closely).

Emirates Palace

You don't have to check in to Abu Dhabi's extravagant **Emirates Palace** (☎ 690 9000; www .emiratespalace.com; Corniche Rd West) to check it out, and unlike Dubai's Burj al-Arab, you're not required to make a booking or spend your dirhams to take a peek. The hotel is so colossal – over 400 rooms and suites, 114 domes, a 2.5km walk around its perimeter –

it's hardly going to get crowded. And nor is your rubber-necking going to disrupt the privacy of VIP guests – the high-security Presidential, Rulers and Royal suites are on floors inaccessible to the rest of the guests, with their own private driveways and entrances. While the enormity of the building impresses, it's the lavish use of marble, gold and crystal (1002 Swarovski chandeliers!) throughout that's the most mind-boggling.

Managed by Europe's Kempinski group and owned by the Abu Dhabi government, the hotel has 2000-plus staff, multilingual welcome ambassadors to personally escort you to your room, and personal butlers to wait on you hand and foot – if you're staying that is. (If you're not, there are state-of-the-art information kiosks around the place in case you get lost.) That kind of personal attention is the kind expected by monarchs, and what would you expect from a hotel that eschewed the seven-star hotel classification adopted by the Burj al-Arab to classify itself as a… 'palace' of course. The palace is located near the Breakwater.

ACTIVITIES
Beach Clubs
Private beach clubs are popular with expats in the UAE, especially in Abu Dhabi, and it's worth experiencing a day at a club at least once, even if you decide it's not your scene. Lounging in the sun, enjoying the beach and pools, playing a game of volleyball and sipping a refreshment as the sun goes down is the order of the day.

The most popular is the Hilton hotel's beautifully landscaped **Hiltonia Health Club & Spa** (☎ 692 4205; male/female/child Fri & Sat Dh120/90/40, Sun-Thu Dh110/70/50; ☼ 8am-6pm) op-

posite the hotel on the Corniche. There's a lovely stretch of white-sand beach lined with palm trees, excellent water sports, three swimming pools, a gym and a good restaurant/bar.

Coming a close second is the club at the **Beach Rotana Hotel & Towers** (☎ 697 9302; s/couple/child Fri & Sat Dh100/140/40, Sun-Thu Dh130/200/40; ☼ 8am-6pm). It has a small but pleasant beach, swimming pools and a wet bar/café. Its PADI-registered **Ocean Diving Centre** (☎ 644 1696; www.oceandivingcenter.com; 1hr dive from Dh200) is also very popular.

Beaches
There is a free public beach, along with a Ladies Beach, at Al Ras Al Akhdar, at the very end of the West Corniche. To get there, continue past Emirates Palace and the Presidential Diwan to the Abu Dhabi Ladies Club and turn right. The beach is at the end of the road, which continues on and connects back to the West Corniche.

Corniche Cruises
The Corniche is stunning and the city skyline is even more spectacular from the sea.

You can hire a small boat from **Al-Dhafra** (☎ 673 2266; Dhow Wharf, Al-Mina) that seats 10 to 15 people for Dh150 to cruise along the splendid Corniche at any time of the day; sunset is sublime. It also run popular two-hour dinner dhow cruises, departing 9pm, with a fixed three-course Arabic menu, including non-alcoholic beverages (Dh120 per person).

For a more refined experience, step aboard the elegant **Shuja Yacht** (☎ 695 0539; The Marina, Breakwater; ☼ cruise 8.30-10.30pm , Mon-Sat) for a fresh seafood buffet (Dh 180 per person), including one drink (alcohol

---

ABU DHABI GETS REVVING

When Abu Dhabi decided to stage a Formula One (F1) festival in early 2007, the rumours started that the F1 circus could be coming to town. With Bahrain already host to a Grand Prix, it appeared unlikely that the Gulf would get two bites at the F1 cherry. However, betting against the UAE on anything is proving futile, and amid the acrid smoke and ear-bleed levels of noise created by the F1 cars flying along the Corniche, a seven-year contract was inked for Abu Dhabi to host a F1 Grand Prix, starting in 2009. The 5.6km circuit being built on man-made Yas Island, close to Abu Dhabi International Airport, will also host a Ferrari theme park, as well as the obligatory golf courses. With the track already under construction, F1 boss Bernie Ecclestone was circling July on the F1 calendar for the race, until someone whispered in his ear that at this time of year the often 45°C heat would see the race reduced to melting rubber rather than burning rubber…

available); after that you buy your own. Board at 8pm, for an 8.30pm start.

Desert Safaris

There's nothing like really experiencing the desert, and if you don't have a 4WD a desert safari is the ideal way to do it. Most tours leave Abu Dhabi in the late afternoon, drive out to the desert, take you on an exhilarating 4WD 'dune-bashing', let you have a go at sand boarding, then put you on a camel for a ride over the dunes in time for sunset. You then get to enjoy an Arabic barbecue while you watch a bit of belly dancing. Safaris start at Dh350 per person. The two oldest and best companies offering desert safaris:

Arabian Adventures (☎ 691 1711; www.arabian-adventures.com; Hamdan St)

Net Tours (☎ 679 4656; www.nettoursdubai.com; Sheraton Abu Dhabi Resort & Towers)

COURSES

If you're still dying of embarrassment after being dragged up to dance by the belly dancer on the desert safari, you can take **belly-dancing lessons** and learn how to shimmy and shake your hips like a pro at the **Hiltonia Health Club and Spa** (☎ 692 4336; members/nonmembers one lesson Dh20/30, 10 lessons Dh180/270; ⏰ 7.40pm-8.40pm Sun) or the **Sheraton Abu Dhabi Resort & Towers** (☎ 677 3333; members/nonmembers one lesson Dh25/30, 10 lessons Dh225/270; ⏰ 6pm-7pm Sun & Tue).

ABU DHABI FOR CHILDREN

Kids love **Café Ceramique** (☎ 666 4412; 26th St, Khalidiya; ⏰ 8am-midnight), where they can paint pots and plates (although their masterpieces can take up to a week to be fired). **Abu Dhabi Mall** (☎ 645 4858; ⏰ 10am-10pm Sat-Wed, 10am-11pm Thu, 3.30-10pm Fri), with Toy Town, roller coaster and video/laser/virtual games will also keep them busy. The new **Al Markaziyah Gardens** on the Corniche and the **Khalidiya Children's Garden** (admission free; ⏰ 9am-noon & 3-9.30pm Sat-Thu, 3-10pm Fri; women & children only) have lots of great playground equipment, including life-size trains and boats they can climb over.

SLEEPING

Unfortunately, Abu Dhabi doesn't have a youth hostel, and there is no budget accommodation available.

Midrange

Al Maha Rotana Suites (☎ 610 6666; almaha.ste@rotana.com; Hamdan St; d Dh400; ▢) The pick of the midrange stays in town, Al Maha is far superior to all other hotels in this category. These spacious, comfortable studios, with kitchenettes and tea and coffee facilities, are excellent value. Rooms are spotless, bathrooms are big, and the Hamdan St location doesn't get more central than this. There's a good 24-hour coffee shop with internet access downstairs.

Al Diar Regency Hotel (☎ 676 5000; www.aldiarhotels.com; cnr Al-Meena & As-Salam Sts; d Dh450; ▢) While the location is good, these gaudy rooms hardly represent a bargain. The rooms are clean, with a small kitchenette: on the plus side, some have good sea views. There's also a gym and sauna.

Al Diar Mina Hotel (☎ 678 1000; www.aldiarhotels.com; Al-Meena St; d Dh650) Offering similar rooms to those at the Regency, yet at an inexplicably higher price, this centrally located hotel should be a last resort. If you have to stay here, ask for a sea-view room. Guests can use the gym and sauna at the Regency.

Top End

Le Royal Meridien Abu Dhabi (☎ 695 0583; www.lemeridien.com; Khalifa St; d Dh600; ▢ ▣) The city's most luxurious hotel is where Arab VIPs stay when they're in town, so it's not surprising to find X-ray machines in the lobby and police escorts waiting out front, adding to the buzz of the place. The supremely comfortable rooms are plush beyond comparison, with big beds you won't want to leave, and all the creature comforts you'd expect, from enormous towels and bathrobes to high-quality toiletries. The views of the Corniche are spectacular and there are lots of great bars and restaurants to keep you busy, including Oceans (p426), SAX (p426), Al Fanar (p426) and Amalfi.

Al Diar Capital Hotel (☎ 678 7700; www.aldiarhotels.com; Al-Meena St; r/studios Dh700; ▢) For a reason that baffles us, this decidedly midrange business hotel charges top-end prices. While it has decent-sized rooms with all the mod cons, and studios featuring kitchenettes, it's looking decidedly worn around the edges. Only stay here if the other hotels are full.

Millennium Hotel (☎ 626 2700; www.millenniumhotels.com; Khalifa St; d Dh780; ▢ ▣) The sleek

Millennium Hotel, with its striking foyer, swish champagne bar Cristal (p426) and elegant Marrakesh restaurant (right), is an altogether stylish address. The spacious, comfortable rooms have stunning sea views and the hotel is in a very central location.

Beach Rotana Hotel & Towers (☎ 644 3000; beach.hotel@rotana.com; d Dh600; 🖵 🖭) This glitzy hotel is immensely popular, with one of the buzziest hotel lobbies in the city. Rooms are snug with little extras like fluffy bathrobes and slippers, tea and coffee facilities, and local magazines. While the narrow white-sand beach is popular despite its size, the real attractions are the many outstanding restaurants – Prego's (right), Finz (right) and Trader Vics to name a few – and the hotel's proximity to the adjoining Abu Dhabi Mall.

Oryx (☎ 681 0001; www.oryxhotel.ae; Khalidiya St; d Dh700; 🖵 🖭) Not completely finished when we visited and with construction sites around it, this smart new hotel can get a tad noisy. The comfortable rooms are extremely spacious, however, with flat-screen TVs, broadband internet, balconies and beautiful city views from the high floors. There's a small rooftop pool area with phenomenal vistas, which turns into an atmospheric *sheesha* café after dark.

EATING
Restaurants

Royal Orchid (☎ 644 4400, 644 1100; As-Salam St; mains Dh28; 🕑 noon-3pm & 6pm-midnight) Perennially popular, the tasty Thai cuisine here is the best in Abu Dhabi. The *gaeng phed lynjee* (duck with lychees in a red curry sauce) is our favourite. The restaurant is rather stylish for an eatery not located in a five-star hotel – there's a fabulous glass walkway in the entrance over a large aquarium – and the service is friendly and efficient. The restaurant is unlicensed.

India Palace (☎ 644 8777; As-Salam St; mains Dh30; 🕑 noon-3pm & 6pm-midnight) You'll feel as if you're in Rajasthan rather than Abu Dhabi when you eat at this expat favourite with its regal Raj interior and fine North Indian cuisine, including lots of vegetarian options and delicious tandoori dishes.

Pars Palace (☎ 681 8600; mains Dh35; 🕑 11am-3.30pm & 6pm-midnight) Tucked away in a Khalidiya backstreet behind Corniche Towers, this excellent Persian restaurant in Orien-

tal surroundings is a hidden gem. Local favourites include the delicious *zereshk polo-ba-morgh* (chicken and saffron with pomegranate seeds; Dh32) and spicy kebabs (average Dh40). The complimentary home-baked flat bread with sheeps'-milk cheese is scrumptious.

Prego's (☎ 644 3000; Beach Rotana Hotel & Towers; mains Dh40; 🕑 noon-midnight) The best of Abu Dhabi's Italian restaurants, Prego's offers up authentic, well-executed Italian fare, including delicious handmade pastas (you can see them being made!) and wonderful wood-fire oven pizza and pasta. The fresh-out-of-the-oven breads and virgin olive oil on arrival are scrumptious, and the staff friendly. But while the interior is buzzy and stylish, there are few better experiences than sitting on the outdoor terrace on a sunny day.

Marrakesh (☎ 626 2700; Millennium Hotel; mains Dh50; 🕑 7pm-2am) If the exotic Moroccan décor and the authentic cuisine, including delicious tajines and couscous, aren't enough to bring you here, there's an excellent Moroccan band and belly dancer. Evenings here are memorable and go late.

Finz (☎ 644 3000; Beach Rotana Hotel & Towers; mains Dh50; 🕑 noon-3pm & 7pm-midnight) With a divine waterfront location in a wooden A-frame beach house with verandas over the azure sea, Finz serves up some of the finest seafood in town. Highlights when we visited were the tuna tartare with lemon capers, crème fraiche and oestra caviar; the sesame crusted oysters with miso; and the grilled sea scallops with tomato and basil ice cream. Sublime.

Jazz Bar (☎ 681 1900; Hilton Abu Dhabi, Corniche Rd West; mains Dh60; 🕑 7.30pm-1.30am Sun-Fri) One of the city's oldest and most consistently fine restaurants serves up fabulous cocktails, clever contemporary fusion cuisine, and live jazz in a modern Art Deco–inspired interior. The South African bands play on a raised platform behind the curved bar, so it's possible to watch from your dining table or from the cocktail bars up close.

Sayad (☎ 690 9000; Emirates Palace, Corniche Rd West; mains Dh70; 🕑 7.30pm-midnight) This swish seafood restaurant at Emirates Palace is a stunner. While the whimsical interior with its fabulous blue-lit interior (designed to make you feel like you're underwater) can be distracting, the creative seafood dishes easily command your attention. The mixed appetiser plate with tuna carpaccio with foie gras and truffles, lobster salad with sevruga caviar, and veal carpaccio was a work of art. From its champagne trolley and caviar menu to its impeccable attentive service, this is a memorable restaurant that you should save for that last night of the trip or special celebration.

Cafés

Café Du Roi (☎ 681 5096; Corniche Rd West, Al-Khalidiya; ☼ 24hr) Affectionately known as 'Roy's', this neighbourhood café is popular with expats and Emiratis alike, from academics calling in for a gossip over lunch to Emirati guys doing deals on their mobiles. The haloumi and *zaatar* (thyme) croissant (Dh8) is delicious while the decent coffee (Dh10) is still the cheapest around.

Hediard (☎ 681 6131; Marina Mall; light meals Dh25; ☼ 10am-10pm) This Abu Dhabi branch of the elegant French chocolatier and patisserie chain, established in 1854, has proven to be popular with Emiratis – the men love to linger and read the paper over lunch, while the wives like to drop in for coffee and petit fours between shops.

Café Firenze (☎ 666 0955; cnr Al Nasr & Tariq ibn Ziyad Sts; ☼ 9am-10pm) Beloved by the expat community, the large alfresco terrace makes this a wonderful choice when the weather is cool. It also makes some of the best coffee (Dh15) around, along with delicious cooked breakfasts (Dh27).

Quick Eats

Automatic Restaurant (cnr Hamdan & Najda Sts; ☼ 11am-1am) This Lebanese eatery is a branch of the successful national chain, and while everything on the menu is good, its tangy *shwarmas* (Dh3.50) are some of the most delicious around.

Lebanese Flower (☎ 665 8700; near cnr Hamdan & 4th Sts; meals Dh25-28; ☼ 10am-2am) Abu Dhabi's most popular Lebanese restaurant does delicious mixed grill meats and garlicky chicken *shwarmas* (Dh3.50). It also sells fabulous Lebanese sweets and pastries.

Idiom (☎ 681 0808; off Corniche Rd West, Al-Khalidiya; ☼ lunch & dinner) Despite being around for a few years, this hip eatery (around the corner from Roy's and opposite Tché Tché), with its minimalist design, is a breath of fresh air. It does delicious soups (Dh15) and a tasty dish of the day (Dh 35).

Self-Catering

Carrefour (☎ 681 7100; Marina Mall; ☼ 10am-10pm Sat-Thu, 2-10pm Fri) has the best bakery and deli counter in Abu Dhabi, with good-quality fruit and vegetables, barrels of delicious olives and Arabic cheeses and a huge range of products from Europe. North American expats prefer **Spinneys** (☎ 681 2897; Khalidiya; ☼ 10am-10pm).

Sheesha Cafés

On the grassy verge next to the Corniche at Kalidiya, these outdoor **sheesha cafés** (Corniche Rd West, Al-Khalidiya; ☼ 24hr) are great for soaking up some local ambience. Emirati men, and the occasional group of Emirati women, chat over *sheesha* (Dh20) and Turkish coffee (Dh10) at white plastic tables on the lawn – well into the early hours of the morning.

Tché Tché (☎ 681 1994; Abu Dhabi Corniche Tower, off Corniche Rd West, Al-Khalidiya; ☼ 9am-midnight) Offers up a true expat Arab experience – with Arabic music videos blaring from the TV and a long *sheesha* menu. This popular café (with a branch in Dubai) also serves delicious Arabic food and good Turkish coffee (Dh10).

DRINKING

The most sublime spot for a sunset drink is at the revolving restaurant **Al Fanar** (☎ 695 0583; Le Royal Meridien; ☼ noon-midnight) for spectacular views over the city. Abu Dhabi's swankiest cocktail bar is **Cristal** (☎ 626 2700; Millennium Hotel; ☼ 4pm-2am) where the speciality is champagne and cigars; expats hog the Chesterfields for the two-for-one happy hour from 6pm.

The place to be during the cooler months is reclining on a sofa on the wooden deck at **Oceans** (☎ 674 1094; Le Royal Meridien; ☼ noon-2am Sat-Wed, noon-3am Thu) listening to chill-out music. The most popular watering hole with long-term expats is still **Hemingways** (☎ 681 1900; Hilton Abu Dhabi; ☼ noon-midnight Fri-Wed, noon-1am Sat), for the good Tex-Mex and live music.

ENTERTAINMENT

There aren't too many places to dance the night away in Abu Dhabi. Your most memorable night in town is the wild Tuesday Lebanese night at swish **SAX** (☎ 674 1286; Le Royal Meridien; ☾ 10pm-2.30am) where you'll meet a sophisticated crowd of friendly Arab expats dancing to the excellent improvisational band and DJ.

Jazz Bar (☎ 681 1900; Hilton Abu Dhabi, Corniche Rd West; ☾ 7.30pm-1.30am Sun-Fri) is the only venue in town to see good live jazz, generally performed by excellent South African bands. Check *Time Out Abu Dhabi* for listings.

Modern multiplex **Century Cinemas** (☎ 645 8988; Abu Dhabi Mall) shows recent Hollywood releases, as do **CineStar Cinemas** (☎ 681 8464; Marina Mall) and **Al Massa Cinemas** (☎ 633 3000; Hamdan St). Tickets at all cost Dh30 for an adult.

You can catch European art films, movies from the Middle East, short films and independent flicks at the Cultural Foundation (p420), along with theatre, ballet and classical music performances.

SHOPPING

Marina Mall (☎ 681 8300; www.marinamall.ae; ☾ 10am-10pm Sat-Wed, 10am-11pm Thu, 2-11pm Fri) The biggest and glitziest mall in town, located on the Breakwater, is shaped like a big-top circus, although its inspiration is supposedly the Bedouin tent. It has several hundred shops, cinemas, a viewing tower, and a snow park is currently under construction.

Abu Dhabi Mall (☎ 645 4858; www.abudhabimall .com; ☾ 10am-10pm Sat-Wed, 10am-11pm Thu, 4-10pm Fri) This more elegant mall is smaller but has a small arcade on the ground level selling Emirati clothes, Arabian perfumes and Middle Eastern crafts.

For more souvenirs (*sheesha* pipes, camel-bone boxes, stuffed leather camels, tapestries, cushion covers etc) head to the **Khalifa Centre** (☾ 10am-1pm & 4-10pm Sat-Thu, 4-10pm Fri), across the road from Abu Dhabi Mall, where you'll find a dozen stores selling handicrafts and carpets.

Carpet connoisseurs should head to **Oriental Carpet House & Antiques** (☎ 632 2459; Al-Nasr St), which specialises in handmade carpets from Iran, India, Turkey and Afghanistan.

If you like the idea of purchasing some of the stuff that glitters, try the **Madinat Zayed Gold Centre** (☎ 631 8555; 4th St; ☾ 10am-1pm & 4-10pm Sat-Thu, 4-10pm Fri).

GETTING THERE & AWAY
Air
Abu Dhabi international airport (☎ 575 7500, flight information 575 7611) is on the mainland, about 30km from the centre.

Golden Class (☎ 575 7466) provides transport to the city for Dh65.

Bus
The **main bus terminal and long-distance taxi stand** (cnr East Rd & Haza'a bin Zayed St) is south of the centre. The large buses near the taxi stand leave for Dubai, while buses for the rest of the emirate run from the left (south) side of the building. From 6.30am to 10pm daily buses leave every 10 minutes for Al-Ain (Dh10, two hours) and Dubai (Dh15, 2½ hours). Buses for Liwa (Dh15, 3½ hours) leave every hour; you need to change at Tarif for Madinat Zayed where there's a connection to Liwa. The last bus leaves at 9pm.

The best bus service between Dubai and Abu Dhabi is the **Emirates Express** (☎ 800 4848) jointly operated by Dubai Public Transport and Abu Dhabi Public Transport. These new, large, comfortable buses depart 24 times a day, from 6.20am until 11.40pm, seven days a week (Dh15 one way). Buses leave every 20 to 40 minutes, taking two hours. These buses are best if you have luggage. Pick up a comprehensive bus timetable from the bus station.

Car
Abu Dhabi has dozens of car-rental agencies, from big international companies to tiny local operations. The former may charge slightly more but you get peace of mind that there's going to be a spare in the boot and 24 hour help if you need it. Europcar offers the best combination of low prices and efficient service in the UAE.
Avis (☎ 575 7180; www.avis.com)
Budget (☎ 633 4200; www.budget.com)
Europcar (☎ 626 1441; www.europcar-dubai.com)
Thrifty (☎ 575 7400; www.hertz-uae.com)

Minibus & Long-Distance Taxi
Long-distance taxis and minibuses also leave from the main bus terminal and long-distance taxi stand. There's little room for luggage in either so these are best for sightseeing/shopping trips. From Abu Dhabi to Dubai, a seat in a shared taxi or minibus will cost Dh25. The taxi is slightly faster

(and the driving pretty terrible), but you could be stuck between two sweaty people without air-conditioning (unless you're a woman travelling alone and the driver will sit you up front). While the bus is more comfortable, it doesn't leave until it's full (so there could be a wait on a slow day), and it has to stay in the slow lane and so takes longer. If you decide to engage a cab for yourself, you'll pay around Dh200 in a regular long-distance taxi which, again, may not have air-conditioning. These can't be booked in advance and the fare is negotiable, so bargain hard.

The plush air-conditioned **Al Ghazal Taxis** (☎ 02-444 7787) provide an efficient and comfortable service from Abu Dhabi to Dubai (Dh275; Dubai to Abu Dhabi return trip Dh175); Abu Dhabi to Al-Ain (Dh275); and Al-Ain to Abu Dhabi (Dh175), and can be booked ahead. Less comfortable but still bookable are **National Taxis** (☎ 02-622 3300): Abu Dhabi to Dubai (Dh225) and Dubai to Abu Dhabi (Dh150); Abu Dhabi to Al-Ain (Dh225); and Al-Ain to Abu Dhabi (Dh150).

GETTING AROUND
To/From the Airport
Most airlines allow you to check in up to 24 hours before departure and get a boarding pass at the **City Terminal** (☎ 644 5599; opposite Beach Rotana Hotel; check-in Dh75, bus Dh38). Shuttle buses leave frequently, two hours before flights, and the trip takes 20 minutes. Local bus 901 (Dh3) runs from the main bus station to the airport around the clock, departing every 30 minutes. A taxi to the airport from the centre should cost around Dh50 if flagged from the street. Negotiate the fare before you get in. To book a taxi to the airport call **Al Ghazal** (☎ 444 7787; Dh75).

Bus
You will notice large municipal buses throughout Abu Dhabi, run by **Abu Dhabi Transport** (☎ 443 1500). These are cheap but the routes aren't very useful to tourists and aimed more at locals going to hospitals, schools and the like.

Taxi
Taxis in the city are metered, usually don't have seat belts, and sometimes don't have air-con. Fares rarely climb beyond Dh10.

WEST OF ABU DHABI

LIWA ليوا
☎ 02

If you're looking for the real desert, not just the one you'll see on an afternoon desert safari with a tour operator, the Liwa Oasis is for you. Positioned on the edge of Saudi Arabia's Empty Quarter (Rub'al-Khali), it lives up to its name, with only the odd roaming camel or small verdant oasis magnifying just how spectacular the vista of incomparable apricot-coloured sand dunes really is. While this is explorer Wilfred Thesiger's Arabia, the area is most famous as the birthplace of the Maktoum and Al-Nahyan families, now the rulers of Dubai and Abu Dhabi respectively. The Liwa Oasis itself is actually a belt of villages and farms spread out over a 150km arc of land and once you visit, you'll understand why the Liwa has a special place in the hearts of locals who come here to get back to their roots, relax and just take in the vastness of the landscape.

The Liwa is best visited in your own vehicle, as the joy of travelling here is to be able to drive through the villages and stop spontaneously to photograph a lone camel on a sand dune or a spectacular 'desert rose' (flower-like crystallised gypsum). The only real 'sight' in the Liwa as such is the 287m-high Moreeb Dune or *Tal Mireb* (the signs will say both). The drive there passes through the most sublime of sand dunes. To get to *Tal Mireb* head for Liwa Resthouse and at the roundabout outside the resthouse, take the fork right. Continue along this well-signposted road for about 20 minutes. The dune is where the road ends – you won't miss it! Also of interest is the restored fort-like Al Hamely tribe residence,. Although it's not signposted and not open to the public, you won't miss it as it's the only elegant old building around here. If heading to *Tal Mireb* it's on the main road on your right, just before Liwa Resthouse.

Locals in 4WDs often camp in the Liwa area on weekends, stopping after the dreary drive from Abu Dhabi to refuel at Madinat Zayed, an artificially greened town that appears rather incongruously in the middle of arid and flat desert.

Al Nafoora (☎ 884 7400; Madinat Zayed; meals Dh20; ۞ 11am-3pm & 5pm-midnight) is popular with locals for its delicious Lebanese mezze, salads, grills and fresh juices. You'll identify Al Nafoora by its yellow-and-white stripes and pretty lanterns – its sign is in Arabic only. It's on the right-hand side of the highway in the first group of shops as you enter from Abu Dhabi.

There are ATMs and grocery stores on both sides of the highway as you enter town. Taxis are in the car park on the left of the highway on the way out of town. The town's bus station is further along on the same side, past the large coffeepot.

If you're travelling to Liwa from Abu Dhabi by bus you'll have to change at Tarif and Madinat Zayed, and from there you'll have to catch a connecting bus on to Liwa, and find a taxi to take you to the Liwa Resthouse or hotel. Once there, however, you're trapped! You're better off hiring a car and driving from Abu Dhabi. It also gives you the freedom to explore. If you catch the bus, the full trip will take around 3½ to four hours and cost Dh15 and a taxi from Madinat Zayed to the Liwa Hotel will cost Dh50. Returning to Abu Dhabi, buses leave Madinat Zayed daily from 6.30am to 10.30pm, running every 90 minutes or so. Two local irregular buses serve the oasis communities.

If driving, the most spectacular scenery can be seen on the route going east from Mezaira'a to the village of **Hameem**. The dunes here are like shifting mountain ranges of sand, with green farms providing an occasional and unexpected patchwork effect. The other route, 40km west to **Karima**, is flatter and more open. The scenery on the 248km sealed road from Hameem back to Abu Dhabi is stunning. There's a petrol station just before Hameem but it's the only one on this road.

Sitting at the top of a hill just outside Mezaira'a opposite the late Sheikh Zayed's palace (itself on a green sand dune!) the **Liwa Hotel** (☎ 882 2000; liwahtl@emirates.net.ae; Dh450; ☒) is fairly comfortable, if outdated. The high-ceilinged rooms are spacious but unfortunately none have views of the spectacular sand dunes. The decent-sized swimming pool is surrounded by lawn and there's a good children's playground. The restaurant is very average but there are no other options, so take some snacks.

The only other accommodation option is the government-run, institutional **Liwa Resthouse** (☎ 882 2075; fax 882 9311; d Dh220). Rooms are clean although a little musty and there's a cafeteria-style restaurant serving three meals daily. You'll find the resthouse about 8km west of the bus station along the road to Arrada and Dhafir. It accepts cash only.

EAST OF ABU DHABI

AL-AIN   العين و

☎ 03 / pop 380,000

The green, tree-lined arrival to Al-Ain (the UAE's half of the Buraimi Oasis) is in stark contrast to the magnificent desert dunes you pass on the way there. Once a five-day camel trek from Abu Dhabi, and now around a two-hour easy drive, it's little wonder that its relatively cool, dry climate has always attracted those looking for respite from the harsh and hot conditions elsewhere in the emirate. The birthplace of Sheikh Zayed, Al-Ain has benefited from his patronage and passion for greening the desert, with its verdant streets and kitschy decorated roundabouts.

But the desert is never far from this capital of the eastern region of Abu Dhabi emirate. The winding road up to the Jebel Hafeet lookout offers a magnificent view of the Empty Quarter in Saudi Arabia, as well as a hotel perched on a precipice. With lively markets, myriad forts and museums to explore, and a famous date-palm oasis, Al-Ain is a breath of fresh air and worthy of a relaxing couple of days.

The oasis' other half, which has kept the original name of Buraimi, is across the border in Oman and is nowhere near as affluent, a telling indicator of what the presence of ample reserves of oil can do for a national economy. The border between the two countries was agreed in 1966, after Al-Ain and Buraimi co-opted the assistance of the British to fend off Saudi Arabia, which had occupied the Buraimi area and laid claim to the entire oasis in 1953. It wasn't until 1974 that the Saudis renounced their claim.

Orientation

The Al-Ain/Buraimi area can be confusing for the visitor to navigate. All of the streets in Al-Ain look pretty much the same, and the presence of so many roundabouts can make getting from point A to point B a nightmare. Fortunately, the local authorities have erected signs throughout the town directing traffic to hotels and major tourist attractions. The main streets are Khalifa ibn Zayed St (known as Khalifa St) and Zayed ibn Sultan St (known as Main St). Most of the town's restaurants and large shops are located on these two thoroughfares. The main north–south cross streets are Abu Bakr al-Siddiq St, which extends into Buraimi and becomes its main street, and Al-Ain St. There is now a check-point here, which only citizens of Oman and the UAE can cross; other travellers need to use the Hilli Checkpoint.

Information

INTERNET ACCESS
Golden Fork Restaurant (Khalifa St; per hr Dh5; ☻ 10am-midnight)
Grand Café (☎ 766 0226; per hr Dh10; ☻ 10am-midnight)

MEDICAL SERVICES
Al-Ain Hospital (☎ 763 5888) At Al Jimi; has an emergency department.
Karim Pharmacy (☎ 764 2725; Khalifa St; ☻ 8am-midnight)

MONEY
There are banks with ATMs on Al-Ain St and the area around the Grand Mosque has several moneychangers. In Buraimi there are several banks on the main road. UAE currency is accepted in Buraimi, but you'll find that Omani currency is not as widely accepted in Al-Ain.

POST
Al-Ain Main Post Office (cnr Al-Ain & Zayed ibn Sultan Sts; ☻ 8am-1pm & 4-7pm Sat-Wed, 8-11pm Thu) At the time of research, the post office was housed in a temporary space on the southeast corner while the main building opposite was being renovated.

TELEPHONE
Etisalat Office (cnr Al-Ain & Khalid ibn Sultan Sts; ☻ 7am-3pm & 6.30-8.30pm Sat-Wed, 8am-1pm Thu)

TOURIST INFORMATION
At the time of research there was no tourist office in Al-Ain, however, word on the street is that the Abu Dhabi Tourism Authority has plans to open one.

Sights

AL-AIN PALACE MUSEUM
This wonderful **museum** (☎ 764 1595; Zayed ibn Sultan St; admission Dh3; ☻ 8.30am-7.30pm Tue-Sun, 3-7.30pm Fri) is situated on the edge of the Al-Ain oasis, in the centre of town. The majestic fort was the birthplace of the UAE's late President, Sheikh Zayed, and is one of the best museums in the country, and a highlight of a visit to Al-Ain. Don't miss Sheikh Zayed's *majlis* and be sure to check out the display of photographs of Al-Ain in the 1960s – it's unrecognisable. There are many splendid rooms, decorated as they probably used to be, and beautiful, verdant gardens.

AL-AIN NATIONAL MUSEUM
The charmingly old-fashioned **Al-Ain National Museum** (☎ 764 1595; Zayed ibn Sultan St; admission Dh3; ☻ 8.30am-7.30pm Tue-Sun, 3-7.30pm Fri) is definitely worth an hour of your time. Highlights include impressive archaeological displays and artefacts from the 3rd-millennium BC tombs at Hili and Umm al-Nar. There are also some black-and-white photos tracing the development of Al-Ain, Abu Dhabi and Liwa from 1962 to the present day, beautiful silver Bedouin jewellery, and traditional costumes. One of the more intriguing exhibits is the circumcision display, with blades and a goat-covered stool. The fort, built in 1910 and located in the same compound as the museum, was the birthplace of Sheikh Zayed. It's quite extraordinary to see these modest surrounds and consider the contrast between them and the life of unparalleled luxury that he was later able to enjoy.

LIVESTOCK SOUQ
Selling everything from Brahmin cows to Persian cats, this chaotic souq (next to the museum car park) attracts people from all over the UAE and northern Oman. Surrounding shops sell veterinary supplies – check out the neon signs of the camel suppliers! The best time to visit the souq is before 9am, when the trading is at its heaviest.

AL-AIN SOUQ
In a series of white buildings next to the bus station and near the flyover, the city's bustling souqs sell amazingly fresh fruit, vegetables and herbs; delicious honey; dates,

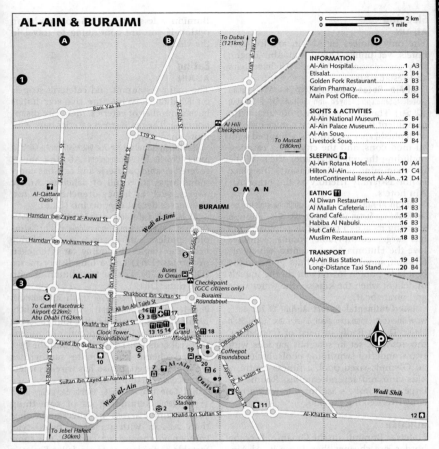

AL-AIN & BURAIMI

To Dubai (121km)

To Muscat (380km)

OMAN

BURAIMI

AL-AIN

Buses to Oman

Checkpoint (GCC citizens only)

Buraimi Roundabout

Shakboot ibn Sultan St
Ali ibn Abi Taleb St
Khalifa ibn Zayed St
Clock Tower Roundabout

Grand Mosque

Zayed ibn Sultan St

Coffeepot Roundabout

Al-Ain Oasis

Sultan ibn Zayed al-Awwal St

Wadi al-Ain

Soccer Stadium

Khalid ibn Sultan St

Al-Khatam St

Wadi Shik

To Jebel Hafeet (30km)

Al-Qattara Oasis

Bani Yas St
Al-Falah St
119 St

Al Hili Checkpoint

Wadi al-Jimi

Hamdan ibn Zayed al-Awwal St

Hamdan ibn Mohammed St

To Camel Racetrack; Airport (22km); Abu Dhabi (162km)

0 — 2 km
0 — 1 mile

INFORMATION
Al-Ain Hospital...........................1 A3
Etisalat.....................................2 B4
Golden Fork Restaurant............3 B3
Karim Pharmacy.......................4 B3
Main Post Office.......................5 B4

SIGHTS & ACTIVITIES
Al-Ain National Museum............6 B4
Al-Ain Palace Museum...............7 B4
Al-Ain Souq...............................8 B4
Livestock Souq..........................9 B4

SLEEPING 🛏
Al-Ain Rotana Hotel.................10 A4
Hilton Al-Ain...........................11 C4
InterContinental Resort Al-Ain..12 D4

EATING 🍴
Al Diwan Restaurant................13 B3
Al Mallah Cafeteria.................14 B3
Grand Café..............................15 B3
Habiba Al Nabulsi....................16 B3
Hut Café.................................17 B3
Muslim Restaurant..................18 B3

TRANSPORT
Al-Ain Bus Station...................19 B4
Long-Distance Taxi Stand........20 B4

date syrup, and date jam; and fresh fish and meat. The tiny shops surrounding it sell everything from textiles to electrical goods.

AL-AIN OASIS

A wander through this atmospheric date-palm oasis is a highlight of a visit to Al-Ain. With its shady stands of date palms, labyrinthine paths and traditional *falaj* systems, it's a great place to spend an hour or so, particularly in hot weather, when it stays deliciously cool. It's also a great place to relax, as the only thing disturbing the extraordinary tranquillity of the oasis is the regular call to prayer from the small mosques within its boundaries. Note that the entrance to the oasis that is near the

museum and fort closes at sunset; you will need to use one of the two other entrances after this time.

CAMEL MARKET

The colourful Al-Ain camel market near Al Hilli had just been levelled by bulldozers when we revisited it for research for this guide. It remains to be seen whether they will relocate the camel souq or build a new one. We hope so – this was the last one of its kind in the UAE and a visit here was a wonderful experience.

There is a **camel-racing track** to the west of the city, just off the road to Abu Dhabi, where races are held early on weekend mornings from October to March.

Sleeping

AL-AIN

The only choices in Al-Ain are five-star hotels, yet unlike Dubai and Abu Dhabi, they are reasonably priced. All have bars and restaurants.

Al-Ain Rotana Hotel (☎ 754 5111; alain.hotel@rotana.com; Zayed ibn Sultan St; d Dh400; 🖥 🏊) The central Al-Ain Rotana, with its opulent lobby, is the best choice in town with plush, spacious rooms, equipped with all mod cons, and the city's best eateries, including the reliable Trader Vic's. While the swimming pool is pleasant, this place is not as family friendly as the other Al-Ain hotels.

Hilton Al-Ain (☎ 768 6666; alhilton@emirates.net.ae; Khalid ibn Sultan St; d Dh550; 🖥 🏊) Though showing its age in parts, this popular hotel has large, comfortable rooms. Families love the Hiltonia leisure centre, which offers golf, snooker, table tennis, gym and the best kids' pool in town (wait for the squeals of delight when the kids see the water slide and pirate boat).

InterContinental Resort Al-Ain (☎ 768 6686; www.intercontinental.com/alain; Khalid ibn Sultan St; d Dh600; 🖥 🏊) Badly in need of renovation, this resort is set in spacious gardens with two wonderful swimming pools, including an Olympic-sized pool, a fitness centre, a kids club and several eateries. Rooms are large and comfy – ask for one with a balcony overlooking the pool.

BURAIMI

Hotels at Buraimi, on the Omani side of the border, are cheaper than those in Al-Ain. Until border formalities were established in late 2006, it was possible to travel freely between the cities, so budget travellers would stay in Buraimi. At the time of research, however, new procedures were being established requiring travellers to purchase a visa at the border for Dh200.

As many Emiratis live in Buraimi (for the cheaper rents) and many Omanis work in Al-Ain (there are more employment opportunities), December 2006 and January 2007 saw daily border chaos and waits of several hours. The authorities are confident that once a new integrated electronic system is established (being trialled at the Hatta border post), problems will be resolved. However, the Dh200 visa makes Buraimi a less attractive accommodation option if you are continuing to travel in the UAE.

Eating

AL-AIN

The main restaurant and cafeteria strip is on Khalifa St. While the five-star hotels have a number of eateries, many are disappointing. The main street eateries have a lot more character.

Habiba Al Nabulsi (☎ 766 9481; Ali ibn Ali Taleb St; pastries Dh5-10; 🕑 9am-midnight) Al-Ain's most-revered Arabic patisserie and café has enormous brass trays full of delicious Arabic sweets, such as honey-drenched *baklava*, and serves decent cappuccino (Dh6).

Al Mallah Cafeteria (☎ 764 4064, 766 9655; Khalifa St; 🕑 11am-3pm & 5pm-midnight) This simple, spotless eatery serves good reliable Lebanese staples, including tangy chicken *shwarmas* (Dh4) and a long list of mezze (Dh7 to Dh75). Try the tasty hummus with pine nuts (Dh17).

Grand Café (☎ 766 0226; Khalifa St; sandwiches Dh10-16; 🕑 10am-midnight) This brightly painted 1950s-inspired coffee lounge serves excellent coffee (Dh10), popular continental breakfasts (Dh14 to Dh16) and the best toasted cheese and tomato sandwiches we've ever tasted. It also has wireless internet access (Dh10 per hour).

Hut Café (☎ 751 6526; Khalifa St; mains Dh20; 🕑 8am-2am) Reminding us of something you'd stumble across in Switzerland rather than Al-Ain with its cosy chalet-style, wooden booths and lacy curtains, this comfortable coffee lounge sees regular Emiratis lingering over their newspapers while they sip the excellent coffee (Dh8) and enjoy the delicious home-cooked breakfasts (from Dh20).

Al Diwan Restaurant (☎ 764 4445; Khalifa St; mains Dh22; 🕑 11am-2am) A big, bright eatery, with floor-to-ceiling glass windows overlooking the busy street, Al Diwan is popular with locals, who love the delicious Iranian and Arabic cuisine. Grilled kebabs are its speciality and the juicy, garlicky *shish tawooq* is particularly good (Dh17 to Dh25).

Muslim Restaurant (☎ 654 158; Al Ghaba St; meals Dh8; 🕑 8am-midnight) This cheap workers' cafeteria dishes up decent-enough dhal and curries, but its piping-hot naan bread is the speciality. Women will not feel comfortable here though.

Getting There & Away

AIR
Al-Ain Airport (☎ 785 5555) is approximately 20km from the centre.

BUS
The bus station is off the Al-Murabba (coffeepot) roundabout opposite the Lulu Centre. Large **Al Ghazal buses** (☎ 751 6565) run from Al-Ain to Abu Dhabi (Dh10, 2¼ hours) every 30 minutes from 6am to 10.30pm. Al Ghazal also runs minibuses to Dubai (Dh20, 1½ hours) every hour from 6.30am to 11.30pm.

Oman's bus company **ONTC** (☎ 708 522, 590 046) runs buses to and from the Ruwi station in Muscat (OR3.600, five hours) via Sohar. These leave Buraimi daily at 1pm and 5pm. On Wednesday and Saturday there's an extra service at 7am. There's also a daily service to Salalah at 5pm. The buses leave from the front of Saeed al-Shamsi Trading on the left-hand side of the main street in Buraimi, just over the Al-Ain border.

LONG-DISTANCE TAXI
Al-Ain's long-distance taxi station is just down from the bus station, near the livestock souq. A seat in a shared taxi to Dubai will cost Dh20, and Dh25 to Abu Dhabi.

Getting Around

TO/FROM THE AIRPORT
An **Al Ghazal taxi** (☎ 751 6565) from the airport to the centre of town costs Dh40.

BUS
All of Al-Ain's buses run roughly every 30 minutes from 6am to midnight. Most fares are Dh1.

TAXI
The gold-and-white Al-Ain cabs are the best bets, as they are metered. Fares are cheap: Dh5 for a short trip.

AROUND AL-AIN
Jebel Hafeet
This majestic, jagged 1350m-high limestone mountain rears out of the plain south of Al-Ain. The views of Oman and the UAE from

the top and on the winding drive up are excellent. The summit is about 30km by road from the centre of Al-Ain with a car park and snack bar at the top of the mountain, often full of local families escaping from the heat closer to ground level.

The Green Mubazzarah park and holiday chalets at the foot of the mountain are popular with Arab families and the impressive new Mercure Grand Hotel is located near the top of the mountain.

To get to the mountain, head south from the clocktower roundabout and turn right at Khalid ibn Sultan St, then follow the signs. A taxi will cost Dh60 for the round trip.

Near the peak of Jebel Hafeet, the décor of the opulent **Mercure Grand Hotel** (☎ 783 8888; www.mercure-alain.com; d Dh350; ☐ ☒) is inspired by the 'Hanging Gardens of Babylon' theme, complete with an indoor garden. It has all of the facilities you could possibly want, including pools, minigolf, tennis, gym and business centre. Children love the outdoor play areas. The rooms are spacious and comfortable, but unfortunately have small balconies that don't really allow you to appreciate the spectacular views. For the price, this is extraordinarily good value. The foyer coffee shop serves good coffee, imported chocolates and Arabic sweets; for a full meal, the Belvedere Restaurant has reasonably priced themed buffets.

THE EAST COAST

FUJAIRAH الفجيرة
☎ 09 / pop 126,000
While Fujairah is the regional centre for this picturesque part of the UAE, it's best to see it as a starting point for the popular domestic tourism spots that dot the east coast up to the Musandam Peninsula. Apart from a visit to Khor Kalba, with its open beaches, bird life and picnicking families, the town of Fujairah itself won't delay you long in heading north. Once past the polluted and unattractive Port of Fujairah, the dramatic mountain scenery delivers a stunning backdrop to the glorious blue of the Arabian Sea and pristine stretches of beach, although development is starting to take its toll on this once clear stretch of coast. While lazing by the pool or on the beach is popular,

the resort hotels around Khor Fakkan and Badiyah also offer the best diving and snorkelling opportunities in the country.

En route to Fujairah from Dubai you'll drive through a strangely desolate dune landscape, punctuated only by power poles. Splendid at dusk, when the sunset on the sand dunes is stunning, the road eventually meets the Hajar Mountains. About 30km before Fujairah on the road from Dhaid you'll drive through Masafi's famous **Friday Market** (Souq al Juma), actually open every day from 8am to 10pm. Here you'll find rugs, fruit and vegetables, household goods and some souvenirs, and though the quality of goods isn't high, it's worth 30 minutes of your time.

Until 1952, Fujairah was a part of the emirate of Sharjah. Even today, neighbouring Khor Fakkan is still a part of that emirate rather than Fujairah.

Orientation

The main business strip in Fujairah city is Hamad bin Abdullah Rd, between the Fujairah Trade Centre and the Corniche.

The coastal road changes its name five times, which can be confusing. Passing through the city from south to north it is called Al-Rughaylat Rd, Al-Muhait Rd, Al-Gurfa Rd, Al-Faseel Rd and Al-Mina Rd. The city's Corniche, a popular promenade with locals, runs from the coffeepot roundabout outside the Hilton hotel south in the direction of Khor Kalba.

Information

The **Etisalat office** (☎ 224 2222) and several banks with ATMs are located on the main business strip. The main **post office** (☎ 222 2235; Al-Sharqi Rd; ⏰ 8am-2pm) is off Hamad bin Abdullah Rd, just near the roundabout. **New Fujairah Hospital** (☎ 222 4611; Al-Nujimat Rd) is on the first roundabout at the entrance to town. The **Fujairah Tourism Bureau** (☎ 223 1436; www.fujaira-tourism.com; 9th fl, Fujairah Trade Centre Bldg, Hamad bin Abdullah Rd; ⏰ 8am-1pm Sat-Wed) has free maps and a few brochures covering local attractions.

Sights & Activities

Fujairah Museum (☎ 222 9085; cnr Al Nakheel & Al Salam Rds; adult/child Dh3/free; ⏰ 8.30am-1.30pm & 4.30-6.30pm Sun-Thu, 2-6.30pm Fri), an old-fashioned archaeology and ethnography museum, is in a run-down building that was once a residence of Sheikh Zayed. Its dusty displays include archaeological finds from Fujairah, including bronze jewellery from the 1st millennium, and 2nd-millennium pottery and stoneware, along with ethnographic exhibits on UAE heritage and traditions, including weapons, costumes and Bedouin jewellery.

The restoration of the 16th-century **Fujairah Fort** was close to completion at the time of research, however, was not yet open to the public. Sitting on a small rocky outcrop overlooking Fujairah's old village and date-palm oasis, the fort looks splendid, especially when floodlit at night. Built from rocks and a lime-based plaster, the fort dates from sometime between 1500 and 1550. The old village is also being restored and reconstructed, and it's possible to walk around the site and take a close look at the architecture of some of the buildings, which really are quite beautiful. You should see mud bricks being made and laid out to dry, as well as other traditional construction methods being used.

The popular spectator sport of **bull butting** (☎ 783 8888; btwn Corniche & Coast Rd; ⏰ 4-7pm Fri, not during eids), held in an unassuming dirt area on the southern outskirts of town (before Al-Rughailat Bridge) has been held in the area for centuries. Bulls are brought here from all over the UAE to lock horns and test their strength against each other. The Emirati families (this is one sport that sees just as many female spectators as male) park their cars in a circle and stand and sit in front of them, forming something of an arena. The five or six Emirati men who judge the event sit cross-legged on the ground quite close to the action. While a wandering bull sees spectators racing for their cars, the judges rarely flinch.

Sleeping

Fujairah Youth Hostel (☎ 222 2347, 050-530 6044; www.uaeyha.org.ae; Al-Basara Rd; dm members/nonmembers Dh25/40) Offering basic segregated accommodation, one block from the beach near the sports club, this grotty hostel mainly sees UAE and GCC students who are in town for sports matches. There's a small grubby kitchen inside and smelly shared bathrooms outside.

Fujairah Beach Hotel (☎ 222 8111; fbm@emirates.net.ae; Al-Mina Rd; d Dh250; ⏷) Situated on the

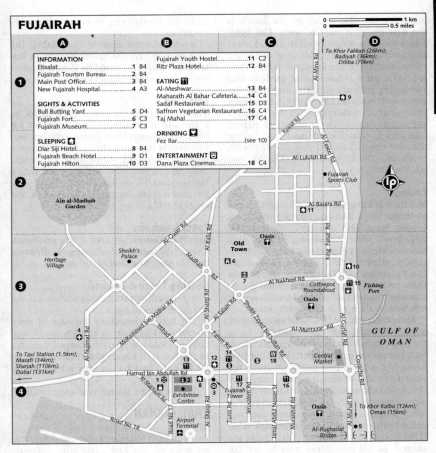

FUJAIRAH

0 ____ 1 km
0 ____ 0.5 miles

INFORMATION
Etisalat...1 B4
Fujairah Tourism Bureau..............2 B4
Main Post Office............................3 B4
New Fujairah Hospital..................4 A3

SIGHTS & ACTIVITIES
Bull Butting Yard..........................5 D4
Fujairah Fort..................................6 C3
Fujairah Museum..........................7 C3

SLEEPING
Diar Siji Hotel...............................8 B4
Fujairah Beach Hotel....................9 D1
Fujairah Hilton............................10 D3

Fujairah Youth Hostel.................11 C2
Ritz Plaza Hotel...........................12 B4

EATING
Al-Meshwar.................................13 B4
Maharath Al Bahar Cafeteria.....14 C4
Sadaf Restaurant.........................15 D3
Saffron Vegetarian Restaurant...16 C4
Taj Mahal....................................17 C4

DRINKING
Fez Bar....................................(see 10)

ENTERTAINMENT
Dana Plaza Cinemas...................18 C4

To Khor Fakkan (26km);
Badiyah (36km);
Dibba (70km)

Ain al-Madhab Garden

Heritage Village

Sheikh's Palace

Old Town

Oasis

Fujairah Sports Club

GULF OF OMAN

To Taxi Station (1.5km);
Masafi (34km);
Sharjah (110km);
Dubai (131km)

Coffeepot Roundabout

Fishing Port

Al-Nakheel Rd

Al-Muntazar Rd

Central Market

Exhibition Centre

Fujairah Tower

Airport Terminal

To Khor Kalba (12km);
Oman (15km)

Al-Rughailat Bridge

---

coast but with no access to the beach (although there's an Olympic-sized swimming pool), this hotel-motel sees the kind of guests checking in who don't have luggage. The tiled rooms are basic (as you'd expect) with simple pine furniture. There is a restaurant and three 'nightclubs' (Arabic, Indian and Pakistani) with 'live shows'. This is really only recommended as a last resort.

Ritz Plaza Hotel (☎ 222 2202; aldiarhotels.com; Hamad bin Abdullah Rd; d Dh345; 🖳) One of only two midrange options in town, the rooms at the Ritz are nothing to write home about. The hotel is better known for its 'entertainment' with five bar/nightclubs, including Sundance Club, Arabic Nightclub, Bang-

ladeshi Nightclub, Russian nightclub 'The Olga', and a live Indian show club. As a result, this is a very busy hotel and women travelling alone might not be comfortable here.

Diar Siji Hotel (☎ 223 2000; sijihotl@emirates.net .ae; Hamad bin Abdullah Rd; r Dh645; 🖳 🛉) Unfortunately the stock standard rooms aren't as glitzy as the lobby, with its marble, polished wood, piano and fountains, although that's probably a good thing. The hotel has a couple of decent eateries, including a popular Italian-cum-seafood restaurant, a coffee shop, a bar and club, along with tennis courts, a bowling alley and a gym.

Fujairah Hilton (☎ 222 2411; rm_fujairah@hilton .com; Al-Faseel Rd; s/d Dh670/700; 🖳 🛉) This attractive low-rise resort on the beach is the best place to stay in town. The light, white rooms are decorated in a sleek contemporary style with balconies with sea views, and there are spacious family chalets. The palm-shaded hotel gardens and swimming pool are pleasant, and while the grey-sand beach isn't very inviting, there's a breezy bar overlooking the sea that's perfect for sunset drinks. The hotel offers airport transfers (Dubai Dh350) and tours along the east coast (half/full day Dh 350/600), to Dubai (Dh 500), Sharjah (Dh700) and Al-Ain (Dh 750).

Eating

Maharath Al Bahar Cafeteria (☎ 222 6963; Hamad bin Abdullah Rd; ⏰ 10am-2am) Popular with local Emirati guys who pull up in their 4WDs and honk their horns for service, this clean cafeteria is a great place for *shwarma* (Dh7), falafel (Dh5), toasted sandwiches (Dh8), wraps (Dh7), burgers (Dh7) and fresh juices (Dh5 to Dh10). Try the multi-coloured 'thabakath' cocktail with layers of avocado, mango and strawberry juice.

Al-Meshwar (☎ 222 1113; Hamad bin Abdullah Rd; mezze Dh6-45, mains Dh22-35; ⏰ 10am-2am) Long the most popular eatery in town, this excellent restaurant (in a bizarre building that looks like a cross between a set from the *Flintstones* and a crusader castle) serves up the best Lebanese food outside of Lebanon. The appetiser plate is delicious (the spicy sausages are scrumptious!) and excellent value at Dh45. Add a *fattoosh* salad (Dh12) and baba ghanooj (Dh10) and it's enough to fill two. Make sure to try the fresh pomegranate juice (Dh10). If you're with a big group, phone ahead and order the house speciality *Ouzie* (a moist tender roast whole lamb with rice and pine nuts). Sit in the *sheesha* section downstairs – the people-watching possibilities alone make a visit worthwhile.

Taj Mahal (☎ 222 5225; Hamad bin Abdullah Rd; mains Dh11-22; ⏰ noon-3pm & 6-11pm) Locals love the Taj, with its rustic Raj interior décor, and extensive Indian and Chinese menu – everything from lamb rogan josh (Dh18) to Manchurian lamb (Dh18).

Sadaf Restaurant (☎ 223 3400; Corniche Rd; mains Dh28; ⏰ noon-3pm & 7pm-midnight) A branch of the popular Sadaf chain, this Persian eatery serves up deliciously moist grilled kebabs

and tasty Iranian rice in rather gaudy surroundings.

If you like the food at Taj Mahal, the owners also run the **Saffron Vegetarian Restaurant** (☎ 222 7752; Hamad bin Abdullah Rd; dishes Dh5-17; ⏰ 10am-midnight) down the street.

Drinking

The nicest place in town for a drink or a *sheesha* is Mediterranean-style **Fez Bar** (☎ 222 2411; Fujairah Hilton; ⏰ 6pm-3am), but unfortunately its lovely alfresco terraces overlook the busy road. While there's no traffic noise inside, you'll be battling it out with a large-screen TV or bad Filipino band. The bar menu spans mezze (Dh12), to fish and chips (Dh18).

Entertainment

Dana Plaza Cinemas (☎ 224 3100) are on Sheikh Zayed bin Sultan Rd, showing Hollywood blockbusters and Bollywood movies.

Getting There & Around

The Fujairah **airport** (☎ 222 6222) is on the southern edge of town.

The taxi station is on the edge of town on the road to Sharjah and Dubai. Shared taxis to Dubai or Sharjah charge Dh25. An engaged taxi to Khor Fakkan can cost up to Dh40, to Kalba Dh15, to Badiyah Dh50 and to Dibba Dh70.

Taxis within Fujairah cost around Dh5.

KHOR FAKKAN خورفكان
☎ 09

An enclave of Sharjah emirate, and the largest town on the east coast after Fujairah, Khor Fakkan (Creek of the Two Jaws) is home to one of the most attractive harbours and busiest shipping ports in the UAE. With a fabulous white-sand beach and a bustling Corniche with beautiful gardens, which is popular for morning and afternoon strolls, it's only the 'dry' aspect of Khor Fakkan (Sharjah has a no alcohol policy) that makes it less appealing to international tourists.

The sweeping Corniche is bounded by the port and fish market at the southern end and Oceanic Hotel at the northern end, with a public beach and port in between. The fort that once dominated the coast is long gone. The Corniche itself features palm trees, lawns, and children's playgrounds and rides. There are refreshment kiosks and lots of spots where you can lay out a picnic. The place is packed with visitors on Fridays.

There are a half-dozen ATMs in the semi-abandoned souq-like shopping centre across the road from the Corniche and at the Adnoc petrol station on the roundabout outside the Oceanic Hotel. There are a number of grocery stores and supermarkets on the busy main road of Sheikh Khalid bin Mohammed Al Qassimi St, which runs perpendicular to the Corniche.

Sleeping & Eating

Khor Fakkan Youth Hostel (☎ 237 0886; www.uaeyha .org.ae; 78 Sheikh Khalid bin Mohammed Al Qassimi St; dm members/nonmembers Dh35/50) In an old, white villa on the busy main road (2km from the Corniche, near the Union National Bank), this clean and simple hostel with bunk-bed rooms only, sees a steady stream of students here for sport and recreation.

Oceanic Hotel (☎ 238 5111; www.oceanichotel .com; d Dh600; 🖳) These old-fashioned 1970s digs may once have had a nautical theme (all rooms have round windows), but now they're just badly decorated, with cheap floral bedspreads and pale 'wood' furniture. The café and buffet restaurants overlooking the beach serve up prawn cocktails and mulligatawny soups. While it sees a steady flow of somewhat dazed-looking German and Russian package tourists ('if it's Saturday, we must be in Sharjah emirate…'), the emirate's 'no alcohol' policy ensures it has an equal measure of families from the GCC and subcontinent. The whole hotel permeates with cigarette smoke, but fortunately there's a pristine white-sand beach on the doorstep offering catamaranning, sailing and waterskiing. Snorkelling and diving are available at nearby Coral Island. A cosy cottage of a spa (☎ 238 7652) in the hotel gardens offers Ayurvedic treatments.

Iranian Pars Restaurant (☎ 238 5631; cnr Corniche Rd & Sheikh Khalid bin Mohammed Al Qassimi St; mains Dh30; 🕓 11am-midnight) Popular with locals for its generously sized Persian cuisine – try the tasty *chelo* kebab – served with enormous plates of delicious rice. Eat inside at tables covered with attractive plastic tablecloths or at plastic tables outside in cooler weather; it also delivers and does takeaway.

Taj Khorfakkan Restaurant (☎ 237 0040; off Corniche; mains Dh22; 🕓 11am-midnight) The only proper restaurant in town apart from the Oceanic's, and sister to the Taj in Fujairah, this place gets busy on weekends with big families on outings from Sharjah and Dubai. Traditionally decorated in a Raj style, it serves up home-cooked Indian and Chinese dishes, with the spicy chicken tikka masala (Dh20) and myriad biryanis (Dh15 to Dh28) proving popular. The restaurant is opposite Al Safeer Centre.

There are a number of *shwarma* stands on the Corniche and fast-food eateries on Sheikh Khalid bin Mohammed Al Qassimi St.

BADIYAH   بادية
☎ 09
The small fishing village of Badiyah (also spelt Bidyah and Bidiya), 8km north of Khor Fakkan but in the Fujairah emirate, is one of the oldest villages in the Gulf. Archaeological digs show that it has been settled continuously since the 3rd millennium BC. Today, it is known mainly for its **mosque** (🕓 7am-10pm), a charming earth-coloured structure of stone, mud brick and gypsum built between 1446 and 1668. The building's roof, with its four pointed domes supported by an internal pillar, is particularly distinctive and its simple interior has a lovely contemplative feel. Thought to be the oldest mosque in the UAE, it now functions mainly as a tourist attraction. Non-Muslims may enter if they are appropriately dressed and have taken off their shoes, but women must cover their heads. The mosque is built into a low hillside along the main road just north of the village.

On the hillside above and behind it are several ruined watchtowers, from where it's possible to admire what must be the most picture-perfect view in the UAE, featuring the Hajar Mountain range to the west, the gloriously blue ocean speckled with small islands to the east and a small palm plantation with *falaj* directly below.

Diving & Snorkelling

The reefs and waters around Badiyah offer the best diving and snorkelling in the UAE. There are nine acknowledged dive sites in the immediate area and six in Dibba, all with world-class coral and marine life. One of the reasons locals and expats maintain an almost religious devotion to the Sandy Beach Hotel & Resort is the fact that it is built in front of Snoopy Island (named after its resemblance to the cartoon character), a lovely, safe reef where guests can snorkel. The following places hire gear and organise dives. All are PADI accredited and offer diving courses.

Sandy Beach Diving Centre (☎ 244 5050; www .sandybm.com; Sandy Beach Hotel & Resort; ☯ 8am-5pm) This PADI five-star dive centre, just a stone's throw from Snoopy Island, offers a full range of courses. Kitted out with custom-built dive boats, it offers a variety of dive trips and caters for experienced divers and novices and knows the coast inside out. Tanks and weights are included in the dive price. If you have your own equipment, a trip to the reef costs Dh75 for the boat trip or Dh50 for beach entry, while a single boat dive including all equipment costs Dh250. There's a long programme of PADI courses and diving packages, from a beginner's 'Discover Scuba Diving' including shore dives (Dh400) to Open Water PADI courses (Dh1750) one/two dives Dh250/350. Hire of snorkelling gear costs Dh60 per day and it offers full services for divers, including Nitrox. The centre can charter boats to Oman and organise full-day and overnight dives.

Al Boom Diving (☎ 244 9000; www.alboomdiving .com; Le Meridien Al Aqah Beach Resort; ☯ 8am-8pm) This long-standing UAE operator offers dive trips leaving twice daily (9am and 2pm). Charters to Oman are available, and

---

EAST COAST 'DEVELOPMENT'

We used to thoroughly enjoy an east coast drive. An easy run from Dubai, the mountains and unspoilt beaches instantly reduced stress levels on arrival. As much as we loved Le Meridien Al Aqah resort when it opened, its incongruous profile always struck us as going against the 'feel' of this area of the UAE. Now, it's partnered by a lower-profile Rotana hotel (that oddly resembles a private school) on the same stretch, with a sea-view-blocking postmodern mash-up of a JAL hotel further along the coast, and still more to come... See the east coast while you can still actually see the coast, or just head to the magnificent Musandam instead.

Terry Carter & Lara Dunston

---

there are snorkelling classes for children. Contact it for prices.

Scuba 2000 (☎ 238 8477; scubaae@emirates.net .ae; ☯ 9am-7pm) Caters mainly to experienced divers. Three trips are offered daily (9am, noon and 3pm) and full equipment hire is included in the dive price (one/two dives Dh160/230). Hire of snorkelling gear costs Dh40 per day and a snorkelling trip costs Dh50.

To get to Scuba 2000, look for the signs in the village and follow the unsealed track running along the beach.

Sleeping & Eating

Many people camp on the stretch of beach next to Le Meridien, providing an incongruous contrast in accommodation choices.

Sandy Beach Hotel & Resort (☎ 244 5555; www .sandybm.com; d Dh400, ocean view Dh550, 1-/2-bedroom chalet Dh600/800; ☒) Located 6km north of Badiyah, near the village of Aqqa, this refreshingly old-fashioned beach resort is beloved by European and Arab expats who prefer its laid-back charm to the ritzy Meridien up the road. The high-ceiling rooms in the hotel wing are basic but spacious, if just a tad run-down: the ground-floor rooms have a terrace while the upstairs room has a big window with view, and an indoor sitting area. The chalets are popular with families who put the private outdoor barbecues to good use in the evenings. There's a verdant garden and children's playground, but most people come for the cream-sand beach (beachcombers will love the seashells), the diving, and snorkelling around Snoopy Island.

The Lebanese chef at the casual brasserie-style restaurant (meals from Dh12 to Dh45) next to the pool serves some of the best Lebanese food we've ever tasted. The mixed grilled meat plate (Dh45) was piping hot, moist and tender while the fried *kibbeh* (Dh12) was simply divine. A new restaurant and bar was about to open at the time of research.

The hotel can organise mountain tours (Dh170), fishing trips (Dh170), and trips to the Musandam (Dh200). It also offers transfers from/to Dubai (Dh250 one way), Fujairah (Dh80 round trip) and Khor Fakkan (Dh50). Accommodation rates include breakfast. Ask about the 20% discount between June and September.

Le Meridien Al Aqah Beach Resort (☎ 244 9000; www.lemeridien-alaqah.com; d Dh700; 🖵 🕿) This swanky hotel to the north of the village is a perfect place to spend an indulgent holiday. Its enormous rooms are lavishly furnished and all have balconies and views of the resort's extensive gardens, private beach and the ocean. From the efficient personalised check-in to the beautiful toiletries in the big rooms, this place is impressive all over. There's a wonderful big pool and myriad activities include diving, windsurfing, water-skiing and tennis. Children will love spending time at the Penguin Club, which has its own pool, playground and activities programme. The eateries are all very good but the highlight is the *sheesha* café near the water, a wonderful place to kick back on a balmy evening.

There are no real alternatives to the restaurants in the two hotels. Those self-catering can shop at the market on the main street, which sells fresh fish, and fruit and vegetables.

DIBBA دبا

☎ 09

The charming fishing village of Dibba, also known as Ras Dibba in the UAE, is enshrined in Islamic history as the site of one of the great battles of the Ridda wars, the reconquest of Arabia by Muslim armies in the generation after the death of the Prophet. The victory at Dibba in 633, a year after the Prophet's death, traditionally marks the end of the Muslim reconquest of Arabia.

Today, Dibba is unique in that it's the only town ruled by two sheikhs and a sultan, because Dibba is actually comprised of the three seaside villages, Dibba Muhallab (Fujairah), Dibba Hisn (Sharjah) and Dibba Bayah (Oman), and you can walk or drive freely across the Omani border. As in most other towns in the UAE there are construction sites everywhere, but the town still has a somewhat sleepy air. With its palm-fringed beach and low-rise buildings with colourful painted doors, it is a joy to wander around.

The town's new **mosque**, spectacularly sited in front of the mountains, is one of the most impressive on the east coast.

There are ATMs, several supermarkets, cafeterias and grocery shops sprinkled throughout town and on the main highway.

Golden Tulip Resort Dibba (☎ 968 26 730888; www.goldentulipdibba.com; d Dh385; 🕿), a new resort at the foot of the mountains, was getting ready to open when we passed through. Stunningly situated at the foot of the mountains with a beautiful private beach, massive grounds, an attractive, round swimming pool, and spacious rooms with balconies overlooking the sea, it promises to be a wonderful east coast escape. It's located at the very end of town; follow the signs.

There is another popular camping spot on the beach north of the hotel.

UAE DIRECTORY

ACCOMMODATION

There are no commercial camp sites in the UAE, but camping in the desert is common, particularly around Liwa, and camping on the beach is very popular on the east coast. Though travellers sometimes camp on the beach at Jebel Ali in Dubai, this is illegal and offenders will be fined.

There are youth hostels in Dubai (p393), Sharjah (p408), Fujairah (p434) and Khor Fakkan (p437) run by the **UAE Youth Hostel Association** (☎ 04-298 8151; www.uaeyha.org.ae). There is no age limit. The association only sells memberships to people living in the UAE, so if you want to use these hostels and benefit from the members-only rate, join HI in your home country. Keep in mind that hostels in the UAE are conservative and do not allow alcohol – don't expect all-night parties! – and because they're often full of young GCC men on sporting trips, women may feel uncomfortable.

The UAE has plenty of decent midrange hotels and an extraordinary number of luxury five-star hotels.

In this chapter, we have defined budget hotels as being those which charge no more than Dh300 for a double room; midrange hotels as those that charge no more than Dh700 for a double room; and top-end hotels as being all those which charge more than Dh700 for a double room. All prices are based on high-season rack rates, including taxes. Hotels will charge rack rates during high season (November to April) but will drop prices – often radically – the rest of the year, by up to 50% over summer (July and August).

UNITED ARAB EMIRATES

From November to April, accommodation in the UAE can be difficult to find. In Dubai and Abu Dhabi, the plethora of special events during this period means that every hotel in town can be booked out for weeks on end. Make sure you book as far in advance as possible.

ACTIVITIES

Desert safaris and dhow cruises are two of the most popular activities for travellers on short stopovers. See the Abu Dhabi and Dubai chapters for details. Those here on longer trips might want to do as the locals/expats do: go diving (see p437), play a round of golf or head to a football match.

The UAE has become the world's number one golfing destination. Emirates Golf Club in Dubai hosts the prestigious 'Dubai Desert Classic' which, with its US$1 million prize money, attracts top golfers from around the world and has become the opening event on the European golfing calendar. Golfing is the most popular activity among expats and most travellers to Dubai are keen to have a swing, even if it's just once. Green fees range enormously, but a round could set you back around Dh300.

Football (soccer) has increased in popularity the world over. If you're in the UAE during winter, head to the nearest stadium on a weeknight to watch a local game. Stadiums get packed with Emirati men (some matches see up to 10,000 spectators), enthusiastically barracking for their favourite teams. Attend a match once and you'll be hooked – the carnival atmosphere is electric! Fans are colour-coordinated and well organised, with a singer and drummers leading choreographed song and dance routines to motivate their team. Try and catch a match between Al Ahli, Sheikh Mohammed's red-and-white jersey team, and the purple-jerseyed Al-Ain. Tempers can flare post-match with riot police with dogs and police on horseback entering the stadium and letting off smoke bombs to restore order. Check *Emirates Today* newspaper or the official website of the **UAE Football Association** (☎ 316 0101; www .uaefootball.org/english) for details.

BOOKS

For an in-depth look at the UAE's major city, check out Lonely Planet's *Dubai* city guide and *Best of Dubai* guide.

Local company Motivate Publishing produces a range of practical guides to the Emirates, including *On Course in the Gulf* and *Off-Road in the Emirates*. Explorer Publishing produces *UAE Off-Road Explorer; Underwater Explorer* (a guide to diving and snorkelling in the UAE); and *Family Explorer* (a 'family handbook' for expats in the UAE). *Sharjah – the Guide* includes information on just about everything there is to see and do in the city.

Frauke Heard-Bey's *From Trucial States to United Arab Emirates* is the most comprehensive history of the UAE. *Mother Without a Mask,* by Patricia Holton, is an engaging account of a British woman's relationship with an Al-Ain sheikh's family, while Emirati Mohammad Al Murr's short stories *Dubai Tales* provides a rare insight into Dubai society and culture.

There are some wonderful coffee-table books including *The Emirates by the First Photographers* by William Facey and Gillian Grant, which features extraordinary images taken over the last 60 years of the 20th century, telling a remarkable story of a nation that has grown from the sand. *A Vanished World,* by Wilfred Thesiger, features portraits of tribal people he took over decades of travel, five years of which he spent in Arabia from 1945 to 1950. Graeme Wilson's *Dubai, A Collection of Mid 20th Century Photographs* and Ronald Codra's *Dubai Life & Times: Through the Lens of Noor Ali Rashid* have wonderful photos showing the extraordinary changes that Dubai has been through.

See p23 for more information about books on the Arabian Peninsula.

BUSINESS HOURS

The UAE weekend changed in 2006 from Thursday and Friday, to Friday and Saturday, but not all businesses had converted at the time of writing. The following information is a guide only. There are variations between each emirate and individual businesses, and there are shorter hours during Ramadan:

Banks 8am to 1pm and 4pm to 7pm Sunday to Thursday, 8am to noon on Friday.

Government offices 7.30am to 3pm Sunday to Thursday and Saturday mornings. Note that they close their doors at 1pm but you can generally find someone on the phone until 3pm.

Private offices 8am to 5pm Sunday to Thursday.
Shopping malls 10am to 10pm. Note that many still close for Friday prayers from 11.30am to 1.30pm, or all of Friday until 2pm or 4pm.
Shops and souqs 9am to 1pm and 4pm to 10pm Saturday to Thursday, 4pm to 9pm on Friday.

CHILDREN

It's easy to travel through the UAE with children. Most top-end hotels pride themselves on the child-friendly facilities they provide, including kids clubs, pools and playgrounds. Every town has at least one public garden with playground equipment and all large shopping malls have some type of amusement centre suitable for children of all ages.

Formula is readily available in pharmacies, and disposable nappies at grocery stores and supermarkets. High chairs are available in restaurants and babysitting facilities are available in some midrange and all top-end hotels, as well as at some shopping malls. Cost is around Dh30 per hour.

See Dubai for Children (p393) and Abu Dhabi for Children (p424) for more information on entertainment for children.

CUSTOMS

The duty-free allowances for tobacco are huge: 2000 cigarettes, 400 cigars or 2kg of loose tobacco. Non-Muslims are allowed to import 2L of wine and 2L of spirits, even in Sharjah, where alcohol is prohibited; duty-free prices on tobacco, alcohol and perfume purchased at all airports are extremely low. You're not allowed to bring in alcohol if you enter the country by land (nor are you officially allowed to take it over the borders between emirates).

DANGERS & ANNOYANCES

As elsewhere on the Peninsula, the main danger is bad driving (see p556). Many drivers in the UAE don't seem to have a concept of other cars, and courtesy on the road simply does not exist. People will cut in front of you, turn without indicating, and race each other on freeways. Out of the cities, the inner lane is for speeding luxury vehicles only – block them at your own risk as speeds of up to 200km/h are not unusual. Drivers have a tendency to zoom into roundabouts at frightening speeds, and try to exit them from inside lanes. Pedes-

trian crossings are no guarantee that drivers will stop or even slow down. Watch out! As per other Peninsula countries, if you have an accident, even a small one, the car must remain *in situ* until the police arrive and make a report. The only exception to this rule is in Dubai, where the crazy traffic means that anything blocking a road constitutes a major hazard. If you have an accident here, pull over to the side of the road and wait for the police.

Although many of the beaches in the country look calm, they often have dangerous rips. If you are swimming at an unpatrolled beach (no public beaches are patrolled), be very careful. There are regular reports of people drowning, particularly at the beaches in Dubai.

EMBASSIES & CONSULATES
UAE Embassies & Consulates

Australia (☎ 02-6286 8802; 36 Culgoa Circuit, O'Malley ACT 2606)
Canada (☎ 613-565 8007; Ste 1800, World Exchange Plaza, 45 O'Connor St, Ottawa K1P-1A4)
France (☎ 01 45 53 94 04; 3 rue de Lota, 75116 Paris)
Germany (☎ 3051 6516; 18-20 Hiroshimastr, D-10785, Berlin)
UK (☎ 020-7581 1281; 30 Princes Gate, London SW1)
USA (☎ 202-363 3009; 3522 International Court, NW, Washington DC 20008)

Embassies & Consulates in the UAE

Opening hours are usually 9am to noon, Sunday to Wednesday. All are closed on Friday and some are also closed on Thursday or Saturday. Embassies tend to be in Abu Dhabi, while consulates are generally in Dubai. The phone book lists them all.

Australia (☎ 02-634 6100; www.austembuae.com; 14th fl, Al-Muhairy Centre, Zayed the First St, Abu Dhabi) Doesn't process visa applications. For this, contact the consulate in Dubai on ☎ 04-331 3444.
Bahrain (☎ 02-665 7500; bahrain1@emirates.net.ae; Baynunah Rd, Abu Dhabi) Closed Tuesday.
Canada (☎ 02-407 1300; 26 St, Abu Dhabi) Near Bateen Palace.
France (☎ 02-443 5100; www.ambafrance.org.ae; cnr 13th & 26th Sts, Abu Dhabi) Near Bateen Palace.
Germany (☎ 02-443 5630; embgermemb@emirates .net.ae; An-Nahyan St, Abu Dhabi) Near Bateen Palace.
Japan (☎ 02-443 5696; embjpn@emirates.net.ae; An-Nahyan St, Abu Dhabi) Near Bateen Palace.
Kuwait (☎ 02-444 6888; fax 02-444 4109; Diplomatic Area, Airport Rd, Abu Dhabi) 10km south of the centre.

Netherlands (☎ 02-632 1920; dba@minbuza.nl; 6th fl, Al-Masoud Tower, Hamdan St, Abu Dhabi)
New Zealand There's no embassy in Abu Dhabi. Contact the consulate in Dubai ☎ 04-331 7500.
Oman (☎ 02-446 3333; omanemb@emirates.net.ae; 19 St, Abu Dhabi) Located behind Immigration Department about 8km south of the centre. For visa inquiries call Dubai ☎ 04 397 2299.
Qatar (☎ 02-449 3300; 02-fax 449 3311; Diplomatic Area, Airport Rd, Abu Dhabi)
Saudi Arabia (☎ 02-444 5700; ksaembas@emirates .net.ae; Diplomatic Area, Airport Rd, Abu Dhabi)
Spain (☎ 02-626 9544; embesbae@mail.mae.es; Union National Bank Bldg, Hamdan St, Abu Dhabi)
UK (☎ 02-610 1100; www.britain-uae.org; Khalid bin al-Walid St, Abu Dhabi)
USA (☎ 02-414 2200; www.usembassy.state.gov/uae; Diplomatic Area, Airport Rd, Abu Dhabi)
Yemen (☎ 02-444 8457; yemenemb@emirates.net.ae; Diplomatic Area, Airport Rd, Abu Dhabi)

EMERGENCY
The following are countrywide numbers:
Ambulance/Police (☎ 998, 999)
Fire Department (☎ 997)

FESTIVALS & EVENTS
Most of the UAE's festivals occur in Dubai. Headliners include:
Dubai Desert Classic (www.dubaidesertclassic.com) A fixture on the international golf calendar; held in February.
Dubai International Film Festival (DIFF; www.dubai filmfest.com) With a mission to bridge cultures and open minds, DIFF provides a wonderful opportunity to see quality films from around the Middle East, good world cinema, and fascinating Emirati short films; held in December.
Dubai Rugby Sevens (www.dubairugby7s.com) British rugby fans arrive en masse for lots of rugby and beers – great for them, scary for the rest of us – held in December.
Dubai Shopping Festival (DSF; www.mydsf.com) Held from December throughout January to early February, with significant discounts (up to 50%) offered in shops throughout the city and events galore, including a multicultural 'Global Village' featuring national pavilions and cultural events.
Dubai Summer Surprises (www.mydsf.com) DSF's more family-focused little sibling, held in July/August.
Dubai Tennis Championships (www.dubaitennis championships.com) The women's WTA is held the first week, followed by the men's ATP event; held in March.
Dubai World Cup (www.dubaiworldcup.com) Watch the gee-gees competing for cash prizes of up to US$6 million per race; held in March.

The other emirates have pale imitations, which include Sharjah's Ramadan Shopping Festival and Al-Ain's spring Flower Festival. However, Abu Dhabi is set to compete in the events stakes, with the first UAE Formula One in 2009 (see p423).

HOLIDAYS
As well as the major Islamic holidays (see p534), the UAE observes the following public holidays:
New Year's Day 1 January
Accession Day (of HH Sheikh Zayed) 6 August
National Day 2 December

When a member of the ruling family or a government head of state from a neighbouring country dies, there is often a three-day period of mourning when government offices, some businesses and state-run tourist attractions such as museums close. When the president or prime minister dies, the country can go into mourning for several weeks.

INTERNET ACCESS
Internet connection is available through Etisalat, the national telecommunications carrier. Internet cafés can be found everywhere in the cities while five-star hotels usually offer internet access from rooms, from the TV with a keyboard, or a broadband plug or wireless. If you're toting a laptop and want to log on, look for an Etisalat 'i-zone' or similar wi-fi sign at cafés and hotel lobbies. You can generally buy a card from the café or get a free code if they're generous.

INTERNET RESOURCES
The following are just a few of the useful websites available for travellers to the UAE:
Abu Dhabi Net (www.abudhabi.net) News and information on city events.
Dubai City Guide (www.dubaicityguide.com) Decent information on happenings in Dubai, plus tourist information.
Dubai Map Site (www.dubailocator.com) Useful map site.
Gulf News (www.gulfnews.com) Website of this English-language newspaper.
Sharjah Online (www.sharjah-welcome.com) Useful tourism information site on everything in Sharjah.
Time Out (www.timeoutdubai.com, www.timeoutabu dhabi.com) Comprehensive listings of restaurants, bars, clubs and cultural events for Dubai and Abu Dhabi.

UAE Ministry of Information and Culture (www
.uaeinteract.com) An excellent website covering every
aspect of life in the UAE.

MEDIA
Magazines
Time Out Dubai (Dh5; weekly) and *Time
Out Abu Dhabi* (Dh10; monthly) have
listings of hot restaurants, bars and clubs.
What's On (Dh10) is another monthly ca-
tering to expats.

Newspapers
Emirates Today, *7 Days* and *Gulf News*
are the better three of the local English-
language daily newspapers available in the
UAE. Each costs Dh2. International news
magazines and newspapers are readily
available in Dubai and Abu Dhabi. Don't be
surprised if your copy has the censor's thick
black mark through articles and pictures
that are considered inappropriate.

Radio
There are a number of English-language
radio stations. Emirates FM1, which caters to a young demographic, is at 99.3FM;
Emirates 2FM, a news, music and current
affairs station, is at 98.5FM. Dubai and
Ajman also have English-language FM
radio stations: Dubai FM is at 92FM, Free
FM is at 96.7FM and Ajman's Channel 4 is
at 104.8FM.

TV
There are many English-language TV
channels, including Abu Dhabi's Channel
48 and Dubai's Channel 33, and scores of
English-language satellite channels.

See also p294 for information on Al-
Jazeera TV, based in Qatar.

MONEY
The official currency is the UAE dirham
(Dh), which is fully convertible and pegged
to the US dollar. One dirham is divided into
100 fils. Notes come in denominations of
five, 10, 20, 50, 100, 200, 500 and 1000. Coins
are Dh1, 50 fils, 25 fils, 10 fils and 5 fils.

Moneychangers sometimes offer better rates than banks. If they don't charge
a commission, their rate is probably bad.
Not all change travellers cheques, though
currencies of neighbouring countries are all
easily exchanged.

There are ATMs on major streets, in
shopping centres and sometimes at hotels.
All major credit cards are accepted.

In each emirate, a different level of municipal and service tax is charged against
hotel and restaurant bills. This is somewhere between 5% and 20%. If a price is
quoted 'net', this means that it includes all
taxes and service charges.

Exchange Rates
The rates below were current at the time
of writing.

Country	Unit		UAE dirham
Australia	A$1	=	Dh2.78
Canada	C$1	=	Dh2.79
euro zone	€1	=	Dh4.62
Japan	¥100	=	Dh3.00
Kuwait	KD1	=	Dh12.53
New Zealand	NZ$1	=	Dh2.43
Oman	OR1	=	Dh9.57
Qatar	QR1	=	Dh1.01
Saudi Arabia	SR1	=	Dh0.98
UK	UK£1	=	Dh6.87
USA	US$1	=	Dh3.67
Yemen	YR	=	Dh0.02

TELEPHONE
Mobile Phones
The UAE's mobile-phone network uses the
GSM 900 MHz and 1800 MHz standard,
the same as Europe, Asia and Australia.
Etisalat was the sole operator until Du
came on the scene. Visitors can buy a prepaid wasel (sim) card for Dh165 from the
airport and Etisalat offices, which can be
recharged with a prepaid mobile charge
card (in denominations of Dh25 and
Dh40, available from most supermarkets
and grocery stores). Etisalat also offers a
special package called Ahlan for short-
term visitors. It costs Dh90 for 90 days
and includes 90 minutes of talk time, nine
SMS messages, missed call notifications,
call waiting, and your first overseas call
for free. For more information call ☎ 400
4101 (international calls) or ☎ 101 (from
within the UAE).

Phone Codes
The country code for the UAE is 971, followed by the area code (minus the zero),
then the subscriber number. In this chapter,

UNITED ARAB EMIRATES

local area codes are given at the start of each city or town section. The international access code (to call abroad from the UAE) is 00. To call a local mobile number first dial the prefix 050. For directory inquiries call 181.

Phonecards

The UAE has a splendid telecommunications system, and you can connect up with anywhere in the world, even from the most remote areas. The state telecom monopoly is Etisalat, recognisable in each city by the giant golf ball on top of its offices.

Coin phones have been almost completely superseded by card phones. Phonecards are available from grocery stores or Etisalat offices for amounts of Dh30 or more. Local calls (within the same area code) are free.

VISAS

Officially, 60-day visit visas are available on arrival in the UAE at air, land and sea ports, to citizens of 34 developed countries, including passport holders of most Western European countries, plus Australia, Brunei, Canada, Hong Kong, Japan, Malaysia, New Zealand, Singapore and the USA. The visa is free of charge and can be extended for another 30 days for Dh500 at a **Department of Naturalisation & Residency office** (☎ Dubai 04-398 0000, Abu Dhabi 02-446 2244). Note that if you overstay your visa, you will be charged a hefty Dh100 per day. The 34 countries are currently under review, however, as they have not extended the same courtesy to UAE citizens. Check the situation before travelling.

Citizens of Gulf Cooperation Council (GCC) countries do not need visas to enter the UAE, and can stay as long as they want. For citizens of countries not included in the list above, a tourist visa must be arranged through a sponsor: a company or a resident of the UAE, or a hotel or travel agency. Charges vary. If you are in transit in the UAE, your airline can organise for you to be granted a free 96-hour transit visa.

Officially, if you have an Israeli stamp in your passport you are not allowed to enter the UAE and will not be given a visa.

See Border Crossings (p547) for information about re-entering the UAE from Oman.

TRANSPORT IN THE UAE

GETTING THERE & AWAY
Entering the UAE

If you are eligible to collect a visit or transit visa when you arrive, entering the country is simple. Proceed straight through the immigration desk or border post and get your passport stamped. If you are entering on a sponsored visa you'll need to go to the clearly marked visa collection counter at the airport when you arrive.

Air

Dubai and Abu Dhabi are the country's main international airports, though an increasing number of carriers serve Sharjah as well. There are also small international airports at Fujairah, Ras al-Khaimah and Al-Ain, primarily used by charter flights. There is no departure tax when leaving by air.

Contact details for all UAE airports can be found under Getting There & Away in each destination section in this chapter.

Emirates Airlines (www.emirates.com) is the Dubai carrier and **Etihad Airways** (www.etihadairways.com) is the UAE's national carrier. Both have an excellent reputation for service and safety, flying to destinations throughout the world. A 'no-frills' airline, **Air Arabia** (www.airarabia.com), was established in 2003 in Sharjah. It flies to Gulf, Middle Eastern and Asian destinations.

OTHER AIRLINES FLYING TO & FROM THE UAE

Air France (AF; www.airfrance.com/ae; Dubai ☎ 04-294 5960, Abu Dhabi ☎ 02-621 5818; hub Charles de Gaulle Airport, Paris)

Air India (AI; www.airindia.com; Dubai ☎ 04-227 8767, Abu Dhabi ☎ 02-632 2300; hub Chathrabathi Sivaji International Airport, Mumbai)

British Airways (BA; www.ba.com; Dubai ☎ 04-307 5555, Abu Dhabi ☎ 02-622 4540; hub Heathrow Airport, London)

Gulf Air (GF; ☎ 800 2200; www.gulfairco.com; hub Bahrain International Airport)

KLM (KL; www.klm.ae; Dubai ☎ 04-335 5777, Abu Dhabi ☎ 02-632 3280; hub Amsterdam International Airport, Netherlands)

Singapore Airlines (SQ; www.singaporeairlines.com; Dubai ☎ 04-223 2300, Abu Dhabi ☎ 02-622 1110; hub Changi Airport, Singapore)

Land
BORDER CROSSINGS

UAE border posts that are open to non-GCC citizens include those at Al Darah (at Tibat, for Musandam), Wajaja (Hatta), Khatmat Malahah (near Jebel Hafeet) and Al Hilli (Al-Ain–Buraimi) Passport Controls. During research, we were informed that only GCC citizens could cross at Gheweifat to Saudi (even if you're only transiting).

Officially, if you're eligible to receive a visit visa on arrival at airports, you should be able to at border posts. The best advice is to cross the border during business hours. If the posts are not staffed and you don't get a visit visa you will have to leave the UAE within 48 hours or be liable for a Dh100-per-day fine.

To travel to Oman, use Al Darah, Wajaja and Khatmat Malahah Passport Controls. At the UAE post, there is a Dh20 exit visa processing fee and a Dh60/OR6 visa fee at the Omani entry point. For reasons not adequately explained to us, at the new Al Hilli Passport Control (Al-Ain–Buraimi, where a border post has just been established and formalities introduced in early 2007), travellers are required to purchase a visa for Dh200. As many Emiratis live in Buraimi and many Omanis work in Al-Ain there is a lot of movement across this border and hence long delays. A new integrated electronic system is being established nationwide, being trialled at the Wajaja (Hatta) border post at the time of research, which authorities promise should speed up formalities everywhere.

See p547 for a summary of border crossings around the region.

BUS

Oman National Transport Company (ONTC) runs buses from Dubai via Hatta to Muscat and vice versa. Buses leave from the **ONTC office** (☎ 04-295 9920; DNATA Car Park, Deira; ✆ 9am-9pm), located near the Caravan Restaurant, two to three times daily. The schedule varies on demand, so call ahead. The trip takes approximately five hours and costs Dh60/100 one way/return. Buses have televisions and toilets on board. Note that this is the only bus company that non-GCC citizens can travel on. The others should not sell you tickets (they don't stop at the border for a start).

Dozens of bus companies have services to Jordan, Syria, Lebanon and Egypt via Saudi Arabia and Jordan, but officially, non-GCC citizens should not be travelling on these and the bus companies are not allowed to sell you tickets. Saudi transit visas are required and at the time of research these were not being given to non-Muslims.

CAR & MOTORCYCLE

If you hire a car in the UAE, you will need to take out extra insurance (usually Dh500 per week) if you plan to take it into Oman.

Sea

The Iranian shipping company Valfajre-8 has twice-weekly services (usually Sunday and Thursday at 9pm, but you'll need to be there at 4pm to go through the formalities) between Bandar-e Abba in Iran and Sharjah's Port Khalid (Dh160 economy, 10 to 12 hours). The local agent is the **Oasis Freight Agency** (☎ 06-559 6325; Kayed Ahli Bldg, Jamal Abdul Nasser Rd, Sharjah; ✆ 8am-1pm & 2-4.30pm).

GETTING AROUND
Air
There are no internal flights in the UAE.

Bus & Minibus
Well-maintained Dubai Transport minibuses or buses serve all the emirates but the only route that takes passengers on the return trip is Sharjah. The rest of the buses go back to Dubai empty. Equally well-maintained Al Ghazal buses travel between Dubai and Abu Dhabi, and Dubai and Al-Ain, as well as within the Abu Dhabi emirate. There is now an excellent frequent inter-Emirate bus service between Dubai and Abu Dhabi. This is the most comfortable way to travel.

Keep in mind that bus journeys taken during Dubai's peak periods (from 7am to 10am, noon to 2pm and 4.30pm to 7pm approximately) can be delayed due to traffic congestion. Trips that might take half an hour outside of peak times or on a Friday could take double that time. And if there's an accident? Triple that time and postpone that dinner reservation!

See Getting There & Away in the relevant destination sections in this chapter for more details.

Car

Driving is by far the best way to see the UAE, allowing you to get off the major highways and onto the more interesting back roads and giving you the freedom to stop as you please. Major roads in the UAE are excellent; multilane highways link the cities and have lighting along their entire length. See the Arabian Peninsula Transport chapter for more information on road rules and hazards (p555).

If you have a breakdown call the **Arabian Automobile Association** (☎ 800 4900).

HIRE

Car rental starts at about Dh150 for one day (including insurance) for a small manual car such as a Toyota Echo. A Mazda 6 will be around Dh270. Rates fall to about Dh107/232 per day for a week, and even more for a month. If you rent a car for more than three days you will usually be given unlimited kilometres. Don't hesitate to negotiate with car rental agencies for dis-

counts. In our experience, Europcar gives the best reductions. It will also drop cars off at your hotel or home.

To hire a car, you'll need a credit card and an international driver's licence; you may also need two passport-sized photos. In some instances rental agencies will hire cars to travellers with only a driver's licence from their own country, but this is happening less often. There are dozens of agencies listed in the phone book; the smaller ones may offer slightly better rates but the more-established ones have bigger fleets and better emergency back up.

Long-Distance Taxi

Shared taxis can be cramped but they are certainly cheap. The main problems are that, aside from the busy Abu Dhabi–Dubai route, they often fill up slowly, and the cars are sometimes not as roadworthy as one would like (ie don't have seat belts). You can take these taxis engaged (ie privately, not shared) if you are willing to pay for all of the seats.

Yemen اليمنية

There can't be many places left in the world that could make God smile, but Yemen is one of them.

Inhabited almost forever Yemen is, in many ways, the birthplace of all our lives. In days past, the sons of Noah knew it as the land of milk and honey, Gilgamesh came here to search for the secret of eternal life, wise men gathered frankincense and myrrh from its mountains and, most famously, a woman known simply as Sheba said Yemen was her home.

Yet since the book of mythology was closed, Yemen has remained largely locked away in a forgotten corner, oblivious to the world that was oblivious to it. Today, like a spring tortoise emerging from hibernation, Yemen is awaking from its slumber and slowly revealing its face. And what a face it is. Sitting at the crossroads of two continents, this country has a little of everything. With its shades of Afghanistan, reflections of Morocco, flavours of Africa and reminders of Arabia, Yemen is utterly unique and deeply romantic. To travel in this most traditional of Islamic countries, surrounded by a people whom the Prophet once described as 'the most gentle-hearted of men', is a privilege you will not quickly forget. But never mind what we have to say about it, let's leave the last word to the man who made it.

Legend tells how one day God decided to check out how his creation was fairing: London, he decided, had changed a lot, Egypt was nothing like he remembered it, but Yemen, 'Well', he smiled, 'that hasn't changed since the day I created it'.

FAST FACTS

- **Official name** Republic of Yemen
- **Capital** San'a
- **Area** 555,000 sq km
- **Population** 21 million
- **Country code** ☎ 967
- **Head of State** President Ali Abdullah Saleh
- **Annual number of tourists** 336,000
- **Stereotypes** Guns and qat chewers, mountains and coffee, frankincense and Sheba
- **Surprises** It's far safer and friendlier than wherever you are from

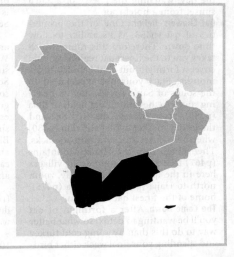

HIGHLIGHTS

- **Old San'a** (p459) Sigh over San'a's icing-cake houses and saunter through ancient alleyways created by the son of Noah and a mischievous bird.
- **Haraz Mountains** (p467) Weave a trail through a tapestry of fortresses and fields in the Haraz Mountains.
- **Wadi Hadramawt** (p505) Wander the sandcastle cities of weird and wonderful Wadi Hadramawt where giants once roamed and scorpions line the entrance to Hell.
- **Ma'rib** (p494) Ponder the palace of the daughter of the Devil and the lover of Solomon in surreal Ma'rib.
- **Suqutra** (p502) Act like a medieval knight and search for dragons and the secret of eternal life in stupendous Suqutra.

ITINERARIES

See the Itineraries chapter (p26) for more Yemen itineraries.

- **San'a Stopover** If time is everything, don't waste it – get lost in the old city. Trying to follow any kind of set walking tour here is impossible so instead allow a cat-like curiosity to lead you through alleyways, up back streets and into interesting corners. The perfect day would involve stopping for tea in any of the numerous teashops, having a *salta* (stew) lunch at Houmald Salta (p464), stuffing your cheeks with qat (p462) and, to round out the day, watching the poetry of a San'a sunset from a hotel roof.
- **Qat Chewers' Delight** One of the properties of qat (p453) is its ability to slow time down. Therefore this route, which takes you to the finest qat regions, should cover a fortnight but could stretch to six months! Start your qat experiment in the souqs of San'a (p462), before heading south to the famous qat fields of Jibla (p485), cross over to the Red Sea and the Friday market of Beit al-Faiqh (p480) where the coast stocks up on its kicks. Then climb into the Haraz Mountains (p467) to explore the numerous villages here in the qat heartland. Finally, zoom north to Hajja (p473) and Sa'da (p475), home of the finest qat in Yemen.
- **The Come Down** After a fortnight of qat you'll be wanting to detox, so what better way to do this than by going cold turkey and spending your final week either bird-spotting in Suqutra (p502) or in magical Hadramawt (p505)?

CLIMATE & WHEN TO GO

Climatically, Yemen can be divided into three main zones: the Tihama (the Red Sea coastal strip); the central highlands (including San'a); and the desert areas of the east and the far north.

The best time to visit the Tihama is between November and February (summertime can be suffocatingly hot). The twice-yearly monsoons bring some rain to the region between mid-March and mid-April, and particularly July to September. Temperatures range from around 21°C in December and January to as high as 40°C in June. Humidity is also high.

The central highlands (which range from 1500m to 3500m) enjoy a temperate climate for most of the year, though it can get hot at noon and chilly at night (particularly between October and February). The monsoons are light in San'a, but heavy (up to 500mm rainfall) in the southwest and can continue into May. San'a ranges in temperature from a minimum of 5°C (from November to January) to a maximum of 25°C (in July).

The desert regions of the east and the far north are hot (particularly between June and September) and very dry, with temperatures from 25°C in December to 37°C or more in June. The southern coastal strip is very hot and humid between May and September.

The island of Suqutra is a special case and is never really too hot or too cold. Wind is the main factor here. During the summer monsoon period from May to September, winds blow constantly from the southwest at severe gale force with frequent gusts up to hurricane force. Don't underestimate how difficult this can make even simple tasks like standing up and walking! Bizarrely, the southern coast of the island and the mountainous interior have much calmer wind patterns than the east, west and north coasts.

Though the monsoons can flood wadis (river beds, often dry) and close roads, they do temporarily turn parts of Yemen into wonderfully green and fertile land.

During the peak season (20 December to 10 January), you're advised to book hotels in popular tourist spots. Travel during the month of Ramadan is not recommended, and during the annual haj pilgrimage (as well as during Ramadan), Yemenia flights are often overbooked or cancelled.

HISTORY
Sabaeans & Himyarites

Aside from legend, a shroud of mystery still envelops the early origins of southern Arabia. The area now known as Yemen came to light during the 1st millennium BC, when a sweet-smelling substance called frankincense first hit the world's markets. Carefully controlling the production and trade of this highly lucrative commodity were the Sabaeans, initially based in eastern Yemen.

Over the ensuing centuries, the Sabaean Empire expanded and came to dominate almost all the rest of modern-day Yemen. The temples and Great Dam at Ma'rib date from this period.

As Sabaean power waned, new powers and empires began to rise in its wake. The greatest of these was the Himyar empire. Initially based in the central highlands, the Himyarites' power grew, and by the late 3rd century AD they had seized control of nearly all the remaining country.

Foreign Powers & the Coming of Islam

Over the succeeding centuries Yemen was invaded many times by hungry regional powers looking for expansion.

Among the powers that passed through its portals – but never managed to fully contain the country – were the Ptolemaic dynasties, the Abyssinians and the Persians (from modern-day Egypt, Ethiopia and Iran respectively). Today Yemenis are still proud of the fact that no foreign power has ever managed to conquer the country completely.

In the early 7th century AD there came a new invasion. It was to prove far more significant than any that had come before: it was the arrival of Islam.

Initially most Yemenis converted to Sunnism, but over the next few centuries individual Shiite sects, such as the Zaydis, were born. For more information on Islam, see p59. During this time, various mini-states grew, ruled by such dynasties as the Sulayhids and Rasulids.

Ottoman & British Occupation

From the 15th century onwards foreign powers, including the Egyptians and Portuguese, vied again for control of the Red Sea coast. But it was the Ottomans (from modern-day Turkey) who made the greatest impact. Occupying parts of Yemen from 1535 to 1638, and again from 1872 to 1918, they ignored, or failed to capture, the remote inland areas ruled by local *imams* (prayer leaders). During the 17th century the Qassimi dynasty ruled over much of this region, but its power declined with the demise of coffee trading, upon which it had relied.

In the middle of the 19th century a new power rocked up. From 1839 to 1967 the British occupied and controlled parts of southern Yemen, including the port of Aden, which was declared a British protectorate. Strategically valuable to Britain's maritime ambitions, the port soon grew into a major staging post.

Meanwhile in the north, after WWI and the defeat of Germany (with whom the Ottomans were allied), a new royal Zaydi dynasty, the Hamid al-Din, rose up to take the place of the former occupiers.

Civil War

Until 1962 central and northern Yemen had been ruled by a series of local *imams*. However, on the death of the influential *imam*, Ahmad, a dispute over succession broke out, embroiling the whole region in a war that dragged on for the next eight years.

On the one side, army officers supported by Egypt proclaimed the Yemen Arab Republic (YAR), while on the other, the royalists based in the north, and backed by Britain and Saudi Arabia, were loyal to Ahmad's son and successor. The YAR forces eventually won.

Following the National Liberation Front's victories in the guerrilla campaign against the British, the colonialists were forced to withdraw from southern Yemen in 1967. Three years later the People's Democratic Republic of Yemen (PDRY) was born. It became the first and only Marxist state in the Arab world.

In the north of the country, meanwhile, Field Marshall Ali Abdullah Saleh had instituted a progressive rule of the YAR with his General People's Congress (GPC). Conflicts between tribes were contained, and the

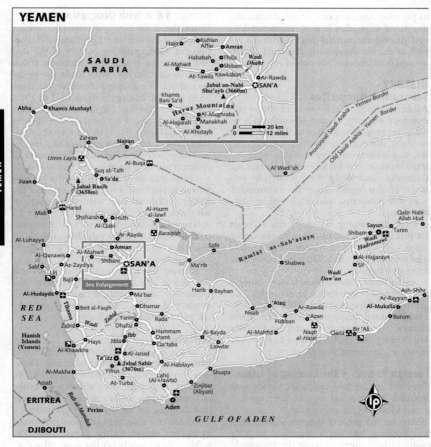

YEMEN

constitution vowed to respect both Islamic principles and Western values, such as personal freedom and private property.

In the PDRY, however, there was turmoil. Power struggles within the Yemen Socialist Party (YSP) had led to rising tension. Finally, in Aden in January 1986, a two-week civil war broke out. The situation was aggravated by the collapse of the Soviet Union, previously the major benefactor of the PDRY. As a result, the south was thrown into a state of bankruptcy.

Additionally, border disagreements between the two states had led to short conflicts in 1972, 1978 and 1979. Yet, despite the political differences, most Yemenis hated having a divided country.

Reunification

On 22 May 1990 a reunified Republic of Yemen was declared and in 1991 Yemen made regional history. The country became the very first multi-party parliamentary democracy on the Arabian Peninsula. Saleh took the position of president and Ali Salim al-Bidh (the leader of YSP, the ruling party of the former PDRY) became vice-president.

Things didn't get off to a good start for the new nation. During the 1990–91 Gulf War, Yemen appeared to side with Iraq (by choosing not to support UN economic sanctions against the country), and in doing so managed to alienate not only the US and its allies, but also its Gulf neighbours, in particular Saudi Arabia

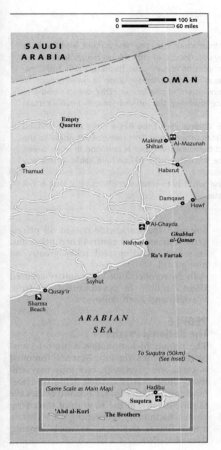

and Kuwait. This led to the expulsion of over one million Yemeni emigrant workers from Saudi Arabia and devastated the economy.

On the home front things also began to sour and the YSP and its members started to feel increasingly marginalised by the GPC and its coalition partner Islah.

Eventually tensions came to a head, and in 1994 civil war again broke out between the north and the south. Bidh's attempts to secede from the north were quashed, and he fled the country.

The country was reunified shortly afterwards. But the path towards democracy was still not smooth. In 1997 the YSP, predicting vote rigging, boycotted the elections.

As a result, the GPC swept into power and Islah became the main opposition party.

In September 1999 the country held its first-ever presidential election, and Saleh was re-elected as the country's president.

In June 2000 a border agreement was signed with Saudi Arabia. Due to come into force in 2007, it has finally settled a decades-old dispute over the two countries frontiers and, the Saudis' hope, will prevent the smuggling of weapons and qat.

Yemen Today

Following the attacks of 11 September 2001, Yemen was viewed with suspicion by the US. With its remote, unruly and little-policed interior, Yemen was suspected of providing – even unwittingly – a refuge for Al-Qaeda members and supporters, as well as supplying a bolt-hole for militant Islamists. A number of incidents encouraged this perception. In October 2000 the US warship the USS *Cole* was bombed in Aden harbour, killing 17 US servicemen. Following this the French supertanker, the *Limburg*, was bombed in 2002. There have been a number of other attempted attacks, the most recent being a foiled attack on oil installations in September 2006. In an effort to avoid further isolation the Yemeni government was very quick to sign up to the US's 'War on Terror', and international fears that Yemen could become a new Afghanistan have proved largely unfounded. Yemen is one of many countries to firmly oppose the current Iraq War.

Prior to the 2006 presidential elections, Saleh announced his retirement from politics, though at the last moment, and under pressure from his party, he opted to stand again. In an election that was seen as largely free and fair he was re-elected by a large margin. The general consensus was that after so many years under his rule it was a case of better the devil you know. There was also fear that without him civil war could erupt as tribal sheikhs with political ambitions vied for the top job.

On the whole the country is the most stable it's been in years, though the Iraq War and the government's continuing cooperation with the US in the 'War on Terror' are proving increasingly unpopular with most Yemenis. A more immediate thorn in the side of the government is the bloody uprising

AN EYE FOR AN EYE

Yemen's tribes still wield a lot of power, sometimes more than the government, and for most Yemenis tribal loyalty comes before national loyalty. Groups of tribes form bigger federations. There are three such federations in the northern part of Yemen – the Hashids, Bakils and Zaraniqs – and no government can be formed without an equal representation of these groups. In the southern part of the country, where the government of the former PDRY did its utmost to erode the powers of the tribes, the tribal structure is weaker, though since reunification a certain amount of 'retribalisation' has taken place.

In the mountainous central regions and the Tihama each tribe has a fairly rigidly defined 'territory', which is still passionately defended from other tribes. This rule doesn't apply to the nomadic Bedouin of the desert regions. Conflict between the tribes is common in many areas. If a person kills someone from an opposing tribe, his entire tribe will be held liable. In this way blood feuds between tribes can continue for years.

Every tribe is led by an elected sheikh, whose job it is to resolve conflicts or, if that is not possible, to raise a tribal army and lead the battle.

that has rumbled on since 2003 between the army and a Zaydi rebel group, based in Sa'da province, who are seeking to overthrow the government and sever links with the West. A tentative truce was reached in 2006, but a sudden return to violence occurred in early 2007, which at the time of writing remained unresolved.

GOVERNMENT & POLITICS

Yemen's first constitution came into force in 1991. Under this system, the president is head of the executive and is elected every seven years; the last presidential election was held in September 2006 (next due 2013). The president also selects the prime minister, who in turn chooses the cabinet. The main legislative body is the Yemeni parliament, which counts 301 members. Parliamentary elections are held every six years (the next election is due to be held in April 2009).

There are more than 12 active political parties, but the main ones are: the GPC (which has the majority), Islah and the YSP. Yemen's legal system is based on Sharia'a (Islamic law).

ECONOMY

Yemen is one of the Arab world's poorest countries, though the economy grew at a rate of 3.5% between 2000 and 2006. Oil is Yemen's economic mainstay and accounts for around 70% of government revenue. Nevertheless, compared to other peninsula countries, Yemen's oil wealth is modest, though revenues increased in 2006 in line with the worldwide rise in oil prices. Yemen struggles to control corruption and excessive spending and relies greatly on foreign aid.

In November 2006 the country secured US$4.7 billion in development aid from Western and Arab donors.

PEOPLE
The National Psyche

The notion of nationality is almost completely lost on a Yemeni. First and foremost is clan, and men with city jobs may still hurry homewards if their tribe or tribal land comes under threat. Second comes the family. Finally, at the bottom of the chain, comes nationality. Pervading all is Islam, a firm fixture and focus in most Yemenis' lives (see p59).

Lifestyle

According to UN figures, the average Yemeni is poor (45% of the population live below the poverty line of US$2 per day), illiterate (just 50.2% are literate) and hardpressed to find a job. Certainly Yemen's late embrace of education has meant its businessmen have real problems finding qualified employees to fill their posts.

Yemeni society is very traditional, conservative and steeped in superstition. With 20 doctors per 100,000 people, many Yemenis still rely on traditional medicine for medical treatment and healing. Keep an eye out for people bearing scars on their head or neck, where bad spirits have been expunged by red-hot pokers.

Women are more 'liberated' than they look. Many work and drive, but on average still have 6.5 babies each.

Population

With 21 million inhabitants Yemen has one of the largest populations on the Arabian Peninsula, and one of the highest growth rates (3.5% annually) in the world. The country's population has increased tenfold in 30 years and San'a is the fastest growing capital in the world. It is a very young country, with nearly half its population (46%) under 15 years old. Yemen is also still a firmly rural society, with 73% of its population living in the country.

Along the Tihama, the population is more closely linked to the African mainland. In the interior, the lighter skin of the Semitic 'Arabs' is visible. Bedouin tribes inhabit parts of the desert region to the east.

SPORT

Yemen's greatest stars have invariably trained abroad. The most famous of these is the boxer Naseen Hamid Kashmim (aka Prince Naseen), born in Yemen in 1966, but brought up in the UK. Nevertheless, he's considered very much a national hero.

Although the country has participated in several Olympic Games, it's yet to return with a medal.

EATING THE FLOWERS OF PARADISE

The first thing every new arrival in Yemen will notice are the bulging cheeks of the qat chewer. Qat, khat, chat or miraa are the leaves of the shrub *Catha edulis*. Originally from Ethiopia, the qat plant has spread across parts of East Africa and into Yemen where the afternoon qat-chewing session has become almost the pivotal point of many Yemeni lives.

Classed by the WHO as a drug of abuse that can produce mild to moderate psychic dependence, it has been banned in most Arab and Western countries, including Saudi Arabia where possession is a serious offence, the US and almost all European nations except for the UK where it's currently legal (though there is talk of this changing). In late 2006 the Yemeni qat world was given a shock when the public chewing of qat was banned in Aden. It remains to be seen whether any other towns will follow suit.

Chewing qat is an important social activity in Yemen and around 80% of the male population are thought to be regular chewers. Women also chew but to a lesser degree and much more discreetly, as do an increasing number of young children. Qat plays an important part in the Yemeni economy, both good and bad. For farmers the profit on qat is five times that of crops, and these profits have done something to slow down the drift to urban areas. On the negative side 17% of the average family's income is spent on qat, and with each chewer often spending four hours every afternoon chewing, over 14,622,000 working hours are lost daily in Yemen.

Environmentally the consequences of qat are bad news. The total amount of land given over to qat has grown from 8000 hectares in 1970 to 103,000 in 2000. Qat is also a thirsty plant and 55% of all the water used in Yemen goes on watering it.

The effects of qat have long been debated – most Yemenis will insist that it gives an unbeatable high, makes you more talkative (at least until the come down when the chewer becomes withdrawn and quiet), suppresses hunger, prevents tiredness and increases sexual performance. Others will tell you that it gives no noticeable high, makes you lethargic, slightly depressed, constipated and reduces sex drive! Most Western visitors who try it report no major effects aside from a possible light buzz and an unpleasant aftertaste.

If you're going to chew qat (and you should try it at least once), you need to make sure the setting is perfect in order to enjoy the experience. Ask for the sweetest qat you can get (most Yemenis regard this as poor quality, but first-time chewers find even this very bitter) and get a good group of people together to chew with, because qat is, above all else, a social drug. Take yourself off to a quiet and comfortable spot (ideally a *mafraj*: literally 'room with a view'), sit back, relax and enjoy the conversation while popping leaves individually into your mouth where you literally just store them in one cheek gently chewing them. All going well you'll be a qat 'addict' by the end of the day, but remember when it comes to the end of the qat session you should spit the gooey mess out – only Ethiopians swallow!

The Yemeni love of football soon becomes apparent as you travel throughout the country. There are stadiums in the largest cities with San'a sitting consistently at the top of the league.

RELIGION

Islam is Yemen's state religion. Most Muslims are Sunnis, many of whom follow the Shafa'i sect. Of the Shiites, most follow the Zaydi sects and are based primarily in the far north. In some parts of Yemen (Hadramawt in particular) many pre-Islamic beliefs have been incorporated into daily life.

The majority of the Jewish population emigrated to Israel in the 1950s. Emigration has continued, and now only a handful of families are estimated to remain in Yemen (largely in the north, in and round Ar-Rayda and Sa'da). In early 2007 the last of the remaining Jewish families were told by Islamic fundamentalists to leave immediately or be killed – most were taking refuge in a Sa'da hotel at the time of writing.

ARTS

For the traveller, Yemen's arts can most easily be appreciated in the varied architecture of its towns and villages, and in its museums. Beautiful examples of ancient art can be found in the latter, as well as more contemporary examples of artisanship. In the larger towns, galleries showcase modern works.

Literature

Poetry – originally oral literature – has been an important art form in Yemen since pre-Islamic times. The most famous Yemeni poet by far is Al Baradouni. Novelists include author of The Hostage, Za'id Mutee' Dammaj, one of the very few writers who have been translated into English.

Cinema

Yemen's cinematic industry is yet to get off the mark, and government funding is nonexistent. A few directors have made films in Yemen, including Passolini (Arabian Nights, 1974). In 2005 Yemen's very first feature film, a romantic drama called A New Day in Old San'a, directed by Bader Ben Hirsi, was premiered at the Cannes Film Festival to positive reviews.

Music

Yemen's music varies greatly from region to region and reflects the different influences of the areas. Tihama music with its frenetic beat, for example, resembles East African music. The best known Yemeni singer is Abu Baker Salem Balfaqih.

Among the most popular instruments are the oud (or lute), played by virtuosos such as Ayoub Taresh, the semsemiya (a kind of five-stringed lyre) and the mizmar (reed or pan pipes). Look out also for the doshan, a kind of minstrel, paid today to entertain at celebrations, such as weddings.

For a time (under the Imam Yahya in the 1940s), music was banned in Yemen.

Architecture

Like Yemen's music, its architecture varies from region to region. Building design depends on available materials (such as mud, reeds or stone), the local climate (seen by thick and high walls to counter the heat or cold) and the region's historical links with other regions or powers (such as Africa, Southeast Asia or the Ottomans).

As Yemen endured a war on average every seven years throughout the 20th century and a similar rate of violence for centuries prior to that, many rural homes are perched on the highest hilltop, sometimes surrounded by walls and towers for added defence.

Water has long played an important part in Yemen, and some of the country's oldest architecture also represents extraordinary civil-engineering feats, such as the Great Ma'rib Dam (p498). For more on Yemeni town houses, see boxed text, p462.

UNESCO WORLD HERITAGE SITES

Old city of San'a (p459): Inscribed in 1986 and described by Unesco as one of the most remarkable urban landscapes in the world.
Shibam (p505): Inscribed in 1982 and described as one of the earliest and most perfect examples of vertical construction.
Zabid (p480): Inscribed in 1993 and added to danger list in 2000. Described as of outstanding historical and historical interest for its significant domestic and military architecture.

Painting

In the past, Yemen's art has been restricted by traditional Islamic taboos, such as the prohibition on the depiction of living things. Consequently, objects were decorated with geometrical patterns and curvilinear forms. Examples of this include the façades of San'a's tower houses and the beautifully illustrated manuscripts found throughout the country.

Today galleries found in the cities exhibit a wider subject matter. The biggest name is Fuad al-Futaih, director and founder of San'a's National Art Centre (Map pp460–1), an artist whose work has been described as 'a wonderful beat to Yemen's heart'.

Dance

Like music, dance forms an important part of Yemeni social traditions. The best known is the *jambiya* 'dance', in which men perform a series of steps and hops in small groups brandishing their *jambiya* (dagger). Technically, this isn't actually a dance but a bond between tribal members, and each region has its own variation. Women and men always dance separately in public.

ENVIRONMENT
The Land

Yemen is about the size of France. Geographically, it can be divided into three main regions.

The Tihama in the west is the desert coastal strip that borders the Red Sea, measuring between 30km and 70km in width.

The central region, which stretches roughly from Sa'da to Ta'izz, is mountainous and rarely drops below 1500m. Jabal an-Nabi Shu'ayb (3660m) is found here, the highest peak on the Arabian Peninsula.

In the east, the Ramlat as-Sab'atayn desert forms part of the Empty Quarter (Rub' al-Khali), which occupies most of southern Saudi Arabia.

Wildlife

Yemen's big wildlife cannot be described as abundant, but if you know where to look there's plenty out there. The country contains a remarkable diversity of habitats and creatures due to its geographic isolation and its position at the crossroads of three 'biological regions': Oriental, Afrotropical and Western Palaearctic.

An excellent booklet on Yemen's wildlife and where to see it is *Wild Yemen – A Guide to Ecotourism Sites Around San'a*, published by the *Yemen Times*. It is sometimes available at bookshops in San'a. Otherwise try another excellent organisation, the **Yemen Ornithological Society** (☎ 01-207059; yos@y.net.ye; PO Box 2002, San'a).

ANIMALS & BIRDS

Yemen is an excellent destination for twitchers. It boasts almost 400 bird species (though many are winterers or migrants), including the 13 'South Arabian endemics'. The island of Suqutra has six endemics of its own. Good places for sightings include verdant wadis, urban rubbish tips and spots around water. For more information, contact the Yemen Ornithological Society (left).

Of the country's 84 species of mammal, many of the larger ones have disappeared, though if you're very lucky you may spot a fox, caracal lynx or striped hyena at night. The Arabian leopard, Arabian wolf and Nubian ibex have been hunted almost to extinction. More abundant and more visible are the 86 species of reptiles, of which 25 are endemic, including the Yemen monitor lizard. Chameleons and agamas are the most commonly seen.

Yemen is also home to over 40 species of snake and 50 species of scorpion, though you're unlikely to come across either. Look out also for butterflies, dragonflies, praying mantises, camel spiders and centipedes.

Yemen's marine life in both of its seas is abundant. Divers can hope to see spiny lobsters, rays, moray eels, octopuses, turtles and sharks. Whale sharks and dolphins are occasionally seen. See also Diving, p512.

PLANTS

Yemen boasts a surprising variety of plant life – around 1750 species in total, of which a high 20% of species are endemic. The plants travellers are most likely to see are the ficus (fig tree), the tamarisk and the ubiquitous but beautiful acacia (loved by Yemen's honey bees). Look out for the 'ilb' tree (*Ziziphus spina-christi*), which is also known as the Crown of Thorns tree because the Bible says Christ's crown of thorns came from it. It is quite easily seen on Suqutra, as are the curious-looking bottle tree (Adenium obesum) and myrrh, frankincense, aloe and balsam trees. Other plants include orchids, ferns and euphorbia. Lucerne, coffee, millet, sorghum – and of course qat – are the crops commonly seen in Yemeni fields.

National Parks

Suqutra has recently become a Unesco biosphere reserve. There are also plans to designate as national parks the forests around Hawf (p511) and the Bura'a Forest in the Tihama.

Environmental Issues

Yemen suffers from typical 21st-century environmental problems: deforestation, soil erosion, excess hunting and desertification (due to salification of the soil). Sand-dune encroachment is also a problem.

The biggest environmental problem the country faces are rapidly dropping levels of ground water, which is only being exacerbated by the nation's huge population growth rate.

Litter is another problem – it wasn't so long ago that everything in Yemen was biodegradable and recyclable and the idea that plastic, tin cans and their ilk don't just disappear overnight has yet to catch on in Yemen. Some of the mountain slopes below villages are knee-deep in old cans and plastic.

FOOD

Yemeni food is simple but good. Breakfast usually consists of little more than a cup of shai (sweet tea) accompanied by bread and honey. Lunch is the main meal of the day and Yemenis tuck in eagerly. A hunk of mutton is the favoured fare, or beef, goat or chicken. Dishes are often served with a thin but delicious broth, such as shurba wasabi (lamb soup), a small salad and a chapati-like flat bread (though over 40 mouth-watering kinds of bread exist in Yemen).

The dish of choice in the highlands is salta, a piping-hot stew containing meat, lentils, beans, fenugreek (giving it its distinctive aroma) and coriander or other spices. For dinner, fasouliya (beans) or fool (a kind of paste made from beans, tomatoes, onions and chilli) often suffices.

Meat is a luxury for the well-off, so there's usually a selection of vegetarian op-

tions. Apart from fool, plates of boiled or fried vegetables, rice or a salad are usually available.

On the coast and in the capital, fresh fish – often cooked in a traditional clay oven – provides a treat not to be missed. Lebanese starters have made it onto many posher menus but generally international cuisine is nonexistent. Meals in Yemen are rushed affairs with little time devoted to lingering conversations.

DRINK

Internationally brewed, nonalcoholic beer (YR100) is readily available throughout Yemen (normally stocked by town grocers). Expensive by local standards, imported alcoholic beer (YR300 to YR350) can be found occasionally in top-end hotels (and some budget bars) in Aden, Al-Hudayda and San'a.

Fresh fruit juices (YR20 to YR70) are filling, healthy and delicious, but are likely to contain tap water at cheaper stalls. Shai is normally hot, black and sweet, and often spiced with mint or cardamom. For some reason the shai served in hotels is usually dreadful. Yemeni coffee is not what you'd expect from the original home of mokha. It's a cloudy, amber and very weak brew made from coffee husks and infused with cloves or other spices. If it's the caffeine buzz you're after, ask for 'Turkish coffee' or buy a jar of Nescafé from any grocery store and just ask for hot water to mix it with. Various saccharine soft drinks are widely available, as is bottled mineral water.

SAN'A صنعاء

☎ 01 / pop 1,707,586

San'a isn't where it was supposed to be. Shem, the son of Noah and founder of San'a, had originally chosen to site his new city a little further west, but just as he set out his guide ropes and prepared for some major DIY a bird dropped out of the heavens, picked up the guide rope and moved it further east. This, Shem knew, was a sign, and so it was there, where the bird had dropped the guide rope, that San'a was born. Today most visitors to Yemen arrive, like that interfering bird, by air. San'a, the world's oldest city, will be their first taste of this most mystical of Arabian countries. It's a good arrival, for this sickly, sweet cake of a city is one of the world's great urban centres, and its many layers, colours and patterns make it the most romantic, living, breathing Islamic city you could ever hope to find.

HISTORY

Though the legend surrounding the founding of San'a may be disputed by a few boring old scientists and archaeologists, what no-one will doubt is that it's a very old city.

Inhabited during Sabaean times, it later became the capital of the great Himyarite dynasty in the early 6th century AD. It also served as a power base for two foreign powers: the Abyssinians and the Persians. In the 7th century AD Islam arrived, altering forever the face of the city, as early mosques and minarets rose up to replace the old churches. The city was later expanded under the Ottomans.

After the civil war in the 1960s, San'a experienced a period of rapid growth, doubling in size every four years. Historically, politically and economically, it was the obvious choice for the capital of the reunited Yemen in 1990. Today San'a is the fastest-growing capital city in the world and this is creating a predictable range of social problems.

ORIENTATION

The old walled city was originally composed of separate parts – east and west – divided by present-day Ali Abdul Mogni St, today one of the principal thoroughfares in the city.

At the crux of the division and still functioning as the administrative heart of the city is Midan at-Tahrir, where the post office, telecoms and internet cafés can also be found. The heart of the old city is Bab al-Yaman.

Many of the travel agencies, Yemenia offices, upmarket shops and better restaurants can be found among the bright lights of Az-Zubayri and Hadda Sts.

San'a's street names are confusing. Many streets have had different names at different periods, some have different names for different sections and few actually have street signs anyway. Unless you've grown up

there, trying to navigate the winding streets of the old city is almost impossible.

Maps

City maps are scarce. Your best bet is to use the inset maps of San'a on the back of some of the country maps (see p515), though not many are more detailed than the San'a maps displayed in this book.

INFORMATION
Bookshops

There are very few bookshops selling English-language publications. Your best bet is the bookshop of the **Taj Sheba Hotel** (Map pp460-1; ☎ 272372; Ali Abdul Mogni St).

Cultural Centres

British Council (Map p458; ☎ 448356; www.british council.org/yemen; Algiers St) Located inside the San'a Trade Center.

Centre Culturel Français (Map p458; ☎ 269472; www.ccdsanaa.com; Al-Qods St; 9am-1pm & 3.30-6.30pm Sat-Wed, 9am-1pm Thu) Near Hadda St.

Emergency

The following emergency numbers apply throughout Yemen:
Fire Brigade (☎ 179)
Police (☎ 199)
Traffic Accidents (☎ 194)

Internet Access

Internet cafés are mushrooming up all over the city centre.
Arab Net (Map pp460-1; 24hr; per min YR2) Off Abdul Mogni St.
Ebhar Net (Map pp460-1; ☎ 284138; per min YR2; 8am-1am Sat-Thu, 3.30pm-1am Fri) Off Abdul Mogni St.
International Telecom Centre (Map pp460-1; ☎ 285030; Midan at-Tahrir; per min am YR1, per min pm YR2; 8am-midnight Sat-Thu, 3pm-midnight Fri)

Laundry

Almost all hotels offer laundry services. Taking your clothes to a laundry may save you some cash. **Bab al-Yaman** (Az-Zubayri St; 7am-midnight) is a good one and charges YR30/40/100 for a shirt/pair of trousers/jacket.

Media

Two English-language weeklies, the *Yemen Times* and the *Yemen Observer* (p515), each cost YR30 and are available from newspaper

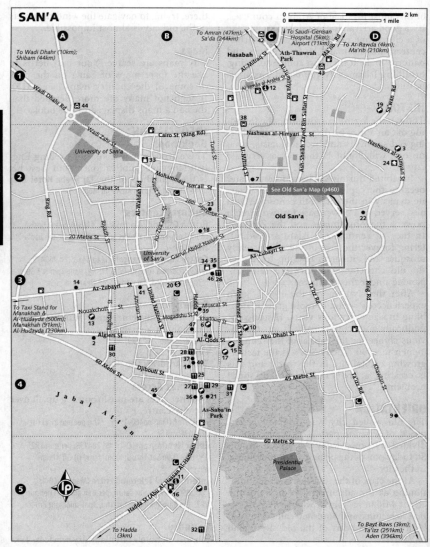

SAN'A

sellers on Midan at-Tahrir. Old copies of *Newsweek* can sometimes be found in the bookshops of some of the top hotels, such as the Taj Sheba.

Medical Services

For minor problems, pharmacies (where English is spoken) provide a good over-the-counter service. The **Saudi-German Hospital** (☎ 313333) is considered to be the best by expats.

Money

Many of the main bank branches in San'a now have ATMs, which accept international cards. There's a freestanding ATM provided by the Yemen Commercial Bank on Midan at-Tahrir. There are several ATMs at the airport. Foreign-exchange offices are found along Az-Zubayri St.

Arab Bank (Map pp460-1-00; ☎ 276585; Az-Zubayri St) Has an ATM.

Crédit Agricole Indosuez (Map pp460-1; ☎ 272801; fax 274161; Qasr al-Jumhuri St) Best place for changing travellers cheques.

Post

Tahrir Post Office (Map pp460-1; ☎ 271180; Midan at-Tahrir; ☺ 8am-2pm & 3-8pm)

Telephone & Fax

Telephone centres can be found all over the city centre, especially along Az-Zubayri St.

TeleYemen (Map pp460-1; Midan at-Tahrir; ☺ 8am-midnight) Centrally located. Calls to Europe/USA/Australia cost YR200 per minute.

Tourist Information

San'a is still awaiting a much-needed tourist office. Tourist Information Centres were supposed to have opened at both the airport and in the city centre years ago, but for the moment you'll continue to find nothing but a veil of secrecy. There are currently no maps or other publications available. The best place for information and maps is at one of the local travel agencies (p520).

Ministry of Tourism (Map p458; ☎ 237131; Al Jamáa al Arabia St; ☺ 8am-8pm Sat-Wed)

Tourism Promotion Board (Map p458; ☎ 252318) Located inside the Ministry of Tourism building.

Travel Agencies

For a list of reputable travel agencies providing a range of services, see Tours (p520).

SIGHTS & ACTIVITIES
Art Galleries & Centres

The **Gallery Al-Bab** (Map pp460–1) and the **Atelier** (Map pp460–1) are both found inside the gates of Bab al-Yaman. The Gallery Al-Bab also offers the chance to clamber up onto the walls of the Bab al-Yaman for memorable views.

NATIONAL ART CENTRE

Housed in a traditional tower house, the **art centre** (Map pp460-1; ☎ 296246; al-futaih@y.net .ye; admission free; ☺ 9am-12.30pm & 4-8pm), north of the Grand Mosque, is good not just for checking out the local art scene, but also for a spot of shopping. In addition to pieces by local artists there are lots of interesting photos of San'a taken in the 1920s.

SHEBA ART GALLERY

Exhibited at this **gallery** (Map pp460-1; ☎ 281415; admission free; ☺ 9am-7pm Sat-Thu, 2.30-7pm Fri) are the paintings of local artist Ali Dahan.

The gallery is located northeast of the Great Mosque, on the 2nd floor of the **National Handicrafts Training Center** (Map pp460-1; ☎ 281415; admission free; ☺ 8am-8pm Sat-Thu). This former *samsarah* (resting/storage house for merchants using the old incense trading routes) also houses a series of other shops selling silverware, woodwork and semiprecious stones.

Old San'a

All these galleries are very nice, but let's be honest, on their own they're not worth traipsing halfway around the world for. However, the Unesco-protected old city of San'a is a different matter altogether. It

YEMEN

OLD SAN'A

INFORMATION		
Arab Bank	1	A6
Arab Net	2	A5
Crédit Agricole Indosuez	3	A5
Ebhar Net	4	A5
International Bank of Yemen	5	B6
International Telecom Centre	(see 8)	
Post Office	6	D5
Radfan Agency Tours	7	C4
Tahrir Post Office	8	B5
Taj Sheba Hotel	9	B6
TeleYemen	(see 8)	
SIGHTS & ACTIVITIES		
Al-'Aqil Mosque	10	E4
Al-Italia	(see 52)	
Andad	11	B5
Atelier	12	E5
Dar al Hayas a Sanania	13	D5

Gallery Al-Bab	14	E5
Great Mosque (Al-Jamaa al-Kabir)	15	E5
Hammam Abhar	16	D5
Horse Riding	17	A4
Military Museum	18	A5
Museum of Traditional Arts &		
Crafts	19	B4
National Art Centre	20	E4
National Handicrafts Training		
Center (Caravanserai)	(see 27)	
National Museum	21	B4
Qat Souq	22	E4
Qubbat al-Bakiriyah Mosque	23	F4
Qubbat Talha Mosque	24	D4
Salah ad-Din Mosque	25	F4
Sana'a Institute for Arabic		
Language	26	C4
Sheba Art Gallery	27	E4

SLEEPING		
Arabia Felix Tourist Hotel	28	C4
Burj al Salam Hotel	29	D4
Dawood Hotel	30	C4
Golden Daar Hotel	31	C4
Old Sana'a Palace Hotel	32	D5
Sanaa Nights Tourist Hotel	33	C4
Say'un Hotel	34	A6
Sultan Palace Hotel	35	C5
Taj Talha Hotel	36	C4
EATING		
Houmald Salta	37	E4
Naeem	38	E5
DRINKING		
Al-Asdeqa	39	A5
Coffeehouse	40	E5

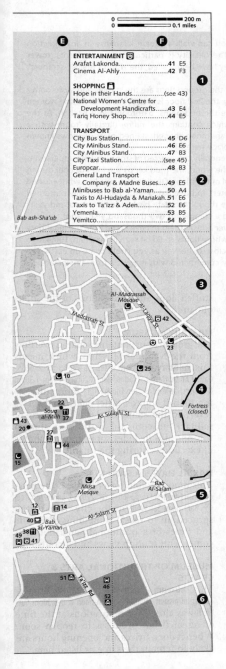

would be fair to say that old San'a is one of the most beautiful cities anywhere on Earth and nothing is likely to prepare you for the moment you first pass through the gates of the Bab al-Yaman. Most people spend days wandering without aim through this enormous work of art and that's certainly the best way to absorb this city.

At the heart of it all is the **Souq al-Milh** (Map pp460–1–00). Though the name indicates that the sole product is salt, this is something of a misnomer. Everything from mobile phones to sacks of sultanas is available here. It's almost impossible to point to individual buildings, souqs or sights, but the qat market, in the centre of the old town, is frenetically busy around lunchtime. The spice souq is every oriental fantasy brought to life and the small cellars where blinkered camels walk round and round in circles crushing sesame seeds to make oil is a glimpse into a bygone age. For many the abiding memory of the city is likely to be of the topsy-turvy, icing-cake houses and the dreamy mosques. Walking the streets of old San'a as the evening prayer call rings out across the rooftops is a deeply romantic and exotic experience and something you're never likely to forget.

Finally, a compulsory activity for tourist and local alike is to climb to the top of one of the tower houses and relish the ravishing views over the city as the sun sinks below the surrounding mountains.

Mosques & Gardens

The mosques in San'a are open only to Muslims, but you can often get a fleeting glimpse inside through a doorway and the majestic minarets are there for all to enjoy. Out of the 50 mosques still standing, the **Great Mosque** (Al-Jamaa al-Kabir; Map pp460-1) north of Bab al-Yaman, is the most significant. For centuries it served as an important Islamic school and centre of learning, and attached to it is a library containing the largest and most famous collection of manuscripts in Yemen.

Of the many other mosques, ones to look out for include the small but elegant **Qubbat al-Bakiriyah Mosque**, built by the Ottomans and renovated in the 19th century; the 17th-century **Qubbat Talha Mosque** (Map pp460–1), with its unusual minaret; the decrepit mid-16th-century **Al-'Aqil Mosque** (Map

YEMEN

A CITY CAUGHT IN TIME

San'a is so perfectly preserved that it is said you can walk a square kilometre in any direction without encountering a single new building. The old city is particularly famous for its 'tower houses'. Reaching up to six or eight storeys, they have been called 'the world's first skyscrapers'; San'a contains no less than 14,000 of them.

Tower houses tend to follow a set design: on the ground floor are the stables and storerooms; on the 1st floor the rooms used for entertaining; the 2nd floor is usually reserved for the women and children; and on the 3rd and 4th floors are the bedrooms, bathrooms and kitchen. At the very top of the house is the *manzar* (attic), which contains the *mafraj* (literally 'room with a view'). Serving often as windows in the *mafraj*, are moon-shaped, stained-glass windows known as *qamariyas*. Today much qat-chewing takes place here.

The ground and 1st floors of the building are generally constructed of stone, and the upper levels of mud brick. Considered the best insulator in the world, the mud keeps the interior cool during the warmth of the day and warm during the cool of the night. Outside, the façade is whitewashed with lime (which protects the mud from rainwater) and decorated with geometrically patterned lines. The stone foundations of some houses are thought to date back at least a thousand years (the oldest building in the city was constructed a staggering two thousand years ago).

The original plan and pattern of the San'a tower house is said to have come from the legendary Palace of Ghumdan, a 2nd-century masterpiece whose lights could be seen in Madinah, 1000km to the north, and which was said to have been as close to heaven as you could come on earth. The Great Mosque is thought to have been partially constructed with materials from this palace.

---

pp460–1) to the north of Souq al-Milh; and the **Salah ad-Din Mosque** (Map pp460–1), due east of Al-'Aqil Mosque, built in the 17th century.

Finally, the city may not look like a lush and green place, but while exploring old San'a keep an eye peeled for the hidden communal vegetable gardens that once made the city self-sufficient.

Qat Souqs

As well as the atmospheric old town qat souq, there's a bigger one further east, near the ring road (Map p458), and another, the **Andad Souq** (Map pp460–1), just to the west of the dry wadi (now a road) that runs through the western fringe of the old city.

Museums

NATIONAL MUSEUM

Claiming to be the largest museum on the Arabian Peninsula, the **National Museum** (Map pp460–1; ☎ 271696; Ali Abdul Mogni St; admission YR500; ☉ 9am-12.30pm Sat-Thu) is certainly one of the best. The ground and 1st floors contain a breathtaking collection of statues, figurines and other artefacts from the pre-Islamic Kingdoms of Saba and Hadramawt. The 2nd floor concentrates on the medieval Islamic period while the top floor features a slightly less rewarding mishmash of

stuffed lions and re-creations of the souqs of San'a.

MILITARY MUSEUM

The ground floor contains Sabaean overflow from the National Museum, which means this **military museum** (Map pp460–1; ☎ 276635; Gamal Abdul Nasser St; admission YR200; ☉ 9am-1.30pm & 3-8pm Sat-Wed, 3-7pm Thu & Fri) is more interesting than it sounds. After that the displays revert to the standard death and guns of military museums the world over, though this one also includes some graphic photos of executions during the Imanic era.

DAR AL HAYAS A SANANIA

This renovated old tower house is the newest **museum** (Map pp460–1, ☎ 270734; admission free; ☉ 8am-noon Sat-Wed) in the city. It has been spruced up to reveal something of the life and times of a traditional San'a home. It comes with rooftop views and a craftshop.

MUSEUM OF TRADITIONAL ARTS & CRAFTS

This **museum** (Map pp460–1; ☎ 271648; Midan at-Tahrir; admission YR500; ☉ 8am-noon & 3-5.30pm Sat-Wed) was closed for renovations at the time of research but promises to reopen soon. When it does, prices and opening hours are likely to remain the same as listed here.

Hammams

At least 20 **hammams** (Turkish bathhouses) dot the city and they are among the best places to mingle with locals and, should you speak Arabic, catch up on the latest gossip. Not all hammams are keen to take foreigners, so ask your hotel to recommend one locally. Most charge around YR300 and are open from 6am to 7pm. Men and women always bathe separately. In the old city, **Hammam Abhar** (Map pp460-1; admission YR300; ⓨ Mon, Wed & Thu for men, Tue, Fri & Sat for women) lies near the Dar al Hayas a Sanania museum.

For a total 'makeover', male travellers might fancy a trip to the **barber**, where for less than US$1 (YR100 to YR150) you'll get a closer-than-close shave and a hair snip.

COURSES

Sana'a Institute for Arabic Language (Map pp460-1; ☎ 284330; info@sialyemen.com; As-Sailah St) Courses cost US$300/570/830 for three/six/nine weeks. Year-long courses are also offered, as are courses in Islamic culture.

Yemen Language Center & Yemen Center for Arab Studies (Map pp460-1; ☎ 270200; www.ylcint.com; 26th September St) Offers group and individual tuition from €1710 for five weeks. The centre is currently merging with the recently formed College of Middle Eastern Studies.

TOURS

City tours of San'a (for around US$40 to US$50) are offered by local travel operators (see Tours, p520).

SLEEPING

The old city might be cramped, noisy and sometimes uncomfortable, but without any doubt its immense character and colour means that it's the best place to stay. Unless you're a businessperson requiring form and functionality, then it's very hard to know why you would opt for the soulless streets and hotels of the ugly new town.

Old City

All of the following are converted tower houses marketed as 'palace hotels', though none were ever anything of the sort.

BUDGET

Old Sana'a Palace Hotel (Map pp460-1; ☎ 280200; Harat al-Abhar; s/d US$10/15) Spartan rooms and one thin, dirty mattress are all you get at this not-too-welcoming hotel. On the plus side it has good views from the roof (nonguests YR100) and a café with a massive wooden sculpture of the Bab al-Yaman.

Sultan Palace Hotel (Map pp460-1; ☎ 273766; sultanpalacehotel@yahoo.com; s/d with breakfast €12/15) Located close to the Qubbat al-Mahdi Mosque in a quiet corner of the old city, this is a friendly budget hotel that is handy to the Midan at-Tahrir and new town. It's the best of the budget options in the old town.

MIDRANGE

Sanaā Nights Tourist Hotel (Map pp460-1; ☎ 482826; www.sanaanightshotel.com; Talha St; s/d from US$15/20) This is a welcome new addition to the accommodation scene. It shares a courtyard with the Golden Daar (p464) but its wobbly white roof beams, bright wall tapestries and clean, simple bedrooms are infinitely preferable to those of its neighbour. It includes a basic free breakfast and as much help and advice as you can handle.

SAN'A FOR CHILDREN

Childcare facilities are lacking in San'a, but entertainment for kids includes the following:

- **Horse riding** Rides costs YR1000 for a five-minute ride around the square, and YR200 for a photograph sitting on a horse. Ask for the bright-orange horse. Its on Midan at-Tahrir, opposite the Honda building.

- **As-Saba'in Park** (70 Park; admission free) Enclosed within this 50,000-sq-metre park are shaded areas for picnicking, as well as swings, slides and a couple of amusement centres.

- **As-Saba'in Amusement Park** (admission free; ⓨ 8.30am-12.30pm & 2.30-7pm) Located in As-Saba'in Park, there are rides (about 18 types) for YR50. If you're not travelling with children, it's worth being a big kid and going anyway, as it's a fun experience that is a real contrast to the exotic souqs of the old city.

Taj Talha Hotel (Map pp460-1; ☎ 287130; www.taj talha-hotel.com.ye; Talha St; s/d with telephone from US$20/25) With possibly the best stained-glass windows in San'a, stunning rooftop views and, just a few metres away, the most tuneful mosque in town, this has all the ingredients for a classic hotel. However, the rooms are dark and gloomy, with bathroom plumbing that seems permanently clogged up. Friendly.

Golden Daar Hotel (Map pp460-1; ☎ 287220; www .almokalla.com; Talha St; s/d with breakfast from US$20/25) The Golden Daar has been providing simple beds to weary travellers for years. The plain rooms have frayed carpets but are very clean, and the giant windows make you feel like you're flying high above San'a.

ourpick Dawood Hotel (Map pp460-1; ☎ 287270; dawoodhotel@yahoo.com; Talha St; s/d from US$20/25) A brash new upstart putting every other hotel in San'a on notice and offering easily the best value for money in town. It's a lovingly restored tower house with shiny clean rooms full of little extras including delightful textiles, Arabian cushion seats and bundles of real and not so real antiques. The beds are soft and comfortable, the views memorable and the sunny courtyard overlooks communal vegetable gardens. The best things, though, are the warm and friendly staff that come a-knocking each evening with frankincense for your room. Try and get one of the better rooms on the upper floors.

Arabia Felix Tourist Hotel (Map pp460-1; ☎ 287330; http://arabiafelix.free.fr; s/d incl breakfast US$22/25) This hotel's best asset is its small but attractive garden. Rooms are small and simple. Some include a bathroom and some don't, but the price is the same! Note that taxi drivers may know the hotel by its Arabic name: Funduq al-'Arabiya as-Sa'ida.

TOP END

ourpick Burj Al Salam Hotel (Map pp460-1; ☎ 483333; www.burjalsalam.com; s/d/ste US$48/84/175) A smart four-star hotel lost in the heart of old San'a. The Italian management ensure European standards but the local staff ensure Yemeni fun and character. The small standard rooms are perfectly presented with heavy wooden furniture, stone floors and large windows, while the suites are big enough to get thoroughly lost in. The biggest attraction might be the arresting rooftop views and the luxurious *mafraj*.

New City

BUDGET

Say'un Hotel (Map p506; ☎ 274838; sayunhotel@ y.net.ye; Ali Abdul Mogni St; r YR2500) The scrappy reception and stairway leads you to fear the worst, but the rooms are actually much cleaner and better than you'd expect. Good for couples on a budget.

TOP END

Mövenpick (Map p458; ☎ 546666; www.movenpick -hotels.com; Nashwan al-Himyari St; s/d from US$180/204; 🖵 🖵) This monster on the hill doing its utmost to ruin the San'a skyline is undeniably the best hotel in the city. It hardly needs saying that the rooms and facilities are of the highest calibre, but the best features are the tempting indoor pool and the huge views. However, you've got to wonder why on earth anyone felt it necessary to build a massive 400-room hotel in such an obstructive place.

EATING

Not surprisingly San'a has the best range of restaurants in the country, including a few serving international dishes.

Restaurants

ourpick Houmald Salta (Map pp460-1; Souq al-Milh; meals YR200; ☼ noon-3pm) Next to the qat market in the heart of the old city. This *salta* (a kind of stew and the traditional lunch dish of the highlands) restaurant is regarded as having the best *salta* in San'a and is a pre-qat-session institution. Buy the accompanying sheets of bread from the women standing around outdoors.

Zeyna Food (Map p458; 14th October St; meals YR250-500; ☼ noon-3pm) Run more as a hobby than a business by an Ethiopian woman, this incredibly popular lunchtime restaurant gives you the opportunity to try Ethiopia's national dish, *injira* and *wat*, a decidedly acquired taste!

Naeem (Map pp460-1; ☎ 771601473; Bab al-Yaman; meals from YR300) This shiny white-tiled restaurant is cleaner than most and does great roast chickens (YR600) and freshly squeezed fruit juices (YR1000). It's right next to the Bab al-Yaman.

Al-Shaibani Modern Restaurant (Map p458; ☎ 505290; Hadda St; meals YR400-700) This is the restaurant that all the other restaurants in Yemen want to take after. All the staples are done to perfection, but it's the oven-baked fish that rules the roost.

Al-Khima (Map p458; ☎ 444705; off Hadda St; meals YR500-800) Its Yemeni and Lebanese food isn't great but it's one of the few places where you might want to linger over a meal. Better than the food are the fruit-flavoured *shee-sha* pipes and the big-screen TV showing all the major sporting events.

Al-Fanoos (Map p458; ☎ 441042; off Hadda St; starters YR200, mains YR600-750) Probably the best Western-style sit-down-and-relax restaurant in Yemen – though don't rely on it being open, as it often only swings back the doors at weekends or when there's a group booking. The food is predominately Middle Eastern and there's occasional live music.

Mumbai Durbar (Map p458; Baghdad St; meals YR1000) Dishing out spicy subcontinental dishes, this is one of Yemen's lonely Indian restaurants.

Quick Eats

Food stalls selling simple but delicious fare that's cheap as chips can be found in the streets immediately south and east of Midan at-Tahrir, such as around the junction of Ali Abdul Mogni and Qasr al-Jumhuri Streets. If you want to see a side of Yemen sitting at the polar opposite of the tourist brochure clichés then head to the bright lights of Hadda Street and its strip of garish Western–style fast-food outlets which culminate in a Pizza Hut and KFC (Map p458).

Self-Catering

Al-Hoda Supermarket (Map p458; Az-Zubayri St) This is good for provisions or picnics, or if you're just hankering after Western goodies, such as chocolate or bikkies. It also stocks shampoo, sanitary towels and – usually – nappies.

DRINKING

Various Turkish-style coffeehouses can be found around Bab al-Yaman, including the coffeehouse next to the wall, immediately to the left of the gate as you enter the old city (look out for the awning).

Open to all are the excellent fruit-juice stalls dotted around town, such as **Al-Asdeqa** (Map pp460-1; Qasr al-Jumhuri St; juices around YR70) not far from the Crédit Agricole Bank.

ENTERTAINMENT

San'a's entertainment is limited to tourist-class restaurants putting on occasional evening shows, such as **Al-Fanoos** (Map p458; ☎ 441042; off Hadda St). The hardcore qat and *sheesha* crowd at **Arafat Lakonda** (Map pp460-1; near Bab al-Yaman) might appeal to some but it's not for the timid (or women).

Cinema Al-Ahly (Map pp460-1; Al-Laqiya St; admission YR100) screens original language films from Egypt, India and America.

SHOPPING

Popular souvenirs include the *jambiya* and traditional jewellery. Prices are negotiable, but note that Yemenis aren't the ardent hagglers found in other Arab countries. Aggressive bartering on the part of the buyer may offend.

The **National Women's Centre for Development Handicrafts** (Map pp460-1; ☎ 482454; Samsarat al-Halaqah; ☷ 9.30am-12.30pm Sat-Thu) and **Hope in their Hands** (☎ 482455; Samsarat al-Halaqah; ☷ 9.30am-12.30pm & 3.30-7pm Sat-Thu) are two non-profit organisations located inside the same building with the joint aim of increasing the financial independence of Yemeni women. This is done through workshops where the women, who are often widowed or divorced, learn skills such as sewing and weaving. The resulting products are then sold in the two downstairs shops, which are the best places in San'a to buy souvenirs. If you're lucky, you might be allowed upstairs to watch the women at work. Even without these centres the building itself, a renovated caravanserai (a traditional lodging house for traders travelling the old trade routes), is worth a visit.

Yemeni honey is well known – and justly so. Honey shops are found throughout the capital (including Az-Zubayri St), though it's not cheap: around YR2500 for 500g, YR5000 to YR6000 for 1kg. Beautiful honeycombs (conveniently packaged in sealed metal discs) cost YR2000 to YR8000 (depending on quality). A decent honey shop in the old city is Tariq Honey Shop, near the Sheba Art Gallery, where the gift of bees is also likely to come with gifts of Islamic literature.

Rows of shops selling gold and silver jewellery can be found on Gamal Abdul Nasser St. Also well worth a look (or a sniff) are the perfume and spice shops. **Yahsob Spice** (Map p458; ☎ 294319; Az-Zubayri St) has a good collection of the latter.

For photographic requirements, **Fuji Film** (Map p458; ☎ 224983; Al-Wahdah Rd) offers products and development services.

GETTING THERE & AWAY

For restrictions on independent travel, see Travel Permits (p518).

Air

The national carrier, **Yemenia** (Map pp460-1 & Map p458; ☎ 201822; www.yemenia.com), has various offices around town. It offers one-way flights to Aden (US$65), Al-Hudayda (US$50), Ar-Rayyan (Mukalla) and Sayun (US$80), Suqutra (US$60), Ta'izz (US$50) and Al-Ghayda (US$60).

Bus

The bus company **Yemitco** (Map pp460-1; ☎ 242366; Az-Zubayri St) runs a service to Al-Hudayda (YR1500, five hours, two daily), Aden (YR1400, six hours, five daily), Al-Mukalla (YR2000, 12 hours, one daily) and Ta'izz (YR1250, five hours, two daily).

General Land Transport Company (Map pp460-1; ☎ 281318; Bab al-Yaman) and **Madne Buses** (Map pp460-1; Bab al-Yaman) have daily services to Say'un (YR1400; 14 hours), which travel via Ma'rib and can, technically at least, be used by foreigners as long as they don't disembark at Ma'rib, which is currently the site of tribal tensions. In reality, though, you probably won't be allowed to travel.

At the time of writing, there was no bus service to Sa'da.

Car

For car hire, **Europcar** (Map pp460-1; ☎ 270751; www.europcar.com; Al-Qiyadiah St), located inside the Sam City Hotel, rents cars/4WDs with limited/unlimited mileage. Similar services (and a franchise of Hertz) are available from **Universal Rent a Car** (Map p458; ☎ 447714; www.hertz.com; 60 Metre St; ☽ 24hr), which also has a branch at the airport.

Taxi

Shared taxis usually leave from spots on the outskirts of the city on the road leading to their destinations (see Map p458 and Map pp460-1 for taxi hub locations). To reach these departure points, take a minibus from Bab al-Yaman (YR20).

Shared taxis run west to Manakhah (YR500, three hours, many daily), and Al-

Hudayda (YR1000, 4½ hours, six daily). North to Amran (YR400, one hour, several daily), Hajja (YR600, two hours, six per day) and south to Ta'izz (YR1000, five hours, lots throughout the day). Tourists are not permitted to travel by taxi to Ma'rib or Sa'da.

GETTING AROUND
To/From the Airport

For the airport (16km from the city centre), minibuses (YR30) depart from outside Al-Shalal restaurant in the Al-Hasabah area. Contract taxis to the airport charge YR2000 from the old town.

Car & Motorcycle

San'a's traffic is frenetic, few road rules are enforced, little etiquette is observed and few vehicle 'appendages' (such as mirrors and indicators) are used. Parking can also be a problem and traffic police (issuing parking fines) patrol the city centre. Almost no signposts (in Arabic or English) exist, so it may be best to leave the car at home unless you know the city well. Accidents are common.

Public Transport

Minibuses (which operate from 6am to 1am) run all around town and are quick and cheap (around YR20). Nippier still are motorbike taxis, which charge YR100 to YR150 for hops around town.

Taxi

Meters are not normally used, so fares should be negotiated in advance. Short hops around town cost YR30 in a shared taxi, YR100 (tourists will be asked YR300 to YR500) in a contract taxi.

AROUND SAN'A

☎ 07

A couple of places just outside town formerly made popular and pleasant excursions. However, the ever-expanding capital has almost swallowed these once separate and tranquil villages. Nevertheless, for those who have limited time but are keen to see something out of town, brief stops are still worthwhile.

Lying 8km north of the San'a city centre is the settlement of **Ar-Rawda**, once known for its high-quality grapes. The area is also known for its distinct, adobe-based architecture and an attractively decorated 17th-century mosque. **Bayt Baws**, 7km south of the San'a city centre, is a naturally fortified village typical of the region.

Wadi Dhahr وادي ظهر

The most popular afternoon excursion from San'a is to the palace of **Dar al-Hajar** (admission YR500; 8am-1pm & 2-6pm) in the fertile Wadi Dhahr. Constructed as a summer residence for Imam Yahya in the 1920s, the palace has become something of a symbol of Yemen, and it's not hard to see why – it erupts forth off its rock table like a giant red-and-white toadstool.

Inside, you will find that few of the rooms are furnished, but for most the main attractions are the great rooftop views and the stunning stained-glass windows throwing flecks of multicoloured light across the floor. Don't miss the ancient subterranean wells that go right through the rock (one is apparently 275m deep).

If you charter a taxi from San'a, your driver will probably take you to one of the viewpoints overlooking the wadi. Most of the time the car park here is loaded with touts and salesmen and is well worth avoiding, but Friday often brings carloads of high-spirited wedding parties out to celebrate by firing their guns into the air.

The palace lies around 1km north of the village of Wadi Dhahr (which is 14km from central San'a). Shared taxis run without much frequency to San'a (YR115, around 20 minutes) or you can get a seat in a shared taxi to **Shemlan** (YR15), from where there are connections every few minutes to the city centre. Alternatively, you can charter a taxi for around YR1000. There are no hotels in Wadi Dhahr, but there is a restaurant in the palace grounds, though it rarely seems to be open.

THE HARAZ MOUNTAINS جبال حراز

Rising abruptly off the steamy Red Sea coastal plains the sheer-sided Haraz Mountains have, for centuries, acted as a cultural fortress protecting the Yemeni heartland from interfering foreigners. Today the suspicion of outsiders is largely a thing of the past, but what hasn't changed one jot is the grandeur of the mountains and the beauty of their tapestry of terraced fields and fortified villages, all huddled together on the most unlikely crags. The Haraz Mountains are prime trekking territory. For those with the spirit of adventure and a little self-sufficiency, it's possible to spend days, or even weeks, weaving along the mule trails that link up the different villages.

SHIBAM شبام

Not to be confused with the town of the same name in eastern Yemen, this ancient village lies 2300m above sea level, at the foot of Jebel Kawkaban (2800m). It's an almost compulsory stop on every visitor's Yemen trip, but despite this it retains a chilled-out, welcoming attitude and makes a good first stop in rural Yemen. Dating from the 2nd century AD, Shibam became an important capital for the local Yafurid dynasty in the 9th century, when its grand mosque – one of the oldest in Yemen – was built.

Sights

Non-Muslims are, as normal in Yemen, forbidden from entering the **mosque**, but even so its exterior walls and solid minaret are pleasing to the eye. Other eye candy is the old **town gate** and the bustling little **souq**, which is the site of a very colourful **Friday market** (6.30am-1pm). Attracting people from all around, it's well worth a visit if you're in the area.

If you're wondering about the little '**caves**' hollowed into the mountainside, they're old tombs – an ancient local tradition. Jebel Kawkaban is also known for its **birdlife**, particularly raptors.

Sleeping & Eating

Hameda Hotel (450480; per person with breakfast & dinner YR1600) This newly built hotel about 1km out of town on the road to Kawkaban offers clean, foreigner-friendly rooms with gorgeous window carvings, ant-sized bathrooms and soft, comfortable beds. A good breakfast and dinner is thrown in with the bargain-basement price.

Hanida Tourist Hotel & Restaurant (450480; lunch YR1000) Lying around 200m south of the taxi stop, this traditional tower-house restaurant is run by the same family as the

Hameda Hotel. Every afternoon its beautiful *mafraj*, full of colourfully carved panels and glowing stained-glass windows, plays host to a lunchtime banquet fit for a king. It's best to reserve in advance.

Getting There & Away
Shared taxis run to Al-Mahwit (YR250, 1½ hours, three to four daily), At-Tawila (YR150, 40 minutes, 10 daily), Kawkaban (YR100, 15 minutes, five to seven daily), San'a (YR150, 30 minutes, four to five daily) and Thilla (YR50, 15 minutes, 10 daily).

KAWKABAN   كوكبان
Perched dramatically on the top of Jebel Kawkaban and lording it over Shibam, some 350 vertical metres below, is the remarkable village and fortified citadel of Kawkaban. During the 15th century, it served as a capital to the Bani Sharaf Al-Deen dynasty and was once renowned for its school of music. In times of conflict the citizens of Shibam would scurry up here to join their brothers and, thanks to some huge grain silos and water cisterns (which can still be seen today), everyone was able to continue going about their life largely unperturbed by any siege. In fact it wasn't until the civil war of the 1960s and the coming of air power that Kawkaban was finally conquered.

Activities
The main activity in Kawkaban is **hiking**. The manager of the Hotel Jabal Kawkaban is a good source of information and can also act as guide (or help find one) and organise camping trips (YR1500 to YR2000 per person per day). Donkeys can also be hired (YR3000 per day). There are no set trekking routes or facilities for foreign walkers and for all except the hour-long hike down the mountain to Shibam, you will need a guide. It's best to explain to your guide how long and difficult you would like to make your hike and let him suggest something suitable. The countryside around here consists primarily of gentle plateaus interspersed with soaring peaks and the hiking is generally fairly easy, though this also means that the scenery doesn't match places such as Manakhah (p470). If the mere thought of a hiking boot makes you puffed out, content yourself with a leisurely stroll through the village to check out both the cisterns and the eagle's-eye view off the edge of the escarpment down to Shibam.

Sleeping & Eating
Hotel Jabal Kawkaban (☎ 733971662; per person incl breakfast & dinner YR1500) Simple dorm-style rooms full of soft cushions and a warm welcome await. The manager, who speaks good English and French, is something of a one-man tourist office. Lunch costs YR900.

Hotel Al-Taj Tourism (Planet's Tower Hotel; ☎ 450170; dm incl breakfast & dinner YR1800, s/d with bathroom, breakfast & dinner YR2600/4000) Small and clean rooms come with larger than average bathrooms, a strangely forlorn atmosphere and a lobster and typewriter on the wall! English speaking and friendly. Sample the lunch for YR800.

Kawkaban Hotel (☎ 450154; fax 450855, s/d incl breakfast & dinner YR2500/3900) It's real luck of the draw here as to whether you get one of the dark and dastardly cell like rooms or one of the spacious and comfortable double rooms. Either way the price remains fixed. Lunch and dinner cost YR900 each.

Getting There & Away
From near the Grand Mosque in Shibam, there is a steep footpath leading 2.5km up to Kawkaban.

Shared taxis use the circuitous 7km road to Shibam (YR100, 15 minutes, five to seven daily). For taxis further afield, go to Shibam first.

THILLA (THULA)   ثلا
Set against a great pillar of rock mounted by a fortress, the chameleon-camouflaged town of Thilla, about 9km north of Shibam, was once an important theological centre. Today it's known more for its lovely architecture than books of learning. An impressive stone wall surrounds the town, making for a memorable arrival through one of its seven gates.

Information
You might be assailed by kids wishing to act as guides, but it's all very low-key and they are just as interested in having a chat as making a sale. Should you want a tour of the town a guide will charge a negotiable YR500.

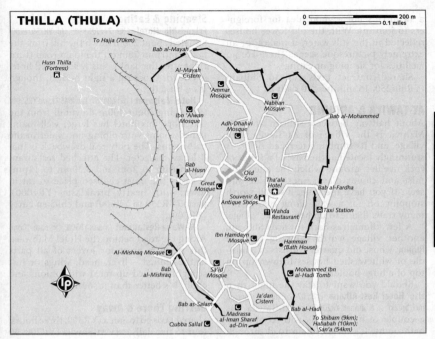

THILLA (THULA)

0 ────── 200 m
0 ────── 0.1 miles

To Hajja (70km)
Bab al-Mayah
Husn Thilla (Fortress)
Al-Mayah Cistern
'Ammar Mosque
Nabhan Mosque
Ibn 'Alwan Mosque
Adh-Dhahiri Mosque
Bab al-Mohammed
Bab al-Husn
Old Souq
Great Mosque
Tha'ala Hotel
Bab al-Fardha
Souvenir & Antique Shops
Wahda Restaurant
Taxi Station
Ibn Hamdayn Mosque
Hamman (Bath House)
Al-Mishraq Mosque
Bab al-Mishraq
Sa'id Mosque
Mohammed Ibn al-Hadi Tomb
Ja'dan Cistern
Bab as-Salam
Bab al-Hadi
Madrassa al-Iman Sharaf ad-Din
To Shibam (9km); Hababah (10km); San'a (54km)
Qubba Sallal

YEMEN

Sights

Thilla is one of those classic Yemeni mountain towns that appears almost organic, so perfectly does it meld into its setting. There are few formal attractions, but a walk through the dusty streets is highly enjoyable. Look out for the 25 **mosques** and **tombs**, which dot the town (some are marked on the map), including the **Great Mosque** (Al-Jami'a al-Kabir Mosque), with its distinctive stone minaret. Many of the houses have added a little razzmatazz to their largely grey-brown exteriors by adding brilliantly whitewashed stone window frames and heavy, carved wooden doors. The little souq also brings some colour to the village.

From town, an old and beautifully constructed stone staircase leads up to **Husn Thilla** (admission YR500; ☼ sunrise-sunset). The fort remained unconquered by the Ottomans, and though the exterior is impressive, the interior is sadly devoid of life. There are memorable views, and inside the fort walls are tombs, cisterns and granaries. It's about a 45-minute uphill (very much uphill!) walk from the village.

Sleeping & Eating

Tha'ala Hotel (☎ 77885095; Main Sq; s/d with shared bathroom, breakfast & dinner YR1600/3200) This traditional tower house is almost the focal point of the village and offers tasty rooms with soft mattresses laid out straight onto the floor. The bathrooms aren't too pretty, but the owner is friendly.

Opposite the hotel is the Wahda Restaurant, where a meal of hummus, *fool* and tea comes in at YR400.

Getting There & Away

Thilla is an easy hike from Shibam or Kawkaban.

Shared taxis (which leave from in front of Bab al-Fardha) run to San'a (YR250, about one hour, five to six daily) and Shibam (YR70, 20 minutes, over 50 daily).

HABABAH

Although similar in style and architecture to Thilla (and lying 10km away), Hababah has a special feature: a large, oval **water cistern**, where people still come to collect water, drive their animals to drink or even have a swim (it's not a good idea for foreigners to join in). With the old tower houses reflected in the still water, it makes for an extremely picturesque scene. There are no facilities for sleeping or eating.

Shared/contract taxis run to Shibam (YR50/250, 15 minutes, 10 daily).

AT-TAWILA & AROUND

About halfway between Shibam and Al-Mahwit is the village of At-Tawila. The village, and its tumbling terraced fields, is stunningly located at the base of a series of rock needles, around which the afternoon mist and clouds play games of hide and seek. If you have the time, it's well worth stopping off for a walk along one of the many trails that lead up behind the village.

A few kilometres back towards Shibam, another village worth stopping at is **Ar Rujum**, whose old quarter consists of a bundle of whitewashed houses thrown up on top of a huge boulder.

Should you want to stay the night then the **Hotel Rest-Alhana** (☎ 07-456369; per person incl breakfast & dinner YR2000) in At-Tawila has a couple of basic rooms with communal bathrooms. It's on the main road through town.

AL-MAHWIT المحويت

The bustling market town of Al-Mahwit is the largest of the mountain towns to the west of the capital, but it has little to offer the traveller bar the beautiful 125km journey from San'a. Al-Mahwit lies in the centre of some of the most fertile country in Yemen and the road from San'a takes you past numerous fruit, coffee, tobacco and qat fields.

Like At-Tawila, Al-Mahwit was once an important coffee-collecting centre, as well as an administrative town during the 16th-century Ottoman rule.

Sights & Activities

The **old town**, perched on a hilltop, marks the site of the Ottoman regional capital and is worth a walk, as is the town's **souq**. There is good **hiking** potential in the attractive surrounding countryside but a guide would be required for anything more ambitious than a quick stroll – the staff at the Hotel Mahweet should be able to sort one out for you.

Sleeping & Eating

Friendship Hotel (☎ 777728530; s/d YR750/1200) Situated about 200m down the hill from the taxi stand and 50m off the main road (turn right after the bank), this well-named hotel is OK for those on a tight budget, though it's a bit tatty.

Hotel Mahweet (☎ 404767; fax 404591; s/d YR5500/6500) Lying about 400m downhill from the taxi stop, this hotel has large, well-maintained rooms with piping-hot water in the bathrooms. The only real drawback is that it lacks character. The attached restaurant (open 8am to 2pm and 3.30pm to 11pm) is easily the most civilised place to eat in town, with hearty breakfasts (YR1000), pasta (YR350 to YR500) and chicken curry (YR700).

Al-Waha Restaurant (meals YR500; ⏱ 6am-10pm) Along the road behind the Hotel Mahweet, this place is great for lovers of all parts of the animal – liver, head, wings or just straight mashed-up meat with onions and chilli. It's better than it sounds!

Getting There & Away

Shared taxis go to San'a (YR500, three hours, four to five daily) via At-Tawila (YR200, 30 minutes) and Shibam (YR400, 1½ hours). There are occasional taxis to Khamis Bani Sa'd (YR1500), where you can change for Manakhah and so save a long backtrack. The route, along a rough wadi bed, isn't always possible after rains.

MANAKHAH مناخة

☎ 01

The largest commercial centre in the high mountains, Manakhah might be a nondescript town, but it's the centre of Yemeni trekking. From here everything from gentle hour-long rambles to serious multiday expeditions fan out across the highlands.

There's no bank in Manakhah, but you can change US dollars and euros (cash) at the foreign-exchange dealers in the market. There's also a telephone centre.

Sights & Activities

Hikes lasting from one hour to three days or more are possible. The Manakha Tourist Hotel is a good source of information about hiking.

Local guides cost YR2000 per day, though they can be hired for shorter hikes, too.

Camping equipment (YR2000 per day per person), including tents, mattresses and all other necessities, can be hired through one of the hotels. A guide and a couple of donkeys to carry everything can be arranged for YR3000 per day. As in Kawkaban, everything to do with trekking here is a bit DIY – there are no set trails, no Nepali-style mountain lodges and no guarantees that everything will go smoothly. However, for those who want to get to know the soul of Yemen, a few days trekking is unbeatable. Trekking is a year-round activity, but during the summer monsoon period it can be uncomfortably hot, not to mention a little damp.

Away from blisters and bivvy bags, attractions in Manakhah include the lively Sunday morning market, which draws in all manner of characters from the surrounding villages. Alternatively, you can kick back in one of the tea shops and admire the views.

Sleeping & Eating

There are currently no restaurants in Manakhah, but the hotels won't let you go hungry (breakfast/lunch/dinner YR400/ 1000/1000). Lunch boxes (YR500 to YR800) can also be prepared and further provisions bought at the market.

ourpick **Manakha Tourist Hotel** (Manakhah Askari Hotel; ☎ 460365; fax 460365; r per person YR800) The homely rooms are simple and pleasing and some have epic views over the valleys and peaks. The English-speaking owners are

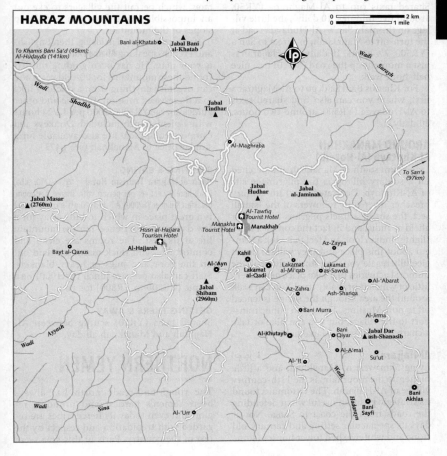

HARAZ MOUNTAINS

YEMEN

very friendly, great cooks and full of trekking information, but take our advice and run away as soon as the musical instruments come out. Otherwise, they'll have you dancing about like a fool before you know it.

Al-Tawfiq Tourist Hotel (☎ 460085; per person with breakfast & dinner YR2200) Lying on the main Manakhah–San'a road, this hotel has slightly fancier rooms than the Manakha Tourist Hotel, but less atmosphere. They also like you to get your dancing shoes on, but if you choose not to you'll be in good company because the president didn't dance either when he came to stay.

Getting There & Away
Shared taxis run to Al-Maghraba (YR50, around five minutes, 10 daily), the little village on the main San'a–Al-Hudayda road at the turn-off to Manakhah, or direct to San'a (YR500, 2½ hours, 10 daily). Al-Hajjarah is just a moment up the road (YR10) or a nice half-hour walk.

For Khamis Bani Sa'd, go to Al-Maghraba first, where you can also find shared taxis to Al-Hudayda (YR500, around two hours, 20 daily).

AROUND MANAKHAH
Al-Khutayb (Al-Hoteib)
Lying 6km south of Manakhah and perched on a solitary hilltop is the pilgrimage site of Al-Khutayb. Dedicated to a 12th-century preacher revered by followers of the Ismaili sect, the shrine attracts pilgrims from as far afield as India, and in fact the complex has a slightly Indian look and feel to it. Ask a Yemeni about this place and they will no doubt gleefully regale you with stories about all the immoral activities that take place here – very little of which is probably true! You can walk around the area, though the shrine is fenced off to non-Muslims. There's no public transport to the village, but you can hike or take a chartered taxi from Manakhah.

Al-Hajjarah
الهجرة

Lying 5km west of Manakhah, and a little higher up the mountain, is the 11th-century village of Al-Hajjarah. The Ottomans found its strategic position useful when defending the roads from the coast to San'a. Nowadays its spectacular setting and century-old stone and whitewashed tower houses (some

up to eight storeys) have caught the eye of visitors with mountain-walking in mind.

INFORMATION
Unfortunately, Al-Hajjarah is one of the very few places in Yemen where you'll be assailed by guides. But they're not exactly persistent, and once in the village proper you'll be left in peace. Some overnight visitors have reported a strange atmosphere here after dark.

SIGHTS & ACTIVITIES
Until recently, the **Al-Ba'aha quarter** was inhabited by Jews. Above this is the old **Muslim quarter**, with its huge entrance gate. Look out for the painstakingly constructed **terraces**, which permit the villagers to eke out an impossible living from the very steep slopes of the mountain.

If you're interested in **hiking**, then English- and French-speaking **Ahamed Ali** (☎ 711901680) is your man. He has been guiding tourists round these mountains for 20-odd years and can organise anything from a one-day hike to a three-week mission. Both he and other guides charge YR3000/5000 per 12/24 hours with a picnic lunch included. Donkeys and camping equipment are also available for a similar price to Manakhah (see p471).

SLEEPING & EATING
Husn al-Hajjara Tourism Hotel (☎ 460210; alhaj jarah-hotel@y.net.ye; per person with shared bathroom, breakfast & dinner YR2000) Al-Hajjarah's only hotel is a great place in which to hide away for a few days and experience Yemeni mountain life at its best. The rooms are clean and comfortable with thick mattresses laid out on the floor and piles of heavy blankets. Staff can also prepare lunch (YR1000) or a picnic (YR200 to YR800) for you.

GETTING THERE & AWAY
Shared taxis (YR10) scuttle between Al-Hajjarah and Manakhah all day.

NORTHERN YEMEN

The rough-and-ready north has always been Yemen's hardest and proudest region and even today its fierce tribes are regarded with trepidation and respect by the rest of the country. Parts of this area seem to plunge constantly in and out of dispute and armed conflict. At the time of writing, almost the entire Sa'da province was out of bounds, though the city itself and the road to San'a were just about open. (The situation is highly unstable and changes on a daily basis.)

North of Sa'da a violent uprising has dragged on since 2003 between government forces and a group of Zaydi fighters calling themselves the 'Believing Youth'. Led originally by Hussein Badreddin al-Houthi and, following his death, by his identically named father, this anti-Western, anti-government group is fighting to overthrow the Yemeni government, which they claim is too pro-Western. The result has been heavy casualties on both sides. The group's support base is north of Sa'da, but areas to the south of the city, including towns and villages on the road to San'a, also show a degree of support for the uprising. Therefore many areas, including the route to Shaharah and anywhere further north, are currently quite tense. Though the government has recently reopened some areas to tour groups, you should consider the situation carefully – there are many equally impressive places in Yemen where the reception is likely to be much warmer.

AMRAN عمران
☎ 07

First impressions of ancient Amran, situated on an old trading route 52km northwest of San'a, aren't good. The town appears to be a rash of half-completed modern developments and seems to offer little reason to stop, but once past this you'll discover a fruity and flavoursome old quarter with something of a wild west feel to it. The town is also known for the quality of its leatherwork.

Sights
The quiet **old town** is in remarkably good shape and the locals do a sterling job of keeping the streets clean. If you've been in Yemen for sometime, you probably won't think much of Amran, but if you're new to the game, you'll think its proud adobe houses and masses of excitable children quite enchanting. The highlights of a visit are walking along the city walls, which virtually surround the old quarter, and inspecting the eastern **entrance gate**. Look out

---

> **STANDING GUARD**
>
> If you're pondering the little watchtowers that dot the landscape with their cylindrical towers and slit windows, they're standing guard over the hectares of qat plantations that spread around them. Inside are armed owners ready to fend off thieves who may come in the night!

for the **ancient stone inscriptions** around the entrance to the town as well as on some of the house façades. The souq in the new town is a riotous affair.

Sleeping & Eating
Most people stop in Amran for only an hour or so en route to Sa'da. There's little reason to stay overnight.

Tourist Goold More Hotel (☎ 604407; Sa'da St; d YR1500) On the noisy main road from Sa'da this hotel certainly doesn't include lots of 'goold', but it's the best of a couple of ropey numbers. It's not at all used to foreign guests and boasts small rooms and smaller bathrooms.

Restaurant Fath Arahman (☎ 604285; meals YR400) Lying on the main San'a to Sa'da road, this place is packed with locals who relish its tasty chicken and meat-based meals.

Getting There & Away
Shared taxis go to Hajja (YR500, 2½ hours, 10 daily) and San'a (YR100, one hour, 20 daily).

AROUND AMRAN
Between Amran and Hajja lies **Kuhlan Affar** and its hilltop fortress, positioned dramatically above the road. Admission to the **fortress** (☏ 9am-6pm) is by donation (YR100 to YR200 is recommended). It's around 15 minutes' walk from the 'car park' above town to the fort, which is one of the most heavily fortified in Yemen. There's not a great deal to see inside, but the walk is pleasant enough.

HAJJA حجة
☎ 07 / pop 24,645

Modern Hajja can't be described as attractive, but the journey there – which takes you over, around and along crest after crest of magnificent mountain – certainly is.

Information

Al-Ikhwah Telecom Centre (Al-Hudayda St)

Al-Manar Internet Centre (Main Rd; per min YR2; ☯ 10am-10pm) Located above a pharmacy 100m west of the main square.

Yemen Bank for Reconstruction & Development (☎ 220401; Main Sq) Can change US dollars and euros in both cash and travellers cheques.

Sights & Activities

Perched on the hill overlooking town is the **Al-Qahira fortress** (admission YR100; ☯ sunrisesunset), which over time both the Ottomans and Zaydi *imams* have used. It's occupied by the army, who will do their utmost to wangle several hundred riyal out of you. Aside from the impressive views over the town, there's not much to see. However, by hunting around, you might find the Britishmade WWII cannons, the water cisterns that could keep the fort going in times of siege and the entrance to the secret passageway (opposite the tower on the eastern side), which allowed the *imam* a swift exit in an emergency.

Sleeping & Eating

Baabel Hotel Tourist (☎ 222075; fax 220818; s/d/ tr YR2000/2500/3000) Despite a general air of rot, the rooms at this cheap hotel are kept fairly clean, and it makes a good budget bet. The Baabel is located just off the main square.

Ghamban Hajja Hotel (☎ 220424; fax 220423; s/d YR3500/4000) Excellent-value midrange hotel with clean, quiet and well-maintained rooms and scorching-hot showers. Breakfast costs YR400, while lunch and dinner cost YR1200. It lacks any character, but its soft beds do guarantee a good night's kip. It has a commanding location on a hill overlooking town.

Golden Al-Nawras Restaurant and Broast (San'a St; meals YR250-500; ☯ 7am-11pm) Tasty and filling portions of all your Yemeni favourites are served in this highly popular streetside restaurant.

Getting There & Away

Hajja makes a good backdoor route to the Red Sea coast if you're coming from Yemen's far north. Shared taxis make the run to Hudayda (YR700, three hours, five daily) and San'a (YR700, three to 3½ hours, 20 daily), via Amran (YR500, 2½ hours).

SHAHARAH شهارة

Fortified mountain villages are two-apenny in Yemen, but Shaharah is the pick of the crop. Incredibly inaccessible, Shaharah has been a thorn in the side of any invading army and a bolthole for retreating *imams* for centuries. It wasn't until the civil war of the '60s that the village was finally conquered through the use of air power. In addition to its defensive fame the village has a long tradition of learning (dating back to the time of the Zaydi dynasty in the 9th century). Its scholars were known throughout south Arabia.

The village lies at 2600m and overlooks mountainous bulging swells to the south and shimmering hot plains to the north. The climb up from these plains to the village takes you through some of the most jaw-dropping scenery in the country. In addition the adventure of getting to Shaharah is half the fun of a trip there.

Most tour operators recommend a stay of just one night. In some ways this makes good sense – aside from admiring the views and walking a little way back down the mountain, there is nothing much to do. However, on the flip side, getting to Shaharah is such a mission (it's six hours minimum from San'a) that when you arrive it's getting dark. You then leave at first light, which doesn't really allow time to appreciate the place. Unfortunately, there is nowhere safe to stay between Amran and Sa'da (drivers of tourist cars don't even like to halt for a photo along some sections of the road), so breaking your journey is also not possible.

Sights

Shaharah's very beautiful 17th-century suspended **bridge** lies around 15 minutes' walk from town. Constructed with limestone blocks, it was commissioned by a local lord, keen to connect two villages separated for centuries by the deep gorge. Every kid in town will want to show you the way.

You can also climb up to the **fort** on the top of the mountain beyond the bridge. The village, including its fat **stone houses** and 23 beautifully constructed **water cisterns**, turns on its charms in the soft light of evening and early morning. Otherwise, Shaharah's a great place for catching up on diaries, postcards and books, curled up with a cup of tea in the cosy confines of your *funduq* (hotel).

Sleeping & Eating

There are no restaurants in Shaharah but all three hotels lay on gut-busting dinners and breakfasts, which are included in the room price.

Funduq Wazir (bed per person YR1000) A friendly, English-speaking woman runs this traditional, though slightly tatty, *funduq*. Some rooms have stunning views over the mountains but the best reason to stay here is for the opportunity it allows to talk with a Yemeni woman.

Funduq Khaled (☎ 07-628133; bed per person YR2000) This is a simple, well-loved *funduq* with a stripy red-and-white interior whose owners will keep you happy. The drivers who bring you up the mountain will automatically drop you off here, as they get paid a commission.

Shahara Bridge Tourist Hotel (☎ 07-628097; fax 07-628248; bed per person YR2500) A new hotel on the edge of town. Though lacking the authentic air of the other two, its sparkly rooms are certainly a lot more comfortable than its competitors.

Getting There & Away

Villagers won't allow any tourist vehicles to travel up to Shaharah, so visitors are obliged to charter a local 4WD (often elderly, battered and not totally safe) for YR8000 (return) per vehicle. The departure point is at the village of Al-Qabi, which lies around 10km (around 1½ hours) below Shaharah. The incline is very steep and the road shocking. Be prepared for a rough journey.

At the time of writing independent travellers were not permitted to travel to Shahara, but the situation changes frequently. When allowed, you should ask any taxi or bus on the San'a–Sa'da road to drop you off at the Huth taxi stand (118km from San'a), from which you may be able to find pick-up trucks going to Al-Qabi or even Shaharah. All tourist cars will be given a police escort for at least some sections of the journey.

SA'DA   صعدة

☎ 07 / pop 21,6721

Ancient Sa'da was once a city of major importance on the trade routes north to Damascus, as well as one of Arabia's original, and most devoted, Islamic cities. It remains to this day the most conservative and traditional town in Yemen. Sa'da (and its region) is known for its particular style of adobe architecture, which gives the houses the impression of having a coat of mud tiles. The town also has some impressive fortifications, including a remarkable 16th-century adobe wall and its original gates. Due to the ongoing troubles in this region, visitors should tread very carefully and women would be advised to stay well covered up.

Information

Al-Hada Exchange (☎ 515261; ☯ 8am-10pm Fri-Wed), next door to the Al-Aokhuah Hotel, can change US dollars. **Top Internet Café** (per min YR2; ☯ 9am-10pm) has slow connections.

Sights

The journey to Sa'da from San'a, over a desiccated and rock-strewn landscape, and the town's raw and wild air are as noteworthy as its physical sights. Indeed, many people find Sa'da to be just another hot and dusty old town, and something of an anticlimax. Certainly, since tourists were banned from the legendary arms market of **Suq at-Talh** (p477) there is far less reason to traipse up here, but that doesn't mean a visit is totally worthless. The old town is one of the few in Yemen that remains completely encased by a **defensive wall**, which you can walk along for nearly 3.5km. It boasts no less than 52 defence towers, four gates, and 16 staircases and is up to 8m high. The souqs are a lot of fun; look out for the livestock market on the western edge of the old town and the *jambiya* sellers, with rows of blades glinting in the sun. If you're looking for an antique *jambiya*, Sa'da is a good place to buy one.

The **Great Mosque** (Al-Hadi Mosque), which dates to the 9th century, is considered one of the oldest in Yemen and is the centre of the Zaydi universe in Yemen. It's home to valuable manuscripts and to a number of important tombs, including that of its namesake, Al-Hadi Yahya bin al-Husain, founder of the Zaydi dynasty in the 9th century. It remains an important centre of Islamic scholarship. Nonbelievers are not allowed to enter, so you will have to content yourself with a surreptitious glimpse through the beautifully inscribed gateway. The city contains many other mosques,

YEMEN

though aside from the minarets there is nothing for non-Muslim travellers to see.

The large **Zaydi cemetery**, close to Bab as-Salam, is famous for its gravestones, which detail the lives and 'virtues' of the deceased below them. It's sometimes possible for respectful foreigners to enter.

Sa'da is also famous for its Jewish population, distinguished by their long, curly side-locks. Sadly, much of this once substantial population has left for better times in Israel, and today you'd be lucky to meet any Jews.

Sleeping & Eating

Rahban Tourism Hotel (☎ 512848; fax 512856; Main St; s/d YR2184/3248) Smelly and stained rooms, which aren't exactly a bundle of laughs to stay in, but are still better than anything the competition can come up with. Some rooms have views over the old town. English speaking.

Al-Jola (Main St; mains YR300) Tasty Yemeni favourites come with a smile in this brightly decorated café full of tacky posters. The café's sign is in Arabic only.

Roma Restaurant (Main St; meal YR400) Easily the town's hottest spot, this narrow and funky restaurant has tables and chairs for the civilised, and floor space for the rebellious. It serves up generous portions of all the basics and there's a beautiful mountain 'backdrop'. Note that the sign is in Arabic only.

Getting There & Away

For almost all the period between 2003 and late 2006, Sa'da was completely out of bounds to all tourists due to the highly unstable security situation. In early 2007 the city, and the city alone, was reopened to foreign visitors, but only to those travelling in a tour group. Even then, the situation was highly unstable and the town and roads leading to it could be opened and closed on a daily basis.

Should the situation ever improve, shared taxis run to San'a (YR650, four hours, 20 to 30 daily) via Amran (YR650, three hours). At the time of research, there were no buses at all connecting Sa'da to the capital.

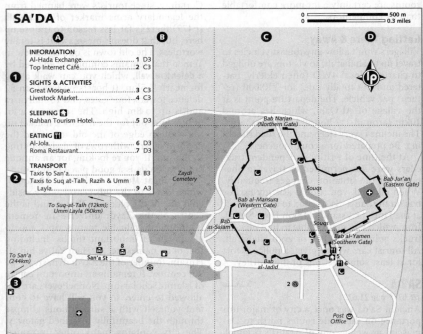

SA'DA

INFORMATION	
Al-Hada Exchange	1 D3
Top Internet Café	2 C3

SIGHTS & ACTIVITIES	
Great Mosque	3 C3
Livestock Market	4 C3

SLEEPING	
Rahban Tourism Hotel	5 D3

EATING	
Al-Jola	6 D3
Roma Restaurant	7 D3

TRANSPORT	
Taxis to San'a	8 B3
Taxis to Suq at-Talh, Razih & Umm Layla	9 A3

0 — 500 m
0 — 0.3 miles

Bab Narjan (Northern Gate)

Zaydi Cemetery

Bab al-Mansura (Western Gate)

Bab Jur'an (Eastern Gate)

Souqs

Bab as-Salam

Souqs

Bab al-Yamen (Southern Gate)

To Suq-at-Talh (12km); Umm Layla (50km)

To San'a (244km)

San'a St

Bab al-Jadid

Post Office

BOYS WITH TOYS

The abundance of weapons in private Yemeni hands is legendary, with estimates of 60 million weapons in the hands of 21 million citizens. The most visible form of gun is the Kalashnikov, but you can also take your pick from a wide assortment of pistols, rifles, hand grenades, large jeep-mounted weaponry, surface-to-air missiles and even anti-aircraft guns. While the trade in such heavy weapons is a little more discreet, the sale of machine guns, grenades and pistols is very open and obvious. For the average Yemeni, with his strong tribal background, guns are an essential of daily life. Blood feuds between tribal groups can continue for years and at times reach levels of almost all-out warfare. These ethnic vendettas result in around 2000 deaths per year.

However, guns are more than just a means of defence: they are a status symbol in the same manner that souped-up cars are for young men in the West. The easy availability of weapons in Yemen stems from the numerous wars fought in and around the country. With the never-ending instability in the larger region, it's no surprise that gun running is big business here. (During the 1994 Civil War, it's thought many of the victorious northern tribal leaders got their hands on all manner of ex-Soviet equipment including tanks.) Even the Yemeni government has recently been caught smuggling weapons into Somalia, and Yemeni firepower has been found throughout eastern Africa. But it's the Middle Eastern market that's proving to be the real headache. The Yemeni/Saudi border has always been a fairly porous and loosely defined affair, and with the tribes holding more power than the central government, in this region smuggling has long been a mainstay of the economy. Though there is no way of knowing where many of these weapons end up, most observers agree that Al-Qaeda can, has and will take advantage of this easy weapons supply. This has been demonstrated on a number of occasions in the past few years when the weapons used in Al-Qaeda–backed terrorist attacks in Saudi Arabia and elsewhere have been found to have originated in Yemen.

It's partially for this reason that in early 2006 the Saudis began construction of a huge security fence along their border with Yemen. Unfortunately, part of the planned route runs through a 20km stretch of disputed no-man's-land, which has so infuriated Yemeni tribesmen that they have vowed to fight any construction work.

AROUND SA'DA

There are many picturesque villages in the environs of Sa'da, and the area is also known for its large number of rock drawings and paintings dating to the Stone Age. However, at the time of research, and for several years preceding that, all the following places, except As-Sinnara and parts of the Wadi 'Abdin, were out of bounds to tourists. Consequently, aside from the two places mentioned above, we have been unable to confirm any practical travel information for the following.

As-Sinnara & Wadi 'Abdin

Visible on a hilltop to the southeast of Sa'da is the ruined 19th-century fortress of As-Sinnara. Built by the Ottomans and also used as a retreat by the *imams* in times of trouble, it continues its military tradition by providing a base for the modern state's army. It's often possible to visit, though you will still need police permission (apparently it's dangerous – despite

or perhaps because of the army occupation!). It makes an enjoyable afternoon's outing, but a bigger draw than the slightly sorry fort is the impressive Wadi 'Abdin, over which it towers. The narrow sides of this wadi are filled with lush green fields and tall mud-brick houses that are in fact much more impressive than many of the houses of old Sa'da. The wadi has a passing resemblance to the Wadi Hadramawt. You will need your own transport to get out here and police will not allow you to walk around any of the villages of the wadi.

Suq at-Talh

The famous Suq at-Talh **market**, which lies around 12km from Sa'da, is the biggest in Yemen. It takes place just off the main road. Friday is the main market day. It's known for its extensive arms market, but as the town is the centre of the uprising it's highly unlikely that any foreigners will be allowed here for some time.

Umm Layla

Lying around 50km to the northwest of Sa'da is Umm Layla, the most important of the castles on the pilgrims' and incense routes and, according to ancient inscriptions, long the site of a settlement.

Jabal Razih

At 3658m, Jabal Razih is one of the highest mountains in Yemen. A trip up to the mountain takes you through some beautiful scenery and isolated mountain villages often cloaked in mist.

TIHAMA (RED SEA COAST)

The flat and featureless Tihama is the chalk next to highland Yemen's mountainous cheese. The contrasts are more than just geographical. With Africa being only a stone's throw away, the flamboyant influence of that continent seems to be present everywhere. The clothing is so bright sunglasses are needed to look at it, the solid stone houses of the mountains have turned into African–style mud-and-thatch huts, the weekly markets are even more animated and the overall attitude is so liberal that unveiled local women feel free to chat and flirt with unknown men. All in all, the final package is a fascinating contrast to the rest of the country – just don't attempt to explore it during summer, when it becomes so hot and steamy that even the deserts of the Empty Quarter start to seem a little chilly.

AL-HUDAYDA الحديده

☎ 03 / pop 298,452

With its wide and clean streets, parks full of shady, snooze-enticing benches and pleasant pavement cafés, Al-Hudayda, capital of Tihama, is probably Yemen's most European-flavoured city and is an enjoyable place to rest up for half a day or so. However, its often-touted description of being the 'bride of the Red Sea' is a little over optimistic and probably says more about the state of someone's wife than the beauty of the town.

History

Settled originally by immigrant fishermen, Al-Hudayda later became known for two

things: the export of coffee (from the 17th century) and the export of pearls. But it wasn't until the Ottomans were looking for a safe port in the southern Red Sea that Al-Hudayda was really developed. The city was largely destroyed during WWI and rebuilding didn't commence with any passion until after the 1994 civil war. Since then the city has boomed and visitors will notice a decidedly more upbeat air to Al-Hudayda than to Aden. Today the town is the fourth largest in Yemen, but the centre has managed to retain a quiet small-town atmosphere.

Orientation

The Hadiqat ash-Sha'b (People's Garden) marks the town centre and it's here that many of the town's restaurants, hotels and facilities are found.

Information

Foreign-exchange offices are found on San'a St. Other services include the post office and, opposite, an International Telephone Centre.

Arab Bank (☎ 201254; San'a St) Changes cash and travellers cheques, and has an ATM.

Arab Net (per hr YR70; ☻ 9am-midnight) Good internet connections.

Bin Thabet Centre (per min YR2; ☻ 9am-11pm) Fast internet connections.

Saba Islamic Bank (☎ 201496) Next to the Hadiqat ash-Sha'b. Has an ATM.

Universal Travels & Tourism (☎ 208691; San'a St; ☻ 8am-12.30pm & 4-7.30pm Sat-Thu) Travel bookings and car hire.

Sights & Activities

The Al-Hudayda **fish market** (☻ 6am-noon), 2km southeast of the centre of town, is a slippery and smelly must-see that's frenetic, cocky and fun. Come early in the morning to watch the day's catch being unloaded in front of a hectic, seagull-like mob of buyers and sellers. The daily trawl nets everything from plump prawns and glistening groupers to huge hammerhead sharks. The traditional dhow boats are also very photogenic. The old and, it must be said, very decrepit Turkish quarter is another possible goal, as are the nearby **souqs**.

Maybe the best way to pass an afternoon in Al-Hudayda is to do as the locals do: buy an ice cream and stroll along the **sea front** (look out for Ottoman and Southeast

Asian–influenced buildings) or laze about with a book in one of the town's parks.

There are some pleasant beaches in the region, such as at **Urj**, 36km north of town on the Salif road.

Sleeping

Hotel Darcum (☎ 226500; San'a St; d YR2500) This excellent budget hotel has clean and comfortable rooms that are kept smelling fresh thanks to liberal use of incense.

Al-Jazera Hotel (☎ 201404; fax 201401; s/d with fridge YR3000/4000) The best feature of this hotel, and one that makes up a lot for the dreary rooms, are the doors that speak to you as you enter the lobby! Centrally positioned and with English-speaking staff.

Dream Hotel (☎ 200381; fax 217986; off San'a St; s/d YR3500/4000) A neat new hotel that comes with clean tiled rooms and a flurry of cushions and sofas to lounge about on. It's on a quiet side street just off the main square, so you might actually get to do some dreaming in this hotel. English-speaking and great value.

Eating

Nana Restaurant (San'a St; meals YR300; ⏱ 6am-1pm) An ideal spot to chill out on one of the outdoor tables while feasting on the delicious *fool*.

Al-Sindbad Broast & Restaurant (☎ 2072720; meals YR400; ⏱ 6am-2am) Clean central restaurant with a wide-ranging menu (in English)

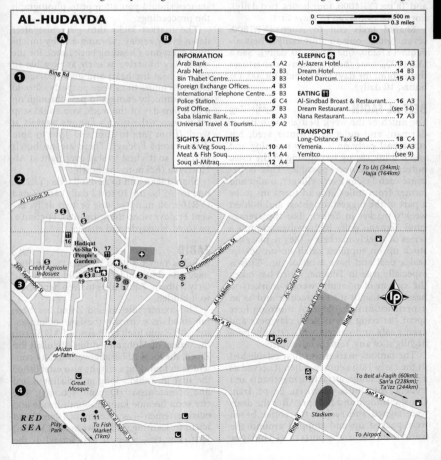

AL-HUDAYDA

0 ——— 500 m
0 ——— 0.3 miles

INFORMATION
Arab Bank	**1** A2
Arab Net	**2** B3
Bin Thabet Centre	**3** B3
Foreign Exchange Offices	**4** B3
International Telephone Centre	**5** B3
Police Station	**6** C4
Post Office	**7** B3
Saba Islamic Bank	**8** A3
Universal Travel & Tourism	**9** A2

SIGHTS & ACTIVITIES
Fruit & Veg Souq	**10** A4
Meat & Fish Souq	**11** A4
Souq al-Mitraq	**12** A4

SLEEPING 🏠
Al-Jazera Hotel	**13** A3
Dream Hotel	**14** B3
Hotel Darcum	**15** A3

EATING 🍴
Al-Sindbad Broast & Restaurant	**16** A3
Dream Restaurant	(see 14)
Nana Restaurant	**17** A3

TRANSPORT
Long-Distance Taxi Stand	**18** C4
Yemenia	**19** A3
Yemitco	(see 9)

Ring Rd

Al Hamdi St

26th September St

Crédit Agricole Indosuez

Hadiqat As-Sha'b (People's Garden)

Telecommunications St

Al-Hakimi St

As-Sulayhi St

Ahmad ad-Dain St

San'a St

Ring Rd

San'a St

To Urj (34km); Hajja (164km)

To Beit al-Faqih (60km); San'a (228km); Ta'izz (244km)

Midan at-Tahrir

Great Mosque

Abd Allah al-Ahmar St

RED SEA

Play Park

To Fish Market (1km)

Stadium

To Airport

YEMEN

that includes some breaks from the chicken and rice routine.

Dream Restaurant (☎ 200381; meals YR600; ☎ lunch & dinner) Located in Dream Hotel, this restaurant is one of the few places outside of San'a where you might like to waste time over a meal. Good seafood and friendly service. A full meal of starter, main and juice shouldn't cost more than YR1000.

Getting There & Away

The national carrier **Yemenia** (☎ 201474; www .yemenia.com.ye) has one-way flights to San'a (US$50, four weekly).

The bus company **Yemitco** (☎ 208668) has services to Aden (YR1300, six hours, two daily), San'a (YR1100, five hours, two daily) and Ta'izz (YR1000, four hours, two daily). For Al-Khawkha, go to Hays first.

Shared taxis run to Aden (YR1800, seven hours, one to four daily), Beit al-Faqih (YR250, one hour, 10 daily), San'a (YR1000, four hours, many departures throughout the day) and Zabid (YR500, 1½ hours, 10 daily).

BEIT AL-FAQIH   بيت الفقيه

For much of the week Beit al-Faqih lies as dormant and quiet as a winter seed, but come past early on a Friday morning and you'll think spring has sprung in the most outrageous manner possible. This is because each Friday every villager, trader and farmer from miles around turns up to be a part of the biggest, brightest and boldest weekly market in Yemen. For the average rural Yemeni, daily life revolves around a series of weekly markets – they're places to stock up on supplies, catch up on gossip, seal a deal and have a bit of fun. This is especially true in Tihama, which has taken the system of nomadic weekly markets to heart. As a sight it's spectacular and as an experience unforgettable. A morning here spent bartering over spices, clay pots and even goats and camels will certainly be a highlight of any Yemeni adventure.

The famous market was first established in the early 18th century, when it served as a coffee exchange, attracting merchants and traders from India, Morocco, Egypt, Iran, Constantinople and Europe. After the deals were signed and sealed, the coffee beans were packed up and shipped around the world from the nearby ports of Al-Hudayda

or Al-Makha. With the collapse of the coffee trade, Beit al-Faqih sought to diversify – today coffee makes up only a tiny fraction of the items on sale. Instead, it's the day-to-day needs of the Tihama villager that form the bulk of the trade.

While wandering around you might be lucky enough to come across the 'cuppers' (due to local sensibilities we won't tell you exactly where in the market they can be found). This ancient form of medical treatment involves bleeding the illness out of a patient through the use of small horns. The doctors involved in this are (just about) tolerant of respectful foreigners stopping by to watch for a few moments, but don't overstay your welcome and under no circumstances should you attempt to photograph the proceedings.

The market kicks into gear just after dawn every Friday morning and by lunchtime everyone's heading back home for the week. Try to arrive as early as possible (if only to beat the heat) and give yourself at least two hours to explore properly. Should you be unlucky enough to pass through on a different day of the week, you could stop off to watch the town's famous **weavers** at work (from 7am to 1pm and 4pm to 6pm daily, except Friday). There are no hotels in town, so it's best to stay overnight at Al-Hudayda (62km to the north).

Shared taxis run to Al-Hudayda (YR250, one to 1½ hours, 10 to 12 daily) and Zabid (YR100, 30 minutes, one or two daily, except Fridays when there are lots). For San'a, go to Al-Hudayda and change.

ZABID   زبيد

Zabid is Yemen's third Unesco World Heritage site, but unlike flirty Old San'a and tarty Shibam, Zabid likes to keep her secrets well hidden.

The countryside around Zabid has been inhabited since virtually the dawn of humanity, with Zabid itself built around AD 819 on the orders of Mohammed ibn'Abdullah ibn Ziyad, the local Abbasid governor. Not content with founding a city, he also established the first in Zabid's long and distinguished line of *madrassas* (Quranic schools). The city soon became known – both inside and outside Yemen – as a centre of Islamic and scientific learning, and between the 13th and 15th centuries, when it also served as the capital of Yemen, Zabid played host to over 5000 students in more than 200 colleges.

The last 500 years have been less kind on Zabid and the town has gradually faded in importance. Don't feel sorry, though, because this is just karma paying Zabid back for the pain caused to school children the world over: it was a scholar from Zabid who was responsible for that refined torture called algebra!

The walled town was declared a Unesco World Heritage site in 1993, and in 2000, with over 40% of the old city houses replaced with new structures, Zabid was registered on the organisation's 'Danger List', requiring urgent funds for restoration.

Finally, as if algebra and Unesco recognition wasn't enough, Zabid has another dubious claim to fame. It's reputedly the hottest town on earth.

Sights & Activities

The dazzling whitewashed, low-rise town is a shy place and keeps most of its best features tucked away out of view. Without a bit of local help, a visitor will probably leave with staid impressions, having seen little but a series of plain exterior walls. Fortunately, help is at hand in the form of a friendly and generous local population. Walk the sweltering streets, stopping to speak with anyone you see and an invitation for tea in somebody's house is almost a given. As soon as this happens, the hidden world of Zabid opens up before you. Plain on the exterior, the interior of the walls, which face onto small courtyards, are nothing short of carved and sculpted works of art in a hundred different patterns and geometrical designs. If you're lucky enough to be invited into someone's home, bear in mind that it's just that, a home, and be discreet with your camera. You should also leave a tip (YR200 for a group of two or three should be sufficient). An even easier way of gaining entry to some of the more beautiful homes, as well as the mosques, is to employ the services of one of the young guides who may greet you on arrival. They can also take you to weaving workshops.

Built around the central souqs, the residential areas of the city were originally divided into different quarters for the different professional classes – merchants, artisans, dignitaries and scholars. The city retains much of its low defensive wall and also some of the original gates, including **Bab as-Siham**, **Bab ash-Shabariq** and **Bab an-Nakhl**. Various ornate buildings, such as the **Nasr Palace**, testify to the town's former prestige and wealth.

Zabid boasts 86 mosques (one for every 10 houses) and two *madrassas,* including the **Al-Asha'ir Mosque** and the **Al-Jami'a Mosque** (Friday Mosque), which dates to the 16th century. Look out, also, for the white, 13th-century **Al-Iskandar Mosque** in the **citadel** on the edge of town. Unusually in Yemen, it's often possible for non-Muslims to quietly enter some of the mosques with a guide.

Formerly the citadel's granary, the restored **Zabid Granary Museum** (admission YR200; ☾ sunrise-sunset) now serves to 'explain the history of Zabid' and exhibits the finds of the archaeological mission working here since 1983. The six sections are themed (mainly historically) and contain a wide range of artefacts, from cannon balls and fragments of fine pottery to Ottoman pipes and lovely Islamic woodcarving.

The Zabid Tourism Resthouse can arrange **camel** or **donkey tours** (per person per day US$75) around the old town, as well as further afield to places such as **Al-Faza**, a beautiful beach around 25km away.

While exploring Zabid, you will probably notice that the women seem to play a much greater role in public life than many other parts of Yemen, and many are not just unveiled but also prepared to start conversations with foreigners of either sex. This is partly to do with the outward-looking attitude common to people all along the Yemeni coast and also the strong, and liberal, African influence.

Sleeping & Eating

Hotel Zabid (☎ 341461; s/d YR2000/2500) Brand-new hotel opposite the Bab ash-Shabariq. The rooms are sterile and the singles have common bathrooms only, but it's more comfortable than the competition and you'll get a much better night's sleep.

Zabid Tourism Resthouse (☎ 340270; s/d with fan & shared bathroom YR2500/5000) Traditional, communal-style rooms are set around a shady central courtyard with rope charpoy beds and walls painted with scenes of everyday Yemeni life. Popular with tour groups and has a good restaurant (meals YR1000).

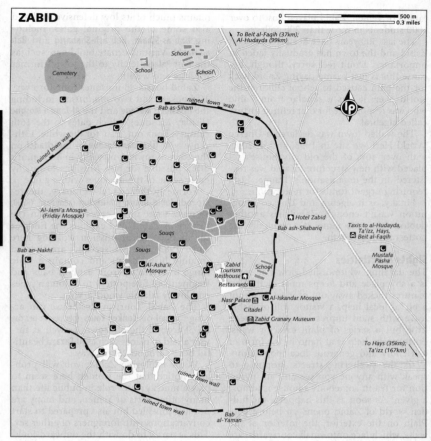

ZABID

To Beit al-Faqih (37km); Al-Hudayda (99km)

Cemetery

School

School

School

ruined town wall

Bab as-Siham

ruined town wall

Al-Jami'a Mosque (Friday Mosque)

Souqs

Souqs

Bab an-Nakhl

Al-Asha'ir Mosque

Zabid Tourism Resthouse

School

Restaurants

Nasr Palace

Al-Iskandar Mosque

Citadel

Zabid Granary Museum

Hotel Zabid

Bab ash-Shabariq

Taxis to al-Hudayda, Ta'izz, Hays, Beit al-Faqih

Mustafa Pasha Mosque

To Hays (35km); Ta'izz (167km)

ruined town wall

ruined town wall

Bab al-Yaman

Getting There & Away

Shared taxis run to Al-Hudayda (YR500, 1½ hours, at least every hour) and Ta'izz (YR1200, 2½ to three hours), Beit al-Faqih (YR100, 30 minutes, every half-hour). For Al-Khawkha, go to Hays (YR200, 30 minutes, every half-hour) and change there; for San'a, change at Al-Hudayda.

AL-KHAWKHA الخوخه

☎ 03

Touted with pride by Yemenis, Al-Khawkha was once an important coffee-exporting port, but today it's Yemen's answer to the Maldives. Well, that's what the tourist board like to think anyway. In reality, it's not a fully fledged beach destination but rather a simple place that offers a relaxing evening after exploring Zabid and the Friday market at Beit al-Faqih.

our pick Moka Marine Village (☎ 362770; mokatours@hotmail.com; s/d YR3000/4000) is the best of the beach 'resorts' by far. Lying on the seafront around 1.5km off the Al-Khawkha–Hays road, the 'village' consists of 10 bungalows, each with a bathroom and two double bedrooms (making them perfect for bickering couples), which are lovingly maintained and set in a pink-and-green garden. The reception area has old granny sofas to lounge about on and the restaurant has a delicious menu of fresh fish (dinner YR1000). In fact, it'd be a perfect place to have a real beach holiday, but for the fact it's missing an essential element: a beach. Instead of soft white sand and clear blue seas you'll find a vast tidal mudflat – excellent for birding but not so good for swimming. Book ahead.

A kilometre or so north, **El Khoka Tourism Village** (☎ 362779; fax 362780; s/d YR3000/3500, with breakfast & dinner YR1800/3600) is definitely the poor relation. It has the air of a '50s Butlins Holiday Camp and the paper-thin walls provide no real privacy. One huge plus is that it almost, and only almost, has a beach where you can swim – though even this involves striding 100m over rocks and mudflats.

In both of these camps snorkelling equipment costs YR1500 per hour, for which you also get a boat ride out to an offshore reef and island. In the past it used to be possible to head out on diving trips to the Hanish Islands by boat, but sadly the government has recently put a halt to such fun and games due to an ongoing dispute with Eritrea over ownership.

Getting There & Away

Nearby Hays (shared taxi YR100) is the main transport hub; shared taxis run from here to Zabid (YR200, 30 minutes).

AL-MAKHA
☎ 04

Ask most people what mocha means and they'll instantly reply, 'coffee' or 'Starbucks'. So it's somewhat ironic that Al-Makha, the original coffee port, is one of the few towns on the planet without a branch of Starbucks or its ilk. In fact, Al-Makha doesn't have a lot of anything these days – except flies and heat.

The history of Al-Makha stretches way back to the days before Islam (and Starbucks), but its heyday was during the 17th century when it became the world's foremost coffee-exporting centre and had a population of some 20,000. Nowadays it's a forlorn and windblown town of a few hundred hardy souls who make their bread and butter through fishing and smuggling. Africa is only a hop and a skip away and the chaos in Somalia provides an endless source of income for the unscrupulous. Alcohol, weapons, drugs, consumer goods and, most disturbingly, people all enter and leave Yemen through this narrow back door.

Al-Makha won't appeal to everyone. To some, it's as close as you can come to the gates of hell. To others, well, it's as close as you can come to the gates of hell, yet it also has a strangely alluring and melancholic air. Either way, it will certainly bring back memories next time you order a coffee.

Sights & Activities

Reminders of past glories are few and far between. The most impressive building is the **Masjid ash-Shadhil**, a blazing white 15th-century mosque. Nearby is an old **minaret**, a few piles of rubble that were once **merchant villas** and, miraculously, one still-standing villa that looks as keen as mustard to join its buddies in a heap on the ground. The newer part of town has a **qat market**, a **beach** with a few garishly painted boats and a large **fish market** and a weighing room, whose floors are ankle-deep in thick, black squid ink.

Sleeping & Eating

If, for some perverse reason, you want to stay the night in Al-Makha, you'll find the

---

THE PECULIAR INCIDENT OF THE GOAT & THE BERRY

Most of us need our early-morning caffeine kick to get going, but have you ever wondered who discovered coffee? Well, according to the Yemenis, it wasn't a person at all but rather a humble goat. It's said that a shepherd was out in the Yemeni hills with his goats when he noticed that one of them, having eaten some peculiar berries, started behaving strangely. Mystified by this sight, the old man took a bite himself and within moments felt 20 years younger. Astonished by this discovery, he raced back to his village and spread the news. One of the people he told was a poet who accompanied the shepherd back into the mountains to try them for himself. After swallowing a few of the berries, the poet felt so enlightened that he immediately composed a poem in praise of this odd shrub. It was this poem that spread the fame of coffee around the world. And the goat we all have to celebrate for our morning rituals? Rumour has it that in thanks he was eaten for lunch the next day.

Al-Rashid Hotel (☎ 4362357; shawky_nagi@yahoo .com; s/d YR2500/3500) on the main road into town. It has small, well-maintained rooms and very uninviting communal bathrooms. The nearby **Al-Waffa Restaurant** (meal YR300) serves oven-baked fish that's way better than its coffee, but be prepared to do battle with the flies over every morsel.

Getting There & Away
Shared taxis run to Ta'izz (YR500, two hours, twice daily).

SOUTHERN YEMEN

Yemen's south is the richest and most developed region of the country. It's also the greenest and most fertile and has long been considered the breadbasket of Arabia. There is a huge amount of historical, cultural and geographic variety in this area. In the far south is the run-down, sweltering port of Aden, the former British colony and old capital of the south. Like many port towns, it's much more liberal and relaxed than the interior (symbolised perhaps by the Adeni women who do not cover their faces, as well as the availability of alcohol).

Further north, and in complete contrast, are the lush and cool highland towns of Ibb, Jibla and Ta'izz, where rain falls year-round and Islam and scholarship are more the keys to life. Overall this is the safest and easiest part of the country in which to travel, particularly for those reliant on public transport.

IBB   إب
☎ 03 / pop 103,312
Situated 194km south of San'a, Ibb boasts a strategic position on a high hill in the western foothills of the Ba'adan Mountains. Settled since early Islamic times, the town grew into an important administrative centre during the time of the Ottomans. Today it's largely, and unjustifiably, ignored by most travellers. This is a shame because its chaotic market area and pretty old town are a pure delight to explore, and when combined with nearby Jibla, Ibb makes for a perfect overnight pause on the journey between San'a and Ta'izz.

Ibb and its governate enjoy one of the highest rainfall levels in Yemen, which

has given rise to the nickname 'the green province'.

The Saba Islamic Bank on the main road has an ATM, which accepts foreign cards.

Sights & Activities
The large and boisterous central **market** area in Ibb is a noisy clash of colours, sounds and smells that feels more Indian than Yemeni. It's one of the most enjoyable markets in the country. Immediately behind the market is the whitewashed old quarter, which, aside from around the qat market, is a much more staid but no less rewarding place to explore. The stone houses, designed in a style unique to Ibb, are typically four to five storeys high, with façades decorated with geometrical friezes and circular *qamiriya* (usually moon-shaped, stained-glass windows).

In the middle of the old town, **Al-Jalaliya Mosque** dates to the time of the Ottomans, while the gaudy nearby **art centre** (☉ 9am-noon Sat-Thu) and dull **museum** (admission fee negotiable but YR100-200 should suffice; ☉ 9am-noon & 3-7pm Sat-Thu) are much more contemporary affairs. The **fortress** perched on the hill nearby is, sadly, closed, but you can get good views of the town from **Jabal Rabi**, around 700m from the town centre. Close to the market area is a small **park** full of fairground rides, a teashop and a depressing row of monkey cages.

Sleeping & Eating
There are a couple of basic hotels in the market area, one being the **Al-Rabie Tourist** (r YR400), which are as cheap as chips. It's much better to stay out on the road to Ta'izz, on the edge of town, where there are a bunch of cleaner, quieter and far superior hotels.

Saba Tourist Hotel (☎ 418892; Al-Wdin St; s/d YR1000/2000) This is eccentrically disorganised and with a highly flexible price, but it's easily the cleanest and best-value budget hotel – even if it does retain the cheap Yemeni hotel requirement of a shower placed directly above the toilet.

Al-Riyad Hotel (☎ 419997; fax 419996; Al-Wdin St; s/d/ste YR2500/3000/6000) Ibb's newest hotel has a memorable reception full of plastic-coated chairs, fake chandeliers and garish wall decorations. The large and comfortable rooms offer great value for money.

Tihama Restaurant (Al-Wdin St; mains YR500) A dozen or so metres from the main roundabout at the entrance to town on the San'a–Ta'izz road is Ibb's favourite restaurant. Its Yemeni standards are anything but standard and all the ingredients are displayed in a hygienic manner on an outside table. Go for the kebabs and hummus – it's ace! The restaurant's sign is in Arabic only.

Getting There & Away

Shared taxis run to Jibla (YR50, 15 minutes, 30 daily), San'a (YR800, four hours, three daily) and Ta'izz (YR300, 1½ hours, 15 daily). For Jabal Rabi and trips around town, taxis charge YR200. The taxi stand lies on the edge of town on the road to Ta'izz. Ask your shared/contract taxi to drop you off at your hotel.

JIBLA   جبله
☎ 04

Situated 8km southwest of Ibb, Jibla is stunningly placed at the summit of a hill. The town served as the capital for much of highland Yemen under the Sulayhid dynasty in the 11th and 12th centuries, and was particularly prosperous under the benevolent and impossibly long-named Sayyida al-Hurra Arwa bint Ahmad as-Sulayhi. Fortunately this mouthful was quickly reduced to plain old Queen Arwa, but by the time of her death at the age of 92, she had proved she was anything but plain. By building numerous schools, roads, bridges and mosques, her policies of investing the kingdom's treasury in projects for the good of the average person mean that she's still remembered fondly today as a 'Little Sheba'.

It was thanks to this investment in education that the town gained a reputation as a centre for Islamic learning, and even today the annexe next to Queen Arwa's Mosque serves as a *madrassa*. More recently, Jibla has attained local fame for its excellent **qat market**.

About 1.5km up from the taxi stand at the southern end of the village are the twin minarets of the 11th-century **Queen Arwa Mosque** (admission by donation). Non-Muslims can normally take a look around if accompanied by the gatekeeper. Take a peek at the lovely, if rather decrepit, carved ceiling of the prayer hall and look out for the exceptionally long string of old, amber beads. Queen Arwa's silver tomb is found inside the mosque.

Across the village from the mosque – and accessible through the narrow lanes of the souq – is the solitary minaret of the 16th-century **As-Sunna Mosque**. The town has an incredible 48 further mosques, 30 of them for men, the remainder for women. Nearby is Arwa's crumbling **Dar as-Sultana Palace**, which was rumoured to have had 365 rooms, one for every day of the year. Some people disagree with this statement, saying that a woman like Queen Arwa would never be so ostentatious as to have such a building, and that it must instead have been constructed by one of her male predecessors. Whatever the truth, due to the dangerous state of the structure, entry is forbidden.

Close to the palace is the **Queen Arwa Museum** (☎ 440900; admission YR500; ⏰ 7am-6pm). It houses a fairly unexceptional collection of items belonging to the queen and her father (but look out for the lovely annotated manuscripts). Opening times are very flexible.

Besides the basic dormitory-style **Asamit Arwa** (☎ 440021), where a mattress on the floor costs YR150, there's no accommodation in Jibla. It's best to come on a day trip from Ta'izz. Shared/contract taxis run to Ibb (YR50/500, 10 minutes).

TA'IZZ   تعز
☎ 04 / pop 317,517

Ibn Battuta, the great 14th-century Arab traveller, once described Ta'izz as 'one of the largest and most beautiful cities'. It's still large – Yemen's third-largest city – but for beauty you need to look a little harder. The city has suffered heavily from unplanned urban growth, which has left it without any real central soul. On a positive note, Ta'izz is one of the most cosmopolitan centres in the country, thanks no doubt to its large student population. It also has one of the most eccentric and interesting museums in the country, as well as an excess of friendly people with time for a chat.

History

The hills around Ta'izz have been occupied virtually forever, but the city itself didn't make any recorded appearance until the 11th century. From the 13th to 15th centuries Ta'izz attained particular prominence when it became the capital of the Rasulid dynasty. Much later, Imam Ahmed bin Yahya Hamid al-Din chose the city as the

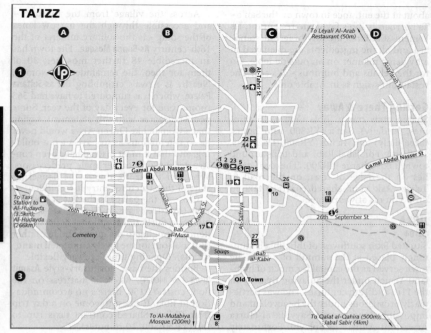

TA'IZZ

To Léyali Al-Arab Restaurant (50m)

To Taxi Station to Al-Hudayda (3.5km); Al-Hudayda (266km)

26th September St

Cemetery

Masallah St

Al-Awadi St

Bab al-Musa

Bab al-Kabir

Souqs

Old Town

At-Saffaya St

Gamal Abdul Nasser St

Asqalani St

26th September St

To Al-Mutabiya Mosque (200m)

To Qalat al-Qahira (500m); Jabal Sabir (4km)

capital, and reigned here from 1948 until his death in 1962. Much of Ta'izz is an entirely modern affair of drab and poorly constructed buildings, which seem to start collapsing before they're even completed. The compact old quarter contains more majestic reminders from the past, including a handful of beautiful mosques.

Orientation

Ta'izz consists basically of three streets. Gamal Abdul Nasser St and 26th September St run parallel to one another, east to west. Bisecting both streets and running north to south is At-Tahrir St, at the end of which lies Bab al-Kabir, the souq and old town.

Information

Al-Hadha Exchange Co (Gamal Abdul Nasser St) Foreign-exchange facilities.
Mamoon Internet (Gamal Abdul Nasser St; per min YR2; ☺ 9am-11pm)
Net Sky (At-Tahrir St; per min YR2; ☺ 10am-10.30pm Sat-Thu)
Post Office (☎ 229618) Lies just north of 26th September St.

Universal Travel & Tourism (☎ 252457; Gamal Abdul Nasser St) Acts as a voluntary tourism service in the absence of a tourist office. Also offers the usual tours.
Yemen Commercial Bank (☎ 251822; Gamal Abdul Nasser St) Has an ATM.

Sights & Activities

Not really a museum at all, but more the petrified palace of Imam Ahmed, the **National Museum** (☎ 215302; 26th September St; admission YR500; ☺ 8am-1pm Sat-Thu) preserves the life and times of its previous and slightly peculiar owner. Among the exhibits – which are intriguing, bizarre and comical in equal measure – are a large collection of gifts and purchases from Europe, including an Etch-a-Sketch, hundreds of bottles of *eau de cologne* (in which the *imam* apparently bathed), a personal cinema (despite TV and films being banned under *Imamic* law) and an electronic rocking bed that must be the envy of Hugh Hefner. Among his many quirks, the *imam* claimed not just to have magical powers that protected him from all evils, but also to be bulletproof. Interestingly, he dropped this claim after someone

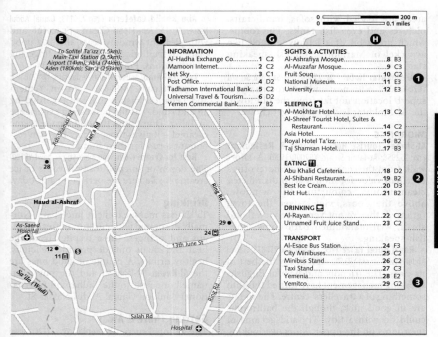

shot him. The results of this attack can still be seen in his bloodstained clothing on display here. Guides speak Arabic only, but some of the signs are in English, French and German.

The impressive **Qalat al-Qahira** is majestically perched on a hilltop like a Lord of the Rings fantasy castle. You can enter the courtyard and gasp over the views, but the interior is undergoing renovations and is off limits.

Ta'izz has a reputation for style when it comes to mosque construction, and at the southern end of the old town are the twin minarets of the beautiful **Al-Ashrafiya Mosque**. Originally constructed in 628, it was rebuilt in the 12th and 13th centuries. Other mosques include the pre-13th-century **Al-Muzafar Mosque**, southwest of Bab al-Kabir, and the Turkish **Al-Mutabiya Mosque**, about 200m south of Al-Ashrafiya Mosque. Non-Muslims are not permitted to enter any of the mosques.

Bab al-Kabir is the main entrance to the **old town**, but only parts of the original 13m-high wall remain, including two of its gates –

Bab al-Musa and **Bab al-Kabir**. Well worth a wander particularly in the early evening are the bright and brash **souqs** spread around Bab al-Kabir. Look out for the local cow's cheese (little white disks laid out in rows) and the sacks of delicious dried dates. Beyond the souqs and mosques, the old town architecture is unlikely to do much for you. Back in the newer streets there's a large and very lively **fruit souq** off Gamal Abdul Nasser St. Ta'izz is a good place to buy textiles and *jambiyas*. Look out also for the famous women merchants of Ta'izz, who traditionally do the buying and selling.

It's not exactly a tourist attraction but the **university**, next to the museum, always has groups of students (men and women) hanging around outside the entrance gates wanting to practise their English and French and make friends with foreigners.

Sleeping

BUDGET

Asia Hotel (☎ 254463; asiahotel@hotmail.com; At-Tahrir St; s/d YR1500/3000) One of the few hotels in Ta'izz with any real character. The communal areas are loaded with sofas, handicrafts, pictures and even fish tanks. The rooms, which are a bit of a letdown, smell like a packet of Marlboros. English-speaking staff.

Al-Mokhtar Hotel (☎ 253643; As-Saifraya St; s/d YR2000/3000) With neat and tidy rooms and a superb location not far from the old town, the Al-Mokhtar is a great budget choice.

MIDRANGE

Al-Shreef Tourist Hotel, Suites & Restaurant (☎ 252958; At-Tahrir St; s/d YR2000/3500) A short walk from the centre, this new hotel offers excellent value for money with disinfected clean rooms, colourful little windows above the doors, views over the town (granted, they're not very nice views) and small, well-maintained bathrooms. English-speaking.

Royal Hotel Ta'izz (☎ 250876; fax 250875; Gamal Abdul Nasser St; s/d YR3500/4200) Easily the best in its class. The friendly and helpful English-speaking management have turned this into something of a travellers' centre. The rooms are in good nick, though the bathrooms could do with a tidy. Try and get one of the rooms on the upper floors overlooking the main road, from where you can watch all the Schumacher wannabes racing about town.

TOP END

Taj Shamsan Hotel (☎ 236513; tajshamsan@y.net.ye; s/d US$61/79; 💻) A sterile but eager-to-please hotel with a good position very close to the old town. Rooms are comfortable and the beds heavenly. In-house health club, restaurant and coffee shop.

Eating

Al-Shibani Restaurant (☎ 251759; Gamal Abdul Nasser St; meals YR500) The fast-talking owner (who speaks brilliant English) will have you ordering everything on the menu in no time at all. Don't let this worry you – it's all top nosh, but the fish is best.

Hot Hut (☎ 265360; Gamal Abdul Nasser St; meals YR700; 💮 9am-1am) You'll probably be craving something a little different by the time you get to Ta'izz, in which case this new and clean restaurant with burgers that aren't a bad imitation of those back home should pass the test. Super sweet ice creams (YR120 to YR140) are another favourite.

Abu Khalid Cafeteria (☎ 226113; Gamal Abdul Nasser St; 💮 7am-11pm) Clean, peaceful and with pleasant window seats, this is a good place for fruit juice and cakes and lingering conversations. Popular with students.

Leyali Al-Arab (Arabian Nights Restaurant; ☎ 210193; Asayfarah St; mains YR150-500) Spot-on Yemeni and Lebanese dishes that are regarded by all and sundry as the best eating experience in Ta'izz. Don't miss the homemade crème caramel – it gives those of any Parisian restaurant a run for their money.

Best Ice Cream (26th September St; per bowl YR100) The dozen or so cool, fruity flavours of ice cream on sale here are perfect on a hot day.

Drinking

Ta'izz has many excellent juice bars. Normally decorated with curtains of fresh mangos and oranges, these respites from the heat and chaos outside provide delicious, healthy drinks. A couple of good ones are the **Al-Rayan** (At-Tahrir St) and the busy, unnamed one next to the Tadhamon International Bank on Gamal Abdul Nasser St.

Getting There & Away

The national carrier **Yemenia** (☎ 217126; Gamal Abdul Nasser St) has one-way flights to San'a (US$50); for a return flight, double the fare. The airport lies around 15km from town and a contract taxi should cost around YR1500.

The bus company **Yemitco** (☎ 233873; Ring Rd) runs services to Aden (YR700, two hours, two daily), Al-Hudayda (YR1200, four hours, two daily) via Zabid (YR500, three hours) and San'a (YR1200, five hours, two daily) via Ibb (YR300, 1½ hours).

Private buses run to most major centres in the highlands from the Al-Esace bus station. For Al-Khawkha and Al-Mukalla, take shared taxis.

Shared taxis run to Aden (YR700, 2½ hours, 20 to 30 daily), Al-Hudayda (YR1000, four hours, 30 daily), Ibb (YR300, 1½ hours, 20 daily), San'a (YR1000, 4½ hours, five daily) and Zabid (YR700, three hours, 30 daily) via Al-Makha (YR500, two hours, two or three daily) and Al-Khawkha (YR700, 2½ hours, two or three daily). The main taxi station is about 4km northeast of the town centre.

Hops around town by contract taxi cost YR150 to YR200, while hops by minibus

are YR30 (just flag one down). A minibus
to the airport costs YR30. Shared taxis to
Al-Hudayda leave from a spot along the
Hodeida Rd, about 4km west of the town
centre.

AROUND TA'IZZ

At 3070m, **Jabal Sabir** is one of the highest mountains in Yemen. A fairly good but
steep road leads the 4km from Ta'izz up to
its summit. Unfortunately, at the time of
research it was only possible to drive three-
quarters of the way up the mountain, as
a police station had been positioned here.
Locals like to cruise up here in the afternoons to chew qat with a view.

ADEN   عدن

☎ 02 / pop 589,419

Aden is where insular Yemen puts on its
cosmopolitan dress and calls out to the
rest of the world to stop by. Since the year
dot, the winter capital has been regarded
as one of the world's finest natural ports,
and in the tradition of fine natural ports, it
has long had a reputation for being seedy
and slutty. However, this reputation is
more than a little overblown – bars and
prostitutes certainly aren't two a penny
here – but what is true is that Aden is more
liberal than anywhere else in Yemen. For
the visitor, this is most noticeable in the
mix of races on the streets and the visibility of unveiled women.

If you are in Yemen for a while, you
shouldn't miss out on Aden, but come at
the end of your trip when you've had time
to adapt to the rest of the country. If, however, you were to visit nowhere else, then
you would leave Yemen with a highly lop-
sided view of the country.

History

According to legend, Noah's Ark was built
and launched in the area, and Cain and Abel
hung out for a while. Inscriptions dating to
the 6th century BC are the first concrete
mentions of the town, but it's clear that it
has long served as an ancient trading centre. Since the 10th century Aden has also
been one of Yemen's largest towns, and by
the 13th century its inhabitants numbered
some 80,000 people.

Initially serving as the capital of a series
of local dynasties, Aden was later taken over
by the Ottomans, followed by the British in
1839. After the opening of the Suez Canal in
the middle of the 19th century, its strategic
importance grew, and it soon numbered
among the largest ports in the world and as
one of the stars of the British Empire.

Aden served as the capital of the PDRY
from 1967 until reunification, when it was
declared a free-trade zone. Although badly
damaged in the 1994 War of Unity, it made
a brief recovery of sorts with the government pouring money into developing and
modernising the port. Just as things began
to look shipshape, disaster again struck
when terrorist groups aligned to Al-Qaeda
attacked the US warship the USS *Cole* and
effectively scared away most international
shipping.

Orientation

Aden spreads around the base of an extinct
551m-high volcano, which is joined to the
mainland by an isthmus. To the west lies
the colonial port of At-Tawahi joined to
the commercial centre known as Crater
(which lies below the volcano) by residential Ma'alla. The airport is found in the area
known as Khormaksar to the north, with
the industrial region of Sheikh Othman
and all the main long-distance bus and taxi
stands lying beyond.

Information

A visit to the **tourist office** (Map pp492–3; ☎ 202580;
Al-Muhsen St) can't be called worthwhile –
a lonely brochure will be your only joy.
Travel agencies, such as Universal Travel &
Tourism (Map pp492–3), may offer more
help and can be found on the main Ma'alla
road.

Centre Al-Ateer (Map p491; ☎ 259683; per min YR2;
🕑 8am-2pm & 4-10pm Sat-Thu, 4-10pm Fri) Provides
internet access.

Crédit Agricole Indosuez (Map pp492–3; ☎ 247403)
In Ma'alla; offers the best foreign-exchange service.

International Telecom Center (Map p491;
🕑 7.30am-midnight) Next door to the post office.

National Bank of Yemen (Map p491; ☎ 259171;
Queen Arwa Rd) Can change euros and US dollars, but not
travellers cheques.

Post Office (Map p491; 🕑 8am-noon & 4-8pm Sat-Thu,
8am-noon Fri) Off Esplanade Rd.

Tahawi Net Centre (Map pp492–3; ☎ 206947; per
min YR1; 🕑 8am-midnight) In At-Tawahi. From 2pm to
midnight, the rate increases to YR2 per minute.

YEMEN

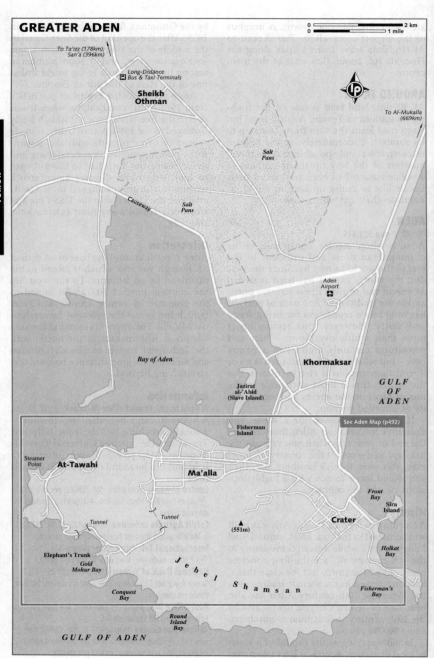

Sights & Activities

On paper Aden appears to have plenty of things to see, but in reality most are of very limited interest and the city's main attraction is its liberal (for Yemen) outlook on life. The boisterous streets and markets of Crater are well worth a wander as are the colonial throwbacks of At-Tahawi. Look out for the bizarre façade of the legendary Crescent Hotel and the Big Ben–style clock tower on the hill above At-Tahawi; but Steamer Point, the entrance and exit gate to Britain's colonial gem, is now nothing more than a collection of out-of-bounds warehouses.

Not exactly overwhelming is the recently renovated **National Museum for Antiquities** (Map p491; ☎ 253161; off Al-Aidrus St; admission YR500; ☒ 8.30am-1.30pm Sat-Wed), which has exhibits dating from prehistoric times to the early Islamic period. The highlights are the wonderful range of Sabaean relics.

Upstairs on the 1st floor is the **Ethnographical Museum** (Map p491; admission free with National Museum ticket; ☒ 8.30am-1.30pm Sat-Wed), which has a musty and poorly displayed collection of traditional dress from across the country.

The **Military Museum** (Map p491; ☎ 253243; Sayla St) was closed at the time of research and seemed unlikely to ever open again, but it's worth cruising past and checking just in case.

Believed to date from the 1st century, **Aden Tanks** (☎ 251409; end of Sayla Rd; admission YR100; ☒ 8am-6pm) were designed not just to collect precious water for the city, but also to remove water in times of flash flooding. A series of ingenious steps, arches and conduits channels the rainwater into a set of beautifully built cisterns. The 13 cisterns (all that remain of the original 53 tanks) have a total capacity of 20 million gallons. Developed by succeeding dynasties, the tanks eventually fell into disuse, until uncovered in the mid-19th century by the British, who, despite their best efforts and modern technology, never did manage to get them to work again.

The **Tourist Harbour** (Map pp492-3; Prince of Wales Bldg/Pier; Al-Muhsen St; admission free) and its **pier** is a colourful place for a stroll, especially early

YEMEN

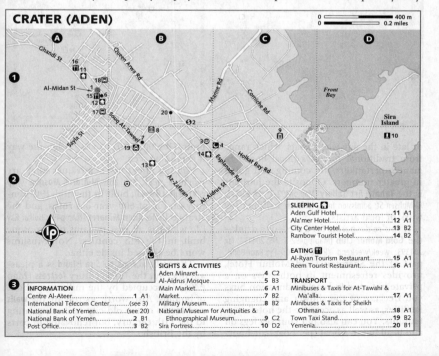

CRATER (ADEN)

0 ———— 400 m
0 ———— 0.2 miles

Ghandi St
Al-Midan St
Queen Arwa Rd
Marine Rd
Corniche Rd
Souq At-Tawcel
Sayla St
Az-Zafaran Rd
Al-Aidrus St
Esplanade Rd
Holkat Bay Rd

Front Bay
Sira Island

INFORMATION
Centre Al-Ateer................................1 A1
International Telecom Center........(see 3)
National Bank of Yemen...............(see 20)
National Bank of Yemen................2 B1
Post Office.....................................3 B2

SIGHTS & ACTIVITIES
Aden Minaret................................4 C2
Al-Aidrus Mosque..........................5 B3
Main Market..................................6 A1
Market..7 B2
Military Museum............................8 B2
National Museum for Antiquities &
  Ethnographical Museum..............9 C2
Sira Fortress.................................10 D2

SLEEPING 🏠
Aden Gulf Hotel...........................11 A1
Ala'mer Hotel...............................12 A1
City Center Hotel..........................13 B2
Rambow Tourist Hotel..................14 B2

EATING 🍴
Al-Ryan Tourism Restaurant..........15 A1
Reem Tourist Restaurant...............16 A1

TRANSPORT
Minibuses & Taxis for At-Tawahi &
  Ma'alla.....................................17 A1
Minibuses & Taxis for Sheikh
  Othman.....................................18 A1
Town Taxi Stand...........................19 B2
Yemenia.......................................20 B1

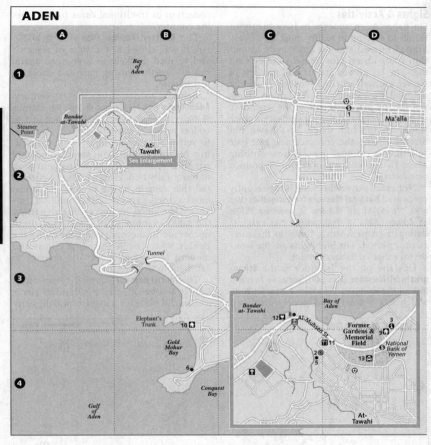

or late in the day when boats, which range from traditional *sambuqs* (local boats) to giant supertankers, are coming and going in greater numbers. Opposite the harbour is the **Tahawi Art Gallery** (Map pp492-3; ☎ 204123; Al-Muhsen St; admission free), which exhibits the work of local artists.

If you're desperate for a dip – or a drink – the **Gold Mohur Club** (Map pp492-3; ☎ 204174; fax 204393; week/weekend YR1000/1500; ☺ 8am-8pm), part of the Sheraton Gold Mohur Hotel, provides refreshment in both ways on a private but muddy beach. Admission buys you free use of the shower and changing facilities, as well as access to the hotel's restaurants. You can also put your sea legs on and head out in a boat (per boat half-hour/

hour YR6000/8000) to view Aden the way it should be seen.

Among the town's mosques that are worth a peek are the **Al-Aidrus Mosque** (Map p491; Holkat Bay Rd), built in the mid-19th century on top of 600-year-old ruins, and the strange little **Aden Minaret** (Map p491; Holkat Bay Rd), which is all that remains of a mosque built in the 8th century. Non-Muslims won't be allowed inside either.

The walk across to **Sira Island** is a pleasant one, but the 11th-century **fortress** (Map p491) is occupied by the military and out of bounds. Also worth a stroll are the **walls** and **towers** of the old city wall, also dating to the 11th century, but renovated in parts by the British.

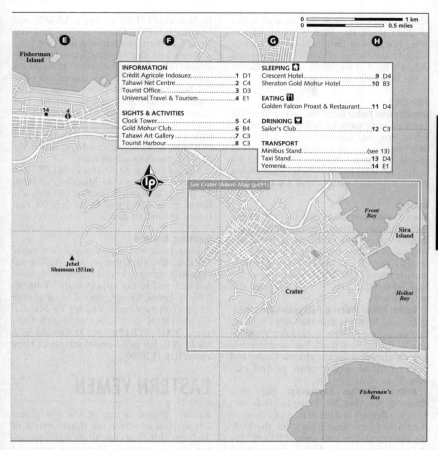

INFORMATION
Crèdit Agricole Indosuez........................1 D1
Tahawi Net Centre...................................2 C4
Tourist Office..3 D3
Universal Travel & Tourism.....................4 E1

SIGHTS & ACTIVITIES
Clock Tower..5 C4
Gold Mohur Club....................................6 B4
Tahawi Art Gallery..................................7 C3
Tourist Harbour......................................8 C3

SLEEPING
Crescent Hotel..9 D4
Sheraton Gold Mohur Hotel..................10 B3

EATING
Golden Falcon Proast & Restaurant.......11 D4

DRINKING
Sailor's Club..12 C3

TRANSPORT
Minibus Stand..................................(see 13)
Taxi Stand...13 D4
Yemenia...14 E1

Fisherman
Island

Jebel
Shamsan (551m)

See Crater (Aden) Map (p491)

Crater

Front
Bay

Sira
Island

Holkat
Bay

Fisherman's
Bay

YEMEN

Sleeping
BUDGET
Aden Gulf Hotel (Map p491; ☎ 253900; fax 251710; Ghandhi St; s/d YR2500) This bog-standard hotel has polished rooms with Qurans and prayer mats provided, and pretty San'a-style stained-glass windows.

Rambow Tourist Hotel (Rimbaud; Map p491; ☎ 255899; Esplanade Rd; r YR2500) This could be one of the better budget hotels in Yemen but any character it may once have possessed has vanished under a layer of rot. Even so, with its high ceilings, carved wooden beds and seedy air, it's precisely the kind of place where you would expect to find a down-at-heel poet like Rimbaud – who is supposed to have made his base here.

MIDRANGE
City Center Hotel (Map p491; ☎ 257700; fax 251056; off Az-Zafaran St; s/d/ste YR3500/4000/7000) Very sterile, but possibly the friendliest hotel in Aden. Rooms are as clean as a whistle and the suite is a good bet if you're travelling in a group.

Ala'mer Hotel (Al-Amer Hotel; Map p491; ☎ 250000; alamer_group@y.net.ye; Al-Midan St; d with breakfast YR4500) Lacks any real zing-zang but the impressively clean rooms and friendly management make this a firm favourite in the midrange category.

Crescent Hotel (Map p490-1; ☎ 203471; fax 204597; Steamer Point; d from US$35) This grand old hotel is a museum piece in the making. With portraits of a very young-looking Queen

Elizabeth II, lazily spinning fans and oodles of character, a stay here is guaranteed to bring the days of Empire to mind. Unfortunately, the rooms, which are large enough to lose a herd of elephants in, are as fading as the memories the place evokes.

TOP END
Sheraton Gold Mohur Hotel (Map pp492-3; ☎ 204010; www.sheraton.com/goldmohur; Gold Mohur Bay; d US$120) Prices vary, but considering it's a five-star they're not bad at all. Even so, it's not one of Sheraton's better offerings. One big bonus is the private beach where sunbathing Western women won't cause a scandal.

Eating
Reem Tourist Restaurant (Map p491; ☎ 254436; Ghandhi St; mains YR200-800; ☺ 7am-midnight) Step into the noisy belly of this local institution and you're in for a treat. Good atmosphere, smartly turned-out waiters and heavenly banana juices (YR150) are just some of the highlights. The kebabs (YR200) are also worth a pop.

Golden Falcon Proast & Restaurant (Map pp492-3; ☎ 206808; Ar-Rayisi St; meals YR400-600) There are two very good reasons to eat here. Number one is the superb fried fish and number two the chance to escape chaotic Crater and relax in the altogether more genteel surroundings of At-Tawahi.

Al-Ryan Tourism Restaurant (Map p491; ☎ 256758; mains YR400-700; ☺ 6am-1am) It doesn't have the Reem's hordes of fans but those in the know keep coming back for the Middle Eastern staples and clean kitchens. Try the excellent *arayesi*, which is more dessert than drink! It's opposite the bus station.

Drinking
Sailor's Club (Map pp492-3; ☎ 203209; Al Muhsen St; admission before 11pm free, after 11pm YR2000; ☺ 8pm-2am Sun-Fri) When in a seedy port, do as is done in seedy ports and come to a smoky, seedy nightclub. This one is full of Somali prostitutes and hard-drinking locals and is hardly representative of Yemen. But for some travellers, a highlight of Aden is the chance to sip a much-missed beer. Spirits cost YR700; beer YR1000.

Getting There & Away
The national carrier **Yemenia** (Map p491; ☎ 253969; fax 252528; Queen Arwa Rd) has flights to Al-Mukalla (US$70), San'a (US$65) and Suqutra (US$50). Quotes are for one-way fares; for return fares, double the cost.

Buses and shared taxis leave from terminals (Map p490) in Sheikh Othman. As is normal, the private bus companies offer the best service and their offices can be found around the main long-distance taxi stand. Sample fares and times include Al-Hudayda (YR1500, seven hours), Al-Mukalla (YR2000, 12 hours, one daily), San'a (YR1400, seven hours, five daily) and Ta'izz (YR600, two hours, two daily).

Shared taxis go to Al-Hudayda (YR1400, six hours, 20 daily), Al-Mukalla (YR1800, 12 hours, five daily), San'a (YR1400, 7½ hours, three daily) and Ta'izz (YR700, two hours, around 50 daily).

Getting Around
Shared taxis and minibuses link Crater, Ma'alla, Sheikh Othman and At-Tawahi regularly from various stations around town. A taxi to the airport costs YR400 to YR500. From Crater, shared taxis charge YR30 (contract taxis YR250) to Ma'alla, YR30 (YR240 to YR300) to Sheikh Othman, YR15 (YR150) to At-Tawahi and YR25 (YR250) to Khormaksar. Short hops cost YR10 (YR100).

EASTERN YEMEN

Eastern Yemen is one of the few places left in Arabia where the desert world of Thesiger still clings on, albeit with increasing precariousness. Home of nomadic Bedouin tribal people, ruined cities of legend, startling oases and more than a hint of danger, this massive chunk of apricot dunes and bleak stonescapes is for many the most romantic corner of Yemen.

MA'RIB   مأرب
☎ 06
It's hard to imagine that this rotting desert town was ever a seat of power, but it was from these very same streets that a woman of intense beauty once came forward and changed the story of Arabia. Bilqis, guardian of the frankincense trade routes, lover of Solomon, mother of the throne of Abyssinia, daughter of the devil and known to the world simply as the Queen of Sheba is

rumoured to have based her capital here. The Quran relates other, equally fantastical stories of Ma'rib, famously describing it as a paradise on the left bank and a paradise on the right bank. Yet by all accounts this was a true description – the city, built on taxes from the incense trade, was impossibly wealthy and, thanks to its famous dam, very fertile. It's said that a person could walk for four days in any direction and not leave the shade of the palm groves and orange trees. However, if you're coming to Ma'rib expecting to find archaeological sites to rival Egypt or Greece, you are going to be sorely disappointed, as almost nothing remains from the glory days of the great queen. This doesn't mean a visit here isn't worthwhile, far from it. Ma'rib is a Yemeni highlight – it's just that around these parts it's all about atmosphere, and that's something Ma'rib has in abundance. A visit here is nothing short of surreal...

Note that because of tribal tension in the area, tourists are given a compulsory police escort while travelling to, around and in the town of Ma'rib. After sunset, a curfew comes into force: you're obliged to remain in your hotel until sunrise.

History

Ma'rib has been inhabited almost since the dawn of time and is one of the world's oldest towns. It is, of course, famous above all else for being the supposed home of the Queen of Sheba (see boxed text p496),

though whether or not she really did grace the streets of Ma'rib is unknown. What cannot be doubted is that the Sabaean capital quickly became the most important staging post on the frankincense trade route, and it was during this period that the dam was constructed (see boxed text p498). The good times couldn't last, though, and with the bursting of the dam the people of Ma'rib scattered across the deserts of Arabia, and the town virtually ceased to exist. It wasn't really until the modern age and the discovery of oil that the fortunes of Ma'rib started to revive – a point that has been made most clear with the construction of a new dam and the greening of the desert. The last few years haven't been all plain sailing, though, and Ma'rib is consistently one of the most troubled places in Yemen. For a visitor this is most obvious in the sheer quantity of serious artillery visible on the streets and a distinct undercurrent of something you cannot quite put your finger on.

Sights

All sights listed here are, theoretically, open from sunrise to shortly before sunset.

In Ma'rib itself, a walk around the threadbare streets and the **market** is well worthwhile. There is nothing much to actually see, but the atmosphere will leave your head spinning for days. Note that the legendary **arms market** has been shut down and the others in the region are highly dangerous and utterly out of bounds to foreigners. You are

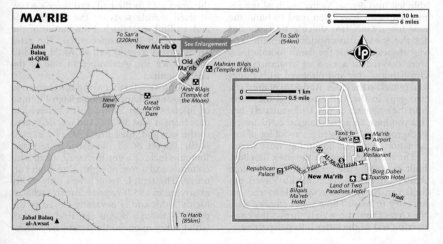

WHO DOES SHE THINK SHE IS?

The most beautiful and alluring woman ever to live had hairy legs and the cloven foot of the devil. Her fame has lasted three thousand years, yet nobody remembers her name. She's a player in the ancient legends of Judaism, Christianity and Islam, yet no-one knows where she lived. She's the most famous daughter of Yemen, mother of the throne of Ethiopia and the original Jerusalem pilgrim. Even today, she remains a household name, and any girl seen to be getting above herself can expect to be compared to her. She is, of course, the Queen of Sheba, but she may never even have existed.

Legend holds that the Queen of Sheba's first public appearance was when she paid a visit to the court of King Solomon in 10th-century-BC Jerusalem. The reasons and results of her visit vary depending on whether you are using Jewish, Christian, Islamic or Ethiopian accounts, but the general consensus is that it was rumours of Solomon's wealth and wisdom that drew her to his court. The best-known story in the West is the Ethiopian tradition that recounts how Solomon became enraptured with her beauty and devised a plan to have his wicked way with her. He agreed to let her stay in his palace unmolested only on the condition that she touched nothing of his. Shocked that he should consider her capable of such a thing, she agreed. That evening the king laid on a feast of spicy and salty foods, and after all had eaten well, Sheba and Solomon retired to separate beds in his sleeping quarters. In the night Sheba awoke thirsty from all the salty food she had consumed and reached across for a glass of water. The moment she put the glass to her lips Solomon awoke and triumphantly claimed that she had broken her

likely to find yourself sent straight back to your hotel if you attempt to walk anywhere around Ma'rib without an escort.

Lying 8km southwest of town is the extraordinary **Great Ma'rib Dam** (admission YR100, payable to the well-armed Bedouin kids sitting by the entrance), justly Yemen's most famous monument. The dam is believed to date to at least the 8th century BC. It was periodically repaired; the last recorded time that major works were carried out was in the 6th century AD, after which it probably fell into disuse. Sadly, much of the remaining walls have been used to build the new town. Only two sluice gates (look out for the Sabaean inscriptions) remain. The vast stones, used for the dam's foundations, were covered in a kind of 'waterproofing' consisting of clay and plastered with stones and gravel on the sides. At the tip of the dam, two gaps in the wall channelled the water into the irrigation canals. Unfortunately, unless you have an archaeological or historical background, you'll need an awful lot of imagination to picture how things once were.

The road continues to the sleek **New Dam**, built in 1986 by the President of the United Arab Emirates (UAE), Sheikh Zayed bin Sultan an-Nahyan, who was able to trace his ancestry to here. Three times smaller than the Great Dam, it certainly throws the engineering feat of the latter into perspective.

Lying on the Safir road, the ancient and enigmatic **'Arsh Bilqis** (Bilqis Palace/Bilqis Throne/Temple of the Moon) is the site of the famous five-and-a-half columns often seen in tourist brochures. Although linked to the legend of the Queen of Sheba, archaeologists now believe that the temple predates the queen and is actually around 4000 years old and was dedicated to the moon.

The temple consists of a square with an open courtyard, at the centre of which lies the old sacred well. Twelve steps lead from the open area to the hall, and there's a row of fixed marble seats on the western side and a plinth on which a 6m statue of the Sabaean Holy Oxen once stood. The gates are normally kept locked so you'll need to track down the gatekeeper in one of the nearby houses.

Around 4km further along the same road is the kidney-shaped **Mahram Bilqis** (Temple of Bilqis/Awwam Temple). It's believed to date from at least 800 BC and was dedicated to the sun god. Measuring 94m by 82m, it is the largest of all the Sabaean temples. Remains include a 9m-high wall, a hall with columns and a row of eight, 12m-high columns. The temple (which was only partly excavated in 1952) requires much archaeological work and is normally closed to the public – though if you can find the man with the key in one of the nearby houses, he

vow. 'But it's only water,' she cried. To which Solomon replied, 'And nothing on earth is more precious than water.'

Ethiopian tradition holds that the child that resulted from the deceitful night of passion that followed was Menelik I, from whom the entire royal line of Ethiopia claim direct descent. Though all the ancient sources agree that a meeting took place between the two rulers, things become a little murky after that point. The Bible doesn't even give Solomon's mysterious visitor a name, Jewish legend kindly gives Sheba hairy legs and a cloven foot and Quranic accounts say that Solomon heard rumours of a kingdom ruled by a queen whose subjects worshipped the sun. He commanded a jinn (spirit) to bring her to him, and when Bilqis, as she is known in the Arab world, arrived at Solomon's crystal palace, she immediately accepted the Abrahamic tradition of worshipping one god alone.

Finding out whether Sheba existed and where her capital was located has not proved easy. The strongest claims have come from Ethiopia, which believes that Axum was her capital, and Yemen, which says it was Ma'rib. Both cities were important trade and cultural centres and it's likely that both were, if not ruled by the same monarch, then closely tied through trade. So far neither has any evidence to suggest that the Queen of Sheba ever existed. For a long time Axum had the edge, but today most scholars believe that Yemen is the more likely candidate. Others claim she came from northwest Arabia or even Nigeria. Whatever the truth, the legend persists and every Yemeni will swear that Ma'rib was the home of the most beautiful cloven-footed woman to ever live.

will be able to open up the exterior gates so you can get a little closer.

Rising like a spectre from the surrounding landscape is the eerie silhouette of **Old Ma'rib**. Originally built long before the 1st millennium BC and sitting on foundations that are vastly more ancient, it suffered much damage from bombs during the 1962 civil war, but for the layperson it's the most romantic of the archaeological sites. A couple of years ago the last family finally moved out (a widow and her children who are often to be seen wandering, ghost-like, across the site) and with their departure one of the oldest inhabited towns on earth effectively ceased to exist.

Sleeping & Eating

Tour guides may try and tell you that foreigners are not allowed to stay anywhere but the Bilquis Ma'reb Hotel out on the edge of town. This is not true. You can stay anywhere you want, but wherever you stay you will not be allowed outside after dark.

Borg Dubei Tourism Hotel (☎ 303850; s/d YR2000/3000) The brightly coloured rooms are worth a look if you're on a very tight budget, but they are somewhat spoilt by a lack of cleaners. Remember to leave your guns at the reception desk.

Land of Two Paradises Hotel (Ardh Al-Jannataun Hotel; ☎ 302309; fax 302306; s/d YR2500/3500) The

rooms certainly won't remind you of the land of milk and honey, but they'll pass for the night and it's easily the best budget bet. Be a little careful in the showers – they can be electrifying! It's recently gained a new manager, the legendary Hassan Mubarak, the best desert guide in Arabia and the man to talk to about a safe escort to Shabwa and Hadramawt. Breakfast costs YR300; lunch and dinner YR800.

Bilquis Ma'reb Hotel (☎ 302372; fax 302371; s/d main bldg US$84/90, d budget annexe YR4800; 🖵 🖭) Popular with tour groups, this huge '70s hotel complex was built for a tourist gold rush that never happened. Nowadays it's fading fast and is overpriced. Highlights are the central courtyard pool and truly memorable portraits of the president 30 years ago! The budget annexe is better value. The restaurant has such unlikely dishes as roast beef with Yorkshire pudding (YR700). There's also a souvenir shop selling a selection of mementos and books.

Ar-Rian Restaurant (meals YR300) On the main road into town from San'a, the Ar-Rian boasts tasty Ma'rib staples such as roast chickens, sheep heads and plenty of friendly tribesmen with Kalashnikovs.

Getting There & Away

The situation changes constantly, but for the past few years a police escort for all

---

THE GREAT DAM & THE IRON RAT

Ma'rib's great dam was enormous, measuring 720m long, 60m wide and about 35m high. It was capable of irrigating about 70 sq km of desert and sustaining a population of between 30,000 and 50,000 people.

The ingenuity of the dam lies not just in the choice of its site (where water collects at the base of a number of valleys), but also in its brilliant and complex construction. Aside from the dam there was a complex and sophisticated series of drains and channels surrounding it.

However, the dam was eventually destroyed by a rat with iron teeth chewing away the base of the dam (apparently the rat made its way down from Syria by jumping from hump to hump along a huge camel caravan). One silver lining to this cataclysmic event was that with the destruction of the dam the people of Ma'rib were turned into nomads who set off to conquer and colonise every corner of Arabia, and if some medieval texts are to be believed, they even got as far as Tibet.

---

tourist cars has been compulsory on the San'a to Ma'rib road. If you are travelling with a tour company, you needn't concern yourself with the logistics of this. But if you are travelling by public transport and are granted a travel permit for Ma'rib (which is normally not allowed), you have to pay a fee of around YR500 at every roadblock, for which the police will then escort you to the next checkpoint. Whatever the case, all vehicles are expected to line up punctually at a police checkpoint to the east of San'a by 9am on the day of travel. If there are sufficient tourist cars, you will travel onwards in a tight convoy to Ma'rib. More often, though, there will only be one or two vehicles, in which case the police will either follow you in their own jeep or they'll pile in beside you.

Travelling eastward to Sayun you have two possible routes – both of which are thrilling desert adventures. The easiest and cheapest route is along the new surfaced road, which takes you through spectacular scenery, past some of the Yemeni oil installations and up towards the Saudi border. Taxis and buses run this route daily (YR1400), but foreigners are unlikely to be granted permission to travel this way. The only exception to this rule might be if you take a bus direct from San'a to Sayun. Once again, an escort is required, and these boys don't mess about; don't be surprised if you're trailed by a couple of cannon-mounted jeeps full of armed soldiers.

The second option takes you, via Shabwa, straight across the middle of the Ramlat as-Sab'atayn desert. To say this is an impressive journey is a major understatement.

Streaming for hours with armed Bedouin escorts over cathedral-sized dunes to the ruined city of Shabwa is something that will live with you forever. En route, you'll get to jeep surf down the side of huge dunes and stop at Bedouin encampments to take tea under their woven, goat-hair tents. The Bedouin are currently charging US$250 per group to take you all the way to Sayun. Yes, it's expensive but as it's one of the most exciting desert crossings in all Arabia, it's worth every penny. To organise this crossing, it's best to either go through one of the San'a tour agencies or call Hassan Mubarak (he only speaks Arabic) at the Land of Two Paradises Hotel. You will need to give at least a day's notice, and remember, the above price does not include the cost of a car and driver.

SHABWA شبوا

Shabwa, situated on the bank of Wadi Arma, has been described as 'a city forever beyond the hills', and it's an appropriate description. Fantastically remote, the seemingly never-ending journey to the political, economic and religious capital of the ancient kingdom of Hadramawt is high adventure even today. When you finally arrive – hot, tired and thirsty – it may come as something of a surprise to learn that time hasn't been kind on Shabwa, and there's little but a few mounds of rubble left. However, further exploration will reveal that this state of affairs is fortunate indeed, for there can be few more romantic ancient ruins anywhere in the world, and certainly none where you can scramble about picking up shards of pottery that have lain in the sand for Sheba knows how long. As for an exact age, nobody really knows for sure, but a foundation date of sometime between 1500 to 1200 BC is generally accepted.

The town was an important collection point for the camel caravans traversing the desert. Traditionally, the caravans were obliged to pay the high priest of Shabwa one-tenth of the total value of their load. As a result, the city grew rich – rich enough to turn the surrounding desert into a 4800-hectare garden of trees, fields and flowers. In modern times Shabwa has been left largely to its own devices, but not so long ago a few Bedouin families built houses here out of the remains of older buildings. It's these that are still just about standing today.

Much of Shabwa awaits further excavation, but for the moment you can see the remains of the old **city walls**, the ruins of an **ancient temple**, various **storerooms** and what is said to be the **royal palace** to the east of the site.

Shabwa is in the proverbial back of beyond, and there are no hotels, restaurants or facilities of any sort. If you want to stay, you'll have to be completely self-sufficient and be prepared to pay a significant additional amount to your Bedouin escorts. The nearest real town is 'Ataq (p501), some 100km to the south, but it's currently not safe to stay there nor to travel from there to Shabwa. Almost all visitors content themselves with a short hour-long pause on the journey over the desert from Ma'rib to Sayun.

AL-MUKALLA المكلا

☎ 05 / pop 122,359

Dating from the 8th century, the shining white capital of Hadramawt, Al-Mukalla, is one of Yemen's most important ports and fastest-growing cities. There's little to encourage the traveller to stay long, but its flavour of faraway lands makes for an interesting change of scene from the conservative interior.

Information

The post office, several banks and foreign-exchange offices are all found along Al-Mukalla St. **M II Internet Cafe** (Corniche; per min YR2; ☉ 9am-10pm) offers internet access.

Dangers & Annoyances

Al-Mukalla's mosquitos can be voracious. Give yourself a good dousing of repellent before going out, and before bed if you're staying at a cheap hotel. Added to this, Al-Mukalla is also a huge holiday destination for zillions of flies who carpet everything throughout daylight hours.

Sights & Activities

Al-Mukalla's **old town** and **corniche** are interesting. The former is reminiscent of Zanzibar and India, and has an exotic (but incredibly dirty) feel to it. It's not at all like an inland Yemeni town. The recently redeveloped Corniche has a more European flavour and makes a great place for an evening walk and a drink overlooking the boats bobbing about in the bay.

Occupying part of the elegant former Sultan's Palace, the **Mukalla Museum** (☎ 303001; Corniche; admission YR500; ☉ 8.30am-noon Sat-Thu) contains displays relating to the sultan and to the town's history. Most explanations are in English, but the huge white building is probably more arresting than its contents.

Based in the Hadhramout Hotel, **Extra Divers** (☎ 777953153; www.extra-divers.de; ☉ 8.30am-5pm 15 Dec-30 Apr) offers diving or snorkelling trips. Reef/boat/night dives cost US$25/35/40 per person. There's a 15% discount if you subscribe to 10 or more dives. Complete equipment hire costs US$25 per day; mask, fins and snorkel is US$15 per day. 'Rocky Banks' is a particularly good dive site. You can also dive a cargo boat wreck. For nonguests, the Hadhramout Hotel charges a 'water facilities admission fee' of US$5, including use of towels, restaurant, showers and the hotel pool.

When arriving or leaving Al-Mukalla, look out for the 19th-century **Husn al-Ghuwayzi** (fortress) perched on a cliff top on the northern airport road. It was only about a decade ago that this building was a fair hike out of town – Al-Mukalla is growing at an extraordinary rate of knots.

Sleeping

Al-Mukalla fills up quickly during the holidays, as many Saudis like to come here to dip their toes in the sea. Book ahead at such times. Many of the cheaper hotels aren't all that keen on taking foreigners, but the following are all tourist friendly.

Half Moon Hotel (☎ 302767; halfmoonhotel@yemen.net.ye; Al-Ghar al-Amar St; r YR2500) Standing head and shoulders above a cluster of

YEMEN

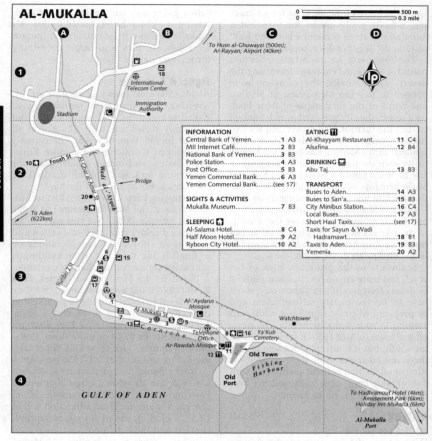

AL-MUKALLA

INFORMATION	
Central Bank of Yemen	1 A3
MII Internet Café	2 B3
National Bank of Yemen	3 B3
Police Station	4 A3
Post Office	5 B3
Yemen Commercial Bank	6 A3
Yemen Commercial Bank	(see 17)

SIGHTS & ACTIVITIES	
Mukalla Museum	7 B3

SLEEPING	
Al-Salama Hotel	8 C4
Half Moon Hotel	9 A2
Ryboon City Hotel	10 A2

EATING	
Al-Khayyam Restaurant	11 C4
Alsafina	12 B4

DRINKING	
Abu Taj	13 B3

TRANSPORT	
Buses to Aden	14 A3
Buses to San'a	15 B3
City Minibus Station	16 C4
Local Buses	17 A3
Short Haul Taxis	(see 17)
Taxis for Sayun & Wadi Hadramawt	18 B1
Taxis to Aden	19 B3
Yemenia	20 A2

nasty neighbours, this hotel offers small and tasty rooms that, for once, aren't suffering from the effects of the tropical heat. Some rooms have views over the redeveloped waterfront.

Al-Salama Hotel (☎ 305210; Al-Mukalla St; s/d YR2500/2800) A solid old-fashioned Al-Salama hotel with a lot more jazz than many of the newer midrange places. It's centrally located, offers excellent value for money and is very friendly. The only minus point is that the staff are big Manchester United fans!

Ryboon City Hotel (☎ 303606; www.Rc-hotels.com; Fouah St; s/d YR4580/5235; 💻) Smart hotel at the top of town. It offers good value for money, but the rooms could do with a lick of paint.

Friendly, English-speaking staff. A filling breakfast is included in the price.

Hadhramout Hotel (☎ 303442; hadmot.htl@y.net .ye; s/d with breakfast US$83/97; 💻 🕱) The overpriced and sloppy rooms have crumbling carpets and as much style and charm as a rotting fish. Despite this, it remains popular with tour groups, and the location, right beside a little cove, is good. Pool is open to nonguests for US$5.

Eating

Along the Corniche are a string of enjoyable teashops/cafés, which get lively in the evenings with locals taking in the sunset views. The Abu-Taj at the western end is one of the better ones.

Al-Khayyam Restaurant (Al-Khaiam Brost Restaurant; ☎ 303552; Al-Mukalla St; meals YR500-900) A noisy and chaotic restaurant that is a long-standing Mukalla institution, and when you taste its gorgeous barbecued fish, you'll understand why.

Alsafina (☎ 380559; mezze from YR200, mains YR900; ☉ noon-11pm) Sail away on this boat-shaped restaurant and enjoy its range of Lebanese starters and dips and seafood mains. If you've emerged from a stint in the countryside, it's probably going to be the first restaurant in a long time where you might want to relax over dinner.

Other cheap-and-cheerful restaurants can be found around the bus stations.

Getting There & Away

The national carrier **Yemenia** (☎ 303444; fax 352365; Al-Ghar al-Amar St) has flights to Aden (US$70), San'a (US$80) and Suqutra (US$50). Quotes are for one-way fares; for return fares, simply double the price.

Buses run to Aden (YR2000, around 10 hours, one daily) and San'a (YR1800, 12 hours, two daily). For Sayun, take a shared taxi.

Shared taxis run to Aden (YR2000, 10 hours, several daily), Bir 'Ali (YR500 or YR3000 contract, two hours, two daily), and Sayun (YR1500, five hours, three daily). Note that for all these journeys a travel permit is required (and should have been obtained in San'a first, though if you've just arrived from Oman you can get one at the police station here), and for the Aden and San'a routes a police escort.

The airport (based at Ar-Rayyan) lies 40km from Al-Mukalla. Contract taxis cost YR1200 (and take 30 minutes), but negotiate the fare before hopping in.

Almost as common as the flies are the minibuses, which provide a cheap form of intercity transport. Travellers might want to make use of them to get from the old centre to the far end of the Corniche. Journeys cost YR20 and to hail one just wave it down.

THE SOUTH COAST

The road between Aden and Al-Mukalla is a long, hard slog taking a minimum of 10 hours. There are few towns in which to stop and fewer still in which a stop is recommended. On the bright side the scenery is wild and spectacular – leaving Aden and the coastal plain, the road traverses a warped volcanic wasteland of searing black rock and volcanic cones. Beyond this the land becomes a little more welcoming and fissured gorges and gravel plains are interspersed with luminous green wadis. It's in this area that the only major settlements between Aden and Al-Mukalla can be found.

The modern and uninspiring centre of **'Ataq**, some distance north of the main road, is the first of these. Despite its enticing status on the map, with roads heading northeast to Shabwa and northwest to Bayhan, it's not a place anyone is likely to either encourage or allow you to visit. The town is generally considered unsafe and the roads leading northward away from it can be plain old treacherous. Back on the main road is attractively placed **Habban**, but at the time of writing it was completely out of bounds due to the threat of kidnapping (a group of French tourists were held captive here in late 2006). Next in line is tiny fly-blown **'Azan**, whose disintegrating old centre police will escort you around if you ask. A few kilometres after the town of 'Azan, are the impressive and rather ghostly looking ruins of **Naqb al-Hajar**. Because of local tension, it's not always possible to visit them; most people content themselves with a photo from the roadside. When it is possible, you can usually contract a 4WD and police escort from 'Azan (YR2000 return, including a half-hour or so visit).

After 'Azan the road wends its way back to the coast and things become less tense. Just before the village of Bir 'Ali, around 128km southwest of Al-Mukalla, you'll come to a side road marked with yellow signs that snakes to the base of a volcanic outcrop at the very edge of the sea. This is the ancient site of **Qana**, the old port of the Hadramawt. The pleasant stretch of beach known by tour agents as **Bir 'Ali** is after the nearby village.

For those with their own transport, it's worth resting here for the night and enjoying the rich turquoise waters and spotless white sands. If you are using public transport, a stop might be more hassle than it's worth, as finding an onward ride the next morning will be difficult. If you have the energy, you can also climb to the top of the outcrop known as **Husn al-Ghurab** (Husn al-Ghurfa), where you'll find the remains of an ancient fortification and control tower, which once overlooked the port. Don't attempt the climb in flip-flops, as the loose scree and sheer drops make it unsafe.

On the beach, the **Qana Tourist Complex** (☎ 211169; per person hut/r YR1500/2000) has basic Thai-style beach huts or stuffy rooms that make for an enjoyable place to stay for a day or so. The staff should be commended for their (successful) attempts to keep the beach clean. Excellent fish dinners (YR800) can be whipped up with a little notice.

SUQUTRA   سقطرى
☎ 05 / pop 160,000

The secret of eternal life shouldn't be something that's easy to stumble across and by cleverly hiding it out on Suqutra the gods have certainly taken that thought to heart. At 3650 sq km Suqutra is easily the largest Yemeni island, as well as one of the most inaccessible. Lying 510km southeast of the mainland, close to the ravaged shores of Somalia, the island has developed in near total isolation from the rest of the world. Rumoured to have once been a refuge for dragons, it continues to provide a refuge for all manner of extraordinary fauna and flora, much of which is found nowhere else. Because of the number of its endemic plants and creatures, it's been described as the 'Galapagos of the Indian Ocean'. While this is a little optimistic, there is no denying that Suqutra is a unique and otherworldly

island. It's the kind of place where people speak a language unknown to anyone else, where the knowledge of how to make fire by rubbing sticks together is still common and where the elderly recall days when money didn't exist.

Until the construction of an airport in 2002, the island remained almost as unknown as it did in the days when adventurers came here to do battle with dragons in their search for the secret of eternal life. Today the dragons might be gone, but the trees are said to still bleed for their memory, and the secret of eternal life remains hidden away in a cave somewhere on stupendous Suqutra.

Information

Most services are found in the capital, Hadibu. Two excellent publications on Suqutra are *Soqotra – the Birds & Plants* and *Saving Socotra – The Treasure Island of Yemen*. Both cost US$10 and are available in Hadibu and at the airport.

The **Soqotra Eco-Tourism Society** (☎ 660132; www.socotraisland.org.com) was set up in early 2003 with the aim of promoting and developing tourism and infrastructure projects on the island in a sustainable manner for the benefit of all. It can advise on itineraries and help in the planning of your trip either by telephone or email in advance of a visit, or in person at the Visitors Information Service in Hadibu (opposite). It also has its own excellent four-night tour of

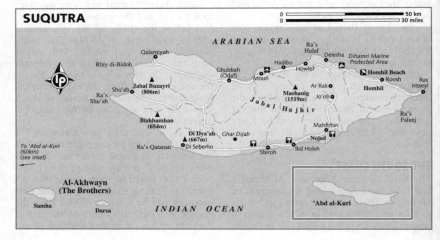

AN ARABIAN EDEN

The remote Suqutran archipelago has been described as an Arabian Garden of Eden and is known for its high level of endemic plants and animals. There are around 850 plant species, of which approximately 230 to 260 species are endemic. The Haggeher Mountains and the limestone plateaus contain the richest variety of endemic plants. The most famous of these is the stumpy Dragons Blood Tree, whose red sap was for years sold as dragon's blood. Another favourite is the Cucumber Tree, the only cucumber plant to grow in tree form. In total 52 of Suqutra's endemic plants are included on the IUCN Red List of Threatened Species.

The fauna also includes a large proportion of endemics. Only seven types of terrestrial mammals call the island home and most of these were introduced. Two, a bat and a shrew, are considered endemic. The bird life is more spectacular and consists of 178 species, six of which are endemic. These are the Socotra warbler, Socotra bunting, Socotra sunbird, Socotra starling, island cisticola and the Socotra sparrow. The most visible bird on the island, though, is the Egyptian vulture. There are 24 reptile species, 21 of which are endemic.

the island (US$320 per person, minimum group size two), which ensures that you get the most out of your stay. Should you have anything more unusual in mind, it can provide guides, jeeps, camping equipment and supplies.

Al-Salami Net (Hadibu; per min YR6; ☺ 9am-9pm Sat-Thu) The island's only internet connections.

National Bank of Yemen (☎ 660192; Hadibu; ☺ 7.30am-2pm Sat-Thu) Changes US dollars and euros cash.

Post Office (☎ 660298; Hadibu; ☺ 7am-1pm & 3.30-5pm Mon-Thu)

Telephone Centre (Hadibu; ☺ 6am-11pm) Calls to the mainland/Europe cost YR20/250 per minute.

Visitors Information Service (☎ 660132; Main St, Hadibu; ☺ 7am-1pm & 4-8pm Sat-Wed) The official HQ for the Soqotra Eco-Tourism Society, it has some maps and brochures. Ring before visiting, as its opening hours are erratic. There's a branch office at the airport, which opens for flight arrivals.

Sights & Activities

Tourism is a new concept to the island, but in a very short space of time an admirable range of tours and activities has become available. There's little to see or do in Hadibu, so try to organise everything in advance to avoid wasting time there. With no organised public transport and, outside Hadibu, no hotels or restaurants, it would be very hard to explore Suqutra in a truly independent manner. Therefore, virtually everyone uses the services of either the Soqotra Eco-Tourism Society or a San'a-based agency (p520).

For most people the island highlights are the exhilarating hiking and divine beaches.

The best beach by far is the deserted bridal-white sands and blissful blues of **Detwah Lagoon** by **Qalansiyah** in the west of the island. There's a small and well-run **camp site** here with pre-erected tents for YR1000. Not far behind on the beach stakes is **Homhil**, in the east of the island, where fresh and salt waters mingle beneath mountainous dunes. The diving (US$35 per dive with all equipment) in Suqutra is world-class, with the attraction being fish rather than corals. Some of these fish grow very big indeed and include curious schools of dolphins, comical turtles (both in the summer only) and lots of very large and decidedly less friendly sharks! Most of the dive sites in Suqutra are virtually unexplored. For the less aquatic, there's excellent snorkelling (YR500 equipment rental), with Dihamri Marine Protected Area, around 15km from Hadibu, being the best place for peering under the waves.

There is great hiking potential, with the green hills and granite outcrops of the 1500m **Haggeher Mountains** providing dragons, cave dwellers and views. Unless you're planning a long trans-island hike, you'll need a vehicle to reach some of the best walking areas.

The following activities are much more specialised and will certainly require the aid of an experienced tour company. Serious naturalists and botanists will appreciate the knowledge of a guide – Soqotra Eco-Tourism Society will be able to sort you out with someone who knows where and what to look for even if they don't know too much detail. Caving is a new activity for which Suqutra (and the Dhofar Mountains around Hawf, p511) has immense potential. The island is thought to boast one of the world's largest cave systems, though they remain almost entirely unexplored to date. The **Dogub Cave** on the south coast has huge stalagmites and stalactites, and is one that everyone can enjoy. With day-in day-out strong to gale-force winds through the May to September monsoon season and heavy swells, Suqutra could one day be a massive name in the windsurfing world. For the moment it's just for the hardcore. Surfers will also find some excellent breaks hidden in the remoter reaches of the island, but the same heavy winds that are such a delight for windsurfers are anything but for surfers. However, wind-related problems will be the least of a surfer's worries. It's the sharks that are the real problem!

A more sedate time can be spent exploring the ramble of half-built streets in Hadibu, as well as the **research centre** (Airport Rd) 2km out of town, which contains a small collection of specimens of Suqutran flora and fauna, that includes shells, shark mandibles and crustaceans, and a small but excellent herbarium. Panels (in English, Italian and Arabic) provide information on Suqutran birds, wildlife and environmental hazards.

Sleeping

Though Hadibu has the only hotels and restaurants, you should aim to spend as little time as possible here.

Camping is not permitted everywhere (so check first). Some good, established spots include Wadi Dae'rho near the fresh-water pool, Nojed on the south coast, Homhil and Dihamri in the east and Detwah Lagoon in the west. Facilities vary in all of these 'camp sites' and go from a toilet and some pre-erected tents and huts (Dihamri and Detwah Lagoon) to nothing at all. At most of these sites someone can be found to cook an evening meal (though not always, so it's good to be prepared). Pitches cost YR1000 per person. It's often possible to arrange to stay in villages, though this sort of thing is hard to organise in advance. If you are invited to do so, be generous with how much you donate (YR2000 per person should be sufficient – more if meals are provided).

If you need to hire camping gear, the Summer Land Hotel and Soqotra Eco-Tourism Society can provide all the standards for US$7 per day.

In Hadibu itself there are a couple of overpriced hotels.

Al-Jazeera Hotel (☎ 660447; fax 660443; Hadibu; d YR4000) A small hotel that offers the cheapest rooms in town. The rooms could do with a sweep more often but otherwise they're perfectly acceptable.

Hafej Hotel (☎ /fax 660469; Hadibu; d YR5000) This clean and conventional 15-room hotel will give you a restful night's sleep, and though it lacks much character it does offer good value for money for those who cannot stretch to the Summer Land.

Summer Land Hotel (☎ 660350; Hadibu; s/d US$25/30) Run by the president's nephew, this travellers' centre has been recently refurbished and is, perhaps not surprisingly, the biggest name in Suqutran tourism. It's a reputation that's well deserved because its rooms, though not memorable, are clean and peaceful. More importantly, the staff know the island well and can sort you out with tours, car hire and camping equipment.

Eating

There are few eating options in Hadibu and none at all outside the town.

Shaboa Restaurant (☎ 660515; Hadibu; meals YR400; ☻ 4am-9pm) Next door to Yemenia, simple and boisterous Shaboa is the local preference. It serves chicken or goat with rice, as well as vegetable-only dishes.

Getting There & Away

The national carrier **Yemenia** (☎ 660123; fax 660510; ☻ 7am-noon & 3.30-5.30pm) flies from Suqutra to Al-Mukalla (US$50), Aden (US$50) and San'a (US$60) twice a week. It's essential to book well in advance.

In theory it's possible to charter a dhow to Suqutra from Al-Mukalla, but doing so is hardly recommended. The weather is unpredictable, the sea high and the dhows often overloaded. No boats operate during the summer monsoon season.

Getting Around

Yemenis say that Suqutra is President Saleh's little baby, and he's certainly enthusiastically promoting the island and pumping cash into it. One of the biggest projects currently under way is the construction of an island ring road, as well as linking trans-island roads. Work is progressing at a rate of knots and the tarmac has already reached Qalansiyah and the Dicksam plateau among other places. By the time you read this there is a good chance that the ring road will be completed. Despite this there is currently no public transport whatsoever, so you will need to rent a jeep (US$70), which can be done through the Soqotra Eco-Tourism Society, Summer Land Hotel or a San'a tour agency (p520).

WADI HADRAMAWT
وادي حضرموت

☎ 06 / pop 1,028,556

After so much sun-blasted desert, arriving in the vast Wadi Hadramawt, a dry river valley lined with lush oases, is like entering another world. In an instant, sterility is replaced by fertility and ochre browns give

way to disco greens. It's the sort of place where stories can grow tall and magic and mystery seem to permeate the very air. It was originally populated by a race of giants called 'Ad who, according to legend, were given wealth unlike anyone else. But instead of thanking God for his generosity, they wasted their time worshipping idols, building fabulous cities and generally running about living life like it was meant to be fun. In retaliation for this behaviour God sent violent winds, tremendous sandstorms and, according to some sources, a plague of dog-sized ants who tore the 'Adites apart limb by limb. With a past like this, it's hardly surprising to learn that this magic kingdom has skyscrapers built of mud, camels that turn into rocks and honey that tastes of liquid gold.

SHIBAM
شبام

As you get closer the heat haze lifts and you realise that what you are looking at is not really a group of fossilised giraffes rearing up out of the palms, but something even more improbable. It's Shibam, a 2500-year-old

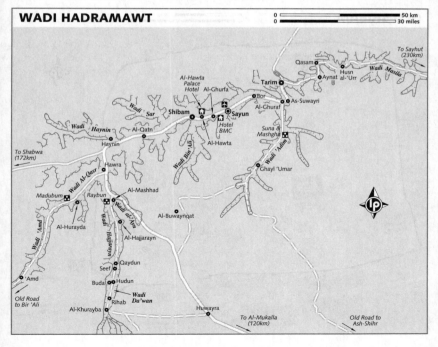

WADI HADRAMAWT

city of seven- and eight-storey tower blocks built entirely out of mud and faith. It will leave you breathless.

History

Shibam is thought to date from the 4th century BC, but was built on the ruins of an even older city. It was later settled by citizens of old Shabwa after their city was destroyed. Later the town grew to boast the most important market in the region, and served for centuries (right up to the 16th century) as an important capital for local dynasties. In 1982 the town was declared a Unesco World Heritage site.

Sights & Activities

Shibam is a silent and reserved place and in the mid-afternoon heat, when everyone else is safely tucked away indoors, it can feel a little like a museum or a library. Don't be mistaken, though, because away from the eyes of nosey travellers the city is alive and kicking. And thanks partially to tourism, it's experiencing something of a revival. Although Shibam covers a

very small area, it manages to pack over 500 dwellings into this confined space. The exterior of the buildings tends to be dull and featureless, but keep an eye open for the magnificent decorative doors and windows. It's worth taking a late evening stroll along the city **walls**, which date from the 17th century, and out into the fields of date palms. Other worthy sites include the **Sultan's Palace** (9am-1pm Sat-Thu), built in AD 1220, and the various **mosques** (none of which are open to nonbelievers), including the **Sheikh ar-Rashid Mosque** (also known as the Al-Jami or Great Mosque), which dates from the 10th century. At the **souq** next to the mosque, look out for the frankincense that has been sold here for centuries and have a game of dominoes with the elderly men who gather outside the teashop every evening. **Bait Jarhum** (420054; 10am-noon & 4-5.30pm Sat-Thu) is a traditional tower house renovated by Unesco. Inside you'll discover a mediocre photo exhibition, some vague views over the town and beautiful window and door frames. Ask for directions locally. Nearby is the similar, but privately run,

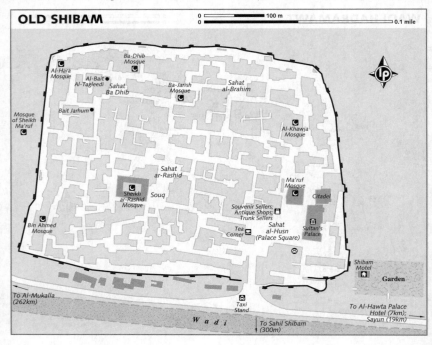

OLD SHIBAM

0 — 100 m
0 — 0.1 mile

Al-Hara Mosque

Ba-Dhib Mosque

Al-Bait Al-Tagleedi

Sahat Ba Dhib

Ba-Jarish Mosque

Sahat al-Brahim

Mosque of Sheikh Ma'ruf

Bait Jarhum

Al-Khawja Mosque

Sahat ar-Rashid

Ma'ruf Mosque

Sheikh ar-Rashid Mosque

Souq

Citadel

Souvenir Sellers; Antique Shops; Trunk Sellers

Bin Ahmed Mosque

Tea Corner

Sahat al-Husn (Palace Square)

Sultan's Palace

Shibam Motel

Garden

To Al-Mukalla (262km)

Taxi Stand

To Sahil Shibam (300m)

To Al-Hawta Palace Hotel (7km); Sayun (19km)

Wadi

Al-Bait Al-Tagleedi (☎ 420400; admission YR300; ⏰ 8.30am-1.30pm & 3.30-5.30pm Sat-Thu). Tea or coffee is included in the price.

A bit of a tourist tradition is to climb the rocky hill above the 'suburb' of Sahil Shibam, opposite the town, to watch the sun fall behind the city.

Sleeping & Eating

Shibam Motel (☎ 420425; alhawtahtl@y.net.ye; s/d/tr US$25/35/45) A quiet hotel with freshly painted and well-maintained rooms that are a step above most Yemeni hotels, as well as just a step from Shibam itself. It's one of the Universal chain's better offerings. You can get breakfast for YR500, and lunch and dinner for YR1200.

our pick **Al-Hawta Palace Hotel** (☎ 425010; alhawtahtl@universalyemen.com; s/d/tr US$100/130/150; 🖳 🖭) Lying around 7km from Shibam and 12km from Sayun centre, the Al-Hawta is probably Yemen's best hotel. It claims the unusual distinction of being the only 1st-class hotel in the world built entirely of mud and clay. Full of domes and arches, it's beautifully designed both inside and out and carefully maintained. The comfortable rooms are sparingly decorated but full of class, and the swimming pool complex and gardens are simply perfect. All in all, it would be hard to imagine a better-value top-class hotel anywhere, but there is a downside – the restaurant. The food is badly cooked and overpriced (breakfast US$5; lunch and dinner US$10), and the 'free' breakfast will be an unexpected and none-too-cheap addition to your bill.

Getting There & Away

The bus and taxi stand lies just outside the entrance to the village. Shared taxis run regularly to Sayun (YR100, 20 minutes, around 20 daily) and Tarim (YR200, one hour, five to 10 daily).

SAYUN
سيؤن
☎ 05

Sayun has a distinguished history. From the earliest days, it was developed by the local Hadramawt clans and dynasties and since the 15th century has been the wadi's capital. Today, despite being the heart and soul of Hadramawt, dusty Sayun is a town with a slow beat and lots of friendly people. For the traveller, Sayun offers a decent range

of accommodation and a picturesque setting of adobe brick houses against a background of hills and palm trees. Aside from the palace/museum there is little to see as all the mosques and graveyards are closed to non-Muslims.

Information

There's a telecommunications office near the post office.

Abdulqadr Mahdami (☎ 406409) For a private guide to the towns of Hadramawt.

Al-Jazirah Restaurant (per min YR2; ⏰ 8am-9pm Sat-Thu) Internet access.

National Bank of Yemen (☎ 402142; ⏰ 7am-1pm Sat-Wed) It's northwest of the cemetery.

Universal Travel & Tourism (☎ 404288; seiyun@universalyemen.com; Central Sq; ⏰ 8am-noon & 4-7.30pm Sat-Thu) Can organise a wide variety of tours and activities in the area.

Sights

Originally built as a 19th-century defensive fort, the **Sultan's Palace** (☎ 402285; Central Sq; admission YR500; ⏰ 8.30am-1pm Sat-Wed) was converted into a residential palace by the Sultan Al-Katheri in the 1920s. The Sultan wasn't a subtle man and his house, containing a mere 90 rooms, towers over Sayun like an exaggerated wedding cake. It now houses one of the best museums in the country.

This treasure trove of relics will stir the imagination of even the most museum-weary and includes Bronze Age statues, such as the 'sphinx', ancient frankincense jars (found buried at a nearby necropolis) and tablets inscribed with beautiful Himyarite and Semitic script (dating from as early as the 8th or 9th century BC). Most of the items on display were found in and around Hadramawt – proving just how long this area has been inhabited.

The 2nd floor of the palace is supposed to house changing exhibitions, though for the past few years it's exhibited a wonderful collection of photographs of the region taken in the 1930s by travellers to the Hadramawt (among them the intrepid British traveller Freya Stark).

The 3rd floor houses the far less interesting **Museum of the Peoples' Customs & Traditions**, which contains staid examples of traditional Hadramawt arts and crafts. Don't leave without a visit to the roof of the palace: there are great views across the town.

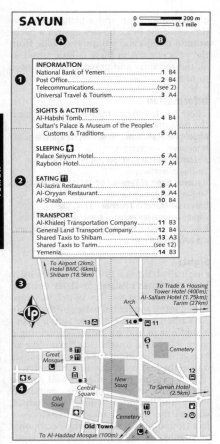

SAYUN

0 ————— 200 m
0 ————— 0.1 mile

INFORMATION
National Bank of Yemen.............................1 B4
Post Office...2 B4
Telecommunications..............................(see 2)
Universal Travel & Tourism........................3 A4

SIGHTS & ACTIVITIES
Al-Habshi Tomb.......................................4 B4
Sultan's Palace & Museum of the Peoples'
    Customs & Traditions............................5 A4

SLEEPING 🛏
Palace Seiyum Hotel................................6 A4
Rayboon Hotel..7 A4

EATING 🍴
Al-Jazira Restaurant.................................8 A4
Al-Oryyan Restaurant...............................9 A4
Al-Shaab...10 B4

TRANSPORT
Al-Khaleej Transportation Company...........11 B3
General Land Transport Company.............12 B4
Shared Taxis to Shibam.........................13 A3
Shared Taxis to Tarim.........................(see 12)
Yemenia...14 B3

To Airport (2km);
Hotel BMC (6km);
Shibam (18.5km)

To Trade & Housing
Tower Hotel (400m);
Al-Sallam Hotel (1.75km);
Tarim (27km)

Arch

Cemetery

Great
Mosque

New
Souq

To Samah Hotel
(2.5km)

Central
Square

Old
Souq

Cemetery

Old Town

To Al-Haddad Mosque (100m)

Sayun is also home to a number of interesting mosques and tombs, such as the **Al-Habshi Tomb**, opposite the cemetery, and the 16th-century **Al-Haddad Mosque**, south of the cemetery. Unfortunately, you won't be allowed to enter any of them. Also well worth a wander are the alleyways of the **old souq**, where you can pick up a *madhalla* – the 'witch's hat' worn by the Hadramawt herders, as well as bright basketry.

Sleeping
BUDGET
Palace Seiyum Hotel (☎ 405566; fax 402371; s/d YR1500/2000) Don't be put off by the prison-cell doors, because the rooms are pretty pleasing. Some come with tiny balconies

and larger than normal bathrooms. The staff think foreigners are hilarious, but you probably won't find the loudspeakers on the nearby mosque quite as funny.

Rayboon Hotel (☎ 405393; fax 402686; r YR1700) Situated in an atmospheric old quarter this new hotel has tatty rooms at a price you can't knock. This place is more accustomed to foreigners and their strange habits than the Palace Seiyum and is therefore a little more welcoming.

MIDRANGE
Al-Sallam Hotel (☎ 403208; fax 403181; Tarim Rd; s/d YR1800/2400) With rooms well past their best, Sayun's original hotel has fallen on hard times, but the staff are friendly and eager to please. The 'pool' is as dry as a Yemeni bar.

Trade & Housing Tower Hotel (Funduq al-Burg/ al-Borg; ☎ 403750; fax 403575; Al-'Aam St; s/d YR2100/ 3000; 🏊) Cheap rooms that sure ain't cheerful, but the swimming pool is the best in town and the towering bougainvillea plants even better. The murky rooms might appeal to a more refined type of backpacker.

Hotel BMC (☎ 428040; fax 428042; Al-Ghorfah St; r YR4000; 🏊) The rooms in this well-maintained hotel a few kilometres west of town are spick-and-span and the receptionists bouncing with enthusiasm. There is a small pool and a restaurant (mains YR300 to YR500) that isn't such a highlight.

TOP END
Samah Hotel (☎ 402777; samahhotel@yahoo.com; s/d US$30/35; 🏊) Sayun's top hotel is 2.5km east of the town centre. The rooms are comfortable and well kept, but the dreary Soviet design doesn't do it any favours. It offers occasional live music and a pool in which swimming is very difficult.

Eating
Al-Oryyan Restaurant (☎ 408330; meals YR80-600) This clean and busy joint is by far the pick of the bunch and its English-language menu makes ordering easy. The crushed beans with egg (YR120) is way better than it sounds!

Al-Shaab (☎ 402486; Central Sq; meals YR200-500; 🕐 lunch only) Located opposite the corner of the park, this brightly coloured restaurant has long served as the pit stop of choice at lunchtime. The menu offers no great surprises

The Al-Jazira Restaurant next door is almost identical, even down to the menu design.

Getting There & Away

The national carrier **Yemenia** (☎ 402550; fax 404388) flies to San'a for US$80.

A good highway connects Sayun to San'a (via Ma'rib). General Land Transport Company runs buses to San'a (YR1400, around 14 hours, one daily). Foreigners are often not allowed to travel this route by bus.

Shared taxis run to Al-Mukalla (YR1500, five hours, six daily), San'a (YR2300, eight to 10 hours, one daily), Shibam (YR70, 20 minutes, 30 daily) and Tarim (YR100, 30 to 40 minutes, around 20 daily). As with the buses, foreigners are often not allowed to travel to San'a via Ma'rib by taxi. For information on crossing the desert to Ma'rib via Shabwa see p497.

New roads have also been constructed heading eastward to Oman and it's now perfectly possible to travel overland to/from Sayun and Salalah in Oman (p247). **Al-Khaleej Transportation Company** (☎ 402188; opposite the Yemenia office) sends buses trundling to Salalah (YR5000, 16 hours) every Saturday and Tuesday morning. Book in advance and prepare for a very long day. The buses use the inland border crossing at Makinat Shihan p512), where Omani tourist visas can be obtained with little fuss for most Western nationalities for US$21. It's also possible to travel to Oman from Sayun via Al-Ghayda (p511) and the coast using local buses and taxis.

TARIM
تريم
☎ 05

Situated 35km northeast of Sayun, the ramshackle town of Tarim has served as the seat of kings since ancient times, and was Wadi Hadramawt's capital before Sayun. It used to be famous as a centre of Islamic learning, as testified to by its library, and at one time had a mosque for every day of the year. During the past century many of the people of Tarim have set off to seek their fortunes abroad, and those who have succeeded have often returned to build sumptuous 'palaces' in and around the city.

Sights

Tarim is famous for the quantity and quality of its mud-brick palaces, many of which were constructed by Yemenis returning to their homeland after making their fortunes in the far east.

As-Sayed Omar bin Sheikh al-Kaf built the **Al-Kaf Palace** ('Ish Shaa Palace; ☎ 417500; admission YR150; ☽ 8am-1pm), Tarim's most flamboyant, apparently using a book of different architectural styles as a template, in a kind of 'pick-your-own' project! The result is an unlikely mishmash of styles – Art Nouveau, Art Deco, baroque, Southeast Asian and Hadrami. Back in its day, it must have been beautiful, but now it's a crumbling relic and a visit here is a little sad as you think about the marvellous lifestyle that this building once represented. Inside, there is a limited display of locally discovered antiques and a collection of old photos recalling happier days. The highlight is probably the stained-glass windows, which are as dazzling as the day they were fitted.

Housed in the back of the Great Mosque (or Masjid al-Jami), **Al-Ahgaf Manuscript Library** (☎ 41522; admission free; ☽ 9am-1pm Sat-Wed) is the second-largest library in the country and contains over 5000 manuscripts, though most are hidden from prying eyes. Some of the more beautifully illustrated manuscripts are on display in glass cabinets. Unfortunately for English speakers, all captions are in Arabic. The large and dazzling-white **Al-Muhdar Mosque** was built in 1915 and boasts the tallest minaret in Yemen; it soars nearly 40m into the air.

Sleeping & Eating

Tarim isn't much of a place to spend the night. There are only a couple of very basic *funduqs* with bare-bones rooms.

Kenya Tourist Hotel Tarim (☎ 417550; kenya_hotel@yemen.net.ye; d YR1700) At the entrance to the town, the Kenya is Tarim's finest hotel, but that isn't saying much. The rooms are noisy and as crumbling as the Al-Kaf Palace.

Al-Kazem Restaurant (meals YR300) On the road into town this is a no-frills joint, but the food is tasty enough with the fried chicken being the star buy.

Getting There & Away

Shared taxis go to Sayun (YR100 to YR150, 30 minutes, 20 daily) and Shibam (YR200, one hour, 10 daily).

AROUND TARIM

Nineteen kilometres east of Tarim, **Aynat** dates from the 16th century and has some lovely old tombstones set in an extensive cemetery; it also boasts some beautifully constructed houses in a style of their own. To get there, take a taxi from Sayun (YR100, 35 minutes, two per day).

On the road west to Sayun, look out for the 10th-century **Tomb of Ahmed bin Eisa the Emigrant**, lying at the foot of the mountain around 10km from Sayun. Its distinctive zigzag shape, leg-aching flight of steps and bright whitewash are unmistakable.

WADI DAW'AN   وادي دوعن
☎ 06

It is hard to imagine how anywhere in the Yemeni desert could be more spectacular and mysterious than the Wadi Hadramawt, but sitting quietly in the sidelines, there is one such place. The Wadi Daw'an might only be small, but it packs one hell of a punch – everything you thought breathtaking about the Wadi Hadramawt is here in force, but unlike the camouflaged mud villages of the main wadi, these villages come in a lush patchwork of shades and colours.

For most people Wadi Daw'an is experienced as a brief glimpse through the windows of a car racing along the back road between Sayun and Al-Mukalla, but it would be much more rewarding to spend a day or so here getting into the slow, agricultural groove of the valley.

Some of the wadi's most attractive villages, in a north to south direction, include **Al-Mashhad**, which, with the 15th-century **Tomb of Hasan ibn Hasan**, is a local pilgrimage site and a near-deserted village. Next down the line, and clambering up the side of a cliff, is maybe the most impressive village of them all, **Al-Hajjarayn**, which is also among the oldest villages in the region. One of the biggest villages in the wadi is **Sif**, whose pastel-fringed houses sprawl across the wadi bed, and whose old quarter sits proudly atop a knuckle of rock. **Al-Khurayba** is the final village in the wadi and is famous for its massive acid-trip 'palace' of rainbow-coloured squares. It was built by a Saudi businessman with roots in the area, who is also responsible for a wave of new schools, clinics and roadworks. It's sometimes possible to spend the night here. The village has another claim to fame that it's a little less keen to promote: it's the ancestral home of the extended Bin Laden family.

Sleeping & Eating

Riboun Hotel (☎ 513590; Main St; r per person with breakfast & dinner YR2000) The only reliable accommodation in the region is this hotel located in the village of Sif. It's English-speaking and has a handful of hot and stuffy rooms.

Riboun Restaurant & Hotel (☎ 73300716; r per person with breakfast & dinner YR2000) Excellent three-course meals (YR850) are provided at this nearby, and confusingly named, restaurant, which is run by relatives of the first

---

OF PETRIFIED CAMELS & TORTURED SOULS

Travel half a day east of Sayun, to the Wadi Masilah, and you will come across an extraordinary sight: a small town of prim and proper houses set at the foot of a tomb. This is the tomb of the Prophet Hud, and this is no ordinary town. The great-great-grandson of Noah, Hud was a giant of a man, the size of a palm tree according to some. He was sent by God to make the 'Adites – the race of giants who were the original inhabitants of Hadramawt – change their immoral and lax ways. This wasn't well received by the 'Adites. They chased Hud and his snow-white camel up to the far end of the wadi, where he eluded his pursuers by riding straight into the cliff face, which parted for him and all of his camel but its hump, which was instantly turned to stone.

It's said that Hud is the father of all south Arabians and his tomb, where the camel's hump can still be seen, is the location of an annual three-day pilgrimage. Aside from these three days, though, the tomb and its surrounding town is utterly deserted and lifeless, haunted it's said only by ghosts.

Not far away is rumoured to be the mysterious Well of Barhut, a bottomless well whose walls are lined with scorpions and snakes. It's said to be the place where fallen angels and the souls of infidels end their days.

Riboun. It also has a couple of brand-new, bright-blue rooms that make you feel as if you're sleeping in a swimming pool.

Getting There & Away

The road between Sayun and Al-Mukalla via Wadi Daw'an is surfaced all the way and in excellent condition, but currently there is no public transport along this route.

AL-MAHRA

Remote even by Yemeni standards, the far eastern province of Al-Mahra is a tough desert landscape populated by an equally tough people, many of whom continue to live a largely nomadic existence. The tribes of this area are the original south Arabians and many inhabitants still speak the ancient language of Mahric, a Semitic language which predates Arabic. It was also in this region that the camel was originally domesticated, an event that was to transform Arabia forever.

Unless you're tackling the Omani border, there is little reason to head to Al-Mahra.

AL-GHAYDA

Sun-baked Al-Ghayda is the state capital, though it's really no more than an overblown fishing village. Attractions are limited to a small but enjoyable fruit-and-vegetable souq and the chance to splash about on the soft white beach a few kilometres to the east of town.

Sleeping & Eating

Facilities in Al-Ghayda are very limited and it's unlikely that you would want to spend more than a night here.

Gulf Hotel (☎ 612498; fax 611466; s/d YR1500/1700) The large rooms here could definitely do with seeing a cleaner on a more frequent basis, but the beds are soft and the atmosphere tranquil.

Almost opposite the Gulf Hotel is an unnamed **restaurant** (meals YR300), where you eat straight off the floor and the food is much better than expected.

Getting There & Away

The **airport** (☎ 612122) is a few kilometres to the west of town. There are flights from here to San'a for US$60.

> ### SEX & THE HIVE
>
> Yemen may not seem like the land of milk and honey, but since ancient times Yemen has been famous for its honey, which you'll frequently be told is the best in the world. The top-quality honey comes from the Wadi Daw'an in the far east of the country, where nomadic beekeepers transport wooden hives around in search of *'ilb* flowers for the bees to feed on. Honey in Yemen is appreciated for more than just its taste and is often used by tribes in order to seal a deal as well as in traditional medical practices. When mixed with myrrh, it provides relief from constipation and with carrot seeds supposedly becomes the perfect aphrodisiac!

Al-Khaleej Co Buses (☎ 05-611222) runs to/from Al-Mukalla every Wednesday (YR2500) and also to Salalah in Oman (YR4000, Tuesday 1pm and Friday 3pm).

HAWF

Sitting between high mountain and deep sea, the little border village of Hawf will either be a fond farewell to Yemen or an enchanting entry. Few people stay more than a couple of minutes and there are no hotels or restaurants, just one small teashop, which seems to have as many camels drop by as tea-drinking customers. It's a shame that Hawf doesn't have more tourist facilities because it's the most alluring coastal town in Al-Mahra, with a sprinkling of idyllic cove beaches (where those with their own transport can camp for a night or two) close by and the fascinating western tip of the Dhofar Mountains rearing up behind the village. Famous for frankincense, these mountains hide a huge slab of forest – the only real forest in Yemen. It's a protected zone and access isn't easy without your own set of wheels. It might be possible to organise something with a driver in Hawf or Al-Ghayda.

Getting There & Away

There's no public transport to/from Hawf and most people will pass straight through the village on the direct Al-Ghayda–Salalah bus. The border is open 24 hours and Omani tourist visas are available for most Western and Arab nationalities for US$21 on the border. If coming the other way, Yemeni tourist visas are available for most for US$30. You don't need a travel permit or to be part of a tour group to cross over this border. Independent travellers can continue on to Sayun or Al-Mukalla on public transport without fuss, though once you reach either of those towns, you will need to register with the police and obtain onward travel permits.

MAKINAT SHIHAN
The inland border village of Makinat Shihan is not a place to linger. Fortunately, the border is open 24 hours and procedures are identical to those at Hawf (p511). There are no facilities for tourists.

YEMEN DIRECTORY

More general information on the following topics can be found in the Arabian Peninsula Directory (p524).

ACCOMMODATION
Camping
There are no established camp sites in Yemen, but it's possible to pitch a tent in most places (bar obvious restricted areas, such as near military bases). Popular places currently include the Haraz Mountains (p467) and the island of Suqutra (p502), where few alternative types of accommodation exist. Camping equipment can be rented from the San'a-based travel agencies (p520).

Hotels
Although rock-bottom places can be unearthed in all of Yemen's towns (for YR400 to YR600), they're not really recommended. The filthy dormitory rooms have rope beds with no mattresses and, if you are lucky, rotten blankets. Qat chewers and itinerant merchants (invariably male) are the main clientele, so foreign men would raise an eyebrow and foreign women will simply be turned away.

Similar but cleaner and more accustomed to travellers of both sexes are the budget hotels, which offer singles/doubles with shared or sometimes private bathrooms for around YR1000/1400. Some of these are converted traditional tower houses,

which offer simple but attractive and cosy dormitory-style accommodation aimed squarely at foreign tourists. In the smaller towns and villages where few eating options exist, these traditional tower houses may also offer half-board for YR2000. TVs are a basic amenity in Yemen and most budget hotel rooms have them (though few offer satellite channels).

In all of the larger towns and in many of the smaller ones, there's usually at least a couple of midrange options where singles/doubles with bathroom cost from YR2500/4000. Cheap but clean, and occasionally well loved, they offer great value.

In the capital and one or two of the larger towns, there are a few top-end options, where rooms cost from YR8000 to just over US$200. Some have all the four- or five-star flourishes you'd expect, including business and fitness centres.

Discounts in the low season (October to November and February to May) are usually negotiable, as well as for stays of a week or more. Don't be afraid to ask for them.

In this chapter, all the rooms listed come with private bathroom (and often a TV) unless otherwise stated.

ACTIVITIES
Diving
Decent diving can be had in both the Red and Arabian Seas. Although coral is less abundant at sites in the Arabian Sea (because of the lower sea temperature) and visibility can be more erratic, fish life is profuse. Visibility ranges from 5m to 25m depending on the season and weather. The best time for diving is between October and April.

Currently the only certified diving centre in Yemen is the German-run **Extra Divers** (☎ 350919; www.extra-divers.de) in Al-Mukalla (p499). Various diving day trips are offered and all diving equipment can be hired. There are decompression chambers in Al-Mukalla and Aden. Various Yemeni-based tour companies also offer diving tours (sometimes using the experience and boats of Extra Divers) to both coastlines and, increasingly, to Suqutra. Try the **ATG travel agency** (www.atg-yemen.com; just off Hadda St, San'a), **FTI Yemen** (www.ftiyemen.com/scuba.htm; Al-Qiada St, San'a) or **Marib Travel & Tourism** (www.marib-tours.com; Hadda St, San'a).

In Suqutra, diving trips can be organised to the unmolested, fish-infested reefs of the island through either San'a-based agencies or the **Summer Land Hotel** (☎ 05-660350; Hadibu) for around US$35 per dive with all equipment.

Hiking
Yemen's highlands offer endless potential for hiking. A popular spot is the Haraz Mountains, southwest of San'a, particularly around the villages of Al-Hajjarah, Kawkaban and Manakhah. There are no official hiking trails or maps, so you may need to rely on local guides. Donkeys (for riding or as pack animals) can also be hired.

Several San'a-based travel agencies specialise in hiking: see p520 for information.

Swimming & Surfing
With two coastlines on two seas, there are many unspoilt beaches in Yemen. Except for those at Aden (p489) and Al-Khawkha (p482), beach resorts are almost nonexistent, and except at Al-Mukalla (p499), very few coastal hotels have private beaches. The waves generated by the summer monsoon have started to grab the attention of a few surfers – conditions are reportedly excellent in the east of the country. For further information on surfing in Yemen as well as occasional tours, see www.oceansurfpublications.co.uk.

BOOKS
For anyone hooked on Yemen's ancient history, *Arabia Felix – An Exploration of the Archaeological History of Yemen* by Alessandro de Maigret is considered the definitive introduction to the subject.

J'étais Médecin au Yemen (I Was a Doctor in Yemen) by Claude Fayein is a classic and charismatic memoir of a female doctor's experiences in Yemen in the 1950s. *Motoring with Mohammed* by Eric Hansen tells of action-packed and amusing travels around Yemen in the late 1980s. Award-winning *Yemen – Travels in Dictionary Land* by Tim Mackintosh-Smith is a modern classic: it's a witty, erudite but very wordy account of contemporary life. *Eating the Flowers of Paradise* by Kevin Rushby is a brilliant and, at times, hair-raising exploration of the world of qat in both Yemen and Ethiopia. *The Zanzibar Chest* by former war correspondent Aidan Hartley focuses primarily on the battles of Africa, but includes many forays into Yemen and is one of the most powerful books you are ever likely to read. *Sheba* by Nicholas Clapp is an interesting and easy-to-read account of his search for the origins of the myth. *The Southern Gates of Arabia* is a travel classic written by English woman Freya Stark, who journeyed through the Hadramawt in the early 1900s.

A good textual and pictorial overview of the country is *Yemen – Land and People* by Sarah Searight. The glossy coffee-table book *Yemen: Jewel of Arabia* by Charles and Patricia Aithie whets the appetite before a trip and serves as a good souvenir after one. For those with a keener interest in art, *Queen of Sheba – Treasure from Ancient Yemen* by St John Simpson (ed), which accompanied the exhibition 'Queen of Sheba', contains 12 fascinating and well-illustrated essays on the country's artistic and cultural heritage. For more travel literature on the Arabian Peninsula, see p23.

BUSINESS HOURS
Hours vary. Outside the central highlands, where the climate is hotter, there is often an extended midday break (but businesses open earlier and close later). Some businesses close at 1pm regardless and reopen around 6pm.

Banks 8am to noon Saturday to Thursday, open only until 11am on Thursday.

Government offices 8am to 3pm, although in practice many close by 1pm or 1.30pm.

Post offices 8.30am to 1pm and 3.30pm to 7pm Saturday to Thursday. Usually open for an hour from 7pm to 8pm on Friday.

Restaurants 7am to 11pm, although they may open earlier and close later in larger towns.

Shops & private businesses 9am to noon and 4pm to 8pm Saturday to Thursday. Some open on Friday as well.

Telecom & internet centres 7am to 11pm.

Yemenia 8am to 1pm or 2pm & 5pm to 7pm or 8pm Saturday to Wednesday, 9am to noon Friday.

CHILDREN
Yemenis love children, and kids of both sexes are permitted freedom and liberties discouraged during adult life.

However, facilities for children aren't greatly developed. There are a couple of amusement parks (see p463) in San'a, and a

YEMEN

few small parks containing swings and slides in other towns. Other possible activities might include donkey or horse riding, swimming in the sea or a hotel pool, and water sports at some of the seaside complexes.

COURSES

Yemen is a great place to learn Arabic. The cost of living is low, school fees are very reasonable, the Yemeni dialect is not too far removed from Modern Standard Arabic (MSA) and relatively few Yemenis speak English. San'a schools (p463), which teach both MSA and the Yemeni dialect, in particular, have a good reputation and some have received glowing reports from travellers.

CUSTOMS

Foreigners are permitted up to 2L of alcohol. Note that there is a prohibition on exporting items of artistic value. Anything that is – or looks like – an antique or is of archaeological value risks confiscation.

DANGERS & ANNOYANCES

Despite salacious press reports to the contrary, Yemen is probably far safer than your own country. Petty crime, even in the big cities, is almost nonexistent and the chances of being caught up in a terrorist attack is highly unlikely. Despite this nobody can say that a trip to Yemen is entirely without risk, and Western governments currently advise against all travel to Sa'da province and also issue regular warnings about the dangers of overland travel in other areas of the country (Ma'rib, Shabwa and 'Amran are the current hotspots) due to the risk of kidnap.

Mines

During the 1994 War of Unity, unknown quantities of land mines were planted. After a sustained anti-mining campaign, many have been cleared, but mines remain, particularly around the old North/South Yemen border. Although the risk may be minimal, hikers in little-explored regions should seek local advice before setting out.

Terrorism

According to the US government, Yemen is home to a significant number of sympathisers and members of Al-Qaeda. However, the chances of being caught up in a terror attack in Yemen are considerably lower than other parts of the peninsula (Saudi Arabia, for example) or even London. Expatriates working for international corporations are at a much higher risk than casual tourists, and dangerous areas of the country are quickly closed to foreigners.

Those arrested in the past for connection with terrorism have almost always turned out to be foreign Arabs living in Yemen illegally. Meanwhile, the Yemeni government has been at pains to express its absolute condemnation of terrorism, and the Yemeni people their disgust and horror of it. The last major terror attack was a foiled double-suicide bombing of the oil installations near Ma'rib and Al-Mukalla in September 2006. Prior to 2001, it's thought that Al-Qaeda maintained some large training camps in the country, but these have been swiftly disbanded and anyone suspected of links to terrorism is dealt with harshly. At least that's the official line, but consistent rumours speak of government and military corruption or even collusion with terror groups, which has allowed suspects to walk away without trial.

The war in Iraq has inflamed passions somewhat, and after his execution Saddam Hussein was turned into a hero. Many Yemenis will ask a foreigner their opinion on the war and the execution, but that's normally as far as it goes. George Bush is almost universally detested in Yemen, and if you're a fan, it would be wise to keep these opinions to yourself. On the whole, though, Yemenis are far too laid-back and hospitable to call their guests to account for the sins or mistakes of their governments.

Traffic Accidents

Although traffic in Yemen is significantly quieter than in its more developed neighbours, drivers should definitely deploy themselves defensively! Mirrors and indicators are not used, car maintenance is practically nil and most road laws, including speed limits, are ignored. See also p522 and p555.

EMBASSIES & CONSULATES
Yemeni Embassies & Consulates

Following are the Yemeni embassies and consulates in major cities around the world. For the addresses of Yemeni embassies in neighbouring Arabian Peninsula countries, see the relevant country chapters.

Canada (☎ 613-729 6627; fax 613-729 6627; 54 Chamberlin Avenue, Ottawa)
France (☎ 01-53238787; fax 01 47234295; 25 rue Georges Bizet, 75116 Paris)
Germany (☎ 030-897305-0; fax 030-897305-62; Budapester Str 37, Berlin 10787)
Italy (☎ 06-44231679; fax 06-44234763; Via Antonio Bosio, 10, 00161 Rome)
Netherlands (☎ 70-365 3936; fax 70-356 3312; Surinamestraat 9, 2585 GG, The Hague)
UK (☎ 020-7584 6607; fax 020-7584 3350; 57 Cromwell Rd, London SW7 2ED)
USA Washington DC (☎ 202-965 4760; fax 202-337 2017; 2319 Wyoming Ave, NW Washington DC 20008); New York (☎ 212-355 1730; fax 212-750 9613; Room 435, 866 United Nations Plaza, New York, NY 10017)

Embassies & Consulates in Yemen

If you're travelling independently, it's not a bad idea to register with your embassy in San'a and inquire about any current security concerns. For those countries without diplomatic representation in Yemen (such as Australia, Canada and Ireland) you can register at your embassy in Riyadh (see p363).

Most embassies and consulates open between around 9am and 1pm from Saturday to Wednesday.

France (Map p458; ☎ 01-268882) Off Khartoum St.
Germany (Map p458; ☎ 01-413177) Off Hadda St.
Italy (Map p458; ☎ 01-269165; Safiah Janubia St)
Netherlands (Map p458; ☎ 01-421800) Off 14th October St)
Oman (Map p458; ☎ 01-208874; Al-Hoboob Corp St)
Saudi Arabia (☎ 01-240429; Al-Quds St)
UAE (Map p458; ☎ 01-248777; Circular Lane)
UK (Map p458; ☎ 01-302450; Thaher Himyari St (Nashwan al-Himyari St), East Ring Rd)
USA (Map p458; ☎ 01-755 2000; Sa'wan St)

HOLIDAYS

In addition to the main Islamic holidays (see the Arabian Peninsula Directory, p534), Yemen observes the following holidays:
May/Labour Day 1 May
National/Unity Day 22 May
September Revolutionary/Anniversary Day 26 September
October Revolutionary/Anniversary Day 14 October
Evacuation/Independence Day 30 November

INTERNET ACCESS

Internet cafés are mushrooming up over Yemen and are found in all the larger towns. However, connections vary greatly from (usually) quite good in San'a to extremely slow in smaller towns. Rates are very reasonable, averaging YR2 per minute.

INTERNET RESOURCES

The following websites provide useful information and links on Yemen:
American-Yemeni Society (www.aiys.org) Contains interesting cultural information about Yemen.
British-Yemeni Society (www.al-bab.com/bys) Includes history and current affairs.
TeleYemen (www.y.net.ye) Yemen's only Internet Service Provider (ISP). It acts as a kind of digital bibliography to all the sites it serves.
US Department of State (www.travel.state.gov/travel_warnings.html) Contains – somewhat alarmist – updates on the security situation and current 'hotspots'.
Yemen Gateway (www.al-bab.com/yemen) An overview of Yemen's attractions, history and culture. Lots of facts and figures, numerous articles on all subjects, as well as great links.
Yemen Times (www.yementimes.com) Good for a quick perusal of what's hitting headlines in the country, plus a very useful archive of past articles.

LANGUAGE

The national language of Yemen is Arabic, and Yemenis are widely regarded as speaking the dialect closest to the pure Arabic of the Quran. Many Yemenis working in the tourist industry speak at least a smattering of English, French or Italian. For more, see the language chapter (p566).

MAPS

Probably the most useful and widely available map is the **Freytag & Berndt** (www.freytag berndt.com) road map *Yemen* (1:1,500,000), which includes insets of San'a. The Reise Know-How Verlag map *Yemen* (1:850,000) is also good.

In Yemen itself (and sometimes available in Europe) the best bet is the *Republic of Yemen Tourist Map* (1:1,2500,000) published by IGN France/Yemen Survey Authority. It also has good insets of the major towns on its reverse side.

MEDIA
Magazines & Newspapers

The English-language weeklies, *Yemen Times* and *Yemen Observer* (YR30 each), are published in San'a and make interesting reading. Both are well regarded, the former for its political commentary and

YEMEN

regular columns, the latter (a more recent addition) for its commentary on social and cultural issues.

Day-old copies of the Saudi newspaper *Arab News* can sometimes be found in bigger towns, as can outdated editions of *Newsweek*.

Radio & TV

Yemen Radio and regional radio stations broadcast English-language news bulletins twice a day (usually once in the evening and morning, though schedules change). **BBC World Service** (www.bbc.co.uk/cgi-bin/worldservice /psims/ScheduleSDT.cgi) can be picked up on short-wave radio (15.57Mhz), as can Voice of America (17.73Mhz).

The two government-run TV channels suffer from underfunding and poor technology. To obtain access to more channels, many homes subscribe to satellite TV. The middle and top hotels invariably receive Al-Jazeera, CNN or BBC News 24.

MONEY

The unit of currency is the Yemeni riyal (YR), divided into 100 fils. Banknotes come in denominations of YR10 (rare), YR20, YR50, YR100, YR200, YR500 and YR1000. Each note is translated into English on one side. Only YR5 and YR10 coins remain, and though both sides of these coins are in Arabic only, they are of different sizes (the YR10 coin is the larger). Many people won't accept ripped or damaged banknotes.

Some midrange hotels, all top-end hotels and most travel agencies quote in US dollars or, increasingly, in euros. Where appropriate this book also quotes in these currencies, but payment is always acceptable in the Yemeni riyals equivalent.

ATMs & Credit Cards

In the past couple of years ATMs have arrived in Yemen and now most of the bigger bank branches in the large towns have ATMs that accept foreign cards. Most will only allow you to withdraw the equivalent of US$200 per transaction up to a daily limit of US$600. Problems with foreign cards are very common and you shouldn't rely simply on them. There are several ATMs at San'a airport.

Credit cards (Visa commonly, Master-Card sometimes and Amex rarely) are ac-

cepted for payment by Yemenia airlines, some tour operators and some top-end hotels, but you'll incur a steep 5% to 10% surcharge.

Cash

Cash is by far the simplest form of carrying your money, and as there is little petty theft, carrying around big bundles of money is not a huge worry. US dollars and euros are the currencies of choice.

Banks offer slightly lower rates for cash than foreign-exchange offices, but are more likely to change travellers cheques. There is no black market, so there's no advantage to changing money on the street.

Exchange Rates

Country	Unit		Yemeni riyal
Australia	A$1	=	YR152.06
Bahrain	BD1	=	YR519.08
Canada	C$1	=	YR166.80
Euro zone	€1	=	YR254.44
Japan	¥100	=	YR160.97
New Zealand	NZ$1	=	YR133.67
Oman	OR1	=	YR508.35
Qatar	QR1	=	YR53.76
Saudi Arabia	SR1	=	YR52.17
UAE	Dh1	=	YR53.28
UK	UK£1	=	YR381.74
USA	US$1	=	YR195.70

Moneychangers

Numerous (and well-signposted) foreign-exchange offices are found in the cities and larger towns. They offer shorter queues than the banks, faster service, longer opening hours (usually 9am to 9pm, except Friday) and almost always offer a better rate of exchange (at least for cash). Check with a couple first, as rates can vary slightly between offices. Commission is seldom charged, but check in advance.

Tipping

Although tipping is not expected in local restaurants, the upmarket tourist establishments often add a 10% to 15% service charge. Service charges and government taxes (totalling 22% or more) are often included at top-end hotels and restaurants, too. Porters and waiters in these establishments will also expect tips (YR100 to YR200). For drivers and guides, travel agencies recommend US$5 to US$10 per day per group. If there are only one or two of you, this can add substantially to the cost of your tour, and drivers can become difficult if they don't feel they have received a sufficient tip. For adults who play tour guides or offer other services, a tip of YR300 to YR500 (YR100 to YR150 for children) is fair.

Travellers Cheques
Travellers cheques can be difficult to change outside the largest towns. Also, changing them generally incurs a 3% to 5% commission or more. If you must use cheques, Crédit Agricole Indosuez is the best bank to change with.

PHOTOGRAPHY & VIDEO
Small memory cards are available in bigger towns, but they are expensive, so bring all you'll need with you. Print film is also available in the larger towns (ISO100/200 from YR300/350), with San'a offering the best selection. You can also find basic slide film there, such as Fujichrome Sensia (YR900), which is very rare elsewhere. Don't expect cards or films to be stored in optimum conditions.

POST
Post offices can be found in the larger towns and villages. Services offered are fairly efficient and cheap: a postcard/letter to Europe costs YR100, USA and Canada YR120, and Australia and New Zealand YR150.

TELEPHONE & FAX
The national telephone system is controlled by the government monopoly, Yemen Communications Company (commonly known as TeleYemen). Every city and town has a plethora of 'telecommunication centres'. Local calls cost around YR30/80 inside/outside town. The standard international charge is about YR200 per minute to anywhere in Europe, North America, Australia and New Zealand. There are no off-peak periods offering discounted rates. Phonecards costing from YR500 to YR4000 are available. Some internet cafés in bigger towns offer internet calling.

Faxes can be sent from any telecommunications centre. Local/international faxes cost YR30/YR500 per page.

Mobile Phones
The only two private suppliers of mobile-phone networks are **Spacetel** (Map p458; ☎ 01-420552; www.spacetelyemen.com; Hadda St) and **Sabafon** (Map p458; ☎ 01-400001; www.sabafon.com; Az-Zubayri St), both in San'a. Reception is good in most areas, though mountain valleys can be problematic.

Phone Codes
The country code for Yemen is ☎ 967, followed by the local area code (minus the zero), then the number. Local area codes are given at the start of each city or town section. For local inquiries, dial ☎ 118; for international inquiries, dial ☎ 152 or 155. The international access code (to call abroad from Yemen) is ☎ 00.

TOURIST INFORMATION
Tourist information is not Yemen's forte. You'll find dated and faded tourist brochures in Yemeni embassies abroad, and little better in Yemen itself. In fact, the capital still awaits its own tourism office, and they're as good as nonexistent in regions around the country. Some of the private travel agents (p520) do a very good job as surrogate tourism offices in the major towns, but it's best to supply yourself with information and maps before you arrive.

VISAS
Over the past couple of years, visa regulations for foreign visitors have changed several times. They may well change again; check with your embassy or consulate.

Currently everyone, except citizens of the Gulf Cooperation Council (GCC) countries, requires a visa to enter Yemen. Tourist visas are easily obtained at San'a and Aden international airports and all land borders (though in reality this means just the Yemen/Oman border) for citizens of all European Union nations, Scandinavian nations, the USA, Switzerland, Australia, New Zealand, Japan, Russia and several other countries. The cost for all nationalities is US$30 (or euro/Yemeni riyal equivalent) and the visa is valid for three months. Obtaining the visa in this manner is fast and painless, but it's still a good idea to check the latest rules with a Yemeni embassy in advance.

Everyone else should obtain visas from an embassy or consulate beforehand. Where there is none, you can obtain one from an embassy/consulate in a neighbouring country (neighbouring your country or neighbouring Yemen). Note that Israelis or travellers to Israel (with an Israeli stamp in their passport) will be denied a visa/entry to Yemen. Very occasionally there are problems at immigration for those with Pakistani or Afghani stamps in their passport. There is no official rule against having these stamps, so if you do encounter problems remain polite and insist on seeing someone higher up the chain of command.

If you're visiting on business or to study, you'll need to apply for a special business/student visa, and provide a letter of introduction from your organisation or college. These must be obtained through a Yemeni embassy in advance of your arrival.

Take note also of the travel-permit restrictions (below).

Visa Extensions

A one-month tourist visa can normally be extended at the **Immigration Authority** (Map p458; ☎ 01-612767; fax 01-618240; Khawlan St; ☺ 8am-2.30pm Sat-Wed) in San'a, where a one-month extension will be granted for YR1500. A tour operator can provide this service, but you may be charged a fee. Alternatively, an exit visa (valid for two weeks) is usually easily obtained on the last working day before the visa expires.

For residents or workers in Yemen, longer extensions can be granted, but you'll need to present a letter from your employer/organisation to the Ministry of Labour, which will then write a letter to the Immigration Authority.

Travel Permits & Closed Areas

Due to tribal tension and conflict in some areas as well as problems with kidnapping, certain areas are completely out of bounds to foreign visitors or require the services of a tour company.

For several years following the September 11 attacks, it was not possible to travel independently in Yemen, and all visitors were required to use the services of a tour company. This has now changed and much of the country is open to independent travellers using public transport, though a travel permit is required. Permits are quick and easy to obtain in San'a and most other big towns (where you should inquire in the police station).

The following table outlines which areas of the country were, at the time of research, closed to all foreigners and which were open only to those travelling with a tour company.

Area	Open to Tour Groups	Open to Independent Travellers
Al-Jawf	no	no
Sa'da city & road to San'a	sometimes	no
Sa'da province	sometimes	no
Shaharah	yes	no
Hajja	yes	yes
Ma'rib town & main roads	yes	sometimes
Barraqish	sometimes	no
Sirwah	no	no
Lahij	yes	yes
Abyan	main roads only	main roads only
Shabwa	normally, but not all areas	main coastal road only
Ah-Mahra	yes	yes
Bab al-Mandab	no	no

Note that the situation changes very fast. For much of 2003 to 2006, all of Sa'da province was closed, but at the start of 2007 the city and main road to San'a were reopened to tour groups only. Also, for a period in 2006, everywhere in Shabwa province was closed to all tourists.

You should not attempt to visit closed areas. Most of Yemen is very safe, but there are a couple of regions where foreigners are not welcome at all, and to attempt to visit them would be very dangerous. Fortunately, the police turn back the occasional foolhardy visitor long before they can put themselves and other people into serious danger.

To travel anywhere else in Yemen you require a permit, which is free and can be obtained from the **Tourist Police** (Map p458; ☎ 01-250203/4; Al Jamáa al Arabia St) in San'a. Although officially open 24 hours, you're best advised to come to the office between 8am to 6pm Saturday to Wednesday, when you're more likely to get somewhere! To gain a permit from the tourist police, you'll need the following:

- passport and photocopy of passport (including personal and visa details)
- itinerary (showing where you're travelling to, and for how long)
- means of transport, eg air, bus, car hire (including the name of the car-hire company or travel agency)
- names of everyone in your group
- details of your return journey home (date of departure, flight etc).

Take wads of photocopies of the permit (around seven or eight per day of travel), as you'll have to dish them out at the checkpoints across the country.

If you significantly change your itinerary, you should inform the tourist police and/or the travel agency within 24 hours. Alternatively, obtain another permit from the nearest major police station. If it's just a minor change, you won't have any problems.

If your first point of arrival is not San'a, try to get a travel permit through the first major police station on your route. Alternatively, you can fly to San'a from wherever you arrive and get a permit in the usual way there.

Note that if you are only flying around Yemen (and not using overland transport), you do not need travel permits.

Police Escorts

At the time of writing, it was compulsory to take a police escort from San'a to Ma'rib and on to Sayun, and from San'a to Sa'da and Shahara, as well as from Aden to Al-Mukalla. However, this may well be relaxed in the future – check in advance. The police normally ask YR2000 to YR3000 per car for this service, though prices seem to be fairly open to negotiation.

WOMEN TRAVELLERS

Yemen's attitude towards and treatment of foreign (and local) women is considerably more relaxed than its northern neighbour, Saudi Arabia. Female tourists can drive rented or private vehicles, and do not have to wear head coverings. In some remote areas as well as northern and eastern provinces, head covering is advised, if only as a gesture of respect (some readers have reported stone-throwing, spitting and glares

from local women and children when not dressed 'appropriately'). Conservative dress is expected. Female toilets can be hard to find, but many restaurants have 'family rooms' with toilet facilities.

See also the general advice for women travellers, p543.

TRANSPORT IN YEMEN

GETTING THERE & AWAY
Entering Yemen

Immigration is an uncomplicated procedure, but slow. If arriving by land, you'll be required to do all paperwork at the border crossing. Proceedings can take hours, particularly if you're with your own vehicle.

Air

Most international traffic arrives and departs from San'a airport. A few airlines, particularly from Middle Eastern countries, also use Aden. Work is currently under way on a new airport for San'a, which is scheduled to be completed by 2009.

Aden Airport (☎ 02-233999)
Al-Hudayda Airport (☎ 03-213254)
Ar-Rayyan Airport (☎ 05-354920)
San'a International Airport (☎ 01-345812)
Sayun Airport (☎ 05-842321)
Ta'izz Airport (☎ 05-218191)

Yemen's national carrier, **Yemenia** (☎ 01-232380; www.yemenia.com.ye; Hadda St, San'a), flies to dozens of destinations across the Middle East, Europe (including London, Paris and Rome), Africa and Asia. Yemenia has a reasonable safety record (see www.airsafe.com for details), though flights sometimes experience delays or cancellations (particularly during Ramadan and the haj pilgrimage), so reconfirmation is essential.

OTHER AIRLINES FLYING TO/FROM YEMEN

EgyptAir (MS; Map p458; ☎ 01-275061; www.egyptair .com.eg; Az-Zubayri St, San'a) Hub Cairo.
Emirates (EK; Map p458; ☎ 01-444442; www.emirates .com; Hadda St, San'a) Hub Dubai.
Gulf Air (GF; ☎ 01-440922; www.gulfairco.com; Hadda St, San'a) Hub Bahrain.
Lufthansa (LH; Map p458; ☎ 01-213400; www .lufthansa.com; Az-Zubayri St, San'a) Hub Frankfurt.
Qatar Airways (QR; Map p458; ☎ 01-506030; www .qatarairways.com; Hadda St, San'a) Hub Doha.

Royal Jordanian Airlines (RJ; Map p458; ☎ 01-446064; www.rja.com.jo; Hadda St, San'a) Hub Amman.
Saudi Arabian Airlines (SV; Map p458; ☎ 01-506574; www.saudiairlines.com; Az-Zubayri St, San'a) Hub Jeddah.
Syrian Air (RB; Map p458; ☎ 01-506020; www.syriaair .com; Hadda St, San'a) Hub Damascus.

Land
BORDER CROSSINGS
Though the border with Saudi Arabia is open to anyone with a visa, it's presently not possible for foreigners to cross the border. This is because of major security problems north of Sa'da leading to the whole area being closed to foreign tourists.

There are two standard border crossings for Oman, both of which are open to foreigners and neither of which present any major problems. Transport from Sayun tends to use the inland crossing at Makinat Shihan, while the coastal route uses the Hawf crossing. Whichever route you choose, the roads are brand new and in excellent condition and visas are available for most on the border. See p511 for further information.

See also information on visas and travel permits (p517) and additional information on border crossings (p547).

BUS
For Oman, buses travel direct from Sayun to Salalah or from Al-Ghayda direct to Salalah. Though it's possible to make the same journey in a series of shorter hops using shared taxis and buses, it will take much longer, cost more and, with very little to see en route, serve little purpose. Two buses a week leave Sayun (YR5000, 16 hours) and two a week leave from Al-Ghayda (YR4000, nine hours). For more information see p509 and p511.

CAR & MOTORCYCLE
The usual documentation is required for border crossings and must be valid for all countries you intend to visit. Crossing borders can be time-consuming (procedures can take between one and two hours). A 'road tax' of around US$55 is usually charged when crossing the Yemeni–Oman border in your own vehicle. Petrol stations are plentiful around the borders, and spare parts can normally be found. Note that unleaded petrol is unavailable in Yemen. See also p556 for information on road rules.

Sea
Although cargo boats sometimes connect Yemen (the ports of Aden, Al-Mukalla and Al-Hudayda principally) to ports on the Peninsula, as well as to Egypt, Eritrea and Sudan, there are currently no regular services or timetables, and finding a vessel willing to take a foreigner can prove very difficult.

One option is to try and persuade a *sambuq* owner to take you aboard, but again your fate will largely be decided by the will and whim of the captain. Note also that *sambuqs* do not have the best health and safety records! Speaking Arabic will considerably increase your chances. Be aware that voyages are generally hot, humid, uncomfortable and time-consuming. There are frequent *sambuqs* between Al-Makha and Djibouti, but many of these are involved in smuggling and recently a number of boats carrying Somali refugees have been attacked by the Yemeni navy, which has resulted in heavy loss of life. For the time being, this is not a safe way of arriving in or leaving Yemen.

Tours
Currently the vast majority of visitors to Yemen travel with a tour agency, and with the constantly changing security situation and travel-permit regulations, this is probably the best way to go. However, few tour operators outside the country offer tours to Yemen. Fortunately, there are a number of good local companies based in San'a that can help organise your trip (as much or as little as you want), from reserving an international flight to organising car hire and renting out full camping equipment.

The standard rate among travel agencies in San'a is US$60 per vehicle per day. This is for a large 4WD and also includes the driver's fee, his food and accommodation, petrol and 230km to 250km free mileage per day. The rate increases to US$75 per day for longer trips (ie more than 250km or about six hours' driving) and to US$100 per day for journeys along desert trails (eg Ma'rib to Wadi Hadramawt) that involve police escorts. Good discounts can usually be negotiated for longer trips.

Guides (costing from around US$30 to US$40 per day, including food and accommodation) speaking English, French, Ital-

---

SIGN & SOUND LANGUAGE

Few tour company drivers speak languages other than Arabic. If you must have one that speaks a language you can understand, request one well in advance of your trip. If you don't get one, don't despair. Most Yemeni drivers are exceptionally obliging, hardworking and eager to please. And you'll be amazed at how far you can get with signs and sounds!

---

ian, Spanish, German and Russian can also usually be organised.

Following is a list of some reputable agencies based in San'a.

Arabian Horizons Travel & Tourism (Map p458; ☎ 01-506007; horizon-tours@y.net.ye; Hadda St) Branches in Aden, as well as in the USA and Canada.

ATG (formerly YATA; Map p458; ☎ 01-441260; www .atg-yemen.com; just off Hadda St) Offers all the standard tours and specialises in diving (see p512).

FTI Yemen (Map p458; ☎ 01-253216; www.ftiyemen .com; Al-Qiada St) A slick professional outfit that can arrange almost any kind of tour almost anywhere in Yemen – including surfing tours in the remote east.

Marib Travel & Tourism (Map p458; ☎ 01-426833/8; www.marib-tours.com; Hadda St). A friendly and well-regarded tour company that values customer service and really goes out of its way to try and help. It can organise standard tours throughout the country as well as specialist trips, including diving in Suqutra, mountain hiking and travel for senior citizens. Highly recommended.

Radfan Agency Tours (Map pp460-1; ☎ 01-272231; fax 01-272231; Talha St) Specialises in hiking off the beaten track, including with camels.

Universal Travel & Tourism (Universal Touring Company; Map p458; ☎ 01-272861; www.universalyemen .com; off Midan at-Tahrir) The largest and oldest travel agency in Yemen, it offers all the usual tours, but specialises in cultural tours. It focuses its efforts on larger groups and there have recently been some complaints from individuals and small groups about the services they have received. There's an office at the airport (open 6am to midnight).

GETTING AROUND

For current travel restrictions outside the capital, see p517.

Air

The only airline offering domestic flights is the national carrier, **Yemenia** (☎ 01-232380; www.yemenia.com; ☉ usually 8am-1.30pm & 4-7pm Sat-Thu). It boasts a pretty extensive network.

See the Yemen country map (Map pp450–1) for Yemenia destinations (marked with an airport symbol).

Note that it's considerably cheaper to buy Yemenia tickets in Yemen through a Yemenia office rather than through a travel agency. For the cheapest fares, book flights well in advance. Yemenia offices can be found in all of Yemen's main towns, and accept Yemeni riyals, US dollars, euros and usually Amex, MasterCard and Visa credit cards.

Yemenia flights are prone to both delays and cancellations. Always reconfirm flights.

Bicycle

As longs as cyclists are reasonably fit (for mountainous terrain), self-sufficient (with lots of spare parts) and able to carry plenty of water, there's no reason not to bring a bike. Punctures are quite common, however, and you'll need to ride extremely defensively. Yemeni drivers aren't used to cyclists, and tend to 'bully' smaller traffic anyway. Make sure that your bike is registered in your passport upon arrival to avoid problems with customs on exiting the country.

Bus

Buses travel to almost all the larger towns (sometimes several a day), and services are pretty punctual and safe.

The longest-established bus company is **Yemitco** (Yemen International Transport Company; ☎ 01-275088; ☉ 5am-8pm, in the south 9am-1pm & 3-8pm Sat-Thu, 4-8pm Fri), which offers comfortable seats in air-conditioned buses. In the last couple of years it seems to be losing out to a multitude of newer companies and now generally only runs a reliable service in the most-populated central areas. The biggest of the rival companies is **General Land Transport** (☎ 01-281318), which also has smooth, comfortable buses that are often a little cheaper than Yemitco.

Yemitco has just one class, but some of the other private companies (such as General Land Transport) offer 1st- and 2nd-class on some services (though the difference in price is usually marginal). Yemitco services work out to be YR3 to YR3.50 per kilometre. Examples of fares include San'a to Aden (YR1400, six hours) and San'a to Al-Hudayda (YR1100, five hours).

You can usually buy tickets in advance, and on Friday and other public holidays this is highly recommended, particularly for longer journeys (when three days in advance is not too soon).

Car & Motorcycle

DRIVING LICENCE

An International Driving Permit is recommended, though not legally required. A driving licence from your country of origin is normally accepted by car-hire companies.

FUEL & SPARE PARTS

Although fuel is fairly widely available (still consider carrying spare fuel in remote parts), spare parts and repair shops are not. Unleaded petrol is unavailable. For general advice and some tips on desert driving, see p554.

HIRE

Most car-hire companies are based in San'a (see p466). Drivers must be over 21 (sometimes 25 years old), and have a valid driving licence from their own country. There's a US$200 deposit payable on all cars as a guarantee. Nowhere in Yemen rents motorbikes.

There are real advantages to hiring a car with a driver. It's safer, cheaper, more comfortable and more convenient. Additionally, a driver acts as navigator, mechanic, interpreter and sometimes guide. See p520 for tour companies that provide car and driver hire.

INSURANCE

Third-party insurance is mandatory and is usually included in car-hire prices – but always check. Rented vehicles cannot be taken out of the country.

ROAD CONDITIONS

In the last five years Yemen's road network has gone from fairly mediocre to something that would leave many Western nations green with envy. This is largely thanks to a huge upsurge in foreign investment, especially from the US government, which sees roads as an essential element in extending the central government's writ to even the most faraway areas. Even the furthest desert trails are starting to get a tarmac coating, and as long as you stick to established routes, it's now quite rare to need to switch into four-wheel drive.

ROAD HAZARDS

The main hazard when driving in Yemen is probably the Yemenis themselves, who demonstrate an almost admirable disregard for road rules, as well as for needless car 'accessories', such as mirrors and indicators. The lack of signposts (in any language) is another problem.

Other hazards include animals wandering onto the road and children playing on them. If you have to drive at night, be extra vigilant. Many vehicles have no lights.

ROAD RULES

Driving in Yemen is on the right side of the road. Seat belts are strongly advised, but are not legally required.

Local Transport

BUS

Minibuses (which run from 6am to around midnight) ply the streets of all the major towns. They're cheap (YR10 to YR30 for a hop), but unless you know exactly where they're heading, taxis are an easier, faster and certainly more comfortable option.

Taxi

In a shared taxi, short hops around town cost YR30 and for a cross-town contract taxi you'll need to negotiate, but Yemeni taxi drivers are generally more honest than most of the world's cabbies! A journey across San'a, for example, would rarely cost more than YR400.

SHARED TAXI

Connecting all the main towns and villages, and operating very much like buses, are the shared taxis (known as *bijou*). Although rarely more comfortable than buses, they tend to be faster, and leave at more convenient times and more frequently. However, they only leave when full, so you can be in for a long wait. When travelling to more remote places, try and catch the first departure.

Fares are fixed (and generally cost about the same as the buses), and payment is made before the journey. Passengers on long-distance trips are often required to write their names and nationalities on a passenger list (English is OK). Foreigners must show their travel permit at each checkpoint.

Some travellers (particularly women) prefer to pay for the two front seats; you'll be a lot more comfortable if you do.

CONTRACT TAXI
Taxis can also be contracted between cities and towns. The word 'special' is commonly used by drivers to describe contracted taxis. To contract your own taxi, you'll need to

pay for all the seats (usually six or 10), so to calculate the fare, multiply the prices quoted for shared taxis in this book.

MOTORCYCLE TAXI
If you want to beat the traffic in the larger towns, you can always hop on the back of a motorbike taxi (YR100 to YR250 depending on the length of the 'hop').

Arabian Peninsula Directory

CONTENTS

The following chapter gives the lowdown on all things practical in the region, and is designed to complement the individual country chapters. It makes a good place to start your search for information (subjects are organised alphabetically), before referring to individual countries for more specific details.

ACCOMMODATION

Throughout the book accommodation options are listed in the following order: budget, midrange and top end, and from cheapest to most expensive within each category. In this book a single/double with bathroom means a room for one/two people with an en suite bathroom. If the bathroom is outside the room, it's 'shared'.

During local holiday periods (particularly over *eid*, the Islamic feast) and popular festivals (such as the shopping festivals in Dubai and Kuwait), as well as Western holidays (Christmas and New Year) and major fixtures (like the Dubai Rugby Sevens), travellers should book well in advance.

Camping

Except in Saudi Arabia's Asir National Park (see p342) and at Ras al-Jinz (see p221) in Oman, there are no specially designated camping areas, although there are organised and generally quite expensive, desert camps in Khor al-Adaid, Qatar (p287), and Sharqiya (Wahiba) Sands, Oman (p225). Wild camping (without any facilities) is one of the highlights of the region, providing you have your own transport and bring all your own equipment. It is very popular among expats, tour groups and Arab families (particularly in Bahrain and Kuwait, where camping is becoming an environmental hazard). It is very important to camp discreetly (away from towns or villages) and responsibly by taking litter away with you and avoiding turtle beaches. Turtle beaches can be identified by the presence of large pits at the top of the tide line.

Hostels

Youth hostels aren't exactly abundant on the Peninsula. Saudi Arabia boasts nine (open to men only) hostels and the United Arab Emirates (UAE) two. All are Hostelling International (HI) members. Cards are required for Saudi Arabian hostels and will secure 50% discounts on prices in the

---

BOOKING ONLINE

For more accommodation reviews and recommendations by Lonely Planet authors, check out the online booking service at www.lonelyplanet.com. You'll find the lowdown on the best places to stay. Reviews are thorough and independent. Best of all, you can book online.

UAE. All bedding is supplied. Hostels cost US$2.50 to US$11 per person per night, depending on whether you're eligible for discounts.

Hotels

As the region is still far from becoming a backpackers' beat, and as local Arabs traditionally stay with relatives when they travel, budget accommodation can be hard to find.

Prices of hotels in the Peninsula are usually high. Bar Yemen, you'll be hard-pressed to find habitable cheap accommodation in any of the Peninsula cities. Outside the cities, there are generally few options to choose from. The good news is that standards are also high. It's rare to find rooms even in the cheapest category that lack air-conditioning, hot water, a telephone and a fridge. Tellingly, a TV (usually with satellite channels, including BBC and CNN) seems to be considered a basic amenity everywhere (even when a bathroom is not).

Prices reflect amenities: US$40 is about the minimum for budget rooms (bar hostels), US$125 to US$175 for midrange (this range has the biggest selection) and from around US$200 for top-end hotels. Of course you can pay many hundreds or even thousands of dollars to stay at the region's star-spangled hotels, such as Burj al-Arab (p389) in Dubai, Emirates Palace (p422) in Abu Dhabi or the Al-Husn Hotel (p212) near Muscat. Competition is often high, however, and it's well worth trying to negotiate discounts, particularly in the low season.

Yemen is the Peninsula's poor relation and its hotels are very cheap: starting from around US$8/14/50 for budget/midrange/top-end accommodation, though several big-dollar, top-end options can also be found.

For those travelling on a tight budget, dormitory-style accommodation is available in some towns, though it's usually very basic, with filthy dorms and worse bathrooms. Such accommodation isn't really an option for women (unless you rent the whole room for yourself). You may even be turned way, or barred outright (as at hostels in Saudi Arabia).

Budget hotel options can normally be found in the souq areas of towns. Increasingly, in some cities, prostitutes (generally from the ex-Soviet Union, Eastern Europe and East Africa) have set up shop and actively ply their trade in these areas. Travellers of both sexes should be aware of this, particularly women travelling alone.

Amenities in the top-end hotels are good and include outdoor pools, business facilities and health centres. Most midrange and all top-end hotels have restaurants. Many serve a wide variety of high-quality food.

In Peninsula countries where restrictions on alcohol apply, drinking is often only officially permitted in the hotels (usually midrange to top end), where bars and nightclubs serving alcohol can be found. Thus hotels often offer the best (or only) entertainment in town for the traveller. Often a second, less than salubrious 'local' bar is attached, which attracts large numbers of rowdy (usually male) merrymakers.

Rental Accommodation

Rental accommodation (most often unfurnished) can usually be found in all the major Peninsula cities, and ranges from modest, purpose-built flats to attractive villas and sumptuous hotel annexes.

Expats on the Peninsula usually opt for one of three types accommodation: a villa (often with garden); an apartment block (often with communal swimming pool and health club); or a residency within a 'compound' (including communal pool, health or sports club, restaurant, children's play park, shops – usually selling Western foods – and ball courts).

Rental accommodation is usually advertised in local English-language newspapers. Embassies, cultural centres, companies and colleagues (if you're working) are another useful source of information. Relocation consultants as well as estate agents can be found in the telephone directories of most countries.

Most employers organise temporary accommodation until employees find their own accommodation. Many of the larger, international companies have a good range of accommodation available for employees on their books.

When looking for accommodation, it's worth bearing the following in mind: make sure each room has some form of air-conditioning; check whether maintenance of shared areas of a compound are included in the rent; opt for properties with mains water as opposed to water delivered by bowser; and look for properties with off-road, shaded parking to protect your car from the sun.

Note that non-Gulf Cooperation Council (GCC) foreigners are not allowed to own property in the Peninsula.

Resorts

With miles of unspoilt coastline on two seas, it's surprising that the concept of seaside resort is only just catching on. Existing resorts range from basic Robinson Crusoe–style constructions (found in Al-Khawkha on Yemen's Red Sea) to sumptuous palace-hotels with underwater restaurants (such as Burj al-Arab in Dubai). Many offer a good variety of water sports and activities, from diving and water-skiing to gentler activities, such as boat trips and fun rides for kids.

ACTIVITIES

Although the Peninsula is a region little known for its activities, it has exceptional potential for more explorative and 'pioneering' activities. The wilderness areas of Oman, Yemen and Saudi, in particular, invite all manner of outdoor pursuits, and the Arabian and Red Seas offer some of the best diving and snorkelling in the world. For more details on all the activities listed below, see Activities in the Directory section of individual countries.

Sporting facilities are quite well developed in most countries on the Peninsula (and particularly in Qatar). If your hotel doesn't stretch to health and sports clubs (and most top-end hotels do), you can usually use the public health and sporting clubs and complexes found in the larger towns of the 'richer' countries. An easy way to keep fit for all visitors to the Peninsula is to pack some running shoes: almost all the seaboard cities of the region have beautiful, landscaped corniches intended for walking, jogging or just catching the breeze.

If on your Peninsula travels the hot weather gets to you, then take heart: for some curious reason, all the countries of the Gulf have an ice-rink! See the boxed text, p204.

Desert Safaris & 4WD Exploration

The Peninsula's most famous topographical feature is the desert, and it comes in several shapes and sizes, each of which offers a different type of activity. There are sand dunes, wonderful for camel rides and sand boarding; rocky plains, giving the best opportunity for spotting wildlife (see Wildlife Watching, p528); and arid mountains and water-catching wadis, where swimming, hiking routes, climbing and caving opportunities are beginning to develop.

Excursions to any of these environments in 4WD vehicles are a long-established pastime among Peninsula Arabs, as well as expats and tour groups. Apart from the challenge of driving and navigating off-road, and the attractions of magnificent scenery, these excursions also offer the chance to see a way of life that is fast disappearing. Indeed, the opportunity to engage with Peninsula Bedu, or the inhabitants of remote, terraced villages, and see how they have refined life under the harshest of circumstances, is a rare privilege.

Be aware that it requires both skill and experience to drive in the desert and it's essential that you're properly equipped, both for the road and for the weather. See the advice and tips offered in the boxed text, p554. In the interests of minimising harmful effects on the environment, it's very important to stick to established off-road tracks and avoid cutting new paths across the desert (see boxed text, p554). In parts of Dhofar (southern Oman) and Yemen, and to a lesser extent in Kuwait, unexploded ordinance is an added incentive to keep to the tracks.

Oman, the UAE and Yemen all offer activities in the desert (see Activities in those chapters for details). Local tour operators can help you organise trips ranging from a short camel ride to expeditions that map uncharted cave systems.

Diving & Snorkelling

The Red Sea is one of the world's top diving sites, teeming with a huge variety of marine life and supported by a magical reef system. Although facilities and 'après-dive' on the Peninsula side of the sea are limited (to say the least), there is the joy of having the pristine reefs to yourself. Arabian Sea diving sites are also good. Because water

---

RESPONSIBLE DIVING & SNORKELLING

Please consider the following tips when diving, and help preserve the ecology and beauty of the Peninsula's reefs:

- Avoid touching or standing on living marine organisms or dragging equipment across the reef. Polyps can be damaged by even the gentlest contact.
- Be conscious of your fins. Even without contact, the surge from fin strokes near the reef can damage delicate organisms. Take care not to kick up clouds of sand, which can smother organisms.
- Practise and maintain proper buoyancy control. Major damage is done by divers descending too fast and colliding with the reef.
- Resist the temptation to collect or buy corals or shells, or to loot marine archaeological sites (particularly shipwrecks).
- Ensure that you take home all your rubbish and remove any litter you may find. Plastics in particular are a serious threat to marine life (turtles often ingest plastic bags, mistaking them for jellyfish).
- Minimise your disturbance of marine animals. Do not feed the fish. Never ride on the backs of turtles.

---

temperatures are lower, there is less coral life, but fish life is profuse.

Many diving opportunities are available throughout the region, although for the best experience balanced against the easiest access, Oman is the frontrunner. Most of the region's diving centres offer beginner diving courses (with either PADI, CMAS or NAUI among others) that take between four to five days and cost US$300 to US$450, depending on the operator and location. A good way of trying out diving before committing to a full course is a 'try dive' (or 'introductory dive'), which costs from around US$80, including all equipment.

For those already certified, a day's diving (two to three dives), including all equipment, costs US$50 to US$100. Divers who want to find their own dive site can hire full equipment from dive centres for around US$25. In some places basic underwater cameras can also be hired. For those on a budget, or pushed for time, snorkelling can still give you an excellent idea of life on the reef. Snorkelling gear usually costs around US$6 to US$10 per day.

Fishing

Fishermen's boats (found throughout the Peninsula) can often be hired by the hour or half/full day for a very reasonable fee. They usually come complete with the fisherman! This is a great advantage to finding the best shoals or haunts of something edible, with some snorkelling and swimming thrown in.

Deep-sea fishing is also possible. Trips need to be booked in advance and usually cost around US$400 per day for two people, including all equipment. Common catches include yellow-fin tuna (which can weigh between 25kg and 60kg), sail fish, barracuda and shark.

Fishing licences are not needed on the Peninsula, but in some countries you may have to register longer boat trips with the local coastguard.

Golf

Despite the blistering heat and chronic water shortages, golf has caught on in a big way in some of the Peninsula countries, including Bahrain, Qatar and particularly the UAE. Today the region boasts several world-class courses. Many more are planned for the future, including at least four in Dubai alone and two in Muscat.

Hammams

Better known in the West as the 'Turkish bath', the *hammam* is one of the great sensual indulgences of the Middle East. Whether you submit to a massage or not (and there's nothing quite like it after days spent on the road), a session in the steam room is worthwhile, if only for a peek at the architecture of some *hammams*, terrific contact with locals and an insight into daily local life.

Although nothing like as popular, famous or indulgent as the baths of Turkey and Syria, *hammams* can be found in many cities and towns of the Peninsula. Just ask at your hotel for a local recommendation.

Trekking

The Peninsula is a fantastic place for wild trekking, particularly in the mountains of Oman, Yemen and Saudi Arabia. Mostly the activity is down to the initiative of the traveller and involves buying a trekking guide in-country, packing more water than you think you'll need, and striking out alone. Tour companies, however, are increasingly able to tailor trips for hikers and some even cater for tour groups. Not wanting to be left behind in the bid to win tourists, some countries (Oman in particular) have mapped walking routes through some of the region's wildest territory.

Considering the Peninsula's particular climatic conditions, the following precautions are worth noting:

- Budget for at least 4L of water per person per day. In the heat of summer (when temperatures can exceed 40°C) hiking can be extremely dangerous. Most hikers will go through 1L of water every hour. Even in the cooler months your main issue will be water.
- Wear light-coloured and lightweight clothing; use a good sunscreen (at least UV Protection Factor 30) and never set off without a hat that shelters your neck and face from direct sunlight. A light, semitransparent veil is useful to protect eyes, nose, mouth and ears from blowing sand and dust.
- Rise before the sun and hike until the heat becomes oppressive. If it's very hot, rest through the heat of midday and begin again after 3pm. During the hotter months consider timing your hike with the full moon, which will allow walking at night.
- Keep an eye on the weather when following wadis. Rain can suddenly render dry wadis impassable and very dangerous. Never camp in wadis or canyons, and always keep to higher ground whenever there's a risk of flash flooding.

Water Sports

The Peninsula boasts long stretches of beautiful, sandy beaches. As such, one would imagine that water sports were a highly developed activity in the region. This in fact is not the case, as for half the year the beach is too hot to stand on, the sea too thick to swim in and the air suffocatingly humid. Added to the climate, local people have traditionally regarded the coast and the sea as a place of work (for fishing, sardine drying, rock collecting). Times are changing, however, and now most seaboard cities on the Peninsula, and some rather exclusive resorts beyond the cities, offer opportunities for sea swimming, sailing, windsurfing, even jet-skiing, particularly in the UAE, where the tourist industry is working hard to promote the country as a winter 'sun and sea' destination.

Many water-sports facilities are attached to either big hotels or private clubs and are not always accessible to nonguests and nonmembers. That said, some hotels are starting to accept short-stay visitors and are usually happy to rent out equipment to guests.

Beaches are generally clean and, save for a very few exceptions – such as in the UAE, where rip tides, especially around Dubai, claim one or two lives each year, and during the turbulent summer *khareef* (monsoon) season in southern Oman – the seas are safe.

The Peninsula boasts many yacht clubs and marinas along its coastline, where everything from diminutive floating dinghies to the famous floating Arab gin palaces and million-dollar power boats can be found. A range of boating activities are possible, from the hiring of small fishing vessels for swimming, snorkelling and picnicking trips, to organised harbour cruises in the Gulf cities, and sailing lessons and crewing for those on an extended stay.

Wildlife Watching

One of the exceptional opportunities of travelling to countries that are seldom visited is the chance to see nature in the raw. The Arabian Peninsula, which is comprised mostly of desert, may seem like an odd place to see wildlife, but it is far from barren land (see boxed text, p104) and offers some exceptional opportunities for the naturalist.

As the Peninsula straddles important migration routes, bird-watching opportunities are legion, from watching raptors scale the escarpments of the Asir in Saudi and rare sightings of the endangered Houbara bustard in the central Peninsula plains, to following the mass migrations of Socotra cormorants on the Hawar Islands in Bahrain and sand grouse in Oman.

Turtles occur along the entire Arabian Sea coast, often in global proportions and night-time excursions can be made to world-important nesting sites, especially in Oman (see p221). Dugongs, whales and easily spotted dolphins are an added joy of the region, and you don't have to be an expert to enjoy the enormous variety of shells along the coasts of the Peninsula.

Animals, and especially mammals, are not as easy to spot, but there are several opportunities for seeing oryx and gazelle in their natural habitat, particularly in Oman, together with fox, hedgehog and gerbil.

More and more tour companies are beginning to offer tailor-made tours around specialist wildlife interests, including botany and geology. Some even offer the chance to monitor the activities of endangered species like leopard, as part of scientific programmes. See also www.responsibletravel .com for information regarding responsible travel.

BUSINESS HOURS

Business hours vary from country to country and sometimes from region to region within a country (depending on climatic differences, such as those in highland/lowland Yemen). They also vary from institution to institution (see the individual country chapters for more details).

An added complication is that traditionally the 'weekend' in the Peninsula used to be Thursday and Friday. Now, in Bahrain, Kuwait, Qatar and the UAE, the weekend has shifted to Friday and Saturday with Oman rumoured to follow suit.

In practical terms this means that Thursday and Friday are holidays for all government offices. Thursday is a holiday for most banks and embassies in Saudi, Yemen and Oman. Saturday is a holiday for most banks and embassies in the other countries. Shops stay open for six days a week in all countries

---

OPEN SESAME

Where possible throughout this book we have given the opening times of places of interest. The information is usually taken from notices posted at the sites. However, often the reality on the ground is that sites open pretty much when the gate-guard feels like it. On a good day he'll be there an hour early, on a bad day he won't turn up at all. Who can blame him when in little-touristed sites, like some of those in Yemen or Oman, he may not see a visitor for days, anyway? All opening hours must be prefaced, therefore, with a hopeful *insha'allah* (God willing)!

---

and many open for a limited period on Friday evening too.

Bank opening hours vary throughout the region, but usually operate from 8am or 9am to noon or 1pm, either five or six days a week. Some reopen for a couple of hours in the afternoon. Foreign-exchange facilities usually keep longer hours.

Hours also vary according to the season or month. All government offices work shorter hours during Ramadan (the month-long fast for Muslims) and businesses tend to open much later and close earlier, or else not open at all during the day but remain open for much of the night. Note that many restaurants close during the day throughout Ramadan – or even remain closed for the month.

One important thing to remember when travelling in the Arabian Peninsula is that you can't rely on many tourist sites opening as prescribed (see boxed text, above). If you're determined to see a particular museum or other attraction and haven't time to waste, it's worth calling ahead to make sure it's open as stated. That, alas, is still no guarantee!

CHILDREN

Taking the kids certainly adds another dimension to a trip to the Peninsula. Children are often made a big fuss of and are allowed liberties unthinkable in Western countries. Travelling with children can help break the ice and permit closer contact with local people. However, there are a few provisos that should be kept in mind.

It's a good idea to avoid travel during the summer months, when the extreme heat can be debilitating for children, particularly babies.

Cleanliness may be another problem when travelling with infants. It's obviously impractical to carry more than about half a dozen washable nappies with you, but disposable ones are not always easy to come by (though they're increasingly available in the larger cities). Infant formula is widely available, however, as is bottled water.

In top-end and some midrange hotels, children can usually share their parents' room for no extra charge. Extra beds or cots are normally available. High chairs are often only available in top-end restaurants.

There are few sophisticated children-oriented entertainments outside of the big cities, but a beach is never too far away, and there are often parks containing children's play areas (including swings and slides) even in small towns. In some cities, babysitting services are also available.

See 'For Children' sections listed under each capital city, for information on interesting diversions.

For more comprehensive advice on the dos and don'ts of taking the kids see Lonely Planet's *Travel with Children* by Cathy Lanigan.

CLIMATE CHARTS

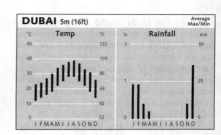

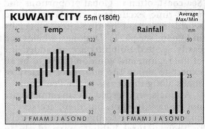

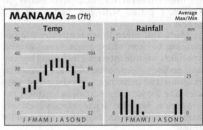

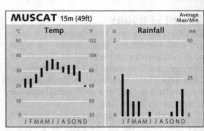

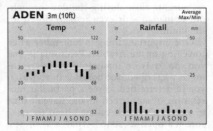

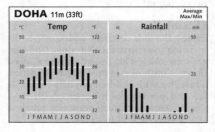

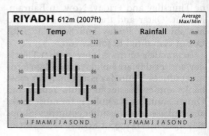

COURSES

The Arabian Peninsula is not the most obvious place to come to learn a skill as a traveller, as there is relatively little tourist-related activity in the region. If you are planning a longer stay, however, or are planning to be expatriate in the region, there are literally dozens of opportunities from learning to line dance in Muscat, public speaking in the cities of the Gulf, to belly dancing in Abu Dhabi.

It is possible on a longer-term stay to learn Arabic at various institutes and colleges throughout the region. Courses generally focus on Classical Arabic (as opposed to local dialect) and vary between six and 10 weeks, with costs starting at US$200.

ARABIC: A COMMON LANGUAGE?

There is nothing more disparaging than polishing up your best phrases in Arabic and having them returned to you by the well-meaning recipient with a crit sheet: 'That was good, but you could have said it this way' is a favourite response, and another is, 'Ah, so you're speaking Arabic, that's great, but that's not how we say it here!' After returning a full volley of greetings (some of which can last up to five minutes) in Arabic, there's then the dismal moment when your companion turns to the main body of the conversation – in English. After a few Arabic courses and endless failed attempts to practise the language, all but the most determined of linguists admit defeat. In short, one has to conclude that learning Arabic in Arabia is neither easy nor encouraged.

Inevitably one begins to wonder whether there's some kind of cultural conspiracy involved. Many people in the region are regretful that their higher studies (especially in health care) are conducted through the medium of English. They regret that the language of the internet is mostly English. They regret too that advertising often involves untranslatable English words and phrases. If you don't speak English, there's a sense that you're missing out on international debate. With the adoption of English at so many different levels, there's the suspicion that a degree of cultural persuasion or even propaganda is subliminally present. Some even suspect the spread of the English language as being part and parcel of a general relaxing of rigid moral codes in the region. Whether or not this is justified, the suspicion of 'cultural colonialism' may be one reason why Arabic people are reluctant to expose their own language to foreign tongues. It raises sensitive questions. Should foreigners and infidels be let loose on the holy language of the Quran? Can language be subverted by meddling foreigners?

A more likely explanation is that Arabic itself is not the common language of the Peninsula that one might expect. Firstly, each country, each region within each country even, has its own dialect. This can pose substantial problems for one national trying to understand another. Secondly, not all Arabs speak Arabic as their mother tongue. In Oman, for example, thanks to their former empires and trading partners, many of them speak Swahili or Baluchi, and some tribespeople speak linguistically unrelated tongues like Kumzari (a mixture of all-sorts) or Jibbali, the arcane 'Language of the Birds'. Thirdly, a considerable number of people living on the Peninsula (over half the population in Qatar) are not Arab. Indeed, most travellers are more likely to come across Hindi, Urdu, Malayalam or Tagalog among the souqs, tour operators, hotels and restaurants in the region than they are Arabic.

Like it or not, English has become the language of cultural and commercial exchange in the region and the younger generation is particularly keen to acquire the basics. Drive up any wadi, ride to any Bedouin settlement and you're sure to hear a stream of 'how-are-yous' following your progress.

So does that mean as a traveller you shouldn't even try to respond in kind? Not at all. Learning Arabic opens windows onto elements of a culture that finds no translation and unlocks the door to meaningful cross-cultural relationships. In fact, ever acquiring a few words gives some interesting cultural insights – like the term *insha'allah* (God willing) and the whole concept of fatalism that lurks behind it, or *mash'allah* (the closest English translation is 'God has willed it'), and the protection from the evil eye that this phrase affords. If nothing else, it'll explain why when you say 'thank you', you won't actually receive anything: *shukran* (thanks in Arabic) usually means 'no thanks'. Never mind opening doors and windows, that one's a cultural minefield!

Some schools additionally offer courses in 'Islamic studies', as well as cultural courses. See Courses in the country chapters and capital city sections for more details.

CUSTOMS

Customs regulations vary from country to country, but in most cases they don't differ significantly from those in the West.

The most important restriction to bear in mind is that it is strictly forbidden to take alcohol into dry regions (Kuwait, Qatar, Sharjah, Abu Dhabi and Saudi Arabia). Alcohol can only be taken into Oman by air. If you're caught attempting to smuggle in even small quantities of alcohol, punishments range from deportation and fines to imprisonment. In most other countries, foreigners (but not Muslims) are permitted a small duty-free allowance.

Those caught in possession of drugs (including ecstasy, amphetamines, cannabis and cocaine) can face the death penalty, which in Saudi Arabia, with its policy of zero tolerance, means what it says. Note that syringes and needles, and some medicinal drugs are also banned (such as tranquillisers and even some antidepressants and sleeping pills), unless you have a doctor's prescription to prove that you need them.

Video cassettes and DVDs are a sensitive subject in Peninsula countries. Censors may well want to examine tapes and then allow you to collect them after a few days. Other custom taboos include pork products (though some countries make allowances for foreigners) and material construed as 'incendiary' (such as books critical of Islam, Peninsula governments or their countries).

There are no restrictions on the import and export of money (in any currency) in and out of Peninsula countries.

All luggage is x-rayed and sometimes opened too. That said, with greater numbers of tourists arriving and in the drive to appear more tourist-friendly, many of the old customs nightmares (like long queues while officials check the contents of your soap box) are things of the past.

See Customs under the directories of individual countries for details, and particularly the boxed text on p362, for the trials and tribulations of Saudi customs.

DANGERS & ANNOYANCES

The Arabian Peninsula has a historical reputation for being a dangerous place, whether for political turmoil, the emergence of Islamic fundamentalism or, more recently, the threat of terrorism. However, the trouble spots are usually well defined, and as long as you keep track of political developments, you are unlikely to come to any harm.

In Saudi Arabia a spate of Al-Qaeda bombings and threats (directed specifically at Westerners) in 2004 was a serious cause for concern. However, the authorities are proving both determined and relatively successful in combating the terrorism threat. Similarly, the hostage threat in Yemen appears to have abated with the authorities threatening zero tolerance of anyone caught messing with the returning tourist trade.

Politics aside, the Peninsula is actually a very safe place compared with much of the West (see boxed text, opposite). The crime rate is extremely low, with the Peninsula boasting one of the lowest average crime rates in the world, and more often than not foreign immigrants (arriving in the Peninsula since the 1970s) turn out to be the

---

GOVERNMENT TRAVEL ADVICE

For info on what's new, as well as updated safety reports, check these websites.

The US State Department's **Bureau of Consular Affairs** (www.travel.state.gov) offers periodically updated Consular Information Sheets, which include entry requirements, medical facilities, crime information and other topics. However, these err heavily on the side of caution and are often out of date.

British Foreign Office travel advisories can be obtained from the **Travel Advice Unit** (☎ 020-7270 4129; www.fco.gov.uk/travel; Foreign & Commonwealth Office, Room 605, Clive House, Petty France, London SW1H 9HD). Regularly updated Foreign Office travel advice is also displayed on BBC2 Ceefax teletext pages pp 564 ff.

Australians can ring the **Department of Foreign Affairs and Trade** (☎ 02-6261 3305) in Canberra for advisories, or visit the **Consular Travel Advice** (www.dfat.gov.au /travel) website.

IS IT SAFE?

Safety is a subjective topic. As far as security in the Peninsula is concerned, most people's perceptions are shaped by the continual news stories of Islamist fundamentalism, terrorism and bombings. It's a picture that bears little relation to reality. Interestingly, Arabs travelling to the US share similar concerns, bearing in mind Al-Jazeera reports of Guantanamo Bay and thinking of *Kill Bill*. Needless to say, day-to-day life in the Peninsula revolves around violence about as often as it does in Wyoming.

Fortunately, the people of the Middle East are ready and willing to distinguish between foreign governments and their policies, and foreign travellers. You might receive the occasional question about politics, but you'll never be held personally accountable. Keep abreast of current events, visit your embassy for travel advice if you're feeling cautious, but otherwise, just go.

---

perpetrators. One reader calculated that he was 97 times more likely to be robbed or killed in his home town (Kansas City, USA) than in San'a, Yemen's capital! That doesn't mean to say you should take unnecessary risks, but it does mean you don't have to worry unduly about mugging and scams designed to part you from your goods.

See the individual country chapters for country-specific dangers and annoyances, as well as Road Hazards, p556.

Climate

The most major hazard of the region is undoubtedly the weather. At any time of year, the high temperatures of midday can quickly lead to heat exhaustion, sun stroke and serious burns. If you are travelling in the summer, breaking down on an empty road without water can literally be life-threatening. You should bear this in mind when planning a trip outside urban areas and think twice about travelling alone.

Avoiding problems is largely a matter of common sense: always carry more water than you think you'll need; cover your head and neck; wear sunglasses; cover up, especially between 11am and 3pm; and avoid too much activity in the summer months – in other words, do as the locals do!

Swimming

The waters of the Red Sea and the northern part of the Arabian Sea are usually calm and safe for swimming and paddling. During the summer in eastern and southern Oman (July to September) and on the northern coast of Yemen, however, huge swells occur making, swimming a very dangerous activity. Every year there are casualties associated with the strong tides and powerful undercurrents. On some stretches of the normally quieter Gulf and Red Sea coasts, lifeguards using internationally recognised flags patrol the beach at weekends.

Litter affects many public beaches, despite the best efforts of local authorities, and tar can be a nuisance on wild beaches, released from irresponsible tankers. The practice is illegal but hard to police.

Most wild beaches are free from pollution and are safe for paddling and swimming. It's important to beware of natural hazards, though, including stone fish (with a highly venomous sting), stingrays and sometimes jellyfish (that deliver a fairly innocuous but persistent sting). These problems can be avoided by wearing shoes and a T-shirt when swimming (also useful against sunburn).

Sharks are common but only very rare incidents of aggressive behaviour have been reported and generally in predictable circumstances (such as in waters where fishermen are gutting fish).

On beaches, foreign women may attract unwanted attention from young Arab males. Generally, the more conservative your swimwear the less attention you'll attract and the more comfortable you'll feel. In some countries 'family beaches' are reserved for females and boys under 10 years.

Note that topless or nude sun bathing on the beaches or in wadi areas is strictly forbidden on the Peninsula; those who flout this law are liable to be arrested, as well as giving grave offense to anyone who chances to see them. Nothing causes more resentment among traditional communities than the behaviour of the few tourists who can't keep their clothes on.

DISCOUNT CARDS

Unfortunately, student, youth and senior citizens cards are of little use anywhere on the Peninsula, though hostelling cards do secure discounts (see p524).

ELECTRICITY

Beware of attaching the wrong appliance to the wrong supply (say a 110V appliance to a 220V outlet) and protect electrical equipment from power surges. See the table below for specific country voltages and plug styles.

Country	Voltage	Plug
Bahrain	220 to 240	3-pin UK style
Kuwait	220 to 240	2- & 3-pin UK style
Oman	220 to 240	3-pin UK style
Qatar	220 to 240	3-pin UK style
Saudi Arabia	220 & 110*	2- & 3-pin UK style
UAE	220 to 240	3-pin UK style
Yemen	220 to 240	3-pin UK style

* Both 220V and 110V are found at various places in the Kingdom, but the latter is more widespread.

EMBASSIES & CONSULATES

Embassies are a fairly good, if somewhat cautious and at times alarmist, source of information on current hotspots and dangers. Many embassies advise travellers to register with them upon arrival, especially if you're staying in the country for an extended period: if you should disappear, have a serious accident, or suddenly need to be evacuated from the country, you will at least be in a better position to receive help.

For the addresses and contact details of embassies and consulates both abroad and in the Peninsula, see Embassies & Consulates in the Directory of the individual country chapters.

GAY & LESBIAN TRAVELLERS

Homosexual practices are illegal in all of the Peninsula countries. Under Sharia'a (Islamic) law, (see p536) in some countries homosexuality incurs the death penalty (though punishment usually ranges from flogging to imprisonment or deportation). In other countries infractions solicit fines and/or imprisonment.

Westerners are unlikely to encounter outright prejudice or harassment so long as they remain discreet. However, this may well change if you become involved with a local. Room sharing is generally not a problem (it will be assumed that you're economising). Condoms are fairly widely available, though may be limited in selection. You're advised to bring your own supply.

For more information on attitudes to gay and lesbian travellers on the Peninsula (and recommendations of bars and hotels), see the *Spartacus International Gay Guide*.

HOLIDAYS

All Peninsula countries observe the main Islamic holidays listed below. Countries with a major Shiite population also observe Ashura. Some of the Peninsula countries also observe the Gregorian New Year (1 January). Every state additionally has its own national days and other public holidays – for details refer to the individual country chapters.

Islamic New Year Also known as Ras as-Sana, it literally means 'the head of the year'.

Prophet's Birthday Known as Moulid an-Nabi, it's 'the feast of the Prophet'.

ISLAMIC CALENDAR

Although most secular activities and day-to-day life are planned in the Peninsula according to the Gregorian calendar (the Western system), all Islamic holidays are calculated according to the Muslim calendar. In Saudi Arabia, however, the Muslim calendar is the principal one used. For visitors this can cause confusion (such as when trying to decipher official documents, including the date of expiry of travel permits and visa). Calendars showing parallel systems are available.

The Muslim year is based on the lunar cycle and is divided into 12 lunar months, each with 29 or 30 days. Consequently, the Muslim year is 10 or 11 days shorter than the Christian solar year, and the Muslim festivals gradually move around our year, completing the cycle in roughly 33 years.

Year zero in the Muslim calendar was when Mohammed and his followers fled from Mecca to Medina (AD 622 in the Christian calendar). This Hejira, or migration, is taken to mark the start of the new Muslim era, much as Christ's birth marks year zero in the Christian calendar. Just as BC denotes 'Before Christ', so AH denotes 'After Hejira'.

ISLAMIC HOLIDAYS 2007–2012

It often comes as some surprise that dates of Islamic holidays are not fixed on a particular day each year, nor are they wholly predictable. This is because dates are dependent on moon sightings and consequently may occur a day later, but not generally earlier, than listed. Not all countries spot the moon on the same day for some reason (cloud cover doesn't count), so regional differences between countries occur each year. In fact, speculation regarding whether or not tomorrow will bring *eid* is the subject of great public debate and private expat exasperation. The following is therefore to be treated as a guide only!

Year Hejira	New Year	Prophet's Birthday	Ashura	Ramadan Begins	Eid al-Fitr	Eid al-Adha
1428	21 Jan 2007	31 Mar 2007	29 Jan 2007	13 Sep 2007	13 Oct 2007	20 Dec 2007
1429	10 Jan 2008	20 Mar 2008	19 Jan 2008	2 Sep 2008	2 Oct 2008	9 Dec 2008
1430	1 Jan 2009	9 Mar 2009	9 Jan 2009	23 Aug 2009	22 Sep 2009	30 Nov 2009
1431	20 Dec 2009	28 Feb 2010	31 Dec 2009	13 Aug 2010	12 Sep 2010	20 Nov 2010
1432	9 Dec 2010	18 Feb 2010	20 Dec 2010	3 Aug 2011	2 Sep 2011	9 Nov 2011
1433	30 Nov 2011	7 Feb 2011	10 Dec 2011	23 Jul 2012	22 Aug 2012	30 Oct 2012
1435	19 Nov 2012	28 Jan 2012	9 Dec 2012	12 Jul 2013	11 Jul 2013	19 Oct 2013

Ashura The anniversary of the martyrdom of Hussein, the third *imam* (religious teacher) of the Shiites.

Ramadan The ninth month of the Muslim calendar, this is when Muslims fast during daylight hours. How strictly the fast is observed depends on the country, but most Muslims conform to some extent. Foreigners are not expected to follow suit, but it is considered very bad form to smoke, drink or eat (including gum-chewing) in public during Ramadan. Hotels make provision for guests by erecting screens for discreet dining. In the more strictly Islamic countries, disrespecting the fast can land you in serious trouble, especially in Saudi Arabia, where jail sentences are handed out to anyone seen so much as smoking during daylight hours. Business hours tend to become more erratic and usually shorter, and in out-of-the-way places you may find it hard to find a restaurant open before nightfall. As the sun sets each day, the fast is broken with something light (like dates and *laban*) before prayers. Then comes *iftar* (breakfast), at which enough food is usually consumed to compensate for the previous hours of abstinence. People then rise again before dawn to prepare a meal to support them throughout the day.

Eid al-Fitr The festivities mark the end of Ramadan fasting; the celebrations last for three days and are a time of family feasting and visiting.

Eid al-Adha This feast marks the time that Muslims make the pilgrimage to Mecca.

INSURANCE

Travel insurance covering accidents and medical problems is strongly advised, particularly as road traffic accidents are a major hazard of the region and problems can easily occur if visiting the desert (particularly on off-road excursions). Although some regional hospitals do not charge for emergency treatment, you cannot rely on this. If you need complicated surgery (for a fracture, for example), it can cost as much as it would to have private treatment in a Western country.

A policy that pays doctors or hospitals directly rather than you having to pay on the spot and claim later is a better option for the region. If you have to claim later make sure you keep all documentation.

Note that some policies specifically exclude 'dangerous activities', which can include activities you may want to engage in on the Peninsula, such as scuba diving, rock climbing, motorcycling and even trekking.

See also Insurance, p553 and the boxed text, p550.

INTERNET ACCESS

The Peninsula has embraced the communications revolution with gusto and it's no longer difficult to keep in touch with home.

Most travellers make constant use of internet cafés and free web-based email such as **Yahoo** (www.yahoo.com) or **Hotmail** (www.hotmail .com). If you're travelling with a notebook or hand-held computer, be aware that your modem may not work in parts of the Peninsula. The safest option is to buy a reputable 'global' modem before you leave home, or buy a local PC-card modem if you're spending an extended time in any one country. Wi-fi hotspots are becoming more common in many hotels, shopping malls and cafés, and plugging a laptop in is usually possible even in small towns.

Bring a universal AC adaptor for your equipment, to enable you to plug it in anywhere without frying the circuit boards. You may also need a plug adaptor for each country you visit (see p534).

Keep in mind that there are a variety of telephone sockets used in each country, so ensure that you have at least a US RJ-11 telephone adaptor that works with your modem.

For more information on travelling with a portable computer, see www.teleadapt.com.

If you access your internet account at home through one of the smaller ISPs or your office or school network, your best option is either to open an account with a global ISP, like **AOL** (www.aol.com), or rely on internet cafés and other public access points to collect your mail.

If you intend to rely on internet cafés, you'll need to carry three pieces of information with you to enable you to access your internet mail account, your incoming (POP or IMAP) mail server name, your account name and password.

You'll find internet cafés throughout the Middle East (even Yemen and Saudi Arabia are now online big time). But while getting access is usually no problem, connection speeds can be painfully slow. Lines often suffer from congestion during the Muslim 'weekend'.

The state telephone companies provide access and act as servers, so can regulate all site access. Much censorship takes place, particularly in Saudi Arabia. See Internet Access in the individual countries for further information.

LEGAL MATTERS

Although the law varies in particulars from country to country, it does share certain similarities. The legal system in all Peninsula countries is based wholly or partly on Sharia'a law, derived mainly from the Quran.

In the West, Sharia'a law is perceived as notoriously harsh and inflexible, but in reality there are basic tenets shared with Western legal values (such as the presumption of innocence until proven guilty). The severest punishment for a crime is in practice rarely exacted (even in Saudi Arabia).

Visitors should remember that they are subject to the laws of the country they find themselves in, and that ignorance of the law does *not* constitute a defence. In Saudi Arabia, in particular, it is vital that travellers (particularly women) acquaint themselves with the local laws.

In other Peninsula countries, note especially the laws concerning alcohol and drugs (see p532), homosexuality (see p534) and the ancient law of 'blood money' in the event of causing injury to another person (see p553).

If you are arrested and detained, call your embassy or consulate and wait until they arrive before you sign anything. In a car accident you mustn't move the car, even if you're causing a traffic jam, until the police arrive.

MONEY

Specific information on money (including details of the currencies used in each country, as well as the best places to change money) are given in the individual country chapters. See also Costs & Money, p22.

ATMs

Most of the larger Peninsula banks in the region now have ATMs linked into one of the big global clearing systems (such as MasterCard/Cirrus or Visa/Plus or Global-Access systems). ATMs are also found in shopping malls. Charges for using cash-advance facilities against a credit card are usually high from these machines.

In all Peninsula countries, except Yemen, it's possible to avoid carrying wads of cash by using your plastic for all transactions (but bring at least two credit cards in case of problems or loss of one). Major credit and credit/debit cards, especially Visa and MasterCard, are readily accepted and many ATMs will also accept bank-issued cash cards (which you use at home to withdraw money directly from your bank account).

Be sure to remember your personal identification number (PIN); if you don't have one, request it from your bank several weeks before travelling. Also check out the transaction fees you're likely to incur from both your own bank and the banks whose machines you will be using when travelling.

Bargaining

Bargaining over prices is still very much a way of life on the Peninsula, although to a lesser extent than in some other Middle Eastern countries. Yemen and Oman are perhaps the exception, where aggressive bargaining can offend.

Western visitors often have difficulty with the concept of bargaining, being more used to products having fixed values. In the Middle East, on the other hand, commodities are typically considered worth whatever their seller can get for them, balanced against whatever the buyer is willing to pay.

Vendors on the Peninsula won't necessarily quote you prices higher than those that the locals pay, particularly for local produce, such as fruit, and especially outside the cities or tourist areas. You needn't be suspicious, therefore, of everybody charging you high prices just, or particularly, because you're a foreigner. Prices rarely come down much below half the original quote, and 25% to 30% discount is more or less the norm. It does help knowing the prices of things, and after the first few days in a country (when you'll inevitably pay over the odds a few times) you'll soon get to learn the usual prices for basic items. Taxis are something of an anomaly: across the region you'll be fleeced.

Cash

Most travellers carry a combination of cash and travellers cheques. Cash is quicker to deal with, can be exchanged almost anywhere and usually gets better rates. However, it obviously cannot be replaced if it's lost.

In small businesses, including cheap restaurants, bus stations, youth hostels and budget hotels, and in rural areas, you will need cash for most transactions. Also, always try to have small bills handy when you travel by taxi – it can be difficult to extract change, especially when bartering over a fare.

Credit Cards

Credit cards are widely accepted on the Peninsula (except Yemen) and almost every-thing can be paid for by plastic, right down to your morning coffee.

Visa and MasterCard are the most popular credit cards; Amex is also accepted but less widely, and in some places it may not be accepted at all.

It's possible to get cash advances on credit cards in several countries in the region. See Credit Cards in the individual country chapters for more details.

Moneychangers

Moneychangers often offer better deals than banks, but they don't always accept travellers cheques. They are also usually quicker, have shorter queues and keep longer opening hours. Always check commission charges and exchange rates before handing over money.

Security

On the whole, the Peninsula is a very safe place and theft is rare. The only real risk of carrying large amounts of cash around is loss. Changing cash outside the big cities can be a hassle, and you may find yourself carrying wads of cash around just to try to avoid this.

In the unlikely event of theft or loss, it's a very good idea to put aside a separate emergency stash, say US$100 for emergency use.

Taxes

The Peninsula used to be world famous as a low-tax area. Nowadays, however, a mixture of taxes, often reaching 17%, is added on top of hotel and restaurant prices.

Tipping

Tips are not generally expected in the Gulf and the concept of 'baksheesh', well known throughout the rest of the Middle East, is little known on the Peninsula. Those who have contact with tourists (such as guides, car-hire drivers or hotel porters) increasingly expect tips, however.

Note that the service charge added to most hotel and restaurant bills is not an automatic gratuity that goes to the waiters. It usually goes into the till and is often the restaurant's way of making the prices on the menu look 10% to 15% cheaper than they really are. Waiters in the Gulf tend to be paid appallingly low wages, so a small tip discreetly left on the table, while not required, is definitely greatly appreciated if the service is good. The practice of automatic lavish tip-giving, however, can backfire as many establishments simply reduce the wages of their employees if they know that tips are expected.

Travellers Cheques

Though not often used by travellers to the region, travellers cheques are widely accepted by banks on the Peninsula, though it can be difficult to cash them in Yemen and with some moneychangers. In some countries hotels offer an exchange service, but rates tend to be poor.

Travellers cheques in US dollars, from major companies such as Amex and Thomas Cook, are the best option, as they're the most widely recognised; both companies have offices in many of the Peninsula cities.

PHOTOGRAPHY & VIDEO
Film & Equipment

Photo studios across the Peninsula were quick to make the transfer to digital and now in most cities (even in Yemen) it's easier to buy memory cards and download images to a CD than it is to find a favourite print film. A full range of batteries are available in most large stores, but if you're planning an extended trip to the interior of Saudi, Yemen and Oman it's worth bringing a few rechargeable spares and the battery charger. Don't forget the adaptor. Prices for all camera equipment are very competitive across the Peninsula, and many people make a special point of stopping off at Gulf airports to buy such goods duty free.

A reasonable range of print film is still available in all the major cities of the Peninsula, but slide and black and white films are getting harder to find and in small-town shops are often out of date. It's still easy to process a colour roll of film.

Cameras and lenses collect dust quickly in desert areas. A dust brush (or even better, compressed air with an outlet tube), lens paper and cleaners are essential photographic equipment.

Technical Tips

In most Peninsula countries, especially in the summer months, early morning and late afternoon are the best times to take photographs (ideally from dawn to 8am, and 4pm to dusk). During the rest of the day sunlight can be too bright, shadows too dark and the sky too hazy, to allow for a crisp, sharp picture.

There are a few remedies for this: a polarising filter (and a lens hood) cuts glare and reflection from sand and water.

A monopod (easier to carry and doubles as a walking stick) or a tripod is recommended if you want to capture the magic of dusk – a particularly beguiling time of day in the seaboard cities as local authorities are fond of illuminations and the sea and sky melt into a single unit of colour.

Restrictions

The basic photographic rules on the Peninsula are simple: do not photograph anything vaguely military in nature (including the police) or anything construed as 'strategic' (including airports, bridges and train stations). In general terms, Bahrain and the UAE are the most relaxed countries on the Peninsula when it comes to photography, while Kuwait, Oman and Yemen seem to have the broadest definitions of what constitutes a 'strategic' site. In Saudi Arabia it often seems that the authorities just don't like cameras.

Most importantly, you should not photograph anyone without their permission, *especially* women. In the more conservative countries, such as Saudi Arabia, Kuwait and some parts of Yemen, you can cause real offence in this way and may risk having stones hurled at you.

By contrast many children love having their photo taken and shouts of 'Sura!' (photo!) in some countries are meant to encourage you. Many men (particularly in Yemen) are often happy to oblige, and may make a terrific joke out of the whole business.

People on the Peninsula are often offended when you take photographs of run-down houses or anything that resembles poverty, as the tendency is to emphasise what the country has achieved in the last few decades.

Photography is usually allowed inside religious and archaeological sites (when entry is permitted), unless there are signs indicating otherwise.

POST

The postal systems in the Gulf vary some-what from country to country. Although most are reasonably efficient, they can be on the slow side. Post offices are found in all the larger towns and cities of the Peninsula.

In some countries incoming packages, even fairly small ones, are still sometimes sent to customs for lengthy searches, during which books, magazines or videos will probably have been vetted for 'inappropriate material'. Note that you may be held responsible for the contents of the parcels sent to you, and sometimes prosecuted (particularly in Saudi Arabia). When picking up parcels you'll need identification.

Receiving Mail

Poste restante services exist in most Peninsula countries. Letters should be addressed in the following form:

Your NAME
Poste Restante
General Post Office
City, Country

You'll need your passport to collect your mail. Letters can take a couple of weeks to work through the system.

Some hotels and tour companies operate a mail-holding service, and Amex customers can have mail sent to most Amex offices.

There is no delivery service for expats; residents must pick up their post from the local post office (where they will be assigned a post office box number).

Sending Mail

Letters sent from a major capital take five days to a week to reach most parts of Europe, and anything from 10 days to two weeks to reach North America or Australasia. Parcels take at least a week longer than ordinary mail (and sometimes up to a month).

If something's urgent the major courier companies, such as DHL or FedEx, have offices in most major Peninsula towns.

SMOKING

Unlike in other parts of the Middle East, smoking is not particularly prevalent in the Arabian Peninsula. This has something to do with the strict interpretation of Islam and the discouragement of dependency on stimulants of any kind; partly to do with the general lack of advertising in most of the region; and partly to do with government drives to dissuade the young from starting the habit.

That doesn't mean to say you won't encounter smoking. The expat communities from India tend to smoke quite heavily and everyone across the region (even fashionably dressed young Arab women in city areas) enjoys a *sheesha* (water pipe filled with scented or fruit-flavoured tobacco) from time to time.

All top-end hotels offer nonsmoking rooms and there are always nonsmoking sections in more expensive restaurants. Curiously, people often assume that all Westerners are smokers; if you are, you'll find it a good way to strike up a conversation, although it is still mostly regarded as a male activity.

SOLO TRAVELLERS

Travel for Arabic people and for most Asian expats entails communal farewells, large convoys of family groups, and great gatherings at the airport on the return. As such, solo travellers are often regarded either with sympathy or with suspicion as it is inconceivable to most Arabian Peninsula people that someone might choose to travel alone.

You might just get away without comment if you're a man, but a woman travelling on her own is bound to be a hot topic of discussion. Women will want to adopt you, men will either ignore you (out of respect) or treat you as a token man. Either way, you will inevitably be showered with well-meaning solicitations for your safekeeping, extra help on public transport and even offers of accommodation. Of course, there are always a few men who will want to take advantage of the fact that you're unaccompanied and for tips as to how to handle that situation, see the section on Women, p542.

Men, on the other hand, will be expected to look after themselves. They will still find that they're the subject of curiosity, however, especially in remote villages and towns, and will get plenty of practice at giving a good account of their purpose and destination before being ushered in to share 'bread and salt'.

Despite the uncomfortable feeling of being conspicuous, there's lots to commend solo travelling. It offers undoubtedly the best way, if not the only practical way, of integrating with the local culture. In pairs, much of the time is spent sharing each other's company. Alone, you're forced to engage with other people, on the buses, in small coffeeshops, strolling along the beach or haggling over goods in the souq. As people are the greater part of the experience of travelling in the Arabian Peninsula, this is a wonderful opportunity. It is particularly rewarding if you can speak some Arabic and engage in a deeper dialogue than the superficial sharing of greetings. Finding out the extent to which Western and Arabic outlooks on life are the same is an education on both sides. Such encounters are also a precious opportunity to be an ambassador for the good things of the West as well as an apologist for the bad. Nothing does more to help improve international relations than one person saying of another: 'Ah, you're from there! Do you know Mr Smith? He was from your country, and he was a very nice person too'.

Without Arabic, however, travelling in the Arabian Peninsula can be quite lonely at times: the roads are long and the deserts wide. Without an established network of tourism facilities, you may spend days without seeing another Westerner and trying to communicate in broken language for days on end can be exhausting.

Single rooms are available in most hotels, though they're often just a few dollars cheaper than double rooms. Walking around alone seldom presents a safety problem.

One word of caution: if you travel away from urban areas in your own vehicle alone, you need to be quite resourceful. Many roads see very little traffic and you could wait hours before help arrives. It is not recommended that you go off-road alone.

TELEPHONE & FAX

The Peninsula boasts some first-rate telecommunications networks (though not all countries, such as Yemen, maintain such high standards). Although state-owned, they're generally well maintained and managed. All the Peninsula countries have International Direct Dialling (IDD) facilities via satellite links.

Most cities and large towns have public telephone offices (either part of the post office, or privately run) from where you can make international calls and send faxes.

Costs for international calls cost up to US$2 per minute for most destinations. Rates don't usually vary during the day or night, but in some countries there are reductions at weekends. Public phones accept coins, phonecards and, in some countries, credit cards.

Faxes are widespread on the Peninsula, even though the internet is gradually making them redundant.

Mobile Phones

The use of mobile phones is widespread throughout the Peninsula and every country has its own (state-owned) national network. Some of these run on the GSM system (as in Europe), so if your phone works on GSM and your account allows you to roam, you'll be able to use your mobile on the Peninsula.

In other places you'll have to buy prepaid SIM cards. Beware though: the cost of using a mobile in some countries is higher than calls made on a land line. See individual country chapters for further details.

TIME

Saudi Arabia, Kuwait, Bahrain, Qatar and Yemen are three hours ahead of GMT/UTC. The UAE and Oman are four hours ahead of GMT/UTC. Daylight-saving time is not observed in any of the Gulf countries (in other words, the time remains constant throughout the year). See also the world map (towards the back of the book) for world time zones.

TOILETS

Outside the midrange and top-end hotels and restaurants of the Peninsula (where Western-style loos are found), visitors will encounter the Arab-style squat toilet (which, interestingly according to physiologists, encourages a far more natural position than the Western-style invention!).

It's a good idea to carry a roll of toilet paper with you on your travels: most toilets only provide water and the use of paper is considered barbaric.

Beyond the towns you're unlikely to find public loos, except poorly maintained ones at filling stations.

TOURIST INFORMATION

Despite the fact that tourism is a growing industry in the Peninsula, there are surprisingly few tourist offices. Staff training and office facilities are equally minimal. Sometimes the most you'll find is a free map (often very outdated) or an aged brochure.

There are two good, unofficial sources of information on the Peninsula: your hotel and the local travel agents (many of whom generously offer information without always expecting you to engage their services in return). Both sources are knowledgeable and resourceful.

Details of tourist offices, as well as tour operators, are given in the individual town and city sections of the country chapters.

TRAVELLERS WITH DISABILITIES

Generally speaking, scant regard is paid to the needs of disabled travellers in the Peninsula. Steps, high kerbs and other assorted obstacles are everywhere, though streets are less rutted and uneven than in some parts of the world. Roads are made virtually uncrossable by heavy traffic, while some doorways are narrow and many buildings (such as Yemen's famous tower houses) have steep staircases and no lifts.

In the top-end hotels facilities are usually better (with lifts, ramps and more accommodating bathrooms) but still leave much to be desired. Trips have to be planned carefully, and may be restricted to luxury-level hotels and private, hired transport. There is an agency in Oman (one of the more enlightened countries in this regard) specialising in making arrangements for disabled travellers; see p256 for details.

Before setting off for the Middle East, disabled travellers can get in touch with their national support organisation (preferably with the travel officer, if there is one) – in the UK contact **RADAR** (☎ 020-7250 3222; 250 City Rd, London EC1V 8AS) or the **Holiday Care Service** (☎ 0845 124 9971; www.holidaycare.org.uk), or try www.disabledtravelers.com.

Elderly people with physical difficulties will find that every effort will be made to welcome them. Arab people are highly respectful of the elderly, and travelling with the aged (even in wheelchairs) is a delightful experience.

VISAS

The flow of foreigners in, out and around the Peninsula is carefully monitored and strictly controlled in most of its countries.

As a result the visa application process ranges from fairly simple and straightforward (Bahrain) to nightmarishly complicated (Saudi Arabia). It also means that if you plan to travel from one country to another, where it involves passing through Saudi, you need to plan ahead. All countries, except Saudi Arabia, issue tourist visas on arrival for most nationalities.

An Israeli passport, or an Israeli stamp in your passport, is a problem. If you have either of these, it's unwise to leave it to chance as to whether an official will notice it or not (see boxed text, below).

Passports need to be valid for at least six months beyond your expected departure date from the region. Note also that most Peninsula countries require you to carry your passport with you at all times. Spot checks occasionally occur.

For more details on each country's visa regulations see Visas in the individual country chapters and the table, p549,

---

THE ISRAELI STAMP STIGMA

The game of wits played between travellers and diplomatic consulars across the Middle East is ratcheted up by what's known as the 'Israeli Stamp Stigma'. In the Arabian Peninsula, all countries refuse to admit anyone whose passport has been tainted by evidence of a visit to the Jewish state – even though, from time to time, rumours abound of a relaxation of this rule in some Gulf countries. Israeli immigration officials will, *if asked*, stamp only a separate entry card and not your passport. This is fine for travellers flying into and out of Israel, but if you are crossing into Jordan or Egypt overland, the entry/exit stamps into those countries (marked, for example: 'taba' or 'aqaba') will be no less incriminating than an Israeli stamp.

The safest option is to arrange your itinerary so that a visit to Israel is the final stop on your tour of the Middle East.

which includes some 'visas at a glance'-type information.

Collecting Visas

If you've arranged your visa in advance of arrival, make sure you have some proof of it with you before setting off (a fax or email with the visa number), or you may not be allowed to board your plane let alone enter the country of your destination.

Transit Visas

Saudi Arabia issues transit visas for people travelling overland between Jordan and Bahrain, Kuwait, Oman, Qatar, the UAE or Yemen (see p177). These transit visas can be sought from Saudi Arabian embassies in any of these countries with proof of onward connections beyond Saudi borders.

Travel Permits

Travel permits are necessary for travelling in Yemen (p518) and Saudi Arabia (p367), and are obtainable in the countries themselves. They're also necessary for Omani residents driving to the UAE.

Visa Sponsorship

If you cannot obtain a visa to the Peninsula on arrival or through an embassy, you can try to obtain one through a sponsor. This can be the hotel where you're planning to stay or a tour company.

In theory, a sponsor is a national of the country you are visiting, who is willing to vouch for your good behaviour and take responsibility for your departure when you're due to leave. You'll need to send details of your passport and itinerary a couple of weeks in advance to your sponsor. Make sure you obtain confirmation that your visa will be awaiting your arrival at the relevant airport before you leave *in writing* (a fax is suitable).

The sponsorship process varies greatly from country to country (and is also liable to change – check current regulations with the local embassy). The documentation required also varies with each country, and processing can take anything from a few days to a few weeks.

WEIGHTS & MEASURES

The metric system is in use throughout the Peninsula. However, there are some local variations where petrol is sold by the imperial gallon not litre. There's a metric conversion table at the front of this book.

WOMEN TRAVELLERS

Many women imagine that travel on the Peninsula is a lot more difficult and traumatic than it actually is. Unaccompanied women will certainly attract curious stares and glances (see Solo Travellers, p539), and occasionally comments, too, but they will receive hospitable treatment almost universally – especially if appropriately dressed.

It's important to be aware that there are 'men areas' and 'women areas' and that this is something that is enforced mainly by women, not by men. As such, it can be quite uncomfortable (and compromising) for both sexes if a woman sits in a male area. Traditional coffeehouses, cheaper restaurants, budget hotels, the back seats of buses all tend to be men-only areas and it's culturally sensitive to avoid them – at some budget Gulf hotels, unaccompanied women may be refused a room. Women areas include family rooms in better restaurants, public beaches on certain days of the week and the front rows of buses.

Sometimes women may be followed or find unwanted visitors at their hotel, but this is far less prevalent than in other parts of the Middle East where there is more exposure to tourists. Sexual harassment in some Peninsula countries is considered a serious crime and the incidence of rape on the Peninsula is extremely low (far lower than in the West). Verbal harassment and sexual innuendo is more common. The best way of keeping trouble at bay is often to engage positively and firmly with potential troublemakers, and above all appear self-confident and keep a sense of humour. For a few simple techniques to help keep hassle at bay, see the boxed text, opposite.

Any specific restrictions on visas, travel or general movement of women (mostly in Saudi Arabia and crossing the border alone by bus in Oman) are covered in Women Travellers in the individual country chapters. For information on the situation for local women, see opposite.

Women's personal requirements (such as tampons and sanitary pads) can be found in some of the larger supermarkets of the bigger cities (which cater for expats), but it's best to come with your own.

TIPS FOR WOMEN TRAVELLERS

In order to avoid misunderstandings and to detract attention from yourself, there are a number of tips that may prove useful. Top of the list is to dress modestly. A woman revealing her knees and shoulders or wearing a tight T-shirt on the street is, in the eyes of the locals, confirmation of the very worst stereotype held of Western women. Generally, if you're alone or with other women, the amount of attention you receive will be directly related to how you dress: the more skin that is exposed, the more attention you'll attract. In some places that are unused to seeing Western women, it may take garbing yourself in full Saudi *abeyya* (a full-length black robe worn by Muslim women) to leave you completely free of unwanted attention. For more on the dress issue, see What to Wear, p544.

Other tips include the following:

- Wear a wedding ring, which will make you appear less 'available'.

- If you are unmarried but travelling in male company, say that you're married rather than girlfriend/boyfriend or just 'friends' (but note the legal restrictions in Saudi).

- Don't say that you are travelling alone or just in the company of another female friend; always say that you are with a group.

- Avoid direct eye contact with local men; dark sunglasses help.

- Don't respond to obnoxious comments – act as if you didn't hear them.

- Be careful in crowds and other situations where you are crammed between people, as occasionally crude things may happen behind you.

- Don't sit on the front seat of taxis unless the driver is a woman.

- On public transport, sit next to a woman if possible.

- Be careful about behaving in a flirtatious or suggestive manner, as it could create more problems than you imagined.

- If you need help for any reason (directions etc), ask a woman first.

- If dining alone, try and eat at Western-style places or those more used to tourists. Ask to be seated in the 'family' section, if there is one.

- It's perfectly acceptable for a woman to go straight to the front of a queue or to ask to be served first before any men that may be waiting. Don't try it if Western men are in the queue or you might find that evil eye isn't the prerogative of Arab men only!

- Going to the nearest public place, such as the lobby of a hotel, usually works if you need to get rid of any hangers-on. If that doesn't discourage them, asking the receptionist to call the police usually frightens them off.

Local Attitudes

Some of the biggest misunderstandings between Middle Easterners and Westerners occur over the issue of women. Half-truths and stereotypes exist on both sides: many Westerners assume all Middle Eastern women are veiled, repressed victims; while a large number of locals see Western women as sex-obsessed and immoral.

The role of a woman on the Peninsula is specifically defined: she is mother and matron of the household (though again, contrary to Western perceptions, may wield much power within that sphere), while the man is the financial provider.

However, as with any society, generalisations can be misleading and the reality is far more nuanced. There are thousands of middle- and upper-middle-class professional women in the Arab world who, like their counterparts in the West, juggle work and family responsibilities.

Among less affluent families, where adherence to tradition is strongest, women may wish to concentrate on home and family, but economic reality means that they are forced to work while being responsible for all domestic chores as well.

The issue of sex is where the differences between Western and Middle Eastern women are most apparent. Premarital sex (or, indeed, any sex outside marriage) is taboo, although, as with anything forbidden, it still happens. Nevertheless, it is the exception rather than the rule – and that goes for men as well as women. Women on the whole are expected to be virgins when they marry, and a family's reputation can rest upon this point. In such a context, the restrictions placed on a young girl – no matter how onerous they may seem to a Westerner – are intended to protect her and her reputation from the potentially disastrous attentions of men.

The presence of foreign women provides, in the eyes of some Arab men, a chance to get around these norms with ease and without consequences – a view reinforced by distorted impressions gained from Western TV. Hence the hassle (see previous section).

What to Wear

Dressing modestly has the following advantages: it attracts less attention to you; will get you a warmer welcome from the locals (who greatly appreciate your willingness to respect their customs); and prove more comfortable in the heat.

Dressing 'modestly' means covering your legs, arms, shoulders and neckline. Baggy T-shirts and loose cotton trousers or long skirts will not only keep you cool but will also protect your skin from the sun. Wearing a bra will detract much attention, and a hat or headscarf (which can be slipped on when you want to look even more inconspicuous or when the situation demands it, such as when visiting a mosque) is also a very good idea.

As with anywhere, take your cues from those around you: if you're in a rural area and all the women are in long, concealing dresses, you should be conservatively dressed. For current dress restrictions on foreign women, see the country chapter directories under 'Women' for details.

WORK

Labour laws throughout the Gulf are extremely strict. It's illegal to seek work in most countries on a visit visa (and there are severe penalties for those caught working illegally). Although some travellers take the chance of applying for ad hoc work (in Dubai, for example), to remain within the law, you should secure a position before arrival. Your 'sponsor' (usually your employer) acts as a kind of guarantor of your good conduct while you reside in the country and will help you obtain a visa.

Working and living conditions are usually of a high standard. Salaries, though not usually significantly higher than those in the West, carry the enormous advantage of incurring no personal taxation. It can be tricky, however, changing jobs if you decide you're not happy with the one you have. It can also be difficult to find long-term employment; many contracts are short term, renewable annually. While it's not necessary to speak Arabic (though it's an advantage), good spoken and written communication in English is a prerequisite.

Those offering professional skills in much-needed services, such as translating, nursing, engineering and teaching (particularly English), stand the best chance of gaining employment: many administrative positions, on the other hand, are beginning to be filled by newly trained local professionals. Recruiting agencies in major European cities still head-hunt for positions in the Peninsula. Note that for English-language teaching, you will need at least a degree and teaching experience to be eligible for most job opportunities.

You can also inquire about job opportunities at your cultural centre (such as the British Council or Centre Culturel Français) and voluntary aid organisations.

For more information and a full discussion of working in the Arabian Peninsula, see the Expats chapter, p91.

Transport in the Arabian Peninsula

CONTENTS

GETTING THERE & AWAY

This chapter explains how to reach the Arabian Peninsula by air, land and sea from other parts of the world. For details of travel between Peninsula countries, see the Getting Around section later in this chapter, and the Getting There & Away sections in the relevant country chapters.

AIR

For thousands of years the Peninsula has served as a kind of commercial crossroads, linking East with West. It still performs the same function, quite apart from attracting considerable international traffic in its own right, channelling commercial activity through some of the world's most modern airports.

All major European, Asian and Middle Eastern airlines (with the obvious exception of El Al, the Israeli airline) serve the principal cities of the Arabian Peninsula. There are also some direct flights between the Peninsula and the US and Australia. Neighbouring regions, such as North and East Africa, also have flights to the Peninsula as do India, Pakistan and the Far East.

The national carriers within the Peninsula itself link one country to another with regular flights at reasonable prices. For more specific information on the Peninsula's airlines, see p550.

Tickets

The Peninsula continues to be viewed by the travel industry largely as a business destination. Tourism, however, is on the increase, especially in the United Arab Emirates (UAE) and Oman, and as such discounted fares are slowly becoming available.

Dubai and Bahrain are major transport hubs. Dubai, the major link between Europe, Southeast Asia and Australasia, is the destination which offers the best hope of picking up cheaper fares. As such, it may be worthwhile to fly into Dubai and arrange onward travel from there.

The following agencies are recommended for online bookings:

Cheap Tickets (www.cheaptickets.com)
Expedia.com (www.expedia.com)
Lowestfare.com (www.lowestfare.com)
Opodo (www.opodo.co.uk)
Orbitz (www.orbitz.com)
STA Travel (www.sta.com) For travellers under the age of 26.
Travelocity (www.travelocity.com)

INTERCONTINENTAL TICKETS

It can often be cheaper to take a transcontinental flight involving a change of planes or a transit stop on the Peninsula, than to buy a ticket directly to the Peninsula. For example, a London–Karachi ticket via Dubai may cost less than the cheapest available London–Dubai ticket, or you could stop off in Dubai on an Emirates package from

---

> **THINGS CHANGE...**
>
> The information in this chapter is particularly vulnerable to change. Check directly with the airline or a travel agent to make sure you understand how a fare (and ticket you may buy) works and be aware of the security requirements for international travel. Shop carefully. The details given in this chapter should be regarded as pointers and are not a substitute for your own careful, up-to-date research.

London to Bangkok. However, check carefully for catches. Sometimes a stopover is only allowed on the return leg, or there may be an extra charge for the stopover.

Most of the region's airline 'stopover packages' include hotel accommodation, airport transfers and a short tour, all for a very reasonable fee.

Australia & New Zealand

Gulf Air and Emirates airlines both fly out of Sydney and Melbourne to Abu Dhabi, Bahrain and Dubai. From these cities, there are connections to most other major Peninsula cities.

Alternatively, it's possible to connect with one of the large Asian carriers, such as Malaysian, Thai, Philippine and Singapore Airlines, which all have regular return flights out of their home ports to Dubai.

No carrier flies direct to the Gulf States from New Zealand. However, there are a number of combination fares available: Air New Zealand and Emirates Airlines, for example, offer return fares to Dubai via Asia.

STA Travel (☎ 1300 733 035; www.statravel.com.au) and **Flight Centre** (☎ 133 133; www.flightcentre.com .au) both have offices throughout Australia.

Servicing New Zealand, both **Flight Centre** (☎ 0800 243 544; www.flightcentre.co.nz) and **STA Travel** (☎ 0508 782 872; www.statravel.co.nz) have branches throughout the country. The site www.goholidays.co.nz is recommended for online bookings.

Europe

There are direct flights to the Peninsula from almost any European city; however, London has the greatest number of flight options closely followed by Frankfurt. Fares from London are usually also cheaper than from other European cities.

The real bargains to the Peninsula used to be with the Eastern European airlines, but for the past few years the best deals have been with Olympic Airways, Air France and Alitalia. All of these involve changes of plane.

MAINLAND EUROPE

All the major European carriers fly to the major cities on the Peninsula (usually several times a week). Conversely, Peninsula carriers usually fly several times a week to various European mainland cities, most commonly Paris, Frankfurt, Rome and Athens.

CLIMATE CHANGE & TRAVEL

Climate change is a serious threat to the ecosystems that humans rely upon, and air travel is the fastest-growing contributor to the problem. Lonely Planet regards travel, overall, as a global benefit, but believes we all have a responsibility to limit our personal impact on global warming.

Flying & Climate Change

Pretty much every form of motor travel generates CO_2 (the main cause of human-induced climate change) but planes are far and away the worst offenders, not just because of the sheer distances they allow us to travel, but because they release greenhouse gases high into the atmosphere. The statistics are frightening: two people taking a return flight between Europe and the US will contribute as much to climate change as an average household's gas and electricity consumption over a whole year.

Carbon Offset Schemes

Climatecare.org and other websites use 'carbon calculators' that allow jetsetters to offset the greenhouse gases they are responsible for with contributions to energy-saving projects and other climate-friendly initiatives in the developing world – including projects in India, Honduras, Kazakhstan and Uganda.

Lonely Planet, together with Rough Guides and other concerned partners in the travel industry, supports the carbon offset scheme run by climatecare.org. Lonely Planet offsets all of its staff and author travel.

For more information check out our website: lonelyplanet.com.

As tourism grows in the region, prices are becoming more reasonable.

Recommended agencies on the mainland include the following:

Barcelo Viajes (☎ 902 11 62 26; www.barceloviajes.com; Spain)

CTS Viaggi (☎ 062 00 400; www.cts.it; Italy)

Expedia (www.expedia.de; Germany)

Nouvelles Frontières (☎ 08 25 00 07 47; www.nouvelles-frontieres.fr; France)

STA Travel (☎ 0697 4303 292; www.statravel.de; Germany)

Voyageurs du Monde (☎ 08 92 23 56 56; www.vdm.com; France)

UNITED KINGDOM

Most of the Peninsula's airlines offer daily flights to London. Competition is driving fares down and most airlines periodically have excellent special offers.

Discount air travel is big business in London and enticing advertisements for many travel agencies appear in the travel pages of the weekend broadsheet newspapers, especially in *Time Out*, the *Evening Standard* and in the free magazine *TNT*. Increasingly, there are more opportunities for reasonable fares to the Middle East, although make sure that prices offered include the hefty airport taxes. As far as the Peninsula is concerned, there are few dedicated specialists and the best bet is to call **STA Travel** (☎ 087 1230 0040; www.statravel.co.uk) and **Trailfinders** (☎ 084 5058 5858; www.trailfinders.co.uk).

Middle East

There are regular flights from Cairo, Beirut, Damascus and Amman to all the major cities in the Peninsula.

Recommended agencies in the Middle East include:

Al-Rais Travels (www.alrais.com; Dubai)

NTT Oman (www.nttoman.com; Oman)

Orion-Tour (www.oriontour.com; Istanbul)

USA & Canada

There are not many flights to/from North America, but most of the big US airlines have some form of code-sharing agreement with one or more of the Peninsula carriers.

Kuwait Airways flies to New York three times a week (stopping in London en route), and Saudia flies to/from Jeddah and Riyadh, linking with both New York and Washington. Yemenia flies to Washington,

Detroit and San Francisco, Chicago, Los Angeles, New York direct, or via Frankfurt or London.

As well as these direct flights, there are also connections with changes for other Middle Eastern airports from various cities in North America.

The cheapest way to get from the US and particularly Canada to the Middle East might be to fly to London and buy a ticket from there.

It's also worth contacting the airlines directly about 'add ons' in which an extra ticket to another destination in the Peninsula is available for a nominal fee.

Discount travel agents in the USA are known as consolidators. San Francisco is the ticket consolidator capital of America, although some good deals can be found in Los Angeles, New York and other big cities.

For Canada, **Travel Cuts** (☎ 1-866-246-9726; www.travelcuts.com) is Canada's national student travel agency. For online bookings try www.expedia.ca and www.travelocity.ca.

LAND
Border Crossings

Border crossings can be slow and may take anything from half an hour to two hours or more. Make certain you have all the required documentation with you. Showing patience, politeness and good humour is likely to speed up the process. For further information see Visas, p541; Bring Your Own Vehicle, p552; as well as the Transport section in the relevant country chapters.

If you are travelling independently overland to the Middle East, you can currently only approach the region from Jordan into Saudi Arabia (see p369). If you want to travel overland between the different countries of the Arabian Peninsula, see the table, p548.

Car & Motorcycle

Anyone who is planning to take their own vehicle with them needs to check in advance what spare parts and petrol are likely to be available (see p552). The following documents are required:

AAA (www.aaauae.com, www.aaaoman.com) Information on car use in Oman and UAE.

Green Card Issued by insurers. Insurance for some countries is only obtainable at the border.

TRAVELLING BY LAND IN THE ARABIAN PENINSULA

To/From	From/To	Border Crossing Notes
Oman	Saudi Arabia	There is no border crossing currently open between Oman and Saudi
Oman (mainland)	UAE	The Wajajah border crossing is the most commonly used (see p242)
Oman (Musandam)	UAE	The Al-Darah/Tibat border crossing is the only one open at present (see p244)
Oman	Yemen	The Sarfait border crossing is the most commonly used (see p254)
Saudi Arabia	Bahrain	The border crossing is on King Fahd Causeway (see p132 and p369)
Saudi Arabia	Kuwait	The border crossing is at Al-Khafji and is usually only used by those on public transport (see p178 and p369)
Saudi Arabia	Qatar	The border crossing is at Salwah and is usually only used by those on public transport (see p296 and p369)
Saudi Arabia	UAE	The border crossing is at Sila (see p369)
Saudi Arabia	Yemen	It is inadvisable to travel between these two countries overland at this time (see p520)
Bahrain	Bahrain	A Saudi transit visa must be obtained before travelling overland between any of these countries
Qatar	Qatar	
Kuwait	Kuwait	**Saudi Transit Visa Details:**
UAE	UAE	▪ Application forms can be downloaded from www.saudiembassy.net.

▪ Travellers must have a ticket with confirmed reservations and/or a visa for the country of final destination.

▪ Transit times cannot exceed 72 hours.

▪ Women can only apply for a transit visa if accompanied by a male relative: proof of kinship is required (ie marriage certificate etc).

▪ Children need a copy of birth certificate.

▪ If travelling by your own vehicle you are required to register your carnet at the embassy.

International Driving Permit (IDP) Compulsory for foreign drivers and motorcyclists in Bahrain and Saudi Arabia. Most foreign licences are acceptable in the other Peninsula States, but even in these places an IDP is recommended.

Vehicle Registration Documents Check with your insurer whether you're covered for the countries you intend to visit and whether third-party cover is included.

SEA

Several ferry services operate to/from the Peninsula. Note that practicality is the priority not pleasure. Even in 1st class you shouldn't expect your voyage to be a cruise, while deck class often means just that. In summer, conditions may be impossibly hot for many people. While food and drink of some sort may be available on board, many passengers prefer to take their own. Vehicles can be shipped on services, but advance arrangements may have to be made.

Ferry destinations and their timetables change frequently. For the latest information get in touch with the head office or local agent of the respective company some time in advance. Most ferry companies have good websites where you can check current fares, routes and contact details.

Cargo boats call erratically at Aden, Muscat and Jeddah on their way to Europe and the Far East. Getting aboard is mostly a question of luck and being in the right place at the right time. Your passage may well be dependent upon the whim of the captain. The best place to inquire about boats is at the port of departure. Be warned that cargo boats are not always a comfortable option. While some offer comfortable passenger cabins (intended for crew family), for others you may need to come equipped with food, drink and bedding.

Visa Obtainable at Border?	Visa Information	Border Crossing Information
n/a	n/a	n/a
yes	see p260 and p444	see p261 and p445
yes	see p260 and p444	see p261 and p445
yes	see p260 and p517	see p261 and p520
to Saudi: no to Bahrain: yes	see p141 and p366	see p142
to Saudi: no to Kuwait: yes	see p177 and p366	see p178
to Saudi: no to Kuwait: yes	see p295 and p366	see p178
to Saudi: no to UAE: yes	see p366 and p444	n/a
n/a	n/a	n/a
to Saudi: no to others: no (you need a visa for your final destination to transit through Saudi)	**General Notes:**	

General Notes:

- Although restrictions are beginning to relax, the rules regarding visas and land crossings in the regionare subject to contradiction, misinformation and frequent change. Check with relevant embassies before travelling.
- You need to have insurance for all countries you're passing through if driving.
- Many car hire companies insist you return cars to country of original hire.

Note from Author of Saudi Arabia Chapter:

Stories are legion of individuals who obtain visas in their country of origin only to find them invalid at the Saudi border: double-check with your local Saudi embassy and, if possible, with the authorities in Saudi Arabia.

Egypt

The Alexandria-based Misr Edco Shipping Company and four Saudi companies sail between Jeddah and Suez. The journey takes about 36 hours direct, about 72 via Aqaba. Misr Edco also sails about twice weekly between Port Safaga (Egypt) and Jeddah. For current schedules and prices contact **Mena Tours** (☎ 202-748 2231; www.mena tours.com.eg) in Cairo (Egypt), and **Ace Travel** (☎ 02-605 6002; www.ace-travel.com) in Jeddah (Saudia Arabia).

Iran

If you're travelling to/from the east and want to avoid Iraq and Saudi Arabia, you can cross the Gulf Sea from Iran into Kuwait and Bahrain.

Ferries only have 1st-class (cabin) accommodation, but are much cheaper than

the equivalent airfare, and most are overnight journeys. They are operated by **Valfajr-8 Shipping Company** (www.irantravellingcenter .com/valfajr8_persian_gulf.htm) in Tehran, which has a good online booking service. See Transport in the Bahrain (p143) chapter for details of sailings from there.

TOURS

Tours to the Peninsula are beginning to gain in popularity, and some attempt multicountry destinations such as the UAE, Oman and Yemen.

In the Peninsula itself there are a host of reputable tour agencies offering good tours at competitive prices. Check under the individual countries for details. Additionally, most regional airlines usually offer short tours of Peninsula cities for a reasonable supplement to an airfare.

CARNETS

A *carnet de passage* is a booklet that is stamped on arrival and at departure from a country to ensure that you export the vehicle again after you've imported it. It's usually issued by a motoring organisation in the country where the vehicle is registered. Many Peninsula countries require carnets, though exact requirements alter frequently.

The sting in the tail with a carnet is that you have to lodge a deposit to secure it. If you default on the carnet – that is, if you don't have an export stamp to match the import one – then the country in question can claim your deposit, which can be up to 300% of the new value of the vehicle. You can get around this problem with bank guarantees or carnet insurance, but you still have to fork out in the end if you default.

Should the worst occur and your vehicle is irretrievably damaged in an accident or breakdown, you'll have to argue it out with customs officials. Having a vehicle stolen can be even worse, as you may be suspected of having sold it.

The carnet may also need to specify any expensive spare parts that you're planning to carry with you, such as a gearbox, which is designed to prevent spare-part importation rackets. Contact your local automobile association for details about all necessary documentation at least three months in advance.

Note that for Saudi Arabia, tours are often the only way of visiting the country (see p326 for more details). Restrictions in Yemen currently allow visitors to travel to most areas outside the capital only with a tour (see p520).

Particularly recommended are the following agencies:

Adventure World (☎ 1800 133 322, 02-8913 0755; www.adventureworld.com.au; 73 Walker St, North Sydney, NSW 2060, Australia) Has branches in Adelaide, Brisbane, Melbourne and Perth and is agent for the UK's Explore Worldwide.

Kuoni (www.kuoni.co.uk; UK) Offers comprehensive tours of the UAE and Oman.

Passport Travel (☎ 03-9867 3888; www.travelcentre .com.au; Suite 11a, 401 St Kilda Rd, Melbourne, Vic 3004, Australia) Middle East specialist which assists in tailor-made itineraries for individuals or groups.

Spirit of Asia Travel (www.spiritofasiatravel.com) Offers multidestination tours of the UAE, Oman and Yemen.

GETTING AROUND

As fuel is cheap throughout the region and vehicles are relatively inexpensive to buy, road transportation is the most popular means of travel within the Peninsula. Car hire (with or without driver) is inexpensive and taxis and bus travel are cheap. Bar the small stretch operating in Saudi Arabia, there is no train service within the region.

Air travel, though a relative newcomer in some Peninsula countries, has developed fast and there's now a good air network linking most major Peninsula cities. It's often easier for the traveller to get about by air, as there is no regional rail network and travel by bus is a test of endurance due to the large distances. Then there's the added complication of obtaining a transit visa for Saudi Arabia, which hampers transport from one Gulf country to another.

AIR

Reputable travel agencies in all major Peninsula cities can advise you about the best intercity deals and it's better to use their services than go directly to the airlines. Note that prices fluctuate considerably according to the season or if there's a public holiday (such as *eid*).

Travel agency addresses are found in the Information sections in the major cities in each country chapter.

Airlines in the Arabian Peninsula

The Peninsula boasts some world-class airlines with good safety records, modern aircraft and well-trained crew. Some, such as Yemenia (the national airline of Yemen), can be less reliable but still offer a good service. For detailed information on safety records (including reams of statistics), visit www.airsafe.com.

Gulf Air is now jointly owned by Bahrain and Oman and has a very good service and safety record. Founded in 1984, Emirates (of the UAE) often wins awards for its excellent service. Newer airlines on the scene also with excellent reputations are Qatar Airways, Etihad and Oman Air.

Most countries (particularly the larger ones such as Saudi Arabia, Oman, the UAE and Yemen) have good domestic flight networks, which are reasonably priced. The Peninsula also boasts some famously slick international airports with good facilities, including 'business centres' and extensive Duty Free sections, particularly in Dubai but also in Riyadh and Bahrain. Other regional airports are adequate, and all are in the process of being modernised and expanded to meet the anticipated increase in tourism.

On the whole, arrival procedures are straightforward and usually remarkably quick and efficient. Note, however, the import prohibition on various items (particularly in Saudi Arabia); see p361 and p532.

Budget Airlines

The arrival of budget airlines in the region has recently revolutionised intercity transport on the Peninsula. As in Europe, they tend to use less-frequented cities as their hubs to avoid the high taxes of major airports. This minor inconvenience is worth considering for the cheap travel they offer.

Air Arabia (www.airarabia.com; Sharjah)
Al-Jazeera Airways (www.jazeeraairways.com; Kuwait)

BICYCLE

The Peninsula offers many good cycling opportunities on long, flat, sealed roads. Cyclists are usually made very welcome (a trademark of the Peninsula), offered food and sometimes accommodation (though you should offer to pay for it). Even the police are helpful and friendly. Many immigrant workers in the richer Peninsula states use bicycles, so repair shops are easy to come by, and the locals often prove fabulous 'bush mechanics'.

There are a few difficulties, however. Drivers are not used to watching out for cyclists and in many cities, especially in the Gulf, you'd be right in thinking cyclists have a death-wish even to consider venturing onto the road.

Most bicycles in the Peninsula are simple machines, and you're unlikely to find spare parts for the latest and slickest mountain or touring bike except in major cities (particularly in the UAE).

The greatest difficulty cited by all cyclists is the heat. The worst months are from June to August, and cycling during these summer months is definitely not recommended. February to mid-April and October to mid-December are the best times in most regions of the Peninsula. Even then you're advised to make an early morning start and call it a day by early afternoon.

If you are considering cycling on the Arabian Peninsula but have a few pressing questions, you can post your query on the Thorn Tree on lonelyplanet.com under the Activities branch. There's a strong likelihood somebody will respond with the information that you're looking for.

Alternatively, you could contact the **Cyclists' Touring Club** (CTC; ☎ 014-8341 7217; www.ctc .org.uk), a UK-based organisation which offers good tips and has a helpful website. It also has some useful information sheets on cycling in different parts of the world.

CYCLING TIPS

■ Carry a couple of extra chain links, a chain breaker, spokes, a spoke key, two inner tubes, tyre levers and a repair kit, a flat-head and Phillips-head screwdriver, Allen keys and spanners to fit all the bolts on your bike.

■ Check the bolts daily and carry spares. Make sure the bike's gearing will get you over the hills.

■ Fit as many water bottles to your bike as you can.

■ Confine your panniers to 15kg maximum. If you can, pack a two-person tent (weighing about 1.8kg) that can also accommodate the bike for when security is a concern.

■ Bring a sleeping bag rated to 0°C and a Therm-a-Rest mattress, a small camping stove with gas canisters, a cooking pot, utensils, a Katadyn water filter (two microns) and Maglite torch.

■ Wear cycling shorts with a chamois bum and cleated cycling shoes (the most comfortable).

BUS

Car ownership levels are so high in some of the Peninsula states that little demand for public bus services exists. It's not too difficult to get between the main towns in Saudi Arabia and Oman by bus, but Bahrain, Kuwait, the UAE and Qatar have fewer if any domestic services.

Of the major regional routes, there are five principal ones: Saudi Arabia to Bahrain; Saudi Arabia and Bahrain to Kuwait in the north; Saudi Arabia and Bahrain to the UAE via Qatar in the south; the UAE to Oman further south; and the UAE to Oman and Yemen in the far south of the Peninsula. For further details of these services see the Getting There & Away sections of the relevant chapters. Note that visas can still be difficult to obtain at borders (see p541).

On the whole, bus travel is reasonably comfortable and fast on the Peninsula and it's very good value. In some countries, such as Saudi Arabia, the UAE and Oman, roads are good and journeys are quick and comfortable on modern, air-conditioned buses. Yemen's services vary according to the company, for example, Yemitco tends to be fast, reliable and quite comfortable. Loud music or videos as well as heavy smoking can cause discomfort for people on some services – it's worth checking before boarding.

In many countries women accompanied by men can sit anywhere, but women travelling alone are expected to sit in the front seats.

For details of costs, bus passes and classes, see the individual country chapters.

Reservations

It's always advisable to book bus seats in advance at bus stations, and it's a must over the Muslim weekend (Friday), as well as during public holidays such as *eid*.

CAR & MOTORCYCLE

Unlike the car, which reigns supreme, motorcycles used as long-distance transport are a rare sight on most of the Arabian Peninsula. In a few cities they're popular for getting around town. If you decide to ride a motorcycle through the Peninsula, take one of the more popular Japanese models if you can. You'll have a better chance of finding spare parts. Even then, make sure

it's in very good shape before setting out. Motorcycles can be shipped ahead of departure. As with cyclists (see p551) try and avoid the summer months.

Bring Your Own Vehicle

Unless you're coming to live on the Peninsula for an extended duration, bringing your own vehicle may prove more trouble than it's worth. Obtaining a *carnet de passage* (see p550) is expensive and progressing through the Peninsula (due to visa regulations and paperwork) can be a major hassle. For most short-term visitors, it would make more sense to hire a car locally. For long-term residents it is cheaper and more straightforward to buy a car in-country and sell it before leaving.

Fuel stations are common throughout the region, both at major roadsides (in the more developed regions) and in towns and villages. On the desert roads they can be few and far between. Away from the main towns it's advisable to fill up whenever you get the chance (sometimes, this involves having your 4WD topped up by hand pump and funnel!). Fuel is extremely cheap throughout the region. Two grades of petrol are often available, but if in doubt buy the more expensive one. Most cars (except in Yemen) run on unleaded petrol.

Garages can be found even in the smallest towns and villages in most countries, but are less common in Yemen. Spare parts (and servicing) are available for the most

---

WOMEN'S LIB OR LIABILITY?

Some drivers are amazed and alarmed at the apparent audacity of local women when crossing roads. Many simply step out apparently oblivious to oncoming traffic. Pedestrians in many Peninsula countries have right of way, and women, who are used to being ushered to the front of a queue, given priority seats on the bus and having doors opened for them, believe this applies particularly to them. Additionally, headscarves or veils may obscure their vision. Note that if you injure someone, you'll be held responsible no matter whose fault it is, the argument being that if you hadn't been in-country, the accident wouldn't have happened.

popular car models (Toyota and Land Rover especially). Parts for other European makes (such as Peugeot) may be more difficult to come by. One tip is to ask your vehicle manufacturer for a list of any authorised service centres in the countries you plan to visit. The length of this list is likely to be a pretty good reflection of how easy it is to get spare parts on your travels.

Signposting (in both Arabic and English) is pretty good throughout the region (bar only Yemen which is notoriously lacking in signs in any language) and uses international symbols. English spelling of place names, however, is highly erratic and seldom matches the maps. Parking is becoming ever more difficult in Peninsula cities, and traffic inspectors and parking meters are now more prevalent.

Driving Licence

Travellers from the West can use their own national driving licences for a limited period in some Peninsula countries (including Oman and Saudi Arabia).

For longer stays an International Driving Permit, obtainable from your own country, is recommended or required by some countries.

To obtain a local licence you'll need to have a residency visa, plus the following documents: a valid foreigner's licence (and sometimes an IDP), a no-objection certificate (NOC) from your employer, your accommodation rental contract, photocopies of your passport, passport-sized photos and sometimes a certificate confirming your blood group. Some countries (such as Saudi Arabia) insist on Arabic translations of foreign documents. For some expats a driving test may also be required.

See individual country Transport sections for details.

Hire

Car hire is possible in all Peninsula countries. Though rarely cheap, it's not unreasonable. International hire organisations such as Hertz or Europcar, as well as local companies, have offices in most of the major cities as well as desks at international airports. Reservations are necessary in some countries during the peak tourism times, particularly during the haj, or major national or religious holidays.

CHECKPOINT CHALLENGE

Travellers often find the number of police checkpoints in many Peninsula countries exasperating. In some states their purpose is pretty pedestrian: to ensure that driver and vehicle papers are in order (note that if they're not, you'll be fined). In other countries there's a more serious purpose: to check for smuggled goods (particularly near the borders of Saudi Arabia and Yemen), illegal immigrants or illegal residents (whose visas have expired). In Yemen the checkpoints are also a means of keeping tabs on unruly tribes and maintaining a conspicuous police presence. Passing through the checkpoints can take time. Showing patience and good humour is always the best way of getting through them unscathed and unruffled.

In a nutshell, the international companies tend to be more expensive, but offer better cars and a better back-up service in case of problems. Local companies offer more competitive rates, but generally offer inferior cars and services, with fewer guarantees. Reputable tour agents are often a good source of cars, offering both competitive rates, plus decent cars and often a driver thrown in for very little extra cost, usually the best option for short-term travellers.

To hire a car you'll need your driving licence and, for some Peninsula countries, an IDP and copies of both your passport and visa. The minimum age varies between 21 to 25. Invariably, credit cards are now a prerequisite.

Some agencies can arrange vans, minibuses and buses for groups, but most deal only in cars; bike or motorcycle hire is near unheard of. Before hiring a self-drive vehicle, seriously ask yourself how well you think you can cope with the local driving conditions and whether you think you can navigate well enough to make good use of one. If going off-road, you also need to be strong enough to change a wheel.

Insurance

Insurance is compulsory. Given the large number of road traffic accidents, fully comprehensive insurance (as opposed to

DESERT DRIVING

The following tips may help if going off-road, but there's no substitute for experience:

Predeparture Planning

■ Travel with another vehicle if you're heading for sandy areas so that you can pull each other out if you get stuck.

■ Don't travel alone unless you can change a tyre (very heavy on 4WD vehicles).

■ Use the services of a local guide if planning an extended dune trip: navigation is not as easy as it seems.

■ Take a map and compass. A GPS and fully charged GSM phone are also useful but remember that GPS is only useful for knowing exactly where you're lost (and not how to find the way out) and phones don't work in some mountainous or remote areas.

■ Bring the equivalent of at least 5L of water per passenger per day and sufficient food to last several days. Dried dates are a good source of energy and keep well in high temperatures.

■ Check oil, tyre condition and tyre pressure before leaving.

■ Bring a tool kit with a tow rope, shovel, sand ladders, spanner, jack, wooden platform (on which to stand the jack), tyre inflator (and preferably a gauge) and jump leads. Also pack a first-aid kit.

■ Tell someone (and in some countries the local authorities, too) where you're going and leave a note detailing passengers, vehicles, itinerary, departure time and expected return time, as well as any mobile phone numbers.

■ Bring a hat, sunglasses and light clothes for the day, and warm clothes and sleeping bags for cold winter nights. Always check clothes, shoes and bedding for scorpions and camel spiders.

Driving Tips

■ In all desert areas follow prior tracks for the sanity of locals and care of the desert, as well as for your own safety.

■ Keep the acceleration up through areas of soft sand and under no circumstances stop!

■ When approaching sandy inclines, engage low gear and increase acceleration.

■ Never camp at the bottom of a wadi (dry river bed), even on a clear day.

third-party) is strongly advised. This covers the ancient law of paying blood money in the event of the injury or death of a person (and sometimes animal). Car-hire companies automatically supply insurance, but check carefully the cover and conditions.

Make certain that you're covered for off-piste travel, as well as travel between Peninsula countries (if you're planning cross-border excursions). If you are taking the car outside Gulf Cooperation Council (GCC) borders, you'll need separate insurance.

In the event of an accident, don't move the vehicle until the police arrive and make sure you submit the accident report as soon as possible to the insurance company or, if hiring, the car-hire company.

Purchase

The Peninsula is a good place to buy a car but note that you can't buy one without a residency permit. Most mainstream makes and models are available, and prices are low (since there's no import duty). As when shopping for other items, bargaining is normal. A down payment of around 10% of the purchase price is usually expected if taking out a loan.

Because cars are cheap, they're also seen as disposable by the wealthy. There is a growing second-hand car market, however, throughout the region. When second-hand car shopping it's essential you ensure that the car you're interested in purchasing has the following:

■ an up-to-date test certificate

- Be very wary of wadis when rain threatens. Flash flooding rips through the narrow channels of a wadi with huge force. Each year many people lose their lives in this way.

- Engage low gear on extended mountain descents even if it slows your progress to walking speed: many people run into trouble by burning out their brakes.

Getting Stuck in Sand

- In sand, the minute you feel the wheels are digging in, stop driving. The more you accelerate, the deeper you'll sink.

- If your wheels are deeply entrenched, don't dig: the car will just sink deeper.

- Partially deflate the tyres (for greater traction), clearing the sand away from the wheel in the direction you want to go (ie behind if you're going to try to reverse out).

- Collect brushwood (you'll wish you brought the sand ladders!) and anything else available, and pack under the tyres, creating as firm a 'launch pad' as possible.

- Plan your escape route or you'll flip out of the sand only to land in the next dune. In most dune areas, there are compacted platforms of sand. Try to find one of these on foot so that you have somewhere safe to aim for.

- Engage low ratio and remember that going backwards can be as effective as going forwards, especially if you stalled going uphill: gravity is a great help.

- Remember that using low ratio consumes a lot of petrol. Make sure you top up when you can and reinflate your tyres before rejoining a sealed road.

What to Do if You're Lost

- Stay with your vehicle, where there's shade and water. The Bedu or local villagers will find you before you find them. It's easier for a search party to spot a vehicle than people wandering in the desert.

- Use mirrors, horns or fires to attract attention, and construct a large sign on the ground that can easily be seen from the air.

- Stay calm, stay in the shade and conserve energy and water. You may think you're alone, but more likely than not, someone will have spotted you travelling through their territory.

- a registration certificate (and that the engine and chassis numbers of the car matches the latter)

Also be sure to give it a thorough check. If you're not a mechanic, bring one. Note that change of ownership has to be completed with the local police and that fines outstanding on the car are usually transferred to the new owner. When buying a vehicle (or importing one), you usually have to register it with the police traffic department.

Road Conditions

Since the oil boom of the 1970s and the growth of the Peninsula economies, road development has been a major priority and much money and effort have been poured into constructing roads. Today, with the exception of parts of Yemen, the Peninsula's road system is one of the best in the world.

Built over the last 25 years, most roads are high-quality two- or four-lane highways. Good highways also connect many of the Peninsula countries to one another. Few roads are unsealed (except in Yemen and Oman) and 4WDs are on the whole only necessary for driving across the desert.

Road building continues both within individual countries as well as between them. Sometimes rich and benevolent sheikhs pay for roads in neighbouring countries, such as Omani sheikhs paying for stretches of road in Yemen. Roads of some form go almost everywhere, even if they are not yet sealed;

TRANSPORT IN THE ARABIAN PENINSULA

DRUNK-DRIVING: A DEADLY SIN

Note that driving under the influence of either alcohol (of *any* quantity) or drugs is not only considered a grave offence on the Peninsula, but also automatically invalidates your insurance and makes you liable for any costs in the event of an accident.

Infractions are punished severely even in the more liberal Peninsula countries. At the least it can lead to a night or two in jail, a fine of around US$1500 and suspension of your licence. More serious cases (such as if you're involved in an accident) can lead to long prison sentences, the loss of your job if you're a resident and even deportation.

---

car tracks even cross the remotest regions of uninhabited desert, leaving only the Empty Quarter (Rub' al-Khali) inviolate.

As such, off-road routes (unsealed roads that have been graded, or levelled, with a roller, or tracks that have simply been made by cars driving along old camel or donkey tracks) provide some of the most exciting ways to explore remote parts of the desert. Off-road driving is a popular pastime in the Peninsula and can be enjoyed by any confident driver with a bit of common sense. Desert driving and navigation require a certain amount of skill, however, and as with all skills they take some practice. It's better to start off with a relatively short and simple trip, and build up to dune driving or extended wadi routes.

Don't economise by taking a sedan when the road conditions require 4WD: it could end up costing you more than you bargained for.

Road Hazards

Prior to the oil boom there was limited vehicular traffic on the Peninsula. Since then the number of vehicles on the road has increased dramatically. Today, some cities suffer from congestion, with rush-hour traffic in Muscat and Dubai rivalling that of Western cities. With the increase in traffic, traffic accidents have become a major issue (particularly in Kuwait, Saudi Arabia and the UAE, which have the highest number of accidents per capita in the world) and as such, it's worth being aware of the main hazards in order to avoid them.

The standard of driving on the Peninsula is poor, largely because driving tests are less exacting or are illegally dodged. Bad driving includes tailgating, queue-jumping, pushing-in, lack of indication, not using mirrors, jumping red lights and turning right across the traffic when sitting in the left lane. Car horns, used at the slightest provocation, take the place of caution and courtesy and no-one likes to give way, slow down or wait.

During Ramadan, drivers (due to the day's fasting) are often tired, thirsty, hungry and irritable, and everyone is in that much more of a hurry – generally to get home for a nap.

The one good news story of the region is Oman, where (on the whole) drivers stick to the speed limits, let people into their lane and thank others for the same courtesy. Use of the horn is forbidden in an emergency and you can be fined for having a dirty car.

Other hazards to look out for are animals on the road (particularly camels). In some countries, such as Yemen, cars are poorly maintained and at night they may travel without any lights. Heavy rain and flash floods frequently wash out sections of road in the mountain areas of the Peninsula, leaving uneven surfaces that damage the tyres. Spare tyres are therefore essential as is a set of jump leads. Batteries are also quickly exhausted in high temperatures.

If involved in an accident, don't move the car until the police arrive. An accident report will be issued (required by law), but it's best to decline to sign anything you don't understand (as you may be accepting responsibility for an accident that wasn't your fault) and call your insurance or car-hire company. If involved in an accident, try at all costs to remain calm. Aggression may be held against you and will only worsen the situation. The traffic police are generally helpful and friendly, and it's customary for men to shake hands with policemen before commencing discussions.

Road Rules

Driving is on the right side of the road in all Peninsula countries, but speed limits vary between 100km/h to 120km/h on highways and 45km/h to 60km/h in towns and built-up areas. Speed cameras are in operation in most city areas and on highways. If you're an expat with a local licence, you can clock up penalty points or hefty fines in some Peninsula countries.

Seat belts are a legal requirement and noncompliance can incur on-the-spot fines (up to around US$30 in some countries).

The use of hand-held mobile phones while driving is also an offence in most countries and may lead to a fine. The use of the horn is banned in Oman except in an emergency.

You should keep your licence with you at all times and carrying a first-aid kit, fire extinguisher and warning triangle is required in some Peninsula countries.

Driving while under the influence of alcohol is a serious offence (see opposite).

Saudi Arabia has many road offences and infractions that can be punished quite severely (fines are high and often accompanied by jail sentences or even lashes); see opposite for more details.

HITCHING

Hitching is never entirely safe in any country and can't be recommended. Travellers who still decide to hitch should understand that they are taking a small but potentially serious risk. This is particularly the case in the Peninsula, where distances are great between towns and you can be marooned in isolated places with literally life-threatening consequences (for example, if you run out of water in the summer months). You may also find that you end up spending days at someone's remote desert settlement because your driver fancied taking you home to show the family. The novelty wears off after the first day and a half of communal living.

Nevertheless, hitching is not illegal in any Middle Eastern country and in many places it is a common practice among the locals. It's considered not so much an alternative to the public transport system as an extension of it. Throughout the Peninsula a raised thumb is a vaguely obscene gesture. The most common means of signalling that you want a lift is to extend your right hand, palm down and wag it up and down briskly.

While it's normal for Arabs, Asians and Africans to hitch, it isn't something Westerners are expected to do. You may attract considerable attention and while this can work to your advantage, it can also lead to suspicion from the local police. It's also considered disappointing by many people: in rural areas there's an expectation that tourism will bring money into the country; watching you hitch along with the locals isn't returning the kind of dividends on their investment that they'd hoped.

HITCHHIKERS FROM HAYL

Only the hardest-hearted driver could leave an old man by the side of the road but don't be fooled: this could be the hitchhiker from Hayl. Hayl is the kind of mountain village that you really hadn't planned on visiting. It's usually at the end of a three-hour detour along a goat track along which most people wouldn't march their boots, and which at more than one point, gives way to precipitous drops to certain death in the wadi below. In fact, there's usually some kind of memorial on the roadside, showing where the last driver reached Hayl earlier than the rest of us. Naturally, when you reach the village you'll be waved in between plantation walls that were intended for slim-line donkeys, not pot-bellied 4WDs. Equally naturally, there's nowhere to turn round, so you'll have to negotiate the tightrope in reverse.

Although giving the old man a ride can be a great way to make friends – as without doubt he'll insist on your returning home for coffee and dates – you may not have had in mind that the entire village would want to make your acquaintance, too. Nor did you reckon on the presents: expect at least a fish, generally smelling a few days distant from the sea, or dates with attendant wasps, and, joy oh joy, company for the return journey. This usually takes the form of two women and a child, none of whom are accomplished car passengers, and nor did they bring a plastic bag. Given their vulnerability, and besides the old man entrusted them personally to your care, you can't possibly leave them at the junction. Unfortunately, they invariably want to go to Hail, three hours in the other direction. Hell, why not just give up the day job and become a taxi driver instead!

Hitching isn't free. The going rate is usually the equivalent of the bus or shared taxi fare, but may be more if a driver takes you to an address or place off their route. However, make sure that any fare is negotiated *before* you get into the vehicle.

Note also that it's safer always to hitch in pairs. Unless accompanied by men, it's unadvisable for women to hitch and out of the question for women travelling alone.

As a driver you'll often be flagged down for a ride: you might need to think what this might entail before offering one (see boxed text, p557). Women drivers should never give a lift to a man.

LOCAL TRANSPORT

As cars are relatively cheap to buy and run, public transport (particularly buses and minibuses in towns) tends to be used by less affluent members of the population.

Minibus & Bus

In most cities and towns, a minibus or bus service operates. Fares are cheap, regular and run on fixed routes. However, unless you're familiar with the town, they can be difficult to use (not all display their destination) and they're often crowded.

In some Peninsula countries, minibus or local bus services tend to connect residential or commercial areas, rather than providing a comprehensive network across the whole city.

Few countries have public minibuses to/from the airport, but top-end hotels and travel agents (if you're taking a tour) can usually provide a complimentary minibus with advance notice. Some hotels provide bus services to city centres too.

Taxi

In the West taxis are usually an avoidable luxury; in the Arabian Peninsula they are often the best way for travellers to get about town. Many cities have no other form of urban public transport, while there are also many rural routes that are only feasible in a taxi or private vehicle.

The way in which taxis operate varies widely from country to country, and often even from place to place within a country. So does the price. Local details are given in the Getting Around sections of the country chapters. See also the boxed text, below.

REGULAR TAXI

The regular taxi (also known as 'contract', 'agency', 'telephone', 'private', 'engaged' or 'special taxi') is an urban phenomenon found in all the main Peninsula towns or cities. In some places no other public transport exists, but usually regular taxis coexist alongside less expensive means of transport (such as shared taxis or minibuses).

Their main purpose is for transportation within a town or on a short rural trip, and their rates can work out competitively even for several hours. They're also often the only way of reaching airports or seaports and are generally considered safe for women travellers.

TAXI TIPS

On the whole, taxi drivers in the Peninsula are helpful, honest and humorous – they're not, however, so scrupulous when it comes to the tariff. New arrivals are particularly tempting bait and a target for minor scams or a bit of overcharging. Here are a few tips:

- Be aware that not all taxi drivers speak English. Generally, in cities used to international travellers they speak enough to get by, but not otherwise.

- *Always* negotiate a fare (or insist that the meter is used if it works) before jumping in. Town taxis sometimes have meters, most of which work only intermittently. This book quotes local rates but if in doubt ask a local, or at hotel reception, what a fair rate is for your destination.

- Don't rely on street names (there are often several versions). If you're not going to a well-known place, find out if it's close to a local landmark. Alternatively, ask someone to write down the name in Arabic.

- Ask the driver to wait while you check you've reached the correct destination.

- Avoid using unlicensed cab drivers at airports.

Taxis range from old Toyota Corolla bangers to fleets of sleek, well-organised, comfortable and metered vehicles (in the larger cities), and even limousine services. For details see the individual country chapters.

SHARED TAXI

A perfect compromise between the convenience of a regular taxi and the economy of a bus is the shared taxi. Known also as 'collect', 'collective' or 'service taxi' in English, and *servees* in Arabic, most shared taxis take up to four or five passengers, but some seat up to about 12 and are as good as indistinguishable from minibuses.

Shared taxis are far cheaper than private taxis and, once you get the hang of them, can be just as convenient. They're usually a little dearer than buses, but run more frequently and are usually faster (they don't stop as often or as long). They also tend to operate for longer hours than buses. Shared taxis function as urban, intercity and rural transport.

Fixed-route taxis wait at the point of departure until full or nearly full. Usually they pick up or drop off passengers anywhere en route, but in some places they have fixed halts or stations. Sometimes each service is allocated a number, which may be indicated on the vehicle. Generally a flat fare applies for each route, but sometimes it's possible to pay a partial fare.

On 'routeless' taxis, you'll quickly find a taxi willing to take you almost anywhere, but if you're prepared to wait a while, or to do your journey in stages, you can get around for almost nothing. Fares depend largely on time and distance.

Beware of boarding an empty shared taxi. The driver may assume you want to hire the vehicle as a 'contract taxi' (see Regular Taxi, p558) and charge accordingly. It's a good idea to watch what other passengers pay and to hand over your fare in front of them. Also, look for a taxi to your destination that's almost full. If a taxi's empty when you board it, you may have to wait a long time (sometimes several hours) for it to leave, particularly if it's destined for a less popular or remote place.

Passengers are expected to know where they are getting off. *'Shukran'* is 'thank you' in Arabic and the usual cue for the driver to stop. Make it clear to the driver or other passengers if you want to be told when you reach your destination.

TRAIN

Because relatively small populations are spread over large areas, as well as the fact that reasonable and inexpensive bus and air services already operate, there's little demand for a train service and no immediate plans to build one.

The only train service currently in the region is that found in Saudi Arabia (see p372) which connects the capital with the east of the Kingdom (running from Riyadh to Dammam, via Hofuf and Dhahran among other places).

Health

Though prevention is always the key to staying healthy while travelling, medical facilities in most Peninsula countries are excellent and as good as anywhere in the West (though emergency and specialised treatment may not be so readily or extensively available).

Problems particular to the Peninsula include respiratory complaints (due to the arid climate and high levels of dust), sunburn and sunstroke, eye problems, and injuries resulting from the high incidence of road accidents (see p556).

BEFORE YOU GO

A little planning before departure, particularly for pre-existing conditions, will save you a lot of trouble later:

- Bring medications in their original, clearly labelled containers with a signed and dated letter from your physician describing your medical condition and the medications (including generic names)
- Carry a spare pair of contact lenses and glasses (and take your optical prescription with you).
- Pack a first-aid kit.

- If carrying syringes or needles, be sure to have a physician's letter documenting their medical necessity (see p532).
- See your dentist before a long trip.

It's tempting to leave it all to the last minute – don't! Many vaccines take time to ensure immunity, so visit a doctor four to eight weeks before departure. Ask your doctor for a 'yellow booklet' (an International Certificate of Vaccination), listing all the vaccinations you've received. This is mandatory for some Peninsula countries that require proof of yellow-fever vaccination upon entry for travellers who have recently visited a country where yellow fever is found.

Travellers can register with the **International Association for Medical Advice to Travellers** (IMAT; www.iamat.org); its website can help travellers find recommended doctors. For travellers about to set off to very remote areas of the Peninsula (to do aid work in Yemen, for example), first-aid courses are offered by the Red Cross and St John Ambulance, and a remote-medicine first-aid course is offered by the **Royal Geographical Society** (www.rgs.org).

INSURANCE

In most Peninsula countries, doctors expect payment in cash on the spot. Find out in advance if your insurance makes payments directly to overseas health providers or reimburses you later. Insist on a receipt for any treatment so that you can claim the money back later.

Ensure that your travel insurance covers evacuation or repatriation, or access to better medical facilities elsewhere (which may be the only way to get medical attention for a serious emergency).

RECOMMENDED VACCINATIONS

The World Health Organization (WHO) recommends that all travellers, regardless of the region they are travelling in, should be covered for diphtheria, tetanus, measles, mumps, rubella, polio and hepatitis B. See your doctor to ensure your vaccination cover is complete and up to date.

MEDICAL CHECKLIST

Consider packing the following items:

- acetaminophen/paracetamol (eg Tylenol) or aspirin
- adhesive or paper tape
- antibacterial ointment (eg Bactroban) for cuts and abrasions
- antibiotics (if travelling off the beaten track)
- antidiarrhoeal drugs (eg loperamide)
- antihistamines (for allergic reactions)
- anti-inflammatory drugs (eg ibuprofen)
- bandages, gauze and gauze rolls
- DEET-containing insect repellent for the skin
- iodine tablets (for water purification if hiking or staying in remote areas)
- oral rehydration salts
- permethrin-containing insect spray for clothing, tents, and bed nets
- pocket knife
- safety pins
- scissors
- steroid cream or cortisone (for allergic rashes)
- sun block
- syringes and sterile needles
- thermometer
- tweezers

INTERNET RESOURCES

There is a wealth of travel-health advice on the internet; **Lonely Planet** (www.lonelyplanet.com) is a good place to start.

The **World Health Organization** (www.who.int /ith/) publishes an excellent book, *International Travel and Health,* which is revised annually and is available online at no cost. Another good website is **MD Travel Health** (www.mdtravelhealth.com), with travel-health recommendations for every Peninsula country. It's updated daily and is free. The website of **Centers for Disease Control & Prevention** (www.cdc .gov) is also a very useful source.

FURTHER READING

Lonely Planet's *Travel with Children* contains useful information for those with kids, including pretrip planning, emergency first aid, immunisation and disease information, and what to do if your kids get ill on the road.

Some other recommended reference books include *Traveller's Health* by Dr Richard Dawood, *International Travel Health*

> ### TRAVEL HEALTH WEBSITES
>
> Consider consulting your government's travel-health website before departing:
> **Australia** (www.dfat.gov.au/travel/)
> **Canada** (www.travelhealth.gc.ca)
> **UK** (www.doh.gov.uk/traveladvice/)
> **United States** (www.cdc.gov/travel/)

Guide by Stuart R. Rose, MD, and *The Travellers' Good Health Guide* by Ted Lankester. The latter is especially useful for volunteer workers and expats on the Peninsula.

IN TRANSIT

DEEP VEIN THROMBOSIS (DVT)

Deep Vein Thrombosis (DVT) occurs when blood clots form in the legs during plane flights, chiefly because of prolonged immobility. The longer the flight, the greater the risk. Though most blood clots are reabsorbed uneventfully, some may break off and travel through the blood vessels to the lungs, where they may cause life-threatening complications.

The chief symptom of DVT is swelling or pain of the foot, ankle or calf, usually, but not always, on just one side. When a blood clot travels to the lungs, it may cause chest pain and difficulty breathing. Travellers with any of these symptoms should immediately seek medical attention.

To prevent the development of DVT on long flights, walk about the cabin, perform isometric compressions of the leg muscles (ie contract the muscles while sitting), drink plenty of fluids and avoid alcohol.

JET LAG & MOTION SICKNESS

Jet lag is common when crossing more than five time zones; it results in insomnia, fatigue, malaise or nausea. To avoid jet lag, drink plenty of nonalcoholic fluids and eat light meals. Upon arrival, seek exposure to natural sunlight and readjust your schedule (for meals, sleep etc) as soon as possible.

Antihistamines such as dimenhydrinate (Dramamine) and meclizine (Antivert, Bonine) are usually the first choice for treating motion sickness. Their main side effect is drowsiness. A herbal alternative is ginger.

HEALTH

IN THE ARABIAN PENINSULA

AVAILABILITY & COST OF HEALTH CARE

At least one modern, well-equipped hospital with well-trained, English-speaking staff can be found in most of the larger towns and cities throughout the Peninsula. Most also have emergency units. In rural regions, treatment may be more limited and hospitals less well equipped. In very remote areas, medicine and even sterile dressings or intravenous fluids may need to be bought from a local pharmacy (signposted with green crosses).

There is a high ratio of doctors to patients in the Peninsula (bar Yemen), and a clinic can usually be found even in rural areas. Due to the high numbers of foreign doctors working in the Gulf countries, you'll probably have little trouble finding a doctor who speaks your language.

Though some Peninsula countries allow travellers access to free state medical treatment in emergencies, you should not rely on this and are strongly advised to have insurance cover. Reciprocal arrangements with other countries don't exist, so you should be prepared to pay for all medical and dental treatment that you receive.

Your insurance company may be able to provide a list of hospitals or clinics; otherwise ask at your hotel or, better yet, your embassy (which will have approved lists). In an emergency, contact your embassy or consulate.

Standards of dental care are also excellent in the larger towns and cities (though again patchy in Yemen). Note that in basic

---

CALL ME A CAB!

If you find you suddenly require urgent medical treatment on the Peninsula, don't call an ambulance, call a cab. The ambulance services – where they exist – are usually reserved for road accidents when the victim is unconscious or immobile (though even they are sometimes popped into taxis!). It's common (and much quicker) to take a taxi.

---

hospitals there is an increased risk of hepatitis B and HIV transmission via poorly sterilised equipment. Note also that your travel insurance will not usually cover you for dental treatment for anything other than an emergency.

For minor illnesses such as diarrhoea, pharmacists (who are usually very knowledgeable and speak good English) often provide valuable advice and sell appropriate medication over the counter. They are also very familiar with local diseases or bugs, and can advise when more specialised help is needed.

Doctors' appointments can usually be arranged within around 24 to 48 hours in the Peninsula (less if it's urgent), and an examination (without clinical tests or prescriptions) typically costs around US$50.

INFECTIOUS DISEASES

Dengue Fever

Also known as break-bone fever, dengue is spread through the bite of the mosquito. It causes a feverish illness, with a headache and muscle pains, that's like a bad, prolonged attack of influenza. There may also be a rash. Take precautions to avoid being bitten by mosquitoes.

Diphtheria

Diphtheria is spread through close respiratory contact. It causes a high temperature and a severe sore throat. Sometimes a membrane forms across the throat, requiring a tracheostomy to prevent suffocation.

Vaccination is recommended for those likely to be in close contact with the local population in infected areas. The vaccine is given as an injection by itself, or with tetanus, and lasts 10 years.

Hepatitis A

Hepatitis A is spread through contaminated food (particularly shellfish) and water. It causes jaundice and, although it is rarely fatal, can cause prolonged lethargy and delayed recovery. Symptoms include dark urine, a yellow colour to the whites of the eyes, fever and abdominal pain.

Hepatitis A vaccine (Avaxim, VAQTA, Havrix) is given as an injection; a single dose will give protection for up to a year, while a booster 12 months later will provide protection for a subsequent period of 10 years. Hepatitis A and typhoid vaccines can also be given as a single dose vaccine in the form of Hepatyrix or Viatim.

Hepatitis B

Infected blood, contaminated needles and sexual intercourse can all transmit hepatitis B. It can cause jaundice, and affects the liver, occasionally causing liver failure. All travellers should make this a routine vaccination – many countries now give hepatitis B vaccination as part of routine childhood vaccination.

The vaccine is given by itself, or at the same time as the hepatitis A vaccine. A course protects for at least five years, and can be given over four weeks or six months.

HIV

HIV is spread via infected blood and blood products, sexual intercourse with an infected partner, and from an infected mother to her newborn child. It can also be spread through 'blood-to-blood' contacts such as contaminated instruments used during medical, dental, acupuncture and other body-piercing procedures, as well as from sharing intravenous needles.

Countries in the Peninsula that require a negative HIV test as a requirement for some categories of visas include Kuwait, Qatar, Saudi Arabia and the United Arab Emirates.

Malaria

The prevalence of malaria varies throughout the Peninsula. The risk is considered minimal in most cities, but may be more substantial in rural areas. Check with your doctor or local travel-health clinic for the latest information. Antimalarial tablets are essential if the risk is significant, and you should also be aware of the disease's symptoms.

Malaria almost always starts with marked shivering, fever and sweating. Muscle pains, headache and vomiting are also common. Symptoms may occur anytime from a few days up to three weeks or more after being bitten by an infected mosquito, and you may still show symptoms even though you are taking preventative tablets.

Meningitis

Meningococcal infection is spread through close respiratory contact.

AIDS ON THE PENINSULA

Though it's strictly illegal for AIDS or HIV sufferers either to visit or to live on the Peninsula (and detection of the disease usually results in instant deportation), the region is not the AIDS-free place you might imagine. In recent years, prostitutes (mostly from Eastern Europe and the old Soviet bloc) have flowed into the area under the guise of tourists. Locals have also returned infected after sexual adventures abroad. Additionally there is something of a cultural taboo about condom use among many Arab men. Travellers who form new relationships should also note that 'fornication', adultery and homosexuality are considered grave crimes in some Peninsula states.

A meningococcal vaccination certificate covering the A and W135 strains is required as a condition of entry if embarking on a haj pilgrimage to Mecca and Medina in Saudi Arabia, and for all travellers arriving from the meningitis belt of sub-Saharan Africa. Visas for pilgrimages are not issued unless proof of vaccination is submitted with the visa application.

Rabies

Spread through bites or licks (on broken skin) from any warm blooded, furry animal, rabies can be fatal. The skin should be immediately and thoroughly cleaned. If there is any possibility that the animal is infected with rabies, immediate medical assistance should be sought. Animal handlers should be vaccinated, as should those travelling to remote areas where a reliable source of postbite vaccine is not available within 24 hours.

Three injections are needed over a month to vaccinate against rabies. If you have been bitten and have not been vaccinated, you will need a course of five injections starting within 24 hours or as soon as possible after the injury. Vaccination does not provide you with immunity; it merely buys you more time to seek appropriate medical help.

Rift Valley Fever

This haemorrhagic fever is spread through blood or blood products, including those from infected animals.

It causes a flu like illness with fever, joint pains and occasionally more serious complications. Complete recovery is possible.

Tuberculosis

Tuberculosis (TB) is spread through close respiratory contact, and occasionally through infected milk or milk products.

TB can be asymptomatic, although symptoms can include a cough, weight loss or fever, months or even years after exposure. An X-ray is the best way of establishing if you have TB.

BCG vaccine is recommended for those likely to be mixing closely with the local population. BCG gives a moderate degree of protection against TB. It's usually only given in specialised chest clinics, and is not available in all countries. As it's a live vaccine, it should not be given to pregnant women or immunocompromised individuals.

Typhoid

Typhoid is spread through food or water that has been contaminated by infected human faeces.

The first symptom is usually fever or a pink rash on the abdomen. Septicaemia (blood poisoning) may also occur. Typhoid vaccine (Typhim Vi, Typherix) will give protection for three years. In some countries, the oral vaccine Vivotif is also available.

Yellow Fever

Yellow-fever vaccination is not required for any areas of the Peninsula, but any traveller coming from a country where yellow fever is found will need to show a vaccination certificate at immigration.

The yellow-fever vaccination must be given at an approved clinic, and is valid for 10 years. It is a live vaccine and must not be given to immunocompromised or pregnant travellers.

TRAVELLERS' DIARRHOEA

To prevent diarrhoea, avoid tap water in rural areas. In areas of uncertain hygiene, eat only fresh fruit or vegetables if they've been cooked or if you have peeled them yourself, and avoid dairy products that might contain unpasteurised milk.

If you develop diarrhoea, drink plenty of fluids and preferably an oral rehydration solution containing lots of salt and sugar.

If you start having more than four or five loose stools a day, you should start taking an antibiotic (usually containing quinolone) and an antidiarrhoeal agent (such as loperamide). You should seek medical attention if the diarrhoea is bloody, persists for more than 72 hours, or is accompanied by fever, shaking, chills or severe abdominal pain.

ENVIRONMENTAL HAZARDS
Heat Illness

Heat exhaustion occurs following heavy sweating and excessive fluid loss. Be aware that in the summer months, temperatures can reach 50°C and in such conditions even a round of golf can be dangerous if you're not protected against the sun and adequately hydrated.

Symptoms include a headache, dizziness and tiredness. Aim to drink sufficient water so that you produce pale, diluted urine. To treat heat exhaustion, drink lots of water, cool down in an air-conditioned room and add a little more table salt to foods than usual.

Heatstroke is a much more serious condition, and occurs when the body's heat-regulating mechanism breaks down. An excessive rise in body temperature leads to the cessation of sweating, irrational and hyperactive behaviour, and eventually loss of consciousness and death. Rapid cooling of the body by spraying it with water or fanning is an effective treatment. Emergency fluid and electrolyte replacement (by intravenous drip) is also usually required.

Insect Bites & Stings

Mosquitoes may not carry malaria or dengue fever, but they can still cause irritation and infected bites. Using DEET-based insect repellents will help prevent bites.

If you have an allergy to bee or wasp stings, carry an adrenaline injection or similar.

Scorpions are frequently found in dry climates. Though their bite can be painful, it's rarely life threatening.

Bed bugs and sometimes scabies are occasionally found in hostels and cheap hotels. They cause very itchy lumpy bites – spray the mattress or find new lodgings!

Water

Tap water is safe to drink in Gulf cities (but not in Yemen or Saudi, nor in rural areas where water is delivered by tanker), but it doesn't agree with everyone. It's easier to stick to bottled water (found everywhere), boil water for ten minutes, or use water-purification tablets or a filter. Never drink water from wadis (valleys or riverbeds) or streams as animals are usually watered in them.

WOMEN'S HEALTH

Emotional stress, exhaustion and travelling through different time zones can all contribute to an upset in the menstrual pattern. If using oral contraceptives, remember that diarrhoea, vomiting and some antibiotics can stop the pill from working. Take condoms with you just in case. Condoms should be kept in a cool dry place or they may crack and perish.

Tampons and sanitary towels are not always available outside of major cities in the Peninsula.

If travelling during pregnancy, have a medical checkup before embarking on your trip. The most risky times for travel are during the first 12 weeks of pregnancy, when miscarriage is most likely, and after 30 weeks, when complications such as high blood pressure and premature delivery can occur.

Most airlines will not accept a traveller after 28 or 32 weeks of pregnancy, and long-haul flights in the later stages can be very uncomfortable.

Excellent obstetric and antenatal facilities are offered throughout the Peninsula (though less so in Yemen), particularly in the larger cities.

Taking written records of your pregnancy, including details of your blood group, is helpful if you need medical attention while away. Ensure your insurance policy covers pregnancy delivery and postnatal care, but remember insurance policies are only as good as the facilities available.

HEALTH

Language

CONTENTS

Learning a few basics for day-to-day travelling doesn't take long at all, but to master the complexities of Arabic would take years of consistent study. The whole issue is complicated by the differences between Classical Arabic (fus-ha), its modern descendant MSA (Modern Standard Arabic) and regional dialects. The classical tongue is the language of the Quran and Arabic poetry of centuries past. For a long time it remained static, but in order to survive it had to adapt to change, and the result is more or less MSA, the common language of the press, radio and educated discourse. It is as close to a lingua franca (common language) as the Arab world comes, and is generally understood – if not always well spoken – across the Arab world.

For most outsiders trying to learn Arabic, the most frustrating thing is understanding the spoken language (wherever you are), as there is virtually no written material to refer to for back up. Acquisition of MSA is a long-term investment, and an esoteric argument flows back and forward about the relative merits of learning MSA first (and so perhaps having to wait some time before being able to communicate adequately with people in the street) or learning a dialect. All this will give you an inkling of why so few non-Arabs, or non-Muslims, embark on a study of the language.

Mercifully, the words and phrases a traveller is most likely to use are fairly standard throughout the Arabian Peninsula, and the words and phrases that follow should be understood anywhere in the region. For a handy guide to the specific variety of colloquial Arabic spoken on the Arabian Peninsula and elswhere, get a copy of Lonely Planet's Middle East Phrasebook.

PRONUNCIATION

Pronunciation of Arabic can be tongue-tying for someone unfamiliar with the intonation and combination of sounds. This language guide should help, but bear in mind that the myriad rules governing pronunciation and vowel use are too extensive to be covered here.

Vowels

Technically, there are three long and three short vowels in Arabic. The reality is a little different, with local dialect and varying consonant combinations affecting the pronunciation of vowels. This is the case throughout the Arabic-speaking world. More like five short and five long vowels can be identified; in this guide we use all of these except the long **o**.

a	as in 'had'
aa	as the 'a' in 'father'
e	short, as in 'bet'; long, as in 'there'
i	as in 'hit'
ee	as in 'beer', only softer
o	as in 'hot'
u	as in 'put'
oo	as in 'food'

Consonants

Pronunciation for all Arabic consonants is covered in the alphabet table (opposite). It's important to note that when double consonants occur in transliterations, both are pronounced. For example, al-Hammam (toilet), is pronounced 'al-ham-mam'.

OTHER SOUNDS

Arabic has two sounds that are very tricky for non-Arabs to produce, the 'ayn and the

STANDARD ARABIC ALPHABET

Final	Medial	Initial	Alone	Transliteration	Pronunciation
ـا			ا	aa	as in 'father'
ـب	ـبـ	بـ	ب	b	as in 'bet'
ـت	ـتـ	تـ	ت	t	as in 'ten'
ـث	ـثـ	ثـ	ث	th	as in 'thin'
ـج	ـجـ	جـ	ج	j/g	as in 'jet'; sometimes as the 'g' in 'go'
ـح	ـحـ	حـ	ح	H	a strongly whispered 'h', like a sigh of relief
ـخ	ـخـ	خـ	خ	kh	as the 'ch' in Scottish *loch*
ـد			د	d	as in 'dim'
ـذ			ذ	dh	as the 'th' in 'this'; also as d or z
ـر			ر	r	a rolled 'r', as in the Spanish word *caro*
ـز			ز	z	as in 'zip'
ـس	ـسـ	سـ	س	s	as in 'so', never as in 'wisdom'
ـش	ـشـ	شـ	ش	sh	as in 'ship'
ـص	ـصـ	صـ	ص	ṣ	emphatic 's'
ـض	ـضـ	ضـ	ض	ḍ	emphatic 'd'
ـط	ـطـ	طـ	ط	ṭ	emphatic 't'
ـظ	ـظـ	ظـ	ظ	ẓ	emphatic 'z'
ـع	ـعـ	عـ	ع	'	the Arabic letter *'ayn*; pronounce as a glottal stop – like the closing of the throat before saying 'Oh-oh!' (see Other Sounds, opposite)
ـغ	ـغـ	غـ	غ	gh	a guttural sound like Parisian 'r'
ـف	ـفـ	فـ	ف	f	as in 'far'
ـق	ـقـ	قـ	ق	q	a strongly guttural 'k' sound; also often pronounced as a glottal stop
ـك	ـكـ	كـ	ك	k	as in 'king'
ـل	ـلـ	لـ	ل	l	as in 'lamb'
ـم	ـمـ	مـ	م	m	as in 'me'
ـن	ـنـ	نـ	ن	n	as in 'name'
ـه	ـهـ	هـ	ه	h	as in 'ham'
ـو			و	w	as in 'wet'; or
				oo	long, as in 'food'; or
				ow	as in 'how'
ـي	ـيـ	يـ	ي	y	as in 'yes'; or
				ee	as in 'beer', only softer; or
				ai/ay	as in 'aisle'/as the 'ay' in 'day'

Vowels Not all Arabic vowel sounds are represented in the alphabet. For more information on the vowel sounds used in this language guide, see Pronunciation (opposite).

Emphatic Consonants To simplify the transliteration system used in this book, the emphatic consonants have not been included.

LANGUAGE

glottal stop. The letter 'ayn represents a sound with no English equivalent that comes even close. It is similar to the glottal stop (which is not actually represented in the alphabet) but the muscles at the back of the throat are gagged more forcefully – it has been described as the sound of someone being strangled. In many transliteration systems 'ayn is represented by an opening quotation mark, and the glottal stop by a closing quotation mark. To make the transliterations in this language guide (and throughout the rest of the book) easier to use, we haven't distinguished between the glottal stop and the 'ayn, using the closing quotation mark to represent both sounds. You should find that Arabic speakers will still understand you.

TRANSLITERATION

It's worth noting here that transliteration from the Arabic script into English – or any other language for that matter – is at best an approximate science.

The presence of sounds unknown in European languages and the fact that the script is 'defective' (most vowels are not written) combine to make it nearly impossible to settle on one universally accepted method of transliteration. A wide variety of spellings is therefore possible for words when they appear in Latin script – and that goes for places and people's names as well.

While striving to reflect the language as closely as possible and aiming at consistency, this book generally spells place, street and hotel names and the like as the locals have done. Don't be surprised if you come across several versions of the same thing.

ACCOMMODATION

I'm looking for ...	ana badawar ala ...
a youth hostel	bayt al-shabaab
hotel	funduq
I'd like to book a ...	ana abga/(abee) eHjaz ... (Kuwait & Bahrain)
Do you have a ...?	fee aindakoum ...?
(cheap) room	ghurfa (rakheesa)
single room	ghurfa muferda
double room	ghurfa muzdawaja
May I see the room?	mumkin ashuf al-ghurfa?
May I see other rooms?	mumkin ashuf ghuraf thaania?

How much is this room per night?	cham ujrat haathil ghurfa fil-leila?
It's very expensive.	hatha ghali jeddan
Do you have any cheaper rooms?	fi ghuraf arkhas?
This is fine.	hatha zein
for one night	lee layla wahda
for two nights	lee layla ten
It's very noisy.	hathee feeha dajeh kaseer
It's very dirty.	hathee waskha kaseer
Where is the bathroom?	wayn el-Hammam?
I'm leaving today.	ana musafer al-youm
We're leaving today.	neHna musafereen al-yom

address	al-anwaar
air-conditioning	mookayif/kondishen
blanket	al-bataaniyya
camp site	al-mukhayam
hot water	al-mayya saakhma
key	al-miftaH
manager	al-mudeer
shower	al-doosh
soap	al-saboon
toilet	al-Hammam

CONVERSATION & GREETINGS

Arabs place great importance on civility and it's rare to see any interaction between people that doesn't begin with profuse greetings, inquiries into the other's health and other niceties.

Arabic greetings are more formal than in English and there is a reciprocal response to each. These sometimes vary slightly, depending on whether you're addressing a man or a woman. A simple encounter can become a drawn-out affair, with neither side wanting to be the one to put a halt to the stream of greetings and well-wishing. As an *ajnabi* (foreigner), you're not expected to know all the ins and outs, but if you come up with the right expression at the appropriate moment the locals will love it.

The most common greeting is *al-salaam alaykum* (peace be upon you), to which the correct reply is *wa alaykum al-salaam* (and upon you be peace). If you get invited to a birthday celebration or are around for any of the big holidays, the common greeting is *kul sana wa intum bikher* (I wish you well for the coming year).

Arrival in one piece is always something to be grateful for. Passengers will often be greeted with *al-Hamdu lillah al al-salaama* (thank God for your safe arrival).

Hello.	*al-salaam alaykum*
Hello. (response)	*wa alaykum al-salaam*
Hello. (informal)	*marHaba/ya marHaba*

It's an important custom in Arab countries to ask after a person's or their family's health when greeting, eg *chayf es-saHa?* (How is your health?), *chayf al-ahal?* (How is the family?). The response is *bikher il-Hamdu lillah* (Fine, thank you).

Goodbye.	*ma'al salaama*
Goodbye. (response)	
(to a man)	*alla ysalmak*
(to a woman)	*alla ysalmich*
(to a group)	*alla ysallimkum*
Goodbye.	
(to a man)	*Hayyaakallah*
(to a woman)	*Hayyachallah*
(to a group)	*Hayyakumallah*
Goodbye. (response)	
(to a man)	*alla yHai'eek*
(to a woman)	*alla yHai'eech*
(to a group)	*alla yHai'eekum*
Good night.	
(to a man)	*tisbaH ala-kher*
(to a woman)	*tisbiHin ala-kher*
(to a group)	*tisbuHun ala-kher*
Good night. (response)	
(to a man)	*wa inta min ahlil-kher*
(to a woman)	*wa inti min ahlil-kher*
(to a group)	*wa inta min ahlil-kher*
Welcome.	*ahlan wa sahlan/marHaba*
Welcome to you.	
(to a man)	*ahlan beek*
(to a woman)	*ahlan beechi*
(to a group)	*ahlan beekum*
Pleased to meet you.	*fursa sa'ida* (also said to people as they are leaving)
Pleased to meet you. (response)	
(by an individual)	*wa ana as'ad*
(by a group)	*wa iHna as'ad*
How are you?	*kief ul-hal?*
(to a man)	*shlonik?/kef Halak?*
(to a woman)	*shlonich?/kef Halik?*
(to a group)	*shlonkum?/kef Halkum?*
Fine, thanks.	*bkher al-Hamdu lillah* or *tammam*
(by a man)	*zein al-Hamdu lillah*
(by a woman)	*zeina al-Hamdu lillah*
(by a group)	*zeinin al-Hamdu lillah*

What's your name?	
(to a man)	*shismak?*
(to a woman)	*shismich?*
(to a group)	*shisimkum?*
My name is ...	*ismi ...*
I'm ...	*ana ...*
Where are you from?	*min wayn inta?*
I'm from ...	*ana min ...*
Do you like ...?	*inta/inti bitHib ...?* (m/f)
I like ...	*ana bHib ...*
I don't like ...	*ana ma bHib ...*
Yes.	*aiwa/na'am*
No.	*la'*
Maybe.	*mumkin*
Please.	
(to a man)	*min fadhlak*
(to a woman)	*min fadhlich*
(to a group)	*min fadhlekum*
Thank you.	*baraka Allah beek* (God bless you) or *shukran* (also *mashkur* in UAE)
You're welcome.	*afwan/al-afu*
Excuse me.	
(to a man)	*lau samaHt*
(to a woman)	*lau samaHti*
(to a group)	*lau samaHtu*
After you.	*atfaddal*
OK.	*zein/kwayyis/tayib*
No problem.	*mafee mushkala*
Impossible.	*mish mumkin*
It doesn't matter/ I don't care.	*ma'alish*

DIRECTIONS

How do I get to ...?	*keef boosal lil ...?*
Can you show me the way to ...?	*mumkin tdallini ala tareeq lil ...?*
How many kilometres?	*cham kilometa?*
What street is this?	*shoo-hatha sharai?*

to/for	*lil*
left	*shimaal/yasaar*
right	*yimeen*
straight	*ala tool/(sida)* (UAE)
street	*shaari'*
number	*raqam*
city	*madina*
village	*qaria*
at the next corner	*thani mafraq*
this way	*matn hina*
here/there	*hina/hinak*
in front of	*chiddaam/(qiddaam)* (UAE)
near	*gareeb*
far	*ba'eed*

EMERGENCIES

Help me!	saa' idoonee!
I'm sick.	ana maareed/mareeda (m/f)
Call the police!	itasell bil shurta!
doctor	al-tabeeb
hospital	al-mustashfa
police	al-shurta
Go away/Get lost!	imshee! (also seer! in UAE)
Shame on you!	istiHi a'la Haalak! (said by a woman)

north	shimaal
south	janub
east	sharg
west	gharb

HEALTH

I'm ill.	ana maareed
My friend is ill.	sadeeyee maareed
It hurts here.	bee yu ja nee hina

I'm ...	andee ...
asthmatic	azmit raboo
diabetic	al-sukkar
epileptic	al-saraa

I'm allergic ...	andee Hasasiyya ...
to antibiotics	min al-mudad alhayawee
to aspirin	min al-asbireen
to bees	min al-naHl
to nuts	min al-mukassarat
to penicillin	min al-binisileen

antiseptic	mutahhir
aspirin	asbireen
Band-Aids	dammad lazeg
chemist/pharmacy	al-sayidaliyya
condoms	kaboot
contraceptive	waseela lee man'al-Haml
diarrhoea	is-haal
fever	sukhooma
headache	suda' ras/waja' ras
hospital	mustashfa
medicine	dawa
pregnant	Haamel
prescription	wasfa/rashetta
sanitary napkins	fuwat saHiyya
stomachache	waja' feel bat-n
sunblock cream	marham wagee min ashat alshams
tampons	tambaks (as in the brand name 'Tampax') or, more formally, fuwat saHiyya leel Hareem

LANGUAGE DIFFICULTIES

I understand.	
(by a man)	ana fahim
(by a woman)	ana fahma
I don't understand.	
(by a man)	ana mu fahim
(by a woman)	ana mu fahma
Do you speak English/ French/German?	titkallam ingleezi/ fransawi/almaani?
I don't speak Arabic.	ma-atkallam arabi
I want an interpreter.	ana abga/(abee) mutarjem (Kuwait & Bahrain)
Could you write it down, please?	mumkin tiktbha lee, min fadlach
How do you say ... in Arabic?	chayf tegool ... bil'arabi?

NUMBERS

0	sifr	٠
1	waHid	١
2	ithneen	٢
3	thalatha	٣
4	arba'a	٤
5	khamsa	٥
6	sitta	٦
7	saba'a	٧
8	tamaniya	٨
9	tis'a	٩
10	ashra	١٠
11	Hda'ash	١١
12	thna'ash	١٢
13	thalathta'ash	١٣
14	arbatash	١٤
15	khamistash	١٥
16	sittash	١٦
17	sabi'tash	١٧
18	thimanta'ash	١٨
19	tisita'ash	١٩
20	'ishreen	٢٠
21	waHid wa 'ishreen	٢١
22	itnayn wa 'ishreen	٢٢
30	thalatheen	٣٠
40	arbi'een	٤٠
50	khamseen	٥٠
60	sitteen	٦٠
70	saba'een	٧٠
80	thimaneen	٨٠
90	tis'een	٩٠
100	imia	١٠٠
200	imiatayn	٢٠٠
1000	'alf	١٠٠٠
2000	'alfayn	٢٠٠٠
3000	thalath-alaf	٣٠٠٠

PAPERWORK

date of birth	tareekh al-welada/al-meelad
name	al-ism
nationality	al-jenseeya
passport	jawaz al-safar/al-bassbor
permit	tasreeh
place of birth	makka al-welada/meelad
visa	ta'sheera/feeza

SHOPPING & SERVICES

I'm looking for ...	ana adawar ala ... ana abHath aa'n ...
Where is the ...?	wein al ...?
bank	el-bank
beach	il-shatt/il-shaat'i
embassy	el-safara
exchange office	maktab el-sirafa
laundry	el-ghaseel
market	el-souq
mosque	el-masjid
museum	el-matHaf
newsagents	el-maktaba
old city	el-madina il-qadima
palace	el-qasr
police station	el-makhfar
post office	maktab al-bareed
restaurant	el-mataam
telephone	el-telefon/el-hataf
telephone office	maktab el-Hatef
toilet	el-Hammam
tourist office	maktab el-seeyaHa

nappies (diapers)	Hafadat leel atfal
disposable nappies	bamberz (brand name)
formula (baby's milk)	Haleeb mujafaf leel atfal

I want to change ...	ana abga/(abee asrif) ... (Kuwait & Bahrain)
money	floos
travellers cheques	sheikat siyaHeeya

I want ...	ana abga/(abee) ... (Kuwait & Bahrain)
Where can I buy ...?	wein agdar ashtiri...?
Do you have ...?	indik (to a man) indich (to a woman)
Is there ...?	fee andakum ...?
What is this?	shoo Hadha?
How much?	bcham/(gedash)? (Saudi & Yemen)
How many?	cham?
It's too expensive.	ghalee/ghalia wa'id (m/f)
There isn't (any).	mafee (walashai)
May I look at it?	mumkin ashoof il?

What time does it open?	
sa'acham yeftaH?	
What time does it close?	
sa'a cham yegfell/(yebannad)? (UAE & Bahrain)	
I'd like to make a telephone call.	
ana abga/(abee) sawee mookalama (Kuwait & Bahrain)	

TIME & DATES

What time is it?	as-sa'a kam?
It's ...	as-sa'a ...
one o'clock	waHda
1.15	waHda wa rob'
1.20	waHda wa tilt
1.30	waHda wa nus
1.45	ithneen illa rob' (literally 'quarter to two')

daily	kil yom
today	al-yom
yesterday	ams
tomorrow	bukra/bacher
early	mbach'ir/badri
late	mit'akhir

Monday	yom al-ithneen
Tuesday	yom al-thalath
Wednesday	yom al-arbaa'
Thursday	yom al-khamis
Friday	yom al-jama'a
Saturday	yom as-sabt
Sunday	yom al-Had

The Western Calendar Months

The Islamic year has 12 lunar months and is 11 days shorter than the Western (Gregorian) calendar, so important Muslim dates will occur 11 days earlier each (Western) year.

There are two Gregorian calendars in use in the Arab world. In Egypt and westwards, the months have virtually the same names as in English (January is *yanaayir*, October is *octobir* and so on), but in Lebanon and eastwards, the names are quite different. Talking about, say, June as 'month six' is the easiest solution, but for the sake of completeness, the months from January are:

January	kanoon ath-thani
February	shubaat
March	azaar
April	nisaan
May	ayyaar
June	Huzayraan
July	tammooz

LANGUAGE

August	'aab
September	aylool
October	tishreen al-awal
November	tishreen ath-thani
December	kaanoon al-awal

TRANSPORT
Public Transport

Where is the ...?	wein al ...?
How far is ...?	cham yibe'id ...?
the bus stop	mogaf al-bas
the bus station	maHattat al-bas
the train station	maHattat al-qatar
a taxi stand	mogaf el-taks
the airport	al-mataar

boat	markab
bus	al-bas
taxi	el-taks
ticket office	maktab al-tathaaker

I want to go to ...	abga/(abee) arouH li ... (Kuwait & Bahrain)
When does the ... leave?	mata yamshi il ...
When does the ... arrive?	mata tusal il ...
What is the fare to ...?	cham il tathkara li ...
Which bus/taxi goes to ...?	ai bas/tax yrouH il ...
Does this bus/taxi go to ...?	Hathal bas yrouH il ...
How many buses go to ...?	cham bas yrouH li ...
How long does the trip take?	cham sa'aa al-riHla?
Please tell me when we get to ...	lau samaHtit goul li mata nosal li ...
Stop here, please.	'ogaf hina, lau samaHt
Please wait for me.	lau samaHt, intethernee
May I sit here?	mumkin ag'id hina?
May we sit here?	mumkin nag'id hina?
1st class	daraja oola
2nd class	daraja thaniya
ticket	al-tathkara
to ...	ee/a ...
from ...	min ...

Private Transport

I'd like to hire a ...	ana abga/(abee) ajar ... (Kuwait & Bahrain)
Where can I hire a ...?	wayn mumkin ajar ...?
bicycle	bisklet/dakaja

camel	jamal
car	sayyara
car baby seat	kursi sayyara leel tefl
donkey	Hmaar
4WD	'four wheel'
horse	Hsaan
motorcycle	motosikl
tour guide	daleel seeyaHe/ murshid seeyaHe

Is this the road to ...?
Hal Hatha al-tarig eela ...?
Where's a service station?
wayn maHattet el-betrol/al-benzeen?
Please fill it up.
min fadhlak fawell Ha
I'd like ... litres.
abga/(abee) ... leeter (Kuwait & Bahrain)

diesel	deezel
leaded petrol	betrol bil rasas
unleaded petrol	betrol khali mina rasas

I need a mechanic.
ana abga mekaneeki
The car won't start.
el-sayyara ma bet door
I have a flat tyre.
nzel el-doolab
I've run out of petrol.
khalas el-betrol/al-benzeen
I've had an accident.
ana a'malt Hads

Also available from Lonely Planet:
Middle East Phrasebook

Glossary

Following is a list of some unfamiliar words and abbreviations you might meet in the text. For a list of common foods you may encounter, see 'Eat Your Words' in the Food & Drink chapter (p88).

abeyya – woman's full-length black robe; also *abaya*
abra – water taxi
agal – black head-rope used to hold a *gutra* in place; also *igal*
ardha – traditional Bedouin dance
attar – rosewater
azan – call to prayer

bachoor – incense (Saudi Arabia)
badghir – wind tower
barasti – traditional Gulf method of building palm-leaf houses; name of the house itself
barjeel – wind tower
Bedouin – (pl Bedu) a nomadic desert dweller
beit ash-sha'ar – Bedouin goat-hair tent
bijou – service taxi
bukhnoq – girl's head covering
burda – traditional Qatari cloak
burj – tower
burka – see *hejab*

caravanserai – travellers' inn, usually constructed on main trade routes; also *khan*
compound – residential area of expats, usually with high security (Gulf States)
corniche – seaside road

dalla – traditional copper coffeepot
dhow – traditional Arab boat rigged with a lateen (triangular) sail; also *sambuq* or *sambuk*
dishdasha – man's long shirt-dress
diwan – Muslim meeting room or reception room
diwaniya – gatherings, usually at someone's home

eid – Islamic feast
Eid al-Adha – Feast of Sacrifice marking the pilgrimage to Mecca
Eid al-Fitr – Festival of Breaking the Fast, celebrated at the end of Ramadan
emir – literally 'prince'; Islamic ruler, military commander or govenor

falaj – traditional irrigation channel
fatwa – religious edict issued by Islamic clerics/scholars
funduq – hotel; also *fondouk*

GCC – Gulf Cooperation Council; members are Saudi Arabia, Kuwait, Bahrain, Qatar, Oman and the UAE
gebel – see *jebel*
gutra – white head-cloth worn by men in Saudi Arabia and the Gulf States; also *shemaag*

haj – annual Muslim pilgrimage to Mecca; one of the Five Pillars of Islam
halal – literally 'permitted'; describes food permitted to Muslims including animals slaughtered according to the prescribed Islamic customs; also *halaal*
hammam – bathhouse
haram – literally 'forbidden'; anything forbidden by Islamic law; also prayer hall
harem – women of the household
hawaja – a term for Westerner
hejab – woman's head scarf or veil, worn for modesty
Hejira – Islamic calendar; Mohammed's flight from Mecca to Medina in AD 622

iftar – the breaking of the day's fast during Ramadan
ilaga – silver, feminine version of an *agal*
imam – preacher or prayer leader; Muslim cleric
insha'alla – 'If Allah wills it'; 'God willing'
iqama – residence permit and identity document (Saudi Arabia)

jalabiyya – see *galabiyya*
jambiya – tribesman's ceremonial dagger (Yemen and southern Saudi Arabia)
jamrah – pillars
jebel – hill, mountain; also *jabal*, *gebel*
jihad – literally 'striving in the way of the faith'; holy war
jizari – people of the Gulf

Kaaba – the rectangular structure at the centre of the Grand Mosque in Mecca (containing the Black Stone) around which haj pilgrims circumambulate; also *Kabaa* and *Qaaba*
khan – see *caravanserai*
khanjar – tribal curved dagger; also *khanja* (Oman and southern Saudi Arabia)
khareef – southeast monsoon, from mid-June to mid-September in Oman
khor – rocky inlet or creek
kilim – flat, woven mat
kohl – eyeliner
Koran – see *Quran*
Kufic – type of highly stylised old Arabic script
kuma – Omani cap

madhalla – 'witch's hat' worn by female Hadramawt herders (Yemen)

madrassa – Muslim theological seminary; also modern Arabic word for school

mafraj – (pl mafaraj) 'room with a view'; top room of a tower house (Yemen)

majlis – formal meeting room; also parliament

mandoos – Omani wooden chest

manzar – attic; room on top of a tower house (Yemen)

mashrabiyya – ornate carved wooden panel or screen; feature of Islamic architecture

masjid – mosque

medina – city, town, especially the old quarter

midan – city or town square

mihrab – niche in a mosque indicating the direction of Mecca

mina – port

minaret – mosque tower

minbar – pulpit used for sermons in a mosque

misbah – prayer beads

muezzin – cantor who sings the call to prayer

mutawwa – religious police charged with upholding Islamic orthodoxy (Saudi Arabia)

Nabataeans – ancient trading civilisation based around Petra in Jordan

oud – wood incense chips; also a stringed musical instrument

qat – mildly narcotic plant, the leaves of which are chewed

qawha – coffee

Ramadan – Muslim month of fasting; one of the Five Pillars of Islam

ras – cape or headland; also head

sabkha – soft sand with a salty crust

sadu – Bedouin-style weaving

salat – prayer; one of the Five Pillars of Islam

sambuq – see dhow; also *sambuk*

shahada – the profession of faith that Muslims publicly declare in every mosque, five times a day; one of the Five Pillars of Islam

shai – tea

sharia – street

Sharia'a – Islamic law

sheesha – water pipe used to smoke tobacco; also *nargileh* or hubble-bubble

sheikh – head of a tribe; religious leader; also shaikh

Shiite – one of the two main branches of Islam

souq – market

stele – (pl stelae) stone or wooden commemorative slab or column decorated with inscriptions or figures

sultan – absolute ruler of a Muslim state

Sunni – one of the two main branches of Islam

suras – chapters of the Quran

tatrees – traditional Bahrani embroidery

tawaf – circling required during the pilgrimage to Mecca

thobe – men's floor-length shirt-dress similar to a *dishdasha*, but more fitting; also *thawb*

umrah – Islamic ritual performed outside of *haj*; literally 'little pilgrimage'

wadi – valley or river bed, often dry except after heavy rainfall

Wahhabi – conservative and literalist 18th-century Sunni orthodoxy prevailing throughout Saudi Arabia and Qatar

wali – regional head in Oman, similar to mayor

wusta – influence gained by way of connections in high places

yashmak – veil

zakat – the giving of alms; one of the Five Pillars of Islam

The Authors

JENNY WALKER
Coordinating Author

Jenny Walker's first involvement with Arabia was as a student, collecting butterflies for her father's book on entomology in Saudi Arabia. Convinced her mother and she were the first Western women to brew tea in the desolate interior, she returned to university to see if that were true. Her studies resulted in a dissertation on Doughty and Lawrence (BA, University of Stirling) and a thesis entitled *Perception of the Arabic Orient* (MPhil, University of Oxford). She has written extensively on the Middle East for Lonely Planet and, with her husband, authored *Off-Road in the Sultanate of Oman*. Although deeply attached to Arabia, Jenny has travelled in 86 countries from Panama to Mongolia, on diverse assignments. For this edition, Jenny wrote the Destination, Getting Started, Itineraries, History, Culture, Islam, Food & Drink, Environment, Bahrain, Kuwait, Oman, Qatar, Arabian Peninsula Directory and Transport in the Arabian Peninsula chapters.

STUART BUTLER
Yemen

English-born Stuart Butler was first inspired to visit Yemen a decade ago after seeing a TV programme about it. Since that first captivating trip he has returned many times, becoming a little more addicted with each visit. He has contributed many Yemeni based articles and photographs to magazines as well as leading tours to Yemen. In 2004 he became one of the first people to surf the wild southern coast of Yemen. He now calls the south of France home and in addition to Yemen, his travels have taken him across the Middle East and beyond, from the desert beaches of Pakistan to the coastal jungles of Colombia. He's still not convinced about qat.

TERRY CARTER
Expats, United Arab Emirates

Terry moved to the United Arab Emirates (UAE) in 1998, after too many years of 60-hour weeks toiling in Sydney's publishing industry. Having erroneously concluded that travel writing and photography was a far more glamorous occupation than designing books or websites, he's been writing and photographing his way around the Middle East ever since. Terry has a Master's degree in media studies and one day hopes to settle down somewhere with his travelling companion Lara, if they could just decide which country to settle down in. Until then Terry's travels have seen him present his passport at immigration counters in over 50 countries.

LONELY PLANET AUTHORS

Why is our travel information the best in the world? It's simple: our authors are independent, dedicated travellers. They don't research using just the internet or phone, and they don't take freebies in exchange for positive coverage. They travel widely, to all the popular spots and off the beaten track. They personally visit thousands of hotels, restaurants, cafés, bars, galleries, palaces, museums and more – and they take pride in getting all the details right, and telling it how it is. Think you can do it? Find out how at lonelyplanet.com.

LARA DUNSTON
Expats, United Arab Emirates

With degrees in film, writing and international studies, and a media background, Lara moved to Abu Dhabi in 1998 to teach film to young Emirati women, living there for five years before moving to Dubai. The job not only gave she and partner Terry the chance to travel throughout the UAE, but through friendships with her students gave them a privileged insight into Emirati life. Lara continues to argue with those who say the country has no culture. As they learnt, it's one that's rich in traditions, rituals, music and dance. Having left to go on the road in January 2006, they were thrilled to return to the country that's the closest place to being a home for Arabian Peninsula.

FRANCES LINZEE GORDON
The Haj, Saudi Arabia

Frances' fervour for travel was sparked by a school scholarship to Venice aged 17. Since then she's travelled extensively in the Middle East, for which she has a special passion. Frances contributes travel articles, books and photos to a variety of publishers, and has completed an MA in African and Asian (Middle Eastern) Studies and Arabic in London. Other work includes radio and TV appearances (including a slot as 'travel advisor' to BBC News 24 programmes). Frances believes passionately in the benefits of travel both for the tourist as well as the country. She encourages women to travel, considering her gender a help not a hindrance, particularly when negotiating hurdles on the road!

Behind the Scenes

THIS BOOK

This second edition of Oman, UAE & Arabian Peninsula was coordinated by author Jenny Walker, who wrote the following chapters: Highlights; Destination Oman, UAE & the Arabian Peninsula; Getting Started; Itineraries; History; The Culture; Islam; Food & Drink; Environment; Bahrain; Kuwait; Qatar; Oman; Arabian Peninsula Directory; and Transport in the Arabian Peninsula. Jenny also contributed to the Health chapter. The balance of the author team consisted of Stuart Butler (Yemen), Frances Linzee Gordon (Saudi Arabia and The Haj: The Ultimate Traveller's Tale), and Terry Carter and Lara Dunston, who worked together on the UAE and Expats chapters. The first edition of this book, titled Arabian Peninsula, was written by Frances Linzee Gordon (coordinating author), Jenny Walker, Anthony Ham and Virginia Maxwell. The Health chapter of both editions was based on the work of Dr Caroline Evans.

This guidebook was commissioned in Lonely Planet's Melbourne office, and produced by the following:

Commissioning Editor Kerryn Burgess
Coordinating Editor Dianne Schallmeiner
Coordinating Cartographers Andy Rojas; Kusnandar
Coordinating Layout Designer Carlos Solarte
Managing Editor Suzannah Shwer
Managing Cartographer Shahara Ahmed
Assisting Editors Carly Hall; Evan Jones; Anne Mulvaney; Rosie Nicholson; Stephanie Ong; Susan Paterson; Laura Stansfeld; Phillip Tang; Simon Williamson
Assisting Cartographers Barbara Benson; David Connolly; Diana Duggan; Jacqueline Nguyen; Malisa Plesa; Andrew Smith
Cover Designer Jane Hart
Colour Designer Pablo Gastar
Project Manager Eoin Dunlevy
Language Content Coordinator Quentin Frayne

Thanks to David Burnett; Sin Choo; Helen Christinis; Sally Darmody; Jennifer Garrett; Raphael Richards; Averil Robertson; Celia Wood

THANKS
JENNY WALKER

Coordinating this project was very much a team effort and I'd like to thank Kerryn Burgess and the participating authors for making it such an enjoyable experience. Numerous thanks are due to sheikhs and officials (especially the Wali of Al-Hashman who saved us from ourselves in Oman's Empty Quarter). It's the generous-spirited everyday encounters with colleagues, friends and acquaintances, however, that demonstrate the principal beauty of Arabia – namely its people. I hope the warmth I feel for them is reflected in my chapters. I couldn't have undertaken this project without my beloved husband, Sam Owen, who was so entirely integral to the research of my chapters that by rights both our names should appear under them.

Dedication

My father fits happily into the tradition of the eccentric, white-bearded, charismatic explorer of hidden worlds – in his case, the world of the insect. He worked for the National Commission for Wildlife Conservation and Development in Riyadh for many years, building a national entomological collection, and co-authored a book on the insects of Eastern Arabia, illustrated by my brother, Allan, and published by Macmillan.

It was a special privilege to accompany my much beloved parents on 'field trips' throughout Saudi Arabia – experiences that instilled in me not only a great love of the Peninsula (my adoptive home) but also the deepest respect for my father's vitality, boundless enthusiasm and profound knowledge of natural history. He died the day after I completed my portion of this book and it is a great honour to be able to dedicate this book to him.

STUART BUTLER

I'm indebted to many people for their advice, help and encouragement with my Yemen chapter. Extra big thanks must go to the following though: Shakib Al-Khayyat of Marib Tours and Safwan Al-Amari from FTI Yemen for the huge help they've provided. For superb driving and good humour thanks to Mujahed Al Sanhani. Thanks are also due for the driving and guiding skills of Ahmed Al Tayib, Abdullah, Abdul and the late Sayeed. For desert expertise and 'boys' games, thanks to Hasan Mubarak and his extended family, especially Hathim (hope the surfing is going ok!); for a warm San'a welcome, cheers to the boys at the Hotel

LONELY PLANET: TRAVEL WIDELY, TREAD LIGHTLY, GIVE SUSTAINABLY

The Lonely Planet tory

The story begins with a classic travel adventure: Tony and Maureen Wheeler's 1972 journey across Europe and Asia to Australia. There was no useful information about the overland trail then, so Tony and Maureen published the first Lonely Planet guidebook to meet a growing need.

From a kitchen table, Lonely Planet has grown to become the largest independent travel publisher in the world, with offices in Melbourne (Australia), Oakland (USA) and London (UK). Today Lonely Planet guidebooks cover the globe. There is an ever-growing list of books and information in a variety of media. Some things haven't changed. The main aim is still to make it possible for adventurous individuals to get out there – to explore and better understand the world.

The Lonely Planet Foundation

The Lonely Planet Foundation proudly supports nimble nonprofit institutions working for change in the world. Each year the foundation donates 5% of Lonely Planet company profits to projects selected by staff and authors. Our partners range from Kabissa, which provides small nonprofits across Africa with access to technology, to the Foundation for Developing Cambodian Orphans, which supports girls at risk of falling victim to sex traffickers.

Our nonprofit partners are linked by a grass-roots approach to the areas of health, education or sustainable tourism. Many projects we support – such as one with BaAka (Pygmy) children in the forested areas of Central African Republic – choose to focus on women and children as one of the most effective ways to support the whole community.

Sometimes foundation assistance is as simple as restoring a local ruin like the Minaret of Jam in Afghanistan; this incredible monument now draws intrepid tourists to the area and its restoration has greatly improved options for local people.

Just as travel is often about learning to see with new eyes, so many of the groups we work with aim to change the way people see themselves and the future for their children and communities.

Dawood. For being great travel companions cheers to Toby Adamson (see his superb photos on www.tobyadamson.co.uk), Gareth Howard (though not for his jokes), Mark Austin and Rachel Bell. Thanks to Rowan and Carl Watts for sharing a Shaharah supper, and to the hundreds who have made Yemen the coolest place on earth – a huge *shukran*! Finally, the biggest thanks of all are saved for Heather, just for being herself.

TERRY CARTER & LARA DUNSTON

No matter how many years you live in a place you still find yourself meeting new people each day who help in some way. A big *shukran* to: Sarah and Saeeda, Ayesha Mubarak Abdulla Obeid and Salman A Bushelaibi at Dubai Museum, Jaylyn Garcia at Dubai Tourism Commerce and Marketing, Sherifa Madgwick, Waleed Nabil and Karen at the Sheikh Mohammed Centre for Cultural Understanding, Amal Harb, Amr Kassem, Nada Sheshtawy, Doaa Amin, Sacha Dandachi, Hamad Buharoon, Dina Sultan, Hoda Beckdash, Eva Cordewener, Fady E Abi Khalil, Abdulfatah Bin Ahmed Al Shehi, Dagmar Weber, Satish Gujaran, Gabor Martin Bors, Aymin Gharib, Angeli Torres, Anne

Deleon, Lejla Charif, Jihane El Fadl, Fuad Al Najjar, Amer Aidi, Farah, Lisandro C Palabrica, Sunil Tandon, Suresh Purohit and Ann Skrilec, and of course our dear family and friends who tolerate our lack of contact during research.

FRANCES LINZEE GORDON

Publishing word-limits sadly prevent me from listing the many, many individuals who helped me daily, so generously and so tirelessly during my wonderful trip to Saudi Arabia. Briefly, thanks for help in particular to Dr Zamil Abuzinada, Abdullah E Motaen and Khaled Al-Ateeq.

For help and hospitality, thanks to Riad Abdullah, Moncef Soltani, Mohammed Ali Ramadan, Ashraf M Hendawi, Sheikh Abdullah Mubark Al-Dosary, and particularly Mahmoud Alim and Ateeq Naif Al-Shamary.

Special thanks to those at the National Commission for Wildlife Conservation including: Mohammed Al-Toraif, Abdulaziz M Al-Mohanna, Borhan A Qary, Khalid Mohammed H Albassri, and particularly Othman Abd-ar-Rahman Llewellyn.

At the Supreme Commission of Tourism, thanks to Talal Fahad A Al-Zaid, Fahad A Alammar, Majed

Al-Sheddi, Ahmed M Al-Eesa, Dr Hussein Ali Abual-hassan, Abdullah S Al-Jehani, and particularly Saad Abdulaziz Al-Mohanna and Mrs Reem Philby for outstanding help with research. Above all, to HH Prince Sultan Bin Salman Bin Abdulaziz, Secretary General, who with a phone call, facilitated any information or interview I desired.

For help with research, thanks in particular to Rawdha Al-Jaizany, Professor ART Al-Ansary, Fahad O al-Faidy, and especially Hamid M Al-Su-laiman and Eric Alexander. Above all, to Ahmed Ali Mostafa of Sadd al-Samallaghi, along with Mr Yusuf and Mr Al-Hadi. Finally, to Hatem A Jameel, the best guide/driver/bank/bodyguard/pretend-husband I ever had, and whose great knowledge, hard work, loyalty, patience and sense of humour made each long day a joy.

Grateful thanks to Hani AZ Yamani for help with my visa; to HE Yusuf Abdullahi Sukkar for generous hospitality; and HH Prince Fawaz Naser Al-Faisal Al-Saud, and HH Prince Sultan Bin Saud Bin Moham-med al-Saud for hospitality and kindness.

Finally, to HH Prince Bandar Bin Saud Bin Mo-hammed al-Saud, Chairman, the National Com-mission for Wildlife Conservation, for help with research, as well as limitless generosity, hospitality, kindness and friendship. May God bless you all.

Thanks lastly to the ever-unsung team at Lonely Planet including Jenny Walker (coordinating au-thor); Shahara Ahmed (managing cartographer); Dianne Schallmeiner (editor), and finally Kerryn Burgess, who as commissioning editor, was quite simply everything an author could want.

OUR READERS

Many thanks to the travellers who used the last edition and wrote to us with helpful hints, useful advice and interesting anecdotes:

Monica Alvaro, Monir Bardouz, David Chaudoir, L Monica Ciabatti, CJ Dippel, Paul Dirks, Osman Durrani, Giulia Favino, Kirstie Feeney, Jens Freyler, Brian Furner, Jonathan Fursland, Dirk Geets, Steve Gracie, Ben Halfpenny, Rainer Hamet, Pasi Hannonen, Nigel Harwood, Michael Kelly, Ken & Lois Kemp, Christoph Kemper, Marnix Koets, Naveed Lasi, Robert Leger, Peter Lindholm, Stuart Maclean, Raf De Meyer, Eugenia Morlans, Robert Nowell, Rob Reid, Barbara Haller Rupf, Christos Shepherd, Leah Silberman, Martin Sobek, Diana Spindler, Ulana Switucha, Harry Turner, Essa van Armesto, Krisztina Varga, Tony Wheeler

ACKNOWLEDGMENTS

BEHIND THE SCENES

SEND US YOUR FEEDBACK

We love to hear from travellers – your com-ments keep us on our toes and help make our books better. Our well-travelled team reads every word on what you loved or loathed about this book. Although we can-not reply individually to postal submissions, we always guarantee that your feedback goes straight to the appropriate authors, in time for the next edition. Each person who sends us information is thanked in the next edition – and the most useful submissions are rewarded with a free book.

To send us your updates – and find out about Lonely Planet events, newsletters and travel news – visit our award-winning web-site: **www.lonelyplanet.com/contact**.

Note: we may edit, reproduce and incorp-orate your comments in Lonely Planet prod-ucts such as guidebooks, websites and digital products, so let us know if you don't want your comments reproduced or your name acknowledged. For a copy of our privacy policy visit www.lonelyplanet.com/privacy.

Index

000 Map pages
000 Photograph pages

Map pages **000**
Photograph pages **000**

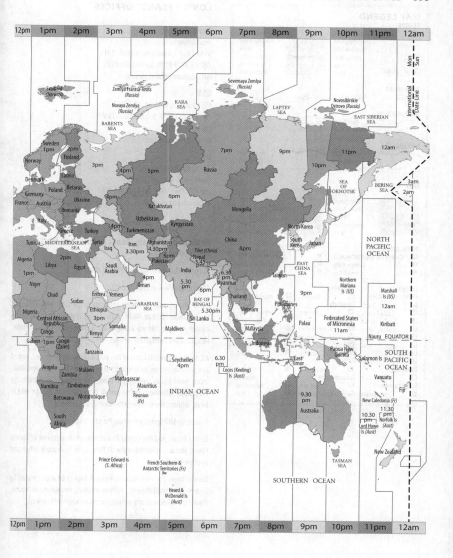

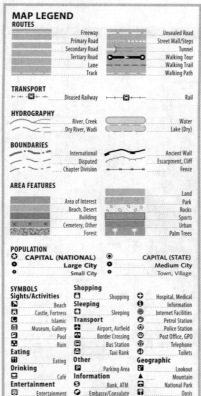

MAP LEGEND

ROUTES

Freeway	Unsealed Road
Primary Road	Street Mall/Steps
Secondary Road	Tunnel
Tertiary Road	Walking Tour
Lane	Walking Trail
Track	Walking Path

TRANSPORT

Disused Railway	Rail

HYDROGRAPHY

River, Creek	Water
Dry River, Wadi	Lake (Dry)

BOUNDARIES

International	Ancient Wall
Disputed	Escarpment, Cliff
Chapter Division	Fence

AREA FEATURES

	Land
Area of Interest	Park
Beach, Desert	Rocks
Building	Sports
Cemetery, Other	Urban
Forest	Palm Trees

POPULATION

CAPITAL (NATIONAL)	CAPITAL (STATE)
Large City	Medium City
Small City	Town, Village

SYMBOLS

Sights/Activities
Beach
Castle, Fortress
Islamic
Museum, Gallery
Pool
Ruin

Eating
Eating

Drinking
Café

Entertainment
Entertainment

Shopping
Shopping

Sleeping
Sleeping

Transport
Airport, Airfield
Border Crossing
Bus Station
Taxi Rank

Other
Parking Area

Information
Bank, ATM
Embassy/Consulate

Hospital, Medical
Information
Internet Facilities
Petrol Station
Police Station
Post Office, GPO
Telephone
Toilets

Geographic
Lookout
Mountain
National Park
Oasis

LONELY PLANET OFFICES

Australia
Head Office
Locked Bag 1, Footscray, Victoria 3011
☎ 03 8379 8000, fax 03 8379 8111
talk2us@lonelyplanet.com.au

USA
150 Linden St, Oakland, CA 94607
☎ 510 893 8555, toll free 800 275 8555,
fax 510 893 8572
info@lonelyplanet.com

UK
72–82 Rosebery Ave,
Clerkenwell, London EC1R 4RW
☎ 020 7841 9000, fax 020 7841 9001
go@lonelyplanet.co.uk

Published by Lonely Planet Publications Pty Ltd
ABN 36 005 607 983

© Lonely Planet Publications Pty Ltd 2007

© photographers as indicated 2007

Cover photograph: Ceremony celebrating the 28th anniversary of the Sultanate of Oman, Maher Attar, Corbis Sygma/APL. Many of the images in this guide are available for licensing from Lonely Planet Images: www.lonelyplanetimages.com.